WHO WAS WHO IN
NATIVE AMERICAN
HISTORY:

Indians and Non-Indians
From Early Contacts through 1900

Carl Waldman

Facts On File

New York • Oxford • Sydney

For Molly…

Whose passion for the
Native American legacy
has been an inspiration

Who Was Who in Native American History:
Indians and Non-Indians from Early Contacts through 1900

Facts On File, Inc.   Facts On File Limited   Facts On File Pty Ltd
460 Park Avenue South   Collins Street   Talavera & Khartoum Rds
New York, NY 10016   Oxford OX4 1XJ   North Ryde NSW 2113
USA   United Kingdom   Australia

Library of Congress Cataloging-in-Publication Data
Waldman, Carl.
   Who was who in Native American history: Indians and non-Indians
from early contacts through 1900 / Carl Waldman.
      p.   cm.
   Includes index.
   ISBN 0-8160-1797-2
   1. Indians of North America—Biography— Dictionaries. 2. Indians
of North America—Government relations—Biography—Dictionaries.
I. Title.
E89.W35   1989
970.004'97022—dc20   89-35088
[B]

British and Australian CIP data available on request from Facts On File.

Facts On File books are available at special discounts when purchased in bulk
quantities for businesses, associations, institutions or sales promotion. Please contact
the Special Sales Department of our New York office at 212-683-2244 (dial 800-322-
8755 except in NY, AK or HI).

Text design by Ron Monteleone
Jacket design by Levavi & Levavi
Composition by Facts On File, Inc.
Manufactured by Maple-Vail Book Mfg. Group
Printed in the United States of America

10 9 8 7 6 5 4 3 2 1

This book is printed on acid-free paper.

CONTENTS

PREFACE

Selecting entries for a Who Was Who in Native American history can be a frustratingly arbitrary process. For every familiar name, there are dozens more whose stories are less discussed, but who are just as fascinating and significant.

Of course, Native American history is *North American* history, a part of it shamefully underemphasized in both United States and Canadian education. Other than at the college level, Indian studies are usually touched upon as a footnote to the political history of the United States or Canada, or as a class's special project, despite great enthusiasm among students about all aspects of the subject. Yet discussion of the growth of the United States and Canada without a thorough discussion of the simultaneous displacement and cultural dispossession of Indian America is incomplete. Likewise, non-Indians, as Indian allies, antagonists, policymakers, and scholars, are an integral part of the Native American story.

The historical record in this reference work is necessarily incomplete. Native American history for every geographical region is overwhelmingly complex. Each tribe has had a succession of leaders who have played important roles in its history. And many other Native Americans have played critical roles in the larger Indian and non-Indian society. Many have had to be omitted from a book of this scope.

As for the non-Indian entries, the information here is again only part of a vast story. There are many more non-Indian officials, reformers, and agents involved in Native American policy decisions; many more anthropologists, archaeologists, historians, writers, painters, and photographers who helped the Indian legacy survive; many more military personnel who fought in the Indian wars; and many more explorers, traders, missionaries, and captives who traveled or lived among Indians than are recorded in this volume.

This Who Was Who covers Native American history from early contacts between Indians and whites through the end of the 19th century, that is to say, individuals who were a significant part of the pre-20th-century Indian story, even though they may have contributed to the story after 1900 as well. Contemporary or recent Native Americans contributing to a tribal or pan-Indian legacy are left out, as are contemporary or recent non-Indians affecting policy and knowledge about Native Americans. Such an approach does not imply that Indian history is relegated to an earlier time. Indian America is a vital, continuing story—so vital, in fact, that it is difficult for a researcher to pass judgment on those people whose current or recent contributions merit study at the exclusion of others. There is enough material for volumes of a Who's Who in 20th-century Native American history, a research project in its own right.

This book further limits itself to Native American history in territory that is now the United States and Canada, omitting the historical record for Central America, South America, and the Caribbean.

What follows is a study aid, not a measure of merit as are some Who's Whos. Famous figures who are likely to be encountered in general readings on Indian history and culture are of course included. Lesser-known figures who participated in an important event have their own entries in some cases to give a fuller version of that event. Other men and women pivotal in a particular area of the Native American legacy also have their own listings. Still others are included because of the representative nature of their stories; others, because of the colorful nature. Consideration was also given to historical, tribal, and geographical distribution.

The decision to cover non-Indians in detail obviously prevents the inclusion of more Native Americans. Having a view of the lives of non-Indians, however, is essential to having an understanding of parallel Indian lives. Quite a few of these non-Indians are famous for other activities. The fact that there is little awareness of how much their careers were intertwined with Indian history points up once again the blind spot most North Americans have about their native peoples.

Alternate names and alternate spellings of names are listed. In some cases, even more versions exist, since, after all, the English versions were attempts to spell unfamiliar Indian sounds phonetically. Translations of names are sometimes given in quotation marks, although many are in dispute. Indian childhood names are generally omitted. Indian names for non-Indians are sometimes given as well.

Some alternate names still prevalent in other current writings are listed alphabetically between entries, and cross-referenced to the primary names used in this book.

Within the Indian entries, tribal names immediately follow individual names. If Native Americans are known to have had non-Indian ancestry as well, the designation "mixed" is added to tribal names.

With many historical Indian figures, birth and death dates are unknown or in dispute. *Circa* (ca.) and *floruit* (fl.) are therefore frequently used.

After the birth and death dates, brief descriptions of significant contributions to Indian history and culture are given as windows into the main text. Family connections are also listed when known and relevant.

A cross-reference to another entry is indicated by capitalization. In some instances, the entry that gives the larger frame of reference for a war, incident, or issue is cross-referenced parenthetically to call special attention to it.

States and provinces are sometimes used to locate events geographically before actual statehood or provinciality was achieved.

The appendix lists by tribes those Indians with their own entries. These are the tribes among whom individuals made their impact, not necessarily their tribes by birth.

Other lists in the appendix organize non-Indians by their most relevant contributions to Indian history: explorers & traders; frontier painters & photographers; officials, agents, & reformers; scholars & educators; soldiers, scouts, & captives. These categories serve as a convenience; there is a great deal of overlapping of these various activities. Missionaries do not have a separate list because so often their primary contributions to Indian history were as explorers, scholars, educators, or reformers.

A final note: A book covering such a wide range of material can be no more accurate than its sources. Much of the material comes from writers who were explorers, missionaries, traders, or army officers first, in addition to amateur historians or anthropologists. Hearsay and legend play a part in what has been passed down. Contradictions abound. Biographers spend lifetimes trying to clear up disputed information about their subjects. In many cases, an attempt at exactitude becomes a means to help illustrate the larger issues of a life or an event. Moreover, a brief summary of a person 's life is by nature misleading. One has to probe deeper, adding details to the skeleton of information presented here, to get to the heart of a person's role in history. These short entries should be viewed as starting points for further study.

Special thanks to my wife Molly Braun for her insight on the subject matter; my father John Waldman for his editorial input; Alan Wexler for his fresh historical perspective and help on the non-Indian entries; Gerry Helferich, associate publisher at Facts On File, for his continuing support and enthusiasm; Wayne Wright and all the other librarians for their assistance; Phillip Loes for finding so many pertinent articles; Frank Coffey of the general advice department; and the many chroniclers and researchers whose earlier efforts have underpinned this book.

A

ABRAHAM (Little Abraham; Teiorhenhsere, Tayorheasere, Teyarhasere, Tiyerhasere, Tyorhansera, Tigoransera). *Mohawk. (d. 1780).* Ally of British in the French and Indian War of 1754–63.

In 1755, Little Abraham, the son of Old Abraham, became chief of his tribe following the death of HENDRICK in the Battle of Lake George in upstate New York. At the Albany Congress of 1754, Abraham served as spokesman for the Iroquois League in meetings with WILLIAM JOHNSON, BENJAMIN FRANKLIN, and other officials. Like Hendrick, Abraham was a gifted orator. He attended a meeting between the Mohawks and American Revolutionary commissioners, again at Albany, in 1755, at which time he indicated that he would remain neutral. The Mohawks later decided to give their support, under JOSEPH BRANT, to the British in the American Revolution.

ADAIR, JAMES. *(d. 1783).* Trader; anthropologist; reformer.

James Adair was an Irish trader out of South Carolina who lived among the Chickasaws for nearly 40 years in the mid-1700s. He took several Indian wives by whom he had many children. He used the Chickasaws, Cherokees, Catawbas, Creeks, and other tribes of the Southeast as informants for his book *The History of the American Indians*, published in 1775 after his return to England. Although he provided much ethnographic information plus valuable suggestions for Indian policy, Adair also made the erroneous case for the Native Americans as descendants of the Ten Lost Tribes of Israel.

ADAMS, JOHN C. *Mixed Stockbridge-Munsee.* *(d. 1895).* Tribal lobbyist.

The Stockbridge Indians were a band of eastern Algonquians, mostly Mahicans from Massachusetts, relo-

cated to New York in 1786 under SAMSON OCCUM, then to Wisconsin in 1822 under JOHN W. QUINNEY. In 1856, they were granted reservation lands along with the Munsee band of Delawares who had also relocated to Wisconsin.

Among this Wisconsin group, John C. Adams was the most important lobbyist for the Citizen Party. The mixed-blood son of a Stockbridge-Munsee and a missionary's daughter, he became one of many tribal delegates who made frequent trips to Washington, D.C. The Citizen Party sought United States citizenship and the allotment of lands to individuals. They supported 1843 federal legislation that ended the tribe's protected status. The Citizen Party was opposed by the Indian Party, represented by John W. Quinney, who worked to have the 1843 act repealed.

Adams eventually sold his Wisconsin farm to help pay for his lobbying efforts, staying for the most part in Washington, D.C., boardinghouses. He died a pauper.

ADARIO (Kondiaronk; Sastaretsi; Gaspar Soiaga, Souoias, Le Rat, The Rat). *Huron-Tionontati.* *(ca. 1650–1701).* Diplomat; orator.

The Tionontati or Tobacco or Petun Indians were a Iroquoian- speaking people whose history became one with the Hurons after the Iroquois invasion of their territory south of Nottawasaga Bay in Ontario in the mid-1600s. Adario was a powerful Huron chief, born a Tionontati, of the late 1600s, who, in the first of the French and Indian Wars (King William's War of 1689–97), proved himself a master of playing the French off against their enemies, the Iroquois, allies of the British. He was also a noted speaker who passionately argued for his people's rights.

In 1688, Adario set out with a war party—armed by the French—southward into Iroquois territory. On the way, he received word from the French garrison at

Cataracouy that an Iroquois peace delegation was heading toward Montreal, and he returned north to set an ambush. On capturing the Iroquois, led by the Onondaga DEKANISORA, he informed them that the French had ordered his attack. To demonstrate his friendship, Adario set the Iroquois prisoners free, keeping one hostage to replace one of his own men killed in battle. Adario and his party then traveled to the French post at Michilimackinac, where the commandant had not yet heard of the peace plans with the Iroquois and, as a result, ordered the execution of Adario's captive.

On returning to his village, Adario released another Iroquois prisoner from an earlier skirmish, sending him home with the message that the French had killed the Iroquois warrior despite the Hurons' efforts on his behalf. The Iroquois, furious with the French, attacked Montreal and other settlements along the St. Lawrence River on August 25, 1689, killing hundreds. Adario's military and trade relationship with the French remained intact and, as far as the Iroquois knew, he was sympathetic to their cause.

Adario later converted to Christianity. In 1701, he headed a delegation of Huron chiefs to Montreal for a peace conference and died while there. The French buried him in the Montreal cemetery with full military honors.

ADOUETTE. See BIG TREE.

AHATSISTARI (Eustache Ahatsisteari). *Huron.* *(d. 1642).* Leader in the Huron struggle against the Iroquois during the mid-1600s.

Ahatsistari led his warriors in two great victories in the early stages of the Huron-Iroquois conflict, 1641–42: one with 50 Hurons against a war party of about 300 Iroquois, the other in war canoes on Lake Ontario. Soon afterward, he was taken captive by a band of Mohawks who raided a combined Huron and French party on Lake St. Peter. He was held prisoner for a time, then killed. Seven years later, in March 1649, the allied tribes of the Iroquois League launched an invasion of Huron territory north of Lake Ontario, driving them from their villages and gaining control of the region.

AKIPA ("meeting"; Tacandupahotanka, "his big-voiced pipe"; Old Indian Doctor). *Wahpeton Sioux.* *(d. 1891).* Medicine man; ally of whites in the Minnesota Uprising of 1862–63.

Akipa led a Christian band of Santee Sioux in the vicinity of the Yellow Medicine Agency near present-day Granite Falls, Minnesota. He was friendly to whites and signed the Traverse des Sioux Treaty of 1851 and traveled to Washington, D.C., to sign the Treaty of 1858. By marriage to Winona Crawford, Akipa was stepfather to some of the white captives taken by LITTLE CROW's warriors during the Santee Sioux revolt known as the Minnesota Uprising.

In August 1862, during the fighting at New Ulm, Akipa journeyed to Little Crow's village, castigated the rebels, and insisted on the release of his relatives. Akipa later joined with others in the antiwar faction, including CLOUDMAN, PAUL MAZAKUTEMANI, MAZOMANI, and GABRIEL RENVILLE, as part of a soldiers' lodge, which negotiated the release of other white captives. As a medicine man with some knowledge of Western medicine, Akipa helped take care of the Indian prisoners, along with RED IRON, after the war.

Akipa and his family later settled on the Sisseton Reservation in South Dakota. He served as an Indian scout with his two sons, Charles Renville Crawford and Thomas Crawford. The former became a noted Presbyterian minister among the eastern Sioux. (See also LITTLE CROW.)

ALCHESAY (Alchise). *Chiricahua Apache.* *(fl. 1870s–1880s).* Army scout.

Alchesay served as a sergeant in the Indian Scouts under General GEORGE CROOK in his Arizona campaign of 1872–73 against the Apaches and Yavapais. He received the Congressional Medal of Honor in 1875 for his service. He also helped Crook track GERONIMO in 1886 along with CHATO, KAYATENNAE, and MICKEY FREE. Despite his military support of whites, Alchesay eloquently pleaded the case of his people. He visited Washington, D.C., in 1886, with an Apache delegation that included Chato and LOCO. In meetings with President Grover Cleveland and other officials, the tribal representatives were unsuccessful in preventing the deportation of Apaches to Florida. In later years, Alchesay became a prominent cattleman. (See also GERONIMO.)

ALEXANDER (Wamsutta, "a warm and loving heart"; Moonanam). *Wampanoag. (d. 1662).* Tribal leader. Son of MASSASOIT; brother of PHILIP; husband of WETAMOO.

The court at Plymouth gave Alexander and Philip English names on their request, after Alexander and Philip of ancient Greece. Alexander was the first in succession as grand sachem of the Wampanoag Confederacy to their father Massasoit, who died in late 1661. Like his father, he advocated continuing peace with the colonists.

Suspecting a Wampanoag conspiracy with the Narragansets against the colonists, Plymouth authorities summoned Alexander for a hearing. When he refused to report, a detachment of 10 men under JOSIAH WINSLOW traveled into Wampanoag country. They located Alexander in the vicinity of present-day Halifax, Massachusetts, where he was feasting with his men in a hunting lodge, their weapons stacked outside. The soldiers seized the arms. Winslow, under threat of an attack, coerced Alexander into coming to trial in Plymouth. His warriors and his wife Wetamoo, along with some other Indian women, were allowed to accompany him. Alexander was offered a horse, but chose to walk with his people.

At Duxbury, Alexander became seriously ill with a high fever. The Wampanoags asked permission to take him home, which was granted. Alexander died on the return trip along the Titicut (now Taunton) River. Wetamoo believed that her husband had been poisoned by the colonists, adding to growing tension between Indians and whites. Embittered by his brother's death, Philip led a revolt of the Wampanoags and Narragansets in what is known as King Philip's War of 1675–76. (See also PHILIP.)

ALFORD, THOMAS WILDCAT (Gaynwah, Gaynwawpiahsika, "the leader"). *Shawnee.* (1860–1938). Tribal leader; educator; lobbyist; Bureau of Indian Affairs official.

Thomas Wildcat Alford was born in the Indian Territory, his mother supposedly the great-granddaughter of TECUMSEH. Alford's parents were both Absentee Shawnees, which were various bands that broke off from the rest of the tribe and settled on the Canadian River. They passed to their son the traditions and legends of their tribe. When 12, he attended a mission school, then won a scholarship to the Hampton Institute in Virginia, where he was converted to Christianity.

On returning to the Indian Territory, Alford found himself in conflict with traditionalists among his people and left again to teach. When offered the position of principal of a new federal school for Shawnee children the following year, he settled permanently in the Indian Territory. He held the post for five years, also working among tribal adults to help them adjust to white society.

In 1893, Alford became chairman of a "Business Committee" of Shawnees and worked to prevent the injustices of the Allotment system. He traveled several times to Washington, D.C., to lobby on behalf of his tribe. In order to convince whites of the Christian-like humanism of the Indian way of life, he drew on his knowledge of traditional customs and frequently quoted the unwritten codes of Shawnee behavior and justice. He became an employee of the Bureau of Indian Affairs in the hope of having more influence on federal Indian policy.

Alford had five children by Mary Grinnell. In 1936, Alford's biography, *Civilization*, as told to Florence Drake, was published.

ALIGHTS-ON-THE-CLOUD. *Southern Cheyenne.* (d. 1852). Warrior; tribal delegate.

In 1844, Alights-on-the-Cloud proved his courage in battle against the Delawares. Wearing a Mexican suit of armor given to him by his father, he walked into battle to draw the enemy fire. After the Delawares had discharged their single-shot, muzzle-loading rifles, the Cheyennes were able to defeat them with bows and arrows and war clubs. Alights-on-the-Cloud signed the Fort Laramie Treaty of 1851 in what is now Wyoming, then traveled to Washington, D.C., with a Cheyenne delegation, including WHITE ANTELOPE, where he met President Millard Fillmore. He died the next year as part of a war party of Cheyennes, Arapahos, Sioux, Kiowas, and Apaches in an attack on a Pawnee buffalo-hunting camp along the Beaver River of Kansas. Although he wore his famous suit of armor, he took an arrow in the eye.

ALLIGATOR (Halpatter Tustenuggee). *Seminole.* (b. ca. 1795). Leader in the Second Seminole War of 1835–42.

Alligator migrated to central Florida with his parents from Creek country. On December 28, 1835, along with MICANOPY and JUMPER, he led about 300 warriors against Major FRANCIS DADE's column of 108 soldiers on their way from Fort Brooke on Tampa Bay, Florida, to reinforce Fort King. All but three soldiers died. That same day, OSCEOLA led an ambush on Indian agent WILEY THOMPSON's party, killing him.

Three days later, on New Year's Eve, Osceola's war party joined up with Alligator and the others in a victory over General DUNCAN CLINCH's force of 300 regulars and 500 Florida militia on the Withlacoochee River.

At Lake Okeechobee in December 1837, Alligator's men, along with ARPEIKA's Miccosukees and WILD CAT's band of Indians and blacks, battled Colonel ZACHARY TAYLOR's force to a draw. With continuing military pressure, Alligator surrendered in March 1838. After an escape attempt that same year, he was sent to the Indian Territory.

Alligator joined an 1843 Seminole delegation to Washington, D.C., to lobby for improved conditions and settlement of land disputes between Seminoles and Creeks in the Indian Territory. (See also OSCEOLA.)

ALLOUEZ, CLAUDE JEAN. (1622–1689). Explorer; missionary.

French-born Claude Jean Allouez entered the Jesuit order in 1639, coming to North America in 1658. He first served along the St. Lawrence River among the Hurons and eastern Algonquians, then was appointed Jesuit vicar-general of the Northwest in 1663. He explored the

Lake Superior region in 1667, providing the information for a Jesuit map. He founded several missions to the western Great Lakes Algonquians, including Chequamegon and De Pere in what is now Wisconsin. After 1676, he was missionary to the Illinois and Miami Indians. He died in what is now Indiana. Allouez is said to have preached to 22 tribes and baptized 10,000 Indians, and is sometimes referred to as the "Founder of Christianity in the West."

AMERICAN HORSE (Iron Shield). *Oglala Sioux. (ca. 1801–1876).* Leader in the Sioux Wars of the 1860s–70s. Cousin of RED CLOUD; possibly uncle of AMERICAN HORSE (the younger).

American Horse, the son of Chief Smoke, joined his cousin Red Cloud in the War for the BOZEMAN Trail of 1866–68. He remained militant after the Fort Laramie Treaty of 1868 and refused to settle at the Red Cloud Agency in Nebraska. In 1870, he accompanied Red Cloud's delegation to Washington, D.C., but took up arms again in the War for the Black Hills of 1876–77 and was present at the Battle of Little Bighorn in June 1876.

The following September, American Horse's band of Oglalas and Minniconjous separated from CRAZY HORSE's band on the Grand River and started south for the winter. A forward detachment from General GEORGE CROOK's force under Captain Anson Mills stumbled upon the Indian camp. In the Battle of Slim Buttes, present-day South Dakota, on September 9, Mills led an unsuccessful attack but managed to trap American Horse, four warriors, and 15 women and children in a cave.

Crook soon arrived and directed the ensuing fighting, in which American Horse was fatally wounded. Those who escaped alerted SITTING BULL and GALL, who rode with about 600 warriors to help American Horse. Having little ammunition, the Indians were unable to break through Crook's rear guard as his main force marched on to the Black Hills. Meanwhile, American Horse emerged from the cave, holding his intestines from a bullet wound. He refused chloroform from army surgeons and silently endured the pain by biting on a piece of wood. On his death, the soldiers scalped him.

American Horse's death and the destruction of the band's tepees and possessions were among a series of setbacks for the Sioux and their allies after their earlier victory at Little Bighorn, and led to their ultimate surrender the following year. (See also RED CLOUD; SITTING BULL.)

AMERICAN HORSE (Wasechun-tashunka). *Oglala Sioux. (1840–1908).* Warrior; negotiator; touring Indian. Possibly son of SITTING BULL; possibly nephew of AMERICAN HORSE (the older); son-in-law of RED CLOUD.

As a young man, American Horse participated with CRAZY HORSE in the FETTERMAN Fight of December 1866 during Red Cloud's War for the BOZEMAN Trail. After the Fort Laramie Treaty of 1868, he lived at the Red Cloud Agency.

In 1888–89, American Horse was one of the proponents of the treaty in which the Sioux ceded about half their land in the Dakota Territory. Before signing, he negotiated with General GEORGE CROOK for two weeks and earned a reputation for endurance and oratorical elegance.

During the Ghost Dance Uprising of 1890, American Horse helped defuse confrontations between his people and whites. The incident at Wounded Knee affected him deeply because he had helped persuade BIG FOOT's band to return to the Pine Ridge Reservation in South Dakota before their massacre. In 1891, he led a delegation of the Sioux chiefs to Washington, D.C., one of several trips to the capital. He spoke passionately of Wounded Knee and helped bring about increased rations and better treatment for his people.

American Horse (the younger). Photo by Edward Curtis. *Courtesy of National Archives of Canada/PA-39293.*

American Horse toured for a time with WILLIAM "BUFFALO BILL" CODY's Wild West Show. He later made a pictographic history of the Oglalas. (See also RED CLOUD; SITTING BULL.)

AMHERST, JEFFREY (Baron Amherst).

(1717–1797). British officer in the French and Indian War of 1754–63, and Pontiac's Rebellion of 1763; governor-general of British North America.

After various European campaigns, English-born Jeffrey Amherst was sent to North America in 1758 to fight the French. He captured Louisburg in Canada that same year; became commander in chief of the British army in North America in 1759; and captured Montreal with WILLIAM JOHNSON and a force of Mohawks in 1760.

Amherst served as governor-general of British North America from 1760 to 1763. When the British took control of New France, Amherst initiated a stricter policy toward the Indian tribes than that practiced by the French. He believed in enforcing regulations through punishment rather than a continuation of the granting of provisions—a policy he considered the equivalent of bribery. His intolerance contributed to the unrest among the tribes of the Old Northwest, who revolted in 1763 under PONTIAC. Amherst encouraged his commander in the West, HENRY BOUQUET, to attempt to spread smallpox to the Indians in revolt, thus introducing biological warfare to North America.

General Amherst was commander in chief of the British army in 1772–95, directing Great Britain's home defenses in the American Revolution. He was granted a baronetcy in 1776. Amherst College is named after him. (See also PONTIAC.)

ANDROS, EDMUND (Corlaer). *(1637–1714).*
Colonial governor.

Sir Edmund Andros, born on the island of Guernsey, served as colonial governor of New York and New Jersey in 1674–81; then of the Dominion of New England, starting in 1686, which, two years later, included New York and New Jersey. Because of Andros's suppression of colonial assemblies and local customs, the colonies revolted in 1689, becoming separate political entities once again. He was imprisoned and sent to England, but was never tried, returning to North America as colonial governor of Virginia in 1692–98, and Maryland in 1693–94. He finished his career in Europe as lieutenant governor of Guernsey.

With regard to Indian affairs, Andros helped bring an end to King Philip's War of 1675–76 by arming the Mohawks of New York to help defeat the Wampanoags and Narragansets under King PHILIP and CANONCHET. He instituted the first multicolonial treaties with the Iroquois League, finalized in Albany in 1677 and known as the Covenant Chain. The Iroquois gave him the name Corlaer, a title of friendship. He also helped make peace with the Susquehannocks, who became a tributary tribe to the Iroquois in the Covenant Chain. (See also PHILIP.)

ANNAWAN (Annawon, Anawon, "commander").
Wampanoag. (d. 1676). War chief in King Philip's War of 1675–76.

Annawan served under MASSASOIT (possibly his brother-in-law) as *missinnege* of the *panseis*, or leader of the war chiefs. During King Philip's War, Annawan also served as PHILIP's leading counselor and strategist.

After King Philip's death in August 1676, Annawan assumed command of the Wampanoag militants and led attacks on the white settlements of Swansea and Plymouth. By having his followers change camp nightly, Annawan successfully eluded men under Captain BENJAMIN CHURCH. Through an informer, Church finally tracked down the remaining rebels on August 26, 1676, at a swamp along the Rehoboth River, a location now known as Annawan's Rock. Church's men were able to divert the Indians long enough to seize most of their arms and trick them into believing they were up against a much larger force. Annawan, considering the situation hopeless, had his men surrender. He turned over the tribe's medicine bundle—deerskin wrapped around a large wampum belt telling of the tribe's history, a smaller wampum belt symbolizing the Wampanoag Confederacy, two powder horns, and a red blanket formerly belonging to Philip—thus marking the official end of the war.

The prisoners were taken to Plymouth for trial, where colonial officials ordered Annawan's execution. Church, who had come to respect his former antagonist, argued for Annawan's life. The war chief was temporarily spared, but while Church was away, a mob seized Annawan and beheaded him. With his death, the Wampanoag Confederacy came to an end. (See also PHILIP.)

ANNE (Queen Anne). *Powhatan. (d. 1725).* Tribal leader; ally of colonists. Wife of TOTOPOTOMOI.

On the death of her husband in 1656, in battle as an ally of the colonists against inland tribes, Queen Anne assumed leadership of the Pamunkey Indians, living at the junction of the Pamunkey and Mattapony rivers in Virginia, part of the POWHATAN Confederacy. In 1675, the governor of Virginia, WILLIAM BERKELEY, asked her help against rebels led by NATHANIEL BACON. She appeared at a council with Virginia officials in full Indian costume, accompanied by her son, and dramatically renounced the colonists for their neglect despite the fact that her husband had died fighting for them. On gaining promises of future compensation, she provided warriors to help suppress Bacon's

Rebellion in 1676. For her help, she was presented a silver badge inscribed to the "Queene of Pamunkey." She came before officials one last time in 1715, to petition for her people. (See also BACON, NATHANIEL.)

ANTONIO, JUAN (Cooswootna; Yampoochee, "he gets mad quickly"). *Cahuilla (Kawia).* *(ca. 1783–1863).* Chief in the post-mission and Gold Rush period.

In 1842, Juan Antonio of the Cahuillas of southern California met with Daniel Sexton, an early Anglo-American traveler, at the San Gorgino Pass, giving him permission to explore the region. During this period, as leader of the Mountain band (after the San Jacinto Mountains), Antonio lent support to a U.S. army expedition under Lieutenant EDWARD BEALE, defending the party against attacks by WALKARA's Utes. In appreciation, Beale presented the Cahuilla warrior with a set of military epaulets that Antonio wore as part of his ceremonial clothing.

During the 1850s, Antonio's Cahuillas competed with ranchers, miners, outlaws, Mormons, and the Cupeno Indians living west of his band, for control of the region. At the request of his friend, the part-Cherokee PAULINO WEAVER, and white ranchers, Antonio helped suppress the Cupeno uprising under ANTONIO GARRA in 1851–52. In spite of his help, the California senate refused to ratify the 1852 treaty giving the Cahuillas control of their lands. In 1854–55, Antonio himself led attacks on settlers, ceasing them only when his attempted alliance with the Quechans and Mojaves failed.

Antonio died from smallpox in 1863. Almost 100 years later, in 1956, an archeological dig at San Timoteo disturbed an Indian grave. On the skeleton's shoulders were military epaulets, verifying Antonio's identity. His remains were reburied with tribal honors.

ANZA, JUAN BAUTISTA DE. *(1735–1788).* Explorer; soldier; Spanish governor of New Mexico.

Juan de Anza was born in northern Mexico, the son of a presidio captain of the same name. When he was four, his father was killed by an Apache.

By 1759, Anza was commander of the presidio of Tubac in what is now southern Arizona. In the 1760s, he led several campaigns against the Apaches. In 1772, he opened an overland route from Mexico, through Arizona, into California. In 1774 and 1775–76, he led other expeditions to California, founding San Francisco during the latter.

In 1777, Anza became governor of New Mexico, serving until his death. He had contacts with many tribes of the Southwest and Far West and led numerous military expeditions against the raiding tribes, including one in 1779 in south-central Colorado against the Comanches

under CUERNO VERDE. In 1780, Anza attempted unsuccessfully to bring the Hopis under Spanish influence. That same year, he also tried to establish a direct route between Santa Fe and Sonora. His expedition reached Mexico, but the route proved impractical because of lack of water. In 1786, Anza established a lasting peace with the Comanches. His alliance with them, and with the Navajos and Utes, helped limit Apache raids.

APACHE KID (The Kid). *Chiricahua Apache.* *(ca. 1865–ca. 1894).* Army scout; outlaw.

The Apache Kid served as an army scout in the campaigns against GERONIMO of the 1880s under ALBERT SIEBER, chief of scouts. Sieber probably first called him the Kid, a nickname that later became the Apache Kid in newspaper accounts about his life as an outlaw.

In spring 1887, Sieber left the Apache Kid in charge of the other scouts while away from the San Carlos Agency, and, on returning, he learned that the Apache Kid and other scouts had killed a fellow Apache for the suspected murder of the Kid's father. Sieber ordered the arrest of those involved in the revenge- killing. A fight broke out in which Sieber was wounded in the foot. The Apache Kid and his companions fled, only to surrender after several weeks. They were tried and convicted; the Apache Kid was sentenced to seven years. While being escorted to jail, however, they escaped. All the fugitives were soon rounded up or killed, except the Apache Kid, who became one of Arizona's most famous outlaws. He preyed on white settlers for their food, and many killings in the region were blamed on him. Fellow Apache army scout MICKEY FREE tracked him for years.

In 1894, an Apache woman claimed she had been with the Apache Kid in the mountains while he was dying from a disease, probably tuberculosis. Free claimed that, in 1897, he located the Kid's remains in the mountains of New Mexico.

ARAPOOSH (Arapooish, Arrapooish, Eripuass, Rotten Belly, Sour Belly). *Crow.* *(ca. 1790–1834).* War chief of the River Crows in intertribal conflicts.

The River Crows lived along the Big Horn, Powder, and Wind rivers in present-day northern Wyoming and southern Montana. Arapoosh was considered the foremost warrior among them in their battles with traditional enemies, especially the Blackfeet, Sioux, and Northern Cheyennes. Before a battle or other tribal project, Arapoosh's shield, bearing a design of his guardian Moon spirit, would be rolled. If it fell face up, the project was undertaken; if face down, the project was abandoned. Arapoosh, suspicious of white intentions, refused to sign his tribe's 1825 treaty of friendship with the United States. The fur trader WILLIAM SUBLETTE met Arapoosh at Pierre's Hole, Idaho, in 1832; ROBERT CAMPBELL met him in 1833; and JAMES BECK-WOURTH, in 1834. Arapoosh died soon afterward in a battle with the Blackfeet.

ARMIJO. *Navajo . (fl. mid-1800s).* Farmer; leader in the Navajo War of 1863–66.

Armijo adopted the name of Manuel Armijo, the governor of New Mexico while it was still Mexican territory, prior to the Mexican War of 1846. The Navajo headman occupied lands in the Chuska foothills of northwest New Mexico where he practiced farming. Although consistently calling for peace between Indians and whites, he supported MANUELITO when fighting broke out in the 1860s. Armijo finally surrendered in April 1864, at Fort Canby, Arizona, and he and his followers were relocated with other Navajos to Bosque Redondo in New Mexico. In 1868, Armijo was one of the signers of the treaty establishing the Navajo Reservation in the Chuska Mountains of Arizona and New Mexico. (See also MANUELITO.)

ARPEIKA (Aripeka, Apayaka Hadjo; Sam Jones). *Seminole-Miccosukee. (ca. 1765–1860).* Medicine man; war chief of the Miccosukees in the Second Seminole War of 1835–42.

Arpeika is thought to have been born in Georgia and to have migrated south to Florida with other Miccosukees. There is a town named after him (Aripeka) located at what was thought to have been his principal village at the Weekwachee River north of Tampa. In 1841, he is known to have had a village north of Lake Okeechobee. Then, at the end of the Third Seminole War of 1855–58, he moved farther south, to Lake Okeechobee in Big Cypress Swamp.

Along with OSCEOLA, ALLIGATOR, and WILD CAT, Arpeika was the most militant of the Seminole chiefs in resisting removal from Florida to the Indian Territory. He counseled Osceola to take revenge on the Indian agent WILEY THOMPSON in 1835. Throughout the war, Arpeika warned his fellow chiefs to beware of white treachery and not to trust truce flags. He fought at the Battle of Lake Okeechobee in December 1837, as did Alligator and Wild Cat. The Indians inflicted heavy damage, but were forced to retreat.

Yet Arpeika and his band were never relocated. He even resisted further white attempts at removal during the Third Seminole War of 1855–58, along with BILLY BOWLEGS. Even when Bowlegs agreed to resettle in the Indian Territory, Arpeika stayed in Florida. He died soon afterward, his exact age uncertain, perhaps more than 100 years old. (See also OSCEOLA; BOWLEGS, BILLY.)

ASHLEY, WILLIAM HENRY. *(ca. 1778–1838).* Trader; explorer; soldier; official.

Born in Virginia, William Henry Ashley moved to Missouri in 1803, settling first in Ste. Genevieve, then in St. Louis. With ANDREW HENRY, he became involved in a profitable lead and gunpowder business during the War of 1812. He also served as a major in the Missouri militia, and, by 1822, he had reached the rank of general.

In 1821, Missouri achieved statehood, and Ashley became the first lieutenant governor. He also became involved in the fur trade with his earlier partner Andrew Henry. In February 1822, Ashley advertised for frontiersmen for an expedition up the Missouri. That spring, he and Henry led a party to the mouth of the Yellowstone River, founding Fort Henry (later the site of Fort Union, North Dakota). Ashley headed a second expedition of 70 in spring 1823. At the Arikara villages, near the present North Dakota–South Dakota border, his men were attacked by Arikara warriors, competitors as middlemen in the fur trade. Ashley sent word for help, resulting in the campaign under Colonel HENRY LEAVENWORTH that dispersed, but failed to pacify, the tribe.

Because of the danger of Indian attacks along the Missouri, Ashley decided to send out small parties of trappers on horseback, the start of the Rocky Mountain fur trade and the brigade system of trapping with regular rendezvous of trappers and friendly Indians, especially the Crows. Ashley employed many of the mountain men, including JAMES BRIDGER, ROBERT CAMPBELL, JAMES CLYMAN, THOMAS FITZ-PATRICK, HUGH GLASS, EDWARD ROSE, JEDEDIAH SMITH, and WILLIAM SUBLETTE, all of whom contributed to the white exploration of the West.

In 1824, Ashley led a wagon and pack train west to supply his trappers at the first rendezvous in the Green River in what is now Wyoming, the first such wagon train crossing through South Pass. Arriving in April 1825, he led an exploratory expedition down the Green River past the mouth of the Uinta River in what is now Utah. Ashley and his party were the first whites to navigate that river. He then attended the rendezvous that July. He attended a second one the next year, at which he sold his business to Jedediah Smith, David E. Jackson, and William Sublette.

Ashley returned to St. Louis, where he continued to develop business interests, but he devoted more and more of this time to politics. He ran unsuccessfully for the governorship of Missouri and for the U.S. Senate, but served in the House of Representatives in 1831–37.

ASPINET. *Wampanoag. (d. 1623).* Sagamore of the Wampanoag Confederacy under MASSASOIT.

Aspinet, sachem of the Nauset Indians of Cape Cod, a subtribe of the Wampanoag Confederacy, was friendly to the Plymouth colonists. He and his ally IYANOUGH rescued a boy, John Billington, who had wandered off from the settlement, returning him to his parents. Aspinet also provided corn and beans to the starving settlers, helping them survive the winter of 1621–22. In spring 1623, however, the Wampanoag grand sachem Massasoit informed the colonists that his sagamores Aspinet and Iyanough were part of a plot against the colonists, supposedly involving their Wampanoag followers as well as Massachuset and Narraganset militants. MILES STANDISH attacked and drove the supposed rebels into the swamps where both Aspinet and Iyanough died, probably of diseases they had caught from the Europeans.

ASSACUMBUIT (Old Escambuit, Nescambiuoit).
Abnaki. (d. 1727). Ally of French in the Abnaki Wars of the late 1600s and early 1700s (part of the French and Indian Wars).

Like other Abnaki chiefs BOMAZEEN, MADOKAWANDO, and MOXUS, Assacumbuit participated in the French offensive against British settlements. He and his warriors joined the French in the attack on Fort St. Johns, New Brunswick, in 1696; the attack on Casco, Maine, in 1703; and several other raids on British settlements in Newfoundland in 1704–05. Assacumbuit visited France in 1705–06, where he was received, knighted, and presented with a sword by Louis XIV. In 1707, back in North America, he joined the French in their raid on Haverhill, Massachusetts, and continued to support the French against the British until his death.

ASSALL, FRIEDRICH W. *(fl. 1820s).* Archaeologist
Friedrich Assall came to the United States from Germany in 1818, where he served as a soldier for nine months before beginning his intended career as a miner. After having lived for a time in Ohio, he eventually settled in Pennsylvania where he became the head mining officer for the state. On a visit to Germany in 1823, he conferred with the Heidelberg professor Franz Joseph Mone on the Indian earthworks he had observed along the Ohio Valley, and Mone encouraged Assall to write about them. Assall's monograph of 1827 was one of the earliest studies of the Mound Builders and helped to make German scholars aware of the subject. Caleb Atwater wrote about the earthworks during the same period.

ASTOR, JOHN JACOB. *(1763–1848).* Trader.
Born in Germany, John Jacob Astor moved to England in the 1770s, where he worked in his brother's musical instrument business. In 1783, he crossed the Atlantic and settled in New York City, where, in 1785,

he married Sarah Todd, the daughter of a prominent and politically well-connected family.

Aided by his wife's knowledge of furs, Astor soon embarked on a career in the fur trade in the Northeast and Old Northwest. Over the next 20 years, he developed a profitable trading enterprise. At that time, his business was dependent on the prices set by the Canadian companies—the Hudson's Bay Company and the North West Company, which dominated the beaver fur industry.

In 1808, following the successful exploration of LEWIS and CLARK into the newly acquired territory of the 1803 Louisiana Purchase, Astor chartered the American Fur Company under the sponsorship of THOMAS JEFFERSON, with the plan of developing a series of fur-trading forts and factories along the Lewis and Clark route. In 1810, he founded the subsidiary Pacific Fur Company, and, the next year, the Southwest Fur Company.

Astor set out to found a trading port at the mouth of the Columbia River in Oregon. Recognizing the vast fur resources of the Rocky Mountains, he planned to establish a trade in furs with China, thus circumventing the Hudson's Bay Company's domination. In 1811, his ship, the *Tonquin*, established the settlement of Astoria, on the Oregon coast, near the site where Lewis and Clark had wintered six years earlier.

Astor also commissioned WILSON PRICE HUNT to undertake an overland expedition from St. Louis to Astoria, starting in 1811. The Iowa woman MARIE DORIAN acted as one of the guides.

Astor's agents soon made plans to involve Indians in the western fur industry, but were unable to induce the Nez Perces, Cayuses, or Shoshones to take part. The Nez Perces did agree to sell surplus horses to Astor's company, however. The Cayuses and Shoshones, after initial hostility, were persuaded only to permit fur trapping by whites on their lands.

The pressures brought on by the War of 1812, attacks by Indians, and the difficulty of supplying Astoria from New York, caused Astor to sell his Oregon coast port to the British North West Company in 1813. In the meantime, the Astoria settlement was reducing the surrounding Indian population by as much as a half because of its introduction of alcohol and European diseases.

Astor chose to concentrate on developing his Great Lakes operation, centered at Green Bay, Wisconsin. In 1817, he obtained full control of the South West Company, in which he had originally invested as a partner. Astor's introduction of liquor into trade with the Indians brought him conflict with local federal Indian commissioners, but his influence with such political leaders as LEWIS CASS helped keep his trade thriving with a minimum of government interference. In 1821, he successfully lobbied Congress to abolish government fur-trading operations in effect since 1796—the "factory system"—to further benefit his empire. He also competed with St. Louis interests headed, during the early 1820s, by WILLIAM HENRY ASHLEY. Other rivals included the Rocky Mountain Fur Company, founded in 1830 by THOMAS FITZPATRICK, JAMES BRIDGER, Milton Sublette, Henry Fraeb, and Jean Baptiste Gervais.

In 1834, Astor sold all his fur company interests and focused his business activities on the speculation and development of New York City real estate and hotels. At his death in 1848, Astor was the richest man in America, leaving an estate worth $20 million.

ATKIN, EDMOND (Edmund Atkin). *(1707–1761).* Colonial Indian superintendent.

Edmond Atkin, who moved to South Carolina from England as a boy, ran a trading company in Charleston during the 1730s. In 1738, he was appointed to the governor's council of South Carolina.

In 1746, Atkin wrote a history of the Choctaw Revolt of that year, involving the activities and death of RED SHOES. In 1755, Atkin published what is known as the Atkin Report and Plan to the Board of Trade. In addition to giving ethnographic information concerning many of the eastern tribes, he advocated the centralization of Indian policy under the direction of the Crown in order to compete with the French. He also recommended a chain of forts to protect British interests.

The British government followed many of his recommendations and established the superintendency system over Indians in 1756, appointing Atkin head of the Southern Department and WILLIAM JOHNSON head of the Northern Department. The Southern Department included territory west of the Appalachian Mountains and south of the Ohio River; the Northern Department, territory also west of the Appalachians but north of the Ohio.

Although the superintendents were supposedly responsible for all relations between the colonists and the tribes, they were often at odds with colonial governors and assemblies concerning economic control of the frontier. Atkin was accused by other officials of being financially self-serving and slow in sending supplies to frontier posts. He was succeeded by JOHN STUART.

ATKINSON, HENRY. *(1782–1842).* Army officer; explorer.

North Carolina–born Henry Atkinson entered the army in 1808, rising to the rank of colonel during the War of 1812.

In 1819, JOHN C. CALHOUN, secretary of War under President James Monroe, planned a series of expeditions to demonstrate the extent of United States military power to the Indians of the upper Missouri River, as well as to British traders. Atkinson was given the command. His force of more than 1,100 soldiers, plus women and children, failed to reach the mouth of the Yellowstone River as intended, but established the first fort west of the Missouri near Council Bluffs—Fort Atkinson in what is now Nebraska—which became an important center of the fur trade. In 1820, Major STEPHEN H. LONG embarked on his expedition to the Rocky Mountains from this post. In 1823, Colonel HENRY LEAVENWORTH set out from Fort Atkinson on a punitive expedition against the Arikaras for attacking a fur-trading party under WILLIAM HENRY ASHLEY.

In 1825, Atkinson sailed up the Missouri with a force of 457 men in eight keelboats on the second Yellowstone Expedition, this time reaching the mouth of the Yellowstone River near what is now the North Dakota–Montana border. Atkinson and Indian agent BENJAMIN O'FALLON negotiated treaties with 12 tribes, including the Cheyennes under HIGH-BACKED WOLF.

In 1826, Atkinson oversaw the founding of Jefferson Barracks south of St. Louis, Missouri, for troops under Leavenworth and Captain STEPHEN WATTS KEARNY. In 1827, Atkinson sent Leavenworth into what is now Kansas, where Fort Leavenworth was established. That same year, Atkinson battled the Winnebagos under RED BIRD.

During the Black Hawk War, as a general and commander of a force of 1,300 regulars and volunteers, Atkinson pursued BLACK HAWK's militant band of Sacs and Foxes, catching up with them on the Bad Axe River, Wisconsin, in August 1832. After the removal of those tribes, Atkinson also directed the relocation of the Winnebagos to Iowa in 1840. (See also BLACK HAWK; RED BIRD.)

ATOTARHO (Atotarhoh, Wathatotarho, Thadodaho, Tododaho, Ododarho). *Onondaga.* *(fl. 1500s).* One of the principal leaders in the formation of the Iroquois League.

The story of the Iroquois League's or Confederacy's beginnings has taken on mythical proportions. As the legend goes, the Mohawk named HIAWATHA, upon inspiration by the Huron mystic DEGANAWIDA, traveled throughout present-day New York among the Mohawks, Oneidas, Onondagas, Cayugas, and Senecas in the late 1500s (or earlier) to preach peace and alliance. According to Iroquois tradition, Atotarho was a powerful sorcerer with serpents growing out of his head, turtle claws for hands and feet, a crooked body, plus other supernatural traits. Of all the sachems, he was the most bitterly opposed to Hiawatha's message. In order to complete the alliance, Hiawatha supposedly had to comb the serpents out of Atotarho's head and straighten his mind and body.

Atotarho insisted that certain conditions be met, including that the Onondagas serve as hosts of the annual Great Council; that they have more representatives at the council than any other tribe; that they keep the wampum belt serving as the record of the meeting; and that they maintain the ever-burning council fire at their village. Atotarho's name was the official title of a hereditary chief; others after him also bore it. (See also DEGANAWIDA; HIAWATHA.)

ATSIDI SANI.   See DELGADITO.

ATTAKULLAKULLA (Attacullaculla, Atagulkalu; Onacona, Oukounaka, Ukwaneequa; Little Carpenter).   *Cherokee. (ca. 1700–ca. 1778).* Peace chief; ally of colonists. Father of DRAGGING CANOE; uncle of NANCY WARD.

In 1730, Attakullakulla accompanied a delegation of Cherokee and Creek chiefs to the royal court in London,

taken there by Sir Alexander Cumming. In 1738, he became the peace chief of the Cherokees. During this period, Standing Turkey was the principal chief and OCONOSTOTA, the war chief. In 1750, Attakullakulla spoke on behalf of the Cherokees at a conference with Governor John Glen of South Carolina. He was friendly to whites and saved the life of William Byrd, one of the treaty commissioners, from militant tribesmen who had planned a surprise attack.

Attakullakulla's efforts on behalf of the colonists led to the Treaty of Broad River and the building of Fort Dobbs in 1756. Three years later, his intercession led to the release of Oconostota, who had been arrested by South Carolina officials. During the subsequent Cherokee War of 1760–61, after the Indian siege and capture of Fort Loudon in present-day Tennessee by Cherokees under Oconostota, Attakullakulla ransomed JOHN STUART and escorted him safely to Virginia. The next year, Attakullakulla helped negotiate the Treaty of Charleston, ending the conflict. After the war, John Stuart became the second Southern Department super-

The Pacification of Atotarhoh. Deganawida and Hiawatha urge Atotarho to join the Iroquois League while other Iroquoi flee. Drawing by Jesse Cornplanter, Iroquois in 1906. *Courtesy of New York State Library, Albany.*

intendent for the British, following EDMOND ATKIN. In 1763, Stuart held a conference in Augusta, Georgia, attended by Attakullakulla and other Cherokees, as well as Creeks, Chickasaws, and Choctaws. The gifts to the Indians and various trade agreements enacted there helped maintain the peace.

Despite these agreements and his friendship with Stuart, Attakullakulla supported the Patriot cause in the American Revolution and raised a regiment of about 500 Cherokee warriors. He continued playing a principal role in negotiations between Indians and whites until his death in 1777 or 1778, probably in Tennessee.

ATTUCKS, CRISPUS ("small deer"). *Mixed Massachuset. (ca. 1723–1770).* First casualty of the pre-Revolutionary Boston Massacre.

Crispus Attucks was the son of a black man and a Massachuset woman who lived in the Indian mission settlement at Natick. He took his name from his mother. It is thought that Attucks was a slave in a Framington, Massachusetts, household who ran away in 1750 and worked as a sailor. The incident known as the Boston Massacre occurred five years before Lexington and Concord and the outbreak of the American Revolution. On March 5, 1770, colonists, upset with tax laws (the Townshend Acts), attacked a detachment of British troops under Captain Thomas Preston in front of the Customs House. The soldiers fired into the rioting crowd, killing five men—three immediately, two later from wounds. Attucks, thought by some to be the leader of the rioters, was the first to fall. In 1888, the Crispus Attucks Monument was erected on Boston Common.

ATWATER, CALEB. *(1778–1867).* Archaeologist.

Caleb Atwater, a native of Massachusetts, attended Williams College, then moved to Ohio where he served as postmaster, state legislator, and state archaeologist. He made a study of the Indian earthworks of Ohio and neighboring states, the earliest archaeological survey of its kind for North America, and traveled to other continents to view and compare mounds. He reached the erroneous conclusion that the Mound Builders had migrated from the Near East and were not the ancestors of the Indians. His *Description of the Antiquities Discovered in the State of Ohio and other Western States* was published by the American Antiquiarian Society in 1820. Atwater later worked for the Bureau of Indian Affairs under President ANDREW JACKSON.

AWASHONKS ("the queen"; Squaw Sachem of the Saconnets). *Wampanoag. (fl. 1670s).* Ally of colonists in King Philip's War.

Awashonks's husband Tolony is thought to have died before King Philip's War of 1675–76 because, at that time, she was ruler of the Saconnet band from the vicinity of present-day Little Compton, Rhode Island. Her band was part of the Wampanoag Confederacy. Early in the conflict, she gave permission for some of her warriors to join King PHILIP's Wampanoags in revolt against the British, but, after a meeting with Captain BENJAMIN CHURCH, she switched her support to the colonists. Some of the Saconnets, including her son Peter Awashonks, subsequently took up arms against former Wampanoag allies. During the fighting, Awashonks led her people to the settlement of Sandwich, Massachusetts. She had other meetings with Church and the two became close friends. (See also PHILIP.)

B

BACON, NATHANIEL. *(1647–1676).* Leader of Bacon's Rebellion of 1676. Cousin of WILLIAM BERKELEY.

An English aristocrat and relative of Francis Bacon, Nathaniel Bacon came to North America in 1673, settling in Virginia, where, soon after, the general unrest between Indians and settlers along the Virginia and Maryland frontier erupted into violence.

The first incident involved a dispute over a debt between the Nanticokes and farmers. Virginia and Maryland militiamen took out their revenge on Susquehannocks as well, killing some of their chiefs when they came to negotiate under a flag of truce. The Susquehannocks in turn also attacked Virginia farmers.

Without permission from William Berkeley, the governor of Virginia and his cousin, Bacon commanded two expeditions against the Susquehannocks, as well as against the peaceful Monacans and Ocaneechis, taking many lives and destroying property.

In June 1676, Bacon led his force to Jamestown, where he coerced the Virginia House of Burgesses into commissioning himself as a commander in chief of the Indian war and into instituting civil and agricultural reforms on behalf of the small farmers. Governor Berkeley himself began raising troops. Bacon moved his force to Williamsburg, where he set out on a campaign against the Pamunkey Indians, who had been loyal to whites for years, killing many.

Governor Berkeley crossed to the eastern shore to raise more troops, and the Pamunkey (Powhatan) leader Queen ANNE, widow of TOTOPOTOMOI, provided warriors for the fight against the force led by Bacon. Berkeley sailed back to Jamestown and occupied it, proclaiming his cousin and his followers rebels and traitors. Bacon's force soon returned, and, after a skirmish, captured Jamestown and put it to the torch.

Bacon died of a disease in October 1676, and, without his leadership, the movement collapsed. The aristocracy regained its power, but some of the civil and agricultural reforms of the rebellion, which protected small farmers, stayed in effect. Meanwhile, the once-powerful Susquehannocks were dispersed and never recovered from Bacon's war on them.

BAIRD, SPENCER FULLERTON. *(1823–1887).* Museum curator.

Spencer Baird was born in Reading, Pennsylvania, and became professor of natural history at Dickinson College. Specializing in ornithology, he was appointed assistant secretary of the Smithsonian Institution's National Museum in 1850, then secretary in 1878. In addition to assembling the Smithsonian's specimens of North American fauna, Baird helped develop its collection of Indian artifacts. JAMES SWAN was his primary collector in the field. Baird was especially active in the acquisition of Northwest Coast Indian objects for the Smithsonian's exhibit at the 1876 Centennial Exposition in Philadelphia. In 1871, he became the first U.S. commissioner of fish and fisheries.

BALDWIN, FRANK DWIGHT. *(1842–1923).* Army officer in the Plains Indian wars; Indian agent.

Frank D. Baldwin, born in Manchester, Michigan, enlisted in the 2nd Michigan Infantry at age 19, soon after the outbreak of the Civil War. In 1862, he became a lieutenant in the 19th Michigan Infantry, and was assigned to the Army of the Ohio. In actions in Tennessee, during 1862–63, he was captured twice by the Confederates and released. Baldwin was later with General WILLIAM T. SHERMAN's army in Georgia, leading a charge at Peachtree Creek. By the end of the war, he had been promoted to the rank of lieutenant colonel of volunteers.

Reenlisting in the regular army in 1866, Baldwin was commissioned a lieutenant. Assigned to Fort Ellsworth, Kansas, he served with troops protecting stagecoaches from attacks by Cheyenne and Arapaho raiding parties. It was during this tour of duty that he first served under colonel NELSON A. MILES. From 1867 to 1874, he was assigned to garrison duty in the New Mexico Territory.

Baldwin was called to serve under Miles again in Kansas during the Red River War of 1874–75, fighting Southern Plains tribes under the Comanche leader QUANAH PARKER. In June 1874, Baldwin was sent to Fort Dodge, Kansas, where his unit joined with General JOHN POPE's forces in their attack on the Indians in the Texas Panhandle. In its campaign, he commanded a company of Miles's scouts, consisting of 20 Delawares, some white volunteers, and about 25 regular army troops. In November 1874, near McClellan's Creek, Texas, Baldwin's company of scouts encountered the village of the Cheyenne chief Grey Beard. Although outnumbered, Baldwin led an attack against the Cheyennes in an engagement that came to be known as the Charge of the Wagon Train. Baldwin managed to rescue two small girls, the German sisters, who had been held captive.

With the onset of the Sioux War for the Black Hills, Baldwin was appointed as battalion adjutant for Miles's unit, and, after the Indian victory at Little Bighorn in June 1876, was sent to join General ALFRED TERRY's force. In December of that year, Baldwin led his company in an attack on SITTING BULL's village and Cheyenne encampments, destroying many of the Indians' winter supplies. In January 1877, at the Battle of Wolf Mountain, in Montana, against Sioux and Northern Cheyennes under CRAZY HORSE, Baldwin led his company in a charge against the Indians who had been attacking Miles's encampment from bluffs above the Tongue River. At Fort Keogh, Montana, Baldwin trained scouts and led his troops in pursuit of Sioux raiding parties throughout the Yellowstone region, as far as the Canadian border.

In 1877, following the Nez Perce War, Baldwin escorted Chief JOSEPH (Young Joseph) and his Nez Perce people to their assigned reservations in the Indian Territory. In 1878, afflicted with tuberculosis, he was assigned emergency medical leave to Fort Marion, Florida.

In 1879, promoted to captain, Baldwin patrolled the Plains north of the Missouri River and arrested hundreds of white traders who had been unlawfully supplying ammunition and whiskey to the Indians. In spring 1880, Baldwin's company destroyed Indian villages and supplies, a strategy that soon led to the surrender of over 1,000 Indians.

Following an assignment in France in 1881, Baldwin was appointed as acting judge advocate and aide to now–General Miles, in the army's Department of the Columbia in the Pacific Northwest. In this capacity, he helped negotiate treaties with Sinkiuse-Salish chief MOSES and leaders of other tribes of the Columbia River region.

In 1885, Baldwin was again assigned to escort Chief Joseph's Nez Perce band, this time back from the Indian Territory to their newly assigned reservations in the Pacific Northwest. In the late 1880s, he served at posts throughout Montana, Texas, Arizona, and the Dakotas.

Following the attack on BIG FOOT's band at Wounded Knee in December 1890, General Miles appointed Baldwin to help supervise the army's inquiry of the incident. Baldwin, along with the other officer in charge of the inquiry, Major John Ford Kent, concluded that Colonel JAMES FORSYTH was responsible for the Wounded Knee tragedy. This determination was subsequently overruled by officials in the War Department.

Between 1894 and 1898, Baldwin, still an army officer, was the agent for the Kiowas and Comanches in the Indian Territory. His duties included evicting "sooners," or whites who had unlawfully encroached upon Indian lands. He also helped protect Indian lands against whites married to Indians, who initiated lawsuits demanding an equal share of reservation allotments.

Baldwin was promoted to major in 1898, then to lieutenant colonel of volunteers in the Spanish-American War. In 1902, he was sent to the Philippines to put down an insurrection. He retired to Denver in 1906, after having reached the rank of brigadier general. He remained active in the National Guard in Colorado, becoming the state's adjutant general and supervising the training of recruits in 1917 for combat in World War I, then retired for the last time in 1919 as a major general. For his actions at Peachtree Creek in Georgia during the Civil War, and for his rescue of the German sisters at McClellan's Creek in the Red River War, Baldwin was awarded two Congressional Medals of Honor in 1891 and 1894.

Baldwin recorded his field experiences in the Indian wars in a diary, and his firsthand account was edited and published by his wife, Alice Blackwood Baldwin, in the 1929 book, *The Memoirs of the Late Major General Frank D. Baldwin*. (See also BIG FOOT; CRAZY HORSE; Young JOSEPH; PARKER, QUANAH; SITTING BULL.)

BANCROFT, HUBERT HOWE. *(1832–1918).*
Historian; publisher.

Hubert Howe Bancroft, born and raised in Granville, Ohio, joined his brother-in-law in Buffalo, New York, when he was 16, and worked with him in his bookselling business. Four years later, Bancroft moved to California, where he worked various jobs, most related to the book trade. In 1856, he started a mercantile business.

In 1859, with the idea of writing an encyclopedia, Bancroft began collecting materials on the Far West, Mexico, and Central America. In 1871, he began work in San Francisco with a staff of researchers and writers on a series of histories that he published and sold by subscription from 1874 to 1890, including the five-volume *Native Races* (1874–75). The principal writers on his studies of the western states were Henry Oak, his librarian, and FRANCES FULLER VICTOR. All told, his firm, the so-called History Factory, employed 600 people, as many as 50 at a time.

Bancroft's method as a historian included the use of interviews and newspaper reports as source materials. The 39 volumes were reissued in 1882–90 as *The World of Hubert Howe Bancroft*. In 1905, he donated his extensive collection of source materials—the 60,000-volume Bancroft Library—to the University of California.

BANDELIER, ADOLPH FRANCIS ALPHONSE. *(1840–1914).* Anthropologist; historian.

Swiss-born Adolph (or Adolf) Bandelier grew up in the farming country of Illinois, but returned to Switzerland for some of his schooling. While supporting himself with clerical work in Highland, Illinois, he studied the history and culture of Mexican and Southwest Indians. He corresponded with LEWIS HENRY MORGAN and was influenced by his views of evolutionary anthropology.

In 1882, Bandelier began his studies in New Mexico and Arizona of the Pueblo Indians, and he began to compare Mayan architecture with the ruins at Pecos Pueblo. He worked at various times with FRANK HAMILTON CUSHING, participating in the Hemenway Southwestern Archaeological Expedition, and with JOHN WESLEY POWELL. He was a close friend of CHARLES LUMMIS, who accompanied him as photographer on an expedition to Peru in 1892.

In addition to his scientific works, Bandelier wrote a novel, *The Delight Makers* (1918), based on his studies of Pueblo peoples. In 1916, the Anasazi ruins in the canyon of Rito de los Frijoles near Los Alamos, New Mexico, were established as the Bandelier National Monument in his honor.

BARAGA, FREDERIC. *(1797–1868).* Linguist; missionary.

Born in Austria, Frederic Baraga came to the United States as a Catholic missionary in 1830. He worked first among the Ottawas in Michigan, then among the Chippewas of Michigan and Wisconsin. In 1843, he founded the L'Anse Mission, and, 10 years later, was made a bishop. Baraga, Michigan, near present-day L'Anse, is named after him. He wrote two works on the Chippewa (Ojibway) dialect of Algonquian: *Practical and Theoretical Grammar of the Otchipewe Language* (1850) and *Dictionary of the Otchipewe Language* (1853).

BARANOV, ALEKSANDR ANDREEVICH (Alexander Andreyevich Baranov or Baranof). *(1747–1819).* Trader; Russia governor of Alaska.

Born in Kargopol, Russia, near the Arctic Ocean port of Archangel, Aleksandr Baranov moved to Moscow in 1762, where he was employed as a clerk for a German company. In the 1770s, he relocated to the Siberian city of Irkutsk, where he first became involved in the fur trade. His business soon fell victim to raids by Siberian Chukchi Eskimo natives, forcing him into bankruptcy.

In 1790, Baranov was hired by GREGORI SHELIKOV to manage his fur company on Kodiak Island in Alaska. Shipwrecked on Unalaska Island in the Aleutians, he arrived at the settlement of Three Saints in spring 1790. Sea otter pelts were the mainstay of the Russo-American fur trade, and Baranov sought to employ the Aleuts to aid in exploiting this valuable resource. He took an Indian woman as his wife and sanctioned relations between Russian males and Aleut women. Under Baranov, a Russian fur interests forcibly employed whole Aleut villages to trap the sea otters, then process and ship the pelts. Baranov also established trade contacts between Russian Alaska, the Hawaiian Islands, and China.

In 1799, the year the Russian Fur Company was granted a fur-trading monopoly charter by Czar Paul I, Baranov established a settlement, New Archangel (Sitka), on what came to be called Baranof Island in the Alexander Archipelago of southeastern Alaska.

Baranov was constantly at odds with the Tlingit Indians of the region. The Tlingits declined to work for Baranov because the Russian trade goods he offered were too expensive and of inferior quality to the trade goods available from the British and the Americans, but they did allow the Russians and their Aleut hunters to trap for furs on their tribal lands in exchange for gifts. The Tlingits under KATLIAN eventually became concerned over the depletion of their own fur resources and attacked and captured Sitka in 1802. Although Baranov returned with an armada and recaptured Sitka two years later, the settlement was subject to Tlingit attacks for the next 20 years. Baranov had to call in ships to patrol Alaskan waters.

In addition to establishing fur-trading stations on Alaska's southeast panhandle, Baranov was instrumental in the founding of Fort Ross in northern California by his associate I. A. Kuskov in 1812. With persistent Pomo Indian resistance, the Russians departed this frontier settlement in 1841.

During his tenure as manager of the Russian-American Fur Company, Baranov was named as

Russia's governor of Alaska. Although he attempted to stabilize relations with the Aleuts and other Alaskan tribes, he developed a reputation for abusive labor and trade practices among the native population. Baranov was terminated as manager of the royally chartered Russian-American Fur Company in 1818. He died on the voyage home and was buried at sea in the Indian Ocean.

BARBONCITA (Barbon; Hastin Dagha, Hastin Daagi, "man with whiskers"; Bislahalani, "the orator"; Hozhooji Naata, "blessing speaker").
Navajo. (ca. 1820–1871). Ceremonial singer; war chief in the Navajo War of 1863–66. Brother of DELGADITO.

Barboncito, born at Canyon de Chelly in what is now Arizona, was a band leader and religious singer among his people. In 1846, during the Mexican War, he signed a treaty with ALEXANDER W. DONIPHAN, agreeing to terms of friendship with whites.

In April 1860, after an incident in which soldiers killed Navajo horses over the issue of grazing lands around Fort Defiance, Arizona, Barboncito joined MANUELITO in an attack on the post. In 1862, Barboncito and Delgadito informed General JAMES H. CARLETON of their peaceful intentions. The following year, however, when ordered to relocate to Bosque Redondo in eastern New Mexico, the brothers joined Manuelito in rebellion.

Barboncito was captured at Canyon de Chelly in September 1864 by troops under Colonel CHRISTOPHER "KIT" CARSON, and then forced to resettle at Bosque Redondo with other Navajos and Mescalero Apaches. On experiencing the terrible conditions, he escaped with about 500 followers in June 1865, rejoining Manuelito. He surrendered a second time in November 1866, leading 21 followers to Fort Wingate.

Barboncito signed the treaty of June 1, 1868, establishing the Navajo Reservation in the Chuska Mountains, where he died three years later. (See also MANUELITO.)

BARNARD, TIMPOOCHEE. *Mixed Yuchi.*
(fl. early 1800s). Ally of Americans in the Creek War of 1813–14).

Timpoochee Barnard's father was Scotsman Timothy Barnard, a friend and employee of BENJAMIN HAWKINS; his mother was a Yuchi.

Although most of the Yuchis were Red Sticks and sided with WILLIAM WEATHERFORD in the Creek War, Timpoochee led 100 Yuchi warriors in support of American forces under General ANDREW JACKSON. In the Battle of Callabee Creek on January 2, 1814, his daring charge enabled outnumbered American forces under Captain John Broadnix to safely retreat. Timpoochee was one of the signers of the Treaty of Fort Jackson, Alabama, in August 1814. He later settled at the Creek Agency on the Flint River in Georgia with his Creek wife.

In 1827, Timpoochee requested that THOMAS McKENNEY, who had visited Creek country for treaty negotiations, take William Barnard, his 13-year-old son, and Lee Compere, the 10-year-old son of another chief, back to Washington, D.C., to be educated. (See also WEATHERFORD, WILLIAM.)

BARRY, DAVID F. *(1854–1934).* Photographer.
Born in Honeoy Falls, New York, D.F. Barry traveled to Osego, Wisconsin, with his family when he was seven years old. In 1878–79, he ran the studio of the frontier photographer ORLANDO SCOTT GOFF at Bismarck in what is now North Dakota, and photographed Sioux Indians of the Standing Rock Reservation. Chief GALL was a frequent subject and became the photographer's good friend. In 1880–83, Barry spent time at Fort Buford, North Dakota, and Fort Custer, Montana, and, in 1889, photographed some of the negotiations involved in the breakup of the Great Sioux Reservation into smaller tracts. Barry later lived in Superior, Wisconsin, and New York City.

BARTLETT, JOHN RUSSELL. *(1805–1886).*
Anthropologist; boundary commissioner.
Born in Providence, Rhode Island, John Russell Bartlett was raised both there and in Kingston, Ontario. In 1836, he moved to New York City, where he operated a bookstore specializing in literature and science. In 1842, along with ALBERT GALLATIN, he helped form the American Ethnological Society and, in 1847, published *Progress of Ethnology*. He also became a close friend of Edgar Allan Poe.

Appointed by the federal government as a boundary commissioner in 1850, following the tenure of JOHN C. FREMONT, Bartlett traveled to the Southwest to help finalize the negotiated border settlement with Mexico, in compliance with the treaty that had ended the Mexican War two years earlier. In this capacity, he made a series of survey expeditions into the region between Tucson in the Arizona Territory and the Mexican provinces of Sonora and Chihuahua, which eventually became United States holdings with the GADSDEN Purchase of 1853.

Bartlett recorded his observations on the history, archeology, and ethnology of Native Americans he encountered. His journal, *Personal Narrative of Explorations and Incidents Connected with the United States and Mexican Boundary Commission*, with illustrations by the author, was published in 1854.

BARTRAM, WILLIAM. *(1739–1823)*. Naturalist; trader; explorer.

William Bartram was born at Kingsessing, Pennsylvania, now part of the city of Philadelphia. His father was the Quaker botanist John Bartram. William studied printing and drawing under the tutelage of BENJAMIN FRANKLIN, then went to work for a Philadelphia merchant. In 1761, he moved south and established himself as an independent trader at Cape Fear, North Carolina.

In 1765–66, Bartram accompanied his father on an expedition along Florida's Saint Johns River, where he had contact with the Seminole Indians. In 1773–77, he undertook an exploration of the Southeast, including the Carolinas, Georgia, and Florida.

After his return to Pennsylvania in 1778, Bartram was associated with the Botany Department at the University of Pennsylvania. He became a member of Franklin's American Philosophical Society in 1786.

Bartram's book, *Travels Through North and South Carolina, Georgia, East and West Florida, the Cherokee Country, the Extensive Territories of the Muscogulges, or Creek Confederacy, and the Country of the Choctaws*, was published in 1791. This work on the flora and fauna of the Southeast, as well as on the ethnology of the Indians of the region, was translated into Dutch, French, and German, and influenced the romantic philosophers and poets of Europe. His father, John Bartram, feared Indians and viewed them as an obstacle to his botanical studies. William Bartram, however, depicted them as living the life of natural men and women in a bountiful paradise. His other work, *Observations on the Creek and Cherokee*, written in 1789, was published in 1853.

BASCOM, GEORGE NICHOLAS. *(fl. 1860s)*. Soldier; instigator of the Bascom Affair.

In 1861, along the Apache Pass through the Chiricahua Mountains of Arizona, Second Lieutenant George Bascom out of Fort Buchanan, under the command of Colonel Pitcairn Morrison, tried to arrest COCHISE for a crime the Chiricahua chief denied committing. Cochise escaped, but Bascom managed to take some of his family hostage and later presided over the hanging of six Chiricahua captives. This incident precipitated the first phase of the Apache Wars of 1861–86. (See also COCHISE.)

BATTEY, THOMAS C. (Thomissey). *(1828–1897)*. Indian agent; teacher.

Thomas Battey was born and grew up on a farm in Starksboro, Vermont. After having attended a Friends' school at Westtown outside Philadelphia, he became a schoolteacher in Viola, Iowa (present-day Springville).

In 1871, during President ULYSSES S. GRANT's Peace Policy to the Indians, Battey applied and was accepted for a teaching position at the Wichita Agency in the Indian Territory (present-day Anadarko, Oklahoma). With the agent A. J. Standing, another Quaker, Battey helped build a schoolhouse where he taught Caddo Indians.

In 1873, Battey transferred to the Kiowa Agency at Fort Sill as teacher and field agent and worked in the camp of KICKING BIRD, leader of the Kiowa peace faction. Known to the Indians as Thomissey, he was trusted by even the militant Kiowas. During the Red River War of 1874–75, he acted as negotiator and played a central role in convincing SATANTA and BIG TREE to honor their parole and report to federal officials in October 1874.

After peace had been achieved, Battey returned to his family in Iowa. On the death of his second wife, he moved to Ohio, where he remarried and lived out his remaining years. His book, *A Quaker Among the Indians*, was published in 1875. (See also SATANTA.)

BEALE, EDWARD FITZGERALD *(1822–1893)*. Indian superintendent; soldier; explorer; surveyor and road builder.

Born in the District of Columbia, Edward Beale graduated from the U.S. Naval Academy at Annapolis in 1842, then served as a lieutenant in the navy in California during the Mexican War of 1846–48 as a courier to Commodore Robert F. Stockton. Beale was with General STEPHEN WATTS KEARNY's forces at San Pasqual, south of Los Angeles, in December 1846, when the Americans were surrounded by Mexican troops. With scout CHRISTOPHER "KIT" CARSON and an Indian friendly to the American cause, Beale slipped through the enemy lines and reached Stockton and the U.S. fleet at San Diego, where a detachment of sailors and marines were dispatched to reinforce Kearny and his command. The following month, American troops went on to win important victories at Los Angeles and the San Gabriel River.

Following the United States victory in the Mexican War, Beale made several overland journeys across the North American continent. He was the first to bring back to the East the news of the California gold strike.

Through the influence of his patron, Missouri senator Thomas Hart Benton, Beale was appointed superintendent of Indian affairs for California and Nevada in 1852, serving for four years. As such, he was one of the first civilian Indian agents on the Pacific Coast. Beale was a friend of the Cahuilla Indian leader JUAN ANTONIO, who helped defend Beale's expeditions from attacks by WALKARA's Utes.

In 1853, at Fort Tejon, near Bakersfield, California, Beale established the Tejon (Sebastian) Indian Reservation, an experiment in concentrating the Indians of the area into one settlement where they could receive instruction in farming and other trades. Beale and his successor, Thomas Henley, established four more small reservations in the coastal ranges of California and in the Central Valley. However, the Tejon Reservation was disbanded 10 years later.

Also in 1853, Beale undertook an independent survey, with Benton's support, for a proposed transcontinental railroad route stretching from St. Louis to the Pacific Coast, along the 38th parallel. He also supervised the construction of frontier roads in the Southwest. In 1857, he used camels as pack animals in a military experiment during the construction of a wagon road from Camp Verde, Texas, across northern New Mexico Territory, to Fort Tejon, California.

At Beale's Crossing, a settlement founded by Beale that year in present-day western Arizona, the route passed through an area on the east bank of the Colorado River inhabited by Mojave Indians. The first immigrants along this leg of the Southern Overland Trail (later the Butterfield Southern Route) turned back when they were attacked by the Mojaves in spring 1858. The government responded to this threat to western migration by sending a large number of troops from Fort Yuma, California. Federal troops established Fort Mohave near Beale's Crossing the following year, and the presence of 700 infantrymen helped deter any further Mojave hostilities. IRATEBA was the Mojave chief who agreed to a lasting peace.

In 1876–77, Beale served as U.S. ambassador to Austria-Hungary. (See also IRATEBA.)

BEAR HUNTER (Wirasuap, "bear spirit").
Shoshone. (d. 1863). Leader of the Shoshone Uprising of 1863.

Bear Hunter's village was located along the Bear River, which feeds the Great Salt Lake of Utah in the north-central part of the desert depression known as the Great Basin.

During the early 1860s, Great Basin Indians resisted white expansion without interference from federal troops, who were then engaged in the Civil War. Warriors made frequent raids on miners and Mormons. They also attacked wagon trains and stagecoaches along the Central Overland Route to California; riders along the Pony Express Trail from Salt Lake City to San Francisco; and crews stringing new telegraph lines. Foremost among the militant Great Basin leaders of this period were NUMAGA of the Northern Paiutes and Bear Hunter and POCATELLO of the Northwestern Shoshones. WASHAKIE of the Wind River Shoshones and TENDOY of the Lemhi Shoshones were friendly to whites.

In order to keep the westward routes open, the 3rd California Infantry of volunteers was raised under PATRICK E. CONNOR and sent across the Sierra Nevada. In 1862, Connor and his men founded Fort Douglas in the foothills of the Wasatch Mountains (part of the Rocky Mountain chain) overlooking Salt Lake City, Utah. From this location, they could patrol parts of Nevada, Idaho, and Wyoming as well.

In January 1863, Connor led a force of 300 men out of Fort Douglas northward toward Bear Hunter's village (the Bear River Campaign). The volunteers marched 140 miles in bitter cold and through deep snow. With ample warning of the invasion, Bear Hunter instructed his people to build barricades of rocks and earth, further reinforcing the steep-walled ravine where his village was located. But the Californians outflanked the Shoshones, and with their superior firepower poured round after round into the village. The fighting on January 27 lasted four hours. As many as 224 Indians, including Chief Bear Hunter, died; 164 women and children were taken prisoner. In comparison, only 21 whites were killed with 46 wounded. That same year, the Indians were forced to sign a treaty, ceding much of the Great Basin.

BEAR'S HEART (James Bear's Heart, Nock-ko-ist). *Southern Cheyenne. (1851–1882).* Warrior; artist.

As a teenager and young man, Bear's Heart, later called James Bear's Heart, earned a reputation among his people as a noted warrior, fighting against other tribes, in particular the Utes; the U.S. army; the Texas Rangers; and the Mexicans. He was arrested at the Cheyenne Agency, in the Indian Territory, in 1875, during the Red River War, which involved Comanches under QUANAH PARKER, Kiowas under LONE WOLF, as well as Southern Cheyennes and Southern Arapahos.

Bear's Heart, along with COHOE, was convicted in the murder of white settlers and sent to Fort Marion in Florida. There, at the encouragement of Lieutenant RICHARD HENRY PRATT, Bear's Heart developed his drawing skills along with Cohoe, HOWLING WOLF, and ZOTOM, who became known as the Florida Boys for their sketchbook work. He served a three-year sentence, then attended the Hampton Institute in Virginia, one of 17 Plains Indians accepted to the otherwise black student body.

In 1881, Bear's Heart returned west to the Indian Territory and began work as a carpenter, but soon died of tuberculosis.

BECKWOURTH, JAMES PIERSON (Jim Beckwourth, Jim Beckwith; The Medicine Calf; Enemy of Horses; Morning Star; Antelope). *(ca. 1800–ca. 1866).* Trader; trapper; scout; interpreter; Crow chief.

Born in Fredericksburg, Virginia, Jim Beckwourth was the son of Sir Jennings Beckwith, a member of the

Irish nobility, and one of his mulatto slaves. Beckwourth moved with his father to the Louisiana Territory in 1810, eventually settling in St. Louis, Missouri.

Freed from slavery by his father, Beckwourth left home in 1822 to work in the lead mines near Galena, Illinois, in the Fever River region. Two years later, he journeyed into the Rocky Mountains as part of General WILLIAM HENRY ASHLEY's 1824–25 supply expedition to the fur trappers on the Green River in Wyoming.

Beckwourth stayed in the West, participating with mountain men JEDEDIAH SMITH and ROBERT CAMPBELL on fur-trapping expeditions into the Rockies. He was with Campbell when his party was attacked by Blackfoot warriors in the Fight in the Willows. According to some accounts, it was Beckwourth who helped summon aid for the beseiged trappers.

In 1828, fellow mountain man Caleb Greenwood persuaded the Crow chief Big Bowl that Beckwourth, with his non-white appearance, was actually the chief's son, captured years before by a Cheyenne raiding party. Big Bowl then adopted Beckwourth, who rose to prominence as a Crow chief. Beckwourth married a succession of Crow, Blackfoot, and Snake women, fathering several families of mixed-blood children. He was known among the Crows by various names: The Medicine Calf, Enemy of Horses, Morning Star, and Antelope. He carried on this deception for the next six years, while taking advantage of his high tribal position to exploit the fur trade on behalf of his associate KENNETH MACKENZIE of the American Fur Company.

In 1837, Beckwourth left the upper Missouri fur trade and accompanied a Missouri militia unit to Florida, serving as a mule driver in the Second Seminole War, during which he took part in the Battle of Okeechobee in December 1837. He then returned to the West, where he became a trader with Andrew Sublette and Louis Vasquez on the newly opened Santa Fe Trail.

In the early 1840s, Beckwourth lived in Pueblo, Colorado, then went to California, where he was swept up in the events leading to the annexation of California by the United States in the Mexican War of 1846–48. With the discovery of gold in the Sierras in 1848, and the subsequent California Gold Rush, Beckwourth became involved in building wagon roads to supply the Sierra Nevada mining camps.

After time in St. Louis, Beckwourth went to Colorado with the Pike's Peak Gold Rush of 1859. In 1861, at the outbreak of the Civil War, Beckwourth was living in Denver, Colorado. In April 1864, he served as a scout and interpreter for troops under Colonel JOHN CHIVINGTON and may have played a role in the raid on BLACK KETTLE and his Cheyennes at Sand Creek the following November.

In 1866, Colonel HENRY B. CARRINGTON employed Beckwourth to undertake a peace mission to the Crows. It is thought that Beckwourth died during this sojourn, perhaps by deliberate poisoning for having brought smallpox to the tribe years before. Other reports claim he died near Denver in 1867.

BEECHER, FREDERICK H. *(1841–1868).* Soldier at the Battle of Beecher's Island.

Frederick Beecher, a nephew of the preacher and abolitionist Henry Ward Beecher, was born in New Orleans and raised in Massachusetts. During the Civil War, he made the rank of second lieutenant, becoming a first lieutenant soon afterward. He was wounded at both Fredericksburg and Gettysburg.

During the SHERIDAN Campaign against the Southern Plains tribes, a party of frontiersmen led by Major GEORGE FORSYTH out of Fort Hays, Kansas, pursued Southern Cheyenne Dog Soldiers under TALL BULL, BULL BEAR, and WHITE HORSE, and Sioux under PAWNEE KILLER, into Colorado. At dawn of September 17, 1868, about 600 Indians attacked the camp. The scouts took up a defensive position on a small sandy island in the middle of a dry streambed of the Arikaree fork of the Republican River. Although numbering only 50, they were armed with Spencer repeating carbines and held off numerous Indian attacks. Beecher died the first day. The siege lasted until September 25, when a relief force of black troopers from the 10th Cavalry arrived. At least six were killed on each side, with many more wounded, Major Forsyth four times.

Although the battle was named after Lieutenant Beecher—the Battle of Beecher's Island—it is more famous for the death of the Cheyenne war chief ROMAN NOSE. (See also ROMAN NOSE; TALL BULL.)

BEESON, JOHN. *(d. 1889).* Reformer; writer.

An English immigrant, Beeson settled in Illinois in 1834. A converted Methodist at the age of 14, he helped runaway slaves along the Underground Railroad. In 1853, he moved with his wife and son to Oregon and farmed along the Rogue River Valley, where he was appalled at the treatment of Indians by fellow settlers.

During the Rogue River War of 1855–56, involving Takelmas and Tututnis under Chief JOHN, Beeson wrote pamphlets on behalf of Indian interests and publicly challenged political candidates to respond. Because of threats by neighbors, Beeson and his family took refuge at Fort Lane. When their home was burned, the Beesons moved back East.

In 1858, Beeson published *A Plea for the Indians* and, in 1860, the only issue of *Calumet*, a journal intended to be the voice of Indians. During the Civil War years,

Beeson met several times with President ABRAHAM LINCOLN to argue for Indian reform. He envisioned a free and distinct Indian nation, a plan he later amended to an Indian territory with elected delegates to Congress.

Beeson was active in PETER COOPER's United States Peace Commission, founded in 1868, and supported President ULYSSES S. GRANT's Peace Policy. He opposed the later attempt of the War Department to regain jurisdiction over Indian affairs and, with Cooper, helped found the Ladies' National League to Protect the Indians in 1878 to lobby against the policy change.

Beeson continued working on behalf of Indians into the 1880s, eventually retiring to his Oregon farm. (See also JOHN.)

BENAVIDAS, ALONSO DE (Alonzo de Benavides). *(fl. 1620s–1630s).* Missionary; explorer.

Originally from the Azores off Portugal, Alonso de Benavidas arrived in Mexico City sometime before 1600. On becoming a member of the Franciscan order that year, he was assigned to the monastery at Puebla. In 1621, he was named to the newly created post of father custodian of New Mexico, and, the following year, began establishing missions throughout New Spain's province of New Mexico.

Benavidas and his contingent of Franciscan friars worked among the Apaches of the upper Gila River and succeeded in winning many converts, including Chief Sanaba. Benavidas also established a church and a convent at Santa Fe. Throughout the 1620s, he founded missions among the Rio Grande Pueblo Indians and sent representatives among the Navajos.

In 1630, Benavidas returned to Spain and presented to King Philip IV a report of his activities among the tribes of New Mexico, known as the *Memorial*. He reported that he had converted 16,000 Indians in less than 10 years. Benavidas's *Memorial* was later expanded, at the request of Pope Urban VIII, to include a history of the missions of New Mexico and a description of the surrounding country.

Benavidas returned to Mexico in 1632 and New Mexico in 1633 or 1634. He later went to India, where he was assigned as assistant to the archbishop of the Portuguese colony of Goa, eventually becoming archbishop himself.

BENNETT, LOUIS DEERFOOT (Hot-tsa-so-do-no, "he peeks in the door").
Seneca. (1830–1896). Athlete who competed in track events in England.

Louis Bennett was born on the Cattaraugus Reservation near Buffalo, New York. As a young man, he earned the name Deerfoot by outrunning a horse. After having established his reputation as a runner in the United States, beating Americans and Englishmen alike, Bennett traveled to England where, at the time, there were more track meets and greater prize money. He ran numerous races in the early 1860s, anywhere from four to 12 miles, usually winning at his five-minute-mile pace. In 1863, Bennett returned to the United States with his substantial earnings and organized a traveling group of runners who raced as entertainment. He retired from running in 1870 and settled on the Cattaraugus Reservation.

BENT, CHARLES. *(1799–1847).* Trader; territorial governor of New Mexico. Brother of WILLIAM BENT; uncle of CHARLIE and GEORGE BENT.

Charles Bent, born in Charleston in what is now West Virginia, moved with his family to St. Louis at the age of seven. His father, Silas Bent, who became a justice of the supreme court of the Missouri Territory, had three other sons, William, George, and Robert.

Charles entered the fur trade in 1822, trading and trapping for the Missouri Fur Company. Three years later, he became a partner in the company with fur entrepreneur JOSHUA PILCHER. Yet JOHN JACOB ASTOR's American Fur Company gained dominance in both the upper Missouri River region and the Rockies, and Bent embarked on a mercantile expedition along the Santa Fe Trail to New Mexico with his brother William Bent in 1829. Using oxen as draft animals, the Bent brothers crossed the Southern Plains from Missouri to Santa Fe by way of the Cimarron cutoff. In the course of their journey, they successfully fought off an attack by Kiowas. The following year, Charles Bent went into the mercantile business with frontiersman Ceran St. Vrain, known as Bent, St. Vrain & Company, and soon established a large trade operation in New Mexico, with stores in Santa Fe and Taos.

By 1833, Bent and St. Vrain had established themselves as major factors in the Indian trade and had founded Bent's Fort near the confluence of the Arkansas and Purgatoire rivers in what is now Colorado. William managed the post. The other Bent brothers, George and Robert, also spent time there. Robert, the youngest, was killed by Comanches in 1841; George died from a disease six years later. In 1842, Bent and St. Vrain established a peace agreement opening up commercial relations with the previously hostile Kiowas and Comanches.

In 1835, Charles married Maria Ignacio Jaramillo, the daughter of a politically prominent Taos family; her sister married CHRISTOPHER "KIT" CARSON, a hunter at Bent's Fort. Bent became a close associate of the Mexican governor of New Mexico, Manuel Armijo.

Following the U.S. invasion of New Mexico in 1846 at the start of the Mexican War, he was named by General STEPHEN WATTS KEARNY as governor of the provisional U.S. territorial government.

When U.S. forces departed New Mexico to attack California and Chihuahua, Mexico, Bent's authority was challenged by powerful Mexican interests, as well as the Pueblo Indians of Taos, for his friendly relations with their traditional enemies, Kiowas and Comanches. A rebellion by these factions erupted in January 1847, and, while on a visit to Taos, Bent was killed and scalped.

BENT, CHARLIE. *Mixed Southern Cheyenne.*
(d. 1868). Warrior in the Plains Indian wars. Son of WILLIAM BENT; nephew of CHARLES BENT; brother of GEORGE BENT.

Charlie Bent, named after his uncle Charles Bent, was the son of William Bent and Yellow Woman of the Southern Cheyennes. Charlie and his brother George were with BLACK KETTLE at Sand Creek, Colorado, in 1864, when attacked by troops under Colonel JOHN CHIVINGTON. George escaped during the fighting; Charlie was captured. But JAMES BECKWOURTH concealed him in a wagon with a wounded officer and later took him to his older brother Robert Bent's ranch.

After Sand Creek, Charlie and George renounced the white world and traveled northward to join the Northern Cheyennes and Sioux in Wyoming and Montana. They acted as interpreters for the Sioux RED CLOUD and the Northern Cheyenne DULL KNIFE, fighting with them along the South Platte and the Powder rivers in the War for the BOZEMAN Trail.

The brothers later split up when George decided to follow the peace chief Black Kettle. Charlie joined the band of the militant ROMAN NOSE and helped carry out raids on stage stations. During a skirmish with soldiers, he was wounded, soon after which he contracted malaria and died.

BENT, GEORGE. *Mixed Southern Cheyenne.*
(1843–1918). Warrior in the Plains Indian wars; interpreter; writer. Son of WILLIAM BENT; nephew of CHARLES BENT; brother of CHARLIE BENT.

George Bent was educated at Webster College in St. Louis. He and his brother were with BLACK KETTLE's band at the 1864 Sand Creek Massacre in Colorado, after which they traveled to the Northern Plains to join the Sioux RED CLOUD and the Northern Cheyenne DULL KNIFE, often acting as interpreters. Charlie later became a follower of ROMAN NOSE; George rejoined Black Kettle and married Black Kettle's niece Magpie. He became an interpreter for the Indian agent EDWARD WYNKOOP and helped negotiate the 1867 Medicine Lodge Treaty in Kansas. His book *Forty Years*

with the Cheyennes (1905–06) and his letters are important resources for the period.

BENT, WILLIAM. *(1809–1869).* Trader; scout; Indian agent. Brother of CHARLES BENT; father of CHARLIE and GEORGE BENT.

William Bent was born in St. Louis, Missouri, and was trapping furs on the upper Arkansas River by the time he was 15 years old. He was employed in his older brother Charles's firm, Bent, St. Vrain & Company, and managed the company's Indian trade center at Bent's Fort in Colorado.

At the outbreak of the Mexican War in 1846, William Bent served as a guide for General STEPHEN WATTS KEARNY's military expedition from Bent's Fort to Santa Fe, New Mexico. He later scouted for Colonel STERLING PRICE.

After the death of his brother Charles in an Indian uprising at Taos in 1847, and the retirement of Ceran St. Vrain two years later, William Bent became the principal owner of Bent, St. Vrain & Company, one of the largest mercantile and Indian trading enterprises in the Southwest.

Increased Indian hostilities, brought on by the influx of white trappers, miners, and ranchers, led Bent to seek a buyer for the company's trade center on the Arkansas River. When the federal government offered Bent an outrageously low price for the Colorado settlement, he chose to blow up the fort in 1849 rather than accept the offer. He then constructed a larger fort farther downstream on the Arkansas, expanding it in 1857, which was the first permanent Anglo-American settlement in Colorado.

With the onset of the Pike's Peak Gold Rush of 1859, encroachment on Indian lands by whites increased tensions with the local Cheyenne bands. Bent, with close ties to the Indians through trade and with three Indian wives, received an appointment as Indian agent to the Cheyennes and attempted to negotiate a peace settlement. Yet hostilities increased throughout the Civil War period.

In 1864, Colorado militiamen forcibly restrained Bent from warning BLACK KETTLE and his Cheyenne people of an impending military action against them at Sand Creek. Additionally, his part-Cheyenne son Robert Bent was forced to guide Colonel JOHN CHIVINGTON's militia units to Black Kettle's encampment, where the notorious Sand Creek Massacre soon occurred. His other mixed-blood sons, George and Charlie, fought alongside both Southern and Northern Cheyenne militants in the subsequent Plains Indian wars.

Bent later retired to Westport, Kansas, where he was a neighbor to mountain men JAMES BRIDGER and Louis Vasquez.

BENTEEN, FREDERICK W. *(1834–1898).* Army officer at the Battle of Little Bighorn.

Born in Petersburg, Virginia, Frederick W. Benteen was raised in St. Louis. When he enlisted in the 10th Missouri Cavalry in 1861, to fight on the Union side in the Civil War, his family, sympathetic to the Confederacy, disowned him. During the war, he rose from the rank of lieutenant to lieutenant colonel of volunteers.

Following the war, Benteen remained in the service as a colonel in command of a black army regiment. In 1866, he was commissioned an officer in the regular army and made a captain in the newly organized 7th Cavalry, under the command of Colonel GEORGE ARMSTRONG CUSTER. After the Battle of the Washita in November 1868 against BLACK KETTLE's Cheyennes in the Indian Territory, Benteen openly criticized Custer's decision to abandon a detachment of his troops, who were subsequently trapped and killed in a Cheyenne ambush.

During the Sioux War for the Black Hills of 1876–77 involving allied bands under SITTING BULL, Benteen was the senior captain of the 7th Cavalry. Before the fighting at the Little Bighorn on June 25, 1876, Custer sent a detachment under Benteen to scout to the west, possibly to prevent a surprise attack from that direction. Benteen later joined up with Major MARCUS A. RENO's detachment after it had been attacked and forced to retreat to a line of bluffs. Benteen commanded most of the fighting from this position. After two days, Benteen's and Reno's besieged men were relieved by the arrival of troops under generals ALFRED TERRY and JOHN GIBBON.

At the military inquiry that was held in 1879 to investigate the battle, Benteen gave testimony that absolved Reno of any negligence, even though other evidence indicated that Reno had panicked and abandoned his command to Benteen.

Benteen led his unit of the 7th Cavalry in the Nez Perce War against warriors under Chief JOSEPH (Young Joseph), taking part in the Battle of Canyon Creek, Montana, in September 1877.

In 1882, Benteen was promoted to major and transferred from the 7th Cavalry to the 9th Cavalry at Fort Duchesne, Utah. In 1886, he was court-martialed for drunkenness and suspended from service for one year. In 1888, he retired to Atlanta, Georgia. He was awarded a brevet of brigadier general in 1890 for the earlier Battle of Little Bighorn. (See also BLACK KETTLE; Young JOSEPH; SITTING BULL.)

BERING, VITUS JONASSEN. *(1681–1741).* Explorer.

Vitus Bering, born in Denmark, entered the Royal Russian Navy in 1703, and, despite his Danish background, rose to prominence.

In 1724, Czar Peter the Great commissioned Bering to explore Siberia and the waterways beyond. Bering crossed the mainland to Kamchatka, then constructed a ship and sailed north in 1728. Although he reached the Bering Strait, later named for him, he failed to sight the coast of Alaska because of heavy fog. He returned to St. Petersburg in 1730, where another expedition was organized. He again crossed to Kamchatka and, in 1733, embarked on a sea voyage during which he determined conclusively that Alaska and Siberia were separated by water.

In 1741, Bering set out on the *St. Peter*, with his associate Aleksei Chirikov as captain of the *St. Paul*. During the voyage, in which the ships were separated, Bering became the first western navigator to sight the coast of Alaska, with a landfall at Cape St. Elias on the Gulf of Alaska. He then sailed west past the Aleutian Islands.

The *St. Peter* was shipwrecked on an island in the Kormandorski group that was named for Bering, who died there from scurvy. Surviving crew members returned to Kamchatka in small boats they built from the wreckage. Chirikov eventually returned to St. Petersburg (present-day Leningrad) with samples of sea otter pelts. Bering's journey led to the development of the Russian fur enterprise in Alaska on Aleut and Tlingit Indian lands by *promyshlenniki*, the private Russian fur traders, and later by the large fur companies under GREGORI SHELIKOV and ALEKSANDR BARANOV.

BERKELEY, WILLIAM. *(1606–1677).* Colonial governor of Virginia. Cousin of NATHANIEL BACON.

The Englishman Sir William Berkeley was appointed governor of Virginia in 1641, arriving in North America the following year. He led a militia force against warriors under OPECHANCANOUGH in 1644, the second rebellion of the POWHATAN Confederacy.

In 1652, Berkeley was deposed by a Puritan faction, whereupon he returned to England. He was reappointed governor following the Restoration of 1660.

Berkeley's economic policies favoring the aristocracy, along with what was considered his inadequate defense of the frontier against Indian attacks, led to Bacon's Rebellion of 1676. With his cousin Nathaniel Bacon's death from illness, Berkeley managed to retain power. Yet he was soon discredited for his policies and for his hanging of rebel leaders in defiance of a royal commission's pardon. He lost the governorship and returned to England in 1677. (See also BACON, NATHANIEL; OPECHANCANOUGH.)

BERLANDIER, JEAN LOUIS. *(ca. 1805–1851).* Anthropologist; naturalist.

Jean Louis Berlandier was born in France near the Swiss border and trained as a botanist in Geneva. When in his early 20s, he was hired as biologist on a Mexican scientific expedition into Texas.

On arrival in Texas via Mexico City in February 1828, Berlandier spent most of his time in the vicinity of San Antonio, collecting plant specimens. He also studied and wrote about more than 40 Indian tribes, especially the Comanches. In fall 1828, he accompanied a party of 60 to 80 Comanches under chiefs Reyuna and El Ronca on a buffalo and bear hunt northwest of San Antonio. Colonel Jose Francisco Ruiz, who, with 30 Spanish soldiers and a number of civilians, also participated in the hunt, acted as an informant for Berlandier.

Berlandier settled in Matamoros in northern Mexico, where he married a Mexican woman and practiced medicine until drowning while crossing the San Fernando River. His comprehensive and detailed writings are among the earliest ethnological studies of the Southern Plains tribes. The Thomas Gilcrease Institute of American History and Art in Tulsa, Oklahoma, possesses one of his manuscripts, completed in 1834.

BETZINEZ, JASON (Batsinas). *Mimbreno Apache. (1860–1960).* Writer. Cousin of GERONIMO.

Jason Betzinez was the son of the Mimbreno Nonithian and the Chiricahua Nah-thle-tla, a cousin of Geronimo. He fought under the war chief as a teenager, and, although he never achieved warrior status, he helped care for the horses of the warrior bands. He was present at Geronimo's surrender talks with GEORGE CROOK at Canyon de los Embudos, Mexico, in March 1886. The following autumn, he was sent to Florida with other Apache prisoners, then attended the Carlisle Indian School in Pennsylvania. He later lived in Oklahoma, where he worked as a blacksmith and joined the Presbyterian church. He wrote about Geronimo and Apache customs in *I Fought With Geronimo* (1959), edited by Wilbur Sturtevant Nye.

BIENVILLE, JEAN BAPTISTE LE MOYNE, SIEUR DE. *(1680–1768).* French governor of Louisiana; military commander against tribes of the lower Mississippi River. Son of CHARLES LE MOYNE; brother of CHARLES LE MOYNE, BARON DE LONGUEUIL and PIERRE LE MOYNE, SIEUR D'IBERVILLE.

Sieur de Bienville was born in Montreal, 12th child of Charles le Moyne. With his elder brother Sieur d'-Iberville, he participated in King William's War of 1689–97, the first of the French and Indian Wars against the British. He accompanied his brother on an expedition to the mouth of the Mississippi in 1698–99 and helped found the post at Old Biloxi (present-day Ocean Springs, Mississippi). While his brother was away, Bienville moved the colony to Mobile Bay in 1702. Iberville was appointed governor of Louisiana in 1703, and, with his brother's continuing absence from the colony, Bienville served as chief administrator, retaining this function after his brother's death in 1706. Bienville founded the settlement of Mobile in 1710. With the appointment as governor of ANTOINE LAUMET DE LA MOTHE, SIEUR DE CADILLAC in 1711, Bienville became second in command.

In 1714, Bienville explored the Alabama River and founded Fort Toulouse at the junction of the Coosa and Tallapoosa rivers, which developed into an important fur-trading post.

Bienville led a successful campaign into Natchez territory in 1716, building Fort Rosalie. The next year, he was officially appointed governor. He founded New Orleans in 1718, and captured the Spanish fort at Pensacola the following year, but his 1723 campaign against the Natchez proved unsuccessful.

Bienville traveled to France in 1725 and was relieved of his governorship the next year. He was sent back to Louisiana in 1732, again as governor.

Meanwhile, the Chickasaws, angered by the French insistence to expel British traders and Natchez survivors from the Natchez Revolt of 1729 under GREAT SUN, increased their raids on traders traveling the Mississippi between Quebec and Louisiana, managing to halt commerce entirely in 1734. In 1736, Bienville launched an expedition northward into Chickasaw territory. One column of 400 French regulars and Choctaw auxiliaries under Major Pierre d'Artaguette approached from the north along the Mississippi; a second column of 600 French and 1,000 Choctaws under Bienville advanced from the south along the Tombigbee. But the two forces failed to meet up as planned and were defeated in separate Chickasaw attacks. In 1739–40, Bienville organized another force, 3,000-strong, against the Chickasaws, which became bogged down in heavy rains and also proved ineffective.

Bienville retired in 1743, returning to Paris. In 1763, he unsuccessfully campaigned against the cession of French Louisiana to Spain.

BIERSTADT, ALBERT. *(1830–1902).* Artist; cartographer.

Albert Bierstadt was born in Germany and brought to the United States as an infant. He grew up in Bedford, Massachusetts, returning to Europe for his studies. In 1858, he joined a military expedition under General Frederick Lander, surveying a wagon road from Fort Laramie to the Pacific. He made several other trips West, traveling on horseback and in covered wagons, sketching landscapes, especially of the mountains, plus scenes of Indians and buffalo for later oil paintings. He had a studio at Tappan Zee just north of New York City, overlooking the Hudson River, where he worked on his large canvases, grand and dramatic in style. His clients included the federal government, which commissioned works from him.

BIG BEAR (Mistahimaskwa, Mistihai'muskwa).
Cree. (1825–1888). Leader in the Second Riel Rebellion of 1885.

Big Bear was born near Fort Carlton in what is now Saskatchewan. By the 1870s, he had become a chief of the Plains Cree.

Government officials first became aware of Big Bear's influence and militance in 1876, when he refused to sign Treaty No. 6 (one of 11 post-Confederation treaties with the Indians of Canada) and gained a following. At a council of 2,000 Indians at POUNDMAKER'S reserve at Cut Knife, Big Bear denounced the whites for dishonesty and called for a united stand by his people.

Big Bear was one of the few Indians of western Canada to lead his people in an uprising, joining LOUIS DAVID RIEL's Metis in their 1885 struggle for lands along the North and South Saskatchewan rivers. Soon after the Metis under GABRIEL DUMONT had battled government troops at Duck Lake on March 26, 1885, Big

Big Bear. Photo by Duffin & Co. *Courtesy of National Archives of Canada/C-17430.*

Bear and the Cree chief Poundmaker joined the conflict. Poundmaker's warriors attacked Battleford on March 28. Warriors from Big Bear's band—Wandering Spirit, Little Bad Man, and 200 others—raided the settlement at Frog Lake on April 2, interrupted a Catholic mass, and captured 13 whites. An Indian agent by the name of Thomas Quinn refused to be taken prisoner and a fight broke out. Wandering Spirit shot Quinn despite Big Bear's efforts to stop him. Other warriors killed eight more whites. Two women and a Hudson's Bay Company clerk survived the incident and were held as captives. Another man escaped and reported the incident to the Mounties at Fort Pitt. When the Mounties abandoned the post because of the overwhelming number of warriors, the Crees ransacked and burned it.

The Canadian government organized the North West Field Force to help the Mounties put down the escalating violence, and, in early May, the Metis suffered a major defeat at Batoche. Before long, troops under Major General Thomas Strange closed in on the Crees. Poundmaker surrendered at Battleford. Assiniboine scouts located Big Bear's band in the vicinity of Fort Pitt, and, on May 28, Strange's men launched an attack on them at Frenchman's Butte. The Indians repelled and outflanked the Canadian cavalry, then escaped northward. The main body of the North West Field Force, under Major General Frederick Middleton, united with Strange's troops and continued their pursuit. A party of Mounties under Samuel Steele caught up with the Crees at Loon Lake on June 3. After a brief firefight and several casualties on both sides, Big Bear's warriors again escaped into the swampy wilderness.

Several days later, on June 18, Big Bear released a group of white prisoners with a note asking for mercy. Many of the Crees surrendered to the garrison at Fort Pitt. Big Bear and some of his most faithful followers remained in the field until July 2, when they showed up at Fort Carlton 100 miles to the east.

In a trial at Battleford, a group of Cree rebels were tried. Eight of them, including Wandering Spirit, were hanged. Big Bear and Poundmaker were sentenced to three years' imprisonment but received early releases. Suffering from sickness and despair, they both died within six months. (See also RIEL, LOUIS DAVID.)

BIG BOW (Zipkiyah, Zipkoheta, Zepko-eete).
Kiowa. (ca. 1830–ca. 1900). War chief in the Kiowa Wars; army scout.

Big Bow established his reputation as a warrior in fights with the Utes and Navajos. In 1867, as one of the most militant of the Kiowa leaders, he refused to sign the Medicine Lodge Treaty. In the 1870s, Big Bow participated in numerous raids on settlers and engagements with troops under the Kiowa leaders SATANTA, SATANK, MAMANTI, LONE WOLF, and BIG TREE.

He was one of the last Kiowa chiefs to surrender. At the urging of KICKING BIRD, he led his followers onto the combined Comanche and Kiowa Reservation in the Indian Territory in 1874. He was granted amnesty and later served as a sergeant in the army's Indian Scouts.

BIG EAGLE (Jerome Big Eagle, Wamditanka, Womditonka, "great war eagle"). *Mdewakanton Sioux. (1827–1906).* Band leader in the Minnesota Uprising of 1862–63; research informant.

Big Eagle was born on the Minnesota River near present-day Mendota, Minnesota. As a young man fought against the Chippewas, wearing a headdress with six feathers for each enemy killed. In 1857, he succeeded his father Mazarota (Gray Iron) as chief of the band of about 200 Mdewakanton Santees on Crow Creek in McLeod County. The next year, he traveled to Washington, D.C., to negotiate with federal officials.

At first Big Eagle argued for peace, but then joined LITTLE CROW in the attacks on Fort Ridgely and on New Ulm in August. He also fought General HENRY HASTINGS SIBLEY's men at Birch Coulee, leading the Santee warriors along with MANKATO, and at Wood Lake, both in September. Mankato was killed at Wood Lake; Little Crow and others fled in disarray. Big Eagle chose to surrender with his people on September 26, 1862. He escaped execution but was imprisoned for three years, during which time he converted to Presbyterianism.

After his release, Big Eagle lived at Granite Falls, Minnesota. He described his experiences during the war in *Big Eagle's Story of the Sioux Outbreak of 1862*, published in 1894. (See also LITTLE CROW.)

BIG ELK (Ongpatonga, Om-Pah-Ton-Ga). *Omaha. (ca. 1772–1846).* Proponent of peace with whites; orator.

Big Elk established his reputation as a warrior in raids on the Pawnees. He became principal chief of the Omahas after the death of Washinggusaba (Black Bird) in 1800 and soon became known among whites for his oratory. He traveled to Washington, D.C., in 1821 and 1837 to sign peace treaties with the federal government. CHARLES BIRD KING painted the chief's portrait during his first visit. GEORGE CATLIN painted him in 1833. Big Elk also signed treaties at Prairie du Chien, Wisconsin, in 1830, and at Bellevue (present-day Omaha, Nebraska) in 1836. He was head chief until 1843, when he was succeeded by his son of the same name. The second Big Elk was succeeded by JOSEPH LA FLESCHE.

BIG FOOT (Si Tanka, Spotted Elk). *Miniconjou Sioux. (ca. 1825–1890).* Chief killed at Wounded Knee.

Big Foot established his reputation through diplomatic rather than military skills. He was known as a compromiser who was called on by other Sioux to settle disputes. On the death of his father, Long Horn, in 1874, he became leader of his Miniconjou band. The Sioux War for the Black Hills in 1876–77 was hard on his people. In 1877, the surviving Miniconjous surrendered and were settled on the Cheyenne River Reservation in South Dakota. During the following years, Big Foot encouraged his band to adapt to the new life. He was one of the first Sioux to successfully plant corn on the reservation and helped build schools for his people. He represented his tribe as a delegate to Washington, D.C.

In 1889, KICKING BEAR brought the Ghost Dance, started by the Paiute WOVOKA, to Cheyenne River. It caught on among Big Foot's and HUMP's Miniconjou bands, now made up mostly of widows, who danced in the hope of bringing their dead husbands back. The size of Big Foot's band increased as other Indians joined them for the Ghost Dance. White officials tried to stop their ceremonial gatherings. Hump agreed. But Big Foot led his more militant followers to a sacred place near Cherry Creek in fall 1890.

After the death of SITTING BULL on December 15, 1890, many of his Hunkpapa followers left the Standing Rock Reservation in North Dakota to take refuge elsewhere. Many joined the Miniconjous at Cheyenne River in South Dakota. On learning that Sitting Bull had been killed, Big Foot set out with his people—230 women and children and 120 men—toward the Pine Ridge Reservation, South Dakota, to seek the protection of RED CLOUD. Big Foot no longer advocated the Ghost Dance, as did Kicking Bear and SHORT BULL, but, concerned for the safety of his people, called for peace with the whites.

On the way, Big Foot contracted pneumonia and was forced to ride in a wagon. His band was intercepted by an army detachment under Major Samuel Whitside, and Big Foot ordered the raising of a white flag. Since his name was on a list of "fomenters of disturbances," he was taken prisoner and led with his followers to a cavalry camp at *Chankpe Opi Wakpala,* Wounded Knee Creek. Big Foot was allowed to ride in the army ambulance. Colonel JAMES FORSYTH soon arrived to take command of the prisoners and ordered his men to place four Hotchkiss cannon in position around the camp.

The next morning, December 29, 1890, the troops approached to disarm the Indians. Big Foot, extremely sick, his breathing labored, was carried outside to sit with a group of old men in front of his tepee. The Indians surrendered their guns. The soldiers further searched the tepees and brought out axes, knives, and tent stakes, as well as sacred bundles. At this, a medicine man by the name of Yellow Bird began dancing and chanting. Only one Indian resisted—a deaf Indian by the name of Black Coyote. When the soldiers tried to disarm him, his rifle reportedly discharged in the air; in response, the soldiers opened up with their carbines. Big Foot collapsed, a bullet in his head. Some of the Indians began to fight back. At first the struggle was at close quarters, but then the soldiers withdrew and let loose with heavy artillery.

In less than an hour, at least 150 Indians were killed and 50 were wounded. Perhaps as many again died later from their wounds. The soldiers lost 25 men, with 39 wounded, most, it is thought, from their own bullets and shrapnel.

The soldiers began clearing the battlefield, but were forced to leave many of the bodies behind because of a blizzard. Three days later, on New Year's Day 1891, a burial party of soldiers and civilians arrived. Big Foot's contorted and frozen body lay where he had fallen. He was buried with the other victims in a communal pit.

The photograph of Big Foot lying dead in the snow, part of the Smithsonian Institution's collection, is perhaps the most widespread visual image remaining from Wounded Knee. (See also KICKING BEAR; SITTING BULL; WOVOKA.)

BIG HAWK CHIEF (Kootahwecootsoolelehoolashar). *Pawnee.* (b. ca. 1850). Army scout; athlete who ran first recorded sub-four-minute mile.

Big Hawk Chief joined the Pawnee Scouts under Captain LUTHER NORTH in 1876 and fought against the Sioux and their allies in Nebraska and Wyoming. That same year, while waiting for his release at Fort Sidney, Nebraska, Big Hawk ran his legendary mile. North realized there were many great runners among the Pawnees; Big Hawk was reputed to be the fastest of all. Along with Hughey Bean, who lived near Fort Sidney, North set up a measured mile course. Each man had a stopwatch. Big Hawk ran the first half of the course in two minutes and the second half in one minute and 58 seconds. Amazed, North and Bean remeasured the track. Big Hawk repeated his feat on a second attempt. At that time in history, the closest recorded mile was over four minutes and 49 seconds. The first official four-minute mile was run by Roger Bannister in 1954.

BIG JIM (Wapameepto; Dick Jim). *Shawnee.* (1834–1900). Tribal traditionalist.

Big Jim was born on the Sabine Reservation in Texas, and, in 1872, he became chief of the Kispicotha band, known as the Absentee Shawnees because they had separated from other Shawnee bands of the Indian Territory. Big Jim strived to preserve the traditional ways of his people and opposed farming, believing that tilling the soil would wound the earth, the mother of the tribe. He refused the land allotments granted to individuals of his band under the General Allotment Act (the DAWES Severalty Act) of 1887. In order to avoid accul-

turation, Big Jim and a small group of followers moved to Mexico, where he died of smallpox.

BIG TREE (Adouette, Adoltay). *Kiowa.* (ca. 1847–1929). Youngest of the Kiowa war chiefs in the Kiowa Wars.

In 1871, at Fort Sill in the Indian Territory, Big Tree was arrested with SATANK and SATANTA for an earlier attack on a freight caravan in Texas and the death of seven whites. Satank attempted an escape on his way to trial in Texas and was killed. Satanta and Big Tree were tried and sentenced to death, but humanitarian groups protested the harsh sentences. Even the Indian Bureau argued for the prisoners' release on the grounds that their act had been one of war and not murder. They were imprisoned at Huntsville, Texas.

LONE WOLF and MAMANTI, leaders of the militants, and KICKING BIRD and STUMBLING BEAR, leaders of the peace faction, argued for the release of the two men. The prisoners were paroled in 1873 with the condition they remain in the Indian Territory. Yet during the period when Kiowa and Comanche war parties began forming for raids on white settlers—the Comanches under QUANAH PARKER—Big Tree and Satanta left the reservation for a hunting trip in Kansas. With 3,000 federal troops in the field, they soon turned themselves in at the Cheyenne Agency. For violating parole, Big Tree was imprisoned at Fort Sill; Satanta was sent back to Huntsville, where he committed suicide.

After his release in 1875, Big Tree lived peacefully on the Kiowa Reservation and ran a supply train from Wichita to Anadarko. He married a Kiowa woman, Omboke, and converted to Christianity, becoming a deacon and Sunday School teacher for the Rainy Mountain Baptist Church.

BIG WARRIOR (Tustennugee Thlocco). *Creek.* (fl. early 1800s). Chief of the White Sticks; ally of Americans in the Creek War of 1813–14.

Considered a Creek Indian, Big Warrior is thought to have had Shawnee or Miami ancestry. Although chief at Tuckabatchee, one of the Upper Creek villages, generally consisting of Red Sticks, he was pro-American, like most of the White Stick Lower Creeks.

Big Warrior helped precipitate the Creek War when his followers captured and executed the Red Stick LITTLE WARRIOR, who had led a pro-British force in the Raisin River Massacre during the War of 1812 and had attacked settlers along the Ohio River on the return trip to Georgia and Alabama.

In the subsequent fighting, Big Warrior supported General ANDREW JACKSON and the White Stick WILLIAM McINTOSH against the Red Sticks WILLIAM WEATHERFORD and MENEWA. The Red Sticks attempted to take his village, a siege that was broken by the White Sticks. During the rest of the conflict, Big Warrior used McIntosh's home at Coweta as his base of operations.

After the war, Big Warrior and Selocta represented the White Sticks in negotiations with Jackson and signed the Treaty of Fort Jackson of August 1814, at which time they were informed that the White Sticks, despite their assistance to federal forces, would also have to compensate the government for the cost of the war. After this betrayal by Jackson, Big Warrior adopted the political views of the militant Red Sticks. (See also WEATHERFORD, WILLIAM.)

BIG WHITE. See SHAHAKA.

BLACK BEAR. *Northern Arapaho. (fl. 1860s).* Leader during the Powder River Expedition of 1865 and in the War for the BOZEMAN Trail of 1866–68.

Black Bear's band suffered an early defeat in the Plains Indian wars—the Battle of Tongue River in 1865 in present-day Wyoming. On the morning of August 29, about 125 cavalrymen and 90 Pawnee scouts of the Powder River Expedition under General PATRICK E. CONNOR surprised Black Bear's camp at the headwaters of the Tongue. The Indians were routed and retreated northward, but then managed to drive the soldiers back to the safety of their artillery in position at the Indian village. The Arapahos had to watch from the hills as the soldiers burned their tepees and possessions, then drove off about 1,000 horses. Black Bear lost a son in the fighting. He joined RED CLOUD's Sioux in the conflict over the next two years, the War for the Bozeman Trail. (See also RED CLOUD.)

BLACK BEAVER (Sucktum Mahway, Sekettu Maquah). *Delaware. (1806–1880).* Trapper and trader; interpreter; army scout; guide; negotiator.

Born in Illinois, Black Beaver traveled West and became one of the mountain men in the early Rocky Mountain fur trade.

In 1834, along with JESSE CHISHOLM, he acted as interpreter for the exploratory expedition under General HENRY LEAVENWORTH and Colonel HENRY DODGE to the upper Red River territory of the Comanches, Kiowas, and Wichitas. In the Mexican War of 1846, he served as an army scout under General WILLIAM S. HARNEY.

At the start of the California Gold Rush of 1849, Black Beaver, along with Captain Randolph Marcy, guided a wagon train of 500 emigrants across the Southwest. On the return trip, Black Beaver blazed a new trail from the Brazos River in northwest Texas, eastward to Fort Smith, Arkansas.

During the 1850s Black Beaver worked as a trader, then in the early 1860s, as a Union scout in the Civil War. In 1865, he served as interpreter, again with Jesse Chisholm, at the Little Arkansas Council with Southern Plains tribes.

Over the ensuing years, Black Beaver became a spokesman for his tribe in their negotiations with federal officials. He died at Anadarko on the Washita River in the Indian Territory, now southwestern Oklahoma.

BLACK ELK (Hehaka Sapa, Ekhaka Sapa). *Oglala Sioux. (1863–1950).* Medicine man; research informant.

Black Elk was born along the Little Powder River in northeast Wyoming; his father was also called Black Elk and his mother was named Sees the White Cow. He experienced his first vision at the age of five and his second at nine, which he later interpreted to mean that his task was to help preserve Sioux religion. As a youth of 13, he participated in the Battle of Little Bighorn of June 1876. Following the army's victories over the Sioux that summer and fall, his family traveled with CRAZY HORSE, a distant cousin. Then, on the war chief's death, they joined SITTING BULL in Canada.

During this period, Black Elk's reputation as a shaman and mystic grew among his people. He and his family eventually returned to the United States, and Black Elk lived on the Pine Ridge Reservation, where tribal members consulted with him for his visions.

In 1886–89, Black Elk toured the eastern United States and Europe with WILLIAM "BUFFALO BILL" CODY's Wild West Show, and he appeared before Queen Victoria in England. On becoming sick, he stayed with a French family until healthy enough to return home.

At first dubious of the Ghost Dance and the message of WOVOKA, Black Elk became a supporter of the movement. The destruction of BIG FOOT's band at Wounded Knee in 1890 affected him deeply and confirmed his belief in a need for harmony among all peoples.

In 1930, the Nebraska poet John G. Neihardt visited Pine Ridge and met Black Elk. The next year, he recorded Black Elk's oral history. At that time, Black Elk was considered the sole living member of his tribe to have a complete knowledge of the metaphysical basis underlying Sioux religious beliefs. This account was first published in 1932 as *Black Elk Speaks: The Life Story of a Holy Man of the Oglala Sioux.* Black Elk also acted as an informant for the anthropologist Joseph E. Brown concerning Sioux ritual and religion, published as *The Sacred Pipe* in 1953.

Black Elk had two wives and two sons. One of them, Ben Black Elk, who acted as interpreter for Neihardt's sessions with his father, became a noted teacher and lecturer.

BLACKFOOT. Crow. *(ca. 1795–1877).* Principal chief.

Blackfoot was a member of the Mountain Crows living north of the Yellowstone River and south of the Musselshell in what is now Montana. He became a chief in the 1850s and head chief in the 1860s. As such, he participated in numerous councils with whites, including the council at Fort Laramie, Wyoming, in 1868, and the council at Crow Agency, Montana, in 1873. At the latter, Blackfoot made several speeches to members of the Board of Indian Commissioners, chaired by Felix R. Brunot, in which he complained of pressures resulting from white settlement and from other tribes. He died of pneumonia near present-day Meeteetse, Wyoming.

BLACK HAWK (Black Sparrow Hawk, Ma-ka-tai-me-she-kia-kiah, Makataimeshekiakiak). *Sac. (1767–1838).* Leader of the Sacs and Foxes in the Black Hawk War of 1832.

Black Hawk, son of Pyesa, was born in the village of Saukenuk (present-day Rock Island, Illinois) at the junction of the Mississippi and Rock rivers. As a young warrior, he led war parties against the Osages and the Cherokees, taking his first scalp at about the age of 17. When he was 19, his father was killed in a raid on the Cherokees, and Black Hawk became the keeper of his

Black Hawk. Lithographic reproduction based on painting by Charles Bird King in Thomas McKenney's Indian Portrait Gallery. *Courtesy of Library of Congress.*

band's medicine bundle. By his wife, Assheweque (Singing Bird), he had three children.

In 1804, some of the southern bands, or the Sacs and Foxes of the Missouri, ceded their tribal lands east of the Mississippi. The governor of the Indiana Territory, WILLIAM HENRY HARRISON, who had traveled to St. Louis for the council, used alcohol as a negotiating tool to cajole tribal representatives into signing the agreement. The Sacs and Foxes of the Mississippi claimed that those who had signed the treaty at St. Louis did not represent all their people.

Black Hawk was receptive to TECUMSEH's message of a confederation of tribes and fought on the side of the British in the War of 1812. Following the war, the pace of white settlement quickened. White officials backed white settlers' claims over Indian claims. In 1816, the army constructed Fort Armstrong at Rock Island, and, in 1818, the Illinois Territory became the twenty-first state of the Union. In 1829, when Black Hawk and his followers left the village for the winter hunt, white squatters moved onto their land, even moving into some of the Indian lodges. That year, Black Hawk's rivals among the Sacs and Foxes, KEOKUK, WAPELLO, and POWASHEEK, agreed to cede the Rock River country in exchange for a tract west of the Mississippi on the Iowa River and a tribal annuity, and departed. Black Hawk and his followers, sometimes called the British Band because of their frequent trading trips to Canada, insisted on staying in lodges that the squatters had not occupied. Despite some quarreling, the Indians and whites endured a planting season together. Black Hawk vowed to return again, which he did in spring 1830 and spring 1831.

State militia were sent by Governor John Reynolds to reinforce General EDMUND GAINES's regulars at Fort Armstrong. They arrived on June 25, 1831, and, the next morning, began a bombardment of Saukenuk. On entering the village, however, they found that Black Hawk's band had slipped back across the Mississippi during the night. War had been avoided for the time being.

In the meantime, WHITE CLOUD, a Winnebago shaman often called Winnebago Prophet, who lived at Prophet's Village about 35 miles to the north along Rock River, preached against the whites and rallied Winnebagos, Kickapoos, and Potawatomis to the Sac and Fox cause. With some Sac blood, White Cloud had followers among that tribe as well as the Winnebagos. His call for a resurgence of the traditional way of life resembled the teachings of other prophets before him, such as DELAWARE PROPHET and TENSKWATAWA (Shawnee Prophet). He predicted that Black Hawk would be aided in his struggle with whites by the Great Spirit and by an army of ancestral warriors. The Sac chief NEAPOPE was also reportedly under White Cloud's influence. Some Kickapoos and Potawatomis indicated their willingness to fight. By spring 1832, Black Hawk's followers numbered more than 2,000, about 600 of them warriors.

Yet pro-peace Winnebagos—such band chiefs as GOOD THUNDER, NAWKAW, SHICKSHACK, and YELLOW THUNDER—countered White Cloud's militancy, dissuading most tribal members from joining the uprising. And key leaders among the Kickapoos and Potawatomis—the Kickapoos KENNEKUK and MECINA, and the Potawatomis LEOPOLD POKA-GON, ALEXANDER ROBINSON, SAGAUNASH, SHABONEE, TOPENEBEE, and WABAUNSEE—took either a neutral or pro-American stance. Keokuk, now in Iowa, also kept his warriors from joining the rebel band. Black Hawk's dream of an Indian confederation never came to pass. And the British, despite his pleas, offered no help.

On April 5, 1832, Black Hawk's people crossed the Mississippi to the south of Saukenuk near the mouth of the Iowa River. Troops were hurriedly called up—militia under General HENRY ATKINSON. There were some young men in this army who later became famous in American history, such as ABRAHAM LINCOLN, ZACHARY TAYLOR, and Jefferson Davis. DANIEL BOONE's son, Nat, was also among them.

Troops arrived at Fort Armstrong by boat on April 12. Black Hawk's band headed overland along the Rock River past Saukenuk toward White Cloud's village farther north. When most of the Winnebagos there refused to help, Black Hawk and White Cloud continued northward to Potawatomi country. Most of that tribe's warriors also declared neutrality.

The first fighting occurred on May 14 when jittery and inexperienced militiamen fired on an Indian party sent to parley under a white flag of truce. Black Hawk had been prepared to surrender, but his warriors attacked and routed the enemy. Major Isaiah Stillman's men fled in panic, leading to the name Stillman's Run for the battle. Black Hawk and White Cloud headed into Wisconsin with their followers.

On June 15, President ANDREW JACKSON gave General WINFIELD SCOTT overall command of the war. Scott organized an army in Chicago. Meanwhile Atkinson's force of regulars and Illinois volunteers was reinforced, and a Winconsin militia was raised under Colonel HENRY DODGE.

The months of June and July were hard on both Indian and white forces. Black Hawk's people suffered exhaustion and hunger in the wilderness. Atkinson's troops, tracking the insurgents northward, became bogged down in the swampy headwaters of Rock River. A cholera epidemic ravaged Scott's troops in Chicago. Minor skirmishes caused additional casualties on both sides.

Aided by Winnebago informers, a combined force of soldiers—Dodge's militiamen and an advance party of Atkinson's men under General James Henry—caught up with the rebels on July 21 at Wisconsin Heights (near Sauk City, Wisconsin). Many Indians died in this battle. The rest managed to escape across the river on makeshift rafts.

Before being intercepted, Black Hawk had hoped to descend the Wisconsin to the Mississippi, from where his followers could reach Keokuk's village in Iowa. Now he decided to push on for the Bad Axe River, which also flowed into the Mississippi. His ragged band began making rafts and canoes to cross the river. On August 1-2, when confronted with the steamship *Warrior* outfitted with cannon, Black Hawk tried to parley a surrender under a flag of truce. But soldiers on the bank and in the steamship opened fire, killing about 28. Running out of fuel, the *Warrior* retreated down the river. Black Hawk now tried to persuade his people to head farther northward to Chippewa country, but most refused. He and White Cloud departed with about 50 faithful.

The next morning, August 3, Atkinsons' force of 1,300 caught up with those who had stayed behind and launched a full-scale attack, firing on women and children as well as warriors. Many were killed while trying to swim the Mississippi. Others who reached islands were shelled by artillery units or picked off by sharpshooters aboard the *Warrior*. Others were killed by Sioux on the west bank. As many as 300 Indians died in the massacre.

Black Hawk and White Cloud were persuaded by the Winnebagos to surrender at Fort Crawford at Prairie du Chien, Wisconsin, on August 27. Keokuk had earlier captured Neapope and delivered him to the army. In subsequent negotiations, Keokuk ceded about six million acres in Iowa to the government.

Black Hawk was imprisoned at Fort Monroe, Virginia. In 1833, as a prisoner of war, he was taken to Washington, D.C., to meet President Jackson. During a subsequent tour of other eastern cities, crowds responded much more enthusiastically to him than to the president. Black Hawk was allowed to return to his people in Iowa under the condition he no longer act as a chief. That same year, he dictated his story to the trader Antoine LeClaire, which was published as *The Autobiography of Black Hawk*. He traveled East a second time in 1837 and had his portrait painted by CHARLES BIRD KING.

Stripped of his homeland and his authority, Black Hawk died at Iowaville on the Des Moines River. His bones were robbed and eventually placed on display in a historical society until it was destroyed by fire in 1855.

BLACK HOOF See CATAHECASSA.

BLACK JIM. *Modoc.* *(d. 1873).* Warrior in the Modoc War of 1872–73.

Along with HOOKER JIM, CURLY HEADED DOCTOR, and SCHONCHIN JOHN, Black Jim encouraged CAPTAIN JACK to assassinate General EDWARD CANBY at the April 1873 parley on the lava beds of northern California. He later surrendered with Captain Jack, BOSTON CHARLEY, and Schonchin John, and was sentenced and executed with them. (See also CAPTAIN JACK.)

BLACK KETTLE **(Chaudiere Noir).** *Onondaga.* *(d. 1697).* War chief in the early French and Indian Wars (King William's War of 1689–97).

Black Kettle, an ally of the British, led his warriors in many engagements with the French and their Indian auxiliaries. He and his men raided numerous settlements and trading posts west of Montreal. He also led attacks on Algonquian trading parties on their way to meet the French. In July 1692, Black Kettle headed a war party that attacked Montreal itself, then escaped southward with many prisoners. Five years later, he negotiated a peace treaty with the French, but before it was finalized, he was killed by an Algonquian during a hunting trip in western New York.

BLACK KETTLE **(Moketavato, Motavato).** *Southern Cheyenne. (ca. 1803–1868).* Peace chief; leader of band attacked at Sand Creek in 1864 and at Washita in 1868. Uncle of WHITE SHIELD.

Black Kettle was an active warrior in his youth, fighting against the Utes, Delawares, and other enemies of the Cheyennes. By the Civil War years, however, he advocated friendship with whites. In 1861, he attended the council at Fort Wise, Colorado, and signed a treaty guaranteeing peace in Colorado and along the Santa Fe Trail. In 1863, he traveled to Washington, D.C., where he met President ABRAHAM LINCOLN.

Governor JOHN EVANS, who, with other Colorado officials, wanted to open up Indian hunting grounds to white settlement and mining, ordered a state militia into the field under the Indian-hating territorial military commander Colonel JOHN CHIVINGTON. In spring 1864, Chivington launched a campaign of violence against the Southern Cheyennes and Southern Arapahos, burning villages and plundering possessions, and forcing further conflict known as the Cheyenne-Arapaho War, or the Colorado War, of 1864–65.

Even when his close friend LEAN BEAR, another proponent of peace, was killed unnecessarily by soldiers, Black Kettle refused to go to war. But many of the Southern Cheyenne warriors chose instead to follow the militant BULL BEAR, TALL BULL, WHITE HORSE, and ROMAN NOSE. Militant Southern Arapahos followed LITTLE RAVEN and LEFT HAND.

With continuing military pressure against them, tribal leaders agreed to a council at Camp Weld outside Denver. Black Kettle, WHITE ANTELOPE, Bull Bear, and other chiefs meeting with Evans spoke for peace. The Indians were led to believe that if their bands camped near army posts and reported regularly, they would be safe from attack by the soldiers. Black Kettle led his followers—about 600 Southern Cheyennes, plus some Southern Arapahos—to Sand Creek near Fort Lyon and informed the garrison of his peaceful intentions. He had chosen this post because the commanding officer was Major EDWARD WYNKOOP, whom Black Kettle trusted. As it turned out, Wynkoop had been replaced by Major Scott Anthony.

Colonel Chivington soon arrived at Fort Lyon with additional troops. Ignoring word of Black Kettle's surrender, he prepared for battle. In the early morning of November 29, 1864, his men, many of them drunk, took up position around Black Kettle's camp. Black Kettle raised both a white flag of truce and an American flag over his tepee. Nevertheless, Chivington ordered the attack, the soldiers opening up with rifles and cannon. Some of the warriors, Black Kettle among them, managed to take shelter behind a high bank and fight back briefly before escaping. But chiefs White Antelope and YELLOW WOLF were killed along with about 200 others, more than half of them women and children.

After a Congressional investigation, Chivington was denounced and forced to resign. But his action convinced many among the Plains Indians that the only way to deal with whites was through warfare. It can be said that Sand Creek began the last phase of the Plains Indian Wars, as Wounded Knee in 1890 ended them.

Black Kettle still encouraged his people to remain at peace with the whites. At the request of his friend Edward Wynkoop, he came to a council at Medicine Lodge and signed the treaty of 1867 in which the Southern Cheyennes and Southern Arapahos, as well as the Comanches and Kiowas, were granted reservations within the Indian Territory.

Yet whites violated the terms of the treaty, settling on Indian lands, and the militant bands continued their raids. General PHILIP S. SHERIDAN launched a three-pronged offensive against the Southern Plains tribes, known as the Sheridan Campaign of 1868–69. Meanwhile, Black Kettle had led his band to the Washita River in the Indian Territory in the hope of avoiding the conflict. He traveled to Fort Cobb with the Cheyenne LITTLE ROBE and Arapaho band leaders to personally assure the garrison under Colonel WILLIAM B. HAZEN that his followers wanted peace. But Lieutenant Colonel GEORGE ARMSTRONG CUSTER discovered the presence of the Indian camp on the

Washita from Osage scouts who had been tracking a small party of militants. Anxious to prove himself after the abortive HANCOCK Campaign the year before, Custer ordered his 7th Cavalry into four surrounding groups.

At daybreak, on November 27, 1868, Black Kettle awoke to learn of soldiers nearby. He fired a warning shot in the air, then rode to meet the soldiers, hoping to prevent the attack through a parley. But the four columns advanced out of the fog and fired on Black Kettle and his wife, killing them both and riding over them. The soldiers then attacked the rest of the camp. They killed about 100 Cheyennes, only 11 of them warriors; captured 53 women and children; and slaughtered several hundred horses. The soldiers suffered 20 dead and 14 wounded.

Custer claimed a major victory in the Battle of Washita, and Sheridan publicly congratulated him. Edward Wynkoop and other friends of the peaceful Black Kettle knew the Cheyenne chief had once again been betrayed.

BLACK PARTRIDGE. *Potawatomi. (fl. early 1800s).*
Ally of British in the War of 1812 who aided settlers on the American side.

Black Partridge's band lived along the Illinois River opposite present-day Peoria, Illinois. He was sympathetic to American settlers during the War of 1812, but was unable to restrain his warriors who chose to follow METEA into battle in support of the British. Black Partridge came in advance to Fort Dearborn, the site of Chicago, Illinois, to warn the settlers of an attack the next day, August 15, 1812, returning a friendship metal from the Americans that he no longer felt he deserved. Captain Nathan Heald and his garrison of 50 regulars led the women and children toward Detroit. When the Potawatomis attacked and routed the column, Black Partridge urged the warriors to show mercy and personally saved the life of at least one of the women. Governor Ninian Evans later led troops in the destruction of Black Partridge's village. The Potawatomi leader, along with other chiefs Metea and WABAUNSEE, participated in his tribe's subsequent peace negotiations.

**BLACKSNAKE (Governor Blacksnake;
Tenwaneus, Thaonawyuthe, Thaowanyuths,
Twyneash, "chain breaker" or "awl breaker").**
Seneca. (ca. 1760–1859). Principal chief; leader of the Longhouse religion; writer. Nephew of
CORNPLANTER and HANDSOME LAKE.

Blacksnake, born at Cattaraugus in the western part of New York, as a young man fought on the side of the British in the American Revolution under the Seneca Cornplanter and the Mohawk JOSEPH BRANT. He was

present at the Battle of Oriskany in 1777, the Cherry Valley and Wyoming Valley raids in 1778, and the Battle of Newtown in 1779.

After the war, Blacksnake participated in negotiations to establish Seneca territory. In 1799, Handsome Lake founded the Longhouse religion; his nephew Blacksnake became one of its most dedicated disciples.

Blacksnake fought as an ally of the Americans in the War of 1812. He later became the Seneca's principal chief, known to his people as Governor Blacksnake. He encouraged education within his tribe, but also the retention of traditional lifeways, and continued to play an important role in the Longhouse Religion.

Blacksnake is thought to have been 99 years of age when he died. His memoirs serve as a source for the American Revolution and for the life of Handsome Lake.

BLAKELOCK, RALPH ALBERT. *(1847–1919).*
Artist.

Ralph Blakelock was born in Greenwich Village, New York City, the son of a doctor. He attended public school, then entered the Free Academy in 1864.

Against his father's wishes, who hoped his son would also become a doctor, Blakelock left college after two years to pursue a career as a painter. He turned down an opportunity to study in Europe, heading West instead in 1869. For the next three to seven years, he traveled in Kansas, Colorado, Wyoming, Utah, Nevada, California, Mexico, Panama, and the West Indies, making numerous sketches of Indians and developing an original impressionistic style for his depictions of their ceremonies and encampments.

After his return East, Blakelock married Cora Rebecca Bailey in 1877. He had difficulties in providing for his family of nine children and suffered a mental breakdown in 1899, at which time he was confined to an institution for the rest of his life. His works eventually became highly valued by collectors.

BLAND, THOMAS A. *(fl. 1880s).* Reformer; editor; lecturer.

Washington, D.C., physician Thomas A. Bland, along with ALFRED MEACHAM, founded the Indian rights magazine *Council Fire*, first published in 1878. When Meacham died in 1882, Bland took over editorship. They were among the few reformers of the 1880s who held that assimilation and detribalization and the breakup of reservations, as called for by other reformers, should occur gradually at a pace determined by the Indians themselves. In 1885, following policy disputes with HERBERT WELSH's Indian Rights Association, Bland formed the National Indian Defense Association. He lectured frequently on the subject of Indian rights.

BLOODY FELLOW (Iskagua, Clear Sky).
Cherokee. (fl. late 1700s). Ally of British during and after the American Revolution.

The Chickamauga Cherokee band of present-day eastern Tennessee, armed by British agents out of Pensacola, raided American frontier settlements in the 1770s–80s. Bloody Fellow was one of the militants, along with DRAGGING CANOE, who led Chickamauga warriors in raids. In 1791, he traveled to Philadelphia to meet with President GEORGE WASHINGTON and Secretary of War HENRY KNOX. Yet he continued his raids, playing the Spanish off against the Americans. He agreed to peace in 1794, signing the Treaty of Tellicoo Blockhouse. (See also DRAGGING CANOE.)

BLOODY KNIFE. *Arikara-Sioux. (ca. 1840–1876).* Army scout.

Bloody Knife was born in North Dakota; his father was a Hunkpapa Sioux and his mother an Arikara. The boy was taunted by his Hunkpapa kinsmen and developed a hatred for them.

After having returned to Arikara country along the upper Missouri with his mother, Bloody Knife worked as a mail carrier between Fort Totten and Fort Stephenson and other Missouri River posts, avoiding attacks by hostile Sioux.

When about 25, Bloody Knife participated in an army attack on the Hunkpapa Sioux GALL's camp south of Fort Berthold, North Dakota, in which Gall was severely bayoneted. The lieutenant in command stopped Bloody Knife from shooting Gall in the head, believing the Hunkpapa already lifeless. But Gall survived to become SITTING BULL's war chief.

Bloody Knife worked as an army scout out of Fort Abraham Lincoln, North Dakota, under General David S. Stanley. His great skill led Colonel GEORGE ARMSTRONG CUSTER to persuade the scout to transfer under his command. The two men reportedly became close friends. Bloody Knife was killed at the Battle of Little Bighorn in June 1876, part of Major MARCUS A. RENO's detachment attacked by Gall and his warriors. It took his wife She Owl four years to collect wages Bloody Knife was owed on his death, less than $100. (See also GALL; SITTING BULL.)

BLUE JACKET (Weyapiersenwah). *Shawnee.*
(d. ca. 1805). Leader in Little Turtle's War of 1790–94.

Along with the Miami LITTLE TURTLE, the Delaware BUCKONGAHELAS, and the Shawnee CATAHECASSA, Blue Jacket helped forge the confederation of tribes that resisted white settlement north of the Ohio River during the 1780s–90s. During Little Turtle's War, Blue Jacket assumed command of the Indian allies for the Battle of Fallen Timbers on August 20, 1794, against troops led by General "Mad" ANTHONY WAYNE. (See also LITTLE TURTLE.)

BLUNT, JAMES GILPATRICK. *(1826–1881).* Army officer in the Civil War campaigns within the Indian Territory.

James Blunt was born in Maine, and, at the age of 15, he went to sea for five years. He then studied medicine at Starling Medical College in Columbus, Ohio, graduating in 1849. Moving his practice to Anderson County, Kansas, in 1856, he became involved in pre–Civil War Kansas politics and was a member of the convention that framed the state constitution.

In 1861, Blunt entered the army as lieutenant colonel of the 3rd Kansas Volunteers. In 1862, he was made a brigadier general and given command of the military department of Kansas, which included a force of infantry, cavalry, and artillery from Kansas, Wisconsin, Ohio, and Indiana, plus Creek followers of OPOTHLEYAHOLO. They advanced along the Grand River to Fort Gibson in the Indian Territory (Oklahoma) and captured the post.

In 1863, a Confederate force of mostly Choctaws, Chickasaws, Cherokees, Creeks, and Seminoles under Colonel Douglas Cooper out of Fort Smith marched toward Fort Gibson. Blunt and his troops intercepted and defeated them at the Battle of Honey Springs on July 17. They then successfully attacked Perryville and Fort Smith. After the Union victories, fighting in the Indian Territory was limited to small raids, many carried out by a regiment under the Cherokee Confederate leader STAND WATIE. On September 25, 1864, Blunt's troops also engaged Cheyenne and Arapaho militants at Walnut Creek, Kansas.

The next year, General ULYSSES S. GRANT removed Blunt from office because of his feuding with fellow officers. In 1873, the Justice Department brought charges against him for conspiracy to defraud the federal government, but eventually dropped them. Blunt was committed to a mental institution in 1879, where he died two years later. (See also WATIE, STAND.)

BOAS, FRANZ. *(1858–1942).* Anthropologist, linguist; museum curator.

German-born Franz Boas studied at the universities of Kiel, Bonn, and Heidelberg, and trained as a naturalist and physicist. In 1883–84, he was part of an expedition to Baffin Island as a cutural geographer, where he came into contact with Eskimo culture. His monograph on the Central Eskimos was published by the Smithsonian's Bureau of Ethnology in 1888.

In 1885–86, Boas witnessed a group of Bella Coola Indians visiting Berlin, and in the latter year, Boas set out to British Columbia on a collecting voyage for the Neues Museum in Berlin.

In 1886, Boas settled permanently in America. In 1893, he began work for the Chicago World Columbian Exposition in arranging the ethnological collections, and went on to work for the American Museum of Natural History in New York City in the same capacity from 1896 to 1905. He pioneered the ethnic as opposed to the typological groupings of artifacts. In 1896, he began his association with Columbia University as a lecturer, becoming its first professor of anthropology three years later.

As museum curator, Boas helped organize the Morris K. Jesup North Pacific Expedition for the purpose of establishing cultural connections between Northwest Coast Indians and Siberian peoples. Two Russian ethnologists, Waldemar Bogoras and Waldemar Jochelson, in exile in Siberia because of revolutionary activities in czarist Russia, provided Boas with materials for the project.

Boas was also one of the earliest anthropologists to apply the principles of linguistic analysis to studies of Indian languages. He was the founder and editor of the *International Journal of American Linguistics*, beginning in 1940.

Although Boas was considered the foremost scholar on Northwest Coast Indians of his day, he also researched and wrote about Pueblo Indians of New Mexico, as well as Mexico's pre-Columbian peoples. Boas's methods of research and that of anthropologists whom he taught or influenced, including GEORGE HUNT—his Kwakiutl-Tlingit collaborator—as well as Ruth Benedict, William Jones, Alfred Kroeber, Robert Lowie, Margaret Mead, Elsie Clews Parsons, Paul Radin, Edward Sapir, John Swanton, and Clark Wissler, relied on field investigation and the examination of individual cultures and are sometimes referred to as the American Historical School of Anthropology. Among Boas's best-known works are *The Mind of Primitive Man* (1911), *Primitive Art* (1927), and *Race, Language, and Culture* (1940).

BODMER, KARL   (Carl or Charles Bodmer).
(1809–1893). Artist.

Born near Zurich, Switzerland, Karl Bodmer first studied art and drafting under his uncle Johann Jakob Mayer. He also studied in Paris. On a sketching trip to Germany, Bodmer met the naturalist and ethnologist Prince ALEXANDER PHILIPP MAXIMILIAN ZU WIED of Prussia, who hired him for a scientific tour of the United States. Arriving in Boston in 1832, they continued to New York City, where they met the fur entrepreneur JOHN JACOB ASTOR.

Starting from St. Louis in April 1833, aboard the American Fur Company's steamer *Yellowstone*, Maximilian and Bodmer traveled up the Missouri. They spent time in various frontier outposts, including Fort

Union (North Dakota), Fort MacKenzie (Montana), and Fort Clark (North Dakota), where they spent the winter on the return trip, arriving back in St. Louis in May 1834.

Bodmer, like GEORGE CATLIN before him, made sketches and watercolors of numerous tribes of the upper Missouri, including the Missouri, Omaha, Ponca, Sioux, Crow, Assiniboine, Blackfoot, Cree, Gros Ventre, Mandan, Hidatsa, and Arikara. Bodmer encouraged Indians he befriended, such as the Mandan MATO-TOPE, to pursue their own art, giving them painting and drawing supplies.

The watercolors and pencil sketches that Bodmer produced provided detailed illustrations of Native American life for Maximilian's later published account of the expedition: *Travels in the Interior of North America*, published in an 1839 German edition and an 1843 English edition.

Bodmer lived the rest of his life in France, in the city of Paris and the village of Barbizon, where many European artists resided. He influenced the French painter Jean Millet. Over 400 of Bodmer's original paintings and drawings were discovered shortly after World War II at Maximilian's family castle in Germany. (See also MAXIMILIAN, ALEXANDER PHILIPP, PRINZ ZU WIED-NEUWIED.)

Karl Bodmer. *Courtesy of Library of Congress.*

BOGUS CHARLEY. *Modoc. (ca. 1850–1880).*
Warrior in the Modoc War of 1872–73; interpreter; principal chief.

Bogus Charley was one of the militants who rebelled with CAPTAIN JACK in the Modoc uprising in California. Because of his excellent English, he regularly acted as interpreter in negotiations. At the April 1873 parley during which Captain Jack killed General EDWARD CANBY, Bogus Charley interpreted along with BOSTON CHARLEY. He surrendered with HOOKER JIM and helped him track down Captain Jack for the army. In the subsequent trial, he testified against Captain Jack. Bogus Charley was principal chief of the Modocs in the Indian Territory for several years before his death. (See also CAPTAIN JACK.)

BOLEK (Boleck, Bowlegs). *Mixed Seminole. (fl. early 1800s).* Chief in the First Seminole War of 1817–18. Brother of King PAYNE. (Bolek is also known as Bowlegs, not to be confused with the later BILLY BOWLEGS.)

During the early 1800s, there was unrest along the Florida-Georgia border between Seminoles and whites, a primary reason being the acceptance of runaway black slaves into the Indian bands. At that time, the two most powerful Seminole leaders were King Payne and his brother Bolek. In 1812, they skirmished with Georgia militiamen under Colonel Daniel Newnan; King Payne was killed and Bolek wounded.

In 1818, ANDREW JACKSON, who had had success against the Creeks in the Creek War of 1813–14, organized a force of 800 regulars and 900 militia, plus Lower Creeks led by WILLIAM McINTOSH, for an invasion of Florida, at that time Spanish territory. Jackson's force, after having taken KINACHE's village of Miccosukee, and then the village of St. Marks, headed for Chief Bolek's village on the Suwanee River. Although the Indians had fled, the troops captured two Englishmen who had been living among the Creeks, Robert Ambrister and Peter Cook. The prisoners were taken back to St. Marks, sentenced to death for aiding and abetting the Indians, and hanged. Jackson then retook Pensacola. A treaty between Spain and Florida the following year, 1819, provided for the sale of Florida to the United States.

Bolek, who had succeeded his brother as principal chief, died soon afterward. He was succeeded by King Payne's grandson, MICANOPY.

BOLON, ANDREW J. *(ca. 1822–1855).* Indian agent.
Born in Pennsylvania, A. J. Bolon moved to the Washington Territory. Following his election to the newly established territorial legislature in 1854, he became the subagent to the Indian tribes living west of the Bitterroot Range and east of the Cascades. During his brief term, he traveled extensively in the unsettled interior of the Washington Territory and held conferences with many tribal leaders on behalf of Governor ISAAC STEVENS.

In September 1855, on learning of impending hostilities against white settlers by the Yakimas under KAMIAKIN, Bolon attempted to negotiate a peace. Ice, Kamiakin's brother and a friend of Bolon, convinced the agent to return to the white settlements to give warning. But Bolon never made it back to The Dalles Indian Agency. On September 25, 1855, he was murdered by the seemingly friendly Ice and three other Yakimas who were traveling with him. (See also KAMIAKIN.)

BOMAZEEN (Bombazine, Abomazine, "keeper of the ceremonial fire"). *Abnaki. (ca. 1675–1724).* Leader in the Abnaki Wars in the late 1600s and early 1700s (part of the French and Indian Wars).

Like ASSACUMBUIT, MADOKAWANDO, and MOXUS, Bomazeen was a prominent sachem of the Abnaki Confederacy. His village of Norridgewock was located along the Kennebec River in Maine.

In 1693, Bomazeen negotiated a treaty with Maine's colonial governor William Phips. The next year, because of continuing land disputes, he went to the post at Pemaquid under a flag of truce for further negotiations. He was seized by the garrison and jailed in Boston. Upon his release, he led his warriors in attacks on colonial settlements, including Chelmsford and Sudbury in Massachusetts in 1706, and Saco in Maine in 1710.

In 1713, Bomazeen signed a peace treaty with the British at Portsmouth, New Hampshire, but before long took up arms again in support of the French. He died in an engagement near Taconnet, Maine. Colonial troops then attacked and destroyed Bomazeen's village, Norridgewock. Bomazeen's daughter was killed and his mother taken captive.

BONGA, GEORGE. *Chippewa. (b. ca. 1802).* Fur trader; interpreter.
George Bonga was the son of a Chippewa woman and a black fur trader. He worked as a canoeman for the American Fur Company and later ran outposts at Lac Platte, Otter Tail Lake, and Leech Lake in Minnesota. He eventually became an independent trader. Fluent in Algonquian, English, and French, Bonga served as interpreter for LEWIS CASS in an 1820 council at Fond du Lac, Minnesota, and, for government agents at a 1837 Chippewa treaty signing at Fort Snelling, Minnesota.

BONNEVILLE, BENJAMIN LOUIS EULALIE DE (Bald Chief). *(1796–1878).* Explorer; trader; army officer.
Born near Paris during the French Revolution, Benjamin de Bonneville's family were friendly with revolutionary supporters, the MARQUIS DE LAFAYETTE,

and Thomas Paine. In 1803, following Napoleon's rise to power, the family left France for America.

Bonneville attended West Point, and, after his graduation in 1815, was commissioned a second lieutenant and stationed at artillery garrisons in New England. He also saw service supervising the construction of a military road in Mississippi. In 1821, he was transferred to the frontier outpost at Fort Smith, Arkansas. When the Marquis de Lafayette made an official visit to the United States in 1825, Bonneville was assigned as his aide. After 1826, promoted to the rank of captain, he then served with the frontier garrison at Fort Gibson in what is now Oklahoma.

In 1831, Bonneville took a leave of absence from the military, and, with the financial backing of JOHN JACOB ASTOR and other Manhattan businessmen, he undertook a fur-trading expedition to the Northern Rockies. Bonneville agreed, as part of the terms of his leave, to explore the area of the Northern Rockies and make a study of the region's Indians for the army. Starting out from Fort Osage on the Missouri River in May 1832, Bonneville and a company of 110 men headed westward. After having led one of the earliest wagon trains through the South Pass of the Rockies, he established Fort Bonneville on the Green River in Wyoming from where he dispatched his guide JOSEPH WALKER on an expedition to explore northern Utah and the Sierras as far as the Pacific Coast. Bonneville himself led two expeditions to the Columbia River in Oregon, at that time territory controlled by British-owned Hudson's Bay Company.

Among the Indians who came to Fort Bonneville, Bonneville was known as the Bald Chief. His fur-trading enterprise proved to be less than a financial success. Most trappers avoided the newcomer's well-fortified trading post, referring to it as "Bonneville's Folly" or "Fort Nonsense," and Bonneville returned East to resume his military career in 1835.

Although cashiered from the military for allegedly overstaying his leave, Bonneville disputed his discharge and was reinstated by direct order from President ANDREW JACKSON in 1836. Although proof does not exist, it has been theorized that Jackson's intercession resulted from the fact that Bonneville had never actually taken a leave of absence, but had been in the army's service as a secret agent to spy on the British in Oregon and the Spanish in California, and seek information on the activities of traders and Indians.

While in Washington, D.C., campaigning for reinstatement, Bonneville sold the story of his western explorations to Washington Irving, who published it as *The Adventures of Captain Bonneville, U.S.A., In the Rocky Mountains and the Far West* (1837).

Bonneville went on to serve in the Mexican War of 1846–48. Promoted to the rank of colonel in 1855, he was sent to the army's Department of New Mexico, which he commanded briefly in 1856–57. He organized the punitive Gila River expedition against the Mogollon Apaches in May 1857. The expedition set out from bases at Albuquerque and Fort Fillmore, supported by Pueblo auxiliaries. Bonneville personally led one of the three columns of Indians that penetrated the Mogollon Mountains in search of those Apaches who had recently killed the Indian agent to the Navajos, HENRY L. DODGE. His force encountered a band of pacified Mimbreno Apaches and killed their chief, Cuchillo Negro. On June 27, 1857, Bonneville's 3rd Infantry regiment was victorious in an attack on a band of Coyotero (White Mountain) Apaches near Mount Graham, an engagement that came to be known as the Battle of Gila River. Bonneville's 1857 military expedition into the western New Mexico Territory (now Arizona), a region newly acquired by the 1853 GADSDEN Purchase, brought the army into contact for the first time with Coyotero, Chiricahua, and Aravaipa Apaches.

During the Civil War, Bonneville commanded garrisons and supervised recruitment in Missouri, reaching the rank of brigadier general. He retired to Fort Smith, Arkansas, in 1866, where he spent the remainder of his life. Lake Bonneville, the ancient lake covering some 20,000 square miles in northeast Utah, is named after him.

BOONE, DANIEL. *(1734–1820).* Explorer; guide; soldier; captive; state legislator.

Born near Reading, Pennsylvania, to a family of Quakers, Daniel Boone and his family headed south in 1749, settling first in the Shenandoah Valley of Virginia, and later in the Yadkin Valley of northwestern North Carolina.

During the French and Indian War of 1754–63, Boone served as a wagoner in British General EDWARD BRADDOCK's abortive attack against the French and their Indian allies at Fort Duquesne (present–day Pittsburgh). He survived the rout of the British and colonial forces by the French and Shawnees on July 9, 1755, and returned to North Carolina.

In 1756, Boone married Rebecca Bryan and worked as a "long hunter," undertaking extended journeys into the western wilderness in search of deer, the hides of which were later sold for cash. In this capacity, he explored the St. Johns River of Florida and, in 1767, made his first expedition across the Alleghenies into Kentucky.

Accompanied by his brother-in-law John Stuart and frontiersman John Finley, Boone returned to Kentucky in 1769. The party crossed the mountains of western Virginia via the Cumberland Gap and explored the Warrior's Trace, an ancient trail used by the Cherokees in their raids on the Shawnees, Wyandots, and Miamis to the north.

Over the next two years, Boone remained in central Kentucky, where he was captured by the Indians for a brief time. After his escape, Boone and his party headed back to North Carolina in 1771, but, as they passed through the Cumberland Gap, they were robbed of their valuable deer hides by Cherokees, who warned them to stay out of their lands.

Defying the Proclamation Line of 1763, and the warnings of the Cherokees not to return to Kentucky, Boone attempted to establish a settlement west of the Alleghenies in 1773. His group of settlers was attacked by the Cherokees at the Cumberland Gap on their way to Kentucky, a raid in which Boone's eldest son was killed. Most of the settlers fled, returning to North Carolina and Virginia, but Boone remained in the region for the rest of the year.

In 1774, Boone served as a messenger to the surveyors working for Virginia governor JOHN MURRAY, EARL OF DUNMORE at present-day Louisville. Following the defeat of the Shawnees in Lord Dunmore's War of 1774, Boone undertook the development of the Wilderness Road from Sycamore Shoals on the Holston River through the Cumberland Gap to the Kentucky River, in order to facilitate the settlement of the newly ceded Shawnee and Cherokee lands in Kentucky and Tennessee. He was also a scout and agent for Richard Henderson's land-development enterprise, the Transylvania Company. Boone established Boonesborough (or Boonesboro) in 1775, near present-day Harrodsburg, Kentucky.

During the American Revolution, after Kentucky had been incorporated as a county of Virginia, Boone was appointed a militia captain. Throughout the war, Boonesborough was subject to attacks by the Shawnee allies of the British. In 1776, Boone succeeded in liberating three young white girls captured by Shawnees, including his own daughter, Jemima. This act of heroism was later incorporated by JAMES FENIMORE COOPER as an episode of his novel *The Last of the Mohicans*.

In 1778, Boone himself was captured by Shawnees at the Blue Licks on Kentucky's Licking River, and was later adopted by Chief Blackfish, who received him into the tribe to take the place of his own son who had died. Following three months of captivity, during which he was exhibited at Detroit by the British and Indians, Boone managed to escape. He provided news of the impending Shawnee and British attack on Boonesborough, and the Kentucky militia forces were able to anticipate the raid and successfully defend the settlement in a siege from March to September. Boone's knowledge of the British and Indian strategy and troop movements also aided Colonel GEORGE ROGERS CLARK in planning an effective offensive against the Tories and Indians in 1778–79. Nevertheless, American military authorities questioned Boone's loyalty because he had led the Indians and the British to believe he could obtain the surrender of the Boonesborough settlement. Boone was court-martialed but exonerated, and, in 1779, he founded a new settlement, Boone's Station, near present-day Athens, Kentucky.

Following the American Revolution, Boone entered politics and became a state legislator, first in Virginia and then Kentucky. He was beset by legal problems, however, and lost his claim to his lands in Kentucky because of improper registry. After having been denied the government contract to develop the Wilderness Road through the Cumberland Gap into a wagon route, he moved with his family to Spanish territory in Missouri in 1799, where he became a Spanish citizen and a district magistrate. When the United States acquired the area through the Louisiana Purchase of 1803, Boone again lost title to his lands. Part of his holdings were restored in 1814 through the intercession of Congress.

BOSOMWORTH, MARY (Mary Musgrove, Mary Matthews; Coosaponakeesa). *Mixed Creek. (ca. 1700–ca. 1763).* Trader; interpreter; "empress" of the Creek Nation.

Coosaponakeesa was born along the Chattahoochee River in Alabama, the daughter of a white trader and his Creek wife. When about seven years old, she was taken to South Carolina by her father, where she was educated and baptized into the Church of England as Mary. She returned to Creek country at about age 16.

Mary married the trader John Musgrove, and, in 1732, they set up a trading post at Yamacraw Bluff on the Savannah River in Georgia. Starting in 1733, JAMES OGLETHORPE, founder of the colony of Georgia, hired Mary as an interpreter for his negotiations with the Creeks, at a salary of $500 per year. The Musgroves established a second trading post at Mount Venture on the Altamaha River. Meanwhile, Mary's influence among the Creeks grew. She advocated Creek support of the British in their colonial struggle with the Spanish for control of the Southeast.

John Musgrove died in 1739, and Mary married a second time, to Jacob Matthews, a British army captain. They moved to Savannah, where he died in 1742.

In 1749, Mary married a third white husband, the Reverend Thomas Bosomworth, taking the last name by which she became widely known to whites. Soon after the marriage, Thomas Bosomworth was assigned agent to the Creeks by the colony of South Carolina. As self-proclaimed "empress" of the Creek Nation, Mary Bosomworth laid claim to several islands off the Georgia coast—St. Catherine's, Ossabaw, and Sapelo—and a large tract on the mainland; the couple moved to St.

Catherine's. Thomas Bosomworth invested in cattle on credit and went further into debt. Demanding payment from the colonists for past services, he and his wife marched on Savannah, Georgia, with a force of Creek warriors in 1749. Colonial officials, ignoring their claims, seized the couple and bought off the warriors with presents.

The Bosomworths were released unharmed and eventually took their claims to England. Finally, in 1759, they received a small settlement and were granted permission to sell Ossabaw and Sapelo. Mary Bosomworth died on St. Catherine's four years later.

BOSTON CHARLEY. *Modoc. (d. 1873).* Warrior in the Modoc War of 1872–73.

Along with BOGUS CHARLEY, Boston Charley acted as interpreter between CAPTAIN JACK and General EDWARD CANBY at the parley on April 11, 1873, at the lava beds of Northern California during the Modoc War. He shot and killed Reverend Eleasar Thomas, one of President ULYSSES S. GRANT's peace commissioners. Boston Charley later surrendered with Captain Jack and was sentenced to hang with him. (See also CAPTAIN JACK.)

BOUCHARD, JAMES (Watomika, "swift foot"). *Delaware. (1823–1889).* First Indian priest; lecturer.

James Bouchard was the son of the Delaware chief Kistalwa and his French wife, Monotowa, who had been captured and raised by the Comanches. On the death of his father in 1834 at the hands of the Sioux, Bouchard converted to Presbyterianism and attended a mission school in Ohio. In 1846, he converted to Catholicism and began studies in Missouri for the Jesuit order. In 1855 he became the first Indian to be ordained a Catholic priest, and in 1861 he began serving as a missionary to miners in San Francisco. Bouchard also gave lectures on his experiences as an Indian and a Christian.

BOUDINOT, ELIAS (Galegina, Buck Watie, Stag Watie). *Mixed Cherokee. (ca. 1803–1839).* Editor of the *Cherokee Phoenix*; writer. Brother of STAND WATIE; nephew of MAJOR RIDGE; cousin of JOHN RIDGE.

Galegina, which translates as "buck," was born in Georgia near the town of Rome, the son of the Cherokee David Uwati and the part-English Susannah Reese. He attended a Moravian school in Salem, North Carolina. Then, in 1818, the New Jersey philanthropist, Elias Boudinot, sent the Cherokee youth to the Cornwall Foreign Mission School in Cornwall, Connecticut, whereupon Galegina took the name of his patron. While at Cornwall, he met a white girl, Harriet Ruggles Gold, whom he married after attending Andover, despite protestations by her family.

On rejoining his tribe, Boudinot served as clerk of the National Council. He was soon appointed editor of the *Cherokee Phoenix*, a tribal newspaper using both English and SEQUOYAH's syllabary, which first appeared in 1828. STEPHEN FOREMAN was associate editor. In 1831, Boudinot lectured in the North to raise money for the publication. He also wrote a novel, *Poor Sarah; or, the Indian Woman*, published in the Cherokee syllabary in 1833. With SAMUEL WORCESTER and Foreman, Boudinot worked on a translation of the Bible.

Like his brother Stand Watie, Boudinot supported the Treaty Party, led by Major Ridge and John Ridge, which held that removal to the Indian Territory was inevitable and that the best possible deal under the circumstances should be negotiated. The opposing Ross party led by JOHN ROSS resisted relocation through legal means. In 1835, Boudinot was one of the signers of the Treaty of New Echota, ceding Cherokee lands.

After relocation to the Indian Territory via the Trail of Tears, Boudinot, Major Ridge, and John Ridge were murdered by tribal members for their support of removal. Boudinot's first wife had died in 1830, leaving six children, whom Boudinot's second wife, Delight Sargent Boudinot, took East with her. One of them, Elias Cornelius Boudinot, studied civil engineering in Vermont, then went on to play a leadership role among the Western Cherokees. He fought with his uncle Stand Watie for the Confederates in the Civil War and was a delegate from the Cherokee Nation to the Confederate Congress at Richmond, Virginia.

BOUQUET, HENRY. *(1719–1765).* British officer in the French and Indian War of 1754–63, and Pontiac's Rebellion of 1763.

Originally from Switzerland, Henry Bouquet was a professional soldier who saw service in Europe with Dutch forces in the War of the Austrian Succession, 1740–48, and also served with the army of Sardinia. In 1756, he became a lieutenant colonel in the British Royal American regiment, and was dispatched for colonial duty in Pennsylvania during the French and Indian War of 1754–63.

In 1758, as second in command to Brigadier General John Forbes, Bouquet helped direct the construction of Forbes Road, the military route through the Alleghenies, north of BRADDOCK's Road, using it to reach the French-held Fort Duquesne, which the French then abandoned. The British renamed it Fort Pitt (present-day Pittsburgh). Bouquet continued to serve on the Ohio frontier, under the command of generals John Stanwix, Robert Monckton, and JEFFREY AMHERST.

During Pontiac's Rebellion of 1763, as commander in the West, Bouquet successfully defended Fort Pitt, and, in the Battle of Bushy Run on August 5–6, defeated a force of Shawnees and Delawares. Bouquet's victory at Bushy Run over an Indian force of superior numbers resulted from his application of European-style tactics to wilderness fighting, including the utilization of rapid troop deployment and massed firepower. Upon Amherst's suggestion, Bouquet ordered the distribution of smallpox-infected blankets as gifts to the Indians near Fort Pitt. A smallpox epidemic soon broke out among them, contributing to the collapse of PONTIAC's alliance of tribes.

In October 1764, Bouquet led a military force to the fork of the Ohio and Muskingum rivers, where he defeated the Delawares and Shawnees. He presented the defeated bands an ultimatum for the return of all white captives, threatening to kill hostages he was holding and to destroy Indian villages. Tribal leaders complied, handing over some 200 captured whites. Most of the captives did not return willingly, however, having been adopted by Indian families and assimilated into tribal life.

In 1765, Bouquet was made a brigadier general in charge of the Southern colonies, but died of fever that same year at Pensacola in British West Florida. (See also PONTIAC.)

BOURKE, JOHN GREGORY (Captain Cactus). *(1846–1896).* Historian; anthropologist; reformer; soldier.

Philadelphia-born John G. Bourke served as a private in the Civil War, then attended West Point, graduating in 1869. He became a second lieutenant and aide-de-camp to General GEORGE CROOK.

At that time, Crook began enlisting Apaches as soldiers to fight their fellow tribesmen. As an officer in the field, Bourke lived and fought alongside the Apaches, becoming interested in their language and culture. The Apaches detached to him called him Captain Cactus.

Bourke was with Crook's combined force of federal troops and Indian auxiliaries when the Apaches suffered a decisive defeat at the Battle of Salt River Canyon in December 1872. In 1874, he lived among the Hopis and made a study of their culture.

Bourke remained with Crook's staff when the general was transferred to the Department of the Platte's headquarters at Omaha, in 1875, to supervise the war against the Sioux and the Cheyennes. In 1875–76, Bourke was involved in four major engagements of the Sioux Wars. At the June 1876 Battle of the Rosebud in Montana, Bourke commanded a force of Crows and Shoshones against Sioux and Northern Cheyennes under CRAZY HORSE. He also took part in the Powder River and Bighorn campaigns of 1876–77 that led to the defeat of DULL KNIFE and his Cheyennes. Bourke was a military observer in the Ute War of 1879, as well as in the Apache Wars of the 1880s.

During his Western assignments, Bourke recorded information about the tribes he encountered. In 1880–81, he was granted an extended leave from the army to make a comprehensive study of the Southwest tribes under the sponsorship of JOHN WESLEY POWELL and the Smithsonian's Bureau of Ethnology. He also produced a dictionary and grammar of the Apache language for the Bureau of Ethnology in 1886. His other works include: *An Apache Campaign* (1886); *Mackenzie's Last Fight with the Cheyenne* (1890); *On the Border with Crook* (1891); *Medicine Men of the Apache* (1892); and *Scatologic Rites of All Nations* (1892).

Bourke's experiences and studies led him to the conclusion that the government was unfair in its treatment of Indians, and he later became an advocate of Indian rights.

BOWL (Diwali, The Bowl, Colonel Bowles). *Mixed Cherokee. (1756–1839).* Early leader of the Western Cherokees.

The son of a Scotch-Irish trader and a Cherokee mother, Bowl probably was born in North Carolina, but grew up in the Cherokee village of Chickamauga in Tennessee. His name was a translation of the vessel used for drinking the Black Drink, the Southeast Indian ritualist purgative. He sided with the British in the American Revolution, along with DRAGGING CANOE.

In 1794, Bowl led a group of warriors in an attack on a white settlement along the Tennessee River, the so-called Massacre of Muscle Shoals in what is now Alabama. When the Cherokee council denounced his act and offered to help in his arrest, Bowl led his followers across the Mississippi River and settled on the St. Francis River in Spanish territory. With the Louisiana Purchase of 1803, Bowl's new homeland in present-day Arkansas was transferred to the United States.

About 1824, because of dissatisfaction with treatment by U.S. government officials, Bowl and his followers crossed the Sabine River into Texas, eventually settling on the Angelina River. Other bands of eastern tribes—Delawares, Kickapoos, and Shawnees—also emigrated to Texas, encouraged by Mexican officials who hoped to protect Texas settlements from both American expansion and from Comanche and Kiowa raids. Mexican officials commissioned Bowl as a lieutenant colonel in 1827.

With Texas independence from Mexico in 1835, the situation again changed for Bowl and the confederated Indian community. The first president of the Texas Republic, SAMUEL HOUSTON, signed a 1836 treaty establishing Indian homelands, but the Senate failed to ratify it. Many Texans, fearing the Indians were conspiring with Mexican inhabitants, wanted removal of all tribes. When Bowl and his followers refused to relocate north to the Indian Territory, the Republic's new president, Mirabeau Lamar, sent in troops. In July 1839, the Indians were defeated in two engagements along the Angelina River. Bowl and his war chief Hard-Mush were killed on the second day of fighting and his followers dispersed. Bowl was found clutching a tin box with a copy of the 1836 treaty.

BOWLEGS, BILLY (Holatamico, Halpatter-Micco, Halpuda Mikko, "alligator chief"). *Seminole.* *(ca. 1810–1864).* Leader in the Second and Third Seminole wars.

In the Second Seminole War of 1835–42, Billy Bowlegs fought in many of the battles with OSCEOLA, MICANOPY, JUMPER, ALLIGATOR, WILD CAT, and ARPEIKA. Even after the death of Osceola and the surrender of the other leaders except Arpeika, Bowlegs led 200 warriors in an 1839 attack on a trading post opened by Colonel WILLIAM S. HARNEY on Seminole land, killing most of the garrison. For almost a year, Bowlegs and his band remained at large in the Everglades, hiding in the swamps during the day and raiding at night. Yet, in 1842, with his followers war-weary and near starvation, he too surrendered and, still refusing to relocate to the Indian Territory, he received a small piece of land. At this time, the federal government officially announced the end of the eight-year Seminole War. The cost to the United States: 1,500 solders killed and $30 million spent. That same year, Bowlegs and other Seminole chiefs visited Washington, D.C.

But violence flared up again in 1855 in what is sometimes referred to as the Third Seminole War. It started when a party of army engineers and surveyors, working in the Great Cypress Swamp, stole crops and destroyed banana trees belonging to Bowlegs's band, then, when confronted, did not offer any apology or compensation. Bowlegs led his warriors in a series of raids on settlers, trappers, and traders. Once again, neither regulars nor volunteers could contain the militants. In 1858, a delegation of Seminoles previously removed to the Indian Territory were brought in to negotiate with Bowlegs's band and made an offer of peace and a large sum of cash on behalf of the whites. Bowlegs and some members of his band eventually agreed to emigrate West. Not all the warriors supported his decision; some stayed behind, joining Arpeika's band.

Bowlegs took his band of now 33 warriors and 80 women and children to lands on the north and south forks of the Canadian River in the Indian Territory. In 1861, he fought for the North in the Civil War under OPOTHLEYAHOLO. (See also OSCEOLA.)

BOWLES, WILLIAM AUGUSTUS (Eastajoca). *(1763–1805).* Trader; director general of the Creek Nation.

William Bowles was born of English parents in Maryland at the close of the French and Indian Wars.

As a teenager, he was a Loyalist soldier in the American Revolution.

After the war, Bowles traveled to Florida (ceded to England by Spain in 1763), joining the Lower Creeks in Pensacola. In 1783, after an attack on West Florida by Bernardo de Galvez, an engagement in which Bowles fought for the British under John Campbell, Spain regained Florida. Bowles, who took both Cherokee and Creek wives and spoke three Indian dialects, continued to play an influential role among the Indians, trading among them and lobbying for the British cause against both Spain and the United States. His pro-British Creeks were opposed by those under ALEXANDER McGILLIVRAY. Bowles traveled to Canada to try to enlist continued British support in the region.

In 1792, during negotiations with the Spanish, Bowles was taken captive. He was imprisoned in Spain, then exiled to the Philippines via South America. On his return trip to Spain, he escaped in Africa and made his way to England, where he stayed seven months.

In 1799, Bowles sailed back to the Americas, organizing the privateer Muskogee navy in Jamaica. Returning to Florida, he set up headquarters among Chief KINACHE's band of Miccosukee Seminoles in West Florida. His assorted force of Creeks, Seminoles, runaway black slaves, and Indians from other displaced tribes of the Southeast, took the Spanish post of St. Marks in 1800. His larger plan, however, was to establish the Indian state of Muskogee, a British protectorate, comprised of both Florida and the Louisiana Territory, with Miccosukee as its capital.

In 1802, when the Seminoles made peace with Spain, and England made peace with France (who had regained the Louisiana Territory in 1800), Bowles lost both Indian and British supporters. At the Hickory Ground Council in 1803, he was betrayed by Upper Creeks and United States representatives and handed over to Spanish officials. He died while imprisoned in Cuba.

BOZEMAN, JOHN M. *(1835–1867).* Explorer; founder of the Bozeman Trail.

Originally from Georgia, John Bozeman traveled to the Colorado goldfields in 1861, and took part in the Montana Gold Rush of 1862.

In the winter of 1862–63, Bozeman left Bannack, Montana, accompanied by trapper John Jacobs and Jacob's mixed-blood daughter, to seek a more direct route to Colorado. They first headed east across the Bighorn Mountains of Wyoming, and then south, avoiding the longer and more circuitous route through Idaho to the Overland Trail. Their shortcut through Wyoming to Colorado, however, passed through lands reserved by treaty for the Sioux and Cheyennes.

In spring 1863, a wagon train led by Bozeman was turned back by Cheyenne and Sioux war parties, who warned the settlers to keep out of their lands, whereupon the majority followed the long route west of the Bighorn Mountains. Bozeman and several others, however, left the wagon train and, traveling mostly at night, traveled to Virginia City, Montana, on the new trail. In spring 1864, he successfully led the first wagon train along the route.

The Bozeman Trail became a popular road north from Colorado into the rich mining regions of Montana. By 1866, the army had built three forts along the Bozeman to protect travelers: Fort Phil Kearny and Fort Reno in northern Wyoming, and Fort C. F. Smith in southern Montana. Sioux and Cheyenne resentment of the white incursion onto their lands led to the War for the Bozeman Trail of 1866–68, also known as RED CLOUD's War.

John Bozeman was killed in a raid by Piegan Indians in 1867. The trail that bears his name was partially abandoned following the Fort Laramie Treaty of 1868, but was reopened as a cattle route following the defeat of the Northern Plains tribes allied under SITTING BULL in the War for the Black Hills of 1876–77. (See also RED CLOUD.)

BRACKENRIDGE, HENRY MARIE.
(1786–1871). Naturalist; writer.

The son of the writer and jurist Hugh Henry Brackenridge, Henry Marie Brackenridge was born in Pittsburgh, at that time still a frontier settlement. His father tutored him in basic skills until he was seven years old, then sent him to Ste. Genevieve in the Louisiana Territory (now Missouri) to learn French. In 1796, he returned to Pittsburgh, where he studied classics with his father and attended the Pittsburgh Academy. Following law studies, he moved to Baltimore to open a practice in 1806. Unable to attract many clients, he went to St. Louis to learn the Spanish language and study Spanish law. He also made studies of the region's Indian antiquities and natural history.

In April 1811, Brackenridge accompanied the trader MANUEL LISA on a keelboat voyage up the Missouri from St. Louis to the Northern Plains country of the Arikaras and Mandans with the purpose of collecting scientific data about Indians and wildlife. Along the way he passed through the lands of hostile Sioux, but his party managed to avoid Indian attacks. In June of that year, Brackenridge arrived at a trading post on the upper Missouri, near Mandan and Arikara settlements along the present-day North Dakota-South Dakota border. After time among fur traders and trappers, he returned to St. Louis in early August, accompanied by fellow naturalist JOHN BRADBURY, who had traveled up the Missouri with the Astorians. In 1814,

Brackenridge's account of this journey, *Journal of a Voyage Up the Missouri River in 1811*, was published.

Brackenridge went on to a career in law and diplomacy that included official positions in the Louisiana and Florida judiciaries, and foreign service work in South America for the U.S. State Department. He wrote additional works, including *Views of Louisiana* (1814) and *Voyage to South America* (1819).

BRADBURY, JOHN. *(1768–1823).* Naturalist; anthropologist.

John Bradbury was born in Scotland and educated in England. Commissioned by the Botanical Society of Liverpool to come to North America to study flora, he was received by former president THOMAS JEFFERSON, who helped plan his trip. In 1809–10, using St. Louis as his base, he made several scientific excursions in the region.

In 1811, Bradbury set out with the expedition sponsored by JOHN JACOB ASTOR up the Missouri River, then departed from the Astorians in what is now South Dakota to accompany a party under trader MANUEL LISA to North Dakota. During the journey, along with Philadelphia naturalist Thomas Nuttall, Bradbury visited Arikara, Hidatsa, and Mandan villages. He returned to St. Louis with the naturalist HENRY MARIE BRACKENRIDGE. The War of 1812 delayed his departure for England, and Bradbury explored the Ohio Valley.

In his work, *Travels in the Interior of North America in the Years 1809, 1810, and 1811*, first published in 1815, Bradbury recorded information about Indian customs in addition to wildlife and geographical features. After a stay in England, Bradbury settled permanently in St. Louis.

BRADDOCK, EDWARD. *(1695–1755).* British officer in the French and Indian War of 1754–63.

Edward Braddock, the son of a Scottish military family, began service in the British army when he was 15 years old, his career sponsored by the Duke of Cumberland, captain general of British forces. He eventually reached the rank of major general.

In February 1755, Braddock arrived in Virginia as commander in chief of British and colonial forces fighting against the French and their Indian allies. Braddock's strategy was to attack French strongholds at Fort Niagara in western New York; Crown Point near Lake Champlain in New York; Fort Beausejour in French Acadia (present-day New Brunswick, Canada); and Fort Duquesne, located at the site of present-day Pittsburgh in western Pennsylvania.

Braddock's campaign against Fort Duquesne began in April 1755, with the construction of a military road extending 100 miles from Fort Cumberland, Maryland, westward to the confluence of the Monongahela and Ohio rivers. The route was originally called NEMACOLIN's Path, after the Delaware Indian who, with Thomas Cresap, had blazed this trail into the Ohio Valley five years earlier. Braddock's command consisted of 700 colonial militia and 1,400 British regulars. His aide on this 100-mile expedition was GEORGE WASHINGTON.

At Washington's suggestion, Braddock advanced with only two-thirds of his forces, with the rest staying behind to complete the road. On July 9, 1755, less than 10 miles from Fort Duquesne, Braddock and his troops were routed by a force of French-allied Wyandots, Algonkins, Ottawas, Delawares, and Shawnees under the command of Captain Hyancinth de Beaujeu. Braddock lost almost 1,000 men in the conflict. Among the Indian participants were the Mingo HALF-KING (Scarouady) on the side of the British, and the Delaware JACOBS on the side of the French. Many of Braddock's troops were ill-trained and fled in panic. Braddock's defeat was due to his adherence to European-style fighting formations, ineffective against the Indians. Among the dead were 63 of his 89 officers.

Braddock, who had four horses shot from under him in the course of the battle, was mortally wounded and died of his injuries four days later at Great Meadows, near the present site of Uniontown, Pennsylvania. While the Indians were preoccupied with looting abandoned British supplies and scalping Braddock's fallen troops, Washington was able to lead the retreating British and colonial forces back to the safety of Fort Cumberland.

As a result of Braddock's defeat, many Indian bands of the Old Northwest defected to the French and began terrorizing British colonial settlers throughout the Ohio Valley and western Pennsylvania.

BRADFORD, WILLIAM. *(1590–1657).* Colonial governor; historian.

Born in England, William Bradford formed the Separatist congregation, apart from the Church of England, and emigrated first to Holland and then to America. Arriving along the New England coast on the *Mayflower* in 1620 with the other Pilgrims, he was one of the founders of the Plymouth Colony. On the death of John Carver in 1621, Bradford became the colony's governor, serving intermittently in that office until 1656. (In the years Bradford did not serve, EDWARD WINSLOW was governor.) Under Bradford's leadership, the Plymouth colonists maintained peaceful relations with the Wampanoags under MASSASOIT and made war on the Pequots under SASSACUS. Bradford encouraged trade with the Indians as well as a colonial economy of fishing and agriculture. The *History of Plimoth Plantation*, written by Bradford between 1630

and 1650, and published in full in 1656, contains some of the earliest accounts of white contact with the Indians of New England. (See also MASSASOIT; SASSACUS.)

BRADY, JOHN GREEN. *(1848–1918).* Alaska territorial governor; reformer; missionary.

John Green Brady was born in New York City and orphaned at a young age. He was sent to Tipton, Indiana, by the Children's Aid Society, where he was adopted by Judge John Green. Having graduated from Yale, he studied to be a minister at New York's Union Theological Seminary.

Brady traveled to Sitka in 1878 to become a missionary teacher to Alaska's Indians, under Presbyterian leader Sheldon Jackson. Three years later, he gave up teaching to enter business. He continued to promote educational opportunities for Alaskan natives by providing jobs at his store and lumber mill for graduates of Sitka's missionary school.

Brady became politically prominent in Sitka, and, in 1897, was appointed governor of the District of Alaska by President William McKinley, at the time of the Gold Rush to Alaska. Throughout this period, he struggled to maintain the rights of Alaskan Indians and sought to expand their educational and vocational opportunities.

Brady opposed the imposition of a reservation system, which he believed would make Indians dependent on the federal government. His administration maintained strict regulations over the sale and distribution of alcohol, including a high licensing fee for sellers. Through Brady's efforts, many Alaskan Indians went on to higher education at RICHARD HENRY PRATT's Carlisle Indian School in Pennsylvania. Brady also encouraged the preservation of Native American culture. He was responsible for the exhibition of Alaskan Indian arts and crafts at the 1904 Louisiana Purchase Exposition in St. Louis.

Even after his resignation from office because of involvement in a financially disastrous mining venture, Brady continued his efforts on behalf of Indian rights. He was active in the Friends of the Indian movement and spoke at conferences held by ALBERT SMILEY at Lake Mohonk, New York. On his death at Sitka, Indians conducted his funeral service.

BRAINERD, DAVID. *(1718–1747).* Missionary; scholar.

David Brainerd was born in the colonial settlement of Haddam, Connecticut, to a prominent family that included several royal officials and clergymen. In 1739, he embraced Calvinism and entered Yale College to study for the ministry. His career at Yale was cut short in 1742, when he was expelled for voicing Separatist views in defiance of school authorities. Following studies under the Reverend Jedediah Mills at Ripton, Connecticut,

Brainerd was commissioned by the main Presbyterian missionary organization of the time, the Society in Scotland for the Propagation of Christian Knowledge, to preach and minister to the Mahican Indians.

In April 1743, Brainerd arrived at the Mahican settlement at Kaunaumeek, located in the woodlands between Albany, New York, and Stockbridge, Massachusetts. At nearby Stockbridge, he studied the Mahicans' Algonquian dialect under fellow missionary JOHN SERGEANT.

After his formal ordination as a Presbyterian minister in June 1744, Brainerd traveled to Delaware Indian country near the fork of the Delaware and Lehigh rivers in Pennsylvania. Most of the Delawares in the area were in the process of leaving their lands, dispossessed by Pennsylvania authorities as a result of the Walking Purchase of 1737. Brainerd preached to the few remaining Unami bands. Although he had learned the Mahican's Algonquian dialect, he was unfamiliar with that of the Delawares. His interpreter to the Indians was the Delaware TATEMY, whom Brainerd subsequently converted.

With Tatemy's help, Brainerd next went to preach among the Delawares of New Jersey at Crossweeksung near present-day Freehold and Cranberry. He attracted many Indians to his prayer meetings and sermons, converting as many as 50 Indians during a 16-month stay. Brainerd frequently made missionary forays into Pennsylvania's Wyoming and Susquehanna valleys. Yet his chronic bad health, probably due to tuberculosis, and repeated bouts of depression hampered his efforts. During his missionary work among the Mahicans and the Delawares, he chose to live among whites rather than Indians.

Brainerd was engaged to marry Puritan leader JONATHAN EDWARDS's daughter Jerusha, but died at Edwards's home in October 1747, leaving behind a record of his short career as a Presbyterian minister to the Mahicans and Delawares. His diaries were published by the Society in Scotland for the Propagation of Christian Knowledge, first as *Mirabilia Dei Inter Indices* and *Divine Grace Displayed*. Collectively known as *Brainerd's Journal*, these memoirs became a handbook for 19th-century Presbyterian missionaries in India and Africa.

David Brainerd's younger brother John was also a missionary to the Delaware Indians.

BRANT, JOHN (Ahyouwaighs, Ayonwaeghs).
Mohawk. (1794–1832). Principal chief. Son of JOSEPH BRANT.

John Brant was the fourth and youngest son of Joseph Brant and his wife Catherine. He attended white-run schools and, like his father, came to feel comfortable with both Mohawk and English customs. He lived for the most part at the Home at the Head of the Lake (also called Willington Square) in Burlington, Ontario.

In the War of 1812, Brant led a contingent of warriors against the Americans, and, in 1821, he traveled to England to argue Mohawk land claims. During his stay, he wrote Thomas Campbell requesting the poet change the depiction of Joseph Brant as cruel and bloodthirsty in the poem "Gertrude of Wyoming."

In 1830, John Brant was selected by his mother to be the new principal chief at the Six Nations Reserve at Brantford, Ontario. He was also elected to the provincial parliament for the county of Haldimand, but had to vacate the seat when landowners contested votes by Indians who, they claimed, were not true landholders. He died of cholera soon afterward.

BRANT, JOSEPH (Joseph Brandt;
Thayendanegea, Thayandanega, "he places two
bets").
Mohawk. (1742–1807). Ally of British in the American Revolution. Brother of MOLLY BRANT; father of JOHN BRANT.

Thayendanegea was born in the Ohio Valley in 1742, while his parents were on a hunting trip away from their New York home. His father Tehowaghwengaraghkwin died shortly after his birth; his mother Margaret remarried another Mohawk who was soon killed in a raid. She then married the Mohawk chief Nikus Brant whose name Joseph took, and the boy grew up at Canajoharie Castle in the Mohawk Valley of New York. Joseph was a frequent visitor to the household of WILLIAM JOHNSON, the land speculator and trader who had built Fort Johnson and later Johnson Hall in Mohawk territory and later married Joseph's sister Molly Brant. Joseph played with William Johnson's son JOHN JOHNSON and nephew GUY JOHNSON, and was educated at the Anglican Mohawk mission school.

When fighting broke out between the British and French in the last of the French and Indian Wars, starting in 1754, William Johnson asked for the help of his Mohawk friends in an expedition to Lake George. Chief HENDRICK led Mohawk auxiliaries. One of the Mohawk braves was Joseph Brant, only 13 at the time. Johnson and his British and Mohawk army won the Battle of Lake George in 1755; Johnson received a knighthood from the king for this victory. In 1756, he was appointed superintendent of Indian Affairs for the Northern Department. In 1759, Brant again accompanied Johnson on a military expedition, this time against Fort Niagara on Lake Ontario.

Brant and two fellow Mohawk youths were recruited by SAMSON OCCUM to attend Moor's Indian Charity School in Lebanon, Connecticut, run by ELEAZAR WHEELOCK. The other Mohawks soon departed, but Brant, in 1761–63, proved himself an excellent student, mastering spoken and written English. He also helped tutor fellow student SAMUEL KIRKLAND, who would become missionary to the Oneidas, in the Iroquoian language.

In 1763, Brant fought for the British against the united Algonquian tribes in PONTIAC's Rebellion. In 1765, he married Margaret, the daughter of an Oneida chief, and settled at Canajoharie, New York, where he had two children by her. On her death from tuberculosis in 1771, he married her half-sister Susanna, but two years later, she too died of tuberculosis. During this period, Brant worked with the Anglican missionary John Stuart in translations of religious texts into the Mohawk Iroquoian dialects.

Joseph Brant later acted as interpreter for Johnson in his negotiations with the Iroquois tribes. When William Johnson died in 1774, his nephew Guy Johnson became the new Northern superintendent of Indian Affairs, and Brant became his interpreter and personal secretary.

Joseph Brant. *Courtesy of New York State Library, Albany.*

At the outbreak of the American Revolution in 1775, Joseph Brant left the Mohawk Valley and went to the British post at Niagara, then to England with Guy Johnson. He met many notables during his visit, such as the writer James Boswell, the painter George Romney, who painted the Mohawk's portrait, and King George III. As legend has it, Joseph Brant did not kneel before the king and grandiosely kiss the queen's hand.

On his return to North America in July 1776, New York was under seige by rebel forces led by General GEORGE WASHINGTON. Brant participated in the Battle of Long Island. Disguised as colonists, he and two companions then slipped through enemy lines and made their way home. He was soon commissioned a colonel by the British and traveled among the Iroquois tribes to win them over to the Loyalist cause. The Mohawks, plus the Senecas, Onondagas, and Cayugas, agreed to support the British in a council at Oswego in July 1777. The Oneidas and Tuscaroras gave their support to the Americans, in large part due to the friendship between the Oneida chief SKENANDOA and the missionary Samuel Kirkland.

Brant led an Indian contingent in support of Colonel Barry St. Leger's force against troops under General NICHOLAS HERKIMER in the Battle of Oriskany on August 6, 1777. In this engagement, royal troops, many of them Hessian professionals, along with Brant's Mohawks and CORNPLANTER's Senecas, battled a makeshift rebel army of farmers, plus Oneidas and Tuscaroras. With many Iroquois losses on both sides, Brant informed the British high command in Montreal that he would henceforth command his warriors in battle his own way.

Brant subsequently led his braves in many successful raids on frontier settlements, many of them Palatine Dutch, as well as on stockades in both New York and Pennsylvania. The Royal Greens, under now–General John Johnson, and Tory Rangers, under Colonel JOHN BUTLER, offered support. In spring and summer 1778, Brant's warriors, operating out of Onoquaga, a Mohawk village on the Susquehanna River, attacked Sacandaga, Cobleskill, Springfield, and German Flats, burning houses and barns and driving away livestock, but sparing the settlers unless they fought back.

That same summer, Colonel Butler led his Rangers plus Senecas and Cayugas in raids along the Wyoming Valley of Pennsylvania, a branch of the Susquehanna. They captured eight outposts with minimal fighting. In an ill-advised counterattack on July 3, 1778, the garrison at Forty Fort lost 227 militiamen and several Continental soldiers, an engagement known historically as the Wyoming Massacre. Many of the settlers who fled the attacks perished from hunger and exhaustion in the Pocono Great Swamp, known as the Shades of Death.

Brant participated in what is known as the Cherry Valley Massacre soon afterward on November 11, 1778. He and Ranger captain WALTER BUTLER, John Butler's son, led approximately 700 troops against outlying settlements, picking off stranded settlers who could not make it back to the fort in time. Then they attacked the stockade, constructed under the direction of the MARQUIS DE LAFAYETTE and defended by the 7th Massachusetts Regiment under Colonel Ichabod Alden. The post held. But since Alden had failed to station guards on the trail, many of the settlers living and working in the surrounding countryside were unable to reach the fort. By the end of the fighting, 32 were dead, including Alden, and 40 more were captured and led off to Fort Niagara. It is said that Brant personally saved the lives of many Cherry Valley settlers, restraining his warriors from further attack.

The persistent frontier raids convinced General George Washington to send an army into Iroquois country. General JOHN SULLIVAN led a column out of Easton, Pennsylvania, and up the Susquehanna into New York; General JAMES CLINTON headed a column out of Albany, New York, along the Mohawk Valley, then across Otsego Lake and down the Susquehanna to join up with Sullivan and push northwestward into the Finger Lakes region; and Colonel Daniel Brodhead led troops from Pittsburgh, Pennsylvania, along the Allegheny to attack from the west. The only major engagement occurred at Newtown on August 29, 1779. Brant and the Seneca OLD SMOKE led their warriors in conjunction with Tories against 4,000 troops, losing 22 and retreating. But the Sullivan-Clinton Campaign succeeded in its goal of conquering the Iroquois by destroying their villages. It is estimated that 40 Indian villages were razed, along with hundreds of acres of crops and orchards.

Brant opposed a separate Iroquois-American peace accord, as attempted by the Seneca RED JACKET, and, in 1781, participated in continuing raids along the Ohio Valley, with SIMON GIRTY and the Delaware HOPOCAN.

Following the Iroquois surrender, many of the Mohawks left the United States for Canada. Brant retained his commission as a colonel, drawing half-pay. In 1784, he arranged for a land grant from the British government to the Iroquois at Oshweken, or Little Oswego, on the Grand River in Ontario (present-day Brantford). He moved there with his third wife, Catherine, daughter of GEORGE CROGHAN and a Mohawk woman. Brant founded a Mohawk Episcopal chapel and finished translating the Book of Common Prayer and Gospel of Mark into the Mohawk dialect.

Brant traveled frequently to Montreal to confer with officials on behalf of his people. In 1792, during LITTLE TURTLE's war, he was received at Philadelphia by President George Washington and his secretary of War, HENRY KNOX, in an attempt to enlist his help as peace envoy to the rebelling tribes. Brant agreed to come only after the Senecas Red Jacket and Cornplanter had departed. The Iroquois leader later spoke for peace at a council of tribes along the Ohio. But the uprising continued until the Battle of Fallen Timbers two years later.

Brant was painted by many other famous artists of the time in addition to Romney: Gilbert Stuart, William Berczy, Charles Wilson Peale, and Ezra Ames. He died in 1807 in a second home at the head of Lake Ontario (present-day Burlington, Ontario). He was buried next to the church he built at Oshweken. JOHN BRANT, his youngest son, one of seven children by Catherine, later became chief at the Six Nations Reserve.

BRANT, MOLLY (Mary Brant, Degonwadonti, Gonwatsijayenni). *Mohawk. (ca. 1735–1796).* Ally of British in the American Revolution. Sister of JOSEPH BRANT; wife of WILLIAM JOHNSON.

Molly Brant was born in the Mohawk village of Canajoharie, New York. She supposedly caught the eye of William Johnson when, in 1753, she responded to an officer's challenge to ride in a sporting event involving British and Mohawks. She married Johnson in a Mohawk ceremony and served as the hostess of Johnson Hall, Johnson's second home in New York, eventually having as many as eight children by him. After Johnson had been knighted for his 1755 victory at Lake George in the French and Indian War, Molly Brant, or "Miss Molly," was referred to as "Lady Johnson." She caught smallpox in 1765 but recovered.

During the American Revolution (after William Johnson's death in 1774), Molly provided intelligence to the British on rebel troop movements in the Mohawk Valley. Because of Oneida attacks on the Mohawks, she took refuge among the Onondagas, eventually joining the British garrison at Fort Niagara, then on Carlton Island. She continued to exert influence among the Iroquois throughout the war. Her brother Joseph acted as principal leader of the Mohawks during the conflict.

After American victory, Molly settled in Cataraui (present-day Kingston, Ontario). She received from the British a yearly pension of 100 pounds, the largest compensation awarded to an Indian at the time. In her later years, she withdrew from tribal affairs to devote herself to her five daughters. (See also BRANT, JOSEPH.)

BREBEUF, JEAN DE (Echon). *(1593–1649).* Missionary; scholar.

Born in the Normandy region of France to a noble family, Jean de Brebeuf began to study under the Jesuits at Rouen, France, in 1617 and was ordained a priest five years later. In 1625, he went to Quebec and began work as a missionary among Quebec's Montagnais Indians.

In 1626, Brebeuf set out with a party of Indians on a canoe expedition to the Georgian Bay region of Lake Huron, where he established an early Catholic mission to the Hurons, who called him Echon. He remained there for most of the next 20 years, with a return to France from 1629–33 during the temporary British occupation of Quebec.

In 1640, following a devastating smallpox outbreak, the Hurons attacked his mission. Brebeuf traveled south to the homeland of the Neutral (Attiwandaronk) Indians between Lake Ontario and Lake Erie, but, considered a sorcerer, had little success among them. He returned to his work among the Hurons around Georgian Bay in 1644, where he was assisted in his Huron mission by Gabriel Lalement, nephew of the Jesuits Charles Lalement and JEROME LALEMANT.

Both Brebeuf and Gabriel Lalement were captured by the Iroquois at the Jesuit mission village of St. Louis near present-day Midland, Ontario, in a raid in March 1649 during the Iroquois invasion of Huronia. They suffered such tortures as a mock-baptism in which scalding water was poured over their heads before being killed. Their bodies were buried by fellow Jesuits at nearby Sainte-Marie, who soon burned and abandoned their palisaded village out of fear of an Iroquois attack.

Brebeuf's head was preserved in a silver bust sent from Europe by his family. It was later declared a religious relic in honor of his martyrdom. He was canonized in 1930, one of the Jesuit Martyrs of North America.

Brebeuf was a scholar of the Huron language, producing a Huron grammar and a catechism in the Hurons' native tongue. He also wrote treatises on the Huron language and on the tribe's customs.

BRIDGER, JAMES (Jim Bridger; Old Gabe).
(1804–1881). Trader; trapper; guide; scout; explorer.

James Bridger was born in Richmond, Virginia. While he was young his family moved to the vicinity of St. Louis. Orphaned by the age of 14, Bridger found work as a blacksmith.

Bridger took part in WILLIAM HENRY ASHLEY's expedition up the Missouri River in 1823. The following year, he was a scout with ANDREW HENRY in the exploration of the middle Rockies. Along with John Fitzgerald, he was left to guard HUGH GLASS, who had been mauled by a grizzly bear. Considering Glass's wounds to be fatal, Bridger and Fitzgerald left him to die. Glass crawled to safety, however, and confronted his former companions, ultimately forgiving them.

In 1825, Bridger became one of the earliest (if not the earliest) white men to see the Great Salt Lake in present-day Utah. He continued trapping for mountain men JEDEDIAH SMITH, WILLIAM SUBLETTE, and David E. Jackson, who had bought out Ashley in 1826, and

then, in 1830–34, as a partner in the Rocky Mountain Fur Company with THOMAS FITZPATRICK, Milton Sublette, Henry Fraeb, and Jean Baptiste Gervais.

Bridger's fur trading brought him into contact with both friendly and hostile Indians of the Northern Plains, Rocky Mountains, and Columbia Plateau. He was a close friend of the Shoshone chief WASHAKIE. In 1832, Bridger and other mountain men, along with the Nez Perce LAWYER and other Indian guides, survived an attack by Gros Ventre warriors in the Battle of Pierre's Hole at the south end of the Teton Mountains near the present site of Yellowstone National Park in Wyoming. Wounded by an Indian arrow in this conflict, he had the point in him for the next three years, until it was removed by frontier missionary MARCUS WHITMAN.

In business with frontier entrepreneur Louis Vasquez in 1843, Bridger founded Fort Bridger on the Green River in southwestern Wyoming, which became an important stopover point for travelers along the Oregon Trail. Bridger sold his share in the post to the Mormons in 1853.

In 1850, Bridger served as a guide for Captain Howard Stansbury's expedition into the Wasatch Mountains of present-day northern Utah and southern Idaho, resulting in the discovery of Bridger's Pass and Cheyenne Pass. In 1855-57, he served as guide for the hunting expedition of Englishman Sir George Gore to the Rockies and Northern Plains.

During the Mormon War of 1857–58, Bridger served as a guide for federal troops. He explored the Yellowstone region of southeastern Montana and northern Wyoming with Captain William Raynolds in 1859–60. The following year, he explored the Rocky Mountain crossing from Denver, Colorado, to Utah's Great Salt Lake. When JOHN BOZEMAN's newly opened trail north from Colorado to the mining country of Montana threatened to incite the Northern Plains tribes to warfare, Bridger explored an alternate route west of the Bighorn range, circumventing the Indians' hunting lands. Bridger also served as a scout for the military in General PATRICK E. CONNOR's Powder River Expedition of 1865 against the Northern Plains tribes. The next year, he helped in the survey for the Union Pacific Railroad.

Bridger was married successively to women members of the Flathead, Ute, and Paiute tribes. He sent his four mixed-blood children to be educated in Missouri. In his later years, with failing health and eyesight, Bridger retired to Westport, Missouri, settling near his former partner Vasquez and fellow trader WILLIAM BENT.

BRIGHT EYES. See LA FLESCHE, SUSETTE.

BRINTON, DANIEL GARRISON. *(1837–1899).* Anthropologist.

Born and raised in Pennsylvania, Daniel Brinton studied literature at Yale, then medicine at Jefferson Medical College and in Europe. He returned to West Chester, Pennsylvania, to practice medicine for a year, then entered the Union army as an assistant surgeon, eventually brevetted to the rank of lieutenant colonel of volunteers. After the war, in Philadelphia, he became editor of the *Medical and Surgical Reporter*.

During his college years, Brinton had pursued anthropological studies as a hobby, living in Florida one winter and publishing *Notes on the Floridian Peninsula* in 1859. He continued his studies and writings in his free time. In 1884, he became a professor of ethnology and archeology at Philadelphia's Academy of Natural Sciences, and, two years later, a professor of American linguistics and archeology at the University of Pennsylvania.

As an anthropologist, Brinton studied the languages, mythology, and literature of the North American Indians and their relationship to Central and South American peoples. He did little fieldwork himself, utilizing that of others in his research. Although some of his conclusions were erroneous, such as his belief in the European origins of Native Americans, his methodology and linguistic classifications, as found in *The American Race* (1891), influenced later anthropologists, such as FRANZ BOAS.

BROCK, ISAAC. *(1769–1812).* British officer in the War of 1812.

Born on the British island of Guernsey, Isaac Brock entered the British army in 1785 as an ensign. He rose to the rank of lieutenant colonel in the 49th regiment, seeing military action in the West Indies, the Baltic, and the Netherlands. He was sent to Canada in 1802 and commanded British forces at York (present- day Toronto), Quebec City, and Montreal.

In 1810, Brock was sent to command the garrisons at Fort George in Upper Canada (Ontario). The next year, he was promoted to major general and made acting lieutenant governor of that province.

In the War of 1812, Brock defended Upper Canada against American troops. Early successes included the attack on Michilimackinac in Michigan. In August 1812, Brock captured American general William Hull and his army at Detroit, for which he was awarded a knighthood. In many of his campaigns, Brock was supported by Indian forces under TECUMSEH, who became his close friend.

While repelling an American offense at the Battle of Queenston Heights in October 1812, Brock was shot and killed. He was replaced by Colonel HENRY PROCTOR. (See also TECUMSEH.)

BRUGUIER, JOHN (Big Leggins). *Mixed Santee Sioux. (b. 1849).* Interpreter for SITTING BULL; army scout.

John Bruguier, the son of the merchant Theophile Bruguier and his second Sioux wife, grew up at the site of present-day Sioux City, Iowa. Along with his brother Billy Bruguier, he attended the College of Christian Brothers in St. Louis.

After the death of his mother and his father's marriage to a white woman, Bruguier went to live with Sioux relatives. In the early 1870s, he found work at the Standing Rock Agency in North Dakota as an interpreter. In 1875, on trying to break up a drunken fight between his brother Billy and an agent by the name of William McKee, Bruguier clubbed McKee to death. He fled the reservation to Sitting Bull's camp. To prove his status as a warrior, Bruguier participated in raids on whites during the War for the Black Hills of 1876–77. He acted as Sitting Bull's interpreter and wrote the chief's messages to the military.

After many of the Sioux had surrendered to forces under Colonel NELSON A. MILES, Bruguier reported to Fort Peck, Montana, and volunteered to help Miles track down Sitting Bull and other fugitives. He personally convinced the Northern Cheyenne TWO MOONS to surrender at Fort Keogh, Montana, in early 1877.

In 1879, Bruguier was brought to trial for the death of McKee. Miles testified on his behalf, stating that his information had helped prevent the joining of Sitting Bull's and CRAZY HORSE's bands in January 1877, and Bruguier was acquitted. (See also SITTING BULL.)

BRULE, ETIENNE. *(ca. 1592–1633).* Explorer; interpreter.

Etienne Brule was born at Champigny-sur-Marne, France, and, in 1608, went to French Canada with SAMUEL DE CHAMPLAIN. Two years later, Champlain sent him to learn about the Indian people of the St. Lawrence region. He lived among Algonquians and Hurons and learned their languages.

With Huron guides, Brule was the first European to explore Lake Huron's Georgian Bay, in 1611–12. On the return journey southeastward, he became the first known white to see Lake Ontario. In 1615, he retraced part of the route with Champlain, separated from him at Lake Simcoe, and became the first white to see Lake Erie.

After having rejoined Champlain at Oneida Lake near present-day Syracuse, New York, the site of Champlain's Huron-backed attack on the Onondagas, Brule embarked in late 1615 on an expedition down the Susquehanna River through what is now New York, Pennsylvania, and Maryland, as far as the Chesapeake Bay. During this exploration, he had contacts with the

Susquehannock Indians. On the return trip, Brule was taken prisoner by the Iroquois, but was released in 1618, after having convinced his captors he could help force an alliance between them and the French.

Brule settled among the Hurons once again, participating in the fur trade in the 1620s. He journeyed as far west as Lake Superior during this period.

When Quebec was captured and held by the British in 1629–32, Champlain suspected Brule of complicity with the British. Brule again returned to live among the Hurons. He was soon killed by tribal members because, it is theorized, of his suspected ties to the Hurons' traditional enemies, the Senecas.

BRUSH, GEORGE DE FOREST. (1855–1941). Artist.

George Brush was born in Shelbyville, Tennessee, but spent most of his boyhood in Connecticut, from where his father sailed as captain of a whaling ship; the family later moved to Ohio. His mother, an amateur portrait painter, encouraged his artistic pursuits. Brush studied at the Academy of Design in New York City, then as a student of Jean Leon Gerome in France.

In 1881, Brush traveled to the American and Canadian Plains and, for four years, lived among various tribes, especially the Crows and Sioux. He was accepted by them and learned many of their skills, including horsemanship and the making of tepees, moccasins, and bows and arrows.

Brush eventually established a studio in Dublin, New Hampshire, creating poetic depictions of Indians. When his Indian paintings stopped selling in the 1890s, Brush returned to Europe for more studies, temporarily settling in Florence, Italy. Once again in New Hampshire, he became known for paintings of the Madonna.

BRUYAS, JACQUES. (1635–1712). Missionary; linguist.

Originally from Lyons, France, Jesuit missionary Jacques Bruyas arrived in Quebec in August 1666. The following July, he embarked on his missionary work among the Iroquois, mainly the Onondagas and the Mohawks. He translated many religious works into the Mohawk language, including a catechism. He also compiled a French-Mohawk dictionary and produced other studies on the Iroquoian language.

Bruyas attempted to bring Christianity to the Oneidas, but his work with this tribe was limited to the conversions of a few elderly Oneidas and some dying children. While among the Oneidas, he was on occasion forced to hide from warriors, intoxicated on British liquor and prone to outbreaks of hostility and violence against the French. On several instances, he had to seek safety among the more sympathetic Onondagas.

From 1693 to 1699, Bruyas, remaining in Quebec, was the father superior to all the Catholic missionaries.

BUCKONGAHELAS (Buckangehela, "breaker in pieces"). Delaware. (d. ca. 1804). Leader in Little Turtle's War of 1790–94.

Buckongahelas was band chief of the Ohio Delawares living along the Miami and White rivers. During the American Revolution, he fought for the British. He again led Delaware warriors against Americans in support of LITTLE TURTLE'S Miamis and BLUE JACKET's Shawnees in the revolt of the tribes of the Old Northwest during the early 1790s. He was furious at the British for not offering refuge at Fort Miami to the fleeing Indians following their defeat in the Battle of Fallen Timbers in August 1794. Afterward, he agreed to peace with the Americans, signing the Fort Greenville Treaty of 1795, the Fort Wayne Treaty of 1803, and the Vincennes Treaty of 1804. (See also LITTLE TURTLE.)

BUFFALO BILL. See CODY, WILLIAM FREDERICK.

BUFFALO HORN. Bannock. (d. 1878). Leader in the Bannock War of 1878.

Buffalo Horn became chief of his Bannock band in the 1870s. He was friendly to whites and even served as a scout for NELSON A. MILES, GEORGE CROOK, and OLIVER HOWARD in various campaigns against the Sioux and Nez Perces.

After the Nez Perce War of 1877, the tribes of the Pacific Northwest were primed for further violence. The issue that set it off was the digging the roots of the camas plant on the Camas Prairie, about 90 miles southeast of Fort Boise, Idaho, a right guaranteed to the Indians by an earlier treaty. The Bannocks and Northern Paiutes, plus a number of Umatillas and Cayuses, angry at the despoliation of their camas root staple by hogs owned by whites, began threatening the settlers. When a Bannock warrior wounded two whites in May 1878, both sides prepared for war.

About 200 Bannocks and Northern Paiutes gathered under Buffalo Horn, who reluctantly agreed to lead them in battle. The Paiute leader WINNEMUCCA argued for peace. The first clash came in June in southern Idaho between Indians and a volunteer patrol from Silver City. Buffalo Horn was killed. His warriors headed westward into Oregon and regrouped at Steens Mountain with Northern Paiutes of the Malheur Reservation. The Paiute chief EGAN then assumed command of the combined force. On his death in July, the Paiute medicine man OYTES led the uprising until his surrender in August. The final party of militants was captured that September.

BUFFALO HUMP (Bull Hump, Pochanaw-quoip).
Comanche. (fl. mid-1800s). Leader in the early
Comanche Wars of the 1830s–50s.

Buffalo Hump proved himself as a war chief in raids
in Texas and Mexico. The Mexicans knew him from his
raids into Chihuahua, with about 1,000 warriors, for
horses and slaves. During the 1830s, Buffalo Hump also
participated in attacks on the Cheyennes and Arapahos,
especially on YELLOW WOLF's Southern Cheyenne
band. A lasting peace between these tribes, the Kiowas,
and the Comanches was established in 1840.

An incident known as the Council House Affair occurred in 1838, when the Texas Rangers tried to force
the release of white hostages by seizing Comanche
chiefs who had come under a flag of truce to parley at
San Antonio, Texas. A fight broke out and a number of
Comanches were killed. As a result, Buffalo Hump led
a war party down from the Comanche homeland north
of the Red River along the Guadalupe Valley, to the Gulf
of Mexico. The Indians attacked the settlements of Linn-
ville and Victoria, killing many and burning houses. On
their return northward, they were attacked by Texas
Rangers at Plum Creek, near Lockhart. Despite some
losses, Buffalo Hump led most of his men to safety.

Buffalo Hump became principal chief of the Penateka
band of Comanches after the cholera epidemic of 1849
throughout the Southern Plains.

In the late 1850s, the Texas Rangers and army regulars
launched a coordinated campaign against the Comanches. In May 1858, Chief Iron Jacket's village north of
the Red River at Antelope Hills (Oklahoma) was attacked
by Texas Rangers. In October 1858, during Major Earl
Van Dorn's Wichita Expedition, Buffalo Hump's band
suffered a major defeat at Rush Springs (Oklahoma).
Fifty-six warriors and two women died; those who
escaped, including Buffalo Hump, left behind 300
ponies and had their tepees and possessions burned. In
May 1859, a Comanche war party of 54 was wiped out
by Major Van Dorn's men at Crooked Creek (Kansas).

In October 1865, Buffalo Hump attended a council
along the Little Arkansas with chiefs from other
Southern Plains tribes. The Comanches, Kiowas,
Kiowa-Apaches, Southern Cheyennes, and Southern
Arapahos were pressured into relinquishing claims to
territory north of the Arkansas River. The struggle for
the Southern Plains would continue, however. Buffalo
Hump's son, who inherited his father's name, would
join the fighting under the war chief QUANAH
PARKER.

BULL BEAR. *Southern Cheyenne. (fl. 1860s–1870s).*
Leader of the Dog Soldiers. Brother of LEAN BEAR.

Along with TALL BULL and WHITE HORSE, Bull
Bear was one of the war chiefs of the Cheyenne military
society known as the Dog Soldiers and generally took a

militant stance against the whites, especially after the
death of his brother Lean Bear in 1864. He participated,
along with BLACK KETTLE and WHITE ANTELOPE,
in the talks with Colorado's governor JOHN EVANS at
Camp Weld in 1864. At that time, he was the most
powerful of the Dog Soldier chiefs.

Bull Bear participated in raids during the HANCOCK
Campaign of 1867. Although he signed the Medicine
Lodge Treaty that same year, he fought in the Battle of
BEECHER's Island, Colorado, during the SHERIDAN
Campaign of 1868, where ROMAN NOSE was killed.
After the death of Tall Bull at Summit Springs, Colo-
rado, in 1869, Bull Bear led his people onto the
Cheyenne and Arapaho Reservation in the Indian Ter-
ritory.

In 1870, Bull Bear took his band northward to join the
Sioux, but returned the next year. He participated with
the Comanches under QUANAH PARKER and Kiowas
under LONE WOLF in the Red River War of 1874–75.
Afterward, Bull Bear accepted life on the reservation.

BULL HUMP. See BUFFALO HUMP.

BURBANK, ELBRIDGE AYER. *(1858–1949).*
Artist.

E. A. Burbank was born in Illinois and studied art in
Chicago and Munich from 1874 to 1892. About 1897, he
was commissioned by his uncle Edward Ayer of the
Field Columbian Museum of Chicago to produce a
series of portraits of Indians. Burbank moved to the
Indian Territory and traveled to other parts of the West
as well, painting mostly portraits, but also scenes and
dwellings.

In addition to the Oklahoma and Plains Indians, Burbank painted Plateau, Southwest, Great Basin, and
California tribes, more than 125 in all. He was known
for his fidelity to actual facial detail, without idealiza-
tion.

Burbank developed lasting friendships with many of
the people he painted, such as Chief JOSEPH (Young
Joseph) and SIMON POKAGON. Some of his subjects
dined with him and occasionally stayed over in his
studio. In 1898, he met GEROMINO, who became a
close friend and who claimed that he liked Burbank
better than any other white man.

Burbank's story is told in *Burbank Among the Indians*
(1944), which he wrote with Ernest Royce.

BURGOYNE, JOHN. *(1722–1792).* British officer
in the American Revolution

A career military officer in the British army, John
Burgoyne was also a popular playwright of his day, and
known in London society as Gentlemanly Johnny. In the
Seven Years War, 1756–63, he led campaigns against the
Spanish in Portugal.

General Burgoyne arrived in Quebec in 1776 to command a British force about 9,000-strong against the rebelling American colonies to the south. Indian auxiliaries—mostly Algonquian-speaking peoples from Canada—made up part of Burgoyne's command, which, in summer 1777, proceeded southward to Lake Champlain in an attempt to isolate New England from the rest of the colonies. He recaptured Fort Ticonderoga in July 1777.

That same month, JANE MacCREA, a woman betrothed to one of Burgoyne's officers, was tomahawked to death and scalped by two Indians, also under Burgoyne's command, while being escorted by them to a British camp. Burgoyne was compelled to pardon the offenders to avoid mass defection of his Indian allies. His pardon became the focus of propaganda in the raising of volunteers for New England militia units that defeated Burgoyne at the Battle of Saratoga in October 1777.

Following the surrender of his 5,700 troops to Continental forces under General Horatio Gates, Burgoyne was released by the Americans. After his return to England, he commanded British forces in Ireland and continued to write plays.

BUSHOTTER, GEORGE (Oteri, "trouble").
Yankton–Miniconjou Sioux. (1864–1892).
Anthrolopologist; teacher; woodworker.

Oteri was born at the confluence of the Moreau and Missouri rivers in what is now South Dakota, the son of a Yankton man and a Miniconjou woman. His father, who had named him Oteri for "trouble" because of jealousy between the boy's mother and a second Winnebago wife, was killed by whites. His mother, Grey Whirlwind, remarried a Brule Sioux who raised the youth to be a warrior on the Lower Brule reservation.

In 1878, at the encouragement of white officials, Oteri was sent to the Hampton Institute in Virginia. He was given the name George Bush, which in combination with his Indian name, soon became George Bushotter. He stayed at Hampton until 1881, returning to the Lower Brule Reservation to work as an assistant teacher at an Indian boarding school. In the winter of 1882–83, he returned to Hampton with some of his Sioux students.

In 1885, Bushotter entered the Theological Seminary of Virginia with the intention of becoming a minister. His poor English caused him to abandon his studies, however. While East, Bushotter met the linguist JAMES OWEN DORSEY of the Smithsonian's Bureau of Ethnology. Dorsey recommended to JOHN WESLEY POWELL that Bushotter be hired as a researcher and informant.

In March 1887, Bushotter began work with Dorsey in Washington, D.C., providing a valuable source of information about Sioux language and culture. He wrote down 258 stories and myths for the Bureau of Ethnology, the first texts recorded by a Sioux in his native language, and helped Dorsey in their translation. Dorsey's health failed, however, and, that June, he went to his wife's parents' home at Hedgesville in the mountains of West Virginia. Bushotter accompanied him in order to continue their collaboration.

While at Hedgesville, Bushotter became known and admired by many of the townspeople, some of whose children he taught archery and woodworking. He became engaged to Evalina Hull, the daughter of the owner of the boardinghouse where he stayed. Bushotter resigned his position at the Smithsonian in December 1887, and was married in March 1888. He applied for a position at the Fort Stevenson Indian School in North Dakota and began work teaching Arikara pupils that same spring. Disputes with the school's superintendent over Bushotter's use of his native language in the classroom and other issues led to his resignation in February 1889, however.

Because of health problems, Bushotter returned to Hedgesville with his wife. He died of tuberculosis in 1892.

BUSHYHEAD, DENNIS WOLF (Unaduti, "wooly head"). *Mixed Cherokee. (1826–1898).*
Principal chief of the Western Cherokees. Great-grandson of JOHN STUART.

Born near present-day Cleveland, Tennessee, Dennis Bushyhead was educated at mission schools in Tennessee and North Carolina at the encouragement of his father Jesse Bushyhead, a Presbyterian clergyman. As a boy, in 1838–39, Dennis traveled the Trail of Tears to the Indian Territory. In 1841, he returned East as part of a Cherokee delegation to Washington, D.C. He started college at Princeton in 1844, but did not finish, leaving to run his deceased father's mercantile business in the Indian Territory.

In 1848, Bushyhead became clerk of the Cherokee National Committee. The next year, he headed to California with the Gold Rush and did not return to the Indian Territory until 1868, after the Civil War, settling at Tahlequah. He became the treasurer of his tribe in 1871, then was elected chief in 1879 as head of the National Party, serving two terms until 1887, the year of the General Allotment Act (the DAWES Severalty Act), which he supported. He later served as tribal delegate to Washington, D.C.

Bushyhead considered himself a compromiser between the traditionalist full-bloods, as represented by the militant Keetoowah Society, and the mixed-blooded assimilationists. He encouraged education among his people and economic development through leasing of Cherokee lands for railroad, mineral, timber, and cattle-grazing rights. He also advocated the acceptance of Eastern Cherokees of at least half-Cherokee lineage into the Western Cherokees.

Bushyhead died at Tahlequah in the Indian Territory, soon to become the state of Oklahoma.

BUTLER, JOHN. *(1728–1796).* Loyalist officer in the American Revolution; Indian commissioner. Father of WALTER BUTLER.

Originally from New London, Connecticut, John Butler moved with his family to the Mohawk Valley region of central New York as a teenager. He learned the Iroquoian language and served as an interpreter between colonial officials and Indian leaders. In the French and Indian War of 1754–63, he was a captain of militia under WILLIAM JOHNSON, often working in conjunction with Indian troops.

Butler remained loyal to Great Britain in the American Revolution. With his son Walter, he departed the Mohawk Valley for the British garrison at Fort Niagara, where he was made deputy Indian commissioner under GUY JOHNSON and instructed to take measures to keep the Iroquois tribes pro-British neutral.

In 1777, Colonel Butler organized a company of Tory militia, called Butler's Rangers, and, along with Iroquois warriors under the Mohawk JOSEPH BRANT, took part in Barry St. Leger's attack on Fort Stanwix in the eastern Mohawk Valley of New York in July–August 1777. Butler and Brant both took part in the related Battle of Oriskany against General NICHOLAS HERKIMER's militia command.

The following year, Butler commanded Tory and Indian raids on settlements in the Mohawk Valley and Wyoming valleys of New York. Among these was the attack on Forty Fort in the Wyoming Valley region of northeastern Pennsylvania, along the west branch of the Susquehanna River. Butler's Tories and Indians killed more than 200 Patriot troops in this engagement, which later became known as the Wyoming Massacre. Butler was unable to restrain the Indians under his command from committing depredations against captives taken in the raids. His son Walter participated in the subsequent raid on Cherry Valley in New York.

Butler's Rangers and Iroquois auxiliaries were defeated by American forces under generals JOHN SULLIVAN and JAMES CLINTON at the Battle of Newtown, near present-day Elmira, New York, in 1779. Butler then rejoined Loyalist and Indian forces under General JOHN JOHNSON and continued to raid the frontier settlements of New York. In 1780, Butler's wife and younger children, held as hostages by the Continental army at Albany, New York, were released at Fort Niagara in exchange for the captives taken at Cherry Valley.

After the war, Butler was made commissioner of Indian affairs at Fort Niagara. He subsequently served in the local government in what is now Ontario. (See also BRANT, JOSEPH.)

BUTLER, WALTER. *(1752–1781).* Loyalist officer in the American Revolution. Son of JOHN BUTLER.

Walter Butler was born at Butlersbury, near Johnstown, New York, and began law school in Albany. With the outbreak of the American Revolution, he departed the Mohawk Valley with his father for Fort Niagara.

As a captain in his father's Tory Rangers, Butler returned with Barry St. Leger's column in its 1777 march along the valley. He worked to raise Loyalist support and was captured at a meeting. Accused of being a spy, he was spared only by the intercession of Continental officers he had known at law school. He became ill while imprisoned, and his friends had him placed in a secretly Loyalist family, who aided him in his escape.

Butler later headed the Tory Rangers in the field while his father was sick. Along with Iroquois warriors under JOSEPH BRANT, he participated in the attack on the settlement at Cherry Valley on November 11, 1778. Although he was feared and despised by pro-Patriot colonists in upstate New York for cruelty in battle, he reportedly, like Brant, attempted to prevent the killing and torture of settlers by warriors. With Butler's Rangers, he carried out subsequent raids in the Mohawk Valley. He died during an action under Major John Ross. (See also BRANT, JOSEPH.)

BYINGTON, CYRUS. *(1793–1868).* Missionary; linguist.

Cyrus Byington was born in Stockbridge, Massachusetts, to a farming family and was educated in Greek and Latin under the tutelage of early 19th-century New England scholar Joseph Woodbridge. He went on to practice law in Stockbridge and Sheffield, Massachusetts, but was soon drawn to a career in the clergy. In 1819, he graduated from the Presbyterian Andover Theological Seminary and was subsequently ordained as a minister and licensed to preach.

Although he originally intended to work as a Presbyterian missionary to the Armenians in Turkey, Byington joined the Presbyterian Mission to the Choctaw Nation, then located in central and northern Mississippi. With a group of about 25 other missionaries, he traveled south from Pittsburgh, via flatboat on the Ohio and Mississippi rivers, to the homeland of the Choctaws in Mississippi, arriving in 1820.

Byington was successful in bringing Christianity to a large portion of the Choctaw people. Among his earliest converts was Chief Tunnapinchuffa. In his missionary work, Byington did not attempt to compromise the tribe's Indian identity, and, as a result, many of his converts retained their native ways and never learned English.

Byington produced a dictionary and grammar of the Choctaws' Muskogean language, as well as biblical translations.

In 1833–34, after the federal government's removal of the Choctaws to reservations in the Indian Territory, Byington relocated his mission to present-day Eagletown, Oklahoma. In 1844, he established a Presbyterian boarding school for Choctaw girls at Ianubbee.

In 1858, Byington became involved in an incident following the murder of a mixed-blood Choctaw by a black slave. The slave was later apprehended, but subsequently committed suicide. Before dying, he had implicated another black, a woman, who was captured and burned to death by an angry Choctaw mob. This woman and the widow of the murdered Choctaw slaveowner were both parishioners of Byington's church. The missionary's pro-abolitionist and outspoken opposition to the lynching caused him to lose favor among many of the Choctaws. With the outbreak of the Civil War and the alliance of most tribal members with the Confederacy, Byington, with his pro-Union views was left with little local support.

Leaving the reservation because of the uncertain political situation and his failing health, Byington continued to work on his Choctaw grammatical and religious studies until his death in 1868. His works on the Choctaw language were subsequently edited by DANIEL BRINTON and other scholars.

C

CABEZA DE VACA, ALVAR NUNEZ.
(ca. 1490–ca. 1560). Explorer.

Born in Spain, the son of a noble family, Alvar Nunez, Cabeza de Vaca, was the treasurer for PANFILO DE NARVAEZ's 1528 expedition to the west coast of Florida and the Gulf of Mexico. With Narvaez and his contingent, Cabeza de Vaca explored northern Florida, where he spent time at Indian villages near present-day Tallahassee, Florida.

The expedition was shipwrecked near an island off the coast of Texas, perhaps Galveston Island or Mustang Island, and Narvaez and most of his party were lost at sea. Cabeza de Vaca was one of a handful of survivors held as slaves on the island. He eventually escaped to the mainland and lived among east Texas tribes until joining up with three other survivors, ESTEVANICO, Andres Dorantes, and Alonso del Castillo Maldonado, in 1532.

Although their exact route westward is uncertain, it is known they wandered through west Texas, New Mexico, and Arizona, possibly crossing into California. They encountered many different Indian peoples during their travels and gained reputations among them as healers. They were probably the first Europeans to see the American bison.

The Spaniards turned southward and reached Culiacan, Mexico, in 1536. Their stories of gold-laden Indian settlements to the north were the beginnings of the legend of the Seven Cities of Cibola and led to subsequent expeditions by MARCOS DE NIZA and FRANCISCO VASQUEZ DE CORONADO. Cabeza de Vaca's account of his adventures among the Indians of Texas was published first in 1542 as *Los Naufragios* ("the shipwrecked men").

In the 1840s, Cabeza de Vaca became the governor of the Spanish colony Rio de la Plata in what is now the country of Paraguay. In 1545, he was arrested and sent back to Spain to face charges of malfeasance in office, but received a royal pardon. He remained in Spain until his death.

CABOT, JOHN (Giovanni Caboto).
(ca. 1450–1498). Explorer.

Born in Genoa, Italy, John Cabot's early career in trade and exploration began with commercial ventures on behalf of Venetian traders. He traveled throughout the eastern Mediterranean and the Middle East, as far as Mecca. In 1484, he journeyed to England where he sought support for a proposed expedition to Asia, which he intended to reach by sailing west across the Atlantic.

With the backing of merchants from the port of Bristol, England, and the sponsorship of English king Henry VII, Cabot sailed from Bristol in May 1497, with a crew of 18 men, one of them probably his son Sebastian Cabot, who also pursued a career in exploration. At the end of June 1497, Cabot reached the coast of North America, probably Newfoundland or Cape Breton Island in what is now Canada. He returned to England in August 1497.

Cabot soon organized a second, larger expedition. With five ships and 300 men, he sailed again from Bristol in May 1498. He reached the coast of Greenland and sailed south, perhaps as far as Chesapeake Bay, before returning northward. Cabot's ship and its entire crew are thought to have been lost at sea. Some accounts relate that he did return to England, where he died in obscurity.

Cabot reported finding traces of Indian settlements on the shores of North America. It is theorized by some scholars that he came into contact with the Beothuks of Newfoundland. British claims in North America were based on his first voyage of exploration.

CABRILLO, JUAN RODRIGUEZ *(ca. 1500–1543)*.
Explorer.

Originally from Portugal, Juan Cabrillo took part in PANFILO DE NARVAEZ's 1520 expedition to Mexico in which the Spanish completed their conquest of the Aztecs.

In 1542, with two ships, Cabrillo led an expedition—originally planned by Pedro de Alvarado, governor of Guatemala, who was killed the year before—from Navidad on the northwest coast of Mexico to the coast of California. In September of that year, Cabrillo reached San Diego, where a shore party was attacked by Indians. Cabrillo made contacts with friendly tribes while following the coast northward, noting the dense Indian population along the coast. He made the first European discovery of Santa Monica Bay, near present-day Los Angeles, California, as well as the islands off the coast of present-day Santa Barbara.

Cabrillo died as the result of an infection from a broken arm on San Miguel Island. The expedition, now under the leadership of his pilot Bartolome Ferrelo, went on to explore the coast of northern California, probably as far as the present Oregon-California border.

CADILLAC, ANTOINE LAUMET DE LA MOTHE, SIEUR DE. *(ca. 1658–1730)*. French
colonial administrator; explorer; fur trader; soldier.

Sieur de Cadillac came to New France in 1683, living first at Port Royal (present-day Annapolis Royal, Nova Scotia), then on a land grant in Maine. He participated in French campaigns against the Iroquois in 1684 and 1687.

In 1694, with the support New France's governor LOUIS DE BUADE, COMTE DE FRONTENAC, Cadillac was appointed to manage the main French fur-trading fort at St. Ignace, near the Straits of Mackinac, the passage between Lake Huron and Lake Michigan. He held this position until 1697, returning to France two years later.

In 1701, with a charter from King Louis XIV, Cadillac founded a new French fur-trading post on the Detroit River, Fort Pontchartrain de Detroit, the present site of Detroit, Michigan. The post was intended to protect the French fur trade from encroachment by the British and their Iroquois allies. To secure French domination of the region's commerce, Cadillac encouraged Algonquian-speaking bands, sympathetic to the French cause, to establish settlements around his new fort at Detroit.

In 1711, Cadillac assumed the governorship of Louisiana, replacing acting governor JEAN BAPTISTE LE MOYNE, SIEUR DE BIENVILLE. The more competent Bienville, with whom he had frequent policy disputes, was his second in command. In 1714, Cadillac commissioned Louis St. Denis to undertake an exploratory expedition of 42 men, mostly Indians, into the Rio Grande Valley of Texas. In 1717, Cadillac lost the governorship to Bienville. On his return to France, he was briefly imprisoned in the Bastille because of accusations by his many enemies in Quebec and Paris. He spent his remaining years in Gascony.

CALDWELL, BILLY. See SAGAUNASH.

CALHOUN, JOHN CALDWELL. *(1782–1850)*.
Secretary of War; vice president.

John C. Calhoun's boyhood home at Abbeville, South Carolina, was on Cherokee lands settled by his Indian-fighter father, a Scottish immigrant. After having graduated from Yale, Calhoun attended law school in Litchfield, Connecticut. His legal career led him to a seat in the House of Representatives at the outbreak of the War of 1812.

Calhoun's support for President James Madison's efforts against the British, and his Jeffersonian sympathies, led to an 1817 appointment as secretary of War by President James Monroe. In this office, he assumed responsibility for the defense of the frontier, as well as matters relating to Indians. In 1824, Calhoun created the Bureau of Indian Affairs within the War Department, with THOMAS McKENNEY as its first director.

Calhoun's frontier policy concentrated on preventing the British from further inciting Indian hostilities against the settlers and on controlling the Ohio and Mississippi valleys. He instituted the Yellowstone expeditions under Colonel HENRY ATKINSON, as well as an expedition to the Rockies under Colonel STEPHEN H. LONG, as a prelude to the building of army roads and a defensive line of forts stretching into the frontier. The military presence on the frontier was intended not only to contain the Indians within treaty lands and convince them to cooperate with federal policies, but also to prevent white settlement of Indian lands.

Calhoun considered the displacement of Indians the primary source of conflict with whites and recommended that unassimilated tribes living in the East be persuaded to relocate to an area beyond Missouri and the Arkansas Territory. His recommendations led to the creation, in 1825, of an Indian Country west of the Mississippi—which came to be called the Indian Territory—supposedly a permanent homeland for Indians, originally containing parts of present-day Nebraska and Kansas as well as Oklahoma. Settlement of this area was barred to all but Indians. The peaceable removal of some eastern tribes was followed by the enforced removal of eastern Indians by subsequent administrations.

Calhoun went on to become vice president under John Quincy Adams and ANDREW JACKSON in 1825–32, and ran unsuccessfully for the presidency. Because of differences with Jackson over states' rights, Calhoun quit the vice presidency to become senator from South Carolina. He served as secretary of State under President John Tyler in 1844–45, and again as senator in 1845–50. A supporter of Southern causes, he became an apologist for slavery.

Calhoun's earlier Indian policies were altered by the outcome of the Mexican-American War and the resulting U.S. expansion into the trans-Mississippi West. He came to perceive the Indians of the newly acquired Mexican Cession as an obstacle to Manifest Destiny.

CALIFORNIA JOE. See MILNER, MOSES EMBREE.

CAMEAHWAIT. *Shoshone. (fl. early 1800s).* Friend to LEWIS and CLARK. Brother of SACAJAWEA.

Cameahwait's band of Lemhi Shoshones subsisted on the salmon that spawned in the Lemhi and Salmon river in what is now Idaho as well as on the buffalo herds of Montana. He was reunited with his sister in August 1805 while she served as a guide and interpreter for the Lewis and Clark Expedition. On recognizing him, she jumped up, ran to him, placed her blanket on him, and wept with joy. He referred to her as *Wadze-wipe*, "lost woman." The reunion proved to be a boon for the explorers because Cameahwait, who had originally intended to attack the party for its goods, provided packhorses, supplies, and guides for the expedition's subsequent trip through the Rockies. (See also SACAJAWEA.)

CAMPBELL, ROBERT. *(1804–1879).* Trader; trapper; peace commissioner.

A native of county Tyrone, Ireland, Robert Campbell first traveled westward to St. Louis, Missouri, in 1824. The next year, he joined a fur-trapping expedition led by WILLIAM HENRY ASHLEY to the Rocky Mountains. Campbell soon became a close associate of such leading fur trappers as JAMES BRIDGER, WILLIAM SUBLETTE, JEDEDIAH SMITH, and THOMAS FITZPATRICK.

While on his way to the 1828 trappers' rendezvous in the Rockies, Campbell and his party successfully fought off an attack by Blackfeet, known as the Fight in the Willows. The following year, Campbell trapped in Crow Indian country.

Following a trip to Ireland in 1830–31, Campbell returned to the Rockies and Northern Plains to trap with William Sublette. In 1832, Campbell and Sublette survived a Gros Ventre attack, an encounter later known as the Battle of Pierre's Hole, at the western end of the Teton Mountains. In 1833, Campbell and Sublette established a trading post, Fort William, near the American Fur Company's trading center at Fort Union in present-

day North Dakota. In 1834, the two men established Fort Laramie in present-day southeastern Wyoming. He remained partners with Sublette until 1842.

Campbell then operated a supply business to the fur trade out of St. Louis. In 1851, he assisted Thomas Fitzpatrick, now Indian agent to the Northern Plains tribes, at the Indian peace conference at Fort Laramie. In 1869, Campbell again served as a peace commissioner to the Indians at the request of President ULYSSES S. GRANT.

CAMPBELL, ROBERT. *(1808–1894).* Explorer; trader.

Born in Scotland, Robert Campbell came to North America in 1830, becoming a trader for the Hudson's Bay Company in North America. In 1834, he was sent on an expedition to explore the Mackenzie River in what is now the Yukon Territory. In 1840, he made the first European discovery of the Pelly River. In 1843, he descended it northwest as far as its confluence with the Lewes River, the start of the Yukon River, where he founded Fort Selkirk five years later. In 1850, the post was destroyed by the Chilkat band of Tlingit Indians, who lived along the Pacific Coast and who wanted to keep the inland Athapascan peoples, such as the Nahanes, out of the fur trade. In 1850–51, Campbell descended the Yukon River as far as the mouth of the Porcupine River. He continued in the employ of the Hudson's Bay Company as a trader among Indian tribes until 1871, whereupon he retired to a ranch in Manitoba. His book, *The Discovery and Exploration of the Pelly River*, was published in 1883.

CANALLA (Canavish; Johnson). *Ute. (fl. 1870s).* Medicine man; leader in the Ute War of 1879. Brother-in-law of OURAY.

The Northern Ute Canalla, who was a shaman to his people and operated a pony-racing track, was originally receptive to many of the ideas offered by NATHAN MEEKER, the agent at the White River Agency in western Colorado. Meeker, however, alienated Canalla by ordering that the tribe's traditional pony-grazing land be plowed for farming. In September 1879, Canalla entered Meeker's house, grabbed the agent by the shoulders, and roughly forced him outside, telling him to leave the agency. Their confrontation influenced Meeker's decision to call in troops. Canalla joined the subsequent fighting with NICAAGAT and COLOROW against troops under Major THOMAS T. THORNBURGH in the Battle of Milk Creek, where he lost a son. Meanwhile, others at the agency, including QUINKENT, killed Meeker and his employees and kidnapped his wife, daughter, and a third woman. (See also OURAY.)

CANASATEGO (Canassatego). *Onondaga.*
(d. 1750). Spokesman for the Iroquois League.

Canasatego of the Onondagas represented the Iroquois Confederacy in numerous conferences with the British: at Easton, Pennsylvania, in 1742, where he chastized the Delaware Indians for signing agreements with the British without the consent of the Iroquois League; at Lancaster, Pennsylvania, in 1744; at Onondaga, New York, in 1745; at Albany, New York, in 1745; and at Philadelphia in 1749. In many of Canasatego's dealings with colonial officials, CONRAD WEISER acted as the liaison. It is thought that Canasatego was killed by a pro-French Iroquois.

CANBY, EDWARD RICHARD SPRIGG.
(1817–1873). Army officer killed in the Modoc War of 1872–73.

Born in Kentucky and raised in Indiana, Edward Canby graduated from West Point in 1839. Commissioned a second lieutenant, he was assigned to Florida and saw action in the Second Seminole War from 1839 to 1842. In the Mexican War of 1846–48, he served under General WINFIELD SCOTT.

In 1855, Canby was assigned to New Mexico. In 1857, he was briefly involved in actions against the Mormons. Promoted to major in 1860, he commanded federal troops and Ute auxiliaries in an expedition out of Fort Defiance, New Mexico, against the Navajos, who had been raiding New Mexican farms and ranches.

The threatened invasion of Confederate forces from Texas into New Mexico in 1861 interrupted Canby's campaign in the Navajo country. Named acting brigadier general, he was placed in command of the army's Department of New Mexico. In February 1862, Confederate troops forced Canby's men to retreat in the battle at Valverde. With support from Colorado volunteers under the command of Major JOHN CHIVINGTON, Canby's forces were able to drive the invading Confederates again into Texas.

In 1863, Canby served briefly in New York City to quell the draft riots. In 1864, he was again in New Mexico where he received the surrender of thousands of Navajos following CHRISTOPHER "KIT" CARSON's Canyon de Chelly expedition against bands under MANUELITO and other chiefs. That same year, Canby was wounded in the Battle of White River in Arkansas. He took command of the Union army's Division of West Mississippi in 1865 and captured Mobile, Alabama.

Canby was appointed commander of the army's Department of the Columbia (Oregon, Washington, and Idaho) in 1870. In April 1873, as part of the federal peace commission seeking to end the Modoc War, he traveled to the lava beds in northern California to confer with the Modoc leaders. At the peace conference near Thule Lake, Modoc chief CAPTAIN JACK killed the unarmed Canby; BOSTON CHARLEY killed Eleasar Thomas; and SCHONCHIN JOHN wounded the Indian superintendent ALFRED MEACHAM. Canby was the only U.S. general to be killed in an Indian war. (See also CAPTAIN JACK; MANUELITO.)

CANONCHET (Cannonchet, Canochet, Quananchit, Quanonshet; Nanuntenoo, Nauntenoo, "dry man"). *Narraganset. (ca. 1630–1676).* Grand sachem; leader of the Narragansets in King Philip's War of 1675–76. Son of MIANTINOMO.

The death of his father, Miantinomo, in 1643, ordered by the colonists and carried out by the Mohegans under UNCAS, caused Canonchet to become militant. He remained hostile toward the colonists, and, years later, after he had succeeded his second cousin MRIKSAH as grand sachem of the Narragansets, he joined King PHILIP's Wampanoags in rebellion. He brought some 3,500 warriors to the conflict and led them in successful attacks on white settlements. His people suffered the worst defeat of the war, however, known as the Great Swamp Fight of December 19, 1675.

On a snowy day, a force of about 1,000 New England colonists, plus some 150 Mohegans, attacked the main Narraganset village near Kingston, Rhode Island. At first, the colonial force was unable to breach the village's thick palisades located on high ground in the middle of a swamp. But the attackers eventually broke through a rear entrance and, setting most of the wigwams on fire, drove the defenders out into the swamp where they were slaughtered—as many as 600, with 400 more captured and sold into slavery.

Canonchet escaped, however, and, in March 1676, he led his warriors in the rout of a detachment under Captain Michael Pierce along the Pawtuxet River. Another detachment captured him in April in the same area. When Canonchet refused to cooperate with the colonists in establishing peace, he was sentenced to death, shot, and beheaded at Stonington, Connecticut. His head was sent as a trophy to officials in Hartford. (See also PHILIP.)

CANONICUS (Qunnoune). *Narraganset.*
(ca. 1565–1647). Grand sachem. Father of MRIKSAH; uncle of MIANTINOMO.

Soon after the Pilgrims' arrival in Plymouth in 1620, Canonicus, grand sachem over the Narraganset bands, sent them a bundle of arrows tied with a snakeskin as a symbol of Narraganset sovereignty; the Pilgrims returned the bundle filled with powder and bullets as a demonstration of strength. Mutual respect and a truce followed.

Canonicus later became a friend of ROGER WILLIAMS, granting him the tract of land where he founded Providence in 1636 after banishment from Massachusetts Bay Colony. Because of his friendship with Williams, Canonicus kept his tribe neutral in the Pequot War of 1636–37. Narraganset warriors under Canonicus's nephew Miantinomo even helped in the attack on the Pequot SASSACUS's village. In 1638, the colonists, Narragansets, and Mohegans, a branch tribe of the Pequots, signed a three-way peace treaty.

Yet, in 1643, the Narragansets and Mohegans under UNCAS went to war. Miantinomo was captured by the Mohegans, who turned him over to the colonists. They in turn sentenced Miantinomo to death, then returned him to the Mohegans for execution. Canonicus felt betrayed by whites in this affair and never trusted them again. He was succeeded as grand sachem by his son Mriksah.

CAPTAIN JACK (Kintpuash, Kintpuas, Kintpoos, Keintpoos, Keintpoees, Pientposes, "having indigestion"). *Modoc. (ca. 1840–1873).* Leader of the Modoc War of 1872–73. Cousin of WINEMA.

Kintpuash was born along the Lost River in California near the Oregon border. His father, a chief, was killed in 1846 in an ambush by whites, whereupon Kintpuash became leader of his band. His people traded with the settlers living to the west in Yreka, California. He took two wives.

The Modoc War was one of the few Indian wars to occur within the boundaries of the state of California. Because California Indians rarely mounted organized rebellions and because the federal government under the post–Civil War administration of President ULYSSES S. GRANT was engaged in a Peace Policy toward Indians, the nation was shocked by the uprising.

The causes dated back to 1864. At that time, the Modocs under principal chief SCHONCHIN JIM signed away most of their territory and retired to the Klamath Reservation in Oregon, northeast of Upper Klamath Lake. Without enough food for both peoples and with disease rampant, tensions mounted between the Modocs and Klamaths over petty issues. The Modocs asked for their own reservation across the California border along the Lost River north of Tule Lake. The federal and California governments rejected their request.

Modocs under Kintpuash, who was nicknamed Captain Jack by whites, left the reservation in 1865 to return to California. In 1869, they were persuaded by officials to return to the reservation. With conditions no better, they departed again the following spring. As white settlement in northern California increased, so did complaints about the Modoc presence. The federal government ordered out troops in 1872.

Captain James Jackson led a detachment from Fort Klamath with instructions to bring back the renegades. On November 29, 1872, when Jackson announced his intentions to the Modocs and ordered the surrender of weapons, a fight broke out. SCARFACED CHARLEY refused to give up his pistol. He and Lieutenant Frazier Boutelle, who was trying to disarm him, fired the first shots. Neither was hit. Scarfaced Charley then grabbed his rifle off the stack of surrendered arms, and the other Modocs followed his example. In the ensuing firefight, called the Battle of Lost River, one soldier was killed and seven wounded, one of whom died later. The Indians suffered one dead and one wounded.

Captain Jack and his followers escaped to a stand of cattails along Tule Lake. They then worked their way farther south to what the Indians called the "Land of Burnt Out Fires," a volcanic highland formed by hardened lava that made for natural fortifications.

Meanwhile, HOOKER JIM and his band were camped on the other side of the river. A posse of ranchers tried to round them up, killing a woman and a baby and wounding several men. In retaliation, Hooker Jim, CURLY HEADED DOCTOR, and others attacked a ranch and killed 12 whites. Then they fled south to the lava beds where Captain Jack and his people had taken refuge. The rebels consisted of about 200 people, 80 of them warriors. On December 22, a Modoc war party ambushed a wagon train, acquiring more ammunition.

On learning of Hooker Jim's actions, Captain Jack gave up hope of a peaceful resolution. Before long, 309 California and Oregon regulars and volunteers under Lieutenant Colonel Frank Wheaton massed near the lava beds. The attack came—the Battle of the Stronghold—on January 17, 1873. While the infantry advanced, the artillery fired rounds into the dense fog enveloping the black rock. But the shells fell closer to the advancing infantry than to the Indians. And the Modoc warriors, moving along lava trenches with sagebrush in their hair as camouflage and protected by lava breastworks, successfully counterattacked. The soldiers, under fire from Modoc sharpshooters, retreated. The count: 11 dead and 26 wounded. No Modocs were injured.

General EDWARD CANBY, the military commander of the Department of the Columbia, decided to personally lead the campaign and massed a force of about 1,000 men. A peace plan was also set in motion. With the help of Captain Jack's cousin Winema and her white husband, Frank Riddle, negotiations were set up on neutral ground. President Grant's peace commissioners—ALFRED MEACHAM, Reverend Eleasar Thomas, Indian agent L. S. Dyer, and Canby himself—met with the dissidents.

At the first parley on February 28, Captain Jack requested the lava beds as a reservation and refused to turn over Hooker Jim for the killing of white ranchers. The standoff continued.

Before the second parley, tribal militants, including Curly Headed Doctor, Hooker Jim, BLACK JIM, and SCHONCHIN JOHN, convinced Captain Jack that if he were to kill the leaders of the army, the troops would be powerless to act. Captain Jack and his friends among the warriors agreed to a plan of treachery. Winema warned the peace commissioners that some among the rebels wanted Captain Jack to kill Canby. Canby ignored the warning and went ahead with the planned meeting on April 11. Captain Jack drew a hidden revolver and shot and killed Canby; another warrior, BOSTON CHARLEY, killed Thomas. Schonchin John fired on Meacham, striking him. Winema threw herself in front of Meacham to protect him and called out that soldiers were coming. Captain Jack and the others fled back to their rock fortifications.

With this attack, any public sentiment in favor of the Modocs ended as well as any hope for their own reservation. Some outraged whites called for the tribe's extermination. The new commander in the field, Colonel Alvin Gillem, launched an assault that was again repulsed. The Modocs managed to steal away to another lava formation farther south.

On April 26, Scarfaced Charley led Modoc warriors in an ambush on a reconnaissance patrol of 63 soldiers under Captain Evan Thomas, who had stopped in an indefensible hollow, killing 25, including all five officers, and wounding 16. Scarfaced Charley reportedly called out to the surviving soldiers to depart before they were all killed.

Yet the Modoc rebellion was winding down. The Modocs lacked food and water and were arguing among themselves. A new commander, General Jefferson C. Davis, organized a relentless pursuit of the now-scattered small bands. On May 18, Hooker Jim and 64 others, while fleeing westward, skirmished with troops, and, four days later, surrendered to Davis. Bargaining for his own life, Hooker Jim offered to help track down Captain Jack. He, Curley Headed Doctor, and BOGUS CHARLEY led the troops to Captain Jack's hideout. Cornered in a cave, Captain Jack, Boston Charley, Black Jim, and Schonchin John surrendered on June 1.

At the court-martial, Hooker Jim served as a witness against the prisoners. Captain Jack and his three warriors were sentenced to hang. The execution took place on October 3, 1873. The death sentences of two other Modocs were changed to life imprisonment in Alcatraz. On the night after the hanging, grave robbers dug up Captain Jack's body, embalmed it, and displayed it in a carnival that toured eastern cities.

The 155 survivors of the insurgent Modocs were exiled to the Indian Territory, but, in 1909, 51 Modocs were allowed to return to the Klamath Reservation. Today Modoc descendants live in both Oklahoma and Oregon.

CAPTAIN PIPE.   See HOPOCAN.

CARDERO, JOSE   (Manuel Jose Cardero, Josef Cordero).   *(ca. 1766–ca. 1810).*   Artist; cartographer.

Jose Cardero, born in Ecija, Spain, was part of the Spanish navy's scientific expedition, led by ALEJANDRO MALASPINA, which departed Europe in 1789 and explored the Northwest Coast in 1791. Cardero had the title of cabin boy, with TOMAS DE SURIA as official artist. For a second reconnaissance to Vancouver Island sent out by Malaspina from Mexico in 1792, Cardero was signed on as official aritst and cartographer. He produced numerous black- and-white drawings depicting customs of the Tlingit, Nootka, and other tribes for the expedition's report. Cardero did not accompany the expedition on its crossing of the Pacific, but returned to Spain from Mexico, after which he continued to serve in the Spanish navy. There is no evidence of continued artistic activity on his part.

CARLETON, JAMES HENRY.   *(1814–1873).* Army officer in the Apache and Navajo wars.

Born in Maine, James H. Carleton began his military career as a lieutenant with the Maine militia during the 1838 boundary dispute with Canada, known as the Aroostook War. The following year, he was commissioned a second lieutenant in the U.S. army.

After cavalry training at Carlisle, Pennsylvania, Carleton was assigned to frontier duty, in 1841, at Fort Gibson in the Indian Territory. In addition to securing the U.S. border, then located along the Red River, he was involved in operations to suppress liquor sales to the Indians. He also recovered slaves that had been taken in Texas raids by Kiowas and Comanches and unlawfully sold to Choctaw and Creek plantation owners in the Indian territory.

In 1842, Carleton supervised the construction of Fort Croghan on the Missouri River in what is now Nebraska. Troops at this installation were intended to maintain a buffer between the Sioux and other eastern tribes being relocated to the Indian Territory, such as the Potawatomis. Carleton and his command at Fort Croghan also intercepted illegal shipments of liquor intended for trade with Indians of the northern tribes on the upper Missouri. With Major Clifton Wharton, he visited Pawnee villages on the Platte River in Nebraska in an effort to improve relations between that tribe and the Sioux. He also led expeditions exploring the Platte River Valley.

During the Mexican War of 1846–48, Carleton served as an aide to General JOHN E. WOOL. In 1850 he was promoted to major, and his cavalry unit was sent to the Department of New Mexico. Two years later, he led military units into eastern New Mexico, seeking to make contact with the Mescalero Apaches. On this expedition Carleton first saw the Bosque Redondo region of the Pecos Valley and recommended the construction of a military post there.

As commander of the cavalry units at Albuquerque in 1853, Carleton led an expedition into the Gran Quivira country to survey a railroad route. He was also ordered to seek out the region's Apaches.

In 1854, Carleton headed a campaign against the Jicarilla Apaches, who had been raiding white settlements. Regular army troops under Carleton, New Mexico militia led by CHRISTOPHER "KIT" CARSON, and Pueblo Indian scouts engaged the Apaches in a surprise attack at Purgatory River in the Raton Mountains. Carleton's forces inflicted heavy economic damage on the Apaches by the capture of their horses and food supplies.

In 1858, Carleton was sent north with his cavalry to investigate the Mountain Meadows Massacre that had occurred in Utah the previous year, involving Mormons under BRIGHAM YOUNG.

At the beginning of the Civil War, Carleton was stationed in southern California, where he was assigned as a colonel in command of a state volunteer regiment. He led his command eastward from Los Angeles to Fort Yuma on the Colorado River and pushed back invading Confederate forces from Texas. While pursuing the Confederates eastward, Carleton's forces won a decisive victory over COCHISE's Chiracahua Apaches and MANGAS COLORADAS's Mimbreno Apaches at the Battle of Apache Pass in July 1862.

The following month, Carleton became commandant of the Department of New Mexico, replacing General EDWARD CANBY. With the Confederate retreat east to Texas, Carleton, now a brevet brigadier general, concerned himself with the orderly military occupation of New Mexico. As commander of Union forces and California volunteers in New Mexico, he controlled the strongest military presence between the Pecos and Colorado rivers. To maintain order in the territory, in anticipation of another Confederate invasion, he instituted martial law and initiated a campaign against Apaches and Navajos. He also established an extensive system of forts throughout the territory.

In August 1862, with New Mexico volunteer units in the field under Carson, Carleton directed an offensive against the Mescalero Apaches. That October, he issued an order suspending further peace councils with the Indians. In addition, he called for the killing of all adult male Mescaleros and the internment of the tribe's women and children on the newly established Indian reservation at Bosque Redondo.

In spring 1863, Carleton ordered his troops to seek out Navajo encampments of MANUELITO and other leaders and destroy their food supplies. In the course of the Navajo War of 1863–66, a total of approximately 9,000 Indians were marched on the Long Walk to internment at Bosque Redondo by the military. Of these, nearly one-fourth died of dysentery, malaria, and malnutrition before gaining their release in 1868. In addition, hundreds of Apache and Navajo women were infected with venereal disease through contact with federal troops stationed at the nearby fort. Most of the 400 Mescaleros sent to Bosque Redondo fled into the mountains soon after their arrival, unable to coexist with the Navajos, who vastly outnumbered them.

In 1864, Carleton ordered Carson and California volunteer units to attack Kiowa and Comanche raiders in the Texas Panhandle, resulting in the November 1864 Battle of Adobe Walls on the Canadian River.

With the defeat of the Confederacy in 1865, Carleton relaxed martial law. Nevertheless, his harsh policies during the military occupation of the territory antagonized many of New Mexico's political leaders, and, in 1866, he was transferred to San Antonio by the federal government.

Carleton was also a naturalist, collecting specimens in the course of his travels; he also wrote short pieces about his military experiences. (See also COCHISE; MANUELITO.)

CARR, EUGENE ASA. *(1830–1910).* Army officer in the Plains Indian wars.

Eugene A. Carr, originally from Erie County, New York, was an 1850 West Point graduate, who, upon receiving his commission as second lieutenant, was assigned to frontier duty with the 3rd Cavalry. In the 1850s, he was involved in military actions against the Apaches, Sioux, Kiowas, and Comanches.

Brevetted a lieutenant colonel in the Civil War, Carr served at the 1862 Battle of Pea Ridge in Arkansas, for which he was awarded the Congressional Medal of Honor in 1894. He also fought at Vicksburg, and joined General EDWARD CANBY in the capture of Mobile, Alabama, in 1865.

Following the war, Carr was reassigned as a major to the western frontier where, in 1868–69, he led cavalry units in actions against the Sioux and Cheyennes in Kansas and the Indian Territory, under General PHILIP H. SHERIDAN.

In July 1869, in charge of a combined force of cavalrymen and Pawnee scouts, Carr launched a successful attack against Cheyenne Dog Soldiers at the Battle of Summit Springs in Colorado.

Carr also commanded cavalry units in the Black Hills country of the Northern Plains, beginning in 1873 as a lieutenant colonel. He served under General GEORGE CROOK in the War for the Black Hills of 1876–77 against Sioux under SITTING BULL.

In April 1879, Carr led units in a campaign against Apaches in Arizona and New Mexico. In August 1881, while in command of Fort Apache, Arizona, Carr arrested Apache medicine man NAKAIDOKLINI near the White Mountain Reservation. The Apaches under NATIOTISH responded with a brief siege of Carr's command at Fort Apache, but were soon driven off. In the attack, Carr's horse was shot from beneath him.

Carr was made a brigadier general in 1892, retiring the following year. (See also NATIOTISH; SITTING BULL; TALL BULL.)

CARR, PADDY. *Mixed Creek. (b. 1808).* Interpreter; guide.

Paddy Carr was born in Alabama of a Creek mother and an Irish father and was reared by the family of the Indian agent John Crowell, among whom he mastered English. In 1826, he interpreted for the Creek delegation to Washington, D.C., headed by OPOTHLEYAHOLO, in its meetings with President John Quincy Adams and other officials on the question of removal, resulting in the Treaty of Washington. On returning to Creek country, Carr married the daughter of a wealthy mixed-blood, receiving a sizeable dowry, and eventually took two more wives. His family lived along the Chattahoochie River, the border between Alabama and Georgia, where he came to own considerable land, slaves, and livestock. He served as an interpreter and guide for General THOMAS JESUP. In 1836, during the Second Seminole War, Carr was second in command to Opothleyaholo, leading about 500 warriors in a campaign against the Creek allies of the Seminoles. Despite his assistance to the white cause, Carr was forced to relocate to the Indian Territory in 1847.

CARRAMANI. See NAWKAW.

CARRINGTON, HENRY BEEBEE. *(1824–1912).* Army officer in the War for the Bozeman Trail.

Connecticut-born Henry B. Carrington graduated from the Yale Law School, after which he began to practice as an attorney in Columbus, Ohio. During the 1850s, he became prominent in Ohio political circles, and was appointed as the state's adjutant general in command of the Ohio militia. He was made a brigadier general of volunteers at the outbreak of the Civil War in 1861, and served as an administrative recruiting officer in Indiana and Ohio.

Following the war, Carrington joined the 18th Infantry regiment with the rank of colonel. He led his regiment from Fort Kearny, Nebraska, into the Sioux lands along the Platte and Powder rivers in summer 1866. At that time, Sioux leaders, including the Oglala RED CLOUD, were engaged in a meeting with Indian Bureau and military officials at Fort Laramie concerning the issue of the encroachment of their hunting lands by travelers on the BOZEMAN Trail. Carrington and his command were assigned to construct a series of forts along the Bozeman Trail to protect travelers on their way to the Montana mining country. The Indians considered Carrington's arrival a sign of deception behind the government's peace efforts, and withdrew from the conference, declaring open hostilities against all who crossed their hunting lands.

Guided by mountain man JAMES BRIDGER, Carrington and his forces proceeded up the Powder River, where they established Fort Phil Kearny near the forks of the Big Piney and Little Piney branches in Montana. From its initial construction, the post was besieged by bands of Oglala, Brule, and Miniconjou Sioux, along with Northern Cheyennes and Arapahos. Carrington, short on actual combat experience, was faced with discipline problems and insubordination by his younger but more experienced officers.

When a wagon convoy returning with wood for the construction of the fort was attacked in December 1866, Carrington consented to let Captain WILLIAM FETTERMAN lead a relief column to drive off the attackers. The Indian attack on the wood train was only a decoy, however. Fetterman and his small command were soon annihilated by an overwhelming force of warriors. News of the Fetterman Fight reached Carrington's superiors at Omaha after frontiersmen John "Portuguese" Philips and Daniel Dixon rode the hazardous 236 miles in a severe blizzard to the telegraph station at Fort Laramie. Carrington was deemed partly responsible for the disaster and relieved of his command. Subsequent military and civilian investigations exonerated Carrington of any negligence or blame.

After transfer to garrison duty in Colorado, Carrington retired from the service due to a hip injury received in the line of duty. He taught military tactics at Wabash College, wrote historical works on the American Revolution, and, in 1889, helped negotiate a treaty with the Flathead Indians. Three years later, he supervised the removal of Northern Plains bands to western Montana reservations. (See also RED CLOUD.)

CARSON, CHRISTOPHER HOUSTON (Kit Carson; Rope Thrower; Father Kit). *(1809–1868).* Army officer; scout; guide; Indian agent; trader.

Originally from Kentucky, Kit Carson moved with his family to the Missouri frontier. At the age of 15, he left an apprenticeship to a saddlemaker to travel westward to New Mexico, later embarking on a career as a trader and trapper in Arizona and California with JAMES BRIDGER and THOMAS FITZPATRICK. He lived among the Indians for extended periods of time, and was known among them as Rope Thrower. The Shoshone chief WASHAKIE became a close friend.

In 1842, while working as a hunter at the Arkansas River trading post BENT's Fort (Colorado), he was enlisted by JOHN C. FREMONT as scout for his expedition into the Northern Rockies. He later served as a guide for two other expeditions with Fremont, in 1843–44 and in 1845–46. Carson was married to an Arapaho woman, who died giving birth to his daughter, and subsequently married a Cheyenne woman, who later divorced him. He married Maria Josefa Jaramillo in 1843, the daughter of a wealthy Taos family and sister-in-law of frontier fur trader CHARLES BENT.

During the Mexican War, Carson served as a courier and guide for General STEPHEN WATTS KEARNY. In 1846, when Kearny's forces were surrounded near Los Angeles, Carson, Lieutenant EDWARD BEALE, and an Indian scout were able to escape and obtain American reinforcements from San Diego.

Carson returned to his home in Taos, New Mexico, in 1849, to take up sheep farming. That same year, he guided federal troops in pursuit of Jicarilla Apache and Ute raiders carrying out attacks along the Santa Fe Trail.

In 1853, Carson was appointed Indian agent to the Mouache Utes and Jicarilla Apaches of northern New Mexico, who came to trust him and called him Father Kit.

As a commander of New Mexico volunteers during the 1850s, Carson fought in U.S. military campaigns against the Apaches, Navajos, and Kiowas. In April 1854, he was a scout for federal forces in their engagement with the Jicarilla Apaches in the Battle of Rio Caliente.

In 1861, Carson resigned his post as agent to serve in the Civil War, taking on a military commission as colonel of New Mexico volunteers. William Arny succeeded him as agent to the Utes and Jicarillas. Carson fought under General JAMES H. CARLETON in campaigns against the Mescalero Apaches and the Navajos. By the end of 1862, he had succeeded in gaining the surrender of almost all the surviving Mescaleros, who were then relocated to Bosque Redondo in eastern New Mexico.

In January 1864, during the Navajo War, Carson led military forces, including Ute auxiliaries, in the assault on the Navajos under MANUELITO at the tribal stronghold of Canyon de Chelly. Destroying their food supplies and confiscating their livestock, Carson forced thousands of Navajos to surrender. They too were marched to Bosque Redondo.

In November 1864, Carson led an attack on Comanche and Kiowa warriors in the Battle of Adobe Walls. Carson's combined force of over 300 New Mexico and California volunteers plus 75 Ute and Jicarilla Apache auxiliaries destroyed the Indian village. But Carson's men found themselves severely outnumbered when the Indians counterattacked. Only the use of two small field howitzers firing grapeshot enabled a retreat with minimal casualties.

Carson, brevetted a brigadier general shortly after the Civil War, represented the army at the Little Arkansas Council in October 1865, in which peace settlements were reached with leaders of the Cheyennes, Arapahos, Kiowas, Kiowa-Apaches, and Comanches. Carson subsequently accompanied a delegation of Utes to a conference in Washington, D.C. He retired from the military in 1867, after brief service as commander of Fort Garland in southern Colorado. He died at Fort Lyon, Colorado. (See also MANUELITO.)

CARTIER, JACQUES. *(1491–1557).* Explorer.
Born in the town of St. Malo, in the Brittany region of France, Jacques Cartier became a sailor and navigator. In 1524, and again in 1528, he reportedly accompanied GIOVANNI DA VERRAZANO on his explorations of the mid-Atlantic coast of North America.

In 1534, at the request of King Francois I of France, Cartier undertook an expedition in search of a Northwest Passage to Asia. During this voyage, he explored the west coast of Newfoundland; Prince Edward Island; the Gaspe Peninsula of Quebec, where he landed and took possession for France; Anticosti Island; and the mouth of the St. Lawrence River. He then returned to France with two Huron Indians, the sons of Chief DONNACONNA.

During a second expedition for France in 1535–36, Cartier sailed up the St. Lawrence River and made contact with Donnaconna's Hurons at their settlements at Stadacona (present-day Quebec) and Hochelaga (present-day Montreal). Wintering in the St. Lawrence River region, Cartier and his men were afflicted with scurvy. They were helped by the Indians who showed them how to treat the nutritional disease with the use of a natural medicine produced from evergreen trees. Cartier brought Donnaconna and several other Indians back to France, where the Huron chief died.

In 1541, on a third expedition, Cartier chose the site at Cap Rouge, Quebec, where Jean Francois de la Rocque de Roberval attempted but failed to establish a permanent colony. After further explorations of the region, Cartier returned to France in 1542, with a shipment of what he thought were precious gems and minerals, but which turned out to be worthless. Cartier spent the remainder of his life in France.

CARVER, JONATHAN. *(1710–1780).* Explorer.
A native of Weymouth, Massachusetts, Jonathan Carver was raised in Connecticut. While working as a

shoemaker from 1746 to 1763, he served in the Connecticut colonial militia in the French and Indian Wars (both King George's War of 1744–48 and the French and Indian War of 1754–63).

In 1766, Carver traveled west to the British garrison and fur-trading center Mackinac Island, in the strait between Lake Michigan and Lake Huron. French and Indian War veteran Major ROBERT ROGERS, assigned to manage the British fur-trading interests there, commissioned Carver to explore the western Great Lakes in order to promote the fur trade among the tribes of the area in what is present-day Minnesota and Wisconsin.

Carver crossed Lake Michigan to Green Bay, then traveled via the Fox and Wisconsin rivers to the Mississippi, which he followed northward. During the winter of 1766–67, Carver and his expedition lived with a band of Sioux at their encampment near the Falls of St. Anthony (present-day St. Paul, Minnesota). He learned the Siouan language and studied the tribe's customs.

Upon arrival at Prairie du Chien, Wisconsin, in spring 1767, Carver's party met up with another expedition, led by Captain James Tute. Tute, who had also been commissioned by Rogers, had orders to search for a water route west to the Pacific from the Great Lakes, the Northwest Passage. Carver and Tute joined their expeditions and explored what is now Minnesota and Lake Superior. Since they did not receive supplies from Rogers as arranged at Grand Portage on the north shore of Lake Superior, they abandoned their explorations in 1768. Additionally, a war raging at that time between the Sioux and the Chippewas made travel farther west dangerous.

Carver went to England in 1769. He faced financial hardship for the remainder of his life, due in part to his not receiving money owed him by Rogers. In 1778, his account of explorations in the Great Lakes region, *Travels Through the Interior Parts of North America in the Years 1766, 1767, and 1768*, was published, one of the earliest English accounts of the Great Lakes frontier, including the life and customs of the Sioux tribes. The book was well received and republished in many editions.

Carver died in England two years later. Reports persisted after his death that he had acquired from the Sioux a vast tract of land in Minnesota and Wisconsin, an area comprising up to 10,000 square miles. His heirs and other parties speculated on this land claim for the next 200 years. Petitions to Congress, as well as to the state governments of Minnesota and Wisconsin, on behalf of beneficiaries of the so-called Carver Deed, continued into the 1950s.

CASS, LEWIS. *(1782–1866).* Governor of Michigan Territory; secretary of War; soldier.

Lewis Cass was born in Exeter, New Hampshire, and, in 1799, he migrated to the Ohio frontier, where he soon began to practice law. In 1806, he was elected to the Ohio Territorial Legislature.

Cass was active in the War of 1812 in the Great Lakes region. With the help of WILLIAM HENRY HARRISON, he recruited Indians to fight the British. In the course of the unsuccessful American campaign at Detroit against a combined force of British troops and Indians under the Shawnee TECUMSEH, Cass was taken prisoner. He was later released, and subsequently fought with the victorious American forces in the 1813 Battle of the Thames, where Tecumseh was killed. Cass made the rank of brigadier general.

At the end of the war, Cass was appointed governor of the Michigan Territory. During his 18 years as governor, 1813 to 1831, he engaged in numerous negotiations with the territory's Indians in an effort to peacefully remove them from their land. He prided himself on the fact that his Indian removal policies did not involve providing liquor to the Indians. Instead, with the help of Superintendent of Indian Affairs WILLIAM CLARK and Indian agent HENRY ROWE SCHOOLCRAFT, he was able to successfully execute treaties that provided cash payments and federal annuities in exchange for Indian lands.

In 1825, Cass helped bring about the Prairie du Chien Treaty, paving the way for the removal of the remaining Old Northwest Indians to the lands west of the Mississippi, including Sacs, Foxes, Potawatomis, and Win-

Lewis Cass. *Courtesy of Library of Congress.*

nebagos. The Chippewas were relocated to northern Wisconsin.

In 1831, Cass became ANDREW JACKSON's secretary of War and continued to pursue his removal policy of eastern Indians. He supported the state government of Georgia in the 1831 U.S. Supreme Court case, *Cherokee Nation v. State of Georgia*. This landmark case, involving the Cherokee leader JOHN ROSS, resulted in the Supreme Court denying the sovereignty of the Cherokee Nation, thus laying the legal basis for their removal to the Indian Territory.

Cass directed the army in the BLACK HAWK War of 1832 against Sacs and Foxes in Illinois and Wisconsin; he also directed the military against warriors under OSCEOLA in the first year of the Second Seminole War of 1835–42.

Following his service as secretary of War, Cass became ambassador to France, serving in 1836–42. He was senator from Michigan in 1845–57, maintaining a policy that favored expansion of the United States. He supported the occupation of Mexico and the takeover from Great Britain of the entire Oregon Territory.

Cass ran for president in 1848 and was defeated by ZACHARY TAYLOR. He ended his political career as secretary of state under President James Buchanan in 1857–60.

CATAHECASSA (Black Hoof). *Shawnee.*
(ca. 1740–1831). War chief; principal chief; orator.

It is thought that Catahecassa was born in Florida and forced to move north with other Shawnees because of white expansion. In the French and Indian War of 1754–63, he fought with the French, helping to defeat General EDWARD BRADDOCK's troops on their way to capture Fort Duquesne in 1755. Catahecassa also supported PONTIAC in his rebellion against the British in 1763, and his exploits in war eventually earned him the position of principal chief among his people.

In 1774, during Lord DUNMORE's War, Catahecassa's men helped defeat troops under Andrew Lewis at Point Pleasant. In the American Revolution, he fought on the side of the British. Along with fellow Shawnee BLUE JACKET, Catahecassa again battled American troops in LITTLE TURTLE's War of 1790–94.

Following the Indian defeat at the Battle of Fallen Timbers, Catahecassa helped keep the peace. He signed the Fort Greenville Treaty of 1795, among other treaties of the Old Northwest. Like his close friend the Wyandot TARHE, he refused to support TECUMSEH in his rebellion of 1809–11. Catahecassa was known as a spellbinding orator. He died at Wapakoneta, Ohio.

CATALDO, JOSEPH. *(1837–1928).* Linguist; peacemaker; missionary.

Italian-born Joseph Cataldo came to North America as a Jesuit missionary and worked among the Plateau Indians from 1865 to 1877, including the Spokanes, Coeur d'Alenes, and Nez Perces. During the Nez Perce War of 1877 under Chief JOSEPH (Young Joseph), Cataldo was called upon to act as a negotiator and peacemaker. From 1877 to 1893, he became superior of the Pacific Northwest missions, and, in 1883, he founded Gonzaga University in Spokane, Washington. After 1893, he was missionary to Alaskan native peoples. He became proficient in numerous Indian languages, about which he wrote several short works.

CATLIN, GEORGE. *(1796–1872).* Artist; writer; explorer.

George Catlin was born in Wilkes-Barre, Pennsylvania, where he grew up on a farm. He studied to be an attorney in Litchfield, Connecticut, and practiced law in Luzerne County, Pennsylvania, before turning to a career in art. He set himself up as a painter of miniature portraits on ivory in Philadelphia in 1823, and, then Washington, D.C., the next year. A visit by a group of Indian chiefs to Philadelphia in 1824 inspired him to paint Native Americans. He made trips to eastern reservations and painted visiting Indian delegations to Washington, D.C.

Catlin traveled to St. Louis in 1830 where he became a friend of the explorer WILLIAM CLARK, then superintendent of Indian Affairs for the territory acquired in the Louisiana Purchase. For two years, Catlin painted Indian delegations to the frontier post.

Clark arranged for Catlin's painting expedition up the Missouri River on the maiden voyage of the American Fur Company's steamer, *Yellowstone*, in spring 1832. Catlin reached Fort Union (North Dakota) near the mouth of the Yellowstone River on June 26. He returned to St. Louis by canoe with two trappers the next fall.

In spring 1833, Catlin traveled to the site of Fort Laramie (Wyoming) on the Oregon Trail, then to the Great Salt Lake (Utah). After his return to St. Louis, he spent time the following winter in Pensacola, Florida, and then in New Orleans.

In spring 1834, Catlin left New Orleans, traveling overland and by canoe to Fort Gibson in the Indian Territory, where he joined up in June with the Dragoon Expedition to the Southern Plains tribes under HENRY LEAVENWORTH and HENRY DODGE. Suffering with fever, he returned to St. Louis the following fall.

In 1835–36, Catlin painted the Indians of Minnesota and Wisconsin. In southwestern Minnesota, he was the first white man to see an ancient quarry used by the Indians as a source of the pipestone from which they carved their ceremonial pipes. The previously unclassified mineral was later named catlinite in honor of the artist. In 1838, Catlin painted the Seminole OSCEOLA imprisoned at Charleston, South Carolina, just prior to his death.

Catlin exhibited his collection of some 600 paintings of 48 tribes, plus thousands of Indian artifacts, in eastern cities in 1837–38, to enthusiastic audiences. He hoped to sell his Indian Gallery to Congress for a national museum, but, because of his criticisms of federal Indian policy, he could not gain support. In 1839, he took the collection to Europe, where his work received great acclaim. By 1852, however, he was in debt and lost his paintings and Indian artifacts to creditors. In 1852–57, he traveled throughout much of Central and South America where he also painted Indians. He also visited the Far West of North America, reaching Alaska.

Many of Catlin's portraits and tribal scenes served as illustrations for his published works on the Indians: *Notes to the Manners, Customs and Condition of the North American Indians* (1841); *North American Indian Portfolio* (1844); and *Last Rambles Amongst the Indians of the Rocky Mountains and the Andes* (1868).

Catlin returned to America in 1870 and died two years later in Jersey City, New Jersey. The heirs of one of Catlin's creditors, the Philadelphian Joseph Harrison, who had acquired many of Catlin's works because of nonpayment in 1852, donated them to the Smithsonian Institution in 1879. Other Catlin originals are held by the American Museum of Natural History in New York City; the Thomas Gilcrease Institute of American History and Art in Tulsa, Oklahoma; and the Joslyn Art Museum in Omaha, Nebraska.

CHALPINICH. *Yokuts. (fl. early 1800s).* Leader of uprising against the Spanish.

Although exact dates are uncertain, 1818 is cited as the year in which several Yokuts bands of the San Joaquin Valley in central California staged an uprising against the Spanish. Chalpinich of the Joyuna Rancheria was the leader of the revolt that threatened the missions east of Monterey, including Soledad, San Miguel, San Antonio, and San Luis Obispo. Governor Vicente de Sola, the last Spanish governor of Alta California before Mexican independence, sent Don Ignacio Vallejo, father of MARIANO VALLEJO, into the field to suppress the uprising. His troops drove off an attack by about 600 warriors along the Nacimiento River—the Battle of El Pleito—and then defeated a force of some 3,000 at San Miguel.

CHAMPLAIN, SAMUEL DE. *(1567–1635).* Explorer; trader; soldier; French colonial official.

Samuel de Champlain was born to a seafaring family in the western French town of Brouage on the Bay of Biscay. He entered the French army and fought in the French wars against Spanish occupation in 1593–97. He then went into the service of Spain, sailing to Spanish settlements in Puerto Rico, Cuba, Mexico, and Central America, from 1599 to 1601.

Under the sponsorship of the governor of Dieppe, France, Ayman de Chastes, Champlain took part in a French fur-trading expedition to Canada in 1603. He sailed southwest up the St. Lawrence River as far as the Lachine Rapids, reaching the Indian village at Hochelaga, later the site of the French settlement of Montreal.

In 1604, Champlain returned to North America and, with Sieur de Monts, established the French colony of Port Royal at the mouth of the St. Croix River, which was moved the next year across the Bay of Fundy (the site of present-day Annapolis Royal, Nova Scotia). In 1605–07, Champlain explored the eastern coast of Canada south of Nova Scotia as far as Cape Cod and Martha's Vineyard.

In 1608, at the Huron village of Stadacona, Champlain founded the settlement of Quebec (present-day Quebec City), as a center for the Indian fur trade. He negotiated trade agreements and military alliances with the local tribes, including the Algonkins, Hurons, and Montagnais.

Champlain and his force of French soldiers took part in several military campaigns against the Iroquois on behalf of the Hurons. In July 1609, while on such a campaign into the Iroquois country of present northeastern New York State, Champlain discovered the large lake there that now bears his name. Soon after, he fought alongside the Hurons in a major conflict against the Iroquois at the site of present-day Crown Point, New York. In this battle, the Iroquois were first introduced to the military power of French firearms.

In 1611, Champlain established a landmark outpost for the fur trade at present-day Montreal.

On one of his trips back to France in 1612, Champlain was given a new grant for the fur-trade monopoly, and, the next year, he embarked on a voyage of western exploration, reaching Allumette Island in the Ottawa River. In 1615–16, accompanied by ETIENNE BRULE and a party of Huron warriors, he explored Georgian Bay on Lake Huron. From there, the party traveled southeastward via Lake Ontario. Champlain then joined a force of Huron warriors and took part in an unsuccessful attack against the Onondagas at their settlement on Lake Oneida, near the site of present-day Syracuse, New York. On being wounded, Champlain wintered in the Indian village and sent Brule southward to the Susquehanna River, which Brule followed all the way to Chesapeake Bay.

Champlain went on to hold a series of French colonial posts in New France, among them lieutenant governor. He sponsored subsequent expeditions in search of a water route from the Great Lakes to the Far East, including JEAN NICOLET's voyage to Wisconsin.

Champlain was forced to leave Canada after 1629, when the principal French settlements were seized by the British-backed Kirke brothers. He returned to Quebec in 1633 when French rule was restored, dying two years later.

In his 1603 book, entitled *Des Sauvages*, Champlain wrote extensively about the Indians of New France, describing at length their customs and politics. His early alliances with the Hurons and Algonquians against the Iroquois affected French policies in North America for over a century after his death. Champlain also produced maps of the Ottawa River, Lake Huron, and other major areas of present-day eastern Canada and New York.

CHARBONNEAU, JEAN BAPTISTE (Pomp, Pompy, Pompey). *Mixed Shoshone. (1805–1866)* Trader; trapper; guide. Son of SACAJAWEA and TOUSSAINT CHARBONNEAU.

Jean Baptiste Charbonneau was the son of Toussaint Charbonneau, an interpreter for the Lewis and Clark Expedition, and his Shoshone wife Sacajawea, who acted as guide. The younger Charbonneau was born on February 11, 1805, while the expedition was camped among the Mandan Indians. Both MERIWETHER LEWIS and WILLIAM CLARK wrote about this event in their journals and described Sacajawea carrying the baby, whom they called Pomp, on her back the rest of the journey to the Pacific and back. Sometime after 1806, at his request, Clark was given care of the boy in St. Louis and eventually sent him to Catholic school.

In 1823, Prince Paul Wilhelm of the German principality of Wurttemberg met Charbonneau at a frontier trading post on the Kansas River and persuaded him to return with him to Europe. Charbonneau spent the next six years abroad, studying foreign languages at Prince Paul's castle near Stuttgart and traveling throughout the European continent and North Africa.

Returning to America in 1829, Prince Paul and Charbonneau explored the upper reaches of the Missouri River. Charbonneau subsequently became a fur trapper in the Rocky Mountain region of what is now Idaho and Utah for the American Fur Company. He became friends with mountain men JAMES BRIDGER, JOSEPH MEEK, and ANTOINE ROBIDOUX and took part in the trappers' rendezvous on the Green River in Wyoming in 1833.

With the decline of the Rocky Mountain fur trade in the 1830s, Charbonneau turned to guiding explorers on the upper Missouri River. In 1839–40, along with Louis Vasquez and Andrew Sublette, he assisted in the establishment of Fort Vasquez on the South Platte River near present-day Denver, Colorado. In 1843, Charbonneau explored the Yellowstone region with the Scottish nobleman William Drummond. He also served as a guide for the U.S. Corps of Topographical Engineers under Lieutenant James Abert's 1845 expedition out of Fort Leavenworth along the Santa Fe Trail.

In 1846, at the outbreak of the Mexican War, Charbonneau was a guide for federal troops heading west from Santa Fe, New Mexico, to San Diego, California. After the war, he prospected for gold with mountain man JAMES BECKWOURTH. Charbonneau stayed in California until 1866. While heading for the gold-mining country of Montana, he died somewhere along the Owyhee River, near the present-day border of Oregon, Idaho, and Nevada. (See also SACAJAWEA.)

CHARBONNEAU, TOUSSAINT.
(ca. 1759–ca. 1840). Trader; trapper; interpreter; explorer. Husband of SACAJAWEA; father of JEAN BAPTISTE CHARBONNEAU.

Toussaint Charboneau was probably born in Montreal of French-Canadian parents. During the 1790s, he was a trader for the Montreal-based North West Company among the Assiniboine Indians. He later worked for JOHN JACOB ASTOR's American Fur Company among the Hidatsas, Mandans, Arikaras, and other Indians of the upper Missouri River. By 1804, he was married to several Indian women and living at the Mandan village near the future site of Fort Lincoln, North Dakota. It was here that the LEWIS and CLARK Expedition hired Charbonneau as an interpreter, and his Shoshone wife, Sacajawea, as a guide. Their son Jean Baptiste was born two months previous to their departure.

After the expedition had successfully reached the Pacific Coast and returned to the East, Charbonneau settled for a time near St. Louis. On leaving his son with William Clark sometime after 1806, he soon returned to live as a trader among the Upper Missouri River tribes, working again for the American Fur Company and for MANUEL LISA. It is not certain whether Sacajawea accompanied him or when she died.

During the War of 1812, Charbonneau was instrumental in keeping the upper Missouri River tribes, such as the Mandans, Sioux, and Gros Ventres, friendly to the United States. After the war, in 1815, he returned to guiding explorers into the Northern Plains and Rocky Mountains. He took part in early trade expeditions along the Santa Fe Trail to Taos, and, in 1820, acted as interpreter for Major STEPHEN H. LONG's expedition in Kansas among the Pawnees. Charbonneau went on to serve as interpreter on the explorations of Prince Paul Wilhelm of the German state of Wurttemberg in 1823, who later took Toussaint's son Jean Baptiste to Europe with him to be educated, and Prince ALEXANDER PHILIPP MAXIMILIAN ZU WIED in 1833. In the course of his travels, Charbonneau went at least as far west as the Great Salt Lake. One of his many Indian wives was a member of the Ute tribe.

In the meantime, during the 1820s–30s, Charbonneau was a government interpreter to the Mandans at their Missouri River settlements in northern Nebraska and the Dakotas, until a smallpox epidemic wiped out that tribe in 1837. He died about 1840, while still living among the Indians.

CHARGER, MARTIN (The Charger, Wa-ana-tan).
Mixed Sans Arc Sioux. (1833–1900). Proponent of peace; rescuer of white captives in the Minnesota Uprising of 1862–63.

Martin Charger was born in the foothills of the Black Hills near present-day Rapid City, South Dakota, the son of Turkey Head and Her Good Road. His father, who was in the employ of the American Fur Company, was reportedly the son of a white man named Lewis—either the explorer MERIWETHER LEWIS or the fur trader Reuben Lewis. When 18, Charger went to war against the Crows, and, the next year, he married Walking Hail, a Yankton Sioux.

In 1860, Charger organized a society of braves, the Fool Soldiers, dedicated to peace among the tribes in the vicinity of Fort Pierre on the Missouri River, including the Sans Arc, Yankton, Yanktonai, and Hunkpapa Sioux, as well as the Arikaras. In November 1862, at the time of the Minnesota Uprising under LITTLE CROW, on learning that Santee Sioux were nearby with white prisoners from the Lake Shetek area in Minnesota, Charger and his Fool Soldiers traveled to the Santee camp opposite the mouth of the Grand River and ransomed the hostages at their own expense.

In 1868, Charger was a delegate to Washington, D.C., to help establish the boundaries of the proposed Great Sioux Reservation. He did not attend the Fort Laramie council that year, fearing for his life at the hands of the Santees. In 1872, he began encouraging the building of log houses and farming among his people. Along with RED CLOUD of the Oglalas and SPOTTED TAIL of the Brules, Charger also represented his people in negotiations in Washington for the Black Hills. He signed the Black Hills Treaty of 1876 and moved his band west of the Missouri. In 1880, the Sans Arcs settled at the Cheyenne River Agency. He returned to Washington, D.C., in 1887 to discuss the federal government's allotment policy. During the Ghost Dance Uprising of 1890, Charger kept his people at peace, encouraging Christianity among them.

CHARLEVOIX, PIERRE FRANCOIS XAVIER DE.
(1682–1761). Historian; explorer.

Pierre Francois de Charlevoix was the son of France's deputy attorney general, Francois de Charlevoix. When 16, he began his Jesuit studies in Paris, and, in 1705–09, he taught at the Jesuit College of Quebec. He was ordained in France in 1713.

Seven years later, Charlevoix received a commission by the French government to find a route to a "Western Sea." He departed Montreal in May 1721, traveled by way of the Great Lakes to the Mississippi River, and descended it to New Orleans, arriving in January 1722. He included his travel experiences and scientific observations—a great deal on the Natchez Indians and other tribes—in his three-volume *History and General Description of New France*, published in 1744, the first such study.

Charlevoix also wrote a biography of MARIE GUYART (Marie de l'Incarnation), founder of the Ursuline order of Catholic nuns in New France and missionary to the Indians.

CHARLOT (Charlos, Slemhakkah, "bear claw").
Kalispel. (ca. 1831–1900). Principal chief who passively resisted removal.

After having signed a treaty in 1855 with the federal government, many of the Kalispels of northern Idaho, northeast Montana, and northwest Washington were settled on the Kalispel and Colville reservations in Washington and the Flathead (or Jocko) Reservation in Montana.

In 1872, a band of Kalispels living in the Bitterroot Mountains of Idaho and Montana signed an agreement for their relocation to the Flathead Reservaton. Their principal chief, known as Charlot after a French trader, resisted passively through passionate oratory, excuses, and delays. White officials then declared Charlot's rival Arly the new chief, and Arly took 71 members of the band to the reservation with him. The remaining several hundred stayed with Charlot in their ancestral valley.

In 1884, the Indian agent Peter Ronan took Charlot to Washington, D.C., in order to negotiate a compromise, but he still refused to relocate. In the following years, with continuing white expansion, many in Charlot's band made the move to the reservation. Charlot and his most faithful held out until 1890, when troops were sent in to relocate them by force.

CHATO (Alfred Chato or Chatto). *Chiricahua Apache. (ca. 1860–1934).* Leader in the last phase of the Apache Wars, 1881–86; army scout.

In 1881, Chato fled the San Carlos Reservation with GERONIMO and hid out in the Sierra Madre in Mexico. The next year, he returned with Geronimo and participated in several raids. In March 1883, while Geronimo and Chihuahua led a war party south to Sonora, Mexico, in search of livestock, Chato and Benito headed north with 24 warriors into Arizona, then New Mexico, to locate ammunition. Before returning to Mexico, they killed at least 11 settlers in a series of raids. In May 1883, troops under General GEORGE CROOK attacked Chato's camp in Mexico, but Chato continued

Chato. *Courtesy of Library of Congress.*

his resistance. He surrendered in February 1884 with and 60 Apaches; Geronimo surrendered in March with 80 more.

Geronimo again fled the reservation in 1885; Chato refused to go and tried to dissuade him. The following year, Chato helped Crook track down Geronimo at Canyon de los Embudos in Mexico along with AL-CHESAY, MICKEY FREE, and KAYATENNAE. He was later part of the Apache delegation to Washington, D.C., in 1886, and pleaded for the prisoners' right to stay in their homeland.

Despite the help he had given the army, Chato was shipped to Florida with other Apache prisoners, including Geronimo. He lost his land allotment at San Carlos and all his livestock. His children were eventually taken from him and sent to the Carlisle Indian School, where they died.

In 1894, Chato, Geronimo, and the other survivors were sent to Fort Sill in the Indian Territory. In 1913, Chato, known to whites as Alfred Chatto, was finally allowed to return to New Mexico, where he settled on

the Mescalero Reservation. He died in an automobile accident. (See also GERONIMO.)

CHICKATAUBUT ("house afire"). *Massachuset.* *(d. 1633).* Sachem.

Chickataubut's territory was in the region of Weymouth, Massachusetts, presently a suburb of Boston. He was at odds with early English settlers because of their destruction of his people's cornfields as well as the desecration of his mother's grave. Yet he came to support the colonists, visiting Governor John Winthrop in Boston in 1631, and helping fight the Pequots in 1632. Chickataubut died in the smallpox epidemic of 1633.

CHIEF JOSEPH. See JOSEPH.

CHILD, LYDIA MARIA. *(1802–1880).* Reformer; writer.

Lydia Maria Francis, born in Medford, Massachusetts, married Boston lawyer David Lee Child in 1828. She edited the first children's monthly in the United States, *Juvenile Miscellany*, in 1826–34, and later edited *The National Anti-Slavery Standard* in 1841–43, and wrote numerous pamphlets in support of abolition and woman suffrage, plus several novels, including *Hobomok: A Tale of Early Times, by an American*, published in 1824, about a New England Indian in the Noble Savage mold and his interracial romance.

During the 1860s, Child also wrote pamphlets on Indian rights, including the famous *An Appeal for the Indians* (1868), in which she called upon governmental officials, as well as ministers and missionaries, especially Quakers, to bring justice to the Indians. Her views helped bring about PETER COOPER's interest in Indian issues and his founding of the United States Indian Commission, and President ULYSSES S. GRANT's subsequent Peace Policy.

CHISHOLM, JESSE. *Mixed Cherokee.* *(ca. 1805–1868).* Trader; guide; interpreter; negotiator; trailblazer of the Chisholm Trail.

Jesse Chisholm was born in Tennessee, the son of a Scottish trader and Cherokee mother. His family emigrated to Arkansas about 1816, settling in a Cherokee community in western Arkansas near Fort Smith. He became active in the fur trade, bartering with the Comanches, Kiowas, Osages, Wichitas, and other tribes in the region that came to be defined as the Indian Territory.

Because of his contacts with tribes, his knowledge of the region, and his language skills (he reportedly knew 14 different Indian tongues), Chisholm found work as guide and interpreter for numerous military expeditions. Along with the Delaware BLACK BEAVER, he worked for the 1834 expedition of General HENRY

LEAVENWORTH and Colonel HENRY DODGE, interpreting at councils with Comanches, Kiowas, and Wichitas. In 1846, he again served as interpreter among the Southern Plains tribes during negotiations at Fort Concho, Texas.

Chisholm eventually operated three trading posts in the Indian Territory, at Oklahoma City, Lexington, and Camp Holmes. At the beginning of the Civil War, he negotiated treaties with Indian tribes for the Confederates, but then accompanied OPOTHLEYA-HOLO's band to Kansas to maintain his neutrality, settling near Wichita. He married the daughter of fellow trader James Edward by whom he had 13 children.

At the war's end in 1865, Chisholm drove a wagon-load of trade goods from his Kansas post through the Indian Territory to the Red River country of Texas to trade with the local tribes. He returned with a wagon-load of buffalo hides, again cutting ruts in the prairie, which became the Chisholm Trail.

Chisholm continued his work as a diplomat to the Indians, helping bring about the signing of treaties at Little Arkansas in 1865 and Medicine Lodge in 1867. He died in 1868 at Left Hand Spring in the Indian Territory (near present-day Oklahoma City).

Other traders made use of the Chisholm Trail, followed by cattlemen. Hundreds of thousands of Texas longhorns were herded from the vicinity of San Antonio, Texas, along the trail to markets and railroads, such as Abilene, Kansas. During the 1880s, with new railway lines and the laying of wire fences, the trail was abandoned.

CHITTENDEN, HIRAM MARTIN. *(1858–1917).* Historian; soldier.

Born in Cattaraugus County, New York, Hiram Chittenden attended West Point, graduating in 1884, and was commissioned an officer in the U.S. Army Corps of Engineers. While stationed in St. Louis, he wrote a history of the fur trade west of the Mississippi covering the years 1806 to 1843. His study, *The American Fur Trade of the Far West*, published in 1902, includes a description of tribal cultures and the Indians' extensive role in the development of the fur industry. With Alfred T. Richardson, Chittenden also edited the letters of the Jesuit missionary to the Plateau Indians, PIERRE JEAN DE SMET, and wrote a biographical summary: *Life, Letters and Travels of Father Pierre-Jean De Smet, S.J., 1801–1873*, published in 1905.

CHITTO HARJO (Crazy Snake; Wilson Jones). *Creek. (1846–1912).* Leader of the Crazy Snake Uprising of 1901 in the Indian Territory.

Chitto Harjo was born in the Indian Territory near present-day Boley, Oklahoma, and lived at Hickory Hills. A traditionalist, he advocated tribal restoration, as the full-blooded OPOTHLEYAHOLO, OKTARSARS HARJO SANDS, and ISPARHECHE had done before him. He also opposed the General Allotment Act (the DAWES Severalty Act) of 1887, calling for redistribution of tribal lands to individuals. With other full-blooded northern Creeks, who called themselves Snakes, he created the alternative Snake Government in 1897, which established laws against accepting allotments and refused enrollment for the allotment process.

In January 1901, in the short-lived Crazy Snake (or Snake) Uprising, some Creeks began attacking Indians who had accepted allotment as well as white settlers in the region. Federal marshals and cavalry rode against the Snakes and arrested Chitto Harjo. In a trial in February, he was found guilty, but allowed to return home.

Chitto Harjo and his followers continued their resistance through legal means, hiring white attorneys and lobbying in Washington, D.C. In 1906, he spoke before the Senate Committee on Land Treaties. Yet, in 1907, Oklahoma became a state; for the time being, the allotment policy continued.

The Snakes were involved in an incident soon after statehood, referred to as the Smoked Meat Rebellion. White police interrupted a council of Creek full-bloods at Hickory Hills in search of the alleged thief of a thousand pounds of smoked bacon. Fighting erupted, leading to the wounding of a white, the death of a Creek, and the arrest of several others. With tension mounting between Indians and whites, the police returned. After another scuffle, Chitto Harjo and several of his followers fled and hid out for his remaining years, in the wilderness and at friends' houses.

CHIVINGTON, JOHN MILTON (The Fighting Parson). *(1821–1894).* Militia officer in the Cheyenne-Arapaho War (Colorado War) of 1864–65.

Originally from Warren County, Ohio, John Chivington became a Methodist minister in 1844, and preached to settlers and Indians in frontier settlements of Kansas, Missouri, and Illinois. He supported the abolitionist movement in Kansas during the 1850s. He moved to Denver, Colorado, in 1860, and, after having preached to miners in the outlying area, he became presiding elder of Denver's First Episcopal Methodist Church.

Chivington became known as the Fighting Parson when he was commissioned a major in the Colorado volunteers by Governor JOHN EVANS in 1861. Dispatched to New Mexico to drive back the invasion of Confederate forces from Texas, Chivington distinguished himself at the 1861 Battle of Glorieta Pass. The following year, promoted to colonel under the command of General EDWARD CANBY, he fought in the decisive drive against Confederate army at Apache Canyon.

In 1863, Chivington was appointed as commander of the Colorado military district. In this capacity, he led Colorado volunteers in combat against the Southern Cheyennes and Southern Arapahos. With the withdrawal of regular army troops to fight in the Civil War, militant bands stepped up their hostilities against settlers and miners. The conflict became known as the Cheyenne-Arapaho War, or the Colorado War of 1864–65.

Many of the Southern Plains bands, including BLACK KETTLE's Cheyennes, sought peace with whites as the winter of 1864–65 approached. By November 1864, Black Kettle had been convinced by Major EDWARD WYNKOOP to lead his people to the vicinity of Fort Lyon, in southeast Colorado, near a tributary of the Arkansas River known as Sand Creek. The location had been decided at a peace conference the month before at Camp Weld, near Denver, at which Chivington was present. At this council, it was Chivington who suggested that the Indians surrender to federal troops at Fort Lyon. Yet, less than two months later, Chivington, with the authorization of Governor Evans, led a surprise attack on the Indians at Sand Creek, killing about 200, mostly women and children. The incident led to increased hostilities on the Plains, including two attacks on Julesburg, Colorado.

In March 1865, the affair, which became known as the Sand Creek Massacre, and alternatively as the Chivington Massacre, was the subject of a joint military-Congressional investigation under Senator JAMES DOOLITTLE, chairman of a Senate committee to investigate Indian affairs on the frontier. Chivington was censured for his conduct at Sand Creek, but efforts to court-martial him failed. In the wake of criticism, he was discharged from the Colorado militia in January 1865, when his term of enlistment expired, thus avoiding a military trial for his role in the massacre.

In the following years, Chivington went into the freight transport business, held public office in Colorado, and worked as a journalist. (See also BLACK KETTLE.)

CHOUTEAU, AUGUSTE PIERRE. *(1786–1838)*.
Trader; Indian agent; officer. Son of JEAN PIERRE CHOUTEAU; brother of PIERRE CHOUTEAU, JR.; nephew of RENE AUGUSTE CHOUTEAU.

The eldest son of frontier entrepreneur (Jean) Pierre Chouteau, Auguste Pierre Chouteau was born in St. Louis, Missouri. He entered West Point, graduating as a commissioned officer in 1806, but, after several years, he left the military to join his family's trading enterprise. In 1809, he joined in the founding of the St. Louis Missouri Fur Company with his father, MANUEL LISA, WILLIAM CLARK, ANTOINE PIERRE MENARD, ANDREW HENRY, and others.

Chouteau served in the War of 1812 as a captain of the territorial militia. In 1815, Chouteau and his business associates expanded their trade to include the Arapahos of the Southern Plains. During an 1817 expedition into Spanish-held New Mexico, he was arrested and held for a short time by Spanish authorities when his group attempted to open up trade with the fur trappers of the Southern Rockies.

Chouteau went on to successfully expand trade throughout the Indian Territory, and also officiated at Indian peace conferences. Between 1834 and 1838, Chouteau helped bring about the first treaties between the federal government and the Comanche and Kiowa tribes.

Chouteau lived at Salina, Oklahoma, where he entertained many notables, including the writer Washington Irving.

CHOUTEAU, JEAN PIERRE (Pierre Chouteau, Sr.). *(1758–1849)*. Trader; Indian agent. Half-brother of RENE AUGUSTE CHOUTEAU; father of AUGUSTE PIERRE CHOUTEAU and PIERRE CHOUTEAU, JR.

(Jean) Pierre Chouteau, also known as Pierre Chouteau, Sr., was born in New Orleans and became active with his half-brother Rene Auguste Chouteau in the upper Missouri fur trade. In 1794, they acquired from the Spanish government exclusive rights to trade with the Osage bands.

In 1804, one year after the United States acquired the vast Louisiana Territory, Chouteau was named the federal government's principal Indian agent to the tribes west of the Mississippi. In this capacity, he advised HENRY DEARBORN, the secretary of War, to take measures against the influx of British Canadian traders, who then began to descend into the newly acquired Louisiana Territory, corrupting and impoverishing the native peoples with whiskey. In the years before U.S. ownership, the Spanish authorities had strictly controlled the liquor trade among the Indians. In 1806, Chouteau became the agent to the Osage Indians and a close friend of Chief WHITE HAIR.

With his son Auguste Pierre, MANUEL LISA, and others, Chouteau was a partner in the St. Louis Missouri Fur Company in 1809, the company that opened up trade with the Crows and Blackfeet. It was reorganized as the Missouri Fur Company in 1812.

Like his half-brother, Chouteau was one of the original trustees of St. Louis, Missouri, and served in the Missouri territorial legislature. Both were among St. Louis's wealthiest and most prominent citizens.

CHOUTEAU, PIERRE, JR. *(1789–1865)*. Trader.
Son of JEAN PIERRE CHOUTEAU; brother of

AUGUSTE PIERRE CHOUTEAU; nephew of RENE AUGUSTE CHOUTEAU.

Pierre Chouteau, Jr., younger son of (Jean) Pierre Chouteau, was born in St. Louis, Missouri. He entered the family fur trade in 1805, then went on to become a partner with Bartholomew Berthold in 1813. In 1831, he helped form Bernard Pratte and Company (later Pratte, Chouteau, and Company), and, in 1834, Chouteau and Pratt purchased the Missouri River interests of the American Fur Company from JOHN JACOB ASTOR. In 1838, his firm became Pierre Chouteau, Jr., and Company, and it was a dominant force in western trade until 1864. Chouteau, who also invested in railroads and mining, lived his final years in New York City.

CHOUTEAU, RENE AUGUSTE. *(1749–1829).*
Trader; territorial official; peace commissioner; militia officer. Half-brother of JEAN PIERRE CHOUTEAU; uncle of AUGUSTE PIERRE CHOUTEAU and PIERRE CHOUTEAU, JR.

Born in New Orleans, (Rene) Auguste Chouteau became a protege of his stepfather, fur-trading entrepreneur Pierre de Laclede in 1763, working as a clerk for Laclede's operation among the Illinois tribes on the upper Mississippi. In February 1764, Chouteau, on orders from Laclede, established the original fur-trading fort on the site of the present-day city of St. Louis, Missouri. In 1768, he became a partner with Laclede, then, on Laclede's death 10 years later, principal owner.

Chouteau and his brother held the trade monopoly to the Osages and served as a diplomat to them for the Spanish government, which controlled the Louisiana country in the late 1700s.

After the United States had acquired the Louisiana Territory in 1803, Chouteau held a series of governmental posts in the new territorial government. In addition to being a judge, serving in Missouri's territorial legislature, and sitting on the first board of trustees of the city of St. Louis, Chouteau was also a commissioner for the U.S. government in treaties with the tribes of the Louisiana Territory. He was also a colonel in the Missouri militia. He spent his last years in St. Louis, where he had extensive landholdings.

CHURCH, BENJAMIN. *(1639–1718).* Colonial militia officer in King Philip's War and the French and Indian Wars.

Benjamin Church was born in the Plymouth Colony and worked as a carpenter until the outbreak of King Philip's War in 1675. His friendship with the Wampanoag AWASHONKS led to her providing warriors against King PHILIP's Wampanoags and CANONCHET's Narragansets.

As a captain in the Plymouth Colony militia, Church led colonial forces against the Wampanoags in the Great Swamp Fight near South Kingston, Rhode Island, in December 1675.

Church became commander of New England colonial troops early in 1676, succeeding JOSIAH WINSLOW. In August of that year, troops under Church's command succeeded in capturing King Philip's family members. That same month, one of Church's Indian scouts killed Philip at his stronghold at Mt. Hope near Bristol, Rhode Island. Church then led his men in pursuit of ANNAWAN, Philip's leading war chief, who, on August 26, 1676, surrendered the Wampanoag Confederacy's medicine bundle to him, marking the end of the war.

Church was active in the colonial militia during the French and Indian Wars. In King William's War of 1689–97, he led a force of 300 into Maine in September 1691 against Abnaki villages until three of their sachems sued for peace, countering efforts by New France's governor-general LOUIS DE BUADE, COMTE DE FRONTENAC to incite the Abnakis to warfare with the British. During Queen Anne's War of 1702–13, Church led a 1704 expedition against the French at Port Royal (present-day Annapolis Royal, Nova Scotia). (See also PHILIP.)

CLARK, GEORGE ROGERS. *(1752–1818).*
Militia officer in the American Revolution; Indian commissioner. Brother of WILLIAM CLARK.

Born in Charlottesville, Virginia, George Rogers Clark worked as a surveyor in an area of western Virginia, now part of Kentucky, during the early 1770s. In 1774, he was a captain of the Virginia militia and participated with the colony's governor, JOHN MURRAY, EARL OF DUNMORE, in his war against CORNSTALK's Shawnees in the Ohio Valley. Clark was present at the 1774 Camp Charlotte Treaty settlement in which Shawnee leaders relinquished all claims to the area that would later become Kentucky.

In 1776, during the American Revolution, Clark persuaded the Virginia government to declare sovereignty over Kentucky. Clark then obtained military supplies to defend the area against attacks by British-allied Indians. Through spies, Clark learned that the Indian uprising in Kentucky was being openly supported by British garrisons in the southern Ohio Valley, now part of Illinois and Indiana.

With the support of Governor Patrick Henry of Virginia, Clark planned a military expedition against pro-British Illinois and Indiana Indians, including Wea, Piankashaw, Miami, and Kickapoo bands. Commissioned a lieutenant colonel in spring 1778, he led a force of 350 Virginia militiamen from Pittsburgh along the Ohio River to Corn Island (present-day Louisville). After having established a base of operations, Clark's expeditionary force moved west against the Indian villages of Kaskaskia and Cahokia, then cut back and captured Vincennes on the Wabash River. Clark had also hoped to advance on Detroit, but because of shortages of men and supplies, withdrew.

About 500 British troops and Indian auxiliaries out of Detroit under HENRY HAMILTON and ALEXANDER McKEE retook Vincennes in October, renaming Fort Patrick Henry as Fort Sackville. Following a winter march through icy waters, Clark and his frontiersmen attacked the post once again on February 23, 1779. His militia reportedly tomahawked to death four captured warriors in front of the fort in order to influence the Indians to abandon their British allies. Hamilton was captured and sent to Virginia in shackles. The next year, because of his successful campaign, Clark was made a brigadier general in the Virginia militia.

Clark continued to defend settlements on the Ohio frontier from attacks by British-armed Indians. From 1780 to 1782, he led campaigns against the Shawnees and Delawares, destroying the villages of Chillicothe and Piqua in southern Ohio. His men also annihilated an Indian army under SIMON GIRTY on its way to reinforce Piqua. He defended Cahokia and St. Louis, at that time a Spanish settlement, against a combined British and Indian siege. He also participated in the defense of Virginia by an invading army under Benedict Arnold.

In the post-Revolutionary years, Clark's victories in the Ohio Valley enabled the newly established United States to maintain sovereignty over the area as part of the terms of the 1783 Treaty of Paris. Clark was appointed Indian commissioner for the Old Northwest Territory. In 1786, he again led an expedition to subdue Illinois bands along the Wabash River. That same year, he was removed from his post as commissioner through the political efforts of General James Wilkinson, probably a Spanish agent. Clark's bitterness on the failures of Virginia and the Confederation to pay him for his services led him to accept commissions from both the French and Spanish in various colonization schemes. He returned to private life in Louisville in 1799. His younger brother William achieved national fame in the LEWIS and Clark Expedition several years later.

CLARK, WILLIAM (Chief Red Hair). (1770–1838).
Explorer; Indian superintendent; territorial governor; soldier. Brother of GEORGE ROGERS CLARK.

William Clark was born on his family's plantation in Kentucky, a younger brother of Revolutionary War officer George Rogers Clark. He was raised on Virginia's frontier. During the 1790s, he fought as a lieutenant under General "Mad" ANTHONY WAYNE in LITTLE TURTLE's War of 1790–94, participating in the final conflict at the Battle of Fallen Timbers. While serving in the army, Clark befriended MERIWETHER LEWIS. In 1796, he left the military and spent the next seven years managing his family's property.

In 1803, on Lewis's request, Clark became co-leader of a government-backed expedition into the newly acquired Louisiana Territory, the Corps of Discovery. In 1803–04, Clark, referred to as Captain Clark by Lewis, was instrumental in organizing the expedition and selecting personnel at its departure point at Camp Wood River, Illinois, on the Mississippi near the mouth of the Missouri opposite St. Louis.

The expedition departed St. Louis in May 1804, heading up the Missouri. Clark, referred to as Chief Red Hair by some of the Indians, acted as the expedition's Indian negotiator and presided over numerous councils. The expedition encountered more than 50 tribes. He became a good friend of SACAJAWEA, the expedition's Shoshone guide, and after the expedition, he helped raise her son JEAN BAPTISTE CHARBONNEAU.

During the expedition to the mouth of the Columbia by November 1805, and back to St. Louis by September 1806, Clark kept a journal containing observations on topography, Indians, and wildlife, and acted as principal cartographer. In 1807, Clark and Lewis reported their findings to President THOMAS JEFFERSON in Washington, D.C.

That same year, Clark was appointed Indian agent for the Louisiana Territory, with his headquarters in St. Louis. In 1808, he became a partner in the St. Louis Missouri Fur Company with MANUEL LISA, ANTOINE PIERRE MENARD, ANDREW HENRY, JEAN PIERRE CHOUTEAU, AUGUSTE PIERRE CHOUTEAU, Reuben Lewis (Meriwether's brother) and others. In 1813, he was named governor of the newly organized Missouri Territory. He was also commissioned a brigadier general of the territorial militia, with the responsiblity of defending the frontier settlements from Indian attacks.

With Missouri statehood in 1820, Clark made a bid for the governorship, but lost the election. He remained superintendent of Indian affairs for the upper Missouri and Mississippi tribes. In this capacity, he was instrumental along with LEWIS CASS, governor of the Michigan Territory, in organizing the removal of the Great Lakes tribes west of the Mississippi. (See also LEWIS, MERIWETHER; SACAJAWEA.)

CLERMONT (Clermore, Claremore, Clermos; Tawagahe, Tawhangage, "town builder"; Gra-Mo'n, "arrow going home"; Manka-Chonka, "black dog").
Osage. (fl. early 1800s). Principal chief of the Arkansas River Osages.

In 1802, a band of Osages under Clermont branched off from the rest of the tribe in western Missouri and settled father west along the Arkansas River in what is now northeastern Oklahoma and southeastern Kansas. WHITE HAIR remained principal chief of the group staying behind. During this period, the Osages maintained trade relationships with the CHOUTEAU family and with MANUEL LISA. With more and more white traders and migrants traveling through their homeland, the way of life of the Osages was threatened. Clermont opposed the use of liquor and dependence on white trade goods, and his efforts to resist alcohol and maintain his people's traditional economy contributed to their prosperity. Subsequent Osage chiefs also bore the name Clermont.

CLINCH, DUNCAN LAMONT. *(1787–1849).* Army officer in the Second Seminole War.

Duncan Clinch was born in North Carolina. He entered the military as a young man and made the rank of first lieutenant in the 3rd infantry in 1808. He was promoted to colonel in the 8th infantry two years later, and, in 1820, he was brevetted brigadier general.

Clinch was in command at Fort King when the Second Seminole War erupted in 1835. Following the December 28 attack on Indian agent WILEY THOMPSON by warriors under OSCEOLA and the attack on Major FRANCIS DADE's column by warriors under MICANOPY, JUMPER, and ALLIGATOR, Clinch led a force of about 300 regulars and 500 Florida militia out of Fort King to locate the militants' hideout in the Wahoo Swamp. The enemy forces met in the Battle of Withlacoochee River of December 31, 1835.

After about 200 of Clinch's regulars had crossed the river, they were ambushed by some 250 warriors under Osceola and Alligator. Because of Seminole sharpshooters, the militia were unable to cross over to the pinned-down regulars. The regulars eventually dispersed the Seminoles with three bayonet charges, but suffered four dead and 59 wounded. Clinch then ordered a retreat, and General EDMUND GAINES subsequently moved on the Seminoles.

Clinch resigned his commisison the following September and settled in Georgia, serving as a congressman in 1844–45. (See also OSCEOLA.)

CLINTON, GEORGE. *(ca. 1686–1761).* Colonial governor.

The Englishman George Clinton entered the British navy in 1708 and became an admiral in 1747. He was appointed New York's governor in 1741, while in England, coming to the colony two years later. During King George's War of 1744–48, Clinton was instrumental in securing the support of the Iroquois against the French. He named WILLIAM JOHNSON as New York's first colonial superintendent of Indian affairs. Recalled to England in 1753, Clinton later became a member of Parliament. His son Henry Clinton served as a British general in the American Revolution.

CLINTON, GEORGE. *(1739–1812).* Continental officer in the American Revolution; first governor of New York State; vice president of the United States. Brother of JAMES CLINTON.

George Clinton was born in present-day Orange County, New York, and he served in the French and Indian War of 1754–63 with his brother James. After the war, George studied law in New York City. In 1768, he was elected to the New York Provincial Assembly, and, in 1775, to the Second Continental Congress.

Clinton then served as a brigadier general in the Continental army during the American Revolution and, with his brother, commanded troops in the defense of the Hudson River. Fort Clinton and Fort Montgomery were captured by British forces under Henry Clinton, son of earlier New York colonial governor GEORGE CLINTON, a different family.

In 1777, Clinton was elected the first governor of New York State and served six successive terms until 1795. He is sometimes referred to as the "Father of New York State." As governor, he negotiated a number of treaties with the Iroquois from 1784 to 1791, extinguishing their land titles. He went on to become vice president from 1805 to 1812, during President THOMAS JEFFERSON's second term and President James Madison's first term.

CLINTON, JAMES. *(1733–1812).* Continental officer in the American Revolution. Brother of GEORGE CLINTON.

James Clinton was born in what is now Orange County, New York. With his brother George, he served in the French and Indian War of 1754–63.

At the start of the American Revolution, he became a colonel in the New York militia and participated in the unsuccessful Quebec campaign with Richard Montgomery. Clinton became a brigadier general in 1776 and, with his brother, helped defend the Hudson River, but was driven from Fort Clinton by British forces.

In 1779, Clinton led a column in the Sullivan-Clinton Campaign against the Iroquois under JOSEPH BRANT and CORNPLANTER. Heading out of Albany along the Mohawk Valley, his men damned up Otsego Lake at Cooperstown to release the water for transport down the Susquehanna River, joining up with General JOHN SULLIVAN at Tioga on the New York–Pennsylvania border. The combined force then marched over Iroquois lands, destroying houses and crops.

In 1781, Clinton commanded a brigade at Yorktown. His brother George and his son DeWitt Clinton both served as governors of New York State. (See also BRANT, JOSEPH.)

CLOUDMAN (Cloud Man, Mahpiyawicasta, Marpiya Wicasta, "man of the sky"). *Mdewakanton Sioux. (ca. 1790–1862).* Friend to whites; Christian convert. Brother of PAUL MAZAKUTEMANI; cousin of LITTLE CROW; great-grandfather of CHARLES EASTMAN.

Cloudman, born near present-day Mendota, Minnesota, was a Mdewakanton Santee by birth, but married a Sisseton woman and became a subchief of that tribe. In 1830, he founded the Lake Calhoun village at present-day Minneapolis, which was later moved to the south side of the Minnesota River after war with the Chippewas in 1839.

Cloudman became a friend to the white settlers and encouraged agriculture and Christianity among his people. With his brother Paul Mazakutemani (Little Paul) and with the help of the missionary STEPHEN RIGGS, he founded the Hazelwood Republic, a constitutional government of Christian Indians, in 1854. During the Minnesota Uprising of 1862–63 under his cousin Little Crow, Cloudman advocated peace and formed a soldiers' lodge with Mazakutemani, AKIPA, MAZOMANI, and GABRIEL RENVILLE to protect themselves and their white friends from the militant faction. (See also LITTLE CROW.)

CLUM, JOHN P. *(1851–1932).* Indian agent.

John P. Clum, born near Claverack, New York, attended Rutgers University in New Jersey for one year, then entered the Signal Service and started a weather station in Santa Fe, New Mexico, in 1871.

With the backing of the Dutch Reformed church, the 23-year-old Clum received an appointment under President ULYSSES S. GRANT's Peace Policy as agent to the Apaches on the San Carlos Reservation in Arizona. He instituted a program that brought the Indians under civilian rather than military control and originated the use of Indian police to enforce law and order.

Clum's policies were so successful that, over the next few years, thousands of Apaches were moved to his jurisdiction from other Arizona reservations: about 1,500 Aravaipas and Pinals from Camp Grant in 1873; about 1,400 Yavapais and other bands from Camp Verde in 1875; about 1,800 White Mountain Apaches from Fort Apache later in 1875; and about 325 Chiricahuas, formerly under agent THOMAS J. JEFFORDS, from the Chiricahua Reservation in 1876. Clum also traveled to the Ojo Caliente (Warm Springs) Reservation in New Mexico in 1877, where he succeeded in arresting GERONIMO and leading him, VICTORIO, and some 450 others to San Carlos.

Clum then proposed to the War Department that he could supervise all the Indians in the Arizona Territory without the help of the army as long as he employed a sufficient number of Indian police, but his offer was rejected.

With continuing military-civil conflict, Clum left the Indian Bureau in July 1877. He went on to establish a newspaper, *The Tombstone Epitaph*, then, after six years, joined the Post Office Department, serving in Texas, Alaska, and New York. (See also GERONIMO; VICTORIO.)

CLYMAN, JAMES (Jim Clyman). *(1792–1881).* Trader; trapper; soldier.

Jim Clyman was born in western Virginia, where his family were tenant farmers on lands owned by GEORGE WASHINGTON. In 1811, he moved with his family to newly opened lands in the northern Ohio Valley. During the War of 1812, he served as a scout, warning outlying settlements of attacks by British-allied Indians.

With the end of hostilities in 1815, Clyman headed west, first settling in the Indiana territory and then in Illinois. He worked as a surveyor and explored the Sangamon River region, near present-day Springfield and Decatur, Illinois.

Clyman traveled to St. Louis in 1823, where he joined WILLIAM HENRY ASHLEY's fur-trading expedition to the upper Missouri tribes. Ashley's 1823 expedition suffered heavy losses in an attack by Arikaras, with 15 killed. Clyman accompanied Colonel HENRY LEAVENWORTH's subsequent punitive military expedition against the tribe.

That same year, Clyman joined Ashley's trappers and guides, JEDEDIAH SMITH, THOMAS FITZPATRICK, and WILLIAM SUBLETTE, on a journey through the Black Hills to the Powder River region of Wyoming, Sioux country. They reached the fur-rich Green River country and confirmed a direct route to it through the South Pass of the Rockies. Following an arduous winter in 1823–24, Clyman was separated from Smith's party, and traveled alone, on foot, over 600 miles to Fort Atkinson in what is now Nebraska.

In spring 1825, Clyman took part in the first trappers' rendezvous on the Green River in Wyoming west of South Pass. Over the next two years, along with William Sublette, he explored the territory around the Great Salt Lake in what is now Utah and Idaho.

Clyman returned to the Midwest in 1827, settling in Danville, Illinois, where he operated a store. He was a volunteer in the Illinois militia in the BLACK HAWK War of 1832. In 1834, with the opening of the Wisconsin Territory, he established a small settlement near present-day Milwaukee. He headed west again in 1844, traveling to Oregon and California by wagon train from Missouri, but returned to Wisconsin with a group led by frontiersman Caleb Greenwood the following year. Three years later, in 1848, Clyman led a wagon train from Wisconsin to California, and later married and settled permanently in the Napa Valley of California.

Clyman's memoirs of his days as a trapper in the Rockies, with numerous observations on Indian peoples, were later edited and published by Clyman's biographer, Charles L. Camp, in *James Clyman, American Frontiersman, 1792–1881* (1928).

COACOOCHEE. See WILD CAT.

COCHISE ("hardwood"). *Chiricahua Apache.* *(ca. 1812–1874).* Leader in the Apache Wars of the 1870s. Son-in-law of MANGAS COLORADAS; father of TAZA and NAICHE.

In February 1861, a rancher reported an Apache raid to the garrison at Fort Buchanan, Arizona, falsely accusing Cochise of having abducted his child—who later became an army scout under the name MICKEY FREE—and having stolen cattle. A lieutenant at the post, GEORGE BASCOM, organized a force of about 50 men and rode to Apache Pass along the Southern Overland (Butterfield) Trail, the heart of Chiricahua country. Bascom set up base at a mail station and sent word to Cochise requesting a meeting. Cochise came under a flag of truce along with members of his family, including his son Naiche. Bascom accused Cochise of the earlier raid. The chief proclaimed innocence, but Bascom told him he was under arrest. Cochise was wounded in the resulting fight, but managed to slash through the tent with a knife and escape. One Apache was killed, and Bascom took the others hostage. In subsequent raids, Cochise took a number of whites hostage. When negotiations broke down, both sides executed prisoners.

The Bascom Affair was the beginning of the Apache Wars. Cochise's followers were joined by Mimbrenos under his father-in-law Mangas Coloradas as well as White Mountain (Coyotero) Apaches. Apache raids threatened to drive both Mexican and Anglo-Americans from Arizona, especially during the early Civil War years, when troops had abandoned their western posts to fight in the East.

In July 1862, to fill the vacuum, some 3,000 California volunteers were sent in under Colonel JAMES H. CARLETON. Cochise and Mangas Coloradas decided to lay a trap for the new troops. They set up breastworks at Apache Pass, and, with about 500 men, held off the larger force until Carleton brought in howitzers. The Apaches then retreated, and Cochise took the wounded Mangas Coloradas to Mexico, where he forced a surgeon to care for his father-in-law.

When Mangas Coloradas was captured and killed the following year by Carleton's men, Cochise became the principal chief of the Apache militants. For 10 years, from his hiding place in the Dragoon Mountains of southern Arizona, known as the Stronghold, the embittered chief led his warriors in raids on white travelers along the Butterfield Trail and on settlements. He was a master at hit-and-run tactics and was feared throughout the region.

In June 1871, Colonel GEORGE CROOK assumed command of the army's Department of Arizona. He established a company of highly effective Indian scouts and managed to track down Cochise and negotiate peace. On learning that his band was to be placed on a reservation at Fort Tularosa, New Mexico, under the system established by VINCENT COLYER, Cochise renounced the agreement.

General OLIVER HOWARD acted as President ULYSSES S. GRANT's peace envoy, as Colyer had done the year before. Howard arranged a meeting with Cochise in fall 1872 through the intercession of the scout THOMAS J. JEFFORDS, who was a close friend of Cochise. After 11 days of negotiations, the general granted Cochise's request to live on a reservation along Apache Pass, with Jeffords as the agent. Cochise, who had promised Howard to keep order along the pass, proved good for his word, his people peaceful until his death in 1874. His elder son, Taza, who succeeded him as chief, attempted to maintain the agreement. On Taza's death, however, the younger son, Naiche, joined forces with the militant GERONIMO. With increasing Apache raids, the Chiricahua Reservation was dissolved in 1876. In ensuing years, VICTORIO and Geronimo would become the most feared chiefs in the Southwest.

COCKENOE ("interpreter"). *Montauk. (d. 1699).* Interpreter; translator.

Cockenoe, born on present-day Long Island, New York, was taken captive by the British when he paid a visit to Massachusetts during the Pequot War of 1636–37. He worked as a servant in the home of Richard Collicot of Dorcester, a sergeant in the army, until JOHN ELIOT heard about Cockenoe's fluency in English and arranged for his help as a tutor. Cockenoe interpreted for Eliot, taught him Algonquian words, and helped him translate the Bible into Algonquian.

CODY, WILLIAM FREDERICK (Buffalo Bill). *(1846–1917).* Army scout; soldier; showman.

Born near Davenport, Iowa, William Cody moved with his family to Salt Creek Valley near Fort Leavenworth, Kansas, in 1854. Cody's father became active in anti-slavery politics in Kansas, and, in 1857, died as a result of wounds he received in a politically motivated attack. Cody then traveled west to Colorado.

After an unsuccessful attempt at prospecting, Cody was a rider for Majors and Russell's Pony Express in 1860. He returned to Kansas in 1861, and in the Civil

"Buffalo Bill" Cody. Spotted Tail is to the right of Cody. *Courtesy of Library of Congress.*

War was active with paramilitary "jayhawkers," who stole horses from Confederate sympathizers for use by the Union. In 1863, he began his career as a military scout with the 9th Kansas Cavalry and guided Kansas cavalry units in engagements with Confederate-allied Kiowas and Comanches. He also led Union forces in campaigns in Tennessee and Missouri.

For about two years, starting in 1866, Cody hunted buffalo under contract to supply meat to workers building the Union Pacific Railroad on the Great Plains. He was dubbed Buffalo Bill by fellow hunters.

In 1868, Cody returned to military service as chief of scouts for General PHILIP H. SHERIDAN's 5th U.S. Cavalry in his campaign against militant Southern Plains bands. On July 11, 1869, along with FRANK NORTH's Pawnee scouts, Cody led cavalry battalions under General EUGENE A. CARR to the Cheyenne encampment at Summit Springs, near Atwood, Colorado. In the ensuing battle, Cheyenne leader TALL BULL was killed, reportedly by either Cody or North.

About this time, writer Edward Zane Carroll Judson, writing under the name Ned Buntline, began producing "dime novels" that glorified Cody's exploits and popularized him as Buffalo Bill, a living legend of the West. Buntline eventually made Cody the hero of more than 1,700 novels. In addition, Prentiss Ingraham be-

came Cody's ghostwriter, producing novels and an 1881 biography of Cody for younger readers. In 1872, Buntline's play, *The Scouts of the Plains*, based on his first novel about Cody, was produced in Chicago, with Cody portraying himself, launching his career as an entertainer.

For the next 11 years, Cody toured with the show throughout the major cities of the East, with fellow scouts, such as JAMES "WILD BILL" HICKOK, also appearing on stage. In between theatrical engagements, Cody returned to the Great Plains, serving as a hunting guide to such notables as Russia's Grand Duke Alexis in January 1872, and as scout for the military.

Serving with the 5th U.S. Cavalry in the War for the Black Hills of 1876–77, under the command of Colonel WESLEY MERRITT, Cody was chief scout at the Battle of War Bonnet Creek in northwestern Nebraska, near the Wyoming border. On July 17, 1876, Merritt's cavalry units intercepted Cheyenne war parties headed for the Powder River region to join the victorious Sioux warriors who had defeated Colonel GEORGE ARMSTRONG CUSTER at the Little Bighorn less than one month earlier. During the confrontation, Cody reportedly killed Cheyenne leader YELLOW HAIR (Yellow Hand) in a gun duel and then scalped him. This event became the subject of a new play, *The Red Right*

Hand, or Buffalo Bill's First Scalp for Custer, in which Cody portrayed himself in productions.

In 1883, as part of the Fourth of July celebration in North Platte, Nebraska, Cody staged his first Wild West Show. Subsequent productions included reenactments of Indian battles, including the Battle of Summit Springs and Cody's fight with Yellow Hair. Indian notables were a regular feature of the show. The Sioux chief SITTING BULL was a featured attraction in an 1885 tour of eastern cities; the Metis leader GABRIEL DUMONT joined the show in 1886.

In December 1890, Cody was sent by General NELSON A. MILES to meet with Sitting Bull at the Standing Rock Reservation in North Dakota to help quell the Sioux uprising inspired by the Ghost Dance religious movement. Yet Sioux agent JAMES McLAUGHLIN refused Cody access to the chief. Sitting Bull was killed a few days later in a skirmish with Indian police attempting to arrest him.

During the 1890s, Cody, his wife Frederici, whom he had married in 1866, and his family settled on a large tract of land granted him by the state of Wyoming in the Bighorn Basin region, near the present site of the city of Cody. He continued to produce and appear in his Wild West shows in the United States and Europe, each season employing scores of Indians to reenact their warrior days in full battle dress. In 1908, Cody's production merged with that of Gordon William Lillie (Pawnee Bill); and, in 1913, with the Sells-Floto Circus. Cody made his final appearance in 1916. He died in Denver the next year and was buried at the top of nearby Lookout Mountain.

COHOE (William Cohoe; Nonicas, Broken Leg, Lame Man; Mohe, "elk"; Maspera Mohe, "water elk"). *Southern Cheyenne. (1854–1924).* Warrior; artist.

Born in Colorado, Cohoe fought in the Red River War of 1774–75 along with the Comanches under QUANAH PARKER and the Kiowas under LONE WOLF, then surrendered at the Cheyenne Agency, Indian Territory, in 1875. He was convicted along with BEAR'S HEART for the killing of whites, and sent to prison at Fort Marion near St. Augustine, Florida.

Encouraged by Lieutenant RICHARD HENRY PRATT, Cohoe became known for his sketchbook drawings and paintings of Plains Indian life along with Bear's Heart, HOWLING WOLF, and ZOTOM, the so-called Florida Boys. In 1878, Cohoe attended Hampton Institute in Virginia and, in 1879, Carlisle Indian School, founded by Pratt.

Cohoe returned to the Indian Territory in 1880 and worked at various jobs. After having received a land allotment the following year, he took up farming. With little success or fulfillment in spite of acculturation, he

rediscovered traditional Cheyenne ways, joining the Native American Church and becoming chief of the War Dancers' Society.

COLBERT, GEORGE. *Mixed Chickasaw.* *(1764–1839).* Ally of Americans in the War of 1812; farmer; businessman. Brother of WILLIAM, LEVI, and PITTMAN COLBERT.

George Colbert fought with U.S. forces against the British in the War of 1812. He lived near present-day Tupelo, Mississippi, where he ran a large farm with about 150 slaves, plus a ferry business. In 1837, he helped pay the expenses of relocation to the Indian Territory of 300 Chickasaws in addition to his own family and servants.

COLBERT, LEVI (Itawamba). *Mixed Chickasaw.* *(d. 1834).* Sponsor of missionaries; chairman of tribal council. Brother of WILLIAM, GEORGE, and PITTMAN COLBERT.

In the 1820s, Levi Colbert encouraged Presbyterian missionaries to settle in Chickasaw country and build the Charity Hall mission school near Cotton Gin Port, Mississippi, so that his people would be better equipped to deal with the pressures of white expansion. He was famous for his hospitality to visitors in his Mississippi homeland. He became unofficial chairman of the Chickasaw Board, or Council, just before his death.

COLBERT, PITTMAN (James Colbert). *Mixed Chickasaw. (fl. 1830s–40s).* Farmer; businessman. Brother of WILLIAM, GEORGE, and LEVI COLBERT.

Pittman, the youngest of six Colbert brothers, was educated in bookkeeping and surveying. Like his brothers, he was a successful businessman and an important tribal leader. During the tribe's removal to the Indian Territory, he took it upon himself to pay the expenses of 50 Chickasaw families. He established a large cotton plantation in the West. During the 1840s, he helped negotiate the separation of the Chickasaw and Choctaw tribal governments, as well as land grants to his people.

COLBERT, WILLIAM (General Colbert). *Mixed Chickasaw. (d. ca. 1835).* War chief; ally of Americans. Brother of GEORGE, LEVI, and PITTMAN COLBERT.

James Logan Colbert, a Scottish trader, settled in Chickasaw country in what is now Mississippi and took three Chickasaw wives by whom he had six sons: William, George, Levi, Samuel, Joseph, and Pittman. William was the oldest. The Colbert brothers were the most powerful Chickasaw leaders of their time.

William Colbert led Chickasaw warriors in support of the rebels in the American Revolution. He also supported General ARTHUR ST. CLAIR against the allied tribes in LITTLE TURTLE's War of 1790–94, and argued against the Chickasaws joining TECUMSEH's Rebellion of 1809–11. In the War of 1812, he fought in the regular infantry for nine months on the side of the Americans, and, in the Creek War of 1813–14, he raised a force of Chickasaws to support General ANDREW JACKSON in Alabama and Florida. Colbert's warriors carried out numerous successful raids against the Creek Red Sticks, killing many and taking 85 prisoners to Montgomery, Alabama.

In 1816, Colbert headed a Chickasaw delegation to Washington, D.C., where he signed several treaties ceding Chickasaw lands. He was known to whites as "General" Colbert.

COLDEN, CADWALLADER. *(1688–1776).* Historian; colonial official.

Scotch-Irish Cadwallader Colden emigrated in 1710 from Ireland to Philadelphia, where he practiced medicine. He moved to New York in 1718, becoming surveyor-general of the colony and a member of the governor's council within three years. He was instrumental in the formulation of the colonial government's policy toward the Indians and was one of the earliest political leaders to advocate protecting the Indians from white exploitation by removing them to their own reservations. From 1761 until his death, he served as New York's lieutenant governor. Colden wrote an early study of the Iroquois, *History of the Five Nations* (1727), which discussed their history and culture, as well as their role in the military balance between England and France and in the colonial economy with regard to the flourishing fur trade.

COLLOT, VICTOR. *(ca. 1751–1805).* Artist; cartographer; soldier.

In the late 1700s, after its earlier defeat in the French and Indian Wars ending in 1763, France continued to harbor hopes of recovering its holdings and influence in North America. In 1796, Victor Collot was sent on a mission along with Joseph Warin, another French officer, to gain information about territory along the Ohio and Mississippi rivers. The spies mapped rivers, settlements, and fortifications, and Collot also sketched Indian peoples, such as the Shawnees. Warin died during their travels from wounds inflicted during an Indian attack. Collot, who later became governor of Guadeloupe, died in Paris. Some of his sketches were reproduced in his *Voyage dans l'Amerique* (1836).

COLORADO. See COLOROW.

COLOROW **(Colorado, "the red"; Toop'weets, "rock").** *Ute-Apache. (ca. 1810–1888).* Leader in the Ute War of 1879.

Colorow's mother was a Jicarilla Apache captured by the Comanches; Colorow was in turn captured by the Mouache Utes and adopted into the tribe. He established his reputation as a warrior while young and became known for the strategy of attacking enemies from high ground.

After the 1868 treaty signed by OURAY in Washington, D.C., Colorow and his band lived on a small temporary reservation outside Denver, Colorado. In 1875, after the reservation had been closed, he and his followers settled on the reservation at White River along with Northern Ute bands under NICAAGAT and QUINKENT. Traditional hunters, the Utes had difficulty in adopting to reservation life and farming.

In 1878, the Indian agent NATHAN MEEKER deposed Colorow, whom he considered too militant, and appointed his rival Sanovik as chief of his band, further adding to ill-feelings.

The next year, after a confrontation with the medicine man CANALLA, Meeker called in troops under Major THOMAS T. THORNBURGH. Colorow led one of the war parties that attacked them in the Battle of Milk Creek in September 1879.

Through Ouray's efforts, the war chiefs Colorow and Nicaagat were pardoned for their roles in the uprising because they had been engaged in what was deemed a fair fight. Quinkent, who was present at the agency when Meeker and his employees were killed, received a jail sentence.

In 1881, Colorow and about 50 of his warriors again threatened to revolt rather than move from White River to the Uintah Reservation in Utah. Colonel RANALD S. MACKENZIE ordered four companies of cavalry to meet the Utes in battle formation; the Utes backed down without violence and were soon relocated.

Colorow eventually left Uintah to settle on the Southern Ute Reservation in the vicinity of Ignacio, Colorado. During a hunting trip off the reservation, he and some of his men were again involved in a confrontation with whites. Sheriff Jim Kendall requested help, and the Colorado National Guard and cowboy volunteers chased the Utes back toward the reservation. In the one skirmish of the so-called Ute War of 1887, two whites were killed and two wounded, and about seven Utes were killed. It is thought that Colorow received a wound in the fight and never recovered; he died the following year. (See also OURAY.)

COLTER, JOHN. *(ca. 1775–1813).* Trader; trapper; explorer; captive.

John Colter was born at Staunton, Virginia, and, in 1803, he joined the LEWIS and CLARK Expedition as a private at its staging camp on the Mississippi River in Illinois. He stayed with the expedition until midway into its return trip from the Pacific in 1806, whereupon he joined two trappers heading up the Missouri.

On his way to St. Louis in 1807, Colter encountered an expedition under MANUEL LISA, who hired Colter as a guide to the mouth of the Bighorn on the Yellowstone in what is now Montana. Lisa established a fort as a base of his trapping operation and sent Colter on a trading mission to the Crow Indians.

Colter's exact route on this solo journey is unknown; he traveled in what is now Wyoming, Montana, and Idaho, returning to the trading post in 1808. His description of an area of intense thermal activity may have been the geyser region of what later became Yellowstone Park.

In autumn 1808, Colter and a trapping companion were attacked by some 500 Blackfeet in central Wyoming. His friend was killed, and Colter was stripped naked and forced to outrun a party of braves, one of whom he killed. Colter eluded the Blackfeet and reached Lisa's fort on the Yellowstone.

In 1810, during an expedition out of Fort Mandan (North Dakota) to the Three Forks region of the Missouri (Montana), with ANTOINE PIERRE MENARD, ANDREW HENRY, and the part-Pawnee GEORGE DROUILLARD, Colter had another near-escape from the Blackfeet and decided to give up trapping. He returned to St. Louis in a solo canoe journey down the Missouri. He conferred with WILLIAM CLARK and provided valuable additions to Clark's maps. Having kept no journal or charts, Colter received little credit for his explorations. The geysers and hot springs he described became known derisively as "Colter's Hell."

COLUMBUS, CHRISTOPHER. *(1451–1506).* Explorer.

Christopher Columbus was born in Genoa, Italy, to a family of weavers and became a seaman in the Mediterranean during the 1470s. He came to Lisbon, Portugal, in 1476, where he studied navigation with his cartographer brother, Bartolomeo. He found work as a sugar buyer in the Portuguese-held islands off Africa, the Azores, Madeira, and Cape Verde, and he visited the west coast of Africa, probably near Ghana, in 1483.

About this time, Columbus devised a plan for reaching the coast of Asia by sailing west across the Atlantic. After numerous appeals, he finally received backing for his expedition from the Spanish court of Ferdinand and Isabella.

In August 1492, Columbus sailed west from Cape de Palos on the coast of Spain with a company of 90 aboard three ships, the *Santa Maria*, commanded by himself; the *Pinta*, commanded by Martin Pinzon; and the *Nina*, under Vicente Yanez Pinzon. After a stopover on the Canary Islands, he sailed due west, then southwest.

On October 12, 1492, Columbus reached the Bahama Islands, landing at an island called Guanahani by the native Arawaks. It was originally thought that the expedition reached Watling Island (now San Salvador), but some scholars now believe he and his men first touched soil on Samana Cay, 65 miles to the southeast. Columbus continued on to discover Cuba, and Hispaniola (now Haiti and the Dominican Republic), on which he left a number of his men to form a colony.

When the *Santa Maria* was wrecked off the coast of Hispaniola, the expedition received help from the Arawaks, led by Chief Guacanagari, who also shared their food and knowledge with the explorers. Columbus triumphantly returned to Spain, believing he had reached the outlying islands of Japan and China. It was Columbus who first dubbed the natives he encountered "Indians."

Columbus's second voyage across the Atlantic began in October 1493, when he left Cadiz, Spain, with 17 ships and 1,200 men and explored the Leewards Islands and Puerto Rico, then returned to Hispaniola. His original settlement had been wiped out by the Arawaks, who had rebelled after being forced by the Spanish to prospect for gold. Columbus established a second colony on the Caribbean island, then explored the southern coast of Cuba and Jamaica. On his return to Spain in 1496, he brought with him a number of Arawaks from Hispaniola, where they remained as slaves, beginning the practice of Spanish slaving raids in the Americas.

Columbus's third voyage to the Americas left Spain in May 1498, during which he explored Trinidad and the coast of Venezuela. On a stopover at the Hispaniola colony, he was arrested by Spanish authorities for his mismanagement and alleged cruelty to the native population. He was returned to Spain in chains, but was subsequently exonerated by his royal sponsors.

Columbus's fourth and final voyage across the Atlantic, in 1502, brought him to the coast of Central America. He was marooned in Jamaica and after having been rescued, returned to Spain, where he died in relative obscurity in 1506.

Columbus believed he had reached the coast of China and Japan, but other explorers and geographers of his time soon concluded that he had in fact "discovered" what came to be called the New World. The resulting exploration and settlement of the Americas led to an accelerating displacement and cultural dispossession of native peoples.

COLYER, VINCENT. *(1825–1888).* Reformer; Indian commissioner; painter.

Vincent Colyer was born in Bloomington, New York, and, in 1844–48, studied art in New York City. In the

Civil War, which interrupted his career as a crayon portraitist, he raised and commanded a black regiment.

After the war, Colyer became involved in Indian as well as black rights and became secretary of PETER COOPER's United States Indian Commission, a private organization formed in 1868. As such, he visited 31 western tribes. In 1869, he was appointed to the congressionally created Board of Indian Commissioners.

In 1871, following the Camp Grant Massacre of ESKIMINZIN's band, Colyer was sent to the Southwest by President ULYSSES S. GRANT to work for peace among the Chiricahua Apaches under COCHISE and help establish a reservation system.

Colyer appeared before Congress on numerous occasions to report on his investigations and also gave lectures sponsored by reform organizations. At his home in Darien, Connecticut, Colyer produced watercolors of Indian scenes from sketches he made during his travels. (See also COCHISE.)

COMCOMLY. *Chinook. (ca. 1765–1830).* Friend to explorers and traders.

In November 1805, Comcomly was one of the Chinook leaders who welcomed LEWIS and CLARK to his homeland, receiving a medal and a flag. In 1811, he provided help to JOHN JACOB ASTOR's fur traders from the shipwrecked *Tonquin*. That same year, he also proved friendly to the Overland Astorians who founded the Astoria trading post at the mouth of the Columbia, offering his daughter in marriage to one of the party's leaders, Duncan M'Dougal.

With Americans and British competing for the region, Comcomly played them off against each other for the best interests of his tribe. In 1812, he offered the Americans military support, but when they sold the post to the British the next year, he maintained good relations with the new owners.

On trips to Vancouver for trade or negotiations, Comcomly was accompanied by a huge retinue of warriors and about 300 slaves, some of whom placed beaver and otter skins over the path as he walked. He died in a smallpox epidemic in 1830. After the traditional Chinook canoe burial, a trader took Comcomly's head and sold it in Edinburgh, Scotland.

CONNOR, PATRICK EDWARD. *(1820–1891).* Army officer in the Bear River Campaign of 1863, and the Powder River Expedition of 1865.

An Irish immigrant, Patrick E. Connor enlisted in the U.S. army at the age of 18, and fought in Florida in the Second Seminole War of 1835–42. In 1844, he left the service and started a mercantile business in New York.

Connor moved his operation to Texas just before the outbreak of the Mexican War of 1846–48. Commissioned a captain, he saw action under General Albert S. Johnston.

Connor then took his business to California. In 1861, with the onset of the Civil War, he was commissioned a colonel of a regiment of California volunteer infantry and given command of fortifications in what is now Utah and northern Nevada. In 1862, he established Fort Douglas in the Wasatch Mountains near Salt Lake City, Utah, as well as Fort Ruby in Nevada.

Connor's command was responsible for protecting the telegraph lines and the Overland Mail Company's stagecoach route across Nevada and Utah, the major communication links between California and the East. He was also to maintain a military presence to keep hostile Mormon factions from inciting the Indians against non-Mormon settlers passing through the area.

Because of continuing Indian raids, Connor embarked on the Bear River Campaign against BEAR HUNTER's Shoshones in January 1863, leading his men on a 140-mile winter march. In the Battle of Bear River of January 27, his soldiers killed more than 200 Shoshones, including Bear Hunter, and took more than 150 women and children prisoner. Connor lost 21 men, with 46 wounded.

In July 1865, Connor was brevetted a brigadier general and placed in command of 2,600 men taking part in the Powder River Expedition. He established Fort Connor, 180 miles northwest of Fort Laramie, present-day Wyoming; it was renamed Fort Reno the following November. The campaign, including the scout JAMES BRIDGER, as well as FRANK NORTH and his Pawnee Indian scouts, was intended to end the Indian raids on travelers along the Oregon and BOZEMAN trails. A combination of bad weather, mutinous troops, and lack of logistical coordination caused the Powder River Expedition to fail in its main objective of subduing the Sioux under RED CLOUD and their Northern Cheyenne and Northern Arapaho allies. The only major engagement of the campaign occurred on August 29, 1865, when Connor's forces attacked BLACK BEAR's Arapahos, who, previous to this engagement, had been one of the peaceful bands. In the Battle of Tongue River, Wyoming, Connor's forces destroyed the village, then were caught in a counterattack. Although outnumbered, his troops managed a successful retreat with a minimum of casualties, aided by the deployment of field howitzers.

Connor left the military in 1866. Developing his mining interests in Utah, he became the most prominent non-Mormon in the territory. (See also BEAR HUNTER; BLACK BEAR; RED CLOUD.)

CONQUERING BEAR (**Whirling Bear, Mahtoiowa**). *Brule Sioux. (d. 1854).* Chief killed in the Grattan Fight of 1854.

Conquering Bear was the chief of a Brule band living along the Oregon Trail in what is now northern Wyoming and southern Montana. In 1851, he participated in the signing of the Fort Laramie Treaty, designed to keep peace along the Oregon Trail. But violence broke out three years later, in an incident known as the Grattan Affair or Grattan Fight.

In August 1854, a Mormon party was traveling along the North Platte River in Wyoming, when one of their cows wandered into a Brule camp along the trail. A Mormon chased after it, sighted the Indians, and fled. He reported to the garrison at Fort Laramie that the Indians had stolen his livestock. In the meantime, a Miniconjou Sioux, High Forehead, who was visiting relatives, slaughtered the cow. Conquering Bear traveled to the post to make restitution, but the commanding officer, Lieutenant Hugh Fleming, insisted on the arrest of High Forehead. He gave the assignment to Lieutenant JOHN GRATTAN, fresh out of West Point.

On August 19, Grattan set out for the Brule camp with the interpreter Lucien Auguste and 29 infantrymen, plus two cannon. Conquering Bear again tried to appease the army, claiming he had no authority over the visiting Miniconjou. But Grattan gave the command to seize High Forehead. Even after a shot was fired and one Indian fell, Conquering Bear still restrained his men. Grattan ordered howitzer fire, and Conquering Bear fell to the ground, mortally wounded in the first volley. His warriors, now led by Little Thunder, counterattacked, killing Grattan and wiping out the detachment. Only one wounded soldier escaped to Fort Laramie. SPOTTED TAIL and other Brule chiefs kept their warriors from attacking the post, hoping to avoid further escalation.

One year later, however, on September 3, 1855, a force of 600 soldiers under General WILLIAM S. HARNEY out of Fort Leavenworth, Kansas, rode into Sioux territory and attacked a Brule camp at Blue Water Creek (Ash Hollow), killing about 80 of the scattering Sioux and wounding five more.

War had come to the Northern Plains. A young Oglala-Brule warrior who had witnessed Conquering Bear's death would become known to whites as CRAZY HORSE.

COOK, JAMES. *(1728–1779). Explorer.*

Although the Englishman James Cook came from a farming family, he went to sea at an early age, sailing on the coal ships from London to North Sea ports. He was already an experienced seaman on entering the Royal Navy in 1755. He saw action against the French in the Seven Years War (known as the French and Indian War of 1754–63 in North America), during which he charted the coasts of the St. Lawrence River region in 1754–60. In 1763–66, he explored and charted Newfoundland and Labrador, his surveys of which later proved valuable for Britain's successful strategy in French Canada.

By 1768, Cook's navigational and maritime skills came to the attention of both the Royal Navy and Britain's Royal society. That year, he was commissioned a lieutenant in the navy and sent on a charting expedition to the Pacific, during which he charted the coast of New Zealand and circumnavigated the globe, returning to England in 1771. He led a second Pacific expedition in 1772–74 that circumnavigated the Antarctic continent.

In 1776, Cook, now a captain, embarked on his third and final voyage of discovery, into the Pacific. His mission was to search the west coast of the North American continent for a maritime passage to the Atlantic, the fabled Northwest Passage. With two ships, the *Resolution*, and the *Discovery*, and a crew of 191 men, Cook reached Nootka Sound on Vancouver Island off the coast of what is now British Columbia in March 1778 after a year in the Pacific. The Nootka Sound Indians they met there eagerly traded the British explorers sea otter pelts for iron and brass tools. During the stopover, members of Cook's expedition recorded the life and customs of the native peoples. Cook and his ships explored the west coast of North America from March until August 1778, traveling from Oregon as far north as Alaska and the Bering Sea, finally turned back by pack ice.

Cook then headed south to winter in the newly rediscovered Sandwich Islands, present-day Hawaii. In early 1779, he was killed by Hawaiian natives in a dispute over the theft of a small boat. His crew continued back to England, stopping at ports in China, where they sold the sea otter pelts they obtained from the Nootka Indians at a fantastic profit. Soon after the expedition's return to England, reports of the profits from the fur trade sparked great commercial interest in the Northwest Coast Indians.

COOPER, JAMES FENIMORE. *(1789–1851).* Writer.

James Fenimore Cooper was born in Burlington, New Jersey, and, when one year old, moved with his family to Lake Otsego at the headwaters of the Susquehanna River in New York. His father, William Cooper, had acquired a land patent for this property five years before and there founded Cooperstown, New York. James Fenimore Cooper attended Yale in 1803–05, then served in the navy as a midshipman in 1808–1811. On ending his service, he married Susan DeLancey. Over the next years, the Coopers lived alternately in Cooperstown and Westchester County and in New York City, and, 1826–1833, they traveled in Europe.

Cooper wrote his first novel in 1820. In his most famous works, collectively known as the *Leatherstocking*

James Fenimore Cooper. *Courtesy of Library of Congress.*

Tales, he related the frontier experience through fiction, from the period of the French and Indian Wars in the mid-1700s to the settlement of the prairies in the early 1800s. The *Leatherstocking Tales* include, in the chronological sequence of historical events: *The Deerslayer* (1841), *The Last of the Mohicans* (1826), *The Pathfinder* (1840), *The Pioneers* (1823), and *The Prairie* (1827). Their central character is the frontiersman Natty Bumppo, known as Leatherstocking, living between the cultures of the Indian and the white. The Indians described include Algonquians and Iroquois, with novels of the prairies depicting also Pawnees and Sioux.

Cooper was the first major American author to use the frontier as the setting for historical fiction and to sympathetically portray the plight of Native Americans in the face of Western civilization. He drew on the earlier writings of the Moravian missionary to the Delawares JOHN HECKEWELDER for his ideal image of the Indian as the Noble Savage, which was in opposition to the prevalent view at the time of Indians as savages without redeeming qualities.

COOPER, PETER. *(1791–1883).* Reformer; philanthropist.

Peter Cooper, born in New York City, worked in various manufacturing jobs for his father when young, then bought a glue factory, leading to a successful career in business. He became an important figure in the iron industry, the railroads, and the use of the telegraph. He

was also the creator of several industrial inventions. In 1859, he founded Cooper Union in New York City for the advancement of science and art.

Before the Civil War, Cooper was active in the anti-slavery movement and promoted his idea that practical Christianity would cure social injustice. Influenced by LYDIA MARIA CHILD's *An Appeal for the Indians* of 1868, he became active in the Indian reform movement. That year, he helped organize the United States Indian Commission, dedicated to the protection and elevation of the Indians and the ending of frontier warfare. WILLIAM EARL DODGE and the Congregational clergyman Henry Ward Beecher were members. JOHN BEESON and VINCENT COLYER also came to be involved. Cooper's efforts helped lead to a subsequent governmental organization, formed by Congress, the Board of Indian Commissioners, which was to oversee President ULYSSES S. GRANT's Peace Policy.

Cooper invited many of the Indian delegations visiting Washington, D.C., to come to New York as well. Among those to speak at Cooper Union were RED CLOUD in 1870 and LITTLE RAVEN in 1871. Cooper presented a gift of 17 horses to Red Cloud's delegation. In 1875, he invited ALFRED MEACHAM and a delegation of Modocs and Klamaths to speak before his Indian Commission.

In 1878, the War Department sought to reassume its administration over Indian affairs from the Department of the Interior. Cooper and Beeson, who believed that only civilian control could maintain lasting peace with the Indians and lead to their social and economic elevation, opposed the intended transfer. They helped form the Ladies' National League to Protect the Indians, in order to campaign against military control.

COPWAY, GEORGE (Kahgegagebow, Kah-Ge-Ga-Gah-Bowh, "stands fast"). *Chippewa (Ojibway). (1818–1863).* Missionary; writer.

George Copway was born in Ontario, where he had a traditional Indian upbringing. He was converted to Methodism as a teenager and became involved in missionary work among his people along with JOHN SUNDAY, both of them influenced by PETER JONES.

When 20 years old, Copway attended Ebenezer Academy in Illinois, and worked on religious translations from English into Algonquian. He next lived in Toronto, where he married Elizabeth Howell, and then New York City, where he found employment with religious publishers. While pursuing a career as a writer, he also lectured extensively in both the United States and Europe.

Copway's works include: *The Life, History, and Travels of Kah-Ge-Ga-Gah-Bowh* (1847, reissued in 1850 as *Recollections of a Forest Life: The Traditional History and Characteristic Sketches of the Ojibway Nation*, then in 1858 as

Indian Life and Indian History); *The Ojibway Conquest* (1850); *The Organization of a New Indian Territory East of the Missouri River* (1850); and *Running Sketches of Men and Places in England, Germany, Belgium, and Scotland* (1851). He eventually returned to his people to work again as a missionary.

CORBITANT (Conbitant, Caunbitant).

Wampanoag. (fl. 1620s). Sachem (sagamore) of the Wampanoag Confederacy under MASSASOIT; enemy of Pilgrims.

Corbitant was leader of the Pocasset and Mattapoiset bands in the vicinity of present-day Tiverton, Rhode Island, and Fall River, Massachusetts. In 1621, when Massasoit, the Wampanoag grand sachem, signed a peace treaty with the Pilgrims, Corbitant sought to form a military alliance with the Narragansets against the colonists. He also plotted against the Wampanoags SQUANTO and HOBOMOK. He finally agreed to a treaty with the colonists that same year after a show of force by soldiers under MILES STANDISH. Corbitant was possibly the father of WETAMOO.

CORNPLANTER (Corn Plant, Gy-ant-wa-ka, Gayentwahga, Gyantwaia, Gaiant-wa'ka, Garganwahgah, Ki-on-twog-ky, Kayehtwanken, Kaiutwaku, "by what one plants," "the planter"; John O'Bail, John Abeel, John O'Beal, John Obeil).

Mixed Seneca. (ca. 1735–1836). Chief; ally of British in the American Revolution; later, ally of Americans. Half-brother of HANDSOME LAKE.

Cornplanter was born at the Seneca village of Conewaugus along the Genesee River in western New York sometime between 1732 and 1740. His father, John O'-Bail, a trader out of Albany, who bartered rum, guns, and other goods for furs, left his Seneca wife and son and became a farmer with a new family in Fort Plain, New York, in Mohawk country. Cornplanter grew up to be a war chief, participating in raids on the British during the French and Indian War of 1754–1763. Some reports have him present at General EDWARD BRADDOCK's defeat near Fort Duquesne (present-day Pittsburgh, Pennsylvania) in 1755.

In the American Revolution, however, Cornplanter sided with the British. He fought at the Battle of Oriskany along with the Mohawk JOSEPH BRANT in August 1777 against a militia force under NICHOLAS HERKIMER, as well as in numerous raids in New York and the Wyoming Valley of Pennsylvania. Probably in 1780, on hearing of the capture of his father by his ally Brant, Cornplanter traveled to O'Bail and identified himself. He gave his father the option of accompanying him to Seneca country or returning to Fort Plain. His father chose the latter. Cornplanter had Seneca scouts escort O'Bail and family safely back to the fort.

Cornplanter. Lithographic reproduction based on painting by F. Bartoli in Thomas McKenney's Indian Portrait Gallery. *Courtesy of Library of Congress.*

Cornplanter took part in Seneca treaty negotiations in 1784 at Fort Stanwix; in 1789, at Fort Harmer; in 1794, at Canandaigua; and, in 1797, at Big Tree; in which huge tracts of Seneca territory were ceded. In some of his policies, he was opposed by his Seneca peer RED JACKET. Cornplanter was on friendly terms with President GEORGE WASHINGTON, whom he visited in Philadelphia in 1790 to present grievances of his people. In 1792, after another meeting with Washington, Cornplanter acted as peace envoy along with Red Jacket and Joseph Brant to the allied Algonquian tribes under LITTLE TURTLE. In 1801–02, he visited President THOMAS JEFFERSON in Washington, D.C., to discuss Seneca land holdings.

Cornplanter encouraged acculturation to white customs among his people, especially the adoption of agricultural techniques. In 1796, he received a personal grant of 640 acres in Pennsylvania near the New York border for his services. By 1800, he had acquired a total of 1,300 acres, which he shared with his followers, the Cornplanter Senecas. Cornplanter's influence among his people led them to support the Americans in the War of 1812. Although he was too old to serve, his son Henry participated and was eventually commissioned a major.

Late in life, Cornplanter experienced a vision—perhaps influenced by his brother Handsome Lake's religious experiences—telling him to end all relations with whites, whereupon he destroyed the gifts he had received from white officials over the years. He died at Cornplantertown in 1836, perhaps more than 100 years old.

In the 1950s, the Senecas became involved in a dispute over the flooding of lands on the Allegany Reservation. They lost their case, however, and the Army Corps of Engineers built the huge Kinzua Dam and flooded 10,500 acres in 1960. Cornplanter's lands and his grave, a sacred site for the tribe, are now under the reservoir.

CORNSTALK (Wynepuechsika). *Shawnee.*
(ca. 1720–1777). Principal chief of Ohio Shawnees; leader against the British in Lord Dunmore's War of 1774.

Born in western Pennsylvania, Cornstalk moved with his parents to a new home on the Sciota River in Ohio in 1730. He became a principal chief of the Ohio Shawnees and a staunch ally of the French, and, in 1759, during the French and Indian War of 1754–63, he led attacks against the British. Cornstalk also threw his support behind PONTIAC in his rebellion of 1763 with raids on settlers along the West Virginia frontier. He became well known as a strategist and orator.

The Proclamation of 1763 and subsequent treaties with Indian tribes imposed an Indian boundary line from Lake Ontario to Florida. Yet Virginia's colonial governor, JOHN MURRAY, EARL OF DUNMORE, ignored the treaties and granted Shawnee territory west of the Appalachian divide to veterans of the French and Indian War who had served under him. As a result, the Shawnees regularly attacked white settlers.

In 1774, Dunmore sent a force of volunteers to quell the insurgents, but it was ambushed and routed along the Kentucky River. Dunmore then organized a 1,500-man militia. The Shawnees appealed to the Iroquois League for help without success, but Mingos under LOGAN, who had recently suffered an attack by white settlers, offered support. CATAHECASSA's Shawnee band and TARHE'S Wyandots also participated, as did some Delaware and Ottawa warriors.

Dunmore's Virginia militia crossed the Appalachians into Shawnee territory to meet the Indians in battle. ANDREW LEWIS led one column along the Kanawha Valley, and Dunmore led the northern column out of Pittsburgh along the Hocking River. Cornstalk and his warriors crossed the Ohio River, launching a surprise attack on Lewis's column at Point Pleasant (in present-day West Virginia) on October 10. After a day of bitter fighting, during which the Virginians suffered about 50 dead and 100 wounded, the Indians, who had lost even more men, finally withdrew. In the meantime, Dunmore led his force to the Shawnee town of Chillicothe, Ohio. Rather than mounting a hopeless defense,

Cornstalk agreed to Dunmore's terms in the treaty of Camp Charlotte.

Despite Cornstalk's efforts to keep the peace, Shawnee militants continued their attacks. In 1777, Cornstalk traveled to Point Pleasant under a flag of truce for a meeting with settlers. They betrayed his trust and took him hostage along with his son Elinipsico and others in his party. After a settler had been killed in a Shawnee raid, angry militiamen stormed the jail and murdered Cornstalk, his son, and a Shawnee by the name of Red Hawk. The killers were subsequently acquitted in a trial. Cornstalk's death contributed to the Shawnee's continuing hostility throughout the Indian uprising of 1790–94 under the Miami leader LITTLE TURTLE and the Shawnee BLUE JACKET.

CORONADO, FRANCISCO VASQUEZ DE.
(ca. 1510–1554). Explorer.

Francisco Vasquez de Coronado was born in the Spanish city of Salamanca and came to Mexico in 1535, as part of the staff of the first royal viceroy, Antonio de Mendoza. In 1538, Coronado was named governor of the northwestern Mexican province of Nueva Galicia.

In the late 1530s, tales of Indian cities rich in gold, lying to the north of Mexico, reached Spanish royal authorities. Among these stories were those of ALVAR NUNEZ CABEZA DE VACA and MARCOS DE NIZA, who told of the wealthy Seven Cities of Cibola.

In April 1540, Coronado left Compostela in northwestern Mexico as captain general in charge of an expedition of 300 Spanish conquistadores and 800 allied Indians. His mission was to locate the fabled cities and claim their treasures for Spain. The group headed north through what is now Sonora, Mexico, and southeast Arizona and reached the region of the present Arizona–New Mexico border, where they encountered the Zuni Indian settlements and took Hawikuh Pueblo by force.

Coronado's lieutenant Pedro de Tovar explored the Hopi pueblos. Another lieutenant, Hernando de Alvarado, reached the Acoma Pueblo and Rio Grande pueblos.

By 1541, Coronado's main party had crossed the Pecos River into what is now Texas and Oklahoma. On the Southern Plains, his men were among the first Europeans to observe the region's Indians engaged in hunting buffalo. In search of the Kingdom of Quivira described by Indian guides the TURK and Ysopete, they reached the homeland of probably the Wichita Indians of present-day Kansas, as well as the Pawnees. Quivira turned out to be a group of mud huts, not a city rich in gold, as their guides had claimed, and Coronado had the Turk executed.

After having spent the winter of 1541–42 on the Rio Grande, the expedition returned to Mexico. For returning empty-handed and for the summary execution of

Turk, Coronado faced an official government inquiry, but he was ultimately exonerated of any wrongdoing. The two years that Coronado spent exploring the American Southwest and Southern Plains provided the Spanish with knowledge of the geography and native peoples of a vast region north of Mexico. Coronado spent his remaining years as a minor colonial official in Mexico.

CORTE REAL, GASPAR (Gaspar Corte-Real or Cortereal). *(ca. 1450–ca. 1501).* Explorer.

Gaspar Corte Real was born in Portugal to a branch of the illustrious Da Costa family. His father was a military official in the Portuguese settlements in the Azors, where Corte Real was raised.

Reports of JOHN CABOT's discoveries on the coast of North America led Corte Real to seek sponsorship for his own voyage of discovery across the Atlantic. He received the support of King Manuel I of Portugal in 1500 for an expedition in search of the Northwest Passage to the Orient. In the spring of that year, he embarked from Lisbon and eventually reached what is thought to have been the coast of Greenland, where his expedition was turned back by pack ice. He may have also touched the North American coast during this voyage. (It is also theorized that this expedition was in fact Corte Real's second trans-Atlantic journey, the first in 1499.)

In 1501, still in search of a Northwest Passage to Asia, Corte Real undertook another voyage west to the coast of North America. He reached the southern coast of Labrador and subsequently landed on Newfoundland, where his party captured more than 500 Beothuk Indians and took them back to Portugal as slaves. One of the three ships of the expedition—Corte Real's own vessel—was lost at sea. Corte Real, his crew, and a number of the Indians chained in the ship's hold, were drowned.

In 1502, Gaspar's older brother, Miguel Corte Real, led an expedition to search for him. Miguel also disappeared somewhere off the coast of North America. There is evidence in the form of rock inscriptions indicating he may have reached the shores of New England, near the present coastal town of Dighton, Massachusetts.

COTA, MANUELITO. *Mixed Luiseno.* *(fl. mid-1800s).* Friend to whites during and after the California Gold Rush.

Manuelito Cota of mixed Luiseno and Spanish descent lived in the village of Paumo on the San Luis Rey River near San Diego, California. He was a rival of the Cahuilla JUAN ANTONIO and the Cupeno ANTONIO GARRA, living to his east. In 1847, he clashed with the former, and, in 1851, he refused the latter support in the Garra Uprising against whites. He acted as head chief of the Luisenos until 1855.

CRANE. See TARHE.

CRAVEN, CHARLES. *(d. 1754).* Commander of militia in the Yamasee War; colonial governor of South Carolina.

Born in England, Charles Craven became secretary of the proprietors of South Carolina colony about 1710, then proprietary governor in 1712. As such, he oversaw the codification of the colony's laws. He also encouraged education among the colonists, founding a free school in Charleston.

The Yamasee Indians, who had fled from Spanish Florida to avoid being sent to the Caribbean as slaves, lived for a time in harmony with the British. By 1715, however, white encroachment onto lands guaranteed to Indians by the colonial government, as well as the exploitive practices of English traders, incited them to revolt in the Yamasee War of 1715–16. Many traders and settlers along the Ashley River were killed in raids by the Yamasees. Others fled to Charleston. Some Apalachees, Catawbas, Creeks, Cherokees, and Choctaws joined the Yamasees in revolt.

Craven organized a militia force of about 1,200, many of them blacks and Indians, and led summer and fall campaigns, attacking Indian villages and tracking war parties through the wilderness. He then forced surviving Yamasees out of the colony. Most settled in Georgia and Florida.

Craven retired from the governorship in 1716, returning to England.

CRAZY HORSE (Tashunka Witco, Tashunca-Uitco, "his horse is crazy"). *Oglala-Brule Sioux. (ca. 1842–1877).* Leader in the Sioux Wars of the 1860s–70s. Nephew of SPOTTED TAIL.

Crazy Horse was born along Rapid Creek near present-day Rapid City, South Dakota, to the east of *Paha Sapa*, the Black Hills. He was the son of an Oglala medicine man of the same name and his Brule wife, the sister of Spotted Tail. His mother died when he was young, and his father took her sister as a wife and she helped raise Crazy Horse. He spent time in both Oglala and Brule camps. His childhood name was Curly.

Before he was 12, Curly had killed a buffalo and received his own horse. About that age, on August 19, 1854, he was in CONQUERING BEAR's camp in northern Wyoming when the Brule leader was killed in the GRATTAN Fight. Although he was away from camp during the Battle of Ash Hollow the following year, he witnessed the destruction of Sioux tepees and possessions by the soldiers during General WILLIAM S. HARNEY's punitive expedition through Sioux territory along the Oregon Trail, experiences that helped shape his militant attitude toward whites.

After the Grattan Fight, Curly underwent a Vision Quest in which he had a vivid dream of a rider in a storm on horseback, with long unbraided hair, a small stone in his ear, zigzag lightning decorating his cheek, and hail dotting his body. Although a warrior, he bore no scalps. People clutched at the rider, but could not hold him. The storm faded and a red-backed hawk flew over the rider's head. When Curly later related the dream to his father, the medicine man interpreted it as a sign of his son's future greatness in battle. At about the age of 16, now bearing his father's name, Crazy Horse rode for the first time as an adult warrior in a raid on Crows. Like the rider in his dream, he wore his hair free, a stone earring, and a headdress with a red hawk feather in it. His face was painted with a lightning bolt and his body with hail-like dots. The raid was successful, but Crazy Horse received a wound in the leg, because, his father interpreted, unlike the rider in the vision, he had taken two scalps. For the remainder of his career as a warrior, it is said that Crazy Horse never again took a scalp.

Crazy Horse became further known to many of the Sioux bands for his courage in the War for the BOZEMAN Trail of 1866–68 under the Oglala RED CLOUD, when the army began building a road in Powder River country from the Oregon Trail to the goldfields of Montana. He was one of the young chiefs, along with the Miniconjou HUMP and the Hunkpapas GALL and RAIN-IN-THE-FACE, who used decoy tactics against the soldiers. Near Fort Phil Kearny, Wyoming, Crazy Horse participated in the Indian victories known as the FETTERMAN Fight of December 21, 1866, and the Wagon Box Fight of August 2, 1867.

With the Fort Laramie Treaty of 1868, in which the army agreed to abandon the posts along the Bozeman Trail, Red Cloud and Spotted Tail settled on reservation lands. Crazy Horse became war chief of the Oglalas, with some Brule followers as well. Moreover, he made friends and followers among the Northern Cheyennes through his first marriage to a Cheyenne woman. He later married an Oglala woman too.

Crazy Horse again waged war in the early 1870s, leading his warriors in raids on Northern Pacific Railway surveyors. The Black Hills Gold Rush, which brought more whites to the region, increased tensions. When the nomadic hunting bands ignored the order to report to their reservations by January 31, 1876, the military organized a campaign against them.

Crazy Horse's band fought in the opening engagement of the War for the Black Hills of 1876–77, the Battle of Powder River. In March 1876, when his scouts discovered an Indian trail, General GEORGE CROOK sent a detachment under Colonel Joseph Reynolds to locate the Indian camp along the Powder in southeastern Montana. At dawn on March 17, Reynolds ordered a charge. The Indians retreated to surrounding bluffs and fired at the troops who burned the village and rounded up the Indian horses. Crazy Horse regrouped his warriors and, during a snowstorm that night, recaptured the herd.

Meanwhile, SITTING BULL of the Hunkpapas, who, during the 1860s, had been active in raids in northern Montana and North Dakota along the Yellowstone and Missouri rivers, came into prominence as the spiritual leader of the allied Northern Plains tribes. Gall acted as his leading war chief. Crazy Horse joined the Hunkpapas on the upper Rosebud. On June 17, 1876, at the Battle of the Rosebud, Crazy Horse, Gall, and other war chiefs led their warriors in repeated assaults that forced Crook's troops to retreat. The Indians then moved their camp to the Bighorn River. On June 25, at the Battle of Little Bighorn, Crazy Horse led the victorious assault on GEORGE ARMSTRONG CUSTER's men from the north and west, while Gall's warriors attacked from the south and west.

Following Little Bighorn, the Indian bands split up, and Crazy Horse led his people back to the Rosebud. The next autumn and winter, Colonel NELSON A. MILES led the 5th Infantry from a base at the confluence of the Tongue and Yellowstone rivers in a relentless pursuit of the militants, wearing them down and making it difficult for them to obtain food. When the Indians attempted hit-and-run strikes, the soldiers responded with heavy artillery to repel them. On January 8, 1877, at Wolf Mountain on the Tongue River in southern Montana, Crazy Horse led 800 braves in a surprise attack. Miles had disguised his howitzers as wagons and opened fire with them. The Indians withdrew to bluffs and, when the soldiers counterattacked, retreated under the cover of a snowstorm.

More and more of the fugitive bands were surrendering. Crazy Horse received a promise from Crook through Red Cloud that if he surrendered, his people would have a reservation of their own in the Powder River country. His people weary and starving, Crazy Horse led some 800 followers to Fort Robinson on the Red Cloud Agency in northwestern Nebraska on May 5, 1877.

But the promise of a reservation fell through. Crazy Horse remained at the Red Cloud Agency, and his presence caused unrest among the Indians and suspicion among the whites. Older chiefs resented the adulation he received from young braves. He remained aloof from whites and refused Crook's request to send him to Washington, D.C., for a meeting with President Rutherford Hayes. Crazy Horse's wife became sick. On hearing unfounded rumors that Crazy Horse was planning a rebellion, Crook ordered his arrest. Taking his family with him, Crazy Horse headed for the Spotted

Tail Agency to the northwest. In a parley with troops sent to capture him, Crazy Horse agreed to return, and the next day, September 5, 1877, he was led back to Fort Robinson. What exactly happened at the Red Cloud Agency is unknown. It is thought Crazy Horse had not expected to be imprisoned. On realizing he was being taken to the stockade, he resisted and, while the Indian police attempted to regain control, he was bayoneted in the abdomen by a soldier.

Crazy Horse died that night. His father and stepmother were given his body and, following their son's request, buried him in his homeland—somewhere near Wounded Knee, according to legend. (See also RED CLOUD; SITTING BULL.)

CRAZY SNAKE. See CHITTO HARJO.

CREMONY, JOHN C. *(1815–1879).* Historian; soldier.

After having served in the 1st Massachusetts Infantry during the Mexican War of 1846–48 and then as interpreter for the United States Boundary Commission in 1849–51, John Cremony was a second lieutenant in the 2nd California Infantry under General JAMES H. CARLETON in the Civil War campaigns in New Mexico and Arizona. He gained firsthand knowledge of the life and culture of the Southwest Indians, which he recorded in his book, *Life Among the Apaches* (1868). Following his military service, Cremony lived in San Francisco.

CROCKETT, DAVID (Davy Crockett). *(1786–1836).* Scout in the Creek War; frontiersman; congressman.

Davy Crockett was born in Greene County, eastern Tennessee, near the Nolichucky River. He received little formal education and sought work as a cattle driver and farmhand. He married in 1805, and, six years later, moved with his family to central Tennessee, where he used his hunting skills to support his family.

On learning of the attack on Fort Mims by Red Stick warriors under WILLIAM WEATHERFORD, at the start of the Creek War of 1813–14, Crockett enlisted in the Tennessee militia. The following November, Crockett served as a scout under General ANDREW JACKSON in the army's counteroffensive against the Creeks, fighting at Tallassahatchee and Talladega.

At the end of the war, Crockett returned to hunting and farming in the frontier regions of western Tennessee, and embarked on a political career in 1821. He served as a justice of the peace, was elected as a colonel of the state militia, and subsequently won a seat in the Tennessee state legislature. In 1827–31, he served two terms in the House of Representatives as a Democrat.

Failing to win reelection in 1831, Crockett changed to the conservative Whig party, in opposition to Jackson, and served again in the House from 1833–35. Defeated in 1835, he left Washington, D.C., to explore Texas and joined the Texas Revolution. He was killed in the Mexican attack on the Alamo on March 6, 1836.

During his years in Congress, Crockett was a popular backwoods figure around Washington, D.C. A magazine, *The Crockett Almanacs*, was first published in Nashville in 1835, continuing after his death. It recounted the exploits of Crockett, the keelboatman Mike Fink, and other frontiersmen, including many stories of escapes from Indian captivity. (See also WEATHERFORD, WILLIAM.)

CROGHAN, GEORGE. *(ca. 1720–1782).* Colonial Indian agent; trader.

George Croghan, no relation to the later military leader of the same name, was an Irish immigrant who settled in western Pennsylvania in 1741. He established a series of Indian trading posts throughout the Ohio Valley, and was known as the "King of the Traders."

In 1748–52, Croghan obtained Wyandot, Delaware, and Shawnee allegiance to the British against the French through treaties negotiated at his trading posts at Logstown and Lancaster on the Pennsylvania frontier. The onset of the French and Indian War in 1754 put an end to his Indian trading business. He became a military scout for General EDWARD BRADDOCK.

In 1756, WILLIAM JOHNSON appointed Croghan as his deputy superintendent of Indian affairs. In this role, he negotiated additional treaties with the Indians of the Ohio Valley that kept them neutral in England's wars with the French.

In 1760, Croghan traveled to the Ohio Valley tribes to explain to the Indian leaders that the garrisons once manned by the French would be controlled by the British, but that the trade relations with the Indians would be maintained. As Indian agent for Major ROBERT ROGERS, and then for General JEFFREY AMHERST, Croghan met with tribal leaders in Detroit in 1760 and 1761. He was one of the first of the colonial officials to report on Indian discontentment in the Great Lakes region that would lead to the outbreak of Pontiac's Rebellion of 1763.

On an official trip to England in the 1760s, Croghan campaigned for the creation of a British governmental department for the administration of Indian affairs that would be independent of the separate colonial governments, but was unsuccessful. Sent to negotiate peace with the Illinois tribes in the mid-1760s, he was taken captive by the Indians for a short time. After his release, he went on to finalize a settlement with PONTIAC in 1765. Three years later, Croghan was instrumental in negotiations for the Fort Stanwix Treaty, which included a restriction on the extent of white settlement in the Appalachians.

Croghan later settled in Pittsburgh, from where he became involved in land speculation enterprises in present-day Indiana. His business ventures were ended by the outbreak of the American Revolution. During the last years of his life, he was impoverished.

Croghan's journals and correspondence are important historical records of the colonial frontier.

CROGHAN, GEORGE. *(1791–1849).* Army officer. Nephew of GEORGE ROGERS CLARK and WILLIAM CLARK.

George Croghan (not to be confused with WILLIAM JOHNSON's deputy Indian agent of the same name) was born in Louisville, Kentucky, and graduated from William and Mary College in 1810. The following year, he began his military career as a volunteer aide-de-camp at the Battle of Tippecanoe in northern Indiana, where he fought under General WILLIAM HENRY HARRISON against the Shawnees led by TECUMSEH's brother, TENSKWATAWA.

With the onset of the War of 1812, Croghan was commissioned an infantry captain by General Harrison and participated in the defense of American forces at Fort Meigs, Ohio. In 1813, he was brevetted a major and assigned as aide-de-camp to Harrison.

Harrison subsequently posted Croghan at Fort Stephenson (present-day Fremont, Ohio) on the Sandusky River. On August 1–3, 1813, Major Croghan led the defense against a combined force of 1,200 British troops and Indians led by British colonel HENRY PROCTOR, as well as 2,000 Shawnee and allied Indian warriors under Tecumseh. Croghan's American forces numbered only 160 men, but with the use of artillery, they were able to repel repeated British and Indian assaults. For his role, Croghan was awarded a commission of lieutenant colonel.

Croghan left the military in 1817, becoming the postmaster of New Orleans in 1824. In 1825, he rejoined the army as inspector general, and, in 1846, he served as a colonel under General ZACHARY TAYLOR in the Mexican War, taking part in the Battle of Monterrey in September. He died in New Orleans three years later. (See also TECUMSEH.)

CROOK, GEORGE (Grey Fox). *(1828–1890).* Army officer in the wars for the West.

George Crook, of Dayton, Ohio, was an 1852 West Point graduate. Although he finished near the bottom of his class, he went on to a distinguished military career that spanned more than 40 years, most of it involved with the Indian wars in the West.

Upon receiving his second lieutenant's commission, Crook was assigned to an infantry regiment on the Pacific Coast. During the 1850s, he was involved in the Yakima War of 1855–56 against allied tribes under KAMIAKIN in the eastern Washington Territory, and the simultaneous Rogue River War involving tribes under JOHN in southern Oregon. While posted in the Pacific Northwest, he was promoted to the rank of captain. Crook was wounded by a poisoned arrow in one engagement.

Brevetted a brigadier general at the outbreak of the Civil War, Crook took command of an Ohio volunteer infantry regiment. He fought in the Battle of Antietam, led Union cavalry units at Chickamauga, and served under General PHILIP H. SHERIDAN in the Shenandoah campaign.

Returning to the regular rank of lieutenant colonel at the war's end, Crook next was assigned to Boise, Idaho, where he launched a successful campaign against the Northern Paiutes under PAULINA and WEAWEA, during the latter part of the Snake War of 1866–68, in the desert regions of eastern Oregon and southern Idaho. Crook, taking command in 1866, began a series of small tracking patrols, forcing about 40 skirmishes and the militants' eventual surrender.

In 1871, Crook was assigned to Arizona to pacify the Chiricahua Apaches. After President ULYSSES S. GRANT's 1872 Peace Commission reached an accord with COCHISE, Crook mounted an offensive against DELSHAY'S Apaches and their Yavapai allies in the 1872–73 Tonto Basin Campaign. He made use of nine small, mobile detachments and used Apache scouts as soldiers in his campaign, forcing about 20 clashes. One outfit under captains William Brown and James Burns won the decisive Battle of Skull Cave at Salt River Canyon on December 28, 1872, against the Yavapais. On March 27, 1873, an outfit under Captain George Randall was victorious in the Battle of Turret Peak. In recognition for his success in breaking Indian resistance, Crook was promoted to brigadier general the next year.

In 1875, Crook was given the command of the Department of the Platte (Iowa, Nebraska, Utah, and parts of Dakota and Montana). By this time, the Sioux and Cheyennes had formed an alliance under the Hunkpapa SITTING BULL to drive out the influx of white settlers and miners who had invaded the Black Hills. In response to the failure of militant bands to comply with the Interior Department's order to return to their reservations, the military mounted major offensives in 1876.

Crook commanded units of infantry and cavalry, as well as Pawnee scouts, a force of about 1,200 men. Heading northward from Fort Fetterman, present-day Wyoming, on the Platte River in the early part of 1876, Crook's forces were part of General Sheridan's three-pronged move against the militant bands. Other components of the campaign were General ALFRED TERRY's column, which included Colonel GEORGE

Council between Geronimo (wearing bandanna) and General George Crook (wearing helmet). Nana is to the right of Geronimo; John G. Bourke is to the left of Crook. Photo by Camillus S. Fly. *Courtesy of Library of Congress.*

ARMSTRONG CUSTER and his 7th Cavalry, moving west from Fort Abraham Lincoln in the Dakota Territory; and General JOHN GIBBON's forces moving east from Fort Ellis in the Montana Territory. All three columns were intended to maintain pressure and converge on Sioux-Cheyenne bands.

On March 17, 1876, Crook's column, headed by Colonel Joseph Reynolds, encountered a Sioux village on the Powder River in southeastern Montana. Units destroyed the village and confiscated the Indians' pony herd, but were forced to withdraw when the Sioux under the Oglala CRAZY HORSE counterattacked and recovered their ponies. This reversal, coupled with severe winter weather, forced Crook to return to Fort Fetterman.

In May 1876, Crook and his column, including more than 250 Crow and Shoshone auxiliaries, proceeded north along the BOZEMAN Trail into Montana. On June 17, 1876, they encountered a force of Cheyennes and Sioux, under Crazy Horse's command at the Rosebud River. The soldiers withdrew when Crazy

Horse's warriors used the area's rugged terrain to gain a tactical advantage. Crook's retreat at Rosebud may have facilitated the Sioux and Cheyenne advance to the Little Bighorn, where they annihilated Custer and his 7th Cavalry eight days later.

On September 9, 1876, Crook led his column to victory over Oglala leader AMERICAN HORSE's warriors at the Battle of Slim Buttes, present-day South Dakota. In the Battle of Dull Knife, present-day Wyoming, on November 25, 1876, Crook's force destroyed the food and clothing supplies of Northern Cheyenne leader DULL KNIFE and his followers. The following spring, many of the Sioux and Cheyennes surrendered at Fort Robinson, Nebraska, marking the end of the War of the Black Hills.

The next year, when Ponca chief STANDING BEAR's son died, he left the tribe's reservation in the Indian Territory, with a wagon train of his people, to bury the boy in the old Ponca lands in Nebraska. Settlers were alarmed by this sudden influx of Poncas, and Crook was dispatched with cavalry units, and arrested Standing

Bear and his people. Crook was sympathetic to the Ponca chief's cause, however, and helped him gain legal representation.

In 1882, Crook was once again assigned to command troops in the Southwest, as head of the Department of Arizona, when the Chiricahua Apaches under GERONIMO left the San Carlos Reservation and raided ranches and other white settlements. For the next four years, Crook pursued Geronimo throughout southern Arizona. His innovative use of Indian scouts and mule trains instead of wagon trains helped him in his tracking of the small bands of militants. Under a diplomatic agreement, Crook obtained permission to lead his troops into Mexico, where he obtained Geronimo's surrender at Canyon de los Embudos in March 1886. Geronimo escaped, however, whereupon Crook was relieved of his Arizona command. He was replaced by General NELSON A. MILES, who managed the final capture of Geronimo.

Crook returned to the Department of the Platte. He was promoted to major general in 1888 and given command of the Division of the Missouri, comprising most of the Great Plains.

Crook campaigned on behalf of Indian rights groups, for the release of Geronimo and the other Apaches held at military prisons in Florida and Alabama. His efforts helped bring about the eventual release of Geronimo and his Apache followers to Fort Sill, Oklahoma.

Even though Crook spent a large part of his military career in armed conflict with the Indians, he was never an advocate of total war, believing that limited strikes would convince militants to cease their resistance to reservation settlement. He advocated diplomacy over warfare, and was trusted by the Indians, who called him Grey Fox. He was also an advocate of the allotment of reservation lands to individual Indian landowners and the granting of full citizenship to Indians. Crook felt that Indian hostilities were caused by the government's failure to comply with the terms of its own treaties. He also voiced an understanding of the Apache life-style, acknowledging that the harsh Arizona environment forced their economy to be based on raiding and stealing. Crook died at the Missouri Division headquarters in Chicago. (See also COCHISE; CRAZY HORSE; GERONIMO; PAULINA; SITTING BULL; STANDING BEAR.)

CROSS, HENRY. *(1837–1918).* Artist.

Henry Cross, born in Flemingville, New York, traveled with a circus while a teenager, where he showed an interest in painting animals. When 16, he went to France to study painting for two years, then settled in Chicago in 1860. Two years later, he traveled to southwestern Minnesota during the time of the Minnesota Uprising of Santee Sioux under LITTLE CROW,

painting portraits of many Indian leaders of that conflict. He returned east and worked as a poster and wagon painter for P. T. Barnum's circus. On subsequent trips west, Cross spent time among the Plains Indians, learning the language of the Sioux and becoming a friend of WILLIAM "BUFFALO BILL" CODY. His paintings of Native Americans include portraits of SITTING BULL and SPOTTED TAIL. He also produced portraits of frontiersmen CHRISTOPHER "KIT" CARSON and JAMES "WILD BILL" HICKOK.

CROW DOG (Kangi Sunka). *Brule Sioux.* *(ca. 1835–1910).* Killer of SPOTTED TAIL; band leader in the Ghost Dance Uprising of 1890.

Crow Dog was the central figure in an 1883 case involving Indian rights. In 1881, in a dispute over a woman or tribal leadership or both, Crow Dog shot and killed Spotted Tail. He was arrested by HOLLOW HORN BEAR, another Brule chief, then serving as a captain of the Indian police. In 1883, the U.S. Supreme Court pardoned Crow Dog in the case of *Ex Parte Crow Dog*, ruling that the federal courts had no jurisdiction over crimes committed on reservation treaty lands. Two years later, Congress passed the Major Crimes Act, providing that an Indian committing a major crime against a fellow Indian, such as murder or burglary, was subject to the laws of the territory or state where the crime was committed.

In November 1890, during the Ghost Dance Uprising, Crow Dog led his band into the South Dakota Badlands

Crow Dog. Photo by Edward Curtis. *Courtesy of National Archives of Canada/C-34804.*

to join the Brule medicine man SHORT BULL at the Stronghold. The army sent a party to negotiate with them, and Crow Dog and Two Strike, another Brule leader, agreed to return to the Pine Ridge Reservation. (See also BIG FOOT; KICKING BEAR; SPOTTED TAIL; WOVOKA.)

CROWFOOT. (Isapo-Muxika). *Blackfoot.*
(1821–1890). Principal chief and spokesman of the Blackfoot Confederacy; peacemaker. Brother-in-law of RED CROW; adoptive father of POUNDMAKER.

Crowfoot was born a Blood Indian, but, after his father's death, moved north to the Blackfoot lodge of his mother's new husband. In 1870, he became one of three tribal head chiefs, but later became the most influential chief in the entire Blackfoot Confederacy because of his great skills as an orator and diplomat.

In 1877, at Blackfoot Crossing on the Bow River, about 80 miles north of Fort Macleod, Crowfoot served as the spokesman for the various Blackfoot, Blood, Piegan, and Sarcee bands. With the other chiefs, including Red Crow, he signed Treaty No. 7, ceding 50,000 acres—what is now most of southern Alberta—to the territorial governor David Laird and the Mountie commissioner JAMES MACLEOD, representing the Dominion of Canada.

During the Second RIEL Rebellion of 1885, Crowfoot kept the Blackfeet out of the conflict, but his adopted son Poundmaker led one of the bands of rebellious Crees. Despite his neutral stance, Crowfoot encouraged

Crowfoot. Photo by J. A. Ross. *Courtesy of National Archives of Canada/PA-134918.*

his people to help any refugee Crees passing through Blackfoot territory.

Crowfoot lost most of his children to smallpox and tuberculosis. In his final years, he traveled among the Bloods, Piegans, Sarcees, Gros Ventres, and Assiniboines in Canada and Montana, continuing to act as a peacemaker in tribal disputes. During his chieftaincy, he witnessed the building of the railroad and the disappearance of the buffalo.

CROW KING. *Hunkpapa Sioux. (fl. 1870s–80s).*
Lieutenant of SITTING BULL; research informant.

Crow King, along with GALL, was one of Sitting Bull's leading war chiefs. He was with his chief at Little Big Horn in June 1876 and later fled with him to Canada. He returned to the United States with Gall in early January 1881, several months before Sitting Bull. Crow King is often quoted as a source for what happened at the Battle of Little Bighorn. (See also SITTING BULL.)

CUERNO VERDE ("green horn"). *Comanche.*
(d. 1778). War chief who fought the Spanish.

During the 1770s, Cuerno Verde led many raids on Spanish settlements along the Rio Grande in New Mexico for food, horses, and slaves. In order to pacify the frontier, the governor of New Mexico, JUAN DE ANZA, led a force of 85 soldiers and 259 Indians against the Comanches in 1779, engaging Cuerno Verde in what is now Colorado. Cuerno Verde, his son, four band chiefs, his medicine man, and 32 other warriors died in a bitter battle against Spanish guns.

CURLING HAIR (Curly Head, Babisigandibe, Babaseekeendase). *Chippewa (Ojibway).*
(ca. 1750–1825). Friend to whites; enemy of Sioux.

Curling Hair was born on the southern shore of Lake Superior, and he moved to upper Mississippi country in present-day Minnesota about 1800. He became both civil and war chief of the Mississippi (or Sandy Lake) band. Along with other Chippewa band leaders, such as NOKA and FLAT MOUTH, Curling Hair fought the Sioux for this reigion and helped prevent Sioux raids on fur-trading posts. To keep his support, traders gave Curling Hair many gifts; he, in turn, welcomed whites to his lodge to share his supply of meat. In 1805, an expedition under ZEBULON PIKE visited him. Curling Hair attended a peace conference of 1825 at Prairie du Chien, Wisconsin. He died on the return trip home and was succeeded by HOLE-IN-THE-DAY.

CURLY (Curley; Ashishishe, Shishi'esh, "the crow"). *Crow. (ca. 1859–1923).* Army scout during the Sioux Wars; research informant.

Curly was born along the Rosebud River in Montana, and, as a young man, he fought on the side of whites, as encouraged by Chief PLENTY COUPS. With his brother White Swan, Curly served as an Indian scout under WHITE-MAN-RUNS-HIM with GEORGE ARMSTRONG CUSTER's 7th Cavalry. He claimed he had been wounded at Little Bighorn in 1876, but managed to escape by hiding his Crow clothing under a dead Sioux's blanket and slipping away. White-Man-Runs-Him and other Indian scouts claimed, however, that they had been sent to the rear before the fighting started, enabling their escape. At the fork of the Bighorn and Yellowstone rivers, Curly met up with an army supply boat, the *Far West*, and reported Custer's defeat. Curly later became an informant on the battle.

CURLY HEADED DOCTOR (Curley-Headed Doctor). *Modoc. (d. 1890).* Medicine man; leader in the Modoc War of 1872–73. Father-in-law of HOOKER JIM.

Curly Headed Doctor, a prominent shaman among his people, played a major role in the Modoc War. He participated with Hooker Jim in the attack on California ranchers, then joined up with CAPTAIN JACK in the lava beds. Before the fighting against troops under Lieutenant Colonel Frank Wheaton, Curly Headed Doctor drew a line beyond which the enemy supposedly could not pass. He performed numerous other rituals to protect the insurgents and gained more influence with each Modoc success. Arguing for continuing militance, he used his oratorical skills to prod Captain Jack into killing the members of President ULYSSES S. GRANT's Peace Commission in April 1873. After his surrender with Hooker Jim and BOGUS CHARLEY, Curly Headed Doctor helped them track Captain Jack for the army. He was forced to relocate to the Indian Territory, where he died. (See also CAPTAIN JACK.)

CURTIS, CHARLES (The Injun). *Kaw-Osage.* *(1860–1936).* Congressman; vice president of the United States.

Charles Curtis was born on the site of present-day North Topeka, Kansas, the son of Oren Arms Curtis and Ellen Pappan Curtis. His mother was a descendant of White Plume, who, although a son of the Osage chief WHITE HAIR, was an adopted member of the Kaw (or Kansa) tribe. Under the care of his maternal grandmother, starting in 1866, Curtis, one-eighth Indian, attended an Indian mission school on the Kaw Reservation near Council Grove. He returned to Topeka, Kansas, in 1868, following an attack on Kaw Indians at Council Grove by Cheyenne militants. As a youth, he spent some of his summers as a jockey in Topeka, and he attended the Topeka High School.

In 1881, Curtis was admitted to the bar and soon entered politics as a Republican. He was elected to the House of Representatives, serving eight terms in 1892–

1906, during which time he sponsored the Curtis Act of 1898, calling for the dissolution of tribal governments and the institution of civil government within the Indian Territory. The act was intended to assimilate Indian peoples and bring the allotment policy to the Five Civilized Tribes, who had been exempt from the General Allotment Act (the Dawes Severalty Act) of 1887, and it authorized the Dawes Commission, organized in 1893 and headed by former senator HENRY DAWES, to extinguish tribal title to lands within the Indian Territory and proceed with allotment of parcels to individuals.

Curtis served on a number of committees while a congressman, including the Committee on Territories; the Committee on Ways and Means; the Committee on Public Lands; the Committee on Expenditures; and the Committee on Indian Affairs. His efforts on behalf of detribalization, allotment, and assimilation led to opposition from many of the tribal leaders of the Indian Territory. His work set the stage for Oklahoma statehood in 1907.

Curtis was later elected to the Senate, serving in 1907–13 and 1915–29. Following an unsuccessful bid for the presidential nomination, he ran on the ticket with Herbert Hoover in 1928, serving as vice president in 1929–33. He was known as a consummate politician who turned his Indian background to an advantage, despite being called "the Injun" by political opponents. He was a fiscal conservative who supported, in addition to the assimilation of Indian peoples into mainstream society, farm and veterans' benefits, women's suffrage, and Prohibition. The Hoover-Curtis ticket was defeated in its run for a second term. When Curtis retired in 1934, he had served longer in Washington, D.C., than any active politician.

CURTIS, EDWARD SHERIFF. *(1868–1952).* Photographer.

Edward Curtis was born near Whitewater, Wisconsin, and, while a young man, he pursued an interest in photography and built his own camera. In 1887, he moved with his family to Seattle and soon began photographing the Indians of Puget Sound. Five years later, he acquired a studio.

In 1898, Curtis helped a lost party of climbers off Mount Rainier, among whom were C. Hart Merriam, chief of the United States Biological Survey, and GEORGE BIRD GRINNELL, editor of *Forest and Stream* magazine. The next year, Merriam arranged for Curtis to be official photographer with the 1899 Edward H. Harriman expedition to Alaska, including John Muir, the naturalist. Then, in 1900, Grinnell invited Curtis to accompany him on a journey among the Blackfeet in Montana, during which time he helped Curtis conceive

Edward Curtis (bearded) with Native American friends. *Courtesy of Library of Congress.*

and plan a definitive pictorial record of Native North Americans.

In 1900, Curtis began documenting the tribes west of the Mississippi. He was unable to finance the project through his studio work and the sale of prints, however. He undertook two trips East, with exhibits and lectures in Washington, D.C., and New York City. His article published by Grinnell in *Scribner's Magazine*, generated further interest. The investment banker J. P. Morgan, at the encouragement of President Theodore Roosevelt, granted Curtis $75,000 to complete the project.

Curtis spent 30 years on his photographic travels in the United States, British Columbia, and Mexico, taking more than 40,000 photos of Indians from 80 different tribes, including many well-known tribal leaders. More than 2,000 were reproduced in *The North American Indian*, published serially in 20 volumes by the Smithsonian Institution, between 1907 and 1930. The work was supervised and edited by the ethnologist FREDERICK WEBB HODGE of the Smithsonian.

In addition to his photographs, Curtis, a pioneer cinematographer, made the first full-length motion picture of Indians with the help of the Kwakiutl-Tlingit GEORGE HUNT. Filmed in 1914–15 among the Indians of the Pacific Northwest, it was originally entitled *In the Land of the Head-Hunters*, and came to be called *In the Land of the War Canoes*.

On completion of his Indian projects, Curtis continued work as a photographer while also developing mining interests. He died in Los Angeles.

CUSHING, FRANK HAMILTON (Tenatsali, "medicine flower"). *(1857–1900).* Anthropologist; archaeologist.

Frank Hamilton Cushing was born in Erie County, Pennsylvania, and, while a young boy, he was given a pre-Columbian arrowhead by a farmer. By the age of 14, he had his own extensive collection.

As a member of the Smithsonian's Bureau of Ethnology under JOHN WESLEY POWELL, Cushing joined the geologist James Stevenson, his wife, MATILDA COXE STEVENSON, and the photographer JOHN K. HILLERS on an expedition to the Zuni Indians in 1879. Over the next five years, he lived among the Zunis, mastered their language, and was accepted into their tribe as a member of the tribal council. He was also initiated into Zuni society, the Order of the Priest of the Bow, receiving the Indian name Tenatsali.

Cushing wrote extensively about Zuni lifeways, including *Zuni Breadstuff* (1884–85), using the Zuni language for many of his ethnological studies.

In 1887–88, while heading the Hemenway Southwestern Archaeological Expedition, funded by the Massachusetts philanthropist Mary Hemenway, Cushing discovered remnants of the Hohokam culture in excavations along the Gila River in Arizona. He left that position because of poor health, and was succeeded by JESSE WALTER FEWKES.

Cushing died in 1900, shortly after having begun work among the Seminoles of Florida.

CUSICK, ALBERT (Sagonaquade, "he who angers them"). *Tuscarora-Onondaga. (b. 1846).*
Christian convert; research informant.

Born on the Tuscarora Reservation in New York, Albert Cusick was the son of a Tuscarora chief and his Onondaga wife. He too became chief, but was deposed on converting to Christianity. He eventually moved to the Onondaga Reservation, where he became known as a valuable informant on Iroquoian language and culture, as well as a church worker.

CUSTER, GEORGE ARMSTRONG (Hard Backsides; Long Hair; Yellow Hair; Son of the Morning Star; Chief of the Thieves). *(1839–1876).*
Army officer in the Plains Indian Wars.

Born in New Rumley, Ohio, George Armstrong Custer attended West Point, his military education sponsored by Congressman John W. Bingham. Graduating in 1861 at the bottom of his class, Custer was immediately thrust into the early engagements of the Civil War, where he gained the attention of his superiors through daring charges and flamboyant behavior. Brevetted a brigadier general of volunteers in 1863, and later a major general in the regular army when just 23 years old, he was the youngest officer in the Union army to attain that rank. He participated in all the major battles of the Army of the Potomac, including a successful cavalry engagement against Confederate general Jeb Stuart at Gettysburg.

Returning to the regular rank of lieutenant colonel at war's end, Custer was assigned to command the 7th Cavalry regiment. In 1867, under General WINFIELD SCOTT HANCOCK, he was the chief commander in the field in the Hancock Campaign. Custer and his men chased Southern Cheyennes under TALL BULL, WHITE HORSE, BULL BEAR, and ROMAN NOSE, plus Sioux allies under PAWNEE KILLER through western Kansas, northeastern Colorado, and southwestern Nebraska. Other than burning an abandoned camp on the Pawnee Fork, Custer was frustrated in his attempts to inflict damage on the militants.

Court-martialed later that year for leaving his command without permission at Fort Wallace, Kansas, and traveling to Fort Riley to visit his wife, as well as for abusive treatment of men and animals, Custer was suspended from the service until September 1868.

Under General PHILIP H. SHERIDAN, Custer and his 7th Cavalry took part in the winter campaign of 1868–69 to drive

George Armstrong Custer. *Courtesy of Library of Congress.*

the Cheyennes and Arapahos back onto their assigned reservations in the Indian Territory. Along the Washita River, near present-day Cheyenne, Oklahoma, Custer's forces attacked BLACK KETTLE's Southern Cheyenne band. The assault, in the midst of a severe November snowstorm, resulted in the killing of over 100 Indians, mostly women, children, and old men. Black Kettle himself was killed. Custer's forces were compelled to withdraw when the Indians launched a counterattack, but managed to destroy their winter supply of food and clothing, as well as their livestock. During the engagement, Custer abandoned a detachment of about 20 of his troops, who died in a Cheyenne ambush.

In 1873, Custer and his 7th Cavalry took part in an exploration of the Yellowstone River region, and, the next year, undertook a scientific and topographic expedition into the Black Hills of the Dakota Territory. Custer's reports of this region led people to believe that gold had been discovered. The area had been reserved for the Sioux, who considered the Black Hills their sacred hunting lands. The influx of miners and other settlers into the region in 1875 gave rise to the Sioux War of 1876–77, sometimes referred to as the War for the Black Hills, or Sitting Bull's War.

In spring 1876, Custer's 7th Cavalry was detailed as part of General ALFRED TERRY's column proceeding west from Fort Abraham Lincoln, Dakota Territory, into Montana. Three columns made up Sheridan's spring offensive against the Sioux and allied tribes under the Hunkpapa SITTING BULL, the other two headed by GEORGE CROOK and JOHN GIBBON.

Breaking off from the main body of Terry's troops, Custer's cavalry regiment advanced as far as the Bighorn River in southeastern Montana on June 25, 1876. When his scouts spotted the Indian camp along the river, he decided to attack rather than wait for reinforcements as instructed. It is theorized that Custer sought the glory himself because of political ambitions, believing that a major victory in the Indian wars would win him the Democratic nomination for the presidency.

Custer divided his men into four groups: the pack train with an escort to stay behind; a detachment under Captain FREDERICK W. BENTEEN to block the Indians from the south; and detachments under Major MARCUS A. RENO and himself to follow the river northward. Unaware of the number of warriors present, with many of them hidden in ravines, Custer sent Reno's men westward across the river in pursuit of a party of about 40, with instructions to strike the Indian camp from the south, while he proceeded along the eastern bank of the river for an attack on the village at its northern end. After a skirmish, Reno's men retreated across the river, where they were joined by Benteen's detachment. The Hunkpapa GALL led an assault from the west, pinning the soldiers down and inflicting severe damage—more than 50 dead and about 60 wounded out of 400. Then, approaching from the south, some of Gall's warriors joined the Oglala CRAZY HORSE's men, advancing from the north and west, in an attack on Custer's detachment. In the ensuing fight, Custer's approximately 200 men were unable to get relief from Benteen or Reno and were all killed. Reno and Benteen's forces were rescued when Terry and his column reached the battle site two days later.

Custer's widow, Elizabeth Bacon Custer, whom he had married in 1864, wrote a series of books about her husband's military career on the Great Plains, including *Boots and Saddles*, published in 1885. Custer himself wrote *My Life on the Plains*, published in 1874.

Custer is more important as a symbolic figure—a man whose ambitions, recklessness, and disregard for Indian peoples made him a victim of the last great Indian victory—than for his actual military contributions. There have been more books written about him than anyone else involved in the Indian wars. (See also BLACK KETTLE; CRAZY HORSE; SITTING BULL; TALL BULL.)

CUTLER, MANASSEH. *(1742–1823).*
Archaeologist; naturalist.

Manasseh Cutler became a pastor of the Congregational church in Hamilton, Massachusetts. He also studied law and medicine, both of which he practiced among church members. With a strong interest in natural science, he worked to classify New England's flora.

In 1787–88, along with Revolutionary War veteran and founder of the Ohio Company Colonel Rufus Putnam, Cutler lobbied the federal government for a land grant and established the town of Marietta in the Old Northwest Territory, present-day Ohio. Here the two men made one of the earliest archaeological investigations of the Indian mounds, helping prevent their destruction by white settlers. Putnam used his knowledge of military surveying to map the mounds. Cutler implemented a form of tree-ring counting to date the earthworks and determined they had been constructed at last 500 years earlier.

In contrast to the popular historical views of the time, Cutler theorized that the origins of the Mound Builder culture in the Ohio Valley were more likely in Mexico than in Palestine or India.

D

DADE, FRANCIS LANGHORNE.

(ca. 1790–1835). Army officer in the Second Seminole War of 1835–42.

Virginia-born Francis Dade was made captain by the time he was 28, and, when 38, he was brevetted major. With increasing tensions between Seminoles and federal officials over the question of removal from Florida to the Indian Territory, Dade was given the command of an expedition from Tampa Bay of about 108 men to reinforce General DUNCAN CLINCH's troops. On December 28, 1835, near Wahoo Swamp, on the route to Fort King, his command was ambushed by Seminoles and blacks under ALLIGATOR, JUMPER, and MICANOPY. Dade and about half his men died in the opening fire. Of those mounting a defense, only three survived and escaped to Fort Brooke. That same day, OSCEOLA led an attack on the agent WILEY THOMPSON. The so-called Dade Massacre and the death of Thompson led to seven more years of hostilities. Counties in both Florida and Georgia are named after Dade. (See also OSCEOLA.)

DARLEY, FELIX OCTAVIUS CARR.

(1822–1888). Artist.

F. O. C. Darley was born in Philadelphia, the son of a well-known English comedian. Although he had no formal art training, in the early 1840s, he embarked on a trip west of the Mississippi and, by the age of 21, had produced the artwork and wrote the text for the book *Scenes of Indian Life…Drawn and Etched on Stone* (1843), depicting the events in the life of an Indian chief. Starting in 1848, Darley was based in New York City, where he executed black-and-white illustrations for the novels of JAMES FENIMORE COOPER, HENRY WADSWORTH LONGFELLOW, Washington Irving, and many other writers. He also produced a series of popular lithographs based on frontier motifs. After 1859, he lived and worked in Delaware.

DATSOLALEE (Datsolai; Louisa Keyser; Dabuda, "wide hips").

Washo. (ca. 1835–1925). Basket maker.

Datsolalee was born in Nevada in the Carson Valley near the California border. As a young girl, she learned the traditional basketry skills of her people, a refined art involving intricate designs and as many as 36 stitches to the inch.

In 1844, Datsolalee was one of the Washos welcoming the expedition of JOHN C. FREMONT to their homeland. She married a Washo by the name of Assu, by whom she had two children. He died soon after, and, years later in 1888, she married another Washo named Charley Keyser.

Starting in the 1850s, the Paiutes, who had defeated the Washos in battle, prohibited Washo baskets in order to increase their own sales to whites. Without this source of income, the Washo people had little to trade and suffered extreme poverty.

In 1895, Datsolalee defied the ban and took several glass bottles woven with willow reeds and fern fibers to Abram Cohn, the proprietor of a clothing store in Carson City. He bought the baskets and told her he would buy any more she produced. Over the years, Cohn bought 120 works from Datsolalee, who is estimated to have woven about 300 in her lifetime. Some of her larger works took more than a year to make and had titles, such as "Myriads of Stars Shine Over the Graves of Our Ancestors."

Datsolalee worked up to her death, even when near-blind. Her pieces came to be highly valued by collectors; one sold for $10,000 five years after her death.

Datsolalee. Photo by Edward Curtis. *Courtesy of National Archives of Canada/PA-39625.*

DAVIS, BRITTON. *(1860–1930).* Army officer in the last phase of the Apache Wars, 1881–86.

Britton Davis, born in Brownsville, Texas, was the son of the Reconstruction-era governor of that state, Judge Edmund J. Davis. Graduating from West Point in 1881, he was assigned to the 3rd Cavalry at Fort D. A. Russell in Wyoming.

In summer 1882, Davis was sent to join General GEORGE CROOK's command in southern Arizona to take part in the suppression of the latest Chiricahua Apache uprising. On the San Carlos Reservation, Davis was assigned the recruitment and training of Apache scouts. Crook's 1882–83 expedition into Mexico succeeded in obtaining the surrender of Apache leaders GERONIMO and NAICHE and their followers. The Apaches were returned to the San Carlos Reservation, where Davis was responsible for the relocation of the fugitives to areas throughout the reservation as farmers.

In June 1884, Davis ordered the arrest of the Mimbreno Apache KAYATENNAE, after the war chief had openly defied the military's restrictions on drinking the Indian intoxicant *tiswin* and attacked Davis. Kayatennae was shipped to Alcatraz prison in San Francisco. In May 1885, Davis was again faced with open

opposition to the army's authority: A number of the Apache chiefs confronted Davis and blatantly announced they had been drinking *tiswin*, in violation of Crook's rules. Davis's request for reinforcements to deal with the threatened uprising was slow in reaching Crook's headquarters. Soon after, on May 17, 1885, Geronimo led a band off the reservation.

Following raids on ranches in southwestern New Mexico and southeastern Arizona, the militants fled into Mexico. They were soon pursued by General Crook and his combined force of regular cavalry and Apache scouts. Under a special diplomatic agreement with the Mexican government, Crook was granted permission to cross the border. During the expedition into Mexico, Davis led a company of Apache scouts.

In early 1886, Davis left the military and became the manager of a New York–owned cattle ranch in Mexico. He later served in the army again for a short time as a major in the Spanish-American War. In his 1929 book, *The Truth About Geronimo*, based on firsthand experience, as well as military records and correspondence, Davis related the Chiricahua's story through his final surrender to General NELSON A. MILES in 1886. (See also GERONIMO.)

DAWES, HENRY LAURENS. *(1816–1903).* Reformer; senator.

Henry Dawes, born in Cummington, Massachusetts, graduated from Yale, taught school and worked briefly as a journalist. He was admitted to the bar in 1842 and eventually became the U.S. district attorney for western Massachusetts. As a Republican, he served in the House of Representatives, 1857–75, as well as the Senate, 1875–93.

Throughout his Congressional career, Dawes promoted legislation and policies aimed at assimilating the Indians and resolving their land claims. In 1870, he campaigned against the types of treaties the government was then entering into with tribes. Rather than paying annuities and resettling tribes on reservations, Dawes favored providing Indians with individual ownership of land and thus creating a base for their eventual assimilation into white society.

In the later 1870s, as chairman of the Senate's Committee on Indian Affairs, Dawes was a major opponent of the plan, sponsored by CARL SCHURZ, secretary of the Interior, for the forced removal of the Poncas from Nebraska to the Indian Territory. With the writer HELEN HUNT JACKSON, Dawes organized the Boston Indian Citizenship Association in 1879, to support the Poncas in their legal struggle.

In 1887, working closely with such Indian reform organizations as HERBERT WELSH's Indian Rights Association, Dawes succeeded in the passage of the General Allotment Act, also known as the Dawes

Severalty Act. This law allowed the government to divide reservations into 160-acre parcels of land, which were then assigned to individual tribal members. The lands assigned to the Indians could be sold to whites only after 25 years. Unappropriated lands on Indian reservations could be sold to whites by the government, however, with the revenue held by the Treasury as a source of interest income to fund Indian development programs.

Although well-intentioned, the law created opportunities for white encroachment on Indian lands and led to problems for Indians, such as multiple heirs holding claims to small tracts of lands because of the prohibition against sales. Additionally, because lands assigned under this program were exempt from taxes, state governments refused to provide basic public services, such as road maintenance and schools. Surplus lands on reservations were sometimes sold to white speculators at very low prices through unscrupulous public officials and Indian agents.

Because of previous treaties, the Five Civilized Tribes of the Indian Territory and the Senecas of western New York were not included under the provisions of the Dawes Severalty Act. After his retirement from the Senate, Dawes became the head of the Dawes Commission in 1893, the purpose of which was to expand the provisions of the General Allotment Act to include these tribes. He served in that capacity until his retirement in 1900.

DEARBORN, HENRY. *(1751–1829).* Army officer; secretary of War.

Originally from North Hampton, New Hampshire, Henry Dearborn was trained as a physician. At the outbreak of the American Revolution, he organized a New Hampshire militia unit and was elected its captain. His command faced British troops at the Battle of Bunker Hill in June 1775. The following December, Dearborn was captured in General Benedict Arnold's abortive assault against Quebec. Released in 1777, he was promoted to major, and, that same year, fought at Ticonderoga and Saratoga against British general JOHN BURGOYNE. He wintered with General GEORGE WASHINGTON's troops at Valley Forge in 1777–78, and was part of General JOHN SULLIVAN's expedition against the Iroquois tribes of New York in 1779. At the Battle of Yorktown in 1781, Dearborn was an officer on George Washington's staff.

After the war, Dearborn settled in Maine. Elected to the House of Representatives, he served during the years 1793–97.

In 1801, Dearborn was appointed as President THOMAS JEFFERSON's secretary of War. During his eight years in the Jefferson cabinet, he was instrumental in formulating the government's plan to remove the Indians to areas west of the Mississippi. In 1804, following the Louisiana Purchase, Dearborn authorized Indian territorial governor WILLIAM HENRY HARRISON to enter into a treaty with Sac and Fox leaders, acquiring lands in the Old Northwest.

In 1803, a military post was established along the Chicago River in northeast Illinois and named in honor of the secretary of War—Fort Dearborn. The fort, defended by a garrison under Captain Nathan Heald, fell to a force of pro-British Indians on August 15, 1812. It was rebuilt in 1816–17; its environs developed into the present-day city of Chicago.

At the outbreak of the War of 1812, Dearborn was named the senior major general of the army, responsible for the nation's northern frontier, stretching from the Niagara River to the coast of New England. The Mohawk ELEAZAR WILLIAMS acted as a liaison to the region's Indians. Dearborn's indecisive tactics and a delay in taking action led to the 1812 defeat of American forces at Detroit by the combined British-Indian forces under British General ISAAC BROCK and the Shawnee TECUMSEH. Although Dearborn captured York (present-day Toronto) in April 1813, subsequent American reverses resulted in Dearborn's removal from command.

Honorably discharged from the service in 1815, Dearborn failed to win Congressional support as President James Madison's secretary of War. Under President James Monroe, he served for a time as United States minister to Portugal before retiring to Roxbury, Massachusetts, in 1824. (See also TECUMSEH.)

DEAS, CHARLES. *(1818–1867).* Artist.

Charles Deas was born in Philadelphia, and, after having failed to win an appointment to West Point, he began art studies about 1836 at the National Academy of Design in New York City. By 1838, he had an exhibition at the National Academy.

Early in his career, Deas had an opportunity to view GEORGE CATLIN's Indian exhibit in Philadelphia and was inspired to travel west to see Native Americans firsthand. In 1841, he visited his brother stationed at Fort Crawford, the outpost at Prairie du Chien, Wisconsin, where he found his first Indian subjects. He also traveled to Fort Snelling and Fort Winnebago, where he painted Sioux and Winnebagos.

Deas established a studio in St. Louis in fall 1841, which became his base of operations. He made annual trips west of the Mississippi in search of Indian subjects. He also depicted French-Canadian voyageurs and mountain men. In 1844, Deas accompanied Major Clifton Wharton on an expedition out of Fort Leavenworth, Kansas, to the upper Platte River region, where he painted Pawnees.

Deas attempted, without success, to raise money by subscription for the establishment of a gallery of Indian art. After his return to New York City in 1847, he suffered a mental breakdown. Few of his canvases have survived.

DECORA, LITTLE (Decoria; Mau-he-coo-sha-nak-zhe, "he stands with head reaching the clouds"). *Mixed Winnebago. (1797–1887).* Friend to whites during the Minnesota Uprising of 1862–63. Grandson of SPOON DECORA; son of WAUKON DECORA.

Little Decora became chief of his band on the death of his father Waukon Decora about 1859. At that time, he and his people lived near Mankato, Minnesota. During the Minnesota Uprising of 1862–63 under the Santee Sioux leader LITTLE CROW, Little Decora helped keep the Winnebagos on the side of the whites. In 1863, because of white hostility following the war, he moved with his people to South Dakota near Fort Thompson. In 1865, he led his band to a new Winnegabo Reservation in Nebraska. He died at Portage, Wisconsin, at his grandfather's tribal home. Little Decora was the grandfather of Angel Decora Dietz, an artist and illustrator prominent in the early 1900s.

DECORA, SPOON (Choukeka, Choo-ghe-ga, "the ladle"; Descarrie, Decori, Decoria, Decorie, Dacorah, DeCorrah, Dekaury, Dekorah, Dekouri, DeKauray, Day Kauray, Day Korah). *Mixed Winnebago. (ca. 1730–1816).* Proponent of peace with whites; father of WAUKON DECORA; grandfather of LITTLE DECORA.

Spoon Decora was the son of Sabrevoie Des Carrie, a French officer, and Hopockaw (The Coming of the Dawn), daughter of a Winnebago chief. He succeeded his mother as leader of his band and married the daughter of NAWKAW, another Winnebago chief. Spoon Decora established his reputation through warfare with the Chippewas, but proved friendly to whites. His band's main village was at Portage, Wisconsin. He signed a treaty in St. Louis in 1816 just before his death. He was succeeded by his son Waukon Decora.

DECORA, WAUKON (Kenoka Dekaury, Old Dekaury; Wau-kon-haw-kaw, White Eagle, Grey Eagle, Bald Eagle; Schachipkaka). *Mixed Winnebago. (d. ca. 1859).* Ally of TECUMSEH in the War of 1812; ally of Americans in the Winnebago Uprising of 1827, and the Black Hawk War of 1832. Son of SPOON DECORA; father of LITTLE DECORA.

Waukon Decora participated in the War of 1812 on the side of the British, as did the Winnebago chiefs FOUR LEGS and NAWKAW. He fought along with Colonel HENRY PROCTOR in the attack on Fort Stephenson on the Sandusky River in Ohio; and under Tecumseh in the Battle of the Thames in Ontario, both in 1813.

Soon after the war, in 1816, Waukon Decora succeeded his father Spoon Decora as chief. His band then lived at Portage, Wisconsin, on the Wisconsin River.

As chief, Waukon proved friendly to American settlers. He signed the 1825 treaty at Prairie du Chien. Yet, during the Winnebago Uprising of 1827, he was seized by whites and held as a hostage at Prairie du Chien, in exchange for the rebel leader RED BIRD. Decora again supported the whites in the Black Hawk War of 1832 and helped capture BLACK HAWK. At the time, his band lived on the Black River near present-day Trempeauleau. Other important band leaders of this time were GOOD THUNDER, LITTLE PRIEST, and WINNESHIEK.

Despite Waukon Decora's aid to whites, his band was forced to relocate several times. In 1840, he moved with his followers to a reservation in northeastern Iowa; in 1846, to Long Prairie, Minnesota; and, in 1855, to a reservation near Mankato, where he died. The band continued to be relocated under his son Little Decora.

DEGANAWIDA (Deganawidah, Dekanawida, Dekanawidah, Dekanahwidah; The Heavenly Messenger). *Huron. (fl. 1500s).* Mystic and lawgiver; founder of the Iroquois League.

Deganawida's story and that of the founding of the Iroquois League or Confederacy have taken on supernatural proportions. It is thought that he was born near present-day Kingston, Ontario, in the early to mid-1500s, one of seven brothers. Legend holds that he was born of a virgin and that his mother saw in a vision he would cause the destruction of the Hurons. As a result, she and his grandmother tried to drown the baby three times in a river, without success.

When grown, Deganawida crossed Lake Ontario—supposedly in a stone canoe—to New York where he met the Mohawk HIAWATHA. Together they planned the Iroquois League. It is thought that Deganawida, with a speech impediment, was the visionary, and Hiawatha the spokesman who traveled among the Mohawks, Oneidas, Cayugas, Onondagas, and Senecas, to spread the message of alliance. ATOTARHO, the Onondaga sachem, proved the biggest obstacle to unification.

After he had helped found the Iroquois League, plant the Tree of Peace, and write the Great Law, Deganawida served as one of the Pine Tree Sachems, chiefs chosen by merit rather than heredity. Deganawida also wanted the smaller Eries and Neutral (Attiwandaronk) tribes as part of the alliance. They declined, leading to their eventual dispersal at the hands of the Iroquois in the 1650s.

The Iroquois tribes also attacked and defeated the Hurons in 1649, as was prophesized by Deganawida's mother. One version of the legend describes how Deganawida, after the formation of the confederacy, departed in his stone canoe, promising to return if the alliance were threatened. (See also ATOTARHO; HIAWATHA.)

DEKANISORA (Decanesora, Dekanisoura, Teganissorens, Connessoa). *Onondaga.* *(ca. 1650–1730).* Spokesman for the Iroquois League.

In 1682, Dekanisora traveled to Montreal to negotiate a peace treaty with the French, becoming known as a powerful orator. Six years later, he was tricked by the Huron chief ADARIO, who wanted to prevent a French and Iroquois trade alliance, into believing that the French had plotted his capture. Dekanisora subsequently participated in an Iroquois attack on the French in Montreal in 1689 and negotiated treaties with the British, including one at Albany in 1726. CADWALLADER COLDEN compared Dekanisora to Cicero, the Roman writer and orator, because of the chief's diplomatic skills and dignity.

DELAWARE PROPHET. *Delaware. (fl. 1760s).* Medicine man; prophet; leader in Pontiac's Rebellion of 1763.

About 1760, the Delaware Prophet had a religious experience in which he claimed he journeyed to the Spirit World, encountered the Master of Life, and received a set of laws. He began preaching among the Delaware Indians of the Muskingum Valley of Ohio and among other tribes in the Lake Erie region of the Old Northwest. In revivalist style, he renounced all white customs and trade goods, especially liquor and firearms, and called for a resurgence in traditional Indian ways, without intertribal warfare, magic, or polygamy. He prepared deerskins with written laws and left them in villages.

The Delaware Prophet also predicted a war with the whites, and his anti-white stand captured the imagination of many tribes of the region. One of his converts was PONTIAC. The Ottawa leader spread the same message of Indian unity, but allowed for friendship with the French as well as the use of guns. Numerous tribes joined Pontiac's Rebellion of 1763 against the British. (See also PONTIAC.)

DELGADITO (Herrero Delgadito, "slender little metalworker"; Beshiltheeni, "knife maker"; Atsidi Sani, Old Smith). *Navajo. (ca. 1830–ca. 1870).* Medicine man and ceremonial singer; participant in

the Navajo War of 1863–66; thought to be first Navajo to take up silversmithing. Brother of BARBONCITO.

Delgadito and his brother Barboncito led 500 followers in the Navajo War in support of MANUELITO. After CHRISTOPHER "KIT" CARSON's scorched-earth offensive in summer 1863, destroying Navajo livestock and grain throughout much of the tribe's Arizona homeland, Delgadito and Barboncito sent a third brother, El Sordo, and another brave to Fort Wingate, New Mexico, under a flag of truce as emissaries. They offered to build hogans near the post, but were told they had to relocate to Bosque Redondo. Some among the band—many of them women and children—surrendered along with Delgadito soon afterward in October 1863. Others remained at Canyon de Chelly with Barboncito until a march by soldiers on the Navajo stronghold in 1864.

Delgadito was among the first Navajos to be taken to Bosque Redondo in eastern New Mexico in early 1864. He later signed the treaty of June 1, 1868, allowing the Navajos to return to their ancestral lands.

Before the war, in the 1850s, Delgadito had learned silversmithing from a Mexican craftsman by the name of Nakai Tsosi. About the same time, the Indian agent at Fort Defiance, Captain HENRY L. DODGE, brought in the blacksmith George Carter to teach the Navajos ironwork. It is thought that, in 1853, Delgadito crafted his first jewelry piece from silver coins. He taught other Navajos, including his son Red Smith, this new skill, establishing a tradition among his people. (See also MANUELITO.)

DELSHAY. *Tonto Apache. (ca. 1835–1874).* Chief of the Tonto band of Western Apaches during the early Apache Wars.

In 1868, Delshay agreed to keep his Tonto band near Camp McDowell on the Verde River in Arizona, reporting to an agent there. In 1871, however, after the massacre at Camp Crant of ESKIMINZIN's Aravaipa Apaches, plus an attack on Delshay by a soldier at Camp McDowell, the chief requested that his band be able to report instead to an agency in the Sunflower Valley, closer to their ancestral homeland. Delshay received no reply.

In 1872, in response to a public outcry about continuing Western Apache raids, General GEORGE CROOK launched the Tonto Basin Campaign, sending nine small, mobile detachments with Apache scouts over the Tonto Basin and surrounding tableland. The army under captains James Burns and William Brown won a victory at the Battle of Skull Cave in December 1872, against Yavapais who had fled the reservation at Camp Verde. Captain George Randall then gained a decisive victory at Turret Peak in March 1873.

The next month, when his band's women and children were surrounded by soldiers, Delshay and his warriors surrendered. Randall took them to Fort Apache on the White Mountain Reservation of Coyotero Apaches to the east. Miserable in confinement, Delshay and his followers fled Fort Apache in July and went to Camp Verde on the Verde River north of Camp McDowell. Delshay was informed by the agent at Camp Verde that the Tontos could stay if they ceased all raiding. They lived peacefully for a time until Apache fugitives from the killing of Lieutenant Jacob Almy on the San Carlos Reservation joined them. Crook ordered the arrest of Delshay. The Tonto leader fled into the Tonto Basin and eluded the soldiers for months. Crook then put a price on his head.

In July 1874, an Apache brought in Delshay's head, or so he claimed; a second Apache brought in what he also claimed was the Tonto leader's head. Crook paid each a reward and displayed one head at Camp Verde and the other on the San Carlos Reservation.

DENIG, EDWIN T. *(1812–1858).* Anthropologist; naturalist; fur trader.

Edwin Denig, born in Stroudsburg, Pennsylvania, began working for the American Fur Company along the upper Missouri in Montana in 1833. Denig married two Assiniboine women and became knowledgeable about the wildlife and Indian tribes of the region. In 1843, he helped John James Audubon collect specimens, and, in 1850, he provided specimens to the Smithsonian. By 1849, he was head administrator of Fort Union, North Dakota.

Denig also provided information on Indian legends to the Jesuit missionary PIERRE JEAN DE SMET, who used much of it in his writings, as well as to HENRY ROWE SCHOOLCRAFT for his study of the Indians. Denig's report to Schoolcraft was later published by the Smithsonian's Bureau of American Ethnology as a book in its own right, *Indian Tribes of the Upper Missouri* (1928–29). It was later established, long after Denig's death in 1858, that much of the material for FERDINAND V. HAYDEN's study of Indian languages, *Contributions to the Ethnology and Philology* (1862), was in fact written by Denig.

DE SMET, PIERRE JEAN (Blackrobe). *(1801–1873).* Missionary; peace commissioner; writer.

Belgian-born Jesuit missionary Pierre Jean De Smet came to the United States in 1821, where he served as a novitiate in Florissant, Missouri, and was ordained in 1827. Catholic church officials sent him to minster to the Potawatomis at Council Bluffs, Iowa, in the early 1830s.

In 1840, after repeated requests by Flathead and Nez Perce delegations to St. Louis for missionaries among them, De Smet traveled to Montana with two Flathead Indians and an American Fur Company caravan. His first mission to the Indians was St. Mary's at present-day Stevensville, Montana, in the Bitterroot Valley. Traveling in territory that now makes up the states of Montana, Idaho, Washington, and Oregon in 1840–46, De Smet and his colleagues, including NICOLAS POINT, succeeded in establishing a chain of interconnected missions, known as the Rocky Mountain Missions. Among his conversions were Flatheads, Coeur d'Alenes, Kalispels, Nez Perces, Cayuses, Yankton and Teton Sioux, and Blackfeet, many of whom referred to the Jesuits as blackrobes.

De Smet also traveled to Europe 16 times to campaign for the continued support of Catholic missions to the Indians of the American West, publishing his entreaties in six languages. After 1846, he used St. Louis as his base of operations, but continued to make trips up the Missouri for missionary purposes or as a peace envoy.

In the course of his work, De Smet established peace between the Blackfeet and the Flatheads. He also served as a government peace commissioner at the Fort Laramie councils in 1851 and 1868, and during the Yakima War of 1855–56 under KAMIAKIN and the related Coeur d'Alene War of 1858.

De Smet wrote several books about his experiences, including *New Indian Sketches* (1863).

DE SOTO, HERNANDO. *(ca. 1496–1542).* Explorer.

Hernando de Soto, born in southeastern Spain's Estremadura region, first came to the Americas in 1514, taking part in the conquest of Panama with Pedro Arias de Avila, then in exploratory expeditions of the coast of Central America. In 1523, he participated in the conquest of Nicaragua with Francisco Hernandez de Cordoba. In 1531–35, De Soto was with Francisco Pizarro in Peru among the Inca Indians. Returning to Spain in 1536, he was named governor of the colony on Cuba, with official approval for the conquest of Florida.

Hearing tales of rich Indian settlements in the inland territory north of Mexico, De Soto undertook an expedition into the present-day southeastern United States, leaving Spain in April 1538 and landing in Cuba in June. At the end of May 1539, with a company of seven ships and 600 men, he landed along Florida's west coast, perhaps at Tampa Bay. He took several Indian hostages to prevent attacks by hostiles, then proceeded north. His expedition spent that first winter in the lands of the Apalachees, near present-day Tallahassee, Florida.

De Soto and his men then headed north into what is now Georgia, sacking an Apalachee settlement along the way. Still seeking gold and other precious minerals, the De Soto party penetrated into the interior of the Carolinas and Tennessee, then headed southward into Alabama. Soon after, in October 1540, they fought a pitched battle with the Alabamas under TASCALUSA. They later came across the settlements of the agriculturally advanced Choctaws in Mississippi, whose fields and food supplies De Soto's men appropriated. In a subsequent battle with the Chickasaws, the expedition lost men and supplies.

De Soto and his men crossed the Mississippi in June 1541, continuing westward into Arkansas and Oklahoma. Failing to find the fabled cities of gold—the seven cities of Cibola for which De Soto's contemporary, FRANCISCO VASQUEZ DE CORONADO, was also searching—De Soto and his men returned southeastward into Louisiana. In May 1542, after nearly three years of exploration in the Southeast, De Soto contracted fever and died. His men secretly disposed of his body in the Mississippi River to prevent the Indians from finding it.

The survivors, now led by Luis de Moscoso de Alvarado, then attempted to reach Mexico by heading southwestward into Texas, probably as far as the Trinity River, but were turned back by the inhospitable environment. They returned to the Mississippi River, built makeshift barges, and sailed into the Gulf of Mexico, heading southward along the coast and reaching the Spanish settlement at Tampico in September 1543. A little more than half of the original expedition had survived. Despite the historical importance of the expedition, it was considered a failure by Spanish officials because no riches were found.

Scientists have speculated that De Soto's early and extensive contact with Indian peoples brought widespread disease to them, decimating many tribes generations before the first extensive white settlement of the area.

DINWIDDIE, ROBERT. *(1693–1770).* Virginia colonial governor during the French and Indian War of 1754–63.

Born in Scotland, Robert Dinwiddie became collector of customs for Bermuda (1727–38); surveyor general for the Bahamas, Jamaica, Pennsylvania, Maryland, Virginia, and the Carolinas (1738–51); then lieutenant governor of Virginia (1751–58). Since the titular governors never came to Virginia, he was in effect the chief colonial administrator.

During Dinwiddie's administration, pro-British tribes of the Ohio Valley were suffering encroachment by Indians allied with the French. Unified support for the Indians against French-backed aggression was hampered by intensive competition for the fur trade between Virginia and the other British colonies. Dinwiddie had a financial stake in the Ohio Company, and his policies in support of the pro-British Indians of the Ohio Valley were considered by private Virginian business interests as a threat to their own trading enterprises.

In 1754, Dinwiddie ordered the militia to undertake an expedition to the confluence of the Ohio, Monongahela, and Allegheny rivers, at the site of present-day Pittsburgh, and there construct a post that would help stem French advancement into the Ohio Valley. The post was soon captured by the French and renamed Fort Duquesne. Colonial troops under the command of GEORGE WASHINGTON, with Indians under the Mingo HALF-KING (Tanacharison), were defeated on July 3 at a nearby entrenchment camp called Fort Necessity and forced to surrender.

The following year, Dinwiddie hired 500 Cherokee warriors to fight on the side of the British colonists in General EDWARD BRADDOCK's campaign to recapture the strategically important Fort Duquesne. The expedition proved a military disaster for the British, with Braddock himself mortally wounded in an attack by French troops and Indian auxiliaries on July 9, 1755.

In failing health, Dinwiddie returned to England in 1758.

DODGE, HENRY. *(1782–1867).* Army officer; territorial governor; Indian superintendent. Father of HENRY LAFAYETTE DODGE.

Born in the Indiana frontier settlement of Vincennes, Henry Dodge was raised in what is now Missouri while the region was still under Spanish dominion. In 1805, following the acquisition of the Louisiana Territory by the United States, Dodge became a district sheriff, and, in 1813, territorial marshal of Missouri. In the War of 1812, he served as a major of mounted volunteer militia, and was subsequently promoted to the rank of major general.

In 1827, Dodge moved to the Michigan Territory in an area now part of Wisconsin, and, that same year, fought in the Winnebago War against RED BIRD's warriors. With the outbreak of the Black Hawk War in 1832, he was made a colonel of a mounted Michigan militia unit, as well as a major in the regular army. In July 1832, he led U.S. Mounted Rangers against BLACK HAWK's followers at the Battle of Wisconsin Heights.

Following the Black Hawk War, Dodge organized the 1st Dragoon Regiment at Jefferson Barracks south of St. Louis. In 1833, the heavily armed mounted unit was sent to Fort Gibson in the Indian Territory to help in the settlement of Iroquois from New York and Ohio and the Five Civilized Tribes from the Southeast.

In June 1834, the army organized a peace mission to the Southern Plains tribes—the Dragoon Expedition, originally commanded by HENRY LEAVENWORTH. Frontier painter GEORGE CATLIN traveled with the Dragoons. By the time the expedition reached Camp Washita, about halfway from Fort Gibson to the Wichita

Mountains, many of the men had become ill, including Leavenworth, who died. Dodge chose 250 healthy men and pushed on to the north fork of the Red River in present-day Kiowa County, Oklahoma. Dodge conferred with Kiowa, Comanche, Wichita, and Caddo leaders and attempted to demonstrate good faith on the government's part by dispensing gifts. In addition, he delivered the Kiowa girl Gunpandama, whom he had earlier ransomed from the Osages, to her people. His efforts soon led to the earliest peace treaties between the tribes of the Southern Plains and the federal government.

In 1835, Dodge carried out another expedition to impress the Plains tribes with the government's military power and to maintain peace on the western routes. Leading three companies of well-armed dragoons, he traveled to the Rocky Mountains via the Oregon Trail and back along the Santa Fe Trail, a total of 1,600 miles. During the expedition, he met with Indian leaders at BENT's Fort to establish peaceful relations.

In 1836, President ANDREW JACKSON appointed Dodge as governor of the newly organized Wisconsin Territory, then comprising Wisconsin, Minnesota, and parts of the present states of North and South Dakota, Iowa, and Michigan. As territorial governor, Dodge was also the area's superindendent of Indian affairs. He was elected to the House of Representatives as Wisconsin territorial delegate, and served from 1841 to 1845, then he was reappointed as territorial governor. When Wisconsin was admitted to the Union as a state in 1848, Dodge became one of its two original U.S. senators, serving until 1857. He was the father of Henry Lafayette Dodge.

DODGE, HENRY CHEE (Hastiin Adits'aii, "man who interprets," "one who hears and understands"; Ashkihih, "boy interpreter"; Kilchii, Kilchee, Chee, "red boy"). *Mixed Navajo. (ca. 1857–1947).* Principal chief; tribal chairman; interpreter.

Chee Dodge, born at Fort Defiance, Arizona, was the son of a Navajo-Jemez mother, Bisnayanchi. The year of his birth, probably either 1857 or 1860, is uncertain, as is the identity of his father. He was originally reported to be the son of a Mexican silversmith and interpreter by the name of Juan Aneas (also spelled Anea, Anaya, Cocinas, Cosinisas, or Goshinashu). Evidence suggests, however, that his actual father was the white agent to the Navajos, HENRY L. DODGE. In any case, he was named after the agent. Aneas or Cocinas, most likely his stepfather, died when he was an infant. His mother died during CHRISTOPHER "KIT" CARSON's 1864 campaign into Navajo country. He was adopted by an old man and his granddaughter and accompanied them on the Long Walk to Bosque Redondo in eastern New Mexico.

On returning to Fort Defiance after 1868, Dodge was reunited with his Navajo aunt, the wife of a white man who was an agency employee, Perry H. Williams, who taught the boy English. He came to live in the family of William F. M. Arny, who was then an Indian agent, and attended the Fort Defiance Indian School, where he learned to read and write and became the official Navajo interpreter. He also found work as an assistant to the ethnologist WASHINGTON MATTHEWS.

In 1885, Dodge was appointed Navajo head chief by the Bureau of Indian Affairs, succeeding MANUELITO. As such he negotiated with federal officials, but was not recognized as a leader by the various bands, who had their own headmen. That same year, Dodge traveled to Washington, D.C., and met President Chester A. Arthur and other governmental officials. In 1890, he became a partner in a trading post and also invested in livestock. His business ventures proved successful and he was able to build a home and ranch near Crystal, New Mexico.

In 1923, Dodge was chosen as first chairman of the newly organized Navajo Tribal Council and served until 1934. He made many trips to Washington, D.C., on behalf of his people. He was reelected to a second term in 1942, then again in 1946, but died the next year.

Dodge was instrumental in the transition of the tribe to an effective modern-day organization, as well as in his people's economic development. At the same time, he encouraged the continuation of traditional Navajo beliefs and arts and crafts.

DODGE, HENRY LAFAYETTE (Red Shirt). *(1810–1856).* Indian agent; interpreter. Son of HENRY DODGE.

Henry L. Dodge was the son of the army officer Henry Dodge. He was born at Ste. Genevieve (Missouri), a fur-trading post on the Mississippi River opposite Kaskaskia (Illinois). He married at the age of 26 and settled in Dodgeville (Wisconsin), serving under his father in the BLACK HAWK War of 1832.

During the Mexican War of 1846–48, Dodge was a captain in the Santa Fe Battalion of Mounted Volunteers. He remained in New Mexico and worked for the military as forage master, as well as interpreter to the Navajos. In 1851, he participated in Colonel EDWIN SUMNER's campaign against the Navajos.

In 1853, Dodge received an appointment as agent to the Navajos, as well as to the Hopi, Zuni, Acoma, and Laguna Pueblo Indians, with instructions to establish his agency headquarters at Fort Defiance in present-day Arizona near the New Mexico border. Over the next years, he conducted agency business from numerous locations in the region. Dodge, whom the Navajos called Red Shirt because of his fondness for the color, established good relations with the tribe's headmen, including ARMIJO, BARBONCITO, DELGADITO, GANADO MUCHO, HERRERO GRANDE, and MANUELITO, showing respect for their way of life. His tenure as agent was a period of peace. He encouraged farming among the Indians and had his blacksmith at Fort Defiance, George Carter, teach them metalwork. Delgadito is thought to have been the first silversmith among his people and passed the art form to his descendants.

In 1865, following a raid on Zuni Pueblo by Apaches, Dodge joined a detachment of troops in pursuit of the hostiles. While hunting away from camp, he was captured and killed by an Apache war party. It has been theorized that if Dodge had lived and continued on as agent to the Navajos, the Navajo War of 1863–66 would not have occurred.

Dodge, who left his first wife in Wisconsin, reportedly married a Navajo woman and might have been the father of HENRY CHEE DODGE, who became tribal chairman of the Navajos in the 20th century.

DODGE, RICHARD IRVING. *(1827–1895).*
Historian; army officer.

Richard Irving Dodge was born in Huntsville, North Carolina, a grandnephew of the writer Washington Irving. He graduated from West Point in 1848, and, during the Civil War, served as aide-de-camp to General WILLIAM T. SHERMAN.

Dodge went on to a military career in the Northern Plains. In summer 1868, he directed the construction of Fort Fred Steele, near the site of present-day Rawlins, Wyoming. This post, situated on the North Platte River, provided protection for workers building the Union Pacific Railway through Indian country. Once the railroad was constructed, Dodge's command protected the tracks and the nearby Oregon-California Trail from Indian attacks.

In summer 1875, the federal government assigned Dodge and his command of 400 troops to escort geologist Walter P. Jenny into the Dakota Territory's Black Hills to confirm Colonel GEORGE ARMSTRONG CUSTER's 1874 report of the discovery of mineral wealth in the region. This influx of troops angered the Sioux and added to the tensions that precipitated the outbreak of the War for the Black Hills of 1876–77.

As part of General GEORGE CROOK's fall 1876 counteroffensive against CRAZY HORSE, SITTING BULL, and the Sioux-Cheyenne confederacy, Dodge commanded the 4th U.S. Artillery Regiment. Operating out of Fort Fetterman, Wyoming, he participated in the November 25, 1876, attack on DULL KNIFE's Cheyenne band on the Powder River.

On leaving the military, Dodge embarked on a career as a historian, producing accounts of the Indian wars on the Great Plains, as well as studies of the Indians and their environment. His works were praised by President Theodore Roosevelt. Among his books on Indian history were: *The Plains of the Great West, and Their Inhabitants* (1877); and his autobiographical work, *Our Wild Indians: Thirty-three Years' Personal Experience Among the Red Men of the Great West* (1882). During the last years of the 19th century, along with writer Jacob Piatt Dunn, Dodge was considered one of the most accurate popular historians of the final Indian wars.

DODGE, WILLIAM EARL. *(1805–1883).*
Reformer; congressman.

William Earl Dodge was born in Hartford, Connecticut, the son of David Low Dodge, founder of the New York Peace Society. When 13, William began work in a wholesale dry-goods store. He went on to establish, in 1833, the merchant firm of Phelps, Dodge & Company. Before the Civil War, he was part of the abolition movement and played an important role in the establishment of the Young Men's Christian Association (YMCA). He also served as a Republican congressman from New York in 1866–67.

Dodge became active in the post–Civil War Indian reform movement and helped institute President ULYSSES S. GRANT's Peace Policy toward the Indians with the hope of bringing them into mainstream American society. Along with PETER COOPER, Dodge helped organize the privately funded United States Indian Commission in 1868.

In 1869, as a member of the government-sponsored Board of Indian Commissioners, Dodge toured the reservations of the Indian Territory and Kansas. He met with Cheyennes and Arapaho chiefs at Camp Supply and advised them to begin to live like whites. At Fort Sill, he met with the Kiowa chief SATANTA, who expressed his doubts about the federal program to assimilate Indians. The next year, a U.S. cavalry battalion under the command of Colonel E. M. Baker killed 173 Piegans—mostly old men, women and children—in Montana. Dodge lobbied for the prosecution of those responsible.

During the 1870s, Dodge unsuccessfully campaigned to have the Bureau of Indian Affairs removed from the Department of the Interior and reestablished as an executive department in its own right. While Congress was enacting the 1883 Indian Appropriation Bill, Dodge made sure that a significant portion of these funds was earmarked for Indian educational programs.

In the early 1880s, Dodge supported the efforts of CARL SCHURZ, secretary of the Interior, in his efforts to forcibly relocate the Ponca Indians of Nebraska to the Indian Territory. Dodge was also a strong advocate of the General Allotment Act (the DAWES Severalty Act) of 1887.

Dodge agreed with the majority of Indian reformers of the 1870s–80s who supported the government's policy of granting citizenship to Native Americans only after they had been "civilized" and lived within white society.

DOHASAN. See LITTLE MOUNTAIN.

DONEHOGAWA. See PARKER, ELY SAMUEL.

DONIPHAN, ALEXANDER WILLIAM. *(1808–18 87)*. Militia officer.

Born near Maysville, Kentucky, Alexander W. Doniphan was an 1826 graduate of Augusta College. He subsequently studied law and was admitted to the bar in 1828. He moved to Missouri two years later and practiced law in Liberty. Becoming active in politics, he was twice elected to the state legislature during the 1830s.

Doniphan was also prominent in the Missouri state militia, holding the rank of brigadier general in 1838, at the height of the Mormon crisis in that state. Doniphan openly defied the orders of the governor of Missouri to carry out the executions of Joseph Smith and other Mormon leaders. Instead, he negotiated a settlement that resulted in the Mormons peacefully leaving Missouri.

At the outbreak of the Mexican War in 1846, Doniphan was elected colonel of the Missouri Mounted Volunteers, a militia unit he had organized. He brought his command to Fort Leavenworth, Kansas, and there joined with General STEPHEN WATTS KEARNY's forces for the invasion of the Mexican province of New Mexico. In November 1846, Kearny, with Doniphan's Missouri volunteers, occupied Santa Fe without any resistance from the Mexicans. Soon after, Kearny claimed the Mexican province of New Mexico for the United States.

Doniphan then drew up a code of laws for the newly acquired U.S. Territory of New Mexico, granting citizenship to all its Mexican inhabitants. Yet Doniphan's New Mexico laws, which came to be known as the Kearny Code, ignored the region's Indians.

When Kearny and his forces headed west to attack the Mexican army in California, Doniphan was left in command of New Mexico. In early December 1846, Doniphan led his Missouri volunteers in an expedition into western New Mexico to pacify Navajo and Ute Indians who had been stealing livestock in their raids on ranches and Pueblo settlements. Doniphan led three columns of his troops, about 330 men, into Navajo country, hoping that a large military presence would discourage the marauding. After a series of minor encounters on the Colorado Plateau, Doniphan concluded peace agreements with 14 Navajo band chiefs at Bear Spring, New Mexico Territory, near the present site of Gallup.

Doniphan then left the military administration of New Mexico to Colonel STERLING PRICE, another colonel of Missouri volunteers. With his command of about 1,000 Missouri Mounted volunteers, he headed south into Texas. In late December 1846, his men defeated a larger force of Mexican troops on the Brazita River, and the Missouri forces soon occupied El Paso.

In January 1847, however, Pueblo Indians and Mexicans, angered by the appropriation of their livestock by the occupying Missouri forces, joined in an armed revolt against the American authorities at Taos. Territorial governor CHARLES BENT was killed along with other Americans. Price was therefore unable to send artillery and other supplies south to aid Doniphan in his invasion of northern Mexico.

Nevertheless, Doniphan's Thousand, as his highly successful but militarily unconventional troops were called, continued their advance into northern Mexico. Near the city of Chihuahua, they faced a 4,000-man Mexican army at the Battle of Sacramento in February 1847. Although outnumbered, Doniphan's Missouri Mounted Volunteers were again victorious.

Doniphan and his command were soon mustered out of the service. The Missouri unit returned to St. Louis by way of New Orleans after having won major victories with a minimum of tactical support and with few casualties.

Doniphan returned to his law practice, and, in 1854, was again elected to the Missouri State Legislature. In 1861, he was a state delegate to the peace conference held in Washington, D.C., that attempted to avert the Civil War. Doniphan opposed secession, but wanted Missouri to remain neutral if war should come. When hostilities erupted, Doniphan held the rank of major general in the Missouri state militia, but resigned after two weeks, returning to private life.

DONNACONNA (Donacona). *Huron.*
(d. ca. 1539). Principal chief; visitor to France.

In 1534, on the Gaspe Peninsula of present-day Quebec, chief Donnaconna and a party of Hurons, on a trip to hunt seals, met the French explorer JACQUES CARTIER. He was persuaded by Cartier to allow his two sons to travel with the expedition as guides. They sailed with Cartier back to France and returned the next year, showing him the way to the Huron homeland.

In 1535, on the second day after the Cartier expedition had anchored in the St. Lawrence River near the Huron village of Stadacona (present-day Quebec City), Donnaconna and his men paddled out in 12 canoes to be reunited with his sons. From Stadacona, Cartier continued up the St. Lawrence to the Huron village of Hochelaga (present-day Montreal).

Back at Stadacona, Cartier, who wanted the chief to help him win backing for further expeditions, had his men take the Huron chief on board the ship by force. Although at first resisting, Donnaconna agreed to go to France when Cartier promised to return him to his homeland within a year. Donnaconna made a speech from the deck of the ship to his warriors, then sent them away.

In France, Donnaconna was presented to King Francis I. Yet the chief and the other Hurons who had accompanied him contracted European diseases and died abroad. Cartier returned to North America in 1541 for further explorations.

DOOLITTLE, JAMES ROOD. *(1815–1897).* Senator; reformer.

James R. Doolittle was born in Granville, New York, attended Hobart College, then studied law in Rochester. He became involved in New York politics, and, after having moved to Wisconsin in 1851, continued his political pursuits. He served as Republican senator from Wisconsin in 1857–69.

In the wake of the 1864 Sand Creek Massacre, in which BLACK KETTLE and his band of Southern Cheyennes were decimated by a Colorado militia force under Colonel JOHN CHIVINGTON, Congress appointed Doolittle as chairman of a joint committee to investigate tribal conditions on the frontier. Doolittle and other committee members toured the tribal lands of the Great Plains to evaluate the situation and determine what measures the government should take to establish a lasting peace.

The Doolittle Committee report, *Report on the Conditions of the Indian Tribes,* published in 1867, provided a picture of the West under the influence of the heavy military buildup following the Civil War. It concluded that armed Indian resistance was the result of unlawful encroachment onto Indian lands by settlers and hunters. In addition, it declared that many outbreaks of armed conflict with the Indians were precipitated by the actions of overly aggressive military officers. Its recommendations included restricting Indians to smaller reservations and discouraging their nomadic life-style.

The Doolittle Report provided a basis for further study, conducted by PETER COOPER's United States Indian Commission, as well as subsequent Indian reform measures of the 1870s and 1880s, culminating in the 1887 General Allotment Act (the DAWES Severalty Act).

DORION, MARIE (Dorion Woman; Marie of the Iowas; Marie Aioe). *Iowa. (1786–ca. 1853).* Guide of Astorians. Wife of PIERRE DORION, JR.

The Iowa Indian Marie Aioe, who would become known as Dorion Woman, was 20 years old and living along the Red River in what is now southwestern Arkansas when she met and married Pierre Dorion, Jr., a mixed French Canadian and Yankton Sioux trader. She accompanied him up the Missouri, and they had two sons, Baptiste and Paul. Her husband, in the employ of the fur trader MANUEL LISA, worked between St. Louis and Mandan (North Dakota).

During a trip to St. Louis, Pierre Dorion left Lisa to join the expedition backed by JOHN JACOB ASTER. To the dismay of WILSON PRICE HUNT, the leader of the Overland Astorians, Dorion insisted that his wife and two boys go along. The expedition set out from St. Louis in March 1811. Like the Shoshone SACAJAWEA, who accompanied LEWIS and CLARK, Dorion Woman proved a valuable guide, interpreter, and peacemaker with the Indians. In December, she gave birth to a third boy, who died within eight days. The expedition reached Astoria, Oregon, at the mouth of the Columbia River in February 1812.

Because of the War of 1812, the post was sold to the North West Company out of Canada. Some of the Astorians departed on a return trip in 1813. Another group, including the Dorions, set out for the Snake River country of what is now Idaho to find an earlier trapping party, collect pelts, then meet up with the Astorians returning to St. Louis. But all were killed in this group—most in attacks by local Indians—except Dorion Woman and her boys. In early 1814, she managed to cross the Snake River, but could not pass through the Blue Mountains in winter. She killed her horses, drying their meat for food and using the hides for a tent. Then, in the spring, she led her boys safely through the wilderness to Wallawalla Indian country where the Snake River meets the Columbia in eastern Washington, about 250 miles. Dorion Woman met the other Astorians here and reported the fate of her party. She did not return with them to St. Louis, however, heading instead for the Okanogan Mountains to the north.

In the following years, Dorion Woman married two more times, first to a trapper named Venier, with who she lived at Fort Okanogon in Washington, then to an interpreter at Walla Walla, Jean Baptiste Toupin. Her eldest son, Baptiste Dorion, became an interpreter attached to the Hudson's Bay Company on the Columbia River. In 1841, Dorion Woman and Toupin moved westward to the Willamette Valley near Salem, Oregon, where she died.

DORION, PIERRE, SR. *(ca. 1750–ca. 1820).* Trader; interpreter; guide. Father of PIERRE DORION, JR.

Born in Quebec to a prominent French-Canadian family, Pierre Dorion, Sr., moved to the Sioux country of the upper Missouri before 1780, where he soon entered the burgeoning Missouri River fur trade. He learned several Indian languages, married a series of

Sioux women, and had several mixed-blood children, including Pierre Dorion, Jr., who also became a guide and fur trader with his Iowa wife MARIE DORION.

By 1799, Dorion was extensively involved in trade with the Iowa tribes who then inhabited the Des Moines River region. In June 1804, he was hired by the LEWIS anc CLARK Expedition as an interpreter to the Sioux bands then living between present-day Glasgow, Missouri, and Yankton, South Dakota. His duties included arranging for delegations of Sioux to visit government officials in Washington, D.C. Moreover, he advised the expedition's leaders on Indian customs and protocol and provided his knowledge of points of Indian cultural interest, such as stone Indian ruins along the Missouri River.

In August 1804, Dorion served as interpreter for Lewis and Clark's conference with five Sioux chiefs and 50 warriors. In 1805–06, he was hired to take a shipment of presents to the Arikaras on the upper Missouri, after an Arikara chief had died on a visit to Washington, D.C., the year before. The presents were intended to indemnify the Indians for the loss of their chief. Dorion was commissioned to get the goods safely past the Sioux tribes living between the Arikaras and the main shipping center at St. Louis. During this venture, he was accompanied by fellow interpreter and guide Rene Jusseaume.

Pierre Dorion, Sr., remained with the Sioux in the Dakotas for the rest of his life. He spent his last days living in a tepee outside of the Missouri River post of Fort Pierre in present-day South Dakota.

DORION, PIERRE, JR. *Mixed Yankton Sioux.*
(d. 1814). Trader; interpreter; guide. Son of PIERRE DORION, SR.; husband of MARIE DORION.

In the early 1800s, Pierre Dorion, Jr., managed a trading post on the Missouri River among the Yanktons in what is now South Dakota for the CHOUTEAU family of St. Louis. He was among the Yankton Sioux in their council of August 31, 1804, with members of the LEWIS and CLARK Expedition, arranged by his father of the same name. He stayed with the expedition for a short time as interpreter.

Then, with his father, Dorion guided a delegation of Yankton chiefs to Washington, D.C. On returning to the Missouri, he worked for the trader MANUEL LISA between St. Louis and Mandan, North Dakota. In 1811–12, Dorion and his Iowa Indian wife, Marie Dorion, accompanied the expedition backed by JOHN JACOB ASTOR from St. Louis to Astoria (Oregon). In January 1814, while on a beaver-trapping expedition at the confluence of the Boise and Snake rivers, about 330 miles east of Astoria near what is now the Oregon-Idaho border, Dorion was killed in an attack by local Indians. His wife and two sons survived him.

DORSEY, JAMES OWEN. *(1848–1895).*
Anthropologist; linguist; missionary.

James Owen Dorsey, born in Baltimore, Maryland, showed an aptitude in languages as a child, mastering Hebrew by the age of six. He studied theology in Alexandria, Virginia, and was ordained into the Episcopal church in 1871. His first contact with western Indians was his assignment as missionary to the Poncas of the Dakota Territory and he soon mastered their language. After having returned East because of illness, Dorsey began to collect ethnographic and linguistic data for JOHN WESLEY POWELL of the Smithsonian's Bureau of Ethnology, especially among the Omahas, Osages, and Sioux, as well as various Athapascan peoples. He was a colleague of the Sioux linguist GEORGE BUSHOTTER. Dorsey's published works include: *Of the Comparative Phonology of Four Siouan Languages* (1883); *Omaha Sociology* (1884); *Osage Traditions* (1888); and *Siouan Sociology* (1897).

DOUGLAS. See QUINKENT.

DRAGGING CANOE (Tsiyu-Gunsini, Tsungunsini, Cheucunsene, Kunmesee). *Cherokee.*
(ca. 1730–1792). Chief of Chickamauga band; ally of British in the American Revolution. Son of ATTAKULLAKULLA; cousin of NANCY WARD.

Dragging Canoe was born along the Tennessee River in what is now eastern Tennessee, the son of the peace chief Attakullakulla. At the Treaty of Sycamore Shoals on the Watauga River (near the present-day boundary between Tennessee and North Carolina) in March 1775, Cherokee leaders exchanged what is now much of Kentucky and northern Tennessee for 10,000 pounds of trade goods. Dragging Canoe led a dissident group that refused to sign the agreement. During the subsequent fighting in the American Revolution, most Cherokees maintained a neutral stance. Attakullakulla, however, leaned toward the rebels, while Dragging Canoe accepted arms from the British.

In July 1776, Dragging Canoe's warriors attacked the trans-Appalachian Watauga settlements, laying siege to two makeshift forts—Eaton's Station and Fort Watauga. His cousin Nancy Ward, council member of the Cherokees, warned the settlers of the attack and saved many lives. When the militia under JAMES ROBERTSON and JOHN SEVIER broke through in a counterattack, Dragging Canoe then led his followers to Chickamauga Creek in the hill country near present-day Chattanooga, Tennessee. The Chickamaugas continued their raids in Tennessee as well as in isolated parts of Virginia, the Carolinas, and Georgia. Militias were raised to destroy Cherokee villages and crops.

In 1777, tribal leaders signed away even more of the Cherokee homeland. Yet Dragging Canoe and his allies, including the Cherokee BLOODY FELLOW and the Creek ALEXANDER McGILLIVRAY, continued their resistance. In 1778, they received a new shipment of arms from British agents out of Pensacola, Florida, and began another wave of attacks on settlers, followed by more destruction on the part of the frontier militias. The deadly cycle continued until all remaining Chickamauga villages were destroyed.

In 1782, Dragging Canoe led his people downriver and established the "five lower towns," one of them Mialaquo, his new home. In 1784, these towns were also destroyed, at which time he agreed to peace.

During Dragging Canoe's final years, he saw more treaties signed, more Cherokee lands ceded, new boundaries formed, and more white squatters. The pattern would repeat itself after his death, leading eventually to the Trail of Tears in the 1830s and the relocation of the Cherokees west of the Mississippi.

DROUILLARD, GEORGE. (Drewyer). *Mixed Pawnee.*

(d. 1810). Guide and interpreter for the Lewis and Clark Expedition; employee of MANUEL LISA.

George Drouillard, the son of a French father and a Pawnee mother, fought on the side of the British in the American Revolution against forces under GEORGE ROGERS CLARK, who later recommended Drouillard to MERIWETHER LEWIS. Drouillard joined Lewis on December 3, 1803, at Fort Massac near present-day Paducah, Kentucky. He was one of the best marksmen on the expedition and shot many of the 131 elk and 20 deer that were killed for food. WILLIAM CLARK also relied on information provided by Drouillard when he drew his map of the West. Because of his knowledge of sign language, the mixed-blood Drouillard also proved invaluable in communicating with many of the tribes encountered.

Drouillard later joined up with Manuel Lisa, representing other partners ANTOINE PIERRE MENARD and William Morrison in the field during the first American trading venture up the Missouri. EDWARD ROSE and JOHN COLTER also joined this expedition, which built the first white trading post in present-day Montana and established trade with the Crows. On his return to St. Louis, Drouillard was arrested, tried, and acquitted for the murder of Antoine Bissonette, who had stolen from and deserted the trading party.

In a subsequent expedition up the Missouri, Lisa built Fort Mandan, and Drouillard, Menard, Colter, and ANDREW HENRY continued upriver to Blackfoot country at Three Forks, where they built a stockade. On one of his beaver-trapping trips, Drouillard and two Shawnee companions were killed by Blackfeet. Legend has it that the warriors mutilated and ate parts of him to partake of his marksmanship and courage.

DUKES, JOSEPH. *Mixed Choctaw. (1811–1861).* Interpreter; translator.

Born in Mississippi, Joseph Dukes attended mission schools, then served as interpreter for various missionaries to his tribe. He also worked on a Choctaw (Muskogean) grammar and dictionary. Dukes stayed in Mississippi after his tribe's removal to the Indian Territory, eventually emigrating himself. In 1851–52, he worked with ALLEN WRIGHT in a translation of the Bible into the Choctaw language.

DULL KNIFE (Tahmelapashme; Wohehiv, Morning Star). *Northern Cheyenne. (ca. 1810–1883).* War chief in the Plains Indian wars; leader of the Flight of the Northern Cheyennes in 1878.

Dull Knife and his Northern Cheyenne warriors were active in the Cheyenne-Arapaho War in Colorado in 1864–65 as well as the Sioux Wars for the Northern Plains. During RED CLOUD's War for the BOZEMAN Trail of 1866–68, Dull Knife fought in the FETTERMAN Fight and other battles. He was one of the signers of the Fort Laramie Treaty of 1868. In 1875, about 400 of his warriors attacked WASHAKIE's Shoshones, allies of the whites.

Dull Knife and his warriors also joined the Sioux under SITTING BULL and CRAZY HORSE in the War for the Black Hills of 1876–77. Many of his warriors, including his son Bull Hump, fought at Rosebud and Little Bighorn in June 1876. Because of Cheyenne involvement, the army escalated its campaign against that tribe.

On July 17, a force under Colonel WESLEY MERRITT out of Fort Laramie intercepted and defeated about 1,000 Cheyennes at War Bonnet Creek, Nebraska, who had left Nebraska reservations to join up with Sioux bands under Sitting Bull and Crazy Horse. Chief YELLOW HAIR died in this battle.

Then, on November 25, Colonel RANALD S. MACKENZIE's 4th Cavalry under the command of General GEORGE CROOK attacked Dull Knife's camp—the so-called Battle of Dull Knife on the Red Fork of the Powder River in Wyoming. The Indians suffered 25 deaths and had 173 tepees destroyed, along with food and clothing, plus 500 ponies captured. The following May, in 1877, Dull Knife, LITTLE WOLF, and their followers, surrendered at Fort Robinson in Nebraska.

The Northern Cheyennes had expected to be assigned to the Sioux Reservation in the Black Hills, but were sent instead to the Indian Territory to join the Southern branch of their tribe on the Cheyenne-Arapaho Reservation near Fort Reno under Indian agent John Miles. The barren Southern Plains were difficult to farm, especially for a former hunting people. The government provided few supplies. With little food and rampant malaria, conditions were so miserable that Dull Knife, Little Wolf, and others resolved to return to their Tongue River homeland in northern Wyoming and southern Montana. On the night of September 9, 1878, nearly 300 men, women, and children, led by Dull Knife and Little Wolf, set out northward.

In a six-week, 1,500-mile flight over lands occupied and developed by whites—railroads, roads, ranches, and farms—the refugees eluded some 10,000 pursuing soldiers and an additional 3,000 civilians. They were cornered on various occasions, with some killed or captured, but the majority escaped. Yet many were too sick and exhausted to continue the flight. It was decided that Dull Knife and the weak would head to Red Cloud's reservation near Fort Robinson, Nebraska, to seek shelter and food from the Sioux. The strong would continue to the Tongue River with Little Wolf.

Dull Knife's group were captured by a cavalry outfit under Captain John Johnson on October 23 and taken to Fort Robinson. On learning they would be sent back to the Indian Territory, Dull Knife led his followers in another breakout on the bitterly cold night of January 9, 1879. Pursuing troops killed about half the escapees, including Dull Knife's daughter. Only Dull Knife, his wife, son, daughter-in-law, grandchild, and another boy escaped capture and made it to Red Cloud's reservation at Pine Ridge, where friends hid them until discovery by the army.

Meanwhile, Little Wolf and his group hid out for most of the winter. They were discovered and induced to surrender on March 27, along the Little Missouri River in the southeastern corner of Montana, by troops under Lieutenant William Philo Clark out of Fort Keogh.

Finally, after a period of bureaucratic wrangling, during which the survivors were allowed to stay in the north, the Northern Cheyennes were officially granted the Tongue River Reservation in Montana in 1884. Dull Knife died the year before and was buried on a high butte near the Rosebud River. (See also RED CLOUD; SITTING BULL.)

DULUTH, DANIEL GREYSOLON, SIEUR
Sieur Dulhut or Du Lhut). *(1636–1710).* Explorer; trader; peacemaker; soldier. Cousin of HENRI DE TONTI.

French-born Daniel Greysolon, Sieur Duluth, served in the French army as a young man. About 1672, he migrated to French Canada with his younger brother, and he settled in Montreal for the next six years.

In 1678, Duluth was sent west by French colonial authorities to explore the Great Lakes and seek a peaceful end to a war then raging between the Sioux and the Chippewas. He led a party into the Lake Huron region, where they spent the winter. In spring 1679, his men continued west to Lake Superior, where they made contact with the Sioux at their settlement at Mille Lacs Lake in what is now Minnesota.

Duluth achieved a peace agreement between the Sioux and the Chippewas and in so doing expanded the influence of France in the lucrative Great Lakes and upper Mississippi fur trade. He also arranged a peace settlement between the Sioux and the Assiniboines.

In 1680, Duluth explored the upper Mississippi River and claimed the territory for France. After this trip, among the Sioux Indians again, he negotiated the release of earlier French explorers in the region LOUIS HENNEPIN and Michel Aco.

On returning to Mackinac with Hennepin, Duluth found himself charged with illegal trading. He subsequently traveled to Montreal, then France to clear himself.

In 1683, French colonial authorities sent Duluth to the northern Lake Superior region, where he established a fort and set up his brother in the fur trade. Along with NICOLAS PERROT, he helped secure the allegiance of Great Lakes Algonquians in the 1683–84 French campaign against the Iroquois, for which he returned east.

In 1686, Duluth was back in the Great Lakes again, establishing trading posts. In 1688, at Rainy Lake, Ontario, he established the westernmost French settlement at that time in Canada. His commitment to the fur trade, as well as his participation in additional service against the Iroquois during the 1690s, in which Duluth commanded Quebec's Fort Frontenac, prevented him from carrying out the exploration of western Minnesota and the Dakotas. He retired to Montreal about 1696.

DUMONT, GABRIEL. *Metis. (1837–1906).*
Hunter; guide; leader in the Second Riel Rebellion of 1885.

The French Canadian Jean Baptiste Dumont was the patron of the Dumont clan. By his Sarcee-Crow wife, he had three sons: Isidore, Gabriel, and Jean. The Dumont family lived along the Saskatchewan River in present-day Saskatchewan, hunting and trading. In the early 1830s, Isidore settled along the Red River in present-day Manitoba and married Louise Laframboise. By her and a later second wife, he had a total of 11 children. The second son by Louise was named after Isidore's brother Gabriel.

In 1839, when Gabriel was two, Isidore Dumont moved his family to the vicinity of Fort Edmonton and Fort Pitt region of present-day Alberta, where he worked as a trader to the Indians. Gabriel was raised a Metis, learning both French Catholic and Cree Indian customs. By the time he was 12, he was a master horseman and sharpshooter with both a gun and a bow and arrow.

Gabriel Dumont. *Courtesy of National Archives of Canada/ C-15282.*

In 1848, the family moved southeast to the region of Regina in Saskatchewan. From this location, Gabriel roamed the Plains of Canada, Montana, and North Dakota with his older brother Isidore as a buffalo hunter. Hs reputation as a guide, hunter, canoeist, drinker, gambler, and fighter of Blackfeet and Sioux became widespread. His mastery of six languages made him valuable as an interpreter.

In 1858, Dumont married Madeleine Welkie, the daughter of a Scotch-Indian trader, and, in 1862, he was elected chief of his Metis band. The next year, he led his followers to a new home near Fort Carlton along the North Saskatchewan River. Over the next years, Dumont worked as a hunter, trapper, trader, and guide to missionaries. In 1868, his band settled permanently in their winter log cabins near Batoche on the South Saskatchewan River.

On learning of the First Riel Rebellion in 1869, Dumont traveled back eastward to the place of his birth, the Red River country, to offer the support of the western Metis. He backed the militant stance of AMBROISE LEPINE as opposed to the more moderate stance of LOUIS DAVID RIEL. After this short-lived uprising in which he saw no action, Dumont returned home and continued to play a prominent role among the western Metis. During the next years, many of the

Red River Metis moved westward to the Saskatchewan River.

In June 1884, Dumont traveled to Montana to ask Louis Riel to lead a second Metis uprising, the Riel Rebellion of 1885. Again, Dumont adopted a militant stance and was made adjutant general in charge of about 300 Metis. His men were victorious at Duck Lake on March 26, at Fish Creek on April 24, and against the gunboat *Northcote* on May 9. After the Battle of Batoche on May 9–12, Dumont escaped to Montana. Before Riel's execution in November, Dumont helped organize relay stations for the escape of his former leader, which never came to pass.

In 1886, Dumont joined the Wild West Show, run by WILLIAM "BUFFALO BILL" CODY, as a crack marksman. He also found employment as a speaker. In 1888, during the Quebec elections, French Canadian politicians brought Dumont to Montreal to give a series of lectures. He spent the next several years among the Metis of Montana before returning to Canada in 1890 and his home at Batoche in 1893. In his last years, he hunted and traded and dictated two memoirs of the rebellion. (See also RIEL, LOUIS DAVID.)

DUNCAN, WILLIAM. *(1832–1918).* Missionary; educator.

A lay Anglican preacher from Yorkshire, England, William Duncan came to Fort Simpson on the coast of British Columbia in 1857, as a missionary to the Tsimshian Indians, whose contacts with whites had led to corruption from alcohol and poverty. Despite hostility from some Tsimshians, Duncan persisted in his efforts to Christianize the tribe and prevent drunken and violent incidents as well as cases of ritualistic cannibalism. Duncan studied the Tsimshian language and mythology and preached to tribal members about the Bible in terms of their own legends.

In 1862, at the Indian village of Metlakatla, 20 miles from Fort Simpson, Duncan established a community for over 1,000 Christianized Tsimshians. For the next 25 years, the community flourished, with the Indians supporting themselves with their own salmon cannery and other businesses. Duncan also ran a school and church for the tribe.

Because of difficulties with the Anglican Church Missionary Society, Duncan and his Tsimshian followers left their British Columbia settlement and relocated to Annette Island, Alaska, where they founded New Metlakatla in 1887. Duncan helped the Indians establish tribally owned businesses, such as a fishing and canning operation, and a sawmill. He also taught them blacksmithing, spinning, and soapmaking. Their businesses prospered even more on American territory. In addition to providing vocational instruction, he taught his followers Western music and baseball. Duncan stayed among the Tsimshians the remainder of his life.

DUNMORE, JOHN MURRAY, EARL OF
(Lord Dunmore). *(1732–1809).* Colonial governor of Virginia during Lord Dunmore's War of 1774.

The Scottish-born John Murray succeeded to his title as fourth earl of Dunmore in 1756 and was a representative peer of Scotland in 1761–69. He was appointed governor of New York in 1770, but was transferred to Virginia within a year.

In 1774, Dunmore, as governor of the Virginia Colony, took possession of the Shawnee lands in the Ohio Valley region of western Pennsylvania and Kentucky. To discourage Shawnee retaliation, he seized a group of chiefs who had come to the colonial authorities at Pittsburgh to seek redress. Dunmore, despite their peaceful intentions, held the Indians as hostages for five months. Upon their release, they were attacked by troops under Dr. John Connolly, Dunmore's western agent. In response, the Shawnees massacred whites at the Yellow Creek settlement. This led to a colonial assault on the family of Mingo chief LOGAN. Further Indian reprisals under the Shawnee CORNSTALK soon brought about what is known as Lord Dunmore's War.

Dunmore sent frontiersmen DANIEL BOONE and Michael Stoner to the Kentucky interior to secure his advance party of surveyors. The diplomatic efforts of WILLIAM JOHNSON, GEORGE CROGHAN, and other colonial officials succeeded in limiting involvement of other tribes. CATAHECASSA's Shawnee band joined Cornstalk's militants, as did TARHE's Wyandots, and some Delaware and Ottawa warriors. A militia force under ANDREW LEWIS defeated the allied Indians at Point Pleasant in October 1774. Meanwhile, Dunmore was able to trap the Indian force at Chillicothe in southern Ohio. Cornstalk surrendered and was forced to agree to the terms of Dunmore's Treaty of Camp Charlotte under which the tribe ceded all claims to Kentucky.

In 1775–76, during the American Revolution, Dunmore led Loyalist troops against the Virginia colonists, but was defeated, whereupon he returned to England. He served as governor of the Bahamas in 1787–96. (See also CORNSTALK; LOGAN.)

DUNQUAT. See HALF-KING.

DUSTON, HANNAH EMERSON (Hannah Dustin or Dustan). *(1657–ca. 1736).* Captive.

On March 15, 1697, during King William's War, Hannah Duston and her nurse, Mary Neff, were captured by Abnaki Indians in a raid on her home in the settlement of Haverhill, Massachusetts. When her newborn baby began to cry, one of the warriors killed the child in front of her, then forced Duston and her nurse to march to an Abnaki encampment on the Merrimack River, near present-day Concord, New Hampshire.

During a stopover, Duston, Neff, and a fellow captive, a 10-year- old boy named Samuel Lennardson, tomahawked 10 of their captors to death as they slept—two warriors, two women, and six children. One Indian woman and a boy escaped. Duston then scalped the victims and escaped to Haverhill, where she learned that her husband and other children had survived the raid. She later applied for a bounty on the Indian scalps, even though the time limit for collecting such rewards had expired. Through a petition to the colonial authorities, she received a special payment, and was further rewarded with a pension as an Indian fighter.

The account of her captivity was later incorporated into the sermons of COTTON MATHER, along with that of HANNAH SWARTON. Mather attributed the evil of the Indians to their Catholic conversion by French missionaries and cited Duston's captivity and escape as an example of the Protestant ideal of divine deliverance from evil. Duston's experiences as a captive later provided the basis for a story by Nathaniel Hawthorne, as well as a moral essay by Henry David Thoreau.

E

EASTERLY, THOMAS M. *(1809–1882).*
Photographer.

Thomas Easterly, born in Brattleboro, Vermont, was an itinerant daguerreotypist. He is known to have worked in the vicinity of Liberty, Missouri, about 1845–46. He may have used a portable tent for his Indian portraits, as indicated by the controlled lighting. He settled permanently in St. Louis, opening a studio about 1847. Easterly is thought to have made the earliest photographic portraits of Sac, Fox, and Iowa Indians, although JOHN H. FITZGIBBON also made early prints of the Sacs and Foxes. Among Easterly's subjects was the Sac chief KEOKUK.

EASTMAN, CHARLES ALEXANDER (Ohiyesa, "victor"). *Mixed Mdewakanton Sioux. (1858–1939).*
Physician; writer; lecturer. Great-grandson of CLOUDMAN; grandson of SETH EASTMAN.

Ohiyesa was born near Redwood Falls, Minnesota, on the Santee reservation, the son of Jacob Eastman (Many Lightnings) and his mixed-blood wife, Mary Nancy Eastman, daughter of the painter Captain Seth Eastman. His mother died when he was born.

As a boy of four, during the Minnesota Uprising of Santee Sioux in 1862–63, Ohiyesa was taken by his grandmother and uncle to what is now North Dakota, then Manitoba, fleeing from federal troops. Eleven years later, Jacob Eastman, who had fought under LITTLE CROW and, after the war, had become a homesteader in Flandreau, Dakota Territory, located his son in Canada. At that time, Charles was reunited with his older brother John Eastman (who went on to be a prominent Presbyterian minister).

Since his father encouraged an education among whites, Eastman attended various mission and preparatory schools, then Dartmouth College, graduat-ing in 1887. He then pursued medical studies at Boston University, graduating in 1890.

As agency physician on the Pine Ridge Reservation in South Dakota for the Indian Health Service, Eastman tended to the wounded from the army's attack on BIG FOOT's peaceful band at Wounded Knee. Following a dispute with the Indian agent Captain George LeRoy Brown over payments to Indians, Eastman resigned in 1893 and had a private practice for a time in St. Paul, Minnesota. In 1900, he was agency physician at the Crow Creek Reservation in South Dakota.

In 1894–97, Eastman, active in the Young Men's Christian Association (YMCA), established 32 Indian YMCA groups. In 1899, he became outing agent for the Carlisle Indian School in Pennsylvania, headed by Captain RICHARD HENRY PRATT. In 1910, Eastman helped found the Boy Scouts of America, along with ERNEST THOMPSON SETON of the Woodcraft Indians and Daniel Carter Beard of the Sons of Daniel Boone.

Eastman, a lobbyist in Washington, D.C., for the Santee Sioux in 1897–99, came to hold several government positions. In 1903, on the recommendation of the writer HAMLIN GARLAND, he was assigned the task by President Theodore Roosevelt of revising the allotment of tribal lands to individuals and assigning the Sioux family names to protect their titles to land. In 1923–25, under President Calvin Coolidge, Eastman was Indian inspector, succeeding JAMES McLAUGHLIN. As such, he verified the burial place of SACAJAWEA on the Wind River Reservation in Wyoming, a controversial finding indicating the Shoshone guide of the LEWIS and CLARK expedition had lived beyond 1812. During the same period, Eastman was a member of The Committee of One Hundred, a reform panel headed by Hubert Work, secretary of the Interior, which made recommendations for the institution of federal measures to expedite Indian claims against the federal government.

Eastman was the recipient of the first Indian Achievement Award, in 1933. He was married to the well-known poet Elaine Goodale, with whom he had six children.

Between 1902 and 1916, Eastman wrote numerous articles and nine books about Indian history and mythology, including the autobiographical *Indian Boyhood* (1902); *The Soul of the Indian* (1911); and *From the Deep Woods to Civilization* (1916). He also gave many lectures about his experiences as an Indian.

EASTMAN, SETH. *(1809–1875).* Artist; surveyor; soldier. Grandfather of CHARLES EASTMAN.

Seth Eastman was born in Brunswick, Maine, and graduated from West Point in 1828. He was first stationed at Fort Crawford, Wisconsin, and, in 1830, he was transferred to Fort Snelling, Minnesota, where he married the daughter of Chief CLOUDMAN in an Indian ceremony. When Eastman was transferred, his Indian wife returned to her people. (Their young daughter would grow up to become the mother of the Sioux writer CHARLES EASTMAN.)

Eastman then served as an assistant teacher of drawing at West Point, and, in 1840–41, he served in the Second Seminole War in Florida against Seminoles under OSCEOLA. He returned to Fort Snelling with his second wife, Mary Henderson Eastman, in 1841, where he remained for seven years, becoming acquainted with the culture and customs of the Sioux and fluent in their language.

Eastman drew upon his frontier experiences to create works depicting everyday life in the Indian encampments—Sioux, Pawnee, and Chippewa—around Fort Snelling. He also depicted Indian rituals, such as the Dog Dance of the Sioux.

In 1848–49, the army sent Eastman to western Texas, and, while stationed at Fort Duncan and Fort Chadbourne, he was able to produce as many as 70 pictures of Comanche scenes. In 1849, the book *Dakotah; Life and Legends of the Sioux—around Fort Snelling* was published, with text by his wife and his illustrations.

In 1850, the government assigned Eastman the task of providing illustrations for the federal publication *Indian Tribes of the United States* (6 vols., 1853–56) with text by HENRY ROWE SCHOOLCRAFT. In 1853, Eastman's illustrations for the Schoolcraft work also appeared in his wife Mary's book, *American Aboriginal Portfolio.*

Brevetted brigadier general in 1866, Eastman, during the next two years, executed a series of paintings of Indian life and western forts to decorate the newly completed Capitol in Washington, D.C.

EDENSHAW, CHARLES (Edensaw, Idansu). *Haida. (1839–1924).* Carver; research informant.

Charles Edenshaw was born at Cape Ball and grew up at Skidegate on Graham Island, the largest of the Queen Charlotte Islands of British Columbia. His uncle was Albert Edward Edenshaw, a chief. On the death of his father, Charles moved to Masset with his mother. He became a skilled carver of wood and argillite, as well as an accomplished silversmith, and his works were valued throughout the region. Through trade with other tribes and whites, he became one of the wealthiest Haidas. Because of his heritage, skill, and wealth, Edenshaw was chosen as chief of the village of Yatza, where he and his wife raised their five children. During the late 1800s and early 1900s, scholars, including FRANZ BOAS and John Swanton, sought him out as informant. Edenshaw provided sketches and model totem poles and information on Haida symbolism and mythology.

EDWARDS, JONATHAN. *(1703–1758).* Missionary; scholar.

Jonathan Edwards was born in East Windsor, Connecticut, the son of that community's Congregational pastor. On graduating Yale College at New Haven when only 17, he continued divinity studies in New York, then returned to Yale as a tutor. In 1726, he joined his grandfather as a pastor at the Congregational church in Northampton, Massachusetts.

In 1734, through his rousing preaching style, Edwards helped bring about the religious revival in New England known as the Great Awakening, spurring on Indian missionary work among such men as DAVID BRAINERD, SAMUEL KIRKLAND, and ELEAZAR WHEELOCK. In 1749, Edwards edited his friend Brainerd's memoirs. He also wrote a biography of Brainerd, describing his religous teachings among the Indians of New Jersey.

In 1750, Edwards was dismissed from his pastorate in Northampton because of a controversy over church membership, with Edwards demanding orthodoxy and zealousness on the part of his followers. The next year, he took charge of a small congregation of whites and a Christian mission to the various Algonquian-speaking Indians, mostly Mahicans, at Stockbridge in the Berskshire Mountains of western Massachusetts. Unlike his predecessor, missionary JOHN SERGEANT, Edwards never learned the Algonquian language and spent his years preaching to them through an interpreter.

Edward's religious studies included natural science and philosophy. He produced many theological works that attempted to use empiricism and science to refute atheism. He strongly believed in the Calvinist precept of predestination. While a missionary at Stockbridge,

Edwards produced an influential work, *Freedom of the Will* (1754).

Edwards remained at the Stockbridge mission until 1757, when he left to become president of the College of New Jersey, now Princeton University. He died the next year of smallpox.

EGAN. *Northern Paiute.* (d. 1878).   Leader in the Bannock War of 1878.

In June 1878, during the Bannock War, following the death of the Bannock chief BUFFALO HORN in a skirmish in Idaho, the insurgent Bannocks headed for Steens Mountain in Oregon to regroup. Northern Paiutes from the Malheur Reservation under Egan and OYTES, as well as a number of Cayuses and Umatillas, joined them. Chief WINNEMUCCA and his daughter SARAH WINNEMUCCA tried to negotiate a peace in the insurgents' camp, but failed. Egan reluctantly agreed to assume the overall command of the militants.

Troops under General OLIVER HOWARD, who had fought in the Nez Perce War the year before, mobilized out of Fort Boise, Idaho. Led in the field by Captain Reuben Bernard, they pursued the Indians through southeastern Oregon, meeting up with them at Silver Creek on June 23. In the skirmish, Egan was wounded and the Indians lost their possessions. Then, on July 8, at Birch Creek, while Howard watched, Reuben's men dislodged warriors from steep bluffs. On July 13, a detachment under Captain Evan Miles battled Indians at the Umatilla Reservation near Pendleton, Oregon.

On July 15, a party of Umatillas supportive of the white cause pretended to join the militants and lured Egan away from his men, killing him. They presented his scalp to Miles; an army surgeon later obtained his head to confirm his identity. Oytes became the principal leader, finally surrendering on August 12. A final party of militants were captured east of Yellowstone Park in Wyoming in September. (See also BUFFALO HORN; OYTES.)

EHNAMANI (Artemus Ehramani, Walks Amongst). *Mdewakanton Sioux.* (1825–1902).
Participant in the Minnesota Uprising of 1862–63; Christian convert.

Ehnamani was born at present-day Red Wing, Minnesota, and was educated by Protestant missionaries. As a young man, he was considered the best deer hunter and most accurate marksman among his people.

Although generally friendly to white settlers, Ehnamani participated in the Minnesota Uprising of 1862–63 with LITTLE CROW and the other militants, but refused to attack whites who did not take up arms. He surrendered to General HENRY HASTINGS SIBLEY after the Battle of Wood Lake in September 1862. He was

convicted and sentenced to be hanged, but was pardoned.

During his imprisonment at Mankato, Minnesota, and later Davenport, Iowa, Ehnamani was converted to Christianity by his friend the Reverend John Williamson. Soon after his release in 1866, Ehnamani became pastor of the Dakota Pilgrim Congregational Church at Santee, Nebraska, the new home of his band. He served there until his death. (See also LITTLE CROW.)

ELIOT, JOHN (Apostle to the Indians).
(1604–1690). Missionary to New England Indians; linguist.

The Englishman John Eliot was educated at Jesus College, Cambridge. He immigrated to North America, arriving in Boston in 1631, where, the next year, he began a lifelong association with the church at the Roxbury settlement.

Eliot's first extended contact with New England tribes was during the Pequot War of 1636–37. The destruction of the Pequots may have prompted Eliot to seek the pacification of the neighboring Massachuset Indians through Christianity. Eliot was of the opinion, popular among theologians and historians of the 17th century, that the Indians were the descendants of Jews who had been led to North America by Satan, and that Indian salvation lay in their embracing the moral philosophy and practices of the Puritans.

In the 1640s, Eliot preached to the Nipmuc chief WABAN, converting him and many of his tribe. His program for Christianizing the Indians involved the establishment of permanent communities in which so-called Praying Indians would settle, giving up their nomadic way of life and turning to farming and conventional colonial trades instead. In these settlements, the Indians lived under biblically inspired codes of behavior drawn up by Eliot. In 1651, Eliot founded a community at Natick. By 1674, he had established 13 more villages, with a total of more than 4,000 Christianized Indians.

With the help of the Montauk COCKENOE, who acted as his interpreter, translator, and tutor, Eliot became proficient in the Algonquian language. The Massachuset NESUTAN also worked with him as a translator. The 1662–63 publication of an Indian-language Bible marked the first printing of any Bible in North America. Algonquian versions of Puritan moral and religious writings soon followed.

Much of Eliot's work was undone by King PHILIP's War of 1675–76, when the Praying Indians were attacked by militant Wampanoags and Narragansets, as well as by revenge-seeking whites. Survivors were treated as prisoners of war by the colonists, and many sold into slavery. Their villages then became white settlements. Eliot's example as the so-called Apostle to the

Indians influenced later generations of missionaries throughout North America, however.

EL MOCHO ("the cropped one"). *Tonkawa-Apache.* *(d. 1784).* Leader of the Tonkawas who attempted an alliance with the Apaches; enemy of Spanish.

El Mocho was born among the Apaches, but was captured by the Tonkawas and taken to their homeland in central Texas. Demonstrating his courage and eloquence to his captors, he soon earned his freedom. He bore his Spanish name because he had lost his right ear in a fight with the Osages. When the chief of the Tonkawas died in 1777 or 1778 during an epidemic, El Mocho was selected as the new chief. In 1782, hoping to unite the Tonkawas and Apaches against the Spanish, he called a council attended by more than 4,000. Despite his efforts, the two tribes were unable to put aside their traditional warring. Fearing his power, the Spanish hunted him, managing to kill him two years after his great council.

EMATHLA, CHARLEY (Charles Emarthla, Amathla). *Seminole. (d. 1835).* Pro-removal leader killed by OSCEOLA.

Charley Emathla, born among the Creeks in Georgia, moved to Florida in the late 1820s, when many in his band were being forced to relocate west of the Mississippi. He established a small farm with a herd of cattle near Fort King and became a leader among the Seminoles. He signed the Treaty of Payne's Landing in 1832, agreeing to relocation to the Indian Territory. Then he traveled westward with a Seminole delegation, including FOKE LUSTE HAJO, to inspect the new homeland, signing the 1833 Treaty of Fort Gibson. In November 1835, after having sold his cattle at Fort King in preparation for removal, Emathla was ambushed and killed by Osceola and other warriors. It is reported that in a symbolic gesture Osceola scattered the cattle money from whites over Emathla's dead body. (See also OSCEOLA.)

EMISTESIGO (Guristersigo). *Creek. (1752–1782).* Pro-British leader during the American Revolution.

In June 1782, a British force marched out of Savannah, Georgia, to meet with Upper Creek warriors under Emistesigo. A rebel force under General "Mad" ANTHONY WAYNE intercepted and defeated them. Emistesigo's warriors surrounded Wayne's men, however, and captured two of his cannon. Emistesigo was killed by bayonet. Seventeen other Creeks died in the close fighting and the rest retreated.

ENDECOTT, JOHN (John Endicott). *(ca. 1588–1665).* Colonial militia officer in the Pequot War; colonial governor.

John Endecott of Devonshire, England, was one of six Puritan founders of the New England Company for a Plantation in Massachusetts, arriving at the Naumkeag settlement, which later became Salem, in 1628. He served as the Massachusetts Bay Colony's first residential governor until 1630.

During his initial term, Endecott tried to maintain peaceful relations with the Indians. On learning that British fur trader THOMAS MORTON was supplying the Indians with guns and ammunition at Merrymount (present-day Quincy), he authorized a military action under MILES STANDISH, which temporarily closed down Morton's settlement.

During the 1630s, Endecott served as an assistant to the governor and also as the colony's military leader. In summer 1636, several Indians, thought to have been Pequots, attacked a Puritan fishing boat from a canoe in the waters near Block Island. Massachusetts Bay Colony governor Henry Vane soon dispatched Endecott on a punitive expedition against the tribe. Endecott and 90 colonial militiamen mounted an attack against the Indian villages on Block Island, destroying every Indian home and killing every male Indian they encountered. As it turned out, most of those killed were Narragansets, not Pequots. Endecott's force then sailed to the nearby Connecticut coast, where they attacked Pequot villages near the Pequot River before returning to Boston.

The attacks by these colonial troops helped precipitate the outbreak of the Pequot War of 1636–37 under SASSACUS, which led to the virtual destruction of the Pequot people of New England. Between 1644 and 1664, Endecott served intermittently as governor and deputy governor of the Massachusetts Bay Colony. (See also SASSACUS.)

ENMEGAHBOWH ("the one who stands before his people"; John Johnson). *Chippewa-Ottawa.* *(d. ca. 1900).* Methodist, then Episcopal preacher and missionary; interpreter.

Born in Canada among the Ottawas, Enmegahbowh was adopted as a boy by the Chippewas (Ojibways). He was educated at a Methodist mission school in Jacksonville, Illinois, and later ordained as Reverend John Johnson. From 1839 to 1844, he served as a missionary to the Chippewas along the upper Mississippi in Minnesota. When the Methodists closed their mission, Enmegahbowh encouraged the Episcopal church to establish one at Gull Lake, which was founded in 1852. He served there as assistant and interpreter and was ordained in 1858. After the Minnesota Uprising of Santee Sioux in 1862–63 under LITTLE CROW, Enmegahbowh remained the only missionary in the region. In 1869, the Gull Lake mission was moved to the White Earth Reservation, and, in 1873, he assisted in the founding of a school to train Indian clergy. He later worked with Reverend HENRY B. WHIPPLE.

ENSENORE. *Secotan. (d. 1585 or 1586).* Friend to Roanoke colonists.

The elderly Ensenore was the principal chief of the Secotans, an Algonquian-speaking tribe living between Albemarle and Pamlico sounds in present-day North Carolina, when WALTER RALEIGH's first colony under Richard Grenville was established on Roanoke Island, present-day North Carolina, in 1585. The painter JOHN WHITE was also part of this expedition and headed the second Roanoke Colony in 1587, which disappeared. Along with his son Granganameo, the acting chief, Ensenore was supportive of the colonists and a friend to Grenville, regularly sending meat, fish, vegetables, and fruit. Granganameo died in 1585, then Ensenore soon after. Ensenore's other son, the militant Wingina, became chief and plotted a strike against the colonists that failed and led to his death as well.

EPANOW (Apanno, Apannow). *Wampanoag. (fl. early 1600s).* One of the first New England Indians to be taken to Europe.

In 1611, a party under Captain Edward Harlow captured Epanow on the island of Martha's Vineyard, part of what is now Massachusetts, and took him to England where he was paraded as one of the wonders of the New World. Epanow accompanied a return crossing as a guide and interpreter and managed to escape by pretending to lead the British to a gold mine. In 1619, he led warriors in an attack on a landing party from Captain Thomas Dermer's ship, driving them off Martha's Vineyard. It is thought that this same Epanow was a sagamore of the Wampanoag Confederacy, a subordinate sachem to the grand sachem MASSASOIT, and that he was one of the signers of the Treaty of Amity at Plymouth on September 13, 1621.

ERICSSON, LEIF (Leif Ericson, Erikson, or Eriksson). *(ca. 970–ca. 1020).* Explorer.

Leif Ericsson, son of Viking leader Eric the Red, was born in the Norse settlement on Iceland. He moved with his family to the Norwegian colony on Greenland about 985, when his father was exiled from Iceland for killing a man.

About A.D. 1000, Ericsson traveled to Norway, where he was converted to Christianity and commissioned by King Olaf I to spread the religion to the Norwegian settlers on Greenland. According to Scandinavian tradition, his ship was blown off course to the shores of what is today believed to have been the New England coast, somewhere between Cape Cod and Nova Scotia. Ericsson and his crew spent the winter here, then returned to Greenland. Some accounts say that Ericsson named this area Vinland or Wineland, but other historians maintain that the New England coastal region

had been known to the Norsemen for at least 50 years prior to A.D. 1000.

Leif Ericsson reportedly returned to Vinland in 1001, with a party of 35 settlers, and they established a community that lasted for three years. After Ericsson's departure for Greenland, the North American settlement disappeared. Some of the surviving Norse settlers may have intermarried with the natives. Ericsson inherited his family estate at Brattahlid, Greenland, where he died about 1020.

Soon after Leif had returned to Greenland, his brother, Thorwald Ericsson, attempted to establish a permanent settlement on the coast of North America, between Newfoundland and Massachusetts. Yet Thorwald's party was attacked by natives, and Thorwald was killed.

The account of Ericsson's travels, contained in the Scandinavian folk legend, "Eric the Red's Saga," in the *Saga of the Greenlanders*, includes a description of the natives of Vinland, which the Vikings called Skraelings. These may have been Eskimos, Beothuks, Micmacs, or other coastal peoples.

ESCALANTE, FRANCISCO SILVESTRE VELEZ DE. *(ca. 1745–ca. 1780).* Explorer; missionary.

Born in Spain, Francisco de Escalante arrived in Mexico City in 1768, where he entered the Franciscan order the following year. He became a missionary priest to the Indians at the Laguna Pueblo and also ministered to the Zunis at their pueblo, both in what is now western New Mexico.

In 1775, the provincial governor of New Mexico commissioned Escalante to explore the overland routes from Santa Fe to Sonora, Mexico, as well as to the Spanish settlement at Monterey in Alta California. He was also to report on the possibility of Christianizing the Hopis of present-day Arizona. His preliminary expedition left Zuni Pueblo in New Mexico in June 1775 and explored the Grand Canyon region of Arizona. Along the way, his men had contacts with the Hopis and Utes. Escalante later recommended the use of force in converting the Hopis.

Escalante's expedition in search of a route to the California coast left Santa Fe in July 1776, consisting of a number of soldiers, Christianized Indians, and a fellow missionary, Friar Francisco Atanasio Dominguez. The party crossed parts of what is now Colorado, after which a Ute Indian guide by the name of Silvestre helped them reach and explore Utah, the first known whites to do so, as far as Utah Lake south of the Great Salt Lake. They were turned back by heavy snows in the Wasatch Mountains and made it back to Santa Fe in January 1777.

In 1779, Escalante produced an account of the Pueblo Uprising of 1680 under POPE, based on archival information no longer available today. After having departed Santa Fe, he was assigned to the Franciscan college at Queretaro in central Mexico.

ESKIMINZIN (Eskaminzin, Hackibanzin, "angry men standing in line for him"; Big Mouth). *Aravaipa-Pinal Apache. (ca. 1825–1890).* Principal chief; proponent of peace whose band was massacred at Camp Grant in 1871.

Eskiminzin, a Pinal Apache by birth, married into the Aravaipas and eventually became their principal chief. (The Aravaipas of the San Carlos group of Western Apaches inhabited south-central Arizona along Aravaipa Creek between the San Pedro Creek and Galiuro Mountains.) In 1871, with increasing tensions between Apaches and whites, Eskiminzin reported to Lieutenant Royal Whitman at Camp Grant near Tucson, expressing his peoples' desire to stay in their homeland, where the agave plant was their staple food, rather than relocate to the White Mountain Reservation. Whitman advised him that if his band surrendered their arms, he could treat them as technical prisoners of war while relaying the request to his superiors.

The band established a new village of wickiups near the post and planted fields of corn and gathered agave. Some of them worked for the soldiers and for local ranchers, cutting hay to feed their horses. Other Western Apaches desirous of peace, especially Pinals, joined Eskiminzin's band.

There were a series of Apache raids in the region in March 1871. Then, on April 10, a party of Apaches raided San Xavier, south of Tucson, stealing livestock. Citizens of Tucson blamed Eskiminin's band and organized a vigilante force of 148 under William Ouray—Anglo-Americans, Mexican-Americans, and Papago mercenaries. At dawn on April 30, they attacked, killing as many as 150 of Eskiminzin's people, mostly women and children. Eight of the victims were members of Eskiminzin's family. Twenty-nine children were abducted into slavery for Tucson whites or Papagos.

President ULYSSES S. GRANT was appalled by the incident and ordered a trial for the vigilantes. He also extended his Peace Plan to the Apaches. Yet the whites were acquitted in December 1871. Meanwhile, militant Apaches stepped up their raids.

Eskiminzin's followers rebuilt their village and replanted their fields, but, in 1873, they were forced to relocate 60 miles southeastward to the San Carlos Reservation on the Gila River. When an uprising occurred the following summer among other San Carlos Apaches, leading to the death of Lieutenant Jacob Almy, the innocent Eskiminzin was blamed by association and ordered arrested by General GEORGE CROOK (just as

the Tonto Apache DELSHAY was blamed for harboring the fugitives). Eskiminzin was imprisoned, but, in January 1874, he managed to escape and led his people off the reservation. Exhausted and starving, they returned to San Carlos the next April. Eskiminzin was again imprisoned as a "military precaution." The new agent to the Apaches at San Carlos, JOHN P. CLUM, arranged that summer for Eskiminzin's release and his return to his band.

Eskiminzin and Clum traveled together to Washington, D.C., in 1886 for negotiations. During that trip, the Chiricahua Apache TAZA, one of COCHISE's sons, died from pneumonia, and his brother NAICHE accused Eskiminzin of not properly protecting his brother. To avoid trouble, Eskiminzin moved off the San Carlos Reservation and established a ranch on the San Pedro River. When it was later destroyed by Apache-hating whites, Eskiminzin again returned to San Carlos. He was arrested in 1888 for associating with the outlaw the APACHE KID—whose wife Chita was probably Eskiminzin's daughter—and sent to Florida, and later Alabama, with GERONIMO's Chiricahuas. At Mount Vernon Barracks, Eskiminzin became the head gardener. He was allowed to return home in 1889.

ESPEJO, ANTONIO DE. *(fl. 1580s).* Explorer.

Antonio de Espejo was a military official in Spanish Mexico when, in 1581, Friar Agustin Rodriguez, accompanied by two other priests, journeyed into the upper Rio Grande region to convert the Pueblo Indians to Christianity. They remained there for over a year, without military support. In 1582, after Spanish authorities had lost contact with the Rodriguez missionary expedition, Espejo and a detachment of soldiers were sent to rescue the priests from San Bartolome, Mexico, leading his party down the Conchos River and then up the Rio Grande. He made contact with the Pueblo Indians of Zuni, Acoma, and other settlements in what is now New Mexico. His expedition also visited the Hopis at their settlements in present-day Arizona. In 1583, Espejo returned to his post with the news that Friar Rodriguez and the two priests with him had been killed by Indians. He also brought back reports of gold and silver deposits in northern New Mexico and Arizona, which provided a basis for JUAN DE ONATE's expedition into the Southwest in 1598.

ESTANISLAO. See STANISLAUS.

ESTEVANICO (Estevan, Estevanito, Esteban, or Estebanico the Moor). *(ca. 1500–1539).* Explorer.

Estevanico was a slave from Azamor in North Africa. Some scholars have described him as a black, and others as a dark-skinned Arab. He went with his master, Andres Dorantes, as part of PANFILO DE NARVAEZ's

1528 expedition to Florida and the Gulf Coast of Texas. After the expedition had been shipwrecked off the coast of Texas, Estevanico and Dorantes were among the survivors who proceeded into the interior of Texas.

In 1532, Estevanico, Dorantes, and another survivor, Alonso del Castillo Maldonado, encountered the expedition's treasurer, ALVAR NUNEZ CABEZA DE VACA. The four men wandered through present-day Texas, New Mexico, Arizona, perhaps eastern California, and Mexico and had contact with numerous tribes. At times they were enslaved by the Indians they met, and at other times they were treated as friends. Estevanico became adept at communicating in sign language.

In 1536, the party reached Spanish settlements in northern Mexico and soon after traveled to Mexico City. They reported to Spain's viceroy, Antonio de Mendoza, stories they had heard through Estevanico of the Indians' fabled Seven Cities of Cibola. Cabeza de Vaca, Dorantes, and Castillo Maldonado declined to return to the north to search for these golden cities. Mendoza purchased the slave Estevanico, and, in 1539, sent him, with Friar MARCOS DE NIZA and a small expedition, into what is now southern Arizona and New Mexico.

The expedition crossed the present U.S.-Mexico border at present-day Lochiel, Arizona, and explored the lower Gila River. De Niza sent Estevanico ahead with a scouting party to contact the Zunis at one of the fabled cities, actually the Indian pueblo at Hawikuh, New Mexico, and to offer presents to any Indians encountered to win their friendship. Along the way, Estevanico attracted a huge following of Indians, especially women, who were fascinated by his appearance—tall and dark-skinned, and adorned with ribbons, badges, feathers, and rattles. Some of the Indian men, apparently resentful of his popularity and overbearing behavior, attacked and killed him.

Before his death, Estevanico sent back reports that De Niza interpreted as definite evidence of the fabled cities of gold. As he approached Hawikuh, De Niza learned of Estevanico's death. He caught a glimpse of the Zuni pueblo, was convinced he had found Cibola, and returned to Viceroy Mendoza in Mexico City to report his findings. News of the supposed riches soon inspired Mendoza to organize the FRANCISCO VASQUEZ DE CORONADO expedition of 1540.

EVANS, JOHN. *(1814–1897).* Governor of Colorado Territory during the Cheyenne-Arapaho War (the Colorado War) of 1864–65.

Evans, born in Waynesville, Ohio, studied medicine in Cincinnati, graduating in 1838. He practiced in Indiana, where, in 1845, he became the first superintendent of the State Hospital for the Insane. In 1848, he became a professor at the Rush Medical School in Chicago, and, in 1851, he helped establish Northwestern University at Evanston, Illinois, a town named after him. He ran for Congress in 1854, but failed to be nominated.

In 1862, President ABRAHAM LINCOLN appointed Evans governor of the Colorado Territory. He was also the *ex officio* superintendent of Indian Affairs for the territory. His policies sought to open up Indian land to white mining and development.

In the Sand Creek Massacre of November 1864, during Evans's governorship, Colorado militia, under colonel JOHN CHIVINGTON, attacked BLACK KETTLE's band of Southern Cheyennes at their Sand Creek encampment, killing over 200, mostly women and children. This led to the conflict, known as the Cheyenne-Arapaho War, or Colorado War, of 1864–65. Evans was held to be partly responsible by a federal investigation undertaken by the Committee on the Conduct of the War. As a result, he was asked to resign his post as territorial governor in 1865.

Evans remained in Denver, becoming active in the organization of a railroad line that connected Denver with the Union Pacific Railway. He was also one of the founders of the institution that eventually became the University of Denver. (See also BLACK KETTLE.)

EWING, GEORGE WASHINGTON. *(1804–1866).* Trader. Brother of WILLIAM GRIFFITH EWING.

George Ewing was born in a settlement on the Raisin River, near present-day Detroit, Michigan. His father soon moved to Piqua in western Ohio, where he engaged in trade with the Potawatomis, Wyandots, Shawnees, Delawares, and Senecas. During the War of 1812, young George Ewing had the opportunity to hear speeches by Shawnee leaders TECUMSEH and TENSKWATAWA (the Shawnee Prophet).

In 1823, Ewing's family moved west to Fort Wayne, Indiana, where his father established a large fur-trading operation with the Shawnees. In 1827, with his older brother William, George Ewing established W. G. and G. W. Ewing and Company, a trading concern that operated a fur business with the tribes of northern Indiana. They soon turned their efforts into providing merchandise to the Indians in exchange for cash payments received by the tribes for the sale of their lands to the federal government. The Ewings were able to gain government approval for the transfer of privately held Indian lands to settle debts owed by tribal members to their trading concern and, as a result, acquired valuable real estate holdings in Indiana, Illinois, and Missouri through their credit transactions with the Indians.

When William died in 1854, George took sole charge of the firm for the next 12 years. George Ewing became involved in lawsuits with Shawnee tribal leader Joseph

Parks and others over claims for past-due Indian debts. He also was continually involved in disputes with GEORGE MANYPENNY, commissioner of Indian Affairs, over Indian policy and regulations that threatened to compromise his position as a creditor to tribal debts.

EWING, WILLIAM GRIFFITH. *(1801–1854).*
Trader. Brother of GEORGE WASHINGTON EWING.

Born in the village of Big Tree in the Genessee Valley, east of Buffalo, New York, William Ewing moved with his family first to the Raisin River in Michigan, and then to Piqua in western Ohio in 1804. His father operated a trading business in Piqua, and dealt with local tribes.

In 1823, his family relocated to Fort Wayne, Indiana, where his father entered the burgeoning fur trade with the Indians. His brother, George Washington Ewing, operated the family's trading post at Kankakee, at English Lake, while William remained at Fort Wayne.

After the death of their father in 1827, the brothers organized W. G. and G. W. Ewing and Company. They continued to trade for furs with the Miami, Potawatomi, and Shawnee tribes at their posts in northern Indiana. They soon began doing business through the American Fur Company, which then held a monopoly on the fur trade. The Ewing enterprise operated independently of JOHN JACOB ASTOR's firm, dealing directly with merchants in New York City.

The decline in the fur trade in the early 1830s coincided with an increased demand for trade goods by the Indians. The tribes of northern Indiana received large cash payments for their lands from the federal government; this flow of money into the region provided a boom for the Ewings' Indian trade. By establishing payment in Indian lands, the Ewings prospered throughout the 1840s and early 1850s. William died in 1854, and his brother George continued the enterprise for the next 12 years.

F

FARMER'S BROTHER. See HONAYAWAS.

FARNY, HENRY F. *(1847–1916).* Artist.

Born in Alsace, France, Henry Farny emigrated when five years old with his parents to western Pennsylvania at the headwaters of the Allegheny River, where he became boyhood friends with Seneca Indians. His family moved to Cincinnati, Ohio, when he was about 11.

In 1878, after having worked as an apprentice in lithography in Cincinnati and having completed art studies in Austria and Italy, Farny set out on a 1,000-mile canoe trip along the Missouri River with the journalist George Smalley in search of western themes for his painting. Then, in 1881, Farny traveled to the Standing Rock Reservation in North Dakota where he sketched Indian subjects to be used for paintings that he completed in his studio in Cincinnati. In 1883, he traveled to Missoula, Montana, for the ceremonies marking the completion of the Northern Pacific Railroad and encountered and painted Crow Indians.

Farny made other trips West during which he searched out subjects for his representations of Indian life, with special emphasis on authentic details of Indian culture. Some of his work provided illustrations for the memoirs of the ethnologist FRANK HAMILTON CUSHING.

FETTERMAN, WILLIAM JUDD. *(ca. 1833–1866).* Army officer in the War for the Bozeman Trail.

William Fetterman, originally from Connecticut, rose to the brevetted rank of major during his Civil War service in the Union army. He remained in the army at the regular rank of captain after 1865.

In 1866, during the War for the BOZEMAN Trail, Fetterman was assigned to Fort Phil Kearny, in what is now Wyoming, near the Montana border. His commanding officer was Colonel HENRY B. CARRINGTON.

On December 21, 1866, Captain Fetterman and 80 troopers were detailed to relieve a wagon train carrying wood that had come under Sioux attack near the fort. Despite Carrington's orders not to proceed over Lodge Trail Ridge, a point beyond which the soldiers would be out of sight of the garrison, Fetterman led his men over the crest in pursuit of a small party of warriors, who were actually decoys drawing him into a trap. Soon Fetterman and his command were ambushed by a force of about 2,000 Sioux, Cheyennes, and Arapahos, headed by RED CLOUD and including CRAZY HORSE. Fetterman and all 80 men under his command were killed in the attack.

The incident, which became known as the Fetterman Massacre, or the Fetterman Fight, led to Carrington's removal from command of Fort Phil Kearny. Fort Fetterman, established in Wyoming in 1867, was named after Captain Fetterman. (See also RED CLOUD.)

FEWKES, JESSE WALTER. *(1850–1930).*
Anthropologist; archaeologist; naturalist.

J. Water Fewkes was born in Newton, Massachusetts. Originally trained as a zoologist at Harvard University, he turned to ethnological studies of Southwest Indians. In 1889, when FRANK HAMILTON CUSHING gave up the position, Fewkes became leader of the Hemenway Southwestern Archaeological Expedition. One of his projects was the first phonograph recordings of Zuni songs, and he also conducted research on the archeology and existing ritual of the Hopis, about whom he wrote extensively. The Hopi potter NAMPEYO became his friend and reproduced the traditional designs uncovered in his excavations in her own work. Fewkes also supervised the excavation of the Casa Grande ruins in southern Arizona, a Hohokam site, and the Mesa Verde ruins in southern Colorado, and Anasazi site. He joined the Smithsonian's Bureau of American Ethnology in 1895, becoming its director in 1918.

FIGUEROA, JOSE. *Mixed Aztec.* *(fl. 1830s).*
Mexican governor of California.

A mestizo of Aztec descent, born in Mexico, Jose Figueroa was appointed as Mexico's California governor in 1834, following the administration of Jose Maria Echeandia. Figueroa instituted the formal secularization of the mission system under which many of the California coastal Indians lived: The authority of the Franciscan priests over the Indians was replaced by the rule of Mexican civilians, known as *mayordomos*, and the missions were transformed into Indian pueblos. Yet the Mission Indians' property and agricultural output were apportioned as they were under the Franciscans, with half going to the Indians and the remainder to the priests and civilian administrators. In many cases, powerful civilian rancheros appropriated jointly held Indian and church property. Secularization of the missions under Figueroa did not result in true emancipation of the Indians, but only a change in their masters, from the Franciscan priests to Mexican civilian officials. Figueroa was succeeded by Juan Bautista de Alvarado.

FINLEY, JAMES BRADLEY. *(1781–1856).*
Missionary; educator.

Born in North Carolina, James Finley was raised in frontier settlements in the Carolinas, Georgia, and Kentucky, becoming familiar with Indian lifeways. His family settled in Chillicothe in southern Ohio, where Bradley was educated in the classics by his father, a Methodist preacher and schoolteacher. He went on to study medicine and was licensed to practice in 1801. However, he soon married, and turned to a life of hunting in the wilderness, removed from white settlements.

At a Methodist revival meeting at Cane Ridge, Ohio, Finley was inspired to dedicate his life to missionary work and preaching. He became a circuit preacher in the backwoods of Ohio, and, after 1812, was formally received into the Western Conference of the Methodist Church. In 1819, he was appointed as an official Methodist missionary.

In 1821, Finley succeeded John Stewart as missionary to the Wyandots at the Methodist mission at Upper Sandusky, Ohio. At Upper Sandusky Mission school, Finely supervised the education of the Wyandot children under the highly organized Lancastrian system of instruction, devised by the Englishmen Joseph Lancaster and Andrew Bell and successfully used by CYRUS KINGSBURY, missionary to the Choctaws and Cherokees. In addition to attending classes, the older Indian boys worked on the school's farm. In 1823, Finley succeeded in persuading the Wyandot tribal council to keep written accounts of meetings, which he considered

a step toward introducing them to organized law and government. He also was instrumental in introducing the practice of branding livestock as a way to avert disputes over ownership. Finley counseled the Wyandots to reject removal proposals by the government, advising the tribe that any relocation would place them in jeopardy of white encroachment and the ravages of alcohol. His evangelical work among the Wyandots at Upper Sandusky lasted until 1827.

Finley rose in the Methodist church organization in Ohio, becoming superintendent of several large rural districts. He also became known for his evangelical work with the prisoners of Ohio's state prison. His book, *History of the Wyandot Missionary at Upper Sandusky, Ohio*, was published in 1840. His other work on Native Americans in 19th-century Ohio, *Life Among the Indians*, was published in 1857, the year after his death.

FISH CARRIER (Ojageght, Ojageghte, Ojageghti, Ojagaghte, Hojawgata, Hojiagede, "he is carrying a fish by the forehead strap"). *Cayuga.* *(fl. late 1700s).*
Peacemaker.

Fish Carrier, a noted warrior among the Iroquois as a young man, became known to whites during the Revolutionary period. He attended various treaty councils in New York and Pennsylvania, including Tioga Point in 1790 and Canandaigua in 1794. In the former, he defused potential violence between the Oneidas, who had supported the Americans in the Revolution, and the Senecas, who had been pro-British. Young warriors who had been drinking rum provided by whites began to boast of their victories against the other tribe during a dance around a war-post. Fish Carrier accused them of being merely boys who had no right to boast until they had reached his age. When he knocked down the post, the braves stopped dancing and dispersed.

FITZGIBBON, JOHN H. *(ca. 1816–1882).*
Photographer.

Born in London, John Fitzgibbon pursued photography in the United States, making his first daguerreotype in 1841 and opening a St. Louis studio in 1846. During the same period as THOMAS EASTERLY, he made early prints of Sacs and Foxes, with exhibits of his works in New York City. Moving to Vicksburg during the Civil War, Fitzgibbon was captured by Union troops and imprisoned in Cuba. He returned to St. Louis in 1866.

FITZPATRICK, THOMAS (White Hair; Broken Hand). *(ca. 1799–1854).*
Trader; trapper; guide; scout; Indian agent.

Born in Ireland, Thomas Fitzpatrick arrived in the United States about 1820. He joined WILLIAM HENRY

ASHLEY's fur-trading expedition to the upper Missouri in 1823.

In 1823-24, Fitzpatrick then traveled to the Rocky Mountain region with JEDEDIAH SMITH and explored the North Platte River and the South Pass as an alternate route to the fur-trapping grounds of what is now Wyoming, Colorado, and Utah. In 1824–25, he accompanied Ashley out of Fort Atkinson up the Platte River and across the Rockies through South Pass.

In June 1825, Fitzpatrick attended the first trappers' rendezvous at Green River, on the way to which he was robbed and chased by Indians. Legend has it that it was this experience that turned his hair white. He was known by some Indians as White Hair; to others he was Broken Hand because of a permanent injury from a firearm accident.

Starting in 1826, Fitzpatrick worked for Jedediah Smith, WILLIAM SUBLETTE, and David E. Jackson after they had bought out Ashley. In 1830, he in turn bought them out with JAMES BRIDGER, Milton Sublette, Henry Fraeb, and Jean Baptiste Gervais, organizing the Rocky Mountain Fur Company. His fur-trading activity brought him into contact with the Crow Indians. In 1834, a new firm was organized, Fontanelle, Fitzpatrick, and Company, working in conjunction with JOHN JACOB ASTOR's American Fur Company until 1837.

In 1831, Fitzpatrick joined a caravan that traveled from St. Louis to Santa Fe, where he obtained trade goods for the Indians to the north. He then headed to eastern Oregon and traded with the Blackfeet. While on a stopover in Taos, Fitzpatrick hired frontiersman CHRISTOPHER "KIT" CARSON as a trapper and guide.

In 1836, Fitzpatrick served as a guide to missionary MARCUS WHITMAN on his journey to the Pacific Northwest. In 1841, he was hired as a guide by the missionary PIERRE JEAN DE SMET, who was accompanying the John Bidwell wagon train west. During an 1842 wagon train expedition, at Independence Rock along the Oregon Trail, Fitzpatrick rescued missionary A. L. Lovejoy from an attack by Indians. He also served as a guide for JOHN C. FREMONT's second expedition into the Rockies in 1843–44 and was a scout for Colonel STEPHEN WATTS KEARNY's 1845 military expedition to the Great Plains west of Fort Leavenworth, Kansas. Later that same year, he was a guide for Lieutenant James Abert's exploration of the Arkansas and Canadian rivers in northern Texas.

In 1846, Fitzpatrick was named U.S. Indian agent to the tribes on the Arkansas and Upper Platte rivers, much of present-day Colorado. His headquarters were located at BENT's New Fort in Colorado. In 1851, he organized a large conference of Indian leaders at Fort Laramie, Wyoming at which many of the important Northern Plains tribes agreed to territorial boundaries that put an end to intertribal warfare. Two years later, in 1853, he negotiated peace treaties with representatives of the Kiowa and Comanche tribes at Fort Atkinson (Fort Mann) near modern Dodge City, Kansas, by which tribal leaders agreed to cease attacks on travelers on the Santa Fe Trail.

In 1850, Fitzpatrick married the part-Indian daughter of Indian trader John Poisal. In his correspondence with the ethnologist HENRY ROWE SCHOOLCRAFT from 1845 to 1853, he presented his views on Indians. Fitzpatrick, though a mountain man, was well-read, and speculated on the parallels between the Indians and the ancient Israelites. He also believed trade would bring civilization to the Indians. He expressed his view that the Indians were a doomed race, condemned not so much by inevitable white encroachment, but by their innate savage nature. He contrasted the Chinook Indians of the Pacific Coast with those of the Northern Plains, commenting that the culture of the Chinooks was more closely akin to that of the natives of Polynesia.

During an 1854 trip to Washington, D.C., to win government approval for the earlier Indian treaties, Fitzpatrick contracted pneumonia and died.

FLAT MOUTH (Wide Mouth, Guelle Plat, Eshkebugecoshe). *Chippewa (Ojibway). (1774–ca. 1860).* Enemy of Sioux.

Flat Mouth's father, Wasonaunequa, used his position as medicine man to become a chief of the Pillager (or Leech Lake) Chippewas of Minnesota by poisoning his rivals. Flat Mouth became chief after his father's death. It is thought that a visit by TENSKWATAWA, the Shawnee Prophet, to Leech Lake turned Flat Mouth against the Chippewa practice of poisoning rivals. Flat Mouth, like NOKA, CURLING HAIR, and HOLE-IN-THE-DAY, led Chippewa warriors in the long-standing struggle with the Sioux for control of the upper Mississippi region. His people suffered many casualties, but Chippewas from other villages joined him in ultimate victory. Despite Tenskwatawa's influence over him, the Chippewa chief remained neutral in TECUMSEH's Rebellion of 1809–11 and the War of 1812, refusing to attack American settlements. The Leech Lake band of Chippewas still live on their ancestral homelands.

FLETCHER, ALICE CUNNINGHAM.
(1838–1923). Anthropologist; musicologist; reformer.

Alice Cunningham Fletcher was born in Cuba during a visit there by her parents from New England. She was influenced in her pursuit of anthropology by FREDERIC WARD PUTNAM of the Peabody Museum of Archaeology and Ethnology at Harvard University in Boston.

In 1879–80, Fletcher met the Omaha Indians FRANCIS LA FLESCHE and SUSETTE LA FLESCHE, who had come east on a speaking tour with the Ponca STANDING BEAR, sparking her interest in Indian issues. In 1883–84, Fletcher was hired by the federal government to oversee the allotment of Omaha tribal lands to individuals. The successful completion of her task was used as evidence in Congress to gain support for the General Allotment Act (the DAWES Severalty Act) of 1887.

While living among the Omahas, Fletcher recorded their songs by notation. Her *Indian Story and Song from North America* was published in 1900. Fletcher worked closely with Francis La Flesche, co-authoring *The Omaha Tribe*, published by the Bureau of American Ethnology in 1911.

Fletcher also helped in the allotment of lands among the Winnebagos in 1887–89 and the Nez Perces in 1890–93, and conducted a government study for the U.S. Senate on Indian education.

FLYING HAWK. *Oglala Sioux. (1852–1931).*
Warrior; touring Indian. Nephew of SITTING BULL; brother of KICKING BEAR.

Flying Hawk was born near present-day Rapid City, South Dakota. He established his reputation as a warrior while in his teens, fighting Crows and Blackfeet. He fought alongside CRAZY HORSE at Little Bighorn when 24 and became a chief eight years later. He spent time away from the Pine Ridge Reservation, South Dakota, as part of WILLIAM "BUFFALO BILL" CODY's Wild West Show, Colonel Miller's 101 Ranch Show, and the Sells-Floto Circus.

FOKE LUSTE HAJO (Foke-Lustee Hadjo, Fuche Luste Hadjo, Black Dirt). *Seminole. (fl. 1830s).*
Pro-removal chief.

Along with CHARLEY EMATHLA, Foke Luste Hajo was one of the signers of the 1832 Treaty of Payne's Landing and the 1833 Treaty of Fort Gibson, agreeing to relocation from Florida to the Indian Territory. In 1835, after OSCEOLA and other Seminoles had decided in council to resist removal, then killed Charley Emathla, Foke Luste Hajo and others fled to Fort Brooke (present-day Tampa), where they encamped under the protection of its garrison. (See also OSCEOLA.)

FOLSOM, DAVID (Colonel Folsom). *Mixed Choctaw. (1791–1847).* Pro-education and
pro-missionary leader; negotiator of removal.

David Folsom, the best known of the large Folsom family of Mississippi, lived in the vicinity of present-day Starkville. Along with PETER PITCHLYNN, he encouraged education among the Choctaws and welcomed Presbyterian, Methodist, and Baptist mis-

sionaries to their homeland. In 1824, Folsom traveled to Washington, D.C., for negotiations with the federal government. His tribal elder PUSHMATAHA died on this trip. In 1826, Folsom was the first leader of the tribe's three districts. Along with GREENWOOD LE FLORE, he worked to achieve what he considered the best possible removal deal, at first opposing land cessions, then signing the Treaty of Dancing Rabbit Creek in 1830. After relocation to the Indian Territory, Folsom established a farm south of the town of Caddo.

FOREMAN, STEPHEN. *Mixed Cherokee.*
(1807–1881). Missionary; translator; editor; educator.

Stephen Foreman was born at Rome, Georgia, one of 12 children of a Scottish trader and his Cherokee wife. His family moved to Cleveland, Tennessee, soon after which his father died. Foreman attended the mission school at Candy's Creek, then continued his studies with SAMUEL WORCESTER, the Congregational missionary at New Echota, Georgia. He went on to the College of Richmond in Virginia and the Princeton Theological Seminary in New Jersey and received his license to preach by the Union Presbytery of Tennessee in 1835.

Foreman worked with Worcester and ELIAS BOUDINOT on translations of the Bible into the Cherokee language. He also worked as associate editor of the *Cherokee Phoenix* and *Cherokee Advocate*, using SEQUOYAH's syllabary. He supported the Ross Party led by Chief JOHN ROSS. Because of his anti-removal stance, Foreman was imprisoned in 1838. Soon afterward, he led a party of refugees along the Trail of Tears.

In the Indian Territory, Foreman continued to act as a tribal and religious leader among his people. In 1841, he helped organized a public school system for his tribe and served as its first superintendent. In 1844, he was elected to the Supreme Court of the Cherokee Nation, and, in 1847–55, he served as executive councilor.

During the Civil War, Foreman avoided choosing sides and worked as a missionary in Texas. On returning to the Indian Territory, he created a church in the former home of Elias Boudinot. Foreman had 14 children by two marriages.

FORSYTH, GEORGE ALEXANDER
(Sandy Forsyth). *(1837–1915).* Army officer in the Sheridan Campaign and the Apache Wars.

Born in Muncy, Pennsylvania, George Forsyth enlisted as a private in the Chicago Dragoons in 1861, at the outbreak of the Civil War. He transferred to the Illinois Cavalry later that year as a lieutenant. He was subsequently involved in 86 Civil War engagements, in which he was wounded four times. He rose rapidly in the ranks, and, by the war's end, had been brevetted a brigadier general.

Forsyth stayed in the regular army following the war, at the regular rank of major in the 9th Cavalry. In 1868, he was on the staff of General PHILIP H. SHERIDAN, then commander of the army's Department of the Missouri. Sheridan had Forsyth organize a company of 50 white scouts for frontier duty, including the protection of the Kansas Pacific Railroad from Indian attack. With a company of 50 frontiersmen, mostly Union and Confederate war veterans, Forsyth pursued Sioux and Cheyenne raiding parties west from Fort Wallace, Kansas, in summer 1868, as part of the Sheridan Campaign.

On September 17, at the Arickaree Fork of the Republican River in eastern Colorado, the Indians counterattacked. Forsyth and his company were forced to take refuge on a small sandy island in the river. For the next nine days, they were besieged by Cheyenne Dog Soldiers led by TALL BULL, WHITE HORSE, and BULL BEAR, as well as Oglala Sioux under PAWNEE KILLER. Forsyth and his company of 50 men fought off the opposing Indian force, numbering about 600 warriors, for more than a week until reinforcements could be summoned from Fort Wallace, Kansas, 125 miles away. By the time a force of black troopers, the so-called Buffalo Soldiers, arrived, nearly half of Forsyth's men were casualties, and Forsyth himself had been wounded four times. The Cheyenne war chief ROMAN NOSE was also killed in the engagement, which came to be known as the Battle of Beecher's Island, after Forsyth's second in command, Lieutenant FREDERICK BEECHER, another fatality.

Brevetted a brigadier general for his role at Beecher's Island, Forsyth eventually reached the regular rank of lieutenant colonel. He continued to serve on Sheridan's staff until 1881, when he was transferred to the 4th Cavalry in command of units campaigning against Apaches in Arizona and New Mexico. In January 1882, Forsyth served under Colonel RANALD S. MACKENZIE guarding the Southern Pacific Railroad through Arizona. In April 1882, following the LOCO Outbreak from the San Carlos Reservation, Forsyth and his cavalry tracked militant Apaches under GERONIMO to the Peloncillo Mountains along the New Mexico–Arizona border. The Battle of Horseshoe Canyon of April 23, 1882, although indecisive, inflicted losses on both sides. The Apaches then fled south into Mexico, with Forsyth and his command in pursuit. Crossing the border into Chihuahua, Mexico, Forsyth soon encountered Mexican troops under Colonel Lorenzo Garcia and was ordered back across the border.

Forsyth served for eight more years, retiring as a colonel in 1890. His memoirs of his military career on the frontier are contained in his books, *Thrilling Days in Army Life* and *The Story of the Soldier*, both of which first appeared in 1900. (See also GERONIMO; ROMAN NOSE; TALL BULL.)

FORSYTH, JAMES WILLIAM. *(1836–1906).* Army officer at Wounded Knee.

Ohio native James Forsyth graduated from West Point in 1856 and served as an infantry officer in the Washington Territory until the start of the Civil War. In 1861, he was appointed a colonel of an Ohio volunteer regiment. He commanded Union forces in the Peninsular campaign under General George B. McClellan. In 1864, he began his long association with General PHILIP H. SHERIDAN when he was appointed to command Sheridan's cavalry division. Following successes in the Shenandoah campaign in 1864, he was brevetted a brigadier general of volunteers.

With the army's reorganization after the war, Forsyth reverted to the regular rank of major. From 1869 to 1878, he was on the staff of Division of the Missouri commander General Sheridan. In 1878, he was made a lieutenant colonel and posted in the 1st cavalry at Fort Vancouver, Washington. He participated in the Bannock War in eastern Oregon and northern Nevada, under General OLIVER HOWARD. After the death of BUFFALO HORN and the defeat of Paiute leaders EGAN and OYTES, Forsyth took command of the army's field headquarters in northern Nevada.

Later that year, Forsyth was assigned as lieutenant colonel in the 7th Cavalry, and, eight years later, was given command of the regiment as a full colonel. In December 1890, during the Ghost Dance Uprising, involving Miniconjou Sioux at the Pine Ridge Reservation, South Dakota, Forsyth ordered his 7th cavalry to surround Teton Sioux leader BIG FOOT's followers at Wounded Knee Creek. When Forsyth ordered his cavalry troopers to disarm the Sioux, gunfire broke out and the army opened fire with carbines and semi-automatic weapons. More than 150 Indian men, women, and children were killed in the crossfire, including Big Foot.

General NELSON A. MILES condemned Forsyth for deploying his troops in such proximity to the Sioux and charged Forsyth with incompetence for not taking precautions against the sudden outbreak of violence. Miles relieved Forsyth of his command and ordered a court of inquiry as a prelude to a court-martial. Over Miles's objections, the court of inquiry, as well as the War Department, absolved Forsyth of any negligence or wrongdoing in the Wounded Knee Massacre.

Forsyth was soon restored to his command of the 7th Cavalry. Promoted to brigadier general in 1894, he retired from the army three years later as a major general. (See also BIG FOOT.)

FOUR BEARS. See MATO-TOPE.

FOUR LEGS (Les Quatres Jambes, Hootshoapkau; Neokautah; The Dandy). *Winnebago. (fl. early 1800s).* Principal chief; ally of TECUMSEH; proponent of peace in the Winnebago Uprising of 1827.

Four Legs's village was located along the Fox River, where it flows out of Lake Winnebago (present-day Neenah, Wisconsin). White travelers who passed through his homeland were forced to pay the chief in trade goods. In the War of 1812, Four Legs supported Tecumseh as did the Winnebagos WAUKON DECORA and NAWKAW, and he participated in the attack on Fort Meigs and Fort Sandusky in Ohio. Following the war, he represented his people in an 1815 peace conference at Mackinaw, Michigan, and, in 1825, he signed the Treaty of Prairie du Chien, Wisconsin. In 1827, he met with Governor LEWIS CASS of the Michigan Territory and federal superintendent THOMAS McKENNEY at a council at Butte des Morts along the Fox River. The chief claimed that western bands near the Mississippi under RED BIRD, not his men, had carried out the raid. Four Legs's and Nawkaw's failure to support the uprising helped force the surrender of the militants.

FOWKE, GERARD. *(1855–1933).* Archaeologist.

Gerard Fowke was born Gerard Smith, in Mayville, Kentucky. After having served as a cavalry officer in the Civil War, he pursued his interest in archeology. He made an extensive tour, on foot, of the mounds of the Ohio Valley, became a collector of Mound Builder artifacts, and wrote about his field research. Fowke also investigated the remains of other Indian cultures in the East and on Vancouver Island, British Columbia.

FRANCIS, JOSIAH (Francis the Prophet; Hillis Hayo, Hillis Hadjo, Hillishago, Hillishager). *Mixed Creek-Seminole. (d. 1818).* Medicine man; leader in the Creek War and the First Seminole War. Father of MILLY FRANCIS.

Josiah Francis's lineage is unknown. He had white ancestry and what was originally thought to be Alabama ancestry, but was perhaps of the Tawasa- or Tuskegee-related tribes. His historical connection is to the Red Stick Creeks, however, and the Seminoles (who had ancestors among a number of different Southeast tribes).

Francis was a friend of TECUMSEH and traveled with him through the Mississippi Valley in 1811, spreading the message of alliance to a number of tribes, including the Osages. In the Creek War of 1813–14, along with WILLIAM WEATHERFORD, Francis fought against General ANDREW JACKSON, who referred to him as "their [the Seminoles'] great prophet." The other name by which Francis is known, Hillis Hayo or Hillis Hadjo, is a Muskogean title mean-

ing "medicine man." In 1815, the Prophet traveled to England for help in the struggle against the Americans.

Francis is famous for the incident at KINACHE's village of Miccosukee in west Florida during the First Seminole War of 1817–18, involving his daughter Milly and a captured Georgia militiaman by the name of Duncan McKrimmon, whose execution he ordered. Milly begged that the American be spared, insisting she was willing to die with him, at which point her father relented.

The next year, 1818, Francis was captured by whites on the St. Marks River and lured onto an American gunboat flying a British flag. His execution was subsequently ordered by Jackson. (See also BOLEK; WEATHERFORD, WILLIAM)

FRANCIS, MILLY HAYO. *Mixed Creek-Seminole. (1802–1848).* Peacemaker who saved a white man from execution during the First Seminole War of 1817–18. Daughter of JOSIAH FRANCIS.

A story surrounding Milly is similar to that of POCAHONTAS, Chief POWHATAN, and Captain JOHN SMITH. In 1817, during the First Seminole War, an Indian war party captured a captain of the Georgia militia, Duncan McKrimmon, and took him to KINACHE's village of Miccosukee in west Florida. Josiah Francis, known as the Prophet, ordered McKrimmon's execution by burning, and the prisoner was tied to a stake. Just before a fire was lit at his feet Milly rushed forward to beg for mercy. Her father ignored her pleas until she insisted she too was willing to die in flames. Francis relented with the condition that McKrimmon shave his head and live with the tribe. It is theorized by some scholars that the execution was symbolic, that the Seminoles carried out the drama as a way to bring McKrimmon into the tribe to stem population loss. In any case, Francis eventually sold his prisoner to the Spanish as a slave.

Soon afterward, Josiah Francis was captured by troops under General ANDREW JACKSON and executed. Several months later, a band of starving women and children, including Milly, her mother, and sister, appeared at an army post asking for food. McKrimmon, since returned to the militia, now saved her life. He asked Milly to marry him, but she refused, believing, as the story goes, that he offered only out of gratitude and obligation because of her earlier deed and not out of love. She returned to live with her people.

Milly was relocated to the Indian Territory with other Seminoles and Creeks. In 1844, she came to the attention of the government while living near present-day Muskogee, Oklahoma. Because of her conduct during the First Seminole War, she was granted a $96 pension and a $20 medal. The funds were delayed, however, and, before receiving any, she died of tuberculosis four years later.

FRANCISCO. *Yuma. (d. 1857).* Rescuer of kidnapped child.

In 1850, a party of Tonto Apaches attacked settlers at Gila Bend, Arizona, killed the adults, and carried off two young girls. Two years later, the Apaches sold the children to the Mojaves. One died soon after. A brother, who had been left for dead in the raid, encouraged the garrison at Fort Yuma, California, to search for his sisters. But all efforts failed. In 1856, while visiting the fort, Francisco claimed knowledge of the surviving girl and requested supplies; he received four blankets and some beads from the soldiers and set off to buy her. The Mojaves tried to conceal her identity by staining her skin with berries, but she let Francisco know who she was. Francisco argued eloquently for her release, then triumphantly brought her to the fort. Soon after this incident, and probably because of the fame resulting from it, Francisco was chosen chief of his tribe. He died the following year. It is thought that his own people killed him for losing 75 out of 78 warriors in a battle with the Maricopas and Papagos.

FRANKLIN, BENJAMIN. *(1706–1790).* Statesman; scholar.

Benjamin Franklin was born in Boston, where he worked with his brother James as a printer. In 1723, he left Massachusetts and settled in Philadelphia, where he continued work as a printer and made his mark on history as an inventor, statesman, and philosopher.

Franklin's earliest contacts with Indians occurred in Philadelphia, where his printing company published the Indian treaties entered into by the colonial Pennsylvania Assembly. He was later a delegate to the 1753 treaty with the Ohio Indians at Carlisle, Pennsylvania.

At the Albany Congress in 1754, Franklin proposed that a plan for colonial union was the only practical strategy to deal with the threat of the French and Indian alliance. When the French and Indian War erupted in western Pennsylvania that same year, Franklin provided logistical support to General EDWARD BRADDOCK's unsuccessful attempt to retake Fort Duquesne. He also led a campaign of Pennsylvania militia that built defensive positions at Gnaddenhutten, where the Moravian mission of Christianized Delaware Indians was located.

Franklin advocated white Protestant settlement of the frontier. In his 1760 essay *The Interest of Great Britain Is Considered*, he maintained that British colonial expansion into the Ohio Valley would create a vast agricultural territory with a tremendous new market for British manufactured goods. Although Franklin had no firsthand knowledge of the Ohio Valley, he had numerous contacts with frontiersmen such as GEORGE CROGHAN and CONRAD WEISER. Franklin's belief in westward expansion was an underlying theme in both his foreign policy pronouncements as an ambassador and his domestic policy views as a colonial legislative delegate and newspaper publisher. Before the American Revolution, he held British colonial domination over the West as the realization of Divine Providence. Franklin viewed the Indians as having a way of life antithetical to the enlightenment ideals of perpetual material and moral progress. Yet he expected moral behavior of whites in Indian affairs.

In his *Narrative of the Late Massacres in Lancaster County*, Franklin condemned the 1763 massacre of Christianized Conestoga Indians by vigilantes from Paxton, Pennsylvania, whom he referred to as "Christian white savages." He also made the point that the ravages of liquor and disease, brought on by increasing white contact, would ultimately result in the Indians' extinction from North America. When the Paxton Boys marched on Philadelphia to exterminate the city's Indians in February 1764, Franklin led a delegation to their camp and acted as peacemaker.

As a delegate to the Pennsylvania Assembly, Franklin advocated payments to Indians for their land rather than military action to remove them for white settlement. He also called for British regulation over frontier traders to protect Indians from exploitative practices.

Franklin helped draft the Declaration of Independence and organized the new American government, basing some political concepts, it has been suggested, on the Iroquois League of Six Nations.

At the 1783 Treaty of Paris, ending the American Revolution, Franklin was instrumental in effecting British recognition of the Great Lakes and the Mississippi as the northern and western boundaries of the newly created United States, thus setting the stage for the future displacement of the Ohio Valley tribes.

While U.S. ambassador to France, Franklin wrote philosophically about the Indians. In his 1784 essay *Remarks Concerning the Savages of North America*, he argued against casually referring to the Indians as "savages." In this work, Franklin sought to compare Indian and white cultures and found value in the Indian way of life.

FRASER, SIMON. *(1776–1862).* Explorer; trader.

Simon Fraser's father, of the Bennington, Vermont, area, was a Loyalist officer during the American Revolution. After his father's capture by Patriot forces and subsequent death, his mother took young Simon to Montreal to live with relatives.

Fraser entered the fur trade in 1792, joining the North West Company. By 1801, he had become a partner in that firm. In 1805, he was chosen to set up fur-trading posts west of the Canadian Rockies.

In 1806, Fraser set out to find a new route from the upper Columbia River to the Pacific. He explored the upper Fraser River, where he established outposts in what is now central British Columbia. In 1808, he followed the river to its mouth, but, because of the many rapids, deemed it impractical for the fur trade. Moreover, he encountered some hostility from the Stalo Indians of the village of Musqueam in the river's delta. The waterway was named the Fraser River in his honor.

Fraser continued to manage the North West Company's fur-trading enterprise in western Canada until he was implicated in an 1816 attack on the Hudson's Bay Company post at Seven Oaks. Although he was acquitted of all charges, he soon retired from the fur trade and lived at St. Andrews in present-day Ontario.

FREE, MICKEY (Mig-ga-n'-la-iae). *Mixed Pinalino Apache. (1851–1913).* Army scout; tracker; interpreter.

Mickey Free was born in Mexico in the Sonoita Hills along the upper Santa Cruz River. His father was probably part Irish; his mother was Mexican. Free had Pinalino Apache ancestry as well. The boy may have taken his adult name himself, in reference to his liberation from the Apaches who had kidnapped him when he was about 10. His abduction helped precipitate the BASCOM Affair and the early Apache wars under COCHISE.

When 14, after having gained his freedom, Free rescued the wife of an army captain at Fort Bowie, Arizona, from a rape, killing two Mexicans with a knife. When 20, he enlisted as an interpreter and scout in the U.S. army under General George Stoneman, then in command of the Department of Arizona.

Free helped the agent JOHN P. CLUM and generals GEORGE CROOK and NELSON A. MILES track GERONIMO throughout Arizona, New Mexico, and northern Mexico in the 1870s–80s. For most of Free's career, ALBERT SIEBER was his chief of scouts; he also worked under the command of Lieutenant BRITTON DAVIS.

Free acted as the Chiricahuas' official interpreter on the San Carlos Reservation. In 1886, he visited Washington, D.C., as interpreter for an Apache delegation including CHATO, LOCO, and ALCHESAY, trying to prevent the sending of Apache prisoners to Florida. After 1886, Free tracked the escaped Indians MASSAI and APACHE KID, as well as numerous outlaws. He never apprehended Massai, but he claimed to have located the remains of the Apache Kid in 1897 in a hideout in New Mexico. Free retired from the army in 1906.

FREMONT, JOHN CHARLES (The Pathfinder). *(1813–1890).* Explorer; soldier; politician.

John C. Fremont, born in Savannah, Georgia, was the son of a French emigré and a mother who was a member of a prominent Virginia family. He studied science at the College of Charleston in South Carolina from 1829 to 1831.

In 1833, Fremont instructed U.S. naval cadets in mathematics aboard the U.S.S. *Natchez.* In 1838, under the sponsorship of U.S. secretary of War Joel Poinsett, he was commissioned a second lieutenant in the U.S. Corps of Topographcal Engineers. He accompanied French mathematician and explorer Joseph Nicollet on an exploratory mission from Fort Snelling on the upper Mississippi in Minnesota, to the Pipestone Quarry on the Minnesota River. The following year, he again joined Nicollet on an expedition up the Missouri River to Fort Pierre in South Dakota. From there, they explored the region to the east as far as Lac Qui Parle.

In 1841, in Washington, D.C., Fremont eloped with Jessie Benton, the 17-year-old daughter of influential Missouri senator Thomas Hart Benton. Benton was eventually reconciled to the marriage. Under his patronage, Fremont was given command of a series of government-sponsored expeditions.

Fremont left St. Louis in spring 1842 on a U.S. expedition that included cartographer Charles Preuss and guides CHRISTOPHER "KIT" CARSON and JOSEPH WALKER. They proceeded north and west to the Oregon Trail via the South Pass through the Wind River Range of southern Wyoming. They were among the first to actually chart the South Pass route.

In May 1843, Fremont's second government-funded expedition into the West embarked from Kansas City on the Missouri River. The expedition, although ostensibly scientific, was also an attempt to assert U.S. claims over the Oregon territory. Guided by THOMAS FITZPATRICK and Kit Carson, Fremont journeyed up the Missouri and then overland across the northern end of the Great Salt Lake in Utah. From the Great Salt Lake, Fremont's party headed north to the Snake River country of Idaho and then into the Oregon Territory, where they encamped at MARCUS WHITMAN's mission settlement at Fort Walla Walla. After having proceeded to the Hudson's Bay Company post at Fort Vancouver, opposite the site of present-day Portland, Oregon, they headed south into California. They crossed the Mohave Desert on their return to Independence, Missouri, which they reached in July 1844.

In July 1845, Fremont, on his third expedition, part of General STEPHEN WATTS KEARNY's military expedition into the Southern Plains, explored the Arkansas River and the upper Rio Grande with Carson and Walker, and then headed west across northern Utah and Nevada. The group, guided by the Northern Paiute TRUCKEE, reached Monterey, California, in summer 1846, and supported the American revolt, the Bear Flag Rebellion, against Mexican rule.

John C. Fremont. *Courtesy of Library of Congress.*

In 1847, with the outbreak of the Mexican War, Fremont became embroiled in the power struggle between General Kearny and Commodore Robert F. Stockton. He was subsequently court-martialed for refusing to obey Kearny's orders. Although his sentence was suspended by order of President James Polk, Fremont soon resigned from the army.

In October 1848, Fremont then embarked on a privately funded expedition, sponsored by Benton and southwestern railroad interests, to chart a proposed railroad across the Rockies into the San Juan Range, as part of a line from St. Louis to San Francisco. This expedition ended in disaster, with severe winter weather and Indian attacks forcing Fremont and his party to seek refuge at Taos, New Mexico. Eleven men died. The naturalist BENJAMIN KERN and guide WILLIAM S. WILLIAMS also were killed when they returned for a cache of possessions the following spring.

In 1850–51, Fremont served as U.S. senator from California, and, in 1853–54, he undertook his fifth and last western expedition, across the Great Basin in search of a railroad pass.

Fremont went on to run unsuccessfully for president as the first Republican Party candidate in 1856. He was defeated by James Buchanan. During the early years of the Civil War, Fremont served as a major general, com-

manding Union troops in Missouri, and later in the early campaign in Virginia. After the war, he became involved in several railroad development ventures, but suffered severe financial losses in 1870. In 1878–83, he served as governor of the Arizona Territory, and published his *Memoirs* in 1887.

Fremont's explorations brought him into contact with numerous trans-Mississippi tribes. His reports of the region dispelled the notion that characterized the West as the Great American Desert, resulting from earlier explorations by STEPHEN H. LONG and ZEBULON PIKE. Fremont's charts of previously unexplored territory on the Northern and Southern Plains provided impetus for the rapid settlement of that area at the conclusion of the Mexican War in 1848.

FRONTENAC, LOUIS DE BUADE, COMTE DE PALLUAU ET DE. *(1620–1698).* Military leader in King William's War; French colonial governor.

French nobleman Louis de Buade, Comte de Frontenac saw early military service as an officer in the armies of Venice, France, and the Netherlands. In 1672, he was appointed governor-general of New France, an area that included what is now Canada and the central Mississippi Valley region.

Frontenac attempted to promote good relations with the Iroquois and Hurons and actively supported the development of French fur-trading posts on the Great Lakes. Yet he drew criticism from Jesuit authorities for allowing the sale of liquor to the Indians. He supported the evangelical missions of JACQUES MARQUETTE and LOUIS JOLLIET to the Indians of the Mississippi Valley and backed the explorations of RENE ROBERT CAVELIER, SIEUR DE LA SALLE. He also encouraged the establishment of frontier posts.

Political and business rivalries led to Frontenac's removal as governor of Canada in 1682. An outbreak of hostilities by the British-allied Iroquois—an attack on Montreal with more than 200 French killed in July 1689, the so-called Lachine Massacre—resulted in his reappointment as Canada's governor-general.

During King William's War of 1689–97, the first of the nearly 75-year French and Indian Wars, Frontenac maintained an alliance with the Abnaki tribes of Maine. Among his troops were also nearly 100 Christianized Iroquois from the Kahnawake (Caughnawaga) settlement near Montreal. Yet Frontenac was never successful in gaining much more than this small number of Iroquois to join him in his war against the British.

In early 1690, with his Indian allies, Frontenac launched a campaign of *petite guerre*—"little war" or guerrilla war—against British settlements in the northern Hudson Valley, including a brutal attack on

Schenectady, New York, in which 60 colonists were killed. Other targets of French-backed Abnaki assaults in 1690 were Salmon Falls, New Hampshire, and Portland, Maine. A campaign against the Abnakis under BENJAMIN CHURCH the next year caused them to sue for a short-lived peace. Although Frontenac lost Port Royal in Acadia (present-day Annapolis Royal, Nova Scotia) to British troops under William Phips, he successfully defended Quebec from an assault by British colonists.

In 1696, Frontenac led punitive campaigns against the Onondaga and Oneida villages in the Mohawk Valley of New York. Hostilities between France and England ended temporarily with the 1697 Treaty of Ryswick.

Before his death in 1698, Frontenac was able to enter into peace agreements with the Onondagas, Oneidas, Senecas, and Cayugas. His successors in the French colonial government effected what also turned out to be a temporary peace settlement with the remaining Iroquois tribe, the Mohawks, in 1700.

G

GADSDEN, JAMES. *(1788–1858).* Minister to Mexico; railroad developer; Indian commissioner; soldier.

James Gadsden was born in South Carolina, the grandson of the American Revolutionary leader Christopher Gadsden. He served in the army under General ANDREW JACKSON in the First Seminole War of 1817–18. Then, in 1832, he served under Jackson's secretary of War LEWIS CASS as commissioner to remove the Seminoles from Florida, meeting with OSCEOLA and other tribal leaders at Payne's Landing and obtaining their signatures on a treaty agreement.

In 1840, Gadsden became president of the South Carolina Railroad Company, a position he held for 10 years. In 1845, at a convention in Memphis, Tennessee, he proposed a southern transcontinental railroad in order to free the South and West from economic dependency on the North.

Jefferson Davis, secretary of War under President Franklin Pierce, arranged for Gadsden's appointment as minister to Mexico. In 1853, Gadsden negotiated the Mexican sale for $10 million of a wedge of territory between Texas and California (including parts of what is now southern New Mexico and Arizona), known as the Gadsden Purchase; the sale was ratified by Congress the following year, bringing more Indian peoples under U.S. dominion. Gadsden's plan for a southern rail system through the new territory was delayed by the Civil War, however.

GAINES, EDMUND PENDLETON. *(1777–1849).* Army officer in the First and Second Seminole wars and in the Black Hawk War; Indian commissioner.

Edmund Gaines was born in Virginia and raised in North Carolina and Tennessee. Joining the army at age 22, he was commissioned a lieutenant, and, in 1807, he was ordered to arrest Aaron Burr for treason. Four years later, he left the service for a short period, but returned to command U.S. troops against the British in the War of 1812, during which he was brevetted a major general.

Gaines was appointed a federal commissioner of Indian Affairs in 1817 and assigned to negotiate a peace treaty with the Creek tribes in the South. Soon after, he was given command of the army's Southern Military District. Also in 1817, because of a dispute over hunting grounds and violence between Indians and whites, as well as the harboring of runaway slaves by Seminoles, Gaines sent 250 men out of Fort Scott, Georgia, across the Florida border to attack NEAMATHLA's village of Fowltown, one of the incidents leading up to the First Seminole War and the invasion of Florida by General ANDREW JACKSON.

In 1821, Gaines assumed command of the army's newly organized Western Department. In 1831, BLACK HAWK's band of Sacs and Foxes resisted white squatters on their lands. In command of federal garrisons in the upper Mississippi Valley, Gaines met with Black Hawk that June at Saukenuk on the Rock River in Illinois. Gaines succeeded in getting Black Hawk to sign "Articles of Agreement and Capitulation," under the terms of which the Sac chief agreed to give up his tribe's claim to Saukenuk, terminate his tribe's relationship with the British on the Great Lakes, and recognize KEOKUK as the supreme Sac leader. In addition, the agreement acknowledged that the federal government had the right to build roads through Sac and Fox country in present-day Iowa. Gaines, in return, ordered the white settlers at Saukenuk to provide the Indians with supplies of corn equal to the amount they would have harvested on their ceded territory. But the settlers soon reneged on their obligation to give corn to Black Hawk's people, leading to the outbreak of the Black Hawk War in 1832. Gaines's agreement later was known as the "Corn Treaty."

In February 1836, following defeat of troops under Major FRANCIS DADE and General DUNCAN CLINCH in the Second Seminole War, Gaines led an unauthorized military expedition by sea from western Louisiana to Tampa Bay, Florida. After having navigated the Alafia River in three steamboats, he led his men overland to Fort King but managed only several inconclusive skirmishes with OSCEOLA's warriors. Gaines's campaign led to a dispute with General WINFIELD SCOTT, who had been given field command in Florida, although the region technically fell within Gaines's department. A court of inquiry censured them both.

Later that year, 1836, Gaines led a force from Louisiana to Texas to participate in the war for independence from Mexico. During the Mexican War of 1846–48, he was involved in a controversy over his recruiting of troops in the South, for which he was court-martialed but subsequently acquitted. He went on to command the army's Eastern Department. (See also BLACK HAWK; NEAMATHLA; OSCEOLA.)

GALL (Pizi). *Hunkpapa Sioux. (1840–1894).* Leader in the Sioux Wars of the 1860s–70s; war chief of SITTING BULL.

Gall was born along the Moreau River in South Dakota; his parents died when he was young, and he was raised an orphan. He reportedly acquired the name Gall as a child when he tried to eat the gallbladder of an animal. On proving himself as a warrior, he was adopted by Sitting Bull as a younger brother. When about 25, Gall was wounded in a skirmish with an army unit, including the Arikara-Hunkpapa scout BLOODY KNIFE, south of Forth Berthold, North Dakota. Bayoneted three times, he was left for dead.

Along with the other young warriors CRAZY HORSE of the Oglalas and HUMP of the Miniconjous and RAIN-IN-THE-FACE of the Hunkpapas, Gall devised decoy techniques in RED CLOUD's War for the BOZEMAN Trail of 1866–68, luring soldiers and settlers into traps. The Fort Laramie Treaty of 1868 called for the abandonment of military posts along the Bozeman in exchange for cessation of raids by the Northern Plains tribes and adoption of reservation life. Gall, like his mentor Sitting Bull, refused to cease the traditional nomadic existence.

In the War for the Black Hills of 1876–77, Gall further proved his military brilliance, acting as Sitting Bull's principal strategist and field commander. He played a key role in the Indian victory over Colonel GEORGE ARMSTRONG CUSTER's 7th Cavalry at Little Bighorn in 1876, leading the counterattack against the troops under Major MARCUS A. RENO. With subsequent Indian defeats, Gall accompanied Sitting Bull to Canada, but, after a quarrel, returned to Montana, surrendering

at a post with about 300 followers at the Poplar River Agency in early January 1881.

Gall settled at the Standing Rock Reservation in North Dakota, where he became a friend of the Indian agent JAMES McLAUGHLIN and eventually accepted the ways of whites, such as farming and public education. In 1889, he became a judge on the Court of Indian Offenses. That same year, he was a member of the Sioux delegation to Washington, D.C., negotiating the treaty in which Sioux lands were further broken up. He was neutral in the Ghost Dance Uprising of 1890. Gall is thought to have died from a drug overdose. (See also RED CLOUD; SITTING BULL.)

Gall. Photo by O.S. Goff; sold to D. F. Barry. *Courtesy of Library of Congress.*

GALLATIN, ALBERT. *(1761–1849).* Anthropologist; linguist; federal official.

Albert Gallatin's first contact with the American Indians occurred in 1780, shortly after his arrival from Switzerland, when he lived for a time in the backwoods of Maine near Abnaki bands.

Throughout his career in public service—several terms as a congressman from western Pennsylvania, secretary of the Treasury to presidents THOMAS JEFFERSON and James Madison, and several diplomatic ministries in Europe—Gallatin pursued an interest in Indian language and culture.

The sources of Gallatin's research were provided in part by the cooperation of the War Department under LEWIS CASS, secretary of War, who sent a circular to all military personnel in command of outposts in Indian territory, requesting examples of Indian vocabulary spoken in their respective areas. Gallatin also received data on tribal customs from WILLIAM CLARK of the LEWIS and Clark expedition, which Gallatin, as secretary of the Treasury under Jefferson, had helped supervise. Moreover, through THOMAS McKENNEY of the Bureau of Indian Affairs, Gallatin came into contact with the Cherokee JOHN RIDGE, who provided firsthand information on the vocabulary and structure of his native language. Gallatin used the Indian delegations visiting Washington, D.C., on official business as subjects of his study.

In 1826, Gallatin completed his study of the Native American languages, *A Table of Indian Languages of the United States*, in which he divided the languages of the 18 known tribes into 28 language families. In his view, primitive languages were thought to contain clues to the development of civilization because they were representative of man at a less-developed level of social evolution. His linguistic groupings were also depicted geographically by a map of the various tribal territories.

In his *Synopsis of the Indian Tribes of North America* (1836), Gallatin theorized that the differences between the societies and levels of civilization between Indians of different regions were based on climatic and environmental reasons rather than racial diffrences. His linguistic research suggested that the Indians of North and South America were one people and had not developed from any displaced European or biblical society. He was also one of the earliest proponents of the theory that the Native Americans had originally migrated from Asia in prehistoric times.

In 1842, Gallatin, along with JOHN RUSSELL BARTLETT, founded the American Ethnological Society. Over the next years, he conducted research on the Pueblo Indians, Pimas, and Maricopas of the Southwest.

Gallatin's research provided the government with a basis for dealing with tribal leaders over the acquisition of their territory. He was against large payments of money for Indian lands and also opposed annuities for Indians who had been displaced by westward expansion. He supported a federal Indian policy of education to assimilate the Indians into the mainstream of white society and economy.

Albert Gallatin. *Courtesy of Library of Congress.*

GANADO MUCHO (Ganodos Muchos, Mucho Ganado, "many cattle"; Aguas Grandes, "big water"; Hastin Totsohnii). *Navajo-Hopi. (ca. 1809–1893).*
Band leader; cattleman; proponent of peace with whites.

Ganado Mucho was the son of Navajo woman and her Hopi husband. He grew up to be a successful rancher in the vicinity of present-day Klagetoh in the northeastern part of Arizona, south of Canyon de Chelly, as well as a band headman.

During the 1850s, because of his large herds, Ganado was accused by whites of cattle theft. He denied all charges and, along with other Navajo ranchers, signed an agreement in 1858 to return any stolen livestock discovered among his people.

In the Navajo War of 1863–66, under MANUELITO, Ganado Mucho encouraged peace. At first, he hid out with his followers from troops under CHRISTOPHER "KIT" CARSON, then, in 1865, led his band to Bosque Redondo as ordered. During this time, he lost his son and two daughters to slave raids by Mexicans and Utes. He was one of the signers of the treaty in 1868, allowing the return of the Navajos to their homeland. Ganado rebuilt his ranch and continued his role as negotiator and peacemaker between his people and the whites. (See also MANUELITO.)

GARAKONTIE, DANIEL (Garakonthie, Garakonke, Harakontie). *Onondaga. (ca. 1600–1676).* Spokesman for Iroquois League; friend to French missionaries; Christian convert.

Garakontie was a spokesman for the Iroquois League in the mid-1600s and was friendly to French missionaries who settled near his village of Onondaga in present-day New York. In 1661, he converted his home into a chapel for the Jesuit missionary Simon le Moyne. Garakontie made several trips to Montreal to negotiate the release of captives, and, in 1669, he was baptized in Quebec as Daniel. Because of his pro-white stance, he was frequently at odds with militant members of the Iroquois League. He also served as spokesman in negotiations with the British colonists. Garakontie used his great oratorical ability to persuade his people to accept the whites' presence and customs, but to reject liquor. In the following years, however, the Onondagas went to war with the French under leaders such as GRANGULA and DEKANISORA.

GARLAND, HAMLIN. *(1860–1940).* Reformer; writer.

Hamlin Garland, the son of farmers, grew up in Wisconsin, Iowa, and South Dakota. Self-educated for the most part, he managed to find work as a schoolteacher. He settled in Boston in 1884.

Garland, with other Boston-based activists in the Indian reform movement, was a critic of the reservation system. During the implementation of the General Allotment Act (the DAWES Severalty Act) of 1887, which distributed plots of land to individuals as an alternative to reservations, he assisted the federal government in the task of renaming Indians with first and last names in order to facilitate the assignment of land titles. Although the allotment policy proved detrimental to the preservation of Indian culture, Garland opposed other governmental measures directed at destroying the Indians' identity as a distinct people. He regarded the culture of the Native Americans as a national resource.

Garland was first published in 1890. Although he related his experience of the hardships of farm life in most of his fiction, verse, and autobiography, he also described the plight of the Plains Indians faced with the encroachment of white civilization. He wrote bleak and despairing portrayals of reservation life, in which poverty and the dissolution of Indian culture was institutionalized by the federal government. His short-story collection, *The Book of the American Indian,* was published in 1923.

GARRA, ANTONIO. *Cupeno. (d. 1852).* Medicine man; leader of the Garra Uprising of 1851–52.

Antonio Garra was chief of the Cupeno Indians living at the headwaters of the San Luis Ray River in southern California. He was a rival of the Cahuilla JUAN ANTONIO to the east and the Luiseno MANUELITO COTA to the west.

With the California Gold Rush of 1849, growing numbers of whites entered the region and competed for Indian lands. Garra tried to organize a general revolt among tribes from the San Diego region to the Colorado River, including the Cahuillas, Luisenos, Kamias, Chemehuevis, Mojaves, Quechans, and Cocopahs. A shaman, he told his followers that he could turn enemies' bullets into water.

The Luisenos under Manuelito Cota remained neutral, as did many of the other area bands. The mountain man PAULINO WEAVER, a friend of Juan Antonio, also worked to keep the peace in the region. Garra's militants carried out numerous raids on ranchers and gained control of the river and desert country. Juan Antonio, whose help was sought by both sides, threw his support to the whites and captured his rival Garra in December 1851. After a court-martial by the state militia, Garra was executed. He had a son of the same name who fought under him in the Garra Uprising.

GELELEMEND ("leader"; Killbuck; William Henry). *Delaware. (ca. 1722–1811).* Leader of tribal peace faction during the American Revolution.

Gelelemend was born in Pennsylvania; his father was Killbuck, a name by which his son also came to be known. In 1778, Gelelemend was chosen chief of his tribe. Like his predecessor, WHITE EYES, he encouraged accommodation with whites.

Gelelemend was opposed by HOPOCAN, the leader of the war faction. When Hopocan's stance prevailed, Gelelemend was encouraged by white officials at Pittsburgh to settle on an island in the Allegheny River with his followers. Yet, in 1782, a party of whites returning along the Allegheny from an attack on peaceful Delaware Indians at the Moravian settlement at Gnaddenhutten also attacked Gelelemend's village. His band suffered several casualties; Gelelemend and others escaped by swimming away from the attackers. During his flight, he lost treaty documents given to his tribe in 1682 by WILLIAM PENN.

Gelelemend later settled at Pittsburgh to avoid the revenge of fellow Delawares, who blamed him for white attacks. There he lived as a practicing Moravian under his baptized name, William Henry.

GENTILZ, THEODORE. *(1819–1906).* Artist.

French artist Theodore Gentilz arrived in Texas in 1843 to serve as surveyor and English interpreter for Count Castro, founder of the French colony of Castroville on the Medina River. In 1846, Gentilz established a studio in San Antonio, where he sold his artwork. He is known to have traded with Indians, exchanging his pictures for buffalo meat. Count Castro sent Gentilz on surveying expeditions into Texas and Mexico, where he made contact with hostile tribes. He gained their confidence and friendship and was successful in getting many tribal members to pose for sketches and paintings.

GERONIMO (Jeronimo; Gokhlayeh, Goyathlay, "one who yawns"). *Chiricahua Apache. (ca. 1825–1909).* Leader of the Apache Wars of the 1880s.

Geronimo was born along the upper Gila River, probably on the Arizona side of the present-day New Mexico–Arizona border. His father Taklishim was a full-blooded Chiricahua; his mother Juana, also full-blooded, had been a captive among the Mexicans. As a young man, Geronimo fought under the Chiricahua COCHISE and the Mimbreno MANGAS COLORADAS. He was not a hereditary chief, but gained prestige within the tribe through skill and courage in battle. He established his reputation against the Mexicans who, in 1858, killed his mother, wife, and three children in an unprovoked attack. He also came to be considered a medicine man by his people because of his gift of "power," the ability to influence people and events.

In 1872, Cochise agreed to peace with white officials on being granted the Chiricahua, or Apache Pass, Reservation along the Butterfield Trail. But, after his death in 1874, the number of Chiricahua raids increased despite efforts by agent THOMAS J. JEFFORDS. War parties rode into Mexico, then returned to use the reservation as a sanctuary. After an incident in which a group of Apaches killed two stagecoach attendants over liquor, the government dissolved the reservation. The Chiricahuas were to be relocated by agent JOHN P. CLUM at the San Carlos Reservation to the north in Arizona with 4,000 other Apaches from other bands. On learning of the plan, Geronimo crossed the border into the Sierra Madre. He joined forces with JUH's Nednhi band and carried out raids on Mexican settlements, selling stolen livestock to New Mexico traders.

In late 1876, Geronimo and his followers appeared at the Warm Springs (Ojo Caliente) Reservation in New Mexico with a herd of stolen cattle. When Clum heard of his whereabouts, he set out from San Carlos to apprehend him, and, after a standoff at the agency, Geronimo allowed himself to be arrested. He was taken to San Carlos in April 1877. The Mimbreno VICTORIO was also transferred with his Warm Springs band at that time, but escaped the following September, starting another phase of the Apache Wars that lasted until his death in 1880. During this period Geronimo resided at San Carlos. He crossed into Mexico once with Juh, but

Geronimo. *Courtesy of New York Public Library.*

returned to San Carlos because of increased Mexican troop activity.

The last phase of the Apache Wars, with Geronimo the pivotal figure, began in summer 1881 and lasted until his final surrender in 1886. On August 30, 1881, the military at Fort Apache northeast of San Carlos made a move to arrest NAKAIDOKLINI, a White Mountain Apache who preached a new religion involving the return of dead warriors to eliminate whites. Fighting erupted at Cibecue Creek and Nakaidoklini was killed. Some of his followers, including Indian scouts for the army, attacked Fort Apache, but were driven back. Additional troops were called up to prevent further violence.

The Chiricahua leaders at San Carlos resented and feared the growing number of troops. One month after the fight at Cibecue Creek, Geronimo, Juh, NAICHE (the son of Cochise and hereditary chief), CHATO, and 74 others departed San Carlos for the mountains of Mexico. They returned in April 1882 in a raid on the reservation in which they killed the chief of police and forced LOCO and his moderate band of Mimbrenos to accompany them across the border, where they united with NANA's militant Mimbrenos. Then, in July 1882, White Mountain Apaches under NATIOTISH battled troops at Big Dry Walsh.

Later in 1882, General GEORGE CROOK, who had campaigned earlier against Victorio's Chiricahuas as well as DELSHAY's Tonto Apaches, was reassigned in the Southwest to pacify the Apaches. Crook promptly organized a number of mobile units, including Apache scouts, who knew how to track fellow Apaches. In May 1883, with permission from Mexican authorities, Crook

led units under Captain Emmet Crawford and Lieutenant Charles Gatewood into the Sierra Madre. They used mules instead of horses, since the former were better suited to desert conditions. The troops managed an attack on Chato's camp on May 15, and, in a follow-up parley, the Apache leaders agreed to return to the reservation. It took about a year for all to comply, however. Juh had been killed earlier in an accident, but the others, including Nana, Naiche, Loco, and Chato, trickled in with their followers. Finally, in March 1884, Geronimo, who by now was the most revered of the war chiefs, also returned to San Carlos.

A little more than a year later, in May 1885, there was more unrest. When reservation officials banned *tiswin*, an Apache alcoholic beverage, Geronimo, Nana, Naiche, and almost 150 followers headed for the Sierra Madre. Crook's soldiers tracked them until they agreed to a parley, this one at Canyon de los Embudos on March 25, 1886. Crook demanded unconditional surrender and imprisonment in the East for two years. Geronimo agreed. But while being led to Fort Bowie by Apache scouts, he, Naiche, and 24 others broke free again.

The army replaced Crook with General NELSON A. MILES, another proven Indian fighter. In order to capture the 24 renegade Apaches, Miles ordered 5,000 soldies into the field with Apache scouts. Captain HENRY W. LAWTON led a unit into Mexico and caught up with the fugitives on July 15, but Geronimo eluded the soldiers. After another month and a half of hiding out, he agreed to surrender, but only to Miles. On September 4, 1886, at Skeleton Canyon, about 65 miles south of the Apache Pass, Geronimo and his few remaining followers surrendered for the final time.

Geronimo and hundreds of other Apaches, not all of them militants, were sent in chains by rail to Fort Pickens and Fort Marion in Florida. After one year, some, including Geronimo, were relocated to Mount Vernon Barracks in Alabama. Many died from tuberculosis and other diseases. ESKIMINZIN's Aravaipas were allowed to return to Arizona, but Geronimo's and Naiche's Chiricahuas were not. They accepted the Comanches' and Kiowas' offer to share their reservation in the Indian Territory, and, in 1894, the remaining Apaches were shipped to Fort Sill.

In his new home, Geronimo took up farming, joined the Dutch Reformed church, and dictated his memoirs *Geronimo's Story of His People* to S. M. Barrett, published in 1906. He appeared at the national expositions in St. Louis and Omaha, where he made money selling his photographs, and in Theodore Roosevelt's inaugural procession of 1905. Although a legend throughout the United States, he was never granted permission to return to his homeland. He died of pneumonia, still a prisoner of war, in 1909. His name has become part of

Geronimo. Photo by Edward Curtis. *Courtesy of National Archives of Canada/C-3870.*

the English language as a war cry, including a jumping call for U.S. paratroopers.

GIBBON, JOHN. *(1827–1896).* Army officer in the Sioux War for the Black Hills and the Nez Perce War.

Originally from Philadelphia, John Gibbon grew up in Charlotte, North Carolina. He graduated from West Point during the Mexican War. Commissioned an artillery officer, he joined U.S. troops in Mexico, although he saw no action.

Gibbon's first Indian engagement occurred in Florida in 1849 during the army's attempt to end Seminole raiding. At the beginning of the Civil War in 1861, Gibbon commanded artillery for General Irvin McDowell's division, and, by 1862, he had been brevetted a brigadier general of volunteers. Gibbon served in numerous battles, including Fredericksburg in 1862, where he was wounded. By the end of the war, he had reached the brevetted rank of major general of volunteers.

Reverting to the regular rank of colonel in 1866, Gibbon was assigned to the 7th infantry at Fort Ellis, Montana Territory. In the first year of the War for the Black Hills of 1876–77, he took part in the June offensive against Sioux and Cheyenne militants led by SITTING BULL and CRAZY HORSE. Advancing east from Fort Ellis, Gibbon led his column in conjunction with columns led by generals GEORGE CROOK and ALFRED TERRY. Colonel GEORGE ARMSTRONG CUSTER's 7th Cavalry, part of Terry's command, engaged the allied bands in the Battle of Little Bighorn on June 25. Gibbon and his column arrived at the battle site two days later and drove off the Sioux and Cheyenne warriors, who had pinned down the surviving portions of Custer's regiment.

During the Nez Perce War of 1877, Gibbon's troops attacked Chief JOSEPH's (Young Joseph's) encampment on the Big Hole River in Montana Territory on August 9, 1877. A Nez Perce counterattack caused significant army casualties, including Gibbon, who ordered his forces to withdraw.

In 1885, Gibbon was promoted to brigadier general and given command of the army's Department of the Columbia (Oregon, Washington, Idaho). He subsequently assumed command of the entire Division of the Pacific. Gibbon retired from the military in 1891. (See also Young JOSEPH; SITTING BULL.)

GIRTY, SIMON (The Great Renegade).
(1741–1818). Scout; Tory leader in the American Revolution; Indian agent; interpreter.

In 1756, during the French and Indian War, Simon Girty's family was attacked by Indians at their home on the western Pennsylvania frontier. His parents were killed; 15-year-old Simon and his two brothers were taken into captivity by the Indians. He eventually was traded to a band of Senecas and lived among them for the next three years.

By the time he was released to the British at Pittsburgh in 1759, Girty had become fluent in the Iroquoian language. For the next 17 years, he worked as a military scout and interpreter for the British in the Ohio Valley. He was a scout in Lord DUNMORE's War of 1774 against the Shawnees under CORNSTALK.

In 1776, Girty was a lieutenant in the Virginia militia, fighting against the British in the American Revolution. Two years later, however, Girty defected to the British. He was assigned to Detroit under ALEXANDER McKEE as an interpreter for Great Britain's Indian allies in the northern Ohio Valley region. He also took an active part in Shawnee raids on white settlements in western Pennsylvania.

Girty was reportedly ruthless in his treatment of pro-Revolutionary captives, making use of traditional Iroquoian methods of torture and execution. In June 1782, Continental army colonel William Crawford was captured after an unsuccessful campaign into the Sandusky River region of Ohio. On orders from Girty, the Shawnees and Delawares burned Crawford alive. Girty did, however, spare the life of the Patriot scout SIMON KENTON several years before.

In August 1782, Girty led a force of Tories and Indians into Kentucky and laid an unsuccessful siege of Bryan's Station. He then battled Kentuckians, at the Battle of Blue Licks, on August 19, 1782. Soon after, Major GEORGE ROGERS CLARK defeated Girty's command on its way to reinforce the Shawnee village of Piqua.

After the war, in 1783, Girty settled in British-held Detroit, from where he continued to act as an agent and interpreter among the Indians of the Ohio Valley. During the U.S. campaign against the tribes of the Old Northwest in LITTLE TURTLE's War of 1790–94, Girty supported the Indians, taking part in the defeat of General ARTHUR ST. CLAIR's forces at an engagement near present-day Fort Wayne, Indiana, on November 4, 1791. Three years later, at the battle of Fallen Timbers, on August 20, 1794, near present-day Toledo, Ohio, he fought with the Indians in their defeat at the hands of American troops under General "Mad" ANTHONY WAYNE.

Girty tried unsuccessfully to dissuade the tribes of the Old Northwest from agreeing to the 1795 Treaty of Greenville. When Britain abandoned its claim to Detroit following the Jay Treaty of 1794, Girty was forced to move to present-day Ontario.

Still wanted for acts against colonists during the American Revolution, Girty was forced to take refuge in a Mohawk village during the War of 1812, when American troops invaded Canada. He died near Amherstburg, Ontario, five years later.

GIST, CHRISTOPHER. *(ca. 1706–1759)*. Explorer; trader; scout.

Born near Baltimore, Maryland, Christopher Gist settled in the Yadkin Valley of North Carolina in 1745, where he became an Indian trader. In 1750–51, employed by the Ohio Land Company, he descended the Ohio River, exploring western Pennsylvania, southern Ohio, and eastern Kentucky, then crossing to North Carolina. In 1752–53, he blazed a trail from the Potomac River in western Maryland through the Alleghenies to Redstone Creek, a tributary of the Monongahela, where he established a settlement.

In 1754, Gist accompanied Ohio Land Company syndicate member GEORGE WASHINGTON on an expedition to the French settlement at Logstown in western Pennsylvania, with plans to order the French out of the region. The resulting skirmishes marked the start of the French and Indian War of 1754–63. During this expedition, Gist saved Washington's life on two occasions.

In 1755, Gist served as a guide to General EDWARD BRADDOCK's abortive expedition against the French at Fort Duquesne (present-day Pittsburgh). Throughout the rest of the war, Gist served as a scout for British forces.

In 1759, Gist traveled to Cherokee country in the western Carolinas to enlist their military support in the war against the French. While among this tribe, he contracted smallpox and died. His account of frontier experiences, *Christopher Gist's Journals*, was published in 1893.

GLASS, HUGH. *(ca. 1785–1833)*. Trader; trapper.

Little is known of mountain man Hugh Glass's early life. Some accounts indicate he may have spent time among Jean Lafitte and his Gulf Coast pirates, and later may have lived among the Pawnees of eastern Nebraska.

In 1823, Glass was a trapper on WILLIAM HENRY ASHLEY's Missouri River expedition. When Arikara Indians attacked Ashley's party in South Dakota, Glass was wounded, but he recovered enough to join ANDREW HENRY's segment of the expedition to the Yellowstone. On the Grand River in what is now South Dakota, he was attacked and mauled by a grizzly bear. JAMES BRIDGER and John Fitzgerald were left to look after Glass, but abandoned him, believing he would die soon. Glass managed to travel hundreds of miles along the Grand River to the Missouri, spending time among the Sioux to recover, then joining another fur-trapping party and proceeding to Henry's new post on the Bighorn River. He eventually found Bridger and Fitzgerald, whom he reportedly chastized, then forgave.

During the late 1820s, Glass was involved in the trade between St. Louis and New Mexico along the Santa Fe Trail. In 1828, at Bear Lake, northeast of the Great Salt Lake on the present border between Idaho and Utah, he was again wounded in an Indian attack.

Glass then settled near Fort Union at the junction of the Missouri and Yellowstone rivers, present-day North Dakota. In winter 1832–33, it is thought he was trapping on the Yellowstone with the part-Cherokee EDWARD ROSE and a third mountain man when the group was attacked and killed by an Arikara war party.

GODFROY, FRANCIS (Francis Godfrey). *Mixed Miami. (1788–1840)*. Ally of British in the War of 1812; trader.

Francis Godfroy, son of the French trader Jacques Godfroy and a Miami woman, grew up in the region of Fort Wayne, Indiana. As a war chief, he was receptive to TECUMSEH's call for an alliance of tribes to drive American settlers from the region. During the War of 1812, General WILLIAM HENRY HARRISON ordered an attack on pro-British Miami villages along the Mississinewa River in present-day Indiana. In mid-December 1812, the soldiers were camped for the night in the nearby countryside, when at dawn on December 18, Godfroy led 300 Miamis in a surprise attack and routed the American troops, killing eight. Godfroy later agreed to peace terms and moved to his father's trading post on the Wabash River where he prospered as a trader. He signed several of the Miami land cessions between 1818 and 1840, for which he received cash and land grants. (See also TECUMSEH.)

GOFF, ORLANDO SCOTT. *(1843–1917)*. Photographer.

O. S. Goff was born in Connecticut, and, following service in the Civil War, lived in New York, then Wisconsin. On relocating to Yankton in what is now North Dakota in 1871, he was hired by STANLEY MORROW to work in his studio. In 1878, Goff opened his own studio in Bismarck and in turn employed DAVID F. BARRY. Goff photographed Plateau as well as Northern Plains Indians, taking possibly the first picture of Sioux chief SITTING BULL. He died in Idaho following retirement.

GOOD THUNDER (Wakuntchapinka). *Winnebago. (ca. 1790–1863)*. Friend to whites.

Good Thunder was considered to have occult powers by his people, which increased his standing among them. Along with WAUKON DECORA, LITTLE PRIEST, and WINNESHIEK, he was a powerful band leader of the Winnebagos. In 1832, during the Black Hawk War in which he participated on the side of the whites, his band had a village at Fond du Lac, Wisconsin. Good Thunder signed treaties in 1832 and 1837. In 1840, his band was relocated to a reservation in the northeast corner of what is now Iowa; in 1848, to Long Prairie, Minnesota; and, in 1855, to Blue Earth County, Minnesota. During the Minnesota Uprising of Santee Sioux in 1862–63 under LITTLE CROW, Good Thunder still supported the whites. Nevertheless, in 1863, his people were relocated again to a reservation in South Dakota. Because of lack of food, they soon departed, settling next to the Omaha Reservation in Nebraska, where Good Thunder died.

GOSNOLD, BARTHOLOMEW. (ca. 1572–1607).
Explorer.

The British-born Bartholomew Gosnold was educated at Cambridge, receiving training in navigation. Under the sponsorship of the Earl of Southampton, he undertook an expedition across the Atlantic in 1602. Commanding the ship *Concord*, Gosnold made the first direct transatlantic voyage to the New England coast.

Off the coast of southern Maine, Gosnold's expedition encountered a small sailboat manned by a group of Indians. Gosnold later reported that a few of these Indians could speak "Christian" words, either English or French. They also wore some items of European clothing, indicating previous white contact.

From the southern coast of Maine, Gosnold sailed southward, charting and naming Cape Cod for its rich fishing grounds. He also explored the island coasts of Martha's Vineyard and Nantucket, journeying as far south along the mainland itself as Narragansett Bay. Gosnold established a fort on Cuttyhunk Island, the westernmost of the Elizabeth Islands off the southeast coast of Massachusetts.

Gosnold's party traded with New England coastal tribes, obtaining furs, lumber, and sassafras bark, which was in great demand in early 17th-century Europe for use as a medicine to treat a wide variety of ailments, especially syphilis.

When James I of England granted a charter to the Virginia Company, Gosnold was appointed a vice admiral of the merchant fleet operated by the London Company, a subsidiary of the Virginia Company. In December 1606, he set out in command of the company's ship, the *God Speed*, reaching the Virginia coast in April 1607. Against Gosnold's objections, the expedition decided to establish its settlement, Jamestown, on a site 30 miles up the James River, near a mosquito-infested swamp. Gosnold was appointed one of the seven original councilors of the Jamestown settlement, where he died a few months later from malaria. JOHN SMITH became president of the colony in 1609.

GRAFFENRIED, CHRISTOPH VON (Christopher, Baron de Graffenried). *(1661–1743)*.
Christian leader; colonizer.

Born in the Swiss city of Bern, Christoph von Graffenried led a group of Swiss and Palatine Germans to North Carolina in 1710. With the help of JOHN LAWSON, they established the settlement of New Bern, at the junction of the Trent and Neuse rivers. The next year, they evicted the native Tuscaroras from their lands without payment, whereupon Graffenried assumed the title of Landgrave of Carolina. The Tuscaroras under HANCOCK soon retaliated with raids on the white settlements near New Bern. Graffenried and Lawson were captured by the Tuscaroras; Graffenried was released when he agreed to peace terms, but Lawson was killed. The Tuscarora War continued until 1713, when the Tuscaroras were defeated by overwhelming colonial forces. Graffenried returned to Switzerland in 1713. An artist, he produced sketches of early colonial North Carolina, as well as a written account of his experiences as a colonizer. (See also HANCOCK.)

GRANGULA (Grande Geule, Haaskouan, "big mouth"; Otreouati). *Onondaga. (fl. 1680s)*.
Spokesman for the Iroquois League.

In 1684, at a conference in Iroquois territory, French officials offered peace on the condition that the Iroquois no longer trade with the British and that they stop all raids on French traders. Grangula spoke on behalf of the League, passionately insisting that the Iroquois could trade with whomever they choose and that they would continue their attacks on French traders as long as the French supplied the Algonquian tribes of the region with firearms. Grangula, like the later Onondaga orator DEKANISORA, helped maintain the longterm trade and military relationship between the Iroquois and the British.

GRANT, ULYSSES SIMPSON. *(1822–1885)*.
President of the United States, 1869–77; reformer.

Ulysses S. Grant, born at Point Pleasant, Ohio, attended West Point and served in the Mexican War of 1846–48, then resigned from the army to pursue a career in business. During this period, he became a friend of the Seneca ELY PARKER in Galena, Illinois. At the beginning of the Civil War, Grant reentered the service as colonel of an Illinois volunteer regiment, eventually rising to command all Union forces. Following the war, he was elected as Republican president.

On assuming the presidency in March 1869, Grant announced a new federal Indian policy, the goal of which was to acculturate Indians and eventually make them U.S. citizens. He appointed Ely Parker as his commissioner of Indian Affairs, the first Native American to hold that post.

Grant's administration first reorganized the Bureau of Indian Affairs by filling the majority of the Indian agent positions with army officers. The remaining Indian agencies were assigned to individuals recommended by the Hicksite Friends, a Quaker denomination, and the Episcopal bishop of Minnesota, HENRY B. WHIPPLE. After the 1870 enactment of federal legislation barring military personnel from holding civil service positions, Grant distributed the Indian agent posts among a wide variety of Christian denominations, with the exception of the Mormons.

The assignment of religiously motivated Indian agents was intended to pacify the Indians and bring an end to frontier conflict. Grant's programs became known as his Peace Policy, or the "Quaker Policy," because of the dominant role played by that group. Grant was reported to have commented that if his policy could make Quakers out of the Indians, it would help take the fight out of them.

Grant encouraged the peaceful relocation of tribes onto reservations and the protection of their territorial integrity by the military. However, Indians who did not restrict themselves to reservations were subject to the military enforcement of federal Indian policy.

At this time, Plains tribes were demanding payment of annuities promised them in exchange for land cessions signed during the previous decades. Funding for these payments had been delayed by corruption and mismanagement of funds, as well as huge federal outlays for the Civil War. In keeping with his Peace Policy, Grant and his Congressional supporters brought about the passage of the Indian Appropriation Act of 1869, under which $2 million in federal funds were designated for Indian matters, including the settlement of treaty claims.

"Friends of the Indian" reform groups flourished during the Grant administration. Money was raised to educate the Indians in preparation for their assimilation into white society, and the federal government made its first allocation of funds for Indian educational programs. Individual Indian ownership of land was encouraged by the passage of the Indian Homestead Act of 1875, which extended the provisions of the Homestead Act of 1862 to Indians who had renounced their tribal affiliations. Prior to 1870, only U.S. citizens were entitled to settle government lands without cost.

Grant received numerous Indian leaders to Washington, D.C., including the Sioux delegation led by RED CLOUD and SPOTTED TAIL. Many Indians toured other cities and appeared before reform groups during his administration. The philanthropist PETER COOPER of the U.S. Indian Commission organized Indian lectures at Cooper Union in New York City, as did Boston groups.

Despite the well-intentioned Peace Policy, Grant's eight years in office were marked by numerous Indian-white conflicts. Other forces were at play, including the accelerating white development of the West and the increased presence of Civil War veterans, such as WILLIAM T. SHERMAN and PHILIP H. SHERIDAN, who sought military solutions. Conflicts of the period included the massacre of ESKIMINZIN's Apache band; the Modoc War of 1872–73 under CAPTAIN JACK; the Red River War of 1874–75 under QUANAH PARKER, the War for the Black Hills of 1876–77 under SITTING BULL; and the Nez Perce War of 1877 under Chief JOSEPH (Young Joseph).

The end of Grant's second term in office saw a public reaction against Indian aggressions and a denunciation of his Peace Policy and the reform movement. Concern over Indian hostilities led to an unsuccessful move by Congress to return the Bureau of Indian Affairs to the supervision of the War Department. (See also PARKER, ELY.)

GRASS, JOHN (Pezi, "grass"; Mato Watakpe, "standing bear"). *Sihasapa Sioux. (ca. 1837–1918).* Spokesman for the Sioux of the Standing Rock Reservation in North Dakota.

John Grass was the son of Grass or Old Grass, the leader of the Sihasapa Sioux during the Sioux Wars of the 1860s–70s. He probably fought under his father in various battles, although this is undocumented. He later achieved prominence in a diplomatic role between the Indians of Standing Rock and white officials, when the agent JAMES McLAUGHLIN purposely negotiated with him and with GALL to diminish the prestige of SITTING BULL. Over Sitting Bull's objections, Grass signed the 1889 agreement that led to the division of the Great Sioux Reservation into four smaller tracts.

GRATTAN, JOHN L. *(1830–1854).* Army officer; instigator of the Grattan Fight of 1854.

On graduating from West Point in 1853, brevet Second Lieutenant John Grattan was assigned to frontier duty at Fort Laramie along the Oregon Trail, near the North Platte River, in what is now Wyoming. That summer, 4,000 Brule and Oglala Sioux arrived at Fort Laramie to collect annuity goods due them by treaty. The Indians had agreed to accept the goods in exchange for a promise not to interfere with travelers along the Oregon Trail, which passed through their hunting grounds.

Following reports that the Sioux had taken and slaughtered a stray cow belonging to a Mormon wagon train, Grattan decided to arrest the perpetrator, a Miniconjou Sioux by the name of High Forehead, visiting among the Brules. Grattan's motivation might have been influenced by a desire for a permanent commission. In any event, in August 1854 he proceeded to the camp of the Brule chief CONQUERING BEAR, with a force of 27 troopers, an interpreter, and two cannon, and demanded the surrender of the Indian responsible for the loss of the cow. Conquering Bear, claiming to have no authority over a Miniconjou, offered to pay for the cow with Indian livestock, or settle the account with annuity goods. In an ensuing dispute, Grattan ordered his men to open fire, and Conquering Bear was fatally wounded. The Indians then attacked and killed Grattan and all but one of his men as they fled back to the post. The only survivor died soon afterward from his wounds.

The incident may have been precipitated by the actions of Grattan's French-Canadian interpreter, Lucien Auguste, who had been drunk during the confrontation and who reportedly mistranslated Grattan's remarks and made unauthorized threats to the Indians in their own language. GEORGE MANYPENNY, commissioner of Indian Affairs under President Franklin Pierce, concluded that the tragedy could have been avoided if Indian annuity funds had been used to pay for the cow. He also concluded that Grattan acted wrongly in trying to arrest the Miniconjou since the military had no law-enforcement authority over the Sioux, an interpretation that strained relations between the recently separated War Department and the Indian Bureau.

The Oglala and Brule Sioux warriors, encouraged by their easy victory over Grattan, embarked on a campaign of pillage of white settlers. The warriors attacked a stagecoach from Salt Lake City, killed its occupants, and made off with $10,000 in gold. The following year, the War Department sent a punitive expedition against the Sioux under the command of General WILLIAM S. HARNEY. (See also CONQUERING BEAR.)

GRAY, ROBERT. (1755–1806). Explorer.

Robert Gray was born at Tiverton, Rhode Island, and served as a navigator in the Continental navy during the American Revolution.

In 1787, in command of the Boston merchant ship the *Lady Washington*, along with Captain John Kendrick in command of the *Columbia*, Gray left Boston and sailed around Cape Horn, arriving at Vancouver Island, where the expedition traded with the Nootka Indians for otter pelts. As commander of the *Columbia*, Gray then sailed across the Pacific to China. In Canton, he traded the otter pelts for tea, and then returned to Boston in August 1790 via the Cape of Good Hope, conducting the first circumnavigation of the globe by an American-flag vessel.

In fall 1790, Gray sailed from Boston aboard the *Columbia* and reached Vancouver Island the next spring. Following a stopover during winter 1791–92, he sailed south along the coast, exploring Grays Harbor. In May

1792, at the border of present-day Oregon and Washington, Gray crossed the bar that had previously halted Spanish and British navigators and sailed 10 miles up the river. He named the river that was central to the lives of so many Indian peoples because of its rich salmon runs, "Columbia's River" (later known as the Columbia River), in honor of his ship. He then returned to the Pacific and proceeded west to China, where he again traded pelts obtained from the Northwest Coast Indians. Following a second circumnavigation of the world, he returned to Boston in 1793.

Although Gray was the first to sail up the Columbia River, he did not publish his findings. Nevertheless, his explorations became the basis for the U.S. claim to the region.

GREAT SUN (Grand Soleil). *Natchez. (d. ca. 1730).* Leader of the Natchez Revolt of 1729. Brother of TATTOOED SERPENT.

"Great Sun" was a hereditary title of the tribe, bestowed upon the principal chief, or emperor. One Great Sun has been recorded in history. He ruled during the early 1700s when the French began settling along the lower Mississippi River. The French built their first mission to the Natchez in 1706, and, 10 years later, in order to keep the peace between Indians and whites and to encourage further settlement and trade, they also built Fort Rosalie. It overlooked the Mississippi and the Great Sun's village.

Tattooed Serpent and Tattooed Arm, the brother and mother of the Great Sun, were devoted allies of the French. When Tattooed Serpent died in 1725, however, the Great Sun began listening to the counsel of the tribe's anti-French faction. Sieur Chepart, recently appointed the new governor of Louisiana, demanded the Great Sun's village site for his own plantation. When the Great Sun refused, Chepart demanded crops in payment for his concession to the Indians.

Then the Great Sun, his priests, and warriors plotted a rebellion. They sent out bundles of sticks to other villages, ostensibly indicating the number of crops to be delivered, but actually giving the time of a planned attack. On the first autumn frost, November 30, 1729, Natchez warriors assaulted Fort Rosalie and other settlements along the Mississippi, inflicting more than 500 casualties. One of those killed was Chepart.

After an army of French soldiers and Choctaw warriors had recaptured Fort Rosalie, the Great Sun agreed to the terms of peace, but managed to escape in the night with some of his followers. He led them up the Red River, where the French located and attacked them a year later. Once again, European firearms proved too much for the defending Natchez, and the Great Sun surrendered.

It is thought that the Great Sun was subsequently taken to New Orleans and executed. His people never recovered their tribal identity. Many Natchez captives were sold into slavery in the Caribbean; other refugees settled among and were absorbed by other tribes.

GREGG, JOSIAH. *(1806–1850)*. Historian; trader; explorer.

Josiah Gregg was born and raised in Missouri. The son of farmers, he supplemented his rural education with extensive reading. In the early 1830s, he set out, because of poor health, for the Southwest and became involved in the fur trade along the Santa Fe Trail. He recorded his experiences and later wrote *Commerce of the Prairies* (1844), the earliest history of the Santa Fe Trail. In 1846, Gregg served in the Mexican War as a member of the Arkansas Volunteers. In 1847–48, he practiced medicine in Saltillo, Mexico, and, in 1850, joined a botanical expedition to Humboldt Bay in California. He died that same year.

GRIERSON, BENJAMIN HENRY. *(1826–1911)*. Army officer in the Red River War and the Apache Wars; leader of Buffalo Soldiers.

Born in Pennsylvania, Benjamin H. Grierson moved to Ohio, then Illinois, where he taught music. At the outbreak of the Civil War, he enlisted as a private in a volunteer regiment, and was soon appointed a major in the 6th Illinois Cavalry and staged raids on railroads and other facilities in Tennessee and Louisiana. By 1863, he had been brevetted a brigadier general.

Grierson remained in the service after the war, and, in 1866, at the regular rank of colonel, took command of the 10th Cavalry, a regiment of black troopers known as the Buffalo Soldiers, headquartered at Fort Concho in west Texas. At the close of the Sheridan Campaign of 1868–69, Grierson's troops began the construction of Fort Sill in the southwestern corner of the Indian Territory, which later became agency headquarters for the Comanche and Kiowa Reservation. Grierson was a supporter of President ULYSSES S. GRANT's Peace Policy and worked with Indian agent LAWRIE TATUM for its implementation among the Comanches and Kiowas.

In May 1871, while at Fort Sill, Indian Territory, Grierson was informed by Tatum that some among the Kiowas boasted of murdering the members of a wagon train party near Salt Creek Prairie, Texas. When General WILLIAM T. SHERMAN, who happened to be visiting Fort Sill at that time, ordered the arrests of SATANTA, SATANK, and BIG TREE, a tense situation developed in which LONE WOLF threatened Sherman with his rifle. Grierson jumped Lone Wolf, spoiling his aim, and probably saved Sherman's life.

In the late 1870s, Grierson was engaged in skirmishes with the Kiowas, Comanches, Apaches, and Kickapoos in west Texas during the 1870s. During summer 1880, he led his 10th Cavalry, operating out of Fort Davis, Texas, in the campaign against the Mimbreno Apache VICTORIO. Grierson and his troops secured strategic waterholes in west Texas and drove Victorio and his followers into Mexico.

Despite his military successes, Grierson was unpopular among fellow officers, especially his superior, General PHILIP H. SHERIDAN, because of his association with black soldiers, his informal relationship with his troops, his sympathy to the Indians, and his lack of West Point credentials.

In 1885, Grierson was transferred to the Department of Arizona. Promoted to the rank of brigadier general in 1890, he retired from the army that same year. (See also SATANTA, VICTORIO.)

GRINNELL, GEORGE BIRD. *(1849–1938)*. Anthropologist; historian; naturalist; writer.

George Bird Grinnell was born in Brooklyn, New York. Originally a zoologist at Yale, he had extensive contacts with the Indians of the Northern Plains, starting with his participation in the last great hunt of the Pawnees in 1872, followed by his service as a naturalist with Colonel GEORGE ARMSTRONG CUSTER's expedition to the Black Hills in 1874. He also served in this capacity the following year in Colonel William Ludlow's expedition to the newly designated Yellowstone Park. Grinnell's association with the Northern Plains tribes would continue for the rest of his life. His best-known works are on the Cheyennes: *The Fighting Cheyennes* (1915) and *The Cheyenne Indians* (1923). Grinnell also wrote about the legends of the Pawnees and the Blackfeet, and related the story of his friends FRANK NORTH and LUTHER NORTH in *Two Great Scouts and their Pawnee Battalion* (1928). He made numerous contributions to magazines, especially *Forest and Stream*, of which he became editor.

GROSEILLIERS, MEDARD CHOUART, SIEUR DES. *(ca. 1618–ca. 1697)*. Explorer; trader. Brother-in-law of PIERRE ESPRIT RADISSON.

Medard Chouart, Sieur des Groseilliers, from Charly-sur-Marne, France, came to French Canada about 1641. From 1641 to 1646, he worked with the Jesuit missionaries among the Hurons in the Georgian Bay region of what is now Ontario.

Following the conclusion of the Iroquois-Huron Wars of 1648–53, Grosseilliers embarked on a career as a *coureur de bois*, a wilderness Indian trader. In 1654–56, he journeyed from the French settlement at Trois-Rivieres on the St. Lawrence River by canoe and overland to the northern Great Lakes, reaching present-day Green, Bay, Wisconsin, on the shores of Lake Michigan. He returned to the Montreal area two years later with

250 Indians from Green Bay and a large shipment of furs.

In 1659–60, accompanied by his brother-in-law Pierre Esprit Radisson (who later made what is considered a false claim to have been present on the first expedition), Groseilliers explored west of Lake Superior, into present-day Minnesota, where he made what was probably the first European contact with the Sioux. However, Groseilliers's and Radisson's unlicensed fur-trading operation ran afoul of French government authorities, who intercepted and confiscated their fur shipment at Montreal. In 1663, seeking new outlets, they were commissioned by a syndicate of Boston merchants to trade for furs with the Indians of northern New England.

In 1665, Radisson and Groseilliers obtained the backing of London business interests. During an 1668–69 expedition, Groseilliers located sites for future trading posts at the mouths of various rivers flowing into the Hudson Bay and, at the mouth of Rupert River on James Bay, founded Fort Charles. His reports led to the chartering of the Hudson's Bay Company the next year. The company established other trading factories on the western shores of Hudson Bay, enabling British seagoing vessels to obtain shipments of furs directly from the Indians, then sail to Boston, New York, or London during the ice-free spring and summer months.

Groseilliers left the Hudson's Bay Company in 1676. He joined the French-owned fur-trading concern, Compaigne du Nord, in 1682, and established a trading post at the mouth of the Hayes River on the shores of western Hudson Bay in what is now northeastern Manitoba. He was subsequently accused of undertaking French-backed raids on Hudson's Bay Company posts and retired after 1684.

GROUARD, FRANK (Standing Bear; The Grabber). (1850–1905). Counselor to SITTING BULL and CRAZY HORSE; army scout.

Frank Grouard was born on the Polynesian island of Tubuai in the South Pacific, south of Tahiti, probably the son of a Mormon missionary and a native woman. Some accounts of his early life describe him as the son of a black steamboat cook and an American Indian woman. In 1858, he was taken to Utah by a Mormon foster mother, and subsequently ran away to the Montana Territory in 1866.

In 1867, while working as a mail carrier on the Northern Plains, Grouard reportedly stole some mail horses and settled among a band of Gros Ventres. He left that tribe the following year, and, after having lived with the Assiniboines and later the Yankton Sioux, he was adopted into the family of Hunkpapa Sioux leader Sitting Bull. Among Sitting Bull's people he was known as Standing Bear because of the furry robe he wore when he first lived with them. He became a trusted counselor to Sitting Bull and may have dissuaded the Sioux leader from entering into a treaty agreement with federal peace commissioners in 1872.

In 1873, Grouard fought on the side of the Sioux against federal troops in the Yellowstone region. He then broke with Sitting Bull and joined with Crazy Horse and his Oglala Sioux followers, where he became known as The Grabber.

Grouard defected from the Indians in 1875, presenting himself to the army at Fort Robinson, Nebraska. He was soon hired as a scout by General GEORGE CROOK. Grouard's knowledge of the Siouan language, as well as his close connections to both Sitting Bull and Crazy Horse, made him Crook's most valued scout in the War for the Black Hills of 1876–77. He also knew Sioux tactics and the locations of the Indians' winter encampments.

Soon after his arrival at Fort Robinson, Grouard accompanied federal Indian commissioners to a peace council with Sitting Bull, receiving instead his former leader's open declaration of war against whites.

Grouard was part of General Crook's offensive in March 1876. He left Fort Fetterman with a small company of civilian scouts and led an advance party of Crook's cavalry to an Indian encampment near the Powder River. A detachment under Colonel Joseph Reynolds attacked the Indian position, but withdrew after a Sioux counterattack. It was theorized at the time that perhaps Reynolds failed to pursue the warriors because he distrusted Grouard and suspected the scout may have deliberately led his troops into a trap. Crook was of a different opinion and later filed court-martial charges against Reynolds.

Grouard located Crazy Horse's encampment on Rosebud Creek, near the site of present-day Kirby, Montana, before the June 17, 1876, Battle of the Rosebud. A few weeks later, Grouard and a detachment of cavalry under Lieutenant Frederick Sibley located Sitting Bull's camp along the Little Bighorn. He was able to safely lead the company's 25 troopers back to Crook's main camp near the Tongue River.

Grouard also scouted for Crook in summer and fall campaigns against the Sioux. In September 1876, he negotiated the surrender of Sioux leader AMERICAN HORSE's band, following the Battle of Slim Buttes in present-day South Dakota.

When Crazy Horse later surrendered to the army at Fort Robinson, Nebraska, in May 1877, Grouard reportedly disappeared from the scene for a time, either fearing the war chief's vengeance, or perhaps what Crazy Horse might inform the army about his past as a Sioux warrior. Grouard was later unsuccessful in persuading Crazy Horse to recruit Sioux scouts for the army's offensive against the Nez Perces. He may have deliberately mistranslated Crazy Horse's reply to this request, leading to rumors of a new Sioux uprising and the attempted arrest and killing of Crazy Horse in September 1877.

Following his scouting for General Crook, Grouard continued to serve in the Dakota Territory under General NELSON A. MILES. He kept federal military authorities posted on the progress of the Ghost Dance religion among the Sioux in 1890–91. Grouard later tracked down outlaws for Dakota territorial law enforcement officers. (See also CRAZY HORSE; SITTING BULL.)

GUERRIER, EDMOND (Ned Geary). *Mixed Southern Cheyenne. (fl. 1860s–1870s).* Interpreter. Son-in-law of WILLIAM BENT.

Edmond Guerrier was the son of a French trader and a Southern Cheyenne mother, and, as a young man, he was part of the militant Dog Soldiers Society. He survived the massacre of BLACK KETTLE's Southern Cheyennes at Sand Creek in 1864 and, during the subsequent wars for the Southern Plains, he served as interpreter for Indian agents and post commanders on numerous occasions. After 1876, he worked as a government employee at Fort Reno, on the Cheyenne-Arapaho Reservation in the Indian Territory.

GUIPAGO. See LONE WOLF.

GUYART, MARIE (Marie Guyard Martin; Marie de l'Incarnation). *(1599–1672).* Historian; linguist; missionary.

Marie Guyart was born in Tours, Frence, and married Claude Martin, a silk marker, at the age of 18. On her husband's death two years later, she turned to Catholicism, eventually entering the Ursuline cloister at Tours in 1632. The next year, she took her vows, then taught among the nuns for six years.

Through visions and her studies of Jesuit writings, Guyart came to the conclusion that she should take her work to New France and volunteered for missionary service. She landed in Quebec in 1639, where she established a convent. As the superior, a position she held until her death, she worked to educate Iroquois and Algonquian girls.

In addition to religious treatises, Guyart wrote about Indian history and customs and produced dictionaries of the Iroquoian and Algonquian languages, plus an Iroquoian catechism. The Jesuit missionary JEROME LALEMENT acted as an informant on Indian customs, as well as her spiritual advisor. The Jesuit historian PIERRE FRANCOIS DE CHARLEVOIX wrote her biography. The Catholic church declared Guyart venerable, a step toward sainthood, in 1911.

GUYASUTA (Guyashusta, Gayashuta, Geyesutha, Gaiachoton, Kyashuta, Kiashuta, Kiyasuta, Kiasola, Keyashuta, Kaiaghshota, Kayahsota, Kayashoton, Quiasutha). *Seneca. (ca. 1725–ca. 1794).* Anti-British chief.

Despite the Iroquois League's alliance with the British in the 1600s and 1700s, the Seneca chief Guyasuta of western New York fought and plotted against them. In 1755, during the French and Indian War, he helped the French defeat General EDWARD BRADDOCK's troops as they advanced on Fort Duquesne (present-day Pittsburgh).

In 1761, with the British capture and occupation of the forts of the Great Lakes country, Guyasuta devised a secret plan for allied tribes to launch concerted attacks against them. The scheme was discovered by the British, however. Although Guyasuta later denied any responsibility for PONTIAC's Rebellion of 1763, in which a similar plan was used, it is assumed that he helped the Ottawa chief plot his uprising and encouraged Seneca warriors to participate.

Guyasuta later served as an intermediary between tribes of the Great Lakes and the British. He originally proclaimed himself neutral in the American Revolution, but then took up arms on the side of his former enemy, the British.

H

HAGLER (Haigler, Haiglar, King Haigler; Arataswa, Oroloswa). *Catawba. (ca. 1690–1763).* Principal chief; ally of British.

It is thought that Hagler was born along the Catawba River in the northern part of South Carolina, and he became principal chief of the Catawbas about 1748. When he assumed power, the Catawbas were greatly reduced in numbers from warfare with traditional enemies such as the Shawnees, Cherokees, and Iroquois; from smallpox, especially during the epidemic of 1738; and from mistreatment by colonists who had settled on their lands and bartered liquor with them for furs. Hagler's efforts helped ensure his people's survival and the maintenance of their traditional ways.

Hagler developed friendly relations with the British colonists, meeting with them on numerous occasions for negotiations. In 1751, he attended a peace conference in Albany, New York. In a meeting with North Carolina officials in 1754, and a letter to the chief justice in 1756, he argued against the sale of liquor to the Catawbas. In 1758, during the French and Indian War, Hagler and his warriors participated with the British in an attack on the French garrison at Fort Duquesne (present-day Pittsburgh). The next year, he helped the British battle Cherokee militants.

Although Hagler became a friend of the Presbyterian missionary William Richardson, he never accepted Christianity and encouraged traditional Catawba beliefs among his tribe. Because of his support, the British built forts along the Catawba River to prevent attacks on Catawbas by other tribes. They also granted a reservation to the Catawbas in 1762, near present-day Rock Hill, South Carolina, the first reservation in the Southeast.

Hagler was killed by a party of Shawnees on his return trip from a visit with the Waxhaw Indians. In 1826, South Carolina erected a statue of Hagler at Camden, considered the first such memorial to an Indian in the United States.

HALDIMAND, FREDERICK. *(1718–1791).* British colonial governor; soldier.

Swiss-born Frederick Haldimand served as a mercenary in several European campaigns, then joined the British army in 1754. He served as an officer in the French and Indian War, starting in 1756 as a lieutenant colonel of the Royal American Regiment. Two years later, he was promoted to colonel after being wounded at Ticonderoga. He helped General JEFFREY AMHERST capture Montreal from the French in 1760.

Haldimand followed this service as military governor of the Trois-Rivieres district of Quebec (1762–66); commander in chief of Florida (1767–73); and commander of the British army in North America in Boston (1773–74). Then, as Great Britain's governor-general of Quebec (1778–84) during the American Revolution, Haldimand provided support for Iroquois raids under the Mohawk JOSEPH BRANT and the Seneca CORNPLANTER on colonial settlements in central New York and Pennsylvania.

At the war's conclusion, Haldimand arranged for Canadian land grants to Brant and other Iroquois when they were expelled from their native territory by the victorious New York colonists. Haldimand returned to England in 1784, where he was knighted. His papers in the British Museum serve as a valuable source for Indian affairs of the period. (See also BRANT, JOSEPH.)

HALE, HORATIO EMMONS. *(1817–1896).* Linguist.

Horatio Hale was born in Newport, Rhode Island; his father David Hale was a lawyer, and his mother Sara Josepha Buell Hale was an editor and writer. Hale served as official linguist with the 1838–42 worldwide naval expedition headed by Lieutenant Charles Wilkes, which explored the Columbia River region all the way to the mouth of the Snake River. Hale conducted research on Northwest Coast Indian languages, as well as the Oregon Trade Language, or Chinook Jargon, that had evolved in this region, a mixture of Indian dialects, French, English, and Spanish. He also studied the language and literature of the Iroquois. His works include: *Biography and Philology* (1846); *The Iroquois Book of Rites* (1883); and *An International Idiom* (1890).

HALF-KING (Tanacharison, Tanaghrisson, Tanaghrishon, Thanayieson, Tenachrisan, Deanaghrison, Johonerissa; Seruniyattha, Scruniyatha). *Mingo. (ca. 1700–1754).* Ally of British in the French and Indian War of 1754–63.

During the 1700s, the Iroquois League of New York controlled territory as far west as the Ohio River and appointed vice-regents to oversee their western holdings. Whites called these chiefs "Half-Kings," and they called the Iroquois living to the west among the Shawnees and the Delawares "Mingos."

The Mingo chief Tanacharison, born a Catawba, was captured and raised by Senecas living on the eastern shore of Lake Erie. He later lived in the vicinity of Logstown (present-day Ambridge, Pennsylvania), where he proved a valuable ally of the British in their struggle with the French along the Ohio River. He met with various frontiersmen, soldiers, and officials, including ROBERT DINWIDDIE, CHRISTOPHER GIST, CONRAD WEISER, GEORGE CROGHAN, and GEORGE WASHINGTON.

Half-King fought with Washington at Great Meadows in 1754, considered the first battle of the French and Indian War of 1754–63 (and the corresponding European Seven Years War of 1756–1763). Half-King later claimed that he killed the French officer Joseph Coulon de Villiers, Sieur de Jumonville, in this battle. After Washington had surrendered Fort Necessity to the French, Half-King moved to Aughwick (present-day Harrisburg), where he died of pneumonia.

HALF-KING (Scarouady, Skaroyady; Monacatoocha). *Mingo. (fl. mid-1700s).* Ally of British in the French and Indian War of 1754–63; successor of Tanacharison, also known as HALF-KING.

Scarouady, an Oneida by birth, inherited the name Half-King when the earlier leader of the Mingos died in 1754. A powerful orator, he urged other tribes of the region, including the Delawares and the Shawnees, to support the British in their struggle with the French for control of the Ohio Valley. He was with British forces under General EDWARD BRADDOCK and his aide GEORGE WASHINGTON in 1755, when they suffered a major defeat on their way to Fort Duquesne (present-day Pittsburgh). In 1756, Half-King spoke at a conference between the Iroquois League and WILLIAM JOHNSON.

HALF-KING (Dunquat, Dunquad, Daunghquat; Petawontakas; Pomoacan). *Wyandot (Huron).* (*fl. late 1700s*). Ally of British in the American Revolution; leader in Little Turtle's War.

The Hurons who moved to Ohio became known as Wyandots. One of them, Dunquat, called Half-King by the whites, became the leader of allied bands of Wyandots, Delawares, Shawnees, Chippewas, and Ottawas who supported the British in the American Revolution and regularly attacked American settlements west of the Allegheny Mountains. Among the tribes, he acted as peacemaker, protecting the Christianized Moravian Delawares from attack by a militant faction. After the Revolution, Half-King joined the Miami LITTLE TURTLE in continued resistance to white expansion. Along with Little Turtle, he signed the Treaty of Fort Greenville in 1795.

HALL, JAMES. (*1793–1868*). Historian; writer.

James Hall, born in Philadelphia, Pennsylvania, served in the army, fighting in the War of 1812. Admitted to the bar in 1818, he spent time in Illinois, then moved to Cincinnati, Ohio, in 1833. Throughout his career as an attorney and judge, Hall pursued a literary career, producing novels and histories of western life. With THOMAS McKENNEY, he coauthored the 1836–44 work, *History of the Indian Tribes of North America*, illustrated with portraits of Indians by CHARLES BIRD KING.

HAMILTON, HENRY (Hair Buyer). (*1734–1796*). British colonial official; officer in the American Revolution.

Henry Hamilton, of Irish descent, entered the British army in 1754 and served in the European Seven Years War. In 1775, he was appointed lieutenant governor of Detroit. During the American Revolution, he supplied the British-allied Shawnees and Delawares with guns, ammunition, and other provisions, and encouraged them to raid American settlements in Ohio and Kentucky by offering a bounty on white scalps. The colonists called him the Hair Buyer.

In October 1778, Hamilton, along with Indian auxiliaries under ALEXANDER McKEE, captured the American settlement of Vincennes on the Wabash River in what is now Indiana. He occupied Fort Patrick Henry, renaming it Fort Sackville. In February 1779, Fort Sackville was attacked by American forces out of Virginia, commanded by Major GEORGE ROGERS CLARK. Outnumbered, Hamilton was forced to surrender, and Clark sent him to Virginia in chains. In 1781, his release was arranged.

In 1782, Hamilton was commissioned lieutenant governor of Quebec, then became chief administrator of the province on Governor FREDERICK HALDI-MAND's departure two years later, serving for a year. Hamilton later served as governor of the Bermudas and Dominica.

HAMILTON, WILLIAM THOMAS (Wildcat Bill). *(1822–1908).* Trader; trapper, scout; guide; Indian agent.

William T. Hamilton, born in the north of England, was brought to St. Louis, Missouri, by his family, in 1824, where he spent his early years. To help improve his frail health, his father arranged for him to travel to the fur-trapping country of the upper Missouri with Indian trader WILLIAM S. WILLIAMS. From 1842–45, Hamilton accompanied Willaims on fur-trading expeditions to the tribes of the North Platte and Green river regions of present-day northern Nebraska and Wyoming. During this period, Hamilton had extensive contact with the Cheyennes and other tribes and became skillful in Indian sign language.

The Gold Rush of 1849 brought Hamilton to northern California, where his knowledge of Indians soon led him to direct involvement in tracking down militant bands. He took part in the Rogue River War of 1855 against the Takelma and Tututni tribes of southern Oregon under JOHN. Then, based at Fort Walla Walla in southeastern Oregon, he was a scout and spy for Colonel George Wright in military actions against the Yakimas, Spokanes, Palouses, and Northern Paiutes during the Coeur d'Alene War of 1858. In later years, he gathered intelligence for the army about the Nez Perces, Blackfeet, and Crows. At one point, while traveling back to Fort Walla Walla in the company of friendly Kootenais, Hamilton survived an attack by a Blackfoot war party.

During his time as a scout and spy, in 1858, Hamilton established a trading post at the Junction of the Indian trails near the Bitterroot River and Hellgate Canyon in Montana, which developed into the modern city of Missoula. In 1864, Hamilton founded a second Indian trading post at Fort Benton, Montana, and subsequently became sheriff of Chouteau County. That same year, he was appointed Indian agent to the Blackfeet. In 1873, he was given special orders to suppress the sale of whiskey to the Indians, and, that year, he was also appointed federal marshal to the Crow tribe.

In the War for the Black Hills of 1876–77, Hamilton again became an army scout, serving under the command of General GEORGE CROOK against Sioux under SITTING BULL and CRAZY HORSE, taking part in the Battle of the Rosebud of June 1876. He later settled in Columbia, then Billings, Montana.

During his later years, Hamilton was a guide for various hunting and scientific expeditions into Montana, and his expertise in Indian sign language enabled him to provide one of the earliest interpretations of the Indian pictographs inscribed on the rocks at Flathead Lake in northwestern Montana. His exploits as an Indian fighter earned him the nickname of Wildcat Bill. Hamilton's autobiographical account of his life as an Indian fighter and fur trader, *My Sixty Years on the Plains, Trapping, Trading, and Indian Fighting*, first appeared in 1905.

HANCOCK (King Hancock). *Tuscarora. (fl. early 1700s).* Leader of the Tuscarora War of 1711–13.

The Iroquoian-speaking Tuscaroras were friendly to British colonists who settled in their homeland in North Carolina, providing crops and knowledge about wilderness survival and helping them fight hostile tribes. Yet Chief Hancock witnessed continuing abuses by whites. Settlers squatted on the Indians' best farmlands; traders cheated them; slavers kidnapped them.

A group of Swiss colonists under Baron CHRISTOPH VON GRAFFENRIED drove Tuscarora families off a tract of land without payment in 1711. Warriors retaliated with a series of bloody raids against settlements between Pamlico Sound and the Neuse River. Granffenried was captured, then released on promising not to raise a militia against the Tuscaroras. The surveyor and explorer JOHN LAWSON, captured with him, was tried and executed, however. A settler by the name of William Brice captured a local chief and had him roasted alive, continuing the cycle of violence; other tribes, such as the Corees, rallied to the Tuscarora cause.

In 1712, North and South Carolina sent troops into the field—many of them Yamasee Indians—under Colonel John Barnwell. They attacked Hancock's main village of Cotechney. Warriors drove off the first attack, then forced a truce by torturing white captives in view of Barnwell, who agreed to depart if the prisoners were released. Barnwell took them back to New Bern, where North Carolina officials ordered him back into the field. After a second siege, Hancock agreed to a lasting peace. However, Barnwell's men violated it by seizing other Tuscaroras as slaves. Indian raids continued.

In 1713, a colonial army under Colonel James Moore, including 1,000 Indian allies, invaded Tuscarora territory and defeated Hancock's warriors, killing and capturing hundreds. In order to finance the campaign, 400 prisoners were then sold into slavery. Survivors fled northward to New York and settled among the five tribes of the Iroquois League. In 1722, the Tuscaroras were formally recognized as the Sixth Nation.

HANCOCK, WINFIELD SCOTT. *(1824–1886).* Army officer; leader of the Hancock Campaign of 1867 on the Southern Plains.

Born in Montgomery County, Pennsylvania, Winfield Scott Hancock was an 1844 West Point graduate. He served under General WINFIELD SCOTT, after whom he had been named, in the Mexican War of 1846–48.

From 1848 to 1861, Hancock took part in actions against militant Seminoles in Florida, and he saw combat also in the Kansas border conflicts of the 1850s. He was appointed a brigadier general of volunteers at the beginning of the Civil War in 1861, and served in most of the major engagements of the Army of the Potomac. By the war's end, he had achieved the rank of major general in the regular amy, and was appointed commander of the army's Department of the Missouri (Missouri, Kansas, Colorado, and New Mexico).

In the wake of the FETTERMAN Fight of December 1866, Hancock was assigned to lead a strong military presence into Kansas to demonstrate the government's willingness to use military force in order to protect workers of the Kansas Pacific Railroad and travelers along the Santa Fe Trail. He met with Southern Cheyenne, Southern Arapaho, Comanche, Kiowa, and Sioux leaders in peace conferences at Fort Dodge and Fort Larned, Kansas, in spring 1867, presenting them with a peace-or-war ultimatum. The military wanted the Southern Plains tribes to restrict their hunting to areas assigned south of the Arkansas River, under the terms of the 1865 treaty negotiated at Little Arkansas.

Southern Cheyenne Dog Soldiers under TALL BULL, WHITE HORSE, and BULL BEAR, and their Sioux allies, wary of Hancock's 1,400 troops, withdrew from their village on Pawnee Fork north of Fort Dodge. Hancock, viewing the move as an indication of a major offensive, ordered his commander in the field, Colonel GEORGE ARMSTRONG CUSTER, to destroy the village: the start of the Hancock Campaign. In retaliation, war parties began a series of raids in western Kansas and eastern Colorado, effectively cutting off transportation through the region for the rest of summer 1867. Custer and his 7th Cavalry pursued Cheyenne and Sioux war parties across western Kansas to Fort Wallace, where they were bogged down by dwindling supplies. The lack of results of the Hancock Campaign led to his replacement as commander of the Department of the Missouri by General PHILIP H. SHERIDAN.

Hancock went on to command army departments throughout the United States, including the Department of Dakota from 1869 to 1872. The democratic Party's candidate for president in the election of 1880, Hancock lost to the Republican James Garfield. He returned to military service and was in command of U.S. forces in the Department of the East when he died in New York City. (See also TALL BULL.)

HANDSOME LAKE (Skaniadariio, Ganeodiyo, Kaniatario, "beautiful lake"; Sedwa'gowa'ne, "our great teacher"). *Seneca. (ca. 1735–1815).* Mystic; founder of the Longhouse religion. Half-brother of CORNPLANTER; uncle of RED JACKET.

Handsome Lake was born at Conawagas, a Seneca village on the Genesee River near present-day Avon, New York. Raised traditionally, he grew up to participate on the side of the British in the French and Indian Wars and the American Revolution. During the post–Revolutionary period, the Iroquois lost most of their land and were forced onto small reservations, and they found it difficult to adapt to this confinement and disruption of their culture. Handsome Lake's personal reformation played a large part in the revitalization of the Senecas and other tribes of the Iroquois League.

In 1799, Handsome Lake, alcoholic and sick, experienced a series of visions in which he claimed he was taken on a spiritual journey by four messengers. Afterward, he stopped drinking and regained his health. He began preaching to his people of what he had learned—*Gaiwiio* or "Good Word." He rejected many white customs, especially the use of alcohol, advocating self-purification through traditional beliefs. He imparted the value of family, community, and sharing, and denounced any form of witchcraft. He also encouraged his people to practice modern agriculture, emphasizing the centrality of land to the tribe.

With his growing prestige and influence, Handsome Lake was elected to the Seneca tribal council in 1801, and, in 1801–02, was one of the Seneca leaders to travel to Washington, D.C., and meet with President THOMAS JEFFERSON. He lobbied against the attrition of remaining tribal lands and the sale of alcohol by whites to his people. However, Handsome Lake's obsession with witchcraft and his accusatory methods cost him support among his people. His nephew Red Jacket was one of his political rivals.

As it came to be defined in the Code of Handsome Lake, published in 1850 with the help of BLACKSNAKE, Handsome Lake's nephew and disciple, and as practiced today, the Longhouse or Handsome Lake religion combines elements of Quakerism and Iroquois beliefs, with an emphasis on good deeds and silent prayer. Followers, who congregate in a longhouse, worship one God as in Christianity, referred to as the Great Spirit.

HANSEN, HERMAN W. *(1854–1924).* Artist.

German-born H. W. Hansen came to the United States in 1877 and studied at the Chicago Art Institute. In 1882, he settled in San Francisco, from where he made sketching trips to Texas, New Mexico, Arizona, Wyoming, and Montana, concentrating on Indian, horse, and buffalo themes. He visited the Crow Reservation, where he produced portraits in oil, showing bead and leather ornaments in detail. His work became extremely prized by European collectors.

HARMAR, JOSIAH. *(1753–1813).* Army officer in Little Turtle's War; Indian agent.

The Philadelphian Josiah Harmar served in the Pennsylvania regiment of the Continental army in the American Revolution. Enlisting in 1776, he rose rapidly from the rank of captain to lieutenant colonel while serving under General GEORGE WASHINGTON in the Northern Campaign, and under General Henry Lee in the South. In 1783, Harmar brought the ratified Treaty of Paris back to France, officially ending the Revolutionary War.

On his return to the United States, Harmar was named commander of the army and assigned to the Old Northwest Territory, where he became the government's Indian agent to the Ohio Valley tribes. He took part in the negotiations of treaties by which the Indians ceded most of present-day Ohio to the United States. For the next five years, Harmar commanded U.S. forces in the region, clearing Indians from ceded lands and evicting white settlers who trespassed on remaining Indian territory in violation of treaty agreements. He was brevetted a major general in 1787.

In 1789, Harmar established a garrison, Fort Washington, on the present site of Cincinnati, Ohio. Because of increased Indian raiding, he was given the order by President Washington to advance into Indian country with an expeditionary force of almost 1,500 men, mostly volunteer militia, against the Miamis and allied tribes under LITTLE TURTLE. On October 18–22, 1790, Harmar's troops, largely untrained and inexperienced, were ambushed and routed on the Maumee River near present-day Fort Wayne, Indiana. A detachment of Kentucky militia under his command panicked when the Miamis they were pursuing suddenly turned in a decoy tactic and began to fight. Harmar's forces were forced to withdraw to Fort Washington, suffering continuous Indian attacks along the way. Nearly 150 of Harmar's men were killed in the October clash.

In 1791, a military court of inquiry cleared Harmar of responsibility for his defeat, citing the inexperience and lack of training of his volunteer troops as the underlying cause of the army's reversal. That same year, Harmar was replaced as the army's senior officer by newly commissioned major general ARTHUR ST. CLAIR. St. Clair would suffer another defeat at the hands of the allied tribes and would be replaced by "Mad" ANTHONY WAYNE. Little Turtle's War, or the Miami War, would last until 1794 and Wayne's victory in the Battle of Fallen Timbers.

Harmar left the army in 1792, subsequently serving as Pennsylvania's adjutant general. (See also LITTLE TURTLE.)

HARMER, ALEXANDER. *(1856–1925).* Artist; soldier.

Originally from Newark, New Jersey, Alexander Harmer studied art during the 1870s between stints of military service. On rejoining the army in 1881, he was stationed in the West and witnessed the Apache Wars. He took this opportunity to produce illustrations of the conflict, which were published in *Harper's Weekly*. His illustrations also appeared in some of JOHN G. BOURKE's books, including *An Apache Campaign* (1886). Many of Harmer's drawings from his army days served as a basis for his later oil paintings and watercolors. On leaving the military in the 1890s, he moved to Santa Barbara, California, where he painted the Mission Indians and other California themes.

HARNEY, WILLIAM SELBY. *(1800–1889).* Army officer.

A native of Haysboro, near Nashville, Tennessee, William S. Harney enlisted in the army's 1st Infantry regiment at age 18. He participated in the Black Hawk War of 1832 against allied Sacs and Foxes under BLACK HAWK, and then in the Second Seminole War of 1835–42 against warriors under OSCEOLA, during which he reached the rank of brevet colonel.

In the Mexican War of 1846–48, Harney served as head of General WINFIELD SCOTT's cavalry units. Harney and Scott clashed, and when Harney refused to give up his command to Major EDWIN SUMNER, he was court-martialed. Although found guilty of insubordination, Harney was restored to command, and participated in major engagements against the Mexicans. At the war's end, he was a brevet brigadier general.

Following the GRATTAN Fight—the confrontation between soldiers and CONQUERING BEAR's Brule Sioux—the army decided to undertake a punitive expedition against the Northern Plains tribes. Harney interrupted his European vacation in 1855 and returned to lead 1,200 infantry, cavalry, and artillery troops out of Fort Leavenworth, Kansas, in a summer offensive against the Sioux. He located a band of about 200 Brules encamped at Ash Hollow, near Blue Water Creek, outside of present-day Lewellan, Nebraska. Despite a Brule attempt to surrender, Harney ordered his men to attack the village, located in a valley, from two directions, on September 3, 1855. The Indians were forced to scatter, and soon were trapped between advancing columns of infantry and cavalry. The soldiers overran the village, and killed more than 80 men, women, and children. The engagement later became known as the Battle of Blue Water.

Harney next took his troops to Fort Laramie, where he conferred with Sioux leaders. The Sioux, faced with an overwhelming military presence, agreed to return to the terms of the Fort Laramie Treaty of 1851 and to surrender those responsible for raids on whites. Among those surrendering at Fort Laramie was the Brule SPOTTED TAIL. Harney and his army then moved through the sacred hunting lands of the Sioux to reach their winter headquarters at Fort Pierre, near present-day Pierre, North Dakota. His bold move alarmed other Sioux bands, and they too sought a peaceful settlement with Harney. In March 1856, Harney met with Sioux leaders once again and entered into another accord guaranteeing safe passage for whites across Sioux lands along the Oregon Trail in Wyoming and Nebraska. Harney soon released all the Indians who had surrendered.

Harney's treaty-making activities put him at odds with the civilian-run Bureau of Indian Affairs under commissioner GEORGE MANYPENNY, and his agreements with the Sioux were not ratified by government officials in Washington, D.C. Meanwhile, the Northern Cheyennes had stepped up hostilities against their traditional enemies, the Pawnees, in violation of the Fort Laramie Treaty of 1851. That summer, 1856, Harney prepared to move against the Cheyennes and Arapahos. Instead, he was promoted to the regular rank of brigadier general and given command of the Department of the West, where he dealt with civil uprisings among the Mormons in Utah, as well as the border clashes in Kansas. He returned to Florida for a time to take part in the final phase of the Third Seminole War of 1855–58 under BILLY BOWLEGS.

In 1859, as commander of the Department of Oregon, Harney caused an international incident by seizing a British-owned island in the Pacific Northwest. Because of his suspected Confederate ties, he was not given a command in the Civil War and was retired from active duty in 1863. (See also CONQUERING BEAR; SPOTTED TAIL.)

HARRISON, WILLIAM HENRY. (1773–1841).
Army officer in Tecumseh's Rebellion and the War of 1812; president of the United States, 1841.

The son of a wealthy family of Southern plantation owners, William Henry Harrison was born and raised in Charles City County, Virginia. He attended Hampden-Sydney College, after which he went to Philadelphia in 1790 to study medicine under Dr. Benjamin Rush.

Following the defeat of Colonel JOSIAH HARMAR and his command by LITTLE TURTLE's Miamis and allied tribes in 1791, Harrison enlisted as a junior officer in the army. He was sent to the frontier post of Fort Washington (present-day Cincinnati), and later served as General "Mad" ANTHONY WAYNE's aide-de-camp at Fort Pitt (Pittsburgh). He served with Wayne at the Battle of Fallen Timbers, on August 20, 1794, and was present when the Indians of the Old Northwest agreed to Wayne's terms in the 1795 Treaty of Fort Greenville, Ohio. In 1797, after his promotion to captain, he commanded Fort Washington.

Two years later, Harrison resigned from the army and became active in territorial politics. In 1799, he was secretary to Northwest Territorial governor ARTHUR ST. CLAIR, and soon after was elected as the territory's delegate in Congress. In Washington, D.C., Harrison was instrumental in establishing new governmental guidelines for the sale of the lands recently ceded by the Indians, and he was appointed governor of the newly organized Indiana Territory in 1800. In this capacity, he entered into 15 treaties with the Shawnees, Potawatomis, Sacs, Foxes, Weas, and Piankashaws. Under these agreements, the Indians ceded vast tracts of their territory, comprising most of the present states of Indiana, Wisconsin, Illinois, and Michigan. Harrison's land acquisitions never cost the government more than one cent per acre.

At a conference held in St. Louis in September 1804, Sac and Fox tribal leaders concluded a treaty under which they ceded their claims to lands comprising large portions of the present states of Missouri, Illinois, and Wisconsin. The Sacs and Foxes were provided liquor during the negotiations in St. Louis, then pressured into ceding their lands as a condition for the release of a warrior the federal officials had in custody. The Indians finally agreed to cede their lands for $2,000, and an annual payment of about $1,000, making one of the government's cheapest acquisitions of Indian territory. The unfair terms of this land cession led to the BLACK HAWK War of 1832.

In spring 1806, Harrison challenged the power of TENSKWATAWA, the Shawnee Prophet, brother of TECUMSEH, chiding him on his inability to perform a miracle. At Greenville, Ohio, before an assembly of Indians, Tenskwatawa accurately predicted an eclipse of the sun on June 16, 1806, before an assembly of Indians. Harrison's challenge to the Prophet only helped to galvanize tribes from as far west as Minnesota into supporting Tecumseh's alliance of tribes. In 1809, under the Treaty of Fort Wayne, the Delawares, Potawatomis, and Miamis gave up their claim to more than 2.5 million acres of land in Indiana, causing dissatisfaction among some factions, especially Tecumseh and Tenskwatawa. In August 1810, Tecumseh met with Harrison at the Indiana territorial capital at Vincennes to voice his objections to Harrison's methods of acquiring Indian lands.

On November 7, 1811, Harrison and a combined force of Indian militia and regular army troops, about 1,000 men, engaged the Shawnees and allied tribes at the Battle of Tippecanoe, near the upper Wabash River in northeast Indiana. Although not a decisive victory, Harrison succeeded in driving off the Indians, led by Tenskwatawa while his brother was away, thus weakening Tecumseh's confederation.

At the onset of the War of 1812, Harrison was appointed a brigadier general in the regular army and took part in the campaign against the British and the Indians on the Great Lakes. He established Fort Meigs on the Maumee River in central Ohio in 1813, and defended the Ohio Valley against British and Indian attacks from nearby Fort Miami. His men suffered a defeat by the British and their Indian allies along the Raisin River in central Michigan in January 1813. He then led an attack against Detroit and reoccupied that site in September 1813. Finally, he commanded American troops in their decisive victory over Tecumseh and Colonel HENRY PROCTOR at the Battle of the Thames, near Lake Erie, in what is now Ontario, on October 5, 1813. The American victory effectively ended the British threat to the Old Northwest.

Harrison retired from the service in 1814, returning to Indiana, where he represented the state in Congress throughout the 1820s–30s. He was the Whig candidate for president in 1836, losing to Martin Van Buren. He defeated Van Buren for the presidency in 1840, successfully using the campaign slogan "Tippecanoe and Tyler Too," but died less than six months after his inauguration. (See also TECUMSEH; TENSKWATAWA.)

HAWKINS, BENJAMIN. *(1754–1816).* Indian agent; senator.

Benjamin Hawkins was born in North Carolina and pursued a career in agriculture. During the American Revolution, he served as a staff officer to General GEORGE WASHINGTON, later becoming a delegate to the Congress of Confederation. After the ratification of the Constitution, he became one of the first senators from North Carolina, serving from 1789 to 1795.

Before 1796, government relations with Indians on the frontier had been maintained through military officers. The federal Indian agency system began with the appointment of Hawkins by HENRY KNOX, secretary of War. Hawkins left his seat in the Senate to begin a 20-year career as agent to the Creeks and superintendent of the Southern Indians.

As agent, Hawkins attempted to transform the Indians' communal way of life to that of farmers with individual landholdings. He negotiated the 1796 treaty of Coleraine with the Creeks which, for a short time, helped stabilize Indian relations on the southern frontier. Hawkins also established schools for Indian children for the purpose of acculturation.

Throughout his tenure, Hawkins was faced with a lack of cooperation on the part of the southern state governments to recognize tribal land claims and prevent white encroachment. Meanwhile, some Southeast Indians did adopt the ways of Southern white planters, obtaining black slaves to work their lands.

The outbreak of the War of 1812, in which many bands sided with the British at the urging of TECUMSEH, followed by the Creek War of 1813–14 under WILLIAM WEATHERFORD, diminished the government's efforts to assimilate the Southeast Indians. In later years, the government instituted a program of relocation of Southeast tribes to lands west of the Mississippi.

HAYDEN, FERDINAND VANDEVEER (Man-Who-Picks-Up-Stones-Running). *(1829–1887).* Anthropologist; geologist; explorer.

Ferdinand V. Hayden was born in Westfield, Massachusetts, and raised by an uncle near Rochester, New York. He attended Oberlin College and Albany Medical School. While obtaining his M.D., he also pursued an interest in geology and paleontology, and, upon graduation in 1853, he began a series of fossil-collecting trips to the Northern Plains for the Smithsonian Institution. In 1859, he was part of Captain William Raynolds's expedition to the upper Yellowstone River.

During the Civil War, Hayden served as a surgeon in the Union army. Afterward, he was on the faculty of the University of Pennsylvania, 1865–72.

In 1867, Hayden was appointed head of the geological survey of Nebraska. In 1869, the project was expanded into the U.S. Geological and Geographical Survey of the Territories, sponsored by the Department of the Interior, including geological and ethnological studies of much of the Great Plains and Rocky Mountain region. Fieldwork lasted from 1870 to 1879, much of it in Colorado.

In 1877, the Department of the Interior gave JOHN WESLEY POWELL, the head of the simultaneous U.S. Geographical and Geological Survey of the Rocky Mountain Region, instructions to specialize in ethnological and geological research. Hayden's survey was to concentrate on geographical and geological information. In 1879, the two surveys, plus two sponsored by the War Department, headed by CLARENCE KING and GEORGE WHEELER, were merged into the United States Geological Survey (U.S.G.S.), first headed by King. Hayden continued to gather specimens for the U.S.G.S. and the Smithsonian until his death.

Hayden's work, along with that of men under him, such as the photographer WILLIAM HENRY JACKSON and the painter THOMAS MORAN, helped lead to the creation of Yellowstone National Park. His scientific expeditions also contributed to both anthropological and archeological knowledge of Indian peoples. To the Sioux, Hayden was Man-Who-Picks-Up-Stones-Running.

HAYS, JOHN COFFEE (Jack Hays). *(1817–1883).*
Texas Ranger in campaigns against the Comanches; officer in the Paiute War.

Frontiersman Jack Hays, originally from Wilson County, Tennessee, worked as a surveyor in Mississippi, then moved to Texas in 1836, at the height of the Texas War of Independence. From 1836 to 1840, he worked as a scout for the army of the Republic of Texas.

In 1840, Hays became a captain in the Texas Rangers. He improved discipline and introduced use of Walker Colt revolving six-shooters. As a result, his detachment found new success as a light cavalry force in campaigns against the Comanches.

During the Mexican War of 1846–48, Hays served under generals ZACHARY TAYLOR and WINFIELD SCOTT. Hays then went to California with the Gold Rush, eventually becoming sheriff of San Francisco County. In 1853, he left law enforcement to pursue business interests.

In 1860, Hays took part in the Carson Valley Expedition against the Northern Paiutes during the Paiute, or Pyramid Lake, War, in what is now western Nevada. Commanding a force of 800 men, comprised of California volunteers, regular army troops, and Texas Rangers, Hays engaged the Paiutes under NUMAGA in an indecisive skirmish on June 3, 1860. The Indians then fled to Pinnacle Mountain, where they lost 25 warriors to Hays's men, and scattered.

Following this brief return to Indian fighting, Hays resumed his California business career. (See also NUMAGA.)

HAYS, WILLIAM JACOB. *(1830–1875).* Artist.
William Jacob Hays was born in Catskill, New York, and studied art at the National Academy of Design in New York City. In 1860, he traveled up the Missouri River by riverboat to Fort Union at the mouth of the Yellowstone in the Dakota Territory. During this journey, he made sketches of trading posts, as well as Indians and fauna. The buffalo is featured in many of his works. His studio was located in New York City.

HAZEN, WILLIAM BABCOCK. *(1830–1887).*
Army officer in the Sheridan Campaign and the War for the Black Hills.

Born in West Hartford, Vermont, William B. Hazen was raised in Hiram, Ohio. On graduating from West Point in 1855, he was assigned as a junior officer in the infantry at frontier posts in Oregon and Texas. In 1859, he was wounded in an engagement with Comanches in Texas and was reassigned to West Point as an instructor.

Appointed a colonel of an Ohio volunteer regiment in the Civil War, he served under General WILLIAM T. SHERIDAN in the 1864 Georgia campaign. By the war's end, he was a major general of volunteers.

In 1866, Hazen returned to the regular rank of colonel of the 6th Infantry regiment. In fall 1868, he was placed in command of Fort Cobb, in the southwestern part of the Indian Territory, to supervise the pacified elements of the Kiowa, Comanche, and Kiowa-Apache tribes, who had been settled on the newly established adjoining reservation. At that time, General PHILIP H. SHERIDAN then planned to wage war on the militant factions of the Southern Plains tribes: the Sheridan Campaign of 1868–69.

In November 1868, Southern Cheyenne leaders LITTLE ROBE and BLACK KETTLE, along with Arapaho chiefs, met with Hazen at Fort Cobb to arrange for the settlement of their people near the post. But Hazen refused the army's protection at Fort Cobb and sent the Indian leaders back to their villages on the Washita. One week later, on November 27, 1868, part of Sheridan's force, the 7th cavalry under colonel GEORGE ARMSTRONG CUSTER, carried out the attack on Black Kettle's people at the Battle of Washita. By the end of November, Hazen had under his supervision over 6,000 reservation Comanches, Kiowas, and Kiowa-Apaches.

From 1872 to 1877, Hazen commanded his infantry regiment at Fort Buford, North Dakota, where he became embroiled in a controversy over the malfeasance of William W. Belknap, the secretary of War, in connection with army supply contracts.

In October 1876, during the War for the Black Hills of 1876–77, Hazen led his infantry command in pursuit of SITTING BULL's Hunkpapa Sioux along the upper Missouri to Fort Peck, Montana, but withdrew when it became apparent that the Indians were too weakened to pose a substantial threat.

In 1880, Hazen was promoted to the rank of brigadier general and was made chief signal officer of the army. He later became involved in a controversy arising out of the army's failure to relieve Lieutenant Adolphus Greely's Arctic expedition in 1882 and 1883. He was court-martialed and subsequently publicly reprimanded for openly criticizing the War Department's lack of a relief effort. Hazen remained in the service until his death in Washington, D.C.

HEARNE, SAMUEL. *(1745–1792).* Explorer; trader.
British-born Samuel Hearne joined the Hudson's Bay Company in 1766 and journeyed to the northwestern shores of Hudson Bay and the company's post, Fort Prince of Wales (present-day Fort Churchill) at the mouth of the Churchill River.

In 1769, Hearne was assigned to explore to the west for a water route from Hudson Bay to the Pacific. The First Coppermine Expedition, improperly supplied, was quickly abandoned. On a second expedition in 1770, he reached only as far as the southern shore of Aberdeen Lake. On the return trip, he was helped by the Chipewyan leader MATONABBEE.

In December 1770, accompanied by Matonabbee and a party of Chipewyans, Hearne left Fort Prince of Wales on the Third Coppermine Expedition, again to search for a route to the Pacific from Hudson Bay and to locate rich copper deposits reported to exist north of Great Slave Lake. With the Chipewyans' help, the expedition reached the Coppermine River and followed it to its Arctic Ocean outlet, establishing that it was not the Northwest Passage to the Pacific. During the expedition, Hearne and his Chipewyan companions encountered a band of Eskimos (Inuits). The Chipewyans attacked and massacred the Inuits, their traditional enemies, in July 1771, against Hearne's protestations. He later named the site of the Inuit massacre Bloody Falls.

Hearne returned to Fort Prince of Wales in June 1772, with no news of a Pacific route and no significant discoveries of copper. Nevertheless, he had accomplished the first overland non-Indian journey across the North American continent to the Arctic Coast.

Throughout the 1770s, Hearne went on to establish inland trading posts for the Hudson's Bay Company, including Cumberland House in 1774, the first inland post of the Hudson's Bay Company and the first permanent white settlement in what is now Saskatchewan. He later was placed in command of Fort Prince of Wales until the capture of the post by the French in 1782. After some time in England, he returned to Canada in 1783–87.

In 1795, three years after his death, his book, *Journey from Prince of Wales Fort on Hudson's Bay to the Northern Ocean*, was first published. In this account of his travels in the Canadian Arctic, Hearne described Chipewyan and Inuit customs. (See also MATONABEE.)

HECKEWELDER, JOHN GOTTLIEB ERNESTUS. *(1743–1823).* Historian; missionary.

John Heckewelder's parents brought him to North America from England to join a Moravian colony in Quebec. He was educated by the Moravians and, as an adult, attempted to carry their message to the Indians. Along with fellow missionary Christian Post, Heckewelder journeyed to the Ohio Valley to help establish a community of Christianized Delawares in 1763. The project was interrupted by the outbreak of PONTIAC's Rebellion of 1763. In 1771, Heckewelder was appointed as an assistant to the missionary DAVID ZEISBERGER. He went on to provide assistance to the U.S. government in the removal of Ohio Valley Indians to Canada, in compliance with Indian treaties entered into during the early 1800s. His written accounts of the Indians of western Pennsylvania and the Ohio Valley include an account of the DELAWARE PROPHET.

HELMER, ADAM. *(1754–1830).* Militia officer during the American Revolution.

During the American Revolution, Adam Helmer was a lieutenant in the colonial militia defending inhabitants of the Mohawk Valley in New York against attacks by British-allied Iroquois warriors under Mohawk chief JOSEPH BRANT. In September 1778, Helmer was given command of a nine-man scouting party to the settlement of Unadilla, then Brant's base of operations, to find out if the Iroquois were planning an attack on settlers for food during the fall harvest. Near Edmeston, the scouts were ambushed by at least 40 warriors. Helmer surivived by hiding beneath bushes, then set out on a run back northward of approximately 50 miles, warning settlers along the way to take refuge at Fort Herkimer against an impending Indian offensive. Because of his efforts, only one settler died in the repeated raids, unlike the Cherry Valley raid the following November in which many perished. The bodies of three of the scouts were later located. Helmer's Run was described in Walter D. Edmonds's novel, *Drums along the Mohawk* (1936). (See also BRANT, JOSEPH.)

HENDAY, ANTHONY. *(fl. 1750s).* Explorer; trader.

A native of England's Isle of Wight, Anthony Henday was in the employ of the Hudson's Bay Company at Fort York, the company's fur-trading fort on the southwestern shore of Hudson Bay in what is now Manitoba. In 1754, accompanied by a party of Creeks, Henday headed south and west from Fort York to expand the company's fur trade to the tribes in the interior. In 1754–55, his expedition explored the Hayes River, then proceeded southwest as far as the foothills of the Rocky Mountains. Along the way, Henday established trade relations with the Assiniboines and a tribe he identified as "Archithinue," what may have been Blackfeet or Gros Ventres. He explored the region lying between the north and south branches of the Saskatchewan River, returning to Fort York in June 1755. Four years later, accompanied by a group of "Archithinue," he again explored northern Manitoba and Saskatchewan. In 1762, he left the Hudson's Bay Company and returned to England.

HENDRICK (King Hendrick, Hendrick Peters; White Head; Theyanoguin, Teoniahigarawe,

Tee-Yee-Ho-Ga-Row, Deyohninhohhakarawenh, Tiyanoga, Aroniateka). *Mohawk-Mahican.* (ca. 1680–1755). Leader in the French and Indian War of 1754–63.

Hendrick, Mahican by birth, but adopted by the Mohawks, was one of four Indians to visit Queen Anne's court in London as "the Four Kings of the New World" in 1710. On returning to New York, he played a major role as a spokesman for the Iroquois League. As an ally of the British and a Protestant convert, he supported the effort against the French. At the Albany Congress of 1754, however, Hendrick spoke out against the failure of the British to defend the frontier. In September 1755, at the battle of Lake George, he led a force of Mohawk warriors along with British troops under WILLIAM JOHNSON against the French and their Indian allies under Baron Ludwig Dieskau. The British were victorious and Johnson received a knighthood for this critical victory, but Hendrick and many of his braves were killed.

HENNEPIN, LOUIS. *(ca. 1640–ca. 1701).* Explorer; missionary; captive.

A native of Belgium, Louis Hennepin became a Franciscan friar, and, in 1675, traveled to France's colony in Canada as a missionary. He was accompanied on this journey by explorer RENE ROBERT CAVELIER, SIEUR DE LA SALLE, who, three years later, enlisted Hennepin as a friar at Fort Frontenac on the eastern end of Lake Ontario.

In 1679, Hennepin accompanied La Salle on his exploration of the Great Lakes and the Mississippi River. He was a part of La Salle's expedition aboard the *Griffon*, the first European sailing vessel west of Lake Ontario, when it sailed from the Niagara River, across Lake Erie and Lake Huron, to Green Bay on the western shore of Lake Michigan. Hennepin then accompanied La Salle to the Illinois Indian village of Kaskaskia on the Illinois River.

From Fort Creve Coeur, which La Salle established near present-day Peoria, Illinois, La Salle sent Hennepin with Michel Aco to find the source of the Mississippi and Minnesota rivers into what is now Minnesota and Wisconsin. During the trip, Hennepin narrowly avoided being caught in the middle of hostilities between the Illinois and invading Iroquois warriors.

In Minnesota, Hennepin and Aco were captured by Santee Sioux and held as prisoners for six months. During his Sioux captivity, Hennepin was taken to and named the Falls of St. Anthony, near present-day Minneapolis. Their release was negotiated by French explorer DANIEL GREYSOLON, SIEUR DULUTH, in 1681.

Hennepin returned to France in 1682, where he published an account of his explorations, including his contacts with the Sioux, Illinois, and Iroquois. In his book, *Description de la Louisiane* (1683), he provided the earliest description of Niagara Falls. He continued to write about his explorations in New France during the 1690s, exaggerating his own role in La Salle's expeditions and claiming to have descended the Mississippi to the Gulf of Mexico. He eventually settled in the Netherlands, where he lived the rest of his life.

HENRY, ALEXANDER. *(1739–1824).* Trader; soldier; captive.

Alexander Henry was born in New Brunswick, New Jersey, and served with colonial forces in the French and Indian War of 1754–63 under General JEFFREY AMHERST. He later became a merchant in Quebec, dealing with the British army.

In 1762, while France and England negotiated for a final settlement to the war, Henry entered the Indian fur trade, journeying to the Great Lakes trading center at Michilimackinac in what is now Michigan. The Chippewas, Ottawas, Potawatomis, and other Great Lakes tribes had been trading with the French for years, and the sudden appearance of a British military and commercial presence in the region in 1762 was a source of unrest among them. The Ottawa chief PONTIAC, falsely representing himself as a Chippewa leader named Menehewehna, met with Henry upon his arrival at Michilimackinac and expressed the Indians' misgivings about having to abruptly change their allegiance from the French to the British.

In 1763, the Chippewas, along with the Ottawas and other allied tribes under Pontiac, rose up against the British throughout the northern Ohio Valley and eastern Great Lakes. Among their first targets was the British fort at Michilimackinac along the Straits of Mackinac. In his 1809 book, *Travels and Adventures in Canada and the Indian Territories Between the Years 1760 and 1776*, Henry gave a firsthand account of this attack, relating how the Indians gained entry to the fort by pretending to hold a lacrosse match with the neighboring Sac tribe, then launching a bloody attack. Henry had befriended a Chippewa named Wawatam, who protected him and later adopted him into his family. He lived with the Chippewas for six months following the capture of Michilimackinac, then escaped to British troops and served under British general John Bradstreet in the campaign to relieve Detroit.

By 1775, Henry had expanded his fur-trading operation to the Indians of present-day Saskatchewan. He united with other Montreal traders, forming the group that would become the North West Company in 1784, under the leadership of SIMON McTAVISH. Henry sold his company interest in 1796, and, for the rest of his business career, was engaged as a general merchant in Montreal.

Henry's nephew of the same name entered the fur trade in the employ of the North West Company. In his journal, edited by Elliot Coues along with the journal of DAVID THOMPSON as *New Light on the Early History of the Greater Northwest* (1897), the younger Henry provided descriptions of the Indian tribes he traded with in both central Canada and on the Oregon coast. He drowned in 1814, while visiting the North West company's newly acquired post at Astoria in Oregon. (See also PONTIAC.)

HENRY, ANDREW (Major Henry).
(ca. 1775–1833). Trader; trapper; soldier.

A native of York County, Pennsylvania, Andrew Henry settled at Nashville, Tennessee, in the early 1800s, and later moved to Ste. Genevieve, Missouri. He worked in the lead-mining business until 1809, when he joined MANUEL LISA, ANTOINE PIERRE MENARD, WILLIAM CLARK, JEAN PIERRE CHOUTEAU, AUGUSTE PIERRE CHOUTEAU, and others as a partner in the St. Louis Missouri Fur Company.

Henry traveled on Lisa's 1809 expedition, establishing Fort Mandan at the mouth of the Knife River near present-day Bismarck, North Dakota. In March 1810, he led an expedition out of Fort Mandan with Antoine Pierre Menard, accompanied by JOHN COLTER as a guide, plus the mixed-bloods GEORGE DROUILLARD and EDWARD ROSE as interpreters, eventually reaching the Three Forks of the Missouri in what is now Montana, where they built a stockade. Henry and his party spent the winter trapping in the region. Because of Blackfoot attacks—in one of which Drouillard lost his life—the party abandoned the post. Colter escaped a Blackfoot attack and returned to St. Louis; Menard returned to his home at Kaskaskia. Henry and Rose proceeded westward over the Rockies, reaching the Continental Divide on the Snake River near present-day St. Anthony, Idaho, where they built another post.

With continuing Indian attacks and minimal success in obtaining furs—even though his trappers had been the first to penetrate the region west of the Rockies—Henry also returned to St. Louis. He took part in the War of 1812, serving as a major in a Missouri militia regiment. During the war, he entered into business with WILLIAM HENRY ASHLEY, supplying lead and gunpowder to American forces.

In 1822, Henry became Ashley's partner in a fur-trading expedition up the Missouri during which they reached the mouth of the Yellowstone River in Montana and established Fort Henry. His trappers continued to operate in the Yellowstone region until they were forced to retreat after an attack by Blackfoot warriors, at Great Falls in what is now north-central Montana.

In August 1823, when JEDEDIAH SMITH delivered word of an attack by the Arikaras on Ashley's expedition, Henry and Smith led a party down the Missouri to aid his partner, but saw no action. He then proceeded to the mouth of the Bighorn River, remaining there until spring 1824. He then trapped and explored the South Pass in Wyoming's Wind River Range and reached the Green River, returning to St. Louis with a shipment of furs in summer 1824.

Henry gave up the fur business to concentrate on his lead-mining interests in Missouri.

HERKIMER, NICHOLAS. *(1728–1777)*. Militia officer in the American Revolution.

Born near present-day Herkimer, New York, Nicholas Herkimer was a lieutenant in the colonial militia during the French and Indian War of 1754–63, taking part in the defense of Fort Herkimer in 1758. He later moved east to the vicinity of Canajoharie, New York, where he became a colonel in the Tryon County militia.

In 1776, Herkimer was appointed brigadier general of militia and placed in command of troops defending the eastern Mohawk Valley against attacks by Tories and British-allied Indians. On August 4, 1777, while in command at Fort Dayton (formerly Fort Herkimer), he embarked on an expedition to relieve Patriot troops at Fort Stanwix, near present-day Rome, New York, under siege by a column led by Barry St. Leger. The invading force of some 1,700 included JOHN JOHNSON's Royal Greens, JOHN BUTLER's Tory Rangers, Hessian mercenaries, and Iroquois under the Mohawk JOSEPH BRANT and the Seneca CORNPLANTER. Herkimer's 800-strong militia was made up mostly of farmers with Oneida and Tuscarora allies.

On August 6, Herkimer's militia was ambushed near Oriskany Creek by Brant's warriors and detachments under Johnson and Butler. Herkimer suffered a leg wound in the battle, but continued to direct operations from the field. In fierce fighting, much of it hand-to-hand, the militia lost about a third of their number, but inflicted damage as well. The Battle of Oriskany further delayed St. Leger's plan to join up with General JOHN BURGOYNE's column advancing against Saratoga from Lake Champlain. On learning that a large Revolutionary force, led by General Benedict Arnold, was on its way, the pro-British Iroquois soon deserted. Diminished in strength, St. Leger's forces withdrew to Canada.

Two weeks after the amputation of his wounded leg, Herkimer died. (See also BRANT, JOSEPH.)

HERRERO GRANDE. *Navajo. (fl. mid-1800s)*.
Blacksmith; principal chief during the Navajo War of 1863–66.

In the 1850s, Herrero Grande lived at Fort Defiance, Arizona, where he learned the art of blacksmithing from

George Carter, a blacksmith brought in by the agent HENRY L. DODGE to teach the Navajos. Herrero became known for his knife blades, bits, and bridle parts, just as DELGADITO became known for his silver jewelry.

In 1861, following a council with whites at Fort Fauntleroy, Herrero was elected principal chief of the Navajos. He refused the order to relocate and hid out early in the Navajo War, but surrendered in February 1864, taking his band to Bosque Redondo in eastern New Mexico—the Long Walk—as ordered. Henceforth, he acted as a peacemaker. He met with MANUELITO on behalf of General JAMES H. CARLETON in February 1865, but failed to convince him to surrender. Along with the other Navajo chiefs, Herrero Grande signed the 1868 treaty establishing the Navajo Reservation in their Chuska Mountain homeland.

HEWITT, JOHN NAPOLEON BRINTON.
Mixed Tuscarora. (1859–1937). Anthropologist; linguist; historian.

J. N. B. Jewitt was born at Lewiston in western New York, the son of a part-Tuscarora mother and a Scottish physician. He attended both public and private schools with the intention of becoming a doctor like his father. In 1880, however, he met the anthropologist Erminie A. Smith, who hired him to help her record Iroquois legends.

On Smith's death six years later, Hewitt was employed by the Smithsonian's Bureau of Ethnology in Washington, D.C., specializing in the study of Iroquoian dialects and tracing their connection to the Cherokees' language. He contributed to FREDERICK WEBB HODGE's *Handbook of the American Indians North of Mexico*, published in 1907–10. He also studied the history and political structure of the Iroquois League in *A Constitutional League of Peace in the Stone Age*, published by the Smithsonian in 1918.

HIAWATHA (Heowenta, "he makes rivers").
Mohawk. (fl. 1500s). Diplomat; legislator; founder of the Iroquois League.

Much of what is known about Hiawatha has been passed down as legend surrounding the formation of the Iroquois League. Probably in the mid- to late 1500s, the Mohawk Hiawatha (some accounts have him as Onondaga) met the Huron mystic DEGANAWIDA and together they planned to end tribal feuding by establishing an alliance among the Mohawks, Oneidas, Onondagas, Cayugas, and Senecas of what is now upstate New York. Since Deganawida had a speech impediment, Hiawatha became the principal spokesman. He traveled from tribe to tribe, preaching his message of unity, and negotiating agreements.

At first he met with great opposition, especially from the Onondaga sachem ATOTARHO, but eventually he managed to forge the alliance. Deganawida's and Hiawatha's visionary confederacy undid generations of intertribal warfare and shaped a framework for lasting peace based on democratic and representative principles. The Founding Fathers reportedly used the League as a model for their concept of democracy: The states were similar to the Five Nations (when the Tuscaroras joined, Six Nations); the senators were like the 50 Iroquois sachems, nominated by clan members and elected by villages; the president and cabinet resembled the honorary Pine Tree Sachems; and Washington, D.C., as the capital, was similar to the central village of Onondaga, where the Great Council was held every year.

It is not known what became of Hiawatha after the League's formation. Among future generations of Iroquois, he took on a legendary status. HENRY WADSWORTH LONGFELLOW borrowed the name for a fictional Chippewa character. (See also ATOTARHO; DEGANAWIDA.)

HICKOK, JAMES BUTLER ("Wild Bill" Hickok).
(1837–1876). Army scout in the Hancock and Sheridan campaigns.

James "Wild Bill" Hickok was born and raised on a farm in Troy Grove, Illinois. In 1855, he headed for the Kansas frontier, where he worked various jobs, including wagon and stagecoach driver. He also participated in the strife in Kansas, as an opponent of slavery. During the early part of the Civil War, he worked for the Union army at Fort Leavenworth, in charge of supply wagon trains. He later served the army as a scout and spy against the Confederates in western Missouri and southern Kansas. During the Civil War years, he gained a reputation as a gunman, after having been involved in several shooting incidents, which were later exaggerated in dime novels.

In 1866, Hickok became a deputy U.S. marshal at Fort Riley, Kansas. The following year, he signed on as a scout under General WINFIELD SCOTT HANCOCK, serving with Colonel GEORGE ARMSTRONG CUSTER and the 7th Cavalry in campaigns against the southern Cheyennes under TALL BULL and other Dog Soldier chiefs. During General PHILIP H. SHERIDAN's subsequent campaign of 1868–69, Hickok was a scout for the 7th Cavalry units taking part in General EUGENE A. CARR's winter offensive out of Fort Lyon, Colorado. It was part of Hickok's duties to carry dispatches between Carr's command in the field and the fort. On his way back to Fort Lyon in early 1869, he was wounded in the leg in an attack by a Cheyenne war party.

That same year, 1869, Hickok returned to law enforcement as marshal at Hays, Kansas, then, in 1871, at

Abilene, Kansas, a cattle town at the end of the CHISHOLM Trail. In 1872–73, he toured as part of theatrical productions with his long-time friend and fellow scout, WILLIAM "BUFFALO BILL" CODY.

In 1876, Hickok traveled to the Dakota Territory with the Gold Rush to the Black Hills. In March of that year, he was shot to death while playing cards in a saloon in Deadwood by Jack McCall, who may have been hired by local lawless elements to prevent Hickok from assuming a law enforcement post. (See also TALL BULL.)

HIGH-BACKED WOLF (Nee-hee-o-ee-woo-tis, "wolf on the hill"). *Cheyenne. (d. 1834).* First principal chief of Cheyennes in the historical record.

In 1825, High-Backed Wolf met with Colonel HENRY ATKINSON and Indian agent BENJAMIN O'FALLON along the Missouri River in what is now South Dakota during the second Yellowstone Expedition up the Missouri, and signed a friendship treaty with them. There later occurred a tribal split in which some of the Cheyenne bands, one of them led by YELLOW WOLF, began frequenting the Arkansas River in Colorado and Kansas and trading with whites. They became known as the Southern Cheyennes as opposed to the Northern branch. In 1832, High-Backed Wolf and his wife, She Who Bathes Her Knees, were painted by GEORGE CATLIN when they came to visit a Sioux camp on the Teton River. High-Backed Wolf was killed two years later in a tribal dispute.

HIGH HORN (Spamagelabe, Spemicalawba; Captain James Logan). *Shawnee. (ca. 1775–1812).* Ally of Americans in the War of 1812. Nephew of TECUMSEH.

High Horn, born among the Shawnees of Ohio, was captured as a boy by a white general in Kentucky, who raised him and gave him the name James Logan (not to be confused with LOGAN the Mingo). High Horn married an Indian woman who had also been captured and raised by whites, and they lived in the Shawnee village of Wapakoneta, Ohio. In favor of peace between Indians and whites, High Horn opposed the attempt by his uncle Tecumseh to form a military alliance of tribes. During the War of 1812, High Horn sided with the Americans and served as a scout and spy. While in the field with two companions, he was wounded in an attack by a British detachment and died two days later.

HILLERS, JOHN K. (Jolly Jack; Bismarck). *(1843–1925). Photographer.*

At the outbreak of the Civil War, at the age of 20, German-born John K. Hillers enlisted in the New York Naval Brigade, and later transferred to the army. At the end of the war, he reenlisted and served in the West until 1870, after which he worked as a cattle driver in Salt Lake City.

The next year, Hillers joined the survey team under JOHN WESLEY POWELL as a boatsman, and volunteered to be an assistant to the photographer Edward O. Beaman. He also learned his craft from Walter "Clem" Powell, Powell's first cousin and Beaman's original assistant. Because of a dispute with Powell, Beaman resigned after 10 months, and James Fennemore, who had been working in Salt Lake City in the studio of CHARLES SAVAGE, was hired and continued to teach Hillers. When Fennemore resigned because of illness, Hillers became the official photographer for Powell's 1872 trip down the Grand Canyon and took numerous Indian photographs, especially of Paiutes. They were first published in 1874.

Hillers became staff photographer under Powell after the merger of the governmental surveys into the U.S. Geological Survey in 1879, as well as for the Smithsonian's Bureau of Ethnology. That year, he joined James Stevenson, MATILDA COXE STEVENSON, and FRANK HAMILTON CUSHING on an expedition to the Zunis of New Mexico, and spent much of his remaining career in the Southwest, photographing Zunis, Hopis, and Rio Grande Pueblo Indians. He also photographed numerous Indian delegations to Washington, D.C.

Hillers retired in 1900. He has been credited with 3,000 negatives for the Powell Survey and 20,000 for the Smithsonian's Bureau of American Ethnology.

HILLIS HAYO. See FRANCIS, JOSIAH.

HITCHCOCK, ETHAN ALLEN. *(1798–1870).* Army officer; reformer.

Born in Vergennes, Vermont, Ethan Allen Hitchcock was an 1817 West Point graduate. The early part of his military career was spent mostly as an instructor, then as commandant of cadets at West Point.

In 1833, Hitchcock served on the frontier at Fort Crawford in the Wisconsin Territory. Three years later, he joined the staff of General EDMUND GAINES, seeing action in the Second Seminole War against warriors under OSCEOLA. In 1836, he was assigned to the Pacific Northwest and was soon promoted to major.

In 1841, the War Department commissioned Hitchcock to undertake an investigation of suspected abuses and fraud committed by government contractors involved in the Cherokee removal operation of 1838. Hitchcock's investigation resulted in an extensive report that uncovered evidence of widespread bribery, perjury, forgery, the issue of spoiled and damaged goods, and other actions aimed at inflating the costs of the Cherokee removal on the Trail of Tears. Cherokees under their chief JOHN ROSS were further cheated through the deduction of relocation costs from the net amount the government had agreed to pay for their lands in the southeastern states. Implicated by Hitchcock's findings were friends of high government officials. As a result, the *Hitchcock Report* was suppressed to avoid causing embarrassment to the incumbent administration.

In 1842, Major Hitchcock was stationed in Florida and subsequently promoted to lieutenant colonel of an infantry regiment. He participated in the last major campaign against the Seminoles.

In the Mexican War of 1846–48, Hitchcock served on General WINFIELD SCOTT's staff and took part in major engagements against the Mexicans. By the end of the war, he was brevetted a brigadier general.

Hitchcock was then assigned to the Division of the Pacific, where in the early 1850s he commanded troops in military actions against the Rogue River Indians of southern Oregon under JOHN. In 1854, Hitchcock was involved in a controversy arising from his seizure of a supply ship intended for political adventurer William Walker's privately backed foray into Mexico. As a result, he resigned from the army in 1855, but returned to duty during the Civil War as a major general of volunteers, and served as a military adviser on President ABRAHAM LINCOLN's Committee on the Conduct of War. He left the service permanently in 1867, settling in South Carolina, then Georgia.

During his military career, Hitchcock wrote and published scholarly works on literature, philosophy, and religion. An account of his experiences with the Indians, based on his notes, A Traveler in Indian Territory, was published posthumously in 1930. (See also ROSS, JOHN.)

HOBOMOK (Hobomoko, Hobbamock).
Wampanoag. (d. ca. 1640). Sagamore of the Wampanoag Confederacy; friend to Pilgrims; Christian convert.

MASSASOIT, the grand sachem of the Wampanoag Confederacy, sent Hobomok as a special envoy to help the Pilgrims after they had landed at Plymouth in 1620. Along with SQUANTO, Hobomok provided food and knowledge of wilderness survival to the colonists. He also acted as a liaison between the colonists and Massasoit, and as a military adviser to MILES STANDISH. In August 1621, Hobomok and Squanto were attacked by warriors under CORBITANT, sagamore of the Pocasset and Mattapoiset bands, but they escaped. Hobomok eventually converted to Christianity and spent his remaining years among the colonists.

HODGE, FREDERICK WEBB (Teluli, "the mouse who digs holes"). *(1864–1956).*
Anthropologist; archeologist; historian.

Born in England, Frederick Webb Hodge came to the United States with his parents while young. He was educated in Washington, D.C., and worked for a short time in a law office.

Throughout the 1880s, Hodge was an executive with the Smithsonian's Bureau of Ethnology, and, in 1886–89, he served with the Hemenway Southwestern Archaeological Expedition, then headed by FRANK HAMILTON CUSHING. He later supervised the excavation of the sites of early Zuni culture in New Mexico, including the ruins of Hawikuh. His Zuni friends called him Teluli, "the mouse who digs holes."

From 1902 to 1914, Hodge was the editor of *American Anthropologist*, the journal of the American Anthropological Association, which he helped found. He also supervised the production of one of the first modern comprehensive books on Native Americans, *Handbook of the American Indians North of Mexico* (1907–10). From 1907 to 1930, Hodge edited EDWARD CURTIS's 20-volume photographic record of the Native Americans, *The North American Indian*. He also undertook expeditions for Heye Foundation's Museum of the American Indian, and was responsible for the acquisition of many Indian artifacts for that institution. In 1932, he became the director of the Southwest Museum in Los Angeles.

Hodge retired to Santa Fe, New Mexico, in 1956. His contributions to Indian studies include 350 published works.

HOLE-IN-THE-DAY (Bugonegijig, "opening in the sky"). *Chippewa (Ojibway). (d. 1846).* Ally of Americans in the War of 1812; war chief in territorial struggle with the Sioux. Father of HOLE-IN-THE-DAY (the younger).

Hole-in-the-Day, who fought in the War of 1812 on the side of the Americans, succeeded CURLING HAIR as the war chief of the Mississippi Chippewas in 1825. Like FLAT MOUTH and NOKA, he led his people in warfare against the Sioux for territory between Lake Superior and the upper Mississippi River in what is now Minnesota. With firearms supplied by white traders, the Chippewas had the advantage. Under Hole-in-the-Day, they succeeded in driving the Sioux west of the Mississippi. To end the cycle of raids and counterraids, the army eventually established boundary lines between the two tribes. On his death, Hole-in-the-Day was succeeded by his son of the same name.

HOLE-IN-THE-DAY (Bugonegijig, "opening in the sky"). *Chippewa (Ojibway). (1825–1868).* Enemy of Sioux; tribal delegate to Washington, D.C. Son of HOLE-IN-THE-DAY (the older).

Hole-in-the-Day was born the same year that his father, whose name he bore, became war chief of the Mississippi Chippewas. The son became chief when his father died in 1846, and he maintained Chippewa territory in Minnesota against Sioux raiding parties from

Hollow Horn Bear. Photo by Edward Curtis. *Courtesy of National Archives of Canada/PA-39269.*

west of the Mississippi. He traveled to Washington, D.C., on numerous occasions to negotiate with the federal government. During a visit East, Hole-in-the-Day married a white reporter, one of eight wives. Some tribal members accused him of using negotiations with whites to profit at the expense of his people. In 1862, at the time of the Minnesota Uprising of Santee Sioux under LITTLE CROW, Hole-in-the-Day was accused of planning a similar revolt among the Chippewas. By the treaties of 1864, 1867, and 1868, his band was settled on the White Earth Reservation. In 1868, Hole-in-the-Day was murdered at Crow Wing, Minnesota, probably because of his role in the earlier treaty negotiations.

HOLLOW HORN BEAR (Matihehlogego). *Brule Sioux. (1850–1913).* Warrior; policeman; negotiator.

Hollow Horn Bear proved himself as a warrior at the age of 16 against the Pawnees. During RED CLOUD's War for the BOZEMAN Trail of 1866–68, he furthered his reputation by participating with CRAZY HORSE in the FETTERMAN Fight of 1866. In 1873, Hollow Horn Bear agreed to settle on a reservation along with SPOTTED TAIL. He became a captain in the Indian police on the Rosebud Reservation and in that capacity arrested CROW DOG for the 1881 murder of Spotted Tail. In the negotiations with General GEORGE CROOK during the Ghost Dance Uprising of 1890, Hollow Horn Bear, known as a skilled orator, served as one of the spokesmen for the Brules. He rode in the inaugural parade of President Theodore Roosevelt in Washington, D.C. After his death from pneumonia, he was buried in Washington, D.C.

HOLMES, WILLIAM HENRY. *(1846–1933).* Anthropologist; archaeologist; geologist; museum director.

William Henry Holmes was born in Ohio and, after having graduated from McNeely College in 1870, he taught school for two years. During the 1870s–80s, he worked first as an artist, then geologist, with the U.S. Geological Survey region of southeastern Utah under FERDINAND V. HAYDEN, then later under JOHN WESLEY POWELL.

In 1875, while surveying the San Juan River region of southeastern Utah, Holmes studied the remains of Anasazi Cliff Dwellers, becoming particularly interested in pottery and shell art. He went on to make studies of ancient Indian art and textiles produced by both ancient and existing Southwest Indians.

As director of the Smithsonian's Bureau of American Ethnology in 1902–09, Holmes investigated the Etowah Mounds of the Mississippian Culture in Georgia. Later in his career, as curator of the U.S. National Museum and also the National Gallery of Art, Holmes was responsible for assembling exhibits of Indian art of the Northwest Coast. His books include *Handbook of Aboriginal American Antiquities* (1919).

HONAYAWAS (Honanyawas, Oghnewigewas; Farmer's Brother). *Seneca. (1725–1815).* War chief; friend to GEORGE WASHINGTON.

Honayawas, who lived at Buffalo Creek in western New York, was called Farmer's Brother by whites because of his friendship with George Washington, who had been a farmer. As one of the most respected Seneca war captains, he signed a treaty at Big Tree in 1797 and at Buffalo in 1801. His warriors gave their support to the Americans in the War of 1812. After the war, Honayawas was buried in Buffalo with military honors by the U.S. 5th Regiment.

HOOKER JIM (Hakar Jim, "let me see" Jim). *Modoc. (ca. 1825–1879).* Leader in the Modoc War of 1872–73; rival of CAPTAIN JACK. Son-in-law of CURLY HEADED DOCTOR.

Hooker Jim was one of the Modoc band leaders opposed to life on the Klamath Reservation in Oregon. Like Captain Jack, he led his followers back to their ancestral homeland in northern California, where they hoped to have their own reservation.

In November 1872, troops under Captain James Jackson came to Captain Jack's camp along the Lost River to return the Indians to the Klamath Reservation, leading to the first firefight of the Modoc War. Hooker Jim and his band were camped on the other side of the river. A posse of ranchers tried to round them up, killing a woman and a baby and wounding several men. In retaliation, Hooker Jim and Curly Headed Doctor led a war party in a raid on a ranch and killed 12 whites. They then fled farther south to the lava beds, where Captain Jack and his people had taken refuge.

Captain Jack still hoped that a peaceful solution could be reached. He refused to turn over the killers of the ranchers, however, as the military demanded. Hooker Jim and others, including Curly Headed Doctor, BLACK JIM, and SCHONCHIN JOHN, encouraged Captain Jack to assassinate General EDWARD CANBY.

After this deed, during the subsequent fighting, Hooker Jim and Captain Jack quarreled over strategy. Hooker Jim abandoned the fight and soon surrendered to General Jefferson C. Davis. He then led soldiers to Captain Jack's hideout. During the trial at Fort Klamath, in order to save his own life, Hooker Jim testified against his former protector. Hooker Jim and his band were eventually relocated to Quapaw lands in the Indian Territory, where he died. (See also CAPTAIN JACK.)

HOPOCAN (Hopokan, "tobacco pipe"; Captain Pipe; Konieschguanokee, "maker of delight").

Delaware. (ca. 1725–1794). Leader of war faction during the French and Indian War and the American Revolution.

Hopocan, or Captain Pipe, was opposed by GELELEMEND's peace faction. He supported the French in the French and Indian War of 1754–63, and PONTIAC's Rebellion of 1763, attempting to take Fort Pitt. He later settled on the Muskingum River in Ohio with his followers.

During the American Revolution, Hopocan took the British side and led many raids on settlers. The Delaware chief WHITE EYES, however, supported the Americans. Hopocan also participated in numerous conferences with whites, including the treaty signing at Fort Pitt (Pittsburgh) in 1778. In 1782, warriors from various tribes of the Old Northwest routed troops out of Fort Pitt under Colonel William Crawford at Sandusky, Ohio. Crawford was turned over to Hopocan's band and was tortured and executed in retaliation for the earlier massacre of peaceful Moravian Delawares by whites at Gnaddenhutten. Since Crawford was a personal friend of GEORGE WASHINGTON, his death led to stepped-up military involvement by American forces along the western frontier.

In 1785, Hopocan signed a treaty at Fort McIntosh, Ohio, and, in 1787, one at Fort Harmar. His band moved several times during the Revolution, eventually settling in what became known as Captain Pipe's Village along the upper Sandusky in Ohio.

HORN, TOM. *(1860–1903).* Army scout in the Apache Wars.

Born in Memphis, Missouri, Tom Horn traveled to the Southwest in the mid-1870s, where he worked as a stagecoach driver and cattle herder.

From 1875 to 1886, Horn was an assistant to ALBERT SIEBER, the chief army scout at the San Carlos Reservation in Arizona, where he learned to speak the Apaches' Athapascan language. He took part in the army's expeditions into northern Mexico to round up GERONIMO and his band of Chiricahua Apaches, assisting in the final surrender of Geronimo and NAICHE to General NELSON A. MILES at Skeleton Canyon, Arizona, on September 4, 1886.

During the 1890s, Horn worked as a deputy sheriff in Arizona and also appeared as a rodeo cowboy. He later worked for the Pinkerton Detective Agency in Arizona, tracking down railroad and bank robbers. He then went to Wyoming in 1894 to exterminate cattle rustlers for the Wyoming Cattlemen's Association. In 1898, he was in Cuba during the Spanish-American War, serving as a mule wrangler for Theodore Roosevelt's Rough Riders.

Horn returned to the Wyoming cattle ranges after the war, where he was soon charged with a murder, arising from a shooting incident in which the 14-year-old son of a sheep rancher was killed. Despite testimony at his trial given on his behalf by both Miles and Sieber, Horn was found guilty of the crime and hanged. (See also GERONIMO.)

HOUGHTON, ARTHUR BOYD. *(1836–1875).* Artist.

British artist Arthur Boyd Houghton was on assignment with the London magazine *Graphic* when he arrived in the United States in 1869 to sketch scenes of American life. In 1870, he traveled west on the Union Pacific Railroad and stopped at an army camp in Nebraska, later named Fort Hartsoff, to make studies of the Pawnees. He was warmly accepted by the Indians, who allowed him to participate in gambling games and other social activities. These experiences he visually recorded, sketching on wood rather than on paper, which gave his work a unique quality that was later to influence the impressionist Vincent Van Gogh. Houghton also worked in oils and watercolors.

HOUSTON, SAMUEL. *(1793–1863).* Indian agent; senator; president of Texas Republic; governor of Texas; Indian rights advocate. Adopted son of JOHN JOLLY.

Sam Houston was born near Lexington, Virginia, and, when about 13, he moved to Maryville, Tennessee, with his family. He lived among the Cherokee Indians for extended periods while growing up as the adopted son of Chief John Jolly.

In 1813, Houston joined the army and served under fellow Tennessean ANDREW JACKSON in the Creek War of 1813–14 against the Red Sticks under WILLIAM WEATHERFORD. At the Battle of Horseshoe Bend in Alabama, he was wounded.

Following his military service, Houston served as a federal subagent overseeing the relocation of Jolly's band to the Arkansas Territory.

Houston went on to a law career, then entered politics. He served in the House of Representatives as a Democrat in 1823–27, then was elected governor of Tennessee in 1827. He resigned his post two years later when his wife left him.

Houston joined John Jolly's band of Cherokees in Arkansas from 1829 to 1833. While serving as the federal government's post trader, he witnessed many abuses by the government's Indian agents, including outright fraud in the payments of federal annuities. Houston appealed to his former army commander, President Jackson, to intercede on behalf of the Cherokees. Jackson then appointed Houston to negotiate with the Indians of Texas, which led to his traveling to that area in 1833 and becoming involved in the Texas independence movement.

When the Texas Republic was established in 1836, Houston became its first president. As president of the republic and later as the governor of the new state of Texas, he sought to establish permanent peace with the Indians. He signed a treaty with the Cherokee leader known as the BOWL, which Congress refused to ratify. Houston opposed secession from the Union, and because of his refusal to take an oath of allegiance to the Confederacy, was deposed in 1861. (See also BOWL; JOHN JOLLY.)

HOWARD, OLIVER OTIS (The Praying General). *(1830–1909).* Army officer; peace commissioner.

Born in Leeds, Maine, Oliver Howard graduated from that state's Bowdoin College in 1850. He went on to attend West Point, graduating as a commissioned officer in 1854.

Howard was a mathematics instructor at West Point when the Civil War erupted in 1861. In June of that year, he was commissioned a colonel in a Maine volunteer regiment and was soon promoted to brigadier general. He saw military action throughout the Civil War. At the Battle of Fair Oaks, near Richmond, Virginia, in May–June 1862, he was wounded and lost his right arm. He continued to command Union regiments, leading troops at Gettysburg and taking part in the final battles of the war in Georgia, Tennessee, and the Carolinas.

Following the war, Howard was appointed head of the newly organized Freedmen's Bureau, and in this capacity established Howard University in Washington, D.C., in 1867. While serving as president of the university in 1872, he was appointed by President ULYSSES S. GRANT as a special peace commissioner, succeeding VINCENT COLYER, to COCHISE's Chiricahua Apaches, who were then raiding settlers in the southern Arizona Territory. With only his aide Captain Joseph A. Sladen and the scout THOMAS J. JEFFORDS, Howard met with Cochise and other Apache leaders at their camp in the Dragoon Mountains in October 1872. He succeeded in obtaining an agreement from Cochise to relocate his people to a newly organized reservation along the Apache Pass in the Chiricahua Mountains, adjacent to the Mexican border, with Jeffords as Indian agent.

In the aftermath of a corruption scandal in the Freedman's Bureau, Howard returned to active military duty in 1874, and was sent to the Department of the Columbia (Oregon, Washington, Idaho) as General EDWARD CANBY's replacement. At Fort Lapwai, Idaho, in May 1877, he met with Nez Perce leaders and presented them with an ultimatum regarding their removal from the Wallowa Valley to the Lapwai Reservation. In attendance at this conference were Chief JOSEPH (Young Joseph), OLLIKUT, WHITE BIRD, LOOKING GLASS, and TOOHOOLHOOLZOTE. During the negotiations, Howard was compelled to order the arrest of the shaman Toohoolhoolzote, who had spoken out strongly against the ceding of Nez Perce lands in the Wallowa Valley and was opposed to the relocation of the Nez Perces. Because of his religious fervor, Howard was known to the Indians as the Praying General.

After the Indians had failed to relocate to the reservation within the 30-day time limit specified in Howard's ultimatum, the Nez Perce War erupted. In the ensuing conflict, Howard's troops, sent to round up the fugitive bands, soon suffered reversals at the Battle of White Bird Canyon, Idaho, in June 1877, and at the Battle of the Clearwater, the following month, where Howard himself saw combat. Howard's command reached the site of the Battle of Bear Paw, Montana, in October 1877, too late to participate in the defeat of the Nez Perces by troops under Colonel NELSON A. MILES.

In 1878, Howard led a campaign against the Bannocks, after a militant faction had departed their reservation at Fort Hall, Idaho, and had begun a series of raids on white settlers who violated Indian lands.

Paiutes, Umatillas, and Cayuses joined in the uprising. The Bannock BUFFALO HORN, then the Northern Paiutes EGAN and OYTES, led the insurgents. Howard mobilized out of Fort Boise, Idaho, and maintained constant military pressure until a final surrender.

In early 1879, the Sheepeaters, a band of renegade Shoshones and Bannocks living in the Salmon Mountains of western Idaho, killed five Chinese prospectors camped on the Salmon River. Howard dispatched troops to round up the warring Indians in what was called the Sheepeater War. A three-month campaign ensued, at the end of which the Sheepeaters, worn out by constant military pressure, surrendered. They were later relocated to the Fort Hall Reservation with the Bannocks.

In 1881, Howard left the Department of the Columbia to become superintendent of West Point. The next year, he became commander of the Department of the Platte (Iowa, Nebraska, Utah, and parts of Dakota and Montana). In 1886, he was promoted to major general and assumed command of the Department of the East (New England, New York, New Jersey, Pennsylvania).

In 1887, Howard, along with General GEORGE CROOK, campaigned on behalf of the Indian Rights Association for the release of the Apache prisoners of war held in Florida. Their efforts led to the transfer of the Apaches to Alabama, and their eventual relocation to Fort Sill, Oklahoma.

Howard retired from the military as a major general in 1894. The year before, he had been awarded the Congressional Medal of Honor for his service at the 1862 Battle of Fair Oaks.

Howard wrote about his experiences with the Indians of the West in his books: *Nez Perce Joseph* (1881); *My Life and Experiences Among Our Hostile Indians* (1907); and *Famous Indian Chiefs I Have Known* (1908). (See also BUFFALO HORN; COCHISE; EGAN; Young JOSEPH; OYTES.)

HOWLING WOLF (Honanisto). *Southern Cheyenne. (ca. 1850–1927).* Warrior; artist; tribal leader. Son of MINIMIC.

By the time he was about 17, Howling Wolf, son of the principal chief Minimic, had counted his first coup. He was active in the wars for the Southern Plains, surrendering in 1875 during the Red River War at the Cheyenne Agency in the Indian Territory. Along with other Cheyennes, he was sent to Fort Marion in St. Augustine, Florida.

At the encouragement of RICHARD HENRY PRATT, Howling Wolf took up art, drawing scenes of Plains Indian life with crayons; he and other artist-prisoners, BEAR'S HEART, COHOE, and ZOTOM, became known as the Florida Boys.

Howling Wolf was released in 1878 and returned to the Indian Territory. He converted to Christianity and tried to earn a living through farming, but eventually reverted to traditional Cheyenne lifeways. In 1884, he became chief of the warrior society known as the Dog Soldiers. As such, he lobbied against the enforcement of the General Allotment Act (the DAWES Severalty Act) of 1887, which called for the redistribution of tribal lands to individuals.

HUDSON, HENRY. *(ca. 1550–ca. 1611).* Explorer.

British-born Henry Hudson earned a reputation as a competent navigator, and, in 1607, was commissioned by a group of London merchants, the Muscovy Company, to find a Northeast Passage to the Orient.

Hudson's expedition left England on the ship *Hopewell* and explored the coasts of eastern Greenland and Spitzbergen, seeking an ice-free route across the Arctic coast of Europe and Asia. Blocked by ice in the Barents Sea north of Norway, the expedition was forced to return to England after a few months. In spring 1608, Hudson again sailed for the Muscovy Company, exploring the coast of Novaya Zemlya in extreme northeastern Russia.

In 1609, Hudson was engaged by the Dutch East India Company for the same purpose: to find a Northeast Passage. He rounded North Cape at the northern end of Norway on the *Half Moon*, but was forced to turn westward toward more favorable weather because of dissension among the crew. Hudson had earlier conferred with Captain JOHN SMITH of the Jamestown Colony, and his decision to turn west was partly based on Smith's navigational reports on the North American coast. Hudson crossed the Atlantic and reached the coast of Newfoundland. From there he sailed south to Chesapeake Bay and Delaware Bay, continually seeking an inland route—the Northwest Passage—to the Pacific Ocean. He then turned back north, eventually anchoring off present-day Sandy Hook, New Jersey. Hudson then entered what is now Upper New York Bay and continued along the river that now bears his name, the Hudson River, as far north as Albany. At Albany, he decided that the river provided no access to the western ocean and he returned to Europe.

While exploring the Hudson Valley of present-day New York and New Jersey, Hudson made contact with various bands of the Delaware, Wappinger, and Mahican confederacies. He traded with the Indians and brought back furs to Europe. His claim of the region for Holland and his reports of the rich fur-trading potential eventually led to a commercial grant to the Dutch West India Company, the establishment of New Netherland, and the resulting displacement of eastern Algonquians.

In England, Hudson was detained by government authorities who enjoined him from continuing his service to the Dutch. In 1610, a group of London merchants hired Hudson to find a Northwest Passage across the northern coast of North America to the Far East. On this voyage, undertaken on the ship *The Discovery*, Hudson sailed through the strait that now bears his name, Hudson Strait, into the great bay known as Hudson Bay. He explored its eastern coast as far south as James Bay, where he and his crew spent the winter.

Severe weather, shortages of food, and resentment of Hudson's leadership resulted in mutiny by his men in spring 1611. With his seven-year-old son, John, and seven or eight other loyal sailors, he was set adrift in a small boat. Hudson and those with him are presumed to have perished at sea. Two leaders of the mutiny, William Wilson and Henry Greene, were later killed by native warriors off Cape Diggs near the northern entrance to Hudson Bay in what is now northern Quebec. Four of the surviving nine members of the 1610–11 expedition were tried for mutiny upon their return to England. Their account of Hudson's mismanagement and food-hoarding, as well as the valuable knowledge they had brought back of the newly discovered Hudson Bay region, led to their acquittal.

HUMP (Etokeah). *Miniconjou Sioux. (d. 1908).* War chief in the Sioux Wars of the 1860s–70s; Ghost Dancer.

Along with CRAZY HORSE of the Oglalas, and GALL and RAIN-IN-THE-FACE of the Hunkpapas, Hump established his reputation as a young warrior in RED CLOUD's War for the BOZEMAN Trail of 1866–68. In the Fetterman Fight of December 1866, Hump led the charge that wiped out the 80-man cavalry unit under Captain WILLIAM FETTERMAN. Hump was also active in the Sioux War for the Black Hills of 1876–77, and was present at Little Bighorn in June 1876.

With unrelenting pressure by the army following the Indian victory at Little Bighorn, Hump and his followers gave up the fight. In May 1877, as a negotiator, he accompanied troops under Colonel NELSON A. MILES in pursuit of the remaining Miniconjou militants under LAME DEER. Hump hoped to induce his fellow Miniconjous to surrender peacefully, but a fight broke out, leading to the Battle of Lame Deer, in which Lame Deer was killed.

Hump joined SITTING BULL in Canada for a time, but eventually returned to settle on the Cheyenne River Reservation in South Dakota. In the early stages of the Ghost Dance Uprising of 1890, he was an active participant along with fellow Miniconjou BIG FOOT at the Cheyenne River, but was soon convinced by Captain Ezra Ewers, an old friend, of the futility of the uprising and took refuge with his followers on the Pine Ridge Reservation. Following the Wounded Knee Massacre, Hump traveled to Washington, D.C., with other chiefs

to lobby for improved conditions on Sioux reservations. (See also BIG FOOT; RED CLOUD; SITTING BULL.)

HUNT, GEORGE (Hau). *Mixed Kwakiutl-Tlingit. (1854–1933).* Anthropologist; guide; interpreter; research informant.

George Hunt was born at Fort Rupert, British Columbia, the son of the Tlingit woman Mary Ebbetts and Robert Hunt, the British administrator of the Hudson's Bay Company's operation on the coast of British Columbia. Although Hunt's mother was Tlingit, he was raised among the Kwakiutls, and married a Kwakiutl woman.

In 1881–83, Hunt was hired as guide and interpreter by JOHAN ADRIAN JACOBSEN to help in the acquisition of Northwest Coast Indian artifacts. Starting, in 1886, Hunt worked with the anthropologist FRANZ BOAS as a guide, interpreter, and informant. He also served as guide and interpreter for the Morris K. Jesup North Pacific Expedition of 1897, which sought to investigate the connections of the Northwest Coast Indians and Eskimos of Alaska with the natives of Siberia.

In 1903, Hunt helped organize the Northwest Coast Indian exhibit of the American Museum of Natural History in New York City. He was Boas's informant and collaborator on *Kwakiutl Texts* (1905–06) and *The Ethnology of the Kwakiutl* (1921).

Other projects included helping secure artifacts of the Northwest Coast tribes for the collection of George Heye, the founder of the Museum of the American Indian in New York City; and helping EDWARD CURTIS in the making of the motion picture *In the Land of the War Canoes.*

Hunt was eventually selected as a chief of the Kwakiutls. He died at his place of birth.

HUNT, WILSON PRICE. *(1783–1842).* Trader; explorer.

Wilson Price Hunt, born in Asbury, New Jersey, and raised in Trenton, became a successful merchant. In 1810, JOHN JACOB ASTOR of the American Fur Company commissioned Hunt to undertake an overland expedition to the mouth of the Columbia River in Oregon, where he was to help establish a fur-trading operation with the Indians, as a complement to Astor's seaborne expedition.

Hunt recruited experienced trappers and voyageurs in Montreal, one of them former North West Company trader Donald McKenzie. The recruits departed Lake Michigan's Mackinac Island, eventually traveling south by way of Green Bay and Prairie du Chien in Wisconsin, then down the Mississippi to St. Louis.

After a winter stopover, Hunt left St. Louis in March 1811, with the Overland Astorians, who came to include the part-Sioux interpreter PIERRE DORION, JR., and his wife, the Iowa Indian MARIE DORION, and, for a time, the part-Cherokee EDWARD ROSE. The naturalist JOHN BRADBURY and botanist Thomas Nuttall accompanied the expedition on the river leg of the journey. Stopping at Osage villages near Council Bluffs, some of the party witnessed the performance of the Scalp Dance. The Astorians then proceeded through the lands of the Sioux, enduring repeated attacks. On this stage of the journey, Hunt was in competition with a party under MANUEL LISA, who sought a trade agreement with the Arikaras living along the Missouri near the present border between North and South Dakota.

After having obtained horses from the Arikaras for cash, as well as from Lisa in exchange for riverboats, the Astorians then deviated from the westward route of the Lewis and Clark Expedition, heading south across the Coninental Divide and then proceeding west to the Snake River region of present-day Idaho. Through the Wind River Range and the Tetons, the Astorians suffered a series of mishaps. Their canoes were wrecked on the rapids of the Snake River in Idaho, with four people drowned. They were also repeatedly attacked by marauding Indians who stole their horses; they ran short of food and other supplies. The survivors finally reached Astoria at the mouth of the Columbia in February 1812.

Hunt remained at Astoria for the next two years, during which he undertook trading expeditions up the Pacific Coast as far as southern Alaska. When Astor sold his Oregon coast fur post to the British in 1814, Hunt returned to St. Louis, where he stayed for the remainder of his life, operating several commercial enterprises and serving as postmaster from 1822 to 1840. (See also DORION, MARIE.)

I

IBERVILLE, PIERRE LE MOYNE, SIEUR D'.
(1661–1706). French colonial military leader; explorer. Son of CHARLES LE MOYNE; brother of CHARLES ME MOYNE, BARON DE LONGUEUIL and JEAN BAPTISTE LE MOYNE, SIEUR DE BIENVILLE.

Sieur d'Iberville was born in Montreal, the third son of Charles Le Moyne. In 1685, he took part in French raids on British fur-trading posts along Hudson Bay, and he continued to raid the Hudson's Bay Company centers throughout the 1690s. In early 1690, during King William's War, he participated in LOUIS DE BUADE, COMTE DE FRONTENAC's combined French and Abnaki offensive against the British settlements in New England and the eastern Mohawk Valley, including the attack on Schenectady, New York. Six years later, Iberville led a combined force of Indians and French colonial militia in raids against Newfoundland settlements.

From 1698 to 1702, Iberville explored the lower Mississippi River region, discovering the Mississippi Delta and building a fort at Old Biloxi (present-day Ocean Springs, Mississippi), thus reestablishing France's claim to Louisiana, originally explored by RENE ROBERT CAVELIER, SIEUR DE LA SALLE. While in the lower Mississippi and Gulf Coast region of what is now Louisiana, Mississippi, and Alabama, Iberville made contacts with the tribes of the Southeast, including the Natchez, Creeks, Chickasaws, and Choctaws, and conducted trade for furs.

In 1703, while away from the colony because of illness, Iberville was appointed governor of Louisiana. His brother Sieur de Bienville served as chief administrator in his absence. In 1706, Iberville returned to the Caribbean on a military campaign. After a series of naval victories against the British at St. Nevis and St. Christopher in the West Indies, he contracted yellow fever and died aboard his ship in Havana, Cuba.

INKPADUTA ("scarlet point"). *Wahpekute Sioux. (ca. 1815–ca. 1882).* Leader of the Spirit Lake Uprising of 1856.

In 1828, after Inkpaduta's father, Wamdesapa, had killed Tasagi, the principal chief of the Wahpekute Santee Sioux, he and his followers became outcasts among the Wahpekutes and other Santee bands. In 1848, on the death of his father, Inkpaduta became chief of the renegade band. The next year, he led an ambush on then-Wahpekute head chief Wamundeyakapi, killing him along with 17 of his warriors.

When his brother was killed by a white bootlegger, Inkpaduta began raiding white settlers, especially in the Spirit Lake region of northwest Iowa. In March 1856, in the Spirit Lake Uprising, his warriors killed 47 settlers and kidnapped four women. PAUL MAZA-KUTEMANI, JOHN OTHERDAY, and Iron Hawk tracked the renegades and managed the release of one of the women. The Mdewakanton Santee LITTLE CROW then led a punitive expedition against Inkpaduta and his followers, and, in a skirmish at Lake Thompson, killed three Wahpekute warriors. In 1862–63, Little Crow himself led a rebellion, the Minnesota Uprising of Santees. Inkpaduta may have played a part in some raids on whites. His warriors fought troops under General ALFRED SULLY at the Battle of Whitestone Hill in present-day North Dakota in September 1863.

Inkpaduta migrated farther westward in later years and reportedly fought with SITTING BULL and CRAZY HORSE at Little Bighorn in 1876, after which he fled to Canada. He died in 1878 or 1882.

IRATEBA (Arateva, Yaratev). *Mojave. (ca. 1814–1878).* Guide; principal chief.

Irateba was born in Mojave territory west of the Colorado River near present-day Needles, California.

He was the hereditary leader of the Huttoh-pah band under the principal Mojave chief Cairook. When white explorers came to his homeland, he welcomed them and even acted as guide. In 1851, he led Captain Lorenzo Sitgreaves' expedition to San Diego; in 1854, he led Lieutenant Amiel Whipple's party to Los Angeles; and, in 1856–58, he accompanied Lieutenant Joseph Ives up the Colorado.

An expedition under Lieutenant EDWARD BEALE established Beale's Crossing of the Colorado and led to increased traffic along the Southern Overland Trail (which later became the Butterfield Southern Route). Mojave militants carried out an attack on a wagon train in 1858, then drove away soldiers sent in to establish a post. The next year, more troops arrived and built Fort Mohave east of the Colorado in present-day Arizona. The army demanded the arrest of those warriors responsible for the attack on the soldiers. Cairook was one of those who surrendered at neighboring Fort Yuma; he died trying to escape, whereupon Irateba became the head chief of all the Mojave bands.

In 1862–63, at the invitation of white officials, Irateba toured eastern cities, including New York, Philadelphia, and Washington, D.C., where President ABRAHAM LINCOLN gave him a silver-headed cane. Irateba was henceforth a proponent of peace with the whites and was opposed by Homoseah Quahorte, who headed a militant faction.

IRON TAIL (Sinte Maza). *Oglala Sioux.*
(*ca. 1850–1916*). War chief; touring Indian; one of three models for the "Indian head" nickel.

Iron Tail fought in the War for the Black Hills of 1876–77 and was an aide to SITTING BULL at Little Bighorn. He later joined WILLIAM "BUFFALO BILL" CODY's Wild West Show and accompanied it to Europe in 1889. The artist James Fraser used Iron Tail, along with the Cheyenne TWO MOONS and the Seneca John Big Tree, as models for the "buffalo" or "Indian head" nickel. (See also SITTING BULL.)

ISATAI (Ishatai, Eschiti; Little Wolf; Coyote Droppings). *Comanche.* (*fl. 1870s*). Medicine man; leader in the Red River War of 1874–75.

Isatai's reputation among his people was established when he correctly predicted that a comet that had appeared in early 1873 would disappear in five days and cause a drought the following summer. He also claimed that in a meeting with the Great Spirit he had learned to make body paint to repel bullets. He prophesied to the war chiefs of the Indian Territory that an allied Indian offensive would drive away the whites and lead to the return of the buffalo on the Great Plains.

In 1874, Isatai called for a Sun Dance in preparation for war and encouraged QUANAH PARKER to invite Kiowas, Cheyennes, and Arapahos. After the Battle of Adobe Walls of June 1874 in Texas, in which buffalo hunters with high-powered Sharp and Remington rifles drove off the Indian attackers, Isatai lost much of his prestige as a shaman. As late as 1890, however, when Quanah Parker was principal chief of the various reservation bands, Isatai was an important figure in Comanche affairs. (See also PARKER, QUANAH.)

ISHI. *Yahi (Yana). (ca. 1862–1916).* Research informant; "last wild Indian in the United States."

During his youth, Ishi witnessed the arrival of numerous whites in the homeland of the Yahis, who were a subdivision of the Yana Indians living in the mountainous country of northeast California. The miners and ranchers took the best lands for themselves and forced the Indians to the parched highlands of the Sierra Nevada. A pattern developed of Indian raids, followed by white retaliation. In 1854, whites attacked a Yahi village on Mill Creek, killing many. They returned in 1868 with plans to exterminate the small band, killing 38 more.

A dozen or so Yahis escaped into the wilderness, one of them a boy about six years old. Over the next decades, the surviving Yahis hid out from whites and lived off the land, occasionally pilfering food from mining camps and ranchers. There were some regional reports of sightings of mysterious Indians and attempts were made to track them. But the Yahis left no footprints and camouflaged their shelters.

By 1908, only four Yahis remained: Ishi himself, his mother, his sister (or cousin), and an old man. They lived on a narrow ledge above Mill Creek. That year, a party of surveyors discovered their hiding place. Ishi's sister and the old man probably drowned while in flight; his mother died soon afterward.

Ishi lived in the wilderness three more years, hunting small game and gathering wild foods. He burned his hair off in mourning for his lost family and friends. Finally, half-starving, he decided to suffer a quick death at the hands of whites rather than the slow death of hunger. He walked to the nearby town of Oroville in the foothills of Mount Lassen.

There, on August 29, 1911, he was found by townspeople, wearing only a tattered poncho and leaning in exhaustion against a fence. The sheriff took him into custody. Ishi, afraid of being poisoned, refused all food.

The anthropologists Alfred Kroeber and Thomas Waterman read about the mysterious Indian in a newspaper. Knowing that the Yanas and a smaller, related but now-extinct Yahi tribe once lived in the region, they made arrangements to meet with him. In Ishi's cell, Waterman tried using a dictionary of the Yana language to communicate with him, without any success. Finally, when the anthropologist used the Yana word for wood while pointing to the frame of a cot, Ishi became animated and asked Waterman if he were of the same tribe. To gain his trust, Waterman told him he was and, with Ishi's help, soon learned how to translate the Yana Hokan dialect into the similar Yahi tongue.

The Anthropological Museum of the University of California in San Francisco took full responsibility for Ishi. When he refused to reveal his name, Kroeber and Waterman gave him the name we know him by, which means "man" in Yahi. He proved a valuable informant of Yahi lifeways for Kroeber and Waterman and many other anthropologists and museum visitors, communicating how to make tools, how to fish and hunt, how to start a fire, and how to prepare foods and herbal medicines. He also narrated Yahi legends and sang songs.

In addition to his ethnological contributions, Ishi became accustomed to white ways and worked as a janitor and groundskeeper at the museum. He became close friends with Kroeber's wife, Theodora, as well as the physician Dr. Saxton Pope of the university hospital. After five years among whites, Ishi died of tuberculosis. Theodora Kroeber wrote about him in *Ishi in Two Worlds: A Biography of the Last Wild Indian in North America* (1961).

ISPARHECHE (Ispahecher, Spahecha). *Creek. (1829–1902).* Leader of faction of full-bloods within the Indian Territory.

Isparheche was born in Alabama and forced to relocate with his parents to the Indian Territory in the 1830s; both his parents died on the trip. In his new home, he grew up to become a farmer.

During the Civil War, Isparheche originally volunteered to fight for the Confederates but changed over to the Union side. After the war, he became an influential leader, first elected to the Creek House of Warriors in 1867. He headed a faction of full-blooded Creeks—as OPOTHLEYAHOLO and OKTARSARS HARJO SANDS had before him—who believed in the restoration of traditional tribal organization and customs.

In 1882–83, fighting occurred between the full-bloods and the mixed-bloods in what is called Isparheche's War, or the Green Peach War. Troops under General Pleasant Porter were forced to intercede.

Isparheche later represented his faction in Washington, D.C., and lobbied against the General Allotment Act (the DAWES Severalty Act) of 1887, which called for the redistribution of tribally held lands to individuals. He was elected principal chief in 1895, serving for four years. The year before Isparheche's death, CHITTO HARJO headed the Crazy Snake Uprising of full-bloods.

IYANOUGH (Iyannos, Yannis, Jannos, Hyannis, Hyanos, Hyanus, Highannus). *Wampanoag. (d. 1623).* Sagamore of the Wampanoag Confederacy under MASSASOIT.

Iyanough was sachem of the Mattakeeset band living on Cape Cod, in the vicinity of present-day Barnstable and Hyannis Port, Massachusetts. He was subordinate to the grand sachem Massasoit to whom his people paid tribute. Along with ASPINET of the Nausets, Iyanough aided the Pilgrims in the early stages of the Plymouth Colony. He helped rescue a boy, John Billington, who had wandered off from the settlement in spring 1621, returning him to his parents. In spring 1623, however, Massasoit informed the colonists that both Iyanough and Aspinet were conspiring against them along with Massachuset and Narranganset leaders. MILES STANDISH attacked and drove the supposed rebels into the swamps, where both Iyanough and Aspinet died, probably from European diseases.

J

JACK. See CAPTAIN JACK.

JACK. See NICAAGAT.

JACKSON, ANDREW (Old Hickory; Sharp Knife). *(1767–1845).* Army officer in the Creek War, the War of 1812, and the First Seminole War; president of the United States, 1829–37.

Born at the Waxhaw frontier settlement along the South Carolina–North Carolina border, Andrew Jackson took part in the Revolutionary War battle at Hanging Rock when 13. Orphaned by the end of the war, he moved to Salisbury, North Carolina, where he studied law and was admitted to the bar in 1787. He later settled in the region that would soon become the state of Tennessee, where he became active in politics.

After Tennessee was admitted to the Union, Jackson served, in 1796–97, as one of the state's first congressmen. In 1797–98, he served in the Senate, and, in 1798–1804, as Tennessee state judge, also becoming a major general in the state's militia.

Following the August 30, 1813, attack on Fort Mims in what is now Alabama, by Creek Red Sticks led by WILLIAM WEATHERFORD, Jackson raised a volunteer militia force. In October 1813, he led his army out of Fayetteville, Tennessee. He engaged the Indians at Tallassahatchee on November 9, 1813, and a few days later at Talladega. Although successful in driving back the Red Sticks in these battles, most of Jackson's troops had departed by December 1813, when their terms of enlistment expired. Jackson received reinforcements in January, many of them Indian auxiliaries, whereupon he resumed his drive against the Creeks. His advance met heavy Creek resistance in engagements at Emuckfaw Creek and Enotachopco Creek, and he was forced to withdraw. On March 27, 1814, he led his men to decisive victory on the Tallapoosa River in the Battle of

Horseshoe Bend. The Indians soon sued for peace terms.

In the Treaty of Fort Jackson of August 1, 1814, Jackson, now known to the Indians as Sharp Knife, demanded that the Creeks reimburse the government for the money expended in the Creek War. The Indians, even the White Sticks who had supported Jackson in his war efforts, were compelled to make reparations in land cessions, giving over 23 million acres, comprising large portions of the present states of Alabama and Georgia.

Following his capture of Pensacola from the British in 1814 and his victory over the British at the Battle of New Orleans in 1815, the final engagements of the War of 1812, Jackson rose to national prominence as a military hero and Indian fighter.

In 1817, Jackson was one of the federal Indian commissioners to meet with Cherokee leaders at the Cherokee Agency in Tennessee, where the tribal leaders agreed to exchange their lands in the East for new territory west of the Mississippi.

In February 1818, Jackson led a campaign against the Seminoles because of their disputes with whites over lands and the harboring of runaway slaves. Among the militant Seminoles and Creeks in the First Seminole War were BOLEK, JOSIAH FRANCIS, KINACHE, NEAMATHLA, and PETER McQUEEN. Jackson used the conflict with the Seminoles as a pretense for invading Spanish Florida.

After the United States had acquired Florida from Spain the following year, Jackson was appointed the new territory's governor, and served for one year, 1820–21. He then returned to Tennessee and resumed his political career, serving again as senator in 1823–25.

Jackson's first run for the presidency as the Democratic candidate in 1824 was unsuccessful, but he was elected in 1828, and again in 1832. As president, Jackson, on the recommendation of his vice president

JOHN C. CALHOUN, supported the Indian Removal Bill of 1830, which provided funding to relocate eastern Indians who had agreed to exchange their lands for new territory west of the Mississippi. He refused to enforce the U.S. Supreme Court's decisions in favor of JOHN ROSS's faction of Cherokees. In 1835–36, Jackson was able to obtain Congress's ratification of treaties with the Cherokees, leading to their enforced removal and the Trail of Tears to the Indian Territory in 1838.

Jackson met with Chief BLACK HAWK in Washington, D.C., in 1833, following the Sac leader's surrender in the Black Hawk War of 1832. Later, after Black Hawk's release, as a condition of the treaty ending the war, Jackson ordered Black Hawk be removed as leader of the Sacs and replaced by KEOKUK.

Throughout Jackson's administration, federal troops were required to contain the sporadic Seminole uprisings in Florida, which developed into a full-scale war during Jackson's last year in office, 1836, under OSCEOLA.

During Jackson's two terms as president, 94 treaties were signed with the Indians of the Old Northwest and the Southeast to further the expansion of U.S. territory. In these years, remaining tribal lands east of the Mississippi were ceded to the government and opened to white settlement. (See also BLACK HAWK; BOLEK; ROSS, JOHN; WEATHERFORD, WILLIAM.)

JACKSON, HELEN HUNT. *(1830–1885).*
Reformer; writer.

Helen Hunt Jackson grew up in Amherst, Massachusetts, where she began her lifelong friendship with the poet Emily Dickinson. She moved to Colorado in 1873, by which time she was a successful author of novels, essays, and poetry under the pseudonym H.H.

Jackson's involvement in the Indian rights movement began during an 1879 visit to Boston when she attended a lecture by THOMAS HENRY TIBBLES on behalf of the Ponca Indians. Tibbles was touring with the Ponca chief STANDING BEAR, plus the Omahas SUSETTE LA FLESCHE and FRANCIS LA FLESCHE, brought to Boston by the reformer WENDELL PHILLIPS. With HENRY DAWES, the chairman of the Senate Committee on Indian Affairs, Jackson organized the Boston Indian Citizenship Association in 1879, to support the Poncas in their legal struggle for a homeland in Nebraska. She entered into an open debate in the New York and Boston newspapers with CARL SCHURZ, secretary of the Interior, and challenged his stand on the issue. Jackson also came to oppose the allotment of tribal lands to Indians, which many reformers supported as a way to assimilate and gain citizenship for Indians.

In 1881, the publication of Jackson's nonfiction work, *A Century of Dishonor*, galvanized public sentiments on Indian issues. The book's discussion of deception and broken promises in U.S. Indian policy in regard to seven tribes, and of three massacres of Indians by whites, had an impact on the Indian rights movement similar to the effect that Harriet Beecher Stowe's *Uncle Tom's Cabin* had had on the antislavery cause, becoming a rallying point. Jackson had a copy sent to every member of Congress.

In 1882, Jackson was appointed by the Department of the Interior as a special agent, assigned to investigate the problem of white encroachment on the reservations of California's Mission Indians. Her report resulted in the Interior Department being granted the authority to use military force to remove white settlers from Mission Indian lands. Her findings also resulted in a Congressional appropriation enabling the Mission Indians to homestead their lands and acquire individual titles without cost.

Jackson's experience as a special Indian agent in California inspired her next book, *Ramona*, published in 1884. The fictionalized account of the Cahuilla Indian RAMONA called attention to the plight of Mission Indians under the impact of white expansion. (See also RAMONA; STANDING BEAR.)

JACKSON, WILLIAM HENRY. *(1843–1942).*
Photographer.

Originally from Keesville, New York, William Henry Jackson crossed the Great Plains to California with a wagon train in 1866–67. His interest in painting western and Indian scenes led to a career as a frontier photographer, including images of Plains, Southwest, Great Basin, and Plateau Indians.

In 1871–72, Jackson served as official photographer with the geological survey of the Yellowstone River region and Rocky Mountains led by FERDINAND V. HAYDEN. He became a close friend of the painter THOMAS MORAN, also part of the expedition. Their work led to the founding of the Yellowstone region as the first national park in 1872.

Jackson's photographs and clay models of the Anasazi cliff dwellings at Mesa Verde in Colorado were exhibited at the Centennial Exposition in Philadelphia in 1876, and after having established a studio in Denver, Jackson produced a series of photographic reports and paintings for *Harper's Weekly*.

In 1924, Jackson moved to Washington, D.C. When in his nineties, he painted murals of the Old West for the new Department of the Interior building. He also acted as a technical adviser for the filming of *Gone With the Wind*. In 1942, at the age of 99, Jackson appeared before the Explorer's Club, where he was commended for his 80,000 photographs of the West. He died that same year.

JACOBS (Captain Jacobs). *Delaware. (d. 1756).*
War chief in the French and Indian War of 1754–63.

In July 1755, Jacobs led one of the war parties in the combined French and Indian victory over British troops under General EDWARD BRADDOCK on their way to attack Fort Duquesne (present-day Pittsburgh). Of Braddock's more than 2,000 regulars and militiamen, fewer than 500 escaped to Fort Cumberland. Braddock himself died from his wounds. Jacobs's band and other pro-French Indians of the Old Northwest kept up their raids on British settlements in western Pennsylvania. In September 1756, troops under Colonel John Armstrong attacked the village of Kittanning and managed to set many of the Delaware wigwams on fire. Jacobs, his entire family, and many of his band members were killed while trying to escape.

JACOBSEN, JOHAN ADRIAN. *(1853–1947).*
Collector of Indian artifacts.

Norwegian-born J. Adrian Jacobsen moved to Germany while young and found work with the impresario Carl Hagenbeck as head of an expedition to Greenland to locate a group of Eskimos to be exhibited at The Tierpark, a private museum and zoo in Hamburg. In 1880, he traveled to Labrador and brought back a second group of Eskimos.

In 1881–83, Jacobsen was employed by the German Adolf Bastian to lead an ethnological expedition to the coast of British Columbia for the purpose of acquiring Indian artifacts for the state-run Neues Museum in Berlin. Jacobsen traveled to the Queen Charlotte Islands, where he visited Haida villages of the Hecate Strait region. He then journeyed to Kwakiutl territory on the west coast of Vancouver Island with the Kwakiutl-Tlingit GEORGE HUNT as his guide and interpreter. The Kwakiutl chief Nagretze was instrumental in his acquisition of both religious and household objects. Jacobsen brought to Europe the largest collection of Northwest Coast Indian artifacts to date, about 2,400 items.

In the year following his return, Jacobsen was again hired by Hagenbeck and undertook another voyage to the Pacific Northwest to locate a group of Bella Coola Indians for a visit to Germany. Hagenbeck arranged a tour of major cities for them, in which they performed dances and demonstrated arts and crafts. On observing them, FRANZ BOAS was inspired to undertake studies of the Northwest Coast Indians.

J. Adrian Jacobsen, along with his brother Fillip, later provided artifacts to other museums, such as the Field Museum of Natural History in Chicago. In 1910, he traveled to North Dakota to recruit Teton Sioux Indians for a show in Germany.

Jacobsen went into the restaurant business late in life. Much of the Berlin collection he had amassed was destroyed during World War II.

JANNEY, SAMUEL McPHERSON. *(1801–1880).*
Indian superintendent; reformer; historian.

Samuel Janney, born in Loudon County, Virginia, was a prominent Quaker and a poet and historian, writing, among other works, a history of WILLIAM PENN and Quakerism.

Janney first became active in the Indian reform movement in 1864 on joining a Quaker committee on Indian concerns. When ULYSSES S. GRANT's Peace Policy went into effect in 1869, ELY PARKER, commissioner of Indian Affairs, appointed Janney as the superintendent for the Northern Superintendency in Omaha. The post involved the administration of nearly 7,000 Nebraska Indians, including Omahas, Winnebagos, Pawnees, Otos, and Santee Sioux.

Janney's success led Quaker leaders to seek additional funding for Indian education and other improvement projects. Their efforts led to Congress's enactment, in 1871, of the first legislation allocating federal funds specifically for the education of Native Americans. It was Janney's recommendations that led to the establishment of boarding schools for all Indian children between the ages of six and 12, providing young Indians with training in white vocational pursuits and domestic life. For all Indians, Janney advocated education in Christian values.

The U.S. Indian Commission, the reform group organized by philanthropist PETER COOPER, adopted Janney's criteria for the appointment of Indian agents, advising that Indian agents be married, of well-attested philanthropic sentiments, and of Christian character.

Janney undertook measures to allot individual plots of lands to reservation Indians under his jurisdiction, and advocated the sale of surplus reservation lands to white settlers, with the proceeds used to finance programs to improve Indian conditions.

JEFFERSON, THOMAS. *(1743–1826).* President of the United States, 1801–09; scholar.

As legislator and president, Virginia-born Thomas Jefferson's policy toward the Indians was shaped by the idea that the United States' survival as a democratic republic required its expansion into the vast areas of land then occupied by the Indians. He believed that only the availability of cheap land for settlement in the West could stem the inevitable development of a tyranny of the rich over the poor.

While serving as a delegate to the Virginia state legislature between 1781 and 1784, Jefferson was instrumental in Virginia's ceding of its claim to a large area of land in the Ohio Valley, thus preparing the way for the establishment of the Old Northwest territories, and the displacement of Indians. He advocated dealing with the Indians as separate tribal entities in their land cessions. He also supported military actions against the Indians of the Ohio Valley, as carried out in LITTLE TURTLE's War of 1790–94.

Jefferson served as vice president in 1797–1801 under James Madison. On assuming the presidency for the first of two terms in 1801, he appointed HENRY DEARBORN as secretary of War in charge of Indian Affairs. He was the first president to propose removal of tribes as a solution to the conflict between Indians and white settlers. The 1803 Louisiana Purchase and the subsequent explorations of the LEWIS and CLARK Expedition served his plan to remove all eastern Indians to lands west of the Mississippi. Jefferson drafted a constitutional amendment that, though never adopted, would have given the president the power to enter into negotiations with Indian tribes to exchange their eastern lands for territory in the trans-Mississippi West. To encourage the Indians to relocate westward, he proposed the settlement of whites as close to tribal areas as possible in the hope of impeding the Indians' hunting-based culture. He hoped the Indians would be protected from white civilization for a period of at least 50 years, time enough for assimilation.

Jefferson directed the territorial governors of the Northwest Territory to promote plans to "civilize" the Indians under their jurisdiction. The Indian Trade and Intercourse Act of 1802, which Jefferson supported, made permanent the federal factory system supervising the western fur trade. The new act included a provision giving the president the power to regulate liquor sales to Indians at frontier trading forts in an effort to control the dishonest practices of agents and traders. In 1806, he created the office of superintendent of the Indian Trade within the War Department, an attempt toward a consolidated Indian policy, with a degree of civilian control as an alternative to the military. Jefferson was also instrumental in obtaining Congressional funding to pay for numerous diplomatic visits of Indian delegations to Washington, D.C., a practice that continued through the 1800s.

As a scholar, Jefferson regarded the Indians in the context of the Noble Savage. He shared the view that societies were hierarchical in their development, and that Indian cultures paralleled earlier stages in the development of Western civilization. He made a study of Indian languages that included a system of classification, and he instructed the explorers Lewis and Clark, as well as ZEBULON PIKE, to return with ethnological data about the Indian tribes they encountered. His interest in Indian culture led Jefferson to a study of the archeological findings at the Hopewell Mounts in the Ohio Valley. It has been speculated that Jefferson's contributions to the 1776 Declaration of Independence may have orignated in the political system of the Iroquois League.

JEFFORDS, THOMAS J. (Taglito, "red beard). (1832–1914). Agent; army scout.

Thomas J. Jeffords, originally from upstate New York, moved to Taos, New Mexico, in 1859. During the Civil War, he was a scout for Union forces under General JAMES H. CARLETON in the New Mexico campaign against invading Confederate troops from Texas.

In 1867, Jeffords came into contact with Chiricahua Apaches when, as the operator of a stagecoach line in southeastern Arizona, he lost 14 of his drivers at the hands of warriors led by COCHISE. He endeavored to meet Cochise, eventually developing a friendship with him. The Chiricahuas gave Jeffords the name Taglito, meaning "red beard" in their Athapascan dialect.

Despite President ULYSSES S. GRANT's Peace Policy, federal authorities were unable to reach Cochise and negotiate an end to Apache raids on white settlers. When President Grant dispatched General OLIVER HOWARD to Arizona in 1872 to establish a peaceful settlement, it was Jeffords, then a scout for the army, whom Howard appointed as his intermediary with Cochise. The Chiricahuas agreed to restrict themselves to a reservation in the Apache Pass region of southeastern Arizona, provided that Jeffords be named their agent.

Jeffords maintained peace between the Chiricahuas and white settlers over the next several years. He was one of the few Indian agents in the Southwest who was not affiliated with a Quaker or other religious group. In addition, he had been appointed by a military officer, which further alienated him from the civilian-run Bureau of Indian Affairs.

Jeffords was with Cochise in 1874 shortly before the Apache chief died, and was the only white man to know the location of his burial site. The death of Cochise and the Apache uprisings under his son NAICHE, as well as GERONIMO and VICTORIO, brought an end to the peaceful settlement of the Chiricahuas on their reservation. In 1876, the Chiricahua Reservation was eliminated and the Chiricahuas were removed to the San Carlos Reservation under the agent JOHN P. CLUM.

In 1880, Jeffords was again active in assisting the army in Apache affairs. He remained in Arizona afterward, tending his mining property. (See also COCHISE.)

JEMISON, MARY (White Woman of the Genesee). (1743–1833). Captive.

Mary Jemison was born at sea during her parents' voyage from Ireland to North America. When she was

15, during the French and Indian War of 1754–63, she was captured by Shawnees in a raid on her family's farm near Gettysburg, Pennsylvania. At Fort Duquesne (present-day Pittsburgh), the Shawnees sold her to two Seneca women who took her to the Genessee Valley of New York. Jemison adopted the Indian life-style and remained with the Indians for the rest of her life. Living with the Indians through the French and Indian War, the American Revolution, and the first decades of the 19th century, she was an eyewitness to many historical events in Pennsylvania and central New York.

Jemison married twice in her life, to a Delaware and to a Seneca. Her second husband, Hiokatoo, was present at General EDWARD BRADDOCK's defeat in the unsuccessful British attempt to take Fort Duquesne at the beginning of the French and Indian War. In addition, during the American Revolution, Hiokatoo was second in command to Chief JOSEPH BRANT at the Cherry Valley Massacre of November 1778.

Jemison openly resisted attempts by whites to rescue her from Indian captivity. She had eight children by her Indian hubands and became a woman of stature in the Seneca tribe, who knew her as the White Woman of the Genesee. Her title to land on the Genesee River, given to her as an Indian in 1797, was upheld by the State of New York in 1817.

An account of Jemison's life as an Indianized captive, entitled *A Narrative of the Life of Mrs. Mary Jemison*, recorded by J. E. Seaver, first appeared in 1824. In this work, Jemison related one of the few Indian captivity accounts that looks upon the Indians with sympathy and understanding.

JESUP, THOMAS SIDNEY. *(1788–1860).* Army officer in the Second Seminole War of 1835–42.

Thomas Jesup was born in Berkeley County, present-day West Virginia. He entered the army at the age of 20, serving as an officer under the command of General William Hull in the War of 1812. By the end of the war, he had been appointed a lieutenant colonel.

In 1818, Jesup became a brigadier general and quartermaster general of the army, then a major general 10 years later. In 1836, he was placed in command of military actions against the Creeks in Alabama when that tribe resisted the government's plan to remove them to the Indian Territory.

That same year, following the outbreak of the Second Seminole War, Jesup assumed leadership of federal forces seeking to suppress militant Seminole bands in Florida. Previous attempts under generals DUNCAN CLINCH, EDMUND GAINES, WINFIELD SCOTT, and Duncan Call had ended in failure for the army. In May 1837, Jesup held a peace parley at Fort Mellon, near Lake Monroe, Florida, attended by Seminole leader OSCEOLA, other Seminole chiefs, and 3,000 warriors.

With plans to forcibly deport the Indians from Florida to the Indian Territory, Jesup assembled a fleet of transport ships near the fort, but Osceola and other Seminole leaders left Fort Mellon under cover of darkness when the army's real intentions became apparent.

Jesup's command was soon bolstered with more than 1,000 Shawnee, Delaware, and Kickapoo auxiliaries. The Seminoles continued raiding white settlements and army patrols, then retreating into the Everglades before the soldiers could engage them in a decisive confrontation.

Another conference with Osceola was arranged through the war chief WILD CAT. On October 21, 1837, the Seminole leader arrived under a white flag of truce at Jesup's headquarters in St. Augustine, with a contingent of 75 warriors. Rather than meet with the Seminoles, Jesup called for their arrest. Although a party of warriors led by Wild Cat soon escaped, Osceola remained incarcerated and was later sent to Fort Moultrie, South Carolina, where he died in January 1838. That same month, Jesup was wounded in a skirmish with the Seminoles.

Jesup's attempt to bring the war to a close through the arrest of Osceola had failed. Moreover, he faced strong criticism among Congressional leaders for his use of treachery, and was relieved of his command in May 1838, replaced by ZACHARY TAYLOR. The Second Seminole War continued for four more years. Jesup remained active as head of the army's quartermaster corps, and went on to take part in the Mexican War of 1846–48. (See also OSCEOLA.)

JEWITT, JOHN RODGERS. *(1783–1821).* Captive.

John Jewitt was a member of the crew of the ship *Boston*, on an 1803 trading voyage from England to Vancouver Island, now part of British Columbia. Sea otter furs obtained from the Nootka Indians in exchange for manufactured goods were then to be sold in China. Jewitt and another man, a sailmaker by the name of Thompson, were the sole survivors of a Nootka attack in which the captain and 24 of the crew were killed, their heads cut off and taken as trophies. Jewitt was spared from death because Chief MAQUINNA valued his skill as a blacksmith and armorer, hoping to have him maintain and repair guns, knives, and other implements. Convincing the Nootkas that Thompson was his father, Jewitt saved his fellow crew member from death.

Jewitt and Thompson were held captive for more than two years. Jewitt was enslaved and then adopted by Maquinna, who bought him a wife from a neighboring tribe. He fought alongside the Nootkas against their enemies, experienced their religious ceremonies, and took part in whaling expeditions.

In 1806, Jewitt and Thompson managed to escape when the fur-trading ship *Lydia* arrived at the Nootka village where they were being held. Jewitt returned to Boston, and his experiences were published as *Narrative of the Adventures and Sufferings of John Rodgers Jewitt* (1815), as told to Roland Alsop. Its appearance brought Jewitt celebrity status and his story was adapted into an 1817 stage play, *The Armourer's Escape* by James Nelson Barker, in which Jewitt portrayed himself.

JOGUES, ISAAC. *(1607–1646).* Explorer; missionary; captive.

Born in Orleans, France, to a prominent family, Isaac Jogues became a professor of literature in Rouen, and, in 1624, entered the priesthood as a Jesuit.

In 1636, on arriving in Quebec, Jogues was sent as a missionary to the Indians of Lake Huron's Georgian Bay region. During his time among the Hurons, he explored north to Sault Ste. Marie in what is now Michigan, which he named in 1641. He also was the first European missionary to reach the shores of Lake Michigan. From the tribes of the region, Jogues heard reports of the Sioux living on the prairies west of the Mississippi.

In 1642, while returning to Quebec, Jogues and several other Jesuits were captured by Mohawks, about 60 miles northeast of Montreal near the St. Lawrence River town of Sorel, Quebec. Two of the Jesuits captured with him were killed; Jogues survived and, in 1643, was ransomed from the Mohawks by the Dutch missionary JOHANNES MEGAPOLENSIS at Fort Orange (present-day Albany, New York). He was taken to New Amsterdam (present-day New York City), from where he sailed to France. Received with great reverence by French royalty and church officials, he celebrated the Roman Catholic Mass at the papal court, even though his hands had been mutilated by Indian torture.

In 1644, Jogues returned to French Canada and became a peace envoy to the Iroquois. He succeeded in reaching an accord with the Mohawks in May 1646. That year, the Indians took Jogues to their land south of Lake Champlain, now in present-day New York, a region uncharted by whites. His captors led Jogues through the narrows between Lake Champlain and Lake George, then known only to the Indians, who called it *Andiatarocte*, meaning "place where the lake narrows." Jogues became the first known white to see Lake George, which he named Lac du Sacrement.

Jogues, along with Father Jean Lalande, attempted to establish a Catholic mission to the Mohawks. Tribal medicine men arranged for the priests to be taken captive and brought to the Iroquois settlement at Caughnawaga near present-day Auriesville, New York, where they were killed. (A second Mohawk settlement known as Caughnawaga or Kahnawake was later established south of Montreal; the Mohawk convert KATERI TEKAKWITHA was from the original Caughnawaga.)

In 1930, Pope Pius XI declared Jogues one of the Jesuit Martyrs of North America and elevated him to sainthood. Near the site of his death, at Auriesville, New York, is a Roman Catholic shrine, Our Lady of Martyrs, which commemorates Jogues and other Jesuit missionaries killed by the Iroquois.

JOHN (Old John). *Rogue River. (fl. 1850s).* Leader of the Rogue River War of 1855–56.

John, or Old John, was a chief of the Takelma and Tututni Indians living along the Rogue River Valley in southwestern Oregon, known to whites as Rogue River Indians. The discovery of gold in the region brought miners and settlers onto Indian lands, forcing the Indians into the foothills.

John managed to arm his followers by having them prospect gold and trade it for guns and ammunition. In spring 1853, his men attacked and killed a party of miners at Cow Creek, then later ambushed others at Applegate and Galice creeks. A company of volunteers was organized under "Fighting Bob" Griffen to pacify the Indians, leading to an engagement on the Applegate on August 12, 1853. John kept his warriors scattered in the woods and, after a feigned retreat, led a counterattack the next day, killing several whites. Because of continuing pressure, several of the Rogue subchiefs, such as Limpy, Sam, and Joe, agreed to the whites' terms of peace. But John remained militant.

In 1855, the Yakima Indians under KAMIAKIN and other tribes living to the east of the Cascade Mountains revolted in the Yakima War. Rumors of a general Indian uprising along the Rogue Valley led the commander of Fort Lane, Captain Andrew Jackson Smith, to open up the post to the local bands in the hope of better controlling them. Before leaving their village, however, the Indians were attacked by Oregon volunteers not under Smith's command. Twenty-three women, children, and old men died in the massacre. In retaliation, a war party killed 27 settlers, setting off a renewed cycle of violence.

In spring 1856, regular troops under General JOHN E. WOOL arrived on the Rogue after their campaign against the Yakimas. The Rogue River chiefs sent word to Captain Smith that they were willing to surrender at Big Meadows, and he and Griffen led a force of about 80 volunteers out of Fort Lane to take the Indians into custody. John made plans for an ambush, however. On being warned of the trap by two Indian women, Smith had his men dig in on a hilltop overlooking the Rogue River. The attack came soon after dawn on May 27. About 20 Indians pretended at first to surrender, with their guns held above their heads, then opened fire. More warriors advanced up the slopes while others fired from flanking hills. Despite overwhelming numbers and heavy casualties, the soldiers held out until reinforcements under Captain Christopher Augur arrived the next day. In a spontaneous pincer operation, the regulars attacked from the rear while militiamen charged from the hilltop, putting John's warriors to flight.

Over the next several weeks, many of the Indians surrendered. John and his faithful held out a month until they were surrounded. Most were relocated to the Siletz Reservation to the north. John and his son Adam were sent to Alcatraz in San Francisco Bay. During the voyage, they attempted an escape, killing a sailor and wounding two before being wounded and overpowered themselves. They were released years later and returned to their homeland, where few remembered them. Old John, it is thought, spent his last days alone in the hills overlooking the Rogue.

JOHNSON. See CANALLA.

JOHNSON, EASTMAN. *(1824–1906).* Artist.

Originally from Maine, Johnson spent the early part of his career as a lithographer in Boston. He went on to become a portraitist, working in New England and Washington, D.C. In 1849, he traveled to Europe, where he was eventually offered a position as an official painter to the Dutch royal court, returning to the United States in 1855.

In 1856–57, Johnson journeyed to Wisconsin to visit his sister. He recorded his observations of Chippewa customs and produced portraits of Chippewa Indians in charcoal drawings and oil paintings. In 1859, after time in Cincinnati and Washington, D.C., he settled permanently in New York, but returned often to the Great Lakes region.

In addition to his Chippewa works, Johnson is known for his 1860 painting *Old Kentucky Home* and his depictions of Civil War battles.

JOHNSON, EMILY PAULINE (Tekahionwake, "double wampum"). *Mixed Mohawk. (1862–1913).* Writer.

E. Pauline Johnson was born at Chiefswood, on the Six Nations Reserve near Brantford, Ontario. Her father was Mohawk chief Henry Martin Johnson (Onwanonsyshon); her mother was an Englishwoman by the name of Emily S. Howells, cousin of the novelist William Dean Howells. Chiefswood was considered the capital of Eastern Indian Canada and, during Emily Pauline's childhood, was visited by Canadian and Enlgish notables.

Johnson attended an Indian day school, then a Brantford central school. Although she had no schooling beyond the elementary level, she was an avid reader who, by the age of 12, had read many of the literary classics.

As a teenager, Emily sold her poems to literary journals. In 1892, she gave her first reading in Toronto, to great acclaim. From that time until 1910, she made numerous public appearances in Canada, the United States, and England. Dressing as an Indian princess, she acted as a cultural ambassdor through her poetry and lectures, celebrating both her Indian heritage and her Canadian background. She eventually settled in Vancouver, British Columbia.

Johnson's collections of poetry, many of them bestsellers, include *White Wampum* (1895); *Canadian Born* (1903); and *Flint and Feather* (1913). She also collected a volume of tales, *Legends of Vancouver* (1911); and produced a novel, *The Shagganappi* (1913).

JOHNSON, GUY. *(ca. 1740–1788).* Colonial Indian superintendent; Loyalist soldier; artist. Nephew of WILLIAM JOHNSON; cousin of JOHN JOHNSON.

Originally from Ireland, Guy Johnson joined his uncle William Johnson in the Mohawk Valley sometime before 1756. He and his cousin John Johnson became close friends with the Mohawk JOSEPH BRANT.

Johnson was a trained topographical artist, and, in 1759, published a drawing of Fort Johnson, the military and trading post his uncle established near Amsterdam, New York.

Serving in the French and Indian War, Johnson came to command a company of rangers under General JEFFREY AMHERST in 1759–60. In 1762, Guy became William's deputy agent for Indian Affairs. The following year, he married Williams's daughter, Mary. They lived at Guy Park near present-day Amsterdam, New York.

When Sir William Johnson died in 1774, Guy Johnson became acting superintendent of Indians of the Northern Department; his position was later made official by England. At the outbreak of the American Revolution, Johnson attempted to maintain the neutrality of the Iroquois, in opposition to the missionary SAMUEL KIRKLAND, who preached pro-Patriot sentiments to the Oneidas and Tuscaroras. Fearing that his position as British liaison with the Iroquois would make him a target for arrest by Patriot forces, Johnson fled the Mohawk Valley to British-held positions at Fort Ontario near present-day Oswego, New York, in May 1775.

The following July, Johnson went to Montreal, where he and his Indian allies carried out campaigns in the Lake Champlain region of northeastern New York. In winter 1775–76, Guy Johnson traveled to England; Brant accompanied him as his secretary. They returned in July 1776, landing at Staten Island.

At Fort Niagara, from 1777 to 1779, Guy Johnson helped direct the Loyalist campaign undertaken by Brant and JOHN BUTLER against settlements in the Mohawk and Wyoming valleys of central New York and northern Pennsylvania. He was present at the Battle of Newtown against Patriot forces under JOHN SULLIVAN and JAMES CLINTON.

At the conclusion of war, Johnson returned to England, where he attempted to secure losses for confiscated property. (See also BRANT, JOSEPH.)

JOHNSON, JOHN. *(1742–1830).* British officer in the American Revolution; Indian commissioner. Son of WILLIAM JOHNSON; cousin of GUY JOHNSON.

John Johnson was born in the Mohawk Valley near present-day Amsterdam, New York. As a youth, he was a friend of the Mohawk JOSEPH BRANT. He fought against allied tribes under PONTIAC in the rebellion of 1763 and, for his services, was knighted two years later.

Upon his father William Johnson's death in 1774, John Johnson inherited the family's huge landholdings in the Mohawk Valley, but declined to assume his father's post as Indian superintendent of the Northern Department, which was passed to Guy Johnson.

During the American Revolution, Johnson remained loyal to the British. In May 1776, he was forced to flee his Mohawk Valley home with 200 other British Loyalists. He joined up with British forces in Montreal and organized the Royal Greens, a Loyalist provincial corps. With General Barry St. Leger and allied Iroquois warriors, Johnson, commissioned a general, took part in the 1777 British offensive into the Mohawk Valley, fighting in the Battle of Oriskany against Patriot forces under NICHOLAS HERKIMER. He later participated in raids in the Mohawk and Schoharie valleys.

In 1782, John Johnson succeeded his cousin Guy Johnson as head of the British Indian Department in Canada. He aided in the post-war resettlement of British-allied Iroquois who had been driven out of New York by the 1779 SULLIVAN-CLINTON Campaign. He later served in the War of 1812 with Canadian militia in engagements against the American forces in Quebec. Johnson was also active in the colonial administration of Quebec. (See also BRANT, JOSEPH.)

JOHNSON, WILLIAM (Brother Warraghiyagey, "one who does much business"). *(1715–1774).* Colonial Indian superintendent; soldier; trader; land speculator. Father of JOHN JOHNSON; uncle of GUY JOHNSON; husband of MOLLY BRANT.

Beginning about 1738, native Irishman William Johnson began the settlement of lands owned by his uncle, Admiral Sir Peter Warren, at the eastern end of the Mohawk Valley near present-day Amsterdam, New York. Through the fur trade with the Indians and purchases of their lands, he became wealthy and a major force in British relations with the tribes of the Iroquois League and their dependent peoples. He built Fort Johnson and later Johnson Hall (present-day Johnstown) on formerly Mohawk lands. Johnson was also deeply involved with Indians in his personal life, marrying Molly Brant in a Mohawk ceremony in 1753 and having eight children by her. Molly's brother JOSEPH BRANT became Johnson's protege. Johnson frequently dressed in Iroquois formal garb and performed dances and other Indian rites. Yet he supported the attempts by missionaries, such as ELEAZAR WHEELOCK, to Christianize the Indians, and was instrumental in the establishment of the Indian Castle Church for the Mohawks at Canajoharie, New York.

During King George's War of 1744–48, Johnson's efforts helped prevent the Iroquois from supporting the French. Colonial governor GEORGE CLINTON appointed him provincial superintendent of Indian Affairs in 1746.

At the 1754 Albany Congress, on the eve of the French and Indian War of 1754–63, Johnson gained Iroquois support for the British cause against the French. The next year, he successfully led a combined British and Iroquois campaign, with Mohawk warriors under HENDRICK, against the French and their Indian allies at Crown Point on Lake Champlain and defended British positions on Lake George. Johnson, for his role in the Battle of Lake George, was awarded a baronetcy by George II.

In 1756, Johnson was named superintendent of Indian Affairs for the Northern Department and colonel

William Johnson. *Courtesy of Library of Congress.*

of the Six Nations. He held frequent meetings with the Iroquois and was often present at meetings at their Council Fire at Onondaga. In 1759, he led British forces and Iroquois auxiliaries in a successful attack on the French at Fort Niagara. He also participated in the occupation of Montreal in 1760.

With the surrender of the French at Detroit in 1761, Johnson became England's main emissary to the Indians of the Ohio Valley. He was named chief Indian administrator after the 1763 Treaty of Paris in which tribes formerly allied with France came under British supervision. As such, he attempted to institute regulation of the fur trade through the appointment of deputies and the establishment of trading forts. His lieutenants were his nephew Guy Johnson, his son John Johnson, GEORGE CROGHAN, and Daniel Claus.

In 1763, Johnson warned the British military leader JEFFREY AMHERST of the impending uprising of tribes of the Old Northwest under PONTIAC. He managed to keep most of the Iroquois neutral in Pontiac's Rebellion, except for some Seneca bands. In 1766, Johnson personally accepted the Ottawa leader's capitulation.

The end of the French threat to British domination in the northern Ohio Valley and New York brought an end to centralized supervision of the fur trade with the Indians. In addition, the end of a large British military presence on the frontier led to uncontrolled white settlement on Indian hunting lands. To stabilize the Indian situation on the frontier, Johnson, on behalf of the colonial authorities, organized the Fort Stanwix Congress in 1768. At this meeting of colonial and Indian delegates representing the Iroquois League and tributary peoples, a demarcation line was established, beyond which all further white settlement was prohibited. Although white traders and land speculators did violate the provisions of this agreement over the next years, Johnson was able to maintain peace with the Indians.

Johnson's legacy of maintaining close British ties with the Iroquois endured after his death in 1774. Under his nephew Guy Johnson, his successor as Indian superintendent, the Iroquois, led by Joseph Brant, supported the British in the American Revolution. (See also BRANT, JOSEPH; BRANT, MOLLY.)

JOLLIET, LOUIS (Louis Joliet). *(1645–1700).*
Explorer; trader.

Louis Jolliet was born in Quebec, Canada, where he prepared for the priesthood at the Jesuit college. His studies included music, in particular the organ, as well as hydrography. Although he took minor orders in 1662, he left the Jesuits in 1667 to embark on a career in the fur trade with the Indians.

In 1669, Jolliet traveled to the western shores of Lake Ontario, near Niagara Falls, where he first met Jesuit missionary JACQUES MARQUETTE at a Seneca village. He continued on to Lake Superior to investigate a reported discovery of copper deposits, and, during his return journey to Quebec, undertook the first successful portage by whites to Lake Erie via the Detroit River.

In 1672, Jolliet was commissioned by French officials to locate the western river described in Indian accounts to earlier explorers. With Jacques Marquette, who knew many Indian languages, Jolliet was to determine if this river flowed into the Pacific Ocean, the Gulf of California, or the Gulf of Mexico.

In May 1673, Jolliet, Marquette, and five voyageurs set out in two canoes from the St. Ignace Mission near Mackinac Island in the strait between lake Huron and Lake Michigan. They paddled south into Lake Michigan and at Green Bay entered the Fox River, then portaged to the Wisconsin River and finally to the Mississippi.

Accompanying Jolliet and Marquette were a number of Miami Indians as guides. Traveling along the Mississippi through what is now Iowa and Illinois, they made contact with numerous Indian tribes. They also spotted large herds of buffalo. On the cliffs overhanging the river at present-day Alton, Illinois, they saw large Indian paintings depicting the slaying of the mythological monster Piasaw by the Indian deity Wassatogo. At present-day Quincy, Illinois, they encountered a friendly band of Illinois Indians with whom Marquette was able to converse in their Algonquian dialect. They were informed of another tribe farther south, called the Arkansas or Quapaws, who dwelled in what is now Arkansas.

On reaching the mouth of the Arkansas River, south of present-day Memphis, Tennessee, they were warned by the Quapaws that they were approaching the lands of hostile Indians, probably the Chickasaws. The party was also concerned about crossing into Spain's territory along the Gulf Coast, fearing arrest by Spanish authorities.

Having ascertained the course of the Mississippi, Jolliet and Marquette headed back north. Along the way, they visited a large village of Kaskaskia Indians, one of the Illinois tribes, and also had contact with Potawatomis. Ascending the Illinois River, they reentered Lake Michigan near present-day Chicago.

Marquette remained in the west, and Jolliet headed for Quebec. At Lachine Rapids on the St. Lawrence near Montreal, Jolliet's canoe overturned, and his notes on the voyage were lost, forcing him to reproduce his journal from memory.

Jolliet returned to the fur trade in the late 1670s, establishing his business in the eastern St. Lawrence River region. In 1679, he expanded his operation with an overland journey to Hudson Bay. However, British raids on his trading posts in 1690 and 1692 undermined his financial position.

In 1694, Jolliet was commissioned to chart the coast of Labrador and provide an account of Labrador's native population. He was named Royal Hydrographer of New France three years later.

JOLLY, JOHN. (Oolooteka, Oolooteskee, Ahuludegi, "he throws away the drum"). *Cherokee.* *(fl. early 1800s).* Leader of Western Cherokees. Adoptive father of SAMUEL HOUSTON.

John Jolly grew up in eastern Tennessee on Hiwassee Island, where the Hiwassee River feeds the Tennessee. About 1806, the young Sam Houston moved to the region and spent three years with the Cherokees; Chief Jolly adopted him into the tribe as his son. Houston later married Jolly's niece. In 1818, at Houston's urging, Jolly and his band of 300 followers, including SEQUOYAH, emigrated west, transporting their possessions in 13 flatboats and 4 keelboats. They crossed the Mississippi and settled along the Arkansas River, joining the Arkansas band led by his brother Tahlonteskee, one of the principal chiefs along with the BOWL. Jolly became a chief of the Western Cherokees on his brother's death.

JONCAIRE, LOUIS THOMAS CHABERT DE (Sonochiez). *(ca. 1670–1739).* French Indian agent; interpreter; soldier.

Born in France, Louis Thomas Chabert de Joncaire came to Canada as an officer in 1687, before King William's War of 1689–97, the first of the series of wars known collectively as the French and Indian Wars. He was taken captive by the Senecas and learned their Iroquoian language; his Seneca name was Sononchiez.

Joncaire later became the principal French Indian agent to the Iroquois, negotiating with them in competition with the British for the lucrative Great Lakes fur trade. He worked to maintain Iroquois neutrality during Queen Anne's War in 1702–13. Joncaire also originated the 1726 French plan to construct Fort Niagara on Lake Ontario as a way to divert a part of the fur trade centered around Albany.

Louis Thomas's son Philippe Thomas Chabert de Joncaire succeeded him as Indian agent in 1735, serving during King George's War of 1744–48. He in turn was succeeded by his brother Daniel-Marie Chabert de Joncaire in 1748, who served in the last French and Indian War, starting in 1754. Like their father, they had close ties to the Senecas and worked to gain their support in the competition with the British for the Ohio Valley. It is thought that WILLIAM JOHNSON captured the Joncaire brothers at Fort Niagara when that French post fell to the British in 1759.

JONES, PETER (Kahkewaquonaby, Kahkewagwonnaby). *Mixed Chippewa (Ojibway).* *(1802–1856).* Missionary; tribal leader; writer.

Peter Jones was the son of a Welshman by the name of Augustus Jones—a friend of the Mohawk JOSEPH BRANT—and Tuhbenahneeguay, the daughter of the Missisauga Ojibway chief Wahbonosay. He was raised traditionally until the age of 16, when he was baptized and began religious studies.

In 1823, Peter and his brother John were converted at a Methodist mission near Rice Lake in Ontario. In 1826, he was sent on a missionary tour throughout Ontario and played a part in converting JOHN SUNDAY and GEORGE COPWAY. During these years, he also worked on translations of religious texts into Algonquian.

In 1830, Jones was ordained into the Wesleyan Methodist church. He continued his travels, both as a missionary and as chief of the Missisaugas, visiting Toronto, New York, London, and other cities. In his double role, he lobbied on behalf of Indian land rights.

Jones was the author of *The Life and Journals of Kah-ke-wa-quona-by* (1860) and *A History of the Ojebway Indians* (1861). He married an English woman who, along with four of his sons, survived him. One son, who bore his name, became editor of an Ontario periodical, *The Indian.*

JOSEPH (Old Joseph, Joseph the Elder; Tuekakas, Tawaitakas; Wallamootkin). *Nez Perce–Cayuse.* *(ca. 1790–1871).* Leader of the Nontreaty Nez Perces. Father of Young JOSEPH and OLLIKUT.

Tuekakas was the son of a Cayuse chief and a Nez Perce woman. Famous as a warrior and buffalo hunter, he became chief of the Wallamwatkin band of Lower Nez Perces who lived in the Wallowa Valley west of the Snake River in northeastern Oregon.

Tuekakas was friendly to whites, as the Nez Perces had been since the LEWIS and CLARK Expedition, and welcomed the Presbyterian missionary HENRY SPALDING, who came to Lapwai in Idaho in 1836. Tuekakas was baptized by Spalding—along with Chief TIMOTHY—and became known to whites as Joseph, or Old Joseph. He was also made a deacon of the church. He spent part of every year at Lapwai, until a quarrel with missionaries in 1846.

In 1855, at the request of ISAAC STEVENS, governor of the Washington Territory, Old Joseph attended the Walla Walla Council involving many tribes of the region. With other Nez Perce leaders, he signed a treaty establishing the Nez Perce Reservation. By the terms of this agreement, Old Joseph's band retained the rights to the Wallowa region. He also accompanied Stevens to Cow Island on the Missouri River in Montana and made peace with the Blackfeet.

With the 1861 Gold Rush to the region and increased settlement, white officials called the Lapwai Council in 1863 and proposed a revised treaty to further reduce the Nez Perce Reservation from 10,000 to only 1,000 square miles in western Idaho, which meant the cession of the entire Wallowa Valley. Old Joseph refused to sign the new treaty. His faction, including TOOHOOLHOOL-ZOTE, became known as the Nontreaty Nez Perces. Those who signed, such as LAWYER, were called the Treaty Nez Perces.

Vowing he would have nothing more to do with whites, Old Joseph destroyed his copy of the Bible and his American flag. He continued to live in his ancestral homeland, maintaining a policy of passive resistance.

Over the next years, Old Joseph and many of his poeple became involved with SMOHALLA's Dreamer cult. When Old Joseph died, leadership of his band passed to his sons Joseph and Ollikut, who participated in the Nez Perce War of 1877.

JOSEPH (Chief Joseph, Young Joseph; Ephraim; Heinmot Tooyalaket, In-mut-too-yah-lat-lat, Hin-mah-too-yah-lat-kekt, Hinmaton-yalatkit, "thunder coming from water over land"). *Nez Perce. (ca. 1840–1904).* Leader of the Nez Perce War of 1877. Son of Old JOSEPH; brother of OLLIKUT.

Joseph was born in the Wallowa Valley of Oregon, the son of Old JOSEPH, or Tuekakas, chief of the Wallam-watkin band, and his wife Khapkhaponimi. Old Joseph was a converted Christian and baptized his son as Ephraim, but the boy later became known by his father's name. Joseph was one of four children.

While Joseph was in his teens, in 1855, at the Walla Walla Council, leaders of various tribes peacefully agreed to the terms offered by ISAAC STEVENS, governor of the Washington Territory. In exchange for Indian lands for white settlement and mining, the Indians were guaranteed reservation tracts, along with homes, schools, livestock, tools, and annuities. Violation of the treaty terms by white settlers led to conflicts within the region, such as the Yakima War of 1855–56 under KAMIAKIN. Old Joseph, friendly to whites and converted to Christianity by the missionary HENRY SPALDING, was satisfied as long as his people could remain in their ancestral Wallowa Valley.

With the 1861 Gold Rush to the region and increased settlement, white officials called the Lapwai Council in 1863 and proposed a revised treaty to further reduce the Nez Perce Reservation from 10,000 to 1,000 square miles, all in western Idaho. Old Joseph and four others refused to sign, however. Their bands became known as the Nontreaty Nez Perces, mostly Lower Nez Perces living along the Snake and Salmon rivers where Idaho, Oregon, and Washington meet. Those who signed, such as LAWYER, were called the Treaty Nez Perces, mostly

Upper Nez Perces living along the Clearwater. Old Joseph, disillusioned with whites and Christianity, became involved with SMOHALLA's Dreamer religion, which held that the Great Spirit had bestowed the lands to the Indians, and whites had no right to them.

On the death of Old Joseph in 1871, leadership of his band passed to his sons: Young Joseph, who later became known to whites as Chief Joseph, and Ollikut. Joseph became principal chief of the Wallowa Valley band, but concerned himself mainly with civil duties. Ollikut acted as war chief. Like their father, they passively resisted relocation to the Nez Perce Reservation near Fort Lapwai, Idaho. Shortly after Old Joseph's death, however, a new group of white homesteaders moved onto Nez Perce lands and claimed a tract for themselves. Joseph's protest led to an investigation by the Bureau of Indian Affairs. Based on the results, President ULYSSES S. GRANT in 1873 formally established the Wallowa Valley as a reservation. The white land-grabbers ignored the finding, however. In 1875, bowing to political pressure, the administration reversed its position, declaring the valley open to white development. In May 1877, General OLIVER HOWARD, army commander of the Department of the Columbia, gave the Nontreaty Nez Perces 30 days to relocate.

Chief Joseph, fearing a major conflict and the loss of Indian life, argued for compliance despite taunts of

Chief Joseph (Young Joseph). Photo by Edward Curtis. *Courtesy of National Archives of Canada/C-19758.*

cowardice from a militant faction. Ollikut, a renowned fighter and hunter, backed his brother. It seemed that peace would be maintained. Yet, on June 12, while Joseph and Ollikut were south of the Salmon River tending their cattle, a brave by the name of Wahlitits (Shore Crossing), publicly shamed for not avenging the earlier killing of his father by whites, attacked and killed four settlers. Over the next two days, other braves joined the bloodletting, killing 15 more whites. Joseph was reportedly heartsick at the developments, but agreed to support his warriors on the condition that there be no slaying of white women, children, and the wounded, and no scalping. He joined th militants at their hiding place at White Bird Canyon along the Salmon River about 15 miles from Grangeville, Idaho.

General Howard at Lapwai sent a detachment of cavalry under Captain David Perry to round up the hostiles. After several Indian boys herding horses outside the camp had spotted the troops' advance, a party of six Nez Perces went out to negotiate with them under a flag of truce. The soldiers, ignoring the white flag, fired at them. The Indians fired back, killing two. In the ensuing battle of White Bird Canyon on June 17, 1877, in which the Nez Perces under Ollikut outmaneuvered the soldiers on the rocky terrain, the Indians killed 34 whites, suffering no fatalities themselves.

General Howard then led a larger force into the field. For almost a month, the warriors and their families evaded the troops along the rugged banks of the Salmon River. In one skirmish, the Nez Perces wiped out an entire scouting party under Lieutenant S. M. Rains. Meanwhile, on July 1, a band under LOOKING GLASS had fled the reservation after an unprovoked attack by jittery troops under Captain Stephen Whipple, and joined up with Chief Joseph's followers. They fought Howard's troops together in the Battle of the Clearwater on July 11–12. The warriors outflanked and outfought the larger white force, giving their families a chance to escape before finally withdrawing themselves.

After this victory, the leaders of the allied bands held a council. Joseph argued in favor of returning to the Wallowa to defend their homeland, but a majority decided to head east through the Bitterroot Mountains to seek a military alliance with the Crow Indians. Looking Glass was given overall command. The Nez Perces who undertook the journey consisted of different bands with respective leaders, such as TOOHOOLHOOL-ZOTE, WHITE BIRD, and POKER JOE. The total number included fewer than 150 warriors and about 500 women and children, and about 2,000 horses. They were pursued by more than 1,900 troops.

Small skirmishes followed. The Indians crossed into Montana through the Lolo Pass, and, on July 25, by guiding their horses along the face of a cliff, they bypassed a barricade hastily built by volunteers from Fort Missoula under Captain Charles Rawn. The failure of the army's operation led to the name "Fort Fizzle" for the barricade.

The Nez Perces then outdistanced the volunteers and peacefully traded for supplies at Stevensville. Afterward, they headed southward along the Bitterroot Valley. Meanwhile, Howard had been telegraphing messages ahead to military posts with instructions to intercept the fugitives.

When the Nez Perces stopped to rest in the Big Hole Valley, about 200 soldiers under Colonel JOHN GIBBON out of Fort Shaw surprised them. At the Battle of Big Hole on August 9, from 60 to 90 Nez Perces were killed before the Indians managed to extricate themselves in a counterattack led by White Bird. Five Wounds and Rainbow, renowned and inseparable buffalo hunters and warriors, who had vowed they would die in battle the same day, were among the dead. Of the troops, 33 had been killed and 38 wounded.

Because of Looking Glass's misjudgment at Big Hole, Poker Joe was chosen as supreme war chief and guide. The Nez Perces headed southeastward, crossing into Idaho again. Howard's troops closed ground. On August 18, Ollikut led 28 warriors in a raid on Howard's camp at Camas Creek, driving away 200 pack mules. While the soldiers were delayed in rounding up the animals, the Nez Perces angled eastward through the Targhee Pass, crossing into Wyoming and the recently established Yellowstone National Park. Vacationing tourists were startled to see the Indians, who, despite their predicament, were nonviolent.

The fugitives continued eastward through the Absaroka Mountains. On meeting with Crows, the Nez Perces learned that some of that tribe were serving as army scouts against them; they received a pledge of neutrality from only one band. They then decided in council to head north through Montana to Canada where they would take refuge with SITTING BULL's band of Sioux, who had escaped across the border the same year.

Colonel Samuel Sturgis, leading 350 cavalrymen out of Fort Keogh, Montana, from the east, managed to intercept the Nez Perces in the Battle of Canyon Creek on September 13. The warriors fought a rearguard action while their families hurried ahead. The soldiers, with 3 dead and 11 wounded, their horses exhausted and their path through the canyon blocked by boulders and brushwood, gave up chase.

The Nez Perces continued northward, but other skirmishes followed. On September 25, at Cow Island on the Missouri River, the Nez Perces raided an army depot for desperately needed supplies, then forged ahead.

About 30 miles from the Canadian border, the half-starving and weary Indians set up camp in a hollow next to Snake Creek in the Bear Paw Mountains. On September 30, still more troops—600 men out of Fort Keogh under Colonel NELSON A. MILES—blocked their escape route.

In the Battle of Bear Paw, Nez Perce sharpshooters, under cover in rifle pits, repelled a series of assaults from different directions. The soldiers used howitzers and Gatling guns to wear them down, and casualties were high on both sides. Howard reached the scene on October 4. By then, White Bird and Joseph were the only surviving chiefs. Ollikut, Toohoolhoolzote, Poker Joe, and Looking Glass had been killed. The final night, while surrender arrangements were being made, White Bird and a group of warriors, including Joseph's nephew YELLOW WOLF, slipped through the ring of soldiers and escaped to Canada. About 80 men remained, with 350 women and children.

During and after the remarkable 1,700-mile flight of the Nez Perces, Chief Joseph received much of the credit for the military victories of the tribe despite the fact that other chiefs had played a larger part in the strategy. His fame among whites resulted in part because of his role as the tribe's spokesman. On the morning of October 5, he delivered a frequently quoted speech.

After a stopover at Bismarck, North Dakota, survivors were taken to Fort Leavenworth, Kansas, then to the Indian Territory. Many died from diseases. In 1883, a group of 33 women and children were allowed to return to the Lapwai Reservation in Idaho, followed in 1884 by 118 more. The next year, Joseph and 150 others were sent to the Colville Reservation at Nespelem, Washington. Despite promises at the time of surrender, Chief Joseph was allowed only a short visit to his ancestral Wallowa Valley.

Chief Joseph visited President William McKinley, accompanied by his former antagonists Howard and Miles, in 1897; and then visited Theodore Roosevelt, along with Miles, in 1903. Joseph encouraged education among his followers as well as abstinence from drinking and gambling. A widower himself, he married two widows at the same time despite the disapproval of white authorities.

Chief Joseph died in 1904. The reservation doctor reported that he died of a broken heart.

JOURNEYCAKE, CHARLES (Johnny-cake; Neshapanasumin). *Mixed Delaware. (1817–1894).* Trapper; guide; preacher; tribal leader.

Charles Journeycake was born on the upper Sandusky River in present-day Ohio, the son of Chief Solomon Journeycake and his Delaware-French wife. Educated in both Indian and white customs, Charles became a Baptist at the age of 16. He worked as a trapper and guide and often preached to those accompanying him in the wilderness.

During the 1830s, many Delawares relocated west of the Mississippi to what was originally the northern part of the Indian Territory. In 1854, by an act of Congress, this land became Kansas and Nebraska territories. By the 1860s, the Kansas Delawares were again being pressured by white settlers to relocate. Journeycake, now a subchief, was one of the Delaware leaders who negotiated with the federal government for a new homeland in the shrunken Indian Territory. He and his Delaware- French wife, Jane Sosha, settled on a former Cherokee holding in present-day northeastern Oklahoma, where he worked as a preacher and farmer.

In the 1890s, Journeycake helped win a Delaware claim against the Cherokees and the federal government for compensation from land sales to white settlers in both Kansas and the Indian Territory.

JUH. *Nednhi Apache. (d. 1883).* Principal chief.

Juh was the principal chief of the Nednhis, a renegade band of mostly Chiricahua Apaches, who, on the dissolution of the Chiricahua Reservation in Arizona in 1876, separated from other Chiricahuas who were relocated to the San Carlos Reservation. Instead, they took refuge in the wilderness country of New Mexico and the Sierra Madre of Mexico. They were joined by Chiricahuas from the Ojo Caliente, or Warm Springs, Reservation in New Mexico, plus other groups.

Juh and his followers, including the Chiricahua GERONIMO, carried out frequent raids on Mexican settlements. In January 1880, most Nednhis, because of pressure from the Mexican army, agreed to settle at San Carlos. The next year, August 1881, after the fighting at Cibecue Creek, Juh, Geronimo, and other Apaches again fled the reservation for the Sierra Madre. They returned in April 1882 in a raid on the reservation, known as the LOCO Outbreak.

The next year, while in Mexico, Juh died, probably from a heart attack, causing him to fall off his horse into water, although some reports hold he was drunk at the time. (See also GERONIMO.)

JUMPER (Ote Emathla, Otee Amathla). *Seminole. (ca. 1790–1838).* Leader in the First and Second Seminole wars. Brother-in-law of MICANOPY.

Jumper was a Red Stick Creek who settled in Florida. He fought against troops under ANDREW JACKSON in 1818 during the First Seminole War, and then, in the 1830s, during the Second Seminole War, he resisted removal from Florida. He served as Micanopy's adviser and, in December 1835, participated with him and ALLIGATOR in the attack on Major FRANCIS DADE's troops as they traveled from Fort Brooke on Tampa Bay to reinforce Fort King. The Seminole force then joined OSCEOLA in an attack on a column under General DUNCAN CLINCH. After having surrendered in

December 1837, Jumper was shipped westward and died during the trip. His son, Jim Jumper (not to be confused with JOHN JUMPER), was elected principal chief of the Western Seminoles in 1848. (See also OSCEOLA.)

JUMPER, JOHN (Hemha Micco; Otee Emathla).
Seminole. (ca. 1820–1896). Leader of Western Seminoles; ally of Confederates in the Civil War.

John Jumper relocated to the Indian Territory from Florida in 1840–41. In 1861, he agreed to support the South and helped the Cherokee STAND WATIE drive pro-Union Indians under the Creek OPOTHLEYAHOLO to Kansas. In 1862–63, however, the Indian Expedition under General JAMES BLUNT achieved victory for the North against Confederate Indian regiments. After the war, John Jumper worked to protect Seminole lands within the Indian Territory, and, in 1877, he became the pastor of the Spring Baptist Church. In 1881, he was elected chief of the Western Seminoles.

JUNALUSKA ("he tries repeatedly but fails").
Cherokee. (ca. 1858). Ally of Americans in the Creek War of 1813–14.

Junaluska led Cherokee warriors in the fight against the Creek Red Sticks under WILLIAM WEATHERFORD. In the Battle of Horseshoe Bend of March 1814, Junaluska is reported to have killed a Tomahawk-bearing Creek just before he struck General ANDREW JACKSON. The Cherokees played a key role in the battle by swimming the Tallapoosa River and attacking the Creek defenders from the rear. Junaluska received his name from other Cherokees because, before fighting, he had boasted he would see to the extermination of the Creeks, and afterward he had to admit that some Creeks remained. He traveled West on the Trail of Tears in 1838, but eventually returned to North Carolina, where he was granted a tract of land for his earlier role against the Creeks. (See also WEATHERFORD, WILLIAM.)

JUNEAU, JOSEPH. *Mixed Menominee. (fl. 1880s).*
Cofounder of Juneau, Alaska.

Joseph Juneau was the son of the French-Canadian Solomon Juneau, the founder and first mayor of Milwaukee, Wisconsin, and his French-Menominee wife. Joseph traveled to Alaska as a gold prospector, and, in 1880, he, Richard Harris, and three Tlingit Indians discovered gold near the site of Juneau, precipitating the Gold Rush. Within a year, about 100 miners had arrived, and, in 1900, Juneau, Alaska, was incorporated.

K

KAMIAKIN (Kamaiakin, Kamiakan, Camaekin, "he will not go"). *Yakima. (ca. 1800–1877).* Leader of the Yakima War of 1855–56 and the Coeur d'Alene (Spokane) War of 1858.

Kamiakin was born near present-day Yakima, Washington, the son of a Yakima woman, but related to the Nez Perces, Palouses, and Spokanes through his father. Because of his ancestry plus other family relationships through marriage, and the force of his personality, he had influence among many different tribes in the area.

In the late 1830s, Kamiakin became known to missionaries in the area as a chief who encouraged education among his people, and, in 1841, he met Captain Charles Wilkes during his expedition to the Pacific Northwest. Kamiakin was supportive of whites as long as they recognized the integrity of Indian lands. He encouraged neutrality among the Indians of the region in the Cayuse War of 1847–50, but the situation changed in the 1850s, however, when gold miners and railroad surveyors began arriving in large numbers.

In 1855, the governor of the Washington Territory, ISAAC STEVENS, organized the Walla Walla Council, where he encouraged the tribes of the region—Yakimas, Nez Perces, Cayuses, Umatillas, Wallawallas, Sinkiuses, and others—to give up most of their lands for reservations, homes, schools, livestock, and annuities. He also promised the Indians a period of two to three years to relocate. But tribal leaders disagreed on a course of action. Many signed, but others distrusted whites because of earlier broken promises. Twelve days after the signing, rather than the promised two years, Stevens declared the Indian lands open to white settlement. His worst fears confirmed, Kamiakin called for an alliance of tribes to contain white expansion. He advised against direct confrontation with superior white forces, however.

Kamiakin's cousin through marriage, QUALCHIN, plus five other braves forced events by killing five prospectors. When the Indian agent ANDREW J. BOLON tried to investigate the incident, he too was killed by another party of warriors. Then a force out of Fort Dalles under Major Granville Haller rode into Yakima country. Kamiakin, considering this an invasion, led 500 warriors against the soldiers, killing five and driving the rest back to the fort. Subsequent expeditions under Major Gabriel Rains and Colonel James Kelly only aroused further hostility. Kelly's volunteers tricked Chief PEOPEOMOXMOX of the Wallawallas into coming to parley in December, but they murdered him and five others, then displayed the victims's scalps and ears to settlers.

General JOHN E. WOOL ordered an offensive into Yakima country for early 1856 under Colonel George Wright. Meanwhile, other tribes—Cayuse, Walla Walla, Umatilla, and Sinkiuse—were raiding white settlements. The Sinkiuse chief MOSES participated in some of these raids. The Nisqually LESCHI led warriors from confederated tribes west of the Cascade Mountains in an attack on Seattle, Washington. Also, in the so-called Rogue River War, the Takelma and Tututni Indians, led by JOHN, were attacking settlers of southwestern Oregon.

With the building of Fort Walla Walla and Fort Simcoe, and the withdrawal of all volunteer forces, there were few other engagements in 1856–57 other than skirmishes. But, in spring 1858, when 164 regulars under Major Edward Steptoe marched out of Fort Walla Walla and across the Snake River into Indian country, the Yakimas and now other tribes—Coeur d'Alene, Spokane, and Palouse—prepared for war. In May, at Pine Creek, in the related Coeur d'Alene or Spokane War, about 1,000 Indian allies routed Steptoe's column.

General Newman Clarke sent out another force of about 600 under Colonel George Wright with instructions to maintain pressure on the hostiles and seek the capture of Indian leaders, especially Kamiakin, Qualchin, and OWHI, Qualchin's father. Because of their earlier victories, the Indians made the mistake of meeting the enemy on an open field in the Battle of Spokane Plain. In that engagement and the Battle of Four Lakes, both in the first week of September 1858, the Indians suffered numerous casualties, whereupon they scattered to their villages. Kamiakin was wounded at Spokane Plain when an artillery shell knocked a tree limb onto him.

Wright's column continued its trek through Indian lands, rounding up dissidents. Fifteen were hanged; many were jailed. Owhi turned himself in, as did Qualchin soon afterward. Qualchin was immediately hanged. Owhi was shot and killed while trying to escape. Kamiakin managed to escape into British Columbia, where he hid out among the Kootenais. He returned in 1861 and lived out his life in peace on the Spokane Reservation. After his death, whites stole his head and displayed it publicly.

KANAPIMA ("one who is talked about"; Augustin Hammelin, Jr.). Ottawa. (b. 1813). Christian convert; tribal leader.

Kanapima was born at Mackinaw, Michigan, and he and his younger brother, the Blackbird (Maccoda Binnasee), attended a Catholic seminary at Cincinnati, Ohio, from 1829 to 1832, after which they were sent to Rome, Italy, for further studies. When his brother died two years later, Kanapima returned to Michigan. Within a year he had become chief of his band, resuming the customs of his people. In 1835, he traveled to Washington, D.C., to negotiate on behalf of the Ottawas with the federal government.

KANCAMAGUS. Pennacook. (fl. late 1600s). Last sachem of the Pennacooks.

The sachem PASSACONAWAY of southern New Hampshire had established relations with the British, maintained by his son Wannalancet. At the time of King PHILIP's War of 1675–76, there was a split among the Pennacooks: Paugus, son of Wannalancet, favored war with the colonists; Kancamagus wanted peace. The colonists, in order to suppress a possible rebellion, tricked some of the peaceful bands into coming to a sporting meet at Dover. The whites killed and captured many of their guests and sold them into slavery.

Kancamagus never again trusted the British and plotted revenge. Years later, in 1689, at the beginning of King William's War, the first in the series of French and Indian Wars, Kancamagus led an attack on Dover. He had his squaws ask permission to sleep in the stockade, and the women then opened the gates at night. Warriors entered and killed the men and babies and headed for Quebec with three groups of women and children to sell into slavery. The British intercepted two of these parties; the third escaped to Canada.

The British then persuaded their Mohawk allies to attack the Pennacooks, who, since their numbers were reduced from disease, could not prevent the destruction of their villages. Kancamagus and his warriors took up position behind log walls at Lake Winnisquam, and managed to repel the first attack, departing that night. Kancamagus led his people through the mountains along what is now called the Kancamagus Highway, to the Connecticut River Valley, and to Quebec, where they settled with other bands of the Abnaki Confederacy.

KANE, PAUL. (1810–1871). Artist; writer.

Born in Ireland, Paul Kane emigrated with his family to York (present-day Toronto, Ontario) when eight. After schooling at Upper Canada College, he left Canada in 1836, traveling between Detroit and New Orleans, working odd jobs. In 1841, he went to Europe and studied art on his own, copying the classics in museums. He also studied furniture decoration in Italy. On viewing an exhibit of GEORGE CATLIN's paintings in London, Kane decided to paint the western Canadian tribes.

In 1845, Kane headed west from Toronto, joining up with fur traders and their fleet of canoes out of Fort William at Thunder Bay, Ontario. Near Fort Garry (Winnipeg, Manitoba), he witnessed a large buffalo hunt of Metis. After having followed the Saskatchewan River to Fort Edmonton (Alberta), he crossed the Rockies on horseback, then descended the Columbia River to Fort Vancouver (British Columbia). He was sponsored in this project by GEORGE SIMPSON of the Hudson's Bay Company, and later by the art patron George William Allan.

Kane returned to Toronto in 1848, established a studio, and began work on more than 100 paintings based on his some 700 sketches of western scenery and the daily activities of about 80 different Indian tribes. He recorded his experiences and illustrated them with his artwork in *Wanderings of an Artist Among the Indians of North America* (1859).

KATLIAN (Kotlian). Tlingit. (fl. early 1800s). Leader of Tlingit resistance against the Russians.

After VITUS BERING's voyage of exploration for Russia in 1741, the *promyshlenniki*, or fur traders, progressed eastward along the Aleutian chain, forcing the Aleuts to trap furs for them. The Russians established their first permanent post at Three Saints on Kodiak Island in 1784. Led by ALEKSANDR

BARANOV, they reached Tlingit lands along the Alexander Archipelago and southern Alaskan coast in the 1790s, establishing a post at Sitka on Baranov Island in 1799.

The Tlingits, with their bows, spears, clubs, and wooden armor and helmets, proved more warlike than the Aleuts. Katlian was the principal chief of the Sitka band. In 1802, he led an attack on Sitka, capturing it and taking back from the Russians the pelts hunted on Tlingit lands.

Katlian's warriors held the post for two years until Baranov returned with an armada of ships and a force of 120 Russians and nearly 1,000 Aleuts. The ships bombarded the defenders with cannon fire, then the soldiers attacked. The Tlingits retreated.

The Tlingits remained hostile to the Russians, however, moving against the post at Yakutat in 1805. Because of the continuing raids, the traders appealed to the Russian navy for protection. Starting in 1818, a warship patrolled the Sitka harbor. Tlingit militance was a factor in Russia's decision to sell Alaska to the United States in 1867.

KAYATENNAE (Kaytennae, Kayatenna, Kaahteney, Ke-e-te-na, Kow-tinne; Jacob). *Mimbreno Apache. (fl. 1880s).* Leader in the Apache Wars of the 1880s; army scout.

Kayatennae, like GERONIMO, was not a hereditary chief but rose to prominence among the Apaches because of his skill and bravery in war. From his hideout in the Sierra Madre of Mexico, he participated with NANA in numerous raids on Mexican and Anglo-American settlements. Unlike many of the Mimbreno and Chiricahua leaders, when he agreed to report to San Carlos, Arizona, in 1883, he had never lived on a reservation. Kayatennae proved unruly during the stay and was arrested in 1884 after an attack on Lieutenant BRITTON DAVIS. He was sentenced to three years at Alcatraz, but was released after about 18 months at the request of General GEORGE CROOK, who employed him as a scout. In 1886, Kayatennae was present at Canyon de los Embudos in Mexico along with Crook and the scouts ALCHESAY, CHATO, and MICKEY FREE, when Geronimo agreed to surrender. (See also GERONIMO.)

KEARNY, STEPHEN WATTS. *(1794–1848).* Army officer; explorer.

Born in Newark, New Jersey, Stephen Watts Kearny attended Columbia College for a year, leaving school to fight in the War of 1812. He was commissioned a lieutenant in the 13th infantry and was wounded and captured in the Battle of Queenston Heights near Niagara Falls. Following his release, he was promoted to captain.

After the war, Kearny was transferred to the 2nd Infantry. In 1819, he headed an expedition sent by the government to explore the Yellowstone region, and, in 1826, along with Colonel HENRY LEAVENWORTH, he helped establish Jefferson Barracks south of St. Louis. Kearny seved under General HENRY ATKINSON in RED BIRD's Winnebago Uprising of 1827 and the BLACK HAWK War of 1832.

In 1837, Kearny became the commander of the elite 1st Dragoon regiment, the forerunner of the cavalry units of the post–Civil War era, which patrolled the Indian Territory and the Northern Plains. By 1842, he was the commander of the army's Third Military Department, which at that time encompassed most of the Great Plains.

Accompanied by frontier scout THOMAS FITZPATRICK, Kearny, now a colonel, undertook an expedition in 1845 to the Rocky Mountains, from Fort Leavenworth, Kansas, to South Pass, in the present state of Wyoming. On June 16, 1845, at Fort Laramie, near South Pass, Kearny met with Arapaho and Sioux leaders. He also invited several thousand members of the Plains tribes to witness a demonstration of U.S. military power. At this event, he had his artillery unit fire howitzers and sky rockets into the air in an effort to impress the Indians and prevent attacks along the Oregon Trail.

With the outbreak of the Mexican War in 1846, Kearny was named as the commander of the Army of the West, with the rank of brigadier general. With a large military force, buttressed by regiments of Missouri volunteers and Mormons, he led an invasion into the Mexican province of New Mexico. After having captured the capital at Santa Fe without Mexican resistance, he established a civilian government over the newly acquired New Mexico territory.

To gain the support of the Mexican settlers, Kearny directed the commander of the Missouri volunteer regiment, Colonel ALEXANDER W. DONIPHAN, to undertake a campaign against the Navajos, Apaches, and Utes, who had been raiding settlements in the western part of the province, unchecked by the former Mexican authorities. Kearny left Doniphan in command of New Mexico, then headed west with troops to take part in the conquest of California. Doniphan in turn passed the military administration of New Mexico to Colonel STERLING PRICE, then advanced into Mexico with troops.

After having suffered heavy losses at the hands of Mexican troops at the Indian village of San Pasqual, near San Diego, California, Kearny was joined by a U.S. force under Commodore Robert F. Stockton. By January 13, 1847, they succeeded in capturing Los Angeles and the rest of the province. Kearny susequently became involved in a controversy with JOHN C. FREMONT and Stockton over who had the authority to establish a civilian government in California.

In 1848, Kearny became the military governor of Veracruz, then Mexico City, where he contracted yellow fever. He died in St. Louis a short time later.

KELSEY, HENRY. *(ca. 1667–1729)*. Explorer; trader.

Henry Kelsey, who was probably born in East Greenwich, England, became an employee of the Hudson's Bay Company in 1684. In 1690, he was stationed at the company's York Factory on the southwestern shore of Hudson Bay, now part of Manitoba.

That year, the company sent Kelsey to solicit furs from the Indians, and he left York Factory in June, accompanied by Indian guides. Kelsey is believed to have proceeded into the interior of Manitoba by canoeing along the Hayes and Saskatchewan rivers. He crossed Lake Winnipeg and later reached The Pas. After a winter there, Kelsey and his guides headed overland across central Canada as far west as Red Deer in present south-central Alberta. He is believed to have been the first European to see the Canadian Plains. During the journey, Kelsey spent time with Plains peoples, presumably the Sioux and the Gros Ventres. He hunted buffalo and attempted, with little success, to establish fur-trading connections with the western tribes.

Kelsey returned to York Factory sometime in 1692. He was present when it was surrendered to French forces in 1694 and 1697 during King William's War. Kelsey remained with the Hudson's Bay Company until 1724, as director of the York Factory post and later as chief trader for the company at Albany, New York. In 1717, he was named governor of all the company's posts on Hudson Bay, and, in 1719, explored the bay's northwest coast.

Kelsey's 1690–92 exploration of western Canada was the last such expedition until the 1750s. An account of the expedition to the Canadian Great Plains, including descriptions of Native Americans, is contained in the 1693 book *The Kelsey Papers*, not known to exist until 1926.

KENNEKUK (Kenakuk, Kanakuk, Kannekuk, "putting his foot down"; Pakaka, Pah-kah-kah; Kickapoo Prophet). *Kickapoo. (ca. 1785–1852)*.
Medicine man; leader of passive resistance to removal.

Kennekuk was the leader of a band of Kickapoos living along the Osage River in Illinois. With increasing white development, he encouraged his people to farm for a living and to maintain friendly relations with settlers. Influenced by the teachings of other holy men before him, such as TENSKWATAWA, the Shawnee Prophet, and claiming he had experienced a vision, Kennekuk preached abstention from liquor and

criminal behavior, as well as the use of meditation, fasting, and wooden prayer sticks to bring about a new tribal paradise, with an abundance of food and no enemies.

White settlers wanted the removal of all Indians, however, even the peaceful bands. In 1819, by the Treaty of Edwardsville, tribal representatives signed away Kickapoo lands amounting to half the state of Illinois. In return they were granted lands in Missouri, which were still occupied by the Kickapoos' traditional enemies, the Osages.

During the 1820s, the various Kickapoo bands responded to forced removal in different ways. Some Kickapoo bands emigrated to Texas and eventually Mexico. Some militants under MECINA resisted through acts of sabotage, destroying and stealing white property. With increasing white patrols, some of Mecina's followers joined Kennekuk's band; others joined the Sacs and Foxes under BLACK HAWK. Kennekuk used passive resistance to hinder relocation. Meeting frequently with white officials, especially WILLIAM CLARK in St. Louis, Kennekuk managed to stall by expressing a willingness to depart westward, while at the same time offering excuses for delays—the harvest, illness, or evil omens. In the meantime, his religious message spread to other peoples as well, such as the Potawatomis of Michigan.

In the volatile period following the Black Hawk War of 1832, Kennekuk was forced to sign the new Treaty of Castor Hill, exchanging his band's land for a tract in Kansas along the Missouri. His band of 350 delayed as long as they could, then finally moved in 1833.

Over the next years, Kennekuk continued to negotiate with officials on behalf of his people. He also continued his preachings of religious renewal. Before dying of smallpox, the Kickapoo Prophet promised to come back to life in three days.

KENTON, SIMON. *(1755–1836)*. Frontiersman; scout; soldier in the American Revolution, Little Turtle's War, and the War of 1812.

Born in Fauquier County, Virginia, Simon Kenton fled to the upper Ohio River region at the age of 16, mistakenly believing he had killed a man in a fight over a woman. For a time, he went under the assumed name Simon Butler.

In 1774, Kenton first saw action against the Shawnees when he served as a scout in Lord DUNMORE's War. He fought alongside SIMON GIRTY, who would later achieve notoriety as a Tory in the American Revolution.

In 1777, Kenton settled at Boonesborough, on the Kentucky frontier, where he again fought the Shawnees with fellow frontiersman DANIEL BOONE. When Boone was wounded in an Indian attack outside the settlement's stockade, Kenton carried him to safety. In

1778, Kenton took part in Colonel GEORGE ROGERS CLARK's successful attack on the British and their Indian allies at Kaskaskia in what is now Illinois. That same year, he was captured by hostile tribesmen on the Little Miami River in Ohio, and was saved from death at the hands of the Indians by the intercession of his former ally, Simon Girty. Kenton was turned over to the British garrison at Detroit, but escaped two years later and again served under Clark in his final Revolutionary campaigns.

Kenton returned to Virginia in 1782, where he learned that he had not killed his rival 11 years before. His name cleared, he settled his family in Kentucky. During the late 1780s and early 1790s, he was the head of a vigilante group known as the Kenton Boys, organized to protect their frontier homes.

Kenton took part in General "Mad" ANTHONY WAYNE's 1793–94 campaign against LITTLE TURTLE's allied tribes of the Old Northwest as a major of a battalion of Kentucky volunteers. In 1798, he settled near Urbana, Ohio, and soon became a brigadier general of the Ohio militia. In the War of 1812, at the age of 58, he was a scout for Kentucky governor ISAAC SHELBY and his militia units, taking part in the American victory at the Battle of the Thames on October 15, 1813, where the pro-British Shawnee TECUMSEH was killed.

After 1820, Kenton settled near Urbana, Ohio. His last years were beset with financial difficulties and legal problems over his ownership of lands in both Kentucky and Ohio.

KEOKUK (Kee-O-Kuck, "one who moves about alert"; The Watching Fox, Watchful Fox). *Mixed Sac. (ca. 1783–1848).* Ally of Americans; rival of BLACK HAWK.

Keokuk was born in 1783, or possibly 1788, in the village of Saukenuk at the junction of the Rock and Mississippi rivers in Illinois. He was not a hereditary chief because his mother was half French, but he obtained his position of influence through his bravery against the Sioux, his role as tribal quest-keeper, and his mastery of political intrigue. Furthermore, since he was receptive to white interests and refused to support the British in the War of 1812, as his rival Black Hawk did, Keokuk became the Sac chief recognized by federal officials.

During the 1820s, whites cultivated Keokuk with flattery, gifts, a tour of eastern cities, and promises of future power if he cooperated with their plans for the region. With the onset of the Black Hawk War of 1832, Keokuk, along with the Fox Indians POWASHEEK and WAPELLO, agreed to cede the Rock River country in exchange for a tract west of the Mississippi on the Iowa River and a tribal annuity of $20,000, which he would administer.

Following the war, in 1833 and 1837, Keokuk made other trips East to Washington, D.C. In negotiations with officials, especially over the issue of Sioux claims to Sac and Fox lands in Iowa, Keokuk earned the begrudging respect of some of his former adversaries who claimed he had earlier sold out his people for personal gain. In 1845, Keokuk ceded Iowa lands for a reservation in Kansas, where he died three years later, probably of dysentery, although there were early reports of murder at the hands of one of Black Hawk's supporters.

Keokuk was buried in Keokuk, Iowa, with a statue erected over him. He was succeeded as civil chief by his son Moses Keokuk, a Baptist minister known for his oratorical abilities. (See also BLACK HAWK.)

Keokuk. *Courtesy of Library of Congress.*

KERN, BENJAMIN JORDAN. *(1818–1849).* Artist; topographer; naturalist. Brother of RICHARD KERN and EDWARD KERN.

Benjamin Kern, a physician and sketch artist from Philadelphia, participated with his two younger brothers on a series of expeditions West in the late 1840s and early 1850s. In winter 1848–49, he was a member of JOHN C. FREMONT's fourth expedition in search of a year-round pass through the Rockies for the railroad. On this journey, Benjamin and his brothers sketched scenes of Indian life and the Rocky Mountain wilderness, surveyed the topography, and collected specimens for the Philadelphia Academy of Natural Sciences.

Although all three Kern brothers survived being lost in the harsh snows and cold of the wilderness, Benjamin Kern and Fremont's scout WILLIAM S. WILLIAMS were killed by Ute Indians when the two went back into the mountains to recover possessions the expedition had previously been forced to leave behind.

Four years later, in 1853, while on a subsequent survey expedition for the railroad, Benjamin Kern's brother Richard met a similar fate at the hands of the Utes.

KERN, EDWARD MEYER. *(1834–1863).* Artist; topographer; naturalist. Brother of BENJAMIN KERN and RICHARD KERN.

In 1845, the Philadelphia-born Edward Kern accompanied JOHN C. FREMONT on his third expedition from St. Louis to California, where a river was named after him. After service in the Mexican War of 1846–48, he joined Fremont's fourth expedition of 1848–49 into the southwestern Rocky Mountain region, serving as a topographer and naturalist. He convinced his two older brothers, Benjamin and Richard, artists and scientists in their own right, to also participate, resulting in death for Benajmin.

Edward and Richard accompanied Lieutenant James H. Simpson's 1849 expedition into the Navajo country of Colorado, Utah, and Arizona. Their drawings included 72 pictures of Indian life. These were later published as illustrations for Simpson's official report: *Journal of a Military Reconnaissance from Santa Fe* (1850). Some were also used to illustrate HENRY ROWE SCHOOLCRAFT's *Indian Tribes of the United States* (1851–57).

Kern, an epileptic, died at the age of 40.

KERN, RICHARD HOVENDON. *(1821–1853).* Artist; topographer; naturalist. Brother of BENJAMIN KERN and EDWARD KERN.

With his brothers, also artists and scientist from Philadelphia, Richard Kern participated in JOHN C. FREMONT's ill-fated 1848–49 winter expedition into the Rockies in search of a pass to use as a railroad route. While serving as a topographer and conducting a scientific servey of the area, Richard made sketches of the Indians he encountered. But the weather and rugged terrain proved too much for the expedition. The Kerns were among the few survivors to reach safety after having been abandoned in the Rockies by Fremont. Benjamin Kern, however, lost his life to the Ute Indians when he returned to the mountains to retrieve abandoned possessions.

Richard Kern then worked for the army as a topographical draftsman. He accompanied various ex-

peditions to Indian lands, including the 1849 survey of a route from Fort Smith to Santa Fe with Lieutenant James H. Simpson, and the subsequent journey into Navajo country. His brother Edward joined the expedition at Santa Fe. Many of their sketches were used in Simpson's published report, *Journal of a Military Reconnaissance from Santa Fe* (1850).

Richard was part of the 1851 expedition, led by Lieutenant Lorenzo Sitgreaves, that explored the Zuni and Little Colorado rivers. His visual records include scenes of the Navajos at Canyon de Chelly.

In 1853, Kern participated in a survey for a central railway, during which, as part of the group led by Captain John Gunnison, he was killed in an ambush by Ute Indians near Lake Sevier in the Utah territory. A sketchbook containing drawings of Indians and other scenes was thought to have been taken by the Indians at the time of his death.

Some of Richard Kern's Indian pictures, like those of his brother Edward, were reproduced in HENRY ROWE SCHOOLCRAFT's *Indian Tribes of the United States* (1851–57).

KIASHUTA. See GUYASUTA.

KICKING BEAR. *Miniconjou-Oglala Sioux.* *(fl. 1870s–1890s).* Medicine man; apostle of the Ghost Dance. Nephew of SITTING BULL; brother of FLYING HAWK; brother-in-law of SHORT BULL.

Kicking Bear, who was an intimate of CRAZY HORSE, fought at the battles of Rosebud, Little Bighorn, and Slim Buttes during the War for the Black Hills of 1876–77. He was an Oglala by birth, but joined the Miniconjous through marriage and became a band chief. After the war, he settled on the Cheyenne River Reservation in present-day South Dakota.

In the winter of 1889–90, Kicking Bear and his brother-in-law, the Brule Short Bull of Rosebud, plus nine other Sioux delegates, traveled to Nevada by train to visit with the Paiute WOVOKA and witness the new religion known as the Ghost Dance. After their return, Kicking Bear, at the request of his uncle, the Hunkpapa Sitting Bull, came to the Standing Rock Reservation in North Dakota in October 1890, to demonstrate what he had learned. Although skeptical, especially about Kicking Bear's claim that the Ghost Dance Shirts would repel the white man's bullets, Sitting Bull asked the medicine man to teach his followers the Ghost Dance. White officials, concerned with the new religious fervor tinged with activism and insurgency, moved to repress the movement. The Indian agent at Standing Rock, JAMES McLAUGHLIN, sent police to escort Kicking Bear off the reservation about a week after his arrival.

By early December, Kicking Bear and Short Bull had led their followers, including bands under the chiefs

Two Strike and CROW DOG of the Brules and Little Wound of the Oglalas, to the escarpment known as the Stronghold in the northwest corner of the Pine Ridge Reservation. Here they conducted continuous dances. During the next weeks, General John Brooke made peace overtures to this group. After the death of Sitting Bull at Standing Rock on December 15, the Ghost Dancers began to abandon the Stronghold. But the incident at Wounded Knee on December 29, where the Miniconjou BIG FOOT was killed, caused further militance.

The remaining hostiles set up camp along White Clay Creek about 15 miles north of Pine Ridge Agency. A party of warriors attacked the Drexel Mission church until driven away by soldiers under colonel JAMES FORSYTH. General NELSON A. MILES, who had earlier assumed command of field operations, ordered his men in place surrounding the White Clay camp and eventually negotiated a surrender without further bloodshed. Kicking Bear gave up his rifle to Miles on January 15. (See also BIG FOOT; SITTING BULL; WOVOKA.)

KICKING BIRD (Tene-angpote, "eagle striking with talons"; Watohkonk, "black eagle"). *Kiowa. (1835–1875).* Peacemaker during the Kiowa Wars of the 1870s.

Kicking Bird's grandfather was a Crow Indian adopted into the Kiowas. While young, Kicking Bird established a reputation as a warrior, but came to accept the viewpoint of the principal chief LITTLE MOUNTAIN, who considered peace with whites the best hope for the tribe. Kicking Bird was one of the signers of the Little Arkansas Treaty of 1865. On the death of Little Mountain in 1866, he represented the peace faction and SATANTA the war faction. The tribe settled on LONE WOLF as the compromise choice for principal chief in 1866, but the split in the tribe continued. Kicking Bird continued to counsel peace and signed the Medicine Lodge Treaty of 1867.

Because of his stance, Kicking Bird was accused of cowardice in 1870 at a Sun Dance held on the North Fork of the Red River. To preserve his influence, he participated in his only raid of the period: He led a war party of about 100 into Texas and purposely lured out the cavalry. A force of 54 under Captain Curwen McClellan met the Indians in battle. Kicking Bird used a flanking strategy to defeat them; he further proved himself by riding straight into soldiers, killing one with his lance.

The death of SATANK in 1871, during an escape attempt, contributed to ill-feelings among the factions. In 1872, Kicking Bird and his cousin STUMBLING BEAR were the principal spokesmen for their tribal delegation to Washington, D.C., and, the next year, they worked for the release from prison of Satanta and BIG

TREE as officials had promised. When Lone Wolf, MAMANTI, BIG BOW, and their militant followers joined QUANAH PARKER's Comanches in the Red River War of 1874–75, Kicking Bird led his band to the Fort Sill Agency in the Indian Territory, where he was treated as principal chief by officials.

Along with the Indian agent THOMAS BATTEY, Kicking Bird worked to bring education to the Kiowas. After the Red River War, he had the difficult task of deciding which of the militants would be sent to exile at Fort Marion, Florida. Lone Wolf and Mamanti were among those he selected. Less than a week later, Kicking Bird died, probably from strychnine poison given by one of the militants. Legend has it that the medicine man Mamanti used his magical powers to will his nemesis dead. Kicking Bird was buried at the Fort Sill graveyard, known as the Indian Arlington.

KIEFT, WILLEM. *(1597–1647).* Dutch colonial governor.

Willem Kieft arrived in North America from his native Holland in 1638 to replace Wouter Van Twiller as director general of the New Netherland colony. His mismanagement of the Indians and his policies of extermination soon provoked a full-scale war.

In 1639, Kieft imposed a tax on the Wappinger and Delaware bands of the lower Hudson Valley, ostensibly to cover the cost of protecting them from hostile tribes. Yet, in February 1643, when a band of Wappingers sought refuge at the Dutch settlement of Pavonia in what is now northern New Jersey from war parties of Mohawks seeking tribute, Kieft allowed the attacking Mohawks to massacre them. Kieft and his colonial troops then annihilated the remaining Wappingers, capturing some and returning them to New Amsterdam for public execution by torture. In retaliation, the Indians began raiding Dutch settlements. A combined British and Dutch force counterattacked under Captain JOHN UNDERHILL. The Wappinger ORATAMIN negotiated the Indian surrender in 1645.

For his role in inciting the Indians to war, Kieft was dismissed as director general in 1647, succeeded by PETER STUYVESANT. On his return voyage to Europe that year, he was lost at sea. (See also ORATAMIN.)

KINACHE (Kinheja, Kinhijah, Kinhega; Capichee Micco, Kapitca Mico, Opie Mico, Lye Drop Mico; Far Off Warrior; Tom Perryman). *Mixed Seminole-Miccosukee. (d. ca. 1819).* Ally of British and WILLIAM BOWLES; leader in the First Seminole War of 1817–18.

Kinache supported the British in the American Revolution, at which time he lived above the forks of the Apalachicola River. After 1783, he relocated southeastward to the village of Miccosukee in western

Florida on the west shore of Lake Miccosukee, which William Bowles used as a base of operations in 1800–02. Kinache participated on the side of the British against ANDREW JACKSON in the Battle of New Orleans in 1815. The next year, he joined in the defense of Negro Fort (later Fort Gadsden) from a detachment of troops who had crossed the border in pursuit of runaway slaves. In 1818, Miccosukee was attacked by Creeks under WILLIAM McINTOSH in support of General Jackson. It was first reported that Kinache was killed in this engagement, but he actually escaped to the Bahamas, dying soon after his return to Florida in 1819. (See also BOLEK.)

KING, CHARLES. *(1844–1933).* Historian; writer; soldier.

Born in Albany, New York, Charles King briefly served in the opening years of the Civil War as a drummer boy and orderly in his army officer father's volunteer regiment, the Iron Brigade. He attended West Point and graduated in 1866 as an artillery and cavalry officer. He served in Louisiana during the Reconstruction Era.

In 1871, Captain King was assigned to the 5th Cavalry in Nebraska, where he became friends with WILLIAM "BUFFALO BILL" CODY, an army scout joining him on buffalo hunts. He then took part under General GEORGE CROOK in the Tonto Basin Campaign against Apaches and Yavapais in Arizona. He was wounded in a skirmish in November 1874–a bullet wound to the arm, as well as an arrow wound to the forehead—and he was forced to take a medical leave from the army until early 1875.

King then rejoined the 5th Cavalry at Fort Riley, Kansas. With the outbreak of the Sioux War for the Black Hills of 1876–77, King again served with Cody on patrols of the northern Plains regions of Wyoming, Nebraska, and Montana. He participated in the army's counteroffensive against the Sioux and Cheyennes following Colonel GEORGE ARMSTRONG CUSTER's defeat at Little Bighorn. Under the command of Colonel WESLEY MERRITT, King fought in the Battle of War Bonnet Creek, Nebraska, in July 1876, in which he was a witness to the famous showdown between Cheyenne warrior YELLOW HAIR and Cody.

In 1877, as regimental adjutant of the 5th Cavalry, King took part in the Wind River Expedition from Fort Washakie, Wyoming, aimed at cutting off the retreat of Nez Perce leader Chief JOSEPH (Young Joseph) and his people to Canada in the Nez Perce War.

The wound King had received in the Apache campaign never properly healed, and, by 1879, he was retired as an officer disabled in the line of duty with the promotion to captain.

Following his service in the cavalry, King turned to a writing career. In 1879–80, his history of the Sioux War,

Campaigning with Crook: The Fifth Cavalry in the Sioux War of 1876, was first published. For the next 50 years, King continued to produce numerous volumes of history and fiction about army life on the frontier during the post–Civil War years. He also wrote hundreds of stories for popular magazines. His books were best-sellers of the period, and King is credited with popularizing stories about the cavalry in the Plains Indian wars.

King settled in Milwaukee, where he served with the Wisconsin National Guard and as superintendent for military academies. In 1898, during the Spanish-American War, he briefly returned to active duty in the Philippines, and later supervised the training of Wisconsin recruits for service in World War I.

In 1913, King attended a reunion at the Pine Ridge Reservation in South Dakota of former army officers who took part in the Indian wars of the last part of the 19th century. William "Buffalo Bill" Cody and General NELSON A. MILES were among those present. It was at this meeting that one of the earliest motion pictures of a re-created Indian battle was made. The W. F. Cody Historical Picture Company filmed a reenactment of the battles of War Bonnet Creek and Summit Springs, Colorado. Recreating their original roles were Sioux from the Pine Ridge Reservation; the 12th Cavalry also appeared. The screenplay was written by King.

KING, CHARLES BIRD. *(1785–1862).* Artist.

Charles Bird King, born in Newport, Rhode Island, studied under Samuel King in Newport; under Edward Savage in New York City; and under Benjamin West in London. He then lived for a time in Philadelphia and Baltimore before settling in Washington, D.C.

Throughout the 1820s, King produced a series of portraits of Indian chiefs visiting the nation's capital, a project undertaken under the auspices of THOMAS McKENNEY, director of the Bureau of Indian Affairs. KcKenney planned to create an Indian portrait gallery with King's portraits as its key element.

In 1865, three years after King's death, the National Indian Portrait Gallery was established as part of the Smithsonian Institution. That year, however, a fire destroyed almost all of King's Indian protraits in the collection.

Reproductions of King's works survived as illustrations in the 1837–44 publication *History of the Indian Tribes of North America* by McKenney and JAMES HALL. A few replicas of the lost paintings, made earlier by King himself, also were preserved. Nine of King's original Indian portraits escaped the flames of the Smithsonian fire and are preserved in Denmark. Years earlier, during his administraiton, President ANDREW JACKSON had made a gift of these works to the National Museum in Denmark.

KING, CLARENCE. *(1842–1901).* Explorer; scholar.

Clarence King of Newport, Rhode Island, was a member of the first graduating class of Yale's Sheffield Scientific School in 1862, whereupon he joined Josiah Whitney's Geological Survey of California. In 1867, although a 25-year-old civilian without a Civil War record, he was given command of his own survey by the War Department, the U.S. Geological Exploration of the Fortieth Parallel, from 1867 to 1879. The photograher TIMOTHY O'SULLIVAN participated in the early stages. In addition to exploration and mapping for the Army Corps of Engineers, King had the secret assignment of reconnoitering Indians of the Great Basin with whom he had numerous contacts, especially Paiutes and Shoshones, producing a photographic record of them as well as compiling ethnographic information. In 1879, when his survey and those under GEORGE WHEELER, FERDINAND V. HAYDEN, and JOHN WESLEY POWELL were merged into the U.S. Geological Survey, King was made the first director. He resigned the next year, however, and was succeeded by Powell. Also a writer, King produced a series of essays about mountaineering.

KING PAYNE. See PAYNE.

KING PHILIP. See PHILIP.

KINGSBURY, CYRUS. (Nashoba Tubikli; "limping wolf.") *(1786–1870).* Missionary; educator.

Cyrus Kingsbury, a native of Alstead, New Hampshire, attended Brown University, graduating in 1812. Three years later he completed his religious training at Andover Theological Seminary and was subsequently ordained a missionary of the Presbyterian church at Ipswich, Massachusetts.

In 1816, Kingsbury was active as a missionary in Tennessee and Virginia. In September of that year, he was sent by the American Board of Commissioners for Foreign Missions, an interdenominational organization run by the Presbyterian and Congregational churches, as a missionary to the Cherokees. He attended a grand council of the Cherokees in October, then subsequently moved to the Cherokee lands, where he established the mission station and school at Brainerd, naming it after DAVID BRAINERD and David's brother John. In June 1818, Kingsbury also established Eliot, a mission to the Choctaws named in honor of the missionary JOHN ELIOT. In 1820, he established his Choctaw mission station, Mayhew, in honor of THOMAS MAYHEW, JR., near present-day Columbus, Mississippi. He was aided among the Choctaws by tribal leader DAVID FOLSOM.

Kingsbury also was an innovator in Indian education techniques. He adopted the highly organized Lancastrian System of education created by the Englishman Joseph Lancaster and Andrew Bell, which facilitated the teaching of reading and other basic skills with a minimum of teachers and books. He also established the first Indian manual-labor boarding schools. Kingsbury advocated teaching Indian students in their native languages, rather than English, to avoid creating a cultural gulf between them and their parents.

When the federal government negotiated the removal of the Choctaws at the Dancing Rabbit Creek Council of 1830, Kingsbury attended on behalf of the tribe. Yet federal officials asked Kingsbury to leave the meeting, fearing his presence would incite dissension among the three main branches of the tribe.

Starting in 1834, Kingsbury toured the lands of the Osage, Creek, and Cherokee tribes, and, in 1836, he reestablished his mission to the newly resettled Choctaws in the southeastern Indian Territory.

In 1859, the American Board of Commissioners for Foreign Missions voted to eliminate Kingsbury's mission and to give him a pension in recognition of his 50 years of work among the Cherokees and Choctaws. Kingsbury declined the pension and arranged to continue his missionary work among the Choctaws under the sponsorship of the Prudential Committee of the Presbyterian Church. He was a lifelong associate of missionary CYRUS BYINGTON, who also ministered to the Choctaws.

KINO, EUSEBIO FRANCISCO (Eusebio Francesco Chino or Chini). *(ca. 1645–1711).* Explorer; missionary; reformer.

Born in Segno, Italy, Eusebio Francisco Kino was educated by Jesuits in Germany, becoming skilled in mathematics and astronomy. In 1665, he was ordained a priest and missionary.

In 1681, Kino traveled in New Spain, where two years later, he received an appointment as royal cosmographer on a colonizing expedition to Baja (Lower) California with Admiral Isidoro de Atondo y Antillon. Kino's explorations and charts of the region established that California was not an island, as had been believed. The colony was eventually abandoned.

In 1687, Kino established a mission to the Pima Indians in what the Spanish called Pima Alteria, now northern Mexico and southern Arizona. At his settlement, known as Nuestra Senora de Los Dolares, he educated the Pimas in ways to improve and diversify their agricultural output. He also introduced livestock to the Indians, including horses, cattle, and sheep.

With Indian guides, Kino undertook more than 50 expeditions, exploring the Gila, Colorado, and Rio Grande rivers for their sources. During an expedition in 1701–02, he made the earliest European contact with the Yumas on the Colorado River in southeastern California. From 1687 to 1711, he established 24 missions throughout the region. Kino also lobbied authorities against policies allowing Indians to be enslaved as laborers in the silver mines of northern Mexico.

Kino wrote the autobiographical *Favores celestiales*, published in 1708.

KINTPUASH. See CAPTAIN JACK.

KIRKLAND, SAMUEL. *(1741–1808)*. Missionary; Indian agent.

Samuel was born in Norwich, Connecticut, the son of Daniel Kirtland, a minister and his wife Mary Perkins Kirtland. He began his formal education at ELEAZAR WHEELOCK's Moor's Indian Charity School in Connecticut, where he became friends with the Mohawk JOSEPH BRANT. In 1762, he entered the College of New Jersey (later called Princeton) as a sophomore. He eventually changed the spelling of his family name to Kirkland.

In 1764, before completing his studies, Kirkland departed New Jersey to do missionary work among the Iroquois of central New York. He traveled with two Seneca guides first to a village of Oneidas, then to a great council of Iroquois at Onondaga, near present-day Syracuse, New York. He spent a year among the Senecas, learning their language. Princeton granted Kirkland a degree *in absentia* in June 1765. He then returned to study with Wheelock at Lebanon, Connecticut, where he was ordained a Congregational minister.

In 1766, Kirkland was comissioned a missionary to the Senecas by the Society in Scotland for Propagating Christian Knowledge, but instead traveled to the Oneida settlement at Kanonwalohule in central New York, from where he also extended his missionary work to the Tuscaroras. He won some converts among the Oneidas, including SKENANDOA.

In his Christianizing efforts, Kirkland refrained from imposing Western European values on the Indians until they requested changes themselves. Nor did he seek to acquire land from the Indians in the name of the church, as was the practice among other missionaries. His aim was to reach the Indians spiritually, without disrupting their indigenous culture. When the Oneidas later requested help in improving their economic condition, Kirkland provided assistance in establishing a sawmill, a gristmill, a blacksmith shop, and a meetinghouse. He also instructed the Indians in techniques to expand and diversify their agricultural output.

In 1774, as a government Indian agent, Kirkland was instrumental in keeping the Iroquois from joining the Shawnees under CORNSTALK in Lord DUNMORE's War. The next year, he also managed to keep the Oneidas and Tuscaroras on the side of the Patriots in the American Revolution, dissuading them from siding with the British as the other Iroquois tribes had done under the Mohawk Joseph Brant and the Seneca CORNPLANTER. Kirkland served as chaplain to Continental army troops at Fort Schuyler near present-day Utica, New York.

In the aftermath of the American Revolution, the Oneidas were confined to a reservation near their homelands in central New York, and Kirkland participated in treaty negotiations on their behalf. In 1788, he was awarded 5,000 acres of land, formerly Oneida lands near Clinton, New York, by the New York state government in recognition for his efforts during the war. He used it as a base of operation for his continued missionary work among the Oneidas. In 1793, with Alexander Hamilton's help, Kirkland established the Hamilton Oneida Academy on his land, where literate Iroquois studied classics and Calvinist theology. White students were attracted to this institution, which, in 1812, was chartered as Hamilton College.

Kirkland was active in keeping the Iroquois neutral in the rebellion of the tribes of the Old Northwest, LITTLE TURTLE's War of 1790–94.

Kirkland lost the financial support of the Society in Scotland for Propagating Christian Knowledge in 1797. Despite financial difficulties and ill health, he carried on his evangelical work among the Oneidas.

KIT CARSON. See CARSON, CHRISTOPHER HOUSTON.

KNOX, HENRY. *(1750–1806)*. Secretary of War.

Henry Knox, born in Boston, was a close associate of GEORGE WASHINGTON. He served in the Continental army, providing artillery support against the British at Boston and in other engagements of the Americna Revolution. He became a brigadier general in 1776 and a major general two years later.

In 1783, Knox succeeded Washington as commander of the army. In 1785, he became secretary of War under the Articles of Confederation, then, in 1789, under the Constitution. In this position, which he held until 1794, he was responsible for formulating the original federal Indian policy.

By the terms of the 1783 Treaty of Paris, ending the Revolutionary War, the United States acquired vast additional territory from England, stretching to the Mississippi River. Yet the new government had to resolve tribal claims to the region. Knox was strongly opposed to a proposal to take these lands by right of conquest, believing that the Indians had a prior and just claim to this territory. Instead, he promulgated the 1789 Fort Harmar Treaties, under which the Iroquois League, as well as the tribes of the Old Northwest Territory, extinguished their claims to these lands in exchange for payment in goods by the federal government. Earlier, in 1785, the Treaties of Hopewell had made similar arrangements with the Creek, Cherokee, Chickasaw, and Choctaw tribes. Knox's negotiations with the Southeast tribes were complicated by conflicting treaties initiated by the Virginia, Georgia, and North Carolina state governments.

Knox was an early advocate of allotting parcels of tribal land to individual Indians. Turning Indians into private landowners, he believed, would assimilate them into white culture. The surplus Indian lands could then be opened for settlement to whites without major conflicts. Under Knox, the first federal laws regulating trade and the purchase of Indian lands were enacted. All acquisitions of Indian lands had to be in the context of federal treaties, and the military was assigned the role of protecting the Indians from the unlawful encroachment of white settlers into their territory. In addition, Knox's Indian policy provided for regulation and licensing of frontier traders.

In 1796, following his return to private life, Knox helped establish the Indian agent system. Upon his recommendaton, Washington appointed the first civilian federal Indian agent, BENJAMIN HAWKINS, who was assigned as Creek agent and superintendent of Southern Indians.

Knox lived out his last years on his estate near present-day Thomaston, Maine, where he died on swallowing a chicken bone.

KONKAPOT (Captain Konkapot, Captain John).
Mahican-Stockbridge. (ca. 1700–ca. 1775). Ally of British in the French and Indian Wars; chief of Stockbridge Indians.

The captital and largest village of the Algonquian-speaking Mahicans was originally Schodac near present-day Albany, New York. In 1664, because of pressure by the Mohawks from the west, the Mahican Confederacy moved their council fire to Westenhuck in the Housatonic Valley of western Massachusetts among the Housatonic band. In 1724, the tribe ceded the Housatonic Valley to the British. Konkapot, one of the signers of this treaty, maintained his friendship with the British and supported them against the French in the French and Indian Wars. In 1734, he was granted a captain's commission.

In 1736, JOHN SERGEANT founded a Calvinist mission, known as Stockbridge, which became the home of the displaced Algonquian bands of the region. In 1744, Konkapot became chief of the Stockbridge Indians, as they were now called. From 1750 to 1757, the missionary JONATHAN EDWARDS worked among them, becoming a friend of Konkapot, who had been baptized by the name John.

The Stockbridges, along with the Brotherton Indians (a community in eastern New York near Stockbridge, consisting of other displaced Mahicans and Algonquians), relocated to New York under SAMSON OCCUM in 1786, and to Wisconsin under JOHN W. QUINNEY in 1822. They were granted lands and eventually merged with the Munsee band of Delawares. Some Mahican descendants still live in Massachusetts and Connecticut, however.

KURZ, RUDOLPH FRIEDRICH (Rudolph Friederich Kurz). *(1818–1871).* Artist; linguist.

In 1846, Swiss artist Rudolph Friedrich Kurz arrived in New Orleans, intent on recording images of the Indians, who he thought embodied the ideal of unspoiled man. Originally, Kurz had planned to travel to the Southwest, at that time a part of Mexico, but, because of the Mexican War, traveled up the Mississippi and Missouri rivers to the Northern Plains. Along the way he made watercolors and drawings of Choctaws, Foxes, Kickapoos, Otos, and Potawatomis.

Among the Iowa Indians, Kurz thought he found the epitome of the ideal man living unencumbered by civilization, mainly because the Iowas he met that summer wore only breechcloths. In winter 1849–50, Kurz became friends with the Iowa chief Kirutsche and soon after married the chief's daughter Witthoe. His marriage ended after a few weeks when Witthoe, dissatisfied with living away from her tribe, left Kurz and moved back to her people.

In June–July 1851, Kurz continued northward, heading up the Missouri to Fort Berthold (North Dakota), where he worked for a time as a clerk to fur trader James Kipp. He continued to make drawings and watercolors of the Indians, now primarily Mandans and Hidatsas. Yet the Indians feared him. Earlier, in the 1830s, artists GEORGE CATLIN and KARL BODMER had visited the Fort Berthold area also to create pictures of the Indians. Soon after their visits, epidemics took a heavy toll on the Indian population.

In September 1851, fearing for his safety, Kurz moved to Fort Union (near the Montana border), where he made secret sketches of the Assiniboines, Crows, Crees, and Blackfeet. He remained there until April 1852, returning to St. Louis in May, then continuing on to Switzerland to make full use of his Indian experiences in his work.

His journal, recounting his life among the Indians along the frontier, was published by the Smithsonian Institution in 1937: *Journal of Rudolph Friederich Kurz: An Account of His Experiences among Fur Traders and American Indians on the Mississippi and Upper Missouri Rivers during the Years 1846 to 1852.* Kurz also produced a dictionary of the Mandan language.

KUTSHAMAKIN (Cutshamaquin, Cutchamekin).
Massachuset. (fl. 1630s–1640s). Christian convert;
interpreter.

At the time of English settlement in the Boston area
of the Massachusetts Bay Colony during the 1630s, Kutshamakin was sachem of the Massachuset band living
in the area of present-day Dorchester, Sudbury, and
Milton, Massachusetts. His people were the first Indians
preached to by JOHN ELIOT. At first wary of the British,
Kutshamakin was eventually converted to Christianity,
becoming one of the so-called Praying Indians and serving as an interpreter for Eliot and colonial officials. He
also fought on the side of the colonists in the Pequot War
of 1636–37, and signed the treaties of 1643 and 1645.

L

LACOMBE, ALBERT (The Man of Good Heart).
(1827–1916). Missionary; peacemaker;
linguist.

Born in Quebec, Albert Lacombe studied to be a priest at L'Assomption College and was ordained into the Oblate order in 1849. After time in Pembina in what is now North Dakota, he accompanied a Hudson's Bay Company expedition as far as Edmonton in present-day Alberta, where he founded the first Canadian school west of Manitoba.

As a traveling missionary for seven years, he also ministered at Lac Ste. Anne, St. Albert, and St. Paul-des-Cris, among Metis, Crees, and Blackfeet. His efforts led to the Canadian government's regulation of the destructive liquor trade to the Indians.

In 1872, Lacombe began service as priest at St. Mary's parish in Winnipeg, Manitoba, returned to Alberta 10 years later as priest of the St. Mary's parish of Calgary, and also ministered out of Fort Macleod.

Lacombe, who probably had a trace of Indian blood, was trusted by the various tribes, who called him The Man of Good Heart. He acted as diplomat for the government in negotiations with the Blackfoot chief CROWFOOT and other Plains Indian leaders. His influence helped prevent the majority of western bands from joining the Second RIEL Rebellion of 1885. In 1898, he traveled north with government officials to the Peace River and Athabasca districts to negotiate treaties with Athapascan bands.

Lacombe produced a dictionary and grammar of the Crees' Algonquian language, published in 1874.

LA DEMOISELLE. See OLD BRITON.

Marquis de Lafayette. *Courtesy of Library of Congress.*

LAFAYETTE, MARIE JOSEPH PAUL YVES ROCH GILBERT DU MOTIER, MARQUIS DE.
(1757–1834). French officer in the American Revolution; statesman.

The Marquis de Lafayette was born at Auvergne, France, to a wealthy French family. He entered the

190

French army in 1771, and, in 1776, withdrew to volunteer his assistance to Patriot forces in the American Revolution. He was commissioned a major general in the Continental army and was involved in major campaigns in the mid-Atlantic region, including the Battle of the Brandywine in Pennsylvania, in which he was wounded. In 1779–80, he returned to France to negotiate French aid for the Patriot effort.

In addition to leading and training the troops, Lafayette designed forts for the defense of frontier settlements against British and Indian attacks. Among these posts was Fort Alden, the stockade at Cherry Valley, New York, which was the scene of an attack by Tories under WALTER BUTLER and Iroquois under JOSEPH BRANT on November 11, 1778, in which every outlying building was destroyed. Thirty-two civilians, unable to reach the safety of the fort, were killed. Yet Lafayette's palisaded fortification withstood the combined Tory and Indian forces.

Lafayette, who obtained a divisional command, served with Patriot forces until the surrender of Cornwallis at Yorktown, Pennsylvania, in 1781, returning to France the next year. During a six-month visit to America in 1784 following the war, he was welcomed as a hero.

Lafayette became an active supporter and political leader of the French Revolution. Supporting a constitutional monarchy, he fled his enemies in the revolutionary government, seeking refuge in Austria, where he was held captive for five years, 1792–97. Although liberated by Napoleon, Lafayette played no active role in his regime, but, in 1815, was instrumental in obtaining Napoleon's abdication.

In 1824–25, Lafayette again visited America. While in Washington, D.C., he met with Choctaw leader PUSHMATAHA just before his death, as well as other Indian notables. Lafayette also toured frontier posts on the Arkansas and Missouri rivers, accompanied by BENJAMIN DE BONNEVILLE.

Upon his return to France, Lafayette again took part in French politics. In the late 1820s, when a touring party of Osages, including MOHONGO, was abandoned by the entrepreneur who had brought them to France, Lafayette arranged for their return passage to North America.

LAFITAU, JOSEPH FRANCOIS. (1681–1746). Historian; missionary.

French-born Joseph Francois Lafitau was sent to New France by his Jesuit superiors in 1713 as a missionary to the Mohawks at the village of Kahnawake (Caughnawaga), south of Montreal. He stayed among them five years and produced a study of their culture in an attempt to understand earlier cultures: *Moeurs des Sauvage Ameriquains, Comparees aux Moeurs des Premiers Temps,* published in Paris in four volumes in 1724. His writing influenced the historian FRANCIS PARKMAN. Lafitau was also the discoverer of ginseng in North America.

LA FLESCHE, FRANCIS (Zhogaxe, "woodworker"). *Mixed Omaha. (1857–1932).* Anthropologist; writer. Half-brother of SUSAN LA FLESCHE and SUSETTE LA FLESCHE.

Francis La Flesche attended the Presbyterian mission school in Bellevue, Nebraska, on the Omaja Reservation. The son of the Omaha chief JOSEPH LA FLESCHE (Inshtamaza) and Elizabeth Esau (Tainne), he also learned the traditional customs of his tribe, participating in buffalo hunts and ceremonials. With his sister Susette, he became involved in the Poncas' struggle to return to Nebraska from the Indian Territory.

In 1879–80, Francis accompanied Chief STANDING BEAR, the journalist THOMAS HENRY TIBBLES, and Susette on a lecture tour of eastern cities, serving as interpreter. In 1881, he was offered a post in the Bureau of Indian Affairs as an interpreter and advisor. He attended the National University Law School, graduating in 1892.

While living in Washington, D.C., La Flesche began a collaboration with the anthropologist ALICE CUNNINGHAM FLETCHER on studies of Omaha and Osage culture. Among their shared studies were: *A Study of Omaha Music* (1893) and *The Omaha Tribe* (1911). In 1910, La Flesche joined the Bureau of American Ethnology. He also wrote *Middle Five: Indian Boys at School* (1900) and created an opera *Da-o-ma* (1912). *A Dictionary of the Osage Language* (1932) was his final work.

LA FLESCHE, JOSEPH (Inshtamaza, Estamaza, Iron Eye). *Mixed Omaha. (ca. 1818–1888).* Principal chief; leader of Progressive Party; research informant.

Joseph La Flesche was the son of a French fur trader and an Omaha (or possibly Ponca) woman. As a young man, he worked as a trade to the Omahas, like his father. In 1853, he succeeded the second Big Elk as head chief, who had succeeded his father, the first BIG ELK, 10 years before.

Joseph La Flesche had several wives and 10 children, some of them famous. With the part-Iowa Mary Gale (Hinnuaganun), he had five children, including SUSETTE LA FLESCHE (Bright Eyes) and SUSAN LA FLESCHE. By Elizabeth Esau (Tainne), he also had five children, including FRANCIS LA FLESCHE.

Leader of the tribe's Progressive Party, La Flesche embraced Christianity as taught by the Presbyterian missionaries on the Omaha Reservation in Nebraska. He encouraged the building of roads on the reservation and the division of lands into lots for individual farming. He also abandoned the traditional Omaha earthlodge to raise his children in a two-story frame house. Believing his children should be assimilated into white culture, he provided education for them in white-run institutions. Yet he taught them traditional customs as well and a sense of pride in their Indian background. He served as an informant for anthropologists JAMES OWEN DORSEY and ALICE CUNNINGHAM FLETCHER.

LA FLESCHE, SUSAN (Susan La Flesche Picotte).

Mixed Omaha. (1865–1915). First female Indian physician; reformer. Sister of FRANCIS LA FLESCHE and SUSETTE LA FLESCHE.

Susan La Flesche was the daughter of the Omaha chief JOSEPH LA FLESCHE (Inshtamaza) and the part-Iowa Mary Gale (Hinnuaganun). She was born in Nebraska and studied with both Presbyterian and Quaker missionaries. In 1879–82, she attended the Elizabeth Institute for Young Ladies in New Jersey; in 1884–86, the Hampton Institute in Virginia; and, in 1886–89, the Women's Medical College of Pennsylvania.

During the next five years, La Flesche served as the government reservation doctor for the Omahas, seeing hundreds of patients and helping stem influenza, dysentery, cholera, conjunctivitis, typhoid, and tuberculosis, all chronic to the reservation. Those patients who could not come to her office, she reached on foot or in a buggy. Starting in 1891, La Flesche also served as the medical missionary to her tribe, sponsored by the Women's National Indian Association, and became a temperance speaker.

In 1894, La Flesche married Henri Picotte, a mixed French-Sioux, and began a practice for both Indians and whites in Bancroft, Nebraska. After her husband's death in 1905, she worked as a missionary at the Blackbird Hills Presbyterian Church in addition to her medical practice, and, in 1906, moved to Walthill, Nebraska. In 1910, she traveled to Washington, D.C, to lobby against those government regulations which made it difficult for tribal members to lease their lands and receive payment.

LA FLESCHE, SUSETTE (Inshtatheumba, Inshta Theaumba; Bright Eyes; Yosette La Flesche Tibbles).

Mixed Omaha. (1854–1903). Lecturer; writer; reformer; painter and illustrator. Sister of FRANCIS LA FLESCHE and SUSAN LA FLESCHE.

Susette La Flesche, or more familiarly Josette, the daughter of the half-French Omaha chief JOSEPH LA FLESCHE (Inshtamaza) and the part-Iowa Mary Gale (Hinnuaganun), attended the Presbyterian mission school on the Omaha Reservation, then the Elizabeth Institute for Young Ladies in New Jersey. She later studied art at the University of Nebraska.

Accompanying her father to the Indian Territory, La Flesche performed volunteer nursing work among the Poncas who had been relocated from Nebraska in 1877–78. When Chief STANDING BEAR led his band back to their homeland in 1879, she assisted their cause as an interpreter. Along with THOMAS HENRY TIBBLES, a minister and journalist for the *Omaha Herald*, who wrote about Standing Bear, she became active in working for the Ponca right to remain in Nebraska. Their work led a group of Nebraskans to volunteer their services to the Poncas.

Susette La Flesche and her brother Francis accompanied Standing Bear and Tibbles on a tour of eastern cities in 1879–80. For public appearances, Susette used the name of Bright Eyes. Their visit to Boston led to the formation of an Indian Citizenship Committee. In 1881, La Flesche spoke before the Association for the Advancement of Women, delivering a paper entitled "The Position, Occupation, and Culture of Indian Women." She was the co-author with Standing Bear of *Ploughed Under; the Story of an Indian Chief* (1882). That same year, she married Tibbles.

La Flesche and her husband continued their public appearances, visiting England and Scotland in 1886–87. In their lectures, they described Omaha and Ponca reservation conditions and argued against removal and in favor of assimilation. The couple lived in Washington, D.C., into the 1890s, appearing before Congress on numerous occasions. They eventually returned to Lincoln, Nebraska, where Susette died.

LA FRAMBOISE, JOSETTE. *Mixed Potawatomi. (fl. mid-1800s).* Sister-in-law of President Franklin Pierce.

Josette La Framboise was the daughter of the French Canadian Alexander La Framboise of Milwaukee, Wisconsin, and his French-Chippewa wife Madiline. In 1817, she married the commander of Fort Mackinac, Michigan, Captain Benjamin Pierce. His brother Franklin Pierce served as president from 1853 to 1857. Because of her marriage and position, Josette was known to both Michigan and Washington, D.C., society circles and was frequently consulted on Indian issues.

LAHONTAN, LOUIS ARMAND DE LOM D'ARCE, BARON DE (Baron de La Hontan). *(ca. 1666–1715).* Explorer; writer; soldier.

Baron de Lahontan first arrived in Montreal in 1683, a 17-year-old member of a company of French marines. He remained in Canada for the next 10 years, participating in campaigns against the Iroquois and undertaking explorations into the area west of present-day Mackinac, Michigan, where he had contact with Indian tribes, the identity of which is uncertain. In 1689, he was back in Montreal.

Deserting the army, Lahontan returned to Europe in 1693. In Holland, in 1703, his account of his explorations, *New Voyages in North America*, was published, including one of the earliest descriptions of Plains Indians on a buffalo hunt. In a supplementary volume, Lahontan recorded conversations with an Indian chief supposedly encountered in his western journeys. Lahontan's dialogues were fictional and his descriptions of Indian life may have been based on secondhand reports. Yet his account influenced other writers, contributing to the Noble Savage concept, as embodied in the works of JEAN JACQUES ROUSSEAU and JAMES FENIMORE COOPER.

LALEMANT, JEROME. *(1593–1673).* Missionary; scholar.

Jerome Lalement was born in Paris, France, and following his studies with the Jesuits, he was ordained a missionary priest. In 1638, he arrived in French Canada and became superior of the Jesuit mission to the Hurons. In 1645, he was named chief administrator of all the Jesuits in Canada, a post his brother Charles Lalement had held in 1634–39. When the Iroquois invaded Huronia in 1649, they destroyed many Jesuit outposts, and a number of Jesuit missionaries were killed, including JEAN DE BREBEUF and Lalemant's own nephew, Gabriel Lalement.

In 1656, Lalemant returned to France, where he taught at the Jesuit college at La Fleche. In 1659, he was back in Canada, again serving as superior of the Jesuit missions. He remained in this office for the next six years, during which he supervised the resettlement of Hurons displaced by the war with the Iroquois. Lalement was known as an authority on Indian ceremonies and religion. He had contact in this regard with French mystic and writer MARIE GUYART (Marie de l'Incarnation).

LAME DEER (Tahca Ushte). *Miniconjou Sioux.* *(d. 1877).* Principal chief; leader in the Sioux Wars of the 1860s–70s.

Lame Deer was principal chief of the Miniconjous during the War for the BOZEMAN Trail in 1866–68 and the War for the Black Hills in 1876–77. He was present at the Battle of the Rosebud and at Little Bighorn in June 1876.

About one year later, troops under Colonel NELSON A. MILES tracked Lame Deer's band to Muddy Creek, a tributary of the Rosebud in Montana. The Miniconjou HUMP, who had previously surrendered, accompanied the soldiers in order to try to induce his people to surrender in what he now considered a hopeless cause after numerous Indian defeats and SITTING BULL's retreat to Canada.

In the Battle of Lame Deer (or the Battle of Muddy Creek), one of the last engagements of the Sioux Wars, the cavalry charged the Miniconjou camp at dawn on May 7, 1877. Many of the surprised Indians fled up a hillside rising from the creek. Hump located Lame Deer and the war chief Iron Star and convinced them to surrender. Placing his rifle on the ground, Lame Deer called out "friend, friend" to demonstrate his intentions and shook General Miles's hand. At that moment, however, a scout rode up with his gun pointed at them and, as some accounts relate, fired at Lame Deer. Lame Deer managed to grab his rifle and killed a soldier behind Miles. The Miniconjou chief then attempted to flee up the slope, but was shot down; Iron Star was shot moments later. Twelve other Indians were killed, as well as three more soldiers. Many Minconjous surrendered. But Lame Deer's son, Fast Bull, and several others managed to escape and continued to elude Miles's men through the summer, finally turning themselves in and settling on the Cheyenne River Reservation in South Dakota.

Lame Deer's great-grandson, also known as Lame Deer or John Fire, wrote a book about his experiences as a medicine man, called *Lame Deer, Seeker of Visions* (1972), with Richard Erdoes. (See also RED CLOUD; SITTING BULL.)

LANGLADE, CHARLES (Charles-Michel Mouet, Sieur Langlade). *Mixed Ottawa. (1729–ca. 1800).* French officer in the French and Indian Wars.

The son of a French noble and trader who had married an Ottawa woman, Charles Langlade grew up learning the ways of both whites and Indians. Like his father, he married an Ottawa woman, with whom he was one of the earliest settlers at Green Bay, becoming known as the "Father of Wisconsin." Before and during the French and Indian Wars of 1754–63, Langlade headed warriors from the Great Lakes region— mostly Ottawas, Chippewas, and Potawatomis—in support of the French. His men defeated the British ally OLD BRITON at Pickawillany, Ohio, in June 1752, and participated in the defeat of General EDWARD BRADDOCK's column as it advanced on Fort Duquesne (present-day Pittsburgh) in July 1755. (See also OLD BRITON.)

LAPPAWINZE ("gathering provisions"). *Delaware. (b. ca. 1700).* Signer of the Walking Purchase.

In 1737, Lappawinze was one of 12 chiefs who met with Pennsylvania proprietor Thomas Penn, WILLIAM PENN's son; Provincial Secretary JAMES LOGAN; CONRAD WEISER; and other white officials in Philadelphia to sign a treaty that confirmed an earlier agreement of 1686, granting to the whites lands extending from the forks of the Lehigh and Delaware rivers as far as a man could walk in a day and a half. Penn and Logan pressured the tribal representatives into agreeing to a retracing of the tract.

Rather than adhering to the Indian custom of slowly pacing out the distance and stopping to rest along the way, the officials had a path cut inland and hired trained runners. The three athletes traveled the first 30 miles in six hours. Two dropped out, but the third, Edward Marshall, spent a short night in Lappawinze's village and continued on at a furious pace, convering 66.5 miles across the Kittatinny Ridge into the Poconos. Then Penn and Logan ordered that the returning line be laid out at a right angle to the Delaware River rather than to the river's closest point, thus claiming 1,200 square miles of Delaware Indian territory.

Lappawinze and other Delawares, including Chief TEEDYUSCUNG, insisted that the whites' methods amounted to fraud. The officials responded by calling in the Iroquois to drive the Delawares off the land. As a result, many Delaware warriors joined the French in the subsequent French and Indian Wars.

LA SALLE, RENE ROBERT CAVELIER, SIEUR DE. *(1643–1687).* Explorer; trader.

Rene Robert Cavelier, Sieur de la Salle, from a prominent family of the village of Rouen in France's Normandy region, originally planned a career in the priesthood and studied under the Jesuits. After nine years, however, he was deemed mentally unfit for the order and was released from his minor vows.

In 1666, La Salle traveled to French Canada and, through family connections, acquired a royal land patent near Montreal, becoming involved in the fur trade with Indians. From visiting Senecas, he heard reports of a great river to the west that flowed to the sea. With an interest in extending trade to unknown tribes in the interior and a desire to discover a water route through North America to the Pacific, La Salle decided to venture into the uncharted lands south and west of New France. Meanwhile, he studied both Algonquian and Iroquoian languages.

La Salle falsely claimed to be fluent in the Iroquoian language, and, in 1689, joined a Sulpitian missionary expedition to the Senecas as an interpreter. Along with two missionaries, he reached the Seneca village at present-day Victor, New York, southeast of modern Rochester, where La Salle had his first contact with an Indian from one of the Ohio Valley tribes, brought to the Seneca village as a captive. He attempted to ransom the Ohio Indian from the Senecas, who declined the offer and killed the captive. It soon became apparent that La Salle had exaggerated his Iroquoian-language skills, and the Sulpitian missionaries departed the Seneca village without him. Instead of returning to Montreal, La Salle headed east to the Iroquois League's headquarters at Onondaga near present-day Syracuse, New York, where he arranged for an Indian guide. He then headed west and south into the upper Ohio valley, reaching the falls of the Ohio River, near present-day Louisville, Kentucky.

Returning to Montreal in 1670, La Salle spent the next few years seeking government and church support for a major expedition to find a river route to the sea. In 1673, LOUIS DE BUADE, COMTE DE FRONTENAC made him commandant of Fort Frontenac (present-day Kingston, Ontario). The next year, La Salle returned to France and received a patent of nobility, obtaining backing for the establishment of a chain of fur-trading posts between the Great Lakes and the Mississippi, which he founded in the western Lake Ontario region in 1674–77. During these years, he returned to France on several occasions.

In 1678, with a company that included Father LOUIS HENNEPIN and HENRI DE TONTI, La Salle explored the Lake Ontario–Niagara Falls region, then headed south to the Ohio River, as far as present-day Louisville, Kentucky.

In 1679, La Salle's ship, the *Griffon*, built by Tonti, the first sailing ship west of Lake Ontario, left its base, near present-day Buffalo, New York, and sailed west to Green Bay, on the western shore of Lake Michigan. La Salle established an outpost there, then proceeded on land, erecting Fort Miami on Lake Michigan (present-day St. Joseph, Michigan) and Fort Crevecoeur on the Illinois River (near present-day Peoria, Illinois). From this latter post, La Salle sent Hennepin and Michel Aco on an expedition to the upper Mississippi River, during which they were captured by Sioux.

La Salle then returned to Fort Frontenac for supplies, leaving Tonti in charge. Tonti's party abandoned Fort Crevecoeur, however, because of attacks by invading Iroquois. Returning to find the post empty, La Salle set out to find Tonti. He and Tonti were reunited at Mackinac Island, located in the strait between Lake Michigan and Lake Huron. During this period, La Salle also arranged for an alliance of the French, Illinois, and Miamis against the Iroquois.

La Salle, Tonti, Father Zenobe Membre, and a small party then explored the upper Mississippi River, and, in 1681–82, followed the river all the way to the Mississippi Delta. La Salle named the territory around the river Louisiana, in honor of King Louis XIV, and claimed it for France.

While Tonti stayed among the Illinois and built Fort St. Louis near present-day Ottawa, Illinois, La Salle returned north to Canada. In 1683, he was back in France, where he was named viceroy of North America and obtained financial support for an expedition to the Gulf of Mexico that was to be the precursor to a proposed conquest of Mexico. Believing that the mouth of the Mississippi was west of its true location, La Salle's backers were attracted to the possibility of appropriating northern Mexico's silver mines.

La Salle sailed from France to the Gulf Coast with four ships of colonists, but was unable to locate the Mississippi's outlet. In 1684, three of the ships landed at Matagorda Bay near present-day Houston, Texas, where La Salle oversaw the building of Fort St. Louis.

La Salle headed two fruitless expeditions overland into south-central Texas in search of the Mississippi Delta. In 1687, with supplies running out, he led a third expedition in search of the river and the Illinois settlements he had found earlier. But somewhere in east Texas, his men rose up in mutiny and killed him.

La Salle's expeditions into the Great Lakes and Mississippi Valley constituted the first white contact with many tribes of the central and southern United States.

LAS CASAS, BARTOLOME DE (Bartholme or Bartholomew de las Casas). *(1474–1566)*. Reformer; historian; missionary.

Born in Seville, Spain, Bartolome de las Casas emigrated with his father to the Caribbean island of Hispaniola in 1502. He became a priest eight years later, the first Catholic to be consecrated in the Americas. In 1512, he became a missionary to the Arawak Indians of Cuba. In 1520–21, he attempted without success to organize a modern Indian colony. In 1523, he joined the Dominican order.

Las Casas wrote numerous tracts critical of Spanish treatment of Indians, including A Relation of the First Voyages and Discoveries Made by the Spaniards in America with an Account of their Unparallel'd Cruelties on the Indians (1552). He was often criticized by Spanish churchmen, officials, and soldiers for his views, but won concessions on behalf of the Indians. Most of the New Laws of 1542, abolishing the chattel slavery of the encomienda system under Charles V, were his conception. In 1550–51, he participated in a series of debates with Juan de Sepulveda, a Spanish lawyer, before the Spanish Royal Court. Sepulveda defended exploitation of the Indians while Las Casas argued that Indians should be given the opportunity to accept Western civilization.

Las Casas also lived in Peru, Guatemala, then Mexico, where, in 1544–47, he was bishop of Chiapa. He dedicated much of his time to his *Historia de las Indias*, published in 1875–76.

Las Casas Bewailing the Cruelty of the Spaniards. A hypothetical photogravure (1801). *Courtesy of Library of Congress.*

LAUDONNIERE, RENE GOULAINE DE.
(fl. 1560s). Explorer; colonizer; historian.

In 1562, the French Huguenot leader Rene de Laudonniere accompanied JEAN RIBAULT on a French colonizing attempt in South Carolina. When Ribault returned to Europe, Laudonniere was given command of the colony, of which the artist JACQUES LE MOYNE was a member. The colonists eventually abandoned their first location and, in 1564, established Fort Caroline on the south bank of the St. Johns River in the country of the Timucua Indians, now part of Florida. Indian hostility and food shortages caused ill will and near-mutiny, a situation that was relieved in 1565, when the English privateer John Hawkins visited the colony and sold a ship and food to the French colonists. When Ribault arrived soon after with additional supplies, Laudonniere abandoned his plans to return to France. PEDRO MENENDEZ DE AVILES of the nearby Spanish settlement of St. Augustine then led an attack on Fort Caroline, killing the majority of the French. One of the few survivors, Laudonniere returned to France in 1566, where he later published his Histoire notable de la Floride (1586).

LAWSON, JOHN. *(d. 1711).* Explorer; colonial official; writer.

British-born John Lawson came to the Carolinas in 1700, and, in December of that year, he helped organize an exploratory expedition of six Europeans and four Indians in Charles Town (present-day Charleston, South Carolina). They started by canoe up the Santee River, proceeding northward through what is now North Carolina over an Indian trading path. Along the way, they stayed among different tribes of the Carolina Piedmont, including the Siouan-speaking Waterees, Congarees, Waxhaws, Santees, and Catawbas. The party eventually broke up: One Englishman turned back for Charles Town; the others continued on the trail to Virginia. Near present-day Hillsboro, North Carolina, Lawson cut eastward with an Indian guide to white settlements near the coast, arriving in February 1701, claiming to have walked 1,000 miles.

In his book, *A New Voyage to Carolina* (1709), written mainly to encourage immigration to the North Carolina colony, Lawson described the Indians' use of herbal medicine to treat illness and injury, as well as the use of herbs by woodland Sioux women as a form of birth control. He also expressed a positive view of Indian culture, condemning the dishonest practices of whites in their dealings with Indians. He defended intermarriage, citing it as the most effective means of resolving cultural conflict between the Indians and Europeans.

Lawson was one of the founders of the settlements of Bath and New Bern in North Carolina and was named surveyor general of the North Carolina colony in 1708. Three years later, during the Tuscarora War of 1711–13, while on a survey, Lawson and the Swiss colonizer CHRISTOPH VON GRAFFENRIED were captured by the Indians under Chief HANCOCK. The Tuscaroras released Graffenried but tried Lawson as a criminal under tribal law, perhaps for the surveyor's role in white encroachment on Indian lands, finding him guilty and executing him. The ensuing conflict resulted in the expulsion of the Tuscaroras from North Carolina and their exodus to New York, where they joined the Iroquois League. (See also HANCOCK.)

LAWTON, HENRY WARE. *(1843–1899).* Army officer in the Red River War of 1874–75, and the Apache Wars.

Originally from the Toledo, Ohio, area, Henry W. Lawton was raised in Fort Wayne, Indiana. He left Fort Wayne Episcopal Methodist College in 1861 to fight in the Civil War, soon becoming a lieutenant in the 30th Indiana Regiment. He was awarded the Congressional Medal of Honor for his service in an engagement near Atlanta, Georgia, in August 1864. By the war's end, he had reached the rank of colonel.

Lawton then attended Harvard Law School, but left in 1867 to serve as lieutenant in the 1st U.S. Infantry, an all-black regiment. In 1871, he was assigned to the 4th Cavalry under the command of Colonel RANALD S. MACKENZIE. He served in this unit as quartermaster in campaigns against QUANAH PARKER's Comanches and other Southern Plains tribes in Texas and in the Indian Territory during the Red River War of 1874–75. He was promoted to the rank of captain in 1879.

In 1886, Lawton was assigned to serve under General NELSON A. MILES in southern Arizona, taking part in the final campaign against GERONIMO that summer. From Fort Huachuca, in southeastern Arizona, he led an army strike force on a 1,300-mile expedition into the Sierra Madre Mountains of northern Mexico in pursuit of Geronimo's band of Chiricahua Apaches; his efforts led to the surrender of Geronimo near Fronteras, Mexico. Lawton and his troops then escorted the Apaches back to the United States, where Geronimo formally surrendered to General Miles at Skeleton Canyon, Arizona, on September 4, 1886.

Two years later, Lawton was promoted to the rank of Major, and subsequently to lieutenant colonel and finally colonel. At the outbreak of the Spanish-American War in 1898, he received appointments as brigadier general and major general of volunteers. He took part in battles against the Spanish in Cuba, later serving as military governor of Santiago, Cuba. In 1899, Lawton was with U.S. forces sent to put down the insurgency in the Philippines, where he was killed.

LAWYER (Aleiya; Hallalhotsoot, Hol-lol-sote-tote, "the talker"). *Nez Perce–Flathead. (1796–1876).* Leader of the Treaty Nez Perces.

Lawyer was the son of Twisted Hair, the Nez Perce chief who welcomed LEWIS and CLARK to his homeland, and his Flathead wife. As a young man, Lawyer followed his father's example, showing friendship to whites, and he worked as a guide and interpreter for explorers and missionaries. Lawyer later became a chief of the Upper Nez Perces living along the Clearwater River in Idaho.

In 1832, Lawyer joined the fur traders JAMES BRIDGER, Milton Sublette, and Nathaniel Wyeth, and their Flathead guides, in a fight against the Gros Ventres known as the Battle of Pierre's Hole, Wyoming. In 1838, he acted as interpreter and teacher for the missionary Asa Smith at Kamiah in northern Idaho and mastered English himself. He henceforth became known among both Indians and whites for his oratorical skills.

At the Walla Walla Council of 1855 in Washington, Lawyer agreed to the treaty terms and land cessions presented by Governor ISAAC STEVENS. He was the only chief who could read and write well enough to sign his name in full rather than with an *X*. After the murder of PEOPEOMOXMOX by soldiers during the Yakima War of 1855–56, Lawyer protected Stevens from attack by warriors seeking revenge.

Lawyer signed a second treaty at the Lapwai Council of 1863, further reducing tribal holdings. His faction, known as the Treaty Nez Perces, was opposed by the Nontreaty Nez Perces, mostly Lower Nez Perces, headed by Old JOSEPH.

In 1868, Lawyer traveled to Washington, D.C., to protest the breaking of treaty terms, and he also wrote numerous letters to officials stating his views. In 1871, he was replaced as principal chief by Jacob. Lawyer died the year before the outbreak of the Nez Perce War of 1877, led by Chief JOSEPH (Young Joseph).

LEAN BEAR (Starved Bear). *Southern Cheyenne.* (d. 1864). Peace chief. Brother of BULL BEAR.

Lean Bear first received historical mention for his involvement in an incident at the Fort Atkinson Council in 1853. At the meeting called by agent THOMAS FITZPATRICK with the Southern Plains tribes near present-day Dodge City, Kansas, Lean Bear took notice of the ring of an officer's wife and grabbed the woman's hand to get a closer look. When she cried out in fear, her husband attacked Lean Bear with a whip. Because of this insult, the Cheyennes threatened warfare and Fitzpatrick had to appease Lean Bear with the gift of a blanket.

In later years, Lean Bear became one of the Cheyenne leaders who strived for peace with whites, as did his close friend BLACK KETTLE. In 1863, he was part of a delegation to Washington, D.C., including TEN BEARS of the Comanches and LONE WOLF of the Kiowas, who met with President ABRAHAM LINCOLN to arrange for a lasting treaty agreement. The delegation also traveled to New York City at the invitation of P. T. Barnum, the entertainer.

The next year, in May, Lean Bear spotted a column of soldiers while on a buffalo hunt—a detachment of troops from the command of Colonel JOHN CHIVINGTON. When the troops moved into battle formation, Lean Bear and another Cheyenne named Star rode forth to state their peaceful intentions. Lean Bear wore a peace medal on his chest and carried papers in his hand signed by Lincoln saying that he was a friend to whites. Nevertheless, Lieutenant George Eayre ordered his men to open fire. Both Cheyennes fell from their horses; the soldiers advanced and shot them again on the ground. Lean Bear's death and the Sand Creek Massacre soon afterward led to increased activity by his brother Bull Bear and other Cheyenne Dog Soldiers in the Cheyenne-Arapaho War (or the Colorado War) of 1864–65 and in later fighting on the Southern Plains.

LEAN ELK. See POKER JOE.

LEATHERLIPS (Shateiaronhia, Shateyaronyah, "two clouds of equal size"). *Wyandot (Huron).* (ca. 1732–1810). Rival of TECUMSEH and TENSKWATAWA.

Leatherlips was a chief of the Ohio Hurons, usually referred to as Wyandots, with a village along the Scioto River. As a friend of the Americans, he aroused the anger of Tecumseh and Tenskwatawa while they were organizing their pro-British alliance of tribes against the United States. They accused him of witchcraft and ordered his execution; another Wyandot chief by the name of Roundhead agreed to carry out the sentence. Leatherlips was informed of the judgment against him in the form of a piece of birch bark with a symbol of a war club, delivered to him by his brother. A number of whites in his village at the time witnessed his death. Leatherlips went to his death willingly, chanting a death song beside his previously dug grave and kneeling to receive the war club's blow. In 1888, a memorial was erected to him on the site.

LEAVENWORTH, HENRY. *(1783–1834).* Army officer.

Born in New Haven, Connecticut, Henry Leavenworth was raised in Vermont and New York. In 1804, he was admitted to the bar in Delhi, New York. He joined the army to take part in the War of 1812, seeing action in engagements at Chippewa Creek and Lundy's Lane in July 1813. By the end of the war, he had reached to the rank of colonel.

Leavenworth served a term in the New York state legislature; however, in 1818, he returned to military service in the 5th Infantry under Colonel Joseph Snelling. The next year, he established Fort Snelling in present-day Minnesota, and, starting in 1821, commanded Fort Atkinson in present-day Nebraska.

In 1823, after WILLIAM HENRY ASHLEY's fur-trading expedition had suffered an attack by a band of Arikara Indians on the upper Missouri in present-day South Dakota, Leavenworth led a punitive expedition against them, the first major military confrontation between federal troops and Plains Indians. His force included 120 regulars, 120 volunteers under fur trader JOSHUA PILCHER, and about 400 Sioux auxiliaries. Leavenworth's assault on the Arikara villages along the upper Missouri drove the Indians from the area, but hostilities with other upper Missouri tribes soon erupted, disrupting travel and trade.

In 1824, as colonel of the 3rd Infantry, Leavenworth was stationed in Green Bay, Wisconsin. Two years later, on the orders of Colonel HENRY ATKINSON, he and Captain STEPHEN WATTS KEARNY founded Jefferson Barracks, south of St. Louis, along with an infantry training school. Then, in 1827, he founded Fort Leavenworth (present-day Leavenworth, Kansas).

In 1834, Leavenworth was made a general and placed in command of the entire southwestern frontier. In June of that year, he commanded the Dragoon Expedition—with Colonel HENRY DODGE's 1st Dragoon Regiment—out of Fort Gibson in present-day Oklahoma, westward, as a peace mission to the Southern Plains tribes. The expedition was beset with illness; Leavenworth himself was stricken with malaria. He died a short time later at a camp on the Washita River. Dodge proceeded to the Wichita Mountains, where he met with tribal leaders in a peace council.

LEDYARD, JOHN. *(1751–1789).* Explorer.

John Ledyard, born in Groton, Connecticut, entered Dartmouth College in 1772, the school established in New Hampshire by missionary ELEAZAR WHEELOCK, where he studied for the ministry alongside Indian students. Ledyard's interest in exploration of the North American interior influenced his decision to leave college after a year. He went to live among the Iroquois of New York, learning their language and customs.

In 1774, Ledyard found work as a common seaman. Traveling to England, he unsuccessfully sought backing for a proposed expedition across the North American continent.

In 1776, as a corporal in the British Royal Marines, Ledyard joined Captain JAMES COOK's expedition to the Pacific. With Cook, he reached Vancouver Island of present-day British Columbia, where he had contact with the Nootka Indians. When Cook sailed north into the Gulf of Alaska and the Aleutian Archipelago, Ledyard was sent along to contact the Russians at their fur-trading settlement on Unalaska Island. He was welcomed by the Russians and had contact with the Aleuts. Ledyard then rejoined Cook's ship and remained with the expedition as it sailed to China and back to London in 1780.

Two years later, in 1782, Ledyard deserted from the British military, spending time in the United States. His book, *A Journal of Captain Cook's Last Voyage to the Pacific Ocean*, published in 1783, contained descriptions of the lucrative fur trade that was waiting to be exploited on the coast of the Pacific Northwest.

For the next few years, Ledyard sought financial backing in America, England, and France for an expedition to the Pacific Northwest. In Paris, THOMAS JEFFERSON, BENJAMIN FRANKLIN, and the MARQUIS DE LAFAYETTE tried to help Ledyard in his endeavor, but to no avail. While in contact with Jefferson in France, Ledyard reportedly related his views that Northwest Coast Indians were physically and culturally unlike the South Pacific islanders, similar instead to the natives of the eastern United States.

Failing to gain support for a seaward trip around Cape Horn, Ledyard next decided to undertake the journey by traveling east across Europe and Asia to the Pacific. With Jefferson's diplomatic help, he secured permission from the Russian government to travel east to Siberia in 1786. From there he intended to sail across the Pacfic to the western shores of America, then travel overland to the Atlantic Coast. For the next year and a half, Ledyard walked across the vast expanse of European and Asiatic Russia. Along the way he sent back dispatches to Jefferson, which included comparisons between the natives of Siberia and the Indians Ledyard had studied in North America.

Ledyard reached Yakutsk in eastern Siberia, 600 miles from Russia's Pacific Coast, where he was arrested by Russian authorities, who sent him back to the Polish border. Reportedly, Ledyard's arrest and expulsion from Russia were the result of intrigues by fur entrepreneur GREGORI SHELIKOV, who feared that the American would encroach on his proposed trading venture to Alaska, the Russian American Company.

From Poland, Ledyard made his way back to London in May 1788, where he was soon commissioned by Britain's African Association to explore the interior of Africa in search of the Niger River. He traveled to Cairo, Egypt, to prepare for his expedition, but died of a fever.

LEE, JASON. *(1803–1845).* Missionary; pioneer.

Jason Lee was a native of Stanstead, Quebec, near the Vermont border. In 1829–30, he attended school at Wilbraham, Massachusetts, and went on to become a Methodist minister and missionary. In 1834, along with his nephew Reverend Daniel Lee, a schoolteacher, and two helpers, he traveled with Nathaniel Wyeth's second fur-trading expedition to the Pacific Northwest, arriving at Fort Vancouver on the Columbia River, near present-day Portland, Oregon.

Lee was commissioned to bring his Methodist missionary work to the Flathead Indians of present-day Montana. On the advice of John McLoughlin, director of the Hudson's Bay Company's enterprise in Oregon, Lee settled instead in the safer Willamette Valley region near present-day Salem, Oregon, from where he could work among the Indians of the Willamette and lower Columbia river valleys, especially the Kalapuyas and Chinooks.

At Lee's request, the mission board sent additional settlers in 1837. Lee departed for the East in 1838, seeking to bring still more Methodists to his colony. Two years later, he returned to Oregon by sea, accompanied by 51 New England settlers.

In 1843, Lee's missionary work ended when he lost the support of the Methodist authorities in New York, who believed he was neglecting missionary work in favor of promoting white settlement in the region. Lee returned to his hometown in Massachusetts, where he died in 1845.

LE FLORE, GREENWOOD. *Mixed Choctaw.*
(fl. 1820s–1830s). Principal chief of the Choctaws during the removal period; Mississippi state legislator.

Greenwood Le Flore was the son of the French trapper Louis Le Flore and the Choctaw Nancy Cravat. He was appointed by THOMAS McKENNEY to head the Choctaw expedition inspecting the Indian Territory in 1828. In the following years, as principal chief of the two northern Choctaw districts, Le Flore, in opposition to MUSHALATUBBEE's faction, resisted removal along with DAVID FOLSOM, holding out for the best deal. He eventually proposed a compromise removal agreement to ANDREW JACKSON, which became the 1830 Treaty of Dancing Rabbit Creek. He himself never relocated, staying in Mississippi along the Yazoo River, and later was elected to the state legislature.

LEFT HAND (Nawat, Newat). *Southern Arapaho.*
(b. ca. 1840). Peace advocate; principal chief.

During the Cheyenne-Arapaho War (or the Colorado War of 1864–65), Left Hand tried to keep his followers out of the conflict. His band of Arapahos were with BLACK KETTLE's Cheyennes at Sand Creek in November 1864, and, although he did not take up arms against Colonel JOHN CHIVINGTON's soldiers and stood with his arms folded when the firing started, he too was wounded. After this incident, many of Left Hand's warriors turned militant despite his continuing efforts for peace. On the death of LITTLE RAVEN in 1889, Left Hand became the principal chief of the Southern Arapahos. He visited Washington, D.C., for various negotiations. In 1890, during one trip, he signed the allotment agreement for lands in the Indian Territory despite opposition from the Southern Cheyennes who shared the reservation with the Arapahos.

LEHMANN, HERMAN. *(1859–1932).* Captive.
Eleven-year-old Herman Lehmann was captured, along with his brother Willie, by Apaches in 1870. Later, on killing an Apache medicine man, he joined the Comanches, among whom he was adopted by the Comanche chief QUANAH PARKER, son of white captive Cynthia Ann Parker. Lehmann spent his teenage years as a Comanche warrior, taking part in raiding parties on cattle drives in west Texas during the Red River War of 1874–75. In 1878, following the settlement of the Comanches on a reservation in the Indian Territory, Lehmann was forced by officials to return to his white family. His story was told to Jonathan H. Jones, who published it in 1899 as *Indianology: A Condensed History of the Apache and Comanche Indian Tribes.* His brother Willie Lehmann, who died in 1951, was the last surviving white captive of Indians.

LE MOYNE, CHARLES (Sieur de Longueuil and de Chateauguay). *(1626–1685).* Soldier; interpreter; trader. Father of CHARLES LE MOYNE, BARON DE LONGUEUIL; PIERRE LE MOYNE, SIEUR D'IBERVILLE; and JEAN BAPTISTE LE MOYNE, SIEUR DE BIENVILLE.

Charles le Moyne, born in Normandy, France, emigrated to New France in 1641. He journeyed to the Huron country of the Great Lakes, where he became an assistant to Jesuit missionaries among the Indians.

During his service with the Jesuits, Le Moyne became fluent in several Indian languages and subsequently became a soldier and interpreter for French troops in the Three Rivers region of New France. He settled in Montreal after 1646, and, over the next 20 years, acquired the largest fortune in New France of his day through the fur trade and through land speculation. He was also a royal attorney and a consultant to Louis XIV on colonial matters, and, in 1668, was granted the seigniory he named Longueuil, one of many he passed to his sons.

Le Moyne participated in the periodic French wars with the Iroquois and was captured by Iroquois warriors in 1665, but won his release through the efforts of the Onondaga leader DANIEL GARAKONTIE. Le Moyne had 12 sons and two daughters by Catherine Thierry-Primot, many of them famous in the history of New France as soldiers, officials, and explorers.

LE MOYNE, JACQUES DE MORGUES.
(d. 1588). Artist; writer.

Jacques le Moyne was part of the French expedition to North America in 1564, headed by RENE DE LAUDONNIERE. As such, he was the earliest painter to visit what is now the continental United States. He accompanied Laudonniere to parts of Florida, Georgia, and the Carolinas, and helped found the Huguenot colony at Fort Caroline near the mouth of the St. Johns River in Florida, where he painted Timucua Indians. In 1565, the Spanish under PEDRO MENENDEZ DE AVILES destroyed the colony. Le Moyne, one of the few French survivors, returned to Europe, eventually settling in England. His watercolors of North American scenes and narrative of his adventures were published by the Flemish engraver Theodore de Bry.

LEPINE, AMBROISE. *Metis.* *(fl. 1860s–1880s).*
Buffalo hunter; aide and general to LOUIS DAVID RIEL.

In the First Riel War of 1869 in present-day Manitoba and the Second Riel War of 1885 in present-day Saskatchewan and Alberta, the buffalo hunters Ambroise Lepine and GABRIEL DUMONT were the leaders in the field and generally took a more militant stance than Riel. After the war, Lepine accompanied WILLIAM "BUFFALO BILL" CODY to France as part of the Wild West Show. (See RIEL, LOUIS DAVID.)

Ambroise Lepine. Photo by Winnipeg Strong. *Courtesy of Winnipeg Strong/National Archives of Canada/PA-139067.*

LESCHI. *Nisqually.* (*d. 1857*). War chief in the Yakima War of 1855–56; leader of attack on Seattle.

During the uprising in Washington involving many of the tribes of the Columbia Plateau, KAMIAKIN was the principal chief of the Yakimas and allied tribes east of the Cascade Mountains while Leschi led insurgents to the west. The Nisqually Indians went to war when the territorial governor ISAAC STEVENS ordered their relocation from grasslands to a reservation on a forested bluff.

In January 1856, Leschi commanded a force of some 1,000 warriors of allied tribes in an offensive on the settlement of Seattle. A ship anchored in Puget Sound managed to drive off the attackers with its cannon. Meanwhile, the Duwamish Indians under SEATTLE remained at peace with whites.

Leschi then fled to the Yakimas. Having recently reached a truce with whites, they would only accept him into the tribe as a slave. Settlers sent a cousin of Leschi to trick the chief into surrendering with a guarantee of his safety, and, in November, he was seized by the army as he approached Fort Steilacoom. In a trial, Leschi was sentenced to death. But the hangman refused to execute an innocent man. Leschi was then taken to Olympia, where, after a second trial, he was executed by the army. (See also KAMIAKIN.)

LEWIS, ANDREW. (*1720–1781*). Militia officer in the French and Indian War, Lord Dunmore's War, and the American Revolution; land speculator.

Andrew Lewis, born in Ireland, moved with his family to the settlement of Staunton in central Virginia in 1732. During the French and Indian War of 1754–63, he was a colonel in command of a Virginia militia regiment, taking part in GEORGE WASHINGTON's assault on Fort Duquesne in 1754; EDWARD BRADDOCK's disastrous campaign the next year; and General John Forbes's successful occupation of Fort Duquesne.

Throughout this period, and in the years following the French and Indian War, Lewis and his family, along with George Washington and Dr. Thomas Walker, actively engaged in acquiring interests in landholdings in southwestern Virginia and present-day West Virginia. Following the imposition of the Proclamation Line of 1763, which limited western settlement, Lewis undertook negotiations with the Indians of the Virginia frontier. He succeeded in gaining territorial concessions beyond the Proclamation Line for the Loyal and Greenbrier companies, landholding syndicates in which he was a principal partner.

Lewis was commissioned a brigadier general of militia in Lord Dunmore's War of 1774 and led his force of 1,100 Virginia militia as part of JOHN MURRAY, EARL OF DUNMORE's invasion of Shawnee lands on the Scioto River. Lewis advanced from the south along the Kanawha River in what is now West Virginia. Chief CORNSTALK led an attack against Lewis's column at Point Pleasant, near the mouth of the Kanawha River, on October 10, 1774. Following a bitterly fought standoff, the Indians withdrew. Lord Dunmore's forces, advancing from Fort Pitt (formerly Fort Duquesne), caught up with the Shawnees at their settlement in Chillicothe in what is now Ohio. The Indians, faced with converging armies, were compelled to sue for peace. The Treaty of Camp Charlotte resulted, which opened more territory in the upper Ohio Valley for Lewis and other land speculators.

Commissioned a brigadier general in 1776, Lewis led his Virginia regiment against the British in the American Revolution and was instrumental in deposing his former commander, Lord Dunmore, as governor of Virginia. He resigned his commission the next year. (See also CORNSTALK.)

LEWIS, JAMES OTTO. *(1799–1858).* Artist.

James Otto Lewis was born in Philadelphia where he trained in engraving. In 1819, he went West at the encouragement of LEWIS CASS, governor of the Michigan Territory. The federal government hired Lewis to make a series of portraits of Indians who attended the treaty councils of the 1820s preceding relocation of Great Lakes tribes west of the Mississippi. He attended the Fond du Lac and Butte des Morts councils in present-day Wisconsin with THOMAS McKENNEY, the director of the Bureau of Indian Affairs. Among the Indians whom Lewis painted for the government were the Sac KEOKUK, the Sioux LITTLE CROW, and the Winnebago FOUR LEGS. Many of Lewis's portraits were copied by CHARLES BIRD KING working out of Washington, D.C. for McKenney. Lewis published *The Aboriginal Portfolio* in 1835, which did not receive as much attention as King's work in McKenney's *History of the Indian Tribes of North America* (1837–44), and he lived the rest of his life in obscurity in Detroit.

LEWIS, MERIWETHER. *(1774–1809).* Explorer; soldier; governor of the Louisiana Territory.

Meriwether Lewis was born to a plantation-owning family near Charlottesville, Virginia. One of his neighbors was THOMAS JEFFERSON. Following his father's death in 1779, Lewis moved with his mother and her second husband to Georgia.

In 1794, Lewis joined the Virginia militia and served in the suppression of the Whiskey Rebellion in western Pennsylvania. He also fought under General "Mad" ANTHONY WAYNE in LITTLE TURTLE's War of 1790–94. In 1795, Lewis joined the regular army, and, by 1800, had attained the rank of captain in the U.S. 1st Infantry. While in the army, Lewis became a friend of Lieutenant WILLIAM CLARK.

On Jefferson's election to the presidency in 1801, Lewis became his private secretary. Jefferson had long contemplated an overland expedition across the North American continent, and he proposed the idea in January 1803 to Congress, while conducting secret negotiations for the Louisiana Purchase, which were completed in April of that year. With the acquisition of the vast region, plans for the expedition were finalized. Lewis, approved by Congress as commander of the expedition, enlisted ex-Indian fighter William Clark as co-leader. Although his friend was only a lieutenant at the time, Lewis henceforth referred to him as a captain. In addition to establishing a land route to the Pacific and strengthening American claims to the Oregon lands, the expedition was to make contact with the Indians of the

newly acquired territory and explain to tribal leaders that the United States had replaced the French as their "fathers and friends." Jefferson hoped to extend American fur trade into the region. He specified that peace overtures to the Sioux were especially important because of that tribe's "immense power." Lewis and Clark were also to gather topographical and naturalist information on the new U.S. holdings.

Lewis departed Washington, D.C., in July 1803, traveling overland as far as Pittsburgh and descending the Ohio River by keelboat. He was met by Clark at the Falls of the Ohio near Louisville, Kentucky, along with a number of recruits. The party then followed the Ohio to the Mississippi River, ascending it to Wood River in Illinois opposite the mouth of the Missouri.

The expedition was mounted at Camp Wood River, Illinois, across the Missouri River from St. Louis. The Corps of Discovery came to include, in addition to Lewis and Clark, 27 soldiers, among them JOHN COLTER and Patrick Gass. Other members were Clark's black interpreter York and the part-Pawnee interpreter GEORGE DROUILLARD. PIERRE DORION, SR., was hired as an interpreter to the Sioux. An additional small party of soldiers and French Canadian boatmen were to

Meriwether Lewis. *Courtesy of Library of Congress.*

accompany the expedition up the Missouri, then return with the first records and wildlife specimens.

The Corps of Discovery departed St. Louis on May 14, 1804, in a keelboat and two pirogues. At the mouth of the Platte River, near present-day Omaha, Nebraska, Lewis spotted large mounds, but believed them to be the work of Kaw (Kansas) Indians and not an earlier Mound Builder culture as later proven. Encountering various Northern Plains peoples, including the Sioux, among them the Yankton SHAKEHAND, the expedition reached the Badlands of what is now southwestern South Dakota, and continued into the lands of the Arikaras and Mandans in what is now North Dakota. Wintering at the Mandan village of SHAHAKA (near present-day Bismarck), Lewis and Clark enlisted the help of the French Canadian TOUSSAINT CHARBON-NEAU and his wife, the Shoshone Indian woman SACAJAWEA. Other Indians of numerous tribes, with whom they held council, provided geographical information essential to the success of the mission.

In April 1805, the Corps of Discovery continued its journey westward into what is now Montana. Sacajawea, meanwhile, had given birth to a baby boy, known as Pomp (JEAN BAPTISTE CHARBONNEAU), and carried the child on a cradleboard. At the Three Forks of the Missouri, which Lewis named Jefferson, Madison, and GALLATIN, the expedition followed the Jefferson River across the upper Missouri headwaters and, with the help of Sacajawea's Lemhi band of Shoshones under her brother CAMEAHWAIT, traveled along the Lemhi Pass of the Rockies, thus crossing the Great Divide. After having followed the Lemhi and Salmon rivers northward, the party headed westward through the Bitterroot Mountains by way of the Lolo Pass. They followed the Clearwater River into the Snake River of present-day Idaho.

Along the way, Lewis and Clark made the earliest contacts with the Nez Perce tribe and other Plateau peoples. From the Snake River they traveled to the Columbia, reaching its Pacific mouth in November 1805. They built a post, naming it Fort Clatsop after the Indian tribe, where they spent a rainy winter.

The expedition started back eastward in March 1806, at first retracing the original route. In July 1806, near the junction of the Clark and Bitterroot rivers, near present-day Missoula, Montana, Lewis and Clark separated. Lewis led his contingent to the Great Falls of the Missouri in central Montana and explored the Marias River. Along the Marias, Lewis and three expedition members encountered a band of what were probably Blackfeet. The Indians at first were friendly and invited Lewis and the others to stay at their encampment, but then attempted to steal their guns. In an ensuing fight, two of the warriors were killed, one shot by Lewis himself. This incident marked the only hostile Indian encounter of the

entire Lewis and Clark Expedition. Only one expedition member lost his life on the entire trip—Sergeant Charles Floyd—from what is thought to have been a ruptured appendix.

Clark and his group, including Sacajawea, reached the Missouri via the Yellowstone and, at their confluence, rejoined Lewis's party in August 1806. Following the Missouri, Lewis and Clark stopped again at the Mandan villages and convinced Chief Shahaka to accompany them to Washington, D.C. They made their triumphant return to St. Louis in September 1806.

Lewis reported his findings to Jefferson in Washington, D.C., in March 1807. Published accounts of the expedition by Lewis, Clark, and Patrick Gass provided the earliest ethnological studies of the numerous Indian tribes encountered in the Northern Rockies and Pacific Northwest, as well as information on fauna and flora.

In 1807, Lewis received appointment as Louisiana's territorial governor, assuming the post the following year. In September 1809, he was called to Washington, D.C., to answer official criticism relating to his governmental and Indian policies; he also planned to make arrangements for the publication of his journals. While on a stopover at a tavern on the Natchez Trace, about 70 miles from Nashville, Tennessee, he died suddenly. Reports of Lewis's death are inconclusive as to whether he was murdered or committed suicide. (See also CLARK, WILLIAM; SACAJAWEA.)

LINCOLN, ABRAHAM. *(1809–1865).* President of the United States, 1861–65.

Born in Kentucky, Abraham Lincoln moved with his family to Indiana in 1816, then to Illinois in 1830. He became a captain of the local militia organized to fight in the BLACK HAWK War of 1832 against the Sac and Fox Indians, but served in the army for less than 80 days, without seeing combat. Following his rise in prominence as a railroad attorney, he was elected to the state legislature and served one term in Congress, in 1847–49.

Elected as the first Republican president in 1860, Lincoln's administration was preoccupied with the conduct of the Civil War of 1861–1865, with Indian affairs regarded as a distraction. While federal troops were engaged in the East, state and territorial militias were forced to carry out campaigns against Indians in the West.

In the Southwest, by spring 1862, Union forces had driven the Confederates from New Mexico, enabling General JAMES H. CARLETON's forces, out of California, to turn their attention to the Apache and Navajos under leaders such as MANGAS COLORADAS, COCHISE, and MANUELITO. Great Basin Indians increased their raids on settlers and travelers, leading to

Colonel PATRICK E. CONNOR's Bear River Campaign of 1863, also out of California, against BEAR HUNTER's Shoshones. Some Civil War-period incidents on the Great Plains, such as the Sand Creek Massacre of BLACK KETTLE's Cheyenne band in Colorado in 1864, set the stage for the next 30 years of hostilities between Indians and whites.

Lincoln's signing of the Homestead Act of 1862, which opened the way for the settlement of Indian lands in Kansas and Nebraska, also contributed to the cycle of violence despite the attempts of a growing reform movement in eastern cities to change the pattern of Indian-white relations.

Meanwhile, in the Indian Territory, some Indians such as the Cherokee STAND WATIE fought for the Confederacy, while others such as the Creek OPOTH-LEYAHOLO sided with the Union. Raids carried over into Texas and Kansas. The Comanches and Kiowas, armed by the Confederates, stepped up raids on white settlements.

In August 1862, the Santee Sioux of Minnesota under LITTLE CROW began carrying out raids on white settlers when supplies and food rations promised them by federal authorities were held up by the corrupt practices of government Indian agents. The conduct of the Civil War had also delayed annuity payments due from the government under previous treaties. Following the conflict known as the Minnesota Uprising, 303 Sioux, taken prisoner by the army, were sentenced to hang for crimes committed against settlers. Lincoln commuted the sentences of a majority of the condemned. Yet, on December 26, 1862, 38 Sioux were hanged, making it the largest mass execution in U.S. history.

LISA, MANUEL. *(1772–1820).* Trader; Indian agent.

Manuel Lisa was probably born and raised in Spanish New Orleans, although some accounts put his birthplace as Cuba. About 1790, he arrived in St. Louis and embarked on a career in the fur trade along the lower Missouri River. In 1802, he had a French government monopoly to trade with the Osage tribe, but this exclusive right ended when the United States took possession of the Louisiana Territory in 1802. He was a supplier for the subsequent Lewis and Clark Expedition.

In winter 1807, shortly after the Lewis and Clark Expedition had returned to St. Louis, Lisa undertook the first U.S. trading expedition up the Missouri to establish commercial relations with the Crow and Blackfoot tribes. His partners in this venture were ANTOINE PIERRE MENARD and William Morrison. The part-Pawnee GEORGE DROUILLARD and part-Cherokee EDWARD ROSE participated in this expedition; JOHN COLTER, who had remained on the upper Missouri after separating from Lewis and Clark, joined later. In 1808, Lisa's upper Missouri expedition succeeded in establishing Fort Raymond (also called Manuel's Fort), a trading post at the mouth of the Bighorn River in what is now Montana.

In 1809, Lisa organized the St. Louis Missouri Fur Company (reorganized in 1812 as the Missouri Fur Company). His partners included his earlier associates, Menard and Morrison, as well as WILLIAM CLARK, Reuben Lewis (MERIWETHER LEWIS's brother), JEAN PIERRE CHOUTEAU, AUGUSTE PIERRE CHOUTEAU, ANDREW HENRY, Sylvester Labadie, and Dennis Fitz Hugh, again with Drouillard as chief interpreter. The company's first expedition established Fort Mandan in 1809, at the mouth of the Knife River near present-day Bismarck, North Dakota (not to be confused with Lewis and Clark's headquarters among the Mandans). Lisa attempted out of necessity to maintain good relations with the Indian tribes, although he generally excluded them from direct participation in his trading ventures, using white and mixed-blood trappers instead.

In 1810, Lisa sent out an expedition under Henry and Menard, along with Colter, Drouillard, and Rose, in an attempt to develop trade father west among the Blackfeet. But the effort failed because of persistent Indian raiding.

In 1811, Lisa competed with WILSON PRICE HUNT of JOHN JACOB ASTOR's American Fur Company in the journey up the Missouri to Arikara country. Soon after, he built Fort Manuel among the Arikaras in what is now North Dakota, near the South Dakota border, while the Astorians continued overland to Oregon.

In 1812, Lisa established Fort Lisa on the Missouri River, north of present-day Omaha, Nebraska. The outbreak of the War of 1812 disrupted the operation of the Missouri Fur Company with increasing Indian attacks and encroachment by British traders from Canada. About that time, Lisa, in order to maintain friendly relations with the tribe, established a sanctuary for old and infirm Sioux at Cedar Island on the Missouri River.

In 1814, the federal government appointed Lisa as the Indian subagent for all the upper Missouri tribes north of the mouth of the Kansas River, with headquarters at present-day Kansas City, Missouri. In this capacity, he encouraged the Omaha, Oto, Pawnee, and Ponca tribes to maintain peaceful relations with the United States. In 1819, Lisa settled at the newly built Fort Atkinson, near Omaha, Nebraska. He brought his wife and her friend with him, the first two white women to settle in the upper Missouri region.

LITTLE ABRAHAM. See ABRAHAM.

LITTLE CROW (Le Petit Corbeau; Cetan Wakan Mani, "the sacred pigeon-hawk which comes walking"; Taoyateduta, Taoyatechata, Tay-oyate-duta, "his red people"). *Mdewakanton Sioux. (ca. 1810–1863).* Leader of the Minnesota Uprising of 1862–63.

Little Crow was the son of a chief of the Kaposia (Kapozha) band of Mdewakanton Santees; his grandfather had also been a chief. On his father's death in 1834, Little Crow assumed leadership of the band. He lived at the present site of South St. Paul, Minnesota and had six wives in the course of his life, several the daughters of a neighboring Wahpeton chief, and, by them 22 children.

Through much of his chieftaincy, Little Crow maintained good relations with whites. In 1846, after a drunken fight with his younger brothers in which he received permanent damage to his hands, he asked the Indian agent at Fort Snelling to send a missionary to help discourage the use of liquor among his people, whereupon Reverend Thomas Williamson moved from Lac Qui Parle to the Kaposia village. In 1851, Little Crow signed the Treaty of Mendota of 1851 by which the Santees ceded much of their land in exchange for a reservation on the upper Minnesota River plus annuities. In 1857, he led 106 warriors against the Wahpekute Sioux INKPADUTA, who had led his renegade band in the Spirit Lake attack on settlers. In 1858, Little Crow was part of a Sioux delegation to Washington, D.C., for further treaty negotiations.

Tensions were mounting between Indians and whites, however. With increased white settlement in the region and a shrinking Sioux land base, the Indians' hunting-and-gathering way of life was disrupted. They were increasingly dependent on government supplies as agreed to by treaty. Moreover, the frontier system of distribution allowed for corruption and fraud. In summer 1862, the Indian agent Thomas Galbraith refused to distribute stockpiled food to the Indians until the traders had been paid by the government and he had received his usual kickback. The hungry Indians broke into a warehouse at the Upper Agency on the Yellow Medicine River. With his people also going hungry, Little Crow demanded food to be distributed at the Lower Agency at Redwood. At a council on August 15, they were told by the trader Andrew Myrick that if they were hungry, they should eat grass or their own feces.

Some of the young Santee braves wanted war against the whites. Little Crow at first argued for peace, but young militants forced the issue by killing five settlers. Little Crow then helped the other Santee chiefs organize a rebellion. He received only partial support from the various Mdewakanton, Wahpeton, Sisseton, and Wahpukute bands of Santee Sioux. Many of the Santee leaders had been longtime friends of whites, men such

as AKIPA, CLOUDMAN, PAUL MAZAKUTEMANI, MAZOMANI, JOHN OTHERDAY, RED IRON, GABRIEL RENVILLE, and WABASHA. Some formed the Friendly Soldiers' Lodge to counter the influence of the insurgents among the Santees, and, during the conflict, they did what they could to warn settlers or free them from captivity. Some even became scouts for the army.

On August 18, 1862, Santee war parties carried out the first surprise raids of the Minnesota Uprising, attacking white settlements and trading posts in southern Minnesota, killing as many as 400 people. Little Crow himself led an attack on the Lower Agency, killing 20 men—one of them Andrew Myrick, whose mouth they stuffed with grass—and taking 12 women captives. After having wiped out a relief force from Fort Ridgely, killing 24, the Santees assaulted the post itself on August 20 and 22. The fort's cannon repelled the Indians, killing and wounding many. Santees also stormed the village of New Ulm on August 19 and 23. The settlers drove the attackers away, but suffered heavy losses—36 dead and 23 wounded—and evacuated the village. Fort Abercrombie was held in a state of siege.

With Little Crow wounded in the second attack on Fort Ridgeley of August 22, MANKATO had assumed command and led the attack on New Ulm of August 23. With BIG EAGLE, he also led the Indian forces at Birch Coulee on September 2, in a raid on an army burial party, killing 22 and wounding 60.

General HENRY HASTINGS SIBLEY engaged the Santees at Wood Lake on September 23, killing many, including Mankato, with heavy artillery. Little Crow, SHAKOPEE, and 200 to 300 others fled northwestward into the wilderness. Big Eagle, EHNAMANI, and others surrendered.

Of those who stayed behind, 303 were sentenced to be hanged for murder and rape. President ABRAHAM LINCOLN took time out from his concerns with the Civil War to review the trial records, and he pardoned the large majority. Still, 38 braves, proclaiming their innocence to the end, were hanged the day after Christmas in 1862, the largest mass execution in U.S. history.

Of the Santees who fled, many settled among the Sioux in Dakota Territory. Some band leaders offered their support; others such as STRUCK-BY-THE-REE of the Yanktons and MARTIN CHARGER of the Sans Arcs protected whites from the militants. Sibley, advancing into North Dakota, was victorious against allied Sioux bands at Big Mound, Dead Buffalo Lake, and Stony Lake in July 1863. General ALFRED SULLY defeated INKPADUTA's warriors at Whitestone Hill in September 1863; then defeated allied bands, including SITTING BULL's Hunkpapas, at Killdeer Mountain in July 1864.

Meanwhile, in May 1863, Little Crow sought British help at Fort Garry (Winnipeg, Manitoba), but was turned away. That June, he led a small party on a horse-stealing expedition to former Santee lands in Minnesota. On July 3, near the town of Hutchinson, while picking berries with his 16-year-old son Wowinapa, Little Crow was attacked and killed by settlers who sought the $25 bounty on Sioux scalps. His son escaped, but was later captured in the Dakota Territory by Sibley's soldiers, and sentenced to be hanged. His sentence was commuted, however, and while in prison in Iowa, he was converted to Christianity and assumed the name Thomas Wakeman.

Little Crow's body had originally been discarded at the dump of a local slaughterhouse. The Minnesota Historical Society later displayed his skeleton and scalp, eventually returning them to the Sioux for proper burial at the Santee cemetery on the Flandreau Reservation, one of three reservations in South Dakota where Minnesota Sioux were relocated.

LITTLE MOUNTAIN (Dohasan, Dohausen, Dohauson, Tohauson, Tohausen, Tohosa, Tehtootsah, "little bluff"). *Kiowa. (ca. 1805–1866).* Principal chief who united the Kiowa bands.

Little Mountain, the son of Doha or Dohate ("bluff"), became chief in 1833 after a defeat by the Osages. He then forged an alliance with the Osages and proceeded to shape the Kiowa bands under him into a power on the Southern Plains. In negotiations with whites, he was both shrewd and blunt. He signed the Fort Atkinson Treaty in 1853 and the Little Arkansas Treaty in 1865, agreeing to settle his people on a reservation in the Indian Territory. On Little Mountain's death, LONE WOLF was the compromise choice for his successor over SATANTA, who headed the war faction, and KICKING BIRD, who headed the peace faction. Little Mountain's portrait was painted by GEORGE CATLIN in 1834.

LITTLE PAUL. See MAZAKUTEMANI, PAUL.

LITTLE PRIEST (Hoonk-hoo-no-kaw, "Little Chief"). *Winnebago. (d. 1866).* Ally of Santee Sioux in the Minnesota Uprising of 1862–63; army scout.

Little Priest took his name from his father (also called Mor-ah-tshay-kaw, or The Traveler), head chief of a village on Lake Koshkonong in Wisconsin, where he was born and raised. In 1840, he relocated with his people to Iowa, at which time he succeeded his father as principal chief. In 1846, he was one of the Winnebago leaders who signed the treaty that exchanged the reservation in Iowa for land at Long Prairie, Minnesota; then, in 1855, he traveled to Washington, D.C., with other tribal members to sign the treaty exchanging those lands for a reservation south of Mankato.

Little Priest, unlike the peaceful LITTLE DECORA and GOOD THUNDER, offered his support to LITTLE CROW in the Minnesota Uprising of 1862–63, forming a soldiers' lodge. He also may have participated in some of the early engagements of the conflict while visiting the Lower Sioux Agency at the time. But general Winnebago support for the Santee Sioux revolt never came about. In October 1862, Little Priest and 11 other Winebagos were arrested for complicity in the uprising and were later tried at General HENRY HASTINGS SIBLEY's camp at West Mankato, but all were acquitted.

In 1863, the Winnebagos were relocated to a reservation on the Missouri River in present-day South Dakota. Because of lack of food, they soon departed, traveling down the Missouri to present-day Nebraska, where they were given lands by the Omahas. In 1865, Little Priest and his son John Priest joined the Omaha scouts; Little Priest was made captain of a company. The Omaha scouts fought the Sioux in RED CLOUD's War for the BOZEMAN Trail of 1866–68.

In March 1866, while stationed on the Powder River of present-day Montana, Little Priest was separated from three other scouts and had to hold off a war party of 32 Sioux from a position between two boulders. He managed to kill three, one of them a Sioux war chief, but took four bullets himself before a rescue party arrived. He died of complications from his wounds the following September.

LITTLE RAVEN (Hosa, "young crow"). *Southern Arapaho. (ca. 1820–1889).* Principal chief; proponent of peace with whites.

Little Raven was born along the Platte River in Nebraska. He proved himself in battle against the Sacs and Foxes, among other tribes, and, in 1855, on the death of his father, he became principal chief of the Southern Arapahos. He signed the Fort Wise Treaty of 1861.

During the Civil War years, he participated in a number of raids in Colorado and Kansas because of white incursions onto tribal lands. When LEFT HAND and his band joined the Southern Cheyenne BLACK KETTLE at Sand Creek previous to the massacre of 1864, Little Raven chose instead to take his followers south of the Arkansas River because he did not trust Colorado governor JOHN EVANS or Colonel JOHN CHIVINGTON.

Little Raven signed the Little Arkansas Treaties of 1865 and the Medicine Lodge Treaty of 1867, establishing the Cheyenne and Arapaho Reservation in the Indian Territory. In 1871, he made a tour of eastern cities with other chiefs, during which he became known to whites for his oratorical abilities. He kept the majority of his warriors out of the Red River War of 1874–75, involving Comanches, Kiowas, and Southern Cheyennes. Little Raven was succeeded as principal chief by Left Hand.

LITTLE ROBE. *Southern Cheyenne. (1828–1886).* Proponent of peace in the wars for the Southern Plains; successor to BLACK KETTLE as leading peace chief.

Little Robe was a noted warrior as a young man in combat with the Utes, Pawnees, and other traditional enemies of the Cheyennes. After the battle with the Pawnees on the Beaver River of Kansas in 1852, in which ALIGHTS-ON-THE-CLOUD and other warriors were killed, Little Robe was given the honor of carrying the Pipe of Mourning from camp to camp. He became a chief about 1863.

Because of the Sand Creek Massacre of 1864, Little Robe briefly joined the hostilities against whites in the Cheyenne-Arapaho (or Colorado) War. Yet, believing warfare with the whites hopeless, he encouraged peace, trying with Black Kettle and GEORGE BENT to induce the militant Dog Soldiers, such as ROMAN NOSE, to sign the Medicine Lodge Treaty of 1867.

After Black Kettle's death in 1868 at the Battle of Washita, Little Robe succeeded him as principal chief of the peace faction and surrendered to General PHILIP H. SHERIDAN at Fort Cobb in the Indian Territory. He toured eastern cities in 1871 with STONE CALF, and traveled again to Washington, D.C., in 1873, with Stone Calf, WHITE HORSE, WHITE SHIELD, and others for a meeting with President ULYSSES S. GRANT. During the Red River War of 1874–75, involving Comanches under QUANAH PARKER and Kiowas under LONE WOLF, Little Robe continued to counsel peace.

Following the war, Little Robe lived on the North Canadian River in the Indian Territory near an army cantonment. Despite his consistent desire for peace, he encouraged the retainment of traditional culture, refusing to send children from his band to white schools. He also worked with Stone Calf and White Shield to keep the whites' herds of cattle off reservation lands.

LITTLE TURTLE (Michikinikwa, Michikiniqua, Meshikinnoquah, Mishekunnoghwuah). *Miami-Mahican. (1752–1812).* Leader of the Miami War (Little Turtle's War) of 1790–94.

Little Turtle was born along the Eel River about 20 miles northwest of Fort Wayne, Indiana. His father, Acquenacke, was a Miami chief, but since his mother was Mahican, he earned his own position within the tribe through merit.

In 1780, during the American Revolution, Little Turtle, an ally of the British, successfully defended his village against a French detachment under colonel Mottin de la Balme.

Following American victory over the British in 1783, more and more settlers began arriving in the region and squatting on Indian lands. The Indians of the Old Northwest responded with many raids, and it is estimated that 1,500 settlers were killed from 1783 to 1790.

In 1790, President GEORGE WASHINGTON ordered an army into the field under General JOSIAH HARMAR to pacify the militant bands. Militiamen from Pennsylvania, Virginia, and Kentucky made up most of the force of 1,453 men, with only 320 regulars. The force organized at Fort Washington (present-day Cincinnati, Ohio).

Little Turtle of the Miamis was principal war chief of the allied tribes. BLUE JACKET and CATAHECASSA of the Shawnees; BUCKONGAHELAS of the Delawares; and TARHE and HALF-KING (Dunquat) of the Wyandots, were some of the other leading war chiefs.

Little Turtle encouraged a strategy of concealment and swift, small strikes to confuse the enemy. He also advised his men, after an ambush, even without any losses, to retreat farther into the wilderness, and to burn some of their own villages in order to make the retreat convincing. Once the soldiers were weary and far from their supply base, Little Turtle then ordered attacks. On October 18 and 22, 1790, along the Maumee River, the allied tribes routed Harmar's force, inflicting more than 200 casualties.

General ARTHUR ST. CLAIR was given the command of the army's offensive. In fall 1791, he mustered an even larger force at Fort Washington. Then, on the way toward the Maumee River, he built new bases for added security, Fort Hamilton and Fort Jefferson. The Indian warriors surprised St. Clair and his 2,000 men on the upper Wabash River, in the Battle of Mississinewa, on November 4, 1791, killed many, then retreated into the forest. The soldiers fell for the ploy and split up into groups. Those who chased the Indians were picked off. Then the Indians surrounded the remaining troops and pressed the attack. After three brutal hours, when the count was taken, there were only a few Indian casualties. But St. Clair's force had 900 casualties—roughly 600 dead, 300 wounded—the greatest single defeat of white forces in all the Indian wars.

Washington ordered a third army into the field, this one 3,000-strong under General "Mad" ANTHONY WAYNE, a Revolutionary War hero. Wayne took two years to organize and train this force before sending it into battle. His men built new, better-equipped posts, Fort Greenville and Fort Recovery. Little Turtle sent his men against Fort Recovery on June 30 and July 1, but they were repelled.

Little Turtle now counseled peace rather than face this huge and well-disciplined force. His advice was ignored and even ridiculed, and he gave up his command to the Shawnee Blue Jacket, leading only a small party of Miamis into battle.

In 1794, the army advanced cautiously, camping near the Indian force along the Maumee River. Wayne delayed a strike for three days. When some of the warriors had departed to find food, he ordered a surprise attack. In the Battle of Fallen Timbers on August 20, the Indians suffered hundreds of casualties, the whites only a few. Some of the fleeing warriors tried to take refuge among the British at Fort Miami, but were refused admission and slaughtered by Wayne's men. The soldiers then marched through Indian country, destroying villages and crops.

A year later, on August 3, 1795, Little Turtle and other chiefs of the allied tribes signed the Treaty of Fort Greenville. The Indians ceded much of their territory to whites, including more than half of Ohio and other tracts for the construction of forts. In exchange they were guaranteed land farther west.

Little Turtle never fought again. He signed later treaties at Fort Wayne in 1803 and 1809 and Vincennes in 1805, and he traveled to eastern cities on numerous occasions in which he was lionized. In Philadelphia in 1797, he met George Washington; Thaddeus Kosciuszko, the Polish general who had helped the rebels in the American Revolution, presented him with a set of pistols; Gilbert Stuart painted his portrait. Little Turtle received an annuity from the government for his diplomacy on behalf of WILLIAM HENRY HARRISON, and even built a house in his village on the Maumee. Despite repeated efforts by TECUMSEH to enlist his support, Little Turtle remained an advocate of peace. He also encouraged farming among his people, smallpox vaccinations, and abstinence from alcohol.

Little Turtle died of complications from gout while under the care of an army doctor at Fort Wayne, Indiana.

LITTLE WARRIOR. *Creek. (d. 1813).* Ally of British in the War of 1812.

Little Warrior and his men fought on the side of the British in the War of 1812, participating in the January 1813 Raisin River Massacre of Americans in present-day Michigan. On the return trip to Creek territory, he and his men attacked and killed settlers near the confluence of the Mississippi River and the Ohio. On learning of the raid, BENJAMIN HAWKINS, the government agent to the Creeks, ordered punishment for those involved, and the Creek Council passed a decree of death for Little Warrior and his men. WILLIAM McINTOSH, who had supported the Americans in the war, was sent with a posse, and they killed five of Little Warrior's men at Red Warrior's Bluff on the Tallahoosa River in Alabama. Captain Isaacs, son-in-law of ALEXANDER McGILLIVRAY, led a party in pursuit of the rest, catch-

ing and killing Little Warrior and two others in a swamp north of Wetumpka. This incident further divided the Creek Nation. In the Creek War that followed, Red Sticks led by WILLIAM WEATHERFORD battled McIntosh and other White Sticks, who gave their support to General ANDREW JACKSON's forces. (See also WEATHERFORD, WILLIAM.)

LITTLE WOLF (Ohkom Kakit). *Northern Cheyenne. (ca. 1820–1904).* Leader in the wars for the Northern Plains.

Little Wolf, a chief of the military society known as the Bowstring Soldiers, established his reputation as a warrior and tactician against Comanches and Kiowas. In later years, he and his Northern Cheyenne warriors fought alongside Sioux and Northern Arapahos in many of the major engagements of the Northern Plains. During the War for the BOZEMAN Trail (or RED CLOUD's War) of 1866–68, he fought with the Sioux CRAZY HORSE, GALL, and HUMP in the FETTERMAN Fight of December 1866. In May 1868, Little Wolf was one of the signers of the Fort Laramie Treaty. But in July 1868, after the Indians had driven the soldiers

Little Wolf. Photo by Edward Curtis. *Courtesy of National Archives of Canada/C-24233*

from the Powder River country, Little Wolf and his followers were among those to occupy Fort Phil Kearny, Wyoming, abandoning and burning it one month later.

Little Wolf was also one of the most active war chiefs in the War for the Black Hills of 1876–77 under the general leadership of the Sioux SITTING BULL. He fought in the Battle of Little Bighorn in June 1876. At the Battle of Dull Knife in November 1876, he was shot seven times, but managed to escape. He held out until the following May, when he surrendered and was sent to the Indian Territory.

Little Wolf joined DULL KNIFE in the Flight of the Northern Cheyennes to their homeland, starting in September 1878. North of the Platte River, they divided into two columns. Dull Knife surrendered in October, but Little Wolf and his followers eluded troops until March 1879, when, after contact with TWO MOONS and other Northern Cheyennes working as army scouts, he was convinced by his friend Lieutenant W. P. Clark to report to Fort Keogh, Montana.

Little Wolf and some of his warriors signed on as army scouts for General NELSON A. MILES and were allowed to remain in the Tongue River country of Montana. In 1880, however, he killed a Cheyenne named Starving Elk in a dispute over the mistreatment of Little Wolf's daughter. Because Little Wolf had killed a fellow Cheyenne, he lost his standing as chief and went into voluntary exile along the Rosebud River until his death. (See also DULL KNIFE; RED CLOUD; SITTING BULL.)

LIVINGSTON, ROBERT R. *(1654–1728).*
Colonial New York secretary of Indian affairs; trader. Brother-in-law of PETER SCHUYLER.

Born in Scotland, Robert Livingston spent much of his youth in Holland. He emigrated to North America in 1673, settling at Albany. Becoming wealthy through the fur trade with the Iroquois, he had acquired a landholding of 160,000 acres, known as Livingston Manor, on the Hudson River by 1686.

Livingston's knowledge of Dutch and the Iroquoian dialects enabled him to provide translations of speeches and treaties pertinent to the administration of the Indians. In 1695, he became the secretary of Indian affairs for the New York provincial government. In 1696, he traveled to England, where he was successful in making the office of secretary of Indian affairs a permanent salaried position.

Livingston administered New York's Indian policy throughout the early French and Indian Wars, King William's War of 1689–97 and Queen Anne's War of 1702–13. He also served as a representative to the New York provincial assembly in 1709–11 and 1716–25. His descendants remained prominent in New York and in national affairs throughout the 18th and early 19th centuries.

LOCO. *Mimbreno Apache. (d. 1905).* Reluctant participant in the Apache Wars of the 1880s.

On the death of VICTORIO in 1880, Loco became the leader of the moderate faction in the Warm Springs band (made up mostly of Mimbrenos) relocated to Arizona from New Mexico. NANA assumed leadership of the militants. On April 19, 1882, a war party under GERONIMO, CHATO, JUH, and NAICHE who had fled San Carlos the year before, returned in a raid, sometimes referred to as the Loco Outbreak. They pressured Loco and his Warm Springs followers to leave with them for Mexico. He participated in guerrilla warfare with the militant Chiricahuas until troops under General GEORGE CROOK tracked them to Mexico in 1883 and, after having attacked Chato's camp, parleyed a surrender. Loco did not take part in Geronimo's 1885 breakout from San Carlos, and, in 1886, he accompanied Chato, ALCHESAY, and others to Washington, D.C., for negotiatons. Despite his desire for peace, he was sent to Florida that same year along with other Apache prisoners. (See also GERONIMO.)

LOGAN (Logan the Mingo, James Logan, John Logan; Tachnechdorus, Tahgahjute, "his eyelashes stick out" or "short dress"). *Mingo (Cayuga). (ca. 1725–1780).* Leader in Lord Dunmore's War of 1774. Son of SHIKELLAMY.

Logan's mother was of the Cayuga tribe; his father, Shikellamy, proconsul of the Iroquois League in Pennsylvania, was either Cayuga or French, but raised by the Oneidas. Born on the Susquehanna River at Shamokin (present-day Sunbury, Pennsylvania, Logan became known historically as a Mingo, the tribal name given to those Iroquois living in Ohio and Pennsylvania. It is assumed he took the name Logan from his friend JAMES LOGAN, a Quaker and colonial secretary of Pennsylvania. Throughout the French and Indian Wars, Logan was regarded as a friend of the British. He supported himself and his Shawnee wife by hunting and fur trading.

About 1770, Logan moved to the Ohio River, and, in 1774, to Chillicothe on the Sciota River in Ohio. In April 1774, a group of settlers attacked and killed some of his family in the Yellow Creek Massacre at Baker's Bottom near present-day Steubenville, Ohio. As a result, Logan turned militant and sought revenge in raids throughout the trans-Appalachian region from the Allegheny River to the Cumberland Gap. In this effort, he was an ally of the Shawnee chief CORNSTALK in what is known as Lord Dunmore's War. After the Battle of Point Pleasant in October, a peace conference was held at Chillicothe between Cornstalk and JOHN MURRAY, EARL OF DUNMORE. Logan refused to attend and sent a letter of defiance—the authenticity of which has been questioned by some scholars—which was read in council.

The Mingo leader continued his raids on American settlers during the American Revolution. He was murdered on a return trip from Detroit, probably by his nephew in a drunken quarrel. (See also CORNSTALK.)

LOGAN, JAMES. *(1674–1751).* Pennsylvania colonial leader; naturalist.

James Logan was an Irish-born Quaker who became WILLIAM PENN's private secretary. In that role he traveled to Pennsylvania with Penn in 1699, when the Charter of Privilege was introduced as the basis for a reformed Pennsylvania colonial government. He rose to political prominence through his association with Penn, becoming a member of the provincial council in 1702 until 1747. He served as mayor of Philadelphia in 1722, and chief justice of the provincial supreme court in 1731–39.

As Pennsylvania's commissioner of property and receiver general, Logan was responsible for the administration of Indian affairs. His Indian policy aimed at maintaining good relations with the Iroquois and promoting their military support against the French. To this end, Logan was a key negotiator with the Iroquois League in the Treaty of Albany in 1722, and later, in the Treaty of Lancaster of 1744. The Oneida SHIKELLAMY and the Indian agent CONRAD WEISER helped shape the Pennsylvania-Iroquois alliance.

Between 1736 and 1738, as acting governor of Pennsylvania, Logan, with Thomas Penn, undertook to enlarge Pennsylvania's holdings through the acquisition of large areas of Indian lands. In 1736, in the midst of a boundary dispute with the neighboring Maryland colony, Logan managed to persuade the Iroquois to cede their Pennsylvania lands west of the Susquehanna River. The next year, he renegotiated the terms of a 1686 treaty by which the Delawares had granted to the Pennsylvania colony the lands between the Delaware and Lehigh rivers that could be covered in a day and a half's walk. This developed into the Walking Purchase of 1737, in which huge tracts of Delaware lands were appropriated despite the protests of LAPPAWINZE, TEEDYUSCUNG, and other Delaware leaders.

Nevertheless, Logan remained an important factor in maintaining colonial Pennsylvania's friendly relations with the Indians until his retirement in 1747. Logan also was a scholar and a natural scientist who did studies of the pollination of corn. His achievements in botany were recognized by Linnaeus, who named an order of herbs, shrubs, and trees in his honor—Loganiaceae. (See also LAPPAWINZE.)

LONE WOLF (Guipago). *Kiowa. (ca. 1820–1879).* Principal chief during the Kiowa Wars of the 1870s.

Lone Wolf grew up to be one of his tribe's most respected warriors and band chiefs. Along with TEN BEARS of the Comanches and LEAN BEAR of the Southern Cheyennes and other tribal leaders of the Southern Plains, Lone Wolf was part of a delegation to Washington, D.C., during the Civil War in 1863, to meet President ABRAHAM LINCOLN.

On the death of LITTLE MOUNTAIN in 1866, Lone Wolf was selected as the compromise choice as principal chief over SATANTA who headed the war faction and KICKING BIRD who headed the peace faction. Lone Wolf was one of the signers of the Medicine Lodge Treaty of 1867, establishing the boundaries of the combined Comanche and Kiowa Reservation in the Indian Territory. When the Kiowas refused to comply with the treaty and report to the reservation, General PHILIP H. SHERIDAN ordered that Lone Wolf and White Bear be taken hostage.

In 1872, following the death of SATANK and the imprisonment of Satanta and Big Tree, Lone Wolf traveled to Washington, D.C., for negotiations, agreeing on peace and securing the promised release of the prisoners. Yet, in 1873, following the death of his son and nephew by soldiers as they returned through Texas from a raid to Mexico for horses, Lone Wolf committed himself to war.

During the Red River War of 1874–75, Lone Wolf, along with MAMANTI and BIG BOW, plus the Comanche QUANAH PARKER, fought Texas Rangers as well as regular troops under Colonel NELSON A. MILES and Colonel RANALD S. MACKENZIE. Lone Wolf's Kiowas participated in the attack on buffalo hunters at Adobe Walls in June 1874 and the defense of Palo Duro Canyon in September against Mackenzie's troops. The latter proved devastating to the Indians, not so much for the loss of life, but for the loss of ponies and tepees. In February 1875, Lone Wolf and Mamanti surrendered at Fort Sill in the Indian Territory. They were among the warriors selected by Kicking Bird, who had been appointed principal chief by white officials, to be sent into exile to Fort Marion in Florida.

Lone Wolf contracted malaria while in exile and was finally allowed to return to his homeland in 1878. He died the following year.

LONG, STEPHEN HARRIMAN. *(1784–1864).* Explorer; army officer.

Stephen H. Long, born in Hopkinton, New Hampshire, was an 1809 graduate of Dartmouth College. In 1814, he entered the army and, the next year, received a commission as second lieutenant in the U.S. Army Corps of Engineers. He taught mathematics at West Point for a year, then transferred to the Corps of Topographical Engineers.

In 1817, Long, now a major, explored the Fox and Wisconsin rivers west of Lake Michigan, as well as the upper Mississippi region. He also founded Fort Smith at the confluence of the Arkansas and Poteau rivers in present-day Arkansas.

In 1819, Long, along with Colonel HENRY ATKINSON, headed out of St. Louis up the Missouri on a government expedition arranged by Secretary of War JOHN C. CALHOUN. The steamboat *Western Engineer* carried the large party, including artists SAMUEL SEYMOUR and Titian Ramsay Peale. The expedition ran into problems, including clogged boilers in the muddy water and scurvy. After the founding of Fort Atkinson at Council Bluffs, Long returned East for the winter and made plans for an overland expedition.

With 19 men, Long headed west out of Fort Atkinson in June 1820, following the Platte River to the Rocky Mountains, where he climbed several peaks, including Longs Peak. He returned via the Arkansas River and Fort Smith, having covered an area comprising what is now Kansas, Colorado, and Oklahoma, over lands of the Pawnees, Arapahos, Cheyennes, Comanches, and other tribes.

Long's report and charts of his 1819–20 expedition referred to the Plains country from the Missouri River to the eastern slopes of the Rockies as the Great American Desert. The concept of the geography of the West as arid and inhospitable led the War Department to propose that the western lands were suited for the resettlement of the remaining eastern tribes—the Indian Territory, as established under President ANDREW JACKSON—rather than for white settlement, delaying development until after the Mexican War of 1846–48.

In 1823, Long undertook another government expedition to determine the source of the Minnesota River, journeying up the Red River to Lake Winnipeg in Manitoba. He also surveyed the border in this region between the United States and Canada.

After 1823, Long remained in the army, serving as engineering liaison to numerous railroad projects in the Northeast and South. He served briefly in the Union army in the Civil War, retiring in 1863.

LONGFELLOW, HENRY WADSWORTH.
(1807–1882). Poet; educator.

Henry Wadsworth Longfellow, a native of Maine, became poet and professor of Romance Languages at Bowdoin College and later at Harvard University. In 1855, he published one of the earliest narrative poems about Indians, *The Song of Hiawatha*, involving the legends of the Chippewas and the Iroquois, and inspired by the writings of the ethnologist HENRY ROWE SCHOOLCRAFT. The work, although a highly fictionalized account, has sparked interest in Native Americans among continuing generations of non-Indians. In addition to *Hiawatha*, Longfellow also published the ballad *The Skeleton in Armor* (1841), a speculative romance of Vikings in pre-Columbian New

England. In his 1858 poetical work, *The Courtship of Miles Standish*, he related a tale about MILES STANDISH, the military leader of the Pilgrims who campaigned against Indians.

LONGUEUIL, CHARLES LE MOYNE, BARON DE. *(1656–1729)*. Soldier; diplomat to Indians; French colonial official. Son of CHARLES LE MOYNE; brother of PIERRE LE MOYNE, SIEUR D'IBERVILLE and JEAN BAPTISTE LE MOYNE, SIEUR DE BIENVILLE.

Baron de Longueuil, eldest son of Charles le Moyne, was born in Montreal. He served in various campaigns against the Iroquois and, in 1690, during King William's War, participated in the defense of Quebec against British troops under William Phips. Longueuil negotiated various accords with the Iroquois. In January 1700, partly in recognition of his great success in maintaining peaceful relations with both the Iroquois and the Algonquians, he was made a baron by French king Louis XIV, the only native-born Canadian to receive such a title while still living in New France. Longueuil was appointed governor of Detroit in 1700; of Trois-Rivieres (Three Rivers) in 1720; and of Montreal in 1724.

LOOKING GLASS (Looking Glass the Younger; Allalimya Takanin). *Nez Perce. (ca. 1823–1877)*.
War chief in the Nez Perce War of 1877.

Looking Glass inherited his name from his father. The name was based on a trade mirror his father wore as a pendant and passed to him. Looking Glass the Elder (Apash Wyakaikt) participated with Old JOSEPH in the Walla Walla Council of 1855 as one of the chiefs who refused to sign the treaty proposed by Governor ISAAC STEVENS of the Washington Territory.

Looking Glass the Younger, leader of the Asotin band, refused to sign a second treaty in 1863 that would have further reduced the tribe's lands. Yet, like Chief JOSEPH (Young Joseph) of the Wallowa band, another Nontreaty Nez Perce, he hoped to avoid war with the whites. He turned militant when, on July 1, 1877, a combined force of army regulars and volunteer militia led by Lieutenant Stephen Whipple, under the command of General OLIVER HOWARD, attacked his camp near the forks of the Clearwater Creek in Idaho.

Looking Glass's band joined up with Chief Joseph's followers, who had suffered a similar attack at White Bird Canyon on June 17. They fought Howard's troops together in the Battle of the Clearwater on July 11. Looking Glass became the principal strategist in the subsequent flight toward Canada until he fell out of favor following his defeat at Big Hole Valley on August 9.

Looking Glass was killed in the final engagement in the Bear Paw Mountains on October 5 when he moved forward to observe what he thought was the arrival of Sioux reinforcements and was struck in the face by a soldier's bullet. (See also Young JOSEPH.)

LOVE, ALFRED HENRY. *(1830–1913)*. Reformer.

Born in Philadelphia, Alfred Love became a leading Quaker and pacifist, and he openly refused to serve in the Civil War or hire a substitute. In 1866, he founded the Universal Peace Union, dedicated to the promotion of international peace through arbitration. Among other endeavors, Love's organization worked on behalf of Indian rights during the administrations of ULYSSES S. GRANT and Rutherford Hayes and was instrumental in the appointment of Quakers as Indian agents to carry out Grant's Peace Policy. Love, a proponent of assimilation, petitioned the Senate for the adoption of a constitutional amendment to make Indians citizens. Although he opposed the forced removal of Indians to reservations, he supported their voluntary relocation along with payments for their lands. He also lobbied against encroachments by white settlers into the Indian Territory. Love was a sharp critic of the army in its dealings with Indians and opposed the return of the Bureau of Indian Affairs from the Department of the Interior to the War Department. He also strongly supported the creation of a separate Department of Indian Affairs within the executive branch.

LOVE, NAT (Buffalo Papoose). *(b. 1854)*. Captive; cowboy.

Nat Love, originally born a slave on a Tennessee plantation, after the Civil War became one of the thousands of black cowboys working the cattle ranches of the West. While rounding up stray cattle near the Gila River in Arizona in October 1876, he was captured by a band of Pima Indians led by Yellow Dog. After his horse had been shot from under him, Love fought the Indians on foot, receiving several bullet wounds in the struggle. The Indians spared his life because they respected his fighting abilities.

The Pimas treated Love's wounds with medicinal herbs and adopted him into the tribe under the name Buffalo Papoose. Yellow Dog intended that Love marry his daughter, but, within 30 days of his capture, Love stole an Indian pony and managed to escape, riding 100 miles in 12 hours to the safety of the west Texas ranch where he was employed.

Love claimed to have been the famous "Deadwood Dick" of dime novel fame. In his 1907 autobiography, entitled *The Life and Adventures of Nat Love Better Known in the Cattle Country as "Deadwood Dick," by Himself*, Love included an account of his month-long captivity by the Pimas. He praised the effectiveness of Indian medicine on his wounds and commented on Indian dances, sports, and warfare techniques.

With the decline of the cattle industry in the Southwest, opportunities for cowboys diminished, and Love became a railroad porter.

LOWRY, GEORGE (Major Lowry, Lowrey, or Lowery; Agili, "he is rising"). *Cherokee.* *(fl. 1820s–1830s)*. Second chief under JOHN ROSS. Cousin of SEQUOYAH.

In 1817, George Lowry was one of the Cherokee leaders who negotiated with officials at the Cherokee Agency in Tennessee and signed a treaty ceding one-third of the remaining eastern lands in exchange for a tract of equal size in Arkansas between the Arkansas and White rivers. By this agreement, emigration was voluntary. After the tribe's later forced removal—the Trail of Tears—Lowry served as chief of council of the emigrants in the 1839 meeting concerning the formation of the new Western Cherokee Nation. (See also ROSS, JOHN.)

LOWRY, HENRY BERRY (Lowrie, Lowery). *Lumbee. (ca. 1856–1872)*. Leader of a revolt in North Carolina during and after the Civil War.

The Lumbee Indians, who officially adopted that name—taken from the Lumber River—in 1953, are descendants of various tribes of the Southeast, of blacks and whites of the region, and possibly of the lost Roanoke colonists from one of the WALTER RALEIGH–sponsored expeditions. Early tribal members of present-day Robeson County, North Carolina, were ill-treated by Southern whites during the Civil War. They were forced to work on Confederate fortifications under terrible conditions—prolonged exposure to the elements, short sleeping hours, and little food. Some hid out to avoid this forced labor; others managed to escape. The Home Guard tracked them down and terrorized the entire Indian community in the process.

In 1864, Henry Berry Lowry, a teenager at the time, established a small guerrilla band made up of Lumbees, blacks, and at least one white. His wife Rhoda's brother, Boss Strong, only 14 at the time, was one of his lieutenants. The band raided plantations and distributed their booty to the region's poor. They fought the Home Guard and the Ku Klux Klan in numerous skirmishes. Their raids continued after the Civil War, whereupon they fought federal troops. Berry escaped capture three times—in 1866, 1868, and 1869, contributing to his legendary status.

In 1871, 18 militiamen ambushed Lowry from a bank of the Lumber River as he paddled by in a canoe. He jumped into the water and, rather than trying to escape, used the boat as a shield and returned fire with his rifle. Slowly advancing toward his attackers, he single-handedly routed them.

The next year, Lowry disappeared and is thought to have been killed. But the bounty on his head was never collected. As late as the 1930s, some tribal members claimed he still lived.

LOWRY, JOHN (Colonel Lowry or Lowrey).
Cherokee. (fl. early 1800s). Ally of Americans in the Creek War of 1813–14.

John Lowry led 400 Cherokee warriors in support of General ANDREW JACKSON against Creek Red Sticks under WILLIAM WEATHERFORD. With Colonel Gideon Morgan, he helped take the village of Hillabee, Alabama, in November 1813. He also fought in the Battle of Horseshoe Bend in March 1814, in which Cherokee warriors helped break Creek defenses by swimming the Tallapoosa River and attacked from the rear. (See also WEATHERFORD, WILLIAM.)

LOYOLA (Etsowich-simmegee-itshin, "grizzly bear standing"). *Kalispel. (d. 1854).* Convert to Christianity.

In 1844, the Jesuit missionary PIERRE JEAN DE SMET established a mission among the Kalispels of northern Idaho and northeastern Washington. Their chief was baptized as Loyola. He encouraged Catholicism among his people and used it to maintain order.

LUMMIS, CHARLES FLETCHER. *(1859–1928).* Anthropologist; photographer; journalist; reformer.

Born in Lynn, Massachusetts, Charles Lummis attended Harvard University for a short time. In 1884–85, he journeyed from Cincinnati to Los Angeles on foot, writing down his experiences and taking photographs.

On becoming a reporter for the *Los Angeles Times*, Lummis provided an eyewitness account of General GEORGE CROOK's 1885–86 campaign against the Apaches. Starting in 1888, he spent much of his time among the Indians of the Isleta Pueblo, becoming fluent in their language and recording their legends. In 1892, he accompanied his close friend ADOLPH BANDELIER, whom he had met in 1888, as photographer on a Peruvian ethnological expedition.

In 1894, Lummis founded and became editor of the magazine *Out West*, and, the next year, he helped establish the Landmarks Club for the preservation of historic California buildings. In 1899, he published a series of articles, entitled "My Brother's Keeper," in which he criticized Captain RICHARD HENRY PRATT of the Carlisle Indian School for his policies of assimilation. In 1901, Lummis founded the Sequoya League to aid the Cupeno Indians of California, and, two years later, he also helped found the Southwest Society as part of the Archaeological Institute of America.

In addition to his articles and photographs, Lummis also produced poetry.

M

MacCREA, JANE (Jane McCrea, M'Crea, or M'Kray). *(1757–1777).* Victim in the American Revolution.

In July 1777, during the Revolutionary War, 20-year-old Jane MacCrea, on her way from Fort Edward, New York, to marry the Tory officer David Jones under British general JOHN BURGOYNE, was abducted, killed and scalped by her two Indian escorts, probably Algonquians. It was reported that her long hair made her a tempting target for scalping. When General Burgoyne, fearing the loss of Indian allegiance, pardoned those who had killed MacCrea, her death became a rallying cry for anti-British and anti-Indian sentiment and helped raise Patriot troops. The incident may have inspired the fictional account of the murder of the character Cora in JAMES FENIMORE COOPER's *The Last of the Mohicans.* The killing of Jane MacCrea was also the subject of a 1784 novel by Michel Rene Hilliard d'-Auberteuil entitled *Miss McCrea; a Novel of the American Revolution,* and the basis for John Vanderlyn's painting, *The Death of Jane M'Crea.*

MACDONALD, JOHN ALEXANDER.
(1815–1891). Prime minister of Canada, 1867–73 and 1878–91.

Born in Scotland, John Macdonald was brought to Kingston, Ontario, by his parents when he was five years old. After having practiced law, he was elected in 1844 to the legislative assembly, where he became a leader in the federation movement and helped develop the British North America Act of 1867, which brought about Confederation, the organization of former British colonies into the Dominion of Canada. He became Canada's first prime minister in 1867 and was knighted that same year.

For the next 24 years, Macdonald was a guiding force in the development of Canadian Indian policy, helping formulate the Indian Act of 1868, in which the Department of Indian Affairs was structured, as well as the Indian Act of 1876, in which individual Indians or bands by majority vote were granted the right to request enfranchisement as Canadian citizens.

Macdonald encouraged development of the Canadian prairies and Far West. During his tenure as prime minister, seven treaties were signed with Canadian tribes, including the Ojibways, Crees, Assiniboines, Chipewyans, Sarcees, Blackfeet, Bloods, and Piegans, in which they conveyed huge tracts of territory in exchange for reserve lands as well as supplies and annuities.

Macdonald's policies of western expansion led to revolts by the Metis—the First Riel Rebellion of 1869 in present-day Manitoba and the Second Riel Rebellion of 1885 in present-day Saskatchewan, both led by LOUIS DAVID RIEL. Macdonald was one of the foremost proponents of the transcontinental Canadian Pacific Railway, the building of which helped bring about the second Metis uprising. The resulting disruption of the Plains Indian way of life led to the participation of some Cree bands under BIG BEAR and POUNDMAKER in the rebellions. After the defeat of the Metis, Riel was found guilty of treason and hanged. Macdonald's role in suppressing the revolt cost him the support of the French-speaking community of Quebec, who regarded Riel as a victim of the government's Anglo-Canadian imperialism against non-English settlers and Indians. (See also RIEL, LOUIS DAVID.)

MACKENZIE, ALEXANDER. *(1764–1820).*
Explorer; trader.

Scottish-born Alexander Mackenzie moved to New York with his parents in 1774. Four years later, he was sent to school in Montreal.

The next year, 1779, Mackenzie joined the fur-trading concern that later became Gregory, MacLeod & Company. He became a partner in 1784, and, when the firm merged with the North West Company in 1787, he was placed in charge of the Athabasca fur district, succeeding PETER POND. At the west end of Lake Athabasca in the extreme northeastern corner of present-day Alberta, he founded Fort Chipewyan in Chipewyan country.

In June 1789, Mackenzie undertook an expedition to search for an outlet to the Pacific Ocean from Great Slave Lake. At the western end of the lake, he entered the mouth of a river that now bears his name, believing it would lead him to Cook Inlet on the Gulf of Alaska near present-day Anchorage. However, after having followed the river's entire 1,100-mile course, he reached the Beaufort Sea, an arm of the Arctic Ocean. He returned to Fort Chipewyan the following September. Although he had little success in obtaining furs from native peoples, he did initiate the first white contacts with some of the Subarctic Athapascan tribes, such as the Slaves (Etchaottine), Dogribs (Thlinigchadinne), and Quarrelers (Kutchin).

In May 1793, Mackenzie, following studies in London, undertook a second expedition in search of a route to the Pacific from Lake Athabasca. With his party—two Indian guides and interpreters, six voyageurs, and the second-in-command Alexander McKay—he traveled by canoe up the Peace and Parsnip rivers, crossed the Rocky Mountains and Continental Divide, followed for a short distance the Fraser River (which SIMON FRASER would rediscover 10 years later), then the Blackwater River through the Coast Mountains to the Bella Coola, which led them to the Pacific Coast at Dean Channel. The last leg of the journey was completed in a borrowed dugout. Along the way, Mackenzie established fur-trading contacts with Subarctic tribes, such as the Beavers (Tsattine), Carriers (Takulli), Sekanis, and Shuswaps, as well as Northwest Coast tribes, including the Tsimshians, Haidas, Kwakiutls, Nootkas, Bella Bellas, and Bella Coolas. Although he encountered many Indians across thousands of miles of uncharted wilderness, he rarely experienced hostility on their part. He returned to Fort Chipewyan in August 1793.

MACKENZIE, KENNETH (Kenneth McKenzie). (1797–1861). Trader.

Originally from Scotland, Kenneth Mackenzie settled in Canada as a teenager and found work as a clerk in the North West Company. In 1821, on the merger between that company and the Hudson's Bay Company, Mackenzie joined the American-run Columbia Fur Company and became its president four years later. Mackenzie and his partners, William Laidlaw and Daniel Lamont, proved successful along the upper Mis-

souri in competition with the Western Department of JOHN JACOB ASTOR's American Fur Company, leading to a merger advantageous to both companies. Mackenzie, granted a free hand by Astor, became the head of the Upper Missouri Outfit.

In 1831, Mackenzie established a series of forts on the Marias, Bighorn, and Yellowstone rivers. The largest of these was Fort Union, on the Missouri, near present-day Williston, North Dakota. From these posts, he sent out fur brigades to compete with the independent trappers of the Rocky Mountains. He also developed extensive trade contacts with the Crows, Assiniboines, and Sioux. With the founding of Fort Mackenzie in western Montana in 1830–31, Mackenzie extended the American Fur Company's trade to the Blackfeet. He also established good trade relations with the Cree tribes of south-central Saskatchewan. Trusted by the Indians, he was called upon to mediate a peace between warring bands of Mandans and Yankton Sioux. Etienne Provost, James Kipp, William H. Vanderburgh, and Andrew Drips worked under him.

The federal government enacted legislation barring the importation of liquor into Indian country in 1822. Yet many traders from St. Louis defied the law and smuggled whiskey to trade with the Indians. Mackenzie arranged to meet this challenge from his competition by having a complete still shipped by steamboat to Fort Union. In 1833, rival traders reported the existence of the still to government authorities, and American Fur Company executives in the East recalled Mackenzie from his command at Fort Union.

In 1834, Mackenzie traveled to Europe where he visited with Prince ALEXANDER PHILIPP MAXIMILIAN ZU WIED. Mackenzie had hosted the prince's 1833–34 tour of the upper Missouri. He soon returned to St. Louis, Missouri, where he spent the remainder of his life in business.

MACKENZIE, RANALD SLIDELL (Bad Hand, Three Fingers). (1840–1889). Army officer in the Plains Indian wars.

Native New Yorker Ranald S. Mackenzie attended Williams College, then West Pont. Graduating first in his class in 1862, he was immediately thrust into the major battles of the Civil War. Only 25 years old at the war's end, he had risen rapidly to the brevetted rank of major general in the regular army. In 1865, reverting to the regular rank of colonel, he was assigned to cavalry duty on the Southern Plains.

In 1871, Mackenzie assumed the command of the 4th Cavalry at Fort Concho in northwestern Texas. During summer 1872, he discovered a series of water holes in the Staked Plains region of western Texas, which allowed his troops to launch an assault against the Kiowa and Comanche bands that had been raiding settlers unchecked since the withdrawal of Confederate troops in 1865. In September 1872, Mackenzie's men attacked the Comanche village of Mow-way, destroyed the Indians' food supplies and livestock, and took 124 Comanche women and children as captives. Using the captured Comanches as a lure, he was able to induce the warring factions to settle on reservation lands near Fort Sill in the Indian Territory.

Mackenzie and his 4th Cavalry were next sent to Fort Clark in the south-central Rio Grande region of Texas, where he soon initiated an offensive against renegade Kickapoos and Lipan Apaches who had been staging raids on white settlements from their villages inside Mexico. Mackenzie crossed into Mexico and attacked the Kickapoos in the Battle of Remolino of May 18, 1873, taking many hostages, a tactic which again succeeded in bringing about the settlement of warriors on reservations in the Indian Territory. Mackenzie's crossing into Mexico had not been sanctioned by any agreement with the Mexican government, however, and the affair became an international incident that had to be resolved by the State Department.

Returning to Fort Concho, Texas, Mackenzie and his 4th Cavalry next took part in the 1874–75 Red River War against the Comanches and Kiowas. On September 28, 1874, Mackenzie's troops attacked a large encampment of QUANAH PARKER's Comanche and LONE WOLF's and MAMANTI's Kiowas at Palo Duro Canyon in the Texas Panhandle. Although most of the Indians were able to scatter, with few casualties, Mackenzie's forces destroyed the tepees and seized supplies. Moreover, in a move aimed at neutralizing the Indians' ability to fight and to support themselves on the Plains, Mackenzie had his men kill all 1,400 captured Indian horses.

With the outbreak of the War for the Black Hills in 1876, Mackenzie and his 4th Cavalry were transferred to the Northern Plains under General PHILIP H. SHERIDAN, where they waged a campaign against Sioux, Northern Cheyenne, and Northern Arapaho war parties under SITTING BULL. On November 25, 1876, near Crazy Woman Creek in the Bighorn Mountains of Wyoming, Mackenzie attacked the village of the Cheyenne chief DULL KNIFE. Along with his usual contingent of Pawnee scouts, Mackenzie, known by the Indians as Bad Hand or Three Fingers because of a Civil War wound, used 350 Cheyenne scouts to raid their own people in this battle. Here too, Mackenzie had his men destroy many of the Indians' horses.

After a brief posting in Washington, D.C., where the 4th Cavalry had been stationed to take action against potential civil unrest resulting from the contested Tilden-Hayes election of 1876, Mackenzie returned to southern Texas. He again crossed into Mexico, this time in pursuit of cattle rustlers. In 1881, he provided the

military presence that compelled the Colorado Utes to relocate to their new reservations in Utah. During 1880–82, he was involved in tracking down Apache raiding parties in New Mexico and Arizona.

Promoted to brigadier general in 1882, Mackenzie was stricken with mental illness soon after, and committed to an institution in New York City. He died on Staten Island, New York, seven years later. (See also PARKER, QUANAH; SITTING BULL.)

Ranald Slidell Mackenzie. *Courtesy of Library of Congress.*

MACLEOD, JAMES FARQUHARSON
(Stamix-otakan, Bull's Head). *(1836–1894).*
Commissioner of Canadian Northwest Mounted Police.

Born in Scotland, James Macleod moved with his family to what is now Ontario while a child. Graduating from the University of Toronto in 1854, he became a practicing attorney after 1860. In 1870, he served as a soldier in the Red River Expedition to what is now Manitoba, sent to negotiate with Metis militants of the First RIEL Rebellion.

In 1873, Macleod joined the newly formed Northwest Mounted Police, and, the next year, became assistant commissioner. As such, he led Mounted Police units against American traders illegally selling whiskey to the Indians in present-day Manitoba, Saskatchewan, and Alberta. Macleod personally hired Blood Indian JERRY POTTS as a scout for the Mounties.

In 1877, Macleod became commissioner of the Mounties and undertook the construction of forts along the Central Plains. His policies, protecting Indian interests from white encroachment, gained him the trust and respect of tribal leaders, who called him Stamix-otakan or Bull's Head.

In September 1877, Macleod was part of the delegation representing the Canadian government at the council in Alberta, in which the leaders of the Blackfeet, Bloods, Piegans, Assiniboines, Sarcees, and Chipewyans agreed to cede most of their territory in exchange for reservations, cattle, farming supplies, food, and cash annuities. The Indian leaders who signed Treaty No. 7 included the Blackfoot chief CROWFOOT and Blood chief RED CROW.

That October, Macleod, Mountie inspector JAMES WALSH, and U.S. general ALFRED TERRY met with Sioux leaders SITTING BULL and SPOTTED TAIL. In the aftermath of the Sioux War for the Black Hills of 1876–77, Sitting Bull had led his people across the Canadian border and settled near Fort Walsh in Saskatchewan, one of the first constructed a few years earlier by the Mounties. Canadian officials were concerned that the influx of Sioux from the United States would strain the fast-vanishing buffalo herds on the Plains. In addition, they feared that the presence of the Sioux would cause renewed conflict with that tribe's traditional enemies, the Blackfeet. In 1881, Sitting Bull, failing to receive support from the Canadian government, was forced to lead his people back to the United States, where they were settled on reservations.

In 1880, Macleod left the Mounties to serve as a judge in the Northwest Territories. His diplomatic skill in dealing with the Indians was again called upon in negotiations with Metis leaders in the Second Riel Rebellion of 1885. (See also CROWFOOT; RED CROW.)

MADOKAWANDO. *Penobscot. (ca. 1630–1698).* Ally of French in the Abnaki Wars of the late 1600s (part of the French and Indian Wars).

The daughter of Madokawando, a sachem in the Abnaki Confederacy, married the Frenchman Jean Vincent d l'Abadie, Baron de St. Castin, who had established a fur-trading post at Castine, Maine, in 1688. When British troops raided and plundered the post, Madokawando joined in attacks on British settlements, including York, Maine, in 1691, where his warriors killed 77 whites and burned all their buildings. He had a reputation for being fierce in battle but humane toward prisoners. Madokawando was succeeded by MOXUS. Other prominent Abnaki leaders during the same period were ASSACUMBUIT and BOMAZEEN.

MAGNUS (Matantuck; Quaiapan, Quaiapen; Old Queen; Saunk Squaw). *Narraganset-Niantic.* *(d. 1676).* Leader of the Narragansets during King Philip's War. Wife of MRIKSAH; sister of NINIGRET; aunt of QUINNAPIN and his wife WETAMOO.

Through marriage to Mriksah, Magnus came to a position of influence among the Narragansets, and her stature grew after her husband's death. Her village, known to the colonists as Queen's Fort, was situated north of the main Narraganset village in Rhode Island. She supported the Narraganset CANONCHET and the Wampanoag PHILIP in King Philip's War of 1675–76. Magnus was captured by colonial troops on July 2, 1676, after a fight near Warwick, Rhode Island, and soon executed. (See also PHILIP.)

MAHASKAH (Mahaskah the Elder, Mahaska, Mashkakahi, White Cloud). *Iowa. (ca. 1785–1834).* Proponent of peace.

Mahaskah's father, Mauhawgaw (Wounding Arrow), the principal chief of the Pauhoochee band, led his people from Great Lakes country to the west bank of the Iowa River in present-day Iowa. On Mauhawgaw's death at the hands of the Sioux, his son Mahaskah refused to accept the leadership of his band until he had proven himself in war. He accompanied a war party into Sioux territory and returned with the scalp of a chief, whereupon he assumed leadership. Mahaskah continued his exploits as a warrior, participating in at least 18 battles, many of them against the Osages.

On a trip to Washington, D.C., in 1824, Mahaskah took all seven of his wives and complained to the agent BENJAMIN O'FALLON about his difficulty in controlling them. He also met with President James Monroe and signed a treaty ceding Iowa lands and guaranteeing peace. Soon after his return home, the youngest and most famous of his wives, RANTCHEWAIME, died when thrown by her horse. In 1834, Mahaskah was killed by some of his own warriors whom he had earlier turned over to white officials for their part in a raid on the Omahas. Mahaskah the Younger, the son of Mahaskah by Rantchewaime, became principal chief upon his father's death.

MALACA. *Patwin. (d. 1817).* Leader of resistance against the Spanish.

In 1817, Vincente de Sola, the Spanish governor of Alta California, instructed Don Jose Arguello, the commander of San Francisco Presidio, to pacify the Indians to the north. Arguello sent Don Jose Sanchez across the Carquinez Straits, where he met Malaca and about 600 Patwin warriors in battle. Malaca then retreated to his village of Suisun. When the Spanish advanced on them, the chief and the majority of his people chose to burn themselves to death rather than live out their lives in slavery. Others escaped to the neighboring village of Chief Motti on the west bank of the Sacramento River. In 1836–37, Chief SOLANO of Suisun became an ally of the Mexicans and helped put down an uprising of Pomo and Patwin bands.

MALASPINA, ALEJANDRO. *(ca. 1755–1810)*. Explorer.

Italian-born Alejandro Malaspina entered Spain's Royal Naval Academy in Cadiz at the age of 14. He rose to prominence in the navy, and, in 1789, was commissioned to undertake a scientific expedition around the world. He was to explore the Pacific Ocean and the western coast of Spain's North American possessions.

Malaspina's expedition departed from the port of Cadiz, Spain, in July 1789. It consisted of two ships, the *Discubierto* (Discovery) and the *Atrevida* (Daring), with a 200-man crew. Malaspina sailed around Cape Horn and reached Acapulco, Mexico, intending to continue west to the Sandwich Islands (Hawaii).

Competition for the Northwest Coast region among Spain, England, and the United States led the Spanish government in Mexico to order Malaspina to provide a Spanish naval presence. His ships headed north and reached the southeastern coast of Alaska in June 1791. At Yakutat Bay, on the eastern shore of the Gulf of Alaska, his two ships made contact with the Tlingit Indians, and his scientists made a comprehensive study of this tribe, which included their social customs, economy, warfare techniques, burial practices, and language. The reception by the Tlingits was generally friendly, although an incident in which a sailor's clothes were stolen by a Tlingit tribesman did lead to a non-violent confrontation. The expedition's artists—TOMAS DE SURIA and JOSE CARDERO—produced pictures of the natives and scenes of Tlingit daily life. A glacier between Yakutat Bay and Icy Bay is named after Malaspina.

Following an unsuccessful attempt to locate the mythical Strait of Anian, which was then believed to be a water route across North America to the Atlantic, Malaspina headed south to Nootka Sound off Vancouver Island. In addition to making the first European circumnavigation of Vancouver Island, the Malaspina expedition made a study of the Nootka Indians of this region of present-day British Columbia. In addition, the expedition explored Puget Sound. Malaspina and his two ships then sailed south for the Spanish settlement at Monterey, California, where mission authorities assisted them in their study of that region's native Chumash Indians.

Following his return to Acapulco for additional supplies, Malaspina sent out a second reconnaissance to Vancouver Island in 1792. He then sailed to the western Pacific, exploring and charting the coasts of the Marshall Islands, the Marianas, New Zealand, Australia, and the Philippines. The expedition then returned to Europe, by way of South America, arriving in Spain in September 1794.

Soon after his return to Spain, Malaspina was embroiled in a political intrigue that resulted in his imprisonment and subsequent exile. Because of the controversy surrounding Malaspina, Spanish government authorities suppressed publication of a seven-volume account of his 1789–94 expedition until the late 19th century. After eight years in a Spanish prison, Malaspina returned to Italy, where he lived until his death.

MALLET, PIERRE ANTOINE. *(1700–ca. 1751)*. Explorer; trader.

French Canadian fur trader Pierre Mallet and his brother Paul traveled up the Missouri River in 1734 to the lands of the Mandans at the mouth of the Heart River near present-day Bismarck, North Dakota. From this location, they opened the fur trade between the Indians of western Canada and the French merchants in the lower Mississippi Valley.

In 1739, while engaged in the fur trade with the Illinois Indians, the Mallet brothers undertook an expedition west across the Great Plains. Aided by Pawnee guides, they ascended the Platte River to its headwaters in the foothills of the Rockies, crossing then-unexplored regions of Nebraska, Kansas, and Colorado.

Traveling south into New Mexico, the Mallets may have traded with Apaches on their way to the Spanish city of Santa Fe. Although French traders were officially barred from operating in Spanish territory at that time, the brothers were treated well by Spanish authorities during a period of detainment.

The following spring, the brothers set out to further explore New Mexico and points east. They traveled into the Texas Panhandle, where they discovered the Canadian River, named in their honor. They eventually entered the Arkansas River in Oklahoma, followed it to the Mississippi, and reached New Orleans in 1741.

At New Orleans, the Mallets were commissioned by French colonial governor JEAN BAPTISTE LE MOYNE, SIEUR DE BIENVILLE to guide the Andre Fabry expedition from New Orleans to New Mexico. During this venture, low water levels prevented them from traveling by river across the Southern Plains.

Paul Mallet probably lived out his life as a trader along the Arkansas River. Pierre took part in an expedition to Santa Fe in 1750, during which he was arrested by the Spanish. He probably died in Spain.

MAMANTI (Maman'te, Sky Walker). *Kiowa.*
(d. 1875). Medicine man; leader in the Kiowa Wars.

In 1871, Mamanti and other Kiowa leaders, including SATANTA, SATANK, and BIG TREE, laid a trap along the Butterfield Southern Route in Texas. They let a small army ambulance wagon train pass because of Mamanti's prophecy that a much larger wagon train would follow. Led by Mamanti, because the raid had been his vision, the Kiowas killed seven of the 12 defenders and plundered the wagons. Unknown to the Indians, General WILLIAM T. SHERMAN had been riding in the ambulance train and, on learning of the attack on the later Warren wagon train, ordered increased efforts against Kiowa and Comanche militants, resulting in the Red River War of 1874–75.

Mamanti and the other Kiowa militants joined QUANAH PARKER of the Comanches in this conflict, much of the activity occurring in the Staked Plain of Texas. Mamanti's band suffered the loss of most of their horses and possessions at the hands of troops under Colonel RANALD S. MACKENZIE at the Battle of Palo Duro Canyon in September 1874. Along with LONE WOLF, he surrendered in February 1875 at Fort Sill in the Indian Territory.

Mamanti was among those selected for imprisonment at Fort Marion in Florida by KICKING BIRD, the leader of the peace faction. The medicine man reportedly prayed for the death of Kicking Bird, who died within a week, perhaps from poison. Mamanti died in Florida, supposedly immediately after learning of the death of Kicking Bird. Tribal legend has it that he willed himself to die because he had used his magical powers to kill a fellow Kiowa.

MAN-AFRAID-OF-HIS-HORSES (Old-Man-Afraid-of-His-Horses, Man-Afraid-of-His-Horses, Tasunkakokipapi). *Oglala Sioux.* *(ca. 1830–1900).*
Lieutenant of RED CLOUD in the War for the BOZEMAN Trail; tribal delegate.

The English version of Tasunkakokipapi's Siouan name is not an accurate translation; the original means that the bearer is so powerful that the sight of his horses inspires fear in others, translating as "young man of whose horses they are afraid." He has been referred to as Old-Man-Afraid-of-His-Horses to distinguish him from his son, who was named after him.

Man-Afraid-of-His-Horses was a war chief in the Powder River country of Wyoming and Montana. He was a hereditary chief, but Red Cloud, by force of character, became head chief of the band. In the War for the Bozeman Trail of 1866–68, both chiefs advocated peace. His son, Young-Man-Afraid-of-His-Horses, was inducted into the Southern Cheyenne warrior society known as the Crooked Lances and rode with them for a time, but he too eventually settled on the Pine Ridge Reservation, where he acted as an unofficial Indian policeman.

Man-Afraid-of-His-Horses served as president of the Pine Ridge Indian Council and made several trips to Washington, D.C., as a tribal delegate. He sought to achieve the best deal possible concerning tribal land cessions. During the Ghost Dance Uprising of 1890, he worked with AMERICAN HORSE (the younger) for peace, opposing KICKING BEAR and SHORT BULL. (See also RED CLOUD.)

MANGAS COLORADAS (Mangos, Mangus, Magnas, or Magnus Colorado, Colorados, or Coloradus; Red Sleeves; Dasoda-hae, "he just sits there"). *Mimbreno Apache. (ca. 1797–1863).* Leader in the early Apache Wars. Father of MANGUS; father-in-law of COCHISE.

The Mimbreno or Mimbres Apaches, closely related to the Chiricahuas, originally inhabited the Mimbres Mountains of present-day southwestern New Mexico. Because of raids on settlements, Mexican authorities in the state of Chihuahua placed a bounty on Apache scalps. In 1837, when a group of trappers invited a number of Mimbrenos to a feast, then murdered them for their scalps, Mangas Coloradas united many of the Apache bands under him for concerted raids. His warriors wiped out the miners in the Santa Rita region.

In 1846, after the United States had gained possession of the New Mexico Territory, Mangas signed a peace treaty with General STEPHEN WATTS KEARNY. He was angered, however, when officials forced his band to return Mexican captives but did not punish a Mexican who had murdered an Apache. With more miners in the region because of the California Gold Rush of 1849, tensions continued to mount. Mangas was seized, bound, and whipped by miners of the Pinos Altos mines. On release, he again began leading war parties on settlers in his homeland and travelers along the Butterfield Southern Route.

In the early 1860s, during the Civil War, troops were called back East, abandoning the forts in Apache country. To protect the northern and southern routes to California, Governor John Downey of California sent two columns east, one to Utah under Colonel PATRICK E. CONNOR, and the other into the Southwest under Colonel JAMES H. CARLETON. In July 1862, Cochise's Chiricahua Apaches and Mangas's Mimbrenos attacked Carleton's advance company headed by Captain Thomas Roberts at Apache Pass in southern Arizona. Mangas took a bullet in the chest. His warriors carried him to Janos, Mexico, and forced a doctor at gunpoint to care for him.

Mangas recovered. With continuing Apache raids, General Joseph West, under the overall command of Carleton, sent a messenger with a flag of truce in

January 1863, offering safe conduct for negotiations at the army camp near Pinos Altos. Mangas agreed to a parley. On his arrival, however, he was seized by West's men and taken to Fort McLane on the Mimbres River. There, as it was later confirmed by a private, West let it be known that he wanted the death of the chief. As witnessed by a miner at the post, two sentinels heated their bayonets in a fire and pressed them to the sleeping Mangas's feet and arms. He jumped up in pain; the soldiers shot him and claimed he had attempted an escape. West himself conducted the follow-up investigation and cleared all the soldiers involved.

The Mimbreno VICTORIO and the Chiricahua GERONIMO, who had both fought under Mangas Coloradas and Cochise would assume the leadership in the later Apache Wars.

MANGUS (Mangas, Carl). *Mimbreno Apache.* *(d. 1901).* Leader in the Apache Wars of the 1880s. Son of MANGAS COLORADAS; son-in-law of VICTORIO.

On the death of his father in 1863, Mangus, although he was hereditary chief of the Mimbrenos, lost influence to his father-in-law Victorio. In 1880, Mangus was present at the Battle of Tres Castillos in Mexico where Victorio died, whereupon LOCO assumed general leadership of the Warm Springs band. Mangus continued to hide out with Chiricahua militants in the Sierra Madre of Mexico and participated in numerous raids. He surrendered in November 1883, followed in early 1884 by CHATO and GERONIMO. The three again led their respective followers from the San Carlos Reservation in May 1885. Mangus remained in the Sierra Madre after all the other chiefs had surrendered, finally being captured without resistance near the border with a small group of followers in October 1886. They were sent to Fort Marion in Florida to join other Apache prisoners. (See also GERONIMO.)

MANKATO (Mahkato, "blue earth"). *Mdewakanton Sioux. (1882–1862).* Leader in the Minnesota Uprising of 1862–63.

Mankato was born on the Minnesota River near present-day Minneapolis. About 1853, he succeeded his father, Tacankuwashtay, as band chief, his village about eight miles up the Minnesota River from Mendota. In the Santee revolt known as the Minnesota Uprising, Mankato was one of the most important war chiefs. After LITTLE CROW had been wounded in the second attack on Fort Ridgely on August 22, Mankato assumed command and led the Indian forces at Birch Coulee on September 2. Mankato died in the Battle of Wood Lake on September 23, killed by a cannonball that struck him in the back. His warriors buried him on one of the bluffs

of the Yellow Medicine River, where the whites would not find him. (See also LITTLE CROW.)

MANUELITO ("little Manuel"; Hastin Ch'ilhajinii, Childhajin, "the man of the black weeds"; Hashkeh Naabah, "the angry warrior"; Pistol Bullet). *Navajo. (ca. 1818–1894).* Leader of the Navajo War of 1863–66.

Manuelito was probably born near Bear Ears Peak in what is now southeastern Utah. He rose to prominence as a warrior and married the daughter of the war chief Narbona. He later acquired a second wife in a raid on a Mexican settlement.

The Americans occupied New Mexico in 1846 during the Mexican War. That winter, Colonel ALEXANDER W. DONIPHAN led his Missouri volunteers into Navajo country to punish the Indians for stealing livestock. In their rugged highlands, the Navajos managed to avoid any major engagements. Most of the winter, they hid out in the deep and jagged Canyon de Chelly, their sacred stronghold. In 1846 and 1849, tribal leaders signed treaties with the U.S. government, but they remained militant into the 1860s.

A point of contention between the Navajos and the soldiers during the 1850s was the territory at the mouth of Canyon Bonito near Fort Defiance. The soldiers wanted the pastureland for their horses. Yet the Navajos had used these grazing lands for generations and continued to do so. The soldiers shot the Navajo horses, whereupon the Navajos raided army herds to make up for their losses. When Zarcillas Largas (Long Earrings) resigned as headman of his band, claiming he could no longer control his wariors, Manuelito was chosen as headman in his place. In 1859, government troops attacked and destroyed Manuelito's home, crops, and livestock because of continuing raids.

In 1860, Manuelito and BARBONCITO led warriors in an attack on Fort Defiance. The Indians nearly captured it, but were driven back. Colonel EDWARD CANBY led troops into the Chuska Mountains in pursuit of the warriors, but the Indians wore them down with hit-and-run raids. In January 1861, Manuelito and other Navajo headmen—including Barboncito, DELGADITO, ARMIJO, and HERRERO GRANDE—met Canby at Fort Fauntleroy (later Fort Wingate), a new post 35 miles to the south of Fort Defiance. They agreed in council to work for peace. At this time, Herrero Grande was selected as principal chief and spokesman of all the bands.

Another fight broke out over a horse race at Fort Fauntleroy in September 1861, during the Civil War. The Navajos claimed that a soldier had cheated them by cutting Manuelito's bridle rein. When the judges refused to hold the race again, the Indians rioted. The soldiers fired artillery into the Indian crowd, killing 10. The Navajos stepped up their raids.

By 1862, Union troops had driven the Confederate troops out of New Mexico. The military then organized Indian campaigns against both Apaches and Navajos. General JAMES H. CARLETON, the new commander of the Department of New Mexico, chose Colonel CHRISTOPHER "KIT" CARSON as his field commander. Carson moved first against the Mescalero Apaches, then the Navajos.

Rather than try to draw the Navajos in direct battle, Carson began a scorched-earth offensive. During a six-month period in 1863, his men destroyed Navajo fields, orchards, and hogans, and confiscated their livestock. In January 1864, his troops moved on Canyon de Chelly, blocked the steep-walled canyon at both ends, and flushed out any pockets of resistance.

Manuelito held out longer than the other chiefs. Delgadito surrendered in October 1863; Herrero Grande in February 1864; Armijo in April 1864; Barboncito in September 1864. By the end of the year, about 8,000 half-starving Navajos had trickled in to army posts, making the Navajo surrender the largest in all the Indian wars. The army carried out its plan to relocate the Navajos, along with Apache prisoners, to the eastern part of New Mexico at Bosque Redondo near Fort Sumner on the barren flats of the Pecos River Valley. About 200 Navajos died on the 300-mile trek eastward, known as the Long Walk. Manuelito reported to Fort Wingate in September 1866 with 23 half-starving warriors. Barboncito, who had fled Bosque Redondo in June 1865, surrendered for the second time in November 1866 with 21 followers.

At Bosque Redondo, the Navajos suffered from outbreaks of disease, shortages of supplies, infertile soil for planting and quarrels with the Apaches. It is estimated that 2,000 of their people died during their stay. A delegation of chiefs, including Manuelito, traveled to Washington D.C., to plead their case for a return to their land. Finally, in the treaty of June 1, 1868, the federal government granted the Navajos 3.5 million acres of reservation lands in their Chuska Mountain homeland.

Manuelito served as principal chief starting in 1870, as well as chief of the Navajo police, starting in 1872. In 1876, he traveled to Washington, D.C., to meet with President ULYSSES S. GRANT. He was succeeded as principal chief by HENRY CHEE DODGE in 1885.

MANY HORSES (Dog, Little Dog; Sits-in-the-Middle). *Piegan. (d. 1867).* War chief; horse breeder.

Many Horses established a reputation among the bands of the Blackfoot Confederacy in Montana and Alberta as a war chief and owner of a huge herd of horses. Acquiring the animals through raids on the Shoshones and in trade with the Kootenais, he became an expert breeder and had numerous herders in his employ. He was one of the signers of his tribe's first treaty with whites in 1855. Many Horses was killed in a fight against Crows and Gros Ventres.

MANYPENNY, GEORGE W. *(1808–1892).* Commissioner of Indian Affairs; peace commissioner; reformer.

Born in Uniontown, Pennsylvania, George Manypenny moved to Ohio, where he practiced journalism, and later oversaw the construction of roads, canals, and dams. He became involved in politics and was admitted to the bar in Zanesville, Ohio, then made an unsuccessful run for governor. In 1853, on the election of President Franklin Pierce, he was appointed commissioner of Indian Affairs. This was four years after the transfer of the Indian Bureau from the War Department to the newly created Department of the Interior.

As director of the Bureau of Indian Affairs, Manypenny's main concerns were the peaceful opening of Nebraska and Kansas to white settlement, and, in that regard, the redefining of the Trade and Intercourse Act of 1834, to eliminate trade monopolies, settle governmental obligations to the tribes, and, at the same time, make Indians less dependent on annuities and, through farming, better prepared to coexist with whites.

Despite his efforts at encouraging peaceful relations, Manypenny's tenure through 1857 saw the beginning of the wars for the West: the GRATTAN Fight of 1854 in Wyoming, in which the Sioux CONQUERING BEAR was killed; the Yakima War of 1855–56 in Washington, involving allied tribes under KAMIAKIN; and the simultaneous Rogue River War under JOHN. And, on the Southern Plains, the Comanches and Kiowas carried out raids on settlers and travelers along the Santa Fe Trail.

In 1876, after the Sioux victory under SITTING BULL and CRAZY HORSE in the Battle of Little Bighorn, Manypenny was assigned by President ULYSSES S. GRANT to a commission to negotiate with RED CLOUD and other Sioux leaders for the cession of the Black Hills. Then, following the Ute War of 1879, Manypenny was named by President Rutherford Hayes as chairman of a special peace commission to the Utes. Along with fellow peace commissioner ALFRED MEACHAM and the interpreter OTTO MEARS, Manypenny traveled to Colorado in summer 1880 to negotiate the cession of the Utes' lands in Colorado in exchange for new lands in Utah.

In his book, *Our Indian Wards*, published in 1880, Manypenny was critical of the military's handling of Indian affairs. Along with HELEN HUNT JACKSON's *A Century of Dishonor* published the next year, it helped bring public attention to the plight of western Indians. (See also OURAY.)

MAQUINNA. *Nootka. (fl. early 1800s).* Leader of the attack on the ship *Boston*.

Maquinna was a chief of the Mooachaht band living on the Nootka Sound of Vancouver Island. In 1803, he led warriors in an attack on the trading ship *Boston* from the port of that name. The Indians killed the entire crew except the blacksmith JOHN JEWITT and the sailmaker Thompson. Maquinna kept them prisoners among his people for two years until they were liberated by the crew of the *Lydia*, also out of Boston. Through Jewitt's captivity narrative, Maquinna and his peoples' customs became known to Easterners.

MARIE DE L'INCARNATION. See GUYART, MARIE.

MARIN. *Pomo. (fl. 1820s).* Leader of resistance against the Spanish and Mexicans.

Marin was a chief of the Gallinomero band of Pomo Indians. In 1815 or 1816, his warriors were defeated in battle by Spanish soldiers, and Marin was captured and taken to San Francisco. He escaped, however, and crossed San Francisco Bay on a balsa, a raft made from reeds.

Regrouping his warriors, Marin launched more raids against the Spanish, keeping them out of Pomo territory. In 1824, after the Republic of Mexico had assumed rule of California from Spain, Mexican troops under Lieutenant Ignacio Martinez plus Indian auxiliaries moved on the Pomos. Marin and his men, including the subchief QUINTIN, took refuge on two islands near the mouth of San Rafael Inlet and held off the soldiers for days before surrendering. Many of the warriors then looked to POMPONIO for leadership. But he too was captured.

After a year-long imprisonment, Marin became Christianized, living at the San Rafael Mission in his homeland. He died there in 1834 or as late as 1848. Marin County, California, is named after him.

MARQUETTE, JACQUES. *(1637–1675).* Explorer; missionary; linguist.

The Frenchman Jacques Marquette began his Jesuit studies in 1654. Shortly after his ordination as a missionary priest in 1666, he traveled to French Canada, where he studied Indian languages at the Jesuit mission at Trois Rivieres, the Jesuit and fur-trading settlement on the St. Lawrence River between Montreal and Quebec.

In 1668, Marquette was sent to minister to the Ottawas. He founded the mission of St. Mary at Sault Ste. Marie in what is now Michigan, where he also ministered to the Chippewas and Hurons. He proceeded to Chequamegon Bay on Lake Superior in northern Wisconsin, where he founded La Pointe Mission. Sioux raiding led Marquette to relocated with his followers to Mackinac Island in the straits between Lake Michigan and Lake Huron, establishing the St. Ignace Mission in 1671. The next year, he moved the St. Ignace Mission to the north shore of the Straits of Mackinac.

Meanwhile, Marquette had received reports from the Indians about the Illinois tribes to the south, unknown to Europeans at that time. He also heard Indian accounts of a great river that ran southward to the sea. In 1672, LOUIS DE BUADE, COMTE DE FRONTENAC, governor of New France, sent LOUIS JOLLIET to St. Ignace, where Marquette was to join him on an expedition in search of this river. It was not known if this river, later referred to as the Mississippi, flowed to the Gulf of Mexico or to the Pacific. Marquette, with his expertise in Indian languages, was to act as interpreter for the expedition and seek new tribes to convert.

Jolliet and Marquette left St. Ignace in May 1673, traveling overland across present-day Wisconsin to the Mississippi River. Led by Miami guides, with a crew of five voyageurs, they paddled and sailed south on the Mississippi River. They eventually determined that they were too far south to be headed for the Pacific and concluded that the Mississippi River led to the Gulf of Mexico. At present-day Arkansas City, Arkansas, they turned back northward. Traveling by way of the Illinois River and Lake Michigan, they reached the French Jesuit mission at present-day De Pere, Wisconsin, in September 1673.

During their journey, Jolliet and Marquette established the initial European contacts with the Illinois, Missouris, Potawatomis, Quapaws, and other mid-Mississippi peoples. They were generally treated with friendship by the Indians. Marquette reported in his journal that among the many gifts bestowed upon them by the Indians were a slave and a calumet pipe.

Marquette returned to St. Ignace, where he worked on his journal of the voyage (first published posthumously in 1681). He headed south in 1674, establishing a mission to the Kaskaskia Indians, La Conception, in present-day southeastern Illinois. Before long, his declining health caused him to set out for St. Ignace. He died en route, near the present site of Ludington, Michigan.

MASON, JOHN. *(ca. 1600–1672).* Militia leader in the Pequot War of 1636–37; colonial official.

Born in England, John Mason was a professional soldier who served in campaigns in the Low Countries during the 1620s. He moved to Massachusetts in 1630, where he was subsequently appointed a captain in the militia unit at the Dorchester settlement. He founded the community of Windsor, Connecticut, in 1636.

With the outbreak of the Pequot War that same year, Captain Mason organized a Connecticut militia force in Hartford, made up of colonists as well as Mohegans provided by UNCAS, moving it to Fort Saybrook at the mouth of the Connecticut River. In May 1637, he embarked on an offensive, joined by militiamen from Massachusetts under Captain JOHN UNDERHILL. Traveling by boat, the expedition first visited friendly tribes east of the Pequot village and recruited Niantics under NINIGRET and Narragansets under MIANTINOMO. Then, traveling back westward overland, the force descended on SASSACUS's Pequot village on the Mystic River and set fire to the wigwams. When the Pequots ran from the settlement, they were cut down by Narragansets, Niantics, and Mohegans; others died in the flames. From 600 to 1,000 Pequot men, women, and children were killed in the raid. Later that day, while returning to their boats, Mason and his command were attacked by a force of 300 Pequot warriors, but managed to extricate themselves.

Mason continued to take part in the final military actions against the Pequots. After the war, he remained in command of the Connecticut militia and also served as a judge in the colonial Connecticut courts. He founded the town of Norwich, Connecticut, in 1660, and served as a deputy governor of the Connecticut colony. His history of the Pequot War was published by Increase Mather. (See also SASSACUS.)

MASON, OTIS TUFTON. *(1838–1908).*
Anthropologist; museum curator.

Otis Tufton Mason, born in Eastport, Maine, specialized in classical studies at Columbian University (now George Washington University). After graduation in 1861, he became a teacher and principal of its preparatory school. With a growing interest in anthropology, he began work for the Smithsonian as a collaborator in ethnology in 1872, and he was one of the founders of the Anthropological Society of Washington in 1879. He gave up teaching to become curator of ethnology for the Smithsonian's National Museum in 1884, becoming head curator of anthropology in 1902. A leader in American museum science, Mason catalogued and wrote about the thousands of Native American artifacts in the Smithsonian's collection. He had a particular interest in Indian technology, especially basketry. In his book, *Woman's Share in Primitive Culture* (1894), he examined the role of women in Indian society.

MASSAI (Big Foot). *Chiricahua Apache.*
(d. ca. 1910). Warrior in the Apache Wars of the 1880s; outlaw.

Massai surrendered with GERONIMO in 1886 and was one of the prisoners to be shipped to Florida. In Kansas, however, he escaped from the train, eventually returning to Arizona. He kidnapped a Mescalero Apache woman and ambushed Mexican and white settlers for food. For more than 20 years, he lived in freedom in Arizona and Mexico. The army scout MICKEY FREE tracked him without success. Massai Point and Massai Canyon at the Chiricahua National Monument in Arizona are named after him.

MASSASOIT (Massassoit, "great chief"; Ousamequin, Woosamequin, Wasamegin, "yellow feather"). *Wampanoag. (ca. 1580–1661).* Grand sachem; friend to Pilgrims; guest at first Thanksgiving. Father of King PHILIP and ALEXANDER.

Massasoit, grand sachem of the Wampanoag Confederacy, ruled over territory and bands from Narragansett Bay to Cape Cod; his main village was near present-day Bristol, Rhode Island. He was introduced to the Pilgrims at Plymouth in March 1621 by the Abnaki SAMOSET. The Wampanoag SQUANTO, who had been taken to Europe as a slave and since returned, acted as interpreter, when Massasoit signed a treaty with the Pilgrims. The acquisition of European trade goods and firearms increased his power among the tribes of the region, despite the dramatic reduction of Wampanoags in the epidemic of 1616–19, brought by earlier explorers.

Massasoit had his people, including Squanto and HOBOMOK, teach the Pilgrims planting methods. In 1621, probably mid-October, Massasoit came to Plymouth with 60 to 100 followers for the first Thanksgiving feast. The Indians supposedly provided five deer for the meal, which included wild turkeys, geese, ducks, eels, shellfish, cornbread, succotash, squash, berries, wild plums, and maple sugar.

In spring 1623, Massasoit became sick and was tended by white doctors sent by Governor WILLIAM BRADFORD. At that time, Massasoit warned MILES STANDISH of a plot against the settlers by militant Indians, including Narragansets, Massachusets, and the Wampanoags ASPINET and IYANOUGH. The insurgents in turn plotted against him. ANNAWAN, Massasoit's leading war chief, carried out raids on competing tribes of the region for his grand sachem. In 1632, Massasoit fled his village to avoid capture by the Narragansets under CANONICUS. ROGER WILLIAMS helped restore peace between the two tribes.

Over the next years, the colonists increasingly settled on Indians lands, and when the Indians tried to regain them, they were punished in white courts as trespassers. Massasoit came to resent the expanding white presence.

On Massasoit's death, his son Alexander became grand sachem briefly, then Philip, who led the uprising known as King Philip's War of 1675–76.

MATHER, COTTON. *(1663–1728).* Historian; church leader.

A member of the prominent Massachusetts Bay Colony family of Puritan clergymen, Mather was born in Boston and educated at Harvard University. The year of his ordination, 1685, he joined his father, Increase Mather, as minister at Boston's North Church.

Cotton Mather was influential in the Puritan-dominated government of the colony, supporting the 1689 revolt against Massachusetts colonial governor EDMUND ANDROS, and serving as adviser to the government of William Phips. He also defended the excesses of the 1692 Salem witch trials.

Like his father, who wrote about New England Indian wars, Cotton Mather was known for his writings, both religious and historical. In his biography of missionary JOHN ELIOT, included in his ecclesiastical history of New England, *Magnalia Christi Americana* (1702), he expressed his opinion that it was futile to attempt to Christianize and civilize the Indians. He included in his writings and sermons the experiences of colonists captured by Indians, in particular HANNAH DUSTON and HANNAH SWARTON, whose sufferings he described as divine punishment for transgressions. Characterizing Indians as descendants of the Ten Lost Tribes of Israel, who had been led to North America by Satan, and Indian ritual as a manifestation of evil in the physical universe, Mather argued in favor of Indian extermination.

MATONABBEE. *Chipewyan. (ca. 1736–1782).* Guide for the Hudson's Bay Company and SAMUEL HEARNE.

Matonabbee was born near Fort Prince of Wales at the mouth of the Churchill River on the west side of Hudson Bay. On his father's death soon after, Matonabbee was adopted and educated by Richard Norton, Hudson's Bay Company governor at the fort. When Norton returned to England, Matonabbee's relatives took him into their hunting band, which roamed the Barren Grounds in what is now northern Manitoba, northern Saskatchewan, and the eastern expanse of the Northwest Territories, where he learned traditional Chipewyan lifeways.

At the age of 16, Matonabbee returned to Fort Prince of Wales and began working for the British as a hunter. He also accompanied them on trading trips along the western shore of Hudson Bay, during which he mastered the Algonquian language of the Cree Indians to the south. He later worked as the company's representative and negotiator among warring tribes. His experiences helped him rise in prominence among his people, and he eventually became a chief.

In 1769, Samuel Hearne set out on the First Coppermine Expedition for the Hudson's Bay Company in the hope of finding the Northwest Passage and a source of copper. This attempt failed when his Indian guides deserted and robbed him of supplies. In a second expedition the following year, Hearne reached the southern shore of Aberdeen Lake and was hard pressed to make it back to the post. In September 1770, Matonabbee entered Hearne's camp and greeted the Englishman, whom he had previously met at the fort, and took charge of getting him safely home.

The two men, now good friends, planned a third expedition. Hearne was to be in charge of charting routes and recording natural history and carrying out the company's objectives; Matonabbee would be in command of actual day-to-day travel preparations and decisions. Chipewyan women would help carry supplies. Moreover, Chipewyan bands, made up of extended families, would be attached to the expedition. They would travel in the same direction as the explorers and set up their own camps. Their number would provide protection against hostile bands and help in the hunting of caribou.

The Third Coppermine Expedition of 1771–72 reached the Coppermine River and followed it to the Arctic Ocean. Hearne, to his disappointment, learned that the river was not the Northwest Passage to the Pacific, and he found only surface samples of copper, not rich mines. Matonabbee, for his part, accomplished one of the Chipewyan goals for the journey—a raid on their traditional enemies, the Eskimos. In July 1771, at Bloody Falls, his warriors, joined by some Copper Indians, wiped out an Eskimo band. On the return trip, however, some of the Chipewyans starved to death.

Ten years later, in 1782, after a smallpox epidemic had killed many of his people after Hearne had surrendered Fort Prince of Wales to the French, Matonabbee committed suicide by hanging himself.

MATO-TOPE (Mah-to-toh-pa, Four Bears). *Mandan. (1800–1837).* Principal chief; friend to painters; artist.

The Mandan Indians of the upper Missouri River near its Big Bend in what is now North Dakota were hospitable to early explorers, traders, and frontier painters. LEWIS and CLARK spent a winter among them in 1804–05. GEORGE CATLIN visited them in 1832, and KARL BODMER, a member of Prince ALEXANDER PHILIPP MAXIMILIAN ZU WIED's expedition, in 1834. A favorite subject for both Catlin and Bodmer was the Mandan chief Mato-Tope, or Four Bears. In addition to posing for both artists, he presented them with his own work on buffalo robes as well as on paper supplied by them. One of Mato-Tope's drawings depicts his fight with a Cheyenne chief in which both were wounded.

Because of his reputation as a warrior, Mato-Tope was chosen as principal chief in 1837. That same year, however, he died of smallpox in the epidemic that killed the vast majority of his people—reportedly all but 125 of 1,600—as well as numerous Arikaras and Hidatsas.

Mato-Tope's son of the same name succeeded his father as principal chief. In 1845, he moved with his people to Fort Berthold, where the reservation for all three upper Missouri tribes was established. In 1851, Mato-Tope, or Four Bears the Younger, signed the Treaty of Fort Laramie.

Mato-Tope. Painting by Karl Bodmer. *Courtesy of New York State Library, Albany.*

MATTESON, SUMNER W. *(1867–1920).*
Photographer.

Sumner Matteson, born in Decorah, Iowa, was originally a salesman out of Denver, selling both photographic equipment and bicycles. He embarked on a bicycle trip in 1898–99, in which he took photos of Native Americans, especially the Pueblo Indians of the Southwest. He returned to the region again in 1900, at which time he photographed a Hopi Snake Dance. The following year, he was attached to an expedition of the Field Musem of Natural History. Starting in 1904, Matteson used his photographs in a series of lectures. He also photographed Assiniboine and Gros Ventre Indians of the Northern Plains.

MATTHEWS, WASHINGTON. *(1843–1905).*
Anthropologist; linguist; translator.

Washington Matthews was born in Ireland; his mother died when he was young and his father took him first to Wisconsin, then to Dubuque, Iowa. He studied to be a doctor at the University of Iowa, and, on graduating in 1864, he entered the army and served as an acting assistant surgeon in the last year of the Civil War.

Matthews reentered the service in summer 1865, receiving a commission as assistant surgeon in 1868. His posting included Fort Union and Fort Berthold, North Dakota, during which time he undertook a study of the Hidatsa people and produced a grammar of their Siouan dialect. He was then transferred to the East.

Matthews's facility with Indian languages came to the attention of JOHN WESLEY POWELL of the Smithsonian's Bureau of Ethnology, who arranged for Matthews to be transferred to Fort Wingate, New Mexico, in Navajo country. Starting in 1884, he spent most of the next six years in the Southwest, for both Powell and the Hemenway Southwestern Archaeological Expedition. He was also on staff as the assistant curator for the Army Medical Museum in Washington, D.C. In 1890–94, he spent additional time among the Navajos.

Matthews retired from the military in 1895. The next year, he became president of the American Folk Lore Society, holding positions in other organizations as well.

Matthews's works on the Navajos range from a study of Navajo weaving and silverwork to translations in verse of traditional chants.

MAXIMILIAN, ALEXANDER PHILIPP, PRINZ DU WIED-NEUWIED. *(1782–1867).*
Naturalist; anthropologist; explorer.

Prince Alexander Philipp Maximilian zu Wied was born to a Prussian noble family from the German city of Coblenz. Following service in the Prussian army during the Napoleonic Wars, he pursued his interest in science and naturalist studies, joining a scientific expedition to Brazil in 1814–17.

Maximilian continued his studies in Europe, and, in 1832, embarked on an expedition to explore North America with the Swiss artist KARL BODMER. They arrived in Boston in 1832, then went to New York City, where they visited with the fur entrepreneur JOHN JACOB ASTOR. They then studied the Indian artifacts at Philadelphia's Peale Museum, acquired by MERIWETHER LEWIS and WILLIAM CLARK on their expedition west nearly 30 years later.

Maximilian and Bodmer continued their ethnological inquiries into Native American culture with scholars at New Harmony, Indiana. They reached St. Louis in spring 1833, where William Clark arranged for their passage up the Missouri aboard Astor's American Fur Company steamer, *Yellowstone*. At Fort Pierre in what is now South Dakota, they transferred to the company's other steamer, the *Assiniboine*, and proceeded to Fort Union in present-day northwestern North Dakota. Along the way they stopped at Fort Clark, present-day Bismarck, North Dakota, from where they continued to the upper reaches of the Missouri River and its tributaries to Fort McKenzie in present-day Montana, traveling at times by keelboat and barge.

Maximilian kept a journal of his travels and made an extensive study of the Northern Plains peoples encountered, especially the Mandans, with whom he and Bodmer spent the winter of 1833–34 at Fort Clark on the return trip. He wrote at length on the Mandans' tribal life, and compiled one of the earliest dictionaries of their Siouan dialect. Maximilian collected items produced by the upper Missouri tribes and brought them back to Europe, including artwork, clothing, and tools. His work, *Travels in the Interior of North America*, with Bodmer's illustrations, was published in an 1839 German edition and an 1843 English edition.

MAY, KARL FRIEDRICH. *(1842–1912).* Writer.

German-born Karl May studied to become a schoolteacher, but was convicted at the age of 20 for stealing a watch. After a series of prison terms for theft and fraud, finally ending in 1874, he pursued a career first as an editor for family magazines, then as a writer. He achieved success with adventure novels of the Wild West and the Orient.

Unlike the other German-language writers Friedrich Gerstack, Heinrich Mollhausen, and Karl Postl (Charles Sealsfield), who also depicted the American West, May never visited North America. Yet he was able to produce a vast amount of fiction of the frontier era based on research in atlases, histories, and ethnological studies.

One of May's major characters was the Apache Indian Winnetou, sidekick to the heroic cowboy Old Shatterhand. Winnetou was depicted as an introspective character, well aware of the inevitable demise of Indian life because of white encroachment. In his writings, May generally portrayed the Indians as victims of injustices and depredations carried out by white settlers and soldiers.

May created a public scandal when he began to claim that his stories were based on his real-life adventures. His popularity endured, however, as did a continuing fascination for America's Old West and Indian peoples among Germans. Among the readers of May's adventure tales were Albert Schweitzer, Albert Einstein, Herman Hesse, and Adolf Hitler.

MAYER, FRANCIS BLACKWELL. *(1827–1899).* Artist; writer.

Baltimore artist Frank Blackwell Mayer was a student of ALFRED JACOB MILLER. In 1851, he was an eyewitness to the council at Traverse des Sioux, Minnesota, between the Sioux Indians and the federal government, and he made sketches of the event as well as of daily Indian life. His written and pictorial accounts were later published in book form, *With Pen and Pencil on the Frontier in 1851* (1932). He journeyed to France in 1862 for art studies, returning to Maryland eight years later.

MAYHEW, THOMAS, JR. *(1621–1657).* Missionary.

Born in England, Thomas Mayhew, Jr., arrived in New England in 1631 with his father, Thomas Mayhew, Sr., as part of the first great wave of Puritan migration to the Massachusetts Bay Colony. In 1641, Mayhew and his father were granted title to Martha's Vineyard, Nantucket, and the adjacent Elizabeth Islands, off the southeast coast of Massachusetts. They established a colony at Edgartown, Martha's Vineyard, where the younger Mayhew became the first pastor of the colony's Congregational church.

Mayhew learned the Algonquian language of the island's Wampanoags and soon began preaching to the Indians in their own tongue. In 1643, he succeeded in converting a Wampanoag named Hiacoomes, then trained him to preach to other members of his tribe. His work with the Indians on Martha's Vineyard preceded JOHN ELIOT's missionary efforts on the mainland by three years. Under Mayhew's direction, a school was established in 1652, where Wampanoag children were taught reading and received religious instruction. Because he used his own resources to support his mission, Mayhew's financial condition increasingly suffered until the mid-1650s, when he gained the financial support of the London-based Society for the Propagation of the Gospel in New England.

In 1657, Mayhew set out for England to take care of family financial matters and to solicit additional support for his missionary work among the Indians of Martha's Vineyard, Nantucket, and neighboring islands. With him on this voyage to England was one of his Indian converts. However, the ship never reached England, and the younger Mayhew and his companion were presumed lost at sea. His father, Thomas Mayhew, Sr., took over his son's mission and also married his son's widow. The elder Mayhew was instrumental in keeping the Martha's Vineyard and Nantucket Indians loyal to the colonists during King Philip's War of 1675–76. Over the next 200 years, three succeeding generations of Mayhews continued their missionary efforts among the Algonquians of the Massachusetts coastal islands.

MAZAKUTEMANI, PAUL (Mazakutamane, "walks shooting iron"; Little Paul). *Mdewakanton Sioux. (ca. 1806–1885).* Spokesman for the peace faction of Santees during the Minnesota Uprising of 1862–63; friend and rescuer of whites; army scout. Brother of CLOUDMAN; cousin of LITTLE CROW.

As a tribal delegate in negotiations with whites, Paul Mazakutemani spoke for the peace faction among the Mdewakantons, Sissetons, and Wahpetons and was one of the signers of the Traverse des Sioux Treaty of 1851. Soon afterward, he was converted to Christianity and supported missionary work among his people. With his brother Cloudman, and help from the missionary STEPHEN RIGGS, Mazakutemani founded the Hazelwood Republic in 1854, a constitutional government of Christian Indians of which he was elected first president.

When INKPADUTA's band of renegade Wahpekutes killed settlers and took captives at Spirit Lake in present-day Iowa in 1856, Mazakutemani, along with JOHN OTHERDAY and Iron Hawk, helped track them. Their efforts led to the release of one of the women.

During the Minnesota Uprising of Santees under his cousin Little Crow in 1862–63, Mazakutemani helped organize the pro-white Friendly Soldiers' Lodge with Cloudman, AKIPA, MAZOMANI, and GABRIEL RENVILLE to work for peace. Mazakutemani also used his oratorical abilities to persuade the militants to release white captives. Later in the conflict, he worked as an army scout. (See also LITTLE CROW.)

MAZOMANI (Iron Walker; Ahanzi, "shade"). *Wahpeton Sioux. (d. 1862).* Friend to whites. Brother of RED IRON.

Mazomani was a subchief to his brother Red Iron. Like Red Iron, he was one of the signers of the Traverse des Sioux Treaty of 1851, and a subsequent treaty signed in Washington, D.C., in 1858. In 1862, at the onset of the Minnesota Uprising of the Santee bands, Mazomani, along with AKIPA, CLOUDMAN, PAUL MAZAKUTEMANI, GABRIEL RENVILLE, and others, organized the Friendly Soldiers' Lodge to oppose the Hostile Lodge of the insurgents. Yet Mazomani was forced to accompany LITTLE CROW and the other militants into battle at Wood Lake on September 23. During the fighting, he tied a white flag to his gun and ran for General HENRY HASTINGS SIBLEY's troops, whereupon he was shot in the leg by a fellow Sioux. He died about two weeks later from his wound. (See also LITTLE CROW.)

McCOY, ISAAC. *(1784–1846).* Indian agent; reformer; historian; missionary.

Isaac McCoy was born near Uniontown, Pennsylvania, the son of a clergyman. When about six years old,

he moved with his parents to Kentucky. He married in 1803 and moved with his wife to Indiana the following year.

McCoy was ordained into the Baptist church and, in 1817, was appointed missionary to the Indians of the Wabash Valley. He became convinced that Indians should be separated from whites and their influences, especially alcohol. In his *Remarks on the Practicability of Indian Reform* (1827), he argued in favor of an Indian state west of the Mississippi. In 1828, he was part of a commission arranging for the relocation of the Miami and Ottawa Indians.

In 1830, McCoy was appointed as Indian agent and surveyor by JOHN C. CALHOUN, secretary of War under President ANDREW JACKSON. McCoy assisted in the removal of eastern Indians, helping choose and survey reservations in the Indian Territory in what is now Kansas and Oklahoma. Despite continuing efforts, he never realized his plan for an Indian state or for the utopian Indian community of New Canaan.

From 1835 to 1838, McCoy published several editions of the *Annual Register of Indian Affairs within the Indian Territory,* and, in 1840, *History of Baptist Indian Missions.* In 1842, he became general agent of the Indian Mission Association at Louisville, Kentucky, where he died four years later.

McGILLICUDDY, TRANT VALENTINE O'CONNELL. *(1849–1896).* Indian agent.

Born in Racine, Wisconsin, T. Valentine McGillicuddy attended the University of Michigan, then the Detroit College of Medicine. Earning his M.D. in 1869, he began a practice in Detroit.

In 1871–74, McGillicuddy served as acting physician and assistant engineer for a federal survey of the Great Lakes; in 1874, he participated in the British-American boundary line survey; in 1875–76, he was chief engineer for a U.S. survey of the Black HIlls; and, in 1876–79, during the Sioux War for the Black Hills and afterward, he was a surgeon for the U.S. Cavalry.

In 1879, McGillicuddy was appointed agent to the Oglala Sioux at the Pine Ridge Agency, located at the western part of the Great Sioux Reservation in the Dakota Territory. He was one of the first agents assigned after President Rutherford Hayes's elimination of religious groups in the selection of agents, a practice established by ULYSSES S. GRANT during the previous administration.

It was McGillicuddy's intention to encourage Indians to engage in an economic system based on labor rather than warfare and hunting, and to diminish the influence of tribal leaders, such as RED CLOUD, over the members of the tribe. Under McGillicuddy's supervision, the Oglalas developed individually held farms on the reservation, erected telegraph lines, constructed sawmills, established six reservation schools, and created local Indian courts plus an Indian police force.

The Oglalas had been receiving rations of food and clothing from the government, under a treaty signed in 1868. McGillicuddy viewed the allotment of these federal rations to the Indians as an obstacle to their development of a self-sufficient economy. Yet he was one of the few Indian agents of that period who administered the distribution of these rations fairly. Despite his reputation for honesty, he was repeatedly investigated for alleged misappropriations of federal rations. These problems stemmed from resistance by the Oglala Sioux chiefs to a government census for the purpose of allocations of government-supplied rations.

Following his resignation in 1886, McGillicuddy remained on the reservation to assist in the overdue census of the Indians, which revealed that significantly fewer Indians lived on the Pine Ridge Reservation than had been thought. Many of the Oglalas formerly under McGillicuddy's jurisdiction were caught up in the Ghost Dance Uprising of 1890.

McGillicuddy continued an active public career and eventually moved to California.

McGILLIVRAY, ALEXANDER (Hoboi-hili-miko, Hippo-ilk-mico, "good child king"). *Mixed Creek. (1759–1793).* "Emperor" of Creeks and Seminoles. Uncle of WILLIAM WEATHERFORD.

Alexander McGillivray was born at a trading post in the Creek village of Little Tallassie along the Coosa River in present-day east-central Alabama. His father was Lachlan McGillivray, a Scottish trader; his mother, Sehoy Marchand, of Creek and French ancestry. As a teenager, Alexander was educated in Charleston, South Carolina, where he was tutored by a relative, Reverend Farquhar McGillivray, and then in Savannah, Georgia. His studies were interrupted by the outbreak of the American Revolution.

Alexander's father, a Loyalist, decided to return to Scotland and left his son lands in Georgia. McGillivray, because of his inherited status, his education, and his abilities, became one of the important Creek chiefs. When Georgia authorities confiscated his property, McGillivray threw his support to the British, who gave him the rank of colonel. Supporting the efforts of the Cherokees DRAGGING CANOE and BLOODY FELLOW, McGillivray led Creek warriors in attacks on American settlements in Georgia and eastern Tennessee. The Frenchman LOUIS LE CLERC MILFORT acted as his adviser and war chief.

After the war, in 1784, McGillivray signed a military and trade agreement with the Spanish, to whom he was known as the "emperor" of the Creek and Seminole Nations and a colonel in their army. His trading concern, with the help of his partner William Panton, grew.

Georgia authorities, meanwhile, had reached a settlement with him for $100,000 in compensation for confiscated property.

McGillivray and his retinue traveled to New York City in 1790, where he was entertained by American officials, including GEORGE WASHINGTON. He signed the Treaty of New York, reestablishing the boundaries of Creek territory. He was given a secret commission as a brigadier general in the U.S. army and an annuity of $1,200. But he also received an annuity of $2,000 and later $3,500 from the Spanish. McGillivray's faction of Creeks, because of ties with both Spain and the United States, were opposed by a pro-British group under WILLIAM BOWLES.

Over the years, McGillivray wrote numerous letters to friends and to public officials. Suffering from various illnesses, he died while visiting Panton's home in Pensacola, Florida.

McINTOSH, CHILLY (Rolly McIntosh or MacIntosh). *Mixed Creek. (fl. 1820s–1830s).* Tribal leader. Half-brother of WILLIAM McINTOSH.

On the death of his brother in 1825, Chilly McIntosh became chief of the Lower Creeks (White Sticks). As such, he was leader of the tribe's minority faction accepting the cession of Creek lands in Georgia and the relocation to the Indian Territory. He made several trips to Washington, D.C., to negotiate with federal officials.

McINTOSH, WILLIAM (William MacIntosh). *Mixed Creek. (1775–1825).* Chief of the White Sticks; ally of Americans to whom he ceded Creek lands. Half-brother of CHILLY McINTOSH.

William McIntosh was the son of a Scottish officer of the same name, who was an agent to the Creeks for England, and a Creek woman. Well-educated, he became a leader of the pro-American White Sticks from the Lower Creek villages. He supported the United States and General ANDREW JACKSON in various military campaigns and was made a brigadier general: against the British in the War of 1812; against WILLIAM WEATHERFORD's Red Sticks in the Creek War of 1813–14; and against KINACHE's and BOLEK's Seminoles in the First Seminole War of 1817–18.

In 1805, a large portion of Creek lands were ceded to Georgia by McIntosh and other chiefs. In the Broken Arrow Council of 1811, attended by McIntosh, Creek leaders passed a tribal law forbidding the further sale of Creek lands. Yet McIntosh and chiefs under his influence ceded additional lands in treaties at Fort Jackson, Alabama, in 1814; Creek Agency, Georgia, in 1818; and Indian Springs, Georgia, in 1821. After another attempt in 1823 to cede 15 million acres, the Creeks reenacted the Broken Arrow Law. When McIntosh and 12 others signed the Treaty of Indian Springs of 1825, reaffirming the cession of 1823 plus 10 million more acres to the state of Georgia, he was sentenced to death in council.

The Red Stick MENEWA led the war party that carried out the execution, shooting McIntosh as he tried to escape from his home. His half-brother Chilly McIntosh succeeded him as chief of the pro-American White Stick faction. (See also WEATHERFORD, WILLIAM.)

McKEE, ALEXANDER. *(ca. 1735–1799).* British Indian agent; trader; Loyalist officer in the American Revolution.

Alexander McKee was the son of the Irish trader Thomas McKee and a woman he met among the Shawnees, thought to have been a white captive raised by them. As a young man, McKee served as a lieutenant in Pennsylvania troops in the French and Indian War of 1754–63.

Beginning in 1760, McKee was an assistant Indian agent to GEORGE CROGHAN among the tribes of the Old Northwest. He married a Shawnee woman and maintained a home in a Shawnee village of the Scioto River, Ohio.

With the outbreak of the American Revolution, McKee, a Loyalsit, fled to Detroit, accompanied by SIMON GIRTY. He was appointed an interpreter for the Indian Department and a captain of Tory forces. As such, he coordinated Indian auxiliaries with British forces in the Ohio Valley. In 1778, his Indian troops, fighting under the lieutenant governor of Detroit, HENRY HAMILTON, helped take Vincennes in what is now Indiana; in 1780, his troops took Rundle's Station in Kentucky, killing about 200 men, women, and children; and, in 1782, he led an unsuccessful attack with Simon Girty on Bryan's Station, near present-day Lexington, Kentucky.

At the end of the Revolutionary War, McKee was granted land in present-day Ontario. In addition to developing his private interests in the fur trade, he served the British as colonel in the militia and as deputy agent. He helped organize Indian resistance to American expansion across the Ohio River and fought along with the Indians against American forces under "Mad" ANTHYONY WAYNE in the Battle of Fallen Timbers in August 1794 during LITTLE TURTLE's War.

Also in 1794, McKee became deputy superintendent and deputy inspector general of Indian Affairs of Upper Canada (now Ontario). His son Thomas McKee became the Indian agent at Amherstburg.

McKENNEY, THOMAS LORAINE. *(1785–1859).* Superintendent of the Indian Trade; director of Bureau of Indian Affairs; organizer of Indian Portrait Gallery.

Thomas McKenney, born in Somerset County, Maryland, studied medicine, but took over his father's mercantile business when 19. About four years later, he opened two dry-goods businesses in Washington, D.C. He became well-known in political circles and went on to become the chief administrator of federal policy toward the Indians during the presidencies of James Madison, James Monroe, John Quincy Adams, and ANDREW JACKSON.

McKenney was first appointed as superintendent of the Indian Trade by JOHN C. CALHOUN, secretary of War, in 1816, following his service as an army officer in the War of 1812. In this capacity, he was responsible for all claims by and against Indians as well as the administration of the federally run trading forts or "factories" throughout the Old Northwest and the Ohio and Mississippi valleys.

When the Bureau of Indian Affairs was created as part of the War Department in 1824, McKenney was named its first director. His policies were aimed at improving the situation of Indians in the face of white expansion, such as helping missionary leaders obtain funding for schools. He also attempted to regulate frontier trade and bar the use of whiskey as a commodity and a means to cheat Indians. He faced opposition by private fur-industry interests, in particular JOHN JACOB ASTOR, for whom McKenney's strict supervision was a major obstacle to his attempted monopolization of the fur trade during the 1820s and 1830s. McKenney's efforts

Thomas McKenney. *Courtesy of Library of Congress.*

were met with Congressional resistance, mainly from the legislative supporters of Astor, especially the Missouri senator Thomas Hart Benton. His opponents in Washington, D.C., convinced Andrew Jackson to remove him from his post in 1830.

Throughout his career, McKenney maintained a grand design of perserving the historical record and cultural legacy of Native Americans in an Indian archive. He continually requested information, sketches, and accounts of Indian life from officials in the western territories, and he provided a great deal of assistance to ALBERT GALLATIN, secretary of the Treasury, for his study of Indian languages.

McKenney also organized the Indian Portrait Gallery of Native American notables who visited Washington, D.C., as delegations from their tribes during the treaty negotiations of the 1820s, commissioning the portrait artist CHARLES BIRD KING to paint the Indian chiefs in their native costumes. After having left government service, McKenney worked on his three-volume *History of the Indian Tribes of North America* (1837–44), with text by historian and novelist JAMES HALL and reproductions of King's paintings as well as those of other artists, such as JAMES OTTO LEWIS.

McKenney continued to promote the rights of Native Americans. Throughout his later career as a lecturer, he donated a share of the proceeds from his speaking engagements to Indian tribes.

McLAUGHLIN, JAMES (White Hair).
(1842–1923). Indian agent.

Originally from Ontario, James McLaughlin was a blacksmith in Minnesota at the time of his assignment as blacksmith and overseer to the Devil's Lake Indian Agency on the Great Sioux Reservation in the Dakota Territory in 1871. Five years later, he was promoted to the position of principal Indian agent at Devil's Lake. Marrying a Sioux mixed-blood, he became fluent in the Siouan language. He was known to the Indians as White Hair.

In 1881, McLaughlin was appointed Indian agent to about 5,000 Sioux of the Standing Rock Reservation. He promoted Indian education, including training in agriculture and other practical skills so that the Indians might become self-sufficient again without government-provided rations. He also helped establish an Indian court of justice to handle reservation criminal matters, and oversaw the founding of day schools for the reservation's children.

With the passage of the General Allotment Act (the DAWES Severalty Act) in 1887, McLaughlin was appointed to the commission assigned to arrange for the allotment of Sioux lands. His efforts were met with opposition by SITTING BULL.

McLaughlin also served as an inspector for the Bureau of Indian Affairs and, in this capacity, negotiated treaties on behalf of the government with Northern Plains tribes, including the Shoshones under chief WASHAKIE. He was succeeded in this position by the Sioux CHARLES EASTMAN.

In 1890, amid concerns over a new Indian war inspired by the spread of the Ghost Dance religion, McLaughlin called for the arrest of Sitting Bull. He urged the use of Indian police rather than federal troops as called for by General NELSON A. MILES. In December 1890, a detachment of Indian police, with army support nearby, killed Sitting bull when he reportedly resisted their attempt to take him into custody, an incident that led up to the Wounded Knee Massacre of BIG FOOT's band several weeks later.

McLaughlin remained active until his death at age 81, while among the Santee Sioux of Minnesota. In his book, *My Friend the Indian*, published in 1910, he related his experiences as an agent. (See also SITTING BULL.)

McQUEEN, PETER. *Mixed Creek-Seminole.*
(d. 1818). Leader in the Creek War of 1813–14 and the First Seminole War of 1817–18.

Peter McQueen, originally from Tallassee on the lower Tallapoosa River in present-day Alabama, fought American troops under General ANDREW JACKSON in two different wars. He helped precipitate the Creek War by leading a force of Red Sticks to Pensacola on the Gulf of Mexico, where the Spanish supplied them with guns, then in a raid on a party of settlers at Burnt Corn Creek in July 1813. After the defeat of the Red Sticks, McQueen joined the Seminoles in Florida. When Jackson invaded Florida and captured St. Marks in the Second Seminole War in 1818, McQueen escaped southward, where he reportedly died on a barren island, probably one of the Florida Keys. (See also BOLEK; WEATHERFORD, WILLIAM.)

McTAVISH, SIMON. *(ca. 1750–1804). Trader.*

Originally from Scotland, Simon McTavish came to North America in 1763. About 1775, he entered the fur trade, working for merchants out of Albany, New York. At the outbreak of the American Revolution that year, he moved to Montreal where he became involved in financing trade expeditions to the tribes of central Canada.

McTavish was instrumental in the series of mergers leading to the establishment of the North West Company in 1784, in order to effectively compete with the Hudson's Bay Company. He oversaw the building of the wilderness post Grand Portage on the north shore of Lake Superior, a stockaded settlement with a dozen buildings that served as a meeting point for Montreal businessmen, voyageurs, and tribal leaders.

In 1787, McTavish also became a partner with Joseph Frobisher in McTavish, Frobisher and Company, which operated principally as a subcontractor to the North West Company. The North West Company soon expanded its operation to much of the Canadian West and Northwest through the explorations of ALEXANDER MACKENZIE, SIMON FRASER, and DAVID THOMPSON, then merged with the Hudson's Bay Company in 1821, under the name of the latter.

MEACHAM, ALFRED B. *(1826–1882)*. Indian superintendent; reformer; historian.

Alfred Meacham was born in Indiana, where his parents had moved from North Carolina because of their objection to slavery. His first experience in managing Indians and promoting their rights was in 1845, when he assisted the Sac and Fox tribes in their relocation to Iowa, following the BLACK HAWK War of 1832. He journeyed to California during the 1849 Gold Rush and then settled in southern Oregon near the Umatilla Reservation.

Meacham became a prominent figure in Oregon politics and was a strong supporter of ULYSSES S. GRANT in the 1868 presidential election. In early 1869, the newly elected Grant appointed Meacham as superintendent of Indian Affairs for Oregon. Meacham conferred with the president and helped formulate the Peace Policy. He stressed a peaceful and humane approach recognizing the economic needs of Indians.

As superintendent for Oregon, Meacham was instrumental in persuading the Modocs to relocate to the Klamath Reservation in Oregon. When a band of Modocs under CAPTAIN JACK departed the reservation in defiance of the treaty agreement, resulting in the Modoc War of 1872–73, Meacham was appointed by President Grant, along with General EDWARD CANBY and Quaker missionary Eleasar Thomas, to a special Peace Commission. The April 1873 parley with the Modocs resulted in an attack by the Indians on the unarmed government delegation, in which General Canby and Eleasar Thomas were both killed. Meacham was severely wounded, shot more than five times, but was saved through the efforts of Captain Jack's cousin WINEMA, who was married to a white man.

On recovering from his wounds, Meacham returned East with a delegation of Modoc and Klamath Indians, including Winema, for a lecture tour to inform the public of the problems Indians faced under the government's removal policy. In Boston, in 1874, Meacham spoke before a group organized by WENDELL PHILLIPS. In Philadelphia, in 1875, Meacham and the Indian delegation addressed ALFRED LOVE's Universal Peace Union. The group also appeared that year at a meeting of PETER COOPER's U.S. Indian Commission in New York City.

Meacham's book *Wigwam and Warpath*, a history of the Modoc War, was published in 1875. Along with THOMAS A. BLAND, in 1878, Meacham established *Council Fire*, a journal dealing with Indian issues. In his magazine and in speeches, Meacham campaigned against the proposed transfer of the Bureau of Indian Affairs from the Interior Department to the War Department. In 1879, he brought Chief JOSEPH (Young Joseph) and other Nez Perces to Washington, D.C., to speak to government officials in support of continued civilian management of Indian affairs.

In 1880, the year after the Ute War, President Rutherford Hayes appointed Meacham to a special commission, along with GEORGE MANYPENNY and OTTO MEARS, to oversee the relocation of the Utes under OURAY from Colorado to new reservations in Utah. (See also CAPTAIN JACK; OURAY; WINEMA.)

MEARS, OTTO. *(1840–1931)*. Treaty commissioner; frontier road builder; railroad pioneer.

Born a Russian Jew, Otto Mears migrated to San Francisco in 1850 with the California Gold Rush. During the Civil War years, he served with CHRISTOPHER "KIT" CARSON in the campaign against the Navajos in western New Mexico and Arizona.

In Colorado during the 1870s, Mears became active in building and operating toll roads through the passes of the San Juan Mountains, achieving fame as "the Pathfinder of the San Juan." He contracted to transport cattle and other supplies to the Ute Reservation at Los Pinos.

After gold had been discovered near Los Pinos in 1871, the Department of the Interior sought to modify the 1868 treaty that had established the Los Pinos Reservation and open the area to white settlement and mining. In November 1872, a delegation of Utes was invited to Washington, D.C., to confer with Indian Bureau officials and President ULYSSES S. GRANT on the question of ceding tribal lands. Mears acted as interpreter for Chief OURAY and other tribal leaders on this trip. With Mears's help, the treaty was completed in 1873 at a subsequent council at Los Pinos. The Utes surrendered their claims to lands in the San Juan Mountains in exchange for goverment annuities and hunting privileges on the ceded tract.

Mears continued to maintain roads for the Indians and contracted to supply the Utes with cattle and provisions at their Uncompahgre Reservation. In the aftermath of the Ute War on the White River Reservation in 1879, and the killing of NATHAN MEEKER, he helped negotiate the release of white captives.

In January 1880, Mears accompanied the Indian agent Charles Adams, Chief Ouray, and a delegation of Utes to Washington, D.C., to face a Congressional committee investigating the Meeker incident and to negotiate new land cessions. That summer, along with GEORGE

MANYPENNY and ALFRED MEACHAM, he was part of the presidential commission to finalize the removal of the White River and Uncompahgre Utes to newly established adjoining reservations in Utah. The signatures of two-thirds of the Utes were required for the treaty to be approved. Mears reportedly offered the Indians $2 each for their signatures. The Ute Treaty of 1880 went into effect, and, under its terms, most of the Utes abandoned their Colorado homes for new reservations in Utah, where Mears was again instrumental in supplying accommodations and provisions.

Angered by Mears's apparent bribery of the Utes, Manypenny, chairman of the presidential commission to the Utes, reported the incident to federal authorities. The following year, Mears was ordered to Washington, D.C., to explain his actions to the Interior Department. The original complaint had been made to CARL SCHURZ, then secretary of the Interior, but by the time Mears reported to Washington, D.C., the newly elected U.S. president James Garfield had appointed Samuel Jordan Kirkwood to that post. On learning that Mears had paid out $2,000 of his own to persuade the Utes to agree to the treaty, Kirkwood, who himself had provided equipment to the Union army with his own money during the Civil War, congratulated Mears on his initiative and offered to help provide federal reimbursement for his expenses.

Shortly after the arrival of the Utes to their reservations in Utah, Mears was attacked and nearly killed by Ute chief Cojoe, who blamed Mears for his band's removal from Colorado.

Mears went on to develop railroads throughout the Southwest, as well as in Maryland. He served for many years in the Colorado legislature and later owned ranching and hotel enterprises in California. (See also OURAY.)

MECINA. *Kickapoo. (fl. 1820s).* Leader of resistance against removal.

In 1819, the Treaty of Edwardsville called for the cession of Kickapoo territory in Illinois in exchange for lands west of the Mississippi. Mecina, like KENNEKUK, the Kickapoo Prophet, believed in TECUMSEH's doctrine that tribal representatives could not sell lands belonging to the entire tribe. Mecina, however, encouraged more aggressive resistance than Kennekuk, and his warriors raided isolated farms on the Sangamon and Illinois rivers, sometimes as far east as the Wabash. They looted houses, killed cattle and hogs, and stole horses, then traded their booty to the Potawatomis for arms, ammunition, and food. In 1824, settlers petitioned to Congress, requesting federal troops, and increased military pressure eventually broke up Mecina's band. Some Kickapoos joined BLACK HAWK's Sacs and Foxes and participated in the Black Hawk War of 1832. Mecina and others joined Kennekuk's band, eventually relocating with them west of the Mississippi.

MEEK, JOSEPH L. *(1810–1875).* Trader; trapper, territorial official.

Originally from Washington County, Virginia, Joseph Meek moved to St. Louis, Missouri, in 1828 to join his brothers, Stephen and Hiram, in the fur trade. In 1829, he was a trapper for WILLIAM SUBLETTE in the upper Missouri and Northern Rockies. In the early 1830s, he joined CHRISTOPHER "KIT" CARSON on hunting expeditions into the Blackfoot country of present-day Montana. At one point, he survived an Indian ambush with Carson in the newly discovered Yellowstone region. In 1833, he crossed the Sierras into California with JOSEPH WALKER's expedition.

Meek continued to trap and trade for furs with the Indians over a territory ranging from the Snake River in what is now southern Idaho, to the mountains in what is now Utah. During this time, he had two different Indian wives, the first killed in a raid by Bannocks.

By 1840, the fur trade in the Northern Rockies had declined, and Meek settled with his second Indian wife at Fort Hall in what is now south-central Idaho. That year, he joined his friend Robert Newell in undertaking one of the earliest wagon train journeys through the mountains to the Oregon country.

Meek settled in the Willamette Valley and became involved in the new territory's political life after 1845; he eventually became marshal for the Oregon Territory. He left his daughter with Narcissa Whitman, wife of missionary MARCUS WHITMAN, to be educated. In 1848, following the outbreak of the Cayuse War under TILOUKAIKT and the killing of the Whitmans at their mission, Meek journeyed to Washington, D.C., to apprise President James Polk—whose wife Sarah Childress was Meek's cousin—of the incidents surrounding the Cayuse War. His visit to Washington, D.C., resulted in federal troops being dispatched to protect the Oregon settlers.

In 1855, Meek served in the territorial militia in the Yakima War. He became an active force in Republican Party politics in the Oregon Territory throughout the Civil War and in the years following. Nevertheless, his mixed-blood children were not accepted by the white community.

MEEKER, NATHAN COOK. *(1817–1879).* Indian agent.

Born in Euclid, Ohio, Nathan Meeker worked as a journalist with Horace Greeley's *New-York Tribune*, specializing in stories about agriculture. He was especially interested in communal farming enterprises of the period, such as the Oneida Community in New York

State. In 1870, with Greeley's support, he established a cooperative farming community, known as Greeley, about 50 miles north of Denver, Colorado.

Eight years later, Meeker attempted to apply his experience in cooperative farm management to the Indians. As Indian agent to the Utes of the White River Reservation in Colorado, Meeker faced tribal resistance to his efforts in transforming the hunting-based economy of the Utes to one of conventional agriculture.

Disputes arose in September 1879, when Meeker's proposal to plow under traditional Ute horse-grazing lands led to a fight with the medicine man CANALLA. Meeker summoned the assistance of federal troops, and a force commanded by Major THOMAS T. THORNBURGH was dispatched from Fort Steele, Wyoming. Warriors under chiefs NICAAGAT and COLOROW attacked the federal troops as they approached the reservation at Milk Creek, believing this was an attempt to forcibly take their lands. Meanwhile, Utes under QUINKENT killed Meeker and 11 other whites, and took a number of women and children hostage, including Meeker's wife and daughter.

Through the mediation of the chief OURAY, a peaceful settlement between the government and the militants was reached and the hostages were released. The government retaliated against the Utes the following year by dispossessing them of their Colorado lands and resettling them on reservations in Utah. (See also OURAY.)

MEGAPOLENSIS, JOHANNES. *(1603–1670).* Missionary; scholar.

Johannes Megapolensis was born of Catholic parents in Holland, but renounced that religion to join the Dutch Reformed church. In 1642 he came to New Netherland with his family. For most of his contracted six-year ministry, he practiced up the Hudson River near Fort Orange (present-day Albany, New York) among Dutch farmers and traders, as well as among the Iroquois who came to the post to trade.

Unlike Jonas Michaelius, the first Dutch missionary to New Netherland, Megapolensis quickly established good relations with the Indians. In his first year, he successfully negotiated the release of the Jesuit captive ISAAC JOGUES.

After two years, Megapolensis had mastered the Iroquoian language and could preach to the Indians in their own tongue. He wrote numerous letters to correspondents in Holland about the Mohawk language, rituals, homeland, and form of government, which were printed without his consent.

Megapolensis intended to return to Holland at the end of his term, but, at the request of the governor of the colony PETER STUYVESANT, stayed on as minister in New Amsterdam (present-day New York City). When New Netherland fell to the British in 1664, Megapolensis swore an oath of allegiance to the king of England in order to continue his work among his congregation.

MENARD, ANTOINE PIERRE   (Pierre Menard). *(1766–1844).* Trader; explorer; Indian commissioner.

Antoine Pierre Menard, known as Pierre Menard, was born in St. Antoine, Quebec, and raised in Montreal. By the time he was 20, he was living at the Indiana frontier settlement of Vincennes, where he worked with Indian trader Francis Vigo. In 1789, he relocated to Kaskaskia, Illinois, where he opened a store with Toussaint DuBois to supply goods to white settlers, as well as to area Indians. In 1795, he became an officer in the Indian territorial militia under WILLIAM HENRY HARRISON, eventually rising to the rank of lieutenant colonel. He subsequenlty was elected to the territorial legislature and was later appointed a territorial magistrate.

In 1806, Menard married a relative of the fur-trading CHOUTEAU family. He also went into partnership with fur entrepreneur and explorer MANUEL LISA and provided financial support and equipment for Lisa's first expedition of 1807 to establish trade relations with the Indians in the Bighorn region of present-day Montana.

In 1809, Menard and Lisa merged their operation with that of Chouteau family, WILLIAM CLARK, ANDREW HENRY, and other St. Louis traders, to form the St. Louis Missouri Fur Company. Menard was part of the company's 1810 expedition to the upper Missouri River and Northern Rockies. In April of that year, Menard and Henry led a contingent, including JOHN COLTER, GEORGE DROUILLARD, and EDWARD ROSE, as far as the Three Forks of the Missouri, near present-day Bozeman, Montana, but attacks by Blackfoot Indians prevented the party from remaining long in the region. Soon after, Menard returned to Kaskaskia, Illinois, where he continued to flourish in the Indian trade.

In the year after the War of 1812, Menard served in the Illinois territorial legislature, and, in 1818, became Illinois's first state lieutenant governor. He left after one term and subsequently served as Indian commissioner to the region's tribes.

MENATONON. *Chowanoc. (fl. 1580s).* Friend to Roanoke colonists.

Menatonon was a chief of the Chowanocs, an Algonquian-speaking tribe living on the Chowan River in what is now northeast North Carolina. In 1585–86, he was captured by a party of English colonists under Ralph Layne, part of WALTER RALEIGH's first Roanoke Colony. Menatonon gave them information concerning the geography, Indians, and wildlife of the region. The colonists came to respect him for his intelligence and released him after a few days. Menatonon later induced the Weapemeoc chief Okiska to help the colonists. When JOHN WHITE reported on the second Roanoke Colony of 1587, he mentioned Menatonon's wife and child, but nothing of the chief, who had perhaps since died.

MENENDEZ DE AVILES, PEDRO. *(1519–1574).* Explorer; colonial governor of Florida.

Pedro Menendez de Aviles was born in Aviles, Spain, to a landed and fairly affluent family. Nevertheless, he ran away from home in 1533 and went to sea. He rose to prominence in Spain's Royal Navy and, in 1549, was assigned to duty against the pirates then disrupting shipping off the Spanish coast.

In 1554, Menendez was named commander of the Spanish fleet operating in its New World colonies, and he made three trips to the Americas between 1555 and 1563. A political controversy led to his imprisonment in 1563–65. Through the influence of King Philip II, he was released and later commissioned to reaffirm Spain's claim to Florida.

French Huguenots under JEAN RIBAULT and RENE DE LAUDONNIERE, had established a colony at Fort Caroline, near present-day Jacksonville, Florida. Shortly after his arrival on the Atlantic coast of Florida in August 1565, with 500 colonists and soldiers aboard 11 ships, Menendez established the settlement and fort at present-day St. Augustine. The following month, he led his forces against the French at Fort Caroline, killing most of the inhabitants. Menendez's forces then occupied the French settlement, which he renamed San Mateo. In 1568, French troops under Dominique de Gourgues, along with Florida Indian allies, including the Saturiba OLOTARACA, assaulted and decimated the Spanish garrison, avenging the earlier attack.

Menendez went on to explore Florida's Gulf coast, where he established friendly relations with various tribes. He then sailed north from St. Augustine to explore the coastal islands of present-day South Carolina, advancing as far north as Chesapeake Bay. The Jesuit missionaries who accompanied the Menendez 1565 expedition to Florida subsequently set about to establish missions to the Indians of the region.

Menendez left Florida in 1567 to oversee Spain's naval operations against the British, returning only briefly in 1571. He died three years later, while still in the service of the Spanish navy.

MENEWA (Manawa, Manauway, "great warrior"; Hothlepoya, "crazy war hunter"). *Mixed Creek.* *(ca. 1765–1865).* War chief of the Red Sticks.

Menewa, born along the Tallapoosa River in what is now Alabama, established his reputation as a daring warrior through numerous raids for horses on settlements in Tennessee. One story relates how, on returning from an expedition, he gave one of the stolen horses to a white traveler who had none, announcing while he made the gift that if the man had owned a horse, he would have stolen it. Menewa became further known to whites when his band was charged for a murder in Georgia, which is thought to have been actually carried out by his rival WILLIAM McINTOSH's band of White Sticks. In retaliation, the settlers burned a Creek village, an incident contributing to Menewa's militant stance against whites.

When TECUMSEH visited Creek country to advocate his alliance, Menewa was receptive, and he joined WILLIAM WEATHERFORD against troops under General ANDREW JACKSON in the Creek War of 1813–14. At the Battle of Horseshoe Bend in March 1814, Menewa, who was in charge of the Red Stick faction after Weatherford's departure from the scene, was shot seven times. Left for dead, he saw a soldier looting the body of a Creek, grabbed a rifle, and shot the soldier, who shot him again. Menewa managed to crawl off to a hidden camp in the swamps where the Creek women and children waited. He later recovered and surrendered, losing all his land and possessions to whites.

Menewa was one of the Creek leaders of the faction opposed to removal. He carried out the execution of McIntosh who was sentenced to death by the Creeks after having signed the Treaty of Indian Springs in 1825, ceding 25 million acres.

Menewa traveled to Washington, D.C., in 1826, along with OPOTHLEYAHOLO and PADDY CARR. In exchange for promises of peace, the Creeks were allowed to retain some parcels of land. As a show of friendship, Menewa led warriors in support of federal troops in the Second Seminole War of 1835–42. Yet, despite his assistance, he too was forced to relocate to the Indian Territory in 1836. (See also WEATHERFORD, WILLIAM.)

MERRITT, WESLEY. *(1834–1910).* Army officer in the Sioux War for the Black Hills of 1876–77.

Originally from New York City, Wesley Merritt was raised in Illinois. On graduating from West Point in 1860, he was commissioned an officer in a dragoon regiment, then at the outbreak of the Civil War, he was brevetted a colonel and eventually a brigadier general of volunteer cavalry. He fought under General PHILIP H. SHERIDAN in the final engagements of the war.

Brevetted a major general of volunteers at the war's end, Merritt reverted to the regular rank of colonel in command of the 9th Cavalry, a black unit, at Fort Davis in west Texas, where he campaigned against raiding Apaches.

In July 1876, during the War for the Black Hills against Sioux under SITTING BULL, Merritt assumed command of the 5th Cavalry. His regiment was sent to join up with General GEORGE CROOK's force in the Powder River country of Montana. Yet he was delayed when he faced a force of 800 Cheyenne warriors, on their way to join CRAZY HORSE's band, in the Battle of War Bonnet Creek, Nebraska, on July 17, 1876. In this engagement, although little actual combat took place, Merritt's scout, WILLIAM "BUFFALO BILL" CODY, killed the Cheyenne warrior chief YELLOW HAIR in a gun duel. Merritt's command then pursued the Cheyennes back to the Red Cloud Reservation in Nebraska.

During the Nez Perce War of 1877, Merritt's regiment pursued Chief JOSEPH (Young Joseph) and his people in the area around Yellowstone National Park, Wyoming. Then, during the Ute War of 1879, the 5th Cavalry relieved Major THOMAS T. THORNBURGH's command at the Battle of Milk Creek, Colorado, in October 1879. It was Merritt and his men who first reached the White River Agency and discovered that Indian agent NATHAN MEEKER and other whites had been killed by the Utes. Following this engagement, through the diplomacy of Chief OURAY, Merritt's forces rounded up the warring Utes.

In 1882–87, Merritt, promoted to the regular rank of brigadier general, served as superintendent at West Point. During the Spanish-American War of 1898, he led the assault on Manila, in the Phillippines. He took part in the peace negotiations in Paris ending this conflict, retiring from the service soon afterward. (See also OURAY; SITTING BULL.)

METACOM. See PHILIP.

METEA ("kiss me"). *Potawatomi. (ca. 1775–1827).* War chief; orator. Ally of British in the War of 1812.

Metea lived in the village of Muskwawasepeotan along the St. Joseph River, about 10 miles from Fort Wayne, Indiana. A friend of the British, from whom his band received supplies during the War of 1812, he led an attack on the inhabitants of Chicago and 50 regulars under Captain Nathan Heald, as they retreated to Fort Detroit on being warned of impending danger by the sympathetic Potawatomi BLACK PARTRIDGE. In a later skirmish against troops on their way to reinforce Fort Wayne, Metea was shot in the arm by General WILLIAM HENRY HARRISON, but escaped. Along with Black Partridge and WABAUNSEE, Metea participated in numerous peace conferences in the following years, becoming known for his oratory. He also encouraged education among Indian youth, sending some from his tribe to the Choctaw Academy in Kentucky. He died soon after a peace council, having mistaken a bottle of poison for liquor.

METHVIN, JOHN JASPER. *(1846–1941).* Missionary; educator.

John Jasper Methvin was born in Jeffersonville, Georgia, and was educated at Auburn Institute. He was a soldier in the Confederate army in 1862–64. Following the Civil War, he studied law and was admitted to the Georgia bar, practicing for only a brief period.

In 1870, Methvin was licensed as preacher in the Methodist Episcopal Church, and four years later, he became a deacon. During the 1870s, he also served as a principal and superintendent of public schools in White County, Georgia. From 1880 to 1885, he was the president of first Gainesille College, then Butler Female College, both in Georgia.

In 1885, Methvin accepted a position as a missionary to the Choctaw Nation in the Indian Territory, and superintendent of the New Hope Seminary, a school for Choctaw girls. His tenure there lasted only one year, and, in 1886, he went on to administer the Seminole Academy.

In 1887, Methvin began his missionary work among the Kiowas, Comanches, and Apaches at the Methodist Episcopal mission and school at Anadarko in what is now Oklahoma. He was a preacher to these tribes, as well as a principal to several Indian boarding schools until 1908.

Methvin believed that evangelical work would ultimately bring Western civilization to Indians. He strongly opposed such Native American Indian religious movements as the Ghost Dance and the ritualistic use of peyote and encouraged the use of camp meetings and revivals. He also sent missionary workers into the Indian community to spread Christian teachings and to teach families about Western domestic living. Notable Kiowas who were influenced by Methvin's work included STUMBLING BEAR and KICKING BIRD.

MEXANNO. See MRIKSAH.

MIANTINOMO (Miantonomo, Miantonomi, Miantunnomoh, "he wages war"). *Narraganset. (ca. 1600–1643).* Sachem. Nephew of CANONICUS; father of CANONCHET; cousin of NINIGRET; uncle of QUINNAPIN.

Miantinomo and his uncle Canonicus were friends of ROGER WILLIAMS and sold land to him; as a result, they were distrusted by Massachusetts authorities with whom Williams had broken. In 1636, Miantinomo was summoned to Boston, at which time he convinced the authorities of his non-militance to whites. In the Pequot War of 1636–37, he aided the colonial force under JOHN MASON in its attack on SASSACUS's village. In 1638, Miantinomo signed a three-way agreement with the colony of Connecticut and the Pequot branch tribe known as the Mohegans under UNCAS. In 1640 and 1642, the Narraganset sachem again had to refute charges of plotting against the colonists, as did his Niantic cousin and ally Ninigret.

In 1643, war broke out between the Narragansets and Mohegans. On capturing Miantinomo, the Mohegans turned him over to authorities in Hartford, Connecticut, who sent him to Boston for trial. He was condemned to death and turned over to Uncas for execution. Uncas's brother Wawequa carried out the sentence. In 1841, a monument was erected on the site where Miantinomo was killed, near present-day Norwich, Connecticut.

MICANOPY (Mikanopy, Micconopy, Micco-nuppe, Michenopah, "head chief"; The Governor, Pond Governor; Sint-chakkee). *Seminole. (ca. 1780–1849).* Hereditary chief of the Seminoles during the Second Seminole War of 1835–42. Grandson of King PAYNE; grandnephew of BOLEK; uncle of WILD CAT.

Micanopy was probably born in the St. Augustine region of Florida. When Bolek, who had succeeded King Payne as head chief of the various Seminole bands, died, Micanopy assumed leadership. He came to have large landholdings, livestock, and slaves.

In 1832, a number of the Seminole chiefs agreed to the Treaty of Payne's Landing, calling for the cession of tribal lands and relocation to the Creek area in the Indian Territory; Micanopy refused to sign, however. Although he tried to maintain peace, he gave his support to the younger warriors preparing to resist forced removal, such as his nephew Wild Cat, ALLIGATOR, and OSCEOLA. Micanopy participated in the attacks on Major FRANCIS DADE's and General DUNCAN CLINCH's columns in December 1835.

In June 1837, Micanopy agreed to relocation, but was kidnapped by Osceola, who hoped to prevent Micanopy's surrender. Later that year, Micanopy finally gave himself up to troops under General THOMAS JESUP. He was at first treated as a prisoner and sent to Charleston, South Carolina, before finally being permitted to emigrate to the Indian Territory.

In 1845, he was one of the signers of the agreement giving the Western Seminoles independence from the Creeks. (See also OSCEOLA.)

MILES, NELSON APPLETON. (1839–1925).
Army officer in the Plains Indian wars.

Nelson A. Miles was born near Westminster, Massachusetts, where he was working as a clerk in a crockery store when the Civil War erupted in 1861. He enlisted in the 22nd Massachusetts Infantry. Rising rapidly in the ranks, he served with the Army of the Potomac throughout the war, seeing action in most of the major battles and serving as a staff officer to General OLIVER HOWARD. He was wounded at the Battle of Fredericksburg in 1862, and again at Chancellorsville in 1863. For his service at Chancellorsville, he was awarded the Congressional Medal of Honor. By the end of the war, he was a major general of volunteers. While in charge of imprisoned Confederate leader Jefferson Davis at Fort Monroe, Virginia, Miles drew criticism from political leaders when he ordered that the ex-Confederate president be kept in shackles.

Miles remained in the military after the war, as a colonel in the regular army, in command of the 5th Infantry at military posts on the western frontier. He was in the field during the Red River War of 1874–75 along with Colonel RANALD S. MACKENZIE and pursued Comanche militants under QUANAH PARKER and their Kiowa, Cheyenne, and Arapaho allies on the Staked Plain of west Texas.

During fall and winter 1876–77, Miles led the 5th Infantry from a base at the confluence of the Tongue and Yellowstone rivers in pursuit of the Sioux and Cheyenne militants of the War for the Black Hills, wearing them down and making it difficult for them to obtain food. When the Indians attempted hit-and-run strikes, the soldiers responded with heavy artillery. In the Battle of Wolf Mountain, Montana, on January 8, 1877, CRAZY HORSE and 800 Sioux and Cheyenne warriors assaulted Miles's camp on the Tongue River. Miles then ordered his howitzers, concealed inside wagons, to open fire, driving off the Indians. Severe winter weather and lack of food and ammunition forced many of the Sioux, including Crazy Horse, to surrender the following spring. Near Fort Keogh, Montana, on May 7, 1877, Miles led his command to victory over Miniconjou Sioux leader LAME DEER at the Battle of Lame Deer (or the Battle of Muddy Creek), one of the last conflicts of the Sioux Wars.

In the Nez Perce War of 1877, Miles and his regiment pursued Chief JOSEPH (Young Joseph) and his followers east out of Fort Keogh while General Oliver Howard advanced from the south. Miles reached the militant band first and, in the Bear Paw Mountains, after prolonged fighting from September 30 to October 5, forced a surrender. In the campaign against the Nez Perces, Miles used over 200 formerly hostile Cheyennes.

In 1878, toward the end of the Bannock War, the uprising led by BUFFALO HORN, EGAN, and OYTES, Miles's soldiers helped prevent Bannocks and Northern Paiutes from fleeing Idaho and Oregon to Canada while they were being pursued by troops under General Howard.

In spring and summer 1879, Miles led his command in pursuit of Sitting Bull and some of his followers when they crossed from Canada, where they had taken refuge, into Montana to hunt near Milk Creek. When Sitting Bull and his people retreated back across the international boundary, federal officials restrained Miles from proceeding into Canada after them. Sitting Bull returned to the United States permanently two years later.

Miles was made a brigadier general in 1880. He commanded the army's Department of the Columbia in 1880–85; the Department of the Missouri in 1885–86; then the Department of Arizona, succeeding General GEORGE CROOK.

In this capacity, Miles launched the final offensive against GERONIMO and the Chiricahua Apaches. He assembled a force of 5,000 regular army troops, nearly 25 percent of the total forces in the regular army, for this expedition in search of less than 30 Apache warriors. A small company of troops and scouts, led by Captain HENRY W. LAWTON and Lieutenant Charles Gatewood, tracked Geronimo into the Sierra Madre country of northern Mexico. Lawton was able to persuade Geronimo to surrender with the condition that none of the renegade Apaches be hanged. Miles agreed to these terms at a meeting with Geronimo at Skeleton Canyon, Arizona, on September 4, 1886, despite President Grover Cleveland's wishes that the offending Indians be handed over to Arizona civil authorities in an unconditional surrender.

Miles then sent Geronimo and his warriors to the military prison at Fort Marion, Florida. Yet Miles also sent Crook's former loyal Apache scouts, as well as a number of the San Carlos Reservation Apaches, to the Florida prison. For this action, he drew the criticism of General Crook and the Indian Rights Association.

Assuming command of the entire Division of the Missouri in 1890, Miles headed federal troops during the Ghost Dance Uprising. He suspected that SITTING BULL, then living at the Standing Rock Reservation, North Dakota, was responsible for the latest Sioux outbreak and ordered his arrest. The Indian agent JAMES McLAUGHLIN had Indian police carry out the mission, in which Sitting Bull was killed. Miles then assembled a force of 3,000 soldiers at the Pine Ridge Reservation, South Dakota, and dispatched the 7th Cavalry under colonel JAMES FORSYTH to bring in BIG FOOT's band. On December 29, 1890, Forsyth's men, in the process of disarming the Sioux under a truce agreement, opened fire in what was to become known as the Wounded Knee Massacre. Miles, whose reputation was tarnished by the events at Wounded Knee, relieved Forsyth of his command, although the War Department later restored it. On January 15, 1891, Miles personally accepted the surrender of the Sioux leader KICKING BEAR, ending the uprising.

Miles went on to command federal troops in the disturbances in Chicago resulting from the 1894 Pullman strike. The following year, he was named commander in chief of the army. He took part in military actions against Puerto Rico in the Spanish-American War of 1898. At the rank of lieutenant general, he retired from the army in 1903. (See also GERONIMO; Young JOSEPH; SITTING BULL.)

MILFORT, LOUIS LE CLERC (Tastanegy, Tastonagi, "great war chief"). *(d. ca. 1814).* War chief of the Creeks; historian. Brother-in-law of ALEXANDER McGILLIVRAY.

The Frenchman Louis Le Clerc Milfort came to North America in spring 1775, landing at New London, Connecticut. In the course of a year, he traveled throughout the East, to the Georgia frontier and the Creek town of Coweta on the Chattahoochee River. Here, at a grand council of the Creeks, he met Chief Alexander McGillivray. Settling among the Creeks, Milfort eventually married MvGillivray's sister. He also became one of the chief's closest advisers and war chiefs, leading Creek warriors in battle against Georgia settlers.

Milfort stayed with the Creeks for two years after McGillivray's death in 1793 and, seeking French military support, vied for power with WILLIAM

Nelson Appleton Miles. *Courtesy of Library of Congress.*

BOWLES, who eventually proclaimed himself director general of the Creek Nation. With his power base weakened, Milfort returned to Europe in 1795.

Because of continuing designs on North America, France conferred upon Milfort the rank of brigadier general in 1796. Napoleon reacquired the Louisiana Territory from Spain, but then sold it to the United States in 1803, ending Milfort's hopes of returning to America in an official capacity.

It is thought Milfort fought on behalf of Napoleon in ensuing European campaigns. He died in 1814, or sometime soon after.

Milfort's *Memoirs or a Quick Glance at my various Travels and My Sojourn in the Creek Nation*, which he hurriedly wrote in 1802 in the hope of influencing Napoleon, are an early, although sometimes inaccurate, source concerning Creek history and culture.

MILLER, ALFRED JACOB. *(1810–1874).* Artist; writer.

Following studies with the American artist Thomas Sully, Alfred Jacob Miller left his native Baltimore to continue art training in Europe in 1833–34. On returning to the United States, he attempted to set up a practice in 1837 as a portrait painter in New Orleans.

That year, the British sportsman and hunter Captain William Drummond Stewart hired Miller to accompany him on a hunting expedition across the Rockies into Oregon, during which Miller was to produce studies for paintings for the Stewart family castle in Scotland. They joined up with an American Fur Company wagon train and journeyed west on the Oregon Trail, through the great South Pass of the Rockies in Wyoming, then to the company's trading post on the Green River in Oregon.

Along the way, Miller made over 100 sketches of Indians as well as mountain men, which served as the basis for oil paintings he completed upon his return to New Orleans. In 1840–42, Miller visited Stewart's family castle in Scotland, where he continued to produce paintings of Western scenes. In 1842, he settled again in Baltimore, where he continued to paint.

A book, with a text by Miller and illustrations drawn from the sketches the artist made on the 1837 expedition, survives today in manuscript form as part of the collection of the Thomas Gilcrease Institute's library in Tulsa, Oklahoma.

MILLY. See FRANCIS, MILLY.

MILNER, MOSES EMBREE (California Joe). *(1829–1876).* Army scout.

Moses Milner, later known as California Joe, left his home near Stanford, Kentucky, in 1843, when he was just 14, to become a trapper in Wyoming. He became a scout for the army in 1846, the first year of the Mexican War, serving under General STEPHEN WATTS KEARNY and Colonel ALEXANDER W. DONIPHAN in New Mexico.

In 1849, Milner went to California to prospect for gold, and, with little success, he established a cattle ranch in Oregon four years later. He returned to the East to fight in the Civil War with the Army of the Potomac, as part of a unit of sharpshooters.

In 1865, frontier artist CHARLES STOBIE was first introduced to the life of a scout when he met Milner during a wagon train trip west to Denver. Milner again found work as an army scout after 1866. Then, in 1868, when Colonel GEORGE ARMSTRONG CUSTER was named commander of the 7th Cavalry, at Fort Dodge, Kansas, he offered Milner employment in his regiment. Milner served very briefly as the regiment's chief scout, but, because of a drunken episode, reverted to the rank of regular scout. After the Battle of Washita of November 1868, in which Custer's command attacked BLACK KETTLE's Cheyenne band, Milner and another scout traveled across 100 miles of hostile Indian country in less than two days to deliver the news to General PHILIP H. SHERIDAN at Camp Supply.

In 1875, Milner was the scout for Colonel RICHARD IRVING DODGE's geological expedition into the Black Hills. The discovery of gold was finally confirmed by this expedition, and Milner stayed to try again his hand at prospecting.

Milner remained a close friend of Custer and his wife, Elizabeth, corresponding with them regularly. Moved by the news of Custer's death at the Little Bighorn in June 1876, he rejoined the army as a scout for the 5th Cavalry at Fort Robinson, Nebraska, under General GEORGE CROOK. That October, he was shot to death in a quarrel with a civilian. (See also BLACK KETTLE.)

MINIMIC (Eagle's Head, Eagle Head). *Southern Cheyenne. (d. 1881).* Peacemaker; negotiator. Father of HOWLING WOLF.

In 1864, before the Sand Creek Massacre, BLACK KETTLE dispatched a letter of peace to Fort Lyon; Minimic volunteered to accompany One-Eye and his wife on this mission. Then he agreed to act as a hostage for agent EDWARD WYNKOOP, to ensure his safety when he rode to a conference with Black Kettle and other Cheyenne leaders at Smoky Hill in advance of the Camp Weld meeting with Governor JOHN EVANS. Minimic later participated in the Little Arkansas Council of 1865 and the Medicine Lodge Treaty of 1867. He led his band to Fort Sill in April 1869 and acted as one of the Southern Cheyennes' chief negotiators for peace. Nevertheless, in April 1875, during the Red River War under the Comanche QUANAH PARKER and other leaders, Minimic was one of the Cheyennes shipped to St. Augustine, Florida. At Fort Marion, he regularly acted as peacemaker and mediator during disputes. He was imprisoned until April 1878, whereupon he returned to the Indian Territory.

MINUIT, PETER (Peter Minnewit).
(ca. 1580–1638). Dutch colonial governor.

Born in the northwestern German city of Wesel, Peter Minuit was a member of the Dutch West Indies Company council that administered the New Netherland colony at the mouth of the Hudson River, now parts of New York and New Jersey. He visited the Dutch settlements at Manhattan and Staten Island in 1625, then returned to Holland.

The next year, 1626, Minuit was appointed the director general of New Netherland. On orders from the Dutch West Indies Company directors, he was sent to negotiate with the Manhattan Indians, a band of Delawares, for the purchase of the island bearing their name in order to establish a legal claim to Dutch settlements. He arranged for the purchase of Manhattan Island for trade goods worth 60 guilders, or $24. New Amsterdam, at the southern tip of Manhattan, soon became a thriving community.

Minuit served as colonial governor of New Netherland until 1631, at which time, he was dismissed by the Dutch West Indies Company in a management dispute. On returning to Europe, he obtained Swedish support to establish a colony in Delaware Bay, and with 50 colonists aboard two ships, he departed Gothenburg, Sweden. Arriving in March 1638, his party landed near the site of present-day Wilmington, Delaware. Minuit soon met with local Indian leaders and arranged for the sale of tribal lands, whereupon he founded a settlement called Fort Christian and established trade relations with neighboring bands.

That year, on a trading voyage to St. Christopher in the Caribbean, his ship was caught in a hurricane, and Minuit was lost at sea. JOHAN PRINTZ became the colonial governor of New Sweden in 1642.

MOANAHONGA ("great walker";
Winaugusconey, "man not afraid to travel"; Big Neck). *Iowa. (d. ca. 1835).* Signer of treaty ceding Iowa lands.

In 1824, Moanahonga was encouraged by WILLIAM CLARK, the former explorer and now Indian superintendent out of St. Louis, to go to Washington, D.C., with other Iowa chiefs, including MAHASKAH. There he signed a treaty ceding his tribe's territory in what is now Missouri for an annuity of $500 and some supplies. On returning to his homeland, Moanahonga was surprised to see white settlers already present and claimed he had not understood the negotiatons. He painted his face black in mourning for having, as he described it, sold the bones of his ancestors.

In 1829, Moanahonga set out to St. Louis with about 60 of his band to meet with Clark again concerning what he considered treaty violations. On the way, his group met up with a party of whites who offered them liquor, and, while the Indians were drunk, stole their possessions. A young Iowa then killed a settler's hog. In response, the settlers not only raised a militia force and demanded that the Iowas depart the region, but pursued them and surrounded their camp. Moanahonga appeared from his tepee holding a peace pipe high, only to be fired upon. His brother and sister were killed in the volley, as were other women and a child. In a counterattack, the Iowas killed the man who had shot the child, wounded several others, and captured the man who had shot Moanahonga's sister, eventually executing him. Troops were sent in to quell the uprising.

After having escaped to the north, where he hid out among the Sacs and Foxes, Moanahonga was induced to surrender. In a trial for murder, a white jury found the chief and others in his band innocent. Moanahonga died about five years later in a fight with a party of Sioux raiding his village for horses.

MOHONGO (Myhangah). *Osage. (fl. 1820s).*
Visitor to Europe.

A Frenchman by the name of David Delaunay, who had been living in St. Louis, induced Kihegashugh (Little Chief), his wife, Mohongo, and four other Osages to take a trip with him to Europe to put them on display for his personal profit. It is not known whether the Indians believed Delaunay was acting in some official capacity or whether they knew they were traveling to Europe or simply New York and Washington, D.C.

The party traveled down the Mississippi River and sailed out of New Orleans in 1827, stopping over in New York, then continuing to Le Havre. Delaunay took the group to Holland, Germany, Paris, and St. Cloud, where they were received by King Charles X.

The Osages were soon abandoned by Delaunay, either because the tour had lost its popularity, or because he was recognized by creditors and arrested. The Osages wandered about Paris, sick and hungry. Moreover, Mohongo was pregnant. They were finally taken to the MARQUIS DE LAFAYETTE, who reportedly paid their fares home.

Kihegashugh and two others in the party died from smallpox during the return trip. The survivors landed in Norfolk, Virginia, and, with the financial help of THOMAS McKENNEY, reached Washington, D.C., in 1830. There Mohongo had her portrait painted with her new child by CHARLES BIRD KING before returning to Osage country in Missouri.

MONCACHTAPE ("killer of pain and fatigue").
Yazoo. (fl. mid-1800s). Indian explorer.

In the mid-1800s, a Frenchman by the name of Le Page du Pratz met a Yazoo Indian in Louisiana and received from him an account of his travels throughout much of North America. Moncachtape described how, after the death of his wife and children, he had set out on a trip to Shawnee country along the Ohio River, then into Iroquois country in New York, and Abnaki country in Maine, all the way to the St. Lawrence. After his return to his homeland along the lower Mississippi, Moncachtape had started out again, he claimed this time northwestward along the Missouri, the same route traveled by LEWIS and CLARK, eventually reaching the Pacific Ocean. He further described how he and a group of local Indians had ambushed and killed 11 bearded white men wearing soft clothes of varied colors. Such an attack has never been verified, nor were his earlier travels, but Moncachtape did demonstrate a knowledge of several different Indian languages.

MONTCALM-GOZON, LOUIS JOSEPH DE, MARQUIS DE SAINT-VERAN (Marquis de Montcalm). *(1712–1759).* French general in the French and Indian War of 1754–63.

French-born Louis Joseph de Montcalm entered the military while a young boy and served as an ensign. He later saw action with the French army in the War of the Polish Succession and the War of the Austrian Succession.

In 1756, the Marquis de Montcalm came to North America to take command of French forces in Canada in the French and Indian War, replacing Baron Dieskau. Montcalm was forced to share his military authority with New France's colonial governor, the Marquis de Vaudreuil, which hampered his military planning.

In 1756, Montcalm led a successful attack against Fort Oswego, near present-day Oswego, New York, on Lake Ontario, and captured that strategic Great Lakes post for the French. His decisive defeat of the British at Oswego led the tribes of the Iroquois League, except the Mohawks, to seek neutrality agreements with the French at Montreal. The withdrawal of these tribes from their alliance with the British left the frontier of northern and western New York open to French colonial troops and their Indian auxiliaries, mostly Abnakis, in attacks on British settlements along the Mohawk Valley.

In 1757, Montcalm's combined force laid siege to Fort William Henry, on the southern end of Lake George, New York. Although Montcalm succeeded in gaining the surrender of the garrison, his Indian troops ignored his promise of safe passage to the captured British and killed many of them.

In 1758, at Fort Carillon (Fort Ticonderoga) on New York's Lake Champlain, Montcalm successfully fought off a siege by British forces led by General James Abercromby. French-allied Algonquian Indians from the Ohio Valley, including Chippewas, Sacs, Foxes, Ottawas, Hurons, Illinois, and Miamis, played a key role in the victory.

Beginning in May 1759, Montcalm defended Quebec City against a British siege led by General JAMES WOLFE and Vice Admiral Charles Saunders. That September, French forces were unable to repel British troops on the Plains of Abraham. Both Montcalm and Wolfe died in this engagement. Montreal also fell to British forces the next year, giving Great Britain control of New France.

MONTEZUMA, CARLOS (Wassaja, Wasajah, Wasagah, "signaling," "beckoning"). *Yavapai. (ca. 1867–1923).* Physician; reformer; editor.

Wassaja was born in the Superstition Mountains of Arizona among the Yavapai Indians, sometimes referred to as the Mojave-Apaches because of their close ties to the Tonto Apaches. His father's name was Cocuyevah.

In 1871, the boy was captured by Pima Indians. He lived with them briefly along the Gila River, then was sold to a photographer-prospector by the name of Carlos Gentile for $30. Meanwhile, his mother, who had left the reservation to search for her son, was shot by an Indian scout. Gentile took the boy—whom he renamed Carlos after himself, and Montezuma after the ancient ruins—to Santa Fe, New Mexico, then East to Illinois and New York. Following his financial ruin because of a fire, Gentile committed suicide in 1877. A family by the name of Baldwin cared for the boy for a short period until George W. Ingalls, a Baptist missionary, placed him with W. H. Stedman, a minister in Urbana, Illinois.

Montezuma was tutored privately for two years, then was enrolled in a preparatory program for the University of Illinois, which he entered as a freshman the next year. He graduated with a bachelor of science degree in 1884. While working part-time for a pharmacist and with a partial scholarship, he attended the Chicago Medical College, graduating in 1889.

For a short time in Chicago, Montezuma attempted a private practice, then accepted an appointment in the Indian Service as physician-surgeon at the Fort Stevenson Indian School in North Dakota. After a year, he was transferred to the Western Shoshone Agency in Nevada, and, three years later, he worked at the Colville Agency in Washington. Frustrated by the conditions on western reservations, he began work in 1894 at the Carlisle Indian School in Pennsylvania, where he became a close friend of RICHARD HENRY PRATT, as well as the Sioux woman Zitkala-sa (Gertrude Simmons Bonnin), who later became a well-known writer.

In 1896, Montezuma returned to Chicago to open a private practice. This time, he was successful as a specialist in stomach and intestinal diseases and was eventually offered a teaching position at the College of Physicians and Surgeons in the Postgraduate Medical School.

Becoming active in Indian affairs, Montezuma gave lectures in which he criticized the Bureau of Indian Affairs (BIA) and the reservation system and advocated citizenship for Indians. Although a proponent of assimilation, he also called for pride in Indianness. He wrote three books, including *Let My People Go*, published in 1914, and founded the Indian magazine *Wassaja* in 1916. Presidents Theodore Roosevelt and Woodrow Wilson both offered him the position of commissioner of Indian Affairs, but he refused and continued calling for the abolition of the BIA.

Montezuma was married twice, both times to white women. Suffering from diabetes and tuberculosis, he returned to his place of birth with his second wife in 1922. The next year, he died at the Fort McDowell Reservation, Arizona, in a brush shelter built especially for him.

MOONEY, JAMES. *(1861–1921).* Anthropologist; reformer.

James Mooney was born in Richmond, Indiana, of Irish-born parents. A newspaperman for the *Richmond Palladium*, he was self-taught in the field of ethnology. Through the efforts of JOHN WESLEY POWELL, he became a staff member of the Smithsonian's Bureau of Ethnology in 1885, and, for the next 36 years, he undertook cultural studies of a wide variety of Indians, including the Cherokees, Kiowas, Cheyennes, and Sioux.

Mooney studied the revivalist and messianic religious movements among the Indians of the West, which had become a widespread phenomenon in the late 1800s and early 1900s. He made an extensive study of the Ghost Dance religion among the Sioux, culminating in *The Ghost-Dance Religion and the Sioux Outbreak of 1890* (1897).

Mooney's *Calendar History of the Kiowa* (1898) was the first such work by an anthropologist to use written Indian sources. He also wrote *The Siouan Tribes of the East* (1894); *Myths of the Cherokee* (1900); and *The Cheyenne Indians* (1907); and did extensive work on FREDERICK WEBB HODGE's *Handbook of the American Indians North of Mexico* (1907–10).

Mooney later examined the peyote-using cults of Oklahoma Indians and was instrumental in the chartering of the Native American Church in that state in 1918. He came into disfavor among members of the Bureau of Indian Affairs who disapproved of his sanctioning of the peyotist Indian religion. As a result, he was banned from conducting further research on the Kiowa Reservation. Among his other efforts were population studies of North American Indians in an attempt to ascertain the impact of white settlement on them.

MORAN, PETER. *(1842–1914).* Artist. Brother of THOMAS MORAN.

British-born painter Peter Moran came to America with his family when he was three years old. He grew up in Maryland and was taught painting by his older brothers, Thomas and Edward. Although remembered for his paintings and etchings of animals, Moran also portrayed Indians in his works, such as the Shoshones and Bannocks, which he encountered while on a trip West with his brother Thomas in 1879. He also participated in a federally sponsored trip West as part of the 1890 Census, providing illustrations for the government report on this expedition.

MORAN, THOMAS. *(1837–1926).* Artist. Brother of PETER MORAN.

British-born Thomas Moran moved to Maryland with his family in 1844. Along with his older brother Edward, Thomas studied painting in Philadelphia and England, then became an illustrator for *Scribner's*.

In 1871–72, Moran was a guest artist with the FERDINAND V. HAYDEN survey of the Yellowstone River region, producing numerous landscapes as well as Indian scenes. The photographer WILLIAM HENRY JACKSON also participated. Moran's paintings and Jackson's photographs helped convince Congress to establish the Yellowstone region as the first national park in 1872.

Moran later accompanied JOHN WESLEY POWELL on his 1873–74 exploration of southern Utah and Arizona during which he produced scenes of Pueblo Indian life. In 1879, accompanied by his younger brother Peter, who also painted Indians, Thomas Moran set out from Fort Hall in Idaho to the Teton Mountains. He established a studio at East Hampton on Long Island, but continued to make trips to the Rockies. Late in life, he settled in Santa Barbara, California.

MORGAN, LEWIS HENRY (Tayadawahkugh, "one lying across"). *(1818–1881).* Anthropologist; political leader.

Lewis Henry Morgan's interest in Indian culture resulted from his early contact with members of the Seneca tribe near his boyhood home in Aurora, New York. Although he went on to a career in law in Rochester, and later served in the New York State legislature in 1861–69, he continued his anthropological studies of Indian society, concentrating mostly on the structure and social fabric of the Iroquois League.

Morgan gained firsthand knowledge of the Senecas through his friend, the Seneca ELY PARKER. In 1847, he was officially adopted as a member of the tribe in recognition of his successful efforts in protecting Seneca lands, and was given the Iroquoian name Tayadawahkugh in honor of his efforts to create bonds between Indians and whites.

In 1851, Morgan published his comprehensive study of the Iroquois, *League of the Ho-de-no-sau-nee or Iroquois*, which was cited by JOHN WESLEY POWELL as the first scientific study of an Indian tribe.

Eight years later, Morgan journeyed to the upper Missouri River and then Hudson Bay, where he undertook a comprehensive study of the societies of 70 different tribes, concentrating primarily on kinship systems. He presented his conclusions in *Systems of Consanguinity and Affinity of the Human Family* (1870).

Morgan applied the newly developed theories of Darwinian evolution to classify cultures into progressive stages. His theories of evolutionary anthropology, as defined in *Ancient Society, or Researches in the Lines of Human Progress from Savagery, through Barbarism, to Civilization* (1877), influenced fellow American ethnologists, such as ADOLPH BANDELIER, as well as European philosophers, in particular Friedrich Engels and Karl Marx.

Morgan also wrote *Houses and House Life of the American Aborigine* (1881), in which he studied Native American shelter in relation to social structure.

MORROW, STANLEY. (1843–1921).
Photographer.

Born in Ohio, Stanley Morrow moved with his family to Wisconsin about 1860. While serving in the army in Maryland during the Civil War, he was a student of photographer Mathew Brady. Following the war, Morrow settled in Yankton in what is now North Dakota, where he made photographic portraits of Indians, especially the Sioux, Mandans, Arikaras, and Hidatsas. The photographer ORLANDO SCOTT GOFF worked for him. In 1876, Morrow traveled with General GEORGE CROOK's men in the War for the Black Hills against the Sioux under SITTING BULL, accompanying them to the Red Cloud Agency in Nebraska. Of particular importance to Native American history are his photographs of the Little Bighorn battle site, taken a short time after Colonel GEORGE ARMSTRONG CUSTER and his men were defeated at the Little Bighorn. In 1878–79, Morrow maintained studios in Montana at Fort Keogh and at Fort Custer.

MORSE, JEDEDIAH. (1761–1826). Missionary; scholar.

Jedediah Morse was born in Woodstock, Connecticut. He graduated from Yale College in 1783, where he remained to study theology for the next two years. During that time, he produced his first work on geography, a school textbook for children. Licensed to preach in 1785, he settled in Norwich, Connecticut, but soon returned to Yale as a tutor.

On being ordained a Congregational minister in 1787, Morse served in the community of Midway, Georgia, for two years. In 1789, he accepted the ministry at Charlestown, Massachusetts, where he remained for the next 30 years. Morse was a conservative force in the church and opposed Unitarianism. In 1816, he was instrumental in organizing the American Bible Society. In 1811–19, he was a director of the American Board of Commissioners of Foreign Missions and also served as secretary to the Society for Propagating the Gospel to the Indians. He had a particular interest in helping the impoverished Abnaki Indians living on Maine's coastal islands.

Starting in 1819, under the sponsorship of the Department of War, Morse undertook a study of various tribes and, in 1822, submitted a report on their condition to JOHN C. CALHOUN, known as the *Report to the Secretary of War*. In his writings, Morse called for a separate Indian state and helped influence federal Indian policy under President ANDREW JACKSON and the formation of the Indian Territory west of the Mississippi River.

Morse's later geographic works on North America were widely published, and earned him a reputation as the "Father of American Geography."

MORTON, THOMAS. (ca. 1590–1647). Trader; writer.

Thomas Morton emigrated from England in 1624, settling at Merrymount (present-day Quincy, Massachusetts) the next year, where he developed trade relations with various New England tribes. In order to prevent his supplying firearms to the Indians and his reportedly indecent behavior, he was arrested by MILES STANDISH under the order of the colonial governor JOHN ENDECOTT and sent to England; he soon returned, however. After a second arrest and a second forced trip to England, he returned again. On his third arrest, he was allowed to settle in Maine. In 1637, Morton published the partly satirical depiction of New England, *The New English Canaan*, in which he expressed admiration for the Indian way of life, unlike most writers of the period.

MOSES (Quelatican, Quelatikan, "blue horn").
Sinkiuse-Salish (Sinkiuse-Columbia). (ca. 1829–1899).
War chief in the Yakima War of 1855–56 and the Coeur d'Alene (Spokane) War of 1858; peacekeeper during the Nez Perce War of 1877 and the Bannock War of 1878; principal chief.

Quelatican was the son of Sulktalthscosum of the Sinkiuses, a Salishan-speaking people of central

Washington State along the east side of the Columbia River. His mother, Karneetsa, was half Spokane, another Salishan-speaking people. He was born near present-day Wenatchee. As a boy, he attended the mission school of HENRY SPALDING, where he was baptized as Moses.

During the 1850s, Moses was a war chief and participated in the Yakima War and Coeur d'Alene (or Spokane) War along with KAMIAKIN. In 1858, he became the principal chief of the Sinkiuses and, during the 1860s, gained influence throughout the region. During the Nez Perce and Bannock uprisings of the 1870s, he helped keep most of the Salishan-speaking tribes at peace.

In 1879, Moses was arrested because he refused to settle his people on the Yakima Reservation near the Big Bend of the Columbia. The agent James Wilbur soon obtained the Sinkiuse chief's release, however. Through Wilbur's further efforts, Moses traveled to Washington, D.C., for negotiations. His band was granted a tract of land west of the Columbia next to the Colville Reservation. Yet, in 1884, the Moses-Columbia band was forced to settle on the Colville Reservation with other inland Salish. Moses took up farming. Over the years, he had wives from various tribes of the region, including the Flatheads, Yakimas, and Nez Perces.

MOUNTAIN CHIEF (Ninastoko). *Blackfoot.* *(1848–1942).* Last hereditary chief of the Blackfeet; research informant.

Mountain Chief was born in southern Alberta along the Old Man River. As a young man, he was active in warfare with neighboring tribes, especially against the Crows and Gros Ventres in 1867; and against the Kootenais the following year. In 1873, Mountain Chief received a leg wound in another fight with the Crows that gave him a limp. In 1886, he agreed to treaty terms offered by the federal government and ceded Blackfoot lands east of the Sweet Grass Hills in Montana. In 1895, he signed a second treaty ceding what is now Glacier National Park. During the early 1920s, Mountain Chief became a well-known public figure in Montana. He made several trips to Washington, D.C., where he met presidents and other officials. He also served as an informant to General HUGH LENOX SCOTT on Plains Indian sign language.

MOXUS (Agamagus). *Abnaki. (fl. late 1600s, early 1700s).* Leader in the Abnaki Wars (part of the French and Indian Wars).

It is thought Moxus was the successor of MADOKAWANDO, who died in 1698. He signed treaties with the English colonists in 1699 and 1702, but led warriors along with the sachem ASSACUMBUIT against the settlement at Casco, Maine, in 1703.

BOMAZEEN was another sachem of the Abnaki Confederacy who was active during the same period.

MOYTOY (Motoy). *Cherokee. (fl. 1720s–1730s).* "Emperor" of the Cherokees.

Moytoy was the chief of the village of Tellico in eastern Tennessee. In order to enlist the support of the Cherokees of all the seven area villages against the French, the Englishman Sir Alexander Cumming wanted a chief in charge that he could control. In a ceremony in 1730, he proclaimed Moytoy the "emperor" of the Cherokees. Yet Moytoy maintained his independence and, over the next years, even led raids against British settlements.

MRIKSAH (Mricksah, Mexanno, Mixanno, Mexam, Mixam, Mixan, Meika, Mikano, Mekanno). *Narraganset. (fl. mid-1600s).* Grand sachem. Son of CANONICUS; cousin of MIANTINOMO; husband of MAGNUS; brother-in-law of NINIGRET.

Mriksah became grand sachem on the death of his father, Canonicus, in 1647, and continued friendly relations with whites. British officials discouraged him from trade with the Dutch, however. He was succeeded as grand sachem by Miantinomo's son CANONCHET, who was supported in his later militant stance by Mriksah's widow, Magnus.

MULVANY, JOHN. *(1844–1906).* Artist.

John Mulvany was born in Ireland and lived in Kansas and New York. His most famous work relevant to Indian history was his internationally celebrated painting *Custer's Last Rally*, one of the earliest depictions of the 1876 Battle of Little Bighorn. In preparation for this project, Mulvany visited the battle site and interviewed army officers active in the area at the time of the battle. He also visited some of the Indians who had participated in the defeat of Colonel GEORGE ARMSTRONG CUSTER's 7th Cavalry.

MURPHY, TIMOTHY. *(1751–1818).* Scout; soldier.

Born in Minisink, New Jersey, Tim Murphy moved to Pennsylvania with his parents when he was six years old. He became a folklore hero of the central New York frontier, known as the "Savior of the Schoharie" for his exploits in the Schoharie Valley region. As the story goes, after his wife and children had been killed by Indians while he was away, Murphy dedicated his life to fighting and killing Indians on the New York frontier. He supposedly fought in the American Revolution against Iroquois allied under the Mohawk JOSEPH BRANT, as well as against Tories and British regulars. Many of the legends surrounding Murphy, similar to those about other frontiersmen such as DANIEL

BOONE, involved his skill in outwitting the Indians and escaping from captivity.

MUSGROVE, MARY.   See BOSOMWORTH, MARY.

MUSHALATUBBEE. *Choctaw. (d. 1838).* Ally of Americans against the British in the Creek War; negotiator.

Mushalatubbee, like the Choctaw leader PUSH-MATAHA, led a contingent of Choctaw warriors in support of General ANDREW JACKSON in the Creek War of 1813–14. As chief of the northeast tribal district, he participated in numerous negotiations with whites, signing treaties at the Choctaw Trading House, Mississippi, in 1816; Treaty Ground, Mississippi, in 1820; Washington, D.C., in 1825; and Dancing Rabbit Creek, Mississippi, in 1830. Pushmataha died on the trip to Washington, D.C., in 1824–25. On that same trip, Mushalatubbee befriended the Frenchman MARQUIS DE LAFAYETTE. Mushalatubbee's tribal opponents on the question of removal and land cessions were GREENWOOD LE FLORE and DAVID FOLSOM. He died of smallpox just after the Choctaw relocation to the Indian Territory.

MUYBRIDGE, EADWEARD JAMES (James Edward Muggeridge). *(1830–1904).* Photographer.

The Englishman Eadweard Muybridge came to the United States and took up photography in 1852. In 1860, he was part of the U.S. Geological Survey along the Pacific Coast. Afterward, he continued to live in San Francisco, where he eventually opened a studio. In 1868, he visited Fort Wrangell, Alaska, with a government military force, where he photographed Tlingit Indians. Again working for the government, he photographed scenes of the Modoc War of 1872–73, involving CAPTAIN JACK, as did the local freelance photographer, German-born Louis Heller. Muybridge is also known for his sequential photographs documenting animal and human locomotion.

N

NAICHE (Na-ai-che, Nahche, Nache, Nachi, Nachise, Nachite, Nachez, Natchez, "the mischievous one"). *Chiricahua Apache. (ca. 1857–1921).* Leader in the Apache Wars. Son of COCHISE; brother of TAZA; grandson of MANGAS COLORADAS.

Naiche was present with his father, Cochise, during the BASCOM Affair and was held hostage for a time before being released to appease the warring Chiricahuas. When his brother Taza died in 1876 from pneumonia after a trip to Washington, D.C., Naiche became militant. From that time on, Naiche's involvement in the Apache Wars closely paralleled that of GERONIMO. Although Naiche was hereditary chief of his band, he deferred to the other chief in matters of war. He surrendered with Geronimo in September 1886. After imprisonment at Fort Marion, Florida, until 1894, Naiche was relocated to Fort Sill in the Indian Territory. He was allowed to return to his Arizona homeland in 1913, dying eight years later of influenza. (See also GERONIMO.)

NAKAIDOKLINI (Nakaydoklunni, Nocadelklinny, Nockay-Delklinne, Noch-ay-del-klinne, Babbyduclone, Bardudeclenny, Bobby-dok-linny). *Coyotero (White Mountain) Apache. (d. 1881).* Medicine man whose death sparked the last phase of the Apache Wars.

Nakaidoklini preached a new religion centering around a dance that would supposedly bring dead warriors back to life to help in the struggle against whites. White officials, alarmed by this militant posturing, ordered his arrest.

On August 30, 1881, 79 Fort Apache cavalry troops under Colonel EUGENE A. CARR, with 23 White Mountain Apache scouts under Lieutenant Thomas Cruse, reached Nakaidoklini's village at Cibecue Creek, about 30 miles to the northwest. After a tense standoff,

Nakaidoklini yielded, but his followers pursued the troops down the valley. When fighting broke out, the White Mounain scouts rebelled and the shaman was killed in the struggle. Later, five of the Apache scouts were tried for mutiny; three were hanged and the others were sentenced to long jail terms.

Nakaidoklini's followers later attacked Fort Apache but were driven back. Some headed for the San Carlos Reservation for refuge with the Chiricahuas. When additional troops were called up, Chiricahua leaders, including GERONIMO, became alarmed and soon fled San Carlos for Mexico, starting a new period of unrest. The White Mountain Apache NATIOTISH, in a subsequent engagement, led warriors against troops in the Battle of Big Dry Wash of July 1882. (See also GERONIMO.)

NAMONTACK. *Powhatan. (d. 1610).* Friend to Jamestown colonists.

In 1608, Captain Christopher Newport placed the youth Thomas Savage with the Powhatan Indians to learn the customs and language of the Tidewater tribes. In return Chief POWHATAN placed Namontack with the English. He proved valuable to the English in obtaining food and preventing attacks from hostile bands. He traveled to England with Newport, where he proved an apt student of English customs. On the return trip, Namontack was killed in a dispute with an Indian companion. (See also POWHATAN.)

NAMPEYO (Nampayo, Nampayu, Snake Woman; Tsu-mana). *Hopi-Tewa. (ca. 1860–1942).* Potter who brought about revival of traditional ceramics.

Nampeyo was born at Hano Pueblo in present-day Arizona. During the 1890s, she became interested in ancient pottery forms and designs, recognizing them as superior to the ceramics produced by Hopis at the time.

Her husband Lesou was employed by the archeologist JESSE WALTER FEWKES at the excavation of Sikyatki and helped Nampeyo find shards showing the old forms.

Nampeyo developed her own style based on the traditional designs. Her work gained the interest of Walter Hough, who purchased her pottery for the Smithsonian Institution; it also began to sell to collectors from around the world. In 1904 and 1907, she made and sold her pottery at the Grand Canyon lodge of the Fred Harvey Company, which operated a chain of hotels and restaurants in the Southwest. She and her husband also traveled to Chicago in 1898 and 1910 to display her work.

Nampeyo's influence led to a renaissance of pottery making among her people and the elevation of pottery to an art form. Her four daughters also became well-known potters.

NANA (Nane, Nanay). *Mimbreno Apache.*
(ca. 1810–1895). War chief in the Apache Wars.

Nana's career as a warrior spanned the entire Apache Wars of the 1860s into the 1880s under many of the

Nampeyo. Photo by Edward Curtis. *Courtesy of National Archives of Canada/PA-39513.*

tribe's famous leaders, first MANGAS COLORADAS, then VICTORIO, then GERONIMO. After the death of Victorio in 1880, Nana assumed leadership of his militant followers while moderates gave their support to LOCO.

In July and August 1881, Nana, as an old man, led 15 Mimbrenos plus 25 or so Mescaleros in numerous raids on settlers and on an army wagon train. Traveling more than 1,200 miles, the small band fought eight battles, killed about 100 whites, and captured 200 horses. In late August, with the 9th Cavalry under Colonel Edward Hatch in pursuit, Nana led his followers back across the Rio Grande into Mexico and joined forces with Geronimo, Loco, JUH, NAICHE, and CHATO who had recently escaped from the San Carlos Reservation in Arizona.

Nana surrendered to General GEORGE CROOK in 1883, fled San Carlos in 1885, then turned himself in for the last time in March 1886. Like the majority of Apache war chiefs, Nana was sent to Fort Marion in Florida. On release, he was relocated to Fort Still in the Indian Territory, where he died. (See also GERONIMO; MANGAS COLORADAS; VICTORIO.)

NANUNTENOO. See CANONCHET.

NARVAEZ, PANFILO DE. *(ca. 1470–1528).*
Explorer.

Spanish-born Panfilo de Narvaez came to the Americas in 1498 and, in 1511–14, took part in the Spanish conquest of Cuba as Diegeo de Valazquez's chief lieutenant. Narvaez's brutal treatment of the Arawak Indians earned him the harsh criticism of Spanish church authorities, including missionary BARTOLOME DE LAS CASAS.

In 1520, Valazquez sent Narvaez to compel Hernando Cortes to return to Cuba from Mexico. In the ensuing armed conflict near Veracruz between Narvaez's forces and Cortes's soldiers, Narvaez was captured after having lost an eye in battle. Most of his men joined Cortes against the Aztecs. After his release in 1521, Narvaez returned to Spain.

In 1526, Spain's king commissioned Narvaez to explore and conquer all the lands between the Rio de las Palmas in northeastern Mexico and the Cape of Florida. Narvaez's expedition to Florida departed Spain in June 1527, with five ships and over 600 colonists. During stopovers in Santo Domingo and Cuba, about a third of the colonists deserted.

The expedition, consisting of colonists and soldiers, as well as Catholic missionary priests and black slaves, landed on the shores of Tampa Bay in April 1528. At Tampa Bay, Narvaez dispatched the ships to explore northward along Florida's east coast, while he journeyed inland with a company of about 300 men to search for the gold-laden cities that explorer JUAN PONCE DE LEON had reported 15 years earlier. While searching for an Indian village called Aute, Narvaez and his party were continually harassed by Apalachee warriors, armed with bows and arrows. His ships failed to rejoin him at Apalachiola Bay near present-day Tallahassee, heading instead to Mexico. Abandoned, Narvaez and his men constructed five barges and headed west along the Gulf Coast toward Mexico.

Off the Texas coast, Narvaez's barge was caught in a storm and he was lost at sea. Some of the survivors reached a coastal island, where they were enslaved by the Indians. Among the members of the expedition who finally reached Mexico after wandering through the American southwest were ALVAR NUNEZ CABEZA DE VACA and ESTEVANICO. Narvaez's expedition was the first inland exploration of the present-day continental United States.

NATAWISTA (Natawista Iksana, "sacred snake woman"; Madame Culbertson). *Blood. (ca. 1825–ca. 1895).* Hostess at upper Missouri River trading posts; diplomat; interpreter.

In 1840, when about 15 years old, Natawista accompanied her father, Men-Es-To-Kos, on a trading trip from Canada to Fort Union at the mouth of the Yellowstone on the Missouri River near what is now the North Dakota–Montana border. At that time, Major Alexander Culbertson, the head of Fort Union, arranged for her marriage to him, which was performed in an Indian ceremony.

Visitors to Fort Union met and wrote about Natawista, including the missionaries PIERRE JEAN DE SMET and NICOLAS POINT, as well as the artist John James Audubon. She was also known in St. Louis, accompanying her husband to the head office of the American Fur Company, then directed by PIERRE CHOUTEAU, JR.

In 1845, Culbertson traveled further up the Missouri to establish a new fort, finding a permanent location for Fort Benton, Montana, two years later. She served as a hostess to white traders as well as a diplomat to the Blackfoot, Blood, Piegan, and Gros Ventre tribes.

ISAAC STEVENS, governor of the Washington Territory, appointed Culbertson as a special agent to the tribes of the Blackfoot Confederacy during his survey, beginning in 1847, for a Pacific railroad through Indian lands. Natawista traveled with her husband and Stevens among the Indian camps, acting as an interpreter and helping maintain peaceful relations.

In 1858, Culbertson retired to Peoria, Illinois, where he built a mansion. The next year, he and Natawista, by whom he had five children, were married in a Catholic ceremony. They lived extravagantly for 10 years until investments, many of them promoted by Missouri senator Thomas Hart Benton, went bad. The Cul-

bertsons returned to the upper Missouri country, where Culbertson again worked as a trader and interpreter.

In the early 1870s, Natawista left Culbertson and lived the rest of her life on Blood lands in Alberta, Canada. Her two surviving daughters married white men from the East; her two sons lived the life of mixed-blood traders in the West.

NATIOTISH (Nantiotish, Nantiatish). *Coyotero (White Mountain) Apache. (fl. 1880s).* War chief at the Battle of Big Dry Wash.

Still bitter over the death of NAKAIDOKLINI near Fort Apache, Arizona, and the fighting at Cibecue Creek in 1881 (the incident that indirectly sparked GERONIMO's return to militancy), some of the White Mountain Apaches continued to hide out. Their leader was Natiotish.

On July 6, 1882, a war party attacked and killed four agency policemen, including the chief of police "Cibecue Charley" Colvig. With additional warriors, Natiotish's band of now more than 50 carried out raids in the Tonto Basin. Troops were sent into the field. Cavalry under Captain Adna Chaffee tracked the Indians to the vicinity of General Springs, a watering place on the Mogollon Rim. On July 17, Natiotish set a trap at the north end of a canyon seven miles to the north of the springs. But the scout ALBERT SIEBER spotted the ambush, and, unknown to the Indians, reinforcements under Major Andrew Evans had joined Chaffee's men the night before. Evans let Chaffee direct the fighting; he formed a skirmish line at the brink of the canyon, effectively pinning down the Apaches, then sent two flanking parties across the canyon. The ensuing strikes killed as many as 27 warriors, probably Natiotish among them. The rest scattered and, over the next weeks, trickled into the White Mountain Reservation.

The Battle of Big Dry Wash, as it became known, was a major defeat for the Apaches, one of the few engagemenst in which their warriors abandoned their guerrilla-style hit-and-run tactics. It led to the end of Apache militancy among most of the bands, except the Chiricahuas and Mimbrenos. (See also GERONIMO.)

NAWAT. See LEFT HAND.

NAWKAW (Nau-kaw-kary-maunie, Carramani, Carrymaunee, Caraminie, Carimine, Karry-Man-ee, Karamanu, "walking turtle"; Onunaka; Wood). *Winnebago. (1735–1833).* Ally of TECUMSEH; later, peace advocate.

Nawkaw's village was at Big Green Lake between Green Bay and present-day Portage, Wisconsin. Like FOUR LEGS and WAUKON DECORA, Nawkaw supported Tecumseh in the War of 1812. He was reportedly at Tecumseh's side at the Battle of the Thames in October 1813 when the latter was killed. Nawkaw later signed the treaties of St. Louis in 1816; Prairie du Chien in 1825; Butte des Morts in 1827; Green Bay in 1828; and Prairie du Chien in 1829. Along with Four Legs, he helped arrange the militant RED BIRD's surrender in the Winnebago Uprising of 1827, then traveled to Washington, D.C., in 1828 to successfully lobby for clemency for the chief. Red Bird died in prison before learning of his pardon, however. Nawkaw also kept his band out of the BLACK HAWK War of 1832. His daughter married SPOON DECORA.

NEAMATHLA (Nehe Marthla, Neah Emarthla, Innemathla). *Seminole (Miccosukee)-Creek. (fl. 1800s).* Leader of Seminoles and Creeks who resisted removal; principal chief.

Neamathla was born a Creek, but first came into historical notice as a Miccosukee, a branch tribe of the Seminoles. In 1817, he insisted that soldiers stop trespassing on Indian hunting grounds. In response, soldiers out of Fort Scott, Georgia, under the command of General EDMUND GAINES, destroyed his village at Fowltown in northwest Florida, one of the incidents that led to the First Seminole War of 1817–18.

After having moved to the Tallahassee region of Florida, Neamathla was decreed principal chief of the Seminoles by government officials in 1821, although most of the Seminoles living father south recognized MICANOPY as their chief spokesman. Neamathla was one of 32 signers of the Treaty of Moultrie Creek (Camp Moultrie) in September 1823, ceding some five million acres of land in Florida. Yet, in 1826, he refused to accept the federal government's payment of $1,000 to build a school to teach Seminole children, believing that the Seminoles should provide their own education.

When Neamathla, known for his oratorical skills, advised the Seminoles not to agree to relocation from Florida, he was deposed as principal chief by officials. He moved to Hatchechubbee Creek in Alabama, where he became part of the Creek tribal council and resisted removal to the Indian Territory, leading raids on settlers and stagecoaches. In 1836, he was captured by Alabama militiamen and shipped West in irons. (See also BOLEK; OSCEOLA.)

NEAPOPE (Napope, Naapope, Nahpope). *Sac. (b. ca. 1800).* Ally of BLACK HAWK in the Black Hawk War of 1832.

Neapope lived along the Rock River near the mouth of the Mississippi. Unlike Black Hawk, he was probably a hereditary chief, but about half his age and less influential. He consistently advocated militancy and never signed a peace treaty. It is said that WHITE CLOUD, the Winnebago Prophet, had a strong influence on him. Neapope led the young warriors in much of the fighting of the Black Hawk War. At the Battle of Wisconsin Heights on July 21, 1832, he and his men stayed behind to cover the retreat of the main body of Indians. He was captured by KEOKUK in the days following the Battle of the Bad Axe River of August 1–2. GEORGE CATLIN painted Neapope's portrait while the chief was imprisoned at Jefferson Barracks, Missouri. After early release, Neapope settled in Iowa. (See also BLACK HAWK.)

NEGABAMET, NOEL (Captain Sillery). *Montagnais. (ca. 1600–1666).* Ally of French.

Negabamet, who lived at Sillery, Quebec, became friends of French settlers in the region, and he and his family were converted to Catholicism, baptized in 1639 as Noel, Marie, and Charles. He supported the French in their wars with the tribes of the Iroquois League, traditional enemies of the Montagnais. In 1645, Negabamet was present at a peace council at Trois Rivieres, Quebec, involving Montagnais, Iroquois, and other tribes. In 1651, he accompanied Father Druilletes on a visit to the Abnaki Indians, and, in 1652, he traveled to New England as a tribal delegate to seek British aid against the League, but without success. He counseled the French and acted as a liaison to other area tribes.

NEGWAGON (Ningweegon, Little Wing, Wing). *Ottawa. (fl. early 1800s).* Ally of Americans in the War of 1812.

Negwagon was an Ottawa chief living near Michilimackinac, Michigan, where he established peaceful relations with American settlers. During the War of 1812, after the British had taken Michilimackinac, he camped near the settlement while on a hunting expedition and displayed an American flag. When British soldiers ordered him to remove it, Neapope wrapped the flag around his arm and, drawing his war club, refused to relinquish it. The soldiers insisted; Negwagon called his warriors to the ready. The British backed down, whereupon Negwagon raised the flag again. After the war, he and his family visited Detroit once a year in two birchbark canoes, an American flag at the stern of each. LEWIS CASS, governor of the Michigan Territory, presented him with new flags on each trip.

NEMACOLIN. *Delaware. (fl. mid-1700s).* Cleared trail that became Braddock's Road.

In 1749–50, Nemacolin and Thomas Cresap, a Maryland frontiersman working for the Ohio Company of Virginia, cleared a trail between the Potomac and Monongahela rivers. It came to be known as Nemacolin's Path, running through the Allegheny Mountains from present-day Virginia, into Maryland, then Pennsylvania. In 1752, the Ohio Company expanded the trail from Fort Cumberland, Maryland, to the Youghiogheny River; and, in 1754, GEORGE WASHINGTON expanded it almost as far as present-day Uniontown, Pennsylvania. Then, in 1755, during the French and Indian War, the British general ED-WARD BRADDOCK used the trail to transport his troops from Fort Cumberland toward French-held Fort Duquesne (Pittsburgh). The force traveled with 300 axmen and carpenters who widened the path to 12 feet, leveled it where possible, and built bridges over rivers and streams. The troops came within 10 miles from the post when they were attacked by French troops and their Indian allies. In the 1780s, Pennsylvania and Maryland improved the road to carry wagons for the growing traffic westward. The town Namacolin, Pennsylvania, is named after the Delaware chief.

NESUTAN (Job Nesutan). *Massachuset. (d. 1675).* Interpreter; translator.

Nesutan was baptized a Christian at the village of Natick in Massachusetts Bay Colony and given the name Job. He worked as an assistant and interpreter for JOHN ELIOT, helping him translate the Bible into Algonquian. He was killed in King PHILIP's War of 1675–76 while fighting on the side of the colonists against the Wampanoags and Narragansets.

NICAAGAT (Jack). *Ute. (fl. 1870s).* Band leader in the Ute War of 1879.

Like OURAY and COLOROW, Nicaagat, known to whites as Jack, is thought to have had some Apache blood. In the late 1870s, at the White River Reservation in western Colorado, he was the favorite leader of the younger Northern Ute warriors. As such, he played an important military role in the uprising.

On learning of the soldiers' approach to the agency, following a dispute between the agent NATHAN MEEKER and the medicine man CANALLA, Nicaagat rode north to meet them. At a parley on Bear River, he informed Major THOMAS T. THORNBURGH that the Utes wanted peace and that there was no need to advance any further. Colorow, another band leader, subsequently rode out to impart the same messages.

But, ignoring Nicaagat's attempt to make peace, Thornburgh and 120 cavalrymen reached Milk Creek on the northern edge of the Ute Reservation, about 15 miles north of the White River Agency on September 29. Nicaagat and Colorow met them with about 100 warriors. After the first shots, the cavalry retreated to their wagon train across the creek; Thornburgh was struck down early in the fighting. Captain J. Scott Payne then took command and organized a defense behind supply wagons. Nicaagat and his warriors laid siege for almost a week. On October 2, a regiment of black cavalrymen under Captain Francis Dodge arrived as reinforcements,

and a larger relief force under colonel WESLEY MER-RITT arrived three days later. The Utes, who had lost about 23 men, retreated southward. Among the whites, 14 soldiers were dead and 43 wounded. In the meantime, at the agency, Meeker and others were killed and his wife, daughter, and another woman taken hostage.

Because of the diplomatic efforts of Ouray, both Nicaagat and Colorow were pardoned for their involvement because they had acted as warriors in a fair fight. QUINKENT, who was present at White River during the killings, received a jail term. (See also OURAY.)

NICOLET, JEAN (Jean Nicollet de Bellesborne). *(ca. 1598–1642).* Explorer; trader; interpreter.

Jean Nicolet, a native of Cherbourgh, France, arrived in French Canada in 1618, with SAMUEL DE CHAMPLAIN. He spent two years with the Algonkins of Allumette Island on the Ottawa River and nine years with the Nipissings on the northern shores of Lake Huron; during this time he mastered various Indian dialects.

In 1634, Champlain sent Nicolet west to the Great Lakes to calm a threatened Indian uprising and to make contacts with Winnebago Indians of what is now eastern Wisconsin. Known by the French at the time as "people of the sea," they were thought to have knowledge of a water route that would lead to the Pacific and the Far East—the Northwest Passage.

With a company of five Indian guides, Nicolet traveled from Georgian Bay on the eastern shore of Lake Huron, through the Straits of Mackinac, and across Lake Michigan. Anticipating the possibility of reaching China, Nicolet brought with him a Chinese ceremonial robe, made of damask cloth. He arrived on the western shore of Lake Michigan, near present-day Green Bay, Wisconsin, where he was welcomed by the Winnebago Indians, and, after having explored the Wisconsin and Fox rivers, he returned east to Quebec. He brought back to Champlain reports of a greater river farther to the south.

Settling at Trois Rivieres, Quebec, Nicolet became a fur trader. He also served as a liaison and interpreter between the Indians of the eastern St. Lawrence River region and Quebec fur-trading interests.

In 1642, Nicolet was sent to rescue a prisoner held by the Iroquois. While he was traveling the St. Lawrence, his boat overturned near Sillery, Quebec, and he was drowned. His account of the rivers beyond Lake Michigan led to the later explorations of JACQUES MARQUETTE and LOUIS JOLLIET.

NINHAM (Daniel Ninham). *Wappinger-Mahican. (ca. 1710–1778).* Ally of British in the French and Indian War of 1754–63; ally of Patriots in the American Revolution.

Soon after Ninham had become sachem of his Wappinger band in 1740, his people were pressured into ceding lands along the eastern Hudson Valley. Starting about 1746, he moved to Westenhuck, known to the settlers as Stockbridge, a village made up mostly of Mahicans, Algonquian relatives of the Wappingers. In 1755, Ninham gave his support to WILLIAM JOHNSON in the French and Indian War. Toward the end of the conflict, probably in 1762, he traveled to England with Mohegan Indians from Connecticut in regard to tribal land claims. The British promised a fair trial and, after long delays, were in the process of settling the claims when the American Revolution erupted. In this struggle, Ninham sided with the Patriots against the British and was killed in the Battle of Kingsbridge on August 31, 1778.

NINIGRET (Nenekunat, Ninicraft, Niniglud; Janemo, Ayanemo). *Niantic. (ca. 1600–1678).* Ally of Narragansets; enemy of Mohegans and Montauks. Brother of MAGNUS; brother-in-law of MRIKSAH; cousin of MIANTINOMO.

Ninigret's village was located on the coast of southwest Rhode Island Colony near present-day Westerly. He was an ally of the Narragansets to the north through intermarriage, a cousin of Miantinomo, and a rival of the Mohegan UNCAS. Although Ninigret provided auxiliaries to colonial troops in the Pequot War of 1636–37, he was accused by Uncas of harboring Pequot refugees. Ninigret was henceforth summoned to Boston to appear before English authorities and was later forced to make annual payments of wampum to demonstrate good faith.

On the death of Miantinomo in 1643, ordered by colonial officials and carried out by Uncas's brother, Ninigret went to war with the Mohegans. Peace was made in 1647. In 1652, Ninigret traveled to Manhattan and met with Dutch officials, whereupon he was again called to Boston to defend his actions. The next year, he made war on WYANDANCH's Montauks of Long Island and was penalized by the English for wampum under the threat of their military involvement. He fought the Montauks again in 1659.

By the outbreak of King PHILIP's War of 1675–76, Ninigret's influence in the region had diminished; he played no part in the uprising in spite of Narraganset involvement under CANONCHET. Ninigret is famous for telling the missionary THOMAS MAYHEW, JR., that before trying to convert Indians, he should make the English good first.

NIZA, MARCOS DE (Marco de Nica, Fray Marcos, Fray Marcos of Nizza; Sayota, "man from heaven"). *(ca. 1495–1558).* Explorer; missionary.

Marcos de Niza, a Franciscan missionary from Nice, France, first came to the Americas in 1531, bringing his religious work to Peru, Guatemala, and then Mexico. At the settlement at Culiacan in northern Mexico, he succeeded in obtaining the freedom of Indians enslaved by the Spanish.

In 1539, Niza was assigned by Mexico's Viceroy Antonio de Mendoza to undertake an expedition to the north to explore what is now Arizona and New Mexico, in search of cities rich with gold—the Seven Cities of Cibola—reported by the earlier explorers ALVAR NUNEZ CABEZA DE VACA and ESTEVANICO, who had survived years of wandering in the Southwest following the disastrous PANFILO DE NARVAEZ expedition of 1528.

Accompanied by Estevanico, several other Franciscan missionaries, and Indian guides, Niza led the expedition to the Zuni pueblos of New Mexico. Estavanico, whom Niza sent ahead of the main party, was soon killed by Indians. Niza viewed the pueblos from a distance and noted how they appeared to glisten like gold in the sun. The glistening effect was probably due to the reflections of the ornamental turquoise the Zunis used to decorate their huts. In any case, Niza returned to Mexico and reported finding Cibola.

Niza then acted as guide on FRANCISCO VASQUEZ DE CORONADO's expedition of 1540. On determining that the Zuni pueblos were normal villages, Coronoado dismissed Niza, who spent his remaining years in missionary work to the Indians of northern Mexico. He was known to the Indians as Sayota for "man from heaven."

NOKA (Old Noka). *Chippewa (Ojibway). (fl. 1760s).* War chief in struggle with Sioux for the upper Mississippi region.

In 1769, the Chippewas battled the Mdewakanton Sioux at Crow Wing in present-day Minnesota. Although the Chippewas held their ground, they suffered many casualties against the larger Sioux force. The next year, Noka headed a war party that attacked the village of SHAKOPEE on the Minnesota River in an indecisive battle. In addition to his fame as a warrior, Noka was known among his people as a great hunter.

NORTH, FRANK JOSHUA (White Wolf; Pawnee Chief). *(1840–1885).* Army officer; scout; interpreter. Brother of LUTHER NORTH.

Originally from upstate New York, Frank North moved west with his family, first to Ohio and then to Nebraska, where his father worked as a surveyor and where he was exposed to the language and culture of the Pawnees. He became fluent in the Pawnee's Caddoan language in addition to Plains Indian sign language and, in 1861, was hired as interpreter and clerk at the Pawnee Agency on the Loup River in Nebraska.

In 1864, General Grenville Mellon Dodge commissioned North a lieutenant and assigned him to raise a unit of Pawnee scouts to protect western Nebraska from

Indian attacks and to rescue white captives taken in raids. Later that year, General Samuel Curtis instructed North to lead a company of 100 Pawnee scouts in a campaign against the Sioux. Pawnee braves were movivated to join up with North's unit of scouts in order to escape the tedium of the reservation and fight against their traditional tribal enemies, Sioux and Cheyennes.

In summer 1865, North was promoted to a captain, and led his Pawnee scouts in the Powder River Expedition, under General PATRICK E. CONNOR. They departed Fort Laramie in late July 1865, in conjunction with other troops. North and a party of Pawnee scouts tracked a Cheyenne war party to their camp on the Powder River, where they killed 22 warriors and one woman. They returned to Connor's camp with the scalps, where they celebrated their victory during which North was rechristened by his men. His Pawnee name had been White Wolf; the Pawnee scouts renamed him Pawnee Chief, the same title they had once bestowed on the explorer JOHN C. FREMONT. The Powder River Expedition had intended to rendezvous at the Rosebud Creek with columns led by General Nelson Cole, but marauding bands of Sioux and Cheyennes, and severe weather had hampered the Black Hills segment of the expedition. In September 1865, North and his Pawnee scouts succeeded in locating nearly 1,200 of these troops. They were without food and supplies, and their horses had frozen to death. North's company escorted the men back to Connor's main column.

In March 1867, North was commissioned a major in command of a battalion of four companies of Pawnee scouts. His younger brother Luther made the rank of captain. They were assigned to protect construction workers on the Union Pacific Railroad in Nebraska from attacks by Cheyennes. In August 1867, a band of 150 Cheyennes under Turkey Leg derailed a train near Plum Creek, Nebraska; North and fewer than 40 scouts waited for the Indians to return to plunder the wrecked train. In the ensuing battle, the Cheynnes lost 17 and retreated. None of the scouts was killed, and only two were wounded.

In June 1869, during the SHERIDAN Campaign against the Cheyenne Dog Soldiers, North's Pawnee battalion was assigned to join General EUGENE A. CARR and his Republican River expedition against TALL BULL. Along with 250 of Carr's troops, North and 50 of his Pawnees attacked Tall Bull's village at Summit Springs, Colorado, on July 11, 1869. In this battle, Tall Bull was killed, shot possibly by North, although other accounts maintain that WILLIAM "BUFFALO BILL" CODY killed the Dog Soldier leader.

In the War for the Black Hills of 1876–77, North organized a Pawnee company for General GEORGE CROOK's campaign against Sioux and Cheyennes under SITTING BULL and CRAZY HORSE. He also provided leadership for Pawnee scouts serving under Colonel RANALD S. MACKENZIE. With Mackenzie on November 25, 1876, North's Pawnee scouts spearheaded the successful attack on Cheyenne chief DULL KNIFE's band.

North left the army in 1877 and went into the ranching business in Nebraska with Cody. He was elected to the Nebraska legislature in 1882. The next year, he joined Cody's Wild West Show, managing the production's Indian participants and leading Pawnees in demonstrations of Indian warfare techniques. He was famous as a marksman with a six-shooter and gave demonstrations.

North was injured in a horseback-riding accident while performing in Hartford, Connecticut, in 1884. The following year, he died from these injuries at his home in Columbus, Nebraska.

NORTH, LUTHER. *(1846–1935).* Army officer; scout; research informant. Brother of FRANK NORTH.

Luther North was born in Richland County, Ohio, and traveled west to Nebraska with his family at the age of 10. He became acquainted with the language and lifeways of the Pawnee Indians and joined his brother's Pawnee scouts. Luther attained the rank of captain under his brother, a major.

Along with his brother, Luther North served in the Powder River Expedition of 1865 against Cheyennes and Sioux. He also led Pawnee scouts in actions against the Cheyennes while guarding the construction of the Union Pacific Railroad through western Nebraska in summer 1867, and against the Cheyenne Dog Soldiers under TALL BULL at the Battle of Summit Springs, Colorado, on July 11, 1869.

At the end of his career, Luther joined his brother in a ranching enterprise in Nebraska with WILLIAM "BUFFALO BILL" CODY. He subsequently became deputy collector of Internal Revenue in the Dakota Territory and eventually retired in Columbus, Nebraska. North was a longtime friend of writer GEORGE BIRD GRINNELL, acting as an informant for Grinnell's works on the history and culture of the Pawnees and Cheyennes.

NORTON, JOHN (Teyoninhokarawen, Te-yo-nin-ho Kalawen). *Mohawk–Mixed Cherokee.* *(ca. 1760–1826 or 1831).* Trader; intrepreter; personal secretary of JOSEPH BRANT.

John Norton, the son of a Cherokee father and Scottish mother, was adopted by a British soldier and taken to England, where he grew up. He returned to North America, where he worked as a trader, then an interpreter for New York officials to the Iroquois. The

Mohawk Joseph Brant, now living on the Six Nations Reserve on the Grand River in Ontario, adopted him as a nephew. Norton became Brant's personal secretary and confidant; on Brant's death in 1807, North was at his bedside. Norton translated the Gospel of St. John into Mohawk in 1805, and, in 1816, he published his Journal about a trip to Cherokee country in 1809–10 and his experiences as a British officer in the War of 1812.

NUMAGA (Young Winnemucca). *Northern Paiute.* *(d. 1871).* Leader in the Paiute (Pyramid Lake) War of 1860. Nephew of WINNEMUCCA; cousin of SARAH WINNEMUCCA.

The Paiute War in western Nevada was the last major western Indian-white conflict prior to the Civil War. The incident leading up to the hostilities involved traders from Williams Station, one of two trading posts serving as Central Overland Mail and Pony Express stations along the Carson Valley, part of the California Trail, running south of Pyramid Lake. Two Paiute girls were abducted and raped by traders. On May 7, 1860, in retaliation, warriors attacked and burned Williams Station, killing five whites and rescuing the girls.

Settlers and miners at Carson City, Virginia, Gold Hill, and Genoa, Nevada, organized 105 volunteers at Buckland Station under Major William Ormsby, and the force advanced northward toward Pyramid Lake. Numaga, chief of a band along lower Mud Lake, counseled peace among his people, like his uncle Winnemucca and cousin Sarah Winnemucca. To prove his sincerity, he fasted for peace. Yet, with the approach of Ormsby's troops, he reluctantly agreed to lead his warriors in battle. He set a trap at the Big Bend of the Truckee River Valley, with his warriors hiding behind sagebrush on both sides of the pass. As many as 46 whites died in the Indian gauntlet on May 12.

Volunteers out of California rushed to Carson Valley, as did a number of regulars, making a force of about 800. The former Texas Ranger JOHN COFFEE HAYS was given the command. On June 3, 1860, the force encountered the Paiutes near the site of Ormsby's defeat. After an indecisive skirmish, Hays's men pursued the Indians to Pinnacle Mountain. There, 25 of Numaga's warriors died; survivors scattered into the surrounding hills. That summer, the army established Fort Churchill near Buckland Station to patrol the valley and keep the Carson Branch of the California Trail open. Numaga negotiated a lasting peace with whites for his people. He died of tuberculosis 11 years later.

OACPICAGIGUA, LUIS. *Pima. (fl. 1750s).*
Leader of Pima Revolt of 1751 against the
Spanish.

Luis Oacpicagigua served the Spanish as a captain general in a campaign against the Seri Indians. On witnessing the growth of mining in his Pima homeland—the Spanish administrative district of Pimeria Alta (present-day northern Sonora, Mexico, and southern Arizona)—and the resulting forced labor among the Indians, he secretly plotted and organized a general uprising, with calls to action among the Papagos, Sobaipuris, and Apaches, as well as his own people.

On the night of November 20, 1751, Oacpicagigua and his rebels killed 18 Spaniards who had been visiting him at his home in Saric. A missionary escaped to Tubutama and spread word of the attack, giving Spanish officials time to prepare. During the following weeks, Indians attacked and plundered a number of missions and rancherias, including Caborca, Sonoita, Bac, and Guevavi. Yet the Sobaipuris and Apaches did not take part. Many Pimas and Papagos also refrained from violence, fearing reprisals.

Spanish officials ordered presidio captains and their troops into the field and managed to subdue rebels over a period of months through both military action and negotiations. They captured and executed a number of militants, including a relative of Oacpicagigua. Oacpicagigua negotiated his own freedom by agreeing to supervise the rebuilding of destroyed churches, although he never carried out his promise.

OCCUM, SAMSON (Occom, Ocum, "on the other side"). *Mohegan. (1723–1792).* Christian convert; educator; first Indian to preach in England.

Samson Occum, the son of Benoni Occum, was born in New London, Connecticut. He was converted to Christianity in 1741 by Reverend ELEAZAR WHEELOCK and educated in Wheelock's family, studying English, Latin, Greek, and Hebrew. Because of health problems, he did not finish his studies at the college level, becoming instead a schoolteacher at New London in 1748.

The next year, he moved to Long Island, where he married Mary Fowler (also known by her tribal name as Mary Montauk), by whom he would have 10 children. In 1759, he was ordained by the Presbyterian church and began serving as minister to the Montauks.

Occum recruited Indian youths on behalf of Wheelock for Moor's Indian Charity School, including JOSEPH BRANT in 1761. In 1765, Occum traveled to England as Wheelock's representative, staying for more than two years, making numerous appearances, and raising considerable funds. The school was moved from Connecticut to New Hampshire and chartered as Dartmouth College in 1769.

On returning to New England, Occum became disillusioned with Wheelock's new emphasis on preparing white missionaries to the Indians rather than educating the Indians themselves. As a result, he began preaching among New England Indians and became minister and teacher at the Brotherton community—consisting of Mahicans, Montauks, Narragansets, and other Algonquian peoples—in eastern New York (near the Stockbridge settlement in Massachusetts). Because of the expanding white population, Occum worked to relocate the Brotherton and Stockbridge Indians to New Stockbridge on Oneida territory in central New York, which he accomplished in 1786. He died there six years later.

OCONOSTOTA ("groundhog sausage").
Cherokee. (ca. 1710–1785). War chief; leader of the Cherokee War of 1760–61.

In 1730, Oconostota was part of a delegation of Cherokees and Creeks meeting King George II in England. ATTAKULLAKULLA, who was also part of the delegation, became the principal Cherokee peace chief in the years to come, and Oconostota, the war chief.

During the 1750s, with increasing numbers of whites coming onto Cherokee lands, the level of violence was escalated. In 1759, Oconostota headed a delegation of 32 chiefs to Charleston, South Carolina, for peace talks. When the Cherokees refused to turn over those warriors accused of an earlier attack on settlers, they were arrested on the order of Governor William Lyttleton. Attakullakulla interceded, arranging the ransom of one of the accused warriors for Oconostota and the other chiefs.

Oconostota now considered warfare the only solution. With support from the Creeks, he led a party of Cherokees in a siege of Fort Prince George, South Carolina, in 1760, the start of the Cherokee War. Oconostota shot Lieutenant Richard Cotymore when he came out of the post for a parley; the garrison in turn killed the Cherokee prisoners they were holding. The Cherokees subsequently carried out raids on frontier settlements, including a siege of Fort Loudon in what is now eastern Tennessee.

It took two armies to defeat Oconostota's Cherokees. The first, under Colonel Archibald Montgomery, consisting of some 1,500 Scottish Highlanders who had recently fought against French forces, relieved Fort Prince George and destroyed many Cherokee towns. Yet the Cherokees offered heavy guerrilla resistance and routed Montgomery's force before it could relieve Fort Loudon. After a long siege of the post, the Cherokees eventually captured the starving garrison.

The next year, 1761, an army of Carolina Rangers, British Light Infantry, Royal Scots, plus Indian auxiliaries, under Colonel James Grant, burned Cherokee towns and their crops. Oconostota and his warriors continued to fight from mountain hideouts, but finally, war-weary and starving, agreed to a peace pact with colonial officials, in which they ceded large portions of their eastern lands and agreed to a boundary separating them from whites.

In 1768, Oconostota traveled to New York with other chiefs to sign a peace treaty with the Iroquois, ending their traditional enmity.

During the American Revolution, Oconostota sided with his old enemies, the British, against the Americans. He was joined in this effort by DRAGGING CANOE, the son of Attakullakulla. Attakullakulla, however, offered his support to the Patriots. Once again, the Cherokees suffered the destruction of many of their towns. Oconostota died at the close of the war, soon after having relinquished leadership of his band to his son Tuksi.

O'FALLON, BENJAMIN. *(1793–1842).* Indian agent; trader. Nephew of WILLIAM CLARK.

Kentucky-born Benjamin O'Fallon was the son of the lower Mississippi land developer, Dr. James O'Fallon, and the nephew of explorer and governor of the Missouri Territory, William Clark. Raised in St. Louis by Clark after his father's death, O'Fallon began trading with the Sioux on the upper Missouri River in his early 20s and eventually became one of the principal owners of the Missouri Fur Company.

In 1817, O'Fallon was appointed Indian agent to the Ponca and Oto tribes at the government agency of Prairie du Chien in present-day Wisconsin. Through his expertise with the Indians and the influence of his uncle, O'Fallon was promoted to Indian agent for the Upper Missouri region. He established his headquarters at Council Bluffs in present-day Iowa after having traveled with Major STEPHEN H. LONG's 1819 Yellowstone Expedition. Two years later, he accompanied a group of Pawnees on a tour of eastern cities. In 1825, with General HENRY ATKINSON, he succeeded in entering into treaties and trade agreements with 15 major tribes of the upper Missouri.

After his 1827 resignation from his agency, O'Fallon devoted himself to Missouri politics, supporting the presidential candidacy of ANDREW JACKSON.

OGDEN, PETER SKENE (M'sieu Pete).
(1794–1854). Explorer; trader; trapper.

Peter Skene Ogden was born in Quebec City to a family who had come to Canada as Loyalists during the American Revolution. He attended school in Montreal.

About 1814, Ogden became involved in the fur trade, first in the Great Lakes region for JOHN JACOB ASTOR's American Fur company, then in the Pacific Northwest for the North West Company. When the Hudson's Bay Company and the North West Company merged in 1821, GEORGE SIMPSON assigned Ogden to the company's trading post at Spokane in what is now eastern Washington, with orders to dominate trapping in the Columbia and Snake river valleys.

In 1824–25, Ogden, as head of a fur brigade, expanded the Hudson's Bay Company's enterprise along the Snake River as far east as the Bitterroot River in present-day Idaho, and as far south as the Bear River in present-day Utah. In 1825, he replaced ALEXANDER ROSS as director of operations in the region.

In 1825–26, Ogden headed a second expedition south from the Columbia River to the Deschutes River in

Oregon, then east through the Blue Mountains to the Snake River.

In 1826–27, Ogden explored south from Walla Walla in present- day Washington to the Deschutes River in Oregon, following it to the Klamath Lake, then proceeding near or into northern California, from where he could see Mount Shasta.

In 1828–29, Ogden undertook an exploration of the Great Salt Lake and traced the course of the Humboldt River to its sink in Nevada. He led his party, including his assistant William Kittson, through the Great Basin along the eastern face of the Sierra Nevada. The group survived an attack by the Mojave Indians before safely reaching the north shores of the Gulf of California, thus completing the north-south journey. They returned via California.

During the 1830s, Ogden managed the Hudson's Bay Company's operation on the southern coast of Alaska, then was assigned to Oregon. He remained in the Oregon country as administrator of the fur post at Fort Vancouver throughout the 1840s. When the Cayuse War erupted in 1847 under TILOUKAIKT, Ogden, experienced in negotiations with Indians, peacefully obtained the release of 50 white captives from the Cayuse militants.

Ogden prospered in the fur trade and retired at Oregon City with one of his several Indian wives. His career had brought him into contact with diverse tribes—in the country of the Great Lakes, Columbia Plateau, Pacific Northwest, California, and Great Basin—and he learned to speak several Indian languages. He recorded his experiences among Indians in his book *Traits of American Indian Life and Character. By A Fur Trader*, which first appeared in 1855, one year after his death.

OGLETHORPE, JAMES EDWARD. *(1696–1785)*. Colonial governor of Georgia.

James Oglethorpe was born in London and educated at Oxford. He served in the military before beginning his 32-year career as a member of Great Britain's House of Commons in 1722. Receiving a charter to establish the Georgia colony in 1733, intended as a buffer between the Spanish in Florida and the British in South Carolina, Oglethorpe founded the first Georgia settlement at Savannah.

Oglethorpe and his colonists, comprised of debtors from England and persecuted Protestants from Europe, were able to obtain a cession of lands from the Yamacraw band of Creeks under TOMOCHICHI. The tract was limited to the Tidewater region, bounded by the farthest upstream points reached by the Atlantic tides. Limitations on the size of individual landholdings, as well as prohibitions against the importation of slaves and liquor, tended to keep white encroachment

on Indian lands at a minimum, and relations with the neighboring Creeks were generally peaceful during Oglethorpe's governorship.

Oglethorpe led military expeditions against the Spanish at St. Augustine in the late 1730s and early 1740s. He won a decisive victory at the Battle of Bloody Marsh, June 9, 1742, which ended Spanish claims to Georgia territory north of St. Marys River.

Oglethorpe returned to England in 1743, resuming his parliamentary career. Settlement beyond the Tidewater did not begin for another 20 years, at which time the western part of Georgia was opened to white settlement by a new treaty with the Creeks. (See also TOMOCHICHI.)

OLD BRITON (Old Britain; La Demoiselle, The Demoiselle). *Miami. (d. 1752).* Trading partner of British.

Old Briton of the Piankashaw band of Miamis originally lived in what is now northwestern Indiana, where his people were traditional allies and trading partners of the French. Convinced of the superiority of British trade goods and hoping to play the British hand to increase his influence among his people, he moved his band eastward to the village of Pickawillany (near present-day Piqua) on the Miami River in Ohio. In 1748, he sent three delegates, including his son Assapausa, to Lancaster, Pennsylvania, to sign a treaty.

In subsequent years, Pickawillany became a central trading post for the British. As many as 50 Pennsylvania traders used the village as their base of operations. Through gifts the traders began winning over bands of the Ohio Valley and western Great Lakes. In addition to Old Briton's Pickawillany band, other Miami bands, such as the Piankashaws and Weas welcomed British traders to their villages. Some Kickapoos and Potawatomis also began relations with the Pickawillany traders.

Their power in the region threatened, the French made various attempts to destroy Pickawillany. In September 1749, a small force out of New France under Pierre-Joseph Celeron advanced on the village; in negotiations, Old Briton avoided conflict by agreeing to lead his followers back to Indiana without any intention of doing so. GEORGE CROGHAN arrived in November to strengthen the British-Miami alliance. The French tried to bribe Old Briton in summer 1750. In February 1751, Croghan once again visited Pickawillany. That same year, another small French force under Sieur de Bellestre unsuccessfully attacked the village while Old Briton was away on an autumn hunt. Old Briton then tried to organize a general uprising of area tribes; in January 1752, he ordered the execution of three French soldiers and cut off the ears of a fourth, sending him back to the governor of New France as a message.

The French responded with a much larger force of mostly Ottawa, Ojibway, and Potawatomi warriors under the part-Ottawa, part-French trader CHARLES LANGLADE out of Michilimackinac in present-day Michigan. In May 1752, they advanced along the shore of Lake Huron to Detroit, from where they moved on Pickawillany, reaching it on June 21. With most of the warriors away from the village on a summer hunt, Old Briton's remaining men and the five traders present were easily defeated. The hoped-for support of the Pennsylvanians against the French never materialized. Langlade's force killed 14 Miamis, Old Briton among them, plus one trader, and captured three other British. Then some of Langlade's warriors boiled and ate the chief.

After the destruction of Pickawillany, surviving Miamis returned to the Wabash River in Indiana. The French constructed a chain of posts to fortify the region. Yet, in the subsequent French and Indian War of 1754–63, the British defeated the French for control of the region, holding it until the American Revolution.

OLD JOHN. See JOHN.

OLD-MAN-AFRAID-OF-HIS-HORSES. See MAN-AFRAID-OF-HIS-HORSES.

OLD SMOKE (Old King, Seneca King; Sayenqueraghta, Siongorochti, Gayahgwaahdoh, Giengwahtoh, Gwuiyahgwaahdoh, Kaienkwaahton, Kayenquarachton). *Seneca. (d. 1786).* Ally of British in the French and Indian War and the American Revolution.

Old Smoke's village was Ganundasaga (present-day Geneva, New York). As a noted warrior and powerful chief, he negotiated treaties with the English at Philadelphia in 1754; Easton, Pennsylvania, in 1758; Johnson Hall, New York, in 1759; and Fort Stanwix, New York, in 1759. He helped WILLIAM JOHNSON take Fort Niagara in 1759 during the French and Indian War of 1754–63. During the American Revolution, Old Smoke fought the Battle of Oriskany in August 1777; participated in raids along the Susquehanna Valley in 1778; and battled American troops again with Brant at the Battle of Newtown in 1779. (See also BRANT, JOSEPH.)

OLLIKUT (Ollokut, Ollokot, Ollicot, Olikut, Alokut, Frog). *Nez Perce. (ca. 1845–d. 1877).* War chief in the Nez Perce War. Son of Old JOSEPH; brother of Young JOSEPH.

Ollikut grew up to be honored for his prowess as a warrior, proving himself against the Blackfeet and other Plains tribes. On the death of his father Old Joseph in 1871, Ollikut took over the duties of war chief, while his brother Young Joseph concerned himself mainly with civil duties. During the Nez Perce War of 1877, Ollikut led charges at White Bird Canyon on June 17 and Camas Creek on August 18, among other battles. He was killed on September 30 in the final battle, in the Bear Paw Mountains, Montana. (See also Young JOSEPH.)

OLOTARACA (Olotoraca, Olotacara, Otocara, Hola'taraca). *Saturiba. (fl. 1560s).* War chief; ally of French against Spanish in Florida.

Olotaraca was the nephew of the chief of the Timucuan-speaking Saturiba Indians living along the lower St. Johns River in Florida. In 1568, as war chief of his people, he joined with the French under Dominique de Gourgues in successful attacks on Spanish forts at the mouth of the river. The first man to scale the Spanish breastwork, he killed a gunner who had slowed the French advance.

ONATE, JUAN DE. *(ca. 1550–ca. 1624).* Explorer; Spanish colonial governor.

It is thought that Juan de Onate, the son of an early Spanish conquistador, was born in Zacatecas, in the western Mexican province of Nueva Galicia. He was married to a granddaughter of Hernando Cortes, the original Spanish conqueror of Mexico.

In 1595, the Spanish king commissioned Onate to establish a new colony north of the Rio Grande, in the region of present-day New Mexico. In 1598, Onate led a 400-man expedition, consisting of soldiers, settlers, and Franciscan missionaries, north to present-day El Paso and proceeded to the confluence of the Rio Grande and Chama rivers. He claimed the region for Spain and established the temporary colonial capital at the Indian pueblo known as San Juan. A more permanent settlement was established the following year at the nearby San Gabriel Pueblo. Onate dispatched Franciscan friars and soldiers to convert the Rio Grande Pueblo Indians to Christianity and inform them of the arrival of their new Spanish rulers.

In December 1598, at the Acoma Pueblo, Keres Indians attacked and wiped out a detachment of soldiers. Several months later, in 1599, Onate initiated a punitive expedition against the Keres at Acoma. Scaling the steep mesa walls, the soldiers captured the pueblo and, in the process, killed nearly 1,500 of its occupants. In public trials, the 80 surviving male captives over 25 years of age were condemned to have one foot lopped off, and were additionally sentenced to 20 years of penal servitude. Boys over 12 were sentenced to 20 years of slavery. Two Hopi tribesmen involved in the revolt each lost a hand as punishment, but were sent home to their people as examples of the severity of Spanish justice. The children under 12 were placed in the care of Franciscan missionaries; most of the surviving Indian women of Acoma were also condemned to 20 years of enslavement.

The allure of the fabled Seven Cities of Cibola, and of the fabled Kingdom of Quivira, led Onate to undertake explorations into the present-day southwestern United States. In 1601, he headed an expedition east across the Texas Panhandle, along the Canadian and Arkansas rivers as far as present-day Wichita, Kansas. Onate's men had contact with the Pawnees and introduced horses to the Southern Plains tribes.

Upon his return to the New Mexico colony at San Gabriel, he discovered that many of his colonists had deserted. Onate continued to explore present-day southern New Mexico and Arizona, still in search of legendary riches. In 1604–05, with a company of about 30 soldiers, he marched westward to the Colorado River and explored as far south as the Gulf of California. Along the way, he had contacts with the Zunis in what is now western New Mexico and the Hopis in eastern Arizona. He also had contact with the Mojaves, Yavapais, and other Indian peoples to the west.

In 1609, two years after Onate had offered his resignation as New Mexico's first colonial governor, he was accused by Spanish authorities in Mexico of employing excessive brutality in putting down the Acoma revolt, as well as for mismanagement in his administration of the New Mexico colony. He was found guilty of these charges in 1614, and exiled from New Mexico. In the early 1620s, he returned to Spain, where his conviction was eventually reversed.

ONEKA (Owanecco). *Mohegan. (ca. 1640–1710).*
Ally of English. Son and successor of UNCAS.

Like his father, Oneka proved an enemy of the other tribes in the region and a friend to the colonists. He supported the English against the Wampanoags and Narragansets in King Philip's War of 1675–76, fighting at Brookfield and Hadley, Massachusetts, and is said to have nearly captured King PHILIP himself. With his father, Oneka signed various land grants to the colonists. On his father's death in 1682 or 1683, Oneka became grand sachem of the Mohegans.

OPECHANCANOUGH. *Powhatan.*
(ca. 1545–1644). Chief of the Powhatan Confederacy; leader of revolts against Virginia colonists in 1622 and 1644. Brother of POWHATAN; uncle of POCAHONTAS.

During much of his brother's reign as chief of the Powhatan Confederacy, the alliance of some 32 Algonquian-speaking Tidewater tribes, Opechancanough of the Pamunkey band of Powhatans was at odds with the Jamestown colonists. In 1607, when a party led by Captain JOHN SMITH explored the upper Chickahominy River, Opechancanough track-ed and ambushed them with 300 warriors. Smith, who had left camp with his Indian guides to hunt, was the only white to survive. On capturing him, Opechancanough took him first to his village on the Pamunkey River, then to his brother's village on the York River where, as legend has it, Pocahontas interceded to save Smith's life. Not long after his release in 1608, Smith, after having been refused a trade agreement by Opechancanough, led his men back to the Pamunkey village, seized the chief by the hair, and took him off as a hostage, whereupon his people ransomed him with food.

On Powhatan's death in 1618, Opitchapan, his brother, became chief in name. Opechancanough became the dominant leader of the confederacy, however.

Tobacco, now popular in Europe, was a lucrative cash crop for the colonists, and boatloads of settlers arrived along the ports of the Chesapeake Bay to cultivate it. Because tobacco depleted the soil, necessitating new fields every several years, the English needed more and more territory to put under the plow. They tricked the Indians into signing away huge tracts, and settlers would then move in and carve the land into plantations, cutting down trees and killing or driving away the game. In the process, Indian hunting grounds were ruined and a way of life destroyed.

Opechancanough wavered in his purpose, uncertain whether his warriors could defeat the numerous colonists. The arrest and execution of a brave by the name of Menatanou for the alleged murder of a white trader led him to decisive action: Opechancanough ordered a surprise attack.

On the morning of March 22, 1622, hundreds of warriors swept out of the forest and through the colony's tobacco fields, killing every white in sight, 347 men, women, and children out of about 1,400 colonists. In response, the English organized a militia army. The troops began a campaign of regular patrols against the Indians, burning houses and crops and pushing the Indians farther inland. Opechancanough agreed to a peace council. But when he and his warriors showed up, they were poisoned and attacked by the colonists. Opechancanough escaped, however. In 1625, a colonial army under Governor Francis Wyatt defeated more than 1,000 Indians at the village of Uttamussick on the Pamunkey River.

Both sides continued their raids for 10 years. Finally, in 1632, they agreed on a peace treaty. Twelve years later, however, on April 18, 1644, when he was supposedly about 100 years old and had to be carried to battle on a litter, Opechancanough ordered another attack. His warriors swept through the colony, killing almost 500 whites out of a population now of approximately 8,000. Again, the colonists responded with a stepped-up military campaign.

Governor WILLIAM BERKELEY and a force of militiamen captured Opechancanough and carried him on his litter back to Jamestown. He was jeered by an angry crowd and later shot by a vengeful guard.

Opechancanough's successor Necotowance granted the colonists the legal right to the lands they presently occupied, and the Powhatan Confederacy ceased to be a major political force in the region.

OPOTHLEYAHOLO (Opothleyoholo, Opothle Yoholo, Opothleyohola, Apothleyahola, Hopothleycholo, Hupuihilth Yahola, Hupuehelth Yahola, "good shouting child"). *Creek.*

(ca. 1798–1862). Tribal leader before and after relocation to the Indian Territory; advocate of traditional Creek customs; Union ally in the Civil War.

Opothleyaholo was born in Georgia, and, as a young Red Stick warrior, he fought in the Creek War of 1813–14 under WILLIAM WEATHERFORD against American forces led by General ANDREW JACKSON. Known for his oratory, he became speaker of the council of the Upper Creek towns under BIG WARRIOR.

In 1825, at Indian Springs, Georgia, Opothleyaholo informed federal officials that the upper Creek leaders would not sign the land cession negotiated by WILLIAM McINTOSH of the White Sticks (or Lower Creeks), many of whom were mixed-bloods. Soon after McIntosh's signing, the Creek council ordered his death for defying the ban on such land cessions. MENEWA carried out the execution.

In 1825–26, Opothleyaholo traveled to Washington, D.C., as a tribal delegate where he met with President John Quincy Adams—the Creek PADDY CARR acting as interpreter—and agreed to the terms in the Treaty of Washington, ceding tribal lands. Opothleyaholo and the other Upper Creek chiefs changed their position because of the threat of civil war. The Upper Creeks still hoped to stay in the East even after the migration of the Lower Creeks. In 1832, with increasing white pressure to relocate, Opothleyaholo headed another delegation to meet President ANDREW JACKSON and signed the second Treaty of Washington.

Although he opposed removal as forced upon his people by the state of Georgia and the federal government, Opothleyaholo remained at peace with the United States. In 1834–35, not wanting to settle in a new home in the Indian Territory with the Lower Creeks, he attempted to buy land in Texas, but met with the opposition of the Mexican government. In 1836, he led a force of about 500 warriors against Creeks and Seminoles who were throwing their support to the insurgent leader OSCEOLA in the Second Seminole War.

Despite his help, Opothleyaholo was forced to relocate in 1836. He led a group of about 2,700 people west of the Mississippi to the Indian Territory. Of those Creeks removed, approximately 3,500 of 15,000 men, women, and children died of disease and exposure during and after the trip west.

Opothleyaholo became head chief of the reunited tribal factions. A full-blooded Creek, he encouraged traditional customs among his people; the mixed-blooded Lower Creeks argued for acculturation.

The Civil War caused a new split in the tribe. Most of the Lower Creeks sided with the Confederacy. Calling for neutrality, Opothleyaholo withdrew from the Creek Nation and established a settlement of about 8,000 followers on the Deep Fork River. When a Confederate Indian cavalry under Colonel Douglas Cooper attempted to drive his people from the Indian Territory, Opothleyaholo led warriors in the Battle of Round Mountain on November 19, 1861, and at Chusto Talasah on December 9. Cooper received reinforcements out of Fort Gibson and Fort Smith and marched on Opothleyaholo's band again on December 26 at Chustenalah. His people were dispersed, fleeing into Kansas without their possessions and livestock. Although Opothleyaholo died the next year, many of his supporters returned to fight as Union soldiers against such Confederate Indian leaders as the Cherokee STAND WATIE, and helped recapture the Indian Territory.

ORATAMIN (Oratam, Oratamy, Oratan, Oraton).

Wappinger. (d. ca. 1667). Leader in the wars between the Hudson River Indians and the Dutch; spokesman and negotiator for numerous bands.

Oratamin was a chief of the Hackensack Indians, who were part of the Wappinger Confederacy of Hudson River bands.

Starting in 1639, the Dutch director-general of New Netherland, WILLEM KIEFT, advocated a policy of harassment and extermination of Indians to make room for Dutch settlers. He paid the Mohawks, traditional enemies of the Algonquian-speaking Hudson River peoples of both the Wappinger and Delaware confederacies, to carry out raids. In February 1643, the Hudson River Indians fled to the Dutch settlement of Pavonia for protection. Dutch soldiers attacked the unsuspecting Indians while they slept, killing and beheading about 80, many of them women and children, and taking 30 more as prisoners. The soldiers brought the 80 heads back to New Amsterdam, where they played kickball with them. They also publicly tortured the remaining prisoners with Kieft's approval.

Following the Pavonia Massacre, about 10 bands of Hudson River Indians from both the Wappinger and Delaware confederacies rose up in rebellion, raiding Dutch settlements in retaliation for the massacre. Trading and farming were disrupted throughout New Netherland as settlers fled to New Amsterdam (present-day New York City), which the Indians held in a state of siege. During this period, the Dutch built a defensive wall in lower Manhattan, where Wall Street is now located. An army of Dutch and English soldiers under Captain JOHN UNDERHILL began a persistent campaign throughout the countryside, tracking down and attacking bands of Indians and destroying villages and crops.

Oratamin spoke on behalf of the Hackensacks, Tappans, Manhattans, and Sintsincks of the allied Wappinger and Delaware confederacies at a peace council in April 1643, but fighting soon broke out again. He participated in a second treaty at Fort Amsterdam on Manhattan Island in August 1645, and a third in July 1649, with the new governor-general PETER STUYVESANT, which led to several years of peace.

An incident in 1655 led to another outbreak of violence. A Dutch farmer killed a Delaware woman for stealing peaches from his orchard, and the Wappingers and Delawares again begin raiding Dutch settlements, including New Amsterdam, and taking hostages. Stuyvesant ordered out a militia force that succeeded in freeing the hostages. The violence shifted up the Hudson. Esophus Indians rebelled against Dutch farmers in their midst, attacking the town of Wiltwyck and surrounding settlements, with the goal of driving away the colonists once and for all. Stuyvesant's soldiers sailed upriver, where negotiations were arranged, but soldiers murdered a delegation of Esophus Indians. In retaliation, the Indians captured eight soldiers and burned them alive.

In 1660, Stuyvesant began a policy of holding Indian children as hostages in New Amsterdam to extort good behavior from the area tribes. He also called in the Mohawks to terrorize the Esophus insurgents, who agreed to peace in May 1664. Once again, it was Oratamin who acted as chief spokesman for the region's Indians and helped negotiate the final agreement. That same year, English troops invaded and captured New Netherland, which became New York, ending Dutch tenure in North America. Oratamin was asked to help in negotiations in the next years, but was too weakened by age.

ORONHYATEKHA ("it is a burning sky").
Mixed Mohawk. (1841–1907). Physician; lecturer.

Oronhyatekha was born on the Six Nations Reserve near Brantford, Ontario, of Mohawk and white ancestry. He attended a mission school near his home, then Wesleyan Academy in Massachusetts, Kenyon College in Ohio, Toronto University in Ontario, and Oxford University in England, from which he graduated a doctor of medicine. On returning to Canada, he settled in Toronto. By his wife, a granddaughter of JOSEPH BRANT, he had a son and a daughter. Oronhyatekha became known among his people as a skilled orator. In 1884, he spoke at the Indian centennial at Tyendinaga, Ontario. He also wrote an article on the Mohawk's Iroquois dialect, published by the Canadian Institute. He participated in numerous societies, including the Good Templars, the Masons, the National Fraternal Congress, and the Independent Order of Foresters.

OSCEOLA (Oseola, Aseola, Asseola, Assiola, Aseheholar, Asi-yahola, "black drink crier"; Talassee Tustenuggee, Talcy; Bill Powell). *Seminole. (ca. 1803–1838).* Leader of the Second Seminole War of 1835–42.

Osceola is thought to have been born near the Talapoosa River along the present-day Alabama-Georgia border. Some scholars maintain he was a mixed-blood. He may have had some white blood on his mother Polly Copinger's side; her spouse, William Powell, by whose name Osceola was sometimes called, is thought to have been his father, but was very likely a stepfather. Osceola himself claimed to be a full-blood.

Osceola moved to Florida with his mother, settling along the Apalachicola River. About 1815, they moved to the St. Marks region. As a teenager, Osceola fought in the First Seminole War of 1817–18. He is thought to

Osceola. Portrait by George Catlin. *Courtesy of Library of Congress.*

have been captured along the Enconfino River by troops under General ANDREW JACKSON, but was soon released. After the war, he moved to the region south of Tampa Bay.

In 1823, some of the Seminole leaders, such as NEAMATHLA, signed the Treaty of Moultrie Creek in which tribal lands were ceded and a reservation created. The Indian Removal Act of 1830 called for the relocation of the Seminoles and other Southeast peoples to the Indian Territory west of the Mississippi. The Treaty of Payne's Landing of 1832, signed by some of the Seminole leaders, such as CHARLEY EMATHLA and FOKE LUSTE HAJO, required all Indians to evacuate Florida within three years in exchange for lands in the Indian Territory, plus grants of money and clothing. It also decreed that any Seminoles with black blood be treated as runaway slaves. In 1833, a delegation of seven Seminoles, again including Emathla and Foke Luste Hajo, traveled west and signed the Treaty of Fort Gibson, accepting a new homeland near the Creeks. By the end of the three-year period, the Seminoles had not complied with the terms of the treaty, however.

Osceola, known to his people as a skillful hunter, warrior, and lacrosse player, was not a hereditary chief, but rose to prominence because of his stand against relocation. He traveled from band to band, urging them to stay on their ancestral homelands.

In April 1835, at Fort King on the Seminole Reservation, the Indian agent WILEY THOMPSON forced a new treaty upon the Seminoles, confirming the terms of removal. Many of the chiefs refused to sign the document or speak to the white official. Seminole tradition holds that Osceola slashed the document with a knife and quarreled with Thompson. The agent had Osceola seized and placed in irons. He angrily protested, but finally agreed to sign. On being released, however, he escaped into the wilderness. In preparation for resistance against forced removal, Seminole leaders began taking their families into the swamps, safe from military roundups.

The following November, in 1835, after having sold his cattle at Fort King in preparation for relocation, the pro-removal chief Charley Emathla was ambushed by a war party under Osceola. As a symbolic gesture, Osceola supposedly scattered the money Emathla had received from whites over his dead body.

On December 28, 1835, Osceola led a party in ambush on the agent Wiley Thompson, killing him along with an army officer and five civilians. The same day, ALLIGATOR, MICANOPY, and JUMPER led about 300 warriors against Major FRANCIS DADE's column of 108 soldiers on their way from Fort Brooke on Tampa Bay to reinforce Fort King. All but three soldiers died. Three days later, on New Year's Eve, Osceola's warriors defeated General DUNCAN CLINCH's force of about 300 regulars and 500 Florida militiamen on the Withlacoochee River. Four soldiers died, with 59 more injured. Only three Indians were killed. Osceola was wounded, but escaped.

Osceola and the other rebel leaders waged an effective guerrilla campaign for two years, attacking isolated settlements and patrols, burning bridges, and driving off horses and cattle. In spring 1837, Micanopy and other chiefs agreed to stop fighting and relocate. They reported to Fort Mellon and Tampa Bay. But Osceola led his men in a raid, forcing Micanopy and others to flee with him into the wilderness. Micanopy surrendered later that year.

General THOMAS JESUP resorted to trickery to capture Osceola. Through WILD CAT, whom he had sent as an envoy, Osceola agreed to attend a peace council at Fort Augustine in October 1837. Jesup, however, ordered the arrest of all the Seminoles and blacks present despite their flags of truce. Osceola was struck on the head, tied up, and imprisoned. Wild Cat and 18 followers soon escaped, but Osceola and the remaining prisoners were moved to Fort Moultrie near Charleston, South Carolina.

There are varying reports on the cause of Osceola's death: mistreatment by or poison from guards; disease, either malaria or quinsy; or simply deep melancholy and loss of will to live. GEORGE CATLIN, who painted a portrait of Osceola in prison, reported that he was ready for his death, embittered at whites for their treachery. After having donned his battle dress and painted himself with war paint, Osceola died on January 30, 1838. The post surgeon Dr. Frederick Weedon displayed his remains in a medical museum until they were destroyed in a fire.

Despite the loss of their leading war chief and the destruction of their homes and possessions, some rebel bands held out for several years. In the course of the long conflict, a series of generals and colonels were given the command against the Seminoles—before Osceola's capture, Duncan Clinch, EDMUND GAINES, WINFIELD SCOTT, Robert Call, and Thomas Jesup; then afterward, ZACHARY TAYLOR, Alexander McComb, Walker Armistead, and WILLIAM WORTH. Small war parties of Seminoles continued to frustrate much larger enemy forces through hit-and-run raids and masterful use of the Everglades as a hiding place. An exception was the Battle of Lake Okeechobee of December 25, 1837, in which Alligator, ARPEIKA, and Wild Cat led their warriors in open combat against Colonel Zachary Taylor's 600 troops. In the bitter fight, the Seminoles gave up the ground but lost only 14 men. The whites suffered 27 dead and 112 wounded.

The long struggle and chronic food shortage gradually wore down most of the remaining insurgents. Jumper surrendered in 1837, then Alligator in 1838. In 1839,

BILLY BOWLEGS led 200 warriors in an attack on a trading post opened by Colonel WILLIAM S. HARNEY within Seminole territory, killing 24. Wild Cat surrendered in 1841, but later participated in the Third Seminole War of 1855–58.

By the time the war petered out, the federal government had lost 1,500 men and spent at least $20 to 40 million, the most costly Indian war ever. For every two Seminoles relocated, one soldier had died.

OSHKOSH (Oshkushi, Oskoshe, Oskashe, Oiscoss, "his hoof," "his nail," or "the brave").

Menominee. (1795–1858). Ally of British in the War of 1812; ally of Americans in the Black Hawk War of 1832; principal chief.

Oshkosh, grandson of Old King, was born at Old King's Village on the Fox River in present-day Wisconsin. At the age of 17, he fought along with TOMAH and SOULIGNY in support of British troops led by Colonel Robert Dickson in the taking of Fort Mackinaw, Michigan. He also joined in the attack the following year on Fort Stephenson, Ohio, which was successfully defended by troops under Colonel GEORGE CROGHAN.

In 1827, when LEWIS CASS and THOMAS McKENNEY, acting as Indian agents for the federal government, needed a representative for the Indians in the treaty negotiations at Butte des Morts in present-day Wisconsin, involving a land dispute between the Menominees and a band of Iroquois under ELEAZAR WILLIAMS who wished to settle in the region, they named Oshkosh principal chief. He later generally supported the American position, joining them in the BLACK HAWK War of 1832 against the Sacs and Foxes. Oshkosh also signed the Treaty of Lake Powahekone in 1848, ceding Menominee lands in Wisconsin.

Oshkosh died in a brawl at Keshena, Wisconsin, and was succeeded by his son. The city of Oshkosh, Wisconsin, bears his name.

O'SULLIVAN, TIMOTHY H. *(1840–1882).* Photographer.

Irish-born Timothy O'Sullivan worked as the photographer Mathew Brady's apprentice during the Civil War, a civilian member of the Union army's Corps of Topographical Engineering. After the war, he participated in the War Department surveys headed by CLARENCE KING and GEORGE WHEELER in the late 1860s and early 1870s. For part of his assignment under King, O'Sullivan used an old mule-drawn army ambulance as a darkroom. His photographs included images of Mojaves, Navajos, Apaches, Paiutes, Shoshones, Hopis, and Zunis, as well as Anasazi ruins and geological features. In addition to photographer, he often acted as mediator to the Indian tribes. O'Sullivan returned to Baltimore in 1875. When

Congress consolidated the four government-sponsored surveys into one in 1879, the U.S. Geological Survey, O'Sullivan was the official photographer under King, then served as chief of the Treasury Department's photographic laboratory. His health forced his retirement after only five months, however.

OTHERDAY, JOHN (Other Day; Am-pa-tu-to-ka-cha, Angpetu Tokecha). *Wahpeton Sioux. (1801–1871).* Christian convert; protector of whites; army scout.

John Otherday was born at Swan Lake, Minnesota, the son of Zitkaduta, and nephew of Big Curly, chief of the Wahpeton band at Lac Qui Parle, Minnesota. As a young man, he was known for his heavy drinking and fights in which he reportedly killed fellow Sioux. He later converted to Christianity under the ministry of Thomas Williamson and married a white woman whom he met in Washington, D.C., in 1858.

Along with PAUL MAZAKUTEMANI and Iron Hawk, Otherday helped rescue one of the female captives from INKPADUTA's band after the Spirit Lake Uprising of 1857. He was one of the members of the Christian Indian Republic at the Yellow Medicine Agency. During the Minnesota Uprising of Santee Sioux in 1862–63 under LITTLE CROW, Otherday again helped whites, leading 62 missionaries, traders, and employees of the Yellow Medicine Agency, plus their families, to safety at Henderson, Minnesota. Little Crow and his followers burned his home and those of other Christian Indians in reprisal.

Otherday then served as a scout for General HENRY HASTINGS SIBLEY, participating in the battles of Birch Coolee and Wood Lake in September 1862, where he gained the attention of his officers for his bravery. He continued work as a scout for two or three years.

In 1867, Otherday traveled to Washington, D.C., to sign a treaty on behalf of the Wahpetons and Sissetons. He received a grant of $2,500 from Congress and used the money to buy a farm near Henderson. Unsuccessful at farming, he sold his house to pay off his creditors and those of his relatives.

Otherday moved with his wife to the Sisseton Sioux Reservation in northwest South Dakota, where the federal government built a home for him. He died of tuberculosis and was buried at Big Coolee with full military honors by fellow Indian scouts. (See also LITTLE CROW.)

OURAY (U-ray, U-re; The Arrow; Willy). *Ute-Apache. (ca. 1820 or ca. 1833–1880).* Spokesman for the seven Ute bands; peacemaker during the Ute War of 1879. Brother-in-law of CANALLA.

Ouray was born in Taos, New Mexico. His father, Guera Murah, was a Jicarilla Apache adopted into the

Utes; his mother was a Tabeguache Ute. Ouray spent much of his youth working for Mexican sheepherders, later establishing his reputation among the Tabeguaches (later called the Uncompahgres) of southwestern Colorado in warfare against the Sioux and Kiowas. Ouray learned Spanish and English in addition to several Indian languges, which were useful in negotiations.

Ouray's son by his first wife was taken by the Sioux in a raid on a Ute hunting camp. In 1859, on the death of his first wife, Ouray married a Tabeguache woman by the name of Chipeta. With his father's death in 1860, he became chief of his band.

In 1863, Ouray first came to the notice of white officials when he helped negotiate a treaty with the federal government at Conejos, Colorado, in which the Utes ceded all lands east of the Continental Divide. In 1867, he helped CHRISTOPHER "KIT" CARSON suppress a Ute uprising under Chief Kaniatse. In 1868, he accompanied Carson, NICAAGAT, and eight other chiefs to Washington, D.C., and acted as the spokesman for the seven bands: the three northern bands, Grand River, Yampa, and Uintah; the three southern bands, Mouache, Capote, and Wiminuche; and his Tabeguache band located between them in the central part of western Colorado. At that time, the Utes retained 16 million acres of land, with agencies for the southern bands at Los Pinos, including Ouray's Tabeguache band and for the northern bands at White River.

With the growth of the mining frontier in western Colorado and eastern Utah, more whites trespassed on Ute lands. In 1872, Ouray, his wife Chipeta, and eight other Utes visited Washington, D.C., with the interpreter OTTO MEARS, where they met President ULYSSES S. GRANT, then went to other eastern cities. In 1873, in a follow-up council at Los Pinos, Ouray and other tribal representatives met with a federal commission headed by Felix Brunot. The Utes were pressured into ceding four million acres for an annual payment of $25,000: the San Juan Cession. For his services, Ouray received an additional annuity of $1,000.

In 1875, the Los Pinos Agency was moved to the Uncompahgre River. The federal government granted Ouray 400 acres near present-day Montrose and built him an adobe house for his services. Because of his friendship with whites and the special favors he received, Ouray made enemies among his people. He was forced to kill at least five Utes in various attempts on his life.

When Colorado achieved statehood in 1876, mining companies tried to expel the three White River bands from their lands. The phrase "the Utes must go" became a political slogan even though Utes had served as guides and auxiliaries for the federal regulars and state militiamen in campaigns against other Indians, such as the Navajos during the 1860s.

In spring 1878, a new Indian agent, NATHAN MEEKER, arrived among the Northern Utes at White River. He advocated agriculture and Christianity among his people. But most of the Indians preferred their ancient ways; many refused to farm. Meeker asked federal troops to help him impose his will; but the government originally ignored his requests. In September 1879, Meeker ordered that a portion of the tribe's land be used for farming. A medicine man named Canalla, brother-in-law of Ouray, grew angry at having to plow lands that had always been used for pony-grazing. He confronted Meeker, grabbing him by the shoulders and telling him to leave the agency. On learning of the incident through correspondence from Meeker, federal officials sent in a detachment of 150 troops under Major THOMAS T. THORNBURGH.

The band leader Nicaagat rode out to meet the approaching soldiers. At a parley on Bear River, he informed Thornburgh that the Utes wanted peace and that there was no need to advance any farther. COLOROW, another band leader, subsequently rode out to insist on the Utes' desire for peace.

When Thornburgh and 120 cavalrymen reached Milk Creek on the northern edge of the Utes Reservation, about 15 miles north of the White River Agency on September 29, Nicaagat and Colorow met them with about 100 warriors. Thornburgh had his men move into battle formation; the Ute leaders ordered the same. Shots were fired before a parley could be arranged, and Thornburgh was killed. The cavalry retreated to their wagon train across the creek, Captain J. Scott Payne took command and organized an effective defense. Nicaagat and his warriors lay siege for nearly a week. On October 2, a regiment of black cavalrymen under Captain Francis Dodge arrived as reinforcements; on October 5, a larger relief force under WESLEY MERRITT arrived. The Utes, with about 23 dead, withdrew southward. The soldiers suffered 14 dead and 43 wounded.

During the Battle at Milk Creek, QUINKENT and others remained at the White River Agency. Some among them killed Meeker and his white employees and kidnapped Meeker's wife and daughter, Arvilla and Josephine, along with Mrs. F. S. Price, wife of the agency's carpenter. The army advanced to the agency, found the bodies, and soon learned of the hostages. Although the generals PHILIP H. SHERIDAN and WILLIAM T. SHERMAN wanted to launch major offensives against the Utes because of the incident, CARL SCHURZ, secretary of the Interior, sent a peace mission under Charles Adams.

Adams met with Ouray in the hope the Ute chief could defuse the situation. Because of his diplomatic efforts, the hostages were released unharmed and

Nicaagat and Colorow were pardoned for their involvement because they had acted as warriors in a fair fight; Quinkent was tried, however. Mrs. Meeker claimed in secret hearings that Quinkent had raped her, although no public charge was made. Nor could it be proven who had actually carried out the killings. Quinkent was imprisoned at Fort Leavenworth, Kansas, but was declared insane after having served a year and was sent back to his people.

Ouray traveled to Washington, D.C., one last time, in 1880. Weakened by illness, he signed the treaty by which the White River Utes were to be relocated to the Uintah Reservation in Utah. The Uncompahgre band was also moved there, and it later became known as the Uintah and Ouray Reservation. In Colorado, the only remaining Ute lands were a small tract in the southwestern corner of the state for the Mouache, Capote, and Wiminuche bands, known as the Southern Ute Reservation (the Wiminuche Utes eventually moved to the western end of this tract, where they came to have a separate piece, the Ute Mountain Reservation).

Soon after his return from Washington, D.C., Ouray died while on a trip to Ignacio, where the Southern Ute Agency had been relocated. He was buried there. His wife, Chipeta, henceforth ignored by the federal government, lived in poverty at the Uintah Reservation in Utah until her death in 1924. Her remains and those of Ouray were eventually brought back to Montrose, Colorado, for reburial.

OWHI (Ouhi). *Yakima. (d. 1858).* Band leader in the Yakima War of 1855–56 and the Coeur d'Alene (Spokane) War of 1858. Father of QUALCHIN; uncle of KAMIAKIN's wife (described as Kamiakin's brother-in-law in many texts).

Owhi, whose village was along the Yakima River, was present at the Walla Walla Council of 1855, convened by Governor ISAAC STEVENS. His son Qualchin helped precipitate the Yakima War that same year, leading to unrest throughout the Washington Territory under the general leadership of Kamiakin. In 1858, during the subsequent Coeur d'Alene War, Owhi surrendered to Colonel George Wright for peace negotiations, but he was immediately placed in irons and used as bait to lure his son, Qualchin, whom Wright considered another of the region's most dangerous leaders. Qualchin appeared soon afterward and was summarily executed. Owhi then was taken with Wright's troops as they crossed the Snake River, but he attacked one of his guards with a whip and managed to ride off. He was chased, shot and wounded, then surrounded. On realizing there was no escape, he sat on the ground to await his death. A soldier then shot him in the head. (See also KAMIAKIN.)

OYTES (Oyte, Oites). *Northern Paiute. (fl. 1870s).* Medicine man; leader in the Bannock War of 1878.

Oytes, a shaman and follower of SMOHALLA's Dreamer religion, took a militant stance against whites, proselytizing among the Northern Paiutes of the Malheur Agency in Oregon. When BUFFALO HORN of the Bannocks was killed early in the Bannock War, June 1878, EGAN assumed command of the combined force of Bannocks, Paiutes, Umatillas, and Cayuses. He was killed in July; Oytes then led the remaining insurgents. With persistent tracking by white forces under General OLIVER HOWARD, Oytes surrendered with a party of 60 on August 12. The Malheur Reservation was terminated and prisoners were settled on the Yakima Reservation in Washington. The Bannocks were eventually allowed to settle on their tribe's reservation along the Snake River in Idaho. (See also BUFFALO HORN; EGAN.)

P

PACOMIO. *Chumash. (fl. 1820s).* Leader of revolt against the Mexicans.

Pacomio was raised and educated by the priests at La Purisima Mission in the Santa Barbara district of California. He became a skilled carpenter under their tutelege. Dissatisfied with the treatment of his people by the Spanish, he planned a general uprising of Mission Indians to drive the Spanish out of Alta California. He visited other missions to promote his cause and encouraged neighboring tribes, including the Yokuts, to move closer to the missions to make a surprise attack easier.

Pacomio sent out messengers to notify his allies of the day of revolt. Some messengers got through to Santa Inez and Santa Barbara Missions, but others, heading to the northern missions, were captured. On the chosen day—it is thought to have been March 19, 1824—he proclaimed himself general-in-chief of the Indians of Alta California and led about 2,000 Indians on La Purisima, capturing it and placing the soldiers in jail. The Indians at Santa Inez and Santa Barbara also rebelled. Yet, with Spanish counterattacks and the failure of other Mission Indians to participate, Pacomio's rebellion came to a gradual end. He surrendered and was allowed to live in peace at Monterey.

PAINTER, CHARLES C. *(d. 1895).* Reformer.

Born in Virginia, Charles Painter was the son of a Virginia planter who freed his own slaves before the Civil War. After graduation from Williams College in 1858, Painter became a Congregational minister. In the post–Civil War years, he served on the faculty of Fisk University, dedicated to the education of blacks.

Starting in 1883, Painter worked for the Indian Rights Association (IRA), founded by HERBERT WELSH and Henry Pancoast the year before. At first, Painter was associated with the IRA's Boston office, but came to be the organization's lobbyist in Washington, D.C. He made frequent trips to Indian reservations to investigate living conditions, as well as the behavior of Indian Bureau personnel. He was widely respected among Washington, D.C., officials for his views on Indian issues. He also made regular reports to the Friends of the Indian conferences sponsored by ALBERT SMILEY at Lake Mohonk, New York.

Painter favored Indian citizenship, the abolition of Indian reservations, and the institution of the allotment in severalty policy introduced in Congress by Senator HENRY DAWES. On Painter's death, his friend Francis Leupp replaced him at the IRA for an interim period; Samuel Brosius replaced Leupp.

PALMA (Salvador Palma). *Quechan (Yuma).* *(fl. 1780s).* Leader of revolt against the Spanish.

In 1774, Chief Palma of the Yuman-speaking Quechans, who lived along the Colorado River where it forms the border of present-day California and Arizona, met with the expedition of JUAN DE ANZA. In 1780, the Spanish established two missions in the region. Instead of founding a presidio with a garrison to protect the missions, 10 soldiers were stationed at each. Within a year, the missions ran short of supplies and gifts for the Indians, who decided to reclaim control of their lands. On July 17 and 18, 1781, Chief Salvador Palma and his brother Ygnacio Palma led their warriors and allies in attacks on the missions, killing perhaps as many as 95 priests, soldiers, and settlers, and capturing 76 women and children. That year and the next, the Spanish launched unsuccessful expeditions against the Quechans, who, along with other area tribes, retained control of the Colorado for years to come.

PALOU, FRANCISCO. *(1722–1789).* Historian; missionary.

Born on the island of Majorca, Spain, Francisco Palou became a student of JUNIPERO SERRA at Lullian University in Palma and was ordained into the Franciscan order in 1747. He came to Mexico with Serra two years later. Starting in 1769, they explored Upper California together and founded several missions. In his *Noticias de la Nueva California* (1774), Palou wrote about Spanish missionaries and California Indians. He has been referred to as the "Father of California History."

PARKER, ELY SAMUEL (Donehogawa, Deioninhogawen, "he holds the door open"; Ha-sa-no-an-da, "coming to the front"). *Mixed Seneca. (ca. 1828–1895).* Chief; research informant; engineer; officer and aide to General ULYSSES S. GRANT in the Civil War; first Indian commissioner of Indian affairs. Grandson of RED JACKET.

Ely Parker was born at Indian Falls near Pembroke, New York, the son of William Parker (Jonoesdowa), a chief at Tonawanda, and his wife, Gaontgwutwus. He attended a Baptist mission school near the Tonawanda Reservation, then spent two years in Canada learning to hunt and fish, with a stint as a stable boy at an army post, where he was teased by British officers because of his failure to understand them. When about 12, he returned to New York with a new determination to master the English language. He attended first Yates Academy in Yates, New York, then Cayuga Academy in Aurora.

In 1844, Parker, while part of a Seneca delegation to Albany, New York, met LEWIS HENRY MORGAN, who introduced himself in a bookstore. As interpreter, informant, and researcher, Parker collaborated with Morgan on the book *League of the Ho-de-no-sau-nee or Iroquois,* published in 1851. The next year, Parker became a chief of the Senecas. He played a central role in the struggle of the Tonawanda Senecas to save their reservation, which was guaranteed in 1857.

Parker had hoped to become a lawyer, but was denied admission to the New York bar because he was not a white citizen. He studied civil engineering at Rensselaer Polytechnic Institute, in Troy, New York, instead. He held various government jobs, including work on the Erie Canal. From 1858 to 1861, he was the superintendent of construction of government works at Galena, Illinois, where he became friends with Ulysses Grant, then a clerk in a harness store.

With the start of the Civil War, Parker hoped to serve the Union. First he tried to convince officials of a plan to raise a regiment of Iroquois. When this failed, he sought enlistment in the Army Corps of Engineers. Once again, he came up against racial prejudice.

Through his friendship with Grant, Parker finally received a commission in May 1863 as captain of engineers in the 7th Corps and joined Grant's army in the Vicksburg campaign. In August 1864, Grant appointed Parker as his military secretary with the rank of lieutenant colonel of volunteers. At Appomattox on April 9, 1865, because of his penmanship, Parker was asked to write out the terms by which General Robert E. Lee surrendered the Confederate army. As of that date, Parker was promoted to brigadier general of volunteers. During the next two years, continuing as an aide to Grant, Parker received a series of commissions from lieutenant to brigadier general in the regular army.

During the next several years, Parker traveled West on commissions to negotiate with militant tribes, such as RED CLOUD's Sioux in the War for the BOZEMAN Trail of 1866–68.

On his election to the presidency in 1868, Grant appointed Parker his commissioner of Indian affairs. Parker resigned his army commission in April 1869 to accept the post. That same year, he married Minnie Sachett, a white woman, by whom he would have a daughter.

Parker helped Grant establish his new Peace Policy toward the western tribes. He cleaned out corrupt bureaucrats from the Bureau of Indian Affairs and hired agents recommended by religious groups, many of them Quakers. He also established a Board of Indian Commissioners to oversee the Indian Bureau. He hoped that both Indians and whites could fill the board, but, because of their lack of political influence, no Indians were appointed.

In order to maintain peace on the Northern Plains, Parker invited the Oglala Sioux Red Cloud and the Brule Sioux SPOTTED TAIL to Washington, D.C., for a council concerning the establishment of Sioux reservation lands. Parker's policies were fair to the western tribes and enlightened for the period. He blocked the Big Horn Association in their efforts to mine Sioux treaty lands, making more enemies among white interests. The so-called Indian Ring of political bosses who had been profiteering through the Indian Bureau plotted Parker's downfall by delaying Congressional appropriations to feed the reservation Indians as agreed by treaty. When western agents urgently requested food for the Indians, Parker broke regulations by buying supplies on credit and transporting them without waiting for competitive bids. A Congressional committee charged him with defrauding the government and held an impeachment trial. Although he was exonerated of all charges and commended for keeping the promises of the federal government, Parker, fed up with prejudice, resigned in 1871.

He moved to New York City where, after having made and then lost money in several business attempts, he was hired as the superintendent for buildings and supplies by the New York City Police Department. He died at his country property in Fairfield, Connecticut, and was buried at the Forest Lawn Cemetery in Buffalo near his grandfather Red Jacket.

PARKER, QUANAH (Quana, Kwahnah, "sweet odor"). *Mixed Comanche. (ca. 1845–1911).* Leader of the Comanche Wars of the 1860s–70s; principal chief; religious leader. Son of PETA NOCONA.

Quanah Parker's mother, Cynthia Ann Parker, had been kidnapped by Comanches as a nine-year-old in 1836. As a teenager, she had become the wife of the Comanche chief Peta Nocono of the Nocona band and had come to prefer the Indian way of life to that of her blood relatives.

Quanah, the son of Cynthia and Peta, also grew up favoring Comanche ways. As a young boy, the mixed-blooded youth proved himself for his horsemanship, bravery, and leadership. He also came to hate whites on the loss of his family. His mother, recaptured by Texas Rangers and returned to her white family, died four years later; his father died from a wound inflicted by whites; and Quanah's brother died of a white disease. Quanah joined the powerful Kwahadie band of Comanches who lived in the Texas Panhandle, and, in 1867, he became one of their war chiefs.

During the years after the Civil War, the army launched new campaigns to pacify the Southern Plains Indians. Under the Medicine Lodge Treaty of 1867, a new reservation was established for the Comanches and Kiowas in the southern part of the Indian Territory between the Washita and Red rivers. Quanah's band refused to be confined on the reservation and give up their nomadic way of life. Most of the action of the subsequent Sheridan Campaign to pacify the Southern Plains was against Southern Cheyennes, led by ROMAN NOSE, TALL BULL, WHITE HORSE, and BULL BEAR, as well as against Southern Arapahos and Sioux, but General PHILIP H. SHERIDAN's southern column under Major Andrew Evans fought Comanches and Kiowas at the battle of Soldier Spring on December 25, 1868. The soldiers drove the Indians away, burned their tepees, and destroyed their food.

Kiowa attacks in May 1871, under SATANTA, SATANK, BIG TREE, and MAMANTI, on travelers along the Butterfield Southern Route (or Southern Overland Trail) led to increased military action against the Kiowas and Comanches. General WILLIAM T. SHERMAN sent the 4th Cavalry under Colonel RANALD S. MACKENZIE against them. After their advance through the reservation, Mackenzie's men invaded the Staked Plain of the Texas Panhandle, where in September 1871, Quanah personally led two charges against them. In the first, his warriors rode through the

army camp at Rock Station, stampeding and capturing many of their horses. In the second, he led an attack on a scouting party. Quanah killed and scalped the single casualty. With the arrival of winter, Mackenzie called off his pursuit of the insurgent bands.

The following spring, by traveling from water hole to water hole in the Staked Plain, Mackenzie's soldiers managed to capture New Mexican traders carrying guns to the Comanches. On September 29, 1872, the 4th Cavalry defeated Mow-way's band of Kotsoteka Comanches at McClellan Creek, killing at least 30 and capturing 124. Yet Quanah's Kwahadies and militant Kiowa bands were still at large.

Meanwhile, another activity by whites threatened the Plains Indian way of life. Before 1870, white hunters had killed buffalo only in wintertime when their furs were long. A new tanning process was developed that enabled furriers to make shorthaired hides workable as well, which called for year-round hunting. Moreover, by the 1870s, white hunters were armed with high-powered telescopic Sharp rifles effective at a range of 600 yards. The buffalo, essential to the Indian economy, were now being slaughtered by whites at a furious pace.

On learning that white hunters had entered the Staked Plain and set up camp at the abandoned trading post of Adobe Walls on the South Canadian River (where Comanches and Kiowas had fought CHRISTOPHER "KIT" CARSON's men a decade before), Quanah called a council of war. At the urging of the

Quanah Parker. *Courtesy of Library of Congress.*

medicine man ISATAI, the Comanches also held a Sun Dance, not a traditional Comanche custom, so that Kiowas, Cheyennes, and Arapahos would come. Preparations were made for an attack, the first strike of the so-called Red River War, or Buffalo War, of 1874–75. On June 27, 1874, Quanah was one of the leaders of an allied force of about 700 warriors against the 28 buffalo hunters at Adobe Walls. Despite their overwhelming numbers, the Indians were repelled by the repeater rifles of the buffalo hunters, losing 15 warriors, with many more wounded.

In the following months, the Comanches—along with Kiowas under LONE WOLF, Mamanti, and BIG BOW; Southern Cheyennes under BULL BEAR; as well as some Southern Arapahos and Sioux—carried out numeous raids on white settlements. The army launched a massive offensive with troops out of Texas, Kansas, and New Mexico. Colonel Ranald Mackenzie was once again in the field, as well as Colonel NELSON A. MILES. They sustained pressure on militant bands, finally dealing a crushing blow to the Indians on September 28 at the stronghold of Palo Duro Canyon. Although the soldiers killed only three braves, they captured or killed most of the Indian horses—an estimated 1,500—and destroyed most of their tepees.

With continuing relentless pursuit by the soldiers, the Indian militants, weary and half-starved, began tricking in to the army posts. The last of the Kiowa militants held out until February 1875. Quanah and his Comanche warriors turned themselves in the following June.

Quanah quickly adapted to his new life. He began using his mother's last name to identify himself among whites, and he studied English and Spanish. By 1878, he was a spokesman for the Kwahadie band in council with Indian agents, among whom he was consistently a favorite (14 different agents from 1878 to his death). He advocated the leasing of surplus pasturelands for grazing rights and for rights-of-way, working deals with white cattlemen and investors. He built a home and became a prosperous rancher himself.

From 1886 to 1898, Quanah Parker served as one of three judges on the Court of Indian Offenses for the Comanches, Kiowas, Apaches, and Wichitas until his polygamy—at the time he had five wives (a total of eight in the course of his life)—led to his dismissal. By 1890, he was principal chief of all the Comanche bands. In 1892, he represented his people in negotiations with the Jerome Commission, which was created in 1889 to apply the General Allotment Act (the DAWES Severalty Act) of two years before to the tribes of the Indian Territory, obtaining what he considered the best deal possible in the inevitable allotment of tribally held lands to individuals.

Parker traveled widely as a tribal delegate, nearly 20 times to Washington, D.C. He was instrumental in ar-

ranging for the return of GERONIMO to the West by offering to share the Comanche reservation with Apache prisoners. The two chiefs rode together in the inaugural parade of Theodore Roosevelt.

Parker also played a major role in spreading the ritual ingestion of the peyote plant. Earlier Comanches had probably helped spread the use of peyote northward when they brought back knowledge of the plant and its properties after raids in Mexico. Parker discovered what is known as the Peyote Road sometime after 1890 and the collapse of the Ghost Dance religion founded by WOVOKA. His work and that of other peyotists, such as Big Moon of the Kiowas, led to the spread of peyote use among Indians throughout North America, especially of the Plains, Southwest, Prairies, and Great Lakes, and the eventual founding of the Native American Church, seven years after his death in 1911.

Quanah Parker was survived by two of his wives. He had earlier brought his mother's remains to Oklahoma to be reinterred and, after a funeral attended by about 1,500 people, was buried next to her at Cache.

PARKMAN, FRANCIS. *(1823–1893).* Historian.

Francis Parkman, born and raised in Boston, had an inheritance from his father, a Unitarian minister, that made him financially independent. He studied at Harvard University and was greatly influenced by the writings of the Jesuit missionary, JOSEPH FRANCOIS LAFITAU, who had lived among the Iroquois of Canada in the early 1700s and who believed that the studies of living Indian cultures would add to an understanding of ancient society.

Shortly after having graduated from Harvard, Parkman spent part of 1846 living among the Pawnees and Sioux in the company of the mountain man Henri Chatillion. He recorded his experiences in *The California and Oregon Trail*, published in 1849 (*The Oregon Trail* in later editions). Parkman went on to write a history of the French and Indian War of 1754–63 and its aftermath, *History of the Conspiracy of Pontiac* (1851); as well as a study of the impact of the Jesuits on the Indians, *The Jesuits in North America* (1867). These works were part of Parkman's history of the struggle of the European powers for control of North America in the 17th and 18th centuries, *France and England in North America*, published as a nine-volume set in 1892.

Parkman contrasted the way in which the French and the British dealt with the Indians. While the British more often had a formal and sometimes blatantly adversarial relationship with the Indians, he characterized the colonial French Indian policy as conciliatory, informal, and friendly. Although he demonstrated a respect for the Indian way of life in his writings, he held that the Indian was ultimately incapable of being civilized.

In addition to his historical studies, Parkman pursued an interest in horticulture and was president of the Massachusetts Horticultural Society in 1875–78. He was also a founder of the Archaeological Institute of America in 1879. He pursued his active career despite severe health problems, including weakness of sight.

PASSACONAWAY ("bear cub"). *Pennacook.* *(ca. 1565–ca. 1665).* Grand sachem; medicine man.

Passaconaway was the most powerful sachem of what is now southern New Hampshire when the colonists arrived. He lived in the village of Pennacook along the Merrimack River near present-day Concord. Under his rule, the various Algonquian bands of the region (grouped together under the name Pennacook by scholars), successfully defended their territory from Mohawk expansion from the west. Passaconaway was considered by his people to have shamanistic powers as well as political wisdom; he reportedly had visions about the British conquest of his people. The Pennacooks at first resisted white settlement in their territory and made scattered raids. Then, in 1642, soldiers moved on Passaconaway's village. He was away at the time, but his wife and son were taken prisoner. When he protested to Massachusetts officials, he gained their release. In 1644, Passaconaway formally submitted to British authority and henceforth encouraged trade relations. On his death, he was succeeded by his son Wannalancet, who was followed by KANCAMAGUS.

PATTIE, JAMES OHIO. *(ca. 1804–ca. 1851).* Trader; trapper; explorer.

James Ohio Pattie, born in Kentucky, was taken by his father, Sylvester Pattie, to the Missouri frontier in 1812. In the early 1820s, he joined his father in trading with the Missouri River trappers and Indians. Eventually they both traveled West to Taos and Santa Fe.

In 1826, Sylvester Pattie became the manager of a copper mine. Meanwhile, the younger Pattie joined a trapping party and ventured into the Southern Rockies. The group was ambushed by Papago Indians near present-day Phoenix; only Pattie and two other whites survived. They later joined up with fur trapper Ewing Young and his party. Their exact route is uncertain, but Young and Pattie may have traveled into the Gila and Colorado river valleys, then headed north as far as the Bighorn and Yellowstone regions of present-day Montana and Wyoming. Along the way, they are thought to have had contact with the Havasupai Indians of the Grand Canyon. Pattie and Young returned to Santa Fe in 1827.

The following year, Pattie, accompanied by his father, undertook a trapping expedition down the Colorado River to its outlet in the Gulf of California. They completed an overland trek across Baja California and reached the Pacific Coast, when they were arrested by the Spanish and imprisoned in San Diego. The elder Pattie died in Spanish custody, but James Ohio Pattie was released in 1830, and returned to U.S. territory.

In Cincinnati, in 1831, aided by journalist Timothy Flint, Pattie published a firsthand account of his explorations in the American West, entitled *The Personal Narrative of James O. Pattie of Kentucky, During an Expedition From St. Louis, Through the Vast Regions Between That Place and the Pacific Ocean.* His account includes descriptions of the great herds of buffalo and wild horses that then played a vital role in the life of the Plains tribes.

Pattie went West again to join the California Gold Rush of 1849. He may have perished in the Sierra Nevadas of California during winter 1850–51.

PAULINA (Pauline, Paunina). *Northern Paiute.* *(d. 1867).* Leader of the Snake War of 1866–68.

Paulina was a chief of the Walpapi band, who were known, along with the Yahuskin band, as the Snake Indians because of their location near the Snake River in present-day northern Nevada, southeastern Oregon, and southwestern Idaho. They also gave their name to the Snake War, sometimes referred to as the Paiute War (but not to be confused with the Paiute or Pyramid Lake War of 1860 in Nevada under NUMAGA).

During the Civil War, with most federal troops drawn from the region, the Indians of the Great Basin, including Paulina's Northern Paiute band, had a relatively free hand in raids on miners and mining camps, stagecoaches and stage stations, ranches and farms, and freight caravans. The Paiutes were active from the Cascade Mountains east to the Snake Valley and from the John Day River south to the Humboldt. Oregon and Nevada volunteers proved unequal to the task of controlling them.

In 1865, former Civil War regulars were assigned to Fort Boise, Idaho, and other posts in the area. But Paulina's warriors managed to regularly outmaneuver these troops as well. The tide turned, however, when Colonel (soon-to-be general) GEORGE CROOK took command of operations in 1866. He began a relentless series of small tracking patrols that kept the insurgents on the run, forcing them into about 40 skirmishes in the course of the war. It is estimated that about 330 Paiutes were killed and 225 taken prisoner.

On the death of Paulina in January 1867, WEAWEA assumed command of the militants. He held out for another year and a half until June 1868, when he surrendered with 800 remaining followers.

PAWHUSKA. See WHITE HAIR.

PAWNEE KILLER. *Oglala Sioux. (fl. 1860s).* War chief of the Southern Oglalas participating in the wars for the Southern Plains.

Pawnee Killer received his name from exploits against the Pawnees, traditional enemies of the Sioux. Like Little Wound, head chief of his Oglala band, plus Little Thunder of the Southern Brules, he was one of the Sioux who drifted southward to the territory between the Platte and Arkansas rivers (in present-day Nebraska, Kansas, and Colorado) starting in the late 1850s, where they became involved in the wars of the Southern Cheyennes and Southern Arapahos. In 1867, along with the Cheyenne TALL BULL and other Dog Soldiers, Pawnee Killer fought against troops of the HANCOCK Campaign, outmaneuvering Colonel GEORGE ARMSTRONG CUSTER. In 1868, during the SHERIDAN Campaign, Pawnee Killer was present at the Battle of BEECHER's Island, where the Cheyenne ROMAN NOSE was killed. His band eventually settled at the RED CLOUD Agency in Nebraska; what happened to Pawnee Killer is unknown.

PAXINOS (Paxinosa, Paxsinos, Paxihos, Paxnos, Paxnous, Paxowan). *Shawnee-Delaware. (d. ca. 1758).* "King" of the Pennsylvania Shawnees.

During the late 1600s, Paxinos was a sachem of the Minisink band of Munsees, a divison of the Delawares in what is now northern New Jersey. Some of the Minisinks merged with the Pennsylvania Shawnees, among whom Paximos became the most powerful leader of the early to mid-1700s, referred to by the colonists as "king." Like TEEDYUSCUNG, the "king" of the Delawares of the same period, Paxinos played the dominant political forces of his time—the British, French, and Iroquois League—off against one another. He was a friend of the Moravian missionaries, who converted his wife with his permission. Along with other chiefs, Paxinos met with Indian superintendent WILLIAM JOHNSON at Fort Johnson, New York, in 1757, and attended a subsequent council the same year at Easton, Pennsylvania. In the mid-1750s, he moved to Ohio with his family, where most of the Shawnees sided with the French against the British in the French and Indian War of 1754–63. Soon after this move, Paxinos died.

PAXSON, EDGAR SAMUEL. *(1852–1919).* Artist; scout; soldier.

Originally from the Buffalo area of New York, E. S. Paxson journeyed West in the 1870s. At various times, while pursuing his career as a painter, he was a soldier, scout, driver for the Overland Stage Company, and telegraph-line rider. In most of his work, he depicted scenes of the Montana frontier, where he arrived in 1877. His most famous painting was his 1899 rendering in oils of the Indian victory over Colonel GEORGE ARMSTRONG CUSTER at the Battle of Little Bighorn in 1876, *Custer's Last Stand.* Paxson also painted murals of Western life that became part of the permanent interior design of the Montana state capitol building in Helena and the Missoula County courthouse.

PAYEPOT. See PIAPOT.

PAYNE (King Payne). *Seminole. (d. 1812).* Principal chief of the Seminoles in the early 1800s. Brother of BOLEK.

Many of the Creeks and Seminoles of northern Florida carried out raids on Georgia settlements at the encouragement of the Spanish. Because of the border unrest, a force of Georgia militia under colonel Daniel Newnan advanced 100 miles into Spanish territory and engaged the Indians in September and October 1812. In one of these engagements, the principal chief of the Seminoles, known to the whites as King Payne, was killed; his brother Bolek was wounded. Newnan's troops were forced to retreat, however. In February 1813, Colonel John Williams led Tennessee militiamen plus some U.S. regulars into Florida and burned hundreds of Indian houses and crops and captured horses and cattle. The repeated border incidents helped bring about the Creek War of 1813–14 and the First Seminole War of 1817–18.

PENN, WILLIAM. *(1644–1718).* Quaker leader; founder of Pennsylvania.

William Penn, son of the British admiral of the same name, was born in London. He attended Oxford, where he studied law, but was expelled for his religious views. He spent time abroad, then managed his family's estates in Ireland, where he joined the Society of Friends. Engaging in political campaigns and writing numerous books and pamphlets, he was imprisoned on several occasions for nonconformity.

Penn first became involved in North American affairs in 1675, when he helped frame the charter for West Jersey; he also, with 11 others, purchased East Jersey in 1681 (West and East Jersey colonies comprising what is now New Jersey). On inheriting from his father a financial claim against Charles II, he petitioned for a grant of land as payment.

In 1682, one year after the charter from King Charles granting him proprietary rights over most of what is now the present state of Pennsylvania, Penn negotiated a treaty with TAMMANY and other Delaware chiefs at Shakamaxon, now part of Philadelphia. At this time, he also communicated with the leaders of the Iroquois League to the north, informing them of his intentions to create a colony based on the principles of peace and harmony.

Penn did not return to the Pennsylvania colony again until 1699 when, with his secretary JAMES LOGAN, he renewed the treaties with the Delawares. Penn was a religious reformer who sought to create in the colony a haven for those persecuted because of their religious beliefs.

Like many religious writers of his day, Penn thought the Indians were descendants of the Ten Lost Tribes of Israel. His policy toward the Indians was characterized by a recognition of Indian land ownership that superceded colonial land claims based on the royal charter. Under Penn's proprietorship, the acquisition of Indian lands was accomplished through governmentally regulated purchase agreements. For the duration of Penn and Quaker domination of Pennsylvania, conflicts with the Indians were at a minimum.

PEOPEOMOXMOX (Peopeo Moxmox, Peo-peo-mox-mox, Peo-peo-mux-mux, Peu-peu-mox-mox, Piu-Piu Mox-Mox, Yellow Bird, Yellow Serpent). *Wallawalla. (d. 1855).* Victim in the Yakima War of 1855–56.

Peopeomoxmox's village, shared by Wallawalla and Palouse Indians, was at the mouth of the Tucannon River in Washington. At the Walla Walla Council of 1855, convened by the governor of the Washington Territory, ISAAC STEVENS, Peopeomoxmox expressed opposition to land sales to whites. Yet he restrained his warriors from joining the uprising that broke out in the Washington Territory that same year, known as the Yakima War. In December 1855, Oregon volunteers under the command of Colonel James Kelly advanced along the Walla Walla Valley in present-day southeastern Washington. After a running skirmish of several days with Wallawallas, Umatillas, and Cayuses, Peopeomoxmox and five of his men came in under a flag of truce for a parley. Their murder and mutilation—the volunteers put the chief's scalp and ears on display—led to greater militancy among the region's tribes. (See also KAMIAKIN.)

PERROT, NICOLAS (Metaminens, "man with iron legs"). *(ca. 1644–1718).* Explorer; trader; interpreter; French colonial official.

Born in France, Nicolas Perrot migrated to French Canada while still young. He worked with Jesuit missionaries around the Quebec settlement and through them acquired a knowledge of several Indian languages.

In 1667, in the service of the French colonial government, Perrot traveled west across the Great Lakes to Green Bay to entreat the tribes west of Lake Michigan to break their exclusive trade agreements with the Ottawas and trade directly with the French. During this expedition, Perrot introduced the first metal trade

goods to the Potawatomis. On this trip, he may also have sighted the Mississippi River. He returned to Montreal with a load of furs.

In 1670–71, Perrot was sent by LOUIS DE BUADE, COMTE DE FRONTENAC to prepare the Indians for the official assumption of French control over the western Great Lakes and beyond. A formal ceremony was held at Sault Ste. Marie.

During the 1680s, along with DANIEL GREYSOLON, SIEUR DULUTH, Perrot established ties with the Miamis and secured the allegiance of that tribe and other Algonquians of the Great Lakes region in France's war with the Iroquois.

In 1684–85, Perrot established French outposts at Prairie du Chien and Lake Pepin, from where he extended the fur trade west of the Mississippi to the Sioux. In 1689, at Fort Antoine on Wisconsin's Lake Pepin, he officiated at the ceremony that formally declared French sovereignty over the Mississippi River Valley. Probably the next year, he discovered lead deposits in what is now southwestern Wisconsin.

In 1696, at the time of a French revocation of all fur-trading licenses, Perrot left the fur trade to return to Quebec where he served as an Indian interpreter.

PERRYMAN, TOM. See KINACHE.

PESHEWAH (The Lynx; John B. Richardville). *Mixed Miami. (ca. 1761–1841).* Principal chief; friend to whites.

Peshewah was born on St. Marys River near present-day Fort Wayne, Indiana; his father was part-French. On the death of LITTLE TURTLE in 1812, Peshewah became head chief of the Miamis. He avoided the Old Northwest conflicts of the period, such as TECUMSEH's Rebellion of 1809–11 and the War of 1812. Fluent in English and French, he offered hospitality to guests at his home along the St. Marys River. At the time of his death, Peshewah was referred to as the richest Indian in North America, with lands worth an estimated $1 million.

PETALESHARO (Pitalesharu, Pitaresharu, Patalacharo, "chief of men," "man chief"). *Pawnee. (ca. 1787–ca. 1832).* Principal chief who abolished Morning Star Ceremony.

Petalesharo was the son of Lachelesharo (Old Knife), principal chief of the Skidi Pawnees. A proven warrior among his people, he took a stand at the age of 30 in opposition to the Morning Star Ceremony.

In Skidi religion, the Sun and Mother Earth conceived the Morning Star, the God of Vegetation. Once a year, the Skidis would raid another tribe for a young girl of about 13. They would keep this girl among them for months, treating her well. At the summer solstice, early in the morning, the Skidi priests would paint half the girl's body in red, for day, and half in black, for night. Then they would tie her to a rectangular frame in a field outside the village. As the morning star rose, three priests would sacrifice her with a torch, arrow, and knife. Then every male old enough to handle a bow would shoot arrows into her body.

In 1816 or 1817, Petalesharo rescued a Comanche girl from the scaffold, stating that his father wanted to abolish the Morning Star ritual and offering himself in her place. When his fellow Pawnees hesitated, Petalesharo untied her, placed her on a horse, and led her to safety. He won the respect of his people for confronting the powerful class of priests, and, on succeeding his father, he proved influential among many of the Pawnee bands.

In 1821–22, Petalesharo headed a delegation of 16 Indians, mostly Pawnees, to Washington, D.C. On New Year's Day, 1822, he led a war dance in front of the White House with an audience of some 6,000. His portrait by CHARLES BIRD KING was one of the first commissioned by THOMAS McKENNEY for the Indian Portrait Gallery.

In 1825, Petalesharo and his father signed the Pawnee Treaty, in which they agreed to cease all raids along the Santa Fe Trail. It is through that Petalesharo died in the early 1830s, possibly in the smallpox epidemic that ravaged his tribe. A Pe-tah-lay-shah-ro, possibly a different chief, signed the Treaty of Grand Pawnee Village on the Platte River in present-day Nebraska in 1833. A Petanesharo signed the Treaty of Table Creek, Nebraska, in 1857.

PETA NOCONA (Nocone, Nokoni, "one who camps along" or "wanderer"). *Comanche.* (*ca. 1812–ca. 1862*). Leader of raiding parties. Father of QUANAH PARKER.

Peta Nocona was the leader of a band of Nocona Comanches, or Noconies, feared by Texans and Mexicans for their wide-ranging raids. In May 1836, he led an assault on Parker's Fort, a stockaded group of homesteads founded by the Parker family near present-day Mexia, Texas. The nine-year-old Cynthia Ann Parker was one of five women and children kidnapped. She was later adopted into the tribe and became the only wife of Peta Nocona, although the Comanches were polygamous.

About 1845, Cynthia gave birth to Quanah Parker, who was to become the most famous of all the Comanche leaders. In December 1860, while Nocona and his warriors were on a buffalo hunt, Texas Rangers under Captain Sul Ross attacked his camp and recaptured his wife. She later tried to return to Nocona but was prevented by her parents. She died four years later, a prisoner in her white home, of a broken heart, it is said.

Nocona, who never saw her again, died about 1862 from an infected wound received in a skirmish with whites.

PHILIP (King Philip; Metacom, Metacomet, Pometacom, Pometacomet, "the faraway place" or "the chief's house"; Philip of Pokanoket; Wagwises, "the circling fox"). *Wampanoag. (ca. 1639–1676).* Leader of King Philip's War of 1675–76. Son of MASSASOIT; brother of ALEXANDER.

Philip's tribal name was Metacomet. He and his older brother Wamsutta requested English names from the colonial court of the Plymouth settlement, and received the classical names of Philip and Alexander. During Philip's revolt, he was called "King" Philip by the colonists.

Massasoit, father of Philip and Alexander and grand sachem of the Wampanoag Confederacy, encouraged peaceful relations with the Pilgrims and subsequent settlers. Nevertheless, over the years, there was a growing militancy among New England Indians. A major contention was that when Indians committed crimes under English law, such as trespassing on lands formerly their own, they were taken before a colonial court to be tried rather than before their own people. Soon after Massasoit's death in late 1661, Alexander, now grand sachem, was arrested. He became sick, however, and soon died. His widow, WETAMOO, of the Pocassets, a

King Philip. A hypothetical rendition; detail from Phelps and Ensign's *Travellers' Guide and Map of the United States*, 1844. *Courtesy of Steve Child.*

Wampanoag tribute tribe, believed that the colonial officials had poisoned him. So probably did Philip, now grand sachem in 1662, in his early 20s.

Philip's main village was located at Mount Hope on the west shore of Mount Hope Bay near present-day Bristol, Rhode Island. His people maintained an appearance of friendship with the colonists for several years. Philip even sold large tracts of land he had inherited from his father and brother to the colonists into the 1670s. Yet, during this period, he was planning a rebellion among area tribes, sending runners to neighboring sachems to ask their help. He held regular councils at Council Oak in present-day Dighton, Massachusetts to win support. Philip's goal was to organize an alliance of tribes that would be strong enough to oust the British settlers from New England. CANONCHET's Narragansets, traditionally suspicious of the colonists' intentions and still bitter over the execution of MIANTINOMO some 30 years before, were receptive, as were certain Nipmuc bands.

On hearing rumors of an uprising, colonial officials called Philip before the court and ordered the confiscation of Wampanoag flintlocks. Philip yielded to their demands in order to buy more time, signing two treaties, and turning in some but not all of the Wampanoag guns.

Fighting came prematurely. In January 1675, the body of a Christian Indian of the Massachuset tribe—John Sassamon, a former aide to Philip, who had betrayed his plan to the English—was found beneath the ice at Assawompsett Pond near present-day Lakeville, Massachusetts. The colonists arrested three Wampanoags, and tried and executed them. In the trial it was concluded that Philip had ordered Sassamon's death. With the increased state of tension, fighting broke out at the settlement of Swansea near Mount Hope. On June 23, a settler fired at and wounded a brave in an argument over cattle. The Wampanoags retaliated, killing 11 colonists.

After the first hostilities of King Philip's War, the Indians began a coordinated campaign of violence against the settlers. Small bands of warriors attacked outlying settlements throughout New England from the Connecticut River to the Atlantic Coast—52 of the 92 English settlements were attacked, and 12 were completely destroyed, including Deerfield, Massachusetts, on September 18, 1675. Over 1,000 settlers lost their lives in the many raids. ANNAWAN, who had served under Massasoit as the leading war chief, also acted as Philip's military strategist.

The New England Confederation of Colonies, including Massachsuetts Bay, Plymouth, Rhode Island, and Connecticut, mustered armies. Their Indian allies—Massachusets, Mohegans, Niantics, and theWampanoag tribute tribes, Nausets and Saconnets—provided auxiliaries. AWASHONKS of the Saconnets at first backed Philip, then, because of her friendship with Captain BENJAMIN CHURCH, gave her support to the colonists.

The colonial troops attacked Indian villages, burning wigwams and destroying crops, and managed to engage the Indians in several major battles. The first occurred on July 19, 1675, at Pocasset Swamp, Wampanoag territory in Plymouth. Philip escaped from Plymouth and Massachusetts troops under Church by rafting down the Taunton River to Nipmuc country. Wetamoo, who also escaped, sought refuge among the Narragansets. Canonchet refused to turn her over that summer to the English, who then sent a punitive expedition against his people, causing undecided Narragansets to join the Wampanoags in revolt.

The next important engagements occurred among Nipmucs along the northern Connecticut River Valley in Nipmuc country—at Hopewell Swamp in August and Bloody Brook in September 1675. That December, Philip traveled to Mohawk territory, setting up base near Albany, in the hope of enlisting Iroquois help. As trading partners with the English, the Mohawks wanted no part of his war and drove the Wampanoags away.

On December 19, 1675, the culminating battle took place in Narraganset territory in southern Rhode Island: the Great Swamp Fight. On a snowy day, a force of about 1,000 New England colonists under Governor JOSIAH WINSLOW of Plymouth Colony, plus a force of about 150 Mohegans, attacked Canonchet's main village near Kingston, Rhode Island. At first, the colonial army was unable to breach the village's thick palisades on the high ground in the middle of a swamp. But the attackers eventually broke through a rear entrance and, setting most of the 600 wigwams on fire, drove the Narragnasts out into the swamp where they were slaughtered—as many as 600, with 400 or more captured and sold into slavery.

Canonchet escaped, however, and, in March 1676, he defeated a detachment of soldiers along the Patucket River. Another colonial force captured him in the same area in April. When Canonchet refused to cooperated in establishing peace, he was sentenced to death, shot and beheaded at Stonington, Connecticut. His head was sent as a trophy to officials in Hartford.

After these colonial victories, troops began tracking down dissident bands. At Peskeompscut on the northern Connecticut River (near Deerfield, Massachusetts), in May 1676, a colonial outfit routed the Indians. In July, Church's men captured Philip's wife Wootonekanuske and his young son. That summer, a Wampanoag informer by the name of Alderman, whose brother had been killed by Philip when he had suggested surrendering, deserted and gave away Philip's location at Bridgewater Swamp to the English. Church led 18 soldiers and 22 warriors to the hiding place and surrounded the camp. At dawn on August 12, 1676, the small force attacked and routed the Indians. It was one of Alderman's bullets that struck down King Philip. His killers cut up his body and kept the parts as trophies.

Annawan now assumed command of the Wampanoags and led attacks on the settlements of Swansea and Plymouth. By changing camp nightly, he successfully eluded men under Church. Through an informer, Church finally tracked down Annawan on August 26, 1676, at a swamp along the Rehoboth River. The soldiers were able to divert the Indians long enough to seize most of their arms and trick them into believing they were up against a much larger force. Annawan, believing the situation hopeless, had his men surrender, whereupon he turned over the tribe's bundle of deerskin, containing wampum belts—a large one telling of the tribe's history and a smaller one symbolizing the Wampanoag Confederacy—plus two powder horns and a red blanket formerly belonging to Philip.

The war had officially ended. Meanwhile, other leaders had been killed, including the Wampanoag Wetamoo, her Narraganset husband QUINNAPIN, and the Narraganset MAGNUS. Survivors were taken to Plymouth for a trial, in which Annawan was condemned to death. Church had come to respect the Wampanoag war chief and argued for his life. But while Church was away, Annawan was seized by a mob and beheaded. He was the last leader of the political alliance known as the Wampanoag Confederacy.

In the aftermath, Philip's wife and son were shipped to the Caribbean to be sold as slaves for 30 shillings apiece. Hundreds of other Indians were also sold into slavery, some as far away as Spain. The colonists took their revenge on peaceful tribes as well, such as the Massachusets, using the opportunity to grab more Indian territory. Philip's head was displayed at Plymouth for 24 years.

The colonists themselves continued to pay the price of war in the years to come since many of their crops had been destroyed, leading to food shortages throughout New England.

PHILIP, JAMES (Scotty Philip). *(1837–1911)*. Army scout; rancher.

James "Scotty" Philip, originally from Scotland, came to the United States in 1853, and soon settled in Colorado, where he operated an overland freight service. In 1876, he traveled to South Dakota as part of the Black Hills Gold Rush. Two years later, he began working for the army as a scout, and in that capacity befriended many Cheyennes and Sioux.

In 1879, Philip married a Cheyenne woman and began ranching near the Pine Ridge Agency in South Dakota. His friendship with the Indians helped him acquire access to the grazing lands of the Lower Brule Reservation. He eventually became one of the West's most successful cattlemen, with a 16,000-acre ranch—the 73 Ranch—near Fort Pierre, South Dakota.

By the end of the 19th century, the American bison was nearing extinction, and Philip took measures to preserve these animals, which had played so vital a role in Plains Indian culture. From a few wild calves, he developed a herd of over 1,000 buffalo, the descendants of which have been placed in zoos.

PHILLIPS, WENDELL. *(1811–1884)*. Reformer; lecturer; writer.

Wendell Phillips, a native of Boston and a Harvard-educated Boston lawyer, was a major force in the antislavery cause. An effective orator, he also lobbied for the rights of women. It was Phillips's contention that racial injustice was the source of all society's ills.

Following the Civil War and the aboliton of slavery, Phillips incorporated the rights of freed blacks and Indians into his crusade for racial equality and universal justice. He proposed that the post–Civil War Andrew Johnson administration create a Cabinet-level post to guarantee Indian rights. In 1869, he unsuccessfully called for the adoption of an amendment to the Constitution that would extend citizenship to all Indians. In his later lectures and in his writings, which appeared in newspapers and periodicals, he argued that the 15th Amendment to the Constitution, ratified in 1870, had granted citizenship not only to those who had been slaves, but to the Indians as well.

Phillips compared the failed federal Indian policy, marked by decades of warfare and uneasy truces, with the successful policy of the British toward the Indians of Canada. At one time, he proposed that the United States abandon the newly completed transcontinental railroad because of its blatant encroachment on Indian lands in the Southwest. In the aftermath of the 1870 Piegan Massacre, in which U.S. troops slaughtered over 170 Blackfoot Indians in Montana, Phillips helped create the Massachusetts Indian Commission with Indian rights activist HELEN HUNT JACKSON and Massachusetts governor William Claflin.

Phillips was not an early supporter of the Peace Policy initiated in 1869 by President ULYSSES S. GRANT. During Grant's first term in office, Phillips, an active temperance advocate, demanded that Grant be investigated for alleged chronic drunkenness while in office. Yet he supported the reelection of Grant in 1872, and later became an influential figure in the presidential appointment of Indian agents.

Throughout the 1870s, Phillips lobbied against military involvement in settling the frontier's Indian problem. He was a critic of General PHILIP H. SHERIDAN, whom he accused of pursuing a policy of extermination of the Indians. He continued to support the claims of the Sioux even after the 1876 Battle of Little Bighorn had caused public opinion to turn against the Indians, deriding those who called the Little Bighorn battle, "the Custer massacre," rather than a battle.

In 1874, Phillips was instrumental in bringing Indian reformer ALFRED MEACHAM and Indians involved in the Modoc War of 1872–73 to Boston to address the public on the injustices of the government's unfair removal policy. In 1879, at the height of the controversy surrounding the forced removal of Poncas to the Indian Territory, Phillips sponsored a trip to Boston for the Ponca chief STANDING BEAR and the Omaha SUSETTE LA FLESCHE.

Piapot. *Courtesy of National Archives of Canada/C-8559.*

PIAPOT (Payepot, "one who knows the secrets of the Sioux"). *Cree. (1816–1908).* War chief; medicine man; leader of resistance against railroad.

Piapot's parents died from smallpox, and he was raised by his grandmother, with whom he was captured by Sioux Indians. He lived among the Sioux for 14 years until a Plains Cree war party freed him. Because of his knowledge of Sioux lifeways and territory, he became a leading Cree war chief in raids on the other tribe.

In 1870, Piapot and his 700 warriors suffered a major defeat at the hands of the Blackfeet. In 1875, he reluctantly signed the Canadian Treaty No. 5, ceding lands in the Qu'appelle Valley of Manitoba, then moved his band west to what is now Saskatchewan.

In 1882, as an act of defiance, Piapot's warriors pulled up survey stakes along a 30-mile stretch of the Canadian Pacific Railway west of Moose Jaw. The next year, at Maple Creek, Piapot had his band erect their tepees in the path of track-laying crews. The Mounties knocked down their tepees and drove the Indians away in a bloodless show of force. Piapot and his band eventually settled near Regina.

Despite his resentment of white settlement in Cree territory, Piapot kept his warriors out of the Second RIEL Rebellion of 1885 unlike the band leaders BIG BEAR and POUNDMAKER. White officials deposed Piapot when his people held a Sun Dance, forbidden under Canadian Law. His band continued to honor his authority, however. In 1901, Manitoba officials sponosored a homage to him.

PIERCE, MARIS BRYANT (Ha-dya-no-doh, "swift runner"). *Seneca. (1811–1874).* Leader of struggle against Seneca removal.

Maris Bryant Pierce was born on the Allegany Reservation in western New York, and was raised on the Buffalo Creek Reservation. He attended various white-run schools and was converted to Christianity in Rochester, New York. At 25, he entered Dartmouth College, under the auspices of the Presbyterian church.

During his college career, Pierce became involved with opposition to the Treaty of Buffalo Creek of 1838. This treaty, which some among the tribe were cajoled into signing, called for the sale of remaining Seneca lands to the Ogden Land Company and the tribe's relocation to Kansas. Pierce made numerous speeches on behalf of his tribe before church and civil groups. He also helped the tribe draft a letter to President Martin Van Buren and hire legal counsel in Washington, D.C. Largely because of his efforts, the treaty was renegotiated in 1842. Some Seneca lands were lost, including the Buffalo Creek Reservation; Pierce and his wife Mary Jane Carroll were forced to move in 1845. But the tribe retained much of the Allegany, Cattaraugus, and Tonawanda reservations.

In later years, Pierce acted as interpreter and secretary for the Seneca Nation and helped bring an elective system of government to the tribe in 1848.

PIKE, ALBERT. *(1809–1891).* Confederate Indian commissioner; Confederate officer; writer.

Massachusetts-born Albert Pike traveled along the Santa Fe Trail in 1831–32, recording his experiences in his book *Prose Sketches and Poems Written in the Western*

Country (1834). In 1832, Pike settled in Little Rock, Arkansas where he edited the *Arkansas Advocate.* He also taught school and practiced law.

Pike became a friend of the Cherokees, taking vacations from his law practice to hunt with his Indian friends. He studied their language and published several books on Indian vocabularies. He also represented the interests of the Five Civilized Tribes of the Indian Territory in several legal actions against the federal government.

During the Mexican-American War of 1846–48, Pike served as a captain in an Arkansas cavalry regiment. In the 1850s, he was an advocate of the South's own railroad to the Pacific. He became a supporter of secession and created some of the lyrics to the Confederacy's national anthem, "Dixie."

In 1861, Pike was appointed chief Confederate representative to the Five Civilized Tribes. He was able to negotiate treaties under which the Indians agreed to terminate their connections with the Union and raise Indian regiments to support Southern forces. The Confederacy, in return, agreed to protect Indian land claims and assume responsibility for annuity payments under earlier treaties, as well as provide military defense against the Union army. Pike was able to gain the support of many Indian Territory bands, including the majority of Cherokees under STAND WATIE. Yet most of the Creeks under OPOTHLEYAHOLO headed north to Kansas, where they joined Union forces.

In 1861, at a grand council with Comanche leaders at Fort Cobb, Pike entered into a treaty that linked the Southern Plains tribes with the Confederacy. Kiowas and Caddos also agreed to concentrate their raids on the Kansas-Missouri border region and not attack Confederate Texas.

Pike was appointed a brigadier general in command of Confederate-allied Indian troops in the Indian Territory. When Confederate forces suffered defeat at the Battle of Pea Ridge of March 1862 in northwest Arkansas, he resigned from the military amid criticism of his ineffective command of the Indian troops.

Pike returned to civilian life and, after the war, worked as a journalist in Memphis, Tennessee, and practiced law in Washington, D.C. He was a prominent Freemason and wrote several studies about the fraternal order. (See also WATIE, STAND.)

PIKE, ZEBULON MONTGOMERY. *(1779–1813).*
Explorer; army officer.

Zebulon Pike was born in Lamberton, New Jersey, now part of present-day Trenton. About 1793, he enlisted in the army and served with his father of the same name—a company leader under General "Mad" ANTHONY WAYNE—in the campaigns against the Indians of the Old Northwest in LITTLE TURTLE's War

of 1790–94. After the war, the younger Pike was assigned to frontier posts in present-day Ohio, Kentucky, and Illinois. By 1799, he was commissioned a second lieutenant.

In 1805, Pike was ordered by his commanding officer, General James Wilkinson, to undertake an exploration to the headwaters of the Mississippi River. Leading a company of 20 soldiers, he left St. Louis by keelboat in August of that year and headed north up the Mississippi. In addition to locating the source of the Mississippi, he was to survey the entire region and report back to Wilkinson information about mineral and fur resources. He was also ordered to contact tribal leaders and negotiate for the purchase of Indian lands for later use as sites for army posts, and was authorized to invite the chiefs of the upper Mississippi tribes to meet with Wilkinson in St. Louis. At present-day Keokuk, Iowa, he negotiated a treaty with leaders of the Sac tribe. Near the mouth of the Minnesota River, he met with Sioux leaders and negotiated one of the earliest peace treaties between that tribe and the federal government, purchasing lands now including the cities of St. Paul and Minneapolis, although the Senate voted against its ratification. Pike's expedition reached the northern Minnesota lakes in the winter. He then traveled over the frozen upper Mississippi as far north as Leech Lake (Cass Lake), erroneously concluding that this was the source of the Mississippi. (The real source was subsequently revealed to be Lake Itasca, to the south and west.) Pike led his expedition down the Mississippi, returning to St. Louis in April 1806.

Less than four months later, Pike again left St. Louis, leading a second expedition, with orders to explore the southwestern regions of the Louisiana Territory, establish peaceful relations with the Comanches, and evaluate the Spanish military presence in New Mexico. He left St. Louis in July 1806 with an expedition including 51 freed Osage captives, whom Pike was to escort to their homelands in western Missouri. From the Osage lands, he headed into present-day Kansas and Nebraska, where he initiated friendly relations with the Pawnees at their village near present-day Red Cloud, Nebraska. The Pike expedition then continued along the Arkansas River into eastern Colorado and beyond the foothills of the Rockies. In November 1806, they sighted the mountain on the edge of the Great Plains that came to be known as Pikes Peak, but were unsuccessful in an attempt to climb it.

After having established an outpost at Pueblo, Colorado, Pike headed southwest to explore the Red River. He mistook the Rio Grande for that river and wandered into Spanish territory in northern New Mexico, where he and his party were arrested. Spanish officials suspected he was on an intelligence-gathering mission into New Mexico, and detained him, first at

Santa Fe, then at Chihuahua, Mexico. The Americans were released at the U.S. border with Spanish Texas, at Natchitoches, Louisiana, in June 1807.

Although later implicated along with Wilkinson in the Aaron Burr conspiracy, Pike was exonerated of any wrongdoing in connection with his Southwest expedition. He remained in the army and went on to fight in the War of 1812 as a brigadier general. During the U.S. attack on York (present-day Toronto, Canada), he was killed in the explosion of a British powder magazine.

Pike's reports of the 1806–07 expedition described the Southern Plains as unsuitable for agriculture. Along with the subsequent reports of STEPHEN H. LONG, Pike's descriptions gave rise to the idea of the Great American Desert, which halted extensive white settlement into the lands of the Plains tribes until after JOHN C. FREMONT's later explorations. Yet his reports of Spanish settlements in the Southwest did spur traders to open up new markets in the Southwest. Spanish authorities discouraged such attempts, but, with Mexican independence from Spain in 1821, the Santa Fe Trail, part of which Pike explored, became an important avenue of trade.

PILCHER, JOSHUA. (1790–1843). Trader; trapper; Indian superintendent.

Born in Culpepper County, Virginia, Joshua Pilcher grew up in Kentucky and became a frontier merchant in Tennessee. In 1815, he moved to St. Louis, Missouri, where he soon entered the fur trade.

About 1819, Pilcher became a partner with MANUEL LISA in the Missouri Fur Company (originally the St. Louis Missouri Fur Company) operating along the upper Missouri River. About 1823, one of his fur-trading expeditions into the Dakota country was attacked and annihilated by an Arikara war party. Pilcher then journeyed upriver, accompanying Colonel HENRY LEAVENWORTH's punitive expedition against the Arikaras, as a federal Indian subagent and with his own detachment of trappers and Sioux warriors. Although Leavenworth sought a peaceful solution, Pilcher had his men attack and burn the Arikara villages on the Missouri, near the present-day North Dakota–South Dakota border. The Arikaras then fled to the Mandan villages on the upper Missouri, in the vicinity of present-day Bismarck, North Dakota.

That year, 1823, another of Pilcher's trapping expeditions was wiped out by Blackfeet near the headwaters of the Missouri River in western Montana. Because of Indian attacks and competition from other traders, such as JOHN JACOB ASTOR, the Missouri Fur Company went out of business in 1825. Three years later, Pilcher began exploring the fur country of the Northern Rockies. By 1830, he had extended his trapping operation across the Northern Plains and through the South Pass

of the Wyoming's Wind River Range. He eventually reached the Hudson's Bay Company post on the Columbia River, opposite present-day Portland, Oregon, then returned to St. Louis.

During 1833, in the employ of the American Fur Company, Pilcher accompanied the naturalist ALEXANDER PHILIPP MAXIMILIAN ZU WIED and artist KARL BODMER on their tour up the Missouri.

In 1834, Pilcher was appointed Indian agent for the upper Missouri tribes. In 1837, he became agent to the Sioux, Cheyennes, and Poncas. He succeeded WILLIAM CLARK as superintendent of Indian Affairs for the Missouri region, serving out of St. Louis in 1839–41, with subagencies at Fort Leavenworth, Council Bluffs, the upper Missouri, and the Osage River.

PIOMINGO (Mountain Leader). *Chickasaw.* *(fl. late 1700s).* Ally of Americans during the post–Revolutionary period.

The Chickasaws of present-day northern Mississippi and western Tennessee, former allies of the British, generally sided with the Americans in the struggle for control of the region between Spain and the United States in the late 1700s. The Creeks under ALEXANDER McGILLIVRAY attempted to force the Chickasaws into joining a Spanish-Indian alliance, but the Chickasaws under Piomingo rejected their proposals and repelled their war parties. During the 1790s, at Piomingo's request, Tennessee officials provided the Chickasaws with abundant arms and ammunition. Chickasaw towns along the Mississippi subsequently served as bases for American agents.

PITCHLYNN, PETER PERKINS (Ha-tchoo-tuc-knee, "the snapping turtle"). *Mixed Choctaw. (1806–1881).* Principal chief; spokesman.

Peter Pitchlynn was born at the tribal village of Hushookwa, Mississippi, the son of John Pitchlynn, a white interpreter for PUSHMATAHA and the federal government, and Sophia Folsom, of the influential Folsom family of Choctaws, among them DAVID FOLSOM. While a boy, on observing a tribal member write a letter, Pitchlynn resolved to seek a white as well as an Indian education and traveled 200 miles to a white-run school for one season. When he first returned home, he was upset to witness his people negotiating a treaty with the government and refused to shake the hand of General ANDREW JACKSON. He soon entered an academy at Columbia, Tennessee, then Nashville University, from where he graduated.

Pitchlynn started a farm and married the mixed-blood Rhoda Folsom. He became involved in tribal politics and was elected to the Choctaw Council. Along with David Folsom, Pitchlynn supported the founding of five English-language schools. He also worked for the end of the practice of polygamy among his people and the enforcement of a ban on liquor. In 1828, he was appointed part of a delegation to inspect lands in the Indian Territory and to make peace with the Osages in preparation for his people's relocation. He spoke out against removal, but helped negotiate what he considered the best possible deal for his people, signing the Treaty of Dancing Rabbit Creek in September 1830.

After the removal of the Choctaws, the first of the Five Civilized Tribes to be relocated, from 1831 to 1834, Pitchlynn, who built a new farm on the Arkansas River, played a major part in reorganizing his tribe and establishing Choctaw schools. He frequently traveled to Washington, D.C., and spoke before the president and Congressional committees. He was elected principal chief in 1860.

During the Civil War, Pitchlynn remained neutral although three of his sons fought with the Confederates. After the war, he spent most of his time in Washington, D.C., where he unsuccessfully lobbied for compensation of his people's land claims. His first wife died, and he married Caroline Lombardy of Washington, D.C., in 1869. He joined the Masonic Order and the Lutheran Memorial Church. He knew many luminaries of his day, including Henry Clay, Charles Dickens, and ALBERT PIKE.

PLENTY COUPS (Aleek-chea-ahoosh, "many accomplishments"). *Crow. (1848–1932)*. Principal chief; friend to whites.

Plenty Coups was born near present-day Billings, Montana. His father, Medicine Bird, was Crow-Shoshone; his mother, full-blooded Crow. At about 14, he climbed into the Crazy Mountains on a Vision Quest and experienced a dream of a chickadee, a sign interpreted by tribal elders to indicate peace with whites. Although a noted warrior against the Crows' traditional enemies, Plenty Coups never made war on whites.

During the War for the Black Hills of 1876–77, Plenty Coups helped supply Indian scouts for General GEORGE CROOK's campaign against the Sioux under SITTING BULL and CRAZY HORSE. Crow warriors such as WHITE-MAN-RUNS-HIM and CURLY were with Colonel GEORGE ARMSTRONG CUSTER at Little Bighorn. Crows also served as army scouts in the campaign against the Nez Perces under Chief JOSEPH (Young Joseph).

Because of his knowledge of English, Plenty Coups represented his people in negotiations with the Northern Pacific Railroad. He also traveled to Washington, D.C., to lobby for Crow land claims.

In 1904, Plenty Coups succeeded Pretty Eagle as principal chief of the Mountain Crows. During World War I, he encouraged enlistment by tribal members to better themselves. In 1921, after the war, he was chosen to represent all other Native Americans at the Tomb of the Unknown Soldier at Arlington, Virginia. To close the ceremony, the aged chief placed his warbonnet and coup stick on the grave.

When 80, Plenty Coups donated his house and surrounding 40 acres to be used as a public park for people of all races. It is presently a state park with a museum about Crow history and customs.

After Plenty Coup's death at Pryor, Montana, the tribe honored him by eliminating the title "tribal chief," making him the last such designated Mountain Crow leader.

Plenty Coups. Photo by Edward Curtis. *Courtesy of National Archives of Canada/PA-39307.*

POCAHONTAS (Pokahantes, Pokahantesu, "my favorite daughter"; Matoaka, Mataoaka, Matowaka, Matoka, Matoax, Matsoaks'ats, "lively one"; Lady Rebecca). *Powhatan. (ca. 1595–1617)*. Peacemaker with Jamestown colonists. Daughter of POWHATAN; niece of OPECHANCANOUGH; wife of JOHN ROLFE.

Pocahontas was the favorite daughter of Powhatan or Wahunsonacock, a powerful chief of about 32 different Algonquian bands and 200 villages—the Powhatan

Pocahontas. *Courtesy of Library of Congress.*

Confederacy—in what is now eastern Virginia. As such, she came into contact with the English colonists who established Jamestown in 1607, the first permanent English settlement in North America.

Although the exact circumstances surrounding the incident are unknown, according to legend, in 1608, when she was probably only 13, Pocahontas saved the life of Captain JOHN SMITH, the Jamestown leader who had been taken captive by her uncle Opechancanough. Supposedly, she intervened just before Chief Powhatan was about to behead his prisoner, although Smith, in his later published account, made no mention of her role.

Relations between Indians and colonists deteriorated after Smith's departure for England in 1609. In 1612, Pocahontas was tricked onto one of the English ships on the Potomac, taken to Jamestown, and held hostage to bargain with Chief Powhatan for the freedom of other prisoners. While at Jamestown, she was converted to Christianity and baptized. Then she was courted by the colonist John Rolfe. On gaining her father's permission, she married the Englishman in April 1613. Their marriage brought about another period of peace between Powhatans and whites.

In 1616, Pocahontas and Rolfe sailed to England with Sir Thomas Dale and several other Indians, including her brother-in-law Uttamatomac. There, received as a princess, daughter of an emperor, Pocahontas met King James I and Queen Anne. She had her portrait painted, a copy of which exists today. She also was reunited with John Smith.

In 1617, while at Gravesend waiting to board a ship to return to her homeland, Pocahontas died of a European disease. She was buried in the yard of St. George's Parish Church, where there are now memorials to her, as there are in Jamestown. Her father, Powhatan, died the following year. In 1622, her uncle Opechancanough went to war with the colonists, during which John Rolfe was killed.

Pocahontas left a son, Thomas Rolfe, who, after an education in London, returned to North America in 1641, where he became a successful businessman. Because of the tensions between Indians and whites, he had to petition Virginia authorities to visit with his Indian relatives. Certain Virginia families have traced their ancestry through Thomas Rolfe to Pocahontas and Powhatan.

POCATELLO (General Pocatello, Pokatello, Pocataro, Pokendara; White Plume; Toniozo, "buffalo robe"). *Shoshone. (ca. 1815–1884).* Band leader who resisted white expansion.

Pocatello was head chief of a band of Shoshones living in the Grouse Creek region in the northwestern corner of Utah near the Idaho and Nevada borders. His band is sometimes referred to as Northwestern Shoshones, a subgrouping of Western Shoshones. Other geographical subgroupings are the Northern Shoshones, including TENDOY's Lemhi band of central Idaho, and WASHAKIE's Wind River, or Eastern, band of western Wyoming.

Pocatello became headman in 1847, the year the Mormons arrived in the Salt Lake area. With increased traffic westward because of the California Gold Rush starting in 1849, Indian raids also increased. Pocatello's band was blamed for much of the violence along the California Trail, Salt Lake Road, and Oregon Trail.

In later years, especially after his capture and imprisonment in 1859, Pocatello worked to maintain a delicate neutrality among the various factions in the region—the different Indian bands, Mormons, miners, ranchers, and missionaries. He left BEAR HUNTER's village one day before the attack by General PATRICK E. CONNOR's California volunteers during the Bear River Campaign of January 1863. He negotiated with Governor James Doty and signed the Treaty of Box Elder in July of that year. From 1867 to 1869, he participated in several buffalo hunts with Washakie's Wind River Shoshones and Taghee's Bannocks.

In 1869, the Union Pacific and Central Pacific railroads met at Promontory Point, Utah, linking the coasts by rail and leading to further white settlement in the region. At the end of 1872, Pocatello's band was forced to settle on the Fort Hall Reservation in Idaho. He converted to Mormonism for a short time in order to be able to live at missionary George Hill's farm on the lower Bear River near Corrine, Utah. But the inhabitants of that town, frightened by the number of Indians—the so-called Corrine Indian Scare—requested federal troops to force the return of the converts to Fort Hall.

Pocatello rejected Mormonism and lived out his life on the reservation. He became known as General Pocatello to distinguish him from brothers and cousins and other tribal members who used the name Pocatello. A city in Idaho is named after him.

POINT, NICOLAS. *(1799–1868)*. Missionary; artist.

The Belgian-born Jesuit priest Nicolas Point traveled West as an assistant to PIERRE JEAN DE SMET, missionary to the Flathead Indians. The wagon train, which departed Westport, Missouri, in May 1841, headed by the guide THOMAS FITZPATRICK, was the first to travel the Oregon Trail. Point kept a journal of his experiences, including numerous sketches, some of which were used to illustrate De Smet's writings. Point founded a mission among the Coeur D'Alenes in 1842, in what is now Idaho. Three years later, he also established a mission to the Blackfeet. On a return trip to St. Louis in 1847, Point made sketches of Missouri River forts and scenes.

POKAGON, LEOPOLD (Pocagin, Pugegun, Pugegin, "rib"). *Potawatomi-Chippewa.* *(ca. 1775–1841)*. Friend to whites; Christian convert. Father of SIMON POKAGON.

Leo Pokagon was a Chippewa captive from present-day Michigan who was reared by Potawatomis. As a youth, he witnessed the work of the Jesuits in the region before the Catholic order was suppressed.

Pokagon eventually became a chief of his people and encouraged Jesuit practices in his village near the St. Joseph River in southern Michigan, close to the Indiana border. He requested a missionary to his people and, in 1830, secured Father Stephen Badin.

Pokagon, a friend to settlers, kept his followers out of TECUMSEH's military alliance and the War of 1812, as well as the BLACK HAWK War of 1832. He signed the Treaty of Tippecanoe River in 1832, in which the site of Chicago was ceded. The following year, despite his pro-white stance, he was forced to relocate from his village to a location outside Dowagiac, Michigan.

Pokagon's wife was the niece of the war chief TOPENEBEE. Their son Paul succeeded Pokagon, but died soon afterward, as did their son Francis; their youngest son, Simon Pokagon, eventually became chief.

POKAGON, SIMON. *Potawatomi. (1830–1899)*. Principal chief; lecturer; writer. Son of LEOPOLD POKAGON.

Simon Pokagon was born in his father Leopold Pokagon's village in Michigan. His father died when he was a young boy. His mother encouraged his education by whites, and Simon began studies at Notre Dame, Indiana, when 14. After three years, he continued schooling at Oberlin College and Twinsburg in Ohio for three more years. He became fluent in five languages and an accomplished organist.

On becoming principal chief, Pokagon used his education on behalf of the Potawatomi bands scattered throughout Michigan. He met with President ABRAHAM LINCOLN on two occasions and President ULYSSES S. GRANT once. Pokagon successfully lobbied for a land claim of $150,000.

Said by some to be the most educated Indian of his time, Pokagon was a noted writer and speaker. He wrote numerous articles on Indian customs, as well as poetry, and he spoke at the World Exposition in Chicago in 1893. The year of his death, his work *Ogimawkwe Mitigwaki: Queen of the Woods* was published, telling the story of his courtship of his first wife.

POKER JOE (Lean Elk; Wahwookya Wasaaw; Kiniknik Hototo). *Mixed Nez Perce. (d. 1877)*. Leader in the Nez Perce War of 1877.

Poker Joe—the name by which he was known to whites—was a renowned buffalo hunter. During the attempted Flight of the Nez Perces to Canada, he served as supreme war chief and guide after LOOKING GLASS's misjudgment at the Battle of Big Hole on August 9 in the Bitterroot Valley in Montana. Poker Joe was killed in the last engagement of the war, at Bear Paw on September 30, along with OLLIKUT and TOOHOOLHOOLZOTE, after which Chief JOSEPH (Young Joseph) surrendered. (See also Young JOSEPH.)

POMPONIO. *Pomo. (fl. 1820s)*. Leader of resistance against the Spanish and Mexicans.

Pomponio lived in the region of San Rafael, California and was missionized by the Spanish at San Francisco. In the early 1820s, he escaped the mission and led a band of warriors in raids on settlements from San Rafael to Santa Cruz. In 1824, he participated with MARIN and QUINTIN in a rebellion against Mexican troops. Pomponio was captured at Novato, imprisoned for a time at the San Francisco Presidio, then sent to Monterey. Receiving a sentence of death, he escaped but was captured several months later at Soledad. During a second escape attempt, in which he may have cut off his heels in order to slip off the iron rings around his ankles, Pomponio killed a guard. He was again condemned to death at Monterey and executed. (See also MARIN.)

PONCE DE LEON, JUAN. *(ca. 1460–1521)*. Explorer.

Juan Ponce de Leon was born to a noble family in the town of Tierra de Campos in Spain's Leon province. He served as a page to the Spanish Royal Court at Aragon, then took part in the reconquest of the Moorish city of Granada in 1490. In 1493, he was a member of CHRISTOPHER COLUMBUS's second voyage. In 1502, he served in the conquest of the Arawaks, on the island of Hispaniola (present-day Dominican Republic and Haiti), where he became deputy to the Spanish governor. In 1508, he established the first settlement on Puerto Rico, becoming governor the next year.

From Caribbean Indians, Ponce de Leon reportedly learned of a legendary Fountain of Youth, and, in 1513, undertook an expedition in search of it. He sailed through the Bahamas, and, on Easter Sunday, 1513, arrived on the North American mainland near present-day St. Augustine, where he encountered Timucua Indians. He named the region La Florida from the Spanish name for Easter (Pascua Florida), then sailed south around the Florida Keys and north along the west coast of Florida, landing on Pine Island at the mouth of Charlotte Harbor, northwest of present-day Fort Myers. His party was attacked by Calusa Indians there, and one of his men was killed. Ponce de Leon then returned to Puerto Rico.

The next year, while in Spain, Ponce de Leon was named governor of Florida and Bimini. He was also commissioned to pacify the Carib Indians of Guadeloupe, an 1514 expedition which proved unsuccessful.

Ponce de Leon returned to Florida's west coast in 1521 with two ships and a company of 200 soldiers. Probably landing at Charlotte Harbor, the expedition was soon attacked by Calusa warriors (or possibly in the vicinity of Tampa Bay by Seminoles). In the conflict, Ponce de Leon was struck with an arrow, later dying in Cuba of his wounds.

POND, PETER. *(1740–1807). Trader; explorer.*

Born in Milford, Connecticut, Peter Pond fought with the British in the French and Indian War of 1754–63, during which he was commissioned an officer.

After the war, Pond went west to trade for furs with the Great Lakes tribes near Detroit. By 1772, he had expanded his operation to Michilimackinac, where he became known as an effective negotiator and peacemaker with the Yankton Sioux.

Starting about 1778, faced with competition from the Hudson's Bay Company, Pond moved his fur-trading operation into what is now southern Saskatchewan and established relations with the tribes of the Saskatchewan River region.

In 1778–79, based on Indian reports, Pond undertook an expedition from the western end of Lake Winnepeg, becoming the first white known to visit the Athabasca River and Lake Athabasca. He initiated trade contacts with the Athapascan Indians, then returned to the eastern Saskatchewan River, where he soon formed a business partnership with SIMON McTAVISH and Benjamin Frobisher, an enterprise that developed into the North West Company.

In 1782, Pond was accused of the murder of a rival trader, but was acquitted. He made several return trips to Lake Athabasca, in 1783–84 and 1785–86.

Pond eventually departed Canada and returned to Milford, Connecticut, where he spent his remaining years. His 1785 map of the Canadian West is one of the earliest detailed charts of the region. His reports and observations were the basis for ALEXANDER MACKENZIE's later expeditions in search of a water route from the interior of western Canada to the Pacific.

PONTIAC (Ponteach). *Ottawa. (ca. 1720–1769).* Leader of the Pontiac Rebellion of 1763.

Pontiac is thought to have been born along the Maumee River, now northern Ohio, of an Ottawa father and Chippewa mother. By 1755, he had become a chief. He had at least one wife, named Kantuckeegan, and two sons, Otussa and Shegenaba. During the French and Indian War of 1754–63, he probably helped defeat British troops under General EDWARD BRADDOCK on their way to Fort Duquesne (present-day Pittsburgh, Pennsylvania).

The four French and Indian Wars from 1689 to 1763 pitted for the most part French and Algonquians against British and Iroquois. By 1760, both Quebec and Montreal had fallen to British forces. French forces in Europe also lost important battles in the Seven Years War (1756–63). In 1760, Pontiac met with Major ROBERT ROGERS on his way to take possession of Fort Detroit for the British. By the time the French signed the Treaty of Paris in 1763, which officially ceded New France to England, British troops had taken control of the forts in the Great Lakes country.

Pontiac had developed a solid trade relationship with the French and resented the less generous policies of the British, established by Lord JEFFREY AMHERST, the British commander in chief for America. No presents were to be given to chiefs and no credit extended in supplies. Moreover, the British, unlike the French, were settling permanently on Indian lands.

Pontiac believed that if the Indian tribes united and won French support, they could drive the British from the Great Lakes region. It is likely he modeled his plan to defeat the British on one conceived two years earlier by the Seneca GUYASUTA. A powerful orator, Pontiac traveled among and sent messages to the Old Northwest tribes to urge Indian unity. The DELAWARE PROPHET helped him in his cause. The Prophet, also an effective orator, claimed that the Great Spirit had communicated with him to bring about a united Indian country where Indians would practice traditional ways. But the Delaware Prophet preached against guns; Pontiac considered them necessary to defeat the British.

Meanwhile, rumors of an uprising had reached Amherst through the extensive network of traders. Amherst sent reinforcements to Detroit under Major Henry Gladwin who took over command from Captain Donald Campbell.

At a council along the Ecorse River on April 27, 1763, Pontiac made final plans for a coordinated campaign involving separate bands throughout the Great Lakes region. On May 5, he visited Fort Detroit with abut 50 braves. While some entertained the garrison with a ceremonial dance, others carried out reconnaissance. On May 7, Pontiac returned with about 300 warriors under the pretense of a peace council, their weapons concealed beneath blankets. Since Gladwin had been warned of a surprise attack by an informer and had his men armed and ready, Pontiac decided not to give a planned signal. On May 8, Pontiac returned with three other chiefs to request another council. Gladwin would now allow only small groups to enter at any one time. With his warriors restless, Pontiac ordered an attack on May 9. The garrison, defending from inside the walls, repelled the warriors. Pontiac then ordered a siege. He also sent messages—wampum belts calling for war—to chiefs of other tribes.

Indians of many tribes west of the Appalachians participated. In addition to Ottawas and Chippewas, Delawares, Hurons, Illinois, Kickapoos, Miamis, Potawatomis, Senecas, and Shawnees carried out attacks on outlying settlements as well as on forts. About 2,000 settlers were killed. Many British posts fell to the various Indian forces: Fort Sandusky (now Sandusky, Ohio); Fort St. Joseph (Niles, Michigan); Fort Miami (Fort Wayne, Indiana); Fort Ouiatenon (Lafayette, Indiana); Fort Michilimackinac (Mackinac, Michigan); Fort Venango (Franklin, Pennsylvania); Fort Le Boeuf (Waterford, Pennsylvania); Fort Presqu'Isle (Erie, Pennsylvania); and Fort Edward Augustus (Green Bay, Wisconsin).

The Indians were also victorious at Point Pelee on Lake Erie on May 28, stopping supply boats on their way to Detroit, and at Bloody Run on July 31, just outside the fort, attacking 54 British soldiers under Captain James Dalyell. At Detroit, however, in early August, the schooner *Huron* broke through Indian lines with fresh men and supplies.

Meanwhile, the defenders at Fort Pitt (Pittsburgh) used an early form of biological warfare to hold out against the siege. At Amherst's suggestion, the defending garrison under Captain Simeon Ecuyer sent out smallpox-infected blankets and handkerchiefs, starting an epidemic among the Indians. Colonel HENRY BOUQUET broke the siege with a victory at Bushy Run south of Lake Erie on August 5–6. Two other western Pennsylvania outposts, Fort Ligonier and Fort Bedford, also held out through the summer.

During the conflict, a Royal Proclamation was finally issued in England on October 7, 1763, establishing an Indian Country west of the Appalachians that was to be protected from white settlement.

The siege of Detroit continued into the autumn. The French never delivered the help they had led the Indians to expect despite urgent requests from Pontiac. With winter coming, the warriors became worried about providing food for their families. On October 20, after a plea to his men for continuation of the siege, Pontiac received a letter from Major de Villiers, the commander of the French Fort de Chartres on the Mississippi River in Louisiana Territory, advising him to cease hostilities. The following day, Pontiac called off the siege.

Some bands remained hostile. In July and August 1764, expeditions under Colonel Bouquet and Colonel John Bradstreet attacked and destroyed Indian villages in Ohio. Pontiac clung to his cause for some time to come. In July 1765, along the Wabash River, he agreed to a preliminary peace pact with GEORGE CROGHAN and signed a treaty at Oswego in 1766 with WILLIAM JOHNSON and was pardoned by the British. He returned to his village on the Maumee River.

Tensions increased between Indians and whites with the influx of settlers who ignored the Proclamation Line of 1763. Pontiac, however, now counseled peace. Young warriors drove him and his small coterie of family and followers from the village because of his stance.

During a trip to the trading post at Cahokia, Illinois, in April 1769, Pontiac was struck on the head from behind and stabbed by a Peoria (Illinois) Indian by the name of Black Dog, probably in the pay of the British, who still feared the Ottawa's influence. Because of his murder by an Illinois Indian, the Ottawas, Chippewas, Potawatomis, Sacs, and Foxes united against the Illinois bands and defeated them.

In the following years, other leaders of the Old Northwest forged Indian alliances, in particular LITTLE TURTLE, TECUMSEH, and BLACK HAWK, against white settlers.

POPE (El Pope, "pumpkin mountain"). *Tewa.* (d. 1690). Medicine man; leader of the Pueblo Rebellion of 1680.

The Spanish came to the upper Rio Grande region under FRANCISCO VASQUEZ DE CORONADO in 1540, and founded the colony of New Mexico in 1598 under JUAN DE ONATE. In 1610, Onate founded the capital of Santa Fe. As dictated by the *repartimiento* system, enforced by well-armed soldiers, the Indians owed Spain taxes in the form of cotton, crafts, and labor. Moreover, the Catholic formula for salvation, as enacted by the missionaries, demanded the suppression of Indian religion and ritual. Spanish officials eventually began punishing practitioners through public floggings. The Indians were forced to practice their kachina religion secretly in the underground ceremonial chambers known as kivas. Disputes between Spanish civil and religious officials over power and influence gradually undermined the authority of both over the Indians. A long series of droughts starting in 1660 caused converted Indians to doubt the effectiveness of the new religion.

Pope, an influential medicine man of the San Juan Pueblo, refused to convert to Christianity, despite harassment by the Spanish. He was seized and punished at least three times and proudly displayed the scars on his back to his people as a symbol of resistance. He also exposed an in-law as a Spanish informer and permitted his death at the hands of his angry followers to demonstrate the strength of his conviction.

In 1675, Pope was one of about 50 Pueblo medicine men rounded up and taken to Santa Fe. Three were hanged and the rest were flogged and imprisoned. A delegation of some 70 Indians, warning of violence by their people, won the release of the captives. Rather than return to San Juan, Pope hid out at Taos Pueblo, where he began organizing a rebellion. Other pueblo leaders joined the cause, including Jaca of Taos, Catiti of Santo Domingo, and Tupatu of Picuris. Even Hopi leaders far to the west became part of the conspiracy. To prevent betrayal to the Spanish, Pope tried to keep word of the plot from anyone who was suspected of being sympathetic to the Spanish. No women were permitted knowledge of it.

Pope's runners carried cords of maguey fibers telling the number of days until the general uprising. The original attack was planned for August 13. On learning that the Spanish had been warned of the plot by Christianized Indians, Pope ordered the attack on August 10 (the change in date might have been planned from the beginning). Warriors from numerous pueblos along the Rio Grande and to the west moved against soldiers and priests stationed in the pueblos as well as ranchers living on outlying haciendas.

After military successes elsewhere, about 500 rebels proceeded to Santa Fe. A garrison of 50 soldiers plus civilians mounted an effective defense, starting on August 14. The Indians climbed on top of the abandoned adobe buildings on the town's outskirts and held siege. The Spanish were able to hold their ground by firing brass cannon from behind the palace walls, where they took refuge with Governor Antonio de Otermin. Intermittent fighting lasted for days. The Indians finally managed to reach the town's water ditch and divert the supply. They also attacked the chapel. With considerable loss of life, the Indians grew tired of the siege and withdrew to their pueblos. On August 21, the Spanish headed south to El Paso. In the week and a half of the revolt, almost 400 of about 2,500 settlers were dead, including 21 of 33 missionaries. Approximately 250 Indians had died in the uprising.

Having regained control of their homeland, the Pueblo Indians were now free to practice their traditional culture and religion. Pope traveled from pueblo to pueblo to oversee the destruction of all elements of Spanish culture—churches, livestock, plants, tools. The use of the Spanish language and names were forbidden. Those Indians who had been baptized by the priests were washed with suds from the yucca plant.

Pope became increasingly tyrannical. Living in Santa Fe, he adopted many of the trappings of the colonial officials before him, including use of the governor's carriage. He ordered the death of many of those who opposed him. A drought contributed to the dissatisfaction, as did Apache and Ute raids on the pueblos. Political and tribal rivalries caused further dissension. Pope was deposed, but soon regained power. Yet, by the time of his death in 1690, his alliance had all but dissolved.

Spanish troops marching north out of El Paso met little resistance: in 1689, they captured Zia Pueblo; in 1692, a force under DIEGO DE VARGAS recaptured Santa Fe. The Pueblo Indians were again wards of the Spanish state.

A lasting cultural trait evolved out of the Pueblo Rebellion and came to influence Indians far and wide. It was during the revolt that the Indians first acquired their own horses, left behind by the fleeing Spanish. The Pueblo Indians traded or lost them in raids to northern tribes, leading to a new way of life on the Great Plains by the mid-1700s.

The Pueblo Indians remained under Spanish rule until 1821, the year of the Mexican Revolution. Mexican rule of the region lasted until 1848 and the Treaty of Guadalupe Hidalgo, ending the Mexican War with the United States.

POPE, JOHN. *(1822–1892).* Army officer in the Plains Indian wars.

A native of Louisville, Kentucky, John Pope graduated from West Point in 1842, and became a topographical engineer for the army. He took part in surveys in Florida and the Northeast until the outbreak of the Mexican War in 1846, when he was assigned to serve under General ZACHARY TAYLOR. He was brevetted a major by the war's end.

In 1849–50, Pope undertook an expedition to the Red River of the North in Minnesota and, in 1851, was named the army's chief topographical engineer for the Department of New Mexico. Between 1853 and 1859, he was involved in explorations in the Southwest, surveying a proposed railroad route to the Pacific Coast.

At the beginning of the Civil War, Pope was appointed a brigadier general of volunteers and led troops in Missouri under the command of General JOHN C. FREMONT. In December 1861, he was victorious against Confederate forces under General STERLING PRICE at the Battle of Black Water, near Warrensburg, Missouri. The following year, he led Union troops to victories on the Mississippi near Cairo, Illinois, and succeeded in gaining control of the mid-Mississippi River for the North. In March 1862, he was promoted to the rank of major general of volunteers and took part in that year's campaign in Virginia's Shenandoah Valley. When his command suffered a significant defeat at Manassas in July 1862, Pope was reassigned to the Minnesota frontier.

Pope took charge of the army's Department of the Northwest and the campaign against LITTLE CROW and his Santee Sioux, then warring against settlers in the Minnesota Uprising, and supervised the offensives of generals HENRY HASTINGS SIBLEY and ALFRED SULLY.

Pope, now at the regular rank of major general, then received the appointment of commander of the Division of the Missouri. In this capacity, he directed the operation against the Northern Plains tribes in the Powder River Expedition of 1865. The Sioux and Cheyennes had been interfering with travelers headed for Montana's mining region, and, to put down the uprising, Pope launched a military offensive from Fort Laramie in present-day Wyoming, and from his division headquarters at Omaha, in present-day Nebraska, under field commander General PATRICK E. CONNOR.

In 1867–68, Pope commanded the Third Military District, including Florida, Georgia, and Alabama; and, in 1868–70, the Department of the Lakes. Then, in 1870, he assumed command of the newly formed Department of the Missouri (Missouri, Kansas, Colorado, and New Mexico), becoming a subordinate of General PHILIP H. SHERIDAN, commander of the larger Division of the Missouri, which had been subdivided into four departments. As such, Pope commanded some columns in the Red River War of 1874–75 and the Ute War of 1879. During the early 1880s, he used federal troops to protect Indian interests against the influx of white squatters, or "Boomers," into the Indian Territory. Pope finished out his career as commander of the Department of California and Division of the Pacific in 1883–86.

Throughout his post–Civil War career in the West, Pope was extremely critical of federal Indian policy and believed the administration of Indian affairs was a military concern. He was in favor of negotiating treaties with the Indians that were essentially nonaggression pacts and was opposed to the use of gifts and annuities to bribe the Indians into remaining peaceful. He further advocated fair treatment on reservations, missionary work among the Indians, and Indian assimilation into white society.

PORTER, PLEASANT (Talof Harjo, "crazy bear"). *Mixed Creek. (1840–1907).* Educator; principal chief.

Pleasant Porter, the grandson of a Creek chief with some black ancestry, was born in Clarksville, Alabama, and later moved to the Indian Territory.

During the Civil War, Porter fought on the side of the South, earning the rank of lieutenant in the Confederate 2nd Creek Regiment, and was wounded in battle. After the war, he became involved in tribal politics, supporting the faction, made up mostly of mixed-bloods, favoring acculturation to white society and a constitutional form of government (although many others of Creek-black ancestry gave their support to the mostly full-blood faction favoring traditional tribal organization).

Porter served his tribe in various capacities. As school superintendent, he was the founder of the modern Creek educational system. He also served as tribal delegate to Washington, D.C., during the allotment period. He was the Creek's principal chief when the Indian Territory became the state of Oklahoma in 1907. He died that same year of a stroke.

POSEY, ALEXANDER LAWRENCE (Chinnubie Harjo). *Mixed Creek. (1873–1908).* Educator; writer.

Alexander Posey, Scotch-Irish by his father, was raised traditionally by his Creek mother near Eufaula, Oklahoma. Mastering English as a teenager, he attended Bacone Indian University, where he learned both library and printing skills. He became active in tribal affairs as a progressive in favor of constitutional government and served as the superintendent of Public Instruction of the Creek Nation. After 1901, Posey devoted more time to his poetry and became editor of the *Indian Journal*. In 1905, he helped write the Creek constitution at Muskogee. He drowned in the Oktahutchee River three years later.

POTTS, JERRY. *Mixed Blood. (1840–1896).* Scout and interpreter for the Northwest Mounted Police.

Jerry Potts was the son of a Scottish clerk and a Blood woman. As a young man of 17, he tracked a man several hundred miles to avenge his father's death. He further built his reputation as a skilled fighter in warfare with the Crees, Assiniboines, and other enemies of the Blackfeet, Bloods, and Piegans. He became known on the Plains of present-day Alberta and Montana as a skilled hunter and guide.

Starting in 1874, Potts served as a guide and interpreter for the Mounties, hired by then–Assistant Commissioner JAMES MACLEOD. He was indispensable in the campaigns against outlaws, including the illegal whiskey traders, guiding Mounties to their frontier stronghold known as Fort Whoop-Up at the confluence of the St. Mary and Oldman rivers near present-day Lethbridge, Alberta. He also acted as interpreter to the Canadian Plains tribes.

The good relations the Mounties generally had with the tribes of the region were due in large part to Potts, who was trusted by Indians and whites alike. He served the Mounties 22 years until his death.

Jerry Potts. *Courtesy of National Archives of Canada/C-17492.*

POUNDMAKER (Opeteca Hanawaywin). *Cree. (ca. 1842–1886).* Leader in the Second Riel Rebellion of 1885. Adopted son of CROWFOOT.

Poundmaker was born near Battleford in what is now central Saskatchewan, and was raised by the Powerful Blackfoot chief Crowfoot. Like Crowfoot, Poundmaker counseled peace with whites. In 1876, although first opposing it, he signed Canadian Treaty No. 6. He was recognized as a chief of the Plains Cree in 1878, and, in 1881, he acted as the guide to the Marquis of Lorne on the viceregal tour of the Northwest, taking him from Battleford to Calgary. During an 1884 incident in which the Mounties disrupted a tribal ceremony in search of a wanted man, Poundmaker talked his warriors out of violence.

Yet, the next year, Poundmaker, fed up with life on the reserve, joined the hostilities in the Second Riel Rebellion led by the Metis LOUIS DAVID RIEL. Two days after the Metis took the trading post at Duck Lake on March 26, 1885, Poundmaker led about 200 warriors on the town of Battleford on the North Saskatchewan River. Some 500 men, women, and children took refuge in the barracks of the Northwest Mounted Police along with 32 Mounties. The Crees killed only one settler, but they ransacked and burned the outlying buildings and laid siege of the fort for three weeks before departing. Another band of Crees under BIG BEAR attacked the

Poundmaker. Photo by O. B. Buell. *Courtesy of National Archives of Canada/C-1875.*

settlement of Frog Lake to the northwest on April 2. One battalion of the North West Field Force under Colonel William Otter relieved Battleford in late April, then moved on the Cree camp at Cut Knife Creek. In a counterattack, the Indians inflicted 23 casualties on the soldiers, then slipped away.

With continuing pressure and the surrender of Riel, Poundmaker and his warriors also turned themselves in at Battleford in June. Along with Big Bear, who held out until early July, Poundmaker was sentenced to three years' imprisonment. He was given an early release the next year, but, suffering from poor health, died while on a visit to Crowfoot's Blackfoot Indian Reserve in Alberta. (See also RIEL, LOUIS DAVID.)

POWASHEEK (Poweshiek, Pawishik, "to dash the water off" or "aroused bear"). *Fox.* *(ca. 1813–ca. 1843).* Ally of KEOKUK.

Powasheek was born at Musquawkenuk (present-day Davenport, Iowa), the grandson of the chief Black Thunder. Along with the Fox WAPELLO, and the Sacs BLACK HAWK and Keokuk, he became one of the most powerful leaders of the two allied tribes. Although some of his followers joined Black Hawk in his rebellion—the Black Hawk War of 1832—Powasheek refused to give complete support to the Sac chief, withdrawing across the Mississippi to Iowa, where he was soon joined by Keokuk's band. Powasheek signed a treaty with the federal government in 1832 and traveled to Washingotn, D.C., in 1833 and 1837 to represent his people in further negotiations. In 1836, he met the Mormon leader Joseph Smith, who failed to convert him, at Nauvoo, Illinois. Powasheek signed another treaty in 1842 and died soon afterward in Kansas.

POWELL, JOHN WESLEY (Karpurats, "one-arm man"). *(1834–1902).* Anthropologist; linguist; explorer.

John Wesley Powell was born in Mount Morris, New York, and grew up in Ohio, Wisconsin, and Illinois. While pursuing studies of natural sciences in various colleges and on his own, he taught school to support himself.

During the Civil War, Powell lost his lower right arm at the Battle of Shiloh. He eventually achieved the rank of major.

After the war, Powell became a professor of geology at Illinois Wesleyan College. In the summers of 1867 and 1868, he led field trips to the Rocky Mountains where he came into contact with Ute Indians, who called him Karpurats.

In 1869, Powell led his first expedition down the Colorado River and Grand Canyon, during which three men were killed by Paiutes. That journey led to funding by the Department of the Interior for the U.S.

Geographical and Geological Survey of the Rocky Mountain Region, 1871–79. Powell headed a second expedition to the Grand Canyon, this time with a photographer, JOHN K. HILLERS. He also led expeditions that explored and charted large areas of Utah and Arizona. Along with collecting geological data on the Southwest, Powell made ethnological studies of Native American peoples.

In 1879, the Interior Department's Powell Survey and the FERDINAND V. HAYDEN Survey, as well as the War Department's CLARENCE KING Survey and GEORGE WHEELER Survey, were merged into the U.S. Geological Survey, with King as the first director, succeeded by Powell in 1881.

Powell also became the first director of the Smithsonian Institution's newly formed Bureau of Ethnology in 1879 (which added American to its name in 1894, i.e., Bureau of American Ethnology), serving until his death. His early projects included a series of anthropological expeditions to study the Pueblo Indians of the Southwest, beginning with the Zunis of New Mexico. Powell worked with leading anthropologists of his day, including ADOLPH BANDELIER, FRANK HAMILTON CUSHING, JAMES OWEN DORSEY, JESSE WALTER FEWKES, WILLIAM HENRY HOLMES, WASHINGTON MATTHEWS, JAMES MOONEY, MATILDA COXE STEVENSON, and WILLIAM ORRIE TUGGLE.

During his career, Powell developed a systematic classification of known North American Indian languages, organizing them into 56 different linguistic families. He also wrote several treatises on geology and made the case for the reclamation of arid western lands through irrigation.

POWHATAN ("hill of the council" or "falls in a flowing stream"; Wahunsonacock, Wahunsonacook, Wa-hun-sen-a-cawh). *Powhatan. (ca. 1547–1618).* Chief of the Powhatan Confederacy; friend to the Jamestown colonists. Father of POCAHONTAS; brother of OPECHANCANOUGH.

Although the name *Powhatan* was really a place name and village name at the falls of the Powhatan River (now the James River near present-day Richmond), Wahunsonacock became known to the English by it. His father had founded the powerful alliance of Algonquian-speaking Tidewater tribes, and Powhatan had further strengthened it into a confederacy of some 32 bands, such as the Pamunkey (Powhatan's people), Mattaponi, Chickahominy, Nansemond, Potomac, and Rhappahanock, and their 200 villages. Powhatan's primary village was Werowacomoco, on the north bank of the York River. He is reported to have had 11 wives and more than 20 sons and 11 daughters; his favorite child was reportedly Pocahontas.

The shaky peace between Powhatan's people and the Jamestown colonists, who had founded the first permanent English colony in the Americas, enabled the whites to survive. Although suspicious of the newcomers, Powhatan had his followers, NAMONTACK for one, provide them with food and teach them how to plant corn. Powhatan's daughter Pocahontas, because of her fondness for the colonists and later marriage to JOHN ROLFE, helped maintain the peaceful relationship. Powhatan and the leader of the colony, Captain JOHN SMITH, apparently had a begrudging respect for each other. In fall 1608, after Powhatan had held him prisoner, then released him—as legend has it at the intercession of Pocahontas—Smith ceremonially crowned Powhatan as "king" of the region in a political maneuver to appease him.

About 1610, when the English began to crowd the village of Werowacomoco, Powhatan took up residency further to the west at Orapax between the Chickahominy and Pamunkey rivers.

Four years after Powhatan's death in 1618, his brother Opechancanough led the confederacy in an uprising against the English.

PRATT, RICHARD HENRY. *(1840–1924).*
Educator; army officer.

Richard Henry Pratt, born in Rushford, New York, was raised in Logansport, Indiana, where he was apprenticed to a tinsmith. In 1861, he began his service in the Civil War, eventually rising to the rank of lieutenant in the Union army. Following his reenlistment in 1867, he was assigned to a black regiment in the Indian Territory, the 10th Cavalry.

In 1875, as commander of the Indian scouts at Fort Sill, Pratt was assigned to round up Indian militants of the 1874–75 Red River War. Seventy-two Indians— Cheyennes, Arapahos, Comanches, and Kiowas—were taken into custody on being identified by army officers, survivors of Indian attacks, and former captives. The selection of the prisoners took into account immunity agreements between the government and some Indian informers. As a result, some Indians who had been guilty of serious crimes were not imprisoned, while others who may have been guilty of lesser crimes were exiled to Florida. Pratt was investigated for alleged irregularities in the prisoner selection process, but was cleared of any wrongdoing.

Because the United States was not officially at war with the Indian tribes, the accused warriors could not be tried by a military court. Nor did the government turn them over to state and territorial authorities because of the difficulty in assuring a fair trial. As an alternative, Pratt was assigned to escort the Indians to the Fort Marion Military Prison at St. Augustine,

Florida, where they would be held for an indefinite time as prisoners of war.

During the next three years at Fort Marion, Pratt established an educational and job-training program for his prisoners. He obtained the services of local teachers, who provided them with instruction in basic academic skills, as well as vocational training in carpentry, baking, masonry, and tailoring. He also encouraged the prisoners to produce artwork. Some of them, including BEAR'S HEART, COHOE, HOWLING WOLF, and ZOTOM, became known for their drawings.

In 1878, the federal government authorized the release of all the Fort Marion Indians. That same year, Pratt began to place some of the Indians in the care of white families, and others under the supervision of the Episcopal church. Seventeen of the former prisoners were sent to the Hamptom Institute in Virginia, a training school for blacks under the direction of General S. C. Armstrong. Pratt himself taught these Indians at Hampton until 1879, at which time he was authorized by the War Department to establish a school at the abandoned military barracks in Carlisle, Pennsylvania, the first federally funded, nonreservation boarding school for Indians. Eleven former prisoners came to Carlisle to help organize the school during its first year.

For the first two years of its operation, the school was self-sufficient, maintaining itself through the work of its students. In 1882, Congress appropriated funding, and, that same year, the first Indian Service hospital was established at Carlisle.

As an army captain, Pratt served as superintendent of the school. Under his direction, an "outing system" was instituted, in which Indian students lived and worked for extended periods of time with white families, who were paid a fee by the government. It was Pratt's belief that, by isolating Indians from life on the reservation and integrating them directly into white communities, they could be assimilated into mainstream society.

The Carlisle Indian School became the model for other Indian boarding schools opened by the government in Oregon, New Mexico, Arizona, Nebraska, and the Indian Territory. Their operation led to certain abuses in the recruitment of students, with charges made that children were sometimes forcibly taken from the reservations to meet boarding school enrollment quotas.

Pratt, who considered the reservation as a place of destruction, encouraged the development of nonreservation schools in the East for the acculturation of Indians. He was at odds with the government program that established boarding schools on or near reservations in the West. Pratt also criticized the Indian boarding schools established by church organizations, charging that the students in those schools were trained only to return to their reservations for missionary work, and were not directed to use their education as a means to integrate into white society.

In 1904, now-General Pratt lost his position at Carlisle for insubordination because of remarks he made in New York City at a conference of Baptist ministers, calling for the abolition of the Indian Bureau. The year before, he had been asked to resign from the army. For the next 20 years, Pratt remained an active force in Indian education and continued to promote his assimilationist views.

PRIBER, CHRISTIAN GOTTLIEB.

(fl. 1730s–1740s). Missionary; reformer; adviser to the Cherokees.

Christian Gottlieb Priber, originally from one of the 18th-century European German states, arrived in South Carolina in 1736 after expulsion from his homeland for his radical socialist views.

Priber befriended the Cherokee chief MOYTOY, becoming his confidant and adviser. Moytoy, who had been recognized as the titular "emperor of the Cherokees" by the British, named Priber as "His Cherokee Majesty's Secretary of State." Priber attempted to apply his socialist theories to the Cherokees and neighboring Southeast Indians, intending to organize the Cherokee, Creek, Choctaw, and Catawba tribes into a socialist utopia. In his proposed Indian state, he planned to abolish private property and introduce the practice of communal marriage. In addition, the state's government was to have custody of all Indian children. There were also to be provisions ensuring equal rights for both men and women.

Priber advised the Cherokees to declare their neutrality in the colonial competition between the British and the French, leading to accusations by British officials that he was a French agent. He also angered British interests by instructing the Cherokees in how to avoid being cheated with false weights and measures.

In the early 1740s, colonial authorities made several attempts to take Priber into custody, but his loyal Cherokee allies protected him. In one incident, South Carolina colonial government agents were detained by the Cherokees and threatened with harm when they entered Indian lands to arrest Priber. Priber himself urged the Cherokees to spare the men, who were released.

In 1743, while en route to Fort Toulouse, the French outpost near present-day Montgomery, Alabama, Priber was taken prisoner by a group of British traders and died while being interrogated by authorities at Frederica, Georgia. Without his influence, the Cherokees supported the British in their subsequent conflict with the French, King George's War of 1744–48.

PRICE, STERLING. *(1809–1867)*. Army officer during the Taos Revolt; Missouri politician.

Born in Virginia, Sterling Price attended Hampden-Sydney College and later studied law. In 1831, he moved with his family to Missouri. He practiced law there and was elected to the state legislature three times, serving in 1836–38 and 1840–44. He was elected to the U.S. Congress in 1844, but failed to retain his seat in the election of 1846. With the start of the Mexican War that year, Price accepted a commission as colonel in the Missouri militia. In the fall, along with Missouri regiments under the command of Colonel ALEXANDER W. DONIPHAN, Price led his regiment into New Mexico as part of General STEPHEN WATTS KEARNY's invasion force.

When Kearny led forces to take California, and Doniphan led troops into Chihuahua, Mexico, Price was left in command of New Mexico. An uprising at Taos, New Mexico, erupted in January 1847, carried out by Pueblo Indians and Mexican allies dissatisfied with the laws imposed upon them by the Americans. The insurgents also resented the extra burden placed on their economy by the occupying troops from Missouri. New Mexico territorial governor CHARLES BENT, installed by Kearny, was killed in the revolt in Taos. Violence against Americans also broke out at Turley's Mill and Mora.

Price and his command advanced on Taos from Santa Fe and attacked the rebels with howitzers and infantry. Over 200 of the militants were killed in Price's offensive, and many more taken prisoner. Price had a number of the Indian ringleaders tried for their crimes against the Americans. Fifteen were found guilty and executed.

Price went on to become military governor of Chihuahua, Mexico, and took part in the Mexican War battle at Santa Cruz de Rosales in 1848. By the end of the war, he had been brevetted a brigadier general.

Price returned to Missouri and was elected governor in 1852. At the outbreak of the Civil War, he was commissioned a general in the Confederate army and served in major campaigns in the Arkansas and Missouri regions. Price's campaigns drew Union forces away from frontier posts to the West and contributed to stepped-up raiding by Plains, Great Basin, and Southwest tribes.

After the war and Union victory, Price fled to Mexico, where he attempted to establish a colony of Confederate veterans. Ill health brought him back to Missouri in 1867, where he died a short time later.

PRINTZ, JOHAN BJORNSSON

(Big Guts). *(1592–1663)*. Colonial governor.

Johan Printz was born in Bottnaryd, Sweden, the son of a minister. He was educated in Sweden and attended universities in Germany. In 1620, while en route to a

German university to study theology, he was pressed into the service of Archduke Leopold of Austria, and went on to fight in numerous campaigns throughout northern Europe as a mercenary in the Thirty Years War of 1618–48. In 1625, he joined the Swedish army, and, by 1638, he risen to the rank of lieutenant colonel.

In 1642, Printz was appointed director general of Sweden's colony in Delaware Bay—New Sweden—established in 1638 by PETER MINUIT. Printz arrived at the colonial capital, Fort Christina (present-day Wilmington, Delaware), the following year. At that time, New Sweden extended from what is now Trenton, New Jersey, on the north, to Cape Henlopen, at the entrance to Delaware Bay, on the south.

During his 10 years as chief administrator of New Sweden, Printz maintained peaceful relations with the neighboring Dutch and English colonies, as well as with the local Delaware bands. Printz weighed perhaps 400 pounds; the Indians affectionately called him Big Guts.

In 1648, tensions arose between Printz and Dutch colonial governor WILLEM KIEFT over conflicting territorial claims. Printz based his claim on Sweden's purchase of the Delaware Bay area from the Indians; the Dutch maintained that they had purchased the same lands from the Indians. The same or different bands may have in fact sold it to representatives of both countries.

Although New Sweden prospered during his governorship, Printz felt compelled to resign in July 1653, when the colonists openly protested his harsh administrative policies. He returned to his hometown of Bottnaryd, Sweden, in 1653, where he died 10 years later as a result of a riding accident.

In 1655, a force under PETER STUYVESANT took control of the colony of New Sweden for Holland.

PROCTOR, HENRY (Henry Procter).
(ca. 1763–1822). British officer in the War of 1812.

Henry Proctor joined the British army in 1781. At the onset of hostilities between the United States and Great Britain in the War of 1812, Proctor was a colonel in charge of British forces on the border between Canada and the western New York State and Ohio region.

In January 1813, Proctor led a successful attack against Kentucky militiamen along the Raisin River, near present-day Monroe, Michigan. Most of the Kentuckians were killed or captured. Although Proctor assured the American prisoners that they would not be harmed, his Indian troops, under the influence of whiskey, killed many of them. Proctor took no action to restrain the Indians from killing captives, unlike his predecessor General ISAAC BROCK.

At Fort Malden, near Detroit, Proctor recruited an army of 1,500 warriors from the tribes of the Old Northwest, under the leadership of the Shawnee TECUMSEH. In May 1813, Proctor led his combined force of British regulars, Canadian militia, and Indian auxiliaries against Fort Meigs, on the Maumee River in what is now northwestern Ohio, founded by General WILLIAM HENRY HARRISON. The post held with assistance from American reinforcements from nearby Fort Defiance. Captives taken in the surrounding countryside were put to death by some of the Indian troops, despite Tecumseh's efforts to prevent such a massacre.

Back at Fort Malden, Proctor organized an army of warriors of Shawnees and allied tribes numbering more than 4,000 men. In July 1813, he led this force in another attack on Fort Meigs. Despite staging a mock battle near the fort to draw American forces into an ambush, Proctor and his overwhelming number of Indians were again unable to take Fort Meigs. In August 1813, Proctor attempted an assault on Fort Stephenson on the Sandusky River, but American forces under Major GEORGE CROGHAN, with the use of a surprise artillery volley, repulsed the British and Indians. Disillusioned, many of the Indians withdrew from the war.

With American naval victories on Lake Erie, Proctor retreated into present-day Ontario, where he was defeated by troops under General Harrison at the Battle of the Thames in October 1813. Many Kentuckians who had lost their comrades-in-arms the previous January, took part in Proctor's defeat. The rallying cry of the Kentucky militiamen in this battle was "Remember the River Raisin!" Tecumseh was killed in the fighting.

After the battle, Proctor fled to eastern Ontario and rejoined the British command. He was suspended from service for six months, but returned to active duty and later reached the rank of major general. (See also TECUMSEH.)

PUSHMATAHA (Apushmataha, "oak tree"; Brother Push; The Indian General).
Choctaw. (1764–1824). Ally of Americans in the Creek War of 1813–14; orator; negotiator.

Pushmataha was born along the Noxubee Creek in present-day Mississippi, of unknown parents. He himself claimed to his people he was sprung from an oak tree. Before he was 20, he established his reputation as a warrior against the Osages and Caddos in forays across the Mississippi. On one expedition, he was captured, then escaped to live and work among the Spanish. On another, he single-handedly killed five men.

By 1805, Pushmataha had earned a chieftaincy. That same year, he signed a treaty ceding Choctaw lands in Alabama and Mississippi. John Pitchlynn, an interpreter for the federal government, fathered by PETER PITCHLYNN of a Choctaw woman, became

Pushmataha's close friend. In 1811, when TECUMSEH visited the southern tribes to seek support for his military alliance, Pushmataha, famed for his oratory, spoke out for support of the United States, influencing many fellow leaders.

In the Creek War of 1813–14, Pushmataha led some 500 warriors in support of American forces under General ANDREW JACKSON against Creek Red Sticks led by WILLIAM WEATHERFORD. He was made a brigadier general (known to whites as "The Indian General") and provided with a full-dress uniform. MUSHALATUBBEE led Choctaw forces as well.

Pushmataha signed treaties in 1816 and 1820. A skillful negotiator, he advocated a policy of conciliation with the federal government and agreed to land cessions. Believing that his people had to learn the skills of whites to protect and preserve the tribe, he helped develop a Choctaw educational system based on white methods. In 1824, he was dismayed to learn of new white demands for Choctaw lands. Pushmataha visited Washington, D.C., in 1824 for negotiations and met with President James Monroe and the MARQUIS DE LAFAYETTE, who was visiting America for the last time. After a one-day illness—a throat infection—the Choctaw leader died. He was buried in Washington with full military honors.

PUTNAM, FREDERIC WARD. *(1839–1915)*.
Anthropologist; museum curator.

Born in Salem, Massachusetts, Frederic Ward Putnam was educated at home and in private schools, then entered Harvard in 1856. He became the curator of Harvard University's Peabody Museum of Anthropology and Archaeology in 1875–1909 (where he influenced the career of anthropologist ALICE CUNNINGHAM FLETCHER), and the American Museum of Natural History from 1894 until his death.

At the latter institution, Putnam applied his skills to organizing the vast Northwest Coastal Indian collection resulting from the work of FRANZ BOAS and his associates. He also organized the ethnological exhibits of Indian life at the 1893 Chicago World's Fair, providing the basis for the establishment of the Field Museum of Natural History in that city the following year. In 1903, he helped establish both the department and museum of anthropology at the University of California at Berkeley. In later years, this institution would come to the forefront of Native American anthropological studies under Alfred Kroeber.

Putnam instituted innovations in the display of Indian tools, boats, housing and ceremonial objects that created an image of the life of Native Americans in their natural surroundings. Rather than classifying items by type, he attempted to use them to communicate the unique culture of each tribe.

Q

QUAIAPAN. See MAGNUS.

QUALCHIN (Qualchiah). *Yakima. (d. 1858).* War chief in the Yakima War of 1855–56 and Coeur d'Alene (Spokane) War of 1858. Son of OWHI.

In September 1855, Qualchin and five other young warriors precipitated warfare with the killing of five miners who were crossing the Yakima River. The conflict known as the Yakima War spread to other tribes in the Washington Territory and evolved into the Coeur d'Alene War. The capture of KAMIAKIN, Owhi, and Qualchin was a high priority of the military. Owhi, Qualchin's father, surrendered after Indian losses to Colonel George Wright's troops in the battles of Spokane Plain and Four Lakes in September 1858, whereupon he was placed in irons and used as bait for his son's surrender. Qualchin appeared soon afterward; it is not known whether he fell for the trap or whether he intended to come for negotiations without knowing of his father's arrest. Qualchin was reportedly hanged 15 minutes after his surrender; Owhi was wounded soon afterward while trying to escape, then executed. (See also KAMIAKIN.)

QUANAH. See PARKER, QUANAH.

QUEEN ANNE. See ANNE.

QUINKENT (Douglas, Douglass). *Ute. (b. 1819).* Band leader in the Ute War of 1879.

Quinkent was a Northern Ute who lived at the White River Reservation in northwestern Colorado. While Ute warriors under NICAAGAT and COLOROW engaged troops at the Battle of Milk Creek starting September 29, Quinkent and others remained at the White River Agency. Some among them killed the Indian agent NATHAN MEEKER and his white employees and kidnapped Meeker's wife Arvilla, and daughter Josephine, along with Mrs. F. S. Price, wife of the agency's carpenter. Mrs. Meeker claimed in secret hearings that Quinkent had raped her although no public charge was made. Nor could it be proven who had actually carried out the killings. Quinkent was imprisoned at Fort Leavenworth, Kansas, but was declared insane after a year, then sent back to his people. (See also OURAY.)

QUINNAPIN (Quinapen). *Narraganset. (d. 1676).* Sachem in King Philip's War of 1675–76. Nephew of MIANTINOMO; husband of WETAMOO.

In December 1675, during King PHILIP's War, Quinnapin, the fifth husband of Wetamoo, the so-called Squaw Sachem of Pocasset, participated in the Great Swamp Fight. He also took part in the attack on Lancaster, Massachusetts, of February 1676, where he purchased MARY ROWLANDSON from her captor. The English captured him on August 24, 1676, and executed him the next day at Newport, Rhode Island. (See also PHILIP.)

QUINNEY, JOHN WAUNNACON (Waun-na-con; Quinequan, "the dish"). *Stockbridge. (1797–1855).* Tribal lobbyist; principal chief.

John W. Quinney was born in New Stockbridge, New York, the second home of the Stockbridge Indians, mostly Mahicans, after they had relocated from Massachusetts under SAMSON OCCUM in 1786. The Quinney family played a central role in tribal affairs before and after John W. Quinney, the most famous among them.

Quinney was educated at white-run schools in New York and eventually became an ordained Presbyterian minister. He quickly rose to prominence among his people and participated in numerous negotiations on their behalf, concerning lands in New York and Wisconsin, where the Stockbridges eventually moved in 1822.

Quinney traveled to Washington, D.C., as a tribal delegate 10 times, his first trip in 1828. A member of his tribe's Indian Party, he lobbied for the repeal of an 1843 act that granted citizenship to tribal members and permitted the allotment of lands to individuals. Quinney wanted his people's federal status restored so that they could retain their traditional customs and form of government, which he accomplished in 1846. In this effort, he was opposed by JOHN C. ADAMS of the Citizen Party.

Quinney was elected principal chief in 1852. In 1856, the year after his death, his tribe merged with the Munsee band of Delawares.

QUINTIN (Quentin). *Pomo. (fl. 1820s).*
Lieutenant of MARIN.

Quintin, a subchief of the Pomo leader Marin, participated in the 1824 rebellion against Mexican troops. After his surrender, he was imprisoned at the San Francisco Presidio for two years. Upon release, he was hired by the priests of Mission Dolores as a pilot on a trading ship in San Francisco Bay. San Quentin is named after him. (See also MARIN.)

R

RADISSON, PIERRE ESPRIT. *(1636–1710).*
Explorer; trader; interpreter. Brother-in-law of
MEDARD CHOUART, SIEUR DES GROSEILLIERS.

Born in France, Pierre Esprit Radisson arrived in the
fur-trading center of Trois Rivieres, Quebec, in 1651. He
was taken captive by the Iroquois the next year, living
as an adoptive member of a Mohawk family until 1653.
During his captivity, he acquired his first knowledge of
Indian languages. On escape from the Iroquois, he spent
time among Dutch fur traders at Fort Orange (present-
day Albany, New York) as an interpreter.

Radisson returned to France in 1654, but soon sailed
again for Canada. Although he later claimed in his
writings to have accompanied his brother-in-law
Medard Chouart, Sieur des Groseilliers on an expedition to the western Great Lakes in 1654–56, it is thought
that only Groseilliers made the first journey.

In 1657, Radisson accompanied a party of Jesuit missionaries to the Iroquois headquarters at Onondaga,
near present-day Syracuse, New York, where he furthered his knowledge of the Iroquoian language and
also took part in a tribal "Dream Contest."

In 1659–60, Radisson and Groseilliers journeyed west
and explored the Lake Superior and Lake Michigan
region. During this time, they had contacts with the
Chippewas, Ottawas, and Potawatomis, as well as
probably the earliest white contacts with the Sioux.

In 1663, Radisson and Groseilliers transferred their
allegiance to the English. In 1668–69, they embarked on
an expedition to the Hudson Bay. Radisson's ship was
forced to turn back; Groseilliers established Fort Charles
at the mouth of the Rupert River in James Bay and
collected furs from the Chipewyan Indians.

In 1670, in England, Radisson gained the support of
merchants for a seaward expedition directly to the
western shore of Hudson Bay. The trading enterprise
was granted a charter as the Hudson's Bay Company.

In a second expedition to Hudson Bay, at the mouth of
the Nelson River in present-day eastern Manitoba,
Radisson established Fort Nelson.

In the early 1670s, Radisson was a leading force in the
Hudson's Bay Company's operations, serving its Nelson River and James Bay posts as interpreter and adviser on Indian relations. He subsequently returned to
serve French fur-trading interests in Quebec, also taking
part in French naval operations against the Hudson's
Bay Company.

In the mid-1680s, Radisson was again employed by
the Hudson's Bay Company, serving as director at the
company's post at Fort Nelson. In 1687, he retired from
the fur trade and settled in London, England.

RAIN-IN-THE-FACE (Iromagaja, Iromagaju, Amarazhu, "face raining"). *Hunkpapa Sioux.* *(ca. 1835–1905).* War chief in the Sioux Wars of the 1860s–70s.

Rain-in-the-Face was born at the forks of the
Cheyenne River in what is now North Dakota. His name
resulted from two incidents: the first, when he was 10,
was a fight with a Cheyenne boy in which he was
wounded and blood streaked down his face; the second,
as a teenager, was a fight with the Gros Ventres in which
rain smeared his warpaint. He earned his position in the
tribe through bravery in battle, not heredity.

During RED CLOUD's War for the BOZEMAN Trail
of 1866–68, Rain-in-the-Face was one of the leading war
chiefs along with the fellow Hunkpapa GALL and the
Oglala CRAZY HORSE in the FETTERMAN Fight in
Wyoming. In 1868, he participated in a raid on Fort
Totten, North Dakota, in which he was wounded.

In 1873, Rain-in-the-Face was arrested and imprisoned at Fort Abraham Lincoln in North Dakota for
the murder of a white surgeon, but one of his guards
helped him escape. He then joined SITTING BULL and

fought in the War for the Black Hills of 1876–77, probably including the Battle of Little Bighorn. He is one of the braves reputed for a time to have dealt the death blow to Colonel GEORGE ARMSTRONG CUSTER, although the matter has never been resolved.

Rain-in-the-Face surrendered in 1880 at Fort Keogh, Montana, after which he lived on the Standing Rock Reservation, North Dakota. In the course of his life, he had seven wives.

RALEIGH, WALTER (Walter Ralegh).
(ca. 1554–1618). Explorer; colonizer.

Walter Raleigh was born to a prominent family in Devon, England. He attended Oxford University briefly, and, in 1569, took part in military campaigns in France backing Protestant Huguenots. In 1578, he joined his half-brother Sir Humphrey Gilbert in a piratical expedition against Spanish ships. In 1580, he achieved stature in the court of Queen Elizabeth I for his triumphs in suppressing rebellions in Ireland. He was granted estates in Ireland, plus royal commercial licenses and monopolies, and was knighted in 1584.

That same year, 1584, Raleigh sponsored an expedition to the Americas, which reached the shores of present-day North Carolina. Upon the return of this expedition, Raleigh named the new lands "Virginia," in honor of Elizabeth, the "Virgin Queen."

In 1585, Raleigh commissioned Sir Richard Grenville to found a colony on the North Carolina coast. Grenville, with seven ships and more than 100 settlers, traveled to North Carolina, establishing a colony on the coastal island of Roanoke. Grenville departed for England later that same year, planning to return with additional supplies. Yet the colonists ran into trouble with the Indians; when Sir Francis Drake visited Roanoke in 1586, they all returned to England with him.

In 1587, Raleigh sent JOHN WHITE and 150 colonists to reestablish the Roanoke colony. White, an accomplished artist, produced watercolors depicting the Indians in the area. He returned to England, intending to bring back additional provisions for the colony, but his return was delayed by the naval war with Spain, highlighted by the battle with the Spanish Armada in 1588. No ships were available for the return voyage to the Roanoke colony until 1590, and when White did return to Roanoke in August of that year, he found no trace of the settlers. The only clue to what had happened was the enigmatic inscription "Croaton," carved into the bark of a tree.

During the mid-1590s, Raleigh explored the northwestern coast of South America in search of the fabled golden city of El Dorado, which had been described by the Indians of the Orinoco River region.

Raleigh's fortunes began to fade in 1603 with the ascendancy of James I. Becoming involved in political intrigues, he was found guilty of treason. While imprisoned from 1603 to 1616, he worked on a history of the world. He later undertook a second voyage of discovery to South America, but failed to find the elusive El Dorado in the Caribbean. He returned to England, where he still faced charges of treason. In 1618, he was again placed in custody and subsequently beheaded.

Through his indirect contact with the Indians of North America, Raleigh learned of tobacco smoking and helped popularize the practice in Europe. His expeditions to the Americas also brought back the potato, which became an important staple crop in the British Isles, especially in Ireland, where Raleigh had once been a major landowner.

RAMONA (Ramona Lubo or Lugo; Ramona Gonzaga Ortega or Ortegna). *Cahuilla (Kawia)*.
(ca. 1865–1922). Research informant; basket maker.

During a trip to Southern California, the reformer HELEN HUNT JACKSON met and interviewed the Cahuilla Indian Ramona (there is some confusion about her parents' name), who lived near the San Diego Mission. Jackson subsequently used her as a basis for the character in her novel *Ramona*, published in 1884. The fictionalized version of Ramona's life included an invented romance. Because of the book and a movie based on the story, the real Ramona became a local celebrity. She sold her baskets and photographs of herself at a souvenir stand. She was married to Juan Diego.

RANTCHEWAIME (Flying Pigeon). *Iowa*.
(d. ca. 1825). Visitor to Washington, D.C. Wife of MAHASKAH.

In 1824, Mahaskah, chief of the Iowas, departed for Washington, D.C., without any of his seven wives. Rantchewaime, the youngest of the seven, followed him as far as the Des Moines River to insist he take her on his journey. Rather than make the other six angry, he returned for them all. Their presence gained a great deal of attention during the visit. Because of her youth and beauty, Rantchewaime made a strong impression on those who met her. CHARLES BIRD KING painted her portrait along with Mahaskah's. Soon after their return to their homeland, Rantchewaime died in a fall from her horse. She left a son, Mahaskah the Younger. Mahaskah the Elder reportedly mourned her until his death in 1834.

RED BIRD (Wanig Suchka; Zitkaduta).
Winnebago. (ca. 1788–1828). Leader of the Winnebago Uprising of 1827.

Red Bird was born near Prairie du Chien, Wisconsin, at the fork of the Mississippi and Wisconsin rivers. Like his father, he grew up to become war chief of the Winnebagos living at Prairie La Crosse, to the north of

Prairie du Chien. It is thought that his adult name resulted from dessicated red birds he wore on his shoulders as epaulettes, or possibly because he wore a red coat.

During the 1820s, with lead prices rising, more and more miners poured into the Galena area where the Fever (Galena) River branches off from the Mississippi near the present-day Illinois-Wisconsin border. When the Winnebagos began digging and selling lead to white traders, government officials became concerned they would resist giving up their profitable land, and they ordered Indian agents to use their influence to prevent the practice.

In the spring of 1826, several warriors attacked and killed members of the Methode family of French Canadians in their maple sugar camp across the Mississippi from Prairie du Chien, at the fork of the Mississippi and Wisconsin rivers. In 1827, two warriors were arrested and charged with murder. A false rumor started by Sioux militants in Minnesota, that the Winnebago prisoners had been turned over to the Chippewas at Fort Snelling for their execution, reached Red Bird's village. Soon afterward, Red Bird, chosen by the tribal council to uphold his people's honor, led two of his braves, Wekau and Chickhonsic, in the arbitrary killing of a farmer, Registre Gagnier, and his hired hand Solomon Lipcap. Gagnier's infant daughter was scalped. Settlers and miners in the region, fearing other Indian reprisals, pressured officials to increase the number of garrisoned troops.

In June 1827, the only actual engagement of the Winnebago Uprising occurred, other than a few more isolated raids. Two Mississippi keelboats, returning from a delivery at Fort Snelling, stopped at a Winnebago village above Prairie du Chien. The boatman drank rum with the Indian men, then kidnapped several Indian women, forcing them onto the boats and raping them. Red Bird organized a rescue party, and his warriors set out for the boats. On June 30, several nights after the incident, at a narrow stretch of water near the mouth of the Bad Axe River, the Indians attacked simultaneously from the riverbank, from an island, and from canoes. Although they were repelled in their attempt to board one of the keelboats, the women captives managed to escape during the melee. Both sides lost several men, with four whites and approximately 12 Indians killed.

Troops converged on the Winnebago militants—from the south, federal regulars under General HENRY ATKINSON, Illinois volunteers sent by Governor Ninian Edwards, and volunteer miners; from the north, regulars out of Fort Snelling under Colonel Josiah Snelling. Officials, including Governor LEWIS CASS of the Michigan Territory and federal superintendent THOMAS McKENNEY, who had come to Wisconsin to negotiate with several tribes, worked to isolate the Winnebago militants. During the first two weeks of August, they met with the Winnebago peace faction—led by FOUR LEGS and NAWKAW—at Butte des Morts along the Fox River in eastern Wisconsin.

With the whites' show of force and the failure of the other Winnebago bands to join the uprising, Red Bird agreed to offer himself to the military to save his people. Expecting to be executed, he sang his death song while surrendering at the portage between the Wisconsin and Fox rivers. Six of his warriors were also arrested—two for the attack at Gagnier's farm and four for the attack on the keelboats—and imprisoned with him in the guardhouse of Fort Crawford at Prairie du Chien. Red Bird suffered through delay after delay in his trial. He died of dysentery while still waiting in early 1828. In the meantime, Nawkaw had traveled to Washington, D.C., to successfully lobby President John Quincy Adams for Red Bird's acquittal, which did not come in time. Because of lack of witnesses to the keelboat incident, the case against four of the Winnebagos was dropped, as was the earlier case against the two warriors accused in the attack on the Methode family. Wekau and Chickhonsic, Red Bird's lieutenants, were convicted, but later pardoned.

In August 1829, Winnebago leaders signed a treaty at Prairie du Chien ceding all tribal lands in Illinois and Wisconsin south of the Fox and Wisconsin rivers.

RED CLOUD (Mahpiua Luta, Makhpiya-luta Makhpia-sha, "scarlet cloud"). *Oglala Sioux.* *(ca. 1822–1909).* Principal chief; leader of the War for the BOZEMAN Trail (Red Cloud's War) of 1866–68.

Red Cloud was born near the forks of the Platte River in north-central Nebraska to Lone Man and his wife Walks as She Thinks; he had a twin brother named Roaring Cloud about whom little is known. Their father died soon after they were born; their maternal uncle helped raise them. Because of his bravery in battle and his leadership qualities, Red Cloud rose to head chief of the Iteshicha (Bad Face) band over the hereditary chief MAN-AFRAID-OF-HIS-HORSES, who became his lieutenant in battle. In the course of his career as a warrior, Red Cloud counted 80 coups, or separate acts of courage.

During the 1860s, the mining fever brought increased traffic to the lands of the western Sioux in Montana and Wyoming, violating the terms of the Fort Laramie Treaty of 1851. In 1862–63, after having traveled to Montana's gold fields, the explorer JOHN BOZEMAN followed a direct route through Teton lands west of the Bighorn Mountains to the Oregon Trail in Wyoming, then south to Colorado, rather than follow a circuitous route through Idaho. Other migrants and miners began to use this new route. In 1865, the government began to build a road from Fort Laramie, Wyoming, on the North Platte by way of the Powder River to Montana.

The various Teton bands—the Oglalas under Red Cloud, the Hunkpapas under SITTING BULL, and the Brules under SPOTTED TAIL—resented the trespassing through prime buffalo hunting grounds. So did their allies, including the Northern Cheyennes under DULL KNIFE and LITTLE WOLF, plus the Northern Arapahos under BLACK BEAR. In 1865, the Indians began attacking miners, wagon trains, and military patrols along both the Bozeman and the Oregon trails. On July 26, in an engagement at Platte Bridge Station along the North Platte stretch of the Oregon Trail, just west of the Bozeman branch, an allied Indian force wiped out a cavalry detachment under Lieutenant Caspar Collins. Accompanying Red Cloud were the Sioux Man-Afraid-of-His-Horses, the Northern Cheyenne Dull Knife, as well as the Southern Cheyennes ROMAN NOSE, CHARLES BENT, and GEORGE BENT, seeking revenge for the Sand Creek Massacre of BLACK KETTLE's band the year before.

In August 1865, General PATRICK E. CONNOR, commanding the Powder River Expedition, sent in three columns to punish the Indians. Their only success against the elusive insurgents, who attacked swiftly then disappeared into the wilderness, was the destruction of a camp of Northern Arapahos under Black Bear in the Battle of Tongue River on August 29.

Some of the chiefs rode into Fort Laramie in June 1866 to sign a nonagression treaty. Red Cloud insisted that no forts be built along the Bozeman, however. When the army refused to comply, he rode off with his warriors to make preparations for war.

Troops under Colonel HENRY B. CARRINGTON reinforced Fort Reno, Wyoming, and built two new posts to keep the Bozeman Trail open—Fort Phil Kearny, Wyoming, and Fort C. F. Smith, Montana. About 2,000 warriors besieged Fort Phil Kearny. The Indian guerrillas used hit-and-run tactics to harass the soldiers. Young warriors of various Teton bands allied under Red Cloud—CRAZY HORSE of the Oglalas, HUMP of the Miniconjous, and GALL and RAIN-IN-THE-FACE of the Hunkpapas—made use of decoy tactics. Their techniques proved disastrous for the cavalry. On December 21, 1866, a few Indians attacked a wood-cutting party, then fled. Captain WILLIAM FETTERMAN led his 80 men after them to their death at the hands of concealed warriors.

After the Fetterman Fight, the army sent in fresh troops with new breech-loading rifles. In the Hayfield Fight of August 1, 1867, near Fort C. F. Smith, and the Wagon Box Fight the next day near Fort Phil Kearny, the Sioux lost many warriors to these modern weapons, but they succeeded in driving the respective hay-cutting and wood-cutting parties back to their posts.

The Indians maintained the pressure. The federal government, realizing the high cost of maintaining the Bozeman forts, yielded to Red Cloud's demands. In the Fort Laramie Treaty, establishing the Great Sioux Reservation, the government agreed to abandon the posts in exchange for the cessation of Indian raids. When the army evacuated the region, the Indians celebrated by burning down the Bozeman forts. Red Cloud signed the treaty on November 6, 1868; the Sioux had won this round of warfare on the Great Plains.

In 1870, Red Cloud and Spotted Tail headed a delegation of Sioux, including AMERICAN HORSE, to Washington, D.C., to meet with President ULYSSES S. GRANT and his Seneca commissioner of Indian affairs, ELY PARKER. Red Cloud also visited New York City during this trip East and spoke at the COOPER Institute. Both Red Cloud and Spotted Tail made subsequent trips and proved effective negotiators. In 1873, agencies bearing their names were established in Nebraska.

In 1874, Colonel GEORGE ARMSTRONG CUSTER violated the terms of the new Fort Laramie Treaty by leading an expedition to the Black Hills to confirm rumors of gold. The subsequent influx of miners led to

Red Cloud. Photo by Edward Curtis. *Courtesy of National Archives of Canada/C-19768.*

a new round of violence, the War for the Black Hills of 1875–76 under Sitting Bull and other chiefs, notably Crazy Horse and Gall.

Despite his warriors' restlessness, Red Cloud advocated peace with whites. After the Indian victory at Little Bighorn in 1876, in which his son Jack and others from his band participated, government officials accused Red Cloud of secretly aiding the militants and appointed Spotted Tail principal chief at both agencies. That same year, the government relocated the Red Cloud and Spotted Tail Cloud agencies to South Dakota within the boundaries of the original Great Sioux Reservation, eventually renaming them the Pine Ridge and Rosebud agencies. Red Cloud and his followers moved to Pine Ridge in 1878.

In 1881, Red Cloud requested the dismissal of Indian agent TRANT VALENTINE McGILLICUDDY, but was himself deposed as chief at Pine Ridge. During the Ghost Dance Uprising of 1890 that swept the Sioux reservtions, he again spoke out in favor of peace and again failed to control his warriors.

Red Cloud, suffering from poor health in his final years and becoming blind, accepted baptism as a Roman Catholic. He died in 1909 in his home, which the government had built for him. His one wife of many years survived him.

RED CROW (Mekasto). *Blood. (ca. 1830–1900).* Principal chief. Brother-in-law of CROWFOOT.

Red Crow, the son of Black Bear, was born on the Belly River in present-day Alberta. As a young man, he participated in numerous raids on the Plains of Alberta, Saskatchewan, Montana, and Idaho. In 1870, he succeeded his father as principal chief of the Bloods, part of the Blackfoot Confederacy.

Red Crow generally cooperated with the Northwest Mounted Police in their efforts to maintain peace on the frontier. Yet he resented that his brother-in-law Crowfoot of the Blackfeet was given preferential treatment by JAMES MACLEOD of the Mounties and that the conference for the Canadian Treaty No. 7 was to be held in Blackfoot territory to the north of Blood lands. As a result, he did not show up until the fourth day and deliberated all night before signing with other chiefs—representing the Piegans, Sarcees, Chipewyans, and Assiniboines as well—on September 21, 1877.

On his Alberta reserve, Red Crow was the first to build a house, plant crops, and purchase cattle. His wives Singing First and Spear Woman were also the first Blood Indians to bake bread with yeast. He stressed the value of both modern education and traditional customs. When the Metis rebelled under LOUIS DAVID RIEL in 1885, Red Crow kept his warriors at peace. He drowned 15 years later while crossing the St. Mary River.

RED EAGLE. See WEATHERFORD, WILLIAM.

RED IRON (Mazasha). *Wahpeton Sioux. (ca. 1810–1884).* Friend to whites in the Minnesota Uprising of 1862–63. Brother of MAZOMANI.

Red Iron was about 35 when he became chief of his band at Traverse des Sioux on the Minnesota River at present-day Carver and St. Lawrence, Minnesota. Advocating peace with whites, he signed the Traverse des Sioux Treaty of 1851 ceding tribal lands in exchange for a reservation on the Upper Minnesota and an annuity. But he protested vehemently concerning an additional agreement in which a portion of the tribe's first annuity from the federal government was to be used to pay off old claims by traders, some of them fraudulent. As a result of a show of force over this issue, he was imprisoned for a day until his warriors disbanded.

Red Iron encouraged farming among his people and opposed the use of alcohol. He accompanied a delegation to Washington, D.C., in 1858, for negotiations in which the tribe ceded additional lands.

In the Minnesota Uprising of 1862–63 under LITTLE CROW, Red Iron refused to participate and offered protection to whites and Christian Indians. After the militants' surrender, he and AKIPA guarded the Indian prisoners for the government. Red Iron then worked as an Indian scout for the army until 1866. For his services he was given a tract of land west of Sisseton City, South Dakota, where he died. (See also LITTLE CROW.)

RED JACKET (Sagoyewatha, "he keeps them awake"). *Seneca. (ca. 1758–1830).* Ally of British in the American Revolution; spokesman. Nephew of HANDSOME LAKE; grandfather of ELY PARKER.

Red Jacket was born near the site of present-day Geneva, New York. At the beginning of the American Revolution, he spoke out for neutrality, but when the Senecas, Mohawks, Onondagas and Cayugas decided in council to support England, he joined the Seneca CORNPLANTER and the Mohawk JOSEPH BRANT in their efforts. He fought little, serving as a dispatch carrier, and was accused of cowardice by both Cornplanter and Brant. It was during this period he became known as Red Jacket because of the British army coat he wore.

After the war, Red Jacket became principal spokesman for the Senecas and at times for the entire Iroquois League of Six Nations. As such, he was present at Canadaigua in 1794 and at Big Tree in 1797 in which many of the Seneca lands were ceded, due largely to the influence of Cornplanter, leaving a number of small reservations. Along with other Iroquois chiefs, he visited President GEORGE WASHINGTON in Philadelphia in 1792 and received a large silver medal, which he later wore when his portrait was painted by

CHARLES BIRD KING for THOMAS McKENNEY's Indian Portrait Gallery in 1828.

Advocating the retention of Iroquois traditional customs, Red Jacket was adamant in his opposition to Christianity, calling for the ban of all missionaries from Seneca territory. He also opposed the Longhouse Religion founded by his uncle Handsome Lake. In 1801, Handsome Lake accused him of witchcraft, damaging his reputation. In 1824, Red Jacket and his traditionalist followers—the so-called "Pagan Party"—succeeded in expelling all Christian missionaries from Seneca reservations for a year.

Red Jacket's influence, under attack by the Christian Party, waned in following years, largely because of a drinking problem. In 1827, he was deposed as chief. His second wife, stepchildren, and many of his friends at Buffalo Creek, his home on Lake Erie, converted to Christianity that same year.

Red Jacket died three years later. Against his wishes, his wife let the local missionary give him a Christian burial. He was later reburied at Forest Lawn Cemetery in Buffalo when his grave—located on the Buffalo Reservation—became part of the city.

RED SHOES (Shulush Humma, Shulush Homa).
Choctaw. (ca. 1700–1746). Pro-British war chief.

Red Shoes, of Choctaw and possibly Chitimacha ancestry, lived in what is now Jasper County, Mississippi. As a young man, he fought as an ally of the French, who were trading partners of his people, against the Chickasaws, allies of the British. In 1734, after one of his wives had been raped by a Frenchman, Red Shoes switched his loyalty to the British, encouraging commerce with traders such as South Carolina's JAMES ADAIR, and became head of a faction supporting peace with the British allies, the Chickasaws. The French governor of Louisiana, Pierre Francois Rigaud, marquis de Vaudreuil, demanded the assassination of Red Shoes by his own people to prove Choctaw loyalty. In 1746, pro-French warriors attacked and killed him as he was returning from a trading trip. His death led to civil war between the two groups, referred to as the Choctaw Revolt and described in detail in the writings of EDMOND ATKIN, who was to become the first superintendent of Indian Affairs for the Southern Department.

RED WING (Koo-poo-hoo-sha; Tatankamani, Tatank'amini, "walking buffalo"). *Mdewakanton Sioux. (ca. 1750–1825).* Ally of British in the War of 1812.

Red Wing was the second in a series of chiefs of that name, taken from a family talisman of a swan's wing dyed scarlet. His father supported the British in the American Revolution. He followed suit and backed them in the War of 1812. On becoming disillusioned

with British strategy, Red Wing declared his neutrality and returned to his home on the upper Mississippi River in Minnesota, where he became known as a friend to settlers. The town of Red Wing is named after him. There were two other chiefs of that name to follow. The last was pressured by fellow Mdewakantons into participating in the Minnesota Uprising of 1862–63 under LITTLE CROW, then forced by whites to resettle in Nebraska, where the Red Wing name died out.

REMINGTON, FREDERIC. *(1861–1909).* Artist; writer.

Born in Canton, New York, Frederic Remington studied at the Yale School of Fine Arts and the Art Students League. When 19 years old, he traveled to the Montana Territory, partly for health reasons and partly to fulfill a desire for adventure. Over the next years, he pursued occupations as gold prospector, cowboy, sheepherder, and salonkeeper. He also accompanied the army on several of the last military campaigns against the Indians and worked as a war correspondent in the Spanish-American War, using Kansas as a base of operations.

Remington originally worked in black and white, selling his first drawings in Kansas City in 1884, but later turned to painting and sculpting. After 1885, he lived in New York, traveling West in the summers. His diverse experiences on the frontier provided material for more than 2,700 paintings and drawings, and 25 bronzes. His illustrations were published in numerous books, including HENRY WADSWORTH LONGFELLOW's *Song of Hiawatha* and FRANCIS PARKMAN's *The Oregon Trail*, as well as in periodicals. Many of his works featured the horse. He also wrote short stories about the frontier, as in the collections *Pony Tracks* (1895) and *Crooked Trails* (1898).

RENO, MARCUS ALBERT. *(1834–1889).* Army officer at the Battle of Little Bighorn.

Illinois native Marcus A. Reno graduated from West Point in 1857. He spent the early years of his military career with the 1st Dragoons regiment on the western frontier. With the onset of the Civil War, he rose quickly to the brevetted rank of major after having led troops in the Peninsula Campaign of 1862. Two years later, he became a brevet lieutenant colonel of volunteers for his service at the Battle of Cedar Creek, fought in Virginia. By the end of the war, Reno had been brevetted a brigadier general of a Pennsylvania volunteer regiment, and was also a brevet colonel in the regular army. Following the reorganization of the regular army, his rank reverted to that of major. He was posted as an instructor at West Point, and then was attached to the federal Freedmen's Bureau in New Orleans.

In late 1868, Reno was assigned as a major with the 7th Cavalry in Kansas, under the command of Colonel GEORGE ARMSTRONG CUSTER. In the War for the Black Hills of 1876–77, Custer's 7th Cavalry was part of General ALFRED TERRY's offensive against the Sioux and Cheyennes under SITTING BULL and CRAZY HORSE. Moving in advance of Terry's main column into the Bighorn country of what is now southeastern Montana, the 7th Cavalry discovered an Indian encampment along the Little Bighorn River. In June 1876, Custer sent three companies under Reno to attack the Indians' southern flank while he led a column to the north. Reno led his command across the river, but was repulsed by an overwhelming Indian force under GALL. Taking up position in front of bluffs, his soldiers were soon cut off by the warriors. They were joined by a third column under Captain FREDERICK W. BENTEEN and held out for two days until a relief force arrived under General Terry. Custer and one-third of the 7th Cavalry were surrounded by the Sioux and Cheyennes and were annihilated.

Reno's conduct at Little Bighorn was called into question, and he was accused of suddenly retreating and leaving half his command to die at the hands of the Sioux. In 1879, a military court of inquiry tried him for cowardice at the Department of the Missouri headquarters in Chicago. He was cleared of these charges but, the following year, faced a court-martial brought by his commanding officer, Colonel Samuel D. Sturgis, whose son had been killed in the battle. Reno was found guilty of minor charges not directly related to the engagement, and was dishonorably discharged from the army. He died in Wasington, D.C., in 1889.

In 1967, a military board of review reexamined the case and reversed Reno's conviction. His discharge was upgraded to honorable, and Reno was reburied at the Little Bighorn military cemetery alongside U.S. soldiers who died in other battles with Plains Indians. (See also SITTING BULL.)

RENVILLE, GABRIEL.   *Mixed Sisseton Sioux.*

(1824–1902). Friend to whites; army scout; principal chief. Nephew of JOSEPH RENVILLE.

Gabriel Renville was born at Big Stone Lake in Minnesota, the son of Victor Renville and nephew of Joseph. In the Renville family tradition, he was friendly to whites and an active Christian. During the Minnesota Uprising of Santees under LITTLE CROW in 1862–63, Renville, a member of a pro-white soldiers' lodge with AKIPA, CLOUDMAN, PAUL MAZAKUTEMANI, and MAZOMANI, used his influence to deter most Sissetons and Wahpetons from joining the Mdewakanton militants. He also helped form and was captain of a company of Indian scouts under General HENRY HASTINGS SIBLEY. In 1867, he traveled to

Washington, D.C., to negotiate the treaty creating the Sisseton Reservation in South Dakota. In 1884, Renville was elected principal chief of the Sisseton-Wahpeton band. (See also LITTLE CROW.)

RENVILLE, JOSEPH.   *Mixed Sisseton Sioux.*

(ca. 1779–1846). Guide; interpreter; trader; ally of British in War of 1812; translator. Uncle of GABRIEL RENVILLE.

Joseph Renville, the son of a French trader and a Mdewakanton Sioux mother, was born in the Indian village of Kaposia, south of present-day St. Paul, Minnesota. He grew up with his mother's Indian family until about age 10, when his father took him to Montreal to be educated by Catholics.

On returning home, Renville worked in the fur trade. When about 19, he was first employed by the Hudson's Bay Company. In 1805, he was guide and interpreter for Lieutenant ZEBULON PIKE and traveled with him to the mouth of the Minnesota River and the Falls of St. Anthony.

In the War of 1812, Renville was a captain under the British. He served as an interpreter to the Sioux, attending the council at Portage des Sioux in 1815. He lived in Canada during and after the war.

Renville returned to Minnesota to help found the Columbia Fur Company, which later merged with the American Fur Company. At his trading post at Lac Qui Parle—sometimes called Fort Renville—he planted crops and kept livestock. He also kept a company of armed Sioux and mixed-bloods to defend against Chippewas.

In 1834, Renville helped the Presbyterian reverend Thomas Williamson found a mission at Lac Qui Parle. Three years later, he aided Williamson and other missionaries in their translation of the Bible into the Siouan language. In 1841, he was made a ruling elder of the church.

Renville's influence extended to all the Sioux bands of the region. His descendants, including his son of the same name and his nephew Gabriel, played an important part in the history of the Sisseton Sioux.

REYNOLDS, CHARLES A.   (Lonesome Charley).

(1842–1876). Guide; army scout at the Battle of Little Bighorn.

The son of a prominent Illinois doctor, Charley Reynolds attended Abingdon College for a time, but traveled to Denver in 1860, working his way west as a teamster on a wagon train. During the Civil War, he enlisted in a Kansas volunteer regiment and saw action against the Confederates in the New Mexico campaign.

In the years after the war, Reynolds worked as a professional hunter, providing meat for army garrisons on the Northern Plains. In 1872–73, he served as a guide for General David S. Stanley's two expeditions into the Yellowstone River region. Reynolds met Colonel GEORGE ARMSTRONG CUSTER in 1873, and, the following year, was hired as Custer's guide in his Black Hills expedition. In the summer of 1874, he delivered Custer's report of the discovery of gold in the Black Hills to the telegraph office at Fort Laramie, Wyoming, successfully making this five-day, 100-mile journey through the heart of hostile Sioux country alone.

In 1876, Reynolds again scouted for Custer, leading the 7th Cavalry out of Fort Abraham Lincoln, in the Dakota Territory, to take part in the major summer offensive against warriors under SITTING BULL, GALL and CRAZY HORSE. On June 25, 1876, Reynolds was assigned to lead Major MARCUS A. RENO and his detachment of troops in an attack on the Indian encampment along the Little Bighorn River. When Sioux warriors counterattacked in overwhelming numbers, Reno ordered a sudden retreat, which resulted in nearly half of his men being cut off by attacking Sioux and Cheyennes. Reynolds was among those surrounded and killed by the Indians in this initial action. (See also SITTING BULL.)

RIBAULT, JEAN (Jean Ribaut). *(ca. 1520–1565).*
Explorer; colonizer.

Born in Dieppe, France, Jean Ribault became a leading naval captain in the French fleet under the command of Admiral Gaspard de Coligny. In 1562, under Coligny's sponsorship, Ribault undertook a voyage to North America to establish a haven for French Huguenots. Accompanied by fellow Huguenot RENE DE LAUDONNIERE and the artist JACQUES LE MOYNE, Ribault led an expedition of three ships and 150 colonists to the east coast of Florida. In May 1562, they arrived at the mouth of the St. Johns River near present-day Jacksonville and claimed the territory for France. To mark the occassion, Ribault had a ceremonial column built at the site of their landing at the mouth of the St. Johns River, which subsequently became an object of worship for the Timucua Indians.

Ribault then sailed north to the coast of present-day South Carolina where, on what is now Parris Island, he established his colony, Charlesfort. Leaving Laudonniere in charge, he returned to France to seek additional support but was soon embroiled in the religious wars between the Catholics and the Protestant Huguenots. He fled to England, where he was imprisoned for a short time on refusing to undertake a joint French and English colonial venture in Florida. While in England, he wrote an account of his experiences in North America, *The Whole and True Discovery of Terra Florida* (1563), including accounts of the Cusabo, Saturiba, Tacatacura, and Timucua Indians.

Laudonniere abandoned the Parris Island settlement when Ribault failed to return. In 1564, he established a second colony at the St. Johns river site on the Florida coast, called Fort Caroline. Spanish authorities, fearing Protestant encroachment into their new colonial empire, dispatched PEDRO MENENDEZ DE AVILES and a large force to remove the French. Ribault returned to Florida with a naval force and planned an attack on Menendez's settlement at St. Augustine. His ships were wrecked in a storm and he and his men took refuge on the Florida coast south of St. Augustine.

Meanwhile, Menendez and his men marched on the French at Fort Caroline, killing most of the Huguenot inhabitants. Menendez next attacked Ribault and his shipwrecked party, capturing and executing them.

RIDDLE, TOBY. See WINEMA.

RIDGE, JOHN. *Mixed Cherokee. (1803–1839).*
Member of the Treaty Party. Son of MAJOR RIDGE; cousin of ELIAS BOUDINOT and STAND WATIE.

John Ridge was born at Rome, Georgia, the son of Major Ridge and Susie Wickett. Along with his cousins Elias Boudinot and Stand Watie, he attended the Cornwall Foreign Mission School in Connecticut, where he met his wife, Sarah Bird Northrup.

On returning to Georgia, Ridge became a tribal leader. He wrote for the *Cherokee Phoenix* and served as interpreter and secretary on several tribal delegations to Washington, D.C.

Like his father, Ridge accepted the federal government's policy of relocation to the Indian Territory as inevitable and signed the Treaty of New Echota in 1835. In this they were opposed by the tribe's antiremoval faction led by JOHN ROSS. In 1836, Ridge wrote a letter to President ANDREW JACKSON, protesting the harsh oppression of his people by citizens of Georgia. After the Trail of Tears, Ridge was murdered in the Indian Territory, along with his father and Boudinot, by members of the Ross Party. His son, John Rollin Ridge, became a successful journalist. (See also ROSS, JOHN.)

RIDGE, MAJOR (Nunna Hidihi, "man on the mountaintop"; The Ridge). *Mixed Cherokee. (ca. 1770–1839).*
Ally of Americans in the Creek War; speaker of Cherokee Council; member of the Treaty Party.
Father of JOHN RIDGE; uncle of ELIAS BOUDINOT and STAND WATIE.

The Ridge was born at Hiwassee, Tennessee, then moved to Georgia with his family. He was educated by relatives and neighbors and was elected to the Cherokee Council when 21, eventually becoming the speaker because of his oratorical ability. He received the title "major" during the Creek War of 1813–14 as an ally of General ANDREW JACKSON. He and his son John by Susie Wickett (Princess Sehoya), as well as his nephew Elias Boudinot, were the foremost members of the Treaty Party in opposition to the anti-removal Ross Party headed by JOHN ROSS. The three signed the Treaty of New Echota in 1835 and, after relocation to the Indian Territory, were killed by their opponents. (See also ROSS, JOHN.)

RIEL, LOUIS (Louis Riel, Sr.). *Metis. (1817–1864).* Leader of the Courthouse Rebellion of 1849. Father of LOUIS DAVID RIEL.

The part-Ojibway Louis Riel was a community leader in the Red River region of what is now Manitoba. He was referred to as the "miller of the Seine" by fellow Metis. With plans to start a woolen factory, he had a nine-mile channel dug from the Red River to the Seine Creek for increased flow on his mill wheel. But the Hudson's Bay Company discouraged industry, which would increase settlement and lessen their hold on the region's fur-trading economy, and enacted regulations that made it difficult for Riel to conduct his business.

The company also tried to regulate Metis fur trading, prohibiting commerce with Americans. Since southern trade with merchants in St. Paul, Minnesota, was essential to Metis survival, Riel and other Metis leaders protested. In 1849, the Hudson's Bay Company brought the Metis Guillaume Sayer to trial for attempting to smuggle his furs across the border. Riel led 300 armed Metis on the Fort Garry (present-day Winnipeg) courthouse and threatened violence. As a result, the jury found Sayer guilty, but recommended his release.

Riel's son Louis David Riel by Julie Lagimodiere continued the struggle for Metis rights in the Riel Rebellions of 1869 and 1885.

RIEL, LOUIS DAVID (Louis Riel, Jr.). *Metis. (1844–1885).* Leader of the Riel (Metis) Rebellions. Son of LOUIS RIEL.

Louis Riel was born along the Seine River at St. Boniface, Red River Settlement (now Manitoba), the son of the French-Ojibway Louis Riel and the French Julie Lagimodiere. He was baptized with the same name as his father, but later added David.

At seven, Riel began studies under the Grey Sisters at St. Boniface. At 13, he received a scholarship to attend the seminary of the Gentlemen of St. Sulpice in Montreal, Quebec, studying French, Latin, Greek, math, philosophy, and the sciences. By the age of 19, he was writing poetry. It was expected he would enter the priesthood, but he never completed his education. Riel quit the seminary in March 1865, just before the end of the term, then left Montreal a year later, in June 1866. The death of his father in 1864, his growing impatience with his teachers, and his rejection by the parents of a white girl he had hoped to marry all contributed to his decision to depart. On his way home, over a two-year period, Riel worked odd jobs in Chicago and St. Paul. Arriving home in July 1868, he became involved in the First Riel Rebellion within a year, also known as the First Metis or the Red River Rebellion.

The French word *metis* for "mixed blood," when used with a lower-case *m*, refers to all peoples with mixed racial ancestry. When used with a capital *M*, however, it refers to a particular group of economically and politically unified people with a special place in Canadian history. Most of the Metis were of French-Cree ancestry; some were Scotch-Cree. Some among them had a parent or grandparent from another Indian tribe, such as the Ojibways (Chippewas), as was the case in the Riel lineage. The white traders who traveled the wilderness in search of furs came to associate with the Indians, their main suppliers of pelts. The men who paddled the trading canoes through the western wilderness for the big fur companies were known as *voyageurs*; those who were independent and unlicensed traders were referred to as *coureurs de bois*. The mixed-blood children of both

Louis David Riel. *Courtesy of National Archives of Canada/C-6688.*

were the Metis, many of whom eventually came to work the same jobs their parents did. By the 19th century, the Metis had developed a unique life-style with elements from both the white and Indian ways of life, speaking French as well as Algonquian dialects, and practicing Catholic and Indian rituals. They farmed and lived in frame houses part of the year, and hunted and lived in tepees the rest.

The Metis of present-day Manitoba led their ox-drawn carts laden with pelts along the Red River of the North valley on annual trips to St. Paul, Minnesota, for trade with the Americans; it is estimated that some years 2,000 different Metis caravans made the long trek. The Metis had had to fight for this right to unrestricted trade. Louis Riel's father had led the Courthouse Rebellion of 1849, demonstrating at Winnipeg with a force of men for the release of a fellow Metis arrested by officials for smuggling goods across the border.

The First Riel Rebellion involved both freedom of trade and land rights. In 1867, the various Canadian colonies united into a Confederation, with a centralized government at Ottawa, that had new independent Dominion status in its relations with its parent country, England. Two years later, the Hudson's Bay Company sold their land holdings—the vast Rupert's Land—to the new Confederation government, which encouraged settlement by Canadians to counter the threat of 800,000 veterans of the United States' Civil War, hungry for land.

Settlers began streaming into the Red River of the North region. Among them were Canada Firsters, led by Dr. John Christian Schultz, annexationist members of the Canada Party. Being Protestant Orangemen, prejudiced against French, Catholics, and Indians, they were insensitive to Metis land rights. The Dominion's first prime minister, JOHN MACDONALD, sent surveyors under Captain Adam Webb to section off square townships of 800 acres apiece. The Metis, however, had always laid out their lands in strips along the river's edge, each lot extending back through stands of woods to fertile fields and then to community-held prairie for livestock grazing. Riel and 16 other Metis drove off the outsiders in October 1869.

Meanwhile, Macdonald's choice as the new territorial governor, William McDougall, was approaching the Red River from Ottawa via Minnesota with a small party. They carried 300 rifles to arm a militia. Louis Riel organized the Comite National des Metis, sent a force of 40 armed men to barricade the border, and led a force of 400 in a bloodless takeover of Fort Garry at Winnipeg. Riel's lieutenant was AMBROISE LEPINE, famous as a hunter and tracker. Riel also issued a List of Rights, including the rights to land, to a voice in the Confederation government, to prior consultation for any decisions pertaining to the Red River country, and to freedom of language and religion.

Despite attempts by McDougall to recruit and arm a militia of Canada Firsters and Salteaux Ojibways, the central government decided to negotiate. Riel and a force of 200 surrounded and forced the surrender of the militia under Colonel John Dennis, McDougall's aide. By the end of December, McDougall had departed the region and the Comite had proclaimed itself a provisional government. Macdonald sent in Donald Smith of the Hudson's Bay Company to meet with the Metis and convince them of the Dominion's fair intentions. The Metis organized a representative government and, in February 1870, elected Riel, then only 25-years-old, president. Riel declared a state of amnesty and released all prisoners. One of them, Thomas Scott, began plotting a Firster attack on Fort Garry, but was intercepted by Lepine and a party of Metis. In a subsequent trial, Scott was sentenced to death by a jury of seven Metis. Riel, who had acted as a prosecution witness, supported the decision, believing it would demonstrate Metis determination and authority. Scott was executed, which turned public sentiment against Riel.

Ottawa passed the Manitoba Act in July 1870, making the Red River area a province and guaranteeing most of the Metis List of Rights, but not amnesty for Scott's death and other actions during the rebellion. In August 1870, the government sent a constabulary force of 1,200 under Colonel Garnet Wolseley, many of whom sought to avenge Scott's death, whereupon Riel fled to the United States. Elected in absentia to the Canadian parliament twice, he was denied his seat and banished from Canada. In 1875, he was pardoned for the rebellion on the condition that he remain in exile five more years. On returning to Canada, from 1876 to 1878, he was committed to mental institutions in Quebec. Upon his release, he went to Keeseville, New York. Eventually becoming a United States citizen, he moved to Montana to teach Indian children in a Jesuit mission school in the Judith Basin, now under the name David Riel.

In the meantime, white Protestants continued to settle Metis lands in violation of the Manitoba Act. Having lost much of what they had fought for, many Metis decided to move westward to the Saskatchewan River, near the buffalo of the Great Plains. Yet the Dominion government was sponsoring the building of the Canadian Pacific Railway linking the East and West coasts. In the 1880s, white settlers sought lands along the Saskatchewan River. Metis rights were again ignored.

The Metis sought Riel's help to lead another struggle for Metis rights to land and freedom of religion. They sent the famed horseman and buffalo hunter, GABRIEL DUMONT, to locate him. In June 1884, Riel agreed to return to Canada to lead the resistance, on the condition the Metis avoid violence.

On his arrival, Riel began preaching to both Metis and Anglos of his divine purpose, using an eclipse of the sun to convince nonbelievers. He also drafted a bill of rights, formed the Provisional Government of the Saskatchewan, and helped Dumont organize the Metis into an efficient cavalry force of some 300 men. When Metis appeals were still ignored, Riel gave his approval for a campaign of sabotage—occupying government property, taking hostages, and cutting telegraph lines. The Metis also sent an ultimatum to the Mounties at Fort Carlton, demanding the surrender of the post in exchange for safe conduct from the region. The Second Riel Rebellion, also known as the Second Metis Rebellion and the North-West Rebellion, had begun.

In spite of Riel's wish for a nonviolent campaign, the situation escalated. At Duck Lake on March 26, 1885, Dumont's men routed a force of Mounties under Leif Crozier. Some of the Cree Indian bands joined the Metis cause: POUNDMAKER led his band in an attack on Battleford on March 28; BIG BEAR's warriors raided Frog Lake on April 2.

The government used the new railroad to send in 8,000 troops, the North West Field Force, from the East. By mid-April, all units had reached their staging points west of Winnipeg. Three battalions moved on the rebels: General Frederick Middleton led a force on Metis headquarters at Batoche; farther west, Colonel William Otter headed for Battleford besieged by Crees; and General Thomas Strange advanced via Calgary toward the Edmonton area.

On April 24, Dumont's men routed Middleton's column at Fish Creek. Taking up position in rifle pits at the bottom of a depression and firing upward at the soldiers, who were silhouetted in plain view at the top of a rise and unable to use their artillery because of the steep angle, the rebels killed or wounded about 50 while suffering only 10 casualties. The same day, Otter's force relieved Battleford, then headed for the Cree camp at Cut Knife Creek. On May 9, Dumont and his men knocked out of commission the *Northcote*, a riverboat converted by government troops into a gunboat, by stringing cable across the South Saskatchewan River, then firing on it. Starting that same day at Batoche, Metis rebels were pinned down by the much larger and better-equipped government force. During much of the engagement, the two sides exchanged only sniper fire. When General Middleton wavered in the decision to order a bayonet charge, Colonel A. T. H. Williams forced his hand by ordering his own attack. Although Middleton ordered a recall, the soldiers ignored the signal, forcing him to send in more troops. The Metis retreated from trench to trench, now firing nails, metal buttons and stones.

By the evening of the fourth day, the Metis finally surrendered. They had suffered 16 dead and 30 wounded; federal troops had lost eight men, with 46 wounded. Riel managed to slip through enemy lines and hide out for three days in nearby woods before turning himself in to a scouting party. After a week in camp, he was taken by steamer to Saskatoon, then by wagon and train to the territorial capital of Regina.

Riel's trial began on July 28. After five days, he was sentenced to death for the murder of Thomas Scott 15 years before, as well as for crimes against the state. His lawyers appealed to Ottawa for clemency. French Catholics voiced their support for him. Dumont organized relay stations for an escape attempt that never materialized. Riel probably could have saved his life by pleading insanity, but he refused to denounce his actions. His execution by hanging was carried out on November 16, 1885, just nine days after the transcontinental railroad was finished. Riel's body was buried in the yard of St. Boniface at Winnipeg. Dumont escaped to the United States. Big Bear and Poundmaker, who by now had also surrendered, were sentenced to jail terms; other Crees were executed.

Metis power and culture were broken. Saskatchewan became an Anglo-dominated province, as Manitoba had earlier. To the Metis, as well as to Catholics all over Canada, Riel was a martyr to their religion and cause.

RIGGS, STEPHEN RETURN. *(1812–1883).* Missionary; linguist.

Originally from Steubenville, Ohio, Stephen Riggs received his early education at the Latin School in Ripley, Ohio. Continuing his studies at Jefferson College and the Western Theological Seminary, he was licensed to preach by the Presbyterian Church at Chillicothe, Ohio, in 1836. He spent the following year as a minister in Hawley, Massachusetts.

In 1837, Riggs received an appointment as a missionary to the Santee Sioux at the Presbyterian mission station, Lac Qui Parle, on the upper Minnesota River, in what is now western Minnesota. While administering at Lac Qui Parle and Traverse des Sioux, he learned Siouan dialects. Starting in 1846, he conducted educational work among the Sioux, producing primers and translations of religious writings in the Siouan language.

In 1854, Riggs helped the Santees, including PAUL MAZAKUTEMANI and CLOUDMAN, organize under a constitutional government, which became known as the Hazelwood Republic. In 1858, when the state of Minnesota was first organized, he petitioned the new government to grant citizenship status to the Indians, but his efforts met with no success. In 1861, he represented eight Sioux who had brought action in the local district court seeking the full rights and privileges of citizens, but the judge refused to hear the case on the grounds that the Indians could not speak English, even though Riggs acted as an interpreter for them.

During the Minnesota Uprising of Santee Sioux under LITTLE CROW in 1862–63, Riggs's life was spared through the efforts of his converts. After the army had suppressed the rebellion, Riggs continued to work on behalf of those Sioux who had been taken prisoner by the military. He traveled with the Sioux prisoners when they were relocated to the upper Missouri River, and also lobbied in Washington, D.C., on their behalf.

In the early 1870s, Riggs settled in Beloit, Wisconsin, where he continued to work on biblical translations and reference works. His Dakota-English dictionary was published after his death, in 1890.

RINDISBACHER, PETER. *(1806–1834).* Artist.

In 1821, Peter Rindisbacher and his family emigrated from Switzerland to western Canada to join the Red River colony established by the Earl of Selkirk, located in the vicinity of present-day Winnipeg, Manitoba. As a teenager, he executed many sketches of the Indians and fauna of north central Canada, some of which he developed into watercolors. His *Inside of a Skin Tent* is one of the earliest drawings of a tepee by a white artist.

After the abandonment of the Red River colony because of starvation and a disastrous flood, Rindisbacher moved first to Wisconsin with his family in 1826, then settled permanently at St. Louis in 1829. There he established a studio where he produced illustrations for magazines. In 1833, he completed his most famous scene, *Blackfeet Hunting on Snowshoes*. One of his drawings, *The Buffalo Hunt*, was used as a frontispiece for the first volume of *History of the Indian Tribes of North America* (1837) by THOMAS McKENNEY and JAMES HALL.

Rindisbacher died when only 28. He is known to have completed 124 artworks; 40 are in the National Archives of Canada.

ROBERTSON, JAMES. *(1742–1814).* Explorer; soldier; Indian agent.

Born in Brunswick County, Virginia, James Robertson was raised in North Carolina. In 1770, he traveled west into what is now Tennessee on behalf of the Watauga Association, a syndicate of colonial land speculators, including JOHN SEVIER. In the upper Tennessee River Valley, Robertson negotiated with the local Cherokees for the leasing of lands to whites in order to circumvent the restrictions placed on colonists against settlement beyond the Proclamation Line of 1763. In 1771, he led the first settlers into Tennessee's Watauga country.

For the next three years, Robertson was a leader of the settlement and acted as diplomat to the Cherokees. His efforts in this regard kept the Cherokees neutral during Lord DUNMORE's War of 1774 against the Shawnees in the Ohio country to the north. Robertson saw action in this conflict under Colonel ANDREW LEWIS and his colonial militia.

During the American Revolution, Robertson helped defend Fort Watauga from attacks by DRAGGING CANOE's Cherokees and other bands allied with the British and Tories.

In 1779, Robertson explored the Columbia River country for Richard Henderson's Transylvania Company, as DANIEL BOONE had done four years earlier, leading a band of settlers through the Cumberland Gap. The next year, he founded the settlement of Nashborough, which developed into modern-day Nashville, Tennessee.

After the Revolutionary War, Robertson was a leading force in early Tennessee politics, and at one point sought an alliance with the Spanish, considering them better able to protect the Tennessee settlements from Indian attacks. He went on to serve in the North Carolina legislature, and, along with Sevier, was instrumental in the organization of Tennessee as a state. Following statehood, Robertson remained active in politics. He also served as Indian agent to the Chickasaws.

ROBIDOUX, ANTOINE. *(1794–1860).* Trader; trapper.

Antoine Robidoux, of French-Canadian descent, settled in New Mexico in 1822, where he embarked on a career as a trader out of Santa Fe and Taos. Two years later, he began trapping in the southwestern Rockies and on the Southern Plains, establishing frontier trading posts, including Fort Uncompahgre on the Gunnison River in southwestern Colorado, and Fort Uintah (Robidoux Rendezvous) on the Uintah River in northeastern Utah. He was joined in his enterprise at various times by his five brothers: Joseph, Francois, Louis, Michel, and Isidore.

In 1844, at Fort Uintah, Robidoux introduced whiskey to the local Utes. Before long, the Utes had attacked and destroyed Robidoux's forts in both Colorado and Utah.

In the Mexican War of 1846–48, Robidoux served as an interpreter for Colonel STEPHEN WATTS KEARNY's campaigns into New Mexico and California. During the California campaign, Robidoux was wounded, but recovered. He eventually retired to St. Joseph, Missouri, a settlement established as a trading post by his brother Joseph.

ROBINSON, ALEXANDER (Cheecheebingway, Cheecheepinquay, Tshee-tsee-beeng-guay, Che-Che-Pinqua). *Potawatomi-Mixed Ottawa.* *(1789–1872).* Peacemaker; interpreter.

Alexander Robinson, the son of a Scottish trader of the same name and an Ottawa woman, was born at

Mackinac, Michigan. Through marriage to Catherine Chevalier, part-French and part-Potawatomi, he became involved in Potawatomi tribal affairs. With other mixed-bloods, such as SAGAUNASH (Billy Caldwell), Francois Bourbonnais, Francois Chevalier, and Claude La Framboise, he rose to prominence within the tribe.

Witnessing the Battle of Fallen Timbers in LITTLE TURTLE's War of 1790–94, at the age of five, made a lasting impression on Robinson, and he worked for peace as an adult. During the War of 1812, after the taking of Fort Dearborn (present-day Chicago), in which he did not participate, Robinson tried to prevent the massacre of the garrison and carried some whites to safety across Lake Michigan in his canoe.

In 1820, Robinson served as interpreter for LEWIS CASS in negotiations with the Chippewas. In the 1829 Treaty of Prairie du Chien, Wisconsin, he was granted two square miles of land on the Des Plaines River in Illinois. During the BLACK HAWK War of 1832, Robinson sided with the whites. When most Potawatomis were forced to relocate to Kansas in 1838, Robinson remained behind, as did fellow chiefs TOPENEBEE and LEOPOLD POKAGON.

ROGERS, ROBERT. *(1731–1795)*. Army officer in the French and Indian War of 1754–63; frontiersman; trader; writer.

Robert Rogers was born in Methuen, Massachusetts, and raised in the frontier regions of New Hampshire. His first fight with Indians occurred in 1746, repelling a raid near his home. In 1755, he was implicated in a counterfeiting incident, but avoided legal penalties by volunteering for service in the colonial militia then involved in the French and Indian War.

Rogers served as a scout with forces under WILLIAM JOHNSON at the attack on Crown Point, near Lake Champlain, New York, in 1755, and later was promoted to captain of a company of Rangers. Rogers's Rangers, as his command came to be known, was made up of frontier mercenaries with extensive knowledge of Indian-style fighting techniques, including the taking of scalps and the torturing of prisoners. The Rangers were also accustomed to living in the wilderness for extended periods without the lines of supply required by a conventional military force. They proved valuable as scouts and as an advance strike force against the French and their Indian allies in the campaigns in the Champlain Valley of New York.

By 1757, Rogers was a major in command of nine companies of Rangers and took part in the British attack on Halifax, Nova Scotia, that year. In 1758, he was part of the unsuccessful British attempt by General James Abercromby to take Fort Ticonderoga on Lake Champlain. When the French and their Indian allies captured Fort William Henry at the south end of Lake George, Rogers reportedly

eluded capture at the hands of the Abnaki Indians by making a daring leap from a high point above the lake, a site now known as Rogers' Rock.

In 1759, with British regulars under General JEFFREY AMHERST, Rogers's Rangers helped capture Fort Ticonderoga from the French. From this base and also from nearby Crown Point, Rogers staged raids against the French-allied Algonquian tribes of northern New England. In September-October 1759, he attacked the Abnaki Indians of the Canadian settlement at St. Francis, losing nearly half of the 180 men. Nevertheless, the Rangers killed about 200 Indians, thus curtailing raids on colonists in Maine and New Hampshire. Rogers also took part in the British attack on Quebec under General JAMES WOLFE in 1759.

Following the end of major hostilities in 1760, Amherst sent Rogers to accept the surrender of the French garrisons at Detroit and other Great Lakes posts. Rogers encountered Ottawas, Hurons, and Potawatomis, including the Ottawa leader PONTIAC, during his trip west.

Rogers became a trader and administrator at frontier posts in New York and South Carolina. His questionable business practices soon led to problems with colonial authorities and an overwhelming personal debt.

In the summer of 1763, during Pontiac's Rebellion, Rogers was part of the force dispatched from Fort Niagara on Lake Erie to relieve the British under attack at Detroit by Pontiac and his allies. He crossed Lake Erie with a company of Rangers and covered the British retreat at the Battle of Bloody Run in August.

In 1765, Rogers traveled to London, where he published his *Journals* and *A Concise Account of North America* about his military experiences. The next year, he wrote and produced a play about Pontiac—*Ponteach: or, The Savages of America*—in which he depicted the nobility of the Ottawa chief in contrast with the duplicity and corruption of whites trading with the Indians. It was the first use of an Indian as a major character in a dramatic work, and was a source for historian FRANCIS PARKMAN's later depiction of Pontiac.

Rogers returned to North America in 1767, where he took charge of the Indian trade at the Great Lakes trading center at Michilimackinac in present-day Michigan. From that post, he sponsored the exploratory expedition of JOHATHAN CARVER into present-day Minnesota in search of the Northwest Passage. Rogers's illegal trading practices and mismanagement soon drew the attention of his former commander, the Indian superintendent William Johnson, who had him removed.

In 1769, Rogers, again in England, was imprisoned for debt. On returning to North America at the outbreak of the Revolutionary War in 1775, he was arrested on GEORGE WASHINGTON's orders as a Loyalist spy. He escaped and raised a company of Loyalist Rangers, who fought the patriots in present-day Westchester County in various engagements, including the Battle of White Plains in 1776, but had little success in the field. Discredited by accusations of dishonesty and dissipation, Rogers returned to England, where he died in poverty. (See also PONTIAC.)

ROLFE, JOHN. (1585–ca. 1622). Farmer; trader; colonial official. Husband of POCAHONTAS.

The Englishman John Rolfe arrived at the Jamestown settlement in the Virginia colony in 1610. Experimenting with Spanish types of tobacco seed, which had been brought to Europe from the Americas by Spanish and Portuguese in the previous century, by 1612 he had produced a tobacco crop and developed a practical method of curing it. Tobacco became a commodity integral to the economic development of Virginia, and its cultivation led to increased demands for Indian lands.

In 1614, the widower Rolfe married Pocahontas, daughter of Chief POWHATAN, thus helping promote peaceful relations between colonists and the Powhatan Confederacy for the next eight years. Rolfe and Pocahontas traveled to England in 1616, where she became ill and died the following year.

Rolfe returned to Jamestown, remarried, and was appointed to several colonial administrative positions. It is believed that he was killed in the uprising of tribes in the Powhatan Confederacy in 1622, led by OPECHANCANOUGH, an uncle of Pocahontas. (See also POCAHONTAS; POWHATAN.)

ROMAN NOSE (Woquini, Waquini, Wokini, "hook nose"; Sautie, Sauts, "bat"). Southern Cheyenne. (1830–1868). Leader in the Plains Indian wars of the 1860s.

Roman Nose was a member of the Crooked Lance Society. There is uncertainty over whether he was a chief. In any case, in the wars with whites, he became a prominent warrior and in battle commanded the respect of a war chief. Whites of his time credited him with leading the Cheyennes in more battles than he actually fought. Although he was possibly born among the Northern Cheyennes, he established his place in history among the Southern branch of the tribe.

The massacre at Sand Creek of BLACK KETTLE's peaceful band during the Cheyenne-Arapaho (or the Colorado) War of 1864–65 confirmed the militance of many of the Cheyenne chiefs. Roman Nose fought in the Battle of Platte Bridge of July 1865 along with Sioux under RED CLOUD, plus Northern Cheyennes and Northern Arapahos, at the start of the War for the BOZEMAN Trail, wiping out a cavalry detachment

under Lieutenant Caspar Collins. In 1866, he traveled south to fight alongside the Southern Cheyenne chiefs of the famous Dog Soldiers military society, such as BULL BEAR, TALL BULL, and WHITE HORSE.

In the spring of 1867, Roman Nose was present at the Fort Larned Council with General WINFIELD SCOTT HANCOCK. Believing that Hancock wanted to force a fight, Roman Nose declared to the Dog Soldiers his intention to kill him, but was dissuaded by Tall Bull and Bull Bear. During the summer of 1867, Roman Nose and the Dog Soldiers, carrying out numerous raids along the Kansas frontier, especially on wagon trains and railroad work parties, managed to stay one step ahead of GEORGE ARMSTRONG CUSTER's 7th Cavalry, part of the Hancock Campaign. In August 1867, Roman Nose led his warriors in the defeat of the cavalry unit under Captain G. A. Armes near Prairie Dog Creek, Kansas.

Roman Nose attended the preliminary talks for the Medicine Lodge Council of October 1867. Yet he refused to participate in the council itself or the signing of the treaty.

Because of renewed Cheyenne raids during the summer of 1868, Major GEORGE FORSYTH and a company of 50 scouts, part of the Sheridan Campaign under General PHILIP H. SHERIDAN, headed into the country of the upper Republican River to locate the hostile Cheyenne, Sioux, and Arapaho bands.

On September 16, Forsyth's men set up camp on the north bank of the Arikaree branch of the Republican, near a camp where Cheyennes under Roman Nose, Bull Bear, Tall Bull, and White Horse, plus Sioux under PAWNEE KILLER, were present. Indian scouts spotted the detachment, and, early the next morning, six braves tried to steal the army's horse herd. They captured only a few mounts and alerted Forsyth, who had his men move to a small island in the Arikaree's dry bed and dig rifle pits.

Roman Nose did not lead the first charge. The night before, his "medicine" had been broken. He was famous for his long feathered warbonnet, which supposedly protected him in battle. While preparing food for the warriors, a woman had broken its power—either by touching the headdress or by preparing food with metal utensils. Roman Nose fully expected to die in battle, and he spent the morning in preparation. During an afternoon charge, he was shot through the spine. He died in the Cheyenne camp that night. The loss of Roman Nose lessened the resolve of the young warriors. They half-heartedly kept the well-armed soldiers pinned down until September 25, finally retreating when a relief force arrived.

The military called the engagement the Battle of Beecher's Island, after Lieutenant FREDERICK BEECHER, one of six army fatalities. To the Indians, it became known as the Fight When Roman Nose Was Killed. (See also RED CLOUD; TALL BULL.)

ROSE, EDWARD (Nez Coupe, "cut nose"; Five Scalps). *Mixed Cherokee. (d. 1832 or 1833).* Trader; guide; interpreter; Crow war chief.

Edward Rose was the son of a white trader and a Cherokee-black mother. As a young man, he was a pirate on the southern Mississippi River near New Orleans. In 1807, he joined MANUEL LISA's fur-trading expedition up the Missouri River, but was fired when he gave away the expedition's trade samples to the Crow Indians, then attacked Lisa on being criticized.

Rose settled among the Crows of what is now southern Montana and northern Wyoming and learned their langauge. In 1811, he was hired by WILSON PRICE HUNT of the Astorians as a guide through Crow territory but was discharged on suspicion of leading the party into a trap.

In the early 1820s, Rose lived among the Arikaras of North Dakota and learned their language as well. He served as interpreter for WILLIAM HENRY ASHLEY's 1823 expedition up the Missouri. Ashley reportedly ignored Rose's warning of an Arikara attack; in the subsequent punitive Arikara Campaign of 1823, headed by Colonel HENRY LEAVENWORTH, Rose again served as emissary and interpreter to the Indians. In September of that year, Rose set out with JEDEDIAH SMITH on his expedition through the Black Hills to the Rockies. Then, in 1825, he acted as interpreter for Colonel HENRY ATKINSON's Yellowstone Expedition.

Rose soon rejoined the Crows and became a noted war chief among them. He was known to them as Nez Coupe because of his scarred nose and also as Five Scalps for single-handedly killing five Blackfeet. It has been theorized that some of the exploits claimed by JAMES BECKWOURTH, who settled among the Crows in 1828, were actually those of his predeccessor.

The exact date of Rose's death is unknown. One theory holds that he was killed by Arikaras on the frozen Yellowstone River along with HUGH GLASS and a third mountain man.

ROSS, ALEXANDER. *(1783–1856).* Trader; explorer.

Born in Scotland, Alexander Ross moved to Upper Canada (Ontario) in 1804, and, for the next six years, worked there as a teacher.

In 1810, he was hired as a clerk to JOHN JACOB ASTOR's seaward expedition to the Pacific Northwest. He sailed with Astor's American Fur Company vessel, *Tonquin*, to the Oregon coast, where he was instrumental in the establishment of Astoria, the first permanent white settlement in the Pacific Northwest. He remained in Astor's employ until the North West Company as-

sumed control of Astoria in 1813, beginning work for the latter company.

In 1818, Ross explored the Columbia River to the mouth of the Snake River in what is now southeastern Washington. Here he established Fort Nez Perces, which later became Fort Walla Walla. After the Hudson's Bay Company had bought out the North West Company in 1821, Ross was appointed director of the Hudson's Bay Company's trading post at Flathead Lake in present-day western Montana. In 1823–24, he undertook an expedition that explored the Snake River region of present-day southern Idaho.

In 1824, a party of Iroquois who trapped for Ross at the Flathead Post in Montana were rescued from an attack by an Indian war party, possibly Flatheads, by American fur trader JEDEDIAH SMITH. Ross then allowed Smith and his Missouri fur traders to remain in the Flathead country, which they explored and later described to WILLIAM HENRY ASHLEY in St. Louis. Ross's superiors in the Hudson's Bay Company, fearing American encroachment into their northwest fur trade, took a dim view of his hospitable treatment of the Americans. The next year, Ross was replaced by PETER SKENE OGDEN as director of operations in the Snake River country.

Ross, with his Okanagan Indian wife, then moved to the Red River settlement in southern Manitoba, where he became sheriff and magistrate.

Ross wrote about his experiences in the fur trade, publishing *Adventures on the Columbia River* (1849) and *The Fur Hunters of the Far West* (1853). He also produced *The Red River Settlement* (1856), a history and commentary on the Metis people of that Manitoba community. His mixed-blood children later became influential in the events involving LOUIS DAVID RIEL and the Metis of Manitoba.

ROSS, JOHN (Coowescoowe, Kooweskoowe, Guwisguwi, "the egret"). *Mixed Cherokee. (1790–1866).* Principal chief and spokesman before and after the Trail of Tears; principal founder of a constitutional government among the Cherokees.

John Ross was born along the Coosa River in Georgia, the third of nine children of Daniel Ross, a Scot, and Mary McDonald, part-Cherokee, part-Scottish. Although raised among other Cherokees, he received schooling in his home from white tutors and attended the academy at Kingston, Tennessee.

In 1809, at the request of the Indian agent to the Cherokees, Ross went on a mission to the Arkansas Cherokees. In 1811, he was a member of the Standing Committee of the Cherokee Council. He fought with other Cherokees in the Creek War of 1813–14 as adjutant of the Cherokee Regiment in support of General ANDREW JACKSON at Horseshoe Bend against Red

Sticks under WILLIAM WEATHERFORD. By leading warriors in a diversion, he played an important role in Jackson's victory.

At the age of 23, Ross married Quatie, a nearly full-blooded Cherokee. In 1814, he established Ross's Landing, a trading post and ferry service on the Tennessee River (present-day Chattanooga).

Following the war, Ross became increasingly involved in Cherokee affairs. In 1816, he participated in a Cherokee delegation to Washington, D.C. In 1818, he became president of the National Committee, as the Standing Committee was now called. The next year, he went to Washington again and negotiated the Cherokee Treaty. He drafted the response to federal officials concerning the exchange of eastern lands for lands west of the Mississippi.

In 1820, the Cherokees established among themselves a republican form of government, similar to that of the United States. Ross advocated education and Christianity among his people in the hope that the Cherokees might one day have their own state under its own constitution. He traveled to Washington, D.C., again in 1824 and 1825. After having helped establish New Echota, Georgia, as the Cherokee national capital, he moved there with his family. In 1827, with Ross serving as associate chief with William Hicks, as well as president of the Cherokee constitutional convention, the Cherokee Nation was founded under a constitution with an elected principal chief, a senate, and a house of representatives. An opposition movement, referred to as WHITE PATH's Rebellion, was suppressed. Ross became principal chief in 1828. GEORGE LOWRY became second chief under him.

Yet the forces of removal were in effect. White interests lobbied for the right to settle on prime Indian farmlands. The discovery of gold near Dahlonega, Georgia, helped influence white officials to call for the relocation of the Cherokees along with other eastern Indians. In 1830, President Andrew Jackson signed the Indian Removal Act to relocate the eastern tribes to an Indian Territory west of the Mississippi.

From 1828 to 1831, the Georgia legislature stripped Cherokees of many of their rights. From 1830 to 1838, Ross headed numerous delegations to Washington, D.C., to argue the case for his people remaining on their ancestral homelands. Despite the fact that Ross argued and won the Cherokee's case before the Supreme Court of the United States, with a strong statement in their favor by Chief Justice John Marshall; despite the fact that Cherokees who had served with Jackson in the Creek War personally pleaded with the president concerning tribal land rights; despite the fact that officials such as Daniel Webster and Henry Clay supported Cherokee claims; President Jackson still called for Cherokee removal.

In 1835, members of the Treaty Party, led by MAJOR RIDGE, JOHN RIDGE, ELIAS BOUDINOT, and STAND WATIE, in opposition to the anti-treaty faction known as the Ross Party, signed the Treaty of New Echota, agreeing to relocation terms. Ross, as part of a campaign to have the treaty reversed, sent a letter to Congress in 1836 asking a review of its legality.

The state of Georgia began forcing the Cherokees to sell their lands for minimal payments. Cherokee homes and possessions were plundered. Whites destroyed the printing press of the *Cherokee Phoenix* because the paper published articles opposing Indian removal. Soldiers began rounding up Cherokee families and taking them to internment camps in preparation for the journey westward. With little food and with unsanitary conditions at these hastily built stockades, many Cherokees died. In the meantime, some Cherokees, such as TSALI, hid in the mountains of North Carolina. Although he failed in his attempts to block relocation, Ross did manage to secure additional federal appropriations for his people.

The first forced trek westward by troops under General WINFIELD SCOTT began in the spring of 1838 and lasted into the summer. On the 800-mile trip, the Cherokees suffered from the intense heat. The second

John Ross. *Courtesy of Library of Congress.*

mass exodus took place during the fall and winter of 1838–39, at first during the rainy season, when the wagons bogged down in the mud, and, in winter, with freezing temperatures and snow. On both journeys, there was death from disease and inadequate supplies of food and blankets. The soldiers drove their prisoners on at a cruel pace, without allowing them to properly bury their dead. Nor did they protect the Indians from attacks by bandits.

During the period of confinement, plus the two separate trips along the Trail of Tears, about 4,000 Cherokees died—nearly a quarter of the total. Ross's wife Quatie was one of the victims of the forced journey. More Cherokees died after arrival in the Indian Territory because of continuing epidemics and shortages of food.

The assassination of the Ridges and Boudinot in 1839, because of their role in removal, threatened to further polarize tribal factions. Some of the Treaty Party members accused Ross of involvement but were unable to produce any evidence. SEQUOYAH, the inventor of the Cherokee alphabet, and other peacemakers sought to reunite the tribe. Ross helped write the Constitution for the United Cherokees and was elected their principal chief in 1839. He rebuilt his own personal fortune with a plantation and slaves, and he remarried a Quaker woman by the name of Mary Bryan Stapler by whom he had three children. Ross traveled to Washington five more times between 1839 and 1846.

At the start of the Civil War, Ross argued for Cherokee neutrality. Most of his supporters were full-bloods who were not slaveholders. In August 1861, however, with many Cherokees under Stand Watie favoring the Confederacy, Ross called a national conference and took a pro-South stand. Watie, who eventually became a general in the Confederate army, contributed to the early Southern victories. After Union troops had invaded and regained control of most of the Indian Territory in 1862, Ross moved his family to Kansas. The Southern Cherokees, unwilling to come to terms with the Union, formed a separate government and elected Stand Watie as their principal chief. Ross traveled to Washington to inform President ABRAHAM LINCOLN of the Cherokees' pact with the Confederacy.

At the close of the war, with the tribe still divided, Ross, now 75 and in poor health, took it upon himself to represent his faction in Washington for new treaty negotiations. He died during the trip. Other delegates for the Northern faction insisted that the wording of the final treaty designate Ross as principal chief.

ROUSSEAU, JEAN JACQUES. (1712–1778).
Philosopher; writer.

Born in Geneva, Switzerland, Jean-Jacques Rousseau spent much of his life in Paris. Throughout his career as

a writer, he was a major force of the philosophical school of Enlightenment. In his works on the human condition, he rejected the concept that man had evolved from savagery to a more refined state, maintaining that man was by nature good and had degenerated through the morally and socially corrupting effects of civilization. He was one of the original popularizers of the idea of the Noble Savage, citing the Indians of North America as examples of man in a pristine state, living unencumbered by the negative forces of society. Rousseau's writings influenced the romanticized portrayals of the American Indian by such later writers as JAMES FENIMORE COOPER and HENRY WADSWORTH LONGFELLOW.

ROWLANDSON, MARY. (ca. 1635–ca. 1678).
Captive.

In February 1676, during King Philip's War, the Narragansets attacked the settlement of Lancaster, Massachusetts. One of the settlers, Mary Rowlandson, a minister's wife, fled from her burning house with her children, one of whom was shot dead in her arms. Along with 24 other English survivors, she was taken captive. Her second child died after nine days of forced marching. Rowlandson spent 11 weeks with her captors, during which she was forced to experience the nomadic life of the Indian in the midst of a harsh New England winter.

The Narraganset QUINNAPIN then purchased Rowlandson from her original captor, and she became a servant to his wife, the Indian woman WETAMOO, Squaw Sachem of the Pocassets and sister-in-law to King PHILIP from an earlier marriage. On two occasions, Rowlandson appeared before King Philip. Quinnapin eventually freed her for a ransom of £20, two coats, half a bushel of corn, and some tobacco, raised by friends in Boston.

Rowlandson's diary was published in 1682 as A Narrative of the Captivity and Restoration of Mrs. Mary Rowlandson (The Sovereignty and Goodness of God) relating her captivity experience in a Puritan religious context. Her work, published in 15 editions by 1800, fostered the great interest in Indian-captivity narratives, which developed into a genre of American literature.

RUSSELL, CHARLES MARION (The Kid).
(1864–1926). Artist. Great-nephew of WILLIAM BENT.

In 1880, Charles M. Russell, from a prosperous family in St. Louis, left home to live in Montana, where he supported himself as a trapper, sheepherder, and cowboy. Starting in 1888, he lived for six months among the Blood Indians of Alberta, Canada, an experience serving as a basis for his later works on Indian life. Over the next years, based in Montana's Judith Basin, Russell lived the life of a roving cowboy, which became the dominant theme in his art. In 1897, he settled in Great Falls, Montana, where he built a studio cabin. Other than brief periods in California and Europe, he lived in Montana the remainder of his life. Although Russell is thought to have had no formal training as an artist, his works, like those of FREDERIC REMINGTON, were well-received.

S

SABEATA. *Jumano. (fl. 1680s).* Ally of Spanish; guide.

Sabeata of the Jumanos or Shumans requested Spanish help in present-day Texas for protection against Apache raids. With the founding of a mission among his people, he adopted Christianity. In 1683–84, he served as guide to a Spanish expedition under Domingo de Mendoza, but departed after a dispute.

SACAJAWEA (Sacagawea, Sakakawea, Sah-cah-gar-we-ah, "birdwoman," "owl woman"; Boinaiv, "grass maiden"; Janey). *Shoshone. (ca. 1784–ca. 1812 or 1884).* Guide and interpreter for the Lewis and Clark Expedition. Sister of CAMEAHWAIT; wife of TOUSSAINT CHARBONNEAU; mother of JEAN BAPTISTE CHARBONNEAU.

Sacajawea was born in 1784 or 1787 among the Lemhi Shoshones of what is now central Idaho and western Montana. While a teenager, she was kidnapped by the Hidatsa Indians, who took her back to their village on the upper Missouri in North Dakota. She was purchased in 1804—or won in a gambling match—by the French-Canadian trader Toussaint Charbonneau.

The exploratory expedition under MERIWETHER LEWIS and WILLIAM CLARK set out up the Missouri from St. Louis in May 1804. They spent the next winter in Mandan villages in present-day North Dakota. During the stopover, the French-Canadian Charbonneau was hired as an interpreter. Charbonneau insisted that Sacajawea, who spoke both Shoshone and Siouan and who hoped to be reunited with her people, come along. In February, less than two months before the expedition set out from Fort Mandan in April 1805, she gave birth to Charbonneau's child, Jean Baptiste Charboneau, known as Pomp during the expedition.

Sacajawea's participation was a stroke of good fortune for the entire undertaking. The only female member of the expedition, cradleboard strapped to her back, she not only showed the explorers the way through the wilderness, but also acted as diplomat to hostile Indians, who viewed the presence of an Indian woman as a token of peace. Moreover, Sacajawea could communicate with the various tribes through sign language. She also contributed to the expedition's success by the introduction of wild plant foods. On one occasion during the voyage, she had the presence of mind to save the expedition's records and journals when her husband accidentally capsized one of the boats.

In August 1805, at the Three Forks of the Missouri in present-day Montana, Sacajawea was reunited with her brother Cameahwait, now chief of his band. At Sacajawea's request, Cameahwait provided horses and supplies for the expedition, as well as guides—an elderly Shoshone, known to the whites as Toby, and his son—to assist in the crossing of the Rockies as far as Nez Perce country.

The expedition followed the Clearwater River, then the Snake, and then the Columbia, successfully reaching the Pacific Ocean in November 1805. On the return journey, Sacajawea traveled with Clark's party along the Yellowstone River, while Lewis's party explored Marias River. Sacajawea and Charbonneau left the expedition at the Hidatsa village at the mouth of the Knife River. Lewis and Clark returned triumphantly to St. Louis in 1806.

It is not known for certain when or where Sacajawea died. One version has it that after she and Charbonneau had come to St. Louis sometime after 1806, leaving their son with Clark to be educated, then returned with the trader MANUEL LISA up the Missouri, where Sacajawea died from disease in 1812. In another version, she lived for a time with the Comanches, then returned to her homeland, settling at WASHAKIE's Wind River Reservation in Wyoming, where she died when about 100 years old.

In addition to the numerous memorials along the explorers' route, Sacajawea has had a river, a mountain, and a pass named in her honor. (See also LEWIS, MERIWETHER.)

SAGAUNASH (Saganash, Sauganash; Billy Caldwell; The Englishman). *Mixed Potawatomi. (1781–1841).* Interpreter; negotiator; secretary to TECUMSEH.

Sagaunash was born in southern Ontario. His Irish father, William Caldwell, was an officer in the British army; his mother was a full-blooded Potawatomi. Sagaunash attended Catholic schools, where he learned to read and write in both English and French. He also developed a mastery of the various Algonquian dialects of Great Lakes tribes.

Starting in 1807, Sagaunash was in the employ of the British and worked as Tecumseh's secretary in the War of 1812. In 1820, he moved to Chicago. Trusted by Indians and whites as an interpreter and negotiator, Sagaunash extended his influence by marrying the daughter of Potawatomi chief Neescotnemeg. In 1826, he was elected a Justice of the Peace in Chicago. Along with SHABONEE, Sagaunash was called upon by white officials to help maintain and negotiate peace in RED BIRD's Winnebago Uprising of 1827 and the BLACK HAWK War of 1832, signing treaties after each conflict and receiving land and cash grants for his family. When the Potawatomis were relocated to Iowa, he went with them, dying at Council Bluffs.

ST. CLAIR, ARTHUR. *(1736–1818).* Army officer in the American Revolution and Little Turtle's War; territorial governor; Indian superintendent; trader.

Scottish-born Arthur St. Clair joined the British army in 1757, entering the service as an ensign. The next year, he was a lieutenant in General JEFFREY AMHERST's forces in Canada, fighting in the French and Indian War of 1754–63. He took part in the British campaigns that resulted in the capture of Louisburg, Montreal, and Quebec.

St. Clair left the army in 1762, settling in western Pennsylvania to engage in farming and the fur trade. Through his own investments and his wife's inheritance, the St. Clair estate in the Ligonier Valley region grew to comprise 15,000 acres. Becoming active in Pennsylvania colonial politics, St. Clair served on the colony's governing council and as a judge. During Lord DUNMORE's War against CORNSTALK's Shawnees in 1774, he was instrumental in keeping Pennsylvania neutral.

In 1775, St. Clair was appointed a colonel in the Continental army and led a regiment of Pennsylvania Infantry against the British. In 1776, he took part in General JOHN SULLIVAN's retreat after his abortive assault on Canada. Later that year, St. Clair and his troops crossed the Delaware with General GEORGE WASHINGTON's forces and took part in the Battle of Trenton, New Jersey, in December 1776. He continued to serve in New Jersey in early 1777, but was then promoted to major general and assigned to command Fort Ticonderoga on New York's Lake Champlain. With British general JOHN BURGOYNE's southward advance toward Saratoga, St. Clair abandoned Ticonderoga; his troops were outnumbered and undersupplied and he chose evacuation over capture. Regrouping at nearby Fort Edward with forces under General PHILIP SCHUYLER, St. Clair led his troops at the Battle of Bennington, Vermont, in August 1777. Relieved of his command, he was criticized for abandoning Fort Ticonderoga, but was exonerated in a 1778 court-martial proceeding. He spent the rest of the war in administrative duties in Philadelphia.

In 1781, St. Clair returned to his estate in western Pennsylvania and became active in politics, representing Pennsylvania in Congress under the Articles of Confederation. In 1787, he was named the first U.S. territorial governor when the Northwest Ordinance of 1787 created the Northwest Territory. As governor, with headquarters in Marietta, Ohio, he was also superintendent of the territory's Indians. In 1789, he finalized the last of the Fort Harmar treaties, under which the tribes of the Northwest Territory agreed to cede their lands in the Ohio region in exchange for a specified dollar amount of trade goods. Yet many bands of the Old Northwest tribes soon renounced the land cessions and began attacking settlers in north central Ohio, leading to Little Turtle's War of 1790–94.

After General JOSIAH HARMAR's army had suffered a devastating defeat by these allied tribes in October 1790, St. Clair was appointed major general in March 1791 by President George Washington. With this commission, St. Clair was then the highest ranking officer in the army. He mustered another expedition to Maumee River Indian country at Fort Washington (present-day Cincinnati, Ohio). Heading northward in early October 1791, St. Clair supervised the construction of Fort Hamilton and Fort Jefferson. His force of some 1,400 men was attacked on November 4 by Indians under LITTLE TURTLE at the headwaters of the Wabash River. St. Clair withdrew to Fort Jefferson, 30 miles away, having seen 630 of his original 2,000 men killed and 283 wounded, compared to minimal Indian casualties. Because of this military disaster, St. Clair soon resigned his commission. Little Turtle's War continued until defeat of the allied tribes at Fallen Timbers by forces under General "Mad" ANTHONY WAYNE in August 1794.

Reassuming an active role as territorial governor, St. Clair opposed statehood for Ohio. His Federalist position led to his removal from office by President THOMAS JEFFERSON in 1802. Retiring to private life, St. Clair lost most of his fortune in land speculation deals and lived in relative poverty until his death. (See also LITTLE TURTLE.)

SAKARISSA (Sagarissa, Saghwareesa, Segwarusa, Sequareesa, Sequareesere, Shequallisere, Achsaquareesory, "spear-dragger").
Tuscarora. (ca. 1730–ca. 1810). Proponent of peace; negotiator.

Sakarissa was born at Niagara Landing, New York. As a chief of the Tuscaroras, he participated in numerous treaty councils, meeting with New York, Pennsylvania, Moravian and Quaker officials. In an age of conflict, including the French and Indian Wars and the American Revolution, Sakarissa was known as a proponent of peace. He signed the Treaty of Fort Stanwix in 1768 and the Treaty of Canandaigua in 1794. At the latter council, he requested that Quaker teachers settle among his people. In 1805, Sakarissa helped found the Tuscarora Congregational Church.

SAMOSET (Samaset, "he who walks over much").
Abnaki. (ca. 1590–ca. 1653). First Indian to greet Pilgrims.

Samoset was a sachem of the Pemaquid band of Abnakis, living on Monhegan Island off the coast of present-day Maine. He is thought to have had early contacts with English fishermen in the region because, by the time the Pilgrims arrived, he knew enough of their language to greet them. He reportedly walked into Plymouth Plantation on March 16, 1621, and announced, "Welcome, Englishman." The Pilgrims fed him and gave him a blanket. He slept on the floor in front of a fireplace in one of their dwellings.

Samoset returned as promised several days later on March 22 with SQUANTO, the Wampanoag who as a slave had been taken to Europe, where he had mastered the English language. He and Squanto arranged a meeting between the colonists and MASSASOIT, grand sachem of the Wampanoag Confederacy, with whom Samoset had been staying the past eight months. Massasoit conferred with the Pilgrims that same day, March 22.

Samoset later had contact with Maine colonists. In 1625, he and Unongoit signed the first deed between the Indians and English in a sale of 1,200 acres of Pemaquid lands to John Brown of New Harbor. In 1653, he sold another 1,000 acres to William Parnell, Thomas Way, and William England, soon after which he died.

SANDS, OKTARSARS HARJO ("sandy place").
Creek. (d. 1872). Leader of the Creek faction of full-bloods.

Oktarsars Harjo Sands supported the North during the Civil War. After the war, he resisted the Creek Reconstruction Treaty by which the federal government appropriated half the Creeks' lands within the Indian Territory (present-day Oklahoma). Like OPOTHLEYAHOLO before him, Sands supported a return to traditional tribal customs. The longstanding dispute between full-blooded Creeks and the mixed-bloods who supported acculturation resulted in violence and the destructon of property. Full-blooded leaders who carried on the struggle for Creek rights in the Indian Territory were ISPARHECHE and CHITTO HARJO.

SASSACUS ("he is wild").
Pequot. (ca. 1560–1637). Grand sachem; leader of the Pequot War of 1636–37. Father-in-law of UNCAS.

It is thought that the Pequots migrated from the Hudson River Valley in present-day New York, to New England, where they fought with other Algonquians, both the Narragansets and Niantics, for territory. Soon after the arrival of the Pilgrims and other English colonists in the first part of the 17th century, the Pequots had gained control of the present Connecticut coastal area from the Connecticut River to Rhode Island. Sassacus was the son of the grand sachem Wopigwooit. As a young warrior, he helped expand the Pequot domain westward to the Hudson River and eastward to Long Island.

Sassacus became grand sachem about 1632 when his father was killed by the Dutch. His main villages were on the Thames (formerly the Pequot) and the Mystic rivers. About 26 sagamores, each with a village, were under his rule. One of these subordinate chiefs, his son-in-law Uncas, broke away from Sassacus's rule in a dispute over a treaty with Massachusetts Bay Colony. Uncas's followers became known as Mohegans and were allies of the colonists.

With an expanding colonial presence, there were frequent disputes over land and trade goods between Pequots and settlers. The death of a coastal trader, John Oldham, in July 1636 caused an outbreak of violence. Another trader, John Gallup, discovered Oldham's hijacked boat off Block Island, skirmished with the Indians aboard, then reported the incident to colonial officials.

Massachusetts Bay Colony ordered out an expedition under JOHN ENDECOTT. His force attacked Indians on Block Island, killing every male they could find, mostly Narragansets, and burning their villages. Then

Endecott's soldiers sailed to the Connecticut mainland. The settlers at Fort Saybrook tried to dissuade him from an attack on the Pequots, fearing Indian reprisals. Ignoring their pleas, Endecott led his men in the destruction of several Pequot villages, then returned to Boston.

Sassacus plotted a retaliatory strike, but he was unable to achieve an alliance with the Narragansets, due largely to the intervention of ROGER WILLIAMS. In the winter of 1636–37, his warriors laid siege to Fort Saybrook and attacked outlying settlements. The following spring, at Wethersfield up the Connecticut River, Pequot warrriors killed nine colonists.

The colonists raised armies under Captain JOHN MASON and Captain JOHN UNDERHILL. Mason was the first in the field, with an army of 80 men out of Hartford, Connecticut, plus Mohegan allies. At Fort Saybrook, Underhill's Massachusetts militia joined him. They sailed westward along the Connecticut coast, then circled back overland from Narragansett Bay, gaining Narraganset and Niantic auxiliaries in addition to their Mohegan allies.

At dawn on May 25, 1637, the army attacked Sassacus's village on the Mystic River. The Pequots repelled the first assault from behind their palisaded walls, but the colonists managed to set the Pequot wigwams on fire. Those who fled the flames were cut down in the surrounding countryside; those who stayed behind, mostly women and children, were burned to death. It is estimated that 600 to 1,000 Pequots were killed that morning. The English lost only two men, with 20 or so wounded. Sassacus, carrying the tribal wampum, led a group to safety.

The survivors were attacked in a swamp west of New Haven the following July, but Sassacus managed to escape once again with a small group, seeking refuge among the Mohawks. Anxious to prove that they had no part in the Pequot uprising, the Mohawks killed the grand sachem and sent his scalp and six others to the English, keeping the Pequot wampum.

Use of the Pequot tribal name was forbidden. Pequot captives were sold into slavery in Bermuda or divided up among the Mohegans, Niantics, and Narragansets in payment for their help. Some Pequots escaped to Long Island and Massachusetts, where they settled among other Algonquians. In 1655, the colonists freed some Pequot slaves and resettled them along the Mystic River.

SATANK (Setangya, Sitting Bear). *Kiowa-Sarcee. (ca. 1810–1871).* Medicine man; leader in the Kiowa Wars of the 1860s–70s.

Satank, or Sitting Bear, was born in the Black Hills region; his mother was part Sarcee. As a prominent war chief among the Kiowas, the leader of the *Kiotsenko*, the Principal Dogs (or Ten Bravest) military society, he

helped establish the peace between the Kiowas and Cheyennes about 1840. In 1846, he was wounded in the face by a Pawnee arrow.

Along with KICKING BIRD, SATANTA, and STUMBLING BEAR, Satank was one of the principal spokesmen for the Kiowas at the Medicine Lodge Council in 1867. After his son had been killed during a raid in Texas in 1870, Satank traveled to Texas, gathered up the bones in a bundle, and carried them on a second horse wherever he went. He also began advocating war with whites.

In May 1871, Satank joined Satanta, MAMANTI, BIG TREE, and other Kiowa warriors in an attack on an army wagon train along the Butterfield Southern Route near Fort Richardson, Texas. The Kiowas killed eight of the 12 defenders and looted the supplies.

At Fort Sill in the Indian Territory, Satank bragged about the raid to Indian agent LAWRIE TATUM and was arrested with Satanta and Big Tree. While on his way to a civil trial in Texas he began singing a death song, freed his wrists, grabbed a knife, attacked a guard, and was shot dead. He was buried at Fort Sill's military cemetery. His fellow prisoners Satanta and Big Tree were later tried and sentenced to death, but were eventually released.

SATANTA (White Bear; The Orator of the Plains). *Kiowa. (1830–1878).* Leader in the Kiowa Wars of the 1860s–70s.

Satanta or White Bear was the son of Red Tipi, the keeper of the *Tai-me*, the tribal medicine bundles. Born on the Northern Plains, he migrated to the Southern Plains with his people. When a young man, Satanta was given a shield by a prominent warrior, Black Horse, which he used in raids in Mexico and Texas. During the early 1860s, while federal troops were fighting the Civil War in the East, he led many war parties in attacks along the Santa Fe Trail.

In November 1864, Colonel CHRISTOPHER "KIT" CARSON under the command of General JAMES H. CARLETON, led his New Mexico volunteers at Adobe Walls, a former trading post in the Canadian River valley of the Texas Panhandle. Using 12-pounder howitzers, Carson's men managed to drive off the Indians and burn their winter stores. The next year, the Kiowas signed a treaty ceding lands in New Mexico, Colorado, and Kansas.

On the death of LITTLE MOUNTAIN in 1866, Satanta was the leading choice of the war faction; his rival was KICKING BIRD of the peace faction. LONE WOLF became the compromise choice as the new principal chief.

Satanta continued his raids into Texas. In April 1867, General WINFIELD SCOTT HANCOCK met with Kiowa leaders at Fort Dodge, Kansas, where he presented Satanta with a major general's dress uniform. The military was incensed when he wore it on a successful raid on the post's horse herd.

Satanta, famed for his eloquence and called by whites "The Orator of the Plains," spoke at the Medicine Lodge council in October 1867, as did Kicking Bird, SATANK, and STUMBLING BEAR. He signed the treaty agreeing to resettle on a reservation within the Indian Territory. Many of the Kiowa bands delayed, however. When Satanta and Lone Wolf came in under a flag of truce to inform the army they had not been with BLACK KETTLE's Cheyennes at the Battle of the Washita, they were taken hostage. General PHILIP H. SHERIDAN held them as hostages until their bands had complied.

In May 1871, Satanta participated in the attack on the Warren wagon train with Satank, MAMANTI, and BIG TREE. Later, at Fort Sill in the Indian Territory, after Satank had boasted of the raid, Satank, Satanta, and Big Tree were arrested. Satank attempted an escape on his way to trial in Texas and was killed; Satanta and Big Tree were tried and sentenced to death. Humanitarian groups protested the harsh sentences, and even the Indian Bureau argued for their release on the grounds that their act had been one of war and not murder. They were imprisoned at Huntsville, Texas.

Lone Wolf and Mamanti, leaders of the militants, and Kicking Bird and Stumbling Bear, leaders of the peace faction, argued for the release of the two men. They were paroled in 1873 on condition that they remain on the Kiowa Reservation in the Indian Territory. At that time, Kiowa, Comanche, Cheyenne, and Arapaho war parties were forming for raids on white settlers under the Comanche leader QUANAH PARKER, the start of the Red River War of 1874–75. Satanta decided to report to officials to prove he was not taking part in hostilities. In September 1874, Big Tree appeared at the Cheyenne agency at Darlington to announce that Satanta wanted to surrender. Satanta himself reported the following October.

Big Tree was imprisoned at Fort Sill; Satanta was sent back to Huntsville. Four years later, sick and feeble, having been informed he would never be released, he committed suicide by jumping from the window of the prison hospital. He was buried in Texas. In 1963, his grandson James Auchiah received permission to bring the chief's remains back to Fort Sill to be buried with other Kiowa leaders.

SAVAGE, CHARLES ROSCOE. *(1832–1909).* Photographer.

In 1858, British-born Charles Savage came to the United States with the Mormons and found work in New York City as a photographer. The next year, he headed west, settling first in Nebraska, then Iowa, and finally at Salt Lake City, Utah, becoming partners in a studio in 1860. He made numerous images of the Great Basin tribes, especially Paiutes and Shoshones. Working as a photograper for the railroad, Savage traveled to California and back in 1866. He also photographed the linking of the Union Pacific and the Central Pacific lines at Promontory Point, Utah, in 1869.

SAVANNAH JACK (John Haig, John Hague). *Mixed Shawnee. (fl. late 1700s, early 1800s).* War chief; enemy of Americans.

Savannah Jack's exact ancestry is not known. He was of mixed descent with either Shawnee or Yuchi blood, perhaps the son of the trader John Haig, or son or younger half-brother of the loyalist trader SIMON GIRTY. Before the American Revolution, Savannah Jack lived for a time in Augusta, Georgia. In 1789, he was in Pensacola, Florida, where he killed a cow keeper and was sought by the Spanish. About 10 years later, he was at Miccosukee with a small band of Shawnee warriors and supported the efforts of the Englishman WILLIAM BOWLES, the director general of the Creek Nation. Savannah Jack was also an ally of WILLIAM WEATHERFORD in the Creek War of 1813–14, fighting at the Battle of Horseshoe Bend, after which he settled permanently in Florida. He was known throughout the Southeast as a fierce fighter.

SCARFACED CHARLEY (Scarface Charley; Chichikam Lupalkuelatko, Chikchackam Lilalkuelatko, "wagon scarface"). *Modoc. (ca. 1837–1896).* War chief in the Modoc War of 1872–73.

Scarfaced Charley was probably a Rogue River Indian who later joined the Modocs. He received his name from a childhood scar received when whites chained his father to the back of a wagon and dragged him until he was dead. The boy either was injured by the wagon during the incident or by a jutting rock.

In November 1872, when troops under Captain James Jackson tracked down the Modocs who had left the Klamath Reservation and ordered their return, Scarfaced Charley refused to give up his pistol. He and Lieutenant Frazier Boutelle, who was trying to disarm him, fired the first shots of the Modoc War. Neither was hit. Scarfaced Charley then grabbed his rifle off the stack of surrendered arms; the other Modocs followed his example. In the ensuing fight, a soldier was killed and seven wounded.

Scarfaced Charley, the principal military strategist among the insurgents, generally took the militant stance in tribal councils. At one point, he had to be restrained from killing two envoys. Yet he was faithful to CAPTAIN JACK's decisions, unlike CURLY HEADED DOCTOR and HOOKER JIM. On April 26, 1873, he led Modoc warriors in an ambush on a reconnaissance patrol of 63 soldiers under Captain Evan Thomas who had stopped in an indefensible hollow, killing 25, including all five officers, and wounding 16. He reportedly called out to the surviving soldiers that they had better depart so that the Modocs would not kill them all.

Scarfaced Charley surrendered with the main body of Modocs. He was called as a witness in Captain Jack's defense. Since he had no hand in the killing of General EDWARD CANBY and Eleasar Thomas or in the wounding of ALFRED MEACHAM, for which Captain Jack, BLACK JIM, BOSTON CHARLEY and SCHONCHIN JOHN were sentenced to death, he was allowed to accompany the 150 or so Modocs sent to first Wyoming, then Nebraska, then the Indian Territory (present-day Oklahoma).

From 1874 to 1881, Scarfaced Charley toured the East on a lecture circuit with Meacham, WINEMA, and other Modocs. He eventually became principal chief of the band in the Indian Territory. (See also CAPTAIN JACK.)

SCAROUADY. See HALF-KING.

SCHONCHIN JIM (Old Schonchin, Sconchin, Shonchin, Schonchis). *Modoc. (fl. mid-1800s).* Principal chief. Brother of SCHONCHIN JOHN.

Although not a hereditary chief, Schonchin Jim assumed leadership of the Modocs about 1846. During the California Gold Rush starting in 1849, he led his approximately 600 warriors in resistance to white incursions onto Modoc lands. In 1864, Schonchin Jim signed a treaty ceding Modoc territory in northern California and southern Oregon and agreeing to settle on the Klamath Reservation in Oregon. He henceforth counseled peace and played no part in the Modoc War of 1872–73 under CAPTAIN JACK, despite his younger brother Schonchin John's involvement. Although he kept the majority of Modocs under his authority during the uprising, he was unable to stop the militants from fighting.

SCHONCHIN JOHN (John Schonchin). *Modoc. (d. 1873).* Leader in the Modoc War of 1872–73. Brother of SCHONCHIN JIM.

Schonchin John, the younger brother of the principal chief Schonchin Jim, was one of the militants among the Modocs despite his brother's efforts to maintain peace. In the Modoc attack of April 11, 1873, on President ULYSSES S. GRANT's peace commissioners, he shot ALFRED MEACHAM, who was saved by WINEMA. Meacham later recovered. Schonchin John surrendered with CAPTAIN JACK, BLACK JIM, and BOSTON CHARLEY, and was sentenced to death and hanged with them. His son Peter Schonchin, who fought under his father, later acted as a research informant on the war. (See also CAPTAIN JACK.)

SCHOOLCRAFT, HENRY ROWE. *(1793–1864).* Anthropologist; Indian agent.

Henry Rowe Schoolcraft grew up near Albany, New York, and attended Union and Middlebury colleges. The son of a glassmaker, he traveled to the lead mines of present-day Missouri and Arkansas in 1817–18, where he came into contact with Indian peoples. In 1820, he accompanied LEWIS CASS, the governor of the Michigan Territory, to the source of the Mississippi River, where he first encountered Chippewas.

In 1822, under Cass's supervision, Schoolcraft conducted a geological survey of the Lake Superior region and shortly afterward was appointed Indian agent to the tribes of the old Northwest Territory, establishing his headquarters first at Sault Ste. Marie and later at Mackinac. He married the mixed-blood granddaughter of a Chippewa chief and began extensive study of Chippewa language and mythology, recording songs and tales. He was one of the earliest ethnologists to base his studies of the Indians on interviews with tribal members.

Schoolcraft concluded that Indians, after the effects of two centuries of white encroachment, were no longer capable of sustaining their hunting society and were incapable of developing agriculture. He was a strong proponent of removing the Indians away from contact with the whites, advocating their relocation to reservations west of the Mississippi. With his help, the federal government and the Great Lakes tribes—the Chippewas, Ottawas, and Potawatomis—entered into treaties that resulted in the cession of much of the Indian-held land in southern Michigan.

In 1841, under some hint of scandal in regard to the misappropriation of federal money, Schoolcraft lost his post as Indian agent in Michigan and moved with his family to New York City. He undertook a study of the Iroquois that attempted to link this tribe, through an examination of their myths, to the classical civilizations of the ancient Mediterranean. In 1845, he conducted the New York State census of Indians.

In 1847, Schoolcraft was commissioned by the federal government to prepare a comprehensive study of all the known Indian tribes of the period. Writing about the tribes he knew personally, Schoolcraft obtained other materials from a 348-page questionnaire sent to persons knowledgeable of Indians—Indian Bureau employes, traders, missionaries, ethnologists, historians, travel writers, etc.—resulting in the publication of the six-volume *Historical and Statistical Information Respecting the History, Conditions, and Prospects of the Indian Tribes of the United States* (1851–57).

SCHREYVOGEL, CHARLES. *(1861–1912).* Artist.

Charles Schreyvogel's interest in Indians developed after 1890, upon his return from three years of art study in Europe. He had the opportunity to make sketches of Indians who were part of WILLIAM "BUFFALO BILL" CODY's Wild West Show, of which the eastern base of operations was located near Schreyvogel's hometown of Hoboken, New Jersey. It was not until 1893 that Schreyvogel, for health reasons, first visited the West and stayed for a time on the Ute Reservation as the guest of an army surgeon. By the time he returned to New Jersey, he had decided to commit himself to portraying the life of the cavalry soldier in his art. Some of his paintings were commissioned by Cody, who sent the artist a Sioux tepee to set up in his studio. Schreyvogel's celebrated reputation as a painter of cavalry and Indian themes eventually led President Theodore Roosevelt to issue him a permit allowing him to enter any army post or Indian reservation in the United States.

SCHULTZ, JAMES WILLARD (Apikuni, Far-off-White-Robe). *(1859–1947).* Writer; trader.

James Willard Schultz was born in Boonville, New York, of socially prominent parents. Although he planned to attend West Point in pursuit of a military career, on hearing stories of the frontier during a visit with an uncle in St. Louis, he undertook instead a trip to the Northern Rockies. He traveled by boat up the Missouri, arriving at Fort Benton, Montana, in July 1877.

Schultz became a partner of the trader Joe Kipp, acquiring buffalo robes from the Indians and selling them to Boston merchants. With the buffalo herds depleted and a diminishing supply of furs, Schultz settled among the Blackfeet in northwestern Montana in the Glacier Park region near the Canadian border, married a Blackfoot woman, and lived off the land. He and his wife Natahki, or Musti Ahwaton Ahki (Fine Shield Woman), had a son, Hart Merriam Schultz, or Nitoh Mahkwi (Lone Wolf) in 1882.

After his wife's death in 1903, Schultz moved to Los Angeles, where he became literary critic for the *Los Angeles Times*. He eventually built a home in the White Mountains of Arizona, but returned often to Montana. In addition to many articles, published by GEORGE BIRD GRINNELL in *Forest and Stream*, Schultz wrote numerous books, including *My Life as an Indian* (1907) and *Blackfeet Tales of Glacier National Park* (1916). His son Lone Wolf, a well-known painter and sculptor, illustrated much of his writing. Schultz remarried in 1931. He died in Wyoming 16 years later and was buried in Montana among the Blackfeet.

SCHURZ, CARL. *(1829–1906).* Secretary of the Interior.

Carl Schurz's involvement in radical political activities compelled his departure from his native Germany. He arrived in America in 1852, became a lawyer, and settled in Milwaukee, Wisconsin.

Active in politics, Schurz campaigned for ABRAHAM LINCOLN in the 1858 senatorial race against Stephen Douglas, and again in 1860 when Lincoln was elected to the presidency. Appointed by Lincoln as ambassador to Spain, Schurz left that post in 1862 to serve in the Union army, eventually rising to the rank of major general. At the war's end, he was a journalist with major newspapers in New York and Detroit, as well as joint owner of a St. Louis German-language daily. He represented Missouri in the Senate for one term, 1869–75, during which he led the liberal Republicans in their opposition to President ULYSSES S. GRANT's programs. Schurz supported Rutherford Hayes in his successful presidential campaign and was named secretary of the Interior in 1877. He was one of the earliest conservationists in government, calling attention to the wastefulness in the lumbering industry and the need to protect the nation's forests.

Schurz inherited the Bureau of Indian Affairs in the wake of the controversey created by eight years of Grant's Peace Policy. The army's defeat by the Sioux at Little Bighorn in 1876 gave rise to a public outcry against the Bureau, charging incompetence in its management of the Indians. Amid allegations of fiscal irregularities, mismanagement, corruption, and waste, Schurz initiated an investigation that resulted in the firing of John Q. Smith, commissioner of Indian Affairs, as well as chief clerk Samuel Galpin. Schurz replaced Smith with Ezra A. Hayt, who was also accused of favoritism, then replaced Hayt with Roland Trowbridge.

Schurz concentrated his reform of the Indian Bureau with a reorganization plan aimed at eliminating the involvement of Quaker and other religious groups, returning the selection process of superintendents and agents to government control. This move was supported by Congressional leaders because it reestablished Indian agency positons as a source for political patronage jobs. Schurz's opposition to the return of the Indian Bureau to military control temporarily gained for him the support of Indian reform groups.

Nevertheless, in 1879, at the height of the national controversy arising from the relocation of STANDING BEAR's Poncas to the Indian Territory, Schurz became embroiled in an open dispute with Indian rights activist HELEN HUNT JACKSON. In an exchange of letters published in the New York and Boston press, Jackson challenged Schurz to clarify his position on whether the Poncas should be allowed to pursue their land claims in federal court. Schurz declined to take a firm stand on the issue and instead put forth his view that reform efforts for Indian rights would be more effective if directed toward making the Indians private land-owners and citizens. That same year, Big Snake, brother of Standing Bear, was killed by government authorities, allegedly while resisting arrest for having threatened an Indian agent. Accusations were made that Big Snake's killing was really a political assassination initiated by Schurz to intimidate the Poncas into withdrawing their lawsuit, with reference made to his European radical political past. In early 1881, these allegations were suggested to Congress by Massachusetts senator HENRY DAWES, even though Schurz was a staunch supporter of the Dawes proposal for the allotment of land to individual Indians. Schurz was later cleared of wrongdoing, although he remained the target of some reformers.

Also in 1879, Schurz interceded in the Ute War in Colorado and appointed a special federal peace commission. The official report concluded that unlawful encroachment of miners into Ute territory was the main factor in precipitating the hostile actions of the Indians. The Utes, represented by OURAY, agreed to cede their Colorado lands to the government in exchange for new reservations in that state and in Utah. These new lands would be allotted to the Indians in severalty when the appropriate legislation was enacted.

After his government service, Schurz became editor in chief of the New York *Evening Post* and published biographies of Henry Clay and Abraham Lincoln. He was a friend of HERBERT WELSH of the Indian Rights Association and continued to serve on various committees on Indian issues. He also served as president of the National Civil Service Reform League from 1892 to 1901. (See also OURAY; STANDING BEAR.)

SCHUYLER, PETER (Quider). (1657–1724).
Colonial New York Indian commissioner; mayor of Albany.

Peter Schuyler was born in Beverwyck, which later became Albany, New York, after the British takeover of Dutch New Netherland in 1664. A skilled frontiersman, he served as lieutenant of cavalry in the Albany militia.

About 1678, Schuyler became commissioner to the Mohawks and other tribes of the Iroquois League. In 1686, when Albany was incorporated, Schuyler was elected its first mayor. In 1690, he led a delegation of British colonial and military officials to the council fire of the Iroquois at Onondaga and succeeded in preventing the formation of an alliance between the Iroquois and the French during King William's War (1689–97).

At the beginning of Queen Anne's War (1702–13), Schuyler brought five Mohawk leaders to London, where they were warmly received by Queen Anne.

Despite assurances of their loyalty to the British cause, the Iroquois League remained officially neutral in the conflict.

Schuyler served briefly as acting governor of New York in 1719–20. The Mohawk pronunciation of his name was Quider.

SCHUYLER, PHILIP JOHN. (1733–1804). Indian commissioner; soldier; senator.

Philip Schuyler was born and raised in Albany, New York, his family among the wealthiest in colonial New York. He was a grandnephew of PETER SCHUYLER. Schuyler fought in the French and Indian War of 1754–63, and, in 1775, at the start of the American Revolution, became a major general in the Continental army. A member of the Board of Indian Commissioners, he campaigned in the Continental Congress for the passage of a resolution urging Indian neutrality in the conflict with England.

Under the 1783 Treaty of Paris, England ceded a large area of unsettled wilderness west of the Appalachians to the United States. Along with GEORGE WASHINGTON, Schuyler urged the new government to adopt a policy of peaceful negotiations with the Indians of the newly acquired territory. He was concerned over the possibility of a new Indian war developing if the United States suddenly began to claim and settle new lands without making boundary agreements with the Indians.

Support of his position by the Continental Congress led to the 1784 Fort Stanwix Treaty with the Iroquois. Under its terms, the Iroquois League recognized United States dominion, ceded lands in western New York, and gave up claims to lands west of Fort Pitt (Pittsburgh) in Pennsylvania. Subsequent treaties were entered into with the Wyandots, Delawares, Chippewas, and Ottawas at Fort McIntosh in 1785, and with the Shawnees at Fort Finney in 1786. Three years later, the Board of Indian Commissioners negotiated the Fort Harmar treaties with the Iroquois and tribes of the Old Northwest, providing for federal payment in trade goods to the Indians for lands ceded under the earlier agreements.

Philip Schuyler went on to become one of the first two U.S. senators from New York State in 1789–91 and 1797–98. His daughter Elizabeth married Alexander Hamilton.

SCOTT, DUNCAN CAMPBELL. (1862–1947).
Canadian deputy superintendent general of Indian Affairs; writer.

A native of Ottawa, Duncan Campbell Scott gave up his ambition to become a doctor for financial reasons and joined the Canadian Department of Indian Affairs when just 17 years old. His early service coincided with the Second RIEL Rebellion of 1885 in the Canadian West. He became the deputy superintendent in 1913, remaining in that position until his retirement in 1932. During his career in Indian Affairs, Scott also wrote prose and poetry. Many of his short stories, as found in the collection *The Circle of Affection* (1947), concern Indian and frontier themes. His narrative poems on Native American subjects are some of his best-known works, such as *The Forsaken* and *The Onondaga Madonna*. As an Indian administrator, Scott was committed to policies of assimilation into white society. Nonetheless, his literary works imply concern over the disappearance of traditional Indian culture.

SCOTT, HUGH LENOX (Mole-I-Gu-Op, "the man who talks with his hands"). *(1853–1934).*
Indian-sign-language expert; soldier; Indian administrator.

Kentucky-born Hugh Lenox Scott attended schools in Princeton and Lawrenceville, New Jersey, before entering West Point. Upon graduation in 1876, he was stationed with the 7th Cavalry at Fort Totten, North Dakota, serving there for 10 yeras. He learned the Siouan language and began a comprehensive study of Plains Indian language that would continue for the rest of his life. Because of his linguistic knowledge, he often acted as interpreter in negotiations.

Scott became a commander of Indian scouts and helped escort Nez Perce prisoners from Montana to North Dakota in the aftermath of the 1877 Nez Perce uprising. At this time, he witnessed an address by Chief JOSEPH (Young Joseph), delivered entirely in sign language.

After a brief period as a recruiting officer in the East, Scott was reassigned to Fort Sill in the Indian Territory, where he came in contact with Comanches and Kiowas.

In 1891, Scott took command of a newly organized army unit of Indian cavalry, and embarked on an unsuccessful hunt with these Indian soldiers after the outlaw APACHE KID. He was often at odds with the Kiowa leader LONE WOLF and became friends with his rival Ahpiatom.

While at Fort Sill, Scott was permitted to take a photograph of a Ghost Dance ritual, one of the few such pictures ever taken. He was sent by the army to the 1892 Chicago World's Fair, where he addressed ethnologists on the subject of Indian sign language. His talk included demonstrations by Oglala Sioux from WILLIAM "BUFFALO BILL" CODY's Wild West Show.

During a Congressional hearing in Washington concerning the opening of Comanche lands to white settlement, Scott represented the interests of those Comanches opposed to the land transfer, in opposition to Comanche leader QUANAH PARKER. In the early 1890s, he helped arrange the transfer of GERONIMO and other Apaches to Fort Sill from their military prison in Alabama.

In 1897, Scott was assigned to the Smithsonian's Bureau of American Ethnology in Washington, D.C., where he began work on a government-sponsored study of Native American sign languages. The project was interrupted for a number of years when he was sent to Cuba and the Philippines for service in the Spanish-American War and its aftermath. In 1906–10, he served as superintendent of West Point.

In 1909, Scott was made assistant to the secretary of War but continued to play an active role in the management of Indians, especially in the Southwest, helping maintain peaceful relations between the Navajos and Paiutes. In 1911, he helped settle a dispute with Hopi medicine man YOUKIOMA over the sending of Indian children to a white-run school. At the outbreak of World War I, Scott was army chief of staff. After the war, he was a member of the government's oversight committee, the Board of Indian Commissioners.

A government-produced sound and motion picture recording of Scott demonstrating Indian sign language was undertaken in the early 1930s, but remained unfinished at the time of Scott's death.

SCOTT, WINFIELD (Old Fuss and Feathers).
(1786–1866). Army officer in the Black Hawk War, the Second Seminole War, and the Cherokee removal operation.

Born in Petersburg, Virginia, Winfield attended William and Mary College and studied law before entering the army in 1807. The next year, he was commissioned a captain of artillery on the recommendation of President THOMAS JEFFERSON and assigned to duty in New Orleans.

At the outbreak of the war of 1812, Scott rose rapidly to lieutenant colonel and led troops in campaigns on the Niagara frontier, including the Battle of Queenston on October 13, 1812, in which he was captured. He was soon released and promoted to the rank of full colonel and named adjutant to General HENRY DEARBORN. In July 1813, he took part in the American victories over the British and their Indian allies at the battles of Chippewa Creek and Lundy's Lane. He was wounded at Lundy's Lane, and saw no action the rest of the war.

In the 1820s, promoted to major general, Scott commanded the army's Northern Department and took part in resolving boundary disputes between the United States and Canada. In 1832, President ANDREW JACKSON gave him charge of military operations in the Black Hawk War that had broken out in the upper Mississippi region. He led a 950-man force to Wisconsin, but, because of a cholera epidemic among his men, arrived too late to take part in the fighting. On his surrender in August 1832, BLACK HAWK was placed under

General Scott's custody before being sent to Washington, D.C. Soon after, Scott negotiated a treaty with the Sacs and Foxes on September 21, 1832. Under the terms of the Fort Armstrong Treaty, the Indians agreed to cede territory comprising most of the present state of Iowa in return for payments in trade goods.

In 1836, Scott took over field command in Florida during the Second Seminole War against insurgents under OSCEOLA but left without mounting an offensive against the Seminoles because of administrative conflicts with his subordinates, General EDMUND GAINES and General THOMAS JESUP. An 1837 court of inquiry investigated Scott's unauthorized departure from his Florida command, but exonerated him of any wrongdoing.

In 1838, Scott, as commander of the Department of the East, supervised the removal of the Cherokees from their native lands in North Carolina, Georgia, and Tennessee to reservations west of the Mississippi in the Indian Territory. Scott's troops enforced the removal of more than 16,000 Cherokees, led by Chief JOHN ROSS, from their ancestral homelands in this mass-relocation operation, which became known as the Trail of Tears.

In 1841, Scott was named commanding general of the army. In the Mexican War of 1846–48, he did not play an active role until February 1847, when he directed one of the earliest American amphibious invasions, at Veracruz, on the coast of Mexico. His army soon advanced inland to victory at Mexico City, and he was installed for a time as military governor of Mexico.

A national hero, Scott was nominated by the Whig party for president in 1852 but was defeated by Franklin Pierce. Still in charge of the military, he supervised the deployment of federal forces in the South until the outbreak of the Civil War. Scott retired from the army in 1861, at the rank of lieutenant general. (See also BLACK HAWK; OSCEOLA; ROSS, JOHN.)

SEATTLE (Seathl, Sealth, See-yat; Noah).
Duwamish-Suquamish. (ca. 1788–1866). Principal chief; friend to whites.

Seattle's father, Schweabe, was Suquamish, his mother Scholitza, Duwamish. In 1792, as a young boy, Seattle witnessed the arrival of whites in Puget Sound in what is now Washington State. During the 1830s, influenced by French missionaries in his homeland, he converted to Catholicism, taking the name Noah. Even with the great influx of settlers during and after the California Gold Rush of 1849, Seattle, principal chief of his people, encouraged friendship and trade between Indians and whites. In 1852, the white settlement in Puget Sound was given his name.

In 1855, Seattle signed the Fort Elliot Treaty with the governor of Washington Territory ISAAC STEVENS, agreeing that his people would relocate to a reservation.

The breaking of treaty terms by whites led to the Yakima War of 1855–56 east of the Cascade Mountains under KAMIAKIN. The Nisqually Indians living west of the Cascades under LESCHI attacked the Seattle settlement in January 1856, but were repelled. Despite continuing unrest in the region, Seattle remained at peace with whites and led his people to the Port Madison Reservation near present-day Bremerton. He lived in a large community building, about 60 by 900 feet, known as the Old Man House. In his two marriages, he had six children, four of whom died young.

Seattle received a small pension in his final years as an advance toward his afterlife because of his people's belief that the use of a man's name—in his case for what was to become the region's largest city—after his death disturbed his spirit.

SEQUOYAH (Sequoya, Sequoia, Sikwaji, Siwayi, Sogwili, "sparrow" or "principal bird"; George Gist, George Guess, George Guest). *Mixed Cherokee. (ca. 1770–1843).* Inventor of Cherokee syllabary.

Sequoyah was born in Taskigi near present-day Vonore, Tennessee, of a Cherokee mother, Wurteh, and a white father, probably the trader and Revolutionary soldier Nathaniel Gist. As a boy of 12, having moved to the vicinity of Willstown, Alabama, with his mother, Sequoyah built a milkshed and learned how to care for cows and make cheese. He also learned how to break horses and plant corn. He then took up hunting and trading in furs. An injury to his leg from a hunting accident troubled him for the rest of his life. There followed a period of heavy drinking, after which Sequoyah became an accomplished silversmith.

Sequoyah served under General ANDREW JACKSON in the Creek War of 1813–14. The next year, he married a Cherokee woman by the name of Sarah (Sally). In 1818, he and his family emigrated to present-day Pope County, Arkansas, as part of Chief JOHN JOLLY's band.

Earlier, in 1809, although he knew little English at the time, Sequoyah had begun working on a written version of the Cherokee language so that his people could have a written constitution, official records, books, and newspapers. In his first attempt, he made use of pictorial writing, but abandoned it after reaching 1,000 symbols. He eventually reduced the Cherokee language to first 200, then 86 characters representing all the different sounds, some similar to English, Greek, and Hebrew characters. His efforts met with opposition among tribal members, some of whom suspected him of witchcraft. Fellow Cherokees burned his home, destroying his notes.

In 1821, 12 years later, Sequoyah finally finished his vast project, becoming the only person in history to

Sequoyah, with his syllabary of the Cherokee language. *Courtesy of New York State Library, Albany.*

singlehandedly invent an entire alphabet (or a syllabary because the symbols represent syllables as we know them). During a trip East in 1821–22, he demonstrated the practicality of his system by carrying messages from the Arkansas Cherokees to their eastern relatives. The Cherokee Council officially adopted the alphabet and later honored Sequoyah with a silver medal. With translations of parts of the Bible into Cherokee by 1825, white missionaries came to support use of the system. In 1827, through the missionary SAMUEL WORCESTER, the Cherokees acquired a printing press made in Boston, equipped with the syllabary font. That same year, the Cherokees wrote down their constitution. In 1828, the first Cherokee newspaper—the *Cherokee Phoenix*—was published in their language, with ELIAS BOUDINOT as editor. Also in 1828, Sequoyah was part of an Arkansas Cherokee delegation to Wasington, D.C., where he was celebrated for his invention.

Sequoyah moved from Arkansas in 1829 with his wife and children to the Indian Territory near Sallisaw in present-day Sequoya County, Oklahoma. As President of the Western Cherokees, he helped unite Eastern and Western factions in the 1839 Cherokee Act of Union. In 1841, the Cherokee National Council voted him a pension, the first member of any Indian tribe to be so honored.

In 1842, Sequoyah organized an expedition to locate through a study of Indian speech patterns a lost band of Cherokees who had migrated west during the American Revolution. The trip through the Southwest aggravated Sequoyah's already poor health and he died near San Fernando, Tamaulipas, in Mexico.

The state of Oklahoma honored Sequoyah by erecting a statue in the national capitol and by making his farmstead a state historical shrine. Furthermore, the giant redwood trees of Coastal California were named Sequoia in his honor by Stephen Endlicher, the Hungarian botanist who discovered that they were a distinct genus.

SERGEANT, JOHN. *(1710–1749).* Missionary; linguist; educator.

John Sergeant, a native of Newark, New Jersey, was a 1729 Yale College graduate. He stayed on as a tutor at Yale until 1735, when he was ordained a Congregational minister.

Sergeant was commissioned as an evangelist to the Housatonic tribe, a subgroup of the Mahicans who lived at that time in the Berkshires of western Massachusetts. Establishing a Christian Indian community at Stockbridge, Massachusetts, he soon became proficient in writing and speaking the Housatonic's Algonquian dialect. In addition to preaching to the Stockbridge Indians in their native language, he also prepared Bible lessons, a catechism, and translations of prayers in Algonquian.

During his 14 years at Stockbridge, Sergeant attempted to instill elements of white culture on the Indian community. He believed that their salvation could only fully be realized if they adopted white "civilization." To this end, he encouraged the adoption of English as their language.

At the time of his death in 1749, Sergeant's converts numbered as many as 130. He was succeeded at the Stockbridge mission by JONATHAN EDWARDS in 1751.

SERRA, JUNIPERO (Miguel Jose Serra). *(1713–1784).* Explorer; missionary.

Junipero Serra was born on the Spanish Mediterranean island of Majorca. He attended the island's University of Palma, and, in 1730, entered the Franciscan order. Until 1749, he was a professor of theology at Palma, but gave up his academic career to journey to Mexico, along with FRANCISCO PALOU, as a missionary. He taught in Mexico City and worked among the Pame Indians in the eastern Mexican region of Sierra Gorda. In 1768, he was appointed head of all the Baja California missions.

In 1769, Serra joined Spanish army officer and explorer Gaspar de Portola on an expedition to Alta California, now the state of California. Portola's objective was to reaffirm Spain's claim on the region, including that based on the 1602 explorations of the California coast by Sebastian Vizcaino. Serra, leading a contingent of Franciscan missionary priests, served as the religious adjunct to the expedition and planned to establish the first missions to the southern California coastal tribes.

In July 1769, the first such mission, San Diego de Alcala, was established on a hill overlooking present-day San Diego, California. Serra remained at San Diego, while Portola led his men northward in search of Monterey Bay, which Vizcaino had discovered 167 years earlier. The expedition missed Monterey Bay, but reached San Francisco Bay.

Serra joined Portola's second expedition to California the following spring. In 1770, on reaching Monterey Bay, Serra established a second mission, San Carlos Barromeo. In 1771, he relocated the San Carlos Mission from Monterey to the nearby site of present-day Carmel, California, in order to insulate his Indian charges from the corrupting influences of the Spanish garrison.

Over the next decade and a half, Serra founded seven more missions along the Califorania coast, including San Antonio de Padua (1771), San Gabriel Archangel (1771), San Luis Obispo (1772), San Juan Capistrano (1776), San Francisco de Asis (1776), Santa Clara de Asis (1777), and Santa Buenaventura (1782). In addition to converting thousands of Indians, the missionaries imported livestock and vegetable seeds from Spanish settlements in northern Baja California, which they used to introduce agriculture to their converts. The missions developed into church-run plantations that made extensive use of forced Indian labor.

During the late 1770s and early 1780s, Serra successfully campaigned for increased military and economic support from Spanish Mexico for his California mission work, which brought white colonization onto the Indian lands of coastal California. He also served as the local administrator of the Spanish Inquisition, and in this capacity condoned harsh punishments against Indian transgressors of Christian rules of conduct, including whippings. Nevertheless, he is credited with protecting the Indians of California from excessive exploitation by the Spanish, and with introducing an "Indian Bill of Rights."

Throughout his work in California, Serra was plagued with ill health, aggravated by his lame leg. In addition, his physical condition was further weakened by his regular practice of self-flagellation to test his faith.

Serra died in 1784 at his mission headquarters in Carmel. In 1985, in recognition of his missionary efforts among the California Indians, he was beatified by Pope John Paul II. Leaders from the Cahuilla tribe protested the act, claiming that Serra's work actually contributed to Indian enslavement in early California.

SETANGYA. See SATANK.

SETON, ERNEST THOMPSON (Ernest Evan Thompson, Ernest Seton-Thompson). *(1860–1946).* Writer; artist; naturalist.

Ernest Evan Thompson was born in England and raised on a farm near Lindsay, Ontario, then in Toronto. He returned to England for art studies. His grandfather, a Cameron by birth, had lived under the assumed name of Thompson and had been heir and successor to a cousin George Seton, earl of Winton. Ernest legally adopted the name Seton in 1898; in the course of his career, he variously signed his art work Ernest E. Thompson, E.S.T., Ernest Seton-Thompson, and Ernest Thompson Seton, the last the most commonly used.

In 1882, Seton joined his brother on his farm in Manitoba, using it as a base for travels in the Canadian and American West for four years. He came into contact with Indian peoples, beginning a lifelong fascination with Indian lore. In 1886, he was the official naturalist for the Manitoba government and wrote and illustrated *Mammals of Manitoba* (1886) and *Birds of Manitoba* (1891).

Seton later lived in New York City. He established the Woodcraft Indians in 1902 (later known as the Woodcraft League), the first outdoors organization for boys and girls in America. He also became chairman of the committee that founded the Boy Scouts of America in 1910, which also included the Sioux CHARLES EASTMAN. Both organizations preserved Indian traditions in their activities. The first Boy Scout handbook was written by Seton, and he produced numerous articles and illustrated books about wildlife and Indians for young readers, such as *The Book of Woodcraft and Indian Lore* (1912).

Seton had a special interest in Native American religion. Late in life, he lived in Santa Fe, New Mexico, near where he founded the College of Indian Wisdom, dedicated to the preservation of Indian culture.

SEVIER, JOHN (Nolichucky Jack). *(1745–1815).* Military officer; frontiersman; land speculator; official.

Born in the frontier region of Virginia, John Sevier became involved in business and land speculation before he was 18. In 1772, along with JAMES ROBERTSON, he helped open up the area of what is now Tennessee to settlement with the formation of the Watauga Assocation.

Sevier fought against CORNSTALK's Shawnees in Lord DUNMORE's War of 1774, taking part in the Battle of Point Pleasant in October. With the outbreak of the American Revolution the next year, Sevier was appointed a lieutenant colonel in the militia. When Cherokees led by DRAGGING CANOE, allied to the British, began raiding settlements in the Watauga region in the summer of 1776, Sevier, with Kentucky frontiersman ISAAC SHELBY, organized defensive fortifications at Sycamore Shoals and at Eaton's Station.

Sevier and Shelby managed to rally the Watauga and Holston River militiamen to counterattack, and the Cherokees were driven back after a three-week siege.

With Shelby and other militiamen, Sevier took part in the victory at the Battle of Kings Mountain, South Carolina, in October 1780, over Tory troops under Major Patrick Ferguson. That same year, with Virginia militia colonel Arthur Campbell, Sevier led a force of 700 Virginia and North Carolina militia against the Cherokees and destroyed their main settlement at Chickamauga. From 1780 to 1782, he undertook raids on Cherokee lands in North Carolina and the region of present-day Tennessee, resulting in the Cherokees ceding additional territory to Sevier and his land speculators.

In 1784, after North Carolina had ceded its western lands to the federal government, Sevier took part in the establishment of the short-lived state of Franklin. As governor, in 1784–88, he was instrumental in negotiating the Treaty of Dumpling Creek with the Cherokees. Under this treaty, the Cherokees ceded nearly all their lands to Franklin. The federal government refused to recognize the new state, however, nor did it recognize the validity of the Dumpling Creek Treaty. Sevier was imprisoned for a time because of his role.

After 1788, Sevier was instrumental in the creation of the state of Tennessee out of the western North Carolina lands. Before becoming Tennessee's first governor in 1796, he served in the North Carolina legislature and also represented that state in Congress. After 1810, he was a congressman from Tennessee. In this capacity, he favored war against England as well as a military campaign against the Indians who were hampering settlement west of the Alleghenies. In 1815, he was appointed a federal commissioner to survey the boundary between Creek territory in Alabama and the state of Georgia, dying while involved in this project.

Sevier's political and military activities, about 30 battles with the Cherokees, contributed to the settlement of this area and the expulsion of Indians from Tennessee, North Carolina, and Georgia. His land speculation activities in the trans-Allegheny region were typical of the frontiersmen who disregarded the terms of the treaties with the Indians that had guaranteed protection from white encroachment onto their lands to the west. Throughout his political career in Tennessee, he was a political rival and personal antagonist of ANDREW JACKSON. (See also DRAGGING CANOE.)

SEYMOUR, SAMUEL. (1797–1823). Painter; illustrator.

English-born artist Samuel Seymour spent most of his career as an engraver in Philadelphia. In 1819–20, he joined Major STEPHEN H. LONG's exploration of the central Plains and Rocky Mountains as official artist. Fellow painter Titian Ramsay Peale served as official naturalist. In 1823, Seymour accompanied a second expedition under Long to the upper Mississippi River and the region of Lake of the Woods and Lake Winnipeg in Minnesota and Manitoba. In addition to his landscape views, Seymour produced miniature portraits of Indians, as well as depictions of their everyday life and customs.

SHABONEE (Shabona, Shabbona, Shaubena, Chambly). *Potawatomi-Ottawa. (1775–1859).* Ally of TECUMSEH and the British in the War of 1812; ally of Americans in the Winnebago Uprising of 1827 and the Black Hawk War of 1832.

Shabonee was born either along the Maumee River in Ohio or along the Kankakee River in Illinois. His father was an Ottawa, perhaps the nephew of PONTIAC, and his mother a Seneca.

In 1807, Shabonee joined Tecumseh's cause and traveled among the Indians of Illinois to persuade them to join the alliance of tribes. He fought in the War of 1812 on the side of the British, but, along with ALEXANDER ROBINSON, SAGAUNASH, and TOPENEBEE, he tried to prevent the massacre of American settlers at Fort Dearborn (present-day Chicago) in 1812.

Following the war, Shabonee settled among his wife's people, the Potawatomis. When his father-in-law, the principal chief, died, Shabonee inherited the leadership. In the following years, he was an advocate of peace between settlers and Indians. During the Winnebago Uprising of 1827 under RED BIRD, he counseled peace and was taken hostage for a time by militants who accused him of being a spy for the federal government. BLACK HAWK twice tried unsuccessfully to convince Shabonee to join his revolt of 1832. When Shabonee could not dissuade the Sac leader from violence at a council of tribes, he and his son went on a Paul Revere-like midnight ride from Princeton, Illinois, to Chicago, warning the white settlements of the coming hostilities. The Sacs and Foxes attempted to kill him for this betrayal and took the life of his son and nephew.

Although Shabonee's followers were granted tracts of lands in Illinois by treaties following both wars, they were forced to relocate west of the Mississippi with other Potawatomis. In 1855, Shabonee returned to Illinois to claim his treaty lands, but found that they had been declared abandoned and sold at a public auction. He was forcibly evicted. Sympathetic whites bought him a tract of land near Morris, Illinois, where he lived with his two wives. He was succeeded as chief by his grandson Smoke.

SHAHAKA (Sheheke, "coyote"; Big White, Le Gros Blanc; Bag of Lies). *Mandan. (ca. 1765–ca. 1815).* Friend to MERIWETHER LEWIS and WILLIAM CLARK; visitor to Washington, D.C.

Shahaka was head chief of Metutahanke, the lower village of the Mandans, near where the Knife River flows into the Missouri in present-day North Dakota. He provided food and lodging to the Lewis and Clark Expedition at Fort Mandan in the winter of 1804–05 and advised the explorers on their mapping of the region. Lewis presented him with a medal.

Eighteen months later, during the expedition's return stopover, Lewis invited Shahaka to Washington. The chief agreed, but insisted on being accompanied by one of his wives, his son, plus his interpreter Rene Jusseaume and his wife and two sons. The party stayed in the East for a year in both Washington and Philadelphia, where the Frenchman Charles Balthasar Julien Fevre de Saint-Memin painted Shahaka's portrait. The chief also paid a visit to President THOMAS JEFFERSON's home to see his collection of Indian artifacts.

Shahaka's first trip up the Missouri from St. Louis with Nathaniel Pryor (formerly of the Lewis and Clark Expedition), AUGUSTE PIERRE CHOUTEAU, and a party of Sioux was delayed because of hostilities among the upper Missouri tribes, in which Jusseaume was wounded. With the protection of the Missouri Fur Company, Shahaka's party reached his village in September 1809, but he never regained his former prestige among his people, who accused him of lying about his travel experiences. He later died in a fight with the Sioux.

SHAKEHAND. *Yankton Sioux. (fl. early 1800s).* Principal chief.

Shakehand first received historical notice when he visited Mackinaw, Michigan, then St. Louis. In August 1804, at the council between MERIWETHER LEWIS and WILLIAM CLARK and the Sioux along the Missouri River near present-day Yankton, South Dakota, Shakehand was the spokesman for the Indians. STRUCK-BY-THE-REE was born among the Yanktons at that time.

SHAKES (Shaikes). *Tlingit. (fl. 1800s).* Principal chief; trading partner of whites.

Shakes was the name applied to a number of hereditary Tlingit chiefs living on Wrangell Island in the Alexander Archipelago off southeast Alaska. The first was mentioned in connection with the 1841–42 expedition of GEORGE SIMPSON. The Shakes family became one of the richest and most powerful among the Tlingits because of the fur trade on their island and up the Stikine River on the mainland conducted by both the Russians and English. Following the purchase of Alaska by the United States in 1867, missionaries arrived at Wrangell but failed to convert Chief Shakes. In the early 1900s, the last of the Shakes line founded a museum with an extensive collection of Northwest Coast Indian artifacts. He died in 1944.

SHAKOPEE (Shakpay, Shakpe, "six"). *Mdewakanton Sioux. (d. 1862).* Friend to whites. Father of SHAKOPEE (the younger).

Several Mdewakanton chiefs bore the name Shakopee. Their village was located along the Minnesota River near where the town Shakopee now stands. The Shakopee who signed the Traverse des Sioux Treaty in 1851 and traveled to Washington, D.C., in 1858, was in favor of peace with whites and was influential among Santee bands throughout the region. According to some sources, if Shakopee had lived longer, the Minnesota Uprising of 1862–63 under LITTLE CROW would not have occurred. His son of the same name participated in the conflict.

SHAKOPEE (Shakpadan, Little Six). *Mdewakanton Sioux. (d. 1863).* Leader in the Minnesota Uprising of 1862–63. Son of Shakopee (the older).

Although his father of the same name was a proponent of peace with whites, Shakopee was under the influence of his militant uncle Hockokaduta (Red Middle Voice). Soon after his father's death in 1862, Shakopee joined LITTLE CROW in his uprising and eventually fled to Canada with other Santees. In 1864, Major Edwin Hatch under General HENRY HASTINGS SIBLEY arranged for Shakopee's and Medicine Bottle's kidnapping across the border. They were brought back to the United States, sentenced to death, and hanged. (See also LITTLE CROW.)

SHARITARISH (Angry Chief). *Pawnee. (ca. 1790–1822).* Tribal delegate to Washington, D.C.

Sharitarish and his older brother Tarecawawaho were the sons of a chief of the Grand Pawnees. In 1806, ZEBULON PIKE met up with them along the Republican River in what is now Nebraska. Tarecawawaho succeeded his father as chief and was invited by Indian agent BENJAMIN O'FALLON to visit Washington with chiefs representing other tribes of the region, including Kaws, Missouris, Omahas, and Oto. Tarecawawaho refused and sent his brother Sharitarish instead. There, on February 22, 1822, Sharitarish delivered a famous speech to President James Monroe and Secretary of War JOHN C. CALHOUN calling for his people's self-determination. During the trip, his portrait was painted by CHARLES BIRD KING. His popularity on his return led to a dispute with his brother; Tarecawawaho died soon afterward and Sharitarish became chief. Within several months, he also died, presumably from cholera.

SHARP, JOSEPH HENRY. *(1859–1953).* Artist.

J. H. Sharp was born in Bridgeport, Ohio, and studied art in Cincinnati, then in Europe. At the age of 24, he journeyed throughout New Mexico, Arizona, California, and the Pacific Northwest, where he made sketches of Indians.

During the following years, Sharp was an instructor at the Cincinnati Art Museum, but almost every summer he traveled west to continue his studies of Indians.

Sharp's well-received exhibition of Indian paintings at the 1900 Paris Exposition soon led to his being commissioned by the federal government to execute additional works depicting Indians for the Smithsonian Institution. He established a studio at the Crow Indian agency in Montana, near the site of the Battle of Little Bighorn, and produced over 200 portraits of Indian warriors believed to have been participants in the conflict.

Beginning in 1909, Sharp made Taos his permanent base, establishing his studio in a building across the street from the former home of CHRISTOPHER "KIT" CARSON. With fellow painters Ernest Blumenschein and Irving Couse, whom he had met in Paris, Sharp helped establish the Taos Society of Artists in 1902.

SHAWANAHDIT, NANCY (Shananditti).
Beothuk. (d. 1829). Last Beothuk on record.

In the culture of the Beothuks of Newfoundland, petty thievery was permitted. The persistent loss of property angered the French fishermen who frequented the island in the 1600s. They armed the Micmacs and placed bounties on Beothuk scalps. As a result of Micmac raids, by the early 1700s, the Beothuks were practically extinct. Those who survived did so by hiding out among other tribes, especially the Naskapis. The last known tribal member, Nancy Shawanahdit, who lived in St. Johns, Newfoundland, died in 1829.

SHAWNEE PROPHET. See TENSKWATAWA.

SHELBY, ISAAC. (1750–1826). Militia officer; land speculator; governor of Kentucky.

Born in Frederick County, Maryland, Isaac Shelby was the son of Revolutionary officer Evan Shelby. In 1773, he settled in what is now eastern Tennessee. The following year, as a member of the Virginia militia, he took part in Lord DUNMORE's War under the command of General ANDREW LEWIS against CORNSTALK's Shawnees of the Ohio Valley.

During the American Revolution, Shelby was involved in fighting British-allied Indians in the outlying regions of North Carolina and what is now Kentucky. His militia unit, along with that of JOHN SEVIER, played a significant role in the defeat of the Loyalists at the Battle of Kings Mountain, South Carolina, in October 1780. He also fought in the American victory at Cowpens, South Carolina, in January 1781.

After the war, Shelby served in the North Carolina legislature. He had worked as a surveyor for the Tran-sylvania Company and became involved in the land speculations surrounding the settlement of Kentucky in the 1780s. He also served as sheriff in western North Carolina and, at the same time, played an active role in the political process that created the state of Kentucky in 1792. He became Kentucky's first governor in that year.

Shelby left public life after 1796, but was elected governor of Kentucky again in 1812. During the War of 1812, he led a company of 4,000 Kentucky volunteers in General WILLIAM HENRY HARRISON's expedition against the British and Indians in northern Ohio. Shelby and his Kentucky riflemen took part in the defeat of the British and their Indian auxiliaries under the Shawnee leader TECUMSEH at the Battle of the Thames in October 1813.

Four years later, Shelby was offered the post of secretary of War by President James Monroe, but declined the appointment because of his age. In 1818, along with ANDREW JACKSON, he negotiated a treaty under which the Chickasaws agreed to sell their remaining lands in Kentucky and Tennessee. After this treaty, Shelby retired permanently to private life.

SHELIKOV, GREGORI IVANOVICH (Grigori Ivanovich Shelekhov). (1747–1795). Trader.

Born at Rylsk in the Ukraine, Gregori Shelikov left his home in 1775 and headed for the frontier region of eastern Siberia. He settled on the Kamchatka Peninsula, part of Siberia's Pacific coast, where he entered the fur trade, eventually expanding his operation seaward to the Kuril and Aleutian Islands. In 1783, he married the daughter of a wealthy family from the Siberian city of Irkutsk, enabling him to raise the capital necessary to extend his fur enterprise to Alaska.

In 1783, Shelikov and his wife led an expedition aboard the ship *The Three Saints* across the Bering Sea into the Gulf of Alaska. They landed on Kodiak Island in August 1784, where they subdued the native Aleuts with a combination of diplomacy and a show of arms and founded the first permanent Alaskan white settlement.

Shelikov returned to European Russia in the mid-1780s to try to obtain a trade monopoly from Empress Catherine the Great, but was denied such exclusive rights. Operating his fur enterprise from Irkutsk, Siberia, Shelikov developed the fur trade into a profitable venture. He appointed ALEKSANDR BARANOV as resident director of Kodiak.

In 1799, four years after his death, Shelikov's widow, sons, and sons-in-law were able to obtain a royal charter for their Alaskan fur enterprise, which then became the Russian-American Company. Under Baranov, the firm established through Shelikov's initial efforts went on to dominate the fur trade with the Aleuts and Tlingits of

Alaska, as well as other native peoples of the Pacific Coast, including the Pomos of California.

SHERIDAN, PHILIP HENRY. *(1831–1888).*
Army officer in the Plains Indian wars.

Philip Henry Sheridan was born in New York and raised in Ohio. He was admitted to West Point in 1848, graduating after five years instead of the usual four because of a one-year suspension for fighting. He was then assigned to frontier duty at military posts in the Rio Grande Valley of Texas, then in the Pacific Northwest, where he took part in the 1855–56 Yakima War against warriors under KAMIAKIN.

Sheridan rose to prominence in the Civil War, achieving the rank of major general after his successes in campaigns in Tennessee and Virginia. In 1864, appointed by General ULYSSES S. GRANT as commander of the 12,000-man cavalry division of the Army of the Potomac, he eventually cut off Robert E. Lee's Confederate forces in Virginia, helping bring about the South's surrender in April 1865.

Following the war, as commander of the Division of the Gulf in 1865–67, Sheridan provided support for the overthrow of the French-supported monarch Maximilian by liberal forces in Mexico. He then commanded the Fifth Military District, including Texas and Louisiana, for six months in 1867, but was criticized for his harsh imposition of Reconstruction programs.

Sheridan was transferred to the Department of the Missouri (Missouri, Kansas, Colorado, New Mexico), replacing General WINFIELD SCOTT HANCOCK. In 1868–69, he directed the war against Southern Cheyennes, Southern Arapahos, Sioux, Comanches, and Kiowas, known as the Sheridan Campaign. Major GEORGE FORSYTH and Colonel GEORGE ARMSTRONG CUSTER were officers in the field against the Cheyenne TALL BULL and other chiefs.

In 1869, Sheridan was made lieutenant general and placed in command of the vast military Division of the Missouri, which, since 1866, included four departments—Department of the Missouri, Department of the Platte, Department of Dakota and Department of Arkansas—comprising most of the Great Plains. That year, WILLIAM T. SHERIDAN succeeded Ulysses S. Grant as general and commander of the entire army.

In 1870–71, Sheridan was a guest of the Prussian government, when he observed engagements against the French in the Franco-Prussian War. He returned to the Great Plains and subsequently directed and coordinated the campaigns of colonels RANALD S. MACKENZIE and NELSON A. MILES against the Comanches under QUANAH PARKER, plus Kiowas, Southern Cheyennes, and Southern Arapahos in the Red River War of 1874–75. Sheridan was also responsible for moving a military presence into Dakota's Black Hills in 1873–74. He directed the campaigns of his subordinate generals GEORGE CROOK, ALFRED TERRY, and JOHN GIBBON in the War for the Black Hills of 1876–77 against Sioux under SITTING BULL and CRAZY HORSE, plus Northern Cheyennes and Northern Arapahos.

In 1883, Sheridan became commander in chief of the army, replacing Sherman, and oversaw the last phase of the Apache Wars under GERONIMO. In 1886, it was his decision to replace General Crook with General Miles in the Department of Arizona.

In 1888, Sheridan was promoted to the army's highest rank, general of the army. He died that year, while still actively in command of all U.S. land forces.

Sheridan took an unsympathetic view of Indian peoples in revolt. His overall strategy against the Plains Indians was based on the idea of bringing "total war" to them. His attacks concentrated not only on warriors, but were aimed at the entire people of those tribes resisting federal authority. The strategy of bringing the war to the people had proved extremely successful in subduing the Confederacy when it was applied by Sheridan in the Shenandoah Valley and by Sherman in his sweep through Georgia. Sheridan and Sherman also adopted the strategy of winter campaigns against the Plains tribes. In the winter, the Indians were forced to stay in concentrated numbers in their villages, having no outside lines of supply as the army did. To support their campaigns against the Indians, Sheridan initiated the construction of a series of new forts throughout the West, such as Fort Sill in the Indian Territory, bases from which troops could be rapidly deployed. (See also GERONIMO; KAMIAKIN; PARKER, QUANAH; SITTING BULL; TALL BULL.)

SHERMAN, WILLIAM TECUMSEH.
(1820–1891). Army officer in the Plains Indian wars.

William Tecumseh Sherman, named in part after the Shawnee leader TECUMSEH, was born in Lancaster, Ohio. On the death of his father, he was raised in the home of the statesman Thomas Ewing. Sherman graduated from West Point in 1840 and served in the Second Seminole War of 1835–42 and the Mexican War of 1846–48. He left the service in 1853, and pursued a short career in banking and law.

At the outbreak of the Civil War, Sherman was the superintendent of the Louisiana state military academy. He resigned from this post upon Louisiana's secession from the Union and received a commission as colonel in the Union army. He rose rapidly in the ranks. Sherman's famous march through Georgia and South Carolina in 1864–65 severely damaged the Confederacy's ability to continue the war and led to the final surrender of the South in 1865.

In 1866, Sherman became commander of the Division of the Missouri out of headequarters in St. Louis. This command included what was formerly the Department of the Missouri, plus Arkansas and the Indian Territory. In the new structure, the subgroupings of Sherman's division were now Department of the Missouri (Missouri, Kansas, Colorado, and New Mexico); Department of the Platte (Iowa, Nebraska, Utah, and parts of Dakota and Montana); Department of Dakota (Minnesota and the rest of Dakota and Montana); and Department of Arkansa (Arkansas and the Indian Territory).

Sherman concluded an inspection tour of the West in 1866 and planned the task of safely opening the frontier to further white settlement. He was also a member of President Andrew Johnson's Peace Commission that met with Southern Plains chiefs at Medicine Lodge, Kansas, in October 1867, and resulted in treaties assigning large reservations to the Southern Plains tribes.

Sherman's overall objective in the late 1860s was to restrict the Northern Plains Indians to areas north of the Platte River and the Southern Plains Indians to reservations south of the Arkansas River. He hoped to create a protected area through the nation's midsection for the construction of the transcontinental Union Pacific Railroad.

In 1869, Sherman was named general of the army, succeeding General ULYSSES S. GRANT, and served thereafter as the supreme commander of U.S. forces during the Indian Wars of the 1870s and early 1880s. At this time, General PHILIP H. SHERIDAN replaced him as commander of the Division of the Missouri. Now working out of Washington, D.C., Sherman found himself frustrated at not being able to influence the course of events in the field. He was also frustrated by the reduction in size of the post–Civil War army. Despite his distaste for politics and bureaucracy, he lobbied for changes in Indian policy, such as the transfer of the Indian Territory back to the War Department from the Interior Department, which was never realized. In 1874–76, Sherman maintained his headquarters again in St. Louis as a respite from the capital's affairs.

In May 1871, during a trip West, Sherman met with Kiowa leaders, including SATANTA, SATANK, and BIG TREE, at Fort Sill in the Indian Territory. At this meeting, he ordered the Kiowa leaders arrested and turned over to Texas civil authorities to answer for depredations committed against whites in Texas, including an earlier attack on a wagon train in advance of his own, along the Butterfield Southern Route.

With his subordinate Sheridan, Sherman brought the concept of advancing lines of forts into the frontier, as well as bringing total war to hostiles, a strategy that had helped defeat the Confederacy in the Civil War. Thus the army fought not only bands of Indian warriors, but attacked the villages of the Plains tribes, destroying their means of survival as well as their ability and will to wage war. Sherman and Sheridan also helped institute a program of winter military offensives against the Plains Indians.

Sherman retired from the service in 1884. All the Indian wars of the post–Civil War era had occurred under his tenure, except the last years of the Apache GERONIMO's resistance through 1886 and the Ghost Dance Uprising of 1890.

Sherman repeatedly rejected offers to run for the presidency on the Republican ticket. His younger brother, John Sherman, served as a congressman and cabinet member.

SHICKSHACK. *Winnebago. (fl. 1820s–1830s).* Friend to whites.

In 1819, because of warfare with the Chippewas, Shickshack led his Winnebago band farther south in Illinois to lands along the Sangamon River in Illinois, where he established a village and maintained peaceful relations with white settlers. During the Winnebago Uprising of 1827 under RED BIRD, Shickshack returned with his people to northern Illinois to avoid hostilities. During the Black Hawk War of 1832, he was at Dixon's Ferry. He was reportedly one of the Winnebagos among whom the Sac leader BLACK HAWK sought refuge. It is assumed that Shickshack and his band were forced to relocate to Kansas along with the militant Winnebago bands following the war.

SHIKELLAMY (Shikallamy, Shikellimy, Shikelimo, Shikellima, Shikellemus, Shickelimy, Shickalamy, Shick Calamy, Shekellamy, Shekallamly, Shakallamy, Shecalamy, Shykelimy, Sicalamous, Swatana, Swatane, Swataney; Takashwangarous; Onkiswathetami, Ongwaterohiathe, Ungquaterughiathe, "he causes it to be light for us," "our enlightener"). *Oneida.*
(d. 1748). Iroquois leader in Pennsylvania. Father of LOGAN.

It is uncertain whether Shickellamy was born a Cayuga or part-French. In any case, he was kidnapped while young by the Oneidas, grew up along the upper Schuylkill River in Pennsylvania, and rose to prominence within their tribe. He was selected by the Iroquois League of Six Nations in council at Onondaga, New York, as their representative or provincial governor for Iroquois holdings along the Susquehanna Valley of Pennsylvania. To carry out this function, he moved to Shamokin (present-day Sunbury, Pennsylvania).

Shikellamy had numerous dealigs with leaders from tributary tribes of the Iroquois—the Delawares, Shawnees, Susquehannocks—as well as with Pennsylvania officials, Moravian missionaries, and representatives of the Susquehanna Land company. In 1736, he was central to the formation of the Pennsylvania-Six Nations alliance in which the Iroquois became responsible for Pennsylvania's Indians. He also worked to reduce the sale of liquor to Indians by white traders and to have a forge established at Shamokin for supplying iron to the Iroquois. When he negotiated the sale by the Iroquois to the English of formerly Delaware Indian lands, he set off a period of Delaware unrest.

The Delaware TEEDYUSCUNG and the Shawnee PAXINOS were other important Indian leaders along the Susquehanna Valley during and after Shikellamy's tenure. Shikellamy was a close friend of the Indian agent CONRAD WEISER and the missionary DAVID ZEISBERGER. The latter nursed him on his deathbed. One of Shickellamy's sons known as Logan, named after the Pennsylvania official JAMES LOGAN, became a leader of the Ohio Iroquois, or Mingos.

SHINGABAWASSIN (Shingaba W'Ossin, "image stone"). *Chippewa (Ojibway). (d. ca. 1832).*
Friend to whites; spokesman for Chippewa bands.

Shingabawassin, living on Michigan's Upper Peninsula, earned his reputation in warfare against the Foxes and the Sioux and rose to be one of the most influential chiefs of the Chippewas in the early 1800s. His daughter married John Johnston, a trader out of Montreal. Shingabawassin signed a treaty at Sault Ste. Marie in 1820. At later conferences with the federal government from 1825 to 1827, negotiated by LEWIS CASS, THOMAS McKENNEY, and HENRY ROWE SCHOOLCRAFT at Prairie du Chien, Fond du Lac, and Butte des Morts, Shingabawassin acted as principal spokesman for the Chippewas. In a show of friendship, he revealed to whites the location of copper deposits at the mouth of the Ontonagon River. He also encouraged the founding of a school among his people.

SHORT BULL. *Brule Sioux. (ca. 1845–1915).*
Medicine man; apostle of the Ghost Dance.
Brother-in-law of KICKING BEAR.

Short Bull was born along the Niobrara River in what is now Nebraska. In the winter of 1889–90, he was part of the delegation of 11 Sioux, including the medicine man Kicking Bear, to travel to Pyramid Lake, Nevada, to meet with the Paiute WOVOKA, the founder of the Ghost Dance religion. Kicking Bear spread the new message at the Cheyenne River Reservation in South Dakota and then at Standing Rock in North Dakota; Short Bull taught the dance at Rosebud, others, at Pine Ridge.

In October 1890, Short Bull led the Ghost Dancers from the Rosebud Reservation to what he proclaimed was a sacred tree at Pass Creek. From there, he led his followers along the White River to the Badlands in the northwest corner of the Pine Ridge Reservation—an escarpment known as the Stronghold—to join up with Oglalas and Miniconjous under Kicking Bear and Little Wound, and Brules under Two Strike and CROW DOG.

The death of the Hunkpapas SITTING BULL and the buildup of troops led to the abandonment of the Stronghold. The massacre at Wounded Knee and the death of the Miniconjou BIG FOOT also reduced the number of dancers. For some time afterward, however, Short Bull and a small group of followers quietly continued practicing the forbidden religion. In 1891, he joined WILLIAM "BUFFALO BILL" CODY's Wild West Show. In his final years, he joined the Congregational church. (See also BIG FOOT; KICKING BEAR; WOVOKA.)

SIBLEY, HENRY HASTINGS. *(1811–1891).*
Army officer in the Minnesota Uprising; governor of Minnesota; peace commissioner; trader.

In 1828, Henry Hastings Sibley, son of a prominent Detroit family, began working for JOHN JACOB ASTOR's American Fur Company at Sault Ste. Marie in the Michigan Territory. In 1834, he was appointed manager of the fur company's operations on the upper Misssissippi near Fort Snelling in what is now Minnesota. His years with the American Fur Company put him in contact with various tribes of the western Great Lakes.

In the 1840s–50s, Sibley became prominent in territorial politics, helping to organize Minnesota as a territory. He also negotiated land cessions by the Sioux in 1851. When Minnesota was admitted to the Union, Sibley was elected its first governor in 1857.

In 1862, following his service as governor, Sibley was appointed as a colonel in the state's volunteer militia and assigned to pacify the Minnesota Uprising of Santee Sioux under LITTLE CROW in southwestern Minnesota. Following the Battle of Birch Coulee on the Minnesota River of September 2, Sibley's 1,400 volunteer forces successfully relieved a burial detachment of regulars who had been surrounded and besieged for almost two days. Sibley's militia then decisively defeated the rebels at the Battle of Wood Lake on September 23. Sibley also recovered 12 white women held captive by the Santees. Little Crow fled to the Dakotas and Canada with a following of militants. The majority of Santees surrendered, however.

Sibley arrested more than 2,000 of the warriors and turned them over to Minnesota civil authorities, who tried them for the crimes of murder and rape. Of those in custody, 303 were sentenced to hang. President ABRAHAM LINCOLN subsequently pardoned all but 38 of them. For his service against the Santee Sioux, Sibley was promoted to the rank of brigadier general.

In June 1863, Sibley, with General ALFRED SULLY, undertook an expedition consisting of over 4,000 men and artillery against the Sioux in the Dakota Territory. During that July, he was successful in military engagements against the bands of Sioux at Big Mound, Dead Buffalo Lake, and Stony Lake in the eastern Dakota Territory.

In 1865–66, Sibley was a peace commissioner to the Sioux, supervising treaty negotiations. After 1866, he settled in St. Paul, Minnesota, where he became a prominent business and social leader. (See also LITTLE CROW.)

SIEBER, ALBERT. *(1844–1907).* Army scout in the Apache Wars.

Al Sieber moved with his family from Germany to Lancaster County, Pennsylvania, as a child of five. During the Civil War, he served as an enlisted man in the Union army, and was wounded twice at the Battle of Gettysburg in 1863.

After his discharge in 1865, Sieber journeyed to the Southwest and settled in southern Arizona. He became fluent in both Spanish and the Apaches' Athapascan language. His linguisitc ability, coupled with his expertise at tracking and his knowledge of Apache-style warfare, brought him to the attention of General GEORGE CROOK, who hired him as his chief of civilian scouts in 1870. He was placed in joint command, with regular officers, of a company of San Carlos Reservation Apaches. Scouts MICKEY FREE and TOM HORN were assistants to Sieber in actions against the Chiricahuas.

Sieber served in the campaign against the White Mountain Apache leader NATIOTISH, leading cavalry troops to the Apaches at the Battle of Big Dry Wash, Arizona, on July 17, 1882. In this engagement, Sieber's scouts warned Captain Adna Chaffee of an impending Apache ambush in a canyon, and Chaffee was able to avert the Apache trap, mounting his own successful assault.

Following GERONIMO's outbreak from the San Carlos Reservation in 1881, Sieber led an advance party of scouts 100 miles into Mexico, and eventually helped obtain the surrender of over 300 Apaches, including Geronimo. After Geronimo and his followers had again fled the San Carlos Reservation in May 1885, Sieber scouted for Lieutenant BRITTON DAVIS's company of regulars and Apache scouts that crossed into Mexico in pursuit. On this expedition, Sieber led a raid on an Apache encampment in which Geronimo's son was killed.

Sieber scouted for General NELSON A. MILES when he relieved Crook in the spring of 1886, again in pursuit of Geronimo. The following year, Sieber was wounded by one of his Indian scouts, the APACHE KID.

In 1907, while supervising a crew of Apache workers building a road near Arizona's Roosevelt Dam, Sieber was killed in a rockslide. (See also GERONIMO; NATIOTISH.)

SIMMS, WILLIAM GILMORE. *(1806–1870).* Writer.

William Gilmore Simms was born in Charleston, South Carolina, where he lived most of his life, except for a period in New York City during the 1830s. He wrote historical novels, as well as nonfiction and poetry, and served as an editor for the Charleston *City Gazette*.

Simms's fiction depicted the early settlement of the colonial south and settlers' relations with Indians. In his novel, *The Yemassee* (1835), he included a description of the ritual killing of an Indian youth, who was punished by his tribe for adopting the vices of the white man. Simms also wrote a biography of the leader of the Jamestown colony Captain JOHN SMITH, in which he included an account of the Powhatan POCAHONTAS. In his short story collection, *The Wigwam and the Cabin* (1845), he classified Indians along with blacks as culturally backward.

In addition to his career as a man of letters, Simms studied and practiced law in his native Charleston and served in South Carolina's state legislature. During the Civil War, his home was destroyed. Because of his historical romances, Simms has been referred to as the South's JAMES FENIMORE COOPER.

SIMPSON, GEORGE. *(ca. 1787–1860).* Administrator of the Hudson's Bay Company; explorer.

George Simpson, originally from Loch Broom, Scotland, was an accountant in London before coming to the Lake Athabasca region of northern Canada in 1820. He was given charge of the Hudson's Bay Company's fur-trading operation in the Athabasca district, much of which involved Indian suppliers and mixed-blood employees.

With the merger of the Hudson's Bay and North West companies in 1821, Simpson became governor of the northern department of Rupert's Land. In 1826, he became governor-in-chief of all the Hudson's Bay Company's territories in North America.

Simpson sponsored many explorations to the Canadian Arctic and, during the 1820s, himself undertook several overland journeys from Hudson Bay to the Pacific and back. His journals of these expeditions were later published as *Fur Trade and Empire* (1931). In 1841–42, he made a round-the-world journey from northern Canada to European Russia, via Siberia.

Simpson was knighted in 1841. He later went into banking and railroad enterprises in Montreal. He reportedly fathered several children by Indian women.

SITTING BEAR.   See SATANK.

SITTING BULL (Tatanka Yotanka, Tatanka Iyotanka, Tatanka Iyotake). *Hunkpapa Sioux. (ca. 1831–1890).* Leader of the War for the Black Hills of 1876–77; principal chief; medicine man.

Sitting Bull was born along the Grand River at Many Caches, a site where the Hunkpapas stored supplies, near present-day Bullhead, South Dakota. He was the son of a chief. As a boy, he was called Hunkesni ("slow"), but proved himself while still young as a hunter and warrior, killing his first buffalo at 10 and counting his first coup in battle against a Crow when 14. During that same period, he completed his Vision Quest. Soon afterward, he was accepted into the Strong Hearts, a warrior society of which he became leader when 22. As a war chief, he led many raids on neighboring tribes, including Crows, Blackfeet, Piegans, Assiniboines, Shoshones, Flatheads, Gros Ventres, Mandans, Hidatsas, and Arikaras. He also gained a reputation among his people for his "medicine."

During the 1850s, the Sioux peoples were beginning to suffer the effects of white expansion: the Santee bands (Eastern Sioux) along the Minnesota River in Minnesota; the Yankton bands (Middle Sioux) along the Missouri River in South Dakota, Iowa, and Minnesota; the Yanktonai bands (also Middle Sioux) along the Missouri in North and South Dakota; and some among the Teton bands (Western Sioux) of western North and South Dakota, eastern Wyoming, and eastern Montana, such as the Oglalas and Brules. With few white incursions on Hunkpapa Teton Sioux lands north of Oglala and Brule territory, Sitting Bull avoided early confrontations. He was not one of the signers of the Fort Laramie Treaty of 1851 in Wyoming, the primary purpose of which was to assure safe passage for immigrants along the Oregon Trail. Nor did he participate in the skirmishes during the period of the GRATTAN Fight of August 19, 1854, in Wyoming, or the Battle of Ash Hollow of September 3, 1855, in Nebraska, in which the Brule CONQUERING BEAR was killed.

Following the Minnesota Uprising in 1862–63 of Santee Sioux under LITTLE CROW, General HENRY HASTINGS SIBLEY and General ALFRED SULLY advanced into the Dakotas in pursuit of Santee Sioux fugitives. Because of this violation of Hunkpapa lands, Sitting Bull and his Strong Hearts carried out hit-and-run raids on army scouting parties. They also fought troops at the Battle of Killdeer Mountain on July 28, 1864.

While the War for the BOZEMAN Trail of 1866–68 involving RED CLOUD's Oglalas raged in the Powder River country of northern Wyoming and southern Montana, Sitting Bull led his men in attacks on small parties in the vicinity of the newly constructed Fort Buford, at the confluence of the Missouri and Yellowstone rivers in northern Montana and North Dakota. The missionary PIERRE JEAN DE SMET traveled up the Missouri to Sioux country on peace missions in 1867 and 1868, meeting with Sitting Bull. The Fort Laramie Treaty of 1868, negotiated by Red Cloud and creating the Great Sioux Reservation, brought temporary peace to the Northern Plains. Some of the Sioux under Red Cloud and the Brule SPOTTED TAIL moved onto reservation lands. Other bands, including that of Sitting Bull, refused to give up their nomadic existence.

The discovery of gold in the Black Hills of Wyoming and South Dakota in 1874 led to renewed tensions between the army and the hunting bands. Sitting Bull came to be recognized as a spiritual leader by those who refused to give up their nomadic way of life, and he was eventually made head of the war council. Among his Teton allies in the War for the Black Hills of 1876–77 were the Hunkpapas GALL, CROW KING, and RAIN-IN-THE-FACE; the Oglalas CRAZY HORSE, AMERICAN HORSE, FLYING HAWK, and IRON TAIL; and the Miniconjous LAME DEER, HUMP, and KICKING BEAR. The Northern Cheyennes DULL KNIFE, LITTLE WOLF, TWO MOONS, WOODEN LEG, and YELLOW HAIR also played a part, as did many other tribal leaders of the Northern Plains, including some Brule, Sihasapa, and Sans Arc Teton Sioux; Yanktonai Sioux; Santee Sioux; and Northern Arapahos.

The military ordered the hunting bands to report to agencies by the end of January 1876. When most failed to comply, General WILLIAM T. SHERMAN, commander of the army, and General PHILIP H. SHERIDAN, commander of the Division of the Missouri, organized two forces for preemptive winter strikes—one under General GEORGE CROOK out of Fort Fetterman, Wyoming; the other under Colonel GEORGE ARMSTRONG CUSTER out of Fort Abraham Lincoln, North Dakota.

The Custer force was delayed because of heavy snows, but Colonel Joseph Reynolds of Crook's force led a cavalry attack against a Teton and Cheyenne camp in Montana on March 17, 1876. In the Battle of Powder River, Reynolds succeeded in destroying many of the tepees and capturing 600 to 800 horses, but, in a counterattack that night, warriors under Crazy Horse retook the animals.

The army organized a new three-pronged offensive: Crook from the south; Colonel JOHN GIBBON out of Fort Ellis and Fort Shaw in Montana from the west; and General ALFRED TERRY and Custer from the east.

Meanwhile, about 10,000 to 15,000 Indians—1,500 to 4,000 of them warriors—congregated along the Rosebud River in Montana. In mid-June, Sitting Bull held a three-day-long Sun Dance in which he had 50 small pieces of skin cut from each of his arms and experienced a vision of soldiers falling dead from the sky into the Indian camp.

In the Battle of the Rosebud on June 17, Sitting Bull's and Crazy Horse's allied warriors went up against General George Crook's force of over 1,000 soldiers and about 250 Crow and Shoshone auxiliaries. The Indians launched repeated, well-organized assaults, causing many casualties and driving away the invading army.

The Indians regrouped at a new camp on a meadow they called the Greasy Grass along the Little Bighorn. On June 21, Terry's and Gibbon's columns united on the Yellowstone River. When a scouting party under Major MARCUS A. RENO reported the general location of the Indian force, Terry sent Custer's 7th Cavalry to intercept them from the south while the rest of the troops advanced from the north.

On June 25, however, after his scouts had reported the Indian camp along the Little Bighorn, Custer, rather than wait for reinforcements, divided his men into four groups: the pack train with an escort to stay behind; a detachment under Captain FREDERICK W. BENTEEN to block the Indians from the south; and detachments under Reno and himself to follow the river northward. On the way, Custer sent Reno's men westward across the river in pursuit of a party of about 40 warriors, with instructions to strike the Indian camp from the valley to its south, while he proceeded along the eastern bank of the river for an attack on the village at its northern end. After a skirmish, Reno's men retreated across the river and joined up with Benteen. Gall led an attack against them from the west, pinning them down and inflicting severe damage—more than 50 dead and about 60 wounded out of 400. Then, advancing from the south, Gall's warriors joined Crazy Horse's men, advancing from the north and west, in the famous attack on Custer's detachment of about 200, killing every man in the party.

The Indian victory in the much-publicized Battle of Little Bighorn led to a stepped-up military campaign. The following engagements proved disastrous for the Sioux and their allies. On July 17, 1876, at War Bonnet Creek in Nebraska, a force under Colonel WESLEY MERRITT intercepted and defeated about 1,000 Cheyennes who were on their way to join up with Sitting Bull and Crazy Horse. On September 9, 1876, at Slim Buttes in South Dakota, General Crook's advance guard captured American Horse's combined Oglala and Miniconjou band of Tetons. On November 25, 1876, in the Battle of Dull Knife in Wyoming, Colonel RANALD S. MACKENZIE's troops routed Dull Knife's band of Northern Cheyennes. On January 8, 1877, at Wolf Mountain in Montana, Colonel NELSON A. MILES's soldiers defeated Crazy Horse's warriors. Then, on May 7, 1877, in the Battle of Lame Deer, Miles's men defeated Lame Deer's Miniconjou band.

Many of the Sioux surrendered at various agencies. Sitting Bull and some of his followers headed for Canada in May 1877. The Canadian government refused to accept responsibility for them and provide supplies, however. Faced with starvation, he led his 187 remaining followers back across the border, surrendering on July 19, 1881, at Fort Buford, North Dakota. Despite promises of amnesty, he was held a virtual prisoner at Fort Randall, South Dakota, for two years. He was finally allowed to settle on the Standing Rock Reservation in North Dakota in May 1883.

For one year, 1885–86, Sitting Bull toured with WILLIAM "BUFFALO BILL" CODY's Wild West Show before he became fed up with the less than respectful audiences and returned to the reservation. In 1888–89, he was outspoken in his opposition to further land cessions and the further break-up of the Sioux Reservation. Because of his resistance to white policies and customs, he found himself in various disputes with the Indian agent JAMES McLAUGHLIN.

In October 1890, after the return of the Sioux delegation to the Paiute prophet WOVOKA of Nevada, Sitting Bull invited his nephew Kicking Bear to come to Standing Rock to demonstrate the Ghost Dance. McLaughlin accused Sitting Bull of inciting the Sioux to militancy and ordered his arrest. Lieutenant Bullhead and sergeants Red Tomahawk and Shavehead surrounded his

Sitting Bull. *Courtesy of National Archives of Canada/C-20038.*

cabin with 40 other Indian police at dawn on December 15. About four times that number of Ghost Dancers gathered outside to prevent Sitting Bull's arrest. When one of them, Catch-the-Bear, pulled a rifle out from under his blanket and shot at Bullhead, the wounded lieutenant fired back, striking Sitting Bull instead. Red Tomahawk also fired, hitting Sitting Bull in the head. In the resulting melee, Sitting Bull's 17-year-old son Crow Foot and six others were killed, along with about the same number of Indian police. The arrival of a support squadron of cavalry prevented further deaths. Because of the incident, the Miniconjou BIG FOOT and his band fled the reservation, culminating in the Wounded Knee Massacre of December 29, 1890.

SKENANDOA (Skenandoah, Skeanendon, Shendau, "deer"). *Oneida. (d. 1816).* Ally of Patriots in the American Revolution.

Skenandoa lived at Oneida Castle, New York. Little is known of his early years as a chief other than a drunken incident in Albany in which he slept on a street and was robbed and henceforth swore off alcohol.

Skenandoa supported the English in the French and Indian War of 1754–63. At the start of the American Revolution, however, he effected an Oneida declaration of neutrality, largely because of his friendship with the Congregational missionary to the Oneidas SAMUEL KIRKLAND. Later he provided the Americans with warriors and military intelligence. The Tuscaroras joined the Oneidas, in opposition to the Mohawks, Onondagas, Cayugas, and Senecas, who sided with the British, causing a split in the Iroquois League.

In September 1778, Skenandoa warned the settlers at German Flats, New York, of an impending attack by Tories and their Indian allies under JOSEPH BRANT. The settlers fled to safety in time, although their homes and barns were burned and their livestock captured.

Following the war, Skenandoa participated in his tribe's negotiations with the federal government and signed numerous treaties. At his request, he was buried next to Kirkland at the Hamilton College cemetery in Clinton, New York. (See also BRANT, JOSEPH.)

SKY CHIEF (Tirawahut Lashar). *Pawnee. (d. 1873).* Friend to whites; enemy of Sioux.

Chief Sky Chief provided scouts for the army under FRANK and LUTHER NORTH, as well as guards for railroad-building crews from among his warriors. The Pawnees' assistance to whites angered other tribes. In 1873, Sky Chief was chosen to lead a buffalo hunt on the plains of southern Nebraska. A Sioux war party ambushed the Pawnees and killed 150, including Sky Chief, before an army detachment rescued the survivors. The site of this battle became known as Massacre Canyon.

SKY WALKER. See MAMANTI.

SLEEPY EYES (Ishtaba, Ishtahumba, Ish-tak-ha-ba). *Sisseton Sioux. (ca. 1780–ca. 1860).* Principal chief; friend to whites.

Born at Swan Lake near present-day Mankato, Minnesota, Sleepy Eyes became principal chief in the early 1820s, succeeding Wakanto. He was a close friend of the Reverend STEPHEN RIGGS. Although not in complete agreement with their provisions, he signed the Treaty of Prairie du Chien in 1825, the Treaty of St. Peters in 1836, and the Traverse des Sioux Treaty in 1851, in order to maintain peace with whites. In 1857, following the Spirit Lake incident, involving INKPADUTA and his Wahpekute Sioux, Sleepy Eyes and his band were pressured into moving to the reservation at Sleepy Eye Lake. He later died in South Dakota while on a hunting trtip. His remains were eventually returned to Minnesota where a monument was erected over them.

SLOCUM, JOHN. *Squakson (Coast Salish). (fl. 1880s).* Medicine man; prophet; founder of Indian Shaker religion.

John Slocum was introduced to Christianity by missionaries in the Puget Sound region of Washington State. Like other Indian prophets of the late 19th century—SMOHALLA, TAVIBO, and WOVOKA— Slocum claimed that while in a trance he was transported to heaven, where he received instructions on how to bring about Indian salvation. In 1881, he founded *Tschadam*, known to whites as the Indian Shaker Religion, named after the shaking or twitching motion participants experienced while "brushing off" their sins in a meditative state. The religion, exclusive to Indians, combined Christian beliefs in God, heaven, and hell with traditional Indian teachings. Slocum and his followers, especially among the Squakson, Skokomish, Nisqually, and Chehalis tribes, were imprisoned regularly by white officials for inciting resistance to assimilation programs. The Indian Shaker religion is still practiced today.

SMILEY, ALBERT KEITH. *(1828–1912).* Reformer; sponsor of Lake Mohonk Conferences.

Albert Smiley was born in Vassalboro, Maine, and grew up on a farm. He attended and taught at Haverford College, in Haverford, Pennsylvania. A Quaker and philanthropist, he became deeply committed to Indian reform.

In 1879, Smiley was appointed by President Rutherford Hayes to the federally sponsored Board of Indian Commissioners. In 1891, he served with CHARLES PAINTER of the Indian Rights Association on a federal commission to select reservations for California Mission

Indians, a cause supported by the writer HELEN HUNT JACKSON.

From 1883 until his death in 1912, Smiley hosted a series of semiannual conferences for leading figures of the Friends of the Indian movement at Lake Mohonk, his resort hotel in the mountains near New Paltz, New York. Prominent at the Lake Mohonk gatherings were HERBERT WELSH, founder of the Indian Rights Association, and Senator HENRY DAWES, sponsor of the General Allotment Act of 1887.

The federal government's policy of replacing the reservation system with the allotment of land to individual Indians originated with resolutions from the Lake Mohonk conferences. Other Lake Mohonk recommendations incorporated into federal Indian policy in the early 1900s were the discouragement of tribalism in Indian political and business affairs, increased federal responsibility in Indian education, and the granting of citizenship to Indians.

SMITH, JEDEDIAH STRONG (Jed Smith).
(1799–1831). Explorer; trader; trapper.

Born in Jericho (present-day Bainbridge), New York, Jedediah Smith was raised in Pennsylvania, and worked briefly as a clerk on a Lake Erie ship.

About 1822, Smith moved to St. Louis, where he joined WILLIAM HENRY ASHLEY's first fur-trading expedition to the Mandans on the upper Missouri River. Smith also took part in Ashley's second expedition the next year. When that party was attacked by Arikaras, Smith was among those dispatched to seek help, heading farther upriver to locate Ashley's partner, ANDREW HENRY, and later took part in the counterattack against the Indians.

Shortly after this 1823 incident, Smith set out westward from Fort Kiowa, on the Missouri River in present-day South Dakota. With THOMAS FITZPATRICK, JAMES CLYMAN, and WILLIAM SUBLETTE, he explored the Black Hills region, surviving a near-fatal mauling by a grizzly bear. The group purchased horses from the Cheyennes and Sioux, then continued westward into what is now Wyoming. They spent the winter of 1824–25 on the Plains near present-day Dubois, Wyoming, then proceeded to the Wind River Range of the Rocky Moutain chain, in the course of which they made the first known westward crossing by non-Indians through the Oregon Trail's South Pass. Returning Astorians had earlier crossed it heading east.

Smith and other mountain men encountered a party of Iroquois trappers of the Hudson's Bay Company, whom they agreed to protect from attacks by Snake war parties in exchange for the Iroquois's furs. They accompanied the Iroquois trappers across present-day Montana to the Hudson's Bay Company's Flathead Post, where they wintered as guests of its director ALEXANDER ROSS and had contact with Nez Perce and Flathead Indians who arrived to sell their furs.

Smith and his party left the Flathead country and headed south to the Green River and the Great Salt Lake, where he learned from Utes in present-day northern Utah of a possible water route, the fabled Buenaventura River, that led from the Great Salt Lake to the Pacific; Smith returned to Ashley at the Green River trappers' rendezvous of 1825 with this information.

Smith became a full partner of Ashley's operation and the leader of the fur brigades. At the rendezvous of 1826, along with William Sublette and David E. Jackson, he bought out Ashley's share of the business.

In 1826, Smith set out from Cache Lake in northern Utah, and headed across the Great Salt Lake desert region south to the Colorado River and the Mohave Desert. His party successfully made the first crossing by an American party of the Southwest, reaching San Gabriel, near present-day Los Angeles, in 1826, where they were detained by Mexican authorities.

On being alllowed to leave California, Smith led his men north through the San Joaquin Valley, and at Ebbett's Pass, made the first non-Indian east-west crossing of the Sierras. His party then re-crossed the deserts of central Nevada and Utah, and reached the fur rendezvous at Bear Lake in northern Utah in 1827.

Smith almost immediately organized a second expedition back to California to rejoin some of his men who had remained in the Sacramento Valley. His party was attacked by Mojave warriors on the southern Colorado plateau, with 10 killed. The survivors reached San Gabriel, California, and traveled northward by ship to San Francisco. In the Sierras, Smith was reunited with the men he had left the year before.

The party headed north into present-day Oregon, and at the Umpqua River, in the summer of 1828, all but Smith and three other mountain men were killed in an attack by an Indian raiding party. Smith and the survivors then found refuge at the Hudson's Bay Company's Fort Vancouver, on the Columbia River, near present-day Portland, Oregon, as guests of John McLoughlin. McLoughlin recovered furs stolen from Smith's party by the Indians, which the Hudson's Bay Company subsequently purchased from the Americans at prices well below market value.

In 1828–29, Smith, in partnership with William Sublette, continued to trap in the Wyoming-Montana region. In 1830, he provided United States secretary of War John Eaton with a firsthand account of the British military and commercial presence in the disputed Oregon country.

Smith returned to St. Louis to take up farming, but, in 1831, he entered the St. Louis-Santa Fe trade with his former partner, Thomas Fitzpatrick. Leading a caravan across the Southern Plains, he went ahead of the main party in search of water. In the region between the Cimarron and Arkansas rivers, he was killed by Comanches.

Smith was known to his fellow mountain men as one of the few practicing Christians among them, a Bible-carrying Methodist. His explorations are considered by some scholars to be second in importance only to those of LEWIS and CLARK in the opening of the American West to white expansion onto Indian lands.

SMITH, JOHN. *(ca. 1580–1631).* Explorer; colonizer; soldier.

John Smith was born in Lincolnshire, England. In his early teens, he was apprenticed to a merchant. In 1596, he embarked on a career as a soldier of fortune, serving with the French army in its war with Spain and later with Austrian forces fighting the Turks in present-day Hungary. He was captured by the Turks and held as a slave until 1604, finally managing to escape and return to England.

Smith then invested in the newly charted London Company, a branch of the Virginia Company, which along with the Plymouth Company, held rights to establish colonies along the North American coast. In December 1606, he led a group of 105 colonists across the Atlantic to the Virginia coast with Captain Christopher Newport. On May 14, 1607, along the James River near present-day Williamsburg, Virginia, Smith and his colonists founded Jamestown, which became the first permanent English colony in North America.

Over the next few months, Smith, as captain in charge of a force of men, explored the Potomac and Rappahannock rivers and Chesapeake Bay. He also journeyed inland, in search of gold and a water route to the Pacific. He was captured by Powhatan Indians under chief POWHATAN. Legend has it that Smith was about to be put to death by the Indians when the chief's daughter, POCAHONTAS, intervened on his behalf.

Smith returned to the settlement at Jamestown, where, after a political struggle, he became president of the colony until 1609. That year, he was injured in the explosion of a gunpowder bag and was forced to return to England.

In 1614, Smith again sailed for North America and explored the coast around Cape Cod, naming the region "New England." He also obtained furs from the coastal tribes and a supply of salted fish, both of which brought substantial profits upon his return to England.

A third voyage to the New World in 1615 ended when Smith was captured by French pirates, then shipwrecked off the coast of France.

In 1616, Smith welcomed visiting Jamestown colonist JOHN ROLFE and his wife, Pocahontas, to England. Smith's final attempted voyage to North America was canceled because of weather delays.

Smith produced a number of accounts of his experiences as a colonizer and explorer of Virginia and New England, which served as impetus for subsequent colonizing efforts, including those of the Pilgrims in Massachusets in 1620–21. (See also POCAHONTAS; POWHATAN.)

SMITH, NIMROD JARRETT (Tsalatihi). *Mixed Cherokee. (ca. 1838–1893).* Leader of the Eastern Cherokees.

Nimrod Jarrett Smith was born near present-day Murphy, North Carolina, to a part-Cherokee father and a full-blooded mother. Smith fought with the Confederates in the Civil War, serving as a sergeant in an Eastern Cherokee company under Colonel W. H. Thomas, a Cherokee trader. He married a white woman by the name of Mary Guthrie. In the 1870s, Smith was first elected principal chief of the Eastern Cherokees, a position he held until his death. He was instrumental in establishing his tribe's title to eastern lands and creating an educational system.

SMITH, REDBIRD. *Cherokee. (1850–1918).* Traditionalist who resisted allotment; principal chief.

Redbird Smith was born near Fort Smith, Arkansas, of a Cherokee father and part-Cherokee mother. He grew up among the Western Cherokees of the Indian Territory.

The original Keetowah Society (from *kituwha*, the Cherokee word for "key") had been formed to protect Cherokee interests in the post–Civil War years, when the federal government appropriated Indian lands in the name of Reconstruction. During the 1890s, a new threat to Cherokee lands emerged. The General Allotment Act (the DAWES Severalty Act) of 1887 called for the dissolution of tribal landholdings and their allotment in 160-acre tracts to individuals, making Indian land more vulnerable to white speculators. In 1893, the federal government removed the exemption of the Five Civilized Tribes of the Indian Territory from allotment and created the Dawes Commission to disperse tribal lands. In 1898, Congress passed the CURTIS Act, abolishing tribal governments and instituting civil governments for the Indian Territory.

Redbird Smith and other traditionalist Cherokees revived the Keetowah Society to resist allotment. His faction became known as the Nighthawk Keetowahs because they did much of their planning and organizing at night. Like the Creek Indian Snakes, led by CHITTO HARJO, the Nighthawks carried out acts of passive resistance against allotment, such as the disruption of the enrollment process. In 1902, federal marshals arrested Smith and forced him to enroll. Smith traveled to Washington, D.C., to plead the case of the Cherokees.

With continuing federal pressure, the tribe eventually signed the allotment agreement. In 1907, the former Indian Territory became the state of Oklahoma. In 1908, Smith was elected principal chief of the Cherokees. In 1912, he and Creek, Choctaw, and Chickasaw leaders founded the Four Mothers Society to continue the political and legal struggle for tribal and cultural restoration.

SMOHALLA (Smohallie, Smokeller, Shmoqula, "the preacher"; Waipshwa, "rock carrier").
Wanapam. (ca. 1815–1907). Medicine man; prophet; founder of the Dreamer Religion.

Smohalla was a Wanapam (or Wanapum or Sokulk) Indian, of the same Sahaptin (or Shahaptian) linguistic family as the Nez Perces. The Wanapams lived in the vicinity of Priest Rapids along the upper Columbia River in present-day eastern Washington State.

As a young man, Smohalla gained renown as a warrior. He was also known to frequent a Catholic missionary, showing an interest in religious teachings. He began to preach his own revelations about 1850. A rivalry with the nearby Sinkiuse chief MOSES led to confrontation on a battlefield, in which Smohalla was wounded and left for dead. Afterward, he departed the area and traveled for several years, as far south as Mexico, then back overland through Nevada. On his return, he claimed he had visited the Spirit world and had been sent back to teach his people.

Smohalla's message was of a resurgence of the aboriginal way of life, free from white influences, such as alcohol and agriculture. Drawing on teachings of the local prophet Sowapso and his son Sohappy, Smohalla established ceremonial music and dancing to induce meditations of a pure, primitive state. He also prophesized the resurrection of all Indians to rid the world of white oppressors. Smohalla claimed that the truth came to him and his priests through dreams; thus, his faith was called the Dreamer religion. His oratory was known as Yuyunipi-Tqana, or "Shouting Mountain."

With growing militance against white influences and white encroachment on Indian lands, Smohalla and his followers traveled to different reservations, denouncing missionaries and government officials. Because of Indian unrest in the region, he was jailed on several occasions. One of his converts, a former Christian, was Old JOSEPH.

Other reservation-era prophets, such as JOHN SLOCUM, TAVIBO, and WOVOKA, were influenced by the Dreamers. Pucklyahtoot, active among the Dreamers after his uncle Smohalla's death, was referred to as "the Last Prophet."

SOLANO (Francisco Solano, Samyetoy). *Patwin.*
(fl. 1830s–1840s). Ally of Mexicans.

In the early 1830s, the Vallejo family of Mexican California, headed by the administrator MARIANO VALLEJO, armed and trained Patwin warriors of the village of Suisun near San Francisco under chief Solano. Meanwhile, Russian traders provided the Pomos to the north with arms in exchange for furs. In 1836, the Pomos, led by Succara, in alliance with Patwin bands under Motti and Zampay, revolted against Mexican rule. Solano's warriors helped Mexican troops put down the uprising. The conflict lasted into the early 1840s.

SOULE, WILLIAM STINSON. *(1836–1908).*
Photographer.

William S. Soule, a native of Turner, Maine, had been working as a photographer in the Boston region, when, in 1861, he enlisted in the Union Army to fight in the Civil War. Wounded and subsequently discharged, he settled for a time in Chambersburg, Pennsylvania, maintaining a studio until a fire destroyed his business.

Plagued by ailments from his war wound, Soule journeyed West to pursue his career. He traveled to Fort Dodge in Kansas and later took a job as the chief clerk at Fort Sill's post store in the Indian Territory, where he supplemented his income by taking pictures of army personnel and their families. He also took pictures of Cheyenne and Arapaho Indians who came to Fort Sill to trade and went on field expeditions to photograph other tribes, such as the Wichitas. He sold his photographs at the Fort Sill store to visitors passing through that frontier outpost, and at his brother's art store in Boston.

Soule eventually returned to Boston and worked with his brother. The Smithsonian Institution acquired a collection of his photographs in 1895.

SOULIGNY. *Mixed Menominee. (1785–1864).* Ally of British in the War of 1812; later, friend to Americans.

Souligny was the grandson of a French trader from whom he took his name. During the War of 1812, he joined other Menominees, such as TOMAH and OSHKOSH, in support of the British and helped capture Fort Mackinaw, Michigan. He also fought alongside TECUMSEH at Fort Meigs, which was defended by troops under General WILLIAM HENRY HARRISON. After American victory, Souligny remained at peace with whites and supported them in the BLACK HAWK War of 1832. His village was on the west side of the Wolf River, near the Great Falls in Wisconsin. In 1855, Souligny and Oshkosh traveled to Milwaukee and personally asked the editor of the *Milwaukee Sentinel* to publicize the kidnapping of an Indian girl by whites.

SPALDING, HENRY HARMON. *(1803–1874).*
Missionary; educator.

Henry Spalding, born in Wheeler, New York, was licensed as a preacher by the Presbyterian Church, becoming a missionary under sponsorship of the Boston-based American Board of Commissioners for Foreign Missions.

In 1836, Spalding and his wife, Eliza Hart Spalding, arrived in the Pacific Northwest with fellow missionary MARCUS WHITMAN. There was professional as well as personal rivalry between the two men, since Spalding had once courted Whitman's wife, Narcissa. The Whitmans founded a mission to the Cayuses at Waiilatpu near Fort Walla Walla in what is now Washington. The Spaldings founded their mission to the Nez Perce Indians at Lapwai near present-day Lewiston, Idaho, establishing in the process the first non-Indian home in what is now Idaho, and, three years later, the first printing press. Spalding eventually baptized Old JOSEPH and TIMOTHY in addition to other Nez Perce leaders.

Amid criticism by Whitman and others, Spalding was dismissed by the mission board in 1840. However, he was reinstated two years later, resuming his missionary work among the Indians.

In 1848, following the death the year before of Marcus and Narcissa Whitman at the hands of TILOUKAIKT and other Cayuses at Waiilatpu, Spalding relocated with his family to Oregon's Willamette Valley, where he took up farming.

Spalding returned to Lapwai in 1862. In 1871, during President ULYSSES S. GRANT's Peace Policy to the Indians, he became a teacher in a federally sponsored Indian school.

Spalding was highly critical of the Catholic missionaries in the Pacific Northwest, such as PIERRE JEAN DE SMET and JOSEPH CATALDO, alleging that they were partly responsible for the 1847 Whitman massacre by encouraging anti-Protestant sentiment among the Indians.

SPEMICALAWBA. See HIGH HORN.

SPOKANE GARRY (Spokan Garry).
Spokane. (1811–1892). Christian convert; principal chief.

Spokane Garry, the son of Chief Illim Spokanee, was born along the Spokane River in what is now Washington State. In 1825, GEORGE SIMPSON, governor-in-chief of the Hudson's Bay Company, asked ALEXANDER ROSS, regional director, to select two boys to attend the Red River Settlement School in what is now Manitoba. Ross asked the Spokane and Kootenai tribes for students; each sent the son of a chief. At the school the boys were given the last names of directors

Spokane Garry. *Courtesy of National Archives of Canada/C-78966.*

of the Hudson's Bay Company—Spokane Garry and Kootenai Pelly. Four years later, when he was about 18, Spokane Garry began preaching among his people and seeking out students for the Red River School. In 1831, his close friend Kootenai Pelly died.

Later, when Spokane Garry became principal chief of his people, he directed them to build a church and a schoolhouse and to conduct Sunday services. In the 1870s, white settlers began arriving in great numbers in the Indian village then called Spokane Falls. In 1881, it was incorporated, becoming known as Spokane. Seven years later, the chief himself was driven from his home by white farmers who wanted his land. He moved to Indian Canyon outside Spokane and lived his final years in poverty.

SPOTTED TAIL (Sinte Galeshka, Sinte Gleska, Zintalah Galeshka). *Brule Sioux. (ca. 1833–1881).*
Proponent of peace; negotiator; principal chief. Uncle of CRAZY HORSE.

Spotted Tail was born either along the White River in what is now South Dakota or near Fort Laramie in Wyoming. His adult name is associated with a raccoon fur given to him by a trapper. Although famed as a warrior, he generally advised peace to his fellow Sioux.

Delegation of Sioux Indians to Washington, D.C., in 1875, including, left to right, Rattling Ribs, Red Cloud, Mandan, Lone Horn, Spotted Tail, Little Wound, Black Bear, and Swan. *Courtesy of New York State Library, Albany.*

In the GRATTAN Fight of August 1854, Spotted Tail participated in the attack on soldiers after the death of CONQUERING BEAR, and defended Sioux territory at Blue Water Creek (Ash Hollow) in September 1855 from troops commanded by General WILLIAM S. HARNEY. Yet, in order to prevent further hostilities against his people, he surrendered at Fort Laramie, chanting his death song. However, the army soon released him. His act of courage increased his prestige among his people, and the Brule council passed over a hereditary chief in his favor.

By the 1860s, Spotted Tail was chief spokesman for all the Brule bands. During the War for the BOZEMAN Trail of 1866–68 under RED CLOUD, he counseled accommodation with whites. He was one of the signers of the Fort Laramie Treaty of 1868, establishing the Great Sioux Reservation.

In 1870, Spotted Tail traveled to Washington, D.C., to meet with President ULYSSES S. GRANT and his Seneca commissioner of Indian Affairs ELY PARKER. He made subsequent trips and proved, like Red Cloud,

a skillful negotiator. In 1873, agencies bearing Spotted Tail's and Red Cloud's names were established in Nebraska. The government offered the Sioux $6 million for the Black Hills after gold had been discovered. Spotted Tail, who had met with miners to determine the land's value, demanded $60 million for their cession. The government rejected this figure.

The influx of miners led to a new round of violence, the War for the Black Hills of 1876–77 under SITTING BULL and Crazy Horse. After the Indian victory at Little Bighorn in 1876, government officials appointed Spotted Tail chief of the Sioux at both agencies instead of Red Cloud. The Brule leader helped negotiate the surrender of the Sioux militants in 1877. That same year, because of the unrest, the government relocated the Spotted Tail and Red Cloud agencies to South Dakota, within the boundaries of the original Great Sioux Reservation. The next year, they were renamed the Rosebud and Pine Ridge agencies, respectively.

Some of the Sioux never forgave Spotted Tail for the consequences of the negotiated surrender, especially the death of Crazy Horse, and plotted his overthrow. One of them, CROW DOG, shot and killed Spotted Tail at Rosebud, in a dispute over a woman. In a landmark decision by the U.S. Supreme Court that state and federal courts had no jurisdiction on Indian land, Crow Dog was freed.

SQUANTO (Tisquantum). *Wampanoag.*
(ca. 1580–1622). Friend to Pilgrims.

Squanto, of the Patuxet band of Wampanoags living on Cape Cod in present-day Massachusetts, is thought to have been first kidnapped by Captain George Weymouth in 1605, then taken to Malaga, Spain, with a group of other Indians and sold into slavery by the English trader Captain Thomas Hunt. After a sympathetic Englishman had ransomed him and taken him back to England, Squanto finally accomplished the ocean crossing back to his homeland in 1618–19 with Captain Thomas Dermer. Few or none of his fellow Patuxets were alive when he returned, having been ravaged by an epidemic, probably smallpox brought to them by Europeans, which broke out in 1616 and lasted three years.

SAMOSET, an Abnaki staying among the Wampanoags, introduced Squanto and MASSASOIT, the Wampanoag grand sachem, to the Pilgrims in March 1621. Squanto used his knowledge of English to instruct the whites in wilderness life, particularly fishing and planting corn, including how to catch herring and use them as a fertilizer. Along with Massasoit, for whom he acted as interpreter, Squanto helped make possible the first Thanksgiving feast in the autumn of 1621.

Squanto was involved to a certain degree in a power struggle among the Wampanoags, perhaps as an agent of a rival sachem, CORBITANT, in an attempt to usurp Massasoit's power. In any case, Corbitant imprisoned Squanto soon thereafter when he attempted to warn the English of a plot against them. The Pilgrim MILES STANDISH secured his release.

In fall 1622, when the Pilgrims decided to seek a trade relation with the Narragansets for food, Squanto volunteered to accompany them on the ship *Swan* to Narragansett Bay as a guide and interpreter. Heavy seas forced the expedition into Chatham Harbor along Cape Cod, where Squanto arranged for barter with the local Indians. While there, however, he succumbed to "Indian fever," probably smallpox, which had previously killed so many of his people.

SQUIER, EPHRAIM GEORGE.
(1821–1888). Archaeologist; anthropologist.

E. G. Squier was born in Bethlehem, New York, the son of a Methodist minister. After a youth spent on a farm, he became a teacher and taught himself civil engineering. On moving to Ohio, he worked as a journalist and became involved in politics.

In 1845–47, along with the physician Edwin Hamilton Davis, Squier made one of the earliest studies of the Indian earthworks of the Ohio and Mississippi valleys. Their 1848 collaboration, *Ancient Monuments of the Mississippi Valley*, more descriptive than speculative, was the first volume published by the Smithsonian Institution. Squier made a similar study of mounds in New York, published as *Aboriginal Monuments of the State of New York* (1849).

In 1849, Squier received a diplomatic posting to Central America, and, in 1863, as U.S. commissioner to Peru. He continued his archeological research and wrote numerous books about Central and South America. In 1871, he became the first president of the Anthropological Institute of New York, which eventually merged with the American Ethnological Society.

In his writings on the origins of the Mound Builders, Squier discounted the prevalent and mistaken view of the time that the Indians had developed their culture from early contacts with ancient civilizations of the Old World. He proposed instead that the Indian culture had evolved from an earlier American culture and was still in a state of evolution at the time of white contact.

Squier also made a study of the myths and religions of a wide variety of Indian tribes, from the Iroquois of New York to the Pueblos of the Southwest, and came to the conclusion that there was an underlying theme to all Indian religion. He believed that the basic sun worship motif indicated a common cultural heritage. He felt that the cultures of the Southwest's Pueblo Indians represented an intermediate stage of Indian civilization, between the civilization of the Aztecs and Toltecs of Mesoamerica and the less evolved society of the Indians to the north in the Ohio and Mississippi valleys.

STANDING BEAR (Mo-chu-no-zhi). *Ponca.*
(ca. 1829–1908). Leader in peaceful resistance and precedent-setting trial.

Standing Bear's village was located at the heart of the Ponca homeland at the mouth of the Niobrara River where it feeds the Missouri River in northern Nebraska. In 1858, the federal government negotiated a treaty establishing a boundary between the Poncas and their traditional enemies, the Sioux. By the terms of that treaty, the Poncas were guaranteed their ancestral lands. Nevertheless, when the federal government established the Great Sioux Reservation, the Poncas' homeland was included. In 1875, the government offered them compensation for the loss of their lands. The next year, Congress passed an act to relocate them from their Nebraska homeland to the Indian Territory.

In 1877, the Poncas were forcibly removed. Soon after the Poncas' arrival in their new home, a third of the tribe died from hunger and disease, including the son of Standing Bear. The Ponca chief, who had also recently lost his daughter, wanted to bury the dead youth with his sister in the land of their ancestors. Carrying the body in a wagon, he set out with an escort of 30 warriors. On spotting the party in country supposedly cleared of Indians, settlers notified the military of a potential uprising. General GEORGE CROOK sent in a cavalry detachment to arrest the Indians. They were held in an army camp near Omaha, during which time Standing Bear was interviewed by the journalist THOMAS HENRY TIBBLES.

When the true purpose of Standing Bear's journey was published, some whites, including Crook himself, showed sympathy. Two attorneys—John Webster and Andrew Poppleton—volunteered their services and applied for a writ of habeas corpus on Standing Bear's behalf. Federal attorneys argued that the writ should be denied because Indians were not persons under the terms of the Constitution and not entitled to habeas corpus. Judge Elmer Dundy ruled in favor of the Poncas, stating that they were indeed persons under the law, with inalienable rights.

Standing Bear and his escort were permitted to proceed to their homeland and bury his son. Because of continuing white sympathy, his party was allowed to stay in Nebraska. In the winter of 1879–80, Tibbles arranged a lecture tour of eastern cities for Standing Bear. Tibbles's wife SUSETTE LA FLESCHE, and brother-in-law FRANCIS LA FLESCHE, Omaha Indians, acted as interpreters. In 1880, Congress appointed a commission to study the Ponca situation, and Standing Bear and his small band were granted a permanent home in Nebraska. The Poncas in the Indian Territory, including his brother Big Snake, were granted better lands and compensation for lost property, but were not allowed to leave.

Nevertheless, Standing Bear's nonviolent resistance and his use of the legal system set a precedent concerning Native American rights. He died when about 80 and was buried in the place of his ancestors.

STANDISH, MILES (Myles Standish). *(ca. 1584–1656).* Colonial officer; negotiator; administrator.

In the early 1600s, English-born Miles Standish was a professional soldier in service to the Dutch in their wars for independence from Spain. In 1620, he was hired by English Puritans living in Holland to assist in their proposed settlement in North America. In December of that year, he arrived in Massachusetts on the *Mayflower* as one of the Pilgrim founders of the Plymouth colony.

On being recognized as a military leader, Captain Standish assumed responsibility for defending the Plymouth colony against Indian attacks and for negotiating with the Indians. The first Pilgrim to learn Algonquian dialects, he established good relations with most of the area sachems, such as the Wampanoag MASSASOIT, who provided him with HOBOMOK as a military adviser. On the advice of Massasoit, Standish led an attack on a Wampanoag faction under ASPINET and IYANOUGH in 1623. That same year, he led an ambush on Massachuset Indians under Witawamet who were rumored to be planning an attack at the Wessagusett settlement (later Weymouth) to the north near present-day Boston. As a warning to other militants, Standish mounted the sachem's head on a wall in front of the Plymouth fort.

In 1625–26, Standish served as agent for the colonists in England, where he negotiated for clear title to the colonial lands for supplies. In 1627, he helped buy out London merchants who had invested in the colony.

In 1628, Standish led an attack against THOMAS MORTON and his Merrymount colony, located on the site of present-day Quincy, Massachusetts. The attack was precipitated when Morton, who was in commercial competition with the Pilgrims, began trading guns to the Indians. Standish captured Morton and sent him back to England under arrest.

With John Alden, Standish founded the settlement of Duxbury, Massachusetts, in 1631, where he later settled. He remained in New England for the remainder of his life, serving as the Plymouth colony's treasurer in 1644–49, as well as in several other govenmental posts. (See also MASSASOIT.)

STANISLAUS (Estanislao). *Mission Indian (probably Yokuts). (fl. 1820s).* Leader of revolt against the Mexicans in 1828–29.

Stanislaus, captured when young, was raised and educated at the San Jose Mission in California. He proved one of the best students and became majordomo (ranch foreman). Yet, dissatisfied with the Mexicans' treatment of his people, he led an escape in 1827 or 1828.

With another leader, Cipriano, Stanislaus then organized refugees from the mission, as well as Indians of the northern San Joaquin Valley, into a general resistance, creating unrest at the San Jose and Santa Clara missions. Father Narciso Duran of San Jose asked help from the commander at San Francisco Presidio, and a small force under Sergeant Antonio Sota was sent into the field in 1828. The warriors repelled the Mexicans, with Sota himself fatally wounded.

There followed an 1829 expedition of 40 soldiers under Lieutenant Jose Sanchez, but this force could not break through the Indian stockade. A third expedition was organized, including about 100 soldiers plus Indian auxiliaries. Artillery fire breached the rebels' defenses, but Stanislaus and others avoided capture by fleeing through a system of tunnels.

Stanislaus fled to San Jose, where Father Duran offered him refuge from the soldiers. Returning to the life of a Mission Indian, he was later pardoned.

STANLEY, JOHN MIX. *(1814–1872).* Artist.

John Mix Stanley was born in Canandaigua, New York. His mother died when he was five and he was raised by his father. Growing up in Iroquois country, he had Indian friends; the Seneca chief RED JACKET reportedly took a liking to him. When 14 years old, Stanley was apprenticed to a wagonmaker. He moved to Detroit when 20 and worked as an itinerant portrait painter in the region. Returning to New York in 1840, he stayed in the East for two years before traveling West to Fort Gibson in the Indian Territory.

In 1843, Stanley attended a council of the Western Cherokees at Tahlequah held by Chief JOHN ROSS. One of Stanley's best-known works is a rendering in oils of this event. He painted Indians of at least 20 different tribes during this period.

In 1846, Stanley accompanied Colonel STEPHEN WATTS KEARNY's expedition from Santa Fe to California during the Mexican War. He then traveled in Oregon and Hawaii. In 1849, he exhibited 152 paintings in the East, including depictions of Indians of 43 different tribes.

In 1853, Stanley traveled with ISAAC STEVENS on an expedition to survey the proposed railroad route from St. Paul, Minnesota, to the Pacific Northwest Coast. The illustrations contained in the report of the Stevens's survey included lithographic reproductions of Stanley's works.

Many of Stanley's Indian paintings were lost in the fire that ravaged the Smithsonian Institution in 1865.

STEPHEN, ALEXANDER M. *(d. 1894).* Anthropologist.

Alexander Stephen, a native of Scotland and a graduate of the University of Edinburgh, emigrated to the United States some time before 1861 and served as a Union officer in the Civil War. In 1881, probably for health reasons, he moved to northern Arizona, staying with trader Tom Keam at Keam's Canyon, where the Hopi Reservation was being established. There he became friendly with both Hopis and Navajos.

In 1882, Stephen provided assistance to the Victor and Cosmos Mindeleff study of Hopi building techniques. By the time JESSE WALTER FEWKES of the Hemenway Southwest Expedition arrived in Hopi territory in 1890, Stephen was knowledgeable about many aspects of Hopi lifeways, not usually open to whites. He had been initiated into three Hopi fraternities and had lived as part of both a Hopi and a Tewa household. Fewkes employed Stephen to provide an inside view of Hopi religious life. His account included a record of Hopi ritual terminology, as well as a listing of kinship terms that was to be of great help to later ethnologists in their understanding of the Hopi clan system. Stephen's observations of the economic life of the Hopis covered such activities as farming, housing, building, cooking, and weaving. The element of humor in Hopi culture was also recorded by Stephen in his account of the Hopi clown tradition.

Before his death from tuberculosis in 1894, Stephen was under the treatment of a Hopi medicine man, Yellow Bear. He recorded his experiences among the Hopis in a journal, edited by the anthropologist Elsie Clews Parsons as *The Hopi Journal of Alexander M. Stephen* (1936).

STEVENS, ISAAC INGALLS. *(1818–1862).* Governor of the Washington Territory; Indian superintendent; soldier.

A native of Andover, Massachusetts, Isaac Stevens was an 1839 West Point graduate. He served as an engineering officer with the army, and, in 1846–47, during the Mexican War, was a member of General WINFIELD SCOTT's staff. In 1847, still with the army, he was named Indian agent for the Washington Territory and chief of the army's survey of that region for a proposed northern railroad route to the Pacific.

Five years later, in 1853, Stevens was appointed by President Franklin Pierce as governor of the Washington Territory, and, as such, superintendent of the region's Indian affairs. In this capacity, he embarked on a territory-wide campaign to sign treaties with Indian tribes. At the Wallawalla Council in May and June 1855, he negotiated treaties establishing territorial boundaries and reservations, with agreement by the tribes to permit whites to cross their lands on establshed trails. Stevens wanted to expedite the agreements with the Indians in order to clear the way for the planned Northern Pacific Railroad. Some of the Indian leaders involved in the seven treaties that Stevens undertook were the Yakima KAMIAKIN, the Wallawalla PEOPEOMOXMOX, and the Nez Perces Old JOSEPH and LAWYER. In exchange for granting land concessions and allowing whites to cross their territory, the Indians were to receive payments of trade goods from the federal government.

Yet unlawful encroachment on Indian lands by miners and settlers, with Stevens's approval, soon led to the Yakima War of 1855–56. Stevens was ruthless in his suppression of the uprising, even persecuting white sympathizers who spoke out on behalf of the Indians; he had a territorial chief justice arrested in his own courtroom for supporting the Indians. Stevens finally agreed to withdraw the territorial militia, and federal troops were successful in suppressing Indian resistance.

In 1857, Stevens served as territorial delegate to Congress. On returning to active military service during the Civil War, he was commissioned a major general. He was killed in the 1862 Battle of Chantilly in Virginia.

STEVENSON, MATILDA COXE (Tilly Stevenson). *(ca. 1850–1915).* Anthropologist; reformer.

Born in Texas, Matilda Coxe moved with her family to Washington, D.C., where she attended Miss Anable's School. In 1872, she married the geologist James Stevenson.

In 1879, along with the ethnologist FRANK HAMILTON CUSHING and the photographer JOHN K. HILLERS, the Stevensons traveled to Zuni Pueblo in New Mexico. Tilly Stevenson learned ethnographic techniques, as well as the Zuni language, and embarked on a study of the role of women in Zuni society.

After her husband's death in 1888, Stevenson became a staff member of the Smithonian's Bureau of Ethnology. She continued her studies of the Zunis, now concentrating on their religious practices. She also conducted research among the Rio Grande Pueblo Indians, at Jemez and Sia, as well as among the Hopis of Arizona, taking photographs of Pueblo Indian ceremonies before such picture-taking was banned in the pueblos. She presented the results of her research in *The Sia* (1894) and *The Zuni Indians* (1904).

Toward the end of her life, Stevenson settled among the Tewas at San Ildefonso Pueblo, New Mexico, where she continued her studies.

Although Stevenson originally supported the policies of assimilation of native peoples into white society, she came to lobby on behalf of the Indians' right to practice their native religions.

STOBIE, CHARLES (Mountain Charlie; Paghaghet, "long hair"). *(1845–1931).* Artist; army scout; buffalo hunter.

Charles Stobie was born in Baltimore, Maryland, eventually moving to Chicago, Illinois. In 1865, he headed west to paint frontier life. He joined a wagon train to Denver, becoming a friend of MOSES MILNER (California Joe), who taught him tracking skills.

In 1866, Stobie settled among the Utes. He joined his adopted tribe in several battles with the Arapahos and Cheyennes, which provided him with material for his paintings of Indian combat. He also painted portraits of Indian chiefs. His Ute nickname was *Paghaghet*, meaning "long hair."

Following his stay with the Utes, Stobie became an army scout and later a buffalo hunter. He was called Mountain Charlie by his white contemporaries. In addition to painting scenes of Indians and scouts of the Great Plains, Stobie made maps showing the Indians' view of their world.

STONE CALF. *Southern Cheyenne. (d. 1885).* Proponent of peace.

Although Stone Calf had been a noted warrior as a young man, he later advocated peace with whites along with BLACK KETTLE and LITTLE ROBE. In 1868, at Fort Larned, Kansas, he met with agent EDWARD WYNKOOP and General PHILIP H. SHERIDAN. In 1870, he met with Quaker Indian agents representing President ULYSSES S. GRANT's Peace Policy in the Indian Territory near the site where the Darlington Agency would soon be founded, then, soon after, accompanied the agent Brinton Darlington there. The next year, he traveled to Washington, D.C., along with Little Robe, as a spokesman for his people, then again two years later.

During the Red River War of 1874–75, Stone Calf attempted to keep his young warriors from joining the Comanches and Kiowas under QUANAH PARKER and other chiefs. His son, however, was killed at the Battle of Adobe Walls in June 1874.

Stone Calf became one of the so-called Cantonment Cheyennes, settling near the army's cantonment post. An active leader in reservation affairs, he strongly opposed a grass-lease program, which allowed white cattlemen to graze their herds on Cheyenne lands. Stone Calf claimed that there was not enough food for tribal horses and that the cowboys mistreated his people. His efforts helped bring about the cancellation of the lease.

STRUCK-BY-THE-REE (The-Man-Struck-by-a-Ricara, Palaneapape). *Yankton Sioux. (1804–1888).* Friend to whites.

Struck-by-the-Ree was born on August 30, 1804, when the LEWIS and CLARK Expedition camped in the Yankton homeland along the Missouri River at the site of present-day Yankton, South Dakota. SHAKEHAND was chief at this time. When Meriwether Lewis learned of the birth, he visited the baby and wrapped him in an American flag and declared him an American. Struck-by-the-Ree earned his adult name in a fight with the Arikara Indians, also known as the Rees. He was a friend to whites, taking pride in Lewis's declaration, and visited Washington, D.C., in 1837. During the Minnesota Uprising of 1862–63 under LITTLE CROW, he placed his warriors between the militants and white settlers to prevent bloodshed.

STUART, GRANVILLE. *(1834—1918).* Artist; writer.

Stuart Granville was born in Virginia. In the late 1850s, after an unsuccessful gold-prospecting trip to California, he traveled up the Missouri River to Fort

Benton, Montana. It was in Montana, near Deer Lodge, that Stuart discovered gold, leading to the 1862 Gold Rush to that area. Stuart eventually settled in the region, becoming active in business and political affairs. He became a major rancher and participated in the vigilante movement against cattle rustlers in the late 1800s. In 1894, Stuart was appointed ambassador to Uruguay and Paraguay by then President Grover Cleveland. Of his approximately 150 drawings of western and Indian life, 42 illustrate his published diary of his travels, *Diary and Sketchbook of a Journey* (1963). He also wrote *Forty Years on the Frontier* (1925).

STUART, JOHN. *(1718–1784).* Colonial Indian superintendent. Great-grandfather of DENNIS BUSHYHEAD.

From 1740 to 1742, Scotsman John Stuart circumnavigated the world with privateer Captain John Anson on a raiding mission against the Spanish colonies in the Americas. He settled in Charleston, South Carolina, in 1750, and began a successful commercial and political career in that city.

In 1762, Stuart was appointed Great Britain's Indian superintendent of the Southern Department, succeeding EDMOND ATKIN. Starting in 1763, he conducted a series of treaty conferences with the leaders of the Cherokee, Choctaw, Chickasaw, and Catawba tribes.

At the Augusta Congress, held in Augusta, Georgia, in June 1763, Stuart lavished the Indians with gifts and rum in order to smooth negotiations. The Catawbas were granted guarantees that their reservation lands would not be violated by white encroachment. The Creeks accepted a boundary line, prohibiting white settlement on their lands along the Georgia frontier, which coincided with the Proclamation Line announced by the British government the following October. The Chickasaws and the Choctaws gave their assurances of continued peaceful relations, as did the Cherokees under ATTAKULLAKULLA, in exchange for British regulation of the Indian trade, assuring fair treatment by frontier traders.

Stuart was especially close to the Cherokees. By a Cherokee woman, he had a son, Oonatata, who was grandfather to DENNIS BUSHYHEAD.

At the outbreak of the American Revolution in 1775, Stuart was assigned the responsibility of keeping Southeast tribes loyal to the British cause. Because of Patriot victories, he was eventually forced to return to England. His South Carolina property was confiscated by the new American government, but the British compensated his loss and rewarded him with a subsidy for his service.

STUMBLING BEAR (Setimkia, "charging bear"). *Kiowa. (ca. 1832–1903).* War chief who became a peace advocate. Cousin of KICKING BIRD.

As a young man, Stumbling Bear was a powerful war chief, famous among his people for raids on Pawnees, Navajos, Sacs, Foxes, and other tribes. In November 1864, he battled troops under Colonel CHRISTOPHER "KIT" CARSON in the first Battle of Adobe Walls in the Texas Panhandle. Along with Kicking Bird, SATANTA and SATANK, Stumbling Bear was one of the principal spokesmen for the Kiowas at the Medicine Lodge Council in 1867. During the Red River War of 1874–75, involving the Kiowas as well as the Comanches under QUANAH PARKER, Stumbling Bear, like his cousin Kicking Bird, called for peace with whites and was a rival of LONE WOLF. In 1872, he and Kicking Bird were the principal representatives for the tribe's delegation to Washington, D.C. In 1878, the federal government built a home for him in the Indian Territory.

STUYVESANT, PETER. *(ca. 1610–1672).* Dutch colonial governor.

Born in Holland, Peter Stuyvesant became governor of the Dutch Caribbean colony of Curacao, Aruba, and Bonaire. He lost his leg during a 1644 campaign on Saint Martin. In 1647, he was named director general of the Dutch West Indian Company's New Netherland colony in what is now New York and New Jersey, succeeding WILLEM KIEFT, whose Indian policy had led to warfare with Hudson River Algonquian bands.

After a period of relatively calm relations with the Indians, the Peach War erupted in 1655 following an incident in which a Dutch farmer killed a Delaware Indian woman for taking fruit from his orchard. The Indian woman's family killed the farmer in retaliation; Stuyvesant authorized the arrest of the Indians responsible for the raid; the Delawares conducted other raids on New Amsterdam (present-day New York City) and outlying settlements around Manhattan Island, taking more than 150 Dutch colonists prisoner; Stuyvesant launched a counterattack, managing to rescue most of the captives. That same year, Stuyvesant wrested control of the Delaware colony from Sweden, thus expanding Dutch dominion over the Indians to the south, as far as Delaware Bay.

Hostilities soon erupted in the upper Hudson region, near the Dutch settlement of Wiltwyck, where the Esophus band raided colonial farms in an effort to drive out the encroaching Dutch. Stuyvesant organized a peace conference and invited the Esophus leaders to meet with Dutch colonial officials at Wiltwyck. While guests of the Dutch, the Indians were slaughtered in their sleep by Stuyvesant's militia. Outraged, the Esophus captured eight Dutch soldiers, whom they burned at the stake.

The Indians continued to lay siege to the Wiltwyck settlement until 1660. Stuyvesant demanded that all the Indian tribes within the New Netherland colony leave some of their children as hostages in New Amsterdam as a guarantee of peace. Stuyvesant also called on his Indian allies, the Mohawks, to terrorize remaining militants into agreeing to a peace settlement. A treaty, under which the Esophus ceded their land and agreed to stay away from Dutch settlements, was concluded in 1664, negotiated by the Wappinger ORATAMIN.

Later that year, Stuyvesant surrendered Dutch control of all New Netherland to the British, who had besieged New Amsterdam with an overwhelming naval force. Stuyvesant retired to private life on his farm in lower Manhattan. (See also ORATAMIN.)

SUBLETTE, WILLIAM LEWIS. *(1799–1845).* Trader; trapper.

William Sublette was born in Kentucky. In 1816–17, his family moved to St. Charles, in the Missouri Territory, where his father opened a tavern.

Orphaned by 1822, Sublette embarked on a career in the burgeoning fur trade with the upper Missouri River Indians. The next year, he joined WILLIAM HENRY ASHLEY's second expedition to the Mandan villages in present-day South Dakota. Along the way, he survived an attack by the Arikaras north of Fort Kiowa. Shortly after, Sublette took part in Colonel HENRY LEAVENWORTH's punitive expedition against that tribe.

Later that year, Sublette was part of JEDEDIAH SMITH's expedition that explored an overland route into the Northern Rockies and through the South Pass of the Wind River Range in present-day Wyoming.

By 1826, Sublette was a partner in the fur trade with Smith and David E. Jackson, having bought out Ashley's interests. Four years later, he pioneered the first wagon route into the Northern Rockies. He sold his shares to the Rocky Mountain Fur Company in 1830, but remained active in the fur trade as a supplier of goods to trappers and traders. He took part in the 1832 fur trappers' rendezvous at Pierre's Hole, on the western slopes of the Teton Mountains. Sublette was wounded there when Gros Ventres attacked the trappers and traders.

In 1833, along with ROBERT CAMPBELL, Sublette founded Fort William in what is now North Dakota to compete with JOHN JACOB ASTOR's American Fur Company. The next year, they founded Fort Laramie in eastern Wyoming, which later became a crucial stopover point on the Oregon Trail and played a vital role in the wars with the Plains Indians.

In 1836, Sublette left the fur trade, going into business in St. Louis. He prospered in commerce and became influential in Missouri politics. In St. Louis, Sublette adopted a family of Indians, who lived in a wigwam inside his store. In 1844, he served as a Missouri state elector in that year's presidential election. He died the following year in Pittsburgh of tuberculosis, while en route to Cape May, New Jersey, with his wife.

William Sublette's four brothers were also involved in the western fur trade: Milton Green Sublette, Andrew Whitley Sublette, Pickney W. Sublette, and Solomon Perry Sublette.

SULLIVAN, JOHN. *(1740–1795).* Army officer in Revolutionary campaigns against the Iroquois.

Born in Somersworth, New Hampshire, John Sullivan studied law, starting a practice in Durham, New Hampshire, in 1760. He was an early supporter of the movement for independence from Great Britain, representing New Hampshire at the first Continental Congress in 1774.

In December 1774, as a major in the colonial militia, Sullivan captured Fort William and Mary at Portsmouth, New Hampshire, from the British. Appointed brigadier general following the second Continental Congress in May 1775, he took part in the siege of Boston and later took command of the Continental army regiments retreating from their unsuccessful campaign against Montreal. In August 1776, he was promoted to major general and placed in command of Continental forces on Long Island. He was captured in the Battle of Long Island that same month, but was released soon after and rejoined General GEORGE WASHINGTON in Westchester County, New York. Sullivan later took part in Washington's victories at Trenton and Princeton, New Jersey, in December and January of 1776–77. In August 1777, he led an indecisive night raid on the British at Staten Island, New York. The following spring, he was placed in command of revolutionary forces in Rhode Island. His campaign of August 1778 against Newport was supposed to be in conjunction with French naval support, but bad weather forced the French warships to withdraw. Sullivan and his command were able to fight off a British counterattack north of Newport, but were forced to pull back to Providence when the British deployed additional troops.

In the summer and fall of 1778, JOHN BUTLER's Rangers joined with Iroquois warriors under JOSEPH BRANT in a campaign of destruction against the American settlers in the Mohawk Valley of New York and the Wyoming Valley of Pennsylvania. The Tories and their Iroquois allies destroyed farms and killed settlers throughout the area, most notably at Cherry Valley, New York, and in northeastern Pennsylvania's Wyoming Valley. Sullivan was directed to lead a punitive expedition against the Iroquois in the spring and summer of 1779.

Starting from Easton, Pennsylvania, in August 1779, Sullivan led a force of about 2,500 men into the Susquehanna and Wyoming valleys of northern Pennsylvania and southern New York. Joining Sullivan on this 1779 expedition against the Iroquois were Continental army regiments under the commands of generals Edward Hand, William Maxwell, and Enoch Poor. Sullivan's column reached Tioga (present-day Athens, Pennsylvania) and built Fort Sullivan. Meanwhile, General JAMES CLINTON led a coordinated assault of 1,500 men down the Susquehanna River Valley from the Mohawk Valley. Clinton's column joined up with Sullivan's at Fort Sullivan in August. A third column under Colonel Daniel Brodhead advanced out of Pittsburgh along the Allegheny River.

The one major engagement of the campaign occurred at the Battle of Newtown, near present-day Elmira, New York, on August 29, 1779, which proved indecisive because the majority of warriors were able to retreat into the wilderness. The Sullivan-Clinton Campaign continued its march over Iroquois lands in small detachments, destroying villages and crops, as many as 40 towns and 160,000 bushels of corn. Suffering few actual casualties, the Iroquois continued their raids. The damage inflicted on their property by the soldiers effectively destroyed their cultural base in New York, however. Many Iroquois settled permanently in Canada at the end of the war.

Sullivan became ill shortly after his campaign against the Iroquois and was forced to leave the military in November 1779. He remained active in state politics in New Hampshire, later serving as the state's chief executive, as well as representing New Hampshire in Congress. He served as a federal district judge in New Hampshire for six years before his death in 1795. (See also BRANT, JOSEPH.)

SULLY, ALFRED. *(1821–1879).* Army officer; Indian superintendent; artist.

Alfred Sully was born in Philadelphia, the son of painter Thomas Sully. Although a painter himself, he embarked on a military career, graduating from West Point in 1841. He served in Florida in 1841–42, the last year of the Second Seminole War under OSCEOLA, and in Oregon in 1853, in the years before the Rogue River War under Chief JOHN. In 1856, he saw action on the Northern Plains in the command of Colonel WILLIAM S. HARNEY.

During the Civil War, Sully served in Virginia and was promoted to brigadier general of volunteers. In 1863, he was given command of the Department of the Dakota. In June of that year, he headed an expedition out of Sioux City, Iowa, up the Missouri River against LITTLE CROW's Santee Sioux, who had fled to sympathetic Yankton and Teton bands in present-day North Dakota during the Minnesota Uprising. Sully's column was supposed to join up with that of General HENRY HASTINGS SIBLEY attacking from Minnesota. Although his troops were delayed, causing him to miss the August rendezvous, Sully inflicted damage on the Sioux, including INKPADUTA's band, in the Battle of Whitestone Hill on September 3. He led another expedition into North Dakota the next year, during which he founded Fort Rice near the mouth of the Yellowstone River and engaged the Sioux, including warriors under SITTING BULL, at Killdeer Mountain on July 28, 1864. Then, in 1865, he headed a third expedition from Fort Rice to Fort Berthold on Devils Lake. These expeditions were designed to send a message to the Sioux concerning U.S. military strength.

In fall 1868, Sully fought in the SHERIDAN Campaign against southern Cheyennes, Southern Arapahos, Comanches, and Kiowas, during which he established Camp Supply on the Canadian River in the Indian Territory. The next year, he became superintendent of Indian Affairs for Montana. During his tenure, he was involved in a controversy concerning the Massacre of the Marias in January 1870 in which federal troops under Colonel E. M. Baker killed about 170 disease-infected Piegans of the Blackfoot Confederacy, leading to criticism of the War Department by eastern reformers.

In the course of his military career, Sully produced watercolors of his experiences, especially views of western forts. (See also LITTLE CROW.)

SUMNER, EDWIN VOSE (Bull Sumner).
(1797–1863). Army officer.

A native of Boston, Massachusetts, Edwin Sumner entered the army in 1819, eventually becoming an officer of dragoon regiments. He served under General WINFIELD SCOTT in the Mexican War of 1846–48, during which he earned the nickname "Bull" Sumner after a Mexican musket ball reportedly bounced off his head.

In the aftermath of the Mexican War, Sumner was a lieutenant colonel in charge of the military in the newly acquired New Mexico Territory. He was responsible for protecting travelers along the Santa Fe Trail from attacks by Apaches, Navajos, and Utes. Sumner moved the American troops out of Santa Fe and garrisoned them in new forts throughout the territory. In August 1851, he established Fort Defiance and led an indecisive campaign against the Navajos at their stronghold at Canyon de Chelly. He continually was at odds with the civil authorities in New Mexico, at one point recommending that the federal government abandon the territory.

In the mid–1850s, the Cheyennes carried out raids on white travelers on the Southern Plains, between the

Arkansas and Platte Rivers, and Sumner was appointed colonel in command of the 1st Dragoons regiment at Fort Leavenworth, Kansas. He undertook an offensive against the Indians in summer 1857. On July 29, he engaged the Cheyennes in a battle on the Solomon River in Kansas. This battle was unique in that it included a classic cavalry charge, with troopers using drawn sabers instead of carbines. The Indians had been led to believe they were protected from the soldiers' bullets after bathing in the waters of a lake with supposed magical powers. Yet they felt defenseless against the army's sabers and retreated. Sumner's 1857 campaign enabled safe passage for miners on their way to the Colorado gold and silver strikes.

In 1858, Sumner became commander of the Department of the West (a pre–Civil War territorial command including all lands west of the Mississippi and east of the Rockies, except Texas and New Mexico). In the Civil War, he rose to the rank of major general.

SUNDAY, JOHN (Shahwundais, "god of the south"). *Chippewa (Ojibway). (ca. 1796–ca. 1855).* Missionary.

John Sunday grew up in Northumberland County, Ontario. In 1826–27, he was converted to Methodism by PETER JONES at a camp-meeting near Coburg. He learned to read and write and was ordained a minister. Along with GEORGE COPWAY, he served as a missionary to his people and helped found missions in Michigan. He toured the United States with Reverend William Case. In 1845, he was present at the general council of Christian Chippewas and Ottawas at Saugeen, Ontario. Sunday was noted for his oratorical abilities.

SURIA, TOMAS DE. *(fl. 1790s).* Artist.

The first two official artists of the Spanish scientific voyage around the world, led by ALEJANDRO MALASPINA, left the expedition at South American ports. Tomas de Suria, living in Mexico City and working as an engraver in the Mexican mint at the time, joined the expedition at Acapulco in February 1791, and participated in the first of two voyages to the Pacific Northwest, where he made drawings of Nootkas, Tlingits, and other Indians. JOSE CARDERO also executed drawings on this and a subsequent journey to the region. Suria, who returned to Mexico following this leg of the expedition, later became known for his portraits, medallions, and religious allegories.

SUTTER, JOHN AUGUSTUS (Johan August Suter). *(1803–1880).* Colonizer; trader.

Born in the German city of Baden of Swiss parents, John Sutter had settled in Berne, Switzerland, by 1839. That year, burdened by debts and a failed marriage, he left Europe for the United States. He lived at various times in New York, St. Louis, and Santa Fe before heading for the Pacific Coast. He went to Oregon, where he became a trader, traveling also to Hawaii and Alaska. In 1839, he arrived in the Sacramento Valley of California.

The Mexican governor of California, Juan Bautista Alvarado, soon authorized a land grant to Sutter of close to 50,000 acres at the junctions of the Sacramento and American rivers. Sutter had military and judicial authority over the territory, which he called New Helvetia, with a capital at Sutter's Fort near present-day Sacramento.

Under the terms of the land grant, Sutter was to help prevent invasions of hostile Indians into the Sacramento Valley. The Mexicans also wanted Sutter's estate to act as a buffer to the increasing encroachment of Russian fur traders from Alaska and British traders from the Columbia River region to the north. There was additional concern about the influx of American fur traders, who at that time were developing routes across the Northern Rockies and into the Sierra Nevada of northern California. Sutter, despite the wishes of Spanish officials, encouraged Anglo-American settlers, who began arriving in the Sacramento Valley during the 1840s.

The Mexican War of 1846–48 and the cession of all of California to the United States brought with it questions concerning Sutter's legal title to his lands. In January 1848, one of Sutter's workmen found traces of gold at a mill under construction on the Sutter property, near present-day Coloma, California. The Gold Rush of 1849 brought thousands of would-be prospectors to the Sacramento Valley, and Sutter's entire opeartion was soon overrun and devastated, as were Indian homelands. Sutter spent much of the rest of his life in the East, lobbying Congressional leaders for financial compensation for his losses.

SWAN, JAMES G. *(1818–1900).* Collector of Indian artifacts.

Born in Massachusetts, James Swan sailed to California in the 1850s in the hope of making his fortune in the Gold Rush. He subsequently settled near Port Townsend, Washington Territory, near the estuary of the Columbia River, where he worked at many different odd jobs, including teaching at an Indian school at Neah Bay.

In 1863, Swan began his relationship with the Smithsonian Institution as a collector, and, during the next four decades, he accumulated artifacts of the Northwest Coast Indians for exhibitions. He specialized in collecting items from the seagoing cultures of the region, especially the Makahs, Bella Bellas, Bella Coolas, and Haidas.

Many of the items Swan obtained from these and other Indians, from Washington Territory to the coast of Alaska, were a major part of the Smithsonian's National Museum displays organized by SPENCER BAIRD. Some were shown at the Centennial Exhibition in Philadelphia as well as the Cotton Centennial Exhibition in New Orleans. Swan also provided Northwest Coast Indian artifacts for the Chicago World's Fair of 1892–93 and the Washington State Exhibition. Toward the end of his life, his efforts were instrumental in building the Northwest Coast Indian collections for FRANZ BOAS of the American Museum of Natural History in New York City.

Swan also kept diaries in which he recorded the culture of the Northwest Coast Indians.

SWARTON, HANNAH. *(fl. 1690s).* Captive.

On May 16, 1690, during King William's War of 1689–97, the first of the French and Indian Wars, Hannah Swarton and her family suffered an attack by a French-led Abnaki party on their home at the settlement of Casco Bay, Maine. Her husband was killed in the raid; she was taken captive, along with four of her children. The Indians soon killed her eldest son. She was held as a slave until the following February, when she was released to French authorities at Quebec. Yet she was not able to return to her home in the Massachusetts Bay Colony until November 1695, when English authorities reached a ransom agreement with the French.

Swarton's captivity became the subject of a sermon by Puritan leader COTTON MATHER, who characterized her ordeal at the hands of the Indians like that of HANNAH DUSTON, as divine retribution for the sin she committed by moving away from an established church community in Beverly, Massachusetts, to a churchless settlement on the Maine coast. Mather paralleled her physical trials at the hands of the Indians with the assault on her Protestant spirituality by the French, who tried to convert her to the Catholic faith while she was in their custody.

T

TAHCHEE (Tatsi; Dutch). *Cherokee. (b. ca. 1790).* Enemy of the Osages and Comanches; army scout.

Tahchee was born at Turkey Town along the Coosa River in what is now Alabama. When a boy, he emigrated with his family west of the Mississippi to the St. Francis River in present-day Arkansas where the BOWL had settled his band of Cherokees.

Tahchee grew up learning the hunting and fighting techniques of the Plains Indians. He participated in raids on the Osages. After a peace was concluded between the Cherokees and that tribe, he lived among them for 14 months, improving his skills. When war broke out again, he headed Cherokee war parties against his former hosts.

In 1828, angry over the treaty between his people and the federal government, Tahchee crossed the Red River into Texas, from where he made war on the Comanches in addition to the Osages. He was declared an outlaw by the army, with a reward of $500 on his head. By this time, he was a legend on the Southern Plains. In defiance of the army, Tahchee carried out a raid on a group of Osages at a trading post near Fort Gibson, scalping one. A bullet grazed his cheek while he made good his escape, his only wound in all his years of warfare.

Tahchee later made peace with the army, who employed him as a scout and hunter against the Comanches. It is said he singlehandedly provided all the game for the troops accompanying him. He built a house along the Canadian River near Fort Gibson and eventually took up farming.

TAIMAH (Taiomah, Tamah, Taima, Tama, "crash of thunder"). *Fox. (ca. 1790–ca. 1830).* Medicine man; friend to whites.

Taimah was a friend to white settlers in Wisconsin and Illinois. He saved the life of an Indian agent by traveling to Prairie du Chien and giving advance notice that a brave seeking revenge was on the way. Pressured by white officials to relocate west of the Mississippi, Taimah founded a village near present-day Burlington, Iowa. In 1824, he was part of a Sac and Fox tribal delegation to Washington, D.C. He had a reputation in the region as a powerful shaman with great curing abilities, and he belonged to the pan-tribal Midewiwin (or Grand Medicine) Society. He died of tuberculosis. Tama, Iowa, is named after him.

TALIAFERRO, LAWRENCE (Four Hearts). *(1794–1871).* Indian agent.

In 1819, Lawrence Taliaferro, a member of a prominent Virginia family of Italian descent, was appointed by President James Monroe as Indian agent to the Sioux and Chippewas at Fort Snelling, the fur-trading post on the site of present-day Minneapolis, at the confluence of the Minnesota and Mississippi rivers.

Taliaferro served five terms as agent, for a total of 20 years. After 1827, the Chippewas were not part of his administration. Taliaferro developed a reputation of honesty in his dealings with Indians. He married a Sioux woman and was known as Four Hearts to her people, for his equal and fair treatment of Indians, French traders, British traders, and American soldiers.

Taliaferro took measures to limit the influence of liquor in the Indian trade, sought to maintain peaceful relations among the tribes under his charge, and was a staunch protector of Indian rights. Yet his efforts to encourage agriculture as an alternative to the fur trade proved unsuccessful.

Taliaferro's journal of his tenure at Fort Snelling provides a detailed account of life on the Minnesota frontier, including descriptions of Indian councils and speeches by Indian leaders.

TALL BULL (Hotoakhihoosis, Hotuaeka'ash, Otoah-hastis). *Southern Cheyenne.* *(ca. 1815–1869).* Leader of the Dog Soldiers.

The most prominent of several Cheyenne chiefs of the same name, Tall Bull was one of the principal leaders, along with BULL BEAR and WHITE HORSE, of the militant Dog Soldier Society active on the Southern Plains during the 1850s–60s.

After the massacre of BLACK KETTLE's peaceful Cheyennes at Sand Creek during the Cheyenne-Arapaho (or Colorado) War of 1864–65, Tall Bull and the other Dog Soldiers increased their raids on white settlements. Following the conclusion of the Civil War, troops under General WINFIELD SCOTT HANCOCK tried to pacify Southern Plains tribes in the Hancock Campaign of 1867. Tall Bull and other Cheyennes met with Hancock at Fort Larned, Kansas, in April 1867, but negotiations broke down. That summer, Colonel GEORGE ARMSTRONG CUSTER and his 7th Cavalry chased the Dog Soldiers and their allies, some of them Sioux and Arapaho, throughout western Kansas, northeastern Colorado, and southwestern Nebraska. Custer succeeded in burning an evacuated village on the Pawnee Fork, but little else, as the Indians continued to raid mail stations, stagecoaches, wagon trains, and railroad work parties.

That autumn, with criticism of both the BOZEMAN Campaign of the Northern Plains against RED CLOUD's Sioux and the abortive Hancock Campaign, government officials launched a commission resulting in two treaties—Medicine Lodge in 1867 and Fort Laramie in 1868. Tall Bull, Bull Bear, and White Horse were all present at Medicine Lodge, as were the prominent Cheyenne peace chiefs.

In the spring of 1868, Tall Bull's warriors carried out an attack on the Kaw (Kansa) Indians at Council Grove, Kansas. Because of this raid, officials refused to distribute to the Southern Cheyennes arms and ammunition for hunting. The angry Dog Soldiers began raiding settlements along the Sabine and Solomon rivers in Kansas. Additional troops, now under the command of General PHILIP H. SHERIDAN, entered the field in the Sheridan Campaign. Tall Bull and the other Dog Soldier war chiefs participated in the Battle of BEECHER's Island on September 17, 1868, in which fellow militant ROMAN NOSE was killed in combat with a 50-man scouting force under Major GEORGE FORSYTH. On November 27, in the Battle of Washita, the peace chief Black Kettle died at the hands of Custer's soldiers.

The Sheridan Campaign continued into the spring and summer of 1869. LITTLE ROBE and other peace chiefs brought their bands into the Cheyenne and Arapaho Reservation in the Indian Territory, but Tall Bull led his followers northward to the Republican River region, from where he carried out raids on the Kansas frontier. Major EUGENE A. CARR organized the Republican River Expedition, and, that spring, attacked Tall Bull's camp along the river. The warriors counterattacked to let the women and children escape, then retreated themselves. After a long pursuit, Carr's men, including Pawnee scouts under FRANK NORTH and WILLIAM "BUFFALO BILL" CODY, located Tall Bull's new camp at Summit Springs in northeastern Colorado. Tall Bull planned an attack the same day—July 11, 1869—but Carr ordered a strike early in the morning. After a bitter fight in which 52 warriors were killed and 17 women and children were captured, the troops destroyed the Cheyenne camp. Tall Bull was shot and killed. Survivors scattered northward to Sioux territory.

The Battle of Summit Springs marked the end of the Dog Soldiers' power on the Great Plains. Some members of the military society later joined Comanches under QUANAH PARKER and Kiowas under LONE WOLF in the Red River War of 1874–75—Bull Bear for one—but not in great numbers.

TAMAHA (Tahama, Tahamie, Tamahaw, "rising moose"; Le Borgne, One Eye, The One-Eyed Sioux). *Mdewakanton Sioux.* *(1775–1860).* Ally of Americans in the War of 1812; scout.

Tamaha was born at present-day Winona, Minnesota. While playing as a boy, he lost an eye, leading to a nickname by which he became known to whites.

In 1806–07, Tamaha became a close friend of Lieutenant ZEBULON PIKE, which led to his decision to support the Americans in the War of 1812, unlike most of the Santee Sioux, such as JOSEPH RENVILLE and RED WING. Tamaha served as a scout and messenger out of St. Louis, Missouri. During one of his voyages, he was captured by Robert Dickson, an Indian trader and a colonel in the British army. He refused to divulge information, however, and was held as a prisoner of war. Upon his release, he returned to St. Louis, where he participated in a council between WILLIAM CLARK and 46 chiefs of Missouri River tribes. Clark commissioned Tamaha as a chief of the Sioux and presented him with a medal.

Tamaha returned to Minnesota, where he became one of the influential Mdewakanton leaders. He died at Wabasha two years before the Santees revolted under LITTLE CROW in the Minnesota Uprising of 1862–63.

TAMAQUE (The Beaver, King Beaver). *Delaware.* *(d. ca. 1770).* Trading partner and sometime ally of both English and French.

Tamaque and his brother Shingass were chiefs of the Unalachtigo Delawares. Their village—Sawcunk or Chingass Town—was on the north bank of the Ohio River near the mouth of Beaver Creek and served as an active fur-trading post. Tamaque also lived part of the time at Kuskuski up Beaver Creek, and at Kittaning along the Allegheny River.

Although Shingass led many raids on settlers, Tamaque was more moderate in his relations with the English and encouraged trade with them. After General EDWARD BRADDOCK's defeat in 1755 during the French and Indian War, Tamaque threw his support to the French from his new home at Tuscararas on the Tuscarawas River in Ohio, due west of Sawcunk; it came to be called The Beaver's Town. He participated in numerous councils with white officials at the end of the war.

Tamaque joined with PONTIAC in raids on British settlements during Pontiac's Rebellion of 1763, finally making a permanent peace with the British because the French failed to provide their promised help. Tamaque was later converted by Moravian missionaries.

TAMMANY (Saint Tammany, Tamanend, Tamenend, Tamany, Taminy, Tamanee, Tamanen, Tamaned, Temane, "the affable"). *Delaware.*
(ca. 1625–ca. 1701). Friend to whites; inspiration for political societies.

Tammany was a Unami Delaware Indian living along the Delaware River, probably in present-day Bucks County, Pennsylvania. Although he was one of the most famous Indians of the colonial period, little is known today of his life. It is thought that he personally welcomed WILLIAM PENN to North America in October 1682. He negotiated and signed two treaties with Penn at Shackamaxon (present-day Philadelphia) in 1683; attended a council between Delawares and settlers in 1694, where he spoke for peace; and signed a third treaty in 1697.

Because of his dedication to friendship with the colonists, Tammany became a symbol of goodness. A legend became widely known among whites in which Tammany is said to have dueled for days with an evil spirit that tried to usurp his power, finally driving it off. Years after his death, during the Revolutionary period, he began to be referred to as Saint Tammany, the Patron Saint of America, and some celebrated the first day of May in his honor. A number of political societies, Loyalist and patriot, took his name. One of these, The Society of St. Tammany, founded in 1789, later became known as Tammany Hall, the infamous Democratic Party organization in New York.

TANACHARISON. See HALF-KING.

TANNER, JOHN (The White Indian).
(ca. 1780–ca. 1846). Trader; interpreter; captive.

In 1789, nine-year-old John Tanner was abducted from his family home on the Kentucky frontier by a Shawnee raiding party. He was later sold to the Ottawas and adopted into the family of the woman Netnokwa.

For the next 30 years, Tanner lived as an Indian hunter and warrior among the Ottawas and Chippewas in the wilderness of western Minnesota and the Lake Superior region of Canada. He married a Chippewa woman known as Red-Sky-of-the-Morning.

In 1817, with the help of Michigan territorial governor LEWIS CASS, Tanner returned to Kentucky and succeeded in locating his brother and other relatives in Kentucky, whom he had not seen for nearly three decades. He brought a second Chippewa wife and two daughters to Mackinac, Michigan, in the 1820s, where he worked for JOHN JACOB ASTOR's American Fur Company.

In 1828, Tanner moved his family to Sault Ste. Marie, Michigan, where he was employed as the interpreter for Indian agent and ethnologist HENRY ROWE SCHOOLCRAFT. About this time, Tanner's second Indian wife left him after she was involved in an attempt to kill him. The Michigan Territorial legislature then took actions that caused him to lose custody of his eldest daughter.

Tanner married a white woman from Detroit in the 1840s, by whom he had a child. But, unable to tolerate his adherence to the Indian life-style, she also soon left him.

In 1846, James Schoolcraft, the brother of Henry Rowe Schoolcraft, was murdered at Sault Ste. Marie. Suspected of the crime, Tanner disappeared soon after and was never seen again. An army officer later admitted having killed Schoolcraft in a dispute over a woman. It was theorized that he had also killed Tanner—a skeleton was eventually found in a nearby swamp—to cover up the first killing.

Dr. Edwin James, who had been the physician and chronicler of the 1820 STEPHEN H. LONG expedition, recorded details of Tanner's years among the Indians in the 1830 book *A Narrative of the Captivity and Adventures of John Tanner.* Tanner was popularly known as The White Indian.

TAPPAN, SAMUEL F. *(fl. 1860s–1870s).* Reformer; peace commissioner; journalist.

Samuel Tappan was a correspondent for Horace Greeley's *New-York Tribune* and covered the antislavery movement in Kansas. An abolitionist, he became an Indian rights activist when he moved to Denver in 1860 to work for the *Daily Herald.* His Civil War military service began in 1861 when he was commissioned a lieutenant colonel in the First Colorado Cavalry, a unit that saw action in the New Mexico campaign against the Confederacy as well as in the Plains Indian wars.

Tappan was appointed head of the military commission that investigated Colonel JOHN CHIVINGTON for his role in the 1864 Sand Creek Massacre of BLACK KETTLE's Cheyenne band. Then, in 1867, he was a member of the presidential Peace Commission that negotiated the Medicine Lodge Treaty in Kansas with the Southern Plains tribes, in which the Indians agreed to relocate to the Indian Territory.

As a leading member of PETER COOPER's United States Indian Commission, founded in 1869, Tappan was active in promoting legislation for the funding of annuities and economic assistance promised to the Indians by the federal Peace Commission two years before.

Tappan was a strong advocate of self-determination for Indians and the removal of military jurisdiction over tribal matters. He proposed that the federal government help institute a form of civil law for the Indians maintained under tribal self-government on the reservations.

Tappan remained active in the cause of Indian rights throughout the 1870s, strongly supporting President ULYSSES S. GRANT's Peace Policy. He openly charged that Congressional railroad and land speculation interests were undermining the efforts of the Peace Policy to reach a final settlement with the Indians of the Plains and the Southwest, and were ultimately responsible for such atrocities against the Indians as the 1871 massacre of ESKIMINZIN's Apache band at Camp Grant, Arizona.

Tappan was married for a time to Pennsylvania abolitionist and Indian rights activist Cora Daniels.

TARHE (Crane, Le Chef Grue, Monsieur Grue).
Wyandot (Huron) (1742–1818). Enemy of whites who became ally of Americans against the British; medicine man.

Tarhe was born at Detroit and became one of the leaders of the Ohio Hurons, referred to as Wyandots. He joined CORNSTALK against the whites at Point Pleasant in Lord DUNMORE's War of 1774, then LITTLE TURTLE at Fallen Timbers in Little Turtle's War of 1790–94. Tarhe was central to the negotiations of the Fort Greenville Treaty in 1795 and was henceforth an ally of the Americans. He was a friend of the Shawnee CATAHECASSA and opposed TECUMSEH's war policy, siding with the Americans against the British in the War of 1812 and fighting at the Battle of the Thames in October 1813. He died at Crane Town, near Sandusky, Ohio. His funeral was attended by Indian and white notables, including the Seneca RED JACKET.

TASCALUSA (Tuscaluca, Tuscaloosa, Taszaluza, Tascaluca, Tastaluca, "black warrior"). *Alabama.*
(fl. 1540s). Leader of the battle against HERNANDO DE SOTO.

The first meeting between the Alabama, or Alibamu, Indians and De Soto's conquistadors in 1540 in what is now Alabama proved peaceful. Tascalusa sat on a raised platform with his son at his side and his notables surrounding him while the Spanish entertained him with a horse-riding display. When De Soto demanded supplies and burden carriers from the Indians, Tascalusa at first refused. De Soto then threatened violence. Although Tascalusa ostensibly agreed to send word ahead to his village of Mabila to comply with the Spaniards' needs, he had his messengers call in his warriors from other villages to his stockaded home.

At Mabila, the Alabamas entertained their guests with dancing, but the soldiers spied weapons concealed among the Indians. When De Soto's men tried to take Tascalusa prisoner, fighting broke out. The Alabamas managed to free the burden carriers of other tribes, who then joined in the fighting and helped drive the conquistadors from the village. The battle continued in open country, where the 580 invaders held the advantage because of their horses and armor. The Battle of Mabila of October 18, 1540, lasted all day, with Indian women and children joining in the conflict. The Spanish eventually managed to set the village on fire, and those Indians not killed by sword and lance were driven into the flames. Some committed suicide rather than be captured. It has been estimated that 2,500 Indians died, as opposed to only 20 Spaniards, with 150 more wounded, including De Soto.

It is not known what happened to Tascalusa. His son's body was found among the dead, stuck with a Spanish lance.

TATANGA MANI (Walking Buffalo; George McLean). *Stoney (Assiniboine). (1871–1967).* Principal chief; lecturer.

Tatanga Mani was named after his grandfather, who had been principal chief of the Stoney Indians, a branch tribe of the Assiniboines, during the 1860s. The boy grew up in Morley, Alberta. When nine, he was adopted by the Methodist missionary John McLean. The missionary John McDougall was one of his teachers. Tatanga Mani became principal chief in 1920, serving until 1935. When in his 80s, he made three goodwill lecture tours on behalf of the Canadian chapter of the Moral Rearmament movement, visiting many European and African countries as well as Australia and New Zealand.

TATEMY (Tattema, Tadema, Titami, Totami, Tundy; Moses Fonda Tatemy, Old Moses). *Delaware. (ca. 1690–ca. 1761).* Interpreter; negotiator; Christian convert.

Tatemy was born on the east side of the Delaware River in what is now New Jersey. In 1737, for services to the English as an interpreter, he was granted a tract of land near Stockertown, Pennsylvania. In the early

1740s, when many of the Delawares were dispersed from the area, Tatemy asked Pennsylvania officials permission to stay on his land and, with the approval of the Iroquois, was allowed to do so. In 1745, he was baptized as Moses Fonda Tatemy by DAVID BRAINERD, for whom he had previously worked as an interpreter.

Tatemy continued to act as an interpreter in the important negotiations during the French and Indian War of 1754–63, helping to secure TEEDYUSCUNG's support for the English. In 1757, Tatemy's son William was shot and killed by a white teenager while accompanying Delaware delegates to Easton, Pennsylvania, for a council. The incident nearly broke down negotiations, but the English promised to bring the youth to justice.

TATTOOED SERPENT (Serpent Pique, Olabalkebiche, Ulabalkebiche). *Natchez. (d. 1725).* War chief; ally of French. Brother of GREAT SUN.

When the French established relations with the Natchez Indians living along the lower Mississippi River in present-day Mississippi and Louisiana during the early 1700s, the Great Sun was their principal chief and Tattooed Serpent was war chief. Although Tattooed Serpent was taken captive by the French under JEAN BAPTISTE LE MOYNE, SIEUR DE BIENVILLE in 1716, he became their trusted ally in the following years. On his death, he was much mourned by the Great Sun, who threatened suicide. By Natchez custom, Tattooed Serpent's wives and servants were killed to accompany him to the next world. Without his influence, the tribe's anti-French faction rose to prominence, and, in 1729, the Great Sun led his warriors in the Natchez Revolt.

TATUM, LAWRIE. *(b. 1822).* Indian agent.

Lawrie Tatum was born in New Jersey and raised there and in Ohio. As one of the earliest Quakers appointed as Indian agent under President ULYSSES S. GRANT's Peace Policy by commissioner of Indian Affairs ELY PARKER, he was responsible for the Kiowas and Comanches at the Fort Sill Agency in the Indian Territory in the late 1860s and early 1870s.

Tatum attempted to adapt the Fort Sill Kiowas and Comanches to agricultural pursuits but could not divert them from their traditional life of hunting and raiding. The fact that Union forces had been raiding Texas settlements during the Civil War made Tatum's task of persuading the Indians to cease hostilities even more difficult.

In May 1871, despite his reluctance as a Quaker to call upon military assistance, Tatum directed the army to arrest Kiowa tribe members SATANK, SATANTA, and BIG TREE for their attack on a wagon train near Jacksboro, Texas.

Tatum related his experiences as agent in his book, *Our Red Brothers* (1899).

TAVERNIER, JULES. *(1844–1889).* Artist.

Soon after his service in the 1870 Franco-Prussian War, Frenchman Jules Tavernier emigrated to New York City, where he became an illustrator for the two most popular illustrated magazines of the day: *Harper's* and *Graphic*. With fellow artist Paul Frenzeney, Tavernier was sent by *Harper's* on a cross-country trip to the Pacific Coast, during which they produced illustrations as part of a promotional campaign. Both men went on to settle in San Francisco where they became known as major California artists of the period. In his work, Tavernier painted Native American scenes. One of his better-known works in this genre, *Indian Camp at Sunrise*, is part of the permanent collection of the Thomas Gilcrease Institute in Tulsa, Oklahoma.

TAVIBO (Tab-be-bo, "sun man," "white man"; The Paiute Prophet). *Northern Paiute. (ca. 1810–1870).* Medicine man; prophet. Father of WOVOKA.

Tavibo was born near Walker Lake in present-day Nevada. As a young man, he was a shaman to his people. Late in his life, after the California Gold Rush of 1849 and subsequent white expansion, he experienced a series of visions concerning the destiny of all Indians. After a period of solitude in the mountains, he received from the Great Spirit a vision of the earth swallowing up whites. Returning to preach his message, he gained only a few converts. After a second vision, he prophesized that an earthquake would kill all humans, but that Indians would return to live in a restored aboriginal enviroment. He later claimed a third revelation that told him only believers would be resurrected. For a time, Tavibo generated interest among Bannocks, Shoshones, and Utes in addition to his own people, but his failed prophesies led to an eventual decline in followers. Wovoka, thought to be his son, carried on and refined his teachings—along with those of other Indian prophets of the Far West, SMOHALLA and JOHN SLOCUM—in the Ghost Dance religion.

TAYLOR, ZACHARY (Old Rough and Ready). *(1784–1850).* President of the United States, 1849–50; army officer in the Black Hawk War and Second Seminole War.

Born in Virginia, Zachary Taylor was raised near Louisville, Kentucky. He entered the army as a short-term volunteer in 1806, but, two years later, was commissioned a lieutenant and assigned to the 7th Infantry in Louisiana. He made the rank of captain, and, in 1811, was placed under the command of General WILLIAM HENRY HARRISON. In the War of 1812, he commanded Fort Knox, and later, Fort Harrison, both in the

Indiana Territory. The latter post, north of Vincennes on the Wabash River, was attacked by a force of Indians allied with the British, on September 4, 1812. After his successful defense, Taylor was promoted to major.

In the summer of 1814, Taylor led a punitive expedition against the Fox and Sac villages on the Rock River, in the upper Mississippi Valley. His force of 430 men suffered an attack by a combined force of 1,000 Winnebagos, Sioux, Fox, and Sac warriors at Credit Island on the Mississippi River, near present-day Davenport, Iowa. His river boats were threatened by a small company of British artillery aiding the Indians, and Taylor was forced to withdraw to St. Louis. One of the Sac chiefs in this engagement was BLACK HAWK, whom Taylor would fight again 18 years later.

Taylor briefly resigned from the army in 1815, but returned as a major in 1816, after which he commanded frontier posts in Wisconsin. At Fort Snelling, Minnesota, in 1829–32, he was in charge of negotiations with Indians.

At the outbreak of the Black Hawk War in 1832, Taylor was made a colonel and led Illinois volunteers and army regulars under the command of General HENRY ATKINSON. He took part in the decisive conflict of the Black Hawk War, the Battle of Bad Axe River, 40 miles north of Prairie Du Chien, Wisconsin. It was Colonel Taylor who delivered the captured Black Hawk to General WINFIELD SCOTT in August 1832.

In 1837, Taylor assumed command of a field force fighting in Florida in the Second Seminole War. By now OSCEOLA was imprisoned, but other militants carried on the resistance. On December 25, 1837, Taylor led a force of 600 men from a staging point on Lake Okeechobee in an attack against the Seminoles under ALLIGATOR, ARPEIKA, and WILD CAT, one of the few pitched battles of the war. The Seminoles, although not suffering heavy losses, withdrew into the Everglades. Taylor was promoted to brevet brigadier general and, in May 1838, was given command of the Department of Florida. He pursued the Seminoles for the next two and a half years, but, by the spring of 1840, had not been able to bring the Second Seminole War to a decisive end. He was relieved of his Florida command at his own request in April 1840.

From that time until 1845, Taylor commanded U.S. forces in Louisiana and Arkansas. In 1845, he took command of the army in Texas. When the Mexican War erupted the next year, Taylor led the first American troops across the Rio Grande. His military victories in northern Mexico in 1847 brought him national prominence, and he was elected president in 1848, running as a Whig in his victory over Democrat LEWIS CASS. He served for less than two years, dying in office from cholera. (See also BLACK HAWK; OSCEOLA.)

TAZA (Tazi). *Chiricahua Apache. (d. 1876).* Hereditary chief. Son of COCHISE; brother of NAICHE; grandson of MANGAS COLORADAS.

As the first son of Cochise, Taza became principal leader on the death of his father in 1874 and worked to maintain his father's peace agreement with whites. He also agreed to the relocation of his people from the Chiricahua Reservation at Apache Pass in Arizona to the San Carlos Reservation to the north in 1876. Yet he was unable to unite the various bands under him as his father had done. About half of them, including GERONIMO, crossed the border into the Sierra Madre of Mexico, which became their base of operations. That summer, Taza also agreed to join the Apache delegation to Washington, D.C., with the agent JOHN P. CLUM, the Aravaipa chief ESKIMINZIN, and others. Taza died of pneumonia during this trip and was buried in the Congressional Cemetery. His death caused his younger brother Naiche to become militant. (See also GERONIMO.)

TECUMSEH (Tecumtha, Tekamthi, "goes through one place to another"; Shooting Star). *Shawnee. (ca. 1768–1813).* Organizer of an Indian confederation and Tecumseh's Rebellion of 1809–11; ally of British in the War of 1812. Brother of TENSKWATAWA.

Tecumseh was probably born in the Shawnee village of Piqua near present-day Springfield, Ohio, the son of Puckeshinwa, a Shawnee war chief, and Methoataske, his wife, who possibly had Creek and Cherokee ancestry. Some reports have Tecumseh the twin of his brother Tenskwatawa; other accounts have Tecumseh as Tenskwatawa's senior by about 10 years. Their father was killed in the Battle of Point Pleasant in Lord DUNMORE's War of 1774. The elder brother who raised him was killed during the American Revolution. Another brother was killed by whites in LITTLE TURTLE's War of 1790–94 in which Tecumseh also fought, participating in the Indian victories over General JOSIAH HARMAR and General ARTHUR ST. CLAIR, and the defeat by General "Mad" ANTHONY WAYNE at Fallen Timbers. Tecumseh earned a reputation for skill in battle as well as compassion, advising fellow Indians to treat prisoners fairly, without degradation and torture.

Tecumseh refused to sign the Treaty of Fort Greenville in 1795 in which tribes of the Old Northwest were forced to cede huge tracts of territory. He maintained that no single Indian or tribe had the right to give up lands to whites because the lands belonged to all Indians and tribes.

It is said that Tecumseh studied world history and literature in order to better understand whites. A white schoolteacher, Rebecca Galloway, reportedly provided him with reading materials—history books and the Bible.

In the early 1800s, Tecumseh, known for his oratorical skills, began spreading a message of a united Indian people. In 1805, following a religious experience, his brother Tenskwatawa, who became known as the Shawnee Prophet, began preaching a return to traditional ways and the elimination of white customs, such as the Christian religion and liquor. In 1808, the brothers moved from Indiana to Ohio and established the former Miami village of Tippecanoe, near the confluence of the Tippecanoe and Wabash rivers in Indiana Territory, as a place where Indians from different tribes could congregate free of white society. About 1,000 to 12,000 Indians came to live in Tippecanoe, or Prophetstown.

The federal government refused to recognize Tecumseh's principle of pan-Indian land ownership. In a second treaty at Fort Greenville in September 1809, WILLIAM HENRY HARRISON, the governor of Indian Territory, forced cessions along the upper Wabash of 2.5 million acres, bringing the number to a total of 33 million acres since 1803. In August 1810, at a meeting with Harrison, Tecumseh repudiated the validity of the agreement. To demonstrate the fate of the Indians, who were crowded by whites, Tecumseh forced Harrison off a bench on which they both were sitting.

Tecumseh's vision had now become one of an Indian nation stretching from Canada to the Gulf of Mexico—a buffer between American, English, and Spanish territory—the different tribes organized into states. He traveled as far west as Iowa, as far east as New York, and as far south as Florida to spread his message. A council of some 5,000 Indians of many tribes, held in Creek country along the Tallapoosa in Alabama in October 1811, influenced a generation of Creek leaders and led to the later uprising known as the Creek War of 1813–14 under WILLIAM WEATHERFORD.

Yet Tecumseh's efforts in achieving Indian unity became unraveled by bad luck and his brother's misjudgment. While Tecumseh was in the South, his brother's hand was forced prematurely. William Henry Harrison ordered a militia force of about 1,000 to march on Tippecanoe, ostensibly because Indians had stolen army horses. He set up camp three miles from the village, his men sleeping in a circular battle formation in case of surprise attack. Tecumseh had warned his brother to avoid a confrontation until the alliance was in place. Tenskwatawa, who claimed to have special "magic" in the fight against whites, followed instead the advice of young hot-blooded warriors and ordered an ambush. That night, the Indians crawled into position under the cover of rain. They attacked just before dawn on November 7, 1811. A sentry managed to fire a warning shot before being killed, and only an advance party of warriors broke through the circle of men into the center

of camp. The main Indian force was repelled with each charge. By full light, the fighting had ended. The militia had suffered 61 dead and twice as many wounded. Despite fewer casualties, the Indians retreated into the wilderness. Harrison's army marched on Tippcanoe and burned the village to the ground, destroying the Indians' supplies.

It was not a major victory in a military sense, although Harrison later claimed so in his victorious presidential campaign ("Tippecanoe and Tyler Too"). But it broke the momentum of Tecumseh's military alliance. Tenskwatawa's "magic" had proven ineffective; the brothers were estranged. Many of the tribes decided to make raids prematurely in their own territories, rather than wait for a united stand. Tecumseh's Rebellion had ended in one indecisive battle.

With the start of the War of 1812 between the United States and England, Tecumseh, who hoped for British help in organizing an Indian homeland, joined the fight

Tecumseh and Tenskwatawa. The pen-and-ink hypothetical drawing by Huyot depicts the seated Shawnee Prophet with his brother, Tecumseh, leaning over him. *Courtesy of Library of Congress.*

against the Americans. Many Indian leaders of the Old Northwest followed his example and provided warriors for the British effort. Others, however, sided with the Americans, further damaging the chances of Tecumseh's hoped-for confederation.

Tecumseh proved himself a skilled strategist. He helped his close friend General ISAAC BROCK take Detroit in August 1812. Because of his role in the British victory at Maguaga against the 4th Infantry under Colonel James Millar, he was commissioned a brigadier general in charge of some 2,000 warriors from the allied tribes.

Colonel HENRY PROCTOR assumed command on the death of Brock in the Battle of Queenston Heights of October 1812. Proctor, unlike Brock and Tecumseh, allowed the killing of prisoners, which served to arouse American anger and resolve, as happened after the Raisin River Massacre of 850 Kentuckians in January 1813. Soon after Raisin River, General Harrison's fresh troops built Fort Meigs along the Maumee River in northern Ohio. British and Tecumseh's Indian forces came close to capturing it in May 1813, but Proctor withdrew his men too early out of unnecessary caution and allowed Harrison a further buildup of troops. An attack on Fort Stephenson in August 1813 also proved unsuccessful.

After a British naval defeat on Lake Erie under Commodore Oliver Hazard Perry, Proctor decided to pull all his men back to Canada. The dejected Tecumseh tried to dissuade Proctor from abandoning land the Indians had fought so hard to hold but Proctor insisted on retreat, which Tecumseh and his men covered.

Tecumseh encouraged Proctor to make a stand at Moraviantown in Ontario against Harrison's invading army of 3,500, despite a reported presentiment of death. He dressed that day in his Indian buckskin rather than his British general's uniform. In the decisive American victory in the Battle of the Thames on October 5, 1813, Tecumseh took bullet after bullet and finally fell dead.

Although a group of Kentuckians skinned a body they thought to be Tecumseh's for souvenirs, they never found his actual corpse, which fellow warriors reportedly hid from the enemy. Rumors persisted among the tribes that Tecumseh would one day return to fulfill his dream of an Indian country on equal footing with the United States.

TEEDYUSCUNG (Tedyuscung, Tedyuskung, Tediuscung, Tediuskung, Tedeuscung, Tydescung, Tydeuscung, Taddyyuscung, Tadeskung, Teedjouskon, Deedjoskon, Detiuscung, "the healer"; Honest John; Gideon). *Delaware. (1700–1763).* War chief in the French and Indian War; "king" of the Delawares.

Teedyuscung was born in the vicinity of present-day Trenton, New Jersey, his father known to the English as Old Man Harris. About 1730, Teedyuscung moved with his band to the upper Delaware River in eastern Pennsylvania and northern New Jersey. His people sold baskets and brooms to settlers throughout the region.

Along with chief LAPPAWINZE, Teedyuscung charged the British with fraud in the Walking Purchase agreement of 1737, a claim he was to repeat often. This early loss of the Delaware lands shaped Teedyuscung's attitudes toward the colonists and led him to play the Indian hand off against both the British and the French.

In 1750, Teedyuscung was baptized as Gideon by Moravian missionaries at Gnaddenhutten. In 1754, he left Gnaddenhutten and settled at Pasigachkunk on the Cowanesque River. He was present at the Albany Congress in 1754, meeting with WILLIAM JOHNSON and the tribal delegates of the Iroquois League.

In the early stages of the French and Indian War of 1754–63, Teedyuscung acted as war chief of allied Delawares, Shawnees, and Mahicans, leading attacks on settlers in the Wyoming Valley along the Susquehanna River. He was known in Pennsylvania as "king" of the Delawares, as PAXINOS was "king" of the Pennsylvania Shawnees. When the British agreed to consider his land claims and provide compensation, as negotiated by the Indian agent CONRAD WEISER with the help of Delaware chief TATEMY, Teedyuscung threw his support to them against the French. The British financed the building of his new home at Wyoming on the north branch of the Susquehanna.

Teedyuscung died there in a fire, which consumed more than 20 homes, rumored to have been set by agents of the Susquehanna Company, seeking to develop the area for white settlement.

TEHORAGWANEGEN (Tehoragwarregen, "he has placed two worlds together"; Thomas Williams). *Mixed Mohawk. (ca. 1758–1849).* Ally of British in the American Revolution; ally of Americans in the War of 1812. Father of ELEAZAR WILLIAMS.

Tehoragwanegen was the great-grandson of the Reverend John Williams, taken captive by the French and Mohawks in a raid on Deerfield, Massachusetts, in 1704. His mother died when he was 15 months old and he was raised by her sister, the wife of a chief at Caughnawaga (Kahnawake), Quebec.

During the American Revolution, when he was only 17, Tehoragwanegen participated in raids on American settlements under General JOHN BURGOYNE and General JOHN JOHNSON. His family had encouraged him to prevent the killing of women and children, which he did on numerous occasions; he also openly complained to his officers of the treatment of captives by Tories and their Indian allies.

Following the war, Tehoragwanegen helped negotiate the Treaty of New York in 1796 between Iroquois who had relocated to Canada and New York State. His son Eleazar Williams was born to him by Mary Anne Rice in 1788. In 1800, Tehoragwanegen led a fur-trading party of Mohawks to the Rocky Mountains on behalf of the North West Company. In the War of 1812, he supported the Americans against the British, as did his son.

TEKAKWITHA, KATERI (Catherine Tekakwitha; the Lily of the Mohawks; La Sainte Sauvagesse). *Mohawk. (1656–1680).* First Indian nun; candidate for Catholic sainthood.

Kateri Tekakwitha, the daughter of a Mohawk chief and a Christianized Algonquian captive, was born near present-day Auriesville, New York, on the south side of the Mohawk River. Her parents and infant brother died in a smallpox epidemic when she was four; she caught the disease and her skin was severely scarred. She was raised by an uncle, also a chief. When the Mohawk villages along the south bank were destroyed in a raid by French and Indians in 1666, the Mohawks moved to the north side of the river. Kateri grew up in the village of Caughnawaga near present-day Fonda, New York. She was known among her people for her industry and her skill in manufacturing wampum.

Kateri witnessed Christianity firsthand when the Jesuit JACQUES BRUYAS visited the Mohawk village. Against her uncle's wishes, she was baptized when 20 years old on an Easter Sunday by the missionary Jacques de Lamberville. She practiced her religion despite ridicule by her people. In 1677, she fled to Canada in a canoe with Christianized Oneidas who had visited her village.

Kateri settled at Sault St. Louis near a Christian community of Mohawks, also called Caughnawaga (or Kahnawake), on the St. Lawrence River outside Montreal. After a visit with nuns in Montreal, she hoped to establish a convent on Heron Island. Church authorities rejected her plan, but she was allowed to make a vow of chastity and become a nun. She was fanatical in her devotions and had a friend flagellate her every Sunday despite her frail condition.

It is said that, when Kateri died, because of her great faith in Catholicism and her dedication to helping others, a miracle occurred—her pockmarks disappeared. She was buried near the La Chine Rapids between La Prairie Mission and Caughnawaga. People visiting her tomb have claimed to experience visions and to be cured of illnesses.

In 1884, Kateri became a candidate for canonization by the Roman Catholic Church; in 1943, she was declared venerable; then, in 1980, she was declared blessed, the second step toward sainthood. The Jesuits have a shrine to her at her first home near Auriesville, New York; the Franciscans maintain a shrine at her

second home near Fonda. She is also honored at the present-day Kahnawake Reserve in Quebec.

TENAYA. *Miwok. (fl. 1850s).* Leader of the Mariposa Indian War.

In 1850, the Miwoks and Yokuts of the Sierra Nevada foothills and San Joaquin Valley mounted an uprising against the settlers and miners who had entered their territory with the California Gold Rush. Tenaya's warriors attacked prospectors and burned the trading posts of James Savage. In 1851, Savage organized a state militia, known as the Mariposa Batallion, which pursued the insurgents into the Sierra Nevada highlands, where they managed to engage them in a number of inconclusive clashes. Because of the increased military activity, however, Tenaya's resistance gradually faded.

TEN BEARS (Parra-Wa-Samen, Parra-wa-semen, Paria Semen, Pariaseamen, Parrywasaymen, Parywahsaymen, Parooway Semehno; Ten Elks). *Comanche. (1792–1872).* Spokesman for his people.

Ten Bears of the Yamparika band was a noted warrior while young, but came to speak for peace and was famous among Indians and whites for his eloquence. In 1863, he traveled to Washington, D.C., as a tribal delegate. He also represented his people at the 1865 Little Arkansas Council, Kansas, and at the 1867 Medicine Lodge Council, Kansas, where he gave a frequently quoted speech. He again visited Washington in 1872, along with TOSAWI of the Peneteka Comanche band plus delegates from other tribes. Ten Bears, rejected by his own people for negotiations with whites, died soon after his return. Many warriors of his band took up arms in the Red River War of 1874–75 under QUANAH PARKER.

TENDOY (Tendoi). *Shoshone-Bannock. (ca. 1834–1907).* Friend to whites; principal chief of Lemhis.

Tendoy was born near Boise River in what is now Idaho, the son of a Bannock war chief and a Shoshone woman. He himself became the leader of a combined Lemhi Shoshone and Bannock band living in the Lemhi Valley of Idaho. His people depended on fishing in the Lemhi and Salmon rivers as well as hunting buffalo in western Montana.

When gold was discovered in the 1860s in Idaho and Montana, the influx of whites altered the Lemhi way of life and they suffered near-starvation. Tendoy established peaceful relations with the Montana mining camps, visiting them on regular trading trips to provide for his people. In 1868, because of the poverty of other Shoshone and Bannock bands, the federal government established the Fort Hall Reservation in southeast

Idaho. Tendoy kept his people in the Lemhi Valley to the north, however.

Like the Wind River band of Eastern Shoshones under WASHAKIE, Tendoy maintained peace with whites even during periods of hostility in the region—the Paiute War under NUMAGA in 1863; raids under POCATELLO, then BEAR HUNTER, of the Northwestern Shoshones in the 1850s and early 1860s; the Nez Perce War of 1877 under chief JOSEPH (Young Joseph); and the Bannock War of 1878 under BUFFALO HORN.

Although President ULYSSES S. GRANT issued an executive order in 1875 granting Tendoy's band permission to remain in their ancestral valley, the government pressured him into signing a new treaty in 1892. He eventually settled on the Fort Hall Reservation, where Lemhi descendants live today.

TENSKWATAWA (Tenskwautawaw, Elskwatawa, "open door"; Shawnee Prophet).
Shawnee. (ca. 1778–1837). Medicine man; prophet; leader in Tecumseh's Rebellion of 1809–11. Brother of TECUMSEH.

Tenskwatawa and Tecumseh were the sons of Puckeshinwa, a Shawnee war chief, and Methoataske, his Creek-Cherokee wife. It is thought the brothers were born at Piqua near present-day Springfield, Ohio. Some reports have them as twins, although Tenskwatawa may have been about 10 years younger.

Tenskwatawa led a dissolute life as a young man, but came into his own as a prophet. He was influenced by the white Shaker religion. In 1805, he experienced a deep trance after which he declared he had visited the spirit world and received a message from the Master of Life. Rejecting intermarriage with whites and white customs—religion, tools clothing, liquor—Tenskwatawa preached a return to traditional Indian ways, such as community ownership of property; he called for an end to intertribal warfare; he also claimed he had recieved the power to cure disease and prevent death on the battlefield. His accurate prediction of the total eclipse of the sun on June 16, 1806, increased his following.

In 1808, the brothers moved from Indiana to Ohio and established the former Miami village of Tippecanoe near the confluence of the Tippecanoe and Wabash rivers in Indiana Territory as a place where Indians from different tribes could congregate free of white society. About 1,000 to 12,000 Indians came to live at Tippecanoe, or Prophetstown. Like DELAWARE PROPHET before him, who helped PONTIAC gain followers for his rebellion of 1763, and WHITE CLOUD (the Winnebago Prophet) after him who preached to BLACK HAWK's warriors in his war of 1832, Tenskwatawa generated support for his brother's efforts in forming a military alliance.

When WILLIAM HENRY HARRISON, the governor of Indiana Territory, moved on Tippecanoe to force a confrontation with the growing number of militants, Tenskwatawa, predicting the soldiers would be routed because of his magic, ordered an attack even though his brother was not present. The defeat, on November 7, 1811, led to the premature break-up of Tecumseh's hoped-for confederacy of tribes. Tenskwatawa's magic had been proven ineffective against the army's might. It also caused an estrangement between the brothers, and Tenskwatawa moved to Canada.

Tenskwatawa played no part in the War of 1812, although his brother was central to British efforts. He stayed in Canada until 1826, after which he returned to Ohio for a year before being forced to relocate with the Shawnees west of the Mississippi River. He lived in Missouri for a short time, then moved to Kansas. GEORGE CATLIN painted his portrait in 1832. (See also TECUMSEH.)

TERRY, ALFRED HOWE. *(1827–1890).* Army officer in the War for the Black Hills of 1876–77; peace commissioner.

Alfred Terry was a native of Hartford, Connecticut. He studied to be a lawyer, but, at the outbreak of the Civil War, became a colonel of a regiment of Connecticut volunteers. After the surrender of the Confederacy in 1865, he remained in the military as a brigadier general in the regular army, and, in 1866, was given the command of the Department of Dakota (Minnesota and parts of the Dakotas and Montana).

Terry was part of the presidential Peace Commission that met with the leaders of the Southern Plains tribes at Medicine Lodge Creek in southwestern Kansas in October 1867. He also supervised exploratory expeditions into the Dakotas during the early 1870s. Under Terry's command, Colonel GEORGE ARMSTRONG CUSTER undertook his 1874 expedition into the Black Hills.

In 1875, Terry was one of the U.S. officials who unsuccessfully tried to buy the Black Hills from the Sioux at a council in June 1875 at the Red Cloud Agency with Sioux leaders RED CLOUD and SPOTTED TAIL. Terry and the other officials offered the Sioux $6 million for the lands, and, failing at that, unsuccessfully tried to lease the region for $400,000 per year.

In June 1876, during the subsequent War for the Black Hills, Terry's command, including Custer and the 7th Cavalry regiment, took part in a three-pronged offensive against Sioux and Cheyennes in the Powder River country. The other columns were led by General GEORGE CROOK and Colonel JOHN GIBBON. Marching west out of Fort Abraham Lincoln in the Dakota Territory, Custer's cavalry advanced too far ahead of Terry's main column and met disaster at the Battle of

Little Bighorn on June 25. Two days later, Terry's command relieved the survivors under Major MARCUS A. RENO and Captain FERDERICK W. BENTEEN. Although later criticized as partly responsible for Custer's loss, he declined to lay the blame on Custer's disobeying of orders. He did, however, order the court-martial of Major Reno for his conduct in the battle.

That fall, Terry's command disarmed the Sioux of the Standing Rock Reservation, North Dakota, and the Cheyenne River Reservation, South Dakota. In October 1877, Terry met with SITTING BULL and Canadian Northwest Mounted Police Commissioner JAMES MACLEOD at Fort Walsh in Canada, but was unable to convince the Sioux chief to lead his people back to a reservation in the United States.

In 1886, as a major general, Terry assumed command of the Division of the Missouri, but retired after two years. (See also SITTING BULL; SPOTTED TAIL.)

THAYENDANEGEA. See BRANT, JOSEPH.

THOMAS, WILLIAM HOLLAND (Will Thomas). *(1805–1893).* Attorney and business agent for the Cherokees; North Carolina legislator; soldier. Adopted son of YONAGUSTA.

Will Thomas was born at Qualla Town near present-day Cherokee, North Carolina, the son of a white trader. His father died while he was young, and he was adopted by the Cherokee chief Yonagusta. Following studies in law, Thomas, in 1838, became attorney and business manager for the Cherokees of the Oconaluftee River region of western North Carolina who had separated from the main body of the Cherokee Nation nearly 20 years before.

In May 1838, while General WINFIELD SCOTT's troops were engaged in removing Cherokees from western North Carolina to the Indian Territory, under the terms of the 1835 New Echota Treaty, a Cherokee named TSALI, his son Ridges, and his son-in-law Lowney were involved in a shooting incident in which a soldier was killed. Thomas used his influence to negotiate the surrender of Tsali and the others.

In the 1840s, Thomas succeeded in obtaining back payments of thousands of dollars for the families of Cherokees, money that was due them under the terms of the New Echota Treaty. In 1848, he was elected to the North Carolina state senate and represented Cherokee interests in the state legislature. Among his constituents was the Cherokee JUNALUSKA, who had fought alongside General ANDREW JACKSON at the 1814 Battle of Horseshoe Bend.

During the Civil War, Thomas served as a colonel in the Confederate army, and led a military unit of 200 Cherokees in military actions against the Union. After the war, he continued to represent the legal and business interests of the North Carolina Cherokees. He oversaw the investment of the Indians' assets in land acquisitions. By 1888, the Cherokees owned 67,000 acres of land in western North Carolina. The legal standing of the North Carolina Cherokees was established after 1886, when the U.S. Supreme Court ruled that they were a distinct people, and separate from the Western Cherokees of the Indian Territory. In 1889, they were officially incorporated under the laws of the state of North Carolina as a legal entity, known as the Eastern Band of Cherokees.

THOMPSON, DAVID (Koo-koo-siut, "the man who looks at the stars"). *(1770–1857).* Explorer; trader.

British-born David Thompson attended school until the age of 14, becoming proficient in mathematics, a skill that would later aid in his explorations. In 1784, he traveled to southwestern Hudson Bay, Canada, where he served as an apprentice to the Hudson's Bay Company.

Thompson undertook a series of expeditions into unknown regions of western Canada, traveling into the Rockies by way of the Saskatchewan River. On the American and Canadian Plains, he established the first white contacts with the Piegan and Blackfoot tribes, introducing them to the use of firearms. He also interviewed their leaders, the earliest such record of the customs.

In 1797, Thompson joined the North West Company, and under their sponsorship continued his explorations of the Canadian West. His journeys took him from Lake Athabasca in the north, as far south as the Mandan villages on the Missouri River in what is now South Dakota. He contacted the tribes living west of the Northern Rockies, bringing them into the British fur-trading sphere, and established the first trading posts in present-day western Montana and Idaho. To the east, he surveyed the headwaters of the Mississippi River.

In 1807-11, Thompson explored and charted the entire length of the Columbia River, all the way to the river's outlet on the Pacific coast. His charts, published after his death, revealed a water route, interrupted by brief portages, that extended from the St. Lawrence River on the Atlantic to the mouth of the Columbia on the Pacific.

In 1812, Thompson left the fur trade and settled with his mixed-blood wife in Montreal, where he worked on a map of the Canadian West for the North West Company, which, as was the case with his charts and journals, was not published until long after his death. In 1816–26, he served on the British Boundary Commission, which surveyed the U.S.-Canadian border.

THOMPSON, WILEY. *(1781–1835).* Indian agent; congressman.

Wiley Thompson was born in Virginia and moved with his family to Georgia when young. Becoming involved in local politics, he was appointed commissioner of the Elbert County school. Following service in the War of 1812, he rose to the rank of major general in the Georgia militia. In 1819, he was part of a commission to determine the boundary line between Georgia and East Florida. He served in the state senate in 1817–19 and the U.S. House of Representatives in 1821–33.

Thompson was a supporter of President ANDREW JACKSON's policies of removal and was appointed Indian agent to the Seminoles in order to carry out the terms of the 1832 Treaty of Payne's Landing and the 1833 Treaty of Fort Gibson. He was also assigned superintendent of emigration. In a council with Seminole leaders in April 1835, Thompson informed them they were to be transported to the Indian Territory by water as one group, rather than by land in three parties as negotiated in the earlier treaties. When OSCEOLA objected, Thompson had him arrested. In December, Osceola led an attack on Thompson's party outside the agent's headquarters at Fort King, Florida. Thompson was shot, stabbed, and scalped. (See also OSCEOLA.)

THORNBURGH, THOMAS T. (Tip Thornburgh).
(ca. 1843–1879). Army officer in the Ute War of 1879.

Tennessee-born Thomas T. Thornburgh rose to the rank of lieutenant during the Civil War, then attended West Point, graduating in 1867 with the rank of 2nd lieutenant of artillery. He was garrisoned in California until 1870, then became a professor of military science at East Tennessee University until 1873. Two years later, he was appointed paymaster with the rank of major, serving until 1878, when he entered the 4th Infantry as major. He was given the command of Fort Fred Steele, Wyoming.

In September 1879, Thornburgh led a company of 150 cavalrymen from Fort Fred Steele to the White River Ute reservation in western Colorado to enforce the policies of Indian agent NATHAN MEEKER. When the troops neared the reservation, Meeker decided that the military presence might incite the Utes to open revolt. He sent word to Thornburgh to halt his column and hold council with the Utes. Thornburgh proceeded onto the reservation lands with 120 of his cavalrymen in spite of Meeker's warning.

On September 29, 1879, he was met by Chief NICAAGAT and COLOROW and about 100 Ute warriors as his command crossed Milk Creek, the northern boundary of the Ute's White River Reservation. While attempting to mediate the situation, a misunderstanding led to shots being fired, and a full-scale battle erupted. Thornburgh was killed in the initial Indian attack, shot in the head. Command was assumed by Thornburgh's subordinate, Captain J. Scott Payne. The soldiers were under attack for six days, losing 13 more men. On October 2, 1879, a company of black caval-

rymen arrived from Fort Lewis, Colorado; on October 5, a large relief column arrived at the White River Agency, commanded by Colonel WESLEY MERRITT, and discovered that Meeker and nine other whites had been killed, and that Meeker's wife and daughter, plus another white woman, had been abducted by the Utes. Chief OURAY of the Utes helped negotiate their eventual release. (See also OURAY.)

TIBBLES, THOMAS HENRY. *(1840–1928).*
Reformer; journalist. Husband of SUSETTE LA FLESCHE.

A native of Athens, Ohio, Thomas Henry Tibbles became a newspaperman after a stint as a circuit preacher. He served in Kansas during the Civil War as a scout for Union troops in pursuit of Charles Quantrill and his raiders.

Tibbles was the assistant editor of the *Omaha Herald* in the late 1870s, when the Poncas were seeking to regain their Nebraska lands following their forced removal to the Indian Territory. Tibbles championed the Ponca cause and rallied local support in Nebraska that succeeded in freeing Ponca leader STANDING BEAR, who had been jailed by federal military authorities for unlawful flight. Tibbles spent a winter with the Poncas, and, after having endured a flesh-piercing ritual dance, was initiated into their Soldier Lodge fraternity.

Tibbles's first wife, Amelia Owen Tibbles, died in 1879, the same year the Standing Bear decision was handed down. The next year, Tibbles's book, *The Ponca Chiefs*, was published under the pseudonym Zylyff. In 1879–80, Tibbles, Standing Bear, and the Omaha brother and sister Susette La Flesche and FRANCIS LA FLESCHE conducted a lecture tour of major eastern cities and gained the support of PETER COOPER, HELEN HUNT JACKSON, and other Indian rights activists. In 1882, Tibbles and Susette La Flesche, also known as Bright Eyes, were married. They continued to lecture on Indian issues, traveling to England and Scotland in 1886–87.

In 1895, Tibbles established a newspaper in Lincoln, Nebraska, *The Independent*, which became known for its populist positions. Tibbles was the People's Party's candidate for vice president, with presidential candidate Thomas Watson, in the election of 1904. The following year, he wrote his autobiography, *Buckskin and Blanket Days* (1957).

TILOUKAIKT (Tilokaikt, Teelonkike). *Cayuse.*
(d. 1849). Leader of the Cayuse War of 1847–50.

Tiloukaikt and other Cayuse leaders allowed the building of a Presbyterian mission in their homeland in the Walla Walla Valley of Oregon Country. Some also sent their children to the school at Waiilatpu to be taught by the missionary MARCUS WHITMAN and his wife, Narcissa.

The Waiilatpu mission also served as a way station for travelers along the Oregon Trail. The emigrants brought diseases to the Indians, especially measles and scarlet fever. Whitman, who was a trained physician, treated both whites and Indians. Many more Indians than whites died, however, and the Cayuses became suspicious that Whitman was poisoning them.

During a measles epidemic in 1847, spread to the tribe's adults by children enrolled in the school, ill-feeling boiled over. On November 29, while Tiloukaikt was visiting the mission for medicine, he had words with Whitman, during which a warrior by the name of Tomahas struck Whitman from behind with a tomahawk, eventually killing him. Other braves joined the violence, killing Narcissa Whitman and 12 others, and taking 53 men, women, and children hostage.

The settlers in the Willamette Valley raised a volunteer militia, headed by Cornelius Gilliam, a fundamentalist clergyman who had fought Indians in the East. A three-man peace commission was also established to meet with other tribes, headed by Joel Palmer. In the meantime, PETER SKENE OGDEN of the Hudson's Bay Company, working to protect fur-trading interests, negotiated the release of the hostages.

However, when Gilliam's troops attacked an encampment of innocent Cayuses, warriors from other area tribes joined the uprising. A Palouse war party retaliated against militiamen who tried to rustle their cattle. Gilliam was killed soon afterward in an accidental firing of his own gun. Since continuing campaigning risked uniting all the Columbia Basin tribes, the troops retired.

Tiloukaikt and Tomahas, plus three other Cayuses, tired of hiding, surrendered two years later. They were taken to Oregon City, hastily tried, and sentenced to hang. Before dying, Tiloukaikt refused Presbyterian rites, accepting Catholic ones instead.

A pattern of raids and counterraids continued in the region. In the following years, most surviving Cayuses joined neighboring tribes, especially the Nez Perces, Umatillas, and Yakimas.

TIMOTHY (Tamootsin). *Nez Perce. (fl. mid-1800s).* Christian convert; friend to whites.

Tamootsin was a band leader of the Nez Perces, with a village on the Snake River near the confluence of the Clearwater in what is now western Idaho. In 1839, he was baptized as Timothy by the Presbyterian missionary HENRY SPALDING and remained a friend to whites. He was the only Cayuse to build a house at Lapwai, as encouraged by Spalding, but used it as a storehouse, continuing to live in his lodge in his village at Alpowa. During the Cayuse War of 1847–50, Timothy

kept his warriors at peace with the settlers and advised whites in the capture of the militants. He was a leader of the Treaty Nez Perces, signing the land cessions in 1855 and 1863. He accompanied LAWYER to Washington, D.C., in 1868. (See also Old JOSEPH.)

TISQUANTUM. See SQUANTO.

TOCQUEVILLE, ALEXIS DE. *(1805–1859).* Writer; French politician.

During his 1831–32 tour of the United States with Gustave de Beaumont, upon which he based his study of American society, *Democracy in America* (1835–40), the Frenchman Alexis de Tocqueville visited the frontier regions of the Great Lakes and the Mississippi Valley, where he viewed Indian culture influenced by nearly two centuries of the fur trade. His views on the American Indian were influenced by the French philosopher JEAN JACQUES ROUSSEAU. What Tocqueville observed confirmed his preconceptions of the Indian as the Noble Savage, subject to the corrupting effects of a rapidly expanding white civilization. Active in French politics, Tocqueville believed that the French would eventually have a democratic system like that of the United States and should therefore study American culture.

TOMAH (Tomau; Thomas Carron). *Mixed Menominee. (ca. 1752–1817).* Principal chief; ally of British in the War of 1812.

Tomah was born near present-day Green Bay, Wisconsin, the second son of the part-French Old Carron and his wife, probably Abnaki. Not a hereditary chief, he was chosen as head chief in tribal council. In 1805, he met and served as guide to Lieutenant ZEBULON PIKE. At first, he resisted TECUMSEH's call for a military alliance agaisnt the Americans, but later joined the British in the War of 1812, as did Chief SOULIGNY and Tomah's protege OSHKOSH, fighting at Fort Mackinaw, Michigan, and Fort Stephenson, Ohio. Following the war, in 1816, Tomah allowed the army to establish a post on Menominee lands. He died the next year at Mackinaw, where he was buried.

TOMOCHICHI (Tomochachi, Temochichi, Tomeychee, Thomochichi, Thamachaychee, Tomo Chachi Mico, Tomo-chee-chee, Bocachee, "the one who causes to fly up"; The King of Yamacraw). *Creek. (ca. 1650–1739).* Ally of British; tribal delegate to London; proponent of trade.

Tomochichi originally lived at the Creek village of Apalachukla along the Chattahoochee River in what is now Alabama. About 1700, he moved to Yamacraw near present-day Savannah, Georgia. In 1733, he was visited there by a party of English colonists under

JAMES OGLETHORPE at which time he signed a peace treaty. The next year, he headed a Creek delegation to England with Oglethorpe, where he was presented to King George II and Queen Caroline. Cornelis Verelst painted a famous portrait of the chief with his nephew Toonahowi. His friendship with the British led to a long-term Creek-British trade alliance.

TONTI, HENRI DE (Henri de Tonty; Bras de Fer).
(ca. 1650–1704). Explorer; soldier. Cousin of DANIEL GREYSOLON, SIEUR DULUTH.

Henri de Tonti, born in the Italian city of Gaeta, served as an officer in the French army and navy in engagements in Europe. During one battle, his hand was blown off in a grenade explosion.

In 1678, Tonti was assigned as a lieutenant to RENE ROBERT CAVELIER, SIEUR DE LA SALLE. Traveling to Canada that year, at Niagara Falls he supervised the construction of La Salle's vessel, the *Griffon*, the first sailing ship to explore the western Great Lakes. He also supervised the construction of Fort Niagara, and sailed west in 1679 on the *Griffon* to Green Bay, on the western shore of Lake Michigan. With La Salle, he explored the St. Joseph and Illinois rivers, establishing Fort Miami (present-day St. Joseph, Michigan) and Fort Crevecoeur (near present-day Peoria, Illinois).

Tonti was a skillful Indian diplomat and he was able to gain the allegiance of the Miami and Illinois Indians of the upper Mississippi Valley. His skill in using his artificial metal hand impressed the Indians, who considered a sign of Tonti's special powers. For this reason, he was known by the Indians as Bras de Fer, the French for "iron arm."

La Salle left Tonti in charge at Fort Crevecoeur, then returned to Fort Niagara on the western end of Lake Ontario to obtain additional supplies. In La Salle's absence, Tonti had to deal with not only Iroquois raiding parties, but with desertions and a mutiny by his own men. He was forced to withdraw, first to Green Bay, then to Mackinac Island at the north end of Lake Michigan.

Tonti was rejoined here by La Salle in late 1681. They embarked on an expedition to reestablish French claims to the Illinois country. Tonti then accompanied La Salle to the mouth of the Mississippi, reaching the Gulf of Mexico in 1682.

Tonti returned to Starved Rock, on the Illinois River, where he established Fort St. Louis, out of which he supervised the fur trade with the Illinois and Miami tribes. A large Indian community, numbering as many as 20,000, soon developed around the French post.

In 1686–87, failing to hear from La Salle, who, after a trip to Europe to raise support for further expeditions, had intended to return to Fort St. Louis by sailing northward from the Gulf of Mexico, Tonti set out on a search mission south. At the mouth of the Arkansas River, he encountered Henry Joutel, a survivor of La Salle's failed colony on the Texas coast. At this site, Tonti was welcomed by the Quapaw Indians and he established the settlement of Aux Arcs (Arkansas Fort) near present-day Gillet, Arkansas. He then returned to Canada with Joulet.

In 1687, Tonti took part in military operations against the Iroquois. With Illinois warriors under his command, he attacked the Iroquois from the west, attempting to drive them back to their homelands in New York.

In 1700, Tonti departed Fort St. Louis on the Illinois and joined PIERRE LE MOYNE, SIEUR D'IBERVILLE in establishing French settlements along the lower Mississippi Valley and Gulf Coast. He contracted yellow fever and died at present-day Mobile, Alabama.

TOOHOOLHOOLZOTE (Toohulhulsote, Tulhulhutsut, "sound"). *Nez Perce. (ca. 1810–1877).* Spokesman; leader in the Nez Perce War of 1877.

Toohoolhoolzote lived along the Snake River near the mouth of the Salmon River in Idaho. Along with Old JOSEPH, he was one of the chiefs who refused to sign the Treaty of 1863 ceding Nez Perce lands to whites. He also encouraged traditional beliefs among his people and participated in SMOHALLA's Dreamer cult. In 1876, Toohoolhoolzote was appointed by officials as spokesman for all the Lower Nez Perce bands. The next year, he was jailed at Lapwai by General OLIVER HOWARD for his refusal to depart ceded lands. When the other Nontreaty Nez Perces agreed to the treaty terms, he was released. Yet violence soon broke out, leading to the Nez Perce War, in which Toohoolhoolzote participated along with Chief JOSEPH (Young Joseph). He was central to the Indian victory at Clearwater River on July 11, 1877, but was killed at Bear Paw on September 30. (See also Young JOSEPH.)

TOPENEBEE (Topenibe, Topinibe, Topnibe).
Potawatomi. (d. 1840). Ally of British in the War of 1812.

Topenebee's village was located along the St. Joseph River in what is now southern Michigan, close to the Indiana border. He was war chief of the Potawatomis at the time LEOPOLD POKAGON, who married his niece, was civil chief. In 1795, following LITTLE TURTLE's War, Topenebbee signed the Treaty of Fort Greenville, Ohio, and, over the next years until 1833, 11 more treaties with whites. He supported TECUMSEH's alliance of tribes and fought on the side of the British in the War of 1812. Nevertheless, along with ALEXANDER ROBINSON, SAGAUNASH, and SHABONEE, he tried to save white settlers after the Indian attack on Fort Dearborn at the site of Chicago,

Illinois. Topenebee stayed on his land grant in Michigan when most of the tribe was removed to Kansas in 1838.

TOSAWI (Tosawai, Toshaway, Toshua, Silver Brooch). *Comanche. (fl. 1860s–1870s).* Band chief in early Comanche Wars; later, proponent of peace.

Tosawi, leader of the Penetaka band, was active in Comanche raids on the 1860s, but agreed to peace in the 1867 Medicine Lodge Treaty. After the Battle of Washita in November 1868, when BLACK KETTLE's band of Cheyennes was attacked, Tosawi was the first Comanche leader to surrender to the military at Fort Cobb in the Indian Territory. When he spoke to General PHILIP H. SHERIDAN, saying "Tosawi, good Indian," the general gave his infamous reply, "The only good Indians I ever saw were dead," passed down as "The only good Indian is a dead Indian." In 1872, Tosawi traveled to Washington, D.C., along with TEN BEARS of the Yamparika Comanche band and delegates from other tribes.

TOTOPOTOMOI (Totopotomoy, Tottopottomoi). *Powhatan. (d. 1656).* Ally of Virginia colonists. Husband of Queen ANNE.

Totopotomoi, a chief of the Pamumkey Indians, part of the POWHATAN Confederacy, maintained peace with Virginia colonists following the death of OPECHANCANOUGH. In 1656, he provided almost 100 warriors to help a force of about the same number of colonists under colonel Edward Hill to repel inland tribes who had occupied what had previously been his band's territory near the falls of the James River. At a parley, Hill had his men seize and execute five enemy chiefs. In the bitter fighting that followed, Totopotomoi and most of his men died. Hill was found guilty and suspended from his military service, but remained active in Virginia politics. In 1675, Totopotomoi's widow, Queen Anne, at first refused to help the colonists in BACON's Rebellion because of what she considered neglect by the colonists despite her husband's sacrifice, but later provided warriors.

TOYPURINA. *Gabrielino. (fl. 1780s).* Religious leader who rebelled against the Spanish.

In 1785, Toypurina, a woman considered to have supernatural powers by her people, along with the neophyte Nicolas Jose, plotted a rebellion against the San Gabriel Mission near present-day Los Angeles, California. They convinced Indians of six villages to participate. On the night of October 25, a war party advanced on the mission. Toypurina was supposed to have killed the occupants with her magic; the priests and soldiers had learned of the uprising, however, and arrested the insurgents. At the subsequent trial, Toypurina denounced the Spanish for trespassing on and despoiling the Indians' ancestral lands. Nicolas Jose assailed them for preventing the practice of traditional ceremonies. Most of the Indians received 20 lashes each. Nicolas Jose and two headmen were imprisoned in the presidio at San Diego. Toypurina was deported to San Carlos Mission in the north, where she later married a Spaniard.

TRUCKEE (Captain Truckee; Winnemucca, Old Winnemucca). *Northern Paiute. (d. 1860).* Guide to JOHN C. FREMONT; interpreter. Father of WINNEMUCCA; grandfather of SARAH WINNEMUCCA.

Truckee was also known as Winnemucca or Old Winnemucca, reportedly after an incident in which he was seen wearing one moccasin, or "one *muck*" in the Paiute form. His son, however, became better known by that name. To John C. Fremont and other whites, the first Winnemucca was Truckee or Captain Truckee. Truckee interpreted the arrival of white explorers and settlers as the reuniting of the Northern Paiutes with lost white brothers, as prophesized in a tribal legend. He guided the Fremont expedition into California in 1845–46 and spent many of the next years working at California settlements in the San Joaquin Valley. Speaking both English and Spanish in addition to his native tongue, he regularly acted as interpreter between whites and other Paiute bands.

TSALI. *Cherokee. (d. 1838).* Leader of resistance against removal.

As Cherokee legend has it, Tsali lived with his family at Valley Town in the Great Smoky Mountains of North Carolina, earning a living through farming and hunting. In May 1838, soldiers came to his cabin to lead him to a stockade at the Bushnell Indian Agency on the Hiwasee River in preparation for removal. On the way, his wife stumbled, and one of the soldiers prodded her with a bayonet. Tsali, speaking Cherokee, which the soldiers could not understand, informed his sons and his brother-in-law Lowney to be ready when he feigned an injury. Shortly afterward, he pretended to hurt his ankle. When the soldiers stopped to help him, Tsali tackled one, and Lowney and Ridges, one of Tsali's sons, grabbed the other. The first soldier was killed by his own gun in the scuffle; the second escaped into the woods.

Tsali hid out that summer with his family in a cave on the peak Clingmans Dome in the Great Smokies. Other Mountain Cherokees, totaling about 300, joined him. The next fall, General WINFIELD SCOTT sent word to Tsali through WILLIAM THOMAS that if those who were responsible for the death of the soldier were to surrender, the army would cease their search for the other fugitives. Tsali, Lowney, and Ridges did so, and, after a military trial, were executed by a firing squad at Bushnell.

Certain events in the story are unproven: the actual circumstances of the soldier's death; the exact role of the adopted Cherokee William Thomas in negotiations; the question of whether Tsali surrendered or was captured by pro-removal Cherokees; and whether white officials would have carried out the costly round-up of the Mountain Cherokees even without Tsali's surrender.

In any case, descendants of Tsali and the other fugitives make up the Eastern Cherokees of North Carolina. He has a special place in tribal history as a martyr and is celebrated for his self-sacrifice in Cherokee festivals.

TSHUSICK (Lucy Cornelia Barbour). *Chippewa (Ojibway). (fl. 1820s).* Visitor to Washington, D.C.

On a winter night in 1827, Tshusick appeared at a tinsmith's forge in Washington, D.C., to warm herself. He sent her to the home of THOMAS McKENNEY, superintendent of Indian Affairs. Tshusick informed him that her home was near Detroit and that she had worked in the household of LEWIS CASS, governor of Michigan Territory. She also related that she knew George Boyd, the Indian agent at Mackinac, and had become a friend of his wife, Harriet Adams Boyd, who was the sister of President John Quincy Adams's wife, Louisa. She explained how her husband had recently died and how, on hearing about the capital and the kindness of the first lady from Mrs. Boyd, she had walked all the way from Michigan, sleeping in the woods and begging for food at farmhouses.

McKenney, drawing on a fund for Indian delegations, arranged for lodging at a boarding house and provided the Chippewa with materials for a new wardrobe. Tshusick, who spoke fluent English and French, met and charmed the president and first lady. Along with Louisa Adams, she appeared at numerous official receptions and other social events, meeting Cabinet members, senators, congressmen, and foreign dignitaries. She was written about in many of the newspapers and had her portrait painted by CHARLES BIRD KING for McKenney's Indian Portrait Gallery. She was also baptized at Christ Church in Georgetown and given the name Lucy Cornelia Barbour in honor of the wife and daughter of Secretary of War James Barbour, now her close friends.

In the course of Tshusick's visit, McKenney wrote a letter to Cass relating how the Chippewa woman had captivated the town. He mentioned this letter to Tshusick, soon after which she announced it was time she return to her people. Despite pleas to stay, Tshusick insisted on leaving. Her passage to the end of the stagecoach line was arranged and she was given money enough for a horse for the remainder of the journey. The president and first lady and many of her other new friends gave her numerous gifts to take with her, one of them a money belt stuffed with cash.

Before long, McKenney received a reply to his letter, in which Cass informed him that Tshusick was a confidence woman, that she was married to a Frenchman who had worked in Boyd's kitchen, and that she had pulled off similar swindles in Montreal, Quebec City, and St. Louis. When word of the Tshusick incident spread, it was used by McKenney's opponents to attack the Bureau of Indian Affairs, the entertainment of Indian delegations and the Indian Portrait Gallery.

McKenney later tried to track down Tshusick in Detroit, Mackinac, Green Bay, and Prairie du Chien. She managed always to stay one town ahead of him, and he never saw her again.

TUGGLE, WILLIAM ORRIE. *(1841–1885).* Anthropologist; lawyer.

William O. Tuggle was a native Georgian. His parents died while he was young and he was raised by foster parents. He attended Brownwood Institute and Mercer University. After having served the Confederacy in the Civil War, he became a successful lawyer in Reconstruction-era Georgia. In 1879, he was appointed by the federal government as legal agent of the Creek Nation and spent most of the next three years in the Indian Territory. While working among the Creeks, Tuggle recorded aspects of their culture, including their medicine songs, tales, and the myths underlying their religious beliefs. He also made detailed observations of many aspects of everyday life among the relocated Creeks, Cherokees, and Choctaws, including their sexual habits, modes of dress, religious practices, and systems of justice. JOHN WESLEY POWELL of the Bureau of American Ethnology helped Tuggle organize his diary and notes. His work influenced the later ethnological studies of JAMES MOONEY and John Swanton.

TURK (The Turk, El Turco). *Pawnee. (d. 1541).* Guide to FRANCISCO VASQUEZ DE CORONADO.

The Turk was a slave at Pecos Pueblo in what is now New Mexico when Coronado's expedition from Mexico arrived in 1540. The Spanish gave him his name because of his style of headdress. The Turk described to Coronado the abundance of gold in the provinces of Quivira and Harahey to the north, probably the homelands of the Kaw (Kansa) and Pawnee Indians. This exaggeration was perhaps contrived by him, in the hope the Spanish would accompany him back to his own people, or perhaps by the Pecos leaders who hoped the militaristic Spanish would leave them alone.

The next year, 1541, with the Turk and another Indian Ysopete as guides, Coronado started out from Tiguex on the Rio Grande for the north country with his army of conquistadors. The Turk led the Spaniards to the barren Staked Plain of west Texas. Coronado, convinced that the guide was trying to trick him, had him placed in irons. He then sent many of the soldiers back to the Rio Grande and headed northward with a reduced party of 30 men and Ysopete as their guide.

The Spanish crossed the province of Quivira (Kansas), and, at the Kansas River, sent messengers ahead to summon Tatarrax, the chief of Harrahey, assumed by scholars to be the Pawnee homeland. Tatarrax arrived with about 200 warriors. The Turk tried to instigate an attack by them and was strangled to death by the soldiers. Coronado returned to Spain without the Turk's promised gold.

TWO CROWS (Lewis Morris). *Omaha.*
(ca. 1826–1894). Tribal leader; research informant.

As a young man, Two Crows had the resonsibility of policing his people during their annual buffalo hunts on the Plains of what is now Nebraska. In 1847, he killed two Sioux in battle and, in 1854, served as war chief of a raiding party in further action against the Sioux. He was an active member of principal chief JOSEPH LA FLESCHE's Progressive Party, although he never converted to Christianity. In 1880, Two Crows was elected a chief of his people, one of seven equal chiefs in a tribal reorganization. Along with La Flesche, he served as an informant for the anthropological studies of the Omahas by JAMES DORSEY and ALICE FLETCHER.

TWO LEGGINGS ("his eyes are dreamy").
Crow. (ca. 1845–1923). Warrior; research informant.

Two Leggings was born along the Montana River and grew up to be a warrior among the River Crows. He joined his people in raids on the Sioux, traditional enemies of the Crows, but never on white travelers or settlers. From 1919 to 1923, he told his life story to Montana businessman and amateur anthropologist William Wildschut under the sponsorship of the Museum of the American Indian and the Heye Foundation. Peter Nabokov edited these notes into the book *Two Leggings: The Making of a Crow Warrior*, published in 1967. Two Leggings died at his home near Hardin, Montana, survived by his wife, Ties-Up-Her-Bundle, and two adopted children.

TWO MOON (Two Moons, Isi'eyo Nissi, Ishaynishus). *Northern Cheyenne. (fl. 1860s).* War Chief in the War for the BOZEMAN Trail of 1866–68. Uncle of TWO MOONS.

Along with DULL KNIFE and LITTLE WOLF, Two Moon was one of the Northern Cheyenne allies of RED CLOUD's Sioux. He was present at the FETTERMAN Fight in Wyoming in December 1866 during the War for the Bozeman Trail. He is often confused with his nephew Two Moons in historical records. (See also RED CLOUD.)

TWO MOONS (Two Moon, Ishi'eyo Nissi, Ishaynishus). *Northern Cheyenne. (1847–1917).* Leader in the War for the Black Hills of 1876–77; army scout; research informant. Nephew of TWO MOON.

The younger Two Moons, or Two Moon, fought with SITTING BULL and CRAZY HORSE in the Sioux Wars of the 1870s. In March 1876, on the Powder River in Montana, he led warriors, including WOODEN LEG, against Colonel Joseph Reynolds's troops, part of General GEORGE CROOK's command. The soldiers managed to destroy the camp before being repelled by the Indians. Two Moons and Wooden Leg were also present at the Battle of Little Bighorn in June 1876.

Two Moons surrendered to Colonel NELSON A. MILES at Fort Keogh, Montana, early the next year. He was recruited as an army scout and served under Miles in the Nez Perce War of 1877, blocking the flight of the Nez Perces to Canada under Chief JOSEPH (Young Joseph). Two Moons was also one of six Cheyennes who

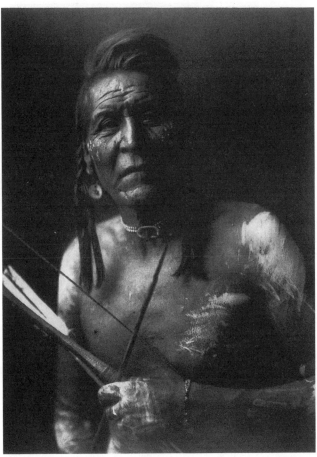

Two Leggings. Photo by Edward Curtis. *Courtesy of National Archives of Canada/PA-39298.*

met up with LITTLE WOLF and his followers in March 1879, following their exodus from the Indian Territory.

Two Moons later acted as an informant to the writer HAMLIN GARLAND, whose article "General Custer's Last Fight as Seen by Two Moon" was published in *McClure's Magazine* in 1898; and as a model for James Fraser, who designed the "buffalo" or "Indian head" nickel, released in 1913. (See also SITTING BULL.)

U

UNADUTI. See BUSHYHEAD, DENNIS WOLF.

UNCAS (Wonkas, "the Fox"; Poquim, Poquoiam). *Mohegan. (ca. 1606–ca. 1682).* Founder of the Mohegans; ally of colonists in the Pequot War and King Philip's War. Son-in-law of SASSACUS.

Uncas was originally a member of the Pequot tribe of Connecticut; his father-in-law, Sassacus, was the grand sachem. Following a dispute with Sassacus over treaty terms with whites and over his attempt to usurp power, Uncas was banished from the Pequot villages. With his followers, he founded his own village along the Thames River in Connecticut. His band, the Mohegans, as they were called, became trade and military allies with the English. After the Pequots had been defeated by the whites and their Indian auxiliaries in the Pequot War of 1636–37, then dispersed, Uncas, who had provided valuable military support, became chief of some of the surviving Pequots as well.

In 1643, war broke out between the Mohegans and the Narragansets under MIANTINOMO. Mohegan warriors captured the Narraganset chief in battle and Uncas turned him over to the colonial authorities at Hartford. Miantinomo was condemned to death, then returned to the Mohegans for execution. Uncas's brother Wawequa carried out the deed.

Uncas supported the whites in King PHILIP's War of 1675–76 and sent his son Oneco into battle. Because of his continuing alliance with colonists, the Mohegan sachem managed to keep power longer than all his rivals among the Pequots, Narragansets, and Wampanoags. Despite his political arrangement with whites, he discouraged the practice of Christianity by his people.

The character Uncas in JAMES FENIMORE COOPER's *The Last of the Mohicans* is a fictionalized version of the Mohegan chief.

UNDERHILL, JOHN. *(ca. 1597–1672).* Colonial militia officer; colonial governor.

British-born John Underhill took up his father's trade as a professional soldier. In 1630, he came to the Massachusetts Bay Colony and was instrumental in organizing the colony's military defenses. He was appointed a captain of militia and was provided with land and an income.

In the Pequot War of 1636–37, Underhill led a company of militia to reinforce colonial forces under Captain Lion Gardiner at Fort Saybrook, Connecticut. In May 1637, he took part in Captain JOHN MASON's raid on SASSACUS's village on the Mystic River in Connecticut, in which hundreds of the tribe were killed.

In 1637–38, Underhill visited England, where he published *Newes from America* about the Pequot War. He then settled in New Hampshire because of a disagreement with Massachusetts church authorities. He became governor of the colony at Dover until 1840.

Underhill fought for the Dutch under WILLEM KIEFT against Algonquian bands of present-day New York, New Jersey, and Connecticut, carrying out a campaign of extermination and eventually forcing negotiations under the Wappinger ORATAMIN.

Underhill later fought against the Dutch in the Anglo-Dutch wars of the 1650s and supported the British in their efforts to take over the Dutch colony of New Netherland in 1664. He retired to Oyster Bay, Long Island, in 1672. (See also ORATAMIN; SASSACUS.)

V

VALLEJO, MARIANO GUADALUPE.

(1808–1890). Army officer in Mexican California.

Mariano Vallejo was born in Monterey, California, at that time under Spanish rule. He was the son of the soldier Don Ignacio Vallejo, who campaigned against CHALPINICH's Yokuts Indians. Following his father's example, Mariano began service in the provincial militia at age 15, soon after Mexican independence from Spain. While posted at the San Francisco Presidio in 1829, he fought against San Jose Mission Indians in revolt under STANISLAUS. During the 1830s, he became a leading military officer in the provincial California government and was part of the movement against the authoritarian rule of Mexico over the province.

Vallejo was responsible for the development of military defenses for Sonoma when that settlement was threatened with attacks by hostile Indians in 1834. Also that year, Vallejo established an alliance with SOLANO, chief of the Suisun band of Patwin Indians. Salvador Vallejo, Mariano's brother, helped arm and train them.

Vallejo and his family established extensive agricultural landholdings throughout the Napa-Sonoma Valley. He required Indian labor to run his ranches, and with Solano, subjugated Pomo Indians into enforced labor on his lands. Pomo bands, armed by Russian fur traders out of Fort Ross, resisted Vallejo's authority and waged war against him until 1843.

When his nephew, Juan Bautista de Alvarado, rebelled from Mexican authority in 1836 and became governor of California two years later, Vallejo was assigned the province's chief military officer. After the Bear Flag Revolt in 1846, Vallejo was placed under arrest by the insurgents, but was released upon the arrival of American troops. After California had been admitted to the Union in 1850, Vallejo served in the state legislature. He donated his lands near Sonoma to the state; Vallejo, California, founded there in 1852, served as the state capital in 1852–53. (See also SOLANO; STANISLAUS.)

VARGAS ZAPATA Y LUJAN PONCE DE LEON, DIEGO JOSE DE. *(ca. 1643–1704).*
Military leader of New Mexico; Spanish colonial governor.

Born in Spain, Diego de Vargas first came to Mexico City as a royal courier in 1673. He remained in the Americas and served in several governmental positions until 1688. That year, he was appointed governor and captain general of New Mexico.

Most of New Mexico had been ruled by Indians since the Pueblo Rebellion of 1680 under POPE. In 1691–92, Vargas, operating out of El Paso, led his Spanish forces in subduing Indians in northern Mexico. Then, starting in 1692, he led an expedition of 60 soldiers and 100 Indian auxiliaries in the reconquest of the Pueblo stronghold at Santa Fe, besieging the town and cutting off the water supply. The Pueblo Indians soon sued for peace. Vargas met some resistance at the pueblos of San Ildefonso and Cochiti, which he repressed.

Vargas used his influence to assuage the resentment of the Pueblos against Spanish occupation in an effort to prevent further uprisings. He reformed the exploitative Spanish economic policies and enjoined the missionaries from persecuting the Indians for practicing their native religion. Except for the Hopis, most of the Pueblo peoples submitted to the reestablishment of Spanish rule under Vargas.

In 1696, Don Pedro Cubero succeeded Vargas as governor and had him arrested for misconduct while in office. Vargas remained in prison until 1700, when he was cleared of all charges. In 1703, he was reinstated as governor of New Mexico. The next year, he died while leading a campaign against the Apaches. (See also POPE.)

364

VENIAMINOV, IVAN (Ioann Veniaminoff).
(1797–1879). Missionary; educator; scholar.

Born Ivan Popov in Siberia, Ivan Veniaminov began studies at the Russian Orthodox seminary at Irkutsk in 1806. In 1821, he was ordained a Russian Orthodox priest. At that time, he assumed the name Veniaminov in honor of a former bishop of Irkutsk.

Three years later, in 1824, at the request of the Russian-American Company, Veniaminov was sent as a missionary to the Aleuts on Unalaska, one of the Aleutian Islands. He learned the Aleut language and prepared a dictionary, grammar, and primer. For the next 10 years, he ministered to the Aleuts and established schools among them. He also made ethnological studies of their culture.

In 1834, Veniaminov moved to the settlement of Sitka on Baranof Island, off the southeastern panhandle of Alaska, where he extended his missionary and educational work to the Tlingits. He returned to Siberia and European Russia in 1834–38. In 1838, on his return to Sitka, he had been promoted to the post of bishop of the Kamchatka region, as well as the Kuril and Aleutian islands. In 1850, he was named Archbishop of Yakutsk, Siberia, a post which he held until 1868. That year, shortly after Russia had sold Alaska to the United States, Veniaminov became head of the Russian Orthodox Church in Moscow.

VERENDRYE, PIERRE GAULTIER DE VARENNES, SIEUR DE LA. *(1685–1749).*
Explorer; trader; soldier.

Pierre Gaultier de Varennes, Sieur de la Verendrye, was born in Trois-Rivieres in what is now Quebec. In 1697, he joined the French army and, during Queen Anne's War of 1702–12, participated in the raid on Deerfield, Massachusetts. He also saw action in Europe and was taken prisoner by the British in 1708. Released in 1710, he returned to Canada two years later. He worked for a time as a farmer, then, in 1726, joined his brother Jacques-Rene, then commandant of posts along the north shore of Lake Superior. He succeeded his brother two years later.

Verendrye received a three-year monopoly on the region's fur trade and, in 1731, began a series of expeditions to expand the fur trade to the more eastern tribes and to find a Northwest Passage to the Western Sea. He and his sons, Louis Joseph, Francois, Pierre, and his nephew La Jeremaye, established several trading posts in the Assiniboine and Red River regions of what is now southern Manitoba.

In 1738, along with his son Louis Joseph, Verendrye traveled into present-day North Dakota, where he helped establish the earliest fur-trading contacts with the Mandans at their settlements on the Missouri River, near modern Bismarck, North Dakota.

In 1742–43, Verendrye sponsored two of his sons—probably Louis Joseph and Francois—on an expedition south and west of the Mandan lands into present-day Montana. The extent of the journey westward is not certain, but they are thought to have reached the Black Hills or perhaps the Bighorn Mountains of Wyoming and Montana. A lead plaque they buried during the return trip was uncovered in 1913 at Pierre, South Dakota.

Verendrye was retired in 1744, but was reappointed as commander in the West in 1746. His sons attempted to continue his planned explorations after his death but failed to obtain government backing.

VERRAZANO, GIOVANNI DA (Giovanni da Verrazzano). *(ca. 1485–ca. 1528).* Explorer.

Italian-born Giovanni da Verrazano was educated in Florence and moved to Dieppe, France. He served the French as a privateer, preying on Spanish ships returning with Aztec gold from Mexico. His success in this enterprise soon led King Francis I of France to sponsor an expedition under Verrazano across the Atlantic in search of a new sea route to Asia.

Verrazano, along with his brother, mapmaker Girolamo da Verrazano, left the port of Dieppe in early 1524, in command of the ship *La Dauphine*. They reached the coast of North America, off the shores of present-day Cape Fear, North Carolina, where a party went ashore and had contacts with Indians, whom Verrazano later described at length in his written account of the voyage, comparing them to the Chinese that he may have read about in the writings of Marco Polo. The expedition then sailed south along the coast as far as present-day Charleston, South Carolina. Along the way, a party landed on the islands of the Outer Banks, where they encountered other friendly Indians.

Still seeking a passage to the Pacific, Verrazano navigated *La Dauphine* northward. At Kitty Hawk, North Carolina, he sent a crew of his men ashore, where they kidnapped an Indian child to bring back to France. *La Dauphine* also entered New York Harbor, which Verrazano later noted was heavily populated with native peoples.

The expedition continued northeast along the coast, and Verrazano and his brother visited the Wampanoag Indians on Block Island. A Wampanoag tribesman helped guide the ship into Narragansett Bay. The Europeans spent over two weeks with the Indians at the site of present-day Newport, Rhode Island. Verrazano later commented extensively on the dress and habits of the Wampanoags, especially noting their copper ornaments.

Off the coast of Maine, Verrazano and his men encountered some hostility from Abnaki Indians. Because of their reluctance to have contact with the explorers, the Abnakis sent their goods down to the awaiting French in a basket, lowered from the top of a seaside cliff. In return, the Indians accepted for trade only metal goods, such as knives, fishhooks, and tools. On his subsequent chart of the Maine coast, Girolamo da Verrazano included an Abnaki place name, "Oranbega," one of the earliest such usages on a European map.

Verrazano explored the coast as far as eastern Newfoundland and was the first European to recognize that the coast of North America was contiguous and belonged to a "New World." He claimed all the land he explored for France, then sailed back to Dieppe.

In 1527, Verrazano made a second voyage of discovery to the coast of Brazil, returning to France with a valuable cargo of tropical lumber. In 1528, he undertook another attempt to find a western route to Asia, and, sailing to the south of his 1524 route, he explored the Lesser Antilles in the Caribbean. Putting ashore with his brother and a small detachment of men on an island—probably Guadeloupe—he was attacked by a party of Carib Indians. Girolamo and the others managed to escape, but watched in horror as the natives seized Giovanni, tore him apart, and devoured him. The party continued to the coast of Brazil, obtained more valuable tropical wood, then returned to France later that year.

VIAL, PEDRO (Pierre Vial). (ca. 1746–1814).
Explorer; guide; interpreter; captive.

Pedro Vial was born in Lyons, France. In the 1770s, he migrated to Spanish Louisiana, where he worked as a gunsmith to the Indians of the lower Missouri River. He also had contacts with tribes of the Southwest and Great Plains and learned their language.

Vial's familiarity with the native peoples and the geography of the region led the Spanish governor of Texas, Domingo Cabello, to commission an expedition under him seeking an overland route from San Antonio to Santa Fe, the provincial capital of Spanish New Mexico. In 1786–87, Vial headed north from San Antonio through the Comanche lands of central Texas, finally reaching Santa Fe.

At Santa Fe, the governor of New Mexico soon engaged Vial to explore a route to Natchitoches, Louisiana, on the eastern frontier of Spanish territory. This expedition led him across 2,500 miles of southwestern territory. He reached Louisiana and returned to Santa Fe, stopping en route at San Antonio.

In 1792, Vial led a third expedition, this one eastward from Santa Fe across the Southern Plains in search of a practical overland route to St. Louis. On this journey, Vial was captured by the Kaw (Kansa) Indians and held for a brief period before he was able to escape or was released. He reached St. Louis in 1794, after having followed a route paralleling the Santa Fe Trail, established in the mid-1820s.

Vial eventually settled in Santa Fe, where he continued to serve as an interpreter and guide for Spanish expeditions to the lands of the Southern Plains Indians.

VICTOR, FRANCES FULLER. (1826–1902).
Historian; journalist.

Frances Fuller Victor was born near Rome, New York. During schooling in Ohio, she published her first poem. With her sister, Metta Victoria, she came to New York City, where both contributed articles to magazines. They moved to Michigan, continuing their writing pursuits in Detroit, then back to New York.

With her second husband, Victor traveled west in 1863, settling in San Francisco, where she worked as a columnist. They settled in Portland, Oregon, the next year. After separation from her husband, Victor began to establish a reputation as a historian, traveling throughout Oregon and Washington to record the stories of surviving early settlers. Her various histories, such as *River of the West* (1870), and articles contain much information about Plateau Indians.

In 1878, Victor began work for HUBERT HOWE BANCROFT, contributing to his histories of the Far West. In 1889, she again embarked on travels throughout Oregon and Washington, and she wrote about MARCUS WHITMAN and the Cayuses. Her *Early Indian Wars of Oregon* was published in 1894.

VICTORIO (Bidu-ya, Beduiat). *Mimbreno Apache.* (ca. 1825–1880). Leader in the Apache Wars.

Victorio was probably born in what is now southern New Mexico. In Mexico, a legend persists that he was of Mexican birth, kidnapped and raised by Apaches, but most scholars reject this theory. There is no mention of his possible Mexican origin in Apache tribal tradition.

As a young warrior, Victorio fought under the Mimbreno MANGAS COLORADAS. On the death of the latter in 1863, Victorio assumed leadership of his followers, who came to include Indians from a number of bands in addition to the Mimbreno (or Mimbres) Apaches: the Warm Springs proper, Mogollon, Copper Mine, Chiricahua, and Mescalero. The various bands came to be known collectively as Ojo Caliente, or Warm Springs Apaches, since their agency was located at Ojo Caliente (Warm Springs) in what is now southwest New Mexico. During the 1860s–70s, Warm Springs Apaches carried out numerous raids in New Mexico and Texas.

Victorio agreed to cease hostilities if granted a permanent reservation at Warm Springs, but negotiations failed, and he and his followers were forced to relocate to the San Carlos Reservation in Arizona among Chiricahua bands. On September 2, 1877, Victorio slipped away with 300 others. Many gave themselves up within a month at Fort Wingate, New Mexico, but

Victorio and 80 warriors remained in the Mimbres Mountains, from where they carried out a series of raids.

In early 1879, the start of what is sometimes referred to as the Victorio War, Victorio again tried to settle at Warm Springs, then in June agreed to settle at the Mecalero Reservation at Tularosa, New Mexico. Here he was indicted on an old charge of murder and horse-stealing. On September 4, fearing a trial, he slipped away with his faithful warriors, this time joined by a substantial number of Mescaleros. Two days later, his war party attacked a cavalry horse camp and killed eight guards. The militants then headed into Mexico, then Texas, then back into New Mexico, and finally Arizona, carrying out attacks.

Both the United States and Mexico mobilized forces: Colonel Edward Hatch in New Mexico and Colonel BENJAMIN H. GRIERSON in Texas, and General Geronimo Trevino in Chihuahua, Mexico. American troops regularly crossed the international border, an exception in policy made because of the Apache threat. Victorio, a master tactitian, eluded all his pursuers, surviving a number of skirmishes.

On October 15, 1880, while fleeing American detachments under Colonel George Buell out of New Mexico and Colonel EUGENE A. CARR out of Arizona into the Chihuahua highlands, Victorio was attacked by a force of 350 Mexicans and Tarahumara Indians under Colonel Joaquin Terrazas. In the two-day battle of Tres Castillos—or "Three Peaks"—about 80 Apaches were killed and about 78 women and children taken prisoner. Only about 30 warriors escaped. Victorio turned up among the dead. It is not known whether he died fighting, killed by a Tarahumara scout, or, as legend has it, he took his own life before the enemy could reach him.

NANA assumed leadership of his band and joined GERONIMO in the Apache Wars of the 1880s.

VROMAN, ADAM CLARK. *(1856–1916).* Photographer.

Born in La Salle, Illinois, Adam Clark Vroman moved to Pasadena, California, in 1892, where he worked as a Kodak dealer as well as a bookseller. In 1895, he took his first of three trips to the Southwest, photographing the Hopis in Arizona. He became a friend of the ethnologist CHARLES LUMMIS, who used Vroman's images to illustrate writings. Vroman also accompanied ethnologist FREDERICK WEBB HODGE of the Smithsonian's Bureau of American Ethnology as official photographer on government-sponsored expeditions in 1887 and 1889 to the Southwest pueblos and ruins. In the course of his career, Vroman also took numerous photographs of the Mission Indians of California.

W

WABAN ("east"). *Nipmuc. (ca. 1604–ca. 1677).*
First "Praying Indian" of Massachusetts Bay Colony.

Waban was born in the Indian village of Musketaquid, the site of Concord, Massachusetts. In 1646, JOHN ELIOT founded his first Christian mission at this location, naming it Nonantum. Waban offered friendship and support and supposedly was the first area Indian to convert to Christianity. In 1651, Eliot founded the mission of Natick to the west. Waban moved there with his family, becoming one of its leaders and a justice of the peace. In 1675, just before the start of King PHILIP's War, he warned Massachusetts authorities of the likelihood of an Indian rebellion. During the conflict, he was arrested by colonial officals along with other peaceful Praying Indians. He became ill during his imprisonment and soon died.

WABASHA (Wapasha, Wapusha, Waapashaw, "Red Leaf"). *Mdewakanton Sioux-Chippewa. (1718–ca. 1799).* Ally and trading partner of British. Father of WABASHA (The Leaf); grandfather (or granduncle) of JOSEPH WABASHA.

The second of five known chiefs of this name, Wabasha was born at the head of the Rum River in what is now Minnesota. He came to be chief of a Mdewakanton Santee band in southeastern Minnesota when the French claimed the region. Little is known of his Mdewakanton father of the same name; his mother was a Chippewa captive.

In 1747, Wabasha negotiated a peace with his mother's people, the Chippewas, traditional enemies of the Sioux. He also agreed to trade relations with the French. In 1759, with French losses during the French and Indian War of 1754–63, Wabasha began a policy of trade with the British. The killing of a trader by a Sioux caused the British to abandon their post in Mdewakanton territory. Wabasha ordered the brave's capture and set out to Canada to deliver him to authorities. When his prisoner escaped, Wabasha offered himself instead, gaining British respect and salvaging the trade relationship.

During the early 1770s, Wabasha battled the Chippewas on several occasions. In the American Revolution, he fought on the side of the Loyalists. After the war, Wabasha established the new village of Kiyuska at present-day Winona, Minnesota. He was succeeded by his son of the same name, called The Leaf by whites.

WABASHA (The Leaf). *Mdwakanton Sioux. (d. ca. 1838).* Friend to whites. Son of WABASHA; father (or uncle) of JOSEPH WABASHA.

The Leaf succeeded his father as chief of the Mdewakanton band at Kiyuska (present-day Winona, Minnesota). In 1805, he met and aided Lieutenant ZEBULON PIKE, who was exploring the region. In the War of 1812, he declared himself for the British along with most Mdewakanton bands, but is thought to have helped the Americans on several occasions. He was a chief negotiator at the Prairie du Chien council in 1825. He traveled to Washington, D.C., in 1837 for further negotiations.

WABASHA, JOSEPH. *Mdewakanton Sioux. (d. 1876).* Reluctant participant in the Minnesota Uprising of 1862–63; principal chief. Son (or nephew) of WABASHA (The Leaf); grandson (or grandnephew) of WABASHA.

On the death of The Leaf, either his father or uncle, Joseph Wabasha became chief of the Mdewakanton band living just west of the Mississippi River on the site of present-day Winona, Minnesota, and eventually head chief of all the bands. In 1858, he signed a treaty at Washington, D.C., ceding tribal lands and moved with his people to a reservation on the upper Minnesota

River. With the outbreak of the Minnesota Uprising in 1862 among the Santee Sioux, Wabasha was forced to accompany LITTLE CROW and other militants into battle to maintain his position in the tribe. Yet he saw little fighting and saved white settlers when he could. He also sent a letter to General HENRY HASTINGS SIBLEY, blaming Little Crow for starting the war and claiming his own peaceful intentions. At the close of the war, Wabasha's band was relocated to the Santee Reservation on the Niobrara River in Nebraska. His son Napoleon Wabasha succeeded him as head chief. (See also LITTLE CROW.)

WABAUNSEE (Waubansee, Wabansee).
Potawatomi. (d. 1848). War chief; ally of British, then Americans.

Wabaunsee lived on the Kankakee River in Illinois, about 40 miles south of Lake Michigan. He was known in the region as a powerful war chief. In the War of 1812, he fought on the side of the British, helping take Fort Dearborn (present-day Chicago). After the battle, however, he protected American captives from death. In 1826, Wabaunsee signed the Treaty of the Wabash ceding Potawatomi lands. In 1832, during the BLACK HAWK War, he joined the Illinois militia against the Sacs and Foxes. In 1835, he traveled to Washington, D.C., ceding the remainder of Potawatomi lands in Illinois and Indiana in exchange for territory west of the Mississippi. He settled on the Missouri River in Iowa near Council Bluffs.

WABOKIESHEK. See WHITE CLOUD.

WAFFORD, JAMES (Tsuskwanunnawata, "worn-out blanket"). *Mixed Cherokee. (1806–1896).* Tribal leader; research informant.

James Wafford was born near present-day Clarkesville, Georgia, the grandson of a Revolutionary colonel of the same name who established a settlement in northern Georgia in 1785. When the Wafford Settlement was found to be on Cherokee lands, the tribe was pressured into ceding about 100 acres by special treaty agreement in 1804. James Wafford's mother had Cherokee, Natchez, and white ancestry and was a cousin of SEQUOYAH. Wafford attended a mission school at Valleytown, where he worked on the translation of a Sunday-school speller. In 1824, he worked for the Census Bureau and gained valuable knowledge about the Cherokees and their homeland, which he later drew upon as an informant. During the Trail of Tears, he was a commander of a party of emigrants and later was a member of the Western Cherokees' tribal council. In 1891, he was interviewed by JAMES MOONEY of the Bureau of American Ethnology at Tahlequah in the Indian Territory.

WAHUNSONACOCK. See POWHATAN.

WALKARA (Wakara, Walker, "yellow"). *Ute.* *(ca. 1808–1855).* Great Basin war chief.

Walkara, one of five sons of a chief of the Timpanogos band, was born along the Spanish Fork River in what is now Utah. He established his reputation as a warrior and horseman and gathered a band of braves, including some Paiutes and Shoshones, who carried out raids on ranches and travelers in the Great Basin region and along the Old Spanish Trail between New Mexico and California.

Walkara's power grew. He learned to speak several different Indian dialects as well as Spanish and English to broaden his power base. Weaker Great Basin bands paid him tribute. He organized raiding parties under his brothers and trusted lieutenants to launch attacks simultaneously. They became a disciplined cavalry force, decorated in bright dyes and silver and other metal ornaments. (Walkara's name, translated as "yellow," referred to his favorite yellow face paint and yellow-dyed leather and hide.) He worked along with the mountain men JAMES BECKWOURTH and Thomas "Pegleg" Smith, who traded weapons and whiskey for horses. Many of the horse-stealing raids went through the Cajon Pass into Southern California. In 1840, Walkara's men supposedly stole 3,000 horses, establishing his reputation in California as "the greatest horse thief in history." In some of these raids, Walkara's warriors fought Cahuilla Indians under Chief JUAN ANTONIO.

After Mormon settlement in the Great Basin, Walkara established a trade relationship with BRIGHAM YOUNG. In 1850, he allowed himself to be baptized into the Latter-Day Saints religion at Manti. During the early 1850s, however, a measles epidemic, raids by Shoshones, and increasing numbers of federal troops led to the decline of his empire.

Walkara turned against the Mormons when he was unable to acquire a Mormon wife. Moreover, several of his people were killed in a fight with whites at Springville. In 1853, he began regular raids on Mormon settlements. In the so-called Walker War, Brigham Young directed the settlers to move from their outlying farms and ranches into forts. Their defense proved successful, and Walkara agreed to peace before winter. Yet, on being offered a 20-acre parcel of land by the Mormons, he pridefully rejected it.

Walkara died two years later at Meadow Creek and was honored by his people in a traditional Ute funeral.

WALKER, JOSEPH REDDEFORD (Joe Walker).
(1798–1876). Explorer; guide; trader; trapper.

Virginia-born Joseph Walker was raised in Tennessee, and, by 1818, had settled on the Missouri frontier at Fort Osage.

In 1820, Walker was a member of a trading parting traveling from Missouri to Santa Fe. He was arrested by Spanish officials for his illegal incursion into Spanish territory, but was released when he offered to help in a campaign against the Pawnees. In 1824, Walker worked for the federal government mapping and marking part of the Sante Fe Trail. Starting in 1827, he served two terms as sheriff of Jackson County, Missouri, including the town of Independence.

In 1832, while on a trip to the Indian Territory to purchase livestock from the Cherokees, Walker met Captain BENJAMIN DE BONNEVILLE, who hired him as field commander on a fur-trapping enterprise in the Middle Rockies of present-day Utah and Wyoming. In 1833, Bonneville commissioned Walker to lead a party of 50 mountain men and trappers from the Green River-Bear Lake region of what is now northeastern Utah to the Great Salt Lake and westward to California.

Walker's party reached the Great Salt Lake, then headed west across the Great Salt Lake Basin to the Humboldt River, seeking a water route to the Pacific. They followed the Humboldt River across what is now Nevada. When they reached the Humboldt Sink in northwestern Nevada, near present-day Lovelock, they were attacked by Great Basin Indians, but managed to fight them off.

Walker led his party of mountain men and trappers south along the Sierra Nevadas. Along the way, they became the first known whites to explore northern California's Yosemite Valley.

The expedition spent the winter of 1833–34 exploring the San Joaquin Valley of central California, then headed south toward present-day Los Angeles. At the southern end of the Sierras, about 120 miles northwest of Los Angeles, Walker discovered a pass through the mountains that now bears his name. He headed east across central Nevada, re-crossed the Great Basin, and rejoined Bonneville at the Bear River rendezvous of 1834.

In 1835–39, Walker trapped in the Rockies for the American Fur Company. He was a guide for JOHN C. FREMONT's 1842–43 expedition across the Oregon Trail into Wyoming, and also was with Fremont during his 1845–46 expedition to California. He was one of the early participants in the California Gold Rush of 1849, settling in Contra Costa County, California, in the 1850s. In 1861–62, he led an expedition into Arizona that resulted in the discovery of gold near the site of present-day Prescott. Walker spent his remaining years as a rancher near Oakland, California.

His brothers—Joel, John, Samuel, and Isaac—were also frontiersmen in the West.

WALKER, WILLIAM. *Mixed Wyandot (Huron).*
(1800–1874). Interpreter; research informant; chief at the time of Wyandot removal; provisional governor of Nebraska Territory.

William Walker was the son of a chief, a white captive raised by the Wyandots (the Hurons of Ohio), and his mixed-blood wife. He received an education among whites, studying languages at Kenyon College, and acted as private secretary and interpreter to the governor of Michigan Territory LEWIS CASS, as well as a later source for the ethnologist HENRY ROWE SCHOOLCRAFT. In 1824, on the death of his father, Walker inherited the chieftaincy. An opponent of removal, he sought the best possible terms in the relocation of his people from northern Ohio west of the Mississippi to Kansas in 1842. Walker became the provisional governor of the Nebraska Territory in 1853, which the following year was divided into the Kansas and Nebraska territories.

WALK-IN-THE-WATER (Myeerah). *Wyandot (Huron). (ca. 1775–ca. 1825).* Ally of TECUMSEH.

Although Walk-in-the-Water signed peace treaties with the United States at Detroit in 1807 and 1808, he came to support Tecumseh's concept of an independent Indian nation and sided with the British in the War of 1812. He and Roundhead were the principal Huron leaders (referred to in the Old Northwest as Wyandots) in the conflict, proving valuable allies in the field. They fought alongside Colonel HENRY PROCTOR against Kentuckians at Raisin River south of Detroit on January 22, 1813. Walk-in-the-Water was also present at the Battle of the Thames on October 5, 1813, where Tecumseh was killed. Following the war, he settled near Brownstone, Michigan.

WALSH, JAMES MORROW. *(1840–1905).*
Officer in the Canadian Northwest Mounted Police.

Born in Prescott, Ontario, James Walsh was educated at the Royal Military College in Kingston. He served in the Canadian militia, reaching the rank of major.

From 1872 to 1883, Walsh was an inspector with the Northwest Mounted Police under Commissioner JAMES MACLEOD, stationed at Fort Macleod (Alberta) and later Fort Walsh (Saskatchewan), which was built and named after him in 1875. While in command of the Mounties at the latter post, he had charge of Sioux chief SITTING BULL and, at their peak, more than 5,000 Sioux refugees following their exodus from the United States in the aftermath of the War for the Black Hills of 1876–77.

Walsh became a trusted friend of the Sioux chief. The Canadian government, fearing further depletion of the buffalo herds and Sioux warfare with the Blackfeet, wanted the Sioux to return to the United States. Considering the relationship between Walsh and Sitting Bull an obstacle to the Sioux's departure from Canada, government officials reassigned Walsh to another post 160 miles away in 1880. Sitting Bull and his remaining followers, refused rations by the Canadian government, crossed back into the United States in July 1881.

Walsh went into the coal business in Winnipeg in 1883, but returned to the Mounties as superintendent during the Yukon Gold Rush of 1897. He became the first commissioner of the Yukon Territory, retiring in 1898. (See also SITTING BULL.)

WAMSUTTA. See ALEXANDER.

WANETA (Wanata, Wanotan, Wahnaataa, Wahnahtah, "the charger"). *Yanktonai Sioux. (ca. 1795–1848).* Ally of British in the War of 1812; later, ally of Americans.

Waneta was born along the Elm River in what is now South Dakota, the son of Red Thunder. With his father, he fought against the Americans in the War of 1812 and, for his bravery, earned the rank of captain. He was wounded in the Battle of Fort Meigs in the spring of 1813. After the war, Waneta was invited to England and presented at court. On his return, he remained pro-British and, in 1820, plotted an attack on Fort Snelling, Minnesota. While visiting the post for military intelligence, he was seized and interrogated, aborting the plan.

Waneta later became a friend of the Americans, signing the treaties of Fort Pierre and Prairie du Chien in 1825. GEORGE CATLIN painted his picture in 1832. To strengthen the Yanktonai position, he made war on the Chippewas, Assiniboines, and Arikaras. Waneta died along the upper Missouri River at the mouth of Beaver Creek in North Dakota.

WAPELLO (Wapella, Wepello, Wapana, "chief," or "he of the morning"). *Fox. (1787–1842).* Friend to whites; ally of KEOKUK.

Born at Prairie du Chien in what is now Wisconsin, Wapello became one of the four most powerful chiefs of the allied Sac and Fox tribes, including the Sacs Keokuk and BLACK HAWK and the Fox POWASHEEK. His village was located on the east side of the Mississippi in present-day Iowa opposite Black Hawk's village of Saukenuk (present-day Rock Island, Illinois). He maintained peaceful relations with whites and signed numerous treaties. In 1829, he led his band farther west to present-day Muscatine, then eventually to Wapello, Iowa. When the Black Hawk War broke out in 1832,

Wapello joined Keokuk and Powasheek in refusing help to Black Hawk. In 1837, he accompanied the Fox delegation to Washington, D.C., and other eastern cities. In Boston, Wapello made a well-received speech at the statehouse. He died near present-day Ottumwa, Iowa, while on a hunting trip.

WARD, NANCY (Nanye-hi, "one who goes about"). *Cherokee. (ca. 1738–ca. 1824).* Beloved Woman of the Cherokees; protector of whites; negotiator; innkeeper. Niece of ATTAKULLAKULLA; cousin of DRAGGING CANOE.

Nanye-hi was born in the old Cherokee capital, Chota, near present-day Knoxville, Tennessee, her father a Cherokee-Delaware and her mother the sister of Chief Attakullakulla. When a teenager, she married a brave by the name of Kingfisher by whom she had two children.

In a fight with the Creeks, Nanye-hi was at her husband's side, chewing the bullets to make them more damaging. When he was killed, she continued fighting with his musket and helped win the day for the Cherokees. The black slaves of the Creeks were divided up among the victors, one of them going to Nanye-hi. She kept the slave and was supposedly the first Cherokee to practice slavery in the fashion of Southern whites. She also earned the tribal title Beloved Woman because of her role in the battle. As such, she was head of the Woman's Council and had a vote on the Chief's Council; she also had the privilege of condemning or pardoning captives.

Nanye-hi gained a reputation as a peace advocate. In 1776, during the American Revolution, she warned the settlers at Watauga and Holston of impending attack by pro-British Cherokees under her cousin Dragging Canoe. She also used her position in the tribe to save white captives. In 1780, she intercepted American troops under colonel Arthur Campbell in a futile attempt to have them cease their attack on her people; they did, however, spare her village of Chota from destruction. In 1785, she participated in treaty negotiations in South Carolina.

Nanye-hi's second husband was an Irish trader by the name of Brian Ward. He returned to his home in South Carolina after the birth of their child and remarried, although reportedly remaining friendly with Nanye-hi. She opened a successful inn along the Ocowee River near the Georgia border, where she introduced the practice of keeping cows to the Cherokees. To whites throughout the South, she was now known by the shortened form of her name, Nancy.

Nancy Ward continued to play a part in tribal decisions, speaking out to her people against further land cessions and relocation to the West.

The Nancy Ward Daughters of the American Revolution chapter honored her with a grave marker that reads: "Princess and Prophetess of Tennessee. The Pocahontas of Tennessee and the Constant Friend of the American Pioneer."

WAR EAGLE (Little Eagle, Huyana). *Yankton-Santee Sioux. (ca. 1785–1851).* Friend to whites; guide; interpreter; principal chief of Yankton Sioux.

War Eagle was born of Santee Sioux parents, probably in present-day Wisconsin. As a young man, he found employment as a guide for steamboats on the upper Mississippi River. During the War of 1812, he was part of the pro-American faction of Santees and served as an army interpreter and courier. Following the war, he journeyed to St. Louis and worked for MANUEL LISA's American Fur Company as a guide and messenger.

War Eagle eventually settled along the Missouri River near present-day Sioux City, Iowa, and became respected among the Yankton Sioux, who elected him principal chief. In 1837, he represented the Yanktons in Washington, D.C., in an unsuccessful effort to protect their lands from white settlement. Despite his disappointment with government officials, War Eagle continued to advocate peace with whites. Local citizens honored him with a memorial after his death.

WARREN, WILLIAM WHIPPLE. *Mixed Chippewa (Ojibway). (1825–1853).* Interpreter; writer; state legislator.

William Warren was born at LaPointe, Minnesota, the son of Lyman Warren—a blacksmith, fur trader, and Indian agent, and the descendant of one of the *Mayflower* Pilgrims—and his part-Chippewa, part-French wife, Mary Cadotte. William was educated by white teachers at various Eastern schools and became fluent in English. In 1842, he married Matilda Aiken and soon moved to Crow Wing, Minnesota. He educated himself in the traditional language and customs of the Chippewas, meeting frequently with tribal elders and found work as a government interpreter. In 1850, he was elected to the Minnesota State Legislature at St. Paul, and the next year, he began writing about Indian life for *The Minnesota Democrat*. He also worked on a history of his people: *History of the Ojibways, Based Upon Traditions and Oral Statements.* Warren was unable to find a publisher before his death at 28 from tuberculosis, and the book was published posthumously in 1885.

WASHAKIE ("gambler's gourd," "gourd rattle"). *Shoshone-Flathead. (ca. 1804–1900).* Principal chief; friend to whites.

Washakie's father was of the Flathead tribe; his mother, Wind River Shoshone. He spent his early years with the Flatheads in the Bitterroot Mountains of what is now Montana. After his father's death, Washakie and his mother settled among her people in the Wind River Mountains of western Wyoming, part of the Rocky Mountain chain. As a young man, he established his reputation on the warpath against Blackfeet and Crows, part of the time fighting alongside Bannocks.

Like the neighboring Lemhi Shoshones in Idaho under Chief TENDOY, the Wind River, or Eastern, Shoshones had a tradition of friendship with whites, beginning with the early explorers, trappers, and traders. During the period of the mountain men in the 1820s–30s, and the great trading rendezvous, Washakie became a friend of CHRISTOPHER "KIT" CARSON and JAMES BRIDGER. He himself hunted and trapped to barter furs with whites for guns, ammunition, tools, cloth, and ornaments, and encouraged his people to do the same.

By the late 1840s, Washakie had become principal chief of his band. His followers proved friendly to immigrants along the Oregon Trail—along its original route through the South Pass and the later 346-mile Lander shoot 20 miles to the north, both through Shoshone territory. Washakie directed regular patrols of braves to provide assistance to whites in the region, helping them ford rivers and recover lost livestock. He also forbade stealing from whites. Washakie became a friend to Mormons in the region, spending part of one winter in the home of BRIGHAM YOUNG.

During Colonel PATRICK E. CONNOR's Bear River Campaign against BEAR HUNTER's band of Northwestern Shoshones in January 1863, Washakie led his people to the safety of Fort Bridger. In July 1863, Washakie signed the Treaty of Fort Bridger, agreeing to allow travelers to pass safely through Shoshone territory in exchange for an annuity for 20 years. In July 1868, he signed a second treaty giving a right-of-way to the Union Pacific Railroad and agreeing to settle his band on the Wind River Reservation near present-day Riverton.

Starting in 1869, after the army had established Camp Brown on the site of present-day Lander, Wyoming, Washakie and his braves served as army scouts in campaigns against the Sioux, Cheyennes, Arapahos, and Utes. Camp Brown was later moved to the junction of the north and south forks of the Little Wind River. In 1876, during the Sioux War for the Black Hills under SITTING BULL, Washakie led 200 Shoshones, Bannock, and Ute warriors across the Rockies to join up with troops under General GEORGE CROOK. His force arrived too late to participate in the Battle of the Rosebud, but they helped pursue CRAZY HORSE's band to the Powder River country. Washakie's two sons also led warriors in support of Colonel RANALD S. MACKENZIE against DULL KNIFE's Northern Cheyennes in November.

In 1878, Camp Brown was renamed Fort Washakie. That year, despite Washakie's opposition, the Arapahos were relocated to Wind River with the Shoshones.

Also that year, President ULYSSES S. GRANT presented Washakie with a saddle decorated in silver in appreciation for his services. In 1883, President Chester Arthur, on a fishing trip to Yellowstone National Park, visited the Shoshone chief.

After the death of a son in a barroom brawl, Washakie converted to Christianity, being baptized into the Episcopal church in 1897. Washakie was still on army rolls when he died three years later at Flathead Village in the Bitterroot Valley of Montana. He was buried in the Fort Washakie cemetery with full military honors, and a monument was erected over his grave. In the course of his life, he had at least two wives and 12 children.

WASHINGTON, GEORGE (Town Destroyer).
(1732–1799). President of the United States, 1789–97; army officer; land speculator.

Born in Westmoreland County, Virginia, George Washington was the son of wealthy, aristocratic parents. His great-grandfather, Colonel John Washington of the Virginia militia, had fought the Susquehannock Indians in Maryland and Virginia in the mid-1670s.

Washington became a surveyor, spending time on the frontier. In 1748, he took part in an expedition to survey the vast holdings of Lord Fairfax in Virginia's Shenandoah Valley. He subsequently became involved in land speculation ventures in the Ohio Valley, becoming a principal in the Ohio Company. In 1752, he inherited Mount Vernon, his half-brother's Virginia plantation. Shortly afterward, he was appointed a major in the Virginia militia by Lieutenant Governor ROBERT DINWIDDIE, a partner in the Ohio Company.

French incursions into the Ohio Company's lands of present-day western Pennsylvania led Dinwiddie to send Washington and a militia company west to evict the French. Washington was aided on this 1754 expedition by the Mingo leader HALF-KING (Tanacharison) and a number of Iroquois warriors. When the French refused to leave at Washington's request, the Virginia colonial government sent in troops to build fortifications at the junction of the Allegheny and Monongahela rivers, near present-day Pittsburgh. Washington, promoted to lieutenant colonel of militia, led an expedition to reinforce this base, called Fort Necessity. His militia force surprised and defeated a small company of French soldiers in 1754, at Great Meadows near Fort Necessity, in the first engagement of what was to become the French and Indian War of 1754–63. Iroquois warriors with Washington on this 1754 expedition disapproved of his seemingly unprovoked attack on the small French force, and withdrew their support. The French soon counterattacked, and Washington, faced with an overwhelming force of soldiers and Indians, was forced to surrender. With his men, he was granted safe passage back to eastern Virginia.

In the summer of 1755, Washington was aide-de-camp to British General EDWARD BRADDOCK in an expedition against Fort Duquesne, near the site of Washington's surrender the previous year. When the French and Indians led an attack on Braddock's column on July 9, 1755, in what later came to be known as Braddock's Defeat, or the Battle of the Monongahela, Washington was able to marshal the surviving British and Virginia colonial troops into an orderly retreat. Yet the engagement cost the British and colonists heavily in men and equipment. In 1758, Washington led a Virginia militia force back to Fort Duquesne under General John Forbes, occupying what was renamed Fort Pitt (present-day Pittsburgh).

Washington soon became a member of the Virginia colonial legislature, the House of Burgesses. He continued to supervise the defense of the Virginia frontier settlements from Indian attack for the duration of the French and Indian War, and, at the same time, developed his extensive landholdings in the Kanawha River Valley. His 45,000 acres there were acquired partly through grants from the Virginia government for his service in the early part of the war.

At the outbreak of the American Revolution, Washington was named commander in chief of the Continental army. His tactics against the British in the mid-Atlantic region included a strategic retreat from New York in 1776, and a counteroffensive into Pennsylvania and New Jersey in 1777–78. Following the British-backed Iroquois raids on wilderness settlements in New York and Pennsylvania, such as the raid on Cherry Valley in the fall of 1778 under JOSEPH BRANT, Washington planned and organized a punitive spring expedition against the Indians. This 1779 offensive into the Wyoming Valley of Pennsylvania and the southern tier of New York was led by generals JOHN SULLIVAN and JAMES CLINTON. The Sullivan-Clinton Campaign laid waste to Iroquois villages and crops and earned Washington the Seneca sobriquet of Town Destroyer. Other important campaigns against the pro-British Indians during the Revolutionary War were headed by Major GEORGE ROGERS CLARK in the Ohio Valley and Kentucky. In the South, Cherokees under DRAGGING CANOE and BLOODY FELLOW, as well as Creeks under ALEXANDER McGILLIVRAY, carried out raids on American settlements in the war years, taking militia forces away from actions against the British.

In 1783, after American victory, Washington recommended that Congress not expel the Indians from United States territory, but instead impose a boundary to restrict white settlement on their lands.

Washington's military success in the American Revolution led to his being elected the nation's first president in 1788. President Washington's Indian policy, formulated by his secretary of war, JOHN KNOX, recognized the Indians' claim to their territory and denied the United States possession of these lands by right of conquest. With Knox, Washington shared the view that the federal government's authority over Indian territory included only an exclusive right to negotiate with the Indians for the purchase of their land.

During his presidency, Indians of the Old Northwest, supported by British military outposts in the Great Lakes, continued to make war on American settlers in the Ohio Valley. LITTLE TURTLE, a Miami chief, led his people, along with warriors from other area tribes, in a war in 1790–94. Washington, amid the objections of many of his supporters, pushed through the ratification of the Jay Treaty of 1794, under which the British agreed to relinquish their Great Lakes forts. While recognizing certain Indian territorial claims, Washington, through the Jay Treaty with Great Britain, isolated the tribes of the Old Northwest from British military support. This diplomatic move by Washington, coupled with military victory in the 1794 Battle of Fallen Timbers by General "Mad" ANTHONY WAYNE, ended Little Turtle's War. At the Fort Greenville Treaty of 1795, the tribes of the Old Northwest were forced to agree to the U.S. purchase of their lands in the Ohio Valley.

During his presidency, Washington established the precedent of meeting with delegations of tribal leaders and treating them with the same respect afforded to visiting foreign dignitaries.

Washington retired to his plantation at Mount Vernon, Virginia, in 1797, where he died two years later. (See also BRANT, JOSEPH; DRAGGING CANOE; LITTLE TURTLE.)

WASSAJA. See MONTEZUMA, CARLOS.

WATIE, STAND (Degataga, "standing together as one," "stand firm," "immovable"). *Mixed Cherokee. (1806–1871).* Tribal leader; Confederate general; research informant. Brother of ELIAS BOUDINOT; nephew of MAJOR RIDGE; cousin of JOHN RIDGE.

Stand Watie, the son of David Uwati and the part-Cherokee Susannah Reese, was born near present-day Rome, Georgia. Like his brother Elias Boudinot, he was educated at mission schools. He returned to the Cherokee homeland to work with his brother on the newspaper *Cherokee Phoenix.*

Accepting the view that resistance to white expansion in the South was hopeless, Stand Watie became an active member of the pro-removal Treaty Party, led by his uncle and cousin, Major and John Ridge. He was one of the signers of the Treaty of New Echota in 1835. Following the Trail of Tears to the Indian Territory, he was marked for assassination by members of the anti-removal Ross

Party, along with Boudinot and the Ridges, but he was forewarned and was the only one of the four to escape. In retaliation, he burned the house of JOHN ROSS.

Stand Watie started a successful plantation on Spavinaw Creek in the Indian Territory, with numerous slaves he had brought from the East. He served on the Cherokee Council from 1845 to 1861, part of the time as speaker.

In August 1861, at the outbreak of the Civil War, ALBERT PIKE convinced Chief John Ross and the Cherokees to give up neutrality and support the Confederacy. Stand Watie organized a regiment of cavalry and, the following October, was commissioned as a colonel in the First Cherokee Mounted Rifles. Opposing him were such leaders as OPOTHLEYAHOLO of the Creeks and BILLY BOWLEGS of the Seminoles, who supported the Union.

Stand Watie is famous for his role in the Battle of Pea Ridge, Arkansas, on March 6–8, 1862, in which his troops captured the Union artillery positions that were inflicting great damage on the Confederates. They then covered the retreat of their allies.

The Union victory at Pea Ridge, the subsequent Indian Expedition of 1862, in which Tahlequah was invaded and tribal leaders were captured, plus the Indian Expedition of 1863, in which Fort Gibson fell, caused many of the pro-Confederate Indians of the Indian Territory to withdraw from the conflict. Stand Watie continued fighting and was promoted to brigadier general by General Samuel Maxey, Pike's successor. He came to command two regiments of Mounted Rifles and three battalions of Cherokee, Seminole, and Osage infantry that fought in the Indian Territory, Arkansas, Missouri, Kansas, and Texas.

Watie's troops were based south of the Canadian River, from where he sent mounted squads north of the river into Union-held territory. They struck at hay-cutting parties sent out to feed the horses at Fort Gibson; when the Union soldiers let the horses out to graze under guard, Watie's men attacked and drove the mounts across the river. In June 1864, he led his troops in the taking of a steamer on the Arkansas River. The following September, he captured a Union supply column of 300 wagons at the Cabin Creek crossing of the road between Fort Scott, Kansas, and Fort Gibson. Watie distributed the booty among Cherokee, Creek, and Seminole refugees displaced from their homes by the war. His force reportedly fought in more battles west of the Mississippi than any other unit.

Watie surrendered to the Union in June 1865, at Doaksville in the Choctaw Nation of the Indian Territory, the last general in the Confederate army to do so. During the war, in 1864, he was elected principal chief of the Southern band of Cherokees.

After the war, Stand Watie participated in negotiations for the 1866 Cherokee Reconstruction Treaty. He worked to rebuild tribal assets as well as his own farming business. In 1868, he purchased with his nephew, Elias C. Boudinot, a tobacco factory in Missouri and moved it to the Indian Territory, where they produced leaf, pipe, and chewing tobacco, as well as snuff. By the terms of the treaty, the Cherokees were exempt from federal taxes, but rival dealers in Arkansas, Missouri, and Texas complained that the Indians were underselling them and ruining their businesses. Watie and Boudinot were arrested and the case taken to federal district court and eventually to the Supreme Court. A landmark decision in the Cherokee Tobacco Case of 1870 ruled that the Cherokees were subject to federal revenue laws, negating the special exemption granted four years earlier by the Cherokee Reconstruction Treaty. The decision had implications for Indian policy at large, deemphasizing the treaty-making process. In 1871, an act of Congress officially impeded further treaties with Indian tribes. Indian policy was henceforth to be settled by acts of Congress or executive order.

Stand Watie later served as an informant for HENRY ROWE SCHOOLCRAFT concerning Cherokee customs. In the course of his marriage to Betsy Bell, he had five children.

WAYNE, ANTHONY ("Mad" Anthony).
(1745–1796). Army officer in the American Revolution and Little Turtle's War; government official.

Born of a prominent country family in Chester County, Pennsylvania, Anthony Wayne attended the Philadelphia Academy and subsequently became a surveyor for new settlements on the frontier. In 1765–67, he conducted surveys for a company partly owned by BENJAMIN FRANKLIN that was developing a short-lived settlement in Nova Scotia. After 1768, Wayne operated his family farming business in Pennsylvania and became active in the Pennsylvania colonial assembly. He was an ardent supporter of independence from Great Britain.

In June 1776, Wayne was appointed a colonel in the Continental army. He joined General JOHN SULLIVAN in his retreat from Canada in 1776 and commanded Fort Ticonderoga on New York's Lake Champlain the following year. In 1777, he was made a brigadier general and took part in major battles in Pennsylvania and New Jersey, including the engagements at the Brandywine and at Monmouth Courthouse. In June 1779, he captured the British position on the Hudson River at Stony Point, New York, and, the next year, delayed British occupation of West Point after General Benedict Arnold's defection. In 1781, he participated in the Yorktown Campaign, and in the summer and fall of 1782, he was in the South, where he accepted the surrender of British forces at Savannah. Wayne also patrolled the Georgia frontier and pacified the Cherokee and Creek tribes.

Wayne returned to farming in Pennsylvania and also in Georgia, where he had been granted lands by the Continental Congress in recognition of his military service. By 1792, he had become active in both Pennsylvania and Georgia politics, but was called back to the service at the request of President GEORGE WASHINGTON after generals JOSIAH HARMAR and ARTHUR ST. CLAIR had suffered defeats at the hands of the Miamis and allied tribes of the Old Northwest under LITTLE TURTLE.

In April 1792, Wayne was appointed a major general. He mounted a force of 3,000 regulars at Pittsburgh and moved them to a camp outside Fort Washington (present-day Cincinnati). After having trained them and having sent out numerous scouting parties, he launched an expedition into northern Ohio. His strategy called for the building of a series of forts in a line extending north from Fort Washington, including Fort Greenville and Fort Recovery. The latter, located near the site of St. Clair's defeat at the headwaters of the Wabash River, was the scene of a sudden Indian attack on June 30, 1794. Soon after the Indians' failure to take this post, Little Turtle withdrew from the war, regarding Wayne as too formidable an enemy for his warriors to face without military support from the British.

Wayne continued his advance into Indian country on the Maumee River and built Fort Defiance. At a place where trees had been felled by a tornado, he surprised the Indians and won a decisive victory in what came to be known as the Battle of Fallen Timbers, on August 20, 1794. The Indians were driven back to Fort Miami, where the British refused to provide them protection or military support. Wayne and his forces next laid waste to the Indians' lands, destroying crops, villages, and fields—more than 5,000 acres. In October 1794, Wayne established Fort Wayne in what is now Indiana.

In August 1795, Wayne helped negotiate the Treaty of Fort Greenville, under which the Indians relinquished their claims to lands comprising the present states of Ohio and Indiana. The Fort Greenville Treaty was significantly different from the earlier Fort Stanwix Treaty of 1784, in that it openly recognized the territorial rights of the Ohio Valley tribes, providing compensation for land cessions as an alternative to possession by right of military conquest.

In 1795–96, Wayne took possession of the forts in the Great Lakes region that the British had agreed to relinquish under the terms of the Jay Treaty of 1794. While completing this mission, he died in present-day Erie, Pennsylvania. His daring military tactics in the American Revolution earned him a reputation as "Mad" Anthony Wayne. (See also LITTLE TURTLE.)

WEATHERFORD, WILLIAM (Lamochattee, Lumhe Chati, Red Eagle). *Mixed Creek.*

(ca. 1780–1824). Leader of the Red Sticks in the Creek War of 1813–14. Nephew of ALEXANDER McGILLIVRAY.

William Weatherford, or Red Eagle, was born and raised among the Creeks near the forks of the Alabama River in what is now Alabama. His parentage is speculative. It is thought he was the son of a Scottish trader by the name of Charles Weatherford and Alexander McGillivray's half-sister, Tait. As the story goes, Charles Weatherford gave his two sons William and John the choice between the Indian and white way of life. William chose the former and John, whose later career is undocumented, the latter.

In October 1811, during one of his many trips south, TECUMSEH appeared before a conference of some 5,000 Creeks and Indians of other tribes along the Tallapoosa River, advocating a confederation of tribes and a military alliance in order to achieve independence from the United States. His message was lost on the Creek White Sticks, the people of peace, most of them from the Lower Creek villages; it reached many of the young Red Sticks, the traditional warriors, the majority from the Upper towns. One of these was William Weatherford.

An incident that further polarized the Creek factions involved a Creek by the name of LITTLE WARRIOR, who had led a band of Red Sticks against the Americans in the War of 1812 and was present at the Raisin River massacre of Kentuckians. On the return trip from Canada after the war, his men killed some settlers along the Ohio River. The White Stick faction under BIG WARRIOR arrested and executed him. Soon afterward, PETER McQUEEN led a force of Red Sticks to Pensacola on the Gulf of Mexico, where the Spanish supplied them with firearms. This group raided a party of settlers at Burnt Corn Creek in July 1813.

The most famous incident of the Creek War occurred the following month on August 30, 1813. Weatherford led a force of about 1,000 Red Sticks against Fort Mims on the confluence of the Alabama and Tombigbee rivers in present-day Alabama. Black slaves reported to the commanding officer of the garrison, Major Daniel Beasley, that Indians were crawling toward the fort in high grass. Beasley ignored the warning and even left the outer gate opened. In the first assault, Beasley himself was killed. The settlers took cover behind the inner walls and held the warriors at bay for several hours. Yet flame-tipped arrows enabled the Indians to break through the defenses. Once inside Fort Mims, they killed about 500 settlers. Only 36 whites escaped. The Red Sticks freed the blacks, however.

Federal and state troops were mobilized. Tennessee raised a militia of some 3,500, including Cherokee auxiliaries under JOHN ROSS, MAJOR RIDGE, SEQUOYAH, JOHN LOWRY, JUNALUSKA, and WHITE PATH. A Chickasaw force was headed by WILLIAM COLBERT; Choctaws, by PUSHMATAHA and MUSHALATUBBEE; and Yuchis, by TIMPOOCHEE BARNARD. The principal leaders of the Creek White Sticks who fought against the Red Sticks were Big Warrior and WILLIAM McINTOSH. Although still recovering from wounds sustained in a duel, General ANDREW JACKSON—"Sharp Knife" to the Indians— was given the command. DAVY CROCKETT was one of his soldiers. There were many more engagements in the so-called Thirty Battles. In one of the most important, on November 5, 1813, Jackson sent an advance detachment under Colonel John Coffee to draw the Red Sticks into a trap at Tallasahatchee. The Indians rushed into a semicircle and lost almost 200 braves. On November 9, Jackson's force relieved the White Stick village of Talladega, where Weatherford led the siege. Jackson again successfully used the decoy tactic killing nearly 300. In December, Weatherford managed to escape white troops at his village of Econochaca on the Alabama River, by leaping off a bluff into a river while mounted on his horse. In January 1814, there were two indecisive battles at Emuckfaw and Enotachopco creeks.

During the winter months, many of the soldiers deserted from Fort Strother in the heart of Creek territory, or departed legally as their short-term enlistments expired. Weatherford was able to regroup his warriors. Peter McQueen, MENEWA, OPOTHLEYAHOLO, JOSIAH FRANCIS, and the Shawnee SAVANNAH JACK fought as Red Sticks. Jackson's force was reinforced by 600 regulars from the 39th Infantry.

The final battle took place at the Horseshoe Bend of the Tallapoosa on March 27, 1814. There, Jackson's men moved into position around the Red Sticks' barricades, took away their canoes and attacked. The Indians defended their position from behind zigzag double-long barricades they had built on a peninsula. Fighting lasted all day. The logs repelled artillery fire. Pro-American Cherokee warriors provided a diversion by swimming the river and attacking from the rear. In a frontal assault, the soldiers eventually managed to set the barricades on fire. By the end of the day, about 750 or 900 Red Sticks lay dead, most on the peninsula, but many also in the river, having been picked off by sharpshooters as they tried to escape. Weatherford survived, however, because he had departed before the attack to inspect other fortifications, leaving his lieutenant Menewa in command.

Weatherford surrendered several days later, walking into Jackson's camp at Fort Toulouse near present-day Montgomery and identifying himself. He expected to be executed but was pardoned by Jackson. Jackson's reasons are unknown: It may have been out of magnanimity and respect for Weatherford's courage and leadership qualities, political motives (because Weatherford agreed to work for peace), or simply out of pride (legend has it that Jackson dared Weatherford to try to fight again).

In subsequent negotiations, Jackson forced Creek leaders to sign the Treaty of Fort Jackson of August 1814, which took away 23 million acres of land from both the militant Red Sticks and the peaceful White Sticks. Because of these harsh terms, many of the Creeks settled among the Seminoles in Florida and participated in the First Seminole War of 1817–18.

Weatherford settled with his large family on a farm near Little River in southern Alabama. He kept his word and henceforth worked for peace between Creeks and whites.

WEAVER, PAULINO (Pauline Weaver). *Mixed Cherokee. (fl. mid–1800s).* Trader.

Paulino Weaver, a fur trader, operated out of Taos, New Mexico, in the 1820s–30s. In 1832, he explored the Casa Grande Mountains of what is now central Arizona. He later settled in southern California, where he became a friend of the Cahuilla JUAN ANTONIO, who, largely because of Weaver's efforts, helped suppress the uprising of 1851–52 under the Cupeno ANTONIO GARRA.

WEAWEA (Old Weawea, Weawa, Weahwewa, Weahwewa, Weahweewah). *Northern Paiute. (fl. 1860s).* Leader in the Snake War of 1866–68 in Oregon and Idaho.

Weawea continued to lead the Walpapi and Yahuskin Northern Paiute bands in the Snake War after the death of PAULINA in January 1867. He surrendered to then-Colonel GEORGE CROOK in June 1868. His people remained in the vicinity of Ft. Harney, Oregon. Old Weawea became one of three head chiefs at the Malheur Agency, founded in 1872, along with EGAN and Wattabelly. (See also PAULINA.)

WEBBER, JOHN E. *(1751–1793).* Artist.

An established artist in 18th-century England, John Webber was a member of Captain JAMES COOK's 1778 expedition to the Pacific Northwest. During the course of the four-year expedition, he sketched scenes of present-day Washington and Oregon that provided illustrations for Cook's official report of the voyage. These studies also served as the basis for the artist's series of paintings and hand-colored etchings of this region, among the earliest glimpses of Northwest Coast Indian life.

WEISER, CONRAD. *(1696–1760).* Colonial Indian agent; interpreter.

Originally from Germany, Conrad Weiser settled with his family on the frontier of southeastern New York in 1710, at Livingston Manor, and, in 1714, at Schoharie. He lived among the Mohawk band of Chief Quagnant, becoming familiar with Iroquois customs and learning the Mohawk language. In 1729, he migrated down the Susquehanna River to Tulpehocken in western Pennsylvania.

Conrad Weiser's proficiency in Iroquoian dialects and ability as a diplomat led him to play a vital role in tribal negotiations with colonial leaders of Pennsylvania, Maryland, and Virginia. In 1731, he became the official interpreter of Pennsylvania to the Indians. He served as interpreter and negotiator in 1737 during the Walking Purchase, in which Pennsylvania Quaker leader JAMES LOGAN acquired a vast tract of land from the Delawares under LAPPAWINZE. Also in 1737, Weiser, with the Oneida SHIKELLAMY, journeyed up the West Branch of the Susquehanna River, from Philadelphia to the Iroquois council at Onondaga, New York. His journal of this voyage describes ancient earthen mounds, similar to those later discovered in Ohio. He was a regular visitor at Iroquois councils, acting as an interpreter in negotiations between the Iroquois and their tributary tribes, including the Susquehannocks and Shawnees.

In 1739, Weiser lived for a time at the Seventh-Day Baptist monastic community of Ephrata, founded by Johann Conrad Beissel. Coming from a strict religious family, he accompanied missionaries on preaching expeditions among the Indians, including the Moravian DAVID ZEISBERGER. Weiser later became a Lutheran.

In 1741, Weiser was appointed Indian agent for Pennsylvania. In 1742, with the Onondaga CANASATEGO, he negotiated an alliance between the Iroquois League and Pennsylvania officials. He also provided his skills as an Indian diplomat and interpreter at the Treaty of Lancaster in 1744, which established peaceful relations with the Indians of the western Pennsylvania frontier. With the aid of WILLIAM JOHNSON's assistant GEORGE CROGHAN, Weiser entered into the Treaty of Logstown with the Ohio country tribes in 1748, an agreement which opened the region's Indian trade to Pennsylvania interests.

Although commissioned a colonel in the Pennsylvania militia in 1755 in the early stages of the French and Indian War, Weiser's declining health prevented him from taking an active role in that conflict, but he did aid in the distribution of gifts used to recruit Indian warriors to fight the French. In 1760, Weiser contracted cholera and died at his home in Reading, Pennsylvania.

WELSH, HERBERT. *(1851–1941).* Reformer; philanthropist. Nephew of WILLIAM WELSH.

Herbert Welsh, grandson of wealthy Philadelphia merchant and statesman John Welsh, attended the University of Pennsylvania. After his return to Philadelphia in 1873 from his European art training, he devoted himself to philanthropic causes and municipal reform.

In 1882, Welsh and Henry S. Pancoast, at the invitation of Episcopal bishop William Hare, made a visit to the agencies to the Sioux Indians of the Dakotas. That same year, they established the Indian Rights Association (IRA).

Under Welsh's direction as executive secretary, the IRA, based in Philadelphia, came to have chapters throughout the United States, sending its agents to reservations to report on conditions. It also worked against corruption and mismanagement in the Bureau of Indian Affairs (BIA) through the application of civil service reform measures. Like his uncle William Welsh, Herbert supported the return of the BIA to the control of the War Department from the Interior Department in order to control corruption. CHARLES PAINTER was the organization's Washington lobbyist. The IRA published numerous pamphlets on Indian issues.

Welsh was a prominent speaker at the Lake Mohonk Conferences sponsored by ALBERT SMILEY. He was a strong supporter of the General Allotment Act (the DAWES Severalty Act) of 1887 and believed the solution to the problems facing the Indians to be their assimilation into mainstream American life.

After 1904, because of failing health, Welsh gave up the day-to-day IRA responsibilities to his former chief clerk Matthew Sniffen, with Samuel Brosius as the Washington lobbyist. Welsh himself continued his efforts on behalf of Indian rights in a consulting role, with the title of president.

WELSH, WILLIAM. *(1810–1879).* Reformer; philanthropist. Uncle of HERBERT WELSH.

William Welsh, born in Philadelphia, became a prominent merchant and philanthropist of that city. Among other posts, he served as director of Girard College and was the owner of several publications, including the *Philadelphia Gazette.* He also became a leading figure in the cause for Indian rights, supporting the work of Episcopalian missionaries. With Bishop HENRY B. WHIPPLE and Reverend Samuel Dutton Hinman, he published *Taopi and His Friends, or Indians' Wrongs and Rights* (1869).

In 1869, Welsh was appointed by President ULYSSES S. GRANT as the first chairman of the Board of Indian Commissioners. But, following a dispute with ELY PARKER, Grant's commissioner of Indian Affairs, over the responsibilities of the board, Welsh resigned almost immediately.

During the remainder of Grant's administration, Welsh was an outspoken critic of the Indian Bureau and the subsequent commissioners of Indian Affairs, Edward P. Smith and John Q. Smith, accusing federal officials of corruption and profiteering. He was one of the few reformers of his day who supported the proposed return of the Bureau of Indian Affairs from the Department of the Interior to the War Department in order to prevent governmental misconduct, a proposal never realized. CARL SCHURZ, who was secretary of the Interior under President Rutherford Hayes, later offered Welsh the position of commissioner of Indian Affairs, but Welsh declined.

Welsh's nephew Herbert Welsh was the founder of the Indian Rights Association.

WETAMOO (Queen Wetamoo, Wetamou, Weetamou, Wetamoe, Weetamoe, Wetemoo, Weetamoo, Weetammo, Weetamore, "sweetheart"; Namumpam, Tatatanum, Tatapanum; Squaw Sachem of Pocasset). *Wampanoag. (ca. 1650–1676).* Leader in King Philip's War of 1675–76. Wife of ALEXANDER; wife of QUINNAPIN; sister-in-law of King PHILIP.

Wetamoo grew up in the vicinity of Tiverton, Rhode Island, close to the Plymouth Colony border. She was the daughter of a sachem of the Wampanog Confederacy, possibly CORBITANT. After the death of her first husband, Winnepurket, she married Alexander, who succeeded MASSASOIT as grand sachem of the confederacy. When her husband died, probably from disease in 1662, after having been summoned before colonial authorities, Wetamoo claimed he had been poisoned. She was King Philip's sister-in-law through Alexander as well as through her sister Wootonekanuske, one of his wives.

Wetamoo became sachem of the Pocasset band of Wampanoags and a sagamore in the confederacy, probably because her father left no son. After Alexander's death, she married Quequequananachet, then Petononowit. When the latter sided with the colonists at the start of King Philip's War in 1675, she left him. Her final husband was Quinnapin, a Narraganset, through whom she expanded her political base to that tribe.

Wetamoo, like the Narraganset woman leader MAGNUS, provided military support to King Philip, commanding her braves in battle. The first major encounter between colonial forces and the insurgents took place in Pocasset Swamp near Wetamoo's village in July 1675. When Philip headed north to Nipmuc country, Wetamoo took refuge among the Narragansets. Their leader, CANONCHET, refused to turn her over to authorities in the summer of 1675, and soldiers attacked his people, leading to the Narragansets' full-scale involvement in the uprising.

During the Great Swamp Fight of December 1675 in Narraganset territory in southern Rhode Island, Wetamoo made brushes of twigs and tied them on her men as camouflage. She also helped build canoes and rafts for escape.

On August 6, 1676, English forces surrounded her camp in Massachusetts. She headed down the Taunton River by canoe. The soldiers fired at it, causing it to sink. Wetamoo then tried to swim ashore, but drowned in the strong current.

The colonists cut off her head and displayed it on a pole at Taunton. Philip, her brother-in-law, was killed the same month. His head was also displayed publicly.

MARY ROWLANDSON, an English captive during the war, bought and freed by Quinnapin, later wrote extensively about Wetamoo, describing her stature among her people and her elaborate clothing and jewelry. (See also PHILIP.)

WHEELER, GEORGE MONTAGUE.
(1842–1905). Explorer; soldier.

Born in Hopkinton, Massachusetts, George Wheeler attended West Point, graduating just after the Civil War. His first assignment was as engineer and surveyor in the San Francisco Bay region of California. He also carried out surveys in Nevada and Utah.

Wheeler hoped to create an extensive collection of topographical maps for military purposes, and, in 1871, as only a lieutenant, he was given command of the U.S. Geographical Surveys West of the 100th Meridian by the War Department. Meanwhile, the civilian geologist CLARENCE KING headed the War Department's U.S. Geological Exploration of the 40th Parallel. Wheeler had the additional secret assignment of military reconnaissance of the Apaches and Paiutes for General GEORGE CROOK's Tonto Basin Campaign. The expedition, mostly in Arizona and Nevada, used Mojave guides. TIMOTHY O'SULLIVAN, who had earlier worked under King, took 700 photographs while with Wheeler, many of Indians.

In 1879, the Wheeler Survey was combined with the King Survey—along with Interior Department surveys under FERDINAND V. HAYDEN and JOHN WESLEY POWELL—into the United States Geological Survey. Wheeler, now a captain, and other army engineers had no function in the reorganization. With failing health, he was placed on disability leave in 1880–84, and retired in 1888.

WHEELOCK, ELEAZAR. *(1711–1779).*
Missionary; educator.

Eleazar Wheelock, a native of Windham, Connecticut, graduated from Yale in 1733. Two years later, he became the pastor of the Congregational church in Lebanon, Connecticut.

Starting about 1743, Wheelock began to tutor Indians in his church-run Moor's Indian Charity School. His first Indian student was the Mohegan youth SAMSON OCCUM. Wheelock developed the academy into a boarding school for training Indians to become missionaries to their own people. His students included Algonquians from New England, as well as Iroquois from New York who had been recommended by WILLIAM JOHNSON, such as JOSEPH BRANT.

In 1765–66, Wheelock's former student Samson Occum, who had been ministering to the Oneidas of western New York, traveled to England and there succeeded in obtaining an endowment for Wheelock to establish a new school for Indian education.

In 1768, Johnson blocked Wheelock's recruitment of students among the Iroquois through provisions of the 1768 Fort Stanwix Treaty. Johnson felt Wheelock may have been using his missionary influence as a way to acquire lands in the Iroquois country. Enrollment had also declined because of his pupils' unwillingness to endure Wheelock's rigorous discipline. That same year, Wheelock closed the school.

In 1769, Wheelock received a charter for the creation of a new college and, the following year, established Dartmouth College in Hanover, New Hampshire. The school's enrollment originally included more than 40 Indians, including some Iroquois recruited from Canada, but to Occum's disappointment, Dartmouth's Indian enrollment only was a small percentage of the school's student population. Wheelock became the first president at Dartmouth, serving in that capacity until his death in 1779. Following the appointment of his son, John Wheelock, as Dartmouth's second president that same year, the college ceased to stress the education of Indians. (See also OCCUM, SAMSON.)

WHIPPLE, HENRY BENJAMIN (Straight Tongue). *(1822–1901).* Reformer; missionary.

Henry B. Whipple was born in Adams, New York, and was educated at local Presbyterian schools, then Oberlin College in Ohio. After a period of work in his father's mercantile business, then as inspector of schools, and then in the military, he studied to be an Episcopal clergyman and was ordained in 1850. Elected as the first Episcopal bishop of Minnesota in 1859, Whipple worked with the Chippewas of the White Earth Reservation, as well as with the Santee Sioux of Minnesota. They came to trust him and dubbed him Straight Tongue.

Whipple advocated restrictions on the sale of liquor to Indians and complained that corruption and mismanagement in federal Indian policy inevitably led to armed conflict. He was an early advocate of the distribution of reservation lands to Indians as private landholders for the purposes of assimilation. It was his further contention that the rights of reservation Indians could only be insured if they were afforded equal protection under the laws of the state in which their lands were situated.

With the outbreak of the Minnesota Uprising of Santee Sioux under LITTLE CROW in 1862–63, Whipple petitioned President ABRAHAM LINCOLN to establish a lasting accord with the region's Indians. He proposed a complete reform of the Indian Bureau and the elimination of the appointment of Indian agents through political patronage.

Whipple was also one of the earliest reform activists to support church supervision of the Indian agent selection process. Although he strongly supported the efforts of the Peace Policy through the early 1870s, he petitioned President ULYSSES S. GRANT on several occasions concerning the need for further reform and a halt to white encroachment on Indian lands in violation of earlier treaties.

During the Rutherford Hayes presidency, Whipple campaigned against the transfer of the Indian Bureau to the War Department, and for the establishment of a cabinet leval post exclusively for the management of Indian policy. He remained a respected voice on Indian issues through six more administrations.

WHITE ANTELOPE. *Southern Cheyenne.*
(1796–1864). Dog Soldier; later, peace advocate.

White Antehope was a noted warrior, fighting Comanches and Kiowas in the 1830s along with YELLOW WOLF. Because of his status in the military society know as the Dog Soldiers, younger warriors listened to his advice to make peace with these tribes in 1840.

During the period of first extensive Cheyenne and white contacts, White Antelope was one of the few Dog Soldiers to counsel peace. He was present at the peace council at Fort Laramie, Wyoming, in 1851, and was part of a subsequent Cheyenne delegation, along with ALIGHTS-ON-THE-CLOUD, to visit Washington, D.C., and meet with President Millard Filmore.

White Antelope was among the Cheyennes attacked by troops under Colonel EDWIN SUMNER at Solomon Fork in western Kansas in July 1857. Three months later, at BENT's Fort in Colorado, White Antelope claimed that Sumner had attacked the wrong band. In 1861, the Cheyenne chief signed the Treaty of Fort Wise.

In 1864, as the oldest of the band leaders, White Antelope was spokesman for the Southern Cheyennes at the Camp Weld Council near Denver, Colorado, with Governor JOHN EVANS, Colonel JOHN CHIVINGTON, and Indian agent EDWARD WYNKOOP. He was with BLACK KETTLE at Sand Creek and, when Chivington's troops approached,

walked out to meet them unarmed. He reportedly held up his hands and yelled to the soldiers, "Stop! Stop!," then folded his arms and sang a death song until shot down. (See also BLACK KETTLE.)

WHITE BEAR. See SATANTA.

WHITE BIRD (Penpenhihi, Peopeo Hihhih, Peopeo Kiskiok Hihih, "white goose"). *Nez Perce.* *(ca. 1807–ca. 1882).* Medicine man; leader in the Nez Perce War of 1877.

White Bird, a shaman and chief, was one of the Nontreaty Nez Perces along with Old JOSEPH, who refused to sign the Treaty of 1863 and move to the Lapwai Reservation in Idaho. He originally advised peace with white settlers, as did Chief JOSEPH (Young Joseph), but when tensions mounted in 1877, White Bird joined TOOHOOLHOOLZOTE and OLLIKUT in calling for war.

At the Battle of Big Hole Valley, Montana, on August 9, against troops under Colonel JOHN GIBBON, White Bird and his warriors, famous for their marksmanship, played a major part in extricating the Nez Perces.

By the end of the final engagement at Bear Paw, which had started on September 30 and turned into a six-day siege, White Bird and Joseph were the only surviving chiefs. The final night, while surrender arrangements were being made, White Bird, YELLOW WOLF, and others slipped through the ring of soldiers and escaped to Canada, where they joined SITTING BULL.

Even after Sitting Bull had returned to the United States, White Bird chose to remain in exile. He was killed by an Indian who was angry because the medicine man had failed to save the life of his two sick sons. (See also Young JOSEPH.)

WHITE CLOUD (Wabokieshek, Wabokieshiek, Waupeshek; Winnebago Prophet, The Prophet).
Winnebago. (ca. 1794–ca. 1841). Medicine man; prophet; leader in the Black Hawk War of 1832.

White Cloud's home, known as Prophet's Village (present-day Prophetstown, Illinois), was located on the Rock River about 35 miles from its junction with the Mississippi. During the Winnebago Uprising of 1827, White Cloud kept his followers at peace. Yet, by the time of the Black Hawk War five years later, he was advocating rebellion.

As the DELAWARE PROPHET had done in PONTIAC's Rebellion of 1763 and TENSKWATAWA (the Shawnee Prophet) in TECUMSEH's Rebellion of 1809–11, White Cloud made prophesies concerning an Indian revolt. He told BLACK HAWK that he would be aided in his struggle with whites for his village of Saukenuk (present-day Rock Island) by the Great Spirit and by an army of warriors. With some Sac ancestry,

White Cloud had followers among that tribe as well as the Winnebagos. The Sac chief NEAPOPE was reportedly under White Cloud's influence. But pro-peace Winnebagos—such band leaders as GOOD THUNDER, NAWKAW, SHICKSHACK, and YELLOW THUNDER—countered White Cloud's militancy, dissuading most tribal members from joining the uprising.

The Prophet stayed with Black Hawk throughout the conflict, surrendering with him at Prairie du Chien, Wisconsin, on August 27. He was imprisoned with Black Hawk and later met President ANDREW JACKSON with him. On being released, White Cloud lived among the Sacs in Iowa until they were relocated to Kansas, then rejoined the Winnebagos, among whom he died in obscurity. (See also BLACK HAWK.)

WHITE EAGLE. *Ponca. (fl. 1870s–1880s).* Principal chief of Poncas in the Indian Territory.

White Eagle, STANDING BEAR, and other band leaders were forced to relocate their people from Nebraska to the Indian Territory in 1876. When Standing Bear returned north, White Eagle became the principal leader of those Poncas who stayed behind. Standing Bear's story, which received national attention, and the work of the Omaha SUSETTE LA FLESCHE and the journalist THOMAS HENRY TIBBLES, helped publicize the plight of the Poncas in both Nebraska and the Indian Territory. In 1880, White Eagle reported to a Congressional investigating committee that conditions were gradually improving and that he and his followers would stay in their new homeland. There are currently Poncas living in both Nebraska and Oklahoma. (See also STANDING BEAR.)

WHITE, EUGENE ELLIOT. *(1854–1908).* Indian agent.

Eugene White studied law and became a district court judge in his native Arkansas, then went on to practice as an attorney in the federal courts of Texas and the Indian Territory. With his brother, he also helped found an Arkansas newspaper, *The Banner*. In 1885, through his friend the congressman Thomas Chipman McRae, White was appointed as a special Indian agent.

After time among the North Carolina Cherokees, White was sent by the Bureau of Indian Affairs to Kansas to investigate a fraudulent real estate transaction that threatened to cheat the Black Bob Band of Shawnees out of their lands. He concluded that the sale of the lands was unfair and unlawful; his recommendation resulted in the nullification of the transaction by the federal government and the restoration of the Shawnee holdings.

In 1886, White was sent to the Ouray and Uintah reservations in Utah because of reports of harassment by whites and the incompetence and corruption of agents. He held councils with Ute leaders and was able to allay their concerns over the presence of federal troops sent to the area to disperse whites. White also dismissed the agents in question and fulfilled their duties until suitable replacements arrived.

While stationed among the Comanches and Kiowas in the Indian Territory, White became a friend of QUANAH PARKER and worked to stem the influx of white encroachers on reservation lands attracted by the oil rush.

In 1893, White's autobiographical *Service on the Indian Reservations*, also known as *Experiences of a Special Indian Agent*, was published. White resigned from the Indian service in 1900, resuming his law practice in Sulphur, Oklahoma.

WHITE EYES (Koquethagechton, Koguethagechton, Kuckquetackton). *Delaware. (ca. 1730–1778).* Chief of the Ohio Delawares; ally of Patriots in the American Revolution.

After having served his band as chief counselor, White Eyes was chosen as chief in 1776. He encouraged his people to maintain a position of neutrality in the American Revolution. The Delaware war chief HOPOCAN sided with the British, however. White Eyes, to prove his bravery, agreed to lead his warriors in battle, but in support of the Patriots. He told his people he would seek to die in battle so that he would not witness the destruction of the Delawares through involvement in the white conflict.

In September 1778, White Eyes signed the Treaty of Fort Pitt, the first treaty between Indians and the new United States government. It promised the eventual formation of a Delaware state with congressional representation.

That November, while acting as guide for General Lachlin McIntosh's expedition against Fort Sandusky, Ohio, White Eyes was shot by American soldiers. The reasons for the shooting are not known. Perhaps White Eyes had forced the incident rather than fight fellow Delawares at Sandusky. To prevent White Eyes's followers from changing sides, the soldiers at first reported that he had died of smallpox, which confused the historical record.

WHITE HAIR (White Hairs, Cheveux Blancs; Cahaga Tonga, Teshushimga, Teshuminga, Gredamanse; Pawhuska, Pahuska, Pauhuska, Pahhueska, Paw-hiu-skah). *Osage. (d. 1808).* Principal chief of the Big Osages.

The first White Hair was probably born at White Hair's Village on the Little Osage River in present-day Missouri. He reportedly received the name by which he was known to whites when he snatched the wig of

General ARTHUR ST. CLAIR in 1791 during LITTLE TURTLE's War and wore it thereafter.

White Hair became a friend of JEAN PIERRE CHOUTEAU and supported his trading endeavors with the Osages. In 1804, the two traveled to Washington, D.C., where White Hair met President THOMAS JEFFERSON. By 1806, at the time ZEBULON PIKE explored what is now western Missouri, White Hair was principal chief of the division of the tribe known as the Big (or Great) Osages. (The Little Osages had settled to the north along the Missouri River during the 1700s for a time before resettling near their kinsmen along the Osage River. Another group broke off from the Big Osages in the early 1800s and settled along the Arkansas River in what is now northeastern Oklahoma under CLERMONT.)

White Hair was one of the signers of the Treaty of Fort Clark (or Fort Osage), negotiated in 1808 by WILLIAM CLARK, in which the Osages ceded half of Missouri and part of Arkansas in exchange for small annuities, houses, tools, the use of a blacksmith shop and mill, and the cancellation of debts. The Clark treaty was never ratified; a similar one renegotiated by Chouteau took effect the same year, however.

A second White Hair, perhaps his son, moved the band from the Little Osage River west to the Neosho sometime before 1822. He died 10 years later. A third White Hair, probably also a relative, was painted by GEORGE CATLIN.

WHITE HORSE. *Southern Cheyenne.*
(fl. 1860s–1870s). Leader of the Dog Soldiers.

White Horse, like BULL BEAR and TALL BULL, was a chief of the militant Dog Soldiers during the 1850s and 1860s. As such, he participated in the Cheyenne-Arapaho (or Colorado) War of 1864–65. Although he signed the Medicine Lodge Treaty of 1867, he remained pro-war, fighting in the Battle of Pawnee Fork in 1867 and the Battle of BEECHER's Island in 1868, where ROMAN NOSE, another Cheyenne militant, was killed. Tall Bull was killed the next year at Summit Springs, and White Horse took his band north, joining the Northern Cheyennes, but soon returned to the Indian Territory. In 1873, White Horse was part of the Cheyenne delegation to Washington, D.C., including LITTLE ROBE and STONE CALF. Despite his attempts to control them, warriors from his band joined the Comanche and Kiowa militants under QUANAH PARKER and LONE WOLF during the Red River War, fighting in the Battle of Palo Duro Canyon in September 1874.

WHITE, JOHN. *(fl. 1580s–1590s).* Artist; governor of Roanoke Colony.

In 1585–86, John White was part of WALTER RALEIGH's expedition to Roanoke Island, headed by Richard Grenville, and painted watercolors of Indians and wildlife, among the earliest European views of North America, 20 years after those of Frenchman JACQUES LE MOYNE. The Indians represented were Secotans under Chief ENSENORE. In addition to his paintings, White brought potatoes back with him, unknown in Europe at the time.

White headed Raleigh's second attempt at a permanent colony in 1587 as governor. His married daughter accompanied him and gave birth to Virginia Dare, the first English child born in the Americas. White returned to England that same year to request additional supplies. Unable to raise funds, he was away three years. When he finally returned to Roanoke in 1590, the colonists, including his daughter and granddaughter, had disappeared, leaving the word "Croatan" carved on a wooden post as the only clue.

Theodore de Bry published 23 of White's watercolors in *A Brief and True Report of the New Found Land of Virginia* (1590). In 1593, White was living in Ireland.

WHITE-MAN-RUNS-HIM (Miastashedekaroos, Mahrstahsheedahkuroosh, Mars-che-coodo, Batsida Karoosh). *Crow. (ca. 1855–1925).* Army scout during the Sioux Wars; research informant.

White-Man-Runs-Him was the son of a Crow warrior of the same name who had been taunted and forced to run by a white man with a gun. As was the case with many other Crows, who were traditional enemies of the Sioux, he served with the army as a scout, a policy encouraged by the Crow chief PLENTY COUPS. He became chief Indian scout in Colonel GEORGE ARMSTRONG CUSTER's 7th Cavalry and was present at Little Bighorn in June 1876. After having spotted the Sioux encampment and reporting it to Custer, he and the other Indian scouts were sent to the rear, which enabled their escape. He later became an informant on the battle, as did CURLY.

WHITE PATH (Nunnatsunega). *Cherokee.*
(1763–1835). Leader of White Path's Rebellion of 1827.

White Path was probably born in the vicinity of Turniptown near present-day Ellijay in northern Georgia. During the American Revolution, he participated in raids on American settlements under DRAGGING CANOE. In the Creek War of 1813–14, however, he sided with Americans against Creek Red Sticks led by WILLIAM WEATHERFORD.

White Path operated a small farm, became a headman at Turniptown, and served on the Cherokee National Council. In November 1825, when he took a stand against his people's rapid acculturation, as indicated by the great number of laws tribal leaders were imposing on the behavior of the people, and the overbearing

White-Man-Runs-Him. Photo by Edward Curtis. *Courtesy of National Archives of Canada/C-34801*

presence of missionaries among them, he was disgracefully expelled from his seat on the council.

In February 1827, White Path and other conservative full-bloods formed a rebel council at Ellijay to oppose the drafting of the Cherokee Constitution as led by JOHN ROSS. By June 1827, White Path's Rebellion had been defused, with certain accommodations by the mixed-bloods in the constitution drafted on July 26, 1827. He was reelected to the National Council on August 28 of that year. (See also ROSS, JOHN.)

WHITE PLUME. See POCATELLO.

WHITE SHIELD (Wopohwats, "white shield owner"). *Southern Cheyenne. (ca. 1833–1883).* Proponent of peace. Nephew of BLACK KETTLE.

White Shield was born along the upper branch of the North Platte River in what is now Wyoming. As a young man, he engaged in warfare on the Great Plains with Pawnees. By the 1860s, however, he was a vocal proponent of peace with whites. In 1870, he was elected to the Cheyenne council of chiefs. The next year, he served as tribal delegate to Washington, D.C., where he met President ULYSSES S. GRANT.

White Shield settled his band permanently near the army cantonment on the North Canadian River in the Indian Territory. He kept his band at peace during the Red River War of 1874–75, when some Cheyennes and Arapahos joined the Comanches and Kiowas in rebellion under QUANAH PARKER and LONE WOLF. After the war, he joined LITTLE ROBE and STONE CALF in opposition to a grass-leasing program to white cattlemen. His son Harvey White Shield (Hishkowits), attended the Carlisle Indian School and became a mission teacher and interpreter.

WHITMAN, MARCUS. *(1802–1847).* Missionary; educator; physician.

A native of Rushville, New York, Marcus Whitman was trained as a physician. In 1832, he received his M.D. degree from the College of Physicians and Surgeons of the Western District of New York, at Fairfield. He practiced medicine in New York and Canada for a number of years.

Whitman was active in the Presbyterian Church, having become a deacon by 1835. That year, he became a missionary to the Indians of the Pacific Northwest for the Boston-based Presbyterian missionary society, the American Board of Commissioners for Foreign Missions.

Also in 1835, Whitman traveled with missionary Samuel Parker to the Indians in what is now Montana and Idaho. He preached to the Flatheads and Nez Perces, then returned East to organize an expedition to establish missions to the Indians of what is now eastern Washington State. He married Narcissa Prentiss, a fellow missionary, in Angelica, New York.

Traveling under the protection of the American Fur Company, and later the Hudson's Bay Company, Whitman, his wife Narcissa, along with missionary HENRY SPALDING and his wife, traveled westward via the Oregon Trail. For part of the journey, THOMAS FITZPATRICK was trail guide. Whitman's pioneering attempt to make the entire journey with wagons failed, but Narcissa Whitman and Eliza Spalding became the first white females to cross the Rocky Mountains. The nearly 4,000-mile trek took six and a half months, with the migrants arriving in September 1836.

Whitman established his mission to the Cayuses near Fort Walla Walla, at Waiilatpu. He instructed tribal members in farming and irrigation techniques and introduced cattle raising; he and his wife also established a school for Indian children. In addition to the Cayuses, the mission had contact with the Nez Perces and Umatillas.

In February 1842, Whitman undertook a winter journey back to Boston in order to convince the mission board to reconsider its decision to close down Waiilatpu and other posts. He was successful in his efforts and returned to the Walla Walla Valley in 1843, bringing with him a large number of white immigrants.

The influx of settlers aroused resentment among the Cayuses. Moreover, the mission attracted many whites coming there for treatment by Whitman, who continued to practice medicine. The Indians were exposed to new white diseases, and, in 1847, the tribe suffered a measles epidemic. Whitman treated both white and Indian children, but the Cayuse children tended to die, while the whites recovered. The Cayuses, led by Chief TILOUKAIKT and the warrior Tomahas, suspected that Whitman was secretly poisoning their children, and, on November 29, 1847, they killed Whitman and his wife along with 12 other whites. The white backlash resulted in a full-blown war between the settlers and the Cayuses that lasted until 1850. (See also TILOUKAIKT.)

WILD BILL HICKOK. See HICKOK, JAMES BUTLER.

WILD CAT (Wildcat, Coacoochee, Coacochee,

Cooacoochee, Coocoochee, Cowacoochee, Coacochu). *Seminole. (ca. 1816–1857).* Leader in the Second

Seminole War of 1835–42; friend to blacks. Nephew of MICANOPY.

Wild Cat was born along the St. Johns River in Florida, the son of Chief Ee-mat-la, who was the brother-in-law of MICANOPY. A twin sister died soon after birth; since Wild Cat was born a twin, however, he was thought to have special gifts.

By the start of the Second Seminole War, the young Wild Cat led a band of Seminoles and blacks, many of them runaway slaves from Georgia. In 1837, after a series of military victories by the Seminoles, his father, Ee-mat-la, was captured by American forces and held at Fort Marion. General THOMAS JESUP sent word to Wild Cat of his father's imprisonment. Wild Cat and a black interpreter came in for a parley in September of that year. He wanted assurances that if the Seminoles agreed to removal to the Indian Territory, their black allies would be allowed to accompany them, but Jesup refused to make such a promise. Wild Cat left to report to his people.

In October 1837, Wild Cat returned carrying a pipe decorated with a white feather of peace from OS-CEOLA, saying that the Seminole war chief would come

for peace talks. At the subsequent parley, Jesup ordered the arrest of all the Seminoles and blacks present. Wild Cat and 18 followers fasted for six days in order to fit through the bars of their cell window and make good their escape. Osceola soon died in prison.

In retaliation for the betrayal, Wild Cat led his warriors in a series of raids. On Christmas Day, 1837, he joined forces with ALLIGATOR and ARPEIKA in the Battle of Lake Okeechobee against troops under Colonel (soon to be general) ZACHARY TAYLOR. Although the army won the ground, the Indians lost fewer men before disappearing into the Everglades. Ee-mat-la died in 1839 during the trip West. The federal government now took the position that blacks would be treated as free Seminoles if they agreed to relocate. Nevertheless, Wild Cat held out for two more years, staying one step ahead of the army in Florida's swamps. In 1841, the year he was listed as the army's most wanted Seminole, he came to a parley at Fort Pierce on the Indian River where he was met by then-Lieutenant WILLIAM T. SHERMAN. His followers war-weary and starving, Wild Cat finally agreed to removal to the Indian Territory.

In 1843, Wild Cat and Alligator returned to the East as tribal delegates to Washington, D.C., asking financial help for their impoverished people. Their request was denied. The situation in the Indian Territory worsened because Creeks were kidnapping his black friends for slave markets. In 1849, Wild Cat and a band of about 100 followers migrated to Texas. They were joined by about 1,000 Kickapoos in their attempt to found a new settlement. The Mexican government eventually granted the Seminoles a tract of land. Wild Cat was commissioned a colonel in the Mexican army and campaigned against Comanches and Apaches. He died in Mexico of smallpox.

WILLIAMS, ELEAZAR. *Mohawk. (1788–1858).* Missionary; creator of plan for a new Iroquois empire; claimant to Bourbon line. Son of TEHORAGWANEGEN.

Eleazar Williams was probably born along Lake George, New York, one of 13 children of Tehoragwanegen (Thomas Williams) and Mary Rice Williams. He grew up at Caughnawaga (Kahnawake) Reserve, outside Montreal, Quebec. In 1800, his father placed him in the care of Nathaniel Ely for Episcopal studies at Long Meadow, Massachsuetts, over the objections of his Catholic mother. Ely died in 1807. With intentions of becoming a missionary to the Indians, Williams continued studies under Reverend Enoch Hale of Westhampton, Masaschusetts, from 1809 to 1812.

In early 1812, Williams began a missionary tour among the Iroquois as an agent of the American Board of Missions. Although he had little luck in converting his people from Catholicism, he gained their respect and he was elected a chief at Caughnawaga. He returned to Massachusetts that July. At the start of the War of 1812, he received an appointment as superintendent general of the North Indian Department in the hope he could keep Canadian Indians from supporting England. Through his Iroquois contacts, he provided valuable information to his superiors, the generals HENRY DEARBORN and Jacob Brown, concerning British troop movements. He was injured at the Battle of Plattsburgh, on September 14, 1814.

From 1817 to 1823, Williams worked among the Oneidas at Oneida Castle, New York. He had some success in converting members of this tribe from their native religion to Protestantism. He procured from them a grant of 100 acres of land and had them sell more property to the state to build a church and school.

In 1820, Williams became involved with the Reverend JEDEDIAH MORSE and other missionaries, the Ogden Land Company and the War Department in a controversial plan to relocate the Iroquois west of Lake Michigan. He wrote a fictitious speech, supposedly given by an Oneida chief in support of the plan, and forged the signatures of council members. Williams hoped to shape a new Iroquois empire with a single leader. He moved to Wisconsin in 1823. His relocation scheme was eventually rejected by most of the Iroquois, led by the Seneca RED JACKET, but many Oneidas, as well as the Mahicans of New Stockbridge under JOHN W. QUINNEY, at that time living among the Oneidas, did move to the Green Bay area in 1832.

Williams's promises to his followers of acquiring large land grants were never realized, nor were his promises to missionary societies of establishing churches and schools, and he lost credibility with both Indians and whites. With his part-Menominee wife, Mary Jourdain, he dropped out of public life.

In 1853, Williams resurfaced with the claim that he was the lost Dauphin of France, Louis XVII, son of Louis XVI and Marie Antoinette, who supposedly had been killed in the French Revolution. Bearing some resemblance to the Bourbon line, Williams claimed that scars on his arms and legs (from childhood play at Caughnawaga and recently enlarged by irritants) resulted from lashings by his jailor during his stay in the Tower of the Temple in Paris, after which he had been secreted to Canada. Williams gained some believers, including the Reverend John Hanson, who wrote a book, *The Lost Prince*, supporting the story, which was soon proved to be false. Williams died five years later.

WILLIAMS, ROGER. *(ca. 1603–1684).*
Colonial leader; clergyman; reformer;
linguist; founder of Rhode Island.

The son of a London merchant tailor, Roger Williams was educated at Pembroke College, Cambridge. Upon his graduation in 1627, he became an Anglican clergyman. Committed to the Puritan religious reform movement of the early 1600s, he emigrated to the Massachusetts Bay Colony in 1631, where he became a minister of the church at the Salem settlement. His outspoken opinion that the Puritans had separated from the main body of the Church of England, and his view that the civil authorities had no jurisdiction over individual religious beliefs, resulted in an open conflict with Puritan leaders. Williams also created controversy when he openly declared that the Massachusetts Bay Colony's charter was invalid. Facing arrest, he left the colony in 1635, traveling south to the Narragansett Bay area.

On land purchased from the Narraganset grand sachem CANONICUS, Williams established the Providence colony in 1636 as a community founded on the principle of religious freedom and toleration. Williams required settlers to purchase their lands from the Indians at fair prices, maintaining that the royal patent for the colonization of New England did not explicitly grant newcomers title to Indian lands. His friendship with Canonicus kept that tribe from joining SASSACUS's Pequots in their uprising against the Connecticut colonists. Williams was also on good terms with MASSASOIT, grand sachem of the Wampanoags.

In 1643, Williams produced a dictionary of Algonquian language and customs, entitled *Key in the Language of America.* He wrote sympathetically of the Indians, citing the advantages of their natural way of life in the New England forests. He respected native culture. In his essay *Christenings Make Not Christians*, he expressed his view that there was no compelling need to convert Indians to Christianity.

Throughout the 1640s and 1650s, Williams journeyed between England and Providence to gain an official patent for his colony. He also had to fend off, in the courts and before Parliament, the claims of Massachusetts and Connecticut on disputed Rhode Island territory. In 1654, the various settlements around Narragansett Bay were unified as a single colony, known as Rhode Island and Providence Plantations, with Williams as its first elected president.

Under Williams, Rhode Island maintained good relations with the Indians, until the 1675–76 rebellion of Narragansets and Wampanoags known as King PHILIP's War. During the conflict, Williams served as a captain in the colonial militia.

WILLIAMS, THOMAS. See TEHORAGWANEGEN.

WILLIAMS, WILLIAM S. (Old Bill Williams).
(1787–1849). Trader; trapper; explorer.

William S. Williams was originally from Rutherford County, North Carolina. He was raised in Missouri, and, during his early years, toured as a Baptist preacher.

Roger Williams Sheltered by the Narragansetts. Courtesy of Library of Congress.

In the 1810s and 1820s, Williams lived among the Osage Indians of the Missouri-Kansas frontier, reportedly marrying an Osage woman. He served as interpreter to the Osages for a government expedition that surveyed the Santa Fe Trail during the late 1820s, then went on to work as an independent trapper in the Rockies. His solo trapping expeditions took him as far north as the Yellowstone River region of present-day Wyoming, and as far south as the fur-trading center at Taos, New Mexico.

Williams was part of JOSEPH WALKER's 1833–34 expedition from northeastern Utah to the Humboldt River and California, probably taking part in the battle with the Great Basin Indians at Humboldt Sink.

Upon his return from California, Williams settled among the Ute tribe in northern Utah and western Colorado. He reportedly continued to practice as a Baptist preacher among such Southwest Indians as the Hopis of Arizona.

In 1842–43, accompanied by WILLIAM T. HAMILTON, Williams trapped and explored the Northern Plains from BENT's Fort on the Arkansas River in southern Colorado, as far north as the Columbia River in the Pacific Northwest. He returned to Santa Fe in 1846, in time to join JOHN C. FREMONT's third expedition across the Rockies and Sierras into California.

Williams returned to Taos in 1848, where he soon joined a military expedition against the Apaches and his former friends the Utes. During this campaign, he was wounded, but recovered enough by the following year to join Fremont's fourth expedition into the Southern Rockies during the winter of 1848–49. During this expedition, poor planning and severe weather wreaked havoc on Fremont and his men. Williams accompanied frontier artist BENJAMIN KERN into the mountains to recover supplies that had been left behind. The two men were ambushed and killed by a Ute war party.

WILSON, JACK. See WOVOKA.

WIMAR, CHARLES. *(1828–1862).* Artist.

Originally from Germany, Charles Wimar came to North America at the age of 15, staying at his father's inn outside St. Louis, where he became friendly with Indians who passed through to trade furs.

Wimar's introduction to art was through an apprenticeship to sign painter and muralist Leon de Pomarede. In 1849, he assisted Pomarede on a journey up the Mississippi, where they made studies of the Indians and wildlife.

Wimar did not begin to produce paintings of Native Americans on his own until he returned to Dusseldorf, Germany, to study art at the age of 24. From memory, he painted portraits of his Indian friends, which he was able to sell in Europe. On his return to the United States in 1856, he found little success in marketing them, however.

Living again in St. Louis, Wimar made at least three trips up the Missouri by riverboat, using a camera as well as a sketchpad. Mandans, Assiniboines, and Crows were among his subjects. In 1859, he was one of the founders of the Western Academy of Art. He died at the age of 34, just after having completed a mural in the rotunda of the St. Louis Courthouse.

WINEMA (Kaitchkona Winema, "strong-hearted woman"; Toby Riddle; Tobey Riddle). *Modoc. (1836–1920).* Interpreter; peacemaker in the Modoc War of 1872–73. Cousin of CAPTAIN JACK.

Winema was born along the Link River in northern California. Because of the reddish-brown cast to her hair, she was originally called Nonooktowa, meaning "strange child." She earned the name Winema, for "strong-hearted woman," as a young girl when she safely guided her canoe through rapids and rocks. She gained the further respect of her people when, as a girl of 14, she rallied Modoc braves to victory after a surprise attack by another tribe.

When 15, Winema refused to marry the Modoc husband chosen for her in favor of a Kentucky miner named Frank Riddle. They settled on a ranch together, and she became known to whites as Toby Riddle. Although her tribe at first rejected her, they later called on her and her husband to act as interpreters in negotiations with whites. On several occasions, she helped defuse tense situations and prevent violence.

After the Modocs under Captain Jack had departed the Klamath Reservation in Oregon for their ancestral lands along the Lost River in California, Winema traveled to their camp to convince her cousin to return to Oregon, where he could safely lobby for a Lost River reservation. Captain Jack reportedly accused her of being dead to the Modocs, of being a white woman.

In the various negotiations that followed, Frank Riddle and Winema acted as interpreters and messagebearers between white officials and the Modoc insurgents, coming and going between the army camp and the chiefs in their natural stronghold, the lava beds along Tule Lake.

In February 1873, after extensive fighting, a peace commission was established, including General EDWARD CANBY, ALFRED MEACHAM, and Eleasar Thomas, and a tent was set up on neutral ground. At the first parley, Captain Jack asked for the lava beds as a reservation and refused to turn over HOOKER JIM for the killing of white ranchers. Before the second parley, Winema told Meacham that some among the rebels wanted Captain Jack to kill Canby. Although Meacham was concerned, Canby ignored the warning and went ahead with the planned meeting in April. As feared by Winema, Captain Jack drew a hidden revolver and shot and killed Canby; another warrior, BOSTON CHARLEY, killed Thomas. SCHONCHIN JOHN fired on Meacham, striking him, but Winema threw herself in front of him to protect him. As Schonchin John began to scalp him, Winema called out that soldiers were coming. After the Modocs had fled, she wrapped Meacham in her saddle blanket and set out for help. During the next weeks, when fighting raged once again, Winema nursed the wounded Meacham back to health.

For her act of courage, Winema became a celebrity in the East. She traveled to Washington, D.C., where a parade was held in her honor and where she met President ULYSSES S. GRANT. From 1874 to 1881, she toured eastern cities with Meacham, her husband, their son Jeff, SCARFACED CHARLEY, and other Modocs, playing herself in the dramatic presentation of Indian issues.

Winema returned to Oregon for the remainder of her life. In 1890, she was granted a pension by the federal government, most of which she donated to her people. Her son by Frank Riddle, Jeff Riddle, used her as an informant for his book, *The Indian History of the Modoc War*, published in 1914. Winema died on the reservation and was buried in the Modoc Cemetery. A national forest is named after her. (See also CAPTAIN JACK.)

WINNEBAGO PROPHET. See WHITE CLOUD.

WINNEMUCCA (Old Winnemucca, Wobitsawahkah). *Northern Paiute. (fl. 1860s–1880s).* Proponent of peace. Son of TRUCKEE; father of SARAH WINNEMUCCA; uncle of NUMAGA.

Winnemucca, or Old Winnemucca, was the second chief of that name. His father, Winnemucca (also sometimes referred to as Old Winnemucca), is better known historically by the name of Truckee. The name Winnemucca supposedly resulted from an incident in which Truckee was wearing only one moccasin. English and Paiute were combined in the name "one muck," which evolved into its present form.

Winnemucca, like Truckee, generally encouraged peace with whites. When his nephew Numaga (sometimes called Young Winnemucca) led an uprising in Nevada—the Paiute War of 1860—Winnemucca kept his band out of the conflict and headed north, where he was held by the army at Yakima, Washington. After a massacre of some of his band members at Mud Lake in 1865, he became disillusioned with whites and avoided them as much as possible. He was drawn into the Bannock War of 1878 under BUFFALO HORN for a time until his daughter Sarah Winnemucca convinced him to return to his neutrality.

In 1879–80, Winnemucca traveled to Washington, D.C., with his daughter to lobby for the right of the Paiutes to live on the Malheur Reservation in Oregon rather than the Yakima Reservation in the state of Washington. The secretary of the Interior, CARL SCHURZ, agreed with them and signed a document to that effect. But western Indian agents ignored Schurz's decree. (See also WINNEMUCCA, SARAH.)

Winnemucca. *Courtesy of Library of Congress.*

WINNEMUCCA, SARAH (Sarah Winnemucca Hopkins, Sally Winnemucca; Thocmectony, Tocmectone, "shell flower").

Northern Paiute. (ca. 1844–1891). Peacemaker; interpreter; lecturer; writer; educator. Granddaughter of TRUCKEE; daughter of WINNEMUCCA; cousin of NUMAGA.

Sarah Winnemucca was born near the sink of the Humboldt River in present-day western Nevada, the fourth of Winnemucca's nine children. Her mother took her as a girl of 10 along with her brothers and sisters to live with her grandfather Truckee, presently on a ranch in the vicinity of San Jose, California. It was here that Sarah had her first extensive contact with whites. Then, when 14, she lived in the home of Major William Ormsby, a stagecoach agent in the Carson Valley of Nevada, where she learned English. On the dying Truckee's request, she and her sister Mary returned to San Jose in 1860 to attend the St. Mary's Convent school. Yet the Paiute students were discharged after a month when white parents objected. Sarah found work at Virginia City, Nevada, as a domestic, spending much of her salary on books.

Meanwhile, in 1860, her cousin Numaga led his band in an uprising known as the Paiute War. With an increased military presence in the region, tribal members were settled on the Pyramid Lake Reservation near present-day Reno, Nevada.

In 1866, at the time of the Snake War, a rebellion of some Paiute bands from the Snake River region under PAULINA and WEAWEA, Sarah and her brother Naches were asked by the military to come to Fort McDermitt, Nevada, in order to discuss Paiute-white relations. She was also asked to persuade her father, Winnemucca, to report to the Pyramid Lake Reservation. Because of her knowledge of English, she was hired as the army's official interpreter to the Paiutes and the Shoshones.

Sarah Winnemucca believed that the military was more competent and fair in management of Indian matters than the Bureau of Indian Affairs. In 1870, she traveled to San Francisco to meet with General John Schofeld, then to Gold Hill, Nevada, to speak to Senator John Jones concerning the mistreatment of Paiutes by Indian agents. Both claimed the problem was not under their jurisdiction.

In 1872, the Paiutes were forced to move to the Malheur Reservation in Oregon. Sarah befriended the agent Samuel Parrish, whose agricultural program she considered beneficial to the Indians. She acted as his interpreter and taught in a local school.

Parrish was replaced after four years by the agent William Rinehart. His failure to pay the Paiutes for their farm work as Parrish had done alienated many of the Paiutes. Some of them, including Sarah's father, joined the Bannock BUFFALO HORN and the Paiutes OYTES and EGAN in the Bannock War of 1878. Sarah was hired by General OLIVER HOWARD as interpreter. She also acted as peacemaker, following the trail of militants from southwestern Idaho into eastern Oregon. She managed to persuade her father and many of his followers to leave the camp and return to the safety of the army post. Despite her assistance, she and the other peaceful Paiutes were ordered to relocate to the Yakima Reservation in Washington.

In 1879, Sarah gave her first lecture in San Francisco, in which she criticized Rinehart and the Indian Bureau. When word of the negative publicity reached federal officials, they sponsored a trip to the capital for Sarah, her father, and other Paiutes. Again, she made the case of government mismanagement and argued for the Paiute's right to return to Malheur and manage their own affairs. Although her views were met with sympathy—the secretary of the Interior, CARL SCHURZ, even providing a document stating the Paiutes' right to return to Malheur—the necessary funding was never provided. Meanwhile, Sarah's criticism of Indian agents drew countercharges about her character, but her friends among the military defended her, including General Howard. In 1881, at Howard's invitation, she taught Indian children at an army post in Vancouver, Washington.

In 1883–84, Sarah toured eastern cities, giving nearly 300 lectures concerning Indian rights. She dressed as an Indian Princess to draw crowds. She met many notables, including Mary Tyler Mann, the widow of Horace Mann, Ralph Waldo Emerson, John Greenleaf Whittier, and Senator HENRY DAWES, whose plan for allotment of Indian lands to individuals she supported. In 1883, her book, *Life Among the Paiutes, Their Wrongs and Claims*, edited by Mary Tyler Mann, was published. In 1887, the General Allotment Act (the Dawes Severalty Act) was passed by Congress. By this time, however, now that so many whites had settled there, Sarah's hope of a permanent Paiute home at Malheur had ended.

Sarah Winnemucca returned to Nevada. With money from private donations, she founded an Indian school near present-day Lovelock, independent of government supervision. She operated her school for almost three years until her health failed and funds became short.

During the course of her life, Sarah Winnemucca had three husbands, two of them whites. She eventually retired to her sister's home in Henry's Lake, Idaho, where she died of tuberculosis.

WINNESHIEK (Winneshiek the Younger; Wa-kan-ja-ko-ga, Coming Thunder). *Winnebago.* (1812–1872). Principal chief.

Winneshiek the Younger was born at Portage, Wisconsin. His father, Winneshiek the Elder (Ma-wa-ra-ga), was chief of a village at present-day Freeport on the Pecatonica River in northern Illinois in 1827; then at present-day Hokah, Minnesota in 1835. Winneshiek the Younger was chosen as head chief in 1845 by government officials. Powerful Winnebago band chiefs at the time were WAUKON DECORA, GOOD THUNDER, and LITTLE PRIEST.

The Winnebagos were removed to a reservation in Iowa in 1850. Winneshiek was part of the delegation that traveled to Washington, D.C., in 1855 and signed a treaty establishing a Minnesota homeland once again, in Blue Earth County. He was deposed as head chief four years later, when he refused to sign a treaty ceding lands to whites, but his people continued to recognize him as such.

After the Minnesota Uprising of Santee Sioux of 1862–63 under LITTLE CROW, the government forced the removal of the Winnebagos to South Dakota on the Missouri River. Winneshiek resisted relocation, leading warriors to an isolated location on Lake Elysian. But after negotiations in which the chief passionately pleaded his case to military representatives, he decided not to make war. The Winnebagos were packed into river boats—about 400 Indians to a boat along with the crews and soldiers—taken down the Minnesota and Mississippi, then up the Missouri to Fort Thompson, South Dakota, where they were left without supplies.

About two months later, the Winnebagos, starving, set out down the Missouri and settled near the Omahas in Nebraska. In 1872, Winneshiek set out for his place of birth in Wisconsin but died on the way in an Iowa Indian village.

WINSLOW, EDWARD. *(1595–1655).* Colonial leader; explorer. Father of JOSIAH WINSLOW.

Born in England, Edward Winslow traveled to North America in the *Mayflower* in 1620 and became a longtime member of the colony's ruling council. In 1621, he negotiated a treaty with the Wampanoag grand sachem MASSASOIT that kept peace between the Pilgrims and that tribe over the next 40 years. Between 1623 and 1625, he was the Plymouth colony's agent in England, where he published an account of the colony's progress. In 1632, Winslow undertook one of the earliest explorations of Connecticut. He was governor for several terms in the 1630s and 1640s, those which WILLIAM BRADFORD declined to serve. Living in England after 1646, Winslow was appointed as a commissioner on an expedition against Spanish holdings in the West Indies. He was with the British forces that captured Jamaica in 1655, but died on the return trip.

WINSLOW, JOSIAH. *(ca. 1629–1680).* Colonial militia officer in King Philip's War; colonial governor. Son of EDWARD WINSLOW.

Josiah Winslow, son of the Pilgrim Edward Winslow, was born in Plymouth colony and grew up to attend Harvard College. He settled in Marshfield, Massachusetts, where he became captain of the local militia.

In 1657, he became assistant to the governor of the Plymouth colony; in 1659, military commander of Plymouth, succeeding MILES STANDISH; and, in 1673, governor of the colony.

In the winter of 1674–75, a Christianized Wampanoag by the name of John Sassamon, a confidant to King PHILIP, informed Winslow of the impending Wampanoag uprising. When Sassamon was found murdered shortly afterward, Winslow supervised the trial of his alleged killers, three Wampanoags, one of them an adviser to Philip. Their subsequent execution by the Plymouth colonial authorities touched off the conflict known as King Philip's War in June 1675.

Winslow became commander in chief of all New England forces. On December 19, 1675, he led militia units from Plymouth, Massachusetts, Connecticut, and Rhode Island in an attack on CANONCHET's Narragansets, allies of the Wampanoags, at their fortified village on Great Swamp Island in Narragansett Bay. The colonists drove the Indians into the adjacent swamp after having destroyed the village. Early in 1676, Winslow relinquished command of colonial troops to BENJAMIN CHURCH, who campaigned until the following August. (See also CANONCHET; PHILIP.)

WOLFE, JAMES. (1727–1759). British officer in the French and Indian War of 1754–63.

The son of a colonel in the Royal Marines, James Wolfe was born at Kent, England. At 14, he entered his father's regiment, but later transferred to the infantry. He saw action in combat in the Low Countries throughout the 1740s and 1750s. In 1742, he fought in the Battle of Culloden, Scotland, the last pitched battle to be fought in Great Britain.

By 1759, he had attained the rank of brigadier general and was assigned to command a British offensive against Canada. In September of that year, following a three-month siege, Wolfe led his command in an amphibious landing above Quebec on the St. Lawrence River. His subsequent victory, on September 13, 1759, over the French on the Plains of Abraham, led to the British occupation of Quebec. Wolfe was mortally wounded in the battle and died soon after, as did his French adversary, LOUIS JOSEPH, MARQUIS DE MONTCALM.

Wolfe's victory at Quebec set the stage for WILLIAM JOHNSON and his Mohawk warriors in their successful assault on Montreal the following year. Artist Benjamin West, in his idealized painting of Wolfe's death on the battlefield, depicted an Iroquois warrior as among those attending the dying general. Yet the Indian allies of the British played no significant role in the Quebec campaign of 1759.

WOOD, ABRAHAM. (fl. mid–1600s). Explorer; trader; soldier; captive.

Captain Abraham Wood, his place of birth unknown, was an early English settler in colonial Virginia. In 1646, under commission by the Virginia Assembly, he established Fort Henry on the Appomattox River near present-day Petersburg, Virginia, on the site of a former Indian village. As payment for his military service, he received a 600-acre land grant near the fort, from which he developed a lucrative farming and trading enterprise.

In 1650, Wood, accompanied by Edward Bland and several companions, set out from Fort Henry and explored south and west into the region between the James and Roanoke rivers. Their objective was to locate a river that might lead them southwest to the silver mines of Spanish Mexico. Political unrest in England and in the Virginia colony forced them to cut the expedition short, however, after having penetrated only 100 miles into the interior.

In 1671, Wood, now a major general, sponsored an expedition by Thomas Batts and Robert Fallam that explored the Blue Ridge Mountains in western Virginia and first discovered a system of streams that flowed into the Ohio and Mississippi rivers.

Wood also initiated the expedition to the trans-Allegheny regions of present-day North Carolina and Tennessee by James Needham and Gabriel Arthur in 1673, with the intention of extending the fur trade to tribes west of the Occaneechi Indians. Needham and Arthur had contact with Indians thought to be Cherokees or Catawbas. Needham was killed by his Occaneechi guide after a return trip to Fort Henry. Arthur was forced to stay among the western band of Cherokees or Catawbas and traveled with them as a member of a raiding party, including a trip through the Cumberland Gap. He was then captured by Shawnees, but gained his release on promising to bring the British fur trade to them. He returned to Fort Henry in 1674.

WOODEN LEG (Kummok'quiviokta, Good Walker). Northern Cheyenne. (1858–1940). Leader in the War for the Black Hills of 1876–77; army scout; research informant.

Wooden Leg was born along the Cheyenne River in what is now South Dakota. He was present with TWO MOONS on the Powder River in March 1876 when their camp was attacked by troops commanded by Colonel Joseph Reynolds. After their possessions had been destroyed, they joined their Sioux allies under SITTING BULL and fought alongside them at the Battle of Little Bighorn that June. Wooden Leg surrendered in the spring of the next year.

Unlike Two Moons, who stayed in the north as an army scout, Wooden Leg was sent to the Indian Territory with the majority of Northern Cheyennes, including DULL KNIFE and LITTLE WOLF. He did not join these two chiefs in their flight north in 1878, however. After six years, Wooden Leg was allowed to return to Montana, where he found work as an army scout. In 1890, he participated in the Ghost Dance movement. In 1908, he converted to Christianity.

Like Two Moons, Wooden Leg is widely quoted on Little Bighorn. His autobiography *Wooden Leg: A Warrior Who Fought Custer*, written with Thomas Marquis, was published in 1931. (See also SITTING BULL.)

WOOL, JOHN ELLIS. *(1784–1869).* Army officer in the Yakima War and the Rogue River War.

Born in Newburgh, New York, John E. Wool was operating a store in Troy, New York, at the outbreak of the War of 1812. He was commissioned a captain in the infantry and distinguished himself at Queenston Heights in what is now Ontario, in 1812, and also in the defense of Plattsburgh, New York, in 1814.

Wool remained in the army after the war, and was appointed colonel and inspector general in 1816. During the 1820s, he supervised the development of a modern artillery force, and, in the 1830s, with General WINFIELD SCOTT, directed the relocation of the Cherokees from their homes in the Southeast to their newly assigned lands in the Indian Territory. In 1841, he became a brigadier general.

In the Mexican War of 1846–48, Wool raised an army of volunteers in the Mississippi and Ohio Valleys, and subsequently took part in General ZACHARY TAYLOR's military conquest of Mexico. He was made a major general and commanded U.S. occupation troops in Mexico after 1848.

Wool was placed in command of the Department of the Pacific in 1854 (at that time the country west of the Rockies, except Utah and part of New Mexico), in which position he supervised campaigns against the Indians in conjunction with Washington militia forces under Governor ISAAC STEVENS. He directed military operations in Washington Territory against allied tribes under KAMIAKIN in the Yakima War of 1855–56, as well as against Takelma and Tututni Indians under JOHN in the simultaneous Rogue River War in Oregon. Wool's efforts to reach peaceful accords with the warring bands were continually frustrated by the actions of territorial militia under Stevens, who supported white incursions on lands guaranteed to the Indians by federal treaties.

Wool returned to command U.S. troops in the East in 1857. During the Civil War, in May 1862, he led Union forces in a successful assault on Norfolk, Virginia. He retired from the military in 1863. (See also JOHN; KAMIAKIN.)

WOOLMAN, JOHN. *(1720–1772).* Reformer; Quaker leader.

Born in western New Jersey, John Woolman attended a Quaker school while working on his family's farm. He became a tailor's apprentice and eventually established his own shop in Mount Holly.

In 1743, Woolman was admitted to the Quaker ministry and began a series of journeys to Pennsylvania, Maryland, North Carolina, Virginia, Rhode Island, and New Hampshire, spreading his doctrine concerning the abolition of slavery. Although he had little success in changing colonial policy, he convinced many individuals to free their slaves. Woolman also was active in Indian issues, speaking out for a fairer Indian land policy and against the trading of liquor to Indians. He backed Moravian missionary attempts among the Indians, visiting bands on the Pennsylvania frontier during PONTIAC's Rebellion of 1763.

Woolman's travels and beliefs are recorded in his *Journal*, published two years after his death. His work influenced a later generation of Quakers active in the reform movement during President ULYSSES S. GRANT's Peace Policy of the 1860s and 1870s.

WORCESTER, SAMUEL AUSTIN.

(1798–1859). Missionary; educator; linguist.

Samuel Worcester was born in Worcester, Massachusetts, and raised in Vermont. He received his early education from his father, who instructed him in the craft of type-making and printing, a skill that would be significant in his subsequent work with the Cherokees. An 1819 graduate of the University of Vermont, he went on to study at the Andover Theological Seminary. In 1825, he was ordained a Congregational minister in Boston and sent as a missionary to the Cherokees at the BRAINERD Mission in eastern Tennessee.

At Brainerd, Worcester was instrumental in creating the typeface used to published written works in the Cherokee alphabet developed by SEQUOYAH, including the *Cherokee Phoenix*, a tribal newspaper. After 1828, he moved to Georgia and settled among the Cherokees on their land near New Echota. He produced and published editions of the Bible translated from Greek into the new Cherokee written language with the help of ELIAS BOUDINOT and STEPHEN FOREMAN.

In 1831, because of his resistance to the forced removal of the Cherokees west of the Msisissippi to the Indian Territory, Georgia officials harassed Worcester, arresting him and other missionaries for violating the state's laws prohibiting whites from residing on Indian lands without a license, and requiring whites living on Indian lands to take an oath of allegiance to the Georgia state government. His case was appealed to the United States Supreme Court, and, in 1832, Chief Justice John Marshall ruled the Georgia statutes were unconstitutional and did not apply on Indian lands. Yet Georgia authorities ignored the ruling, as did President ANDREW JACKSON. Worcester was not released from prison until the following year, whereupon he urged Cherokee leaders to accept the terms of what he now considered inevitable removal. In 1835, Boudinot, MAJOR RIDGE, JOHN RIDGE, STAND WATIE, and other leaders soon signed the Treaty of New Echota, despite continuing resistance to removal by Chief JOHN ROSS.

Worcester moved to the Indian Territory, where he headed the Park Hill Mission and ministered to the Cherokees who had been relocated from Georgia and the Carolinas along the Trail of Tears. Over the next 25 years, he established schools, a gristmill, and publishing house for Cherokee-language publications, including the *Cherokee Almanac*, which was published annually from 1838 to 1861. He also supervised the publication of written works for the Choctaws and Creeks of the Indian Territory. In 1841, he established the Cherokee Bible Society, which distributed 5,000 Bibles in the Cherokee language. Worcester campaigned against the use of alcohol by the Cherokees, serving as an officer of the Cherokee Temperance Society.

WORTH, WILLIAM JENKINS. *(1794–1849).*
Army officer in the Second Seminole War of 1835–42.

Born in Hudson, New York, William Worth was a store clerk in nearby Albany at the onset of hostilities in the War of 1812. He entered the infantry as a lieutenant in 1813, serving under generals Morgan Lewis and WINFIELD SCOTT. He was aide-de-camp to Scott in the American victories at Chippewa Creek and at Lundy's Lane, both in present-day Ontario, Canada.

Worth remained in the army after the war at the rank of major. In 1820–28, he served as commandant of cadets at West Point. In 1832, he was assigned to the army's newly organized Ordnance Corps.

In 1838, at the rank of colonel, Worth was sent to Florida for action in the Second Seminole War. He was placed in command of U.S. forces in Florida in the spring of 1841. Although OSCEOLA was now dead, other Seminole leaders continued the resistance from their camps deep in the Everglades.

Worth launched a successful campaign against the remaining militants, culminating in the defeat of the Indians at the Battle of Palatka, Florida, on April 19, 1842. Unlike his predecessors, who merely pursued the retreating Seminoles into the Everglades, Worth led his forces on a campaign of destruction against the Indians' villages and crops. He also took captives, including some Seminole chiefs, and threatened to hang them if the Seminoles did not surrender. Faced with starvation, over 3,000 Seminoles surrendered, many of whom were relocated to the Indian Territory. Nevertheless,

sporadic uprisings among the Seminoles continued into the 1850s under BILLY BOWLEGS.

Worth was next assigned to General ZACHARY TAYLOR's command in Texas, and, in 1846, crossed the Rio Grande into Chihuahua in the early engagements of the Mexican War. He took part in all the major campaigns throughout Mexico, serving under Taylor at Palo Alto in 1846, and took part in Winfield Scott's amphibious invasion of Veracruz in 1847. At the war's end, in November 1848, he was given command of the army's newly organized Department of Texas. He died the following May while on duty at San Antonio. (See also OSCEOLA.)

WOVOKA ("the cutter"; Jack Wilson; Wanekia, "one who makes life"). *Northern Paiute.*
(ca. 1856–1932). Medicine man; prophet; founder of the Ghost Dance religion. Son of TAVIBO.

Wovoka was born along the Walker River in Mason Valley, Nevada. He is generally thought to have been the son of Tavibo. In any case, Wovoka grew up in the same area as the earlier Paiute shaman and was influenced by his teachings, as well as those of other reservation prophets, such as SMOHALLA and JOHN SLOCUM. For part of his youth, he lived on a ranch near present-day Yerrington, Nevada, with a white family named Wilson, who were devout Christians. Among whites, he became known as Jack Wilson.

In late 1888, Wovoka became sick with a fever. He was in this state during an eclipse of the sun on January 1, 1889. On recovery, he related that he had been taken to the spirit world for a visit with the Supreme Being and had returned to spread the message that the earth would soon perish and then come alive again in a pure, aboriginal state, with the messiah present. The new world would be inherited by all Indians, he preached, including the dead, for an eternal existence free from suffering. To earn this new reality, Indians had to live harmoniously and honestly, cleanse themselves often, and shun the ways of whites, especially alcohol, the destroyer. He also discouraged the practice of mourning, because the dead would soon be resurrected, instead calling for the performance of meditation, prayers, singing, and especially dancing, through which one might briefly die and catch a glimpse of the paradise-to-come, replete with lush prairie grass, herds of buffalo, and Indian ancestors.

The new religion spread to the Indians of the West confined to reservations, especially the Shoshones, Arapahos, Cheyennes, and Sioux. Some of his followers came to consider Wovoka himself the messiah and he was referred to as the Red Man's Christ. Some of the Sioux bands, desperate in defeat for any glimmer of hope, found a new militance after their representatives KICKING BEAR, SHORT BULL, and nine others made the pilgrimage to Nevada in the winter of 1889–90. They gave Wovoka's gospel their own interpretation, choosing to emphasize the possible elimination of whites. Special Ghost Dance Shirts, they claimed, could even stop the white man's bullets. The Sioux began gathering in great numbers to hold the dances, with men and women holding hands in large circles and moving slowly around while singing without accompaniment. The Ghost Dance Uprising made white officials nervous and led to military intervention and the death of SITTING BULL and the massacre of BIG FOOT's band at Wounded Knee in December 1890.

Wovoka, shocked by the bloodshed, henceforth emphasized peace with whites. The religion gradually died out, although some tribes, such as the Arapahos and Cheyennes, retained elements of Ghost Dance rituals in their other tribal dances. Wovoka lived well into the 20th century with his wife, Mary, by whom he had four children, dying at the Walker River Reservation near Schurz, Nevada.

WRIGHT, ALLEN (Kiliahote, Kilihote, "let's kindle a fire"). *Mixed Choctaw. (1825–1885).* Minister; translator; principal chief.

Kiliahote was born along the Yaknukni River in Mississippi, the son of nearly full-blooded Choctaws. When seven years old, he was relocated to the Indian Territory with his family. His mother died just before removal; his father died soon after arrival in the West, leaving him only with a sister.

The Presbyterian missionary CYRUS KINGSBURY took an interest in the boy, giving him the name Allen Wright and providing him with an education at local missionary schools. He continued his education in New York, graduating from Union College in 1852, and from Union Theological Seminary in 1855, with a mastery of English, Greek, Latin, and Hebrew. He married a white missionary from Ohio, Harriet Newell Dayton, by whom he had eight children.

In 1856, Wright was ordained into the Presbyterian church after which he began work among his people. He became involved in tribal affairs and was elected to the Choctaw house of representatives and the senate, eventually becoming his tribe's treasurer. In 1862, during the Civil War, he served the Confederacy.

After the war, Wright was elected principal chief, serving for two terms, from 1866 to 1870. In 1866, during negotiations for Choctaw and Chickasaw treaties, he suggested the name *Okla-homma* for the region, meaning "red people," which became the official name of the state of Oklahoma in 1907. During the 1870s and 1880s, Wright translated numerous works, including the Chickasaw constitution and codes of law into English, and the Psalms from Hebrew to English. In 1880, his *Chahta Leksikon*, a Choctaw dictionary, was published.

WYANDANCH (Wyandance, Wiantance). *Montauk. (ca. 1600–1659).* Grand sachem of the Montauk Confederacy.

Wyandanch lived at Montauk Point on the tip of Long Island, New York. In 1639, he received historical notice when he sold land to the Englishman Lion Gardiner for trade goods—the island of Manchonack, henceforth known as Gardiner's Island. In 1653, he became grand sachem when his brother Pogattacut died. That same year, Niantics out of Rhode Island and Connecticut under NINIGRET raided the marriage ceremony of Wyandanch's daughter Quashawam (or Momone for "heather flower") and kidnapped her. Gardiner put up the ransom to free her. Wyandanch rewarded his friend by giving the English the right to graze cattle on 7,000 acres in the vicinity of Smithtown for seven years. In the late 1650s, a smallpox epidemic ravaged Long Island's Indians, killing as many as a third of the population. Wyandanch died in 1659, probably from the disease, although there was a rumor of his having been poisoned. His son Wyancombone, who succeeded him as grand sachem, died three years later.

WYNKOOP, EDWARD (Tall Chief). *(1836–1891).* Indian agent; reformer; soldier.

Originally from Philadelphia, Edward Wynkoop arrived in Colorado in 1858 to take part in the Pike's Peak Gold Rush, where he became one of the founders of the city of Denver.

At the beginning of the Civil War, Wynkoop was commissioned a major in the 1st Colorado Cavalry under Colonel JOHN CHIVINGTON. In 1862, he took part in the defense of New Mexico from an invasion of Confederate forces at Apache Canyon and Glorieta Pass.

In July 1864, Wynkoop, known to the Indians as Tall Chief, brought Cheyenne chief BLACK KETTLE to Camp Weld near Denver to negotiate a peace treaty with Colorado governor JOHN EVANS. The following November, Black Kettle's people were attacked by Colorado cavalry under Chivington at the Sand Creek Massacre. Wynkoop was an outspoken critic of Chivington's actions.

In 1866, Wynkoop was appointed agent for the Upper Arkansas Agency on the Cheyenne-Arapaho Reservation, but resigned the next year in protest of General PHILIP H. SHERIDAN's Indian policy. In December 1868, he appeared before PETER COOPER's United States Indian Commission to decry the unnecessary attack on Cheyennes by troops under Colonel GEORGE ARMSTRONG CUSTER in the Battle of the Washita, resulting in the death of his friend Black Kettle. His criticism of the military's handling of Indian issues and the government's breaking of treaty agreements helped spur the movement to block the return of the Indian Bureau to the jurisdiction of the War Department.

In the 1870s, Wynkoop went to the Black Hills after the discovery of gold in that area. He then settled in New Mexico, where he served as adjutant general and warden of the state penitentiary.

Y

YELLOW HAIR (Nape-zi; Yellow Hand).
Northern Cheyenne. (ca. 1850–1876). Leader in
the War for the Black Hills of 1876–77; killed by
WILLIAM "BUFFALO BILL" CODY.

On July 17, 1876, soon after the Battle of Little Bighorn,
a force under Colonel WESLEY MERRITT out of Fort
Laramie, Wyoming, intercepted about 800 Northern
Cheyennes who had left the RED CLOUD Agency in
Nebraska to join up with SITTING BULL and CRAZY
HORSE along the Powder River in Wyoming and Mon-
tana. In the so-called Battle of War Bonnet Creek (or Hat
Creek) in northwestern Nebraska, there was little fighting.
At the end of the encounter, however, most of the Chey-
ennes retreated to the reservation and were discouraged
from participating in subsequent engagements.

The only casualty of the day was Yellow Hair, killed by
the army scout William "Buffalo Bill" Cody. In advance of
their respective groups, the two men came face to face. They
circled each other on horseback and fired simultaneously.
Yellow Hair's shot missed; Cody's went through Yellow
Hair's leg and killed his horse. Cody's horse stumbled and
he jumped off. On foot, each fired again and Yellow Hair
was struck in the head. Cody finished him with a knife,
scalping him. The encounter was later embellished by the
press, dime novels, and Buffalo Bill's Wild West Show. In
most accounts, the inaccurate name Yellow Hand was used
instead of Yellow Hair. (See also SITTING BULL.)

YELLOW HAND. See YELLOW HAIR.

YELLOW THUNDER (Wa-kun-cha-koo-kah,
Wakunchakukah, Waunkauntshawzeekau).
Winnebago. (ca. 1774–1874). Proponent of peace who
passively resisted removal.

Yellow Thunder was born on Lake Winnebago in
Wisconsin. He was known to settlers as a Catholic convert and a peace advocate, not joining RED BIRD's

Winnebago Uprising in 1827 or the BLACK HAWK War
of the Sacs and Foxes in 1832.

Yet Yellow Thunder passively resisted relocation to
reservation lands in Minnesota and Iowa. In 1837, he
was induced to travel to Washington, D.C., as part of a
tribal delegation, where he was pressured into signing
a treaty ceding Winnebago lands in Wisconsin. On
returning home, the Wisconsin Winnebagos were given
eight months to relocate west of the Mississippi. Yellow
Thunder claimed that he had been led to believe his
people could stay eight more years. In 1840, at the
rumors of an armed Indian revolt, officials sent in troops
and ordered Yellow Thunder's arrest. He was soon
released, then forcibly removed.

Within a year, however, Yellow Thunder and his wife
had returned to the Portage region, where he home-
steaded along the Wisconsin River. They were allowed
to stay until their deaths. In 1909, a monument was
erected to his memory.

YELLOW WOLF. *Southern Cheyenne. (d. 1864).*
Early leader of southern branch of tribe.

About 1830, some of the Cheyenne bands began
camping in Arkansas River country of present-day
Colorado and Kansas. They eventually became known
as the Southern Cheyennes to distinguish them from
their relatives who stayed to the north in present-day
Nebraksa, Wyoming, and Montana. Yellow Wolf was a
chief of a southern band. During the 1830s, Yellow Wolf
had frequent contacts with the fur traders CHARLES
and WILLIAM BENT and Ceran St. Vrain at Bent's Fort,
Colorado. He also became friends with Lieutenant
James Abert during his visits to Bent's Fort in 1845 with
expeditions under JOHN C. FREMONT and STEPHEN
WATTS KEARNY in 1846. Abert sketched him with a
pencil and was criticized by Yellow Wolf because of the
lack of color, which Abert explained he would add later.

During the 1830s, Yellow Wolf's Cheyennes, along with Arapaho allies, participated in numerous raids on Comanches and Iowas, especially on the Comanche chief BUFFALO HUMP's band. Peace was established among the tribes at a council at Bent's Fort in 1840. Yellow Wolf, who had always shown friendship to whites, was killed by Colonel JOHN CHIVINGTON's men in their attack on BLACK KETTLE's camp at Sand Creek in 1864.

YELLOW WOLF (Hermeme Moxmox). *Nez Perce.* *(1856–1935).* Warrior; research informant. Nephew of Young JOSEPH.

As a warrior of 21, Yellow Wolf participated in the Nez Perce War of 1877. Before the surrender at Bear Paw, Montana, on October 5, he joined WHITE BIRD's group which fled to Canada and joined up with the Sioux under SITTING BULL. Yellow Wolf returned to the United States in a band of about 25 the next year, heading for the Lapwai Reservation in Idaho. They were captured and sent to the Indian Territory instead, where Chief Joseph and others had previously been relocated. In 1895, a number of Nez Perces were allowed to return to Lapwai. Others, including Chief Joseph and Yellow Wolf, were forced to settle on the Colville Reservation in the state of Washington. In 1908, Lucullus McWhorter recorded Yellow Wolf's experiences, published as Yellow Wolf: His Own Story (1940). (See also Young JOSEPH.)

YONAGUSTA (Yonaguska, Drowning Bear). *Cherokee. (ca. 1760–1839).* Principal chief of the Mountain Cherokees; orator; medicine man. Adoptive father of WILLIAM THOMAS.

Yonagusta was a peace chief of the Mountain Cherokees of North Carolina, known for his diplomacy and oratory. His band originally lived along the Tuckaseigee River, then, after 1819, moved to the Oconaluftee River. When about 60 years old, he became seriously ill and slipped into unconsciousness. He was mourned as dead by his people. After a day, he revived, claiming he had visited the spirit world. He was henceforth considered a prophet. In his teaching he denounced tribal use of alcohol. In 1829, Yonagusta and 58 other Mountain Cherokees legally broke off from the Cherokee Nation to become citizens of what was at the time Haywood County in western North Carolina. They purchased a tract of land through Yonagusta's adopted son Will Thomas, who had become an attorney, and managed to avoid removal to the Indian Territory.

YOUKIOMA (Youkeoma, Yukeoma, Yukioma, "almost perfect"). *Hopi. (ca. 1835–1929).* Leader of traditional faction during tribal split.

Youkioma lived in the ancient village of Oraibi on Third Mesa in Arizona. In the late 1800s, when the federal government advocated a policy of assimilation and acculturation of Indian peoples, the pueblo Oraibi was divided between two factions: the Friendlies (or Progressives), favoring accommodation with whites; and the Hostiles (or Conservatives), rejecting white values. The hereditary chief Lololoma (Lolulomai) backed the Friendlies; his principal rival was Lomahongyoma.

Lololoma died in 1902 and was succeeded by his nephew Tewaquaptewa, who also supported the Friendlies. About that time, Youkioma became the leader of the Hostile faction. The split between the two groups intensified. Separate religious ceremonies were sponsored by each.

In late summer 1906, with the approach of the important Snake Dance, the rivalry reached its climax. It appeared as if the arguments and fights would boil over into a civil war. White officials threatened military intervention. On September 7, angry Hostiles and Friendlies faced one another outside the village. It was Youkioma who proposed the solution to the standoff and prevented bloodshed. He drew a line in the earth, stood on it, and announced that if the Friendlies pushed the Hostiles across it, the Hostiles would leave once and for all. But if the Hostiles pushed their way across it, they would stay in Oraibi. The Friendlies triumphed in the "push-of-war," and the Hostiles, as promised, departed Oraibi to form their own pueblo on Third Mesa, Hotevilla.

Youkioma was jailed by white authorities on several occasions, once for a year at Alcatraz, for civil disobedience in resisting the education of Hopi children at white boarding schools. He was also sent to the Carlisle Indian School in Pennsylvania for rehabilitation. In 1911, he traveled to Washington, D.C., to lobby for Hopi self-determination, meeting President William Taft.

YOUNG BEAR (Maqui-banasha). *Fox. (ca. 1868–1933).* Reservation leader who encouraged tribal restoration.

Young Bear was one of several Fox chiefs to bear that name. The son of Pushetonequa, he became chief of the Iowa Foxes, who, after having moved to Kansas from Iowa in 1842, purchased a tract of land in Tama County, Iowa, and returned in 1856. In the late 1800s and early 1900s, when federal Indian policy called for assimilation of Indians into white society, Young Bear worked to maintain traditional customs. He encouraged the recording of tribal legends and lore and a revival of arts and crafts. He died at Tama just before the federal government under President Franklin Roosevelt and his commissioner of Indian Affairs John Collier officially recognized the failure of assimilation and the importance of tribal restoration with the Wheeler-Howard Act (the Indian Reorganization Act) of 1934.

YOUNG, BRIGHAM. *(1801–1877).* Mormon leader; governor of Utah Territory.

A native of Whittingham, Vermont, Brigham Young moved to western New York in 1824, and, eight years later, was converted to Mormonism. He became an active force in the Church of Jesus Christ of Latter-Day Saints, founded by Joseph Smith in 1830. Young was active in organizing Mormon communities in Ohio, Missouri, and Illinois, also traveling to Canada and England to gain new converts. In 1846–47, he led the Mormon church in its westward migration from Nauvoo, Illinois, including a winter stopover on Indian lands at Council Bluffs, Iowa, and Winter Quarters, Nebraska.

In July 1847, Young founded the Mormon settlement at Salt Lake in Utah. Before long, nearly 16,000 Mormon immigrants entered the area, with thousands following over the next 20 years. Young, who had become president of the Mormon church, was named as the newly organized Utah Territory's first governor and superintendent of Indian Affairs in 1851.

Under Young's territorial governorship, the Mormon settlers were involved in a conflict with the Ute Indians under WALKARA known as the Walker War of 1853. Young managed to maintain good terms with some of the region's bands, including the Shoshones under WASHAKIE, who was a guest in his home.

In August 1857, the Mormons were threatened with an invasion by federal troops in reaction to the rebellious policies of Young's administration. At this time, a wagon train of non-Mormons was attacked by a combined force of Mormons and Paiutes under Indian agent John D. Lee near Mountain Meadows, Utah. Whites in the area, fearing the federal invasion, had agreed to help the Indians attack the wagon train rather than contend with both federal troops and Paiute warriors. Following nearly three days of siege by the Paiutes, the emigrants had been falsely advised by the local Mormons to proceed to Cedar City unarmed and on foot. As they moved out, they were set upon by the Indians and shot down by the Mormons, resulting in death of more than 120 men, women, and children. Young, who had not encouraged his followers to take part in the raid, authorized an investigation of the Mountain Meadows Masacre but instituted no action against those involved.

In 1858, Young was removed as Utah territorial governor by President James Buchanan, but remained a major force in Utah politics for the next 20 years. It was not until 1877 that federal authorities were able to implicate the Indian agent John D. Lee for his role at Mountain Meadows. He was tried and executed on the site of the incident. Young died the same year. (See also WALKARA.)

Z

ZEISBERGER, DAVID. *(1721–1808).*
Missionary; scholar.

David Zeisberger was born in the central Czechoslovakian region of Moravia and moved with his parents to the German principality of Saxony in 1727. When his family migrated to the newly established English colony in Georgia, he stayed behind in Saxony to finish school. He subsequently worked for a time in Holland as a merchant's apprentice, then went to London. From there, he obtained aid from Georgia's colonial governor JAMES OGLETHORPE, who helped him rejoin his family in the Moravian community of Savannah, Georgia.

In 1739, with the rest of the Georgia Moravians, Zeisberger moved to Pennsylvania and helped establish the Moravian community of Bethlehem. In 1745, Iroquois chief HENDRICK invited Zeisberger to live with his people. That year, Zeisberger assisted Indian diplomat CONRAD WEISER in negotiating an alliance between the English and the Iroquois at the council fire in Onondaga, near present-day Syracuse, New York. Zeisberger learned the Onondaga's Iroquoian dialect and worked at maintaining peaceful relations with white settlers. He officially began his missionary work in 1749, the year in which he was ordained a Moravian minister.

In 1762, Zeisberger began concentrating his missionary work among the Delaware Indians of Pennsylvania, learning their Algonquian dialect and leading a group of converts to the site of a former village in the upper Lehigh Valley known as Gnaddenhutten. At this time, even the peaceful bands on the Pennsylvania frontier suffered at the hands of whites who, because of PONTIAC's Rebellion, viewed all Indians as a threat. When a large number of Delawares were interned in Philadelphia in 1762–63, Zeisberger remained with his charges during the entire 16-month imprisonment.

Zeisberger then took his Delaware converts into the frontier of western Pennsylvania, where he established the Indian community of Friedenshutten in the Wyoming Valley. In the face of increasing white encroachment, he established in 1772 the Indian community of Schoenbrunn in the Tuscarawas Valley region of what is now southern Ohio along with the first church west of the Ohio River. Other Moravian communities he established in the region with his assistant JOHN HECKEWELDER came to include Shawnees, Wyandots, Nanticokes, Conoys, and Cherokees, as well as Delawares.

During the American Revolution, Zeisberger's activities among the Indians were viewed with suspicion by British military authorities on the southern Great Lakes. In 1781, he was arrested by the British and held at Detroit. Although he was soon released, his Christian Indian settlements soon disbanded in the face of increasing hostility from British-allied tribes. Moreover, in 1782, a force of American militiamen attacked Zeisberger's Christian Delaware settlement at Gnadenhutten and massacred all of its Indian inhabitants, including women and children.

In 1782, Zeisberger migrated westward with Delaware followers to new settlements in present-day Michigan and Ontario. In 1798, he settled at the Christian Delaware settlement of Goshen in Ohio, where he spent his remaining years.

Zeisberger produced dictionaries and religious works in Iroquoian and Algonquian. He also wrote studies of the Indians. In his book, *History of the American Indians*, he provided one of the earliest descriptions of the Indian mounds of southern Ohio.

ZIPKIYAH. See BIG BOW.

ZOTOM (**"the biter," "hole biter"; Podaladalte, "snake head"**). *Kiowa. (1853–1913).* Warrior; artist; Christian convert.

As a young man, Zotom established a reputation as a warrior on the Southern Plains, participating in numerous horse-stealing raids. He was captured in 1875 during the Red River War and sent to Fort Marion in St. Augustine, Florida. At Fort Marion, with the encouragement of Lieutenant RICHARD HENRY PRATT, Zotom became a skilled artist, one of the so-called "Florida Boys," along with BEAR'S HEART, COHOE, and HOWLING WOLF. Zotom was known especially for his painted fans. He was also the camp bugler. In 1878, he attended Hamptom Institute in Virginia, then Paris Hill near Utica, New York, where he studied for the Episcopalian ministry. In 1881, he was ordained a deacon and sent to the Indian Territory to work among his people.

At home, Zotom tried to strike a balance between his two cultures. He was reprimanded by the Episcopal church for participating in a Sun Dance, and a second time when the bishop found him in traditional clothing. In 1894, Zotom lost his deaconship and tried the Baptist religion before finally joining the Native American Church. He continued his art, painting model tepees for the 1898 Omaha Exposition and later a series of shields.

APPENDIX

NATIVE AMERICANS LISTED BY TRIBES (historically relevant tribes; not necessarily tribes by birth)

ABNAKI (See also PENNACOOK, PENOBSCOT)
Assacumbuit
Bomazeen
Moxus
Samoset
ALABAMA
Tascalusa
APACHE
ARAVAIPA
Eskiminzin
CHIRICAHUA
Alchesay
Apache Kid
Chato
Cochise
Geronimo
Massai
Naiche
Taza
COYOTERO (WHITE MOUNTAIN)
Nakaidoklini
Natiotish
MIMBRENO (MIMBRES)
Betzinez, Jason
Kayatennae
Loco
Mangas Coloradas
Mangus
Nana
Victorio
NEDNHI
Juh
PINALINO
Free, Mickey
TONTO
Delshay
ARAPAHO
NORTHERN
Black Bear
SOUTHERN
Left Hand
Little Raven
ARIKARA
Bloody Knife

ASSINIBOINE
Tatanga Mani
AZTEC
Figueroa, Jose
BANNOCK
Buffalo Horn
BEOTHUK
Shawanahdit, Nancy
BLACKFOOT (See also BLOOD, PIEGAN)
Crowfoot
Mountain Chief
BLOOD
Natawista
Potts, Jerry
Red Crow
CAHUILLA
Antonio, Juan
Ramona
CATAWBA
Hagler
CAYUSE
Tiloukaikt
CHEROKEE
Attakullakulla
Bloody Fellow
Boudinot, Elias
Bowl (The Bowl)
Bushyhead, Dennis, Wolf
Chisholm, Jesse
Dragging Canoe
Foreman, Stephen
Jolly, John
Junaluska
Lowry, George
Lowry, John
Moytoy
Oconostota
Ridge, John
Ridge, Major
Rose, Edward
Ross, John
Sequoyah
Smith, Nimrod Jarrett
Smith, Redbird

Tahchee
Tsali
Wafford, James
Ward, Nancy
Watie, Stand
Weaver, Paulino
White Path
Yonagusta

CHEYENNE
NORTHERN
  Dull Knife
  High-Backed Wolf
  Little Wolf
  Two Moon
  Two Moons
  Wooden Leg
  Yellow Hair (Yellow Hand)
SOUTHERN
  Alights-on-the-Cloud
  Bear's Heart
  Bent, Charlie
  Bent, George
  Black Kettle (2)
  Bull Bear
  Cohoe
  Guerrier, Edmond
  Howling Wolf
  Lean Bear
  Little Robe
  Minimic
  Roman Nose
  Stone Calf
  Tall Bull
  White Antelope
  White Horse
  White Shield
  Yellow Wolf (1)

CHICKASAW
Colbert, George
Colbert, Levi
Colbert, Pittman
Colbert, William
Piomingo

CHINOOK
Comcomly

CHIPEWYAN
Matonabbee

CHIPPEWA (OJIBWAY)
Bonga, George
Copway, George
Curling Hair
Enmegahbowh
Flat Mouth
Hole-in-the-Day (the older)
Hole-in-the-Day (the younger)

Jones, Peter
Noka
Shingabawassin
Sunday, John
Tshusick
Warren, William Whipple

CHOCTAW
Dukes, Joseph
Folsom, David
Le Flore, Greenwood
Mushalatubbee
Pitchlynn, Peter Perkins
Pushmataha
Red Shoes
Wright, Allen

CHOWANOC
Menatonon

CHUMASH
Pacomio

COMANCHE
Buffalo Hump
Cuerno Verde
Isatai
Parker, Quanah
Peta Nocona
Ten Bears
Tosawi

CREE
Big Bear
Piapot
Poundmaker

CREEK
Big Warrior
Bosomworth, Mary (Mary Musgrove)
Carr, Paddy
Chitto Harjo
Emistesigo
Isparheche
Little Warrior
McGillivray, Alexander
McIntosh, Chilly
McIntosh, William
McQueen, Peter
Menewa
Opothleyaholo
Porter, Pleasant
Posey, Alexander Lawrence
Sands, Oktarsars Harjo
Tomochichi
Weatherford, William (Red Eagle)

CROW
Arapoosh
Blackfoot
Curly
Plenty Coups

Two Leggings
White-Man-Runs-Him
CUPENO
Garra, Antonio
DELAWARE
Black Beaver
Bouchard, James
Buckongahelas
Delaware Prophet
Gelelemend
Hopocan
Jacobs
Journeycake, Charles
Lappawinze
Nemacolin
Tamaque
Tammany
Tatemy
Teedyuscung
White Eyes
DUWAMISH
Seattle
FOX
Powasheek
Taimah
Wapello
Young Bear
GABRIELINO
Toypurina
HAIDA
Edenshaw, Charles
HOPI
Nampeyo
Youkioma
HURON-WYANDOT
Adario
Ahatsistari
Deganawida
Donnaconna
Half-King (Dunquat) (WYANDOT)
Leatherlips (WYANDOT)
Tarhe (WYANDOT)
Walker, William (WYANDOT)
Walk-in-the-Water (WYANDOT)
IOWA
Dorion, Marie
Mahaskah
Moanahonga
Rantchewaime
IROQUOIS
CAYUGA
Fish Carrier
MINGO
Half-King (Scarouady) (ONEIDA)
Half-King (Tanacharison)

(CATAWBA-SENECA)
Logan (ONEIDA)
MOHAWK
Abraham
Brant, John
Brant, Joseph (Thayendanegea)
Brant, Molly
Hendrick
Hiawatha
Johnson, Emily Pauline
Norton, John
Oronhyatekha
Tehoragwanegen
Tekakwitha, Kateri
Williams, Eleazar
ONEIDA
Shikellamy
Skenandoa
ONONDAGA
Atotarho
Black Kettle (1)
Canasatego
Dekanisora
Garakontie, Daniel
Grangula
SENECA
Bennett, Louis Deerfoot
Blacksnake
Cornplanter
Guyasuta
Handsome Lake
Honayawas
Old Smoke
Parker, Ely Samuel
Pierce, Maris Bryant
Red Jacket
TUSCARORA
Cusick, Albert
Hancock
Hewitt, John Napoleon Brinton
Sakarissa
JUMANO
Sabeata
KALISPEL
Charlot
Loyola
KAW (KANSA)
Curtis, Charles
KICKAPOO
Kennekuk
Mecina
KIOWA
Big Bow
Big Tree
Kicking Bird

Little Mountain (Dohasan)
Lone Wolf
Mamanti (Sky Walker)
Satank (Sitting Bear)
Satanta (White Bear)
Stumbling Bear
Zotom

KWAKIUTL
Hunt, George

LUISENO
Cota, Manuelito

LUMBEE
Lowry, Henry Berry

MAHICAN
Konkapot

MANDAN
Mato-Tope
Shahaka

MASSACHUSET
Attucks, Crispus
Chickataubut
Kutshamakin
Nesutan

MENOMINEE
Juneau, Joseph
Oshkosh
Souligny
Tomah

METIS
Dumont, Gabriel
Lepine, Ambroise
Riel, Louis
Riel, Louis David

MIAMI
Godfroy, Francis
Little Turtle
Old Briton
Peshewah

MIWOK
Tenaya

MODOC
Black Jim
Bogus Charley
Boston Charley
Captain Jack (Kintpuash)
Curly Headed Doctor
Hooker Jim
Scarfaced Charley
Schonchin Jim
Schonchin John
Winema (Toby Riddle)

MOHEGAN
Occum, Samson
Oneka
Uncas

MOJAVE
Irateba

MONTAGNAIS
Negabamet, Noel

MONTAUK
Cockenoe
Wyandanch

NARRAGANSET
Canonchet
Canonicus
Magnus
Miantinomo
Mriksah
Quinnapin

NATCHEZ
Great Sun
Tattooed Serpent

NAVAJO
Armijo
Barboncito
Delgadito
Dodge, Henry Chee
Ganado Mucho
Herrero Grande
Manuelito

NEZ PERCE
Joseph, Old
Joseph, Young (Chief Joseph)
Lawyer
Looking Glass
Ollikut
Poker Joe
Timothy
Toohoolhoolzote
White Bird
Yellow Wolf (2)

NIANTIC
Ninigret

NIPMUC
Waban

NISQUALLY
Leschi

NOOTKA
Maquinna

OMAHA
Big Elk
La Flesche, Francis
La Flesche, Joseph
La Flesche, Susan
La Flesche, Susette (Bright Eyes)
Two Crows

OSAGE
Clermont
Mohongo
White Hair

OTTAWA
Kanapima
Langlade, Charles
Negwagon
Pontiac
PAIUTE
Egan
Numaga
Oytes
Paulina
Tavibo
Truckee
Weawea
Winnemucca
Winnemucca, Sarah
Wovoka
PATWIN
Malaca
Solano
PAWNEE
Big Hawk Chief
Drouillard, George
Petalesharo
Sharitarish
Sky Chief
Turk (The Turk)
PENNACOOK
Kancamagus
Passaconaway
PENOBSCOT
Madokawando
PEQUOT
Sassacus
PIEGAN
Many Horses
PIMA
Oacpicagigua, Luis
POMO
Marin
Pomponio
Quintin
PONCA
Standing Bear
White Eagle
POTAWATOMI
Black Partridge
La Framboise, Josette
Metea
Pokagon, Leopold
Pokagon, Simon
Robinson, Alexander
Sagaunash
Shabonee
Topenebee
Wabaunsee

POWHATAN
Anne (Queen Anne)
Namontack
Opechancanough
Pocahontas
Powhatan
Totopotomoi
QUECHAN
Palma
ROGUE RIVER
John (Old John)
SAC
Black Hawk
Keokuk
Neapope
SATURIBA
Olotaraca
SECOTAN
Ensenore
SEMINOLE-MICCOSUKEE
Alligator
Arpeika
Bolek
Bowlegs, Billy
Emathla, Charley
Foke Luste Hajo
Francis, Josiah
Francis, Milly Hayo
Jumper
Jumper, John
Kinache
Micanopy
Neamathla
Osceola
Payne (King Payne)
Wild Cat
SHAWNEE
Alford, Thomas Wildcat
Big Jim
Blue Jacket
Catahecassa
Cornstalk
High Horn
Paxinos
Savannah Jack
Tecumseh
Tenskwatawa (Shawnee Prophet)
SHOSHONE
Bear Hunter
Cameahwait
Charbonneau, Jean Baptiste
Pocatello
Sacajawea
Tendoy
Washakie

SINKIUSE
  Moses
SIOUX
  SANTEE
    Bruguier, John
    MDEWAKANTON
      Big Eagle
      Cloudman
      Eastman, Charles Alexander
      Ehnamani
      Little Crow
      Mankato
      Mazakutemani, Paul
      Red Wing
      Shakopee (the older)
      Shakopee (the younger)
      Tamaha
      Wabasha
      Wabasha (The Leaf)
      Wabasha, Joseph
    SISSETON
      Renville, Gabriel
      Renville, Joseph
      Sleepy Eyes
    WAHPEKUTE
      Inkpaduta
    WAHPETON
      Akipa
      Mazomani
      Otherday, John
      Red Iron
  TETON
    BRULE
      Conquering Bear
      Crow Dog
      Hollow Horn Bear
      Short Bull
      Spotted Tail
    HUNKPAPA
      Crow King
      Gall
      Rain-in-the-Face
      Sitting Bull
    MINICONJOU
      Big Foot
      Hump
      Kicking Bear
      Lame Deer
    OGLALA
      American Horse (1)
      American Horse (2)
      Black Elk
      Crazy Horse
      Flying Hawk
      Iron Tail

      Man-Afraid-of-His-Horses
      Pawnee Killer
      Red Cloud
    SANS ARC (ITAZIPCO)
      Charger, Martin
    SIHASAPA
      Grass, John
    YANKTON
      Bushotter, George
      Dorion, Pierre, Jr.
      Shakehand
      Struck-by-the-Ree
      War Eagle
    YANKTONAI
      Waneta
SPOKANE
  Spokane Garry
SQUAKSON
  Slocum, John
STOCKBRIDGE-MUNSEE
  Adams, John C.
  Quinney, John Waunnacon
TEWA
  Pope
TLINGIT
  Katlian
  Shakes
TONKAWA
  El Mocho
UTE
  Canalla (Johnson)
  Colorow (Colorado)
  Nicaagat (Jack)
  Ouray
  Quinkent (Douglas)
  Walkara
WALLAWALLA
  Peopeomoxmox
WAMPANOAG
  Alexander (Wamsutta)
  Annawan
  Aspinet
  Awashonks
  Corbitant
  Epanow
  Hobomok
  Iyanough
  Massasoit
  Philip (King Philip, Metacom)
  Squanto
  Wetamoo
WANAPAM
  Smohalla
WAPPINGER
  Ninham

Oratamin
WASHO
Datsolalee
WINNEBAGO
Decora, Little
Decora, Spoon
Decora, Waukon
Four Legs
Good Thunder
Little Priest
Nawkaw
Red Bird
Shickshack
White Cloud (Winnebago Prophet)
Winneshiek
Yellow Thunder

YAHI
Ishi
YAKIMA
Kamiakin
Owhi
Qualchin
YAVAPAI
Montezuma, Carlos (Wassaja)
YAZOO
Moncachtape
YOKUTS
Chalpinich
Stanislaus
YUCHI
Barnard, Timpoochee
YUMA (See also QUECHAN)
Francisco

NON-INDIANS LISTED BY THEIR MOST RELEVANT CONTRIBUTIONS TO NATIVE AMERICAN HISTORY

EXPLORERS & TRADERS
Allouez, Claude Jean
Anza, Juan Bautista de
Ashley, William Henry
Astor, John Jacob
Baranov, Aleksandr Andreevich
Beckwourth, James Pierson
Benavidas, Alonso de
Bent, Charles
Bent, William
Bering, Vitus Jonassen
Bonneville, Benjamin Louis Eulalie de
Boone, Daniel
Bowles, William Augustus
Bozeman, John M.
Bridger, James
Brule, Etienne
Cabeza de Vaca, Alvar Nunez
Cabot, John
Cabrillo, Juan Rodriguez
Campbell, Robert (1)
Campbell, Robert (2)
Cartier, Jacques
Carver, Jonathan
Champlain, Samuel de
Charbonneau, Toussaint
Chouteau, Auguste Pierre
Chouteau, Jean Pierre
Chouteau, Pierre, Jr.
Chouteau, Rene Auguste
Clark, William
̇ ̇man, James
̇ . John
̇ ̇s, Christopher

Cook, James
Coronado, Francisco Vasquez de
Corte Real, Gaspar
De Soto, Hernando
Dorion, Pierre, Sr.
Duluth, Daniel Greysolon, Sieur
Ericsson, Leif
Escalante, Francisco Silvestre Velez de
Espejo, Antonio de
Estevanico
Ewing, George Washington
Ewing, William Griffith
Fitzpatrick, Thomas
Fraser, Simon
Fremont, John Charles
Gist, Christopher
Glass, Hugh
Gosnold, Bartholomew
Gray, Robert
Groseilliers, Medard Chouart, Sieur des
Hamilton, William Thomas
Hearne, Samuel
Henday, Anthony
Hennepin, Louis
Henry, Alexander
Henry, Andrew
Hudson, Henry
Hunt, Wilson Price
Jogues, Isaac
Jolliet, Louis
Kelsey, Henry
Kino, Eusebio Francisco
Lahontan, Louis Armand de Lom d'Arce, Baron de
La Salle, Rene Robert Cavelier, Sieur de

Laudonniere, Rene Goulaine de
Lawson, John
Ledyard, John
Lewis, Meriwether
Lisa, Manuel
Long, Stephen Harriman
Mackenzie, Alexander
Mackenzie, Kenneth
Malaspina, Alejandro
Mallet, Pierre Antoine
Marquette, Jacques
McTavish, Simon
Meek, Joseph L.
Menard, Antoine Pierre
Menendez de Aviles, Pedro
Morton, Thomas
Narvaez, Panfilo de
Nicolet, Jean
Niza, Marcos de
Ogden, Peter Skene
Onate, Juan de
Pattie, James Ohio
Perrot, Nicolas
Pike, Zebulon Montgomery
Pilcher, Joshua
Ponce de Leon, Juan
Pond, Peter
Radisson, Pierre Esprit
Raleigh, Walter
Ribault, Jean
Robertson, James
Robidoux, Antoine
Rolfe, John
Ross, Alexander
Serra, Junipero
Shelikov, Gregori Ivanovich
Smith, Jedediah Strong
Smith, John
Sublette, William Lewis
Sutter, John Augustus
Tanner, John
Thompson, David
Tonti, Henri de
Verendrye, Pierre Gaultier de Varennes, Sieur de la
Verrazano, Giovanni da
Vial, Pedro
Walker, Joseph Reddeford
Williams, William S.
Wood, Abraham

FRONTIER PAINTERS & PHOTOGRAPHERS
Barry, David F.
Bierstadt, Albert
Blakelock, Ralph Albert
Bodmer, Karl

Brush, George de Forest
Burbank, Elbridge Ayer
Cardero, Jose
Catlin, George
Collot, Victor
Cross, Henry
Curtis, Edward Sheriff
Darley, Felix Octavius Carr
Deas, Charles
Easterly, Thomas M.
Eastman, Seth
Farny, Henry F.
Fitzgibbon, John H.
Gentilz, Theodore
Goff, Orlando Scott
Hansen, Herman W.
Harmer, Alexander
Hays, William Jacob
Hillers, John K.
Houghton, Arthur Boyd
Jackson, William Henry
Johnson, Eastman
Kane, Paul
Kern, Benjamin Jordan
Kern, Edward Meyer
Kern, Richard Hovendon
King, Charles Bird
Kurz, Rudolph Friedrich
Le Moyne, Jacques de Morgues
Lewis, James Otto
Matteson, Sumner W.
Mayer, Francis Blackwell
Miller, Alfred Jacob
Moran, Peter
Moran, Thomas
Morrow, Stanley
Mulvany, John
Muybridge, Eadweard James
O'Sullivan, Timothy H.
Paxson, Edgar Samuel
Remington, Frederic
Rindisbacher, Peter
Russell, Charles Marion
Savage, Charles Roscoe
Schreyvogel, Charles
Seymour, Samuel
Sharp, Joseph Henry
Soule, William Stinson
Stanley, John Mix
Stobie, Charles
Stuart, Granville
Suria, Tomas de
Tavernier, Jules
Vroman, Adam Clark
Webber, John E.

White, John
Wimar, Charles

OFFICIALS, AGENTS, & REFORMERS
Andros, Edmund
Atkin, Edmond
Battey, Thomas C.
Beale, Edward Fitzgerald
Beeson, John
Berkeley, William
Bland, Thomas A.
Bolon, Andrew J.
Bradford, William
Brady, John Green
Cadillac, Antoine Laumet de la Mothe, Sieur de
Calhoun, John Caldwell
Cass, Lewis
Child, Lydia Maria
Clinton, George (1)
Clinton, George (2)
Clum, John P.
Colyer, Vincent
Cooper, Peter
Croghan, George (1)
Dawes, Henry Laurens
Dinwiddie, Robert
Dodge, Henry Lafayette
Dodge, William Earl
Doolittle, James Rood
Dunmore, John Murray, Earl of
Evans, John
Franklin, Benjamin
Gadsden, James
Garland, Hamlin
Graffenried, Christoph von
Grant, Ulysses Simpson
Haldimand, Frederick
Hamilton, Henry
Hawkins, Benjamin
Hitchcock, Ethan Allen
Houston, Samuel
Jackson, Andrew
Jackson, Helen Hunt
Janney, Samuel McPherson
Jefferson, Thomas
Jeffords, Thomas J.
Johnson, Guy
Johnson, William
Joncaire, Louis Thomas Chabert de
Kieft, Willem
Knox, Henry
Las Casas, Bartolome de
Lee, Jason
Lincoln, Abraham
Livingston, Robert R.

Logan, James
Love, Alfred Henry
Macdonald, John Alexander
Macleod, James Farquharson
Manypenny, George W.
McCoy, Isaac
McGillicuddy, Trant Valentine O'Connell
McKee, Alexander
McKenney, Thomas Loraine
McLaughlin, James
Meacham, Alfred B.
Mears, Otto
Meeker, Nathan Cook
Minuit, Peter
O'Fallon, Benjamin
Oglethorpe, James Edward
Painter, Charles C.
Penn, William
Phillips, Wendell
Pike, Albert
Priber, Christian Gottlieb
Printz, Johan Bjornsson
Schurz, Carl
Schuyler, Peter
Schuyler, Philip John
Scott, Duncan Campbell
Simpson, George
Smiley, Albert Keith
Stevens, Isaac Ingalls
Stuart, John
Stuyvesant, Peter
Taliaferro, Lawrence
Tappan, Samuel F.
Tatum, Lawrie
Thomas, William Holland
Thompson, Wiley
Tibbles, Thomas Henry
Washington, George
Weiser, Conrad
Welsh, Herbert
Welsh, William
Whipple, Henry Benjamin
White, Eugene Elliot
Williams, Roger
Winslow, Edward
Woolman, John
Wynkoop, Edward
Young, Brigham

SCHOLARS & EDUCATORS
Adair, James
Assall, Friedrich W.
Atwater, Caleb
Baird, Spencer Fullerton
Bancroft, Hubert Howe

Bandelier, Adolph Francis Alphonse
Baraga, Frederic
Bartlett, John Russell
Bartram, William
Berlandier, Jean Louis
Boas, Franz
Bourke, John Gregory
Brackenridge, Henry Marie
Bradbury, John
Brainerd, David
Brebeuf, Jean de
Brinton, Daniel Garrison
Bruyas, Jacques
Byington, Cyrus
Cataldo, Joseph
Charlevoix, Pierre Francois Xavier de
Chittenden, Hiram Martin
Colden, Cadwallader
Cooper, James Fenimore
Cremony, John C.
Cushing, Frank Hamilton
Cutler, Manasseh
Denig, Edwin T.
De Smet, Pierre Jean
Dodge, Richard Irving
Dorsey, James Owen
Duncan, William
Edwards, Jonathan
Eliot, John
Fewkes, Jesse Walter
Finley, James Bradley
Fletcher, Alice Cunningham
Fowke, Gerard
Gallatin, Albert
Gregg, Josiah
Grinnell, George Bird
Guyart, Marie
Hale, Horatio Emmons
Hall, James
Hayden, Ferdinand Vandeveer
Heckewelder, John Gottlieb Ernestus
Hodge, Frederick Webb
Holmes, William Henry
Jacobsen, Johan Adrian
King, Charles
King, Clarence
Kingsbury, Cyrus
Kirkland, Samuel
Lacombe, Albert
Lafitau, Joseph Francois
Lalemant, Jerome
Longfellow, Henry Wadsworth
Lummis, Charles Fletcher
Mason, Otis Tufton
Mather, Cotton

Matthews, Washington
Maximilian, Alexander Philipp, Prinz zu
   Wied-Neuwied
May, Karl Friedrich
Mayhew, Thomas, Jr.
Megapolensis, Johannes
Methvin, John Jasper
Milfort, Louis Le Clerc
Mooney, James
Morgan, Lewis Henry
Morse, Jedediah
Palou, Francisco
Parkman, Francis
Point, Nicolas
Powell, John Wesley
Pratt, Richard Henry
Putnam, Frederic Ward
Riggs, Stephen Return
Rousseau, Jean Jacques
Schoolcraft, Henry Rowe
Schultz, James Willard
Scott, Hugh Lenox
Sergeant, John
Seton, Ernest Thompson
Simms, William Gilmore
Spalding, Henry Harmon
Squier, Ephraim George
Stephen, Alexander M.
Stevenson, Matilda Coxe
Swan, James G.
Tocqueville, Alexis de
Tuggle, William Orrie
Veniaminov, Ivan
Victor, Frances Fuller
Wheeler, George Montague
Wheelock, Eleazar
Whitman, Marcus
Worcester, Samuel Austin
Zeisberger, David

SOLDIERS, SCOUTS, & CAPTIVES
Amherst, Jeffrey
Atkinson, Henry
Bacon, Nathaniel
Baldwin, Frank Dwight
Bascom, George Nicholas
Beecher, Frederick H.
Benteen, Frederick W.
Bienville, Jean Baptiste le Moyne, Sieur de
Blunt, James Gilpatrick
Bouquet, Henry
Braddock, Edward
Brock, Isaac
Burgoyne, John
Butler, John

Butler, Walter
Canby, Edward Richard Sprigg
Carleton, James Henry
Carr, Eugene Asa
Carrington, Henry Beebee
Carson, Christopher Houston "Kit"
Chivington, John Milton
Church, Benjamin
Clark, George Rogers
Clinch, Duncan Lamont
Clinton, James
Cody, William Frederick "Buffalo Bill"
Connor, Patrick Edward
Craven, Charles
Crockett, David "Davy"
Croghan, George (2)
Crook, George
Custer, George Armstrong
Dade, Francis Langhorne
Davis, Britton
Dearborn, Henry
Dodge, Henry
Doniphan, Alexander William
Duston, Hannah Emerson
Endecott, John
Fetterman, William Judd
Forsyth, George Alexander
Forsyth, James William
Frontenac, Louis de Buade, Comte de Palluau et de
Gaines, Edmund Pendleton
Gibbon, John
Girty, Simon
Grattan, John L.
Grierson, Benjamin Henry
Grouard, Frank
Hancock, Winfield Scott
Harmar, Josiah
Harney, William Selby
Harrison, William Henry
Hays, John Coffee
Hazen, William Babcock
Helmer, Adam
Herkimer, Nicholas
Hickok, James Butler "Wild Bill"
Horn, Tom
Howard, Oliver Otis
Iberville, Pierre le Moyne, Sieur d'
Jemison, Mary
Jesup, Thomas Sidney
Jewitt, John Rodgers
Johnson, John
Kearny, Stephen Watts
Kenton, Simon

Lafayette, Marie Joseph Paul Yves Roch Gilbert du Motier, Marquis de
Lawton, Henry Ware
Leavenworth, Henry
Lehmann, Herman
Le Moyne, Charles
Lewis, Andrew
Longueuil, Charles le Moyne, Baron de
Love, Nat
MacCrea, Jane
Mackenzie, Ranald Slidell
Mason, John
Merritt, Wesley
Miles, Nelson Appleton
Milner, Moses Embree
Montcalm-Gazon, Louis Joseph de, Marquis de Saint-Veran
Murphy, Timothy
North, Frank Joshua
North, Luther
Philip, James
Pope, John
Price, Sterling
Proctor, Henry
Reno, Marcus Albert
Reynolds, Charles A.
Rogers, Robert
Rowlandson, Mary
St. Clair, Arthur
Scott, Winfield
Sevier, John
Shelby, Isaac
Sheridan, Philip Henry
Sherman, William Tecumseh
Sibley, Henry Hastings
Sieber, Albert
Standish, Miles
Sullivan, John
Sully, Alfred
Sumner, Edwin Vose
Swarton, Hannah
Taylor, Zachary
Terry, Alfred Howe
Thornburgh, Thomas T.
Underhill, John
Vallejo, Mariano Guadalupe
Vargas Zapata y Lujan Ponce de Leon, Diego Jose de
Walsh, James Morrow
Wayne, Anthony
Winslow, Josiah
Wolfe, James
Wool, John Ellis
Worth, William Jenkins